Dedication: To LTJG Douglas M. Webster, *USS Ticonderoga* (CVA-14), VA-56, A-4, *Skyhawk* pilot who gave his life for his country, on December 5, 1965, while insuring readiness for nuclear war. To my forty-two shipmates listed within these pages who lost their lives serving their country. I was honored to have served with these heroes—may they never be forgotten.

Acknowledgements:

My mom, Imogene Sylvester Little. She kept all the letters I sent to her over a thirty-year period. If she hadn't, this book would not have been possible. Also, had it not been for her, my existence would not be possible. I love you, Mom.

My wife, Carmen Little. She's not only my love and perfect wife, but also held the toughest job in the Navy for thirty-three years: that of a Navy wife. I love you, Carmen.

My sister, Linda Little Wilson, who was anxious to see the completion of this book, but left for heaven before it was done. I love you, Linda.

The sailors of the United States Navy who served their country in one of the most vital, demanding, and unique jobs ever to exist: Navy Nuclear Weaponsman.

Editing of this book was completed by editing.com.

TABLE OF CONTENTS

FORWARD IX
CHAPTER 1: DUCK AND COVER 1
CHAPTER 2: DECK APES AND PIKE QUEENS 19
CHAPTER 3: LEARNING ABOUT THE "BOMB" 26
CHAPTER 4: THE ROCK 39
CHAPTER 5: THE "INDY" 50
CHAPTER 6: BEGINNINGS OF THE VIETNAM WAR 79
CHAPTER 7: THE "O.H.T." 120
CHAPTER 8: GUAM IS GOOD 137
CHAPTER 9: TONKIN GULF YACHT CLUB 150
CHAPTER 10: FIRST CLASS REST HOME 200
CHAPTER 11: GUAM IS GOOD (AGAIN) 233
CHAPTER 12: LAND OF ENCHANTMENT 283
CHAPTER 13: MIDWAY MAGIC 302
CHAPTER 14: ONE-THIRD OF THE NATION'S STOCKPILE 369
CHAPTER 15: INSIDE THE BELTWAY 386
CHAPTER 16: SUBMARINES AND SALMON 405
CHAPTER 17: I REQUEST PERMISSION TO GO ASHORE SIR 415
IN MEMORIAM 423
ENDNOTES 425

Forward

Ever feel like a dinosaur? Well, due to the current world situation, we have become a dinosaur of a sort. But there is another way of looking at the passing of the nuclear age. We have been members on a unique government project that may well be the only government action that we not only saw in its infant development, but also have watched it grow through its years of peaceful deterrence, and now watch it die from lack of need. Don't ever sell yourself short shipmates. If it was not for each and every one of your efforts, dedication, and years of hard work in somewhat less than desirable conditions, this great nation of ours would never be in the position to negotiate the arms reduction treaties that are now in front of Congress for ratification. We have always worked under the veil of secrecy, and we will never be publicly thanked for this effort, but you have one thing you can always do. That is simply look into the mirror in the morning and know that you, aside from everyone else, have made it one of the biggest contributions that this country and mankind will ever know.

LCDR Thomas H. Best, Sr., U.S. Navy-Retired

Chapter 1: Duck and Cover

Our teacher screamed at us
"Duck and cover."

As obedient seven year olds, we immediately scurried under our desks amid horrific visions of flesh burning and melting off our young bones as a huge mushroom cloud rose over our small California country school.

As a boy growing up in the late 1940s and 1950s, this shouted command was very familiar. Nuclear war was a real threat, and "duck and cover" drills were common in our classroom. A blinding white flash meant an atomic bomb had exploded, and we were to scurry under our desks (duck), place our arms and hands around our heads, and tightly close our eyes (cover). Often during these years there would be announcements of atomic bomb tests conducted at the Nevada Test Site, usually during the early morning hours. I remember watching awestruck as the eastern sky would light up for many minutes at a time. As a boy, I never imagined how my adult life would be intertwined with these atomic bombs we feared and were told would be used in World War III, which could begin at any time.

As I begin my memoirs of a thirty-year career in the United States Navy and take a pen in hand, I'd like to clarify something: I'll write of events from June 1960 to January 1991. I should acknowledge these memoirs would be impossible if my mother had not saved every letter I sent to her during my Navy career. I'm very grateful that she did, although it's sometimes painful to read what I wrote at the ages of seventeen and eighteen.

First the basics. I was born 8 December, 1942, in Porterville, California, to Stewart Little and Imogene Sylvester Little, of Strathmore, California, the oldest son of four children. Strathmore is located near the foothills of the Sierra Nevada Mountains in the fertile San Joaquin Valley, surrounded by orange groves, olive groves, and cotton fields. From a very young age I was interested in the U.S. Navy; I remember excitedly reading a World War II vintage book describing the Navy and Marine Corps. I was also very impressed by my cousin, Howard Worley, when he visited my parents when he was stationed on a ship in California. I thought he was very inspiring in his blue bell-bottom Navy uniform. At the time, I was eight years old.

When television was new in the early 1950's, I looked forward to watching military based programs such as the *Big Picture*[1] and *Navy Log*[2]. One of my favorites, *The Silent Service*[3], was about the Navy submarine service.

While in high school, several of the boys ahead of me including Lloyd Van Antwerp and Calvin Keith joined up. I talked to them when they returned to Strathmore on leave and they spoke of the Navy in glowing terms. I made a pact with a couple of friends (Butch Coley, and Frank Caudle) that we would join the Navy after graduation. Our slogan was: "After we graduate its Navy blue for me and you." In the 1950s and 1960s, the draft was in effect and everyone expected to get a letter in the mail after age eighteen, inviting him to a physical examination and into the Army. Not many wanted to go into the Army, the services of choice were the Air Force and Navy, and the Marines were a different matter. I worked after school and on weekends at a Chevron gas station in Lindsay, California. A guy, who was older than I, also worked at the station. He joined the Air Force. I began to think after talking to him that the Air Force might be a good choice for me after graduation. In May, 1960, I was staying with classmates Don and Shirley Bradford who had gotten married right after high school graduation. I had been Don's best man, and the girl I had been dating, Donna, was the Maid of Honor. I searched for a job, but there wasn't much choice. Don was working as a butcher, but that wasn't for me.

One day I went to the nearby city of Porterville to see about joining the military. I wasn't sure at the time which service. I went first to the Air Force office but it was closed. The Navy office was open so I went in and talked to the chief petty officer there. He was very friendly and said I could take the written entrance exam, which took about an hour and half. I passed with satisfactory marks. Next I would need a physical at a service induction center. I was scheduled for a trip to Fresno, 60 miles away, the following week of 24 June.

I traveled there by car; there were three other men who were also getting physicals. At the induction center I was introduced to the military's way of doing things. There I learned how the saying, "Hurry up and wait" came about. We stood in line waiting for our eye tests, hearing tests, urine samples, blood tests, etc. We stood around in our underwear for most of the day. The majority of people were getting physicals for the Army. A doctor listened to my heart, and lungs, and then asked if I had any problems.

"No." I said.

At five feet ten inches tall, I was the least impressive of my group—very thin, and about 127 pounds. Still, the other three guys with me didn't pass their physicals.

I needed a parent's signature to join because I was seventeen and half. My father agreed, so we went to the recruiting office, and the paperwork was signed just two days before I was to go to boot camp in San Diego. I was not officially in the Navy until I was sworn in. My enlistment was a special type: if you enlisted prior to the age of eighteen, and after seventeen and a half, you only served until your twenty first birthday. My discharge date would be 7 December, 1963, the day before I became twenty-one. Those who enlisted under these conditions were called "kiddy cruisers," and only served three years six months instead of the usual four years.

I asked Donna, my girlfriend, if she would marry me. The day of my enlistment was her fifteenth birthday. Donna was a pretty blonde, blue-eyed girl, with an exceptionally beautiful white complexion. We had dated for over two years. I gave her an engagement ring the day before I was scheduled to leave. The night of the twenty-ninth I stayed at my parent's house. I was anxious and nervous about this new life I was about to begin.

I had to meet the chief petty officer from the recruiting office in Strathmore in front of the firehouse at 7:00 a.m. on the 30th. My father drove me into town. My mother was not happy about my enlistment and was upset about my leaving, so she stayed home. I said goodbye to my father and climbed into the car with the chief. He had to pick up a guy named Steven in the nearby town of Dinuba before we could travel on to Fresno.

When we arrived at the Fresno Receiving Center, the chief wished us luck and left Steven and me at an office that had six sailors working behind desks. Everyone was very kind to us; they even brought us cokes to drink. We were told an officer would come and administer the enlistment oath. At noon a Lieutenant (LT), came in and ask us to stand; a couple of sailors that hadn't gone to lunch also stood at attention. The LT asked us to raise our right hand, and to repeat after him: "I, James Stewart Little do solemnly swear (or affirm) that I will bear true faith and allegiance to the United States of America; that I will serve them honestly and faithfully against all their enemies whomsoever; and that I will obey the orders of the President of the United States and the orders of the officers appointed over me, according to regulations and the Uniform Code of Military Justice."

Immediately after the Oath, the lieutenant's attitude changed from friendly and congenial to stern and businesslike. Steven had been chewing gum. The officer barked at him: "Spit that gum out, you don't chew gum in an officer's presence." "Okay," Steven stuttered. The LT said, "You address me as Sir." Steven turned pale and replied, "Yes Sir." Then the LT said: "Both of you stand over by the door at attention, and no talking." We stood by the door in a stupor. A sailor came over, gave us bus tickets to San Diego, our orders, and a phone number to call when we arrived. "Welcome to the Navy, boots," he said.

A Greyhound bus arrived at 1:00 p.m., and we got onboard. We didn't have any luggage. After we had been on the bus about an hour, we discovered that there were a couple of sailors on the bus in civilian clothes. They were returning to San Diego. We asked them about boot camp, and what it was like. They said, "It's O.K., just be sure to keep your locker locked." A little after 10:00 p.m., we arrived at the San Diego bus station, and we dialed the telephone number we had been given in Fresno. We were told a van would pick us up in about fifteen minutes. The bus station was full of men in uniform and we wondered how we would look in ours.

A sailor driving a van arrived. There were six other men waiting as well. We all climbed into it and, after a twenty-minute ride, arrived at the gate of the San Diego U.S. Naval Training Center. The marine gate guard looked inside, and before waving us through, said, "Ah, fresh meat!" The van stopped in front of a long row of wooden benches under a roof supported by steel poles. There were two of these areas with a large concrete slab between. On the concrete slab were more than one hundred numbered squares outlined in yellow. There were about forty men standing on it, each within a numbered square. A sailor with an insignia on his arm (which we were to learn later was a first class petty officer) met us. He shouted at us to get off the bus, and stand at attention. He said, "Welcome to San Diego U.S. Naval Training Center. From this point on you will not speak unless told to, as far as I'm concerned you are all are useless, lower than whale s***, and you have a long way to go before you can be considered human beings, etc., etc." He went on for a long while, generally telling us how worthless we were. He then said that we were to march two blocks to a barracks, where we would sleep. We tried to march, but judging from his groans and expressions of disgust our attempts were pathetic.

Inside the barracks were single beds with bare mattresses, and a folded wool blanket on each one. We were all bewildered: Where were the sheets, pillows, and pillowcases? Another first class who said, "Lights out, and I don't want to hear any noise" had joined the other who had marched us to the barracks. So we went to bed without a shower, but we were allowed to brush our teeth quickly. At least those that had a toothbrush. Luckily, I'd brought toothpaste and toothbrush on the advice of the recruiter.

As I lay on the bare mattress, and pulled the wool blanket over my shoulders, (I'd always disliked wool), the thought ran through my mind *"What have I got myself into?"* This same thought raced through my mind when the lights came back on at 4:00 a.m., to a loud banging from a trashcan that was being beaten upon by a first class petty officer. He was shouting for us to get up, hollering "Reveille, reveille." He said, "You have ten minutes to assemble outside." We dressed, stumbled around, and went outside. It was dark and cold. We marched back to the area of the wooden benches. Men were marching to the same location from all directions. Eventually about 400 men were assembled.

At 5:30 a.m., groups of sixty of us were marched a few blocks, and I was introduced to a Navy chow hall. We formed a line, each person selected a metal-compartmented tray and silverware, and then as we moved down the chow line, men standing behind the serving line dumped food in the compartments of the tray. We sat at long tables, and were watched over by petty officers who maintained order. We were permitted to get up and get glasses of milk from large metal boxes holding milk cans with plastic dispensing tubes hanging down. After we finished eating (the food was very good), we took our trays and silverware to a window labeled "scullery." We then assembled outside until everyone was ready to return to the wooden bench area. Throughout that day we watched new people arrive, as we had arrived the night before.

The loud, stern-talking petty officers amazed us with the derogatory names that they used on the new arrivals. Very seldom did they repeat themselves. When we were allowed to smoke, and almost everyone did, one guy made the mistake of crushing his cigarette on the ground instead of putting it in the cans filled with sand that were placed near the benches. The petty officers made him stand at attention all morning.

We tried to stay quiet and only whispered. Different sailors with bullhorns shouted orders all day. We were told to stand on a block with a number on it and told to memorize the number. My number was eighty-three. From then on we were to remain in a certain section of the benches, which were within colored sections of blue, green, red, and white. When your section was called out you had to immediately run to your square and stand in it. In the evening after dinner, it was my section's turn to assemble around a large U-shaped table that we stood up at.

Everyone was told to empty their pockets and all pocketknives and pocket combs were collected. The petty officers joked, "You won't be needing a comb for a while." We had seen a few bald newcomers during our marches and we all wondered when our haircuts would take place. We had to turn in any pictures of girls and girl friends from our wallets, although pictures of families could be kept. All jewelry, except wedding rings, had to be turned in as well. We signed paperwork that assigned a seven-digit service number to each of us. This number was very important, as it remained a sailor's identification number during his Navy career. The men who wore glasses had to turn them in, and were given eye exams so that Navy-issued glasses could be given to them. We felt sorry for them, many were blind without glasses, and had to wait a few days until their glasses were ready. We all helped these "blind ones." We also filled out postcards to our next of kin telling them what our address was. I was assigned to "Boot Camp Company 303." My address was written: Company. 303/U.S. Naval Training Center/San Diego 33, California.

One of the first things we were issued was a ditty bag. It contained soap, toothbrush, toothpaste, razor, razor blades, shoe polish, shower shoes (called "flip-flops"), and writing material. I was assigned a billet number within Company 303. My billet number was fifty-six. There were initially about eighty men in my company. Our company commander was a career first class petty officer, named Ship's Serviceman First Class (SH1) C.E. Bohlen. We were all terrified of him. All the company commanders wore a red braided rope on their right shoulder.

The days wore on; the boot camp process was slow as a large number of recruits had enlisted at once. Most of us were high school graduates. We were assigned the lowest rank in the Navy, "Seaman Recruit," which is written: "SR," and is indicated by three-inch diagonal mark on the left upper sleeve. However, at this time we didn't have uniforms. We were able to take showers, but couldn't change clothes. So, speaking of rank—our clothes were becoming very rank!

It soon was apparent the Navy had a new language. All the petty officers (all of them first class, or chief petty officers) used unfamiliar words. One phrase we learned immediately was "A-TEN-HUT," which was "attention" and meant you were to stand absolutely still, eyes straight ahead, shoulders back, with back straight, arms down your sides with your thumbs aligned down the outside seams of your pant legs, both heels together, with toes pointed outward, so your feet formed a forty-five-degree angle. We were at attention much of the time.

One trick we learned to prevent from passing out was to slightly bend your knees and wiggle your toes inside your shoes. But because this wasn't explained until after a few days, occasionally someone would "hit the deck," which is a Navy term for the floor or ground. One term we all looked forward to was "at ease," which meant you could relax, and move your body, but had to keep your left foot in place, and depending on what the petty officer said, you might be permitted to talk. The first basic marching skill began by stepping out with your left foot, (to determine if someone has been the military, watch them walk; if they lead with their left foot, it's a good bet that they've marched before). The petty officers leading us would continually scream for us to "keep in step," and would shout cadences, usually "your left – your left – your left – right – left." Each time he said "left," your left foot was to strike the pavement (deck). We were all out of synchronization the first few times we tried to march and stepped on the heels of the person ahead of us. The petty officers would scream at us to get in step, yelling things like: "You all march like little girls, you're all useless," and other derogatory comments. In order to stop when you arrived at your destination, the command "company halt" was given. It meant you stopped the left foot first and brought the right foot up with the right heel against the left. Thus, you stopped in the "attention" position. In order to get out of the marching formation the command "fall out" was given. If you were "at ease," the company had to be called to "attention" before you could be given the command to "fallout." These are some of the first basic marching skills we were taught. We also were taught (not too gently), how to skip to get back in step. Another of the unfamiliar words we heard were "taps" which meant lights out. "Reveille" was not a welcome term. It meant wake up and get out of bed.

"Colors" signified the flag raising on the base. Every morning at 8:00 a.m. the flag was raised and we had to immediately stand at attention and face toward the flag. We stood at attention, while all the petty officers saluted and the National Anthem was played over loudspeakers. At the completion of the National Anthem, a bugle was blown, and the command "carry on – carry on" was issued. "Colors" were also held in the evening at sundown. The petty officers also used terms such as "overhead," (which meant the ceiling), and "bulkheads," (which were walls), "ladders" (for stairs), "a chow hall," (the dining area). The "head," was a bathroom, and "lid," was a hat. "Port," was left, and "starboard," meant right. There were many other terms we struggled with at first.

By the fifth day our clothes were becoming unbearable and rumors started to fly around. We heard about guys who tried climbing the fence after only a day or two. We also heard they were placed in a jail where conditions were horrible. The waiting was making us all apprehensive and anxious. We all looked shabby and our constantly worn civilian clothes were becoming smelly. We were anxious for the day we would get our uniforms (had we known what a miserable day it turned out to be, we might not have been so anxious.) We were not permitted to eat anything but what we consumed at the chow hall. A cigarette machine was in the bench area. Everyone commented how cheap cigarettes were, the cost being ten cents a pack.

Most were homesick; many of the conversations were about home. I must admit I was very homesick, being in such a foreign and threatening environment. We all admired the uniforms of the petty officers and their controlled and commanding presence. They all wore khakis, (in the case of chief petty officers), or spotless whites, (as in the case of the first class petty officers.) But with this admiration there was also fear. There were instances where a recruit would be kicked in the behind if they were out of step, or a finger would be poked repeatedly in the chest for some infraction. At times we saw men break down and cry when being hollered at. None of us wanted to be humiliated to the point of tears. I think we all were in shock from all the orders, and drastic change in our treatment.

By the fifth day we had our ditty bag, containing basic toilet articles, but were still wearing the clothes we arrived in. Thankfully the weather was pleasant, although cool at night. After our section's color was called out, we were ordered to stand on our square. Then we marched to a building, and were told to get in a single file. We waited in a corridor and suddenly we were all frightened by a scream. We were there to get a dental exam and the shriek had come from a room further down the hall.

One by one we would get into a chair, with two recruits standing on each side—they were two of the biggest recruits in our company. These two would hold the arms of the person being examined, while a dentist examined his teeth. The dentist described his findings to a corpsman standing nearby, who wrote down the comments on a dental chart. While we were in the dental clinic, one guy said he didn't want to be examined. The company commander slammed him against the wall, and took him to the head of the line. We were very somber and quiet after that. I'll never forget another poor guy. After he was examined, the doctor directed him to another section of the building. When we marched back to the wooden bench area, he wasn't with us.

About an hour later he was escorted back with a swollen jaw and blood spattered on his shirt. He mumbled to us that they had pulled three teeth without any painkiller. He was miserable for a couple of days.

On 6 July, seven days after I arrived, we'd become a company of eighty men. We were marched to a medical clinic, told to roll up our sleeves, and given two shots—one in each arm. After waiting for an hour we were marched back around to the front door again, and given five more shots. I have no idea what they were. We all had seven shots each that morning. The ones who went in first would come out grimacing and complaining how painful they were; this terrified the ones waiting to go in. Afterwards, most of the recruits would laugh and try to be macho, but I remember it hurt. Getting the inoculations took all morning; we had to wait to see if anyone would get an adverse reaction.

In a letter I wrote that day to my parents, I included instructions on how to contact the Red Cross in the event of an emergency, and what to do if I was needed at home. I also wrote that I couldn't have any visitors for six months. This was false, as boot camp only lasted a little more than two months. We had been told this to increase our sense of isolation.

The afternoon of shot day we marched to a building to receive our uniforms. The first-order of business was to get out of our filthy clothes. Sailors measured and examined us before they gave out the clothing. Skinny guys were given clothes of larger sizes, and fat guys were given clothes of smaller sizes. My socks could stand up by themselves. We were given "skivvies" (a term for underwear), T-shirts, and boxer shorts, and then dungaree shirts, and bell-bottom dungaree pants. We were given large black lace up boots, called "boon dockers." There were muttered complaints (not loud enough for the company commander to hear). We all looked very odd in ill-fitting uniforms. We were not given white hats as we had expected. We all dressed, and were given black knit caps, but told not to put them on. We were all given cardboard shipping boxes, and instructed to address them to our home of record (parents), and we mailed our filthy clothes. I imagined the parent's shocked expressions when they opened them.

So now we were out of our filthy clothes, but the new dungarees we had on were stiff, and we all smelled like mothballs. After we assembled outside, and the smelly packages were gathered, we marched to the barbershop. One by one we sat down in a barber's chair (six barbers working at once), and our heads were shaved. It wasn't a gradual haircut, but a couple of passes with electric razors and your hair was on the floor (deck), and some down your back. The barbers seemed to be enjoying themselves as they joked and said things like: "Would you like a little off the top and sides?" When we all assembled outside again, we were in a daze; we all looked alike, bald white skulls (a few brown and black also). Everyone felt miserable, from the shots, the uncomfortable clothes, the haircut, and the hot afternoon sun bearing down with strands of cut hair inside our shirts. We were directed to put on our black knit caps so our heads wouldn't get sunburned.

After we had our evening meal and returned to the barracks, we discovered when we took off our dungaree pants that our legs were blue. The blue dye from the pants had colored our legs. The next day we were to get our complete sea bag (all our required uniform items), and then relocate to the other side of the training center for two weeks. The other side was called "the Nimitz side." This was an ominous place; it was where we were to begin boot camp in earnest, and it was called "Hell's Island."

Hell's Island was only spoken about in hushed tones, but we'd heard what a terrible place it was. Because this was a time of rampant speculation, no one slept very well. I was pleased with myself, because I'd been able to take what had been thrown at me so far. It was comforting to know that there were eighty other guys in the same boat as me. I'd certainly been experiencing a lot of things I never imagined growing up in the small country town of Strathmore. I'd never been around people who had so many different accents, or mannerisms. I was making friends with one of the black guys in our company; I'd never even spoken to a black person before.

The next day was full of surprises… and pain! When everyone got up, there were moans and groans; our arms were sore from the shots we'd gotten the previous day. After breakfast we were marched to a large building where the issue of our sea bag would take place. We were becoming a little better in our marching efforts. A few days prior to "shot day" we had been assembled in a large square, and our company commander had asked if anyone had a military education, or had been in military school. A number of hands went up. One guy had four years of military school. His name was Edward L. Stephen. He was assigned as company leader. Also selected were platoon leaders, and there were eight of these. Also there were two guide-on bearers; they would eventually carry the flags that were carried whenever we marched anywhere, which was a naval training center flag, and our Company 303 flag. Stephen also had helpers that he selected, an executive officer, and administrative assistants. I did not have any military experience or training, so I was not assigned any specific duties, which was all right with me.

The platoon leaders marched at the very front of company, with a guide-on bearer at both sides of the formation. Company leader Stephen marched with the company commander, at one side of the company. We were all assigned positions within a platoon. We were arranged according to height, shorter men to the rear. Some of the platoon leaders were picked because they were taller than most. I was in platoon number seven, three positions behind the platoon leader. There were eight men in each platoon. Friendships were usually closest within a platoon, as we were always in close proximity to one another.

Various days at the wooden bench area were spent learning commands such as "attention," and marching, and formation commands. One of the more complicated movements was "about face" this meant placing your right foot behind you, and swiveling 180 degrees so you were facing the direction behind your back. Many of us almost fell over the first time we attempted this! It took many hours of practice before we could "about face." We struggled to learn all the strange commands, and tried to control our bodies and arms and legs during these odd contortions. These first few days were an intense learning experience. One of the commands "Parade dress," was a position of change from standing at attention. Both hands were placed in the small of the back, and legs spread to shoulder width. I had to work on this, as the right hand (open) was always placed in the left hand. I was always being corrected because I had positioned my hands the wrong way.

We marched about the base and learned how to turn a corner at the command: "Company, right turn, march," or "company, left turn, march." Prior to arriving at the intersections, the command "road guards, post" was given. Two men from the outside platoons would run out of formation ahead of the company and stand at parade rest to stop vehicles that might be approaching the intersection. After the company passed through the intersection, the command "Road guards, in" would be given. The two men would then run back into formation. Some of the more complicated maneuvers such as "To the rear, march," and "Left oblique" or "Right oblique, march" we learned later. We also practiced marching "double time," at which time we moved along twice as fast as our normal marching pace.

Returning to the day of our uniform sea bag issue, we arrived at a large open building, and were given all of our uniforms, one by one. We all stood behind large upright tables. Upon the tables were stencil brushes, stencil ink, and stencil board. We were all instructed on how to use the stencil machine, and we cut ½ inch letters and numbers into four different stencil boards to stencil our clothes. I made stencils: "Little J. S." on two boards, the other two were: "Little J.S. (followed by my service number)" We were amazed at all the clothes we were given: dress blues; undress blues, white jumpers, socks, underwear, white hats, and so on. It all had to be given in the proper size. Once each man had all the pants he was to be issued, we stood on a platform and a chalk mark was made for hemming up the pants. A mark was made on the dungarees we had been issued the previous day. The pants were the first items we stenciled our names on. The stencil had to be placed in a specific place on all the pants. We had both black and white ink. The white ink was for the dungarees, and the blues. The black ink was for the white pants. The dungarees we'd been given, and worn the day before had been rolled up at the cuffs. After stenciling, all the pants were collected in a large bin with rollers, and taken away. We stood around "pant-less" for the rest of the stenciling work. We each stenciled: One sea bag, two belts, (one black, one white), one brass belt buckle, one blue cap (with gold lettering "U.S. Navy"), one blue hat, and a multitude of uniform and underwear items. All of these items were stenciled in a specific area, and folded the way our company commander directed. Some items such as the jumper tops, and pants were folded while inside out. This job took most of the morning, after folding the items; we placed them in our sea bag. Near the completion of the stenciling, and folding, all of the pants were returned, all hemmed. Apparently there was an area where a group of seamstresses had been working? Surprisingly all the items fit into the canvas sea bag we had been issued. We assembled outside with our sea bags (about 60 pounds), and were told to put them on our shoulders. A few of the smaller guys had trouble with this, so we helped each other. Our arms were still sore from the shots.

Then we went on a long march toward Nimitz Island (Hell's Island). There was a bridge we'd need to pass over. When a company of men march over a bridge, you cannot march in step, as the vibrations of simultaneous footsteps might damage the bridge, so the command "route step, march," is given. Everyone marches out of step at this command. Marching out of step was difficult and a big change from the previous week.

Our first glimpse of our destination filled us with foreboding, and sent chills down our spines. The buildings we had been in and around thus far in boot camp, had been painted light yellows and browns. All the buildings we now saw were unpainted huge, dark concrete structures.

Blacktop and concrete covered the ground, and there was no vegetation. A huge fence encircled all the ominous looking buildings. It looked like a prison. We marched to a two-storied building that was to be our barracks. There were long clotheslines in front, and on the sides of all the buildings there were two large concrete tables, sloping toward each other, which would channel water to drains in the ground. We went inside the barracks; we were to be on the ground floor (lower deck) another company was to live on the top floor (topside). Along the walls were rows of double stacked beds. Steel lockers were against the wall between the beds. At the foot of each double-stacked bed, there were two buckets; inside each bucket there was a scrub brush. That afternoon after leaving our sea bags, we marched back to the other side of the base. We each were issued a rifle. The rifles were heavy old World War I 30-06's with lead plugged barrels. The company commander said we were not to call the 30-06's guns or rifles, in the Navy they were called "pieces." He then recited a raunchy descriptive slogan. Holding a 30-06 up, he said, "This is a piece," and then grabbing his crotch he said, "This is a gun." Then holding the 30-06 with both hands, he said, "This is for shooting," once again grabbing his crotch, he said, "This is for fun." Carrying these pieces on our shoulders, while marching was awkward, and painful to our sore arms, in which we had received shots the previous day.

We also were issued lace up ankle leggings. One pair was khaki and the other white. We would not wear these leggings until we had completed our two weeks on Hell's Island.

That afternoon we were introduced to the "sixteen count manual." It was an exercise with the heavy 30-06's (pieces), which we were expected to master in boot camp. It was painful and tiring going through various contortions that were unfamiliar to us.

Supper in our new chow hall left us all exhausted, but our day was far from over. It was then that the company commander told us that the Navy considered new clothes dirty clothes. We were directed to collect all our sea bag clothing, except the wool blues, dungaree jacket, belts, and leather gloves, and carry them outside to the concrete tables. Then with the buckets, scrub brushes, and soap, we washed all the clothes while wearing T-shirts, dungaree pants, and shower shoes. After washing, we then hung the clothes on the huge clotheslines in front of the barracks. We attached clothes on the clothesline with small pieces of line called "clothes stops." All items were attached as directed by the company commander. For example, the bottom two corners of the T-shirts were looped with two clothes stops, and then both clothes stops were tied to the clothesline with a square knot. It took a lot of clothes stops to hang our laundry on the clothesline that night. We worked late into the night until 10:30 p.m.

There were always two men on watch any time we were at the barracks. One man was a fire watch inside the barracks, and another man was a watch stander outside near the clothesline and trash bin (dumpster). The watches lasted two hours, and went from the 4:00 p.m. to 6:00 p.m., 6:00 p.m. to 8:00 p.m., and so on until 8:00 a.m. in the morning. Watch standers wore helmets the inside fire watch had a club, called a nightstick, and a flashlight; the outside watch carried his piece (rifle). Watch standers had to maintain watch logs, and write down the happenings during their watch.

Watch standing was serious business—being derelict in this duty was unforgivable, and sleeping on watch during wartime could mean standing before a firing squad. Everyone was usually assigned a watch every other day. The company leader, and platoon leaders didn't stand watch. As watch standers we had to memorize the eleven general orders of a sentry, such as "Take charge of this post and all government property in view, walk my post in a military manner, etc. We could be called upon anytime to recite these eleven general orders. While on watch, anytime our company commander, or any sailor other than a recruit walked into a room, or through an outside area near our watch area, we had to scream "Attention on deck," and everyone would leap to attention. Everyone was to remain at attention until the people left, or they said, "Carry on."

Returning to our first night on Hell's Island, we were exhausted that evening, and we collapsed into our beds (I slept on a bottom bunk). The lights were turned out, and the company commander said, "No talking, you all have a big day tomorrow." (I couldn't imagine a day "bigger" than the one we had just had!) About 1:00 a.m., all the lights suddenly blazed on, and our company commander started screaming: "Everyone up, hit the deck, and stand at attention!" We were all dazed. He said, "Who was talking?" He was very angry. After we'd all scrambled in front of our bunks to stand at attention, he again asked, "Who was talking?" No one said a word. He yelled again: "If we don't find out who was talking, we'll stay up all night!" He and the company leader, then walked down the line of men, and stopped in front of each person, looked him up-and-down and asked "Was it you talking?" After he had asked each person in the company, he then gave us a lecture on how we were all responsible for ourselves, and each other, what one person did, (or did not do) reflected on the reputation of Company 303.

This lecture went on for a long while. He then put us "at ease," and said he was going to leave the room we were permitted to talk, and he said, "If I don't find out who was talking, then all of you will stay up all night!"

After he left, we all started talking, and complaining, "Come on, whoever you are that was talking, confess so we can get some sleep." The previous day had been exhausting, and we all wanted to get some rest. Finally the company commander returned, we snapped back to attention, and two men immediately confessed they had been talking. After he chewed them out, he then gave them both toothbrushes, and said they were to scrub the entire deck of the barracks head for the rest of the night. We then were permitted to return to bed, and the lights were turned off. The company commander then said, "Maintain silence about the deck." The guilty talkers began scrubbing the deck of the head on their hands and knees. The time was about to 2:45 a.m. It didn't seem like the lights had been off very long, when they were turned on at 4:30 a.m. We were given thirty minutes to dress, brush our teeth, and fold our blankets in the acceptable manner that we had been taught on our first morning in boot camp. Our bunk mattress only had a cotton mattress cover, and a wool blanket was used for covering at night. The same blanket was to stay with us throughout our time in boot camp. After we assembled outside, we were told that we were going for a little run. We had to run all the way around Hell's Island, a distance of about two and a half miles. Running in the heavy boots (boon dockers), was difficult, but it was something we would do each morning on Hell's Island.

That first morning run many guys got very sick! All during the run company commanders, harassed, urged, and threatened, the runners. There were many companies running at the same time. Huffing and puffing I made it all the way around. It was a lot like the football team conditioning runs I made in high school. After our company completed the run, a few men were completely exhausted. We formed into ranks and marched toward the chow hall. It was about 6:00 a.m. We were to undergo the first of our morning personnel inspections. We stood at attention in ranks, and were instructed to hold the neck of our T-shirts inside out with the thumb of our left hand, so the company commander could inspect the inside neck of the T-shirt for cleanliness! He also told us that we were to be clean-shaven and absolutely clean. Cleanliness was emphasized over and over, we would live in close quarters in the Navy, especially onboard ship, and good hygiene was important to everyone.

After the personnel inspection it was an hour before the company could enter the chow hall and eat. There were many companies ahead of us. This chow hall was different from the one we had been using on what we called the "main side." The Hell's Island chow hall had high concrete walls, and we could not talk while eating.

A system that greatly motivated and inspired us to learn, and do the best we could was a merit system. It would have more properly been called a "demerit" system. Our goal was to graduate from boot camp, and join the real Navy. The demerit system meant if you gained twenty-five demerits within one week you were set back, and then being in a different company you would repeat the previous week's training.

Our company, Company 303, (75 sailors) was in a battalion—Battalion 33, (750 sailors). Battalion 33 was in a brigade, which was the 568th Brigade (1,500 sailors). Each week during the summer of 1960, 1,500 men began training at San Diego Naval Training Center. San Diego was one recruit training center; there was also a boot camp at Great Lakes, Illinois. A woman's recruit training center was located at Bainbridge, Maryland that trained women sailors, or Women Accepted for Volunteer Emergency Service (WAVES).

Each day after we ate breakfast on Hell's Island, we would practice the "sixteen count manual" with our heavy rifles. This was a vigorous workout, and the first few days our muscles were sore.

As time progressed, we could tell what phase of training a company was in by their uniforms; the first two weeks the uniform was dungarees with white hats, without leggings. The succeeding weeks companies wore khaki-colored leggings.

We were issued a book with our sea bag we were expected to study, and in some cases memorize. This book *The Bluejackets' Manual*[4] has often been called "The Sailor's Bible." The book was originally written in 1902, by Lieutenant (later Rear Admiral) Ridley McLean, USN, for the United States Naval Institute. The book has served the Navy for almost ninety-three years. The copy we were issued in 1960, had been revised in 1959, and was the fifteenth edition. The forward of *The Bluejackets' Manual* reads:

> To all Navy men: You are a Navy man, part of the largest and
> strongest seagoing force in the world. When you were sworn in and put
> on your uniform for the first time, you became part of a great tradition.
> All the brave men who have gone before you, and those who will follow
> you, make up an unbroken chain of courage and devotion to duty that
> should make you proud to wear your uniform.

> As a Navy man you are, in a special sense, a good citizen of these United States. Your uniform alone does not entitle you to special privileges, rather it obligates you to set high standards of conduct and performance of duty. At home, and on duty abroad in foreign countries, you'll be under constant observation as a representative of the United States government. Be sure that no careless act of yours brings discredit to your uniform or to your countries flag.
>
> Service in the Navy can be whatever you make it. It takes some time to understand and become adapted to the ways of the Navy, for going to sea in ships and aircraft is a tough, serious business, particularly in these troubled times. If you must work hard and at times miss a leave period or a few liberties in your homeport, remember that you chose a man's job when you joined the Navy.

The words were very impressive; we read and reread one page entitled "The United States Navy." It reads:

> Guardians of our country - The United States Navy is responsible for maintaining control of the sea and is a ready force on watch at home and overseas, capable of strong action to preserve the peace or of instant offensive action to win in war. It is upon the maintenance of this control that our country's glorious future depends; The United States Navy exists to make it so.
>
> We serve with honor - Tradition, valor, and victory are the Navy's heritage from the past. To these may be added dedication, discipline, and vigilance as the watchwords of the present and the future. At home or in distant stations we serve with pride, confident in the respect of our country, our shipmates, and our families. Our responsibilities sober us; our adversities strengthen us. Service to God and country is our special privilege. We serve with honor.
>
> The future of the Navy - the Navy will always employ new weapons, new techniques, and greater power to protect and defend the United States on the sea, under the sea, and in the air. Now and in the future, control of the sea gives the United States her greatest advantage for the maintenance of peace and for victory in war. Mobility, surprise, dispersal, and offensive power are the keynotes of the new Navy. The roots of the Navy lie in a strong belief in the future, in continued dedication to our tasks, and in reflection on our heritage from the past. Never have our opportunities and our responsibilities been greater.

The Bluejackets' Manual contained 639 pages that had information about everything concerning the Navy. One chapter we used often was "Naval Words and Phrases," in order to learn the language of the Navy. At the end of each chapter of *The Bluejackets' Manual* there were quizzes with eight to fifteen questions. We were expected to read, and know the answers to a specific number of chapters each week.

It should be understood that we were living in a time when it was felt that nuclear war was inevitable. In high school and grammar school we had been taught atomic attack drills by diving under our desks when told to, and to "duck and cover." Russia and communist nations were declared enemies. A clarification of this is reflected in the following statement in our *The Bluejackets' Manual*:

> The record of communism is a record of deceit, dishonesty, and tyranny. The evil of communism is not static; it is a cancer that grows ruthlessly. Unless it is checked, it expands and chokes off all other forms of government and all freedom of belief, thought, and speech. Our moral obligation to fight communism includes the necessity to maintain a strong Navy. The Communists, and for that matter any enemy, bow only to force. To force that they see and fear.

The Russian Premier Nikita Khrushchev, had declared, "We will bury you" (referring to the United States). President Eisenhower was in office, and an intense election campaign between Vice President Nixon, and Senator John Kennedy, was prominent in the news. A frequent campaign statement was that our nation needed a strong military to defend against communist expansion.

Many of our fathers, and relatives had been in the military, and fought in World War II. We felt that we were carrying on in the footsteps of the previous generation, and defending our great nation against the forces of evil (Russia).

Most of the company commanders, especially the chief petty officers, had served in the Navy during the Korean conflict, and many during World War II. The Korean War had taken place only eight years previously. World War II had ended in 1945, fifteen years earlier. American U-2 pilot Gary Powers was captured by the Soviets after his spy plane was shot down over Russia. As a result, Premier Khrushchev canceled a planned summit conference. Cuban and American relations continued to deteriorate as Castro signed an economic agreement with Russia.

A time we looked forward to was "mail call." This occurred daily, except Sunday, in the early afternoon. One recruit was assigned as the company mail man. He would report to the base post office each day, and was accompanied by a different person from the company assigned that day. The two men would collect all the mail for Company 303 in a large gray mailbag, and upon returning to the barracks, would sort the mail. "Mail call" would then be held, and all the mail handed out. We were given twenty minutes to smoke and read our mail. Some recruits would get handfuls of letters; others never received any mail. I was one of the fortunate ones; my parents, fiancée, and sister Linda, were wonderful about writing and telling me news of home. I cherished these letters and would read them over, and over. My father had a minor operation I was anxious about, and my brother Joe, who was two years old, had been sick. We all would compare news from home; "mail call" was definitely a pleasurable time.

If "mail call" was a time we anticipated, the daily morning personnel inspection was a time we dreaded! Cleanliness was emphasized over and over. We were expected to shower and shave every day. Many of the guys had "peach fuzz" instead of whiskers. However, it was expected that we be clean-shaven. When we would stand in ranks for our morning personnel inspection, after our daily run, the company commander would look closely at each man. We would stand at attention, with the thumb of our left hand hooked under the neck of our T-shirt, holding the shirt neck out so it could be inspected.

In our right hand we would hold our white hat, with the inside oriented up, so the inside rim could be inspected for any trace of dirt. The company leader, Stephen would accompany the company commander, with a clipboard, and paper, and document the name of anyone who received demerits. Most infractions rated five demerits. We were all terrified of receiving twenty-five demerits, which meant being assigned to a company a week behind us (as I previously said), and repeating the weeks training. The repeat of training was dreaded, but more than that, it meant training with strangers, and losing the friendships we had made with each other in Company 303. We learned very quickly that any hint of dirt was not tolerated. The company commander carried a blade type razor, and I don't believe it was very sharp. If the company commander discovered one whisker, the guilty person would be given the dull razor, and he had to dry shave standing there in ranks. Most would have bloody cheeks, or necks after this dry shave seeing this; we were very conscientious about shaving from then on. Another incident that shocked us was when a recruit spit on the blacktop while we were in ranks. SH1 Bolen made him kneel, and lick the spittle off the blacktop. When standing in ranks, we had to keep our eyes looking straight forward. It was difficult to keep your eyes from wandering. Our company commander was always yelling at one person or another, for not looking straight ahead.

Since we were a group of mostly teenagers, with raging hormones, the company commander addressed a delicate subject: he said there was to be no masturbation, but he jokingly added, "When you take a shower, I don't care how fast you wash." Our uniforms had to be washed daily. We washed our clothes nightly with our scrub brushes, at the concrete tables by our barracks.

If a recruit received five demerits during the personnel inspection, not only were the demerits documented, but the recruit also had to march in the rear of the company, carrying not only his rifle, but also a bucket full of sand, for as long as the company commander directed. I remember a few occasions when one recruit wasn't complying with orders, and cleanliness, the company commander had him lay his rifle aside and carry two sand filled buckets.

The first week I was proud that I received no demerits during the morning personnel inspections. I never forgot something that happened my second week on Hell's Island.

While standing in ranks, the company commander had not yet gotten to me. I dropped my hat. It had accidentally slipped from my grasp. He inspected six people before he got to me. When he stood before me, he said, "Pick up your hat." It had dropped on the bottom of the headband, and blacktop had left black marks on the inside. He said, "I saw you drop your hat sorry, but that's five demerits." I had to carry one bucket of sand for an hour that morning. It was humiliating marching in the rear of the company, and the bucket was very heavy. I then understood why the guys that had to carry the buckets of sand would be wringing wet with perspiration after our marches.

The first two weeks we were taught the basics concerning the proper way to wear our uniforms. We wore dungarees, and all buttons had to remain buttoned, on shirts, and pants. The white hat had to set square on the head, with the bottom of the brim of the hat set "two fingers" above the eyebrows. With the hat on your head you lay your index finger, and second finger horizontally against your forehead and with the other hand adjusted your hat. Our boots (boon dockers) were spit-shined. Some guys had difficulty shining shoes; others seemed to be able to do it naturally. We could have no threads on our uniforms, we looked our shirts and pants over carefully, as they were new, and many threads were left over from the manufacturing process. These threads were called "Irish pennants," if one was found during the morning personnel inspection, we were awarded demerits.

Our pieces (rifles) had to be spotless. Although the pieces were not in shooting condition, no rust was permitted on the metal. We would clean them nightly with steel wool and polish them with metal polish.

We had much to learn in the area of military protocol; for instance, we would wear our hats anytime we were outside, but the second we stepped inside a building, we were to remove them. Some confusion existed about whether to wear, or remove the hat while under a covered walkway. The rule was that if there were four walls, the hat came off; otherwise, the hat was to remain on. Saluting was even more confusing; first the manner in which to salute was to bring the right arm up smartly with the forearm and wrist straight, the fingers formed in a straight line with the forearm, the index and second fingers touched the forehead above the right edge of the right eyebrow. The upper arm and the forearm formed a forty-five-degree angle; at the conclusion of the salute the right arm came down smartly to the right side. The next confusing matter was when not to salute. We were to salute only when we were "covered" (hat on), so unlike Army personnel, who render salutes inside buildings, without hats on, we did not.

Some of the basics of saluting were: accompany a salute with a cheerful, respectful greeting: "Good morning Sir," "Good evening Commander," etc.; Always come to attention; Don't bow your head, look directly at the officer as you salute; If both hands are occupied, and you're unable to salute, face the officer as though you were saluting him and greet him with "Good morning sir" and so on. Don't salute with pipe, cigar, or cigarette in your mouth. If you're accompanying a commissioned officer do not salute another officer until the officer with you salutes, then salute at the same time he does. Salute an officer even if his hands are engaged and he cannot return the salute. Enlisted men salute officers and junior officers salute senior officers when meeting, passing near, and addressing or being addressed. All salute (if not in formation) during honors to the flag or playing of the national anthem. When several officers are saluted, all shall return it. When over-taking a senior, the salute shall be given when abreast with the senior; state: "By your leave sir." Salute when reporting with a hat on. Guards salute all officers passing close by. There were many, many other situations we had to learn, such as saluting officers in cars, and other circumstances. We also had to learn when not to salute, such as when part of a work detail, in public conveyances when obviously inappropriate, and engaged in games or athletics. We soon learned that saluting was an important part of Navy life. As recruits we saluted enlisted persons such as the company commanders, as well as officers, and were told to salute anyone who was not a recruit.

One day during our second week on Hell's Island, we each were given two shots. That same day we assembled in a large room, and were given a number of written exams. None of us was feeling well because of the shots. If we'd known how important the exams were, it might have frightened us! The exam results would be used to determine if we'd be given additional school, and basically classify each person so it could be determined what his job might be in the Navy. The most important exam was a General Classification Test, or G.C.T., next was arithmetic, mechanical, and clerical, also a special test for sonar, and radio. The exams took all day.

We all were being paid sixty-four dollars a month. One hundred and twenty dollars of this was used for the initial issue of our uniforms. This was somewhat of shock to us that we had to buy our own uniforms. Our first two-month salary was used to pay for our uniforms.

After six months in the Navy we were to be given four to six dollars a month clothing allowance. In a letter that I wrote to my parents on 16 July, I asked to borrow two dollars. They sent me five.

While on Hell's Island, we were introduced to mess cooking; our company worked a full day at the chow hall, cleaning, and serving three meals. Not many liked this duty.

After two weeks on Hell's Island, the daily morning runs, inspections, marching, and rifle drills, our company moved to a barracks on the main side of the base. This barracks would remain our home until graduation. The move also brought about a change in our uniforms we now wore leggings, which wrapped around our lower legs, and laced up the side. We also wore a canvas webbed belt around our waist.

With the change of location and barracks, our training changed somewhat; we now had more mental work in the classroom. We were also told to start thinking about what job, or rating, we wanted in the Navy. I always thought that submarine duty would be exciting. I had gotten a high score on my sonar test, and sailors on submarine duty got an additional fifty dollars a month. The Sonarman description of duties read: Operate sonar detection equipment, underwater fire control equipment, and harbor defense detection equipment; perform operational and preventive maintenance on sonar and harbor defense detection equipment.

I was also interested in the Torpedoman's Mate job, whose duties read; perform upkeep and repair of torpedoes and ASW (antisubmarine warfare) ordnance other than mines and antisubmarine rockets. The Sonarman School was a ten-week school that I would attend after boot camp.

The whole company felt wonderful when we finally moved off Hell's Island. The island had a depressing effect on all of us; it had felt like being in a huge, cold, prison. Our new barracks were much nicer, made of wood instead of concrete, and better living conditions, nicer lockers and bunks. Our clothes had to be stored in specific locations in our lockers, and folded in accordance with *The Bluejackets' Manual*. Our lockers were to remain locked at all times, we wore the key to our locker around our neck on a chain, with the dog tags we'd been issued on the day we'd gotten our sea bags. The chain consisted of one large chain and one dog tag along with the key to our locker, and a smaller chain around the large chain, which contained an additional dog tag. My dog tags read: Little, J. S., (service number), USN, Bapt., and B. The "B" was my blood type, and the "Bapt." my religion preference of Baptist. We were expected to wear our dog tags at all times, when showering, and sleeping, they were not to be taken off. We were told a gruesome tale about the purpose of our dog tags. They are used in battle to identify sailors that had been killed. The dog tag on the smaller chain was removed and notched between the front upper, and front lower teeth, then a blow (or kick) was given to chin of the dead person, and the dog tag was wedged in the teeth for body identification. The person discovering the body kept the other removed dog tag. One disadvantage of wearing dog tags - they jingled and made noises when a person walked or moved. The marines, and soldiers, wear rubber noise eliminators on their dog tags. The dog tags would also entangle and pull the hair on your chest. This wasn't a big problem for me at this time, as I had little hair on my chest at the age of seventeen.

Everyone was expected to learn how to tie knots. Each of us had a length of line, (rope is called "line" in the Navy) tied at the end of our bunk. We were shown a different knot every few days, such as a square knot, single bolen, half hitch, clove hitches, an overhand knot, etc. I didn't do well tying knots, and struggled.

We were all anxious to discover what our job or rating would be in the Navy. One morning we were directed to a building where first and second class petty officers sat behind desks. These petty officers talked to us about the scores we'd gotten on our classification exams, and what job we might have in the Navy. I told the petty officer who talked to me about my choices of Sonarman and Torpedoman's Mate. He said that my GCT score of sixty-five was very good, and made me eligible for an A school, which was additional schooling after boot camp. I also told him that I was interested in submarine duty. He said that with my high scores I would also qualify for the Nuclear Weaponsman rating. He asked questions about my background. I explained that I had lived in the same community all my life. He seemed pleased about that, and said it should be easy for me to get a security clearance. He also said that I would have to have an evaluation by a psychiatrist.

A few days after this discussion, I was told one morning that I was to report to the base hospital for an evaluation for submarine duty. I was given directions about how to get to the hospital, and that afternoon I was excused to go to my appointment. I was anxious about what I would be asked, and it was also a time for anxiety, because I had not been off by myself for about four weeks. I made it to the hospital without mishap, saluting everyone I met. I was directed to a hallway with a bench outside an office door. At the appointed time an officer, a lieutenant commander, asked me to come into the office.

I went in and, stood at attention in front of the desk, as I had been instructed to. The officer said, "Please take a seat."

There were two chairs in front of his desk, one straight back, wooden chair, and a plush, well-stuffed leather chair. I selected the wooden chair, and sat down. He said, "Good, you selected the right chair." He then asked me if being in closed in spaces bothered me, and if I got along with my fellow recruits. I said "no" and "yes." He then said, "Okay, you're dismissed." I left amazed that the interview was so short.

Three days later, the company returned to the building where we talked to the petty officers about what we wanted to do in the Navy. I was in for a couple of surprises. First I was told I was going to be a Nuclear Weaponsman, and second, that I'd qualified for submarine duty. The petty officer briefing me said that very few men are selected to be a Nuclear Weaponsman, and only one in 300 qualifies for submarine duty. He said I would have to get a security clearance before I could go into the nuclear weapons field. He gave me a long application to fill out for my security clearance. He also said the FBI would be talking to my character references, and asking questions in my hometown. I was quite pleased with all this, and felt special about being selected for this type of duty, but I didn't have a clue what a Nuclear Weaponsman did in the Navy. I knew the job had something to do with atomic and H-bombs. *The Bluejackets' Manual* said that Nuclear Weaponsman duties are to maintain, adjust, repair, inspect, test, and package nuclear weapons, components, and associated equipment.

On 2 August, I wrote my parents telling them about my future job in the Navy. I asked for information I needed to fill out my security clearance application, such as birth dates, and birthplaces of all family members. I also had to list five character references, who had to be more than twenty-one years old, neither relatives, nor former employers and not connected with the military. I listed a high school teacher, neighbors and family friends such as Iva Milam, and Greta Stewart. I was thankful, as my parents suggested these references, and provided the information immediately. I was told to complete all the forms within ten days, and keep them until called for. If I were not called to bring the forms to the classification building, this would mean that I was not selected for a school requiring the security clearance. Luckily, about two weeks after the classification visit, the forms were asked for.

Recruit training continued six days a week on Sundays we had a day off although, everyone was required to attend a Sunday morning church service. We were told as long as we were in boot camp we would attend church services every Sunday morning. Some men in our company had never been to church services before. I had attended church all my life, so I enjoyed the Sunday mornings, and also the free time in the afternoons. I especially liked the church service singing of the Navy Hymn.

My parents, sister, and brother had taken a two-week vacation to Kansas. They wrote me often, and sent pictures, which I enjoyed very much.

A few of the men who started with Company 303 could never master the things we were taught in classes, the marching and rifle drills, and never seemed to be able to remain clean or neat. Instead of being set back, some of these individuals were assigned to a "remedial company." This company was for the "slow learners," or people that didn't stay clean or squared away. This company did not carry a company flag and didn't stay in the same recruit training area. They were billeted on Hell's Island, and were called the "Mickey Mouse Company." No one wanted to end up here. If after a few weeks a recruit didn't get out of Mickey Mouse Company, he would be given either an administrative or undesirable discharge.

After a month, one of the guys in our company tried to commit suicide by cutting his wrists. He did this late at night in the head. The watch found him and called for help. It awakened us all. The corpsmen came and took him to the hospital. We never heard from him again. A few guys got ill with one thing or another, if you stayed sick, and out of the company training for over a week, you were set back. We were all anxious to stay in good health. I remember one recruit, who was always in trouble, dirty, and constantly receiving demerits. He was finally assigned to the Mickey Mouse Company. He didn't seem to understand anything he was told. I remember a couple times, after the company commander had lost patience with him, he had to empty all of the clothes out of his locker, take them outside, put them on the ground, and the entire company marched back and forth stepping on his clothes. He then stayed up most the night washing his clothes for inspection by the company commander in the morning.

If someone had trouble folding clothes in the regulation way, or had trouble shining shoes, wearing the uniform properly, we would try to help each other out. In our battalion an honor company was to be selected. Company commanders, who graded companies on their marching skills, and the highest company average in classroom exams, would select this company. We worked hard to improve our marching skills, and sixteen count manual, as well as our classroom scores.

A guy in his late twenties seemed very ancient to seventeen and eighteen year olds. We called him "Pappy." My best friend was from Alabama, and another friend was from Montana. There wasn't much racial diversity in our company, only four black sailors in the eighty-man company. One recruit was an Indian from the southwest, he was called "chief" and he was always commenting on the abundance of water when we took showers.

The men who had positions of authority, such as company leader, and platoon leaders, wore a small version of a petty officer's eagle (crow), and chevrons on their left upper uniform sleeve. A peon such as me, was "slick-armed," or wore nothing on the left sleeve. Some of the petty officers had very poor leadership skills and liked to "Lord it" over us. They were not popular. The recruit company leader and his assistant slept in a separate section of the barracks. This separation had a tendency to erect a barrier of something akin to respect, or dislike between us. The company commander passed many of his orders to us through Company Leader, Stephen. He always emphasized that Stephen was in charge in his absence.

One evening, we were washing our clothes and tying the washed clothes on the clothesline with clothes stops. I might add company commanders planted the animosity we would feel toward the marines! They directed us to tie our pants on the clotheslines with the fly of the pants toward the Marine Corps Boot Camp, which was west across the freeway from the naval training center. Anyway on this evening, our company commander walked into our barracks. At this point in our training, this was unusual, because unless he had duty, which was every twelve days, he would leave the base on liberty daily at around 5:00 p.m. This was about 8:30 p.m., and he was extremely inebriated. One of the company commanders who had duty would come around our barracks at 10:00 p.m. every evening to ensure we were squared away and there were no problems. We were afraid our company commander would be in trouble if he were discovered in such a drunken condition. He was so intoxicated, he passed out. From what we could understand, he had a fight with his wife. We hid him behind some lockers, when the duty company commander arrived for his inspection. After the barracks inspection, we put him in a bunk, and kept an eye out for anyone that might be trouble. He apparently sobered up enough before we were awakened in the morning, to get up and leave. He showed up a little late in the morning, bleary, and red eyed. Not a word was ever said about the incident.

Much of our training revolved around a landlocked ship named *USS Recruit*, also called *USS Never Sail*. It was a ship that was built in the middle of a large blacktop square. It was four stories high, and had all the hatches, ladders (stairs), firefighting equipment and fittings of a Navy ship. We also learned that all vessels in the Navy are called ships, except for submarines, which are called boats. The *"USS"* stood for "United States Ship." The *USS Recruit* was our classroom for many days. We practiced the correct way to go aboard, and depart a Navy ship. We saluted the flag, which was flying from the fantail (rear of the ship), from 8:00 a.m. until evening colors, and would then request permission from the Officer of the Deck (OOD) to come aboard. We would reverse the procedure when leaving the ship, asking the OOD permission to leave the ship (while saluting), and then salute the flag prior to departure.

We were also shown the proper way to respond to General Quarters (GQ). We had to run on the ship in a clockwise direction, and go up ladders on the port side (left) and down ladders on the starboard side (right). This was to prevent traffic jams.

We were taught that Navy ships were made up of many, many spaces or compartments, which are all watertight. When hatches (doors) were dogged (closed with levers), the gaskets on these hatches made the compartments leak-proof. If all the compartments were closed, this increased the water integrity of the ship, and made the ship very difficult to sink. We also learned the unique way that compartments within a ship are numbered. This rather complicated system identified compartments within a specific section of the ship; the numbering system also told what the compartment was used for.

An example would be 3-75-4-M which meant that the compartment was on the third deck, it was 75 frames from the front (bow) of the ship, and was the second compartment outboard of the centerline of the ship, to the port side, and the space was used as an ammunition magazine. We had to identify each compartment of the *USS Recruit*, and were required to master this identification system.

We learned about firefighting equipment, such as one ½ inch, and two ½ inch fire hoses, applicators, spanners, and much more. We also learned how to use an Oxygen Breathing Apparatus (OBA), which allowed you to breathe, and fight fire in a smoke-filled compartment. We became familiar with the all-purpose water nozzle, a nozzle that could produce either water fog, or a solid stream of water. The nozzle could also be used with a four-foot applicator. We learned that fire was a fearful thing at sea, as often the nearest land is straight down, at the bottom of the ocean.

We were taught the basics of "ABC" warfare defense. ABC stood for Atomic, Biological, and Chemical warfare. We were given gas masks, taught how to wear them, and marched into a gas chamber. The gas chamber was flooded with tear gas we then were told to take our masks off. Our exposure to tear gas was very painful, my eyes hurt for hours afterwards.

One day we were taken by bus to a shooting range. We were given classes of introduction to the M-1 rifle, and the thirty-caliber carbine. We also were given classes on the forty-five-caliber pistol. After the safety lessons, and directions on how to follow instructions on a firing range, half the company took positions on the firing line; the other half of the company was taken 100 yards down range, and into a deep trench, with targets on rope pulleys that went up-and-down. The rope on the pulleys had cardboard squares attached to them that had removable paper targets with full-size bulls-eyes on them. Behind the targets when they were hoisted into position, was a high mound of dirt. Each recruit fired fifteen rounds, five shots at a time with a M-1 rifle. Each man in the trench was assigned a target, and after the firing line completed a five round volley, we would pull the targets down and examine where the bullets struck the target. We each had a long pole, with red rags tied on the top, and we would signal to the shooter where he hit the target. If the target was missed, we would wave the pole from side to side this was called "waving Maggie's drawers." Why it was called this I didn't learn. It was a lesson about what it's like to be under fire, being in the trench with the bullets whistling over our heads hitting the bank of dirt above us. I fired well when it was my turn to shoot; at least I didn't get Maggie's drawers waved from my target spotter. We also fired a Browning automatic rifle, called a "BAR," and the Thompson machine gun. The most thorough instruction was on the M-1 rifle. Some of the commands we were given on the firing range were "Ready on the right", "Ready on the left", and "Ready on the firing range." "Commence firing" and "Cease-fire" Anytime we heard the command "Silence," we were to immediately cease-fire. After shooting we had to collect all the spent cartridges of brass, and clean the M-1 rifles we'd fired. Some of the men had never fired a weapon (piece) before, and had to shoot extra times, until the company commander was satisfied with their performance.

The next day we marched to an area that had various gun mounts positioned on the blacktop. There were anti-aircraft guns, five-inch guns, and the huge sixteen-inch guns in a large steel turret. Many of large gun mounts onboard ships have a fire control system, consisting of radar, and electronic aiming and firing systems, however some gun mounts that were smaller in caliber were fired manually, and required a minimum of three people to operate: A "trainer" who turned a hand wheel that moved the gun barrel in a horizontal direction, and a "pointer" who turned a hand wheel that moved the gun barrel in a vertical direction. The third person was the "mount captain" who aimed and fired the gun.

We were also instructed in the mechanics required to fire the largest guns in the Navy, the sixteen-inch guns. It was a manual loading procedure. The projectile was placed in the gun breach, and then black powder, in bags, was placed behind the projectile prior to firing. We had to keep our mouths open to prevent our eardrums from breaking when the big guns fired. A gun this size can fire an explosive projectile weighing more than 2,000 pounds accurately up to twenty miles. Gun mounts of varying calibers are mounted on different ships for different purposes. Guns are arranged on a ship in a specific manner in batteries, and are used against specific targets. For example the "main battery" on a ship is the largest caliber gun on the ship and used mainly against ships and shore positions. There are also dual-purpose batteries that are of intermediate caliber used against either surface or air targets. There also are anti-aircraft batteries that are used against air targets.

We also had classes on torpedoes, mines, and depth charges. I paid close attention in these classes, as I looked forward to being on a submarine. Also, classes were given on rockets and guided missiles. Nothing was said about atomic bombs, or nuclear weapons.

One day five of us were assigned to clean a building in the main administration area of the base. The petty officers here treated us like "human beings". One petty officer taught me how to use a buffer (a large electric type, common in the Navy). The handle had to be pressed up-and-down to move back and forth, this took practice to master.

One Sunday we were given a few hours of freedom and were permitted to walk, instead of march, to the base Navy Exchange to do some shopping. We were permitted to buy soft drinks at a snack bar.

We all looked forward to our first day of liberty, which was to take place in the latter part of August on a Saturday. In a letter I wrote on 20 August, I told my parents I would have liberty from 11:00 a.m. to 9:00 p.m. The big day arrived; I met my mom, sister, brother Joe, and fiancée, Donna, at the visitor's gate. It was wonderful to relax off base, and I appreciated them driving to see me. It was about a 300-mile drive from Strathmore. We went to the San Diego Zoo, and had a picnic.

I wore my white uniform, and told them all of my experiences in boot camp. I returned to the base that afternoon, and bid them goodbye. Everyone talked about his liberty for days. The guys who didn't have visitors, toured downtown San Diego. Only two recruits were twenty-one they visited a few of the numerous San Diego bars. Pappy returned to the barracks a little drunk.

An important skill for a sailor to master is swimming. We had a complete week dedicated to swimming, in one of the largest swimming pools I'd ever seen. I enjoyed the classes, as I loved to swim. I felt sorry for the non-swimming recruits. The swim instructors had long poles (twelve feet long), and they would push the guys that couldn't swim away from the side of the pool into the deep end of the pool. We saw a lot of "near-drowning" men! The recruits that couldn't swim or swam poorly received intense swimming lessons. It amazed me that anyone would join the Navy, not knowing how to swim. We jumped off a high platform into the pool simulating a jump off the side of a sinking ship. The platform was about twenty feet high, we had to step off this twenty foot platform feet first with legs crossed, nose pinched with fingers, the other arm held straight into the air. We also were taught how to swim through burning oil on the surface of water. You had to swim underwater, and before surfacing, flay your hands around to make an opening in the oil burning on the surface, take a breath, then continue again underwater until you had to surface for another breath. We were taught how to make a life jacket out of our dungaree pants, shirts, and even white hat. We had to jump in the pool, remove our pants, tie a knot in each leg, slap the waist opening against the water trapping air inside, and use the pants as a water float. We did the same thing with shirts and hats. I was designated a "First Class Swimmer" because of my swimming skills. Only two other recruits out of the 160 recruits swimming that week qualified for this designation. We had to swim constantly for over an hour, and complete a few other tests. I was very proud of this achievement.

We were issued more clothes for our sea bag, a raincoat, pea coat, and more blues, also a few other odds and ends. One guy, who was with us throughout our training, was discharged about this time. He had trouble wetting his bed at night, and the doctors were unable to help. He was upset and embarrassed, he was a well-liked guy, and we were sorry to see him go.

Our preparation for the graduation ceremony intensified and our marching improved dramatically. One day all our blue and white jumpers (tops) were turned in so rate insignias could be sewn on the left sleeve. We were to be Seaman Apprentices (SA), Fireman Apprentices (FA), Constructionman Apprentices, Airman Apprentices (AA), Hospitalman Apprentices, Dentalman Apprentices, or Stewardsman Apprentices. We were identified as Apprentices or E-2's by two stripes on our left sleeve.

Some recruits such as recruit company leaders, and some sailors that had previous military training or experience would be promoted to Seaman (SN), (E-3), identified by three stripes upon graduation. Seaman Apprentices like me had to wait six months before being considered for Seaman. With the promotion to Seaman came a slight increase in pay of about eight dollars a month.

There are nine rates for enlisted men in the Navy, from E-1 to E-9, and a comparable number of ranks for officers, and four ranks for chief warrant officers. We struggled to memorize all the insignias, and rank identifications for not only the Navy, but also the other armed services. Each branch of the military identified enlisted men's rates, and officer's ranks, with different names, and insignia, to further complicate our attempts at memorization.

We had an intense final exam on the *USS Recruit*. One afternoon the company went throughout the landlocked ship, and was required to demonstrate the knots we had learned. We also had to demonstrate how to use the equipment that was positioned at various stations about the ship.

The last week prior to the graduation ceremony, we practiced the ceremony daily. This included the sixteen-count manual, a physical drill medley, which were a number of movements with our pieces. We were treated a little more kindly by our company commander. I was anxious for my parents to see the graduation, and anxious to get out of boot camp. Carrying the pieces around all the time, and daily exercises had put more weight on some of us, and gotten rid of fat on others.

An exciting event was the issuing of our "dummy orders." This was a piece of paper that told us where we were to be stationed following boot camp. My orders were to go to *USS Haven* (AH-12) stationed in Long Beach, California, then to U.S. Naval School, Nuclear Weaponsman's Course, Phase One, Naval Training Center Great Lakes, Illinois. I learned the *USS Haven* was a hospital ship. I was somewhat confused, because there was no mention of submarine school.

It is against Navy regulations for juniors to give seniors gifts, or vice versa, seniors to juniors, however, we took up a collection and bought Company Commander SH1 Bolen a butane cigarette lighter. We got a thank you card, which we all signed, and one day it was placed in his car, which was parked on the base. This was the morning of the day of our graduation.

The graduation took place Friday, 9 September 1960 at 1530 (3:30 p.m.). The entire ceremony took a little over an hour. From my position on the parade field I could see my mom and dad, my sister Linda, brother Joe, my fiancée, and Uncle Hubert and Aunt Kay. I was very pleased that they came to my graduation.

A few things in the graduation handout pamphlet[5] state in part:

> The Recruit Training Command takes pleasure in welcoming you to its weekly Recruit Brigade Review. At these Reviews, the Brigade is Officered entirely by recruits, none of whom have been in the Navy more than ten weeks. Their ability to directed drills and maneuvers included in the parade procedure is a tribute to American youth. To assist us in presenting the parade, the following is requested:
> 1. As a matter of courtesy, please remain seated until the band has passed in review.
> 2. Please do not pass in front of the podium (reviewing stand).
> 3. While the taking of pictures is permitted, please do not move onto the parade field for that purpose.
> 4. During the playing of the national anthem, foreign anthems, passing of the colors, and military honors, all persons please rise to their feet. Men with hats should place their hats over their hearts.
>
> In the course of today's ceremonies, the following presentations will be made; The American Spirit Honor Medal will be awarded to the outstanding recruit of the graduating companies. Honor man certificates to the Honor man of each graduating company, and the Brigade Award to the Honor Company of the week. We hope that you share our pride in the young men participating in Recruit Brigade Review.

Company 303 was an average company. We didn't receive any awards, but we all were very proud of ourselves, and our company, as we marched by the reviewing stand. We stood at attention during the playing of the national anthem, and we stood a little taller, and straighter, realizing that now we all were truly sailors in the United States Navy. After marching past the reviewing stand, we marched back to our barracks. While standing in front of the barracks, our company commander told us all congratulations, and thanks for the cigarette lighter we had given him. He then said that we were one of the best companies he had taken through boot camp. His voice cracked, and his eyes were moist. It was surprising to see him show such emotion, and it touched us all. After he said "fall out," we threw our hats into the air, and cheered. We were permitted to visit the guests that came to see the graduation, so after finding my hat, I left the barracks, and visited with my family for about an hour. They then left to return home.

That weekend we were to prepare our sea bags, and get ready to leave boot camp. Everyone was anxious to go home, we were to have fourteen days' leave, that is most of us, some sailors had to report directly to various "A schools" (additional training). I was one of the lucky ones; I was to have fourteen days leave, then report to the *USS Haven*. It's hard to describe the feelings we had after graduation, and throughout that weekend. We were full of pride, and the thrill of accomplishment and achievement. We had survived all the rigors of boot camp; we had become a disciplined unit as Company 303. We were proud to be in the service of our country, and we felt we were invincible. Combined with feelings of pride, were the sad thoughts of all the friendships we had made coming to an end. This was the first of many bittersweet partings that make up a Navy career, the end of friendships that are bound together by the completion of difficult tasks and hard jobs. We had helped each another, encouraging one another when the going got tough. The cutting of our hair, the humiliations, the times we all suffered for the mistakes of one of our number, served to teach us that we had to work together as a company, and that there was no place for "loners" in the Navy. We learned to work together as a team. Departure also meant anxiety about what the future held. We were not sure what the real Navy would be like.

That weekend we relaxed, and prepared for departure the only ones that worked, were the men that stood watch. The watches were stood twenty-four hours a day. Standing watch is a hallmark of the U.S. Navy, ever since the attack on Pearl Harbor when the ships were under-manned during that Sunday on 7 December 1941. From then on, all ships maintain a third of the crew onboard, and on watch. This standard was also maintained on shore stations. As I mentioned before, standing watch was serious business.

In the days to follow we turned in the unique boot camp items we'd used, our pieces, buckets and scrub brushes, webbed belts, clothes stops, and, items we were pleased to be rid of, two pairs of leggings. The khaki and white colored leggings had been difficult, and time-consuming to put on each morning. We would never again wear leggings unless on shore patrol, or assigned to a special flag detail. We packed the black ankle high lace up boots called "boon dockers" in our sea bags. We would be wearing our black dress shoes, on our departure. The heavy boots had been worn and shined daily, and they contributed to our fitness, because marching in the heavy boots had strengthened our legs.

Company Leader Stephen attempted to be overly friendly to everyone during this weekend, because since graduation, he was just another one of the crew. Most of the company didn't care for him. He had let his position go to his head, and rode roughshod over the rest of us. I remember he commented to me, he had not had many dealings with me, and I would probably go far in the Navy.

On Monday night we were not able to sleep, we whispered conversations long after lights-out, talking about what we would do on leave. We were to have a busy week, on Monday, and Tuesday the items I mentioned were turned back in, and orders were finalized. We were permitted to go anywhere on the base, except recruit training areas.

On the days we had to turn items back in, we would march, other than that, we could walk freely about the base. Looking at the group picture that was taken of Company 303, I can't remember names, but I remember the personalities of each person. Some were cheerful, some serious, or easy to get along with, or unfriendly etc. I ran across two of them in the future, but for the rest, our paths never crossed again.

Thursday, 15 September, we gathered at an area where buses were parked. We had purchased tickets for our various destinations the previous day. In the morning, we had marched to the chow hall, marching together for the last time. We carried sea bags to the departure area. Our company commander went around and shook everyone's hand, wishing each of us good luck. Everyone was saying goodbye, and I boarded the bus. I sat next to the same guy that I'd been with on the way to boot camp, Steven from Dinuba. We'd made it all the way through boot camp. We were pleased to leave together through the same gate we'd entered, what seemed like a lifetime ago. The bus was destined for Bakersfield; from there I would make further connections home. Our orders had been given to us just prior to boarding the bus. We had been paid the day before. With our orders we had been given our service record, medical and dental records, and pay records. These records were in a large manila envelope that was securely taped and was not to be opened until we reported to our new duty station, at which time the personnel office would open the envelope.

It was not a sad sight seeing the front gate of the San Diego Naval Training Center fade from view, as I looked through the rear window of the bus. In the late 1990's the San Diego Boot Camp was closed, and its service of giving birth to sailors of the U.S. Navy ended.

Chapter 2: Deck Apes and Pike Queens

After a 300-mile ride on the bus, I was back home. I was no longer the naive teenager I'd been two and a half months previously. I enjoyed wearing my uniform, and the pride I felt following graduation from boot camp remained with me. It was wonderful being with my family, and fiancée, away from the restrictions, and regulations of boot camp. My leave went by quickly, and fourteen days after I arrived home, it was time to report to my new duty station.

On 29 September, I boarded a bus at Tulare, California, headed for Long Beach, California, where I would report to the *USS Haven*. I was anxious to see my ship, and hoped I would do a good job. I arrived at the Long Beach bus station at 7:00 p.m. that evening. I got a taxi, and directed the driver to go to the Long Beach Naval Base. At the base gate, I showed the marine sentry my ID, and he waved the taxi through. The cab driver dropped me off in front of a large pier. Alongside the pier was a huge white ship, with large red crosses painted on the sides. I had practiced and practiced the proper way to go aboard a Navy ship. I lifted my sea bag on my shoulder, walked up the steep gangway. At the quarterdeck, I faced the aft section of the ship, saluted, then faced the petty officer standing there, and said, "Request permission to come aboard sir." He said, "Permission granted you don't salute the fantail after dark, because the flag is taken down at sunset." So much for doing things right, this was an embarrassing moment for me!

A sailor on the quarterdeck escorted me down a passageway and down two ladders to a berthing compartment. It was a large room with steel lockers for clothes' storage, and bunks, which were steel frames with canvas stretched between them. Mattresses were laid on top of the stretched canvas. There were more than 100 bunks, stacked four high, within the berthing compartment. I was directed to an empty bunk, given a mattress cover, and an empty locker in which to store my clothes. The petty officer on the quarterdeck had taken my orders after stamping, and signing them with my arrival time. He also took the manila envelope containing my records.

It was a weekend, so reveille wasn't held in the morning. I was told I could go on liberty if I wanted, but I was broke, and payday was Monday. I busied myself putting my uniforms in my new locker, and I asked questions of the sailors in the berthing compartment. One sailor showed me how to get to the chow hall, and I memorized the route, because it was confusing to go anywhere below decks, up and down ladders, I ate breakfast and then went straight back to the berthing compartment. I spent the weekend exploring the ship and sleeping.

Reveille was at 6:00 a.m. (0600) on Monday morning. I was told to be on the fantail (rear section of the ship) a little before 0730. I went to breakfast, which meant standing in line, going down a ladder to the mess line. You first got a metal tray with food compartments, and then moved along the mess line. On the mess line a mess cook stood at each food station dishing out food onto your tray, serving such things as bacon, potatoes, pancakes, etc. You could have scrambled eggs, or eggs cooked to your preference. After you filled your tray, you selected silverware, and then sat at tables that had seats for four men. The tables had a metal lip around the edges that would prevent food trays from sliding off the table, should the ship be at sea rolling on the waves. Positioned around the mess deck were metal boxes that held steel cans containing milk. The metal boxes were refrigerated to keep the milk cool. Plastic tubes extended down from the steel milk cans, you moved a handle, and holding your glass under the tube, were dispensed milk. There were also large pots that held coffee. After eating you placed your tray and silverware, and drinking glass, through a window identified as a scullery. Later on during my assignment to the *USS Haven* I was to become very familiar with the mess decks.

My first few days on the ship, I noticed there were men throughout the ship dressed in blue cotton shirts and pants, with white robes and slippers. I was to learn later that these were patients being treated on this floating hospital.

I made my way to the fantail following breakfast. A little before 0730 a group of about fifty sailors and I formed ranks, while a first class, and second class petty officer stood facing us. We were brought to attention, and roll call was held. Each man's name was called out, and each sailor responded either "here," or "present."

The second class petty officer then read aloud the "Plan of the Day," or as it was called the "POD." The plan of the day was published daily in the evening prior to the day it applied. It was published each day during the life of a Navy ship, or each day at a Navy shore station. All hands are expected to know the contents of, and be responsible for information published in the daily plan of the day. Typical information includes: the name of the commanding officer, executive officer, and name of the command duty officer of the day. A listing of the names of quarterdeck watches and times of watch, listing what section has duty, and what sections have liberty.

The time of sunrise, and sunset is listed, as well as a chronological listing of the events of the day, such as time liberty expires, times for morning muster, any special training events, medical inoculations, special visitors and officials, power outages, lunch time, knock off work time, liberty commencement time, etc. The POD also listed advancement information, such as rating tests, any information received from higher authority, the name of the evening movie, and many, many other topics. The POD is an important document onboard ship, and is signed and authenticated daily by the executive officer. After the POD was read, we remained in ranks until morning colors. Whistles blew, and we faced the rear of the ship while the flag was raised. We stood at attention, while those out of ranks saluted. The National Anthem was played on loudspeakers throughout the base. From the fantail (it was actually a helicopter landing platform) we could see many Navy ships alongside piers, conducting morning quarters. While the flag was being raised on the fantail, on the forecastle (front of the ship), the Union Jack was being raised. This flag is flown daily on commissioned Navy ships while in port, or at anchor.

After quarters we fell-out, and I was assigned to another sailor, who was to take me around while I "checked in." First we went to the personnel office, where I was given a check-in sheet that had spaces for each office to sign. Along with the check-in sheet were few copies of my orders. The sailor who was with me took me to the disbursing office where I got thirty-two dollars or two weeks pay. After turning in my pay records, we went to sickbay where I turned in my medical record. We then went to the Deck Department Office, and an officer, a lieutenant, who was the Division Officer of Deck Division, welcomed me. His title was First Lieutenant. He explained to me that I would be assigned to his division, and I would be working for a Boatswain's Mate Chief. He dismissed us, and my guide took me to the boatswain's locker, and I met the chief. He was definitely in charge. He said to continue checking in. He had a "commanding presence." We continued going to the library, chaplain's office, and other various offices.

The *USS Haven* was the naval hospital for Long Beach Naval Station. It was a full service hospital, even conducting surgeries. There were actually two commands combined on the ship. The ship's company had our own commanding officer, and a Navy doctor (captain) commanded the hospital portion of the ship. The *USS Haven* had seen action during Korea. She had been tied to the pier at Long Beach since 1957. She never got underway, although she was capable of it. Once a month she was untied from the pier, and repositioned, as far as I could tell this was so the sailors assigned to the *USS Haven* could get sea pay. The "AH" in AH-12 meant Auxiliary Hospital, and the twelve was her hull number. Other hospital ships in the Navy were named *Mercy*, *Hope*, and *Recluse*, and other names of compassion, and healing.

A few vital statistics about the *USS Haven*[6]:

> Her length was 520 feet, 71 feet 6 inches across her widest part (beam), her top speed was eighteen knots, and she was capable of accommodating 564 persons, including crew, hospital, and patients. *USS Haven*, an 11,141-ton hospital ship, was built in 1944 at Chester, Pennsylvania, as the U.S. Maritime Commission's C4-S-B2 freighter *Marine Hawk*. She was acquired by the Navy in June 1944 and commissioned, after conversion, in May 1945. *Haven* reached Pearl Harbor in July 1945 and carried patients back to San Francisco, arriving just before the Japanese surrender in August 1945. She then sailed to Nagasaki, Japan, where in September she received on board a group of Allied ex-prisoners of war, some of whom were suffering from the effects of the atomic blast. During the rest of 1945 *Haven* transported patients from various Pacific locations to San Francisco. During much of 1946 she supported the atomic bomb tests at Bikini Atoll, operating for part of this period as a transport for the evacuation of wounded personnel under the temporary designator APH-112. She resumed duties as a regular hospital ship (AH-12) in late 1946, carrying patients from the Western Pacific to California, but began inactivation in February 1947 and decommissioned at San Diego that July.

In September 1950, following the sinking in a collision of her Sister, *USS Benevolence* (AH-12) in August, *Haven* recommissioned to help respond to the great need for hospital ships during the Korean War. Ten days after commissioning she sailed from the west coast for Inchon, Korea, where she remained until advancing Chinese Communist forces forced her to move south in January 1951. For the next three years she supported U.S. forces in Korea, primarily from Pusan and Inchon, with maintenance periods in the United States between October 1951 and January 1952, between September 1952 and January 1953 when a helicopter flight deck was fitted aft, and between September 1953 and January 1954. With Korea in an uneasy state of truce, *Haven* sailed for French Indochina in September 1954 to support the withdrawal of French troops after the partitioning of the former colony. She delivered French personnel to Oran and Marseille before returning to Long Beach, California, in November 1954. After supporting the Pacific Fleet in California during 1955 and 1956, *Haven* decommissioned at Long Beach in June 1957. She remained there as a stationary floating hospital.

The sailor escorting me around during my check-in was not anxious to complete his job as an escort, because it was a much easier task than sweeping or swabbing the deck, or chipping, and painting. It was obvious to me that the shipboard environment was much more relaxed than boot camp. I noticed many sailors did not pay attention to their appearance. Most of the sailors wore dungarees that were wrinkled, and un-ironed! I vowed that I would always try to wear a pressed, and proper uniform, and spit-shined shoes. I was assigned to the deck division, which was responsible for the maintenance of the ship's hull, painting, rust prevention, maintaining the lines that held the ship to the pier, and attending to the thousand and one things that make up "housekeeping" on board ships. Sailors in the Deck Division were called sailors in the "deck force" A derogatory name for us was "Deck Apes," but we took pride in being the hardest workers on the ship. In addition to the jobs I was assigned in the deck force, I had duty section responsibilities. The ship was in four-section duty, which meant every fourth day I was required to remain onboard for twenty-four hours in the "duty section." One of the duties of the duty section was standing various watches. We in the Deck Division stood quarterdeck watches. Non-rated men (E-2/E-3's) such as I stood the quarterdeck watch with a petty office.

The watches on the quarterdeck were busy during the workday, and we had to be in the "uniform of the day," which during this time of year meant undress blues, blue wool uniforms without the white piping. During the workday off watch we wore dungarees. Daily at 1800 (6:00pm) everyone had to change from dungarees to the uniform of the day. I learned to pass the word with the ship's loudspeaker, and announce various events, and daily happenings throughout the ship. One important task was to watch for the captain of the ship arriving, and departing. When he arrived, the announcement would be "*Haven* arriving," preceded by ringing the ships bell four times, and when his foot hit the quarterdeck; the bell would be struck one time. When the commanding officer left the ship there would be four bells, "*Haven* departing," and one bell when his foot hit the pier. We also had to watch for the captain of the Medical Department. The bells would be the same, and the announcement "Hospital arriving" or "Hospital departing." I enjoyed learning the proper way to use the announcement system, or as it's called the, "1-MC". Often during a duty night I would be on a working party that set up chairs on the fantail under the helicopter-landing platform for the evening movie. Another duty task was the daily 8:00 a.m. (0800) flag raising each morning, of the National Flag, and the Union Jack.

The Union Jack was a blue flag with stars, and was hoisted up on the forecastle, as I explained previously. Each flag detail consisted of two sailors. At sundown the flags were taken down during the playing of the National Anthem. The days and duty nights were always busy sweeping, cleaning up, or performing various tasks. It was winter, so the weather was mostly wet and cold. I would try to go home every weekend that I could. If I had duty on Saturday, or Sunday it was impossible to go all the way to Strathmore, and back in one day. Sometimes I would try to get a "standby," which was someone who would take your duty so you could go on liberty, it usually cost five dollars.

When we left the ship on liberty, we had to be dressed in the liberty uniform. No one was permitted to wear civilian clothes on the ship, or base, other than officers. Prior to going on liberty we had to have our liberty card, and military identification (ID) card. The military ID card was kept in your billfold and on your person at all times. The section leader gave the liberty card to us; he was a first class petty officer.

In order to request your liberty card you had to be in the liberty uniform, and inspected by him before you could get the liberty card, and leave the ship. When you returned from liberty in the evening or morning, you returned your liberty card, by placing it in a box that was kept on the quarterdeck. My section leader was somewhat sadistic; he enjoyed giving us a hard time when we requested our liberty card. He would take his time inspecting haircuts, shoeshine, uniforms, and so on. He appeared to enjoy making the sailors that requested their liberty card from him uncomfortable. I always dreaded asking him for my liberty card. We were at his mercy, because he was a First Class Petty Officer Electrician, and if he wasn't in his workspace, the Electric Shop, you had to search for him. If he happened to be at chow or elsewhere, you had to wait for him. He also approved or disapproved standby requests.

Long Beach was what is called a "sailor town." There was a permanent carnival that was a tourist attraction called "the Pike." There were Ferris wheels, rides, carnival shows, carnival booths, and a huge roller coaster. The carnival covered several city blocks, and there were also a large number of bars, within the carnival complex. I was much too young to go in the bars. There were shady, rough characters that hung around the "pike." The women who frequented the pike were called "pike queens." There were also many homosexuals that frequented an area called "Lincoln Park"; my shipmates warned me about this. Some of the sailors would rob the homosexuals, to make extra money by rolling them! I was naive, and had lived a sheltered life in my small country community it was hard for me to come to terms with some of these harsh realities.

There were twenty-four-hour movie theaters in Long Beach; they showed one movie after another for the cost of fifty cents. Many sailors would sleep overnight in these theaters. We couldn't keep civilian clothes on the ship, so locker clubs were popular. For a monthly fee you could rent a locker, and have a place to change out of your uniform into civilian clothes or as they were called "civvies."

The middle of October saw me assigned to mess cooking for three months. I moved from the deck department berthing compartment to the mess cooks' berthing compartment and had to wear a white T-shirt, with white pants, and a white mess cook hat while working. I discovered I was to have a long workday. Each day, we had to be up in time to be on the mess deck by 5:00 a.m., and worked until 6:00 p.m., every fourth day I would get off at 2:00 p.m. It was hard work, sweeping, swabbing, cleaning, and also serving food. There was a little variety to the work, and I sometimes worked preparing salad, peeling vegetables, making soup and other various cooking tasks. The ship's baker had a sadistic streak. When he would bake rolls (all bread was made aboard the ship), and prepare a baking pan of about sixty rolls, in one roll he would put a cockroach he caught (cockroaches were thick on the ship.) This was somewhat like "roll Russian roulette!" I never ate a roll while on the *USS Haven* and warned my shipmates not to.

In a letter that I wrote on 25 November to my parents I was not happy. We could not have weekends off. I could not be home on Thanksgiving, but my parents called me, and also mailed a nice package full of candies and food. About this time I started filling out the seaman's correspondence course. If you completed a Navy wide correspondence course of twelve lessons, then you took a locally prepared exam, and if you passed both, after six months as a seaman apprentice, you became a seaman.

I was very tired each evening, during my mess cooking tour. I had decided to work as hard as I could while mess cooking. I soon enjoyed a reputation as a hard worker, and made friends with many of the cooks. I remember lifting a milk can and feeling a terrible pain my back. This may have been the beginning of my life long back troubles. I didn't go to sickbay, but continued working.

Mess cooking was distasteful work, but within mess cooking duties there was a job that was disliked above all others! That job was working in the scullery. The scullery was where all the cooking utensils, metal serving trays, glasses, coffee cups, and silverware were washed. It was hot, dirty work; the scullery was located on the mess deck. Sailors and patients would leave their trays, silverware and drinking glasses at the scullery window after eating meals. A trashcan was located under the window, food that was not eaten, apple cores, etc., was dumped into the can before placing the metal trays, with utensils at the window. The scullery workers would scrape off excess uneaten food, and then place the items to be washed in segmented trays. The filled trays would then be placed on a conveyer belt, which moved through a large machine that sprayed scalding hot water on the items, and thus cleaned and sterilized them. We who worked in the scullery had to wear rubber gloves, and rubber aprons to keep from being scalded by the hot water. As I said, this was a hot, dirty job, and we wore dungarees. The hot water was destructive to our shoes, so I had to take extra time daily to shine my shoes. The steam washing machine was very noisy. All the items that went through the machine had to be inspected for cleanliness, and if necessary re-cleaned.

Another reason the scullery job was disliked was because the scullery workers were usually the last ones to finish work in the evening after everyone else on the mess deck had knocked off work for the day. Another mess cook job was delivering trays of food to patients that were bed-ridden. We were not the only mess cooks on the ship; the officer's wardroom was separate from the enlisted mess decks. Stewards served the officers. I thought it was odd that there were no white stewards; they were all Filipino, or black sailors. The chief petty officers also had their own mess deck, so there were three different areas on the ships where meals were prepared and served.

Another sailor and I were assigned to the scullery for a few weeks. Everyone had to rotate through this undesirable job. I determined early in my Navy career that what I had been told in boot camp, about success in the Navy had a "ring of truth," and I had taken it to heart. This wise statement was, "if you can't take orders, and carry them out to the best of your ability, then you'd never be able to give orders". So I never grumbled (at least not too often), and tried to do all jobs as well as I could, in the hope that someday I would have more responsibility, along with more authority.

I had been working in the scullery for a couple of weeks. One morning, my co-worker was especially quiet. He was usually very talkative. When we started washing the morning dishes, he was told to deliver food trays to the hospital wards. He returned a short time later pale and shaking. He said, "I'm in big trouble!" He then quickly explained that the night before he had gone to Lincoln Park, looking for a homosexual to roll. He said a guy had suggested that they go to his apartment, so he went with him, planning to rob him. It should be explained at this point that sailors who preyed upon homosexuals seldom got in trouble. The Long Beach police "looked the other way," when a homosexual was robbed or attacked. My co-worker said after they arrived at the guy's apartment, they had a few drinks, and the guy started making advances, he got scared, pulled out a knife, stabbed the man in the stomach and ran out of the apartment. He said when he walked into one of the hospital wards a moment ago a patient in bed had started screaming at him; it was the guy he had stabbed! It was not very long before my co-worker was told to report to the captain. He was gone all day, and I worked in the scullery alone. That evening when I spoke to him, he was very relieved. He said it was discovered that the victim of the stabbing was a retired chief petty officer.

The chief was told by the captain if he insisted on pressing charges, because of Navy disapproval of his lifestyle, the captain would take action to have his retirement pension taken away. The chief said he would not press charges. The captain told the sailor, he couldn't go on liberty for a month. All of this wasn't quite legal, but that's how it was resolved. I don't think my scullery co-worker ever went "homosexual bashing" again.

I was invited to go once with sailors who planned to roll these people, but I declined. It was an illegal, dangerous pastime. I definitely felt it was wrong to harm or injure innocent people regardless how much their lifestyle was disliked.

One day a cook, who was a second class petty officer, invited me to go on liberty with him that night. He was heavily tattooed, and he was going into town to get another tattoo. He had befriended me on the mess deck, and he said that I should be tattooed like a "real sailor." We went to the pike, walked around for a while, and went to a coffee shop that was a *Haven* sailor's hangout. I went with him to the tattoo parlor planning to have my fiancée's name tattooed on my arm, but I didn't have enough money. That was the closest I ever came to getting a tattoo.

Around the first of December my fiancée and I began discussing marriage, as I was scheduled to go to Great Lakes to begin nuclear weapons school in March. I had missed her terribly during boot camp, and the times I was not able to travel home. I was almost eighteen, and she was fifteen, which meant that we would have to have parental consent to marry. Love also blinded me to many of the realities of life.

On one occasion on the *Haven*, the reality of the restrictions of liberty, such as freedom of speech we in the Navy lived under, was made very real to me. One evening I was in the ship's TV lounge, this was a room in which about forty people could watch television. November had been the presidential election; Kennedy had been elected over Nixon. Someone in the lounge was saying how he felt the country would be ruined now that a catholic was going to be president. This was a seaman talking, a second class petty officer in the back of the lounge said, "Watch your mouth, you could be put on report and go to court martial for saying disrespectful things about our Commander-in-Chief." The seaman immediately became quiet.

The first of December I was told I would have Christmas off, and could travel home. This privilege was being given to me because of my hard work on the mess decks. On 8 December, I turned eighteen years old. I went into Long Beach on liberty and treated myself to a movie.

My parents had sent me a very nice birthday package. In mid-December, I went into town and completed my Christmas shopping. I had asked my parents if they would give their consent for Donna and me to be married around the first of January. Our plan was to pay my fiancée's mother rent while Donna finished school. My pay was to be $150 a month, with a marriage allotment. Looking back at this it's painful to realize how shortsighted my plans as a teenager were. I got to spend Christmas with my parents, fiancée, and relatives. It was a wonderful Christmas, although cold and foggy.

Around the first of January I had a coat and sweater stolen from a small locker in my berthing space, in which I was allowed to keep a few civilian clothes. This privilege of a small locker with civilian clothes was illegal, but the chief of the division gave it to me because I was to become the leading seaman as soon as I put on my third stripe. A thief is despised in the Navy. All your possessions are accessible to everyone, so you must trust each another. A thief is viewed in almost the same light as a murderer. In the early Navy and most navies of the world, the penalty for theft onboard ships was death. This theft of my coat and sweater was disheartening.

On New Year's Eve 1961, I remember about midnight sitting in a Long Beach city bus waiting to head back to the ship. A girl suddenly came on the bus walking down the aisle, kissing all the sailors on the bus happy New Year. We were all amazed.

I was relieved from mess cooking the latter part of January. I enjoyed being back in Deck Division; I was being assigned positions of authority. Many new sailors reported aboard in December. I was becoming a senior non-rated sailor in deck department. I was being groomed as the Leading Seaman. We were doing a lot of hull side cleaning, and painting. The ship was painted white, which took much more work and upkeep than the standard Navy gray painted ships' hulls. We worked on boards suspended by lines hung from the railing, high over the water, called "a boatswain's chair". I was not too comfortable about heights, so was not very enthusiastic about side cleaning and painting the hull. We also kept an eye on the lines that tied the ship to the pier, and the camels or floats, which were buffers between the ship hull, and pilings of the pier.

We also made sure the rat guards on the ships mooring lines were kept in place. These were large flanges of metal placed on the lines to prevent rats from climbing up the mooring lines and boarding the ship. I truly enjoyed working in Deck Division, and was seriously considering becoming a Boatswain's Mate I was mastering knots, and the many job tasks required of a Boatswain's Mate.

Many of the petty officers on the *USS Haven* were completing their twenty-year Navy careers, and were veterans of World War II. One First Class Boatswain's Mate, we all highly respected, had been stationed on a couple of ships that had been sunk during the war. When he spoke of his experiences, everyone would be silent and listen carefully. One story was how his ship had been torpedoed, and rolled upside down prior to sinking. He was below decks and, to abandon ship, he had to go down in order to get topside and off the ship. We all had tremendous respect for these veterans of World War II and Korea, and considered them role models.

Money was scarce, and often I would hitchhike home, which was a trip of more than 200 miles. I had to get approval from my division officer by submitting a request chit asking for an out of bounds pass. Any sailor leaving his ship or duty station beyond a radius of fifty miles needed "out of bounds permission" that was so sailors could return to their ship or duty station quickly in the event of a recall. Any sailor caught more than fifty miles away from the ship without an out of bounds pass would be punished by the captain, or court martial. Hitchhiking, in those days was common, and in uniform, we seldom had any trouble catching a ride. The Navy permitted hitchhiking, and there was no formal policy against it.

We also could not leave the ship on liberty carrying anything. In order to take any personal items off the ship such as clothes, radio, etc., a property pass was required, and had to be shown at the quarterdeck. Division officers signed property passes.

Prior to one weekend, I looked up a guy who joined the Navy, the year before I had from my hometown. His name was Lloyd Van Antwerp, and he was stationed on the aircraft carrier *USS Hornet*, which was in Long Beach for a couple of weeks. That weekend we traveled home together, as he had his car at Long Beach. I had considered bringing my car to Long Beach, but it never worked out, which was probably best, as I would never have been able to afford it. I had a 1950 Plymouth, and a 1952 Chevrolet, my parents kept at their house.

There are honorable ceremonies in the Navy, but I never forgot one occasion when I participated in a ceremony of dishonor. A sailor in the deck division had gone to a court martial for stealing, and a few other charges. He had been found guilty and was to be taken off the ship, spend prison time at the Long Beach brig, and then be dishonorably discharged. When the time came for him to leave the ship, the Deck Division Chief directed all of deck department to man the rail near the quarterdeck.

We stood along the side rails of the ship at attention, in dungarees with white hats, as two master at arms brought the convicted sailor to the quarterdeck. He was carrying his sea bag and was being led off the ship to the pier and eventually to the brig. As he walked down the gangway the chief passed over the loudspeaker, "Deck Division, about face," so as the soon-to-be prisoner walked down the gangway and along the pier we all had our backs to him.

In February I learned I was scheduled to leave the ship on 3 March, and be in Great Lakes, Illinois on the tenth. I had a few days' leave. The wedding plans were to either go to Las Vegas, or have a small wedding at my parents' house.

One weekend, my mom, sister, fiancée, and brother Joe came to Long Beach for a day, and visited the ship. I enjoyed showing them the ship. My mom took a beautiful picture of the ship on that visit. Thirty-three years after that visit this same picture was greatly appreciated by ex-members of the *USS Haven* (see photograph page) who adopted it as the ship's reunion official photograph of the ship.

Before long it was almost time to leave the *Haven*. The last of February, I was assigned two hours' extra duties, for something I didn't do! We could smoke in only one area of our berthing space. One morning someone crushed a cigarette on the deck by my bunk. The chief gave me two hours extra duty, although he said I probably didn't do it (it was a brand of cigarette I didn't smoke), he said that he had to set an example! I felt this marred my effort to stay out of trouble, and felt this was an injustice, but I accepted the punishment.

After I had gotten off mess cooking, I looked forward to sleeping until 6:00 a.m. each morning, but the Deck Division Officer decided that Deck Division would get up at 5:30 every weekday morning and holy stone, and swab the *Haven*'s teak wooden quarterdeck area. Teak wooden decks were mostly on battleship main decks, unfortunately we had this one deck that no one had thought to holy stone, and swab every day, until our division officer thought of it. A holy stone was a piece of sandstone rubbed back and forth on the teal deck. After the stone was pushed back and forth, the deck was washed down with salt water, and the deck then took on a smooth almost white appearance. It was nicknamed a holy stone at some time in the Navy's past, perhaps because its use brought a sailor to his knees, thus it must be holy. So every morning at 5:30 a.m. before breakfast we worked on this deck.

I was enjoying being one of the senior non-rated sailors. I didn't look forward to leaving the *Haven*. I thought of canceling my school, and striking for Boatswain's Mate. One evening, while requesting my liberty card from my First Class Petty Officer Section Leader, I told him of my desire to stay on the *Haven*. He had gradually become more friendly to me, he launched into a long lecture about how fortunate I was to have the opportunity to attend an "A school," and I shouldn't even consider not going, and becoming a "deck ape." His intense attitude and serious talk impressed me. Before, it seemed like he was aloof and stern toward all who came to him to request their liberty card, and didn't discuss anything other than appearance and uniform discrepancies.

I got a blood test at sickbay in preparation for the wedding, and began to say farewell to all my friends. I began the checkout procedure, which was reverse of the check-in procedure six months before. Many people were shocked that I was leaving so soon, and many wished me good luck at A school. Most had never heard of Nuclear Weaponsman School. The evening before I left, I had mixed feelings; it was sad to leave the ship, yet I was anxious to learn what my school would be like. I had learned much, worked hard, and matured as a sailor.

I left the ship early in the morning with my sea bag on my shoulder. The Deck Division sailors were out scrubbing the quarterdeck; they all shouted "goodbye." I saluted the OOD, and the flag, walked down the gangway, onto the pier. I looked back at the *USS Haven* for the last time.

She remained in Long Beach as a stationary floating hospital until stricken from the Navy List in March 1967, In June of that year she was transferred to the Maritime Administration reserve fleet. C4 cargo ships of her type were then in demand for commercial service because of their relatively large size and engines-aft configuration, and *Haven* was sold by the Maritime Administration in 1968, lengthened by 145 ft., and converted into the chemical carrier *Clendenin*. Renamed *Alaskan* upon completion of conversion, she served the Union Carbide Corporation until scrapped in 1987.

Chapter 3: Learning about the "Bomb"

I spent five days on leave; the planned wedding did not take place. I was to be in Great Lakes, Illinois by midnight 8 March. I intended to catch a bus in the town of Tulare, about one hundred fifty miles north of Los Angeles, and go to the L.A. airport on the seventh. I stayed at my friends, Don and Shirley, the evening of the seventh; however I fell asleep on their couch, and missed my bus! Don and Shirley drove me to Los Angeles and I caught a later plane. This was to be my first airplane ride. The trip was eight hours long. When the plane landed in Chicago there was a snowstorm, which hampered ground transportation. I became worried about getting to the Navy base on time. I hailed a taxi at the airport, and after a long ride, and a cost of twenty dollars, a small fortune to me, almost one third of a month's salary, I made it to the base and checked in with fifteen minutes to spare.

After getting my orders stamped with the date and time I reported in. Leaving my records at the check-in window of the personnel office, I was directed to a brick barracks. There was two feet of snow on the ground and it was very cold. The inside reminded me of boot camp— same barracks, same bunks, same lockers.

The next day a few other sailors and I were given an exam to determine our level of knowledge in mathematics. Most of us qualified for night school. We had refresher courses in math and algebra all day, and classes at night from 1800 (6:00 p.m.) to 2100 (9:00 p.m.). We had homework that was due in the morning. I stayed up until after midnight struggling with the problems. At this point I wished I'd studied harder in high school.

The school course I was in was entitled: Nuclear Weaponsman Course Phase I, Electricity and Electronics. I noticed immediately that I was more experienced in the Navy than my classmates. I had just come from six months duty aboard ship, whereas, with the exception of one other sailor, they had all just graduated from boot camp. Most had just moved from the other side of the base, which was the Great Lakes Naval Recruit Training Command, the boot camp for the east coast.

I'd been in Great Lakes for a couple of days, when a snowstorm hit, and dumped an additional foot of snow on the ground. All of the students were assigned to working parties shoveling snow off the base roads and sidewalks. Living in the snow was a new experience for me, as I'd grown up in California where it never snowed. In a letter I wrote home shortly after arriving, I said I had a case of "homesickness," I missed my fiancée and parents, I was in a foreign environment, and I was depressed about being back in what appeared to be boot camp.

I continued remedial math classes, and was told that the school course would begin 20 March, and would last until 12 May. Every third day I stood a four-hour barracks fire watch, which included patrolling the barracks watching for fire hazards. Everything on the base was widely spread. The brick-built chow hall, exchange, movie theater, and classrooms were at considerable distances, which meant long walks from the barracks.

The weekend prior to starting school, I had a Saturday off, so a few of us decided to visit Chicago. We wore dress blues and pea coats, and it was very cold. We took a train to Chicago. The train station was close to the main gate of the base. On weekdays and on Sunday nights we had "Cinderella liberty," which meant your liberty expired at midnight, and you had to be through the main gate by 2400.

I remember six of us going to a large downtown Chicago drug store that had a café. We had hamburgers and French fries. What was most memorable was a very large (fat) security guard that roamed among the tables, and as soon as he saw you were finished eating he would order you out. He was very rude, and seemed to enjoy ordering sailors out of the café! After a little sightseeing, looking at the huge buildings, and girls bundled in fur coats, we went to a movie. After the movie we returned to the base

On Monday morning, in our first class we were told that only fifty percent of the sailors that began the course would graduate. This was not encouraging to me, as I wanted desperately to get back to the west coast, closer to my family and fiancée. If I flunked out of the course, it was doubtful that the Navy would spend the transfer money so I could get back to the west coast.

The course started with the subject "basic electricity." We had four hours of homework each evening. We didn't have much time for anything but study, study, and more studying. We were told that this eight-week course in electronics was the equivalent of a two-year college electronics course. We studied series circuits, parallel circuits, power supplies, transistors, and more. I sincerely wished I'd paid closer attention during my high school algebra classes.

In a letter I wrote 26 March, I asked my parents if I could borrow seven dollars, as I had sent my fiancée twelve dollars; this underscored the fact that it was fortunate that I had not gotten married.

I needed the money in order to buy some uniform items prior to a sea bag inspection, which was an inspection to insure we had all our required uniform items. Along with the homework, we had many personnel inspections, and sea bag inspections. The middle of March, I was promoted to Seaman (E-3), as I had passed all the requirements for promotion on the *USS Haven*. I also got a pay raise to seventy-four dollars a month. A sailor named George Holden and I were the only seaman in our class, all others were seaman apprentices.

Typically we would have class for an hour, or an hour and a half, and then take a ten-minute break. Most smoked, so we would stand out in the passageway. Petty officers would roam the passageway, and watch for any "horse play," or improper conduct. You were not permitted to lean against a wall, if you're caught leaning on the wall (bulkhead), you got two hours extra duty, which meant after classes you had to pick up trash, swab and sweep decks, or whatever menial job might be assigned to the violator. One chief petty officer, who was much younger-looking than the usual chief, was particularly diligent trying to find someone he could assign extra duty. He would patrol the passageways continually, and he had a reputation for being "hard-nosed." It was rumored that he was a dropout from Annapolis. He had apparently been a plebe at Annapolis for a couple of years, then, for some reason was not able to graduate and receive a commission as an ensign. He was made a chief petty officer. I guess he enjoyed taking out his frustrations on the younger students.

Our first class subject was D.C. or direct current electricity, how to measure voltage, ohms, current, and how to use ohmmeters, amp meters, and voltmeters. These were the subjects of the first four weeks. Weeks five and six were A.C. or alternating current electricity, and the last two weeks were learning about rotors, motors, and transistors, and the practical application of all we had been taught. Each week we had a final test. I was maintaining a grade of B plus.

After the fourth week of school, a group of us went into Chicago. We went to a movie that had just come out titled *"Ben Hur[7]"* starring Charlton Heston. Six of us walked around town, and through the east side of Chicago. We rented a couple of cheap hotel rooms, just to spend a night off base. We stayed overnight, some even sleeping on the floor.

In mid-April there was a failed invasion of Cuba by U.S. backed Cubans in an incident that became known as the *Bay of Pigs*. We wondered if America might invade Cuba at some point in the future.

The weekend prior to beginning AC electricity, a group of us visited Milwaukee; the people of Milwaukee were much friendlier toward sailors than Chicagoans.

There were thirty-four people who started our class, two flunked out. Not all sailors in the class were striking for Nuclear Weaponsman. Some students were striking for Fire Control Technician (FT); they maintained and used radar, and weapons firing systems.

I was assigned as the class master at arms, as I was one of the only seaman in class. I was expected to maintain order when the instructor was out of class, and also march the class to and from the barracks, and chow hall.

One morning the last week of April, while in class, a chief petty officer walked into our classroom, and said he had announcement. He said, "All of you striking for Nuclear Weaponsman are now striking for Gunner's Mate Technician," he said the reason was for added security. Our rating badge (a device wore on the left upper sleeve indicating what your job is in the Navy) would be changed to crossed cannons, or the Gunner's Mate insignia. Our old insignia had been a bomb encircled by two electrons. We were all shocked by this announcement, and somewhat dismayed, because the Nuclear Weaponsman (NW) rating badge was distinctive, and set us apart from the common sailor. The chief said he didn't know the specific reason behind the change, other than it was to keep the Nuclear Weaponsman rating secret. Later on in New Mexico we were to learn some reasons behind the change. There had been a number of kidnappings of nuclear weaponsmen by the Soviets. Sailors had disappeared in Mexico, and in Japan. Also it was a sore point with the Japanese when they saw the rating badge of a Nuclear Weaponsman, because of Hiroshima and Nagasaki. Apparently the victims of the kidnaps were never heard from again, but they were traced to Russia and Mexico where their trail ended. So we, as potential kidnap, and torture victims, should have appreciated the anonymity of the rating badge. No one could distinguish a Nuclear Weaponsman from a common Gunner's Mate.

The last part of April, a friend, Jerry Hecko, got into trouble. Anytime you left your base you had to remain within a fifty-mile radius of the base, as I described previously, anything further than that required an "out of bounds" pass. Jerry traveled home to Indiana one weekend, and was stranded by a snowstorm. He did not have an out of bounds pass. He was set back in class two weeks.

The last weeks of school were very busy. The class material was much more difficult, and my additional duties as class master at arms kept me busy. I was nervous about passing the course.

I was anxious to get out of Great Lakes (the climate was not to my liking), and the base was too much like boot camp. On 12 May 1961, I passed my final exam, and had a class standing six of twenty-two.

We were all to leave for New Mexico on 14 May. I was ecstatic about passing; we spent the weekend, and Monday preparing to leave for New Mexico. We were to travel by train. There were twenty-two of us. George Holden and I were assigned co-leaders of the class. We were given all of the service records, and orders were written stating George and I were in charge.

We boarded a bus Tuesday morning, which took us to the train station. We boarded the train, and were directed to the last car. It was a Pullman sleeper with beds; the conductor said we must remain in this car except when we had meals in the dining car. We pulled out of Chicago Station at 10:00 a.m. I felt no remorse, and I was happy to be leaving Chicago. We did not know what to expect in New Mexico. I had visited Albuquerque in the past with my parents on summer vacations.

It was an adventurous trip. George and I as class leaders had all the meal tickets, which were used in the dining car. We gave the meal tickets out at meal times. The train food was good, and the scenery was interesting as the train moved across the country. Many sailors played card games of blackjack, or "twenty-one". I played a little, but preferred watching the sights pass by the train window.

The train had a long stop of four hours in Kansas City, from 1800 (6:00 p.m.) to 2200 (10:00 p.m.), on Wednesday. All passengers had to disembark, and enter the train station. One of our classmates was twenty-two years old. The rest of us were less than twenty-one. The twenty-two-year-old left the train station with six others, and returned thirty minutes later. All had bottles of whiskey, or vodka hidden under their jumpers (uniform tops). At 2130 (9:30 p.m.), we were told to re-enter the boarding area of the station. Suddenly four policemen appeared, and told us to line up. They began to search us, patting everyone down. The policemen took all the bottles of liquor. The policemen were smiling and good-natured. George Holden and I were afraid that since we were in charge, we would be held accountable. The police directed us to get on the train, and wished us a good trip. They kept the bottles, and looking back at the incident, they acted like this was a regular occurrence. These appropriated bottles probably ended up in their liquor cabinets. We all boarded the train frightened and somewhat angry about being searched. After the train had left the station, it was discovered that one guy had managed to smuggle one bottle on the train, so we felt a little better outsmarting the police. It had been humiliating to be searched in public.

Our trip continued, and the train arrived in Albuquerque 1700 (5:00 p.m.) on Friday afternoon. Compared to Chicago it was hot! The temperature was in the 80s. George was disgusted with the conduct of the class during the trip, and mumbled, "We should let you guys find your own way to the base." We called the base, and shortly a bus arrived at the train station, and after a fifteen-minute ride we were at Sandia Base. It was an Army base, we were to discover that the services took turns managing the base for two-year periods; during this time frame it was the Army's turn.

The bus stopped at the Navy barracks, which was across the street from the base movie theater. We off-loaded our sea bags and a petty officer took our orders, and records, and assigned us rooms. We were in for a pleasant surprise. The rooms were like college dorms. It was a far cry from the Great Lakes barracks. The rooms were huge. We had big single beds, and huge clothes lockers. We were told we had liberty until Monday morning. After we'd gotten somewhat settled, most of the class went to the exchange cafeteria. It was then we discovered that if you were eighteen years old you could drink beer on the base. We also learned that civilian clothes were permitted to be worn when we were off duty. We were very excited about all this news, along with the rumors that civilians in Albuquerque liked sailors. Chicago and New Mexico were as different as night and day. I enjoyed the warm weather, and relaxed atmosphere. The barracks was located right next to the chow hall. It was much like being in college, instead of the Navy. I think I appreciated being in this school environment much more than my classmates. I had been in the Navy longer, and experienced shipboard life, all of them, except George, had come directly out of boot camp into the school at Great Lakes. We were encouraged to wear civilian clothes off base. I had a problem. I had no civilian clothes. I wrote my parents asking them to mail me some of my civilian clothes.

Classes didn't start until 2 June, so for two weeks we did very little other than having pictures taken for our security badges, and work occasionally on different work details. One day we worked in the chow hall, other days we picked up trash, or did yard work about the base. About this time I was given news that my mom and dad were expecting an addition to our family. The baby was expected in September.

There were six of us assigned to each room. A sailor who had graduated left his television in our room, so we had a TV to entertain us. One roommate was from New Jersey, one from Texas; George Holden was from Maine, two others, and me from California.

Many in the class hung out at an Albuquerque coffee shop called "The Purple Turk." It was located across from the University of New Mexico College. "Beatniks" were fashionable then, and The Purple Turk featured espresso coffee, poet readings, and ballad singers. The weather was perfect, except for infrequent winds, and the chilly nights. During this time frame, I began doing the correspondence course, Military Requirements for Third Class Petty Officer.

A letter dated 22 May 1961, by Captain P.R. Belcher, who was the Commanding Officer of the U.S. Navy Administration Unit, was sent to my parents, it said:

> As your son's Commanding Officer, I'm writing to explain why he has been sent here to Sandia base, Albuquerque, and to express my interest in his welfare.
>
> This command is a part of the Defense Atomic Support Agency, a joint command, which was established to support the Army, Navy and Air Force in the field of advanced weapons.
>
> Your son is here to receive a technical course in advanced weapons, to prepare him for the on-job training onboard ship or at a Navy shore station as a Gunner's Mate Technician. The duration of this course is about eleven weeks.
>
> It is greatly to his credit that he has been selected for this training and I hope he will successfully complete the course. I also hope he will enjoy his stay here at Albuquerque.
>
> In case he has forgotten to furnish you his current mailing address, all mail should be addressed to him at: U.S. Naval Administrative Unit, Sandia Base, Albuquerque, New Mexico. I assure you that I am interested in all aspects of the welfare of personnel attached to my command. If I can be of assistance please feel free to contact me.

My mother answered the letter, expressing appreciation for the captain's interest. There were differences in military protocol between the Navy, Air Force, and Army that sometimes caused friction. An example, sailors always remove hats when entering, and while inside a building, and we don't salute with a hat off. The Air Force and Army saluted indoors, and hatless. We were told, if in doubt salute, in order to "keep the peace".

On 2 June 1961, I entered a world different from any I'd imagined, the world of nuclear weapons. We were directed to report to a large fenced compound five blocks from our barracks. We all had been issued badges that had our picture, birth date, physical description, signature, and a distinctive Sandia Base decal. This badge was given to an armed civilian guard at the gate guardhouse. The guard would examine the badge, compare badge pictures with faces, then obtain an identical badge from a storage rack, which had a clip for fastening on clothes, and he would give this badge to the person requesting entry. The badge he took from the person was then placed in a storage rack. The badge issued was to be worn in view on the upper left area of your shirt at all times when within the fenced complex. When we exited the compound, we returned the badge with the clip to the guard, and he would return our "outside badge". We were warned to take extra care not to lose this badge, and were forbidden to remove this badge from the base, and were not to take it with us while on liberty.

I was assigned as a student in Navy Nuclear Weaponsman Course, Class Seventy-three. Our courses were grouped in specific "phases". We had ten phases to complete. Each phase had a final exam that had to be passed in order to graduate. One incentive we had for doing well in class was the choice of assignment after graduation for those who graduated at the top of the class. We were told that eighty percent of a graduating class was assigned to sea duty on aircraft carriers. Students who excelled at the top twenty percent got assignments other than sea duty, such as shore duty, and overseas shore duty. I was hopeful that I would be assigned to the west coast near my family.

The topics of our first class were security, the method of classifying classified material, and what was expected of us, as far as the safeguarding of the nation's classified information. It was explained to us why our rating badges (which we wouldn't get until graduation), had been changed. As I've explained previously this change was made so we would blend in with other sailors in the Navy.

We were also told that Juarez, Mexico, which was a one-day trip to the south, was "off limits". Apparently a sailor attending school had visited Juarez, and disappeared. It was thought that the soviets had him. We were cautioned about telling anyone off base that we were in nuclear weapons school. We were to report anyone who questioned us, or asked inappropriate questions. There were known Russian spies in Albuquerque, and Los Alamos who were anxious to obtain information about nuclear weapons.

We had notebooks, and took notes during our classes, but could not remove the notebooks from the class area. Our notes were classified so they remained locked in safes when not in use. The levels of classification beginning from the lowest to the highest were: "For Official Use Only," "Confidential," "Secret" and "Top Secret". A description of each level was as follows; For Official Use Only: Just as the title implies, this information was for officials with a "need to know". Confidential: Information if improperly revealed could be prejudicial to the defense of the nation. Secret: Information if improperly revealed could cause serious damage to the defense of the nation. Top Secret: Information if improperly revealed could cause grave damage to the defense of the nation. Nuclear weapons information is further protected by a special statute called "The Atomic Energy Act of 1954", which placed all nuclear weapons information in a category called "Restricted Data," or "Formerly Restricted Data". These categories prohibited the release of nuclear weapons information to any foreign national, or our allies. We were told just because a person has a security clearance doesn't mean he can have access to any classified material. He or she had to have a "need to know"; an example might be a Nuclear Weaponsman could not be given a classified document about radio transmission codes, unless he or she could establish a "need to know." The covers of classified documents, or cover sheets are color-coded to indicate classification. Confidential: yellow, Secret: blue, and Top Secret: red. Most of the material we were to be taught was Secret, Restricted Data. Each of our classes began in the same manner, the instructor would tell us what level of classification the information was that he was about to discuss.

We were told the penalty for unauthorized disclosure of classified material was what was called the "20/20 punishment". This meant twenty years in prison, and $20,000 fine. If caught giving information to the Russians, the punishment could be life in prison, or death.

Our first classes were physics, covering atoms, neutrons, protons, electrons, and the mechanics of atomic fission. We also learned the history of the development of nuclear weapons. New Mexico is considered the birthplace of the atomic age. The Manhattan Project, which was partially based in Los Alamos, New Mexico, was north of Albuquerque. The first nuclear detonation was at Alamogordo, south of Albuquerque. We learned what materials were used in atomic bombs, the most basic material being enriched uranium. We learned about non-sustaining chain reactions, sustaining chain reactions, and multiplying chain reactions. We studied equations, the most basic being Einstein's formula $E=MC^2$. We were taught the two primary methods of creating a nuclear explosion, or fission reaction: 1. Rapidly bringing together two non critical masses of radioactive material to form a critical mass or as this method is called a "gun type" weapon. 2. Compressing a non critical mass to form a critical mass, or as this method is called an "implosion type" weapon. We were also taught the basics of "H bombs" or thermonuclear weapons. We learned that the thermonuclear process was one of fusion. In order to have fusion you have to intense heat. Fission is a method used to create intense heat. So an H-bomb was actually two bombs in one, a primary or fission bomb, as a "spark plug" and secondary material to cause fusion. We studied the health hazards of radiation. We had all grown up on a diet of horror movies that featured monsters that had been created because of the atomic bombs, and the effects of radiation. We discovered that the public image of radiation was much overstated, and unrealistic.

The types of radiation we studied were alpha, beta, gamma, and x-ray. We learned the methods of protection from radiation, and the effects of radiation on the human body. I recall one story of a worker in Los Alamos in the 1950s, who was carrying two pieces of uranium that he accidentally brought together in a laboratory. There was a blue flash, and his body absorbed a huge dose of radiation. His condition was critical, and he was the subject of intense medical study. Unfortunately he only survived a few weeks. This Los Alamos worker, and the Japanese of Nagasaki, and Hiroshima were the only human subjects who had been exposed to radiation studied by the medical profession. Exposure limits were much higher in the 50s and 60s. Many military people that were exposed to nuclear detonations in the 50s, and 60s, now in the twenty-first century are experiencing medical problems.

My classmates and I studied the types of nuclear detonations, and their effects upon targets, and people. The different types of nuclear bursts are: airburst, surface-burst, subsurface, and underwater bursts. An airburst is described as a nuclear detonation with a fireball created by the explosion that does not touch the earth's surface at its maximum expansion. A surface burst occurs when the fireball touches the surface of the earth, or water.

A subsurface or underwater burst occurs when the center of the fireball is below the surface of the earth or water. A blinding white flash characterizes a nuclear detonation. A nuclear explosion might be compared to what would happen if the sun in miniature were to suddenly appear on the earth's surface momentarily. The thermal blast causes blindness, and intense heat burns, and melts earthly material. A nuclear explosion on, or above the surface of the earth creates immense overpressures, which spread out from the center of the explosion. As the heat and shock wave expand outward, air rushes back toward the void created by the explosion. This is called a negative phase. An example of the negative phase; the effect that is seen in pictures of houses being blown away from an atomic blast, the siding, roof, and material of the house can be seen blowing away from the blast, then reversing and going inward toward the blast center. This inward movement is cooler air rushing back toward the center of the explosion. This double blast effect is one reason for the devastation of a nuclear blast, which is much more destructive than that of a conventional explosive blast. This is also reason for the familiar mushroom cloud. Tons, upon tons of dirt, rock, and material are sucked upward toward the stratosphere as the fireball rises and diminishes. Just as hot air rises, so does the very hot fireball. When all the material sucked up through the stem created by the rising fireball hits the colder, thinner, upper atmosphere, it spreads out and begins its long fall back to earth; thus the familiar mushroom shape is created. This material falling back to earth is also radioactive. The blast from a nuclear detonation causes the most damage; damage is also caused by intense thermal heat. At the instant of a nuclear detonation there's a pulse of radiation, mostly gamma, x-ray, and neutrons, (a small amount of beta), this radiation is capable of penetrating many feet of shielding material such as dirt, metal, etc. There are usually two major pulses of radiation that expand outward from ground zero (or center of the explosion). The radiation strength levels decrease as the distance increases from ground zero. The bomb material and much of the dirt dust, and rocks that fall back to earth are called "fallout." This material is a radiation hazard, and is mostly alpha and beta radiation. This material must be inhaled, ingested, or absorbed through cuts in the skin to be harmful, or deadly.

An air burst detonation is the most destructive of all the nuclear blasts. One effect that causes this great amount of destruction is the creation of the phenomenon called a precursor. This is created when the shock wave bounces off the surface of the earth, and combines with the expanding shock as it moves across the surface of the earth. A precursor as it moves across and through a target has double the destructive force of a single shock wave. A surface burst cannot create a precursor shock wave, and it has diminished explosive power since the fireball touches the surface of the earth or water. In a surface burst there is, however, much more fallout because the fireball touches the ground and irradiates more material. The subsurface bursts and the surface bursts cause huge craters on the surface of the earth, and in water, they create huge radioactive base surges, or tidal waves.

We learned that the size of a nuclear detonation is measured by comparison to the power, or size of an explosion that occurs when 1,000 tons, or two million pounds, of TNT explosives explode. This unit of measure is called a kiloton. Therefore, one kiloton equals 1000 tons of TNT. Another measurement is a megaton; a megaton is 1,000 kilotons, or an explosion equal to two billion pounds of TNT. A weapon's explosive power is expressed either in kilotons or megatons. It has become standard to compare weapon explosive power to the weapon that was dropped on Hiroshima, which was twenty kilotons, or the equivalent of forty million pounds of TNT. An example of the use of the standard might be a statement such as: "The weapon detonated was three times the size of the weapon detonated over Hiroshima," which would be twenty kilotons times three equals sixty kilotons. The destructive force of nuclear weapons was mind boggling to us! A one-megaton blast would have a fireball many miles across, and the radius of destruction would extend more than one hundred miles. We were in awe of the destructive power of these weapons; deaths and injuries were not spoken of in the hundreds or thousands, but in millions. This had the effect of de-sensitizing a person. We did not question the morality or justness of nuclear weapons. Our instructors stated the position that it was hoped these weapons would never be used, but if they were we had to make sure they worked, because it was either us or them, "them" being the Soviet Union. In 1961 the feeling was, as I've said before, that nuclear war was only a matter of time, we as a generation didn't expect to reach middle, or old age!

We learned there was a definite "chain of command" in the world of nuclear weapons. The Atomic Energy Commission (AEC), later to be renamed the Department of Energy (DOE), maintained ownership of all radioactive material within the nation. The Army, Navy, and Air Force owned and developed delivery systems, and those components other than the warhead, which was owned by AEC. The final authority on matters of nuclear weapons was the AEC.

The Defense Atomic Support Agency (DASA), later to be renamed Defense Nuclear Agency, headquartered in Washington, D.C., was the liaison agency between AEC and the armed services.

We were told the history of nuclear weapons' development. One interesting story we were told was of Julius and Ethel Rosenberg, who were tried in 1951 and executed in 1953 for spying for the Soviet Union. They provided the Russians with an explosive system called the "lens system," which created an "implosion" force during a nuclear weapon detonation cycle.

Explosives were arranged in a sphere so the force of the explosion was directed inward, versus outward, and thus causing a "squeeze" on the active material within the sphere, and ultimately causing a multiplying chain reaction, or blinding white flash, and a nuclear detonation.

One of the foremost considerations during the development of nuclear weapons was safety. The weapons had to be safe to maintain, handle, and transport, and not detonate until the desired time over a target. Nuclear weapons contain conventional explosives of varying sensitivity. This sensitivity is determined in a laboratory by a drop test. Explosive sensitivity is expressed in inches. For example, TDX3 explosive has a sensitivity of twenty-four inches. This meant if TDX3 were dropped from a height of twenty-four inches, it would detonate fifty percent of the time.

Detonators were devices of high sensitivity that set off explosives of lower sensitivity. We learned that explosives are also classed by the speed that they explode. Class A explosives are high explosives, class B explosives are slower burning explosives, class C explosives are pyrotechnics, fireworks, etc. One method of maintaining safety was to store highly sensitive detonators separate from a warhead, and install them just prior to the bombs' use. Another safety consideration was to keep the active material or nuclear component separate, or out of position until just prior to a nuclear detonation. One example is an In-Flight Insertion Device (IFI), which I'll discuss later on. Other safety features include keeping power supplies, and batteries separate until preparation of weapons for use.

Thinking back about the sequence of classes, I realized they were structured purposely. First we were told of the immense destructive power of nuclear weapons, then to ease our fears, and possible concerns, we were told of the many safety devices incorporated in weapons that made them safe to work on and handle.

We were told of the many different methods of delivering nuclear weapons, by aircraft carried both internally and externally. There were missiles, or rockets, which were delivered from silos, and launchers, and aircraft. They were launched from submarines such as torpedoes, Regulus missiles, and Polaris missiles. They were fired by artillery guns, shipboard sixteen-inch guns, and as depth charges, and there were also atomic demolitions carried in backpacks.

Something that had to be taken into account when a nuclear weapon was delivered by airplane was the survival of the pilot and aircraft. Different methods of delivery were developed to ensure that the plane and pilot survived the powerful detonation of an atomic bomb. One method called a loft delivery, involved the pilot flying toward the target and near the target placing the aircraft in the steep climb and during the climb, releasing (or lofting) the bomb to the target so the bomb remained in the air long enough to give the pilot time to turn and immediately fly away. This put enough distance between the detonation and his plane to ensure his survival. Another method was to have a rocket, or jet assist on the bomb so the bomb traveled away from the plane toward the target, which permitted the pilot to put distance between him and the bomb prior to detonation.

We were introduced to fusing, and firing components. Most nuclear weapons, we learned, used electricity for fusing, firing, and detonation. The fusing and safety devices included timers, altimeters, velocity sensing devices, hydrostats, impact crystals, and radars, just to name a few.

We had to learn a completely new language. For instance all nuclear weapons have a mark number, such as Mark 7, Mark 27, Mark 28, etc. The mark numbers were assigned as weapons were developed. Many weapons had nicknames such as Mark 90 depth bomb: "Betty," Mark 30.5 rocket: "Boar," Mark 101: "Lulu," Mark 105: "Hot Point," and so on.

There were three sections of a bomb, a nose, warhead, and tail. The right and left sides of a bomb were determined by standing at the rear of the bomb looking toward the nose, the right and left side corresponding to the person's right and left side. Bombs, and missiles, had "station numbers," used for location identification. For example, "station number twelve", meant exactly twelve inches from the front of the bomb or missile nose, "station number 42.5"= 42 ½ inches, etc. A letter or combination of letters and numbers identified large sections of bombs.

Examples follow, MC-290, MC stood for Major Component, N-43, N stood for Nose, SC-43, SC stood for Shape Component, W28, W stood for Warhead, F-62, and F stood for a Fuze component. We had a maze of terms, and a number of designations to learn. Anything that was used to handle, or test weapons, and weapon parts, had either a "T" or "H" number, the "T" standing for test equipment, the "H" standing for handling equipment. These pieces of equipment had undergone extensive development and research, and had to be approved, or "blessed" by AEC and the services before they could be used on a weapon. An example is an H-12 hand truck that was used for handling the F-7 Fuze, and other components. This hand truck cost as much as two Cadillac's in 1961, which was more than $10,000. Many items of Test equipment, or "T" gear were used to insure that the electric circuitry of bomb's parts, and that bombs themselves were in working condition.

We were told that nuclear weapons have a specific life span of seven phases, beginning with Concept, then Development, Manufacturing, Quality Assurance and Testing, Stockpile, Modification, and finally Retirement.

When a nuclear weapon system is active it is considered to be "in the stockpile." There are different classes of weapons used for different purposes. The "real ones" are called "War Reserves". Bombs used for quality assurance, usually without nuclear components are called "Quality Assurance Weapons." Weapons used by maintenance crews to practice maintenance, and handling, are called "Trainers". There are also classifications for bombs used by aircraft loading crews to practice aircraft loading called Bomb Dummy Units, or "BDU's".

We learned that maintenance operations on nuclear weapons were every bit as strict, and disciplined, and often even more so, as surgery operations on human beings. Maintenance manuals governed all the maintenance operations. Any handling or maintenance operation on a nuclear weapon was in strict compliance with written procedures within manuals that were written and published by AEC, and the services. Defense Atomic Support Agency (DASA) accomplished the actual publishing and authentication of these manuals. The manuals covered different subjects concerning nuclear weapons, and the subject was identified by a number system. A manual entitled TP (Technical Publication) B7-1 would cover the topic of assembly and maintenance on the B-7 bomb. Each service had its own terminology. In the Navy the manuals were called "Special Weapons Ordnance Publication," or "SWOP." A "-4" manual was an illustrated parts breakdown manual showing nuts, bolts, and individual parts that makes up a bomb. As I described "-1" manuals were assembly and maintenance operations, "-0" manuals were weapon summaries, "-6" Explosive Ordnance Disposal (EOD) procedures; "-7" covered fusing options. The manual system called "Joint Nuclear Weapons Publication System" or "JNWPS', is a complicated, exact system that each Nuclear Weaponsman had to master in order to do his job. Every detail of weapons maintenance was described, and accomplished exactly as directed by the "written word" within these manuals. Some typical maintenance operations are as follows, "Removal from Storage, and Preparation for Strike," "Inspection and Test Following Removal from Strike Aircraft," "Inspection and Test Following Removal from Strike Aircraft," "Parachute Removal and Replacement," and many more.

We were to discover that manuals, records and reports, and paperwork were the lifeblood of the nuclear weapons' program. At the time of manufacture each nuclear weapon had a card initiated called an Inspection Record Card (IRC). This was somewhat like a birth certificate, and life history. The IRC remained with the weapon throughout its life. All maintenance operations and significant events that occurred on the weapon were recorded on the IRC. Some weapons had Pressure Test Record Cards (PTR's) that reflected a weapon pressure history. Some weapons were pressurized to prevent high altitude electric arcing, and to maintain watertight integrity in depth bomb applications. The paperwork involved with nuclear weapons was immense. It seemed there was more paperwork than the "nuts and bolts" work.

We had classes on Radiation and Detection Instruments and Computation equipment, or "RADIAC" instruments. These instruments detect radiation. One of the most common instruments was used to detect alpha radiation, which would be used to monitor "fallout" material. Alpha radiation is harmful only if absorbed into the body through cuts in the skin, by breathing, or ingesting. Alpha radiation only traveled in air a little over an inch, so the probe of an alpha detector had to be held very close to the surface being surveyed. We also studied gamma and beta radiation detection equipment.

Another subject we studied was what to do in the event of fire in the vicinity of a nuclear weapon, and what to do if the weapon was engulfed in fire. The older weapons systems had explosives that could possibly detonate if overheated, so it was required to try and determine how long a weapon case had been exposed to fire, and attempt to keep it cool with water spray. The possibility of a nuclear detonation was very low when a weapon was involved in a fire. Future technical advances made the possibility of nuclear detonation in a fire impossible.

One day the class was taken to a remote location on base, and we were given a demonstration. We watched some explosions, which were very impressive. One memorable demonstration was when the instructor placed a small blasting cap under a turned over bucket. The bucket soared into the air when the blasting cap was set off.

I enjoyed the "college atmosphere" of the school. We had weekly final exams, and night school study sessions were available to us. I attended these a few times prior to exams. Most of the time; however after class we had freedom to do, as we liked. We had infrequent duty days. Once every two weeks, we stood a four-hour barracks fire watch.

One day while returning to the barracks after the day's classes, there was a commotion. The Navy barracks was a two-story building. A sailor had gone out on the second story balcony, tied a plastic water hose, around his neck, and the railing, and then jumped in an attempt to commit suicide. His attempt was a failure, the hose stretched until his feet touched the ground. He ended up with a sore neck. He had been depressed because he'd gotten word that his parents were getting a divorce. Normally such an attempt would have gotten him removed from school, but he remained in school. I won't reveal his name, but he went on to have a successful Navy career, even becoming a commissioned officer!

My fiancée and I again planned on being married after I graduated from school. I tried to save money. I did ironing for my classmates in the barracks. I charged ten cents for a shirt, and twenty-five cents for a pair of pants.

The first part of July we began doing in class what we would be doing after we graduated, actually working on weapons. The weapons we worked on were not the "real thing" or "war reserves," but "trainers". The trainers had the physical components, and circuitry of war reserves, but did not have high explosives or nuclear components installed. The bomb shop classes were held in Quonset huts. Each weapon we studied had its own trainer shop work area.

The first weapon we worked on was the Mark 7 bomb. We were shown all the applicable operation steps by the instructors, then we were split into teams performing the operations with the instructor observing. A team consisted of a sailor, or as he was called a "Team Leader," or "Hook Leader," reading the manual step by step, while five or six sailors called "Assemblymen or Team Members" carried out the read steps. An example of the operation procedure follows: Team leader reads, "While supporting the tail, and using a 5/16" allen, unscrew four bolts holding the clamp rings together." The team assemblymen would perform the steps, and upon completion, loudly proclaim, "Check". The operation would not continue until a "check" had been stated. It's not accurate to say the team leader read from a manual, because he actually read steps from "check sheets," which had been prepared by someone reading the manual, and placing operation steps in order in a check sheet format. The check sheets were encased in plastic cover sheets, for use over and over again. As the assemblymen completed the steps read by the team leader, and proclaimed, "Check," the team leader would place a check by the step with a grease pencil. If an assemblyman saw something unsafe, or wrong, he was to proclaim "silence," and everyone was supposed to freeze, until the unsafe, or incorrect procedure was corrected. Speaking of "silence," no one was to talk during the operation other than the team leader. We all took turns being a team leader; other times we were assemblymen.

The first shop work was on the Mark 7 bomb. We were told about the Mark 5, but did not work on it, as it was scheduled for retirement. The Mk 7 (see photo page) warhead was used in a number of weapons systems, the Betty depth bomb, the Boar rocket, the air-dropped bomb, and the Genie air-to-air rocket, and a number of others, but we only worked these four applications. The Mk 7 warhead had an In Flight Insertion (IFI) device. The nuclear material, which was in the form of a capsule ball, was not inserted in place in the middle of the explosive sphere until just prior to detonation. This was a safety device, as there could be no nuclear detonation until the capsule ball was in place. The bomb dropped on Hiroshima had the nuclear material inserted manually by a Navy Captain on the plane just prior to the bomb drop. An electrical motor operated the IFI device in the Mark 7 warhead. The Mark 7 warhead was a large warhead, and the operations we conducted on this warhead took longer than those on other weapons. The warhead required unique operations that we did not do on more modern warheads. We removed and installed the detonators on the high explosive sphere, and conducted inspections on the nuclear sphere, or ball, which was stored in a metal canister. The metal canister was surrounded by metal tube frame, and was nicknamed a "birdcage". The Mark 7 bomb contained nickel-cadmium (NiCad) batteries that required frequent maintenance, radars, timers, impact crystals, altimeters, and many other components that required maintenance and testing.

There were many associated test sets with the Mark 7. Test sets were called T-gear. A test set designation might be T-128, T-79, etc. Electrical cables used for nuclear weapons testing purposes were identified as (Cable Test) "CT" cables. Electrical cables within a bomb were identified as (Cable Functional) "CF" cables.

The Mark 7 bomb was unattractive, or ungainly. It had three fins. The fin on the bottom of the tail was retractable, in order to provide ground clearance when the large bomb was hung under small planes that needed ground clearance when on the ground, and during takeoffs and landings. The fin was extended, and retracted by an electrical motor, or manually on the ground with a hand crank. The bomb had two suspension lugs, and an electrical connector for plane power, and assembly tests. There was also an arming wire that was extracted at the time of drop from the aircraft. The yield (or explosive power), of the bomb was determined by the size of the nuclear capsule ball at the time of assembly on the ground before the plane took off. The bomb was detonated by radars or upon impact with the ground by impact devices.

One interesting test we performed on the Mark 7 was, "ringing in the radars". With the bomb assembled, in a maintenance stand, and power applied to the radars, an assemblyman would cover the nose radome with a special nylon bag, and rub the bag back and forth until the radars rang in, and a green light on the test set lit.

The Mark 7 bomb shop class lasted two weeks. It was one of the more primitive bombs, not too far removed from Little Boy, and Fat Man bombs dropped on Japan. The electrical testing of the bomb took many hours. There was a Completely Assembled Test called a "CAT Test," a Final Assembly Test called a "FAT Test," and a Completely Assembled for Strike Test called a "CAS Test".

During some of the tests we did in the shop, the bomb was cycled through its complete drop sequence electrically. At the end of the test, a light on the test set would flash simulating detonation of the bomb. During this test the high explosives were not connected, nor was the nuclear capsule ball installed, but had they been, a nuclear detonation would have occurred. A common saying in school, instead of saying detonation, or explosion, was to say;"There is a rapid disassembly of the bomb with an accompanying blinding white flash"!

We performed "hands on operations" with the nuclear components of the Mark 7 warhead. As stated previously, the nuclear capsule ball was stored within a metal canister. This canister was airtight. The nuclear ball was encased in a metal cover, two hollow spheres of specific metal. Uranium "spalls" over time, and small specks of the uranium "pop off". This is a characteristic of radioactive material. At specific time frames it was required that the capsule balls (considerably larger than a softball), be inspected for spalling. The capsule ball was unpackaged, and placed on a table. The ball was placed within a paper sack. The sack containing the capsule ball was placed within a clear plastic box, which had two rubber gloves that extended into the box from both sides. An assemblyman placed his hands in the gloves, and rubbed the capsule ball vigorously rubbing off any loose material on the surface of the capsule ball. After completion of rubbing, the capsule ball was removed, and any material within the paper bag, and box were considered radioactive waste, and treated as such.

After shop work on the Mark 7 bomb we worked on the "BOAR" which stood for Bomb Ordnance Assisted Rocket or as it was also called, the 30.5 inch Rocket. This was a Mark 7 bomb with a rocket motor; the rocket motor was primarily to give the pilot a safe separation distance. The Boar was launched from the aircraft toward the target, while the plane rapidly departed in the opposite direction. We had classroom lessons, but no shop classes on the Mark 90 "Betty" which was a depth bomb that used the Mark 7 warhead.

We studied the Mark 101 "Lulu" which was also a depth bomb, using a W34 warhead. This was the depth bomb that was to take the place of the Betty, with many advanced features. One thing that stands out in my mind about our Mark 101 shop work is that during our shop instruction, part of the operation called for the tail to be removed. One of the sailors in class always did very well in the classroom but wasn't very mechanically inclined, and had trouble in the shop work. The shop operation had progressed to a point just before tail removal when the instructor told us to take a break. We all left the assembly shop area, except for the one guy I mentioned. After we left and had been in the break room for short while, we heard a huge bang! We all rushed into the assembly shop, and there stood the guy, red faced, with the tail lying on the deck (floor). He had decided to continue working in our absence, but skipped a step, which required having four assemblymen support the tail while the clamp rings holding the tail to the weapon body were removed. The tail was thick gauge steel and quite heavy. Nothing was damaged, but he was embarrassed, and the instructor was upset. This incident emphasized the importance on us of following the check sheets exactly. The Mark 101 tail had holes and a shroud ring, which caused the weapon to sink properly in water. The nose was weighted to ensure a nose down sinking posture. Hydrostats or, timers detonated the bomb. It was normally dropped into water by P2V *Neptune* aircraft (antisubmarine aircraft, or helicopters).

In the assembly phases we discovered that many screws, bolts, and nuts in nuclear weapons were tightened to exact tightness by using torque wrenches. We then had to safety wire the screws, bolts, and nuts. The safety wire was to prevent loosening by vibration, such as might be experienced while the bomb was hanging on aircraft, or at the impact of hitting the water, or ground, etc. Safety wiring, torque procedures, and tool use, was detailed in a publication called TP 45-51 General Maintenance Procedures. It's a true statement that any operation, procedure, or any task involved with nuclear weapons was written in detail in some publication, or instruction, nothing was left to personal interpretation.

After the Mark 101, we were introduced to and worked the trainer on the Mark 105 (Hot Point), which used the same warhead as the Mark 101. This bomb, which was used primarily for airstrip, or runway destruction, was one of the first parachute retarded lay-down weapons. It had a specially constructed nose nicknamed a "cookie cutter". The nose dug into concrete, or blacktop when dropped. The nose was manufactured by General Mills and had the label "General Mills" on the nose. This label "General Mills," which was normally seen on breakfast cereal boxes, looked somewhat out of place on one of the most destructive weapons on earth. We studied both the internal and external version of the bomb. The internal version was carried inside the aircraft bomb bay; the external version was carried on aircraft wing stations or the underside of the plane. The internal and external versions had their own "fairing kits". The fairing kits included nose covering, tail, and other components, such as fins, etc. The Mark 105 was my least favorite weapon, and was very difficult work on.

We had classroom work on the Mark 44 Astor Torpedo, but no shop work. The Astor also used the W34 warhead, and was launched from submarines. The torpedo was guided, fused, and fired, by wire. When the torpedo was launched, an unbelievably long spool of wire unrolled, and trailed behind the torpedo.

The next weapon we studied was a giant not only in physical size but also in yield size. It was the Mark 27 bomb, the largest in the Navy arsenal, excluding the Polaris missile. The A3 *Skywarrior* aircraft, which was the Navy's largest aircraft carrier-based aircraft, carried the Mark 27 internally (see photo page).

Following classes on the Mark 27, we studied the Mark 28 bomb. Aircraft carried the Mark 28 both internally and externally. An interesting feature on the external version, was folding fins on the tail. The fins would unfold at the time the bomb was dropped from the aircraft. The Mark 28 had varying yields from ten kilotons, up to the megaton range. (see photo page)

We studied the Regulus missile, which was launched from submarines, and followed by a "chase airplane" that transmitted commands to the missile. The chase aircraft transmitted all guidance, fusing, and firing commands.

A surface to air missile we worked on was the Talos, which used the W30 warhead. We also were given classroom instruction on the "Genie," which was an air-to-air missile, and used the Mark 7 warhead. I believe this was the only air-to-air missile developed, and when you consider that a missile explosion in the range of kilotons was used to knock a plane out of the sky, this was an example of "overkill!"

We had classes on the Polaris submarine launched ballistic missile, and "SUBROC," and "ASROC," which were antisubmarine weapons. We also had classes on atomic demolition devices. These devices are called "suit case bombs." The variety of weapons was amazing! It was a standard nuclear weapons community joke that the only nuclear device we didn't have in the arsenal was a nuclear hand grenade, and that would be developed as soon as we found a marine dumb enough to throw it!

We had classes on what was considered a modern "wooden bomb". Wooden bombs contained many advanced features and required much less maintenance by nuclear weaponsmen than their predecessors, such as the Mark 7 and W34 warhead, and others. The Mark 43 (see photo page) was delivered by aircraft, and in the Navy normally carried externally on a wing pylon, or the aircraft centerline. We were also told of new developments in the world of nuclear weapons. A new airdrop weapon was expected in the fleet. It was the Mark 57 bomb (see photo page).

Each of the weapons system we studied required not only electrical and mechanical hands-on-training, but we also had to learn the "drop sequence" of each weapon. This meant we had to know the sequential operation of each bomb component when the bomb was dropped, the missile launched, or weapon initiated, until detonation. The drop sequences were diagramed in the technical publications, showing for example, in the case of an air-dropped weapon numbered actions until detonation such as; 1.Bomb release, batteries start. 2. Radar ringing begins 3. Timer T1 ends, firing capacitor charged…and so on until the final numbered event, detonation. Something interesting, the person who illustrated these drop sequences always showed a miniature city as the target, which had Russian spires, such as the ones in Moscow, and other Russian cities.

All the weapons' systems had many, many safety devices incorporated in their designs. It was very apparent that the United States considered safety to be of great importance. It was even expressed at times that our weapons have so many safety devices built in, that their reliability was degraded. Each safety device prevents an inadvertent nuclear detonation, or a saboteur's detonation. The more safety devices, the less assurance the weapon will detonate when desired, over an enemy target. Of course another very important reason to consider safety devices during handling, shipment, and storage of nuclear weapons was the safety of the people working on the weapons and the safety of innocent civilians that might live or be near the storage vicinity of weapons. Any serious accident, especially involving the nuclear detonation of a weapon, could cause a public outcry, and outrage, that might seriously hamper our country's ability to deploy, store, and transport weapons, and thus hamper our defense, and ability to wage war.

Reliability was also an important issue. Nuclear weapons are "dual channeled". This means components are installed in weapons in "pairs," and all electrical circuits are dual and in parallel, so if one should fail, there's always a "back up".

I'll list a few safety devices, which were also called "ground handling safety devices." A complete list could fill volumes of books. Many safety devices interrupt electricity flow, in circuits. Most circuits remain open until the desired time of electrical detonation. Items called differential pressure switches, usually located on the external skin of a weapon, sensed airflow. The differential pressure switch has to sense wind velocities in excess of 250 miles per hour, before it closes the circuit it controls. This wind velocity would only be sensed at the time of airdrop from an aircraft, and would be difficult to duplicate on the ground. Other safety devices sense changes in velocity, such as a sudden G-force change that might be sensed during a parachute deployment, or sudden direction changes by a missile. Another safety device is called a "Strike Enable Plug," or SEP. This is a plug in certain weapons that is stored in separate safes, and only installed when the weapon is being prepared for loading on a strike aircraft. Without the SEP installed it is impossible to complete the fusing circuits. All weapons have Ready/Safe switches. These switches are normally visible to all who look at the skin of the weapon. While on the ground Ready/Safe switches are always kept in the Safe position, this switch indicator was colored green. The only time a Ready/Safe switch was placed in the Ready (red) position was just prior to drop from an aircraft. Some weapons had high voltage batteries that were in storage positions until preparation for loading on strike aircraft, at which time they would be placed in the operating position. Safety devices sense velocities, or forces that can only be sensed in a drop from aircraft, or firing environment, and are almost impossible to duplicate on the ground. We also were told of built in devices that provide safety in the event a weapon is exposed to fire. These devices open, and prevent electricity flow if they are exposed to extreme heat conditions, as would be experienced in a fire.

I enjoyed the daily classes, and the relaxed life. There was always anxiety as Fridays approached, as each week we were required to pass a final written exam on the weapon, or weapons we had studied that week. These exams usually contained sixty questions or more.

I relaxed at the base swimming pool one weekend, and got a Southwest sunburn, I suffered with it for a week. Another weekend a group of us stuffed ourselves into the car of my roommate, and visited Sandia Crest, which overlooked Albuquerque. It was a beautiful view. I remember much vacant land near the base, which in years to come would be priceless real estate as the city grew.

During this time frame there was a mystery in the barracks. We had laundry rooms in the barracks with washers and dryers for cleaning our soiled clothes. From time to time, if someone left clothes in the dryer, and neglected to check on them for an hour or so, upon returning to the laundry room he would find his clothes removed from the dryer and neatly folded. We all wondered who the "phantom clothes folder" was. Eventually the mystery was solved: the "phantom" was a guy in a class a few weeks behind ours, who was secretly dating an Army captain (male), in a homosexual affair. We guessed his feminine side prompted this folding behavior. He and the captain were discharged.

On 27 July we all filled out Duty Preference Sheets, also called "dream sheets," listing where we desired to be stationed after graduation. I was maintaining a class position of fourth, in twenty-two, so it was a good chance that I would not be going to sea duty. The preferred choices I put down were: Shore duty in San Diego or Long Beach. Preferred ship duty was an aircraft carrier home ported on the west coast. Preferred overseas duty: Hawaii.

Nationally this was a time of great world tension. In July everyone was talking about Russia beating us into space with the sputnik satellite. President Kennedy had made a number of speeches about the diversity between the U.S. and Russia.

The president had also extended the enlistment of all in the military service who had less than a year left to serve. There was a sense of something about to happen. There was talk of a national emergency being declared. Many thought that nuclear war was right around the corner.

Our graduation day was scheduled for 15 August 1961. Prior to graduation we all sewed our rating badge of crossed cannons above our rate, on our upper left uniform sleeves. In my case it was above my three Seaman stripes. We were all to become Gunner's Mate Technicians. After graduation my rate would be written "GMTSN".

Throughout school, George Holden and I had been class leaders. Each day after class we would assign people to clean up, dump trash, and do other menial tasks. We both had learned a few leadership skills, and gotten a few headaches from the stress of being "responsible".

Everyone was anxious to learn where his duty station would be. A few days before graduation we were told our duty assignments. I could not believe my assignment; I could never have guessed it! My future duty assignment was Keflavik, Iceland! I could not have been assigned further from home, and in what I thought was the most isolated part of the world! Most of my classmates were assigned to aircraft carriers home ported on the east coast. At this point I'd been in the Navy a little over a year. After graduation we were all granted two weeks leave before going to our new duty station. I began making plans to travel home. One of my roommates had a 1953 Mercury, and was from San Francisco. He and I, and two others planned to drive to California; it was to cost us ten dollars each for gas.

On 15 August, the twenty-two sailors that made up our class, formed into ranks, and the Captain of the Naval Barracks handed us our diplomas and shook our hands. The course had been from 5 June to 15 August. We were all now proud finally to be GMT's. After we were congratulated, we left the fenced and guarded training area for the last time, and handed in our badges. We spent the next day checking out, getting our orders, and records, and saying goodbye. We all felt sad to be leaving Albuquerque, but we also felt fortunate to be leaving at this time. Things at the barracks were changing. It seems there had been some concerns and complaints by the Army about how the Navy walked about the base. We did not march back and forth as a group going between the barracks and the training side of the base, or back and forth to the mess hall. We walked casually, and often not as a group. Future classes would be marching when they went to and from classes.

We all had fond memories of New Mexico, and for many years anytime a GMT spoke about where he'd like to be stationed, it was more than likely Albuquerque. In the personnel office there was a First Class Yeoman named Adams, who was highly liked by everyone. He was one of the most helpful, personnel administrators I ever met. I heard that he died of cancer a couple of years later. He was admired and respected by all the students.

On 17 August at 7:00 a.m. in the morning, four of us checked out on leave. On this same day in Berlin, Germany, construction of the Berlin Wall began. This visible barrier, called the "Iron Curtain", against freedom built by communism between East and West Germany was to remain in place for almost thirty years.

With our four sea bags in the back of the 1953 Mercury, we drove off the base, and headed for California. One sailor was going to Los Angeles, then I was getting off at Lindsay, and then the owner of the car and the other passenger were going on to San Francisco. I expected to get home in about twenty-three hours. We were taking turns driving. We made good time through New Mexico, and Arizona, anxious to get to our respective homes. Then about 2:30 a.m. in the middle of the Mojave Desert, we had a flat tire on the left rear. We were on Route 66, and it was very dark. We checked the spare and it was flat too! Two guys hitchhiked to a gas station we had passed about twenty-five miles back, with the flat tire. I and another sailor stayed with the car. Luckily the two with the tire got a ride right away, and the station was able to repair the tire, and we were on our way before daylight. We stopped again at another station, and had the spare flat tire repaired. After dropping off the first guy, we went on another 150 miles to Lindsay. I told them to drop me off, and then go on up Route 99, but they insisted on taking me to Lindsay, which was about fifteen miles out of the way. I arrived in the town of Lindsay about 3:00 p.m., and after a kiss and embrace was reunited with my fiancée. I bid my classmates farewell, and they continued on to San Francisco.

I had an enjoyable two weeks leave. Once again the planned wedding did not take place. My mom was expecting a baby in September; I was disappointed that I would not be home when the baby arrived. The only complaint I had about my leave was that it went by much too quickly.

Chapter 4: The Rock

The first of September I bid my family, and fiancée goodbye. I boarded a plane at Fresno, California, and flew to San Francisco. From there I boarded a plane to New York. I took a taxi from the New York Airport to the Brooklyn Naval Station. The taxi cost was a dollar fifty, much better than the twenty dollar taxi fare I'd paid in Chicago. My first experience in a New York City cab was a thrilling, careening ride, speeding in and out of traffic!

The Brooklyn Naval Station was what is called a Transit Station. Sailors reported there for further transportation connections overseas. Transit stations have a bad reputation, somewhat like being in purgatory, in limbo between duty stations. You're not treated well, usually treated much like a recruit in boot camp. You have to muster many times throughout the day and night, and live out of your sea bag. You have to be ready to leave at a moments notice to catch your plane or bus for further transportation to your ultimate duty station. My transfer orders which I'd been given in Albuquerque, listed Brooklyn Naval Station as my intermediate duty station. Keflavik, Iceland was listed as my ultimate duty station for a period of twelve months.

The first morning at the Brooklyn Naval Station, I was called up to a window, and asked if I were a Nuclear Weaponsman. The personnel office had seen my rate "GMTSN" on my orders. The first class petty officer who talked to me seemed very impressed. He said, "I heard about you guys, but never met one. You work on all that secret stuff". He directed me to the Fleet Reserve Association (FRA) Office, which was near the personnel office. The FRA is a fraternity of enlisted personnel of the Navy, Marine Corps, and Coast Guard. This office was within the transit barracks office area. I wasn't to do anything. The people in the office said I could help myself to coffee, and read magazines all day. I felt rather privileged, because about forty other sailors who had reported in the same day I had, were mess cooking, sweeping, swabbing, and doing other menial tasks.

Since graduating from Nuclear Weaponsman School, I had felt a sense of accomplishment, and was very pleased to have joined an elite group of people that were involved with a job very few people were permitted to do. I felt it was one of the most important jobs in the defense of our country. In our school classes, we were constantly told that we were the "cream of the crop," as only a small percentage of people in the Navy were permitted to work on nuclear weapons. We were also told our school was one of the most difficult enlisted A schools.

While at Naval Station Brooklyn, I learned of a situation that was very irritating to all the sailors stationed there. The wife of the commanding officer of the Brooklyn Naval Station demanded that she be saluted just as though she were a naval officer! Apparently the captain complied with her wishes, because he ordered all enlisted men to salute her when she was on the base. Her picture was posted throughout the base so sailors would recognize her, and salute. There was much resentment over this illegal situation.

Although I was granted liberty, I did not leave the base the five days I was there. On the afternoon of the sixth day, sixty of us boarded a bus and rode north to McGuire Air Force Base. On the way I saw the Statue of Liberty through the bus window. The whole group stayed overnight in an Air Force transit barracks. The Air Force barracks seemed much nicer than Navy barracks.

I had no idea what Iceland would be like. I'd never met anyone who had been stationed there. About all I knew was that I'd be working in an Advanced Undersea Weapon (AUW) Shop. I was to learn the following about Iceland after I'd been on the island for a while. Iceland is an island in the North Atlantic Ocean, located 185 miles east of Greenland, and 620 miles west of Norway. The island is about 190 miles from north to south, and 300 miles from east to west; the island has an area of 39,800 square miles. I had visions of a land covered in ice as the name implies, but that was not the case. Eric the Red (950–1001), Norwegian Explorer, was the first European to explore Iceland and Greenland. I was told that both Iceland and Greenland were both named in opposite contrast to their climates? Greenland was mostly covered with snow and ice. The average temperature was around forty-one degrees, rising to around fifty-one degrees in the summer, to thirty-one degrees in the winter, with occasional severe windstorms in the winter. In Iceland the annual rainfall was between sixty and eighty inches. The island is riddled with volcanoes, and is mostly barren rock and soil. A joke that circulated among sailors was "On Iceland there's a woman behind every tree." There are very few trees on Iceland!

The history of Iceland says Irish Monks may have been the first on the island around AD 800. A Norwegian Viking named Ingo'lfur Arnarson is considered to be the first permanent settler.

He established his farm at Reykjavik, which is now Iceland's capital city. Settlers came from Scandinavian countries, and the British Isles. Leif Eriksson, the Icelandic explorer, reached the mainland of North America (Vineland), but attempts to establish settlements there failed.

Iceland was ruled by Denmark for many centuries, until Denmark was occupied by Nazi Germany in 1940. In 1944 Iceland declared independence. Iceland has had foreign troops on its soil since World War II, and is a member of the North Atlantic Treaty Organization (NATO). While American troops have been at the Keflavik Air Base since the 1940's, and Iceland is sympathetic to western democracies, there has always been controversy about having Americans stationed on Iceland.

After remaining overnight at the McGuire Air Force transit barracks, we boarded a plane the evening of the following day. The plane was a large four-engine propeller driven aircraft. After an hour and a half flight we landed in Greenland.

After our lay over, the plane reloaded and we took off headed for Iceland. After an hour into the flight the plane hit very rough weather, with thunder booming, and the plane bounced wildly up and down. It was one of the most terrifying plane rides of my life! The thunder of the storm boomed throughout the cabin of the plane, everyone was pale with fright. I did my share of praying!

We landed, to everyone's relief at 0630 in the morning. We had a pleasant surprise awaiting us. A Navy band was playing, welcoming us as we got off the plane. The landscape was dreary, a flat rocky plain with mountains in the distance. The sky was gray and stormy, and it was a chilly forty degrees.

I was directed to the Navy personnel office where I turned in my records, and then I was assigned to a barracks. I began to settle in. It was hard to adjust my sleeping and waking hours, as there were ten hours' difference between California and Iceland. I learned that there was very little leave or liberty. The Icelandic police manned the base main gate and restricted many items you could take off the base. I also learned the communist party was a force in Iceland.

I asked my parents in the first letter written from Iceland if they would send me some warm civilian clothes. I was also concerned about the birth of my brother or sister that was to take place soon. Sailors were assigned three to a room in the barracks. We had large wooden clothes storage lockers. There were two beds stacked one atop the other, and a single bed. Also, within the room was a sink and medicine cabinet. There was a radio in the room. There was only one English speaking broadcast station operated by the Armed Forces Radio and Television System (AFRTS). We used a common bathroom and shower area. There were three stories in the barracks; I lived on the first floor. I shared my room with two Torpedomen. Both Seamen recently graduated from Torpedoman A School in Florida. I learned we would be working in the same AUW Shop. Before I could go to work, however, my security clearance had to be confirmed. This confirmation involved letters or messages being sent to naval administration commands in order to confirm that I was who I was supposed to be. This could take as long as a month or more. I hoped it wouldn't be too long because I was anxious to go to work. I completed my check-in process on the base, and while waiting security clearance confirmation was assigned to the base armory. This was where small arms such as M-1 pieces (rifles), pistols, machine guns, grenades, etc., were stored and maintained. I cleaned rifles and pistols and did housekeeping chores around the armory. The Air Force and the Navy jointly occupied the base. The Air Force maintained the chow halls, and the meals were excellent.

In mid-September I sent eighty dollars home. I owed my parents twenty dollars I had borrowed during my leave period. I began saving money for marriage after I completed my Iceland assignment. I knew this was to be a lonely year, but I saw this assignment as an opportunity to prepare for a financially solid married life with Donna. Normally payday took almost all morning. We were paid twice a month, and three days before payday (which was on the first or fifteenth) a pay list would be posted at various locations about the base. This list was alphabetical, and you could find your name and listed amount. My pay was normally thirty-seven dollars. You had to get a pay chit, which was a form about the size of a dollar bill, which contained spaces for your name, service number, and the amount of your pay, both in numbers and written form. On payday prior to 9:00 a.m., we had to line up alphabetically and approach a desk behind which an officer and two disbursing clerks were usually seated. These sailors worked in the disbursing office and handled pay records, and payrolls. You first handed your filled out pay chit, and your identification card to the officer. The officer looked at your ID card, compared your face to the card, and then examined your pay chit. If your pay chit was filled out incorrectly, when he compared it to your ID card, and the pay list, then you had to step out of line, and wait until stragglers were paid. This was after all the alphabetical line had been paid.

If your pay chit was correct, the next disbursing clerk would count out your pay, recheck the pay list, hand the next disbursing clerk, the money, and he would return your ID card. The last clerk would recount the money and hand it to you. We frequently received two-dollar bills, which were common. On paydays there were often problems with pay chits, as many sailors were poor spellers. Commonly miss-spelled words and numbers were posted at the beginning of the pay line. Also, masters at arms roamed up-and-down the pay line maintaining order. We were not allowed to talk in the pay line.

A week after I arrived on Iceland, I was on television. The Armed Forces Television Station had a short weekly program after the daily news that showed interviews and introduced newcomers to the island. The interviewer was cautious about saying what my job was. He asked where I was from. I responded "California". He said I was a Gunner's Mate who worked on guns. The television station began broadcasting daily at 4:00 p.m., and went off the air midnight.

Mail call was an anxiously awaited event; the mail only came once a week. A nickname for Iceland, coined by sailors was "the Rock." The question asked often of one another was, "How long have you been on the Rock?"

Fortunately I only waited a few days before my clearance paper work was complete and my access badge was made. I was then permitted to begin working at the AUW Shop. The shop was miles from the main base, reached by a gravel road. The shop was in the middle of a desolate flat plain, covered with rocks. Two fences surrounded the shop, and these were ten feet high with barbed wire strung along the top. The entire compound covered about three acres. Marines guarded it. To gain access to the compound we had to exchange badges. The badges were worn all the time within the compound. Four marines were always on watch and armed with forty-five caliber pistols, and M-1 rifles. The AUW compound had a vehicle gate, and a pedestrian gate, which was a large steel revolving door that only permitted one person through at a time. We also had to turn in all spark-producing devices, such as matches and cigarette lighters.

I was introduced to my Division Officer, Lieutenant Mack, and the Leading Chief Petty Officer. I had already met my Leading Petty Officer (LPO), Torpedoman First Class Smith. They seemed please to meet me. I had taken special pains to ensure that I had on a well-pressed uniform, good haircut, and shined shoes for this first meeting. I was quickly scheduled to attend driving school so I could obtain a Navy driving permit, and drive the ¾ ton pickup, stake truck, and bomb truck that was used by the sailors stationed at the AUW Shop.

In September there was less and less daylight. Iceland is close to the Arctic Circle, and during the middle of a winter we would have only one hour of daylight daily.

There was only one other GMT at the AUW Shop, a Second Class named Shewe. There was a Second Class Mineman named Stanwick, and an Electrician named Jones. All the rest of the sailors were Torpedomen. We had a Third Class Storekeeper who managed supplies.

The AUW Shop was really two shops in one. Shop 1 was where torpedoes were assembled and maintained. Also within Shop 1 was a battery shop, where torpedo batteries were worked on. Shop 1 contained a break room, with coffee pots, refrigerator, and small cooking stove. Located also within this room were a television, and two bunks. The coffee break room was one of the areas within the fenced compound where smoking was permitted. In the break room there were electric grids on the wall that would get hot when a button was pressed. You placed the end of your cigarette against the hot wire that was behind a silica plate about the size of a silver dollar to light up. The other rooms in the front of the AUW Shop entrance were the offices of Lieutenant Mack, and the Leading Chief Petty Officer. There was also a head, and shower. In the rear section of the shop was Shop 2. This was the area I was assigned to work in. It was a classified area that only the GMT's, and others assigned to Shop 2 could enter. The door entering Shop 2 was a thick armored steel door with a peephole. There was an electric alarm system on all the AUW compound doors. The alarm board was monitored twenty-four hours a day by marines. Prior to opening certain doors, and magazines, we used a daily code word that was stated over a phone to the marines. We also had a "duress" word that changed each month. Duress words were to be used over the phone within a sentence to alert the marines to respond with force because we were being forced by hostile person(s) to open an alarmed area.

All the electrical outlets within the shop were specially constructed so there would not be an electric spark upon connection and disconnection of electrical cords. All hammers and some other hand tools were made of beryllium, or metal that would not cause sparks. We wore safety shoes with rubber soles that would not conduct electricity. Positioned at the entrances of Shop 1 and Shop 2 were "slap plates," which were grounded conductive plates you touched before entering in order to dissipate any static electricity that might be in your body.

Since high explosives were handled and worked on within this building, sparks and exposed flames were avoided. Although modern explosives are not as susceptible to accidental detonation, safety precautions from the days of black powder were still in force. The entire building was constructed of reinforced concrete, and was built with a roof "sitting" on the walls. This special construction was to insure in the event of an explosion that the roof would blow away, and the majority of the blast would be directed upwards and not destroy the walls of the building. After an explosion, the inside of the shop would be cleaned up (equipment, body parts, etc.), a new roof placed on the walls, and the shop would be back in business.

In addition to the rooms I mentioned there was an emergency generator room, and storage room. Next to the AUW Shop was a large building that served as a garage for vehicles. Also within the fenced compound there were two magazines. There was a marine guard shack, and alarm control building within the fence.

In a letter written by my parents, shortly after 30 September 1961, I got the news I had been waiting for. I had a new brother named Jeremy Douglas Little. It would be a year before I saw him.

I was studying for my third class petty officer's exam to be conducted in February. I also passed my Navy driver's license exam, after a short three-day driving school. The Navy driver's license permitted me to drive a government vehicle on base. During the short driving school, I had to learn Icelandic traffic signs. I also had to learn to drive on the left side of the road, which took some getting used to. My license permitted me to drive vehicles up to two ½ tons.

I had some discouraging news in mid-October, while filling out my duty preference card, which detailed my assignment preferences, or as I mentioned is called a "dream card." After my assignment in Iceland was over, I was told I couldn't request duty on the west coast, because I was assigned duty on the east coast. It was almost impossible to transfer from the east coast to the west coast, and vice versa. This was due primarily because of the cost involved transferring a sailor across country. One way sailors got around this, is something called a "duty swap." Two sailors on opposite coasts with exactly the same rate, qualifications, and the same transfer dates could request a duty swap. Also, the sailors had to pay for the travel expenses' cross-country. It was rare when all these circumstances came together. Duty swap requests were commonly listed in such publications as the *Navy Times*[8]. So it appeared I had escaped sea duty after A school graduation because of my high marks in class, but I was now stuck on the east coast!

I and the other GMT's were in charge of the magazines located within the fenced compound. The magazines were two large earth-covered bunkers, with two large twelve-foot high by eight-foot wide steel doors, locked by two huge padlocks. We recorded magazine temperatures each morning, seven days a week. The thermometers were located just inside the doors. We recorded the maximum and minimum temperatures daily. The thermometers had a metal sliver that moved up-and-down on top of the mercury, and indicated to us, the warmest and coldest temperatures experienced within the magazine. Taking the temperatures involved driving from the shop to the magazine, after checking out the keys, calling the marine located within the alarm center, and requesting entry with proper code word, before unlocking the padlocks.

Upon arrival in Iceland, I was issued a foul weather coat, and a parka. I was cautioned about venturing outside alone during storms, as it was very easy to become disoriented in a snowstorm and freeze to death. The buddy system was used: if you went outside in bad weather, there had to be two sailors together.

About mid-October light snows began. I started thinking about Christmas. This would be the first Christmas of my life away from home. I had pangs of homesickness. I was halfway around the world from my family. My fiancée was hardly writing at all. I had only received a couple of letters from her since arriving in Iceland, although I wrote to her every day.

I was anxious to take my third class petty officer exam. Becoming a petty officer was called "putting on the crow," the "crow" being the eagle above the chevrons of a petty officer. A third class petty officer was considered the first step in becoming a leader and supervisor.

In mid-October the sun would rise about 0930, and set at 1530, so we had roughly six hours of daylight. The married sailors who lived off base did not talk kindly about the Icelandic natives. They were very limited about what they could take off base. They were only permitted to take groceries they could consume within a week. Icelandic police searched automobiles as they left the base. The black-market was a problem; cigarettes were popular items that were smuggled. The Icelandic people for the most part were big in stature, blond, blue eyed, with fair skin. A slang word for Icelandics was "Moe Jacks," it was a term not appreciated by the Icelandics.

It snowed heavily on Thanksgiving. The Air Force chow hall prepared a wonderful Thanksgiving meal, but it wasn't like being at home.

My two roommates and I went in together and bought a set of weights, bar bells and dumb bells. We started working out in the evenings. My parents were wonderful about writing letters; so once a week at mail call I had a few letters to read.

A typical day consisted of getting up at 6:00 a.m., breakfast at the chow hall, and catching the truck to the shop at 7:15 a.m. We mustered inside the AUW Shop at 7:45; Leading Petty Officer TM1 Smith would lead morning muster, read the plan of the day (POD), and give out any special orders; we would then go to work. I and another seaman usually took magazine temperatures. We then worked in Shop 2, sometimes training, or painting, cleaning, etc. At 11:30 we knocked off for lunch, went to the chow hall on base, and returned by 1300. We would continue working until 1630 (4:30 p.m.), at which time we returned to the barracks. After supper, we worked out with weights, or wrote letters. The lights were turned out at 10:00 p.m. We had liberty on the base, and we could go to the movie theater, or enlisted club. I stayed in the barracks trying to save money. In order to leave the base single sailors had to have special permission. This was the routine Monday through Friday. Normally we had weekends off, but every fourth day we had duty for twenty-four hours. This meant staying at the AUW Shop overnight. Two persons, sometimes three, would sleep inside the shop, and open the shop in the morning, if it were a workday. The shop was alarmed, and the duty sections remained inside the shop after we secured for the day. If an alarm went off after hours, the marines manning the alarm panel would notify us, and we would arm ourselves with forty-five-caliber pistols and investigate.

I was assigned responsibility for cleaning Lieutenant Mack's office, and the Leading Chief's office. I took this job seriously, and often, when I had duty, I would clean their offices although I was not required to do so. I took pride in working a little longer, and harder than asked to. I was paid a nice complement in November. One afternoon Lieutenant Mack and the chief asked me to come into the office. I had no idea why they wanted to talk to me. They said that I was the best, hardest working seaman in the shop, and they would give me all the help they could to help me to prepare for my third class exam. I didn't tell anyone about this praise, especially the other seaman.

A Torpedoman Second Class, named Walker took me under his wing, and invited me to his home on the base a number of times for supper. He and his wife had a baby girl born on the same day my brother Jerry was born. I baby-sat for them for a number of times. This helped me relate to how my new baby brother was growing up half way around the world in California.

In November GMT1 Puterbaugh checked in. He was a married first class petty officer, but had opted for an unaccompanied tour, which was twelve months. Married sailors who brought their wives to Iceland had a twenty-four month assignment. GMT1 Puterbaugh was to become the Leading Petty Officer of Shop 2. At this point there were four of us assigned to Shop 2. Another GMTSN was scheduled to report in at any time.

The Leading Chief of the AUW Shop was a Torpedoman, and he knew nothing about Shop 2. Shop 2 was much smaller than Shop 1 where the torpedoes were worked on. Within Shop 2 we had what we called a "swimming pool". This was a large square tub in the concrete floor that was normally covered with a steel lid. The tub had a faucet for filling the tub with water, and a drain in the bottom. This tub was used with our Mark 90 "Betty" trainer. When the trainer was assembled, the weapon would be pressurized; using a hoist we would lower the trainer into the water filled tub. We would then watch for bubbles, which would reveal unwanted leaks. The Betty was notorious for having more bolts, screws, and nuts requiring safety wire, than any other weapon in the stockpile. It was said you could tell a GMT who works on a Mark 90 Betty by all the bandages on the ends of his fingers from being stuck by the safety wire during the countless safety wiring jobs.

GMTSN John Gaffey reported aboard in November. He had been a few weeks behind me in A school. John was from Florida. We concluded there must be someone in the duty assignment branch in Washington with a sadistic sense of humor, to assign two sailors from the sunshine states of California and Florida to Iceland.

This time of year everyone's thoughts were turning to Christmas. I was thankful for the letters from my parents and sister. On 8 December, I turned nineteen years old. I received a birthday package from home, which contained a nice sweater, and warm clothes.

Shop 2 had been preparing for an inspection that was to take place on 12 December. This was to be the first of a long list of technical inspections I was to experience in the coming years. An inspection in the world of nuclear weapons was a frequent event. A Navy Technical Proficiency Inspection, or NTPI, is conducted every twelve months at all nuclear capable activities. The inspection teams were from Albuquerque, New Mexico, and in later years, from San Diego, California, and Norfolk, Virginia. A Technical Safety Inspection or TSI was an inspection that was conducted every four years, or more frequently, by Defense Atomic Support Agency, and the Joint Chiefs of Staff.

At times new weapons systems were introduced; a command had to undergo a Nuclear Weapons Acceptance Inspection, or NWAI. The inspectors for this type of inspection were stationed at McAlester, Oklahoma. The passing of these inspections meant a command was "certified" to store, handle, and maintain weapons for a specific period of time, normally twelve months. If an inspection was failed, then the command was "decertified," and lost its nuclear capability. A failure had serious consequences, at the least reprimands and intense efforts to correct whatever deficiencies had been discovered. A serious failure could mean the end of careers, from the commanding officer of the command down. Inspection times were a very tense and anxious time for a nuclear capable command. A nuclear weapons technical inspection could last as long as two weeks, but normally was a one-week affair. Absolutely everything was examined, security, administration, technical operations, safety, emergency procedures, and much more.

Our inspection in December was to certify our ability to transport weapons to an aircraft loading area one mile from the AUW Shop. To demonstrate this we pulled a wooden dummy torpedo, simulating a weapon, loaded on a bomb trailer, connected to a large bomb truck. A convoy of thirty armed marines guarded the bomb truck pulling the bomb trailer.

We were watched closely by the inspectors, (mostly GMT chief petty officers), during all our preparations for transporting the dummy weapon, and the entire operation to the loading area and return to the AUW Shop. The evolution went off without a hitch, much to our relief. We had practiced and practiced prior to the inspection.

The planes we would provide weapons to in the event of war, were P2V *Neptunes*, which were dual propeller, jet assist aircraft, with a crew of five to seven sailors. These were antisubmarine warfare planes. If a hostile submarine were suspected to be in an area, the plane would over-fly the area dropping electronic buoys until the sub's location was pinpointed, and then a weapon would be dropped.

The Air Force flew frequent air reconnaissance flights out of Keflavik Air Base. The planes were large four propeller driven aircraft, with huge radomes rising up from the body of the plane. Looking at a globe, a person would immediately recognize the strategic location of Iceland. The island guarded North American approaches through the North Atlantic Ocean.

In a letter I wrote to my parents on 16 December, I told of being tired, because the night before, John Gaffey had come into our barracks room around midnight drunk and threatening to kill himself! I stayed up with him until 0400. He was upset over his parent's divorce. I was obligated to tell my Shop 2 supervisor, GMT1 Puterbaugh, that John was having some emotional problems. We were expected to "inform" on each another if there was anything observed that might be dangerous behavior, considering the importance of our job. GMT1 Puterbaugh counseled John, and had him work in Shop 1 for a week.

The weather was strange. Often it would snow during night hours, and then rain during the day, causing mud. The wind blew continually. It didn't appear that we would have a "white Christmas". This time of year, we lived in darkness, except for a couple of hour's daylight around noon. I was scheduled to have duty on Christmas Day, which was all right with me. This permitted the married sailors to spend Christmas with their families.

On Christmas Day, TM2 Walker brought a Christmas dinner that his wife had prepared out to the Shop for the duty section. The day after Christmas I got a nice, (as we called them), "care package", from home. My parents and sister sent long-john's, shirts, and much needed toilet articles. I received a radio from my fiancée and a nice package from my Aunt Lois and Uncle Dean. I received a nice "scribbled" Christmas card from my brother Joe; brother Jerry was too young to do any writing. My parents included a Scrabble board game in the package. This game became very popular in the barracks; someone was always asking to borrow it.

I was sending most of my paycheck home, as I planned on having one thousand dollars for a wedding in September when I returned home. I continued studying for my third class exam in February. John Gaffey and I studied together, as he was also taking the exam.

In January a P2V *Neptune* disappeared while out over the Atlantic on patrol. The plane was never found, and it was never determined what happened. One thing that was always on the minds of aircrews was the short survival time in the frigid North Atlantic water.

A couple of days in February, everyone was restricted to the barracks, because of bad weather. It was snowing heavily, and the wind was blowing in excess of sixty miles an hour. It was actually snowing horizontally! Sandwiches were delivered to the barracks so we would not have to go to the chow hall. The duty section at the AUW Shop was stranded there for a few days. They had C-ration meals that were stored for this very purpose.

On 16 February, about 150 sailors and I reported to the chow hall at 0800. It was time to take the third class petty officer exam. Small tables that would seat four each were positioned throughout the chow hall. Sailors taking the same rate exam could not sit together. The rate exams were given every six months, and were held Navy-wide. The exams were mailed to commands from Washington, D.C., and San Diego, California, and kept under lock and key until the appointed day of the exam. The exam consisted of 150 to 200 multiple-choice questions. Answer sheets were mailed to Washington, D.C., and San Diego for grading, after the exam. This grading and notification process took a month and a half, or more. The exams that John and I were to take that morning were classified secret. GMT2 Shewe was assigned as an exam monitor, and he handed John and me our exams. We were given four hours to complete the exam. I finished in less than three hours. I knew many of the questions, and I felt good about the exam. John and I compared answers after the exam.

The isolation and boredom were difficult to live with. I was a teenager, and I thought of the kids I'd grown up with at home, that were going to college, or enjoying themselves with their families, and not living with the daily discipline, and isolation I found myself in. I thought of taking a few days' leave and visiting England. We were permitted to catch "hops" (free military aircraft rides), to England for rest and recreation, but I decided against it, I needed to save money. I saved every penny I could, and was becoming concerned because my fiancée wasn't making much of an effort to save money. I asked my mother in a letter if she would talk to her. I was also concerned because I was not hearing from her very often, she only wrote a couple of times a month, while I wrote almost every day.

All the sailors, marines, and Air Force people stationed in Iceland, were considered to be the "Icelandic Defense Force". Every few months we would be given helmets, and pretend to set up defensive posts around the base. We would receive lectures on combat basics. In the event of an invasion we would all be issued M-1 rifles, and defend the base. I often thought that we sailors would be good targets among the rocks in our blue dungarees! As March arrived, it appeared spring was on the horizon. The sun rose at 8:00 a.m. and set at 6:00 p.m. I continued working out with weights at the barracks and succeeded in gaining about fifteen pounds.

From letters I received, it appeared my brother Joe was growing up; his latest comment was he'd "like a dangerous gun." My parents were concerned that he might have rheumatic fever. I hoped he didn't. I began to drink coffee regularly, as most sailors did; the coffee pot was a constant fixture at most Navy commands.

On 30 March we had a farewell party for our shop chief petty officer. He was retiring after twenty years in the Navy. He had joined the Navy in 1942, the year I was born.

In mid-April I received a letter from my Aunt Edna. She mentioned in her letter that she thought my fiancée was dating someone else. This was very discouraging, but I was helpless to do anything about it. My Aunts Edna, Lois and Pearl, were faithful letter writers, as well as a family friend, Iva Milam. I looked forward to their letters.

On the 21st of April a few of us from the AUW Shop were conducting loading practice with a Mark 101 trainer, called a Mark 104. Armed marines had set up a perimeter around the P2V *Neptune* aircraft that was being loaded. We had been at the loading site for a couple of hours. A taxiway to the landing strip went by the loading site. A couple of planes had taxied by during our loading practice. A plane was approaching, and Lieutenant Mack went wild, and screamed for us to cover up the trainer with a tarp. We rushed over, and covered up the trainer. The plane approached, it was a large four-engine passenger plane, and on the tail was a red hammer and sickle. It was a Russian plane. Iceland's international airport, shared the runway with the American base. People at the plane windows waved, we noticed that some of them had cameras. We were much more cautious about planes that approached our loading site from then on.

The latter part of April we had a command personnel inspection of all sailors on the base. We all mustered in a large hanger in our dress uniforms and stood in ranks at attention, while the captain walked by and inspected each sailor. An embarrassing thing happened to John Gaffey. The captain stopped in front of John and asked him if he knew the name of his commanding officer. John didn't know. We all got a lecture when we got back to the AUW Shop. We were told to learn the names of all the officers in our chain of command.

The last of April I got word that I had passed my third class petty officer test. I would become a GMT3 on 16 May. John Gaffey also made third class, and GMT2 Shewe had made GMT1. I was very excited about putting on a crow. The crow I would wear on my left upper sleeve was an eagle with crossed cannons underneath and one chevron. I would wear a crow on all my uniforms, including dungarees.

GMT1 Shewe and I put in a special request chit asking permission for liberty on 19 May. We wanted to celebrate our promotions. This would be the first time I set foot off the base in nine months. We planned to visit the capital of Reykjavik.

The first of May, I mailed my parents a cuckoo clock, which I bought at the Navy exchange. On 16 May, I was promoted to GMT3. I had sewn a crow on all my uniforms. We wore dungarees on workdays at the shop. John Gaffey and I wore crows for the first time that day. It was then that we learned of the tradition of "tacking on a crow". All senior petty officers (second class and above) were permitted to hit you on the left arm, where your new crow was worn, with their fist. John Gaffey's arm and mine were very sore that night, but we were very happy. We both had a bit of a "port (left) list" walking around with our new crows on our arms.

The 19th of May was a Saturday. GMT1 Shewe and I had our liberty request approved by Lieutenant Mack. He discouraged liberty, because of our classified work, however he felt we should celebrate our promotions. On Friday we went to the base personnel office and picked up liberty cards that had to be carried while we were off base. We also had to wear our uniforms (dress blues). We had to observe a curfew from 2200 (10:00 p.m.) to 0600 (6:00 a.m.), while in Reykjavik. We were not permitted on the streets or in public view at these times.

Saturday morning we left the base on a bus. We arrived at Reykjavik an hour later. We walked around sightseeing, and had lunch in a small café. All the streets were cobble stoned, the buildings were mostly made of bricks, some made of wood, and the predominant house color was white. After lunch we went to a hotel and rented a room, the clerk said we would have to return in the evening to get our room key. We paid for the room, then left and strolled around. We visited a bar, Shewe had a drink, but I was not twenty-one, so I had a coke. The bartender told us about a dance that was going to take place that afternoon a few blocks away. After leaving the bar we went to where the dance was going to be held; however, the people there treated us coldly, and we didn't feel welcome, so we left.

While walking down the street, we noticed a crowd of about 200 people coming toward us. All in the crowd seemed agitated and excited. As they approached, we saw in the middle of the crowd, a black man in civilian clothes. He saw us, and said "Boy am I glad to see you guys, I'm on a merchant ship, and all these people started following me, jabbering Icelandic. I'm scared; would you two please walk with me back to my ship?" We said "of course," although we were a little scared also. The crowd seemed very curious about him, trying to touch his skin, and hair. We walked with him about half a mile back to the pier where his ship was. He thanked us, and said "I'm not going ashore again in this crazy place." Shewe and I were baffled. Talking about it however we noted that we'd not seen any black sailors, marines, or Air Force people since we'd been on Iceland. We were to learn later it was a Navy and Air Force policy that black military personnel not be assigned to Iceland, because of the social disruption possibility. The Icelandics had never seen black people before. The Icelandics were not overly friendly to any outsider. That's understandable from the isolated part of the world in which they live. As I said before, the Icelandic men were very large in stature. Most of the police were well over six tall. They did not like firearms. The police carried nightsticks. On those occasions that assigned workers came into the AUW Shop compound to do work, we escorted them. We were armed with forty-five-caliber pistols; they were very nervous about this escort situation, so we tried not to appear threatening to them.

Shewe and I returned to the center of town, had dinner in a nice restaurant, and then took a few pictures. We walked around for a while and noticed there seemed to be more and more people on the streets. It was getting close to 2200, our curfew time, so we went back to the hotel. It was then we got a shock, there was a different man behind the desk, he said there were no rooms. We explained we had already paid for a room. At that point he said he didn't understand English! Shewe was very upset. We left and checked a few nearby hotels; none had vacancies. It was well after curfew, when a police van drove by us. The van stopped, and these huge policemen got out. Shewe was more than six feet tall, but he looked like a midget next to these policemen. One policeman spoke English, he said we were not supposed to be on the street, and we were under arrest. They put us in the back on the police van. I was disgusted, I'd never been in trouble in the Navy, and now I'd just become a petty officer and was being arrested. I visualized my crow "flying off my arm" after going to captain's mast.

We explained what had happened at the hotel, so they took us to the hotel, after a lengthy discussion in Icelandic, the hotel clerk admitted he had a room, but it would cost an additional five dollars. We had no choice but to pay, then the police left. In the morning we got up, had breakfast, and returned to base. My one and only liberty on Iceland was not enjoyable. I had no desire to visit Reykjavik again.

The isolated duty was difficult for the younger single sailors. Prior to our third class exam John Gaffey and I had gotten into an argument in the barracks. It began when he started teasing me, while I was shaving in our room. We got into a fight, no blows were thrown, but we had a vicious wresting match. We both had a few bruises, and didn't talk to each other for a few days.

This was an example of "cabin fever". Most people counted the days until they got off the "Rock".

John Gaffey and I were friends (except when we got on each other's nerves), and we pulled practical jokes on each other, such as short sheeting each other's bunk, etc. This was something that helped us maintain our sanity in the isolated environment in which we found ourselves.

One very cold morning, John and I boarded the shop's bomb truck, to take morning magazine temperatures. The bomb truck was a 2-½ ton truck, with a large boom crane on the bed. The crane was operated from a seat on the crane, and was used to hoist bombs from storage containers, onto bomb trailers, and other ordnance lifting jobs. We used the bomb truck to drive back and forth from the AUW Shop to the two magazines in the compound. This was a drive of about one block, and the four-wheel drive was used when snow was on the ground or when it was muddy. When it was cold, often the padlocks would freeze, so we would take a bucket of hot water, and soak a rag in it, wrap the rag around the padlock prior to inserting the key and unlocking it. As I mentioned, John was from Florida, and had never lived in a cold climate. We got out of the truck at the first magazine; I put the hot rag around the first padlock, and mentioned to John, "On a cold day like today, you'd be in trouble if you put your tongue on a metal door like this." I then removed the rag, and turned to take it back to the truck. I heard a strangling sound, and turning, I saw John with his face stuck to the door! I dipped the rag in the bucket of water, and wrung the warm water from the rag so it ran down the magazine door, loosening his stuck lips, and tongue. His nose, lips, and tongue were raw. After we returned to the shop he went to sickbay, and was given some salve to use for a few days.

John had "no neck". In order to look back when backing up the bomb truck, he had to turn his whole upper body to ensure the road was clear. There was an area near the magazines we used to turn around and return to the AUW Shop after taking magazine temperatures. Occasionally on cold days when John was driving the bomb truck, he would look to his left out of the driver's window. While he was looking, I would slip the floor-mounted gearshift out of reverse. He would step on the accelerator and race the engine. Then he would step on the clutch, and I would slip the gearshift back into reverse. He would assume the wheels were slipping on ice. This would repeat about three times, I'd then say, "I'll get out and push". When I pushed of course the truck moved. I managed to pull this about six times, and he never caught on! Twenty-six years later, I talked to John and confessed this trick to him. He said he had wondered why the truck wheels never spun in reverse when I was driving.

Torpedoman Petty Officer First Class (TM1) Smith was a bachelor, and lived in a section of the barracks called the "First Class Section." Often he would invite me down to his room. Although he was the leading petty officer of the shop, and my boss, we became friends. He would tell me stories about his experiences during World War II, and also blow off steam about some of the problems he had with sailors at the shop. He liked Scotch whiskey, and he would always give me a glass of it. I would sip it to be hospitable, although it tasted like kerosene to me! I was the only seaman, and later only third class that he invited to his room, so I felt honored. All who knew him respected him, and he was fair to everyone. I learned a lot about leadership watching him, and listening to him. I heard after I left Iceland that he made chief, which was long overdue; he had more than twenty years in the Navy.

Mineman Second Class Petty Officer Stanwick, who worked in Shop 2, was president of the base chapter of the Fleet Reserve Association (FRA). This was the same fraternal organization with the office in Brooklyn where I had relaxed while waiting for transportation to Iceland. Stanwick invited John and me to a meeting one month, and we joined. The dues were five dollars a year. Everyone wanted to buy us a drink. Not knowing anything about mixed drinks, I said I'd have a rum and coke. After four or five I got terribly sick. To this day when I smell rum I get nauseous!

In June I received advance word about my next duty station. I was going to the aircraft carrier *USS Independence* (CVA-62), home ported in Norfolk, Virginia. It was not what I wanted, but what I had expected. In July I was planning the leave I would have before reporting to the ship. I still planned on getting married, and then my bride Donna and I would travel across country to Norfolk. I had been sending money home each payday. The money I sent to my parents was going into a savings account, and I was also sending my fiancée "spending money". Since making third class I had received a raise of twenty-five dollars per month. I also had taken a "proficiency pay" exam. The GMT rating was undermanned, along with other technical ratings in the Navy, so proficiency pay was offered to sailors in these undermanned ratings. Proficiency pay was given in two steps; P-1 was twenty-five dollars per month, and P-2 was fifty dollars per month. I was only eligible for P1, but had to pass an exam. I was pleased to discover I passed the exam, and my P-1 pay would begin in July.

Proficiency pay was a subject of resentment for the Torpedomen in the AUW Shop since they were not eligible for it.

In June a GMT1 named Charles Ross, from Nuclear Weapons Training Center Atlantic, Norfolk, Virginia, visited Shop 2 for a week, and gave refresher classes on the Mark 90, and Mark 101. He also conducted classes on safety, and security. This was a welcome break from our daily routines.

I felt I was doing well in the Navy. This feeling arose partially from the marks I was getting on a report that was filled out at normal intervals on all sailors. This was the "Report of Enlisted Performance Evaluation/NAVPERS 792," or as they were commonly called "Quarterly Marks". A sailor's immediate supervisor filled out this report; it was then reviewed through the chain of command, and finally signed by the sailor's commanding officer. The report was extremely important, as the document is made a permanent part of a sailor's service record, and referred to for recommendations for promotion, transfers, special programs, and a host of other things. The reports covered every day of a sailor's life in the Navy. As a sailor is promoted upward through the ranks, the report format changes. As a seaman and third class the specific categories I was evaluated in were: Duties (except supervisory), Military Behavior (How well the seaman accepts authority and conforms to standards of military behavior), Leadership and Supervisory Ability (His ability to plan and assign work to others and effectively direct their activities.). Military Appearance (His military appearance and neatness in person and dress), Adaptability (How well he gets along and works with others). Within each category there were levels of marks ranging from a high of 4.0 to the lowest mark of 2.0.

To show the importance of quarterly marks, at the end of a sailor's enlistment, if the averages of all his marks in Military Behavior are less than 3.0, he will not receive an Honorable Discharge. Also any mark in Military Behavior less than 3.0, makes a sailor ineligible for a Good Conduct medal. All the marks I had received thus far on the *USS Haven*, A School, and Iceland were averaging 3.7. The reverse of the form described service schools attended, special educational achievements, awards, and other achievements during the reporting period. At the end of each evaluation period a sailor was supposed to be counseled by his immediate supervisor, and given praise where praise was due, and also told how to improve any marks he was given. At this point in my career I realized that evaluations were important, but as time went on I appreciated much more the impact of this piece of paper upon a sailor's career. I was to learn generally that many supervisors, who filled them out, did not take the time they should with them, and often looked upon evaluation work as just another piece of paperwork that imposed upon their time. As I gained more experience as a supervisor, I campaigned to increase awareness about how very important evaluations were not only to the individuals, but also to the Navy.

In July, all was not well in the AUW Shop. Since the leading chief had retired, TM1 Smith had been standing in as the shop leading chief. A chief reported to the AUW Shop who was an Aviation Electrician. It soon became obvious that the new chief had never worked with ordnance men before, and that he had very little experience supervising sailors. He would give orders, and then reverse them. He was a recently promoted chief, and very impressed with himself. He was not respected by the troops. In addition to the chief, the shop had six first class petty officers, three second class, and four third class (myself included).

Reflecting on my time in Iceland I felt good about what I had learned and accomplished. I'd learned a good deal about human nature, and felt I'd proven myself in an isolated difficult environment. There was a lot of "squabbling," and "back stabbing" that went on from time to time, and I'd managed to stay clear of it. I'd watched good leaders, and bad, and noted the traits of each. I was not sure if I would make the Navy my career. I'd had a lot of time to reflect on my life, the Navy, and my maturity. The first of August, I'd not heard from my fiancée for a number of weeks. I received a letter from my aunt saying my fiancée was dating a high school classmate of mine. This was the equivalent of a "Dear John Letter". I was devastated over this news. All the marriage plans were gone, and all I'd worked for was dissolved. I felt betrayed. I had dated Donna for more than four years, she had been my "first love," and this rejection was very painful. I finally rationalized that I was too young to be married. I told my parents that I intended to buy a car while I was home on leave, then when I returned to Norfolk, I would leave the car for my sister to use.

About this time the single guys who lived in the barracks, moved to a different barracks. Since being in Iceland, I had changed rooms five times, for repainting and various other reasons. This was not good for my morale, to play "musical rooms." The time for my transfer was drawing near. My parents were on a two-week vacation to Kansas, and they continued to write faithfully. My aunts also wrote often. These letters were encouraging to me since receiving my "Dear John Letter".

When a person is close to transfer, he is called a "short timer". I was scheduled to leave Iceland on 12 September. A popular "short timer calendar" was a drawing of a nude girl, with thirty sections numbered one through thirty. Each day the sections were colored in until the last three, which were on her obvious body parts that interested sailors most.

I called my parents on 18 August; it was late at night in Iceland, and 0300 in California. The phone call cost me twelve dollars. I purchased my plane tickets on the first of September that I would use to go on my thirty days leave. I was to go by military plane from Iceland to McGuire Air Force Base. I had to buy my ticket from McGuire to Philadelphia, then to San Francisco, and onto Fresno.

On 8 September, John Gaffey and I contributed ten dollars each, and the AUW Shop gave us a going away party. John was transferring shortly after me to a submarine tender in Norfolk. Everyone seemed truly sorry to see me go. The party was held at the base enlisted club. Everyone wished us "good luck". I began the checkout process on the ninth. I had sent a large box containing my civilian clothes home earlier in the month.

On 12 September, I went to the Keflavik Air Terminal, boarded a plane, looked out the window and bid the barren rock landscape of Iceland goodbye. I was not sad to leave; it had been a tough year, although I had learned much about my job and myself. I was anxious to get home. The plane trip to Greenland was much smoother than the trip twelve months' previously! My trip across country was uneventful.

The AUW Shop was destined to be closed in a few years when all of the worldwide AUW Shops ceased to exist. On September 8, 2006 the Keflavik Naval Station was disestablished, ending 45 years of operations in support of the defense of Iceland.

Chapter 5: The "INDY"

I had a wonderful homecoming seeing my parents, sister Linda, and baby brothers. It was an emotionally painful time however, as my ex-fiancée Donna did not care to see me. One day my mom and I went car shopping, and found a red and white 1956, two-door Chevrolet convertible for $900. It was a beautiful car, and I enjoyed driving it while on leave. I had to readjust to driving on the "right" side of the road, having driven on the left side in Iceland for a year. I discovered while on leave that many of the kids I attended high school with had since moved away from my small country community, either attending college, or pursuing careers. My thirty-day leave went by quickly, and before I knew it I was preparing to fly to the east coast. My plans had been to be married at this point. This was a painful time, and I remained heart-broken.

I left California on 11 October, 1962. When I arrived at the Norfolk Receiving Station, Virginia I was told the *USS Independence* was at sea. She was supposed to be in port during this time, but had gotten underway unexpectedly. There were a lot of stranded *Independence* sailors at the receiving station who had been left behind. This was a time of national tension, because of the discovery of Russian missiles on the island of Cuba pointed at America. There was a lot of speculation about what was going to happen. It looked like the war everyone had been dreading was about to start.

Norfolk Naval Station had a "rustic" look, much like the Great Lakes Naval Base where I'd gone to electronics school. All the buildings were made of brick. Once again I found myself in the least desirable position in the Navy, in a transit status at a naval receiving station, living out of a sea bag, ready to leave at a few moments notice, with constant musters, and rude treatment. One night while feeling sorry for myself, I went on liberty to the Norfolk YMCA, and called my ex-fiancée. I told her if her boyfriend would not marry her, then I would. It was not meant to be, however; as it developed she was eventually happily married, had two sons and settled down in my hometown of Strathmore.

On 15 October, eighty sailors awaiting the *Independence* were told we would be flown out to the ship. On the 16th we had an early reveille, and were taken to the Norfolk Naval Air Station. We boarded a transport plane at 0700, and at 1400 in the afternoon landed at Naval Air Station, Mayport, Florida. It was hot and humid, especially since we were wearing our wool dress blue uniforms. I was also miserable because I was suffering from a cold.

The plan was to fly a few of us at a time out to the ship on the ship's Carrier Onboard Delivery (COD, see photo page), plane, which was a two-engine plane that could carry as many as twenty passengers. We would land on the flight deck. The weather did not cooperate with this plan, however; there were hurricane warnings that prevented flying. Five days later we were still stuck at Mayport. *Independence* sailors kept arriving at Mayport from Norfolk, trying to catch the ship.

While in Norfolk, and Mayport, I began to enjoy the prestige of being a petty officer. I was put in charge of a number of seamen during cleanup times, and working parties. I stood barracks master at arms duty, and held taps and reveille. I was giving orders for the first time.

I was going to be in W Division on the ship. I met a guy who had been in Albuquerque the same time I had, who had been on leave when the ship got underway. He said there were a lot of our classmates on the *Independence*. The barracks at Mayport were wooden, with large screened windows. The mosquitoes were plentiful, huge, and hungry. Every evening a sprayer would go around the base spraying a fog of insecticide. About all I did in Mayport was eat meals and wait in the barracks. We were not permitted to go on liberty. As I said, I was suffering from a bad cold; I'd gotten from all the sudden climate changes during the last month. My cold seemed worse in the hot humid climate of Florida. All this did not improve the depression I felt from the loss of my fiancée.

On 21 October, President Kennedy gave a speech concerning the Soviet missiles in Cuba, and our embargo of Cuba. There were a lot of rumors of impending war. On the 22nd, twelve of us boarded a "COD" and along with eight other COD's, we flew from Mayport to West Palm Beach, Florida. We stayed overnight at a big exclusive hotel; one President Kennedy was rumored to have stayed in when he vacationed at West Palm Beach. I shared a room with a second class cook, who was headed for the ship. We were supposed to get up at 4:00 a.m. in the morning on the 23rd and re-board our planes. The cook went out on the town, and came into our room drunk about 2:30 a.m. I got up at 4:00, and tried to awaken the cook, but he was passed out cold. I dragged him into the shower and turned the cold water on, but he refused to get dressed, and fought me when I tried to help him.

I told an officer traveling with us that the cook refused to get ready, and he said, "Don't worry about him." I felt bad, but I could not do anything to get him moving. Missing ship or plane movement was a serious offense.

At the airport there were more than one hundred sailors assembled to board eight planes. We were told that we would fly in a tight formation, with fighter escorts, A-1 *Skyraiders*, single engine prop planes, guarding our flight. The Cuban Air Force was supposed to have fighters roaming the airspace in which were going to fly. We took off, and everyone's nose was pressed to the plane windows, watching for hostile airplanes. We landed on a small island called Grand Turk, refueled, and then took off. After flying for about thirty minutes we were told to tighten our seat belts. We were going to land on a carrier. The seats faced the rear of the aircraft. The seat belts consisted of two straps across your chest and one across your lap. We also wore life jackets, in the event the plane went into the sea. I looked out the window, and saw the carrier far below. It looked very small. The plane dropped lower and lower, and then we were on our approach. Everyone was very quiet; the plane floated toward the carrier deck, there was a sudden bump, the plane slammed to the sudden stop, pushing us into the cushions of our seats, while the engines roared. We were told prior to landing in the event the plane's arresting hook hanging down from the tail, missed the arresting wire on the carrier deck, then we would take off immediately for another landing try. Luckily we made it on our first try, and we were aboard. I was relieved, but not for long, we discovered that we had landed on the *USS Enterprise*, the world's first nuclear powered aircraft carrier. We were to wait for about an hour, and then we would take off again, and fly onboard the *USS Independence*. For landing and taking off a carrier deck, we were instructed to place our arms across our chest, and lean into the seat belt shoulder straps. After an hour it was time to take off again. We boarded the plane, put on our life jackets, strapped in, and the plane taxied to the catapult. The plane jolted to a stop, and the catapult was attached. The plane engines revved up full speed. We could feel the ship rise and fall with waves. Then there was a jolt, and we were hurled toward the bow of the ship. It was a terrific acceleration. My legs and feet were forced off the floor of the plane; my body was pressed into the straps, away from the nose of the plane. There was a sickening drop downward as the plane cleared the flight deck, after what seemed like a long time dropping toward the surface of the ocean, we began slowly to climb skyward. After twenty minutes, we began circling; I looked down and far below was my new home, the *USS Independence*. The landing was a repeat of the landing aboard the *Enterprise*. I was finally aboard my new duty station.

We got off the plane, each sailor carrying his sea bag. One constant inconvenience being in transit was that you carried your sea bag everywhere. A sea bag weighed about sixty pounds. The easiest way to carry it was slung over your shoulder. Another very uncomfortable aspect of transferring was that you were required to wear dress blues while moving from one place to another. For example from Norfolk to Mayport and, from Mayport to West Palm Beach, and onto the ship, we wore dress blues. The dress blues were made of thick wool, and very uncomfortable in hot tropical climates. Dress whites, which are made of white cotton, and worn in hot climates, and during summers, could not be worn when a sailor was in a transfer status. This regulation was eventually changed, but I suffered with it for many years, as did all sailors.

The *USS Independence* flight deck was a beehive of activity. We were ushered off the flight deck into the island superstructure. We were taken down an escalator that went down many decks, to the hangar deck; we walked across the hangar deck, and then down a ladder to the personnel office. My service record, health, and pay record, along with transfer orders were turned in. I was told I would be assigned to W Division. A third class GMT came to the personnel office, and directed me to the W Division berthing compartment. There I saw a berthing compartment, which was much more modern than the one I had lived in on the *USS Haven*. The bunks were three high, and made of metal with privacy curtains and air-conditioning vents in each one. The bottom bunk was constructed so it could be latched up off the deck, to permit sweeping and swabbing of the deck. Within the individual bunk compartments were lockers, for storage of uniforms and personal items. The mattress could also be raised up to reveal an additional storage area. Each bunk had a light for reading. I was very impressed with the berthing arrangements. The *Haven* had bunks four high, with stretched canvas, and a thin mattress. A crude term for the sheet bag that was placed on the mattress, and served as a sheet, was nicknamed a "fart sack." I took an "in-between" bunk, one in the middle of a top and bottom bunk.

The *Independence* was one of the modern carriers of the Navy. The newest in the Navy at the time was a *USS Enterprise*, whose hull number was CVN-65, (the carrier I had landed on prior to *Independence*.) The *Independence*'s hull number was CVA-62.

I was tired from my travels; I slept well that first night as the ship rolled gently on the sea. I quickly gained my "sea legs." The first day the division chief and leading first class petty officer introduced themselves to me. As it always is being the new guy, I was an object of curiosity to everyone. I recognized many of the sailors as classmates and those that had been in classes behind me in New Mexico.

The first morning I began checking in, with a guide from W Division. The ship was huge. It didn't take long for me to become turned around and confused about where I was on the ship. I learned it would be a while before I could go to work. I could not enter W Division spaces until my security clearance was confirmed. While awaiting confirmation, I was assigned as the berthing compartment supervisor. Each day I supervised a couple of seaman cleaning the W Division berthing compartment, which contained bunks for forty-five men.

There was much speculation about the world situation. We were told that there were Russian ships headed toward Cuba, and we would be enforcing the blockade that the president had ordered. In the event our marines invaded Cuba, our aircraft, operating as fighters, and bombers would be instrumental. As is often the case during wars or times of tension, we had less information in the combat area, about what was happening than did the ordinary citizen on the street who had access to daily news that we did not have.

I learned that most of the places I frequented on the ship, such as the mess decks, sickbay, small stores, head, berthing, and others, were on the second deck, or the deck immediately under the hangar deck. This was the "main street" on the aircraft carrier.

One day while going through the chow line, I saw the cook I had tried unsuccessfully to awaken, and urge to get going at the Palm Beach Hotel on the way to the ship. He was sheepish, and said he had been put on report for missing movement. I told him I tried my best to get him up that morning. He said he knew that, and was sorry he had gotten so "plastered". After going to captain's mast, he was busted from second class to third class petty officer.

Being "put on report," was something feared by sailors. It was comparable to getting a serious traffic ticket, or being placed under arrest in civilian life. A sailor put on report meant he had violated a ship's regulation, or an article listed in the "Uniform Code of Military Justice," (UCMJ). Unlike the civilian communities of our country where you are considered innocent until proven guilty, in the Navy you are considered guilty until proven innocent. The junior ranks have few rights, or freedoms. Any petty officer or commissioned officer can place those junior to him or her on report. The judging authorities an accused might be brought before have authority to impose increasing amounts of punishment, beginning at the lowest level, Executive Officer's Inquiry; next Captain's Mast; then Summary Court Martial; and the highest court, that can give capital punishment, or the death penalty, a General Court Martial. Petty officers could also assign hours of "extra duty," which was extra work performed outside normal working hours, often during hours of liberty.

When an American citizen enters the military, many freedoms and privileges enjoyed by that person are either curtailed or taken away because of the nature of military life. Examples of restricted American privileges are freedom of speech, freedom of movement, treatment of equality, etc. At sea a ship is a monarchy; the captain is the final voice of authority.

The number of men on the *USS Independence* was about 5,500. The ship was divided into two groups, "Ship's Company," and the "Air Wing". Ship's company operated the ship, while the air wing was involved with the maintenance and operation of the airplanes. This has been the basic make up of carriers since the aircraft carrier's beginning.

The sailors in the air wing are called "airedales," or "brown shoes," while ship's company sailors are called "black shoes". The "brown shoes" referred to a time when aviators in the Navy were permitted to wear brown shoes. We GMT's in W Division were a part of ship's company, so we were "black shoes".

The captain is the overall boss of the ship, and the air wing has a commanding officer called the "Air Wing Commander," or as he is called "Air Boss". When the ship is operating, the air wing sailors have their own working and berthing areas. When the ship is in the yards, or not "battle ready," the air wing, and planes are normally moved off the ship, to a nearby ashore naval air station. In the *USS Independence*'s case this was Norfolk Naval Air Station.

The air wing was further divided into squadrons; these squadrons were grouped by aircraft type, such as fighter squadrons, bomber squadrons, reconnaissance squadrons, and support squadrons. The ships' company was divided into departments, and further divided into divisions. Each squadron had a commanding officer, and each department had a department head. A commander normally held these positions. It may be helpful to the reader if I list the naval officer ranks beginning with the lowest.

Ensign (ENS, O-1), Lieutenant Junior Grade (LTJG, O-2), Lieutenant (LT, O-3), Lieutenant Commander (LCDR, O-4), Commander (CDR, O-5), Captain (CAPT, O-6), Rear Admiral (Lower Half) (RDML, O-7), Rear Admiral (Upper Half) (RADM, O-8), Vice Admiral (VADM, O-9), Admiral (ADM, O-10), Fleet Admiral (FADM, O-11). A unique officer rank is the Chief Warrant Officer ranks, which I'll write about in detail later on. These ranks are: Warrant Officer One (WO-1), Chief Warrant Officer Two (CWO-2), Chief Warrant Officer Three (CWO-3), and Chief Warrant Officer Four (CWO-4).

Officers headed divisions on the ship from the rank of warrant officer to commander. An example of a department and the divisions within a department is Weapons Department which included: G-1 Division, G-2 Division, G-3 Division, G-4 Division, EOD Division, 1st Lieutenant Division, and W Division. Each division had a specific job, with all division officers accountable to the Weapons Department Head, who was normally a commander.

After I had completed the check-in process, my days were spent overseeing the cleaning of the division berthing space, and sitting around. I was anxious to go to work in the W Division spaces. One job I was given in the berthing compartment was looking for clothing, or personal items left out, or as said in the Navy, "left adrift". When the word was passed to commence ships work, everything, clothing, etc., was supposed to be stowed within personal lockers. If anything was found adrift, I was to turn it over to the Division Police Petty Officer, GMT1 Frankie Ramsey. He would lock up the item(s) in a special locker called the division "Lucky Bag". In order to reclaim the item, the person who owned it had to perform a specific amount of extra work, or duty in order to get it out of the lucky bag. If the item, or clothes went unclaimed, then eventually the items were turned into the ship's lucky bag, and it would either be sold or disposed of.

All aspects of life and work were regulated. Some examples of ships' regulations[9] follow:

Haircuts – All persons are required to keep their hair neatly trimmed. Any person whose hair does not present a neat appearance shall be ordered to the ship's barbershop for a haircut.

Berthing – No person shall: 1. Sleep in any spaces or use any bunk or berth other than that to which he has been assigned except as may be authorized by proper authority. 2. Sleep in or lie on any bunk or berth while clothed in dungarees or working clothes or while wearing shoes. 3. Smoke while sitting on or lying on any bunk or berth, or smoke in any space during the night hours between taps and reveille. 4. Remove any mattress from any bunk or place of storage, or place such mattress on the deck or in any place other than a bunk except as may be authorized by proper authority. 5. Create a disturbance or turn on any white light in any berthing space or living spaces during the night hours between taps and reveille except as may be necessary for the performance of his duty. 6. Fail to turn out of his bunk at reveille except when he is on the sick list or authorized to bunk late. 7. Be authorized late bunk privilege unless he has stood a midwatch, performed ships' work, or made a boat trip as a crewmember after 2200 the previous day, or is specifically authorized late bunk privileges by competent authority. All late sleepers shall turn out at 0700. 8. Lie down in a bunk occupied by another person.

There were many other ship's regulations to be complied with. More examples follow, concerning shoes:

Shoes–1. All persons shall wear shoes equipped with rubber heels on board this vessel and in ship's boats except boat crewmembers shall wear rubber-soled canvas shoes when embarked in ship's boats. 2. No person shall wear shoes with taps, cleats, or other metal devices on the heels or soles on board this vessel or in the ship's boats.

When I reported aboard, I was given a substantial booklet containing the ships regulations I was to comply with. I had to get a camera pass immediately for a small brownie camera I had. In order to use a camera on board *Independence* you had to have a camera pass, which verified that you knew what areas you were permitted to have a camera. Cameras were definitely not allowed in W Division working spaces.

The ship had its own internal police force that roamed throughout the ship maintaining order, and enforcing regulations. This police force was called the Master at Arms Division, and worked directly for the officer who was the second in charge of the ship, the Executive Officer. The Master at Arms, or "MAA's" as they were called, wore arm badges emblazoned with orange letters "MAA". I might add the MAA's were held in contempt by many sailors, as they had the authority to place sailors on report, and hand out violation slips, as well as prevent sailors from going on liberty if they were not squared away. An aircraft carrier can best be described as a large city with its own police force, hospital, fire department, restaurants, and even its own internal radio and television station.

While I was adjusting to life at sea, I was catching up on what my former classmates had been doing. One friend Jerry Hecko was in the brig! He had been an Unauthorized Absentee, (U.A.) for a couple of days, and after going to captain's mast he had been given a couple of weeks in the ship's brig. The ship's Marine Detachment ran the ship's brig, and it was a much worse environment than any civilian jail. It wasn't known if he would be going back into W Division or not after his brig time. Normally a GMT who underwent disciplinary action such as brig time would lose his security clearance. Jerry was the sailor who had been caught out of bounds in school at Great Lakes. As it developed, he did come back to W Division, mostly because of his personality. He was a very personable guy, and well liked by everyone. He just had the unfortunate ability to occasionally get into trouble.

Many of my classmates had come to the ship after A school, instead of going as I had, to an overseas shore duty assignment. I had gone to Iceland because of my higher graduation standing, but I didn't feel more "fortunate," since I had ended up on the east coast.

There was a lot of talk about a proclamation from President Kennedy. All those in the military scheduled to be discharged between 11 November, and 28 February, had their enlistment extended twelve months. Everyone hoped something like this didn't happen to him when his time to get out of the Navy was near.

There were two "subcultures" on the ship. We, who were "first-termers," had come into the Navy with the idea of completing our military service obligation, and then returning to civilian life as quickly as possible. There was also the group of sailors who had "shipped over," or signed up for additional enlistments, which were career sailors, or as first-termers called them "lifers". First-termers were not too respectful of lifers, at least behind their back; much of this disdain was because most of the lifers were our supervisors.

Before the Cuban Crisis the *Independence* had been scheduled to go into the Norfolk shipyard for overhaul on 20 December. It was not sure if this shipyard date would be met. We were told that the Russian ships that had been steaming toward Cuba had turned around. This was a relief as a dangerous confrontation had been avoided. One evening before we got word about the Russian ships, rumors had been flying, because the ordnance divisions had been mixing napalm liquid for use, and this was an indication that bombing was to start soon!

During this time we were shown photographs that had been taken of fighter aircraft in flight that had been taken by U.S. planes. These planes had American markings on the fuselage, but squadron number identification numbers that were not in existence, the pilots of these planes would not respond to radio calls. It was assumed these were Cuban or Russian planes painted to look like ours. These planes were not permitted to fly near the naval task groups.

Speaking of airplanes, there were a variety of planes on the ship, each type designated for specific jobs. Each different type of plane was grouped in its own squadron. We had A-4 *Skyhawks* (see photo page), which was the smallest, single seat jet on the ship. This was a fighter/bomber. We had the A-1 *Skyraiders*, a prop-driven bomber that could carry its weight in bombs and ordnance. We also had the A-5 *Vigilante*, which was the fastest plane on the ship and flew at mach (700 mph) plus speeds. It was a two seated, dual engine jet, which was a bomber, and photo plane. The A-6A *Intruder* (see photo page), a dual jet engine, two seated all-weather bomber, was the newest plane onboard. We had F-4B *Phantoms*, and F-8 *Crusader* jet fighters. We had Carrier Onboard Delivery or COD planes that flew people, equipment, and the all-important mail, back and forth from land. I had flown aboard *Independence* in a COD. This plane was very popular with the crew, especially when we had not received mail for a few days. There were helicopters used for rescues at sea during flight quarters or in the event of a man overboard. Helicopters were also used to transport material and people from ship to ship and ship to shore. There were also Special Airborne Warning & Control Systems (AWACS) aircraft, which extended the radar coverage of the ship when these planes were airborne flying around the ship.

The *USS Independence* was a "*Forrestal* Class Carrier," which meant it was one of our country's newest aircraft carriers with an angled flight deck. The only larger carrier in 1962 was the *USS Enterprise*.

The *Kitty Hawk* and *Constellation* were under construction, and would be larger. An angled flight deck on these carriers permitted simultaneous takeoffs and landings.

The first of November, my security clearance was confirmed. I had my badge pictures taken, badges prepared, and the captain signed the access list that permitted me to enter W Division spaces. W Division had a forward magazine area, and an aft magazine area. Each magazine area had its own supervisor. The W Division Officer's office was in the forward magazine area. The rationale behind having widely separated magazine areas, splitting W Division in half, were in the event of a torpedo, bomb hit, or battle damage that took out one section of the ship, there would still be an undamaged magazine able to deliver weapons for aircraft loading.

I was first taken to the forward magazine area. In order to gain access, I gave my wallet sized- entry badge to the armed marine sentry who guarded the entrance. He compared my face and the photo on my badge, and keeping the badge, gave me an identical badge with a clip on it that I attached to my left shirt pocket, so it would remain visible at all times while I was within W Division spaces. Another term for W Division spaces was Special Aircraft Service Stores, or "SASS Spaces".

The W Division entrance was on the 2nd deck, or the deck immediately below the hangar deck. After the marine opened the electronically locked door, a ladder went down to the 3rd deck. The 3rd deck contained the W Division Officer, and Leading Chief's office, as well as a coffee locker and break room, also a head. A ladder went down to the next deck, which was the magazine area. At the head of this ladder was a logbook with names, and columns titled "time-in," and "time-out". Prior to going down the ladder, a person had to log the time, and upon exiting the lower space, the time was entered. This was the same system that we had used in the Iceland AUW Shop, to record person's entry and exit time within Shop 2.

I was introduced to the W Division Officer, who was Lieutenant William Johnson. I met the Leading Chief Petty Officer GMTC Tom Reese, and the Leading Petty Officer, GMT1 Robert Diedolf. I was also introduced to the Technical Monitor and Officer in Charge of the aft spaces, Chief Warrant Officer Three White.

On the third deck was a T-329 Air Monitor Air Sampler, which ran twenty-four hours a day monitoring the air in the 4th deck magazine. This test equipment had a stylus that marked a chart on a spool. The chart paper was changed every seven days. In the event a loud buzzer sounded, along with a flashing red light, evacuation procedures were initiated.

The aft magazine area spaces were laid out almost identically to the forward space layout, but somewhat smaller. A marine sentry also guarded the aft spaces. All of the W Division spaces were protected by an electronic alarm system. A Marine Response Team would investigate in the event of an alarm. The forward office spaces were manned twenty-four hours a day. After normal working hours, from 1600 to 0800 there was a watch of two people posted. This watch lasted four hours, and we all stood this watch on a rotation basis.

I discovered I was to be assigned as the Calibration Petty Officer, and was to supervise two seamen. I had a shop located within the forward magazine, on the 4th deck. My job would be to insure that all test equipment within W Division was maintained and calibrated properly. As I explained previously, a "T" number, such as T-329, T-290, etc., identified test equipment associated with nuclear weapons. Much of this equipment required periodic calibrations. The calibration would be completed at calibration laboratories ashore. Part of my job was to ensure our entire test equipment inventory was calibrated and useable during those times the ship was at sea when taking the equipment to a calibration laboratory was impossible. I was also responsible for "H-Gear," or handling equipment. Many items of H-Gear such as hoisting slings, and hook devices used for lifting weapons and components, were required to periodically be "load tested". This involved attaching a heavier weight than the one they were designed to lift, to ensure they would not fail, or break. One task that kept the seaman and me busy was ensuring that the many torque wrenches used by the assembly teams, or "hooks," as they were sometimes called, were properly calibrated. This task was complicated by the fact that the brand, or maker of a torque wrench determined how often it had to be calibrated, and there were a wide variety of torque wrenches used within the division.

I was anxious to try my hand at supervising the two men that were assigned to me. Our working area was a sixteen by twenty foot enclosed wire cage within the forward magazine. A desk, workbench, and storage shelves were in the cage. We kept the cage locked when it was not occupied. It was a pleasant working area, as all the magazines were kept at a constant temperature by air conditioning and the humidity was maintained at low levels. Magazine temperatures were recorded twice daily, in the mornings, and evenings.

In the Navy there is always a "chain of command". Orders and commands generally flow down the chain of command. Requests flow up the chain of command. It's a serious matter for anyone to "jump the chain of command".

An example might be a magazine supervisor going to the W Division Officer with a request, without first going to the leading petty officer, and skipping the two links of chief petty officer, and technical monitor. Anytime the chain of command is "blurred" or not clearly defined, it's difficult to have a smooth functioning organization. If there's a weak link in the chain of command that does not pass orders and commands down, or requests upward, poor morale is sure to follow.

As well as primary duties of W Division sailors, there was a lengthy list of "collateral duties". Examples of collateral duties are Damage Control Petty Officer, Flammable Locker Petty Officer, Publications Control Petty Officer, Safety Petty Officer, and many more. As I began my job as Calibration Petty Officer, I discovered there was not a system in force that tracked the calibration periods of test gear and torque wrenches. There also was not a good inventory of all the test sets and equipment I was responsible for. The first thing I did was hold a complete inventory of all of W Division test and handling gear, and torque wrenches. I set up a system much like one I had set up at the Iceland AUW Shop, used to track calibration, and test times of all the equipment within division spaces.

There was much speculation about whether the ship would be back in Norfolk for Christmas. The ship had been steaming off the coast of Cuba for over a month. Word was received the latter part of November that we would make it home for Christmas. We celebrated Thanksgiving off the coast of Cuba, and were relieved by the aircraft carrier *USS Lexington* a couple of days later. On 30 November, we pulled into Mayport, Florida for a couple of hours, and then steamed north along the east coast. We pulled into Norfolk on the 7th of December. The following day, the 8th was my birthday. I had turned twenty years old; I was no longer a teenager. I went on liberty into Norfolk; it was definitely a "sailor town," much more so than Long Beach. Every other downtown building was a bar catering to sailors. I noticed something I'd not seen before, all the black people rode in the rear of the public buses, and there were distinct black and white sections in Norfolk. I went into town to do some Christmas shopping. I'd been jostled on the street, and soon discovered my wallet was gone! My pocket had been picked. I'd lost seventy dollars, and had to have my ID card replaced.

The ship pulled out a few days later. The ship was busy preparing for an explosive off-load. The ship was scheduled to go into the yards for repair and upkeep. There would be welding; the ship's power, and water supply would sometimes be turned off. For all these reasons, and the increased possibility of fire, all conventional explosives and ammunition had to be offloaded during the yard period. This was a huge undertaking. Anytime a weapon was moved out of W Division magazines, it was guarded by armed marines, who were authorized to use deadly force, or had "shoot to kill orders." In order to move bombs out of the magazines, bomb elevators were used. Bomb elevators had flat platforms measuring twelve by twenty feet that moved up and down between decks. On the hangar deck, ordnance was lifted by crane down to an ammunition barge, and from there taken to storage magazines ashore. One thing we had to always keep in mind any time that an ordnance item was unbolted from its storage location, and wheels installed, was the need to keep positive control of the ordnance and prevent it from moving about as the ship rolled on the sea. Tie down chains were used to prevent uncontrolled movement. Finally the offload was complete, and we pulled into the Portsmouth Naval Shipyards.

The ship was placed in its designated dry dock. This meant the ship was positioned in a huge "bath tub," with support blocks. The locks of the dry dock were closed, the water pumped out, and the entire hull of the ship was exposed.

The weather this time of year in Norfolk was cold, although not quite as cold as Iceland, it was still very cold. We wore pea coats, anytime we were outside. I learned that I would be taking the second class petty officer Navy wide examination in February.

My parents, sister, Aunt Lois and Uncle Dean sent me a nice Christmas package. My church in Strathmore sent a wonderful package containing cookies and candy, which didn't last very long sharing it with my shipmates. My parents sent me an iron, which I needed badly. I had Christmas dinner on the ship mess deck. I called California from a phone on the pier, and had a good conversation with my parents.

The yard period was to be a busy time. Small numbers of the division were scheduled to attend refresher school at Norfolk Nuclear Weapons Training Center Atlantic for a four-week course. When one group completed the course, they would return to the ship, so another group could attend. I was scheduled with the first group to begin school.

Gary King a friend of mine from California, had been a golden gloves boxer in Los Angeles, and some evenings we would spar in the empty magazines. I would usually be the loser in these sparring matches, but it helped "blow off steam". I was making plans to go home to California on leave in March.

Money was always in short supply, as I was making $156 a month. I was hoping to make second class and get a raise. My 1962 W-2 form showed that I made a grand total of $1,651.00, and owed $2.90 federal income tax. On board ship I was receiving an additional fifteen dollars sea pay each month.

The weekend before the refresher school was to begin, I and five other GMT's moved off the ship to the Norfolk Naval Base. We moved into a barracks near the school we would be attending. The course we were taking was called, CVA Refresher Course. This was to be a condensed A school course on all the weapons peculiar to aircraft carriers. We would have classroom work, and assembly bay work, or "hands on work" with the school's weapon trainers. The atmosphere was more relaxed than on the ship. We had liberty every night, and were not required to stand watches. We could also wear civilian clothes on liberty. As on the *USS Haven*, we were not permitted to keep civilian clothes on the *Independence*. Many sailors paid a monthly fee for a locker in which to keep civilian clothes, in the many locker clubs that catered to sailors in Norfolk. The school was much like Albuquerque. We had a badge exchange system at the gate. Our class workshop area was set up like our magazine work area on the ship. We also had written exams we were expected to pass.

My sister Linda was a junior in high school, and she wrote me often. She was enjoying driving the Chevy convertible I had left at home. She was dating a guy named Frank Perkins. While I was answering a letter from her one evening in the barracks, a friend of mine from South Carolina, Dave Underwood, came in and asked me what I was doing. I told him I was writing my sister. He said he had always wanted to write a California girl, so he sat down and wrote her a long, rambling letter. The first of 1963, I complained because the cost of stamps went from seven cents to eight cents!

A trait common among a group of sailors is the assigning of nicknames. Sometimes the nicknames stayed with a person from duty station to duty station, other times the nicknames changed from place to place. For instance our division officer, Lieutenant William Johnson, was overweight, so his nickname was "Billy Big Hips," (never was he called this to his face). An older second class, about forty years old named Warren, was called "Pappy". Bob Zarate was "Z"; Jim Zielsdorf was also "Z" so sometimes he was "Z-1". Everett Shine was "Shoe Shine," Richard King was "Gary," Jerry Hecko was "George," often the nickname made little sense, but never the less it stuck. Anyone from Texas was often called "Tex.," my nickname was "Uncle Lenny," why, I don't know. When referring to *Independence*, we often shortened it to *"Indy."*

One of the first class in the division GMT1 Frankie Ramsey was black. This was unique, because in the early days of the nuclear weapons program there were very few black sailors. In future years it was more common for black sailors to become Nuclear Weaponsman, but the percentages never came close to those of the general population of the Navy. There were a lot of racial comments made about him behind his back, and inappropriate prejudice toward him. I heard of a few occasions when a black marble was put under his pillow in the berthing compartment. To his credit, he never said anything about it. I think I know who was doing this. It was a cowardly thing to do, and I'm ashamed that something like that was done to a shipmate that I served with. On a sad note, the next year 1964, Ramsey died of lung cancer; he was in his mid-thirties.

Enlisted men always addressed officers without exception by rank, or as "Sir." Chief Warrant Officers were addressed as "Sir," or "Mister," or if in the ordnance field, as was CWO White, "Gunner". No other military service has such a wide gulf as exists in the Navy between officers and enlisted men. Also, no other service treats their E-7 through E-9 rates with such deference as the Navy. All chief petty officers were addressed as "Chief". There was a wide separation between chiefs, and first class petty officers (E-6's), and below. The chiefs had their own berthing, and mess decks on the ship, and the gulf of separation was further emphasized by the fact that Chiefs (E-7 through E-9) wore khaki, and dress uniforms similar to officers. When a sailor made chief petty officer he went through a secret initiation that was never spoken of, and was a mystery to all those that never experienced it. A common refrain throughout the U.S. Navy is, "Chiefs are the backbone of the Navy."

I completed the refresher school course with a grade of B+. The weekend before we completed the school, a group of us spent a weekend at Virginia Beach. This was a summer resort area, but this being winter (the temperature was below freezing) it was a deserted town. Four guys in the division had gone in together and rented an apartment in Virginia Beach. There were about ten of us in the small apartment on this weekend, we slept on the floor, or anywhere we could find a place. I remember one guy had a record player, but only one record. The record was *"Moon River*[10]*,"* by Andy Williams. He played it over and over again until we threatened to break it!

Rumors circulated on the ship were that we were scheduled to cruise around Cuba in July and head for the Mediterranean in February 1964. I was scheduled to be discharged in December, a day before my twenty-first birthday. It looked like I would not be going overseas with the ship, which suited me, because I was anxious to get back to California. My shipmate; Gary King and I were the only ones in the division from California, and we had a common bond, we both had fiancées we'd known for a long time, and a "Dear John letter" had ended the relationship for us both. We talked endlessly of returning to California. The east coast seemed foreign to us.

The yardwork on the ship continued twenty-four hours a day. Being on a ship during a yard period is not a pleasant experience. Heating was intermittent, and it was often cold in the berthing spaces. Often there was no hot water for showers, it was dirty, and dusty throughout the ship, and there was the constant noise of air powered chipping hammers banging against the ship's steel hull. Fire hoses and cables were strung through passageways. Walking through passageways was difficult, dodging hoses and cables, and brushing against things that dirtied your uniform. Many of the compartments were secured for painting. All of W Division spaces were repainted, and many of the decks that had tile, were retiled. We worked long hours painting, and I was busy having all of the weapons hoisting equipment in the magazines weight tested.

The first of February I was assigned Shore Patrol duty for the first time. I was assigned duty with another third class on the ship. We were picked up on the pier in front of the ship at 2100 (9:00 p.m.) by the base shore patrol. We were given a black armband with the orange letters "SP," to wear on the right upper arm of our pea coats. We were also given a web belt with a holstered billy club, to wear around our waist. We were assigned to patrol a street on base that led from the enlisted club to the ship. We were told if we saw a fight, let the sailors fight until they were tired, then take them into custody and call Shore Patrol Headquarters. It was a cold dark night. We both walked the street from 2200 (10:00 p.m.) until 0230 (2:30 a.m.). There were no incidents, so my first shore patrol duty was unremarkable.

A group of W Division sailors began hanging out in a place downtown called "The Peppermint Lounge". It was what was called a "three two beer lounge." Anyone eighteen years and older was permitted in these places. They served beer that did not exceed 3.2 % alcohol. The Peppermint Lounge had a restaurant, and a rock and roll band that played nightly. A singer in the band sounded like the popular singer Buddy Holly. Many divisions would establish a bar as their hangout. W Division's was The Peppermint Lounge. I began dating a girl who was often in The Peppermint Lounge; her name was Barbara. She worked for an insurance company. I told her a "white lie," that I was twenty-two years old. We had a serious relationship, but just as I had fibbed about my age, she had fibbed about her marital status. I discovered she was married! She said she was getting a divorce. She was a nice girl, but I was skeptical about some of the things she told me. After a couple of months the relationship was over. I dated a number of girls in The Peppermint Lounge.

On 16 February, I took my second class petty officer exam. Just like my GMT3 exam, this exam had 150 multiple-choice questions. I did not feel very confident after I'd completed it. I was scheduled for a three-day aircraft loading school at the Norfolk Air Station beginning on 23 March. After this school I was to go to another aircraft loading school at Sanford Naval Air Station, Florida, for one week. These schools were to qualify me as a "Technical Monitor". A few W Division petty officers performed duties as a technical monitor, which involved overseeing aircraft loading operations carried out by aircraft loading crews. Crews consisted of six to eight squadron sailors led by a first class, or chief, and supervised by a loading officer, usually a squadron pilot. A W Division technical monitor, who watched for technical mistakes or safety violations, observed each loading operation. The technical monitor also graded the operation. The job of a technical monitor placed an enlisted man in one of the few situations where he had authority that exceeded that of an officer, or those petty officers senior to him. A technical monitor had the authority to stop an aircraft loading operation at any time.

On 25 March, seven of us from W Division began school at the Norfolk Naval Air Station. The loading school was in an isolated section of the base. We had classes on the A-1 *Skyraider* prop-driven bomber, the A-4 *Skyhawk* fighter-bomber single engine jet, and the A-3 *Skywarrior* dual jet engine bomber. We had class work, and practiced loading different weapons on the aircraft. The class hours were long, and five of us who were going to Florida didn't go on liberty. We were saving our money for the trip. We all passed the school, and the five going to Florida had to report back to the ship before 1600 on Friday so that we could be issued our orders to school.

We left early Saturday morning, and flew from Norfolk Naval Air Station to Sanford Naval Air Station. It was hot and humid in Florida, a welcome change from the cold in Norfolk.

We checked into the barracks, and were given liberty until our class began on Monday. Tim Mcenaney (Mac), Richard King (Gary) and I went into the town of Sanford. The town was very small, and it reminded me of my hometown of Strathmore. We went to the USO, and had coffee and cookies. I remember being fascinated by a new toy at the USO, called an "Etch a Sketch". There wasn't much to do in the little town, and the streets were "rolled up". We went back to the base and prepared for school on Monday morning.

This loading school provided instruction on loading one of the newest planes in the Navy, the A-5 *Vigilante*, a dual jet bomber. It had two seats, one for the pilot, and a rear seat for the bombardier/navigator. It was capable of speeds over mach one, or 700 miles per hour. The problem with a plane that flew faster than sound was the heat generated on the fuselage and any weapon attached to a wing pylon. A weapon hanging on a wing would experience high temperatures, which could affect the electronics of the weapon, and heat and high explosives were a dangerous combination. So the *Vigilante* had been designed around the bomb, literally! The interior of the tail of the plane contained a tunnel complete with miniature "railroad tracks". A loading crew would fit a weapon with "railroad train type wheels" that rolled on the tracks, and screw the weapon onto fuel tanks that also had wheels. This cylindrical tube of weapon and fuel tanks would be slid into the plane's tail tunnel on the tracks, and the plane's tail end cap was secured. During flight the weapon was protected from the outside environment by the aircraft fuselage. The plane would approach the target at a low altitude, and supersonic speeds. At the target the pilot would punch the release button, and the bomb, and fuel tanks (usually empty at this time), would roll down the tracks, pop open the tail end cap, and the bomb and fuel tanks would drop out of the tail of the plane toward the target. The mechanics of preparing the weapon for insertion into the plane involved, installing the wheels, screwing on the fuel tanks, and making all the electrical connections. A crew of well-trained men could complete a loading operation in about four and a half hours, compared to an external loading operation on an aircraft wing which took as little as fifteen to twenty minutes. One of the complexities of the loading operation was that the weapon had to be rolled upside down from its normal storage position. There was a lot of unique expensive equipment that had been designed for this difficult loading operation. I believe this was the first time a plane had been designed around a bomb. I could not estimate how much of the taxpayer's money was spent on this system. It was a huge shock to hear what happened to this delivery system about a year after we attended this loading school, which I'll explain later.

The school only lasted three days, and as it was Easter weekend, we had four days liberty before we were to fly back to Norfolk. Mac, Gary and I heard from some sailors on the base that Daytona Beach was supposed to be full of college kids on spring break over the upcoming weekend. College kids from all over the nation were supposed to be on spring break, and the news we were excited about was that there was a ratio of ten girls to one guy! We each packed a small bag, but we didn't have civilian clothes, and we bought bus tickets to Daytona Beach. The bus went through Orlando, and we got off, because I wanted to call John Gaffey's Mom, (I'd been stationed in Iceland with him). I had promised him I'd call his mom if I were ever in Orlando. I called but there was no answer. We continued on to Daytona Beach. When we arrived, it was amazing: the streets were packed with kids our age, eighteen to twenty-one. We were wearing our summer white uniforms, and people were looking at us oddly. We got a room at the Daytona Streamline Hotel. We then formulated a plan. We didn't have any civilian clothes, but we each had a set of dungarees. We put on a white T-shirt, dungaree pants, with the legs rolled up, and we wore shower shoes. We then went out and walked around town and the beach gawking at all the girls. We blended in with the crowd with our outfits. That afternoon we met a group of kids who invited us to their motel. The motel and swimming pool had been taken over by a large group of college kids from Ohio.

Our story was that we were college students from Los Angeles, and we had hitch hiked across country to be here! We were famous; there was no one else from California, and everyone thought we were very heroic for coming all the way from the west coast. Everyone wanted to meet us. We had all the free food, and drink we could handle. Mac and I were together, and Gary went off in another group. We had a great time, and about midnight Mac and I called it a night and went back to our hotel room. In the morning Gary still hadn't shown up. Mac and I were worried so we went back to the motel we'd been at the night before. We asked around, but no one had seen Gary. They said it had been a great party but the police broke it up a little after 2:00 a.m. Mac and I went back to our hotel room, and called the local hospitals, they had no Richard (Gary) King. We called the police station, and, sure enough, they had him! We left immediately and found the police station and jail. We were permitted to see Gary. We talked to him over a phone; there was a thick panel of glass between us. He looked worried. He said around 2:00 a.m. he had been talking a long while with a girl and her boyfriend had gotten mad and tried to fight him. He punched him, and he fell into the pool.

The police were called, and he was arrested. It turned out the guy's nose was broken. As I mentioned Gary had boxing experience in the golden gloves program. Mac and I got a bondsman, pooled our money, and paid the ninety dollars bail (which was a small fortune to us!). Gary was released, and we checked out of our hotel room the next morning. Our weekend was over, and we were broke. The day before we left Florida, I got a butch haircut. On that day we couldn't afford to do anything, so we checked out a football from special services and threw it around. We all got a bit of a tan. We left Sanford and were flown back to Norfolk.

Gary had to go to captain's mast. He paid a fine to the Florida court, and was required to pay the college kid's medical bill. He also received a suspended reduction in rate for six months, which meant for six months he was on probation. We also learned that the Navy placed the motel where the party was held, "off limits." Gary eventually repaid Mac and me the bail money.

When I returned to the ship, I had a wonderful surprise. I had passed my second class petty officer exam! On 16 May 1963, I would become a GMT2. I was pleased that I had made E-5 in less than three years. As a third class I was making $142.00 a month, as a second class my pay would jump to $220.00 a month. I was sending money home monthly for my car payments. I planned on taking leave in April. The ship's schedule had changed, she was not going to remain in the yards until February 1964, but get underway the last of May 1963.

We had personnel inspections during which the captain inspected sailors' uniforms and appearance, and as the shipyard period was almost over, we had material inspections. A material inspection was an inspection of all the ship's compartments, for cleanliness, and proper damage control equipment, as well as watertight integrity, such as gaskets around hatches, dogs (handles), on doors, and all ship's equipment within the compartment. Material inspections were normally held on Fridays. Field day, or concentrated cleaning would take place on Thursdays, and Friday mornings, and the inspection would be held on Friday afternoon. In each compartment a sailor from the division responsible for the space would be required to "standby". There were hundreds of compartments to inspect, so a large number of officers were assigned to conduct the material inspection, and record their findings. When an inspecting officer entered a space, the sailor standing by would render a salute; this was one of the few times a sailor saluted indoors. While he held the salute, he would make a statement along this line: "Good afternoon Sir. W Division berthing compartment A-215-L, open for your inspection. GMT3 Little, standing by for your inspection." The inspecting officer would then examine the compartment. A sailor who would record his comments accompanied him. He would make departing comments to the sailor who was standing by. I had presented spaces to inspecting officers in Iceland a number of times during material inspections. One motivating factor to do well on material inspections was the practice of excluding compartments from the next material inspection if a grade of "outstanding" was awarded to a compartment. W Division always did well on material inspections. It was always a hassle during preparations for these inspections, as heads, and berthing spaces were secured, and it was difficult to move about the ship or get any normal work completed.

I ran across a sailor I had gone to school with in Albuquerque. He was on the aircraft carrier *USS Saratoga*, which was tied up to a pier near us. While in Albuquerque he had dated a girl, and they were married just prior to graduation. He invited me to their home one evening. They lived in base housing, and had recently had a baby girl. I had a nice evening. They wanted to set me up with a blind date. I agreed, and after a few days the couple introduced me to a girl, and the four of us visited a botanical garden called Azalea Gardens. She was a true southern girl. Her southern accent was so thick I could barely understand her! It was not a successful date, and we never dated again.

On 10 April, the Navy was saddened over the loss of the submarine *USS Thresher* and her crew of 129, during a test dive in the Atlantic.

I was having trouble coming up with the plane fare I needed to go from Norfolk to Fresno on leave. I needed $150.00; I asked my parents if I could borrow seventy-five dollars, and I would pay them back while at home. I was going to have two paychecks mailed to me from the ship. This points out that I was not a very good financial manager at this time in my life, mostly because I had so little finances to manage. Navy pay at the lower rates was at the poverty level! I was thankful, and always will be thankful for my parents, and their understanding, and help.

I departed on thirty days leave the 27th of April. I enjoyed flying across country. I took two sets of uniforms, and two second class "crows." My promotion date was 16 May, during my leave period, and I asked my mom to sew my new crows on. My left arm now had two chevrons under the eagle.

I had a wonderful time on leave. I enjoyed being temporarily free of the military regulations and restrictions. I enjoyed driving my car, and the weather was perfect for a convertible.

My Aunt Edna was a "matchmaker," and set me up with a number of dates, one, which was with a past Miss California! I also visited my ex-fiancée's Mom, who worked in a restaurant in Lindsay, and who had a special place in my heart. I also visited my ex-fiancée's grandparents. Although these visits reopened the heartache I had from the break-up I'd gone through, I enjoyed seeing these whom I loved and respected. My parents let me use their gas credit card, which I used and ran up a substantial bill, which I paid when I got back to the ship. I drove to the Pacific coast near Pismo Beach and visited my Uncle Dean and Aunt Lois and their family. I also visited a high school friend, Butch Coley and his wife Janice. I enjoyed seeing all the people at the church I had attended with my parents for many years.

Shortly after 16 May, my mother received a letter from my Division Officer, Lieutenant Johnson, which said:

> Dear Mrs. Imogene Little,
>
> Today marks an important step forward in your son's Naval Service. His advancement to Gunner's Mate Technician Second Class has required extensive study, training and preparation. The skills required are unique in that they cover a broad spectrum of specialties; I.E. mathematics, electronics, physics, etc.
>
> More important however, are the added responsibilities as a Petty Officer in the United States Navy. James will be responsible for supervising the work and training of men junior to him.
>
> He is a member of a highly skilled team, but above all he is a loyal, dedicated member of the Naval Service.
>
> More so than ever before, it is during these trying times that our country needs men who are willing to serve their country and fight to defend our freedoms and ideals. I sincerely wish to express my congratulations to you and James on this occasion.

I thoroughly enjoyed my leave. It was great being with my parents, sister, and two baby brothers. One day I went "cruising" the main street of a nearby town with my brother Joe, who was four years old. He asked me how the radio worked in my car. I told him there was a little man inside. He asked what he ate. I said, "I feed him once in a while." The next day I caught him sitting in my car holding a cracker under the radio! I realized then that I needed to be cautious about what I told my little brother.

I flew back across country on 28 May. On the ship I had a few people waiting to "tack on" my crow, as I'd had my crow "tacked on" in Iceland. My arm was once again sore from the punches on my left arm. While promotions were exciting times, they were also times of expressed and unexpressed emotions, and often are a somewhat traumatic time. In the civilian world, your status, and authority is shown by the way you dress (or don't dress), your house, your car, your political position, etc. In the Navy your position is shown on your sleeve, or in the case of officers, on your collar or shoulders. When a sailor's promotion time comes, there are congratulations, and also scrutiny to see how the promoted sailor behaves. Some humbly accept the promotion, and gradually exercise their increased authority. Others let it "go to their head," and lord it over subordinates immediately, or desert friendships with those of their peers who did not get promoted with them. Promotion time is often a time of difficult adjustment. You are suddenly elevated to a new supervisory position, and expected to give orders to, and lead men that the previous day had been equal to you.

As I mentioned before, the most drastic, dramatic change in promotion was from first class petty officer to chief petty officer. To become a "Chief" was the pinnacle of promotions for an enlisted man. Chiefs are the "backbone" of the Navy, and a common statement is "Go ask the Chief". The rate of second class petty officer (E-5), is often called the "in between rate". A second class has more authority than a third class, but not the responsibility of a first class. Many sailors have fond memories of their time as a second class, as it is a "comfortable rate". One of the men in W Division, Pappy Warren, had been a second class for almost twenty years. I met other men in the Navy who retired as a second class. Many said they couldn't get promoted because they couldn't take a written test well. I suspect in some cases they just wanted to remain a "comfortable" second class petty officer.

Upon my return to the ship following leave, as I was being congratulated on my promotion, I was also told I had a new job. I was being relieved as the Calibration Petty Officer, and reassigned to the aft magazine as an Assembly Team Leader, or Hook Leader.

I would be supervising five men when performing operations on weapons, and supervising their daily work. The two seamen, who worked for me in the calibration office, were unhappy to see me leave. One had made third class, and would take my old job. I had gained experience supervising the two seamen, but I was somewhat anxious about supervising five sailors. I had tried to be consistent supervising the two seamen, so they would know what to expect from me. I had observed during my time in the Navy, up to this point, that there were "people managers" and "mission managers". The first type of manager, being one of those supervisors with the philosophy that "people" if possible, be given the first consideration in day-to-day work. They gave extra attention to the men that worked for them, and tackled any problem their men might have that would affect their daily work. The "mission" supervisors placed first priority on the completion of jobs, and tasks regardless of the effect these efforts had on the men that worked for them. They supervised with strict discipline, and often placed a high priority on how high they could boost their standing with their superiors. One saying about a "mission supervisor" was "He got the job done, or he got his promotion standing on the bodies of his men." Probably the best supervisor would use a combination of the two styles. I decided that I would try to be a "people manager." Some confirmation that I was on the way to becoming a people manager was that the two seamen who had worked for me were truly sorry to see me going to the aft magazine. I had tried to be liberal with praise when it was deserved. I had tried to remain true to the rule: praise in public, correct in private.

Since boot camp, it had become obvious to me that those sailors who paid attention to their appearance, got along well in the Navy, compared to those who were continually being told to "get a haircut," "shine your shoes," or "square away your uniform." I also noticed an officer with a well-pressed uniform, and who remained squared away gained more respect than an officer who paid little attention to his appearance. One example was "Billy Big Hips," the assignment of this nickname to him revealed the lack of respect from the crew. He was overweight, often in wrinkled uniforms, and seldom shined his shoes. Gunner White on the other hand, was always in a sharply pressed uniform, with shined shoes, and he always looked sharp, and maintained a constant military bearing. He had the respect of all in the division. He had this respect not only because of his appearance, but also for other reasons, which I'll explain later.

The ship's laundry cleaned our clothes. We had two large laundry bags in our berthing compartment. One bag was for blue dungaree shirts and pants, and black socks. The other bag was for whites, such as underwear, and white hats. It was important that each item of clothing you put in the laundry bag was clearly stenciled with your name, as the clean clothes returned from the ship's laundry was sorted and placed on your bunk. Socks were placed in sock bags, made of fish net material that permitted washing and drying in the ships laundry machines. The sock bags had an area for a name stencil. The ship's laundry also pressed and ironed the uniforms of chiefs and officers, but not first class and below. These sailors used either the Navy Exchange Laundry, or the commercial laundries that had pickup and delivery trucks on the pier each morning, or the men ironed their own uniforms. Few second class and below bothered to iron their uniforms. I spent a lot of time ironing my dungaree working uniforms; I don't believe I ever wore a wrinkled shirt, whereas many of my fellow second class petty officers wore wrinkled clothes daily. I also tried to keep my shoes well shined. Whereas many of my shipmates wore neglected shoes that were scuffed and never shined.

Each sailor wore the white hat, often called a "Dixie cup." Although regulations required it to be worn in a specific way, each sailor wore it somewhat differently. In the movies sailors are often shown wearing the white hat pushed way back on their head. It was seldom worn this way, especially if the shore patrol, or a chief or officer was around. The white hat was to be worn as we were taught in boot camp, two fingers above the eyebrows. We all wore the same uniforms, haircuts, etc., one purpose being to discourage individuality, emphasize equality, and encourage teamwork. Sailors still tried to express individuality in the way they wore their white hat. Sailors that seemed to be unable to shape the hat into any recognizable style wore the "crooked" style. There was the "wings" style, with the sides of the hat flared out on both sides. The "rim" style was perfectly round with a pronounced rim around the top, and I preferred this style. There was the "stove pipe" that was round without a rim. To properly shape your hat you placed it over your knee and stretched it into shape. Some sailors wore the hat at a slight angle toward one side or the other, at whatever angle they thought they could get away with. This angle they felt gave them a "salty" look. No one wanted to look like a "boot," or wet behind the ears! Although lifers were sailors held in disdain by the first termers, we still wanted to have an experienced or salty look. Another area sailors pushed the limits, or tried to express their individuality was with the silk neckerchief worn with dress blues, and dress whites.

The neckerchief is tightly rolled, tied with a string or rubber band, placed around the neck under the flap of the jumper, and then a square knot is tied with both bitter ends hanging free. The top of the knot is supposed to be even with the bottom of the "V" neck of the jumper. A salty look was when the knot was tied higher. A sailor would often rearrange the tie after he had gotten through the uniform inspection by the chief on the quarterdeck before leaving on liberty. Many sailors tried to roll the neckerchief as tightly as possible, some rolled an illegal double roll which resulted in a very thin neckerchief. Some sailors would place a roll of dimes in the middle of the neckerchief, so it could be used as a "billy club".

The flap on the back of jumpers is a style left over from the old days when sailors would tar their hair, often with a pigtail down the back, and a canvas flap would be placed under their hair to prevent soiling their uniform, before they went ashore. The bell-bottom pants were made for quick removing and donning of pants (as during the sinking of a ship). The dress blues had a flap with thirteen buttons, supposedly after the original thirteen colonies. Efforts to individualize uniforms were discouraged, but continued nevertheless. On dress blues, designs of dragons, confederate flags, women, etc., were sewn on the inside of the buttoned cuffs, which were supposed to always remain buttoned. Out of sight of the shore patrol or officers the cuffs were rolled up exposing the designs. Also jumpers were tailored so tightly that a zipper was sewn into the side so they could be put on. Pants were tailored tightly around the thighs, and flared out into extreme bell-bottoms. Many tailored blues were made of non-regulation material. Many tailor shops in sailor towns thrived on the business of making tailor-made uniforms. They had a booming business built on the desire of sailors to achieve a "salty look". 1963 was before the days of corfram shoes; so much time was spent spit-shining shoes.

All of the Gunner's Mate Technicians felt like an elite group of sailors in the Navy and on the ship. No one could get past the marines guarding our spaces, unless he had a badge. This situation irritated the MAA's, as they had access to all areas of the ship in their enforcement duties, except ours. Our berthing compartment was purposely isolated from others on the ship to prevent the inadvertent disclosure of classified information. No one knew what our job was on the ship. We were shrouded in secrecy, and were told constantly that we were the "cream of the crop". We were entrusted with the most powerful, deadly weapons on earth, and on our shoulders rested the fate of democracy, and our country. Our families, and loved ones lives depended on how diligently we performed our job. The failure of one weapon during nuclear war could determine whether we survived or perished. We had to be ready to go to war if "the button was pushed". We didn't dwell on the gruesome realities, but the fact was we would be the very first to know if nuclear war was declared, when we began pushing weapons out of the magazines onto the bomb elevators, and up to the loading crews. A question that was frequently asked of us during reliability briefings was; "If war were to begin in the next five minutes, and you knew that the weapon you were helping push out of the magazine, was going to be dropped on a city where millions of innocent women and children might be killed, would you hesitate, or have moral reservations?" I always said I would not hesitate and would do my duty. I reconciled this in my mind, by deciding it was the honorable and right thing to do protecting my loved ones, and country, and my fellow shipmates. I had to do the best job I could, and not dwell on the horrible end results of a nuclear war. In the depths of my soul I prayed that God would not permit these weapons to be used, but I also realized the importance these weapons played in preventing war. They were a constant deterrent, to those who desired global domination. There was always pressure to do our jobs flawlessly. Mistakes could not be tolerated.

The majority of the sailors in W Division were between the ages of nineteen to twenty-two years old. Only one sailor in the younger group was married, and that was Donn Green. He had married a girl from Albuquerque. There were many different social levels on the ship. Officers were the "upper class"; enlisted men did not associate with them except during the performance of division work. The officers lived in staterooms, and ate in a wardroom. Officer's quarters were luxurious, carpeted, and much larger than enlisted berthing. Officers had stewards, who acted almost like servants, serving them, making their bunks, and catering to their needs. The staterooms and wardroom were located in areas of the ship called "Officers Country." Enlisted men were not permitted in this area except on business. The captain and executive officer both had an armed marine escort with them at all times on board ship. Officers could store civilian clothes on the ship, and could wear civilian clothes, while departing, and arriving on the ship.

Chiefs had their own berthing compartment, and own gallery where they ate. All other first class and below ate in the crew's mess, and berthed in berthing compartments. First class petty officers had their own secluded area within the berthing compartments, which sometimes included second class. On the mess decks there was a First Class Mess where only first class petty officers could eat.

This area was also used by the first class as a coffee break area, and an area in which to socialize. First class petty officers also had head of the line privileges in the chow line, and ships store.

On bases the clubs were separated into Officer's Club, Chief's Club, Acey Ducey Club (first and second class), and Enlisted Clubs (third Class and below). On the mess decks black sailors tended to congregate together. I was shocked to learn how much animosity there was between sailors from the south, and sailors from the north. They called each other Rebels, and Yankees.

The divisions with good morale often went on liberty together, and frequented the same places. A division with poor morale tended to fracture into small groups, and went separate ways. Those of the same rate formed friendships, as did those from the same geographical area of the country.

In W Division we were expected to observe the behavior of each other, as we all held security clearances and had to be alert for espionage, or suspicious activity. We were also aware that from time to time The Naval Investigative Service (N.I.S.) would place undercover agents in W Divisions. These agents would transfer onto a ship just like a regular GMT, and would investigate, and report security violations, etc. We watched each other, and were watched!

GMT's needed a degree of mechanical ability, as there was a lot of tool handling during weapon operations, as well as unique mechanical methods we had to master. It was also required that we have an above average intelligence and good social adjustment. It was interesting that often those who had higher IQ's were the least mechanically inclined. These sailors were usually assigned paperwork duties, or as publication custodians, or anything that kept them away from tools.

We all wanted to be accepted by our peers, and most had three or four closest friends. I hung out with Richard King (Gary) from California, Jerry Hecko (George) from Indiana, Tim Mcenaney (Mac) from Ohio, and Jim Zielsdorf (Z) from Wisconsin. I counted many, many others as my friends, but was closest to these four.

The older sailors looked upon those of us who were under twenty-one as "kids". We were all idealistic and thought of ourselves as the guardians of freedom. Many of us had not been away from home very long, and were anxious to be considered adults. There is some basis for the saying "cuss like a sailor"; much of the profanity used was an effort to appear more "adult." I resisted this urge. I'd not been raised around profane talk, and I had noticed that those in authority, and leaders who used no profanity were listened to, and respected above those who sprinkled their speech with profanity.

Upon my return to the ship following my leave to California, I had been issued a new ID card with my new rate on it. As well as a change in jobs, as a second class, I no longer had to have a liberty card when off the ship on liberty. I was assigned as a Section Leader, which meant I made up the watch assignments for my duty section; I had eight men in my duty section. We were in four-section duty, which meant I remained on board for twenty-four hours every fourth day.

As a Hook Leader I had a lot of work to get up to speed. My team was assigned the Mark 27 and Mark 28 bombs. I had two third class, and three seamen who worked on my assembly team. We had a big inspection, an NTPI only a few weeks away. Failure of this inspection would mean the ship would not get underway, and possibly the captain would be relieved (and everyone below him!).

We put in long hours training. The inspectors came onboard, and the ship got underway steaming off the coast of Virginia. Every aspect of our job was examined; the inspectors, chiefs from Nuclear Weapons Training Center Atlantic, watched over our shoulder during all the operations. While W Division was going through our inspection, the rest of the ship was training in damage control, and battle readiness. Finally, after five days, our inspection was over. We passed with flying colors. I was very proud of my assembly team.

The ship anchored in Guantanamo Bay, Cuba (the base was commonly called "Gitmo"). The crew was permitted to go on liberty on the base. We were permitted to wear dungaree pants and T-shirts on liberty. We rode a liberty boat from the ship to the pier on base. A group of us from W Division went swimming and then to a large open-air club. I took some 8mm movies of this liberty, which I still have. A newsletter[11], which was written on the ship after this time reads:

> The Story of the Fence
>
> Those of you who have been aboard *Independence* for ten months or more will undoubtedly never forget the tension, the excitement, the long hours, and the endless days of waiting while we fulfilled our role during the crisis of October and November.

Those of you who have joined our ranks since that time are undoubtedly familiar with our participation in that operation. As *Independence* steamed on station for forty days during that campaign every man was intensely aware of the communist threat, which lay just beyond our horizon. That threat which we could not see with our eyes, we learned of by radio and Teletype contact. No spot seemed under more intense threat than did the Naval Base at Guantanamo. Eight months after leaving Cuban waters, *Independence* returned to the Guantanamo area, underwent an intensive refresher-training period and enjoyed weekend liberty at the many fine recreational facilities afforded the fleet. Swimming, boating, golfing, and even horseback riding were relaxing diversions enjoyed on base seemingly as free from tensions as any liberty port. The facts are that not far beyond the hills which rim the populous area of the Naval Base runs a wire fence mounted with barbed wire, stretching for twenty-four miles around the Cuban border, a fence that divides freedom from communism. This border area has in recent months fallen from the front pages of the newspapers and the coverage given this area is indeed small compared with the attention constantly focused on the Berlin border area. But for many of us this has been our closest point of approach to a system of government and a political philosophy so directly opposed to our own. Even now as we steam toward new duties in lands and waters far distant from the Caribbean it might be well to remember that which we have seen, and in remembering become more fully aware of the obligations and duties that are ours to fulfill throughout our deployment to the sixth fleet.

In order to walk back to the pier in Cuba, a black top path led through the base housing area. Every few yards shore patrol sentries were posted to make sure sailors didn't stray from the path. This path on the base is nicknamed "The Bloody Mile." This is because sailors often drank too much in the clubs, and the combination of hot tropical sun and heat, and no female diversions, led to fights along the path. Many sailors had stitches, bruises, and cuts from the bloody mile.

June and July were busy months. We trained in preparation for our deployment to the "Med." After working hours while at sea, our activities were limited. A big topic of discussion was "What's for chow?" The food on board *Independence* was good; the only complaints being that there was occasionally a shortage of fresh fruit or lettuce, and at sea we drank recombined milk, which few people liked. Standing in line was also disliked. So you learned to time your visit to the mess decks when the line was the shortest, but the line was often long as thousands of sailors ate at the same mess deck area. It wasn't unusual to stand in line for thirty minutes or longer. As I said, first class petty officers could go to the head of the line. This was a much-desired privilege.

After working hours many sailors would read, going through many books during an at sea period. Some played cards, cribbage, and acey ducey, which was played with dice, and poker chips on a playing board. A few in W Division played chess. Gambling was forbidden, but it was rampant. Poker games were played in out of the way places; poker chips were used without any money showing. Dice games were more "underground." A dice game could continue for many weeks at different locations.

Some sailors lifted weights, and most wrote letters. A popular past time was to go to the hangar deck or areas exposed to the sea, and get a breath of fresh air. Within the berthing compartment, W Division Coffee Locker (both forward and aft), the air was thick with cigarette smoke, as almost everyone smoked. Most of the sailors assigned aft hung out in the aft spaces, and the forward sailors hung out in the forward spaces. We all stood alarm panel and magazine security watches in the forward office. Officers and chiefs very seldom came into the spaces after working hours, so it was a comfortable atmosphere for the enlisted men.

As of 30 June, 1963, I'd been in the Navy for three years. I was beginning to be pressured to remain in the Navy. These pressures came in the form of "shipping over lectures." To "ship over," meant an enlisted man signed an agreement to serve for a specific number of years, normally four or six years. The thought of becoming a lifer did not appeal to me, and I was anxious to return to California, and find a job. I assumed that the unique training I'd received in the Navy, and with a security clearance, I'd be an attractive employee.

In readiness for our Med deployment, all the sailors on the ship were issued Geneva Convention Identification Cards. This was a paper card that was entitled Armed Forces of the United States Geneva Convention Card. This card had the statement "This card is issued in accordance with the provisions of the Geneva convention of 12 August 1949." It had my name, rate PO2, branch of service USN, my service number, and date of birth. We would carry this card while overseas, and in the event of capture by hostile forces; we were to reveal only name, service number, rate, and date of birth. We were not to reveal that we were nuclear weaponsmen.

In mid-July the ship was off the coast of Cuba, and Lieutenant Johnson was told there were component storage containers that needed to be transferred from Gitmo to Puerto Rico. He selected Tim Mcenaney and me to accompany him. These containers are most often referred to as "bird cages," because of their appearance. The birdcages were component storage and shipping canisters that were pressurized, and airtight. The frame surrounding the canisters prohibited the storage or shipping of the birdcages closer than three feet together, measured from center to center of the canister. The "three foot rule" was a constant precaution throughout the nuclear weapons program. We never positioned a weapon or nuclear component closer than three feet to another weapon or component measured from center to center. Maintaining this distance prevented any possible nuclear activity, or possible nuclear interaction. The job of relocating the birdcages had a sense of urgency about it. Mac and I were told one morning we had an hour to pack a few things. In the company of Lieutenant Johnson we boarded a COD on the flight deck. We were catapulted off the flight deck, and as we were not far off the coast of Cuba, after a few minutes we landed. It was about 1300 in the afternoon. The birdcages, ten of them were positioned in a large hangar bay. We noticed that the base was in the state of high alert. Whether this was a drill, or a real alert no one seemed to know. Everyone seemed nervous. The missile crisis had occurred less than eight months before. Lieutenant Johnson told us we would not be flying on to Puerto Rico until the next day. We were in an isolated section of the hangar bay, and we stood guard over the birdcages. We sat there, and watched all the activity. It seemed as if everyone was armed with some kind of firearm. Since we had to spend the night, and one of us had to remain awake, a sleeping cot was setup within the roped off area containing the birdcages. We took turns going to eat, and then about 2100 Lieutenant Johnson said, "I'm going to the BOQ (Bachelors Officers quarter), and get a room. You two take turns standing watch, and I'll see you in the morning". Lieutenant Johnson had the only firearm among the three of us, a forty-five-caliber pistol. He left the pistol, in a holster, on the cot. He then left. After a few minutes, I picked the pistol up, to do a safety check, and to ensure that a round was not in the firing chamber. It was then I discovered the magazine clip in the handle of the pistol was empty, and we had no bullets for the gun. We called the BOQ, but Lieutenant Johnson wasn't there, (probably at the officers club?). A couple of marines said they would get bullets for us, but never got back to us. Mac and I did not sleep that night, we imagined the Cuban army attacking the base, and we had a useless pistol. In the morning when Lieutenant Johnson showed up, he thought the empty gun was funny; we did not.

We placed the birdcages on the plane. We tied them down with life jackets on each one in the event the plane went down in water. We took off from Gitmo late in the afternoon. We circled above Roosevelt Roads Naval Air Station, Puerto Rico, after dark. Mac and I, Lieutenant Johnson, and the Plane Crew Chief, were strapped in our seats, when the aircraft landing wheels touched the runway. Suddenly the plane swerved violently back and forth, the brakes squealed. The copilot shouted back to us "hang on." The pilot said, "I don't think we're going to stop in time." We were hanging onto our seat armrests tightly; luckily the birdcages did not break free from their tie downs. The plane finally came to rest, after what seemed like a long time. The pilot said that the control tower had brought us in on a runway that was too short for the plane! He just barely had enough time to stop before the end of the runway. We taxied to a hanger, where a crew of sailors unloaded the birdcages, and our job was complete. We were to fly back to the ship in the morning. The LT went to the BOQ. Mac and I went to the enlisted barracks, and then to the enlisted club. We had dinner and talked about leaving the base on liberty, but we were tired, we'd had more than enough excitement, so we stayed on the base. From what I could see of Puerto Rico, it was tropical, green, and beautiful. We took off in the morning and landed back on the flight deck of our home.

The ship was undergoing an intense training period in order to ensure that it was battle ready prior to our Med deployment. A number of new GMT's reported aboard, many fresh out of Albuquerque school. We also got aboard a GMT named Dave Wiesenhahn; he had been regular Gunner's Mate before converting to GMT. He was a strict disciplinarian and not too well accepted. Many of the sailors in other Weapons Department Divisions were jealous of W Division.

As I said no one knew what we did, and no one could walk into our spaces because of the marine guards. They looked upon us as "prima donnas." Some of the younger sailors did have spoiled, superior, attitudes, that were irritating to other sailors. Much of this was from being told continually that GMT's were the "cream of the crop" in the Navy, and we were the guardians of freedom, against the evil communists. I was of the opinion that it would be much better if sailors' fresh out of boot camp went to an interim duty station, such as a ship, as I did for a few months prior to going to the Nuclear Weaponsman A School. I appreciated the better working conditions, and more intelligent leadership we enjoyed in W Division. I had "tasted" the life of the "deck ape," and had no complaints, comparing that hard-working life to the life of a GMT.

The ship was usually at sea Monday through Friday and in port at Norfolk Naval Base over the weekend. There was a colony of bars outside the main gate that lived off the patronage of sailors. The bars catered to eighteen to twenty year old sailors who could drink 3.2% beer. Most of the bars had young girls as barmaids who would sit with sailors, and ask them to buy them a drink, which was often a glass of weak tea. The girls would sit with sailors, and talk, as long as drinks were bought, which were very expensive. They were good conversationalists, and for each drink bought for them, they received a credit, and extra pay in their salary. Some of the drinks of choice for younger sailors were Black Label and, Pabst Blue Ribbon beer, and a cheap wine made in Virginia called Sly Fox. This wine was "rot-gut" and most of the labels on the bottles were crooked. Any trouble ashore was dealt with harshly by our superiors. We kept an eye on each other as often when we had too much to drink we were wild, and sought fights, and trouble.

Independence in 1963 was one of the newest aircraft carriers in the Navy. She'd been commissioned 2 February, 1959. She was built at the New York Naval Shipyards, Brooklyn. She was the fifth United States vessel named *Independence*. The flight deck had an overall length of 1,046 feet; the angled deck was 678 feet.

The flight deck appeared to be chaotic, but it wasn't. It was one of the more skillfully organized, and complex operations of the ship. The experience necessary in spotting, handling, and servicing aircraft so that each is ready and in position at the scheduled time makes flight deck operations the veritable "art" of carrier performance. To help facilitate efficiency each man on deck wore a jersey indicating by color his particular job, Red: Gasoline, Ordnance, and Repair Crews. Green: Catapult, Electronics, and Arresting Crews. Blue: Plane Handlers. Yellow: Flight and Hangar Deck Directors. White: Oxygen, and Medical. When W Division Technical Monitors performed duties on the hangar deck or flight deck, we wore red jerseys.

Each department on the ship had a mission statement. Weapons Department's mission statement was: "To defend the ship from enemy attack utilizing AA armament, to support the Air Group with ordnance-both conventional and nuclear. To provide for security of the ship and conduct all seamanship evolutions." There were 16 officers, and 632 enlisted men in Weapons Department.

Those GMT's in W Division who had qualified to become technical monitors by graduating from loading schools were kept busy watching and supervising the squadron loading operations. Each squadron had loading crews that underwent certification inspections just as W Division did. The loading operations involved marines, firefighters who stood by with fire hoses, Explosive Ordnance Disposal (EOD) crew, and many others.

Squadron loading crews trained loading their squadron's aircraft with nuclear weapon trainers that W Division supplied. The loading operations were conducted on the hangar deck or flight deck. Loading operations on the flight deck were often noisy, with jet engines turning up. We wore red jerseys while on the flight deck, and inflatable life vests. We also carried clipboards, and flashlights with red lenses. After dark all exposed lights, such as those in passageways, and other areas were red, so that pilots and others who worked on the flight deck would not ruin their night vision. As technical monitors, we carried the appropriate aircraft loading checklists. As with all nuclear weapons operations, the loading of aircraft was conducted using standardized, approved checklists. Navy Nuclear Weapons Evaluation Facility (NWEF) of Albuquerque, New Mexico, prepared the aircraft loading checklists. The loading crew chief read operation steps, just as the hook leaders in W Division read steps. After the read steps were completed, the crewmembers would respond, "check."

The weapons in W Division were bolted to the magazine decks in their storage containers. When a weapon was to be loaded on an aircraft, it had to be removed from its storage container, and placed in a special truck, called a bomb truck. This truck with the bomb was used to move from the magazine to the hangar deck, and flight deck, and used to position the bomb underneath the plane's loading attachment points. Using either a hydraulic system on the bomb truck, or an aircraft bomb hoist, the bomb was hoisted up and attached to the plane.

As I described before, the loading of a nuclear weapon into the A-5 *Vigilante* airplane was unique. The bomb was loaded into the tail, so the bomb would be protected from the heat that the plane's surfaces were subjected to at speeds above 700 mph. We, who completed the loading school in Florida, were only to see a couple of loading operations of this type on the ship.

A shocking discovery had been made, shortly after a few practice bombing runs had taken place, at naval bombing ranges. As the *Vigilante* approached the target at extremely high speed, the bomb release button was pushed; a small explosive charge would activate a mechanism to push the bomb, with empty fuel tanks attached, backwards down the railroad tracks inside the tail, popping opening the tail cap, and out of the plane. The bomb was then supposed to drop down toward the target. It was discovered however, when the bomb exited the plane, instead of falling toward the target the bomb would remain in the "slip stream" behind the plane, and would follow the *Vigilante* all over the sky. So instead of dropping toward the target, the bomb would then detonate behind the aircraft stuck in the vacuum created by speeding plane. The system was a failure! I've often wondered how many millions of dollars were wasted on this effort. The intentions were good. The A-5 was still considered a nuclear weapons delivery system. The bomb was loaded on the plane's wing pylons, and delivered at slower speeds. Because of the plane's superior speed, its primary use was changed to photo reconnaissance, and cameras were positioned in the aircraft nose.

The newer generation of nuclear bombs had special epoxy paint covering bomb cases that resisted the high heat experienced by a bomb hanging out in the wind stream of a speeding aircraft. We as GMT's were constantly touching up the epoxy paint, and inspecting to ensure that there were no scratches, or chips on the bombs painted surfaces. The bombs were kept spotless, and were cleaned endlessly.

All weapons of *Independence* and other carriers were classified as "air-dropped weapons." In other words these weapons were dropped from aircraft. A statement from the ship's welcome aboard booklet[12], talking about *Independence*'s air wing mission, states:

> In the present day as in days gone by, the primary mission of the
> Navy is to control the sea. The coming of the atomic age has not
> changed the basic concept, but has broadened it to the extent that the
> Navy must now have the capability to project its power against the
> enemy, not only on the sea, but in the air as well. This is the job of
> attack carriers like *Independence*.

Each aircraft squadron had their own commanding officer that reported to Commander Air Group Seven when embarked on the ship. Each squadron averaged about 20 officers, 200 enlisted men, with twelve aircraft. Considering only the planes that were nuclear load capable, there were about forty-eight planes capable of launching off the ship, and delivering a weapon to a target.

Because of the rapidity of events that would occur in nuclear war, it was doubtful that our planes would be able to launch, drop their weapons, and return to the ship to have another weapon loaded. The carrier would probably be sunk by the time the plane returned. We heard it said if we could launch at least six nuclear loaded aircraft, then we would have accomplished our mission in nuclear war! The pilots had somewhat of a "kamikaze" attitude. After they launched off the flight deck and flew to their designated target, through probable intense anti aircraft fire, and enemy fighter aircraft, they had to worry about escaping the intense blast of the bomb. The airplanes had special visors or canopy shields to prevent flash blindness. After they escaped all this they had to worry about where to land, because it was almost a surety that the ship would be at the bottom of the ocean by then, and they would no longer have a home to return to. We in W Division lived with this reality always in the back of our minds. If we were told to start loading our weapons, our life expectancy was probably no more than a couple of hours! Our survivability was lessened by the fact that as a surface ship *Independence* would be high on the list of targets of Russian submarines. The Soviet Navy had a huge submarine force, almost four times larger than the U.S.

W Division magazines were located below the waterline of the ship, on the 5th or 6th deck, five or six levels below the hangar deck. Bomb elevators brought the weapons up and out of the magazines. Huge electrical motors reeled large spool wound steel cables attached to the elevator platform, and thus moved the platform up and down. A matter of concern, when positioning a weapon on the elevator was the possibility of the nose or tail overhanging the platform and being crushed during the up or down operation of the elevator. When a weapon was placed on the elevator, it was tied down, and the wheels of the bomb truck were chocked. The elevator cables were heavily greased, and most GMT's had the unpleasant experience of rubbing against the cables and soiling uniforms with the thick black grease of the elevator cables.

We called this "getting kissed" by the elevator. A petty officer made a last second check before the elevator doors were closed, and the elevator up button was pushed. I always held my breath listening to the elevator move until it reached the deck level it was ascending to. There were elevator operators in communication with each other at each level, ready to push the emergency stop button in the event an unusual noise was heard.

In the event a weapon is damaged, the accident is classified according to the severity of the damage, and placed in a category. The code words for the categories were beginning with the most severe, "Broken Arrow," "Bent Spear," and "Dull Sword."

There was an important rule that we as GMT's had to observe, a rule called "the two man rule." This rule had gone into effect a couple of years earlier because of an incident at Midway Island, which I'll describe later. Anytime a room, compartment, or an area containing a nuclear weapon (called an exclusion area), was entered, there had to be two people. Never was a lone individual permitted to be in an exclusion area. The two people in the exclusion area had to be two persons of equal knowledge, in other words if any work was to be done each sailor had to know exactly what was being done. The two-man rule was a precaution against any possible sabotage, and to prevent a lone individual from trying to detonate a weapon. The two persons enforcing the two man rule had to keep each other in sight at all times. The two-man rule was relatively new in 1963, but as time passed more emphasis was placed on it.

In preparation for the ship's deployment to the Med we were very busy. There was a blur of activity, loading team training, inspections, assembly team training, flight operations, working parties loading supplies, inspections, and more inspections. In order to insure the ship was battle ready, we often went to "General Quarters" or "Battle Stations." General Quarters were announced over the 1MC (ship's main loudspeaker). The announcement was a pulsating ringing tone followed by, "This is a drill, this is a drill, general quarters, general quarters, all hands man your battle stations, condition Zebra will be set in five minutes." This announcement always got your heart pounding. My battle station was the after magazine. All sailors had to move very quickly to their battle station, because setting condition "Zebra" meant all hatches, and doors would be dogged tight so the ship would be compartmented, and more difficult to sink. If you were caught in a compartment after the five-minute time limit, you were stuck there. It was a serious offense if someone opened a hatch or door after a material condition was set. All sailors had personal gas masks held in storage bags attached to their belts. Everyone remained in battle dress during general quarters, with shirts buttoned all the way up to the neck, shirtsleeves rolled down, and pants legs tucked into socks. This covering up gave sailors some protection against flash burns, and fires. The smoking lamp was out during general quarters, which meant absolutely no smoking. One sailor in each compartment manned a sound-powered phone, which was the method of communications within ships departments, and also with Damage Control Central, which was the nerve center of the ship. Damage Control Central kept the captain updated on the battle readiness of the ship, and informed him of any battle damage that might occur. The sound powered phones did not require electrical power to operate; they used crystals that were powered by the phone talker's voice. Sound powered phone talkers had to be trained in the proper way to speak over a sound powered phone circuit. Strict speech discipline was used. If the ship were going to war this meant we in W Division would be sending weapons up to the loading crews for loading on aircraft. This would involve the marines, pilots, squadrons and many others. The coordinating authority for this effort was a division in the operation department called "Strike Operations." They planned and executed war plans.

With the arrival of summer our uniforms changed from blues to whites. This usually prompted a captain's personnel inspection, and this summer was no exception. We did not look forward to personnel inspections, standing for hours at a time, worrying about getting hit for unshined shoes, haircuts, or some small detail. The corpsmen always stood by to tend to sailors who passed out from the long stand at attention. W Division had a good reputation as having squared away sailors; a big help was our "in-house barber" GMT3 Donn Green, who cut our hair. One thing we looked forward to was that we were usually given liberty immediately after the inspection.

The W Division sailors assigned to the aft magazine enjoyed better working conditions, and had higher morale than the sailors who worked in the forward spaces. From my viewpoint this was primarily because of Chief Warrant Officer White. He had been an enlisted man in the aviation ordnance field, before he was commissioned. We felt he understood us, and could relate to us as enlisted men much more so than Lieutenant Johnson, who had started his Navy career as an officer. Mr. White asked that we address him as "Gunner," which is an option for a chief warrant officer in the ordnance field. He was a tall athletic, white-haired man in his 40's. His uniforms were always immaculate, and he always seemed to be in control of his emotions.

He treated us with respect, and we in turn respected and admired him. We would have quarters in the after magazine each morning before "turn-to," or going to work. After the magazine supervisor read the plan of the day, Gunner White would often speak to us, telling us the latest word on the ship's schedule, or whatever the news might be on the ship. He would often publicly praise individuals during our morning quarters.

I recall an incident prior to one of W Division's technical inspections. My assembly team wanted to paint our Mark 28 trainer that we would be using to demonstrate operations on during the inspection. We didn't have a spray paint gun to paint with, so I invented a spray gun with a ballpoint pen, and a small glass jar, the repainting, and stenciling of the trainer turned out very good. Gunner White gave my team and me high praise for this job. I never forgot this recognition, and I greatly appreciated this public praise not only for me, but also for my crew. I don't recall Gunner White ever correcting or disciplining anyone in public. Correction was done in private, and he did so quietly, and firmly. No one wanted to displease him, and we were more than willing to do anything he asked. As I think of him today, he stands out as one of the most outstanding leaders I knew in the Navy. He worked the same hours as we did; he was technically knowledgeable, dedicated to the Navy, and most important, lead by example. Gunner White passed away in 1978. He was a model of leadership I've never forgotten. Only on one occasion did I see Gunner White angry.

One day in August at morning quarters, I was surprised when Gunner White called me out of ranks by saying, "GMT2 Little, front and center." I went forward, and he read a certificate that said I was being awarded a Good Conduct Medal. This medal was issued every three years in recognition of faithful, zealous, and obedient naval service (later the periodicity was changed to four years). This was my first medal; I was now authorized to wear a burgundy colored ribbon on my dress uniforms. The award was two months late, as I had been authorized the medal on 30 June 1963; also the certificate listed my rate as "GMT3" instead of "GMT2." After quarters, Gunner White called me into his office, and apologized for the late issuance of the medal, and the mistake on the certificate. He then closed the door to his office, and with me sitting there called the Personnel Officer. The personnel officer was a LCDR, and technically senior to Gunner White, but Gunner White talked to him like a seaman recruit! I don't remember much of the conversation, but I remember being thankful that I was not on the receiving end of Gunner White's anger. He was outraged by the sloppy work the personnel office had done with my medal certificate. He did not raise his voice, but very thoroughly corrected the Personnel Officer. There was nothing the LCDR could say because Gunner White was right.

We younger sailors were amazed at the authority and respect accorded chief warrant officers. Even the captain often solicited their advice. Although the chief petty officers are considered the "backbone of the Navy," chief warrant officers hold the unique position of being the ultimate source of information, and undisputable professional experts, as well as the most experienced leaders in the Navy. They truly had "positional authority." Chief warrant officers and limited duty officers were those officers that came up through the ranks. Very few enlisted men ever achieved officer status. Annually out of an eligible group of over half a million sailors, only about 300 are selected for officer status. They were called "Mustangs."

On 5 August, 1963 a nuclear test ban treaty was signed by the USA, USSR, and UK prohibiting the testing of nuclear weapons in the atmosphere, outer space and underwater. This was a step forward toward world peace, but it was also a small disappointment for us as nuclear weaponsmen, as we all had hoped to see a test shot some day in the future.

During 1962 and 1963 we were required to demonstrate that we were physically fit by doing a certain number of sit ups, pushups, and running in place for a specific time (the number and length of time of the exercises were dependent upon the tested sailor's age). This was one of the first mandatory physical fitness tests that U.S. sailors had to undergo. The nickname of the tests was "JFK's," because it was President Kennedy's idea. He had said in December 1961 that the "United States was becoming a nation of spectators rather than a nation of athletes." The physical fitness tests were not wholeheartedly accepted, especially by the chief petty officers, who were well known for their substantial "pot bellies." There was much false documentation or "railroading" when recording the completion of the JFK required number of pushups, sit ups, etc., for the older sailors. We younger sailors had no problem completing our JFK's. I remember in Iceland GMT1 Shewe, although he was a big man, had a terrible time doing pushups. No one seemed to take the fitness programs that came and went in the Navy very seriously. There would come a time when this would change, but in the 1960's and 1970's, efforts to insure that the Navy was physically fit were laughed at by most sailors. Very few officers even tried to create an image of complying with physical fitness requirements. On paper the Navy was fit, but in reality most were heavy smokers, drinkers, and enjoyed the good Navy chow too much! On the topic of physical fitness the Marine Corp. was as different from the Navy as night is from day.

The marines lived for physical fitness, running for miles first thing in the morning, and constantly exercising. Many sailors were secretly thankful that the Navy didn't have the same attitude toward physical fitness that the marines did. Sailors and marines are somewhat like oil and water, and often don't mix well. We in W Division were the exception; since we worked together daily, many marines and W Division sailors were close friends. marines called sailors "squids," or "swabbies," while we sailors called marines "jar heads," or "grunts" (never did a junior call a senior these names!).

It is said that a marine on watch has no friends. This refers to the single-minded devotion to orders while a marine is assigned a post, or four-hour watch. The marines are "first in battle," and their heritage is one of sacrifice and honor. Marines are trained to follow orders blindly and without questions. I appreciated this devotion to duty when they stood guard over me, and the weapons that required the strictest security possible. Anyone who has served in the Marine Corps, frequently say "Once a Marine always a Marine." I had the highest respect for marines, and with few exceptions never spoke ill of them or teased them. I treated them as men of honor, and tried to emulate their devotion to duty. I tried to remain physically fit by lifting weights and exercising. I tried to stop smoking (often), and when I wore the U.S. Navy uniform, I realized the importance of appearing presentable.

There was something mischievous some sailors used to do to the marines, often late at night, around 0200, returning from liberty. They would go to the head of a ladder that led down into the marines berthing compartment, which was near W Division berthing. There was a huge steel hatch, supported by an upright bar, in the open position. The upright bar would be removed, and the hatch would be dropped, making a horrendous noise, awaking the sleeping marines. The W Division sailors would then run to their bunks, and jump under the covers with clothes on, as the MAA's would soon be investigating with flashlights through the berthing compartment. This was thought to be a hilarious prank, and I must confess I may have done it once. I'm sorry for the sleepless nights we caused the marines.

As a second class petty officer I was a Section Leader. This job involved preparing a watch bill assigning junior men to stand watch after working hours, and on weekends. This meant rotating the sailors so they didn't stand the same four-hour watch two duty days in a row. My other duties as section leader included insuring that sailors carried trash from W Division spaces to the dumpsters located on the pier, and insuring that sweepers (a nightly cleanup) were held. On weekends I helped, or filled out the daily morning muster report. This report was required daily at 0800, to be turned into the personnel office. The report showed any unauthorized absentees, sailors on the sick list, or anyone off the ship undergoing special training, etc.

I was becoming a "short timer," my enlistment as a "kiddy cruiser," meant my obligated service was to end the day before my 21st birthday, which was only five months away. I was anxious to return home. I questioned my parents about employment opportunities. I thought about returning to school, working in the electronics field, or perhaps applying for a job at the state mental hospital where my mom had worked for a number of years. I missed my sister and brothers. During the summer my sister had gone to visit our aunt and uncle who lived on the coast at Arroyo Grande, California. In one letter to my parents, I asked them to buy some candy for my baby brothers, and tell them it was from me. I hadn't saved much money for my transition to civilian life, so I didn't feel very secure about my uncertain future.

As an Assembly Team Leader by necessity I'd become more involved with the paperwork associated with nuclear weapons maintenance. One big job was extracting the electrical and mechanical steps out of the technical manuals, and putting them in sequence in check sheet form. I used the check sheets during operations, by reading the steps and checking them off with a grease pencil. Any time a change came out from Albuquerque for the technical manuals, the check sheets had to be updated. The check sheets were type written, so I had to teach myself the "chicken" method of typing "hunt and peck" with two fingers. Any time the check sheets were changed, it was a requirement that they be reviewed by the chain of command up to the division officer. There were numerous other pieces of paperwork. One was a form called an Unsatisfactory Report, or "UR." This report was submitted to report any discrepancy in technical publications, material problems with weapons, Test sets, handling gear, and anything that interfaced with the nuclear weapons program. This report was submitted to McAlester, Oklahoma, and then forwarded by them to the appropriate agency for resolution. I agreed wholeheartedly with the UR program, as it was a tool to cleanse the nuclear weapons program of errors, and helped us all on the elusive path to perfection.

One night returning to the ship on liberty, I spied a familiar sailor in the back of the city bus I was riding. It was John Gaffey, who I'd been with on Iceland. It was good to see him.

He was stationed on a submarine tender home ported in Norfolk. We only had about twenty minutes to talk before he got off the bus. We exchanged addresses, and would write to each other from time to time.

When a W Division sailor was assigned to a working party bringing food from the pier on board the ship, often large cans of peanut butter, fruit, etc., would disappear into W Division spaces where they would be devoured without fear of being caught by the MAA's, as they could not get past the marine sentry.

W Division magazines were kept at a constant cool temperature of 65–75 degrees, and were cooler than most spaces on the ship. Often when the ship was steaming in the hot tropical climate of the Caribbean, after lunch was eaten, many of us would take a noon nap, sleeping on the deck of the magazine. In retrospect this was not a wise thing to do from a radiation exposure viewpoint.

It was interesting to see the expressions on the faces of those who would enter W Division magazines on visits, perhaps officers inspecting, or others doing repair work on vents, plumbing, etc. It was an awesome sight to see row upon row of gleaming white and silver weapons that contained unimaginable power. I would almost say it was like entering a cathedral, but that's not accurate; it was more like being in the arsenal of a spaceship of another world. This feeling of unreality became dulled after being in the magazines day after day. You couldn't dwell on the fact that megatons of destructive force were just inches away from you. We cleaned, polished, pampered, and tended to these weapons of mass destruction, as precious spoiled children that we hoped would never be unleashed.

As GMT's performing our job, we had to be above reproach. The consequences of sloppy or indifferent work could not be tolerated. The very existence of our nation might depend on our attention to detail. There was a tale of a candy bar wrapper found inside the warhead of a weapon. This certain weapon was required to be inspected internally with a flashlight and mirror, when the candy bar wrapper was found. I don't recall if it was in the Air Force or Navy. It was not a story that was "chuckled at"; someone may have considered it a practical joke, but this could not be tolerated in the nuclear weapons program. This meant someone entrusted to complete critical maintenance, and inspections on weapons could not be trusted. I remember an incident that caused us in W Division to suspect each other. Some of our weapons had been off-loaded to an AEC facility for disassembly and retirement. The ship was informed that upon disassembly of a small interior foam pad held in place with a screw, it had been discovered that someone had drawn a "smiley face," with a felt tip pen. While this had no impact on the functioning of the weapon, it did mean someone was not taking his responsibilities seriously. If a person did something like this, who knew whether he would leave a cable disconnected, a screw loose, or skip an important step? The weapon had been in the custody of a number of different commands, so AEC had notified all of them. I don't believe it was anybody in *Independence*'s W Division, but I could not say for sure.

Our new captain was Captain Swanson. He introduced something new to *Independence*, the use of bugle calls for chow, mail call, general quarters, and many other announcements over the ship's loudspeaker. Life on board ships is somewhat like living on a spaceship. Your boundaries are where the hull of the ship ends, and the expanse of the ocean begins. An aircraft carrier is one of the largest ships in the world, it is immense; very few people go into all the spaces, and it's easy to get turned around and lost. However after being on board for a while the ship seems to "shrink" and become smaller, especially after being at sea for a few weeks. Privacy was a rare luxury, we as enlisted men had less personal space than prisoners were given in jail. You were never completely alone, even on watch in W Division there were always two sailors.

The first week in August the ship remained in port prior to our departure for overseas. News from home was that my parents, sister, and brothers were spending two weeks in Kansas on vacation. This was a busy time, loading supplies, and needed material. Married men of the crew were arranging affairs, as they would be apart from their families for eight months. The married sailors naturally were not as anxious as the single sailors to get underway. I was the envy of many of the younger sailors as I had so little time left before I was to be discharged. I was anxious to see Europe, I was anxious to see the Med, and I was anxious to get out of the Navy.

On 8 August, the ship got underway for a Mediterranean deployment. Most of W Division, and many other divisions on the ship, "manned the rail." This meant sailors in dress whites stood along the sides of the flight deck, while the mooring lines were cast off, and the ship got underway. A band was playing on the pier; a huge crowd of family and friends were waving, holding up "I Love You" signs, and screaming "goodbye." The ship quickly moved away from the pier, and soon land was out of sight, and we began the long transit across the ocean.

We were scheduled to pull into Cannes, France on 31 August. One thing I had discovered when the ship anchored off Cuba, or pulled into Florida, or Norfolk after being at sea for a week or so, you could smell land. Cuba smelled different from the United States. I was to discover that each country had its own distinctive smell. One day we began to smell land. We were entering the Mediterranean.

We sailed past the Rock of Gibraltar. Prior to arriving at this point we had set up the "Pig Pen." This was the nickname of an alert plane positioned on the flight deck. The plane was kept on alert with a pilot standing by. The plane was guarded twenty-four hours a day by the marines. Each day at noon power was hooked up to the plane and an electrical continuity test was run with a W Division technical monitor and a pilot observing. The plane engines were also fired up momentarily.

The ship dropped anchor off the coast of Cannes, France, 31 August. We younger sailors were anxious to see France, and French girls! On the way over from Norfolk, we had received a number of lectures on the hazards of overseas liberty. We were told there were communists in each port who had the goal of getting American sailors in situations that would cause bad publicity for our country. They would try to start fights between sailors and the citizens of whatever country we were visiting, or take pictures of drunken sailors, or do whatever they could to cast America in a bad light. It was emphasized over and over to us that we were representatives of America. We might be the only Americans some Europeans would ever see, and they would judge America by our good or bad actions. We were to be ambassadors of our homeland.

As the ship was anchored off the coast, we caught liberty launches, called motor whaleboats, to go ashore, just as we had in Cuba. Each boat held about 100 men, and had a coxswain (driver), two deck hands, and a Boat Officer, usually an ENS or LTJG to maintain order. There were six boats working. The boat trip took twenty-five minutes one way, so it would take a long time to shuttle a few thousand sailors anxious to go on liberty. Rank has its privileges, so senior ranks were permitted to leave the ship first. Officers first, then chiefs, first class, second class (me included), then third class, and lastly seaman. A long ladder extended down the hull from the after brow (gangway where enlisted men departed and arrived), and down from the quarterdeck (were officers departed and arrived). The ladders were attached to floating platforms, which the boats pulled alongside of. The ladders were steep and precarious, and when the sea was rough, it was necessary to be careful lest you fell over the side. This was more of a matter of concern when sailors returned from liberty after enjoying French wine, and their sense of balance was affected.

Each time we left the ship on liberty, our uniform, and appearance was carefully inspected by the Junior Officer of the Deck (JOOD), a chief petty officer, and also any MAA's standing near the liberty line. If you were pulled out of line, because you needed a haircut, a shoeshine, dirty uniform, etc., you had to correct the problem before getting in line again. This could mean a delay of hours before you could go on liberty. In some cases a chit was filled out that had to be given to the sailor's division officer before he could try again to go on liberty. Luckily, I was never stopped for a uniform infraction. Here are some statements about liberty in the ships welcome aboard booklet:

> Wear your uniform correctly and with pride. Maintain a smart
> military appearance; keep your cuffs buttoned, and your hat squared.
> 1. Obey any orders of the shore patrol.
> 2. Have a good time-but be sure it is the kind that leaves no regrets.
> 3. Don't talk shop-what is happening, or will happen in
>   *Independence* is nobody's business but those in *Independence*.
> 4. Don't drink to excess-don't speed when driving and don't
>   overstay your leave or liberty.

Some of the sailors who had been on a previous Med Cruise said, while in Cannes a movie was being filmed called "*Where the Boys Are*[13]," starring Connie Francis. They also said when the ship visited Monaco, Prince Rainer and Princess Grace Kelly had come aboard the ship for a visit.

We could not take American currency off the ship, so prior to going on liberty we would change our money into francs. Disbursing clerks would exchange money on the hangar deck.

A few others from W Division, and I made it onto a liberty launch, and headed for the pier. The weather was nice; the blue sea, the expanse of white beach, behind which were white buildings with brightly colored flags flying combined to make a beautiful scene. We walked around Cannes a long while taking in the sights. Some of the most interesting sights for us were on the beach, girls wearing bikinis, many without tops! There were huge resort hotels, and crowds of people. Many sailors gravitated toward the bars. Looking out toward the sea, the *Independence* looked very impressive and powerful.

She overshadowed all the other vessels at anchor near her. Many of the shops and bars catered to American sailors so there were no language problems. One of the most delightful smells came from the French bakeries. We stuffed ourselves with French bread and pastries. W Division laid claim to one particular bar, as most divisions did. The Marine Detachment would usually be in the same bar as W Division.

Odd sights to us were the urinals that were on the sidewalks in public view. Frenchmen would relieve themselves at these urinals without a thought of the crowds on the sidewalk. Thankfully there were a few public toilets with enclosed walls that we modest Americans could use.

Red wine was served in all restaurants, to everyone regardless of age. We were asked constantly if we had a cigarette. If you ever smelled a French cigarette, you'd know why the French loved American cigarettes. French cigarettes smelled like old burning rags, and tasted terrible. Our first impressions were that the Frenchmen were very rude (very few said, "please" or "thank you"), and the French women were beautiful.

We had been in Cannes for a week, when I and two other guys discovered that there was to be a five-day tour to Paris the ship's chaplain was putting together. We would be given five days "basket leave" (the days would not be credited against our leave totals). The tour cost forty-nine dollars. Tim Mcenaney, Jim Zielsdorf, and I packed a small bag each, and with 200 other *Independence* sailors, left the ship, and boarded a train headed for Paris. I had borrowed a movie camera, and took pictures of the countryside, as we traveled past the farms and fields. Most houses were white washed with thatched roofs. We finally reached Paris after four hours. We took a bus to our hotel. We stayed at "Hotel De L' Ocean," located at 7 Rue Mayran. We stayed on the eighth floor, which was reached by an old, slow elevator. The room was nice, although we were confused why there were two toilets in our room. We learned one was a bidet. We had two beds, one large, and one small. The forty-nine dollar tour cost was for five nights, and three meals a day. We had to eat our meals at specified times of the day, or else pay for them out of our own pocket. Tours left daily, in the morning, or we were permitted to sight see on our own. One night we sat in the hotel bar, and flirted with some German girls who were tourists. We sampled cognac, but it tasted terrible to our American palate.

The first few days, we three set out on our own. The streets were narrow, and cobble stoned. There were many outdoor cafes, and from our viewpoint many pretty girls. We stood out like sore thumbs in our white uniforms. We went to a large clothing store, and each bought a shirt, and pair of pants, so we could get out of our uniforms. We explored many streets and got lost often. The outdoor markets were crude and unsanitary by our standards, chickens and meat hanging in the open, and the smells were not too appetizing.

We went to the famous Paris Follies, which was an extravagant show that lasted a couple of hours. This was near Pigalle, an infamous street where each evening prostitutes of every description imaginable would stand on the sidewalk. There was a woman every ten feet or so, as we walked down the sidewalk. They called to us trying to entice us. We said we were just looking. One morning we caught the scheduled tour, and went to the Eiffel Tower, Arc de Triumph, Notre Dame, Sacred Heart Church, and the Seine River.

One night, we three were in a bar in Pigalle, when a guy struck up a conversation. He was older, about twenty-eight, and he was asking us a lot of questions. He told us he lived in Paris, although we had no French accent. He also said that he used to work for the Atomic Energy Commission. He was very friendly, and bought us drinks. We were very cautious, and didn't reveal our jobs, or anything specific about the ship. We got out of the bar quickly; it scared us, and we reported the incident when we got back to the ship. Our jaws ached from eating so much good French bread. All in all, it was forty-nine dollars well spent. It was an interesting tour, and I took 100 feet of movie film. The five days were a nice respite from the rigors of shipboard life. Upon our return to the ship, a day later we got underway.

We continued to tend to the "Pig Pen," performed various maintenance jobs, and continued day-to-day work. I wrote a letter to my sister congratulating her on becoming a senior in high school. We were scheduled to pull into Naples, Italy in mid-September. In Naples we once again anchored in the bay. We had to change our money to lire. Italian money was unique, the larger the denomination, the larger the size of the bill. A twenty-dollar equivalent was about six inches by ten inches; I imagined a $100 bill would be about the size of a newspaper!

The smell of Naples was very different from Cannes. The smell was bad, and there was much evident poverty. In the streets there was a constant sewer smell. Near the boat landing there were a very popular café and bar. A few of us stopped in, and an older man came over and introduced himself as "Boston Blacky." He was very friendly and seemed truly pleased to see American sailors. He said he owned the place, and he bought us drinks, and asked questions about the United States. It was said that he was a mafia member who had been deported from the U.S.; anyway he treated us like royalty.

Everywhere we walked in Naples we were accosted by small dirty, children begging, and saying things like, "Hey G.I. do you have money for me?" or "Hey Joe do you have a cigarette?" It was pathetic to see children in this condition. We had been warned not to give them anything, because once you did, it would bring hordes of them out, and they would mob you trying to grab your billfold, watch, and cigarettes. We had to harden our hearts, which was difficult for me, because my brother Joe was the same age as many of them. In uniform we carried our packs of cigarettes inside the top of our socks, out of sight under our pants leg, as there were no pockets on our uniforms in which to carry a pack of cigarettes. I remember being in an outdoor café sitting at a table with a large hanging tablecloth on it. There were four of us at the table; I felt something on my ankle. We all looked under the table, and there were three children trying to pick the packs of cigarettes from our socks. We shouted, and the waiters shooed the children away.

There were vendors everywhere trying to sell their wares. The most commonly sold object is embarrassing to relate. It was a replica of a male penis and scrotum with attached wings. This was in various shapes, in the form of necklaces, jewelry, rings, etc. I didn't even consider buying one---what would be the reaction of a mother or wife who found one of these among sailors' mementoes? Naples seemed to be a poverty ridden, dirty city. All the women we saw were older and unattractive; older men or women closely guarded all the girls our age. Italy was very different from France. A few *Independence* sailors were rolled and robbed in Naples.

I was anxious to be discharged, and very uncertain about what I wanted to do in the future. In a letter written to my parents 17 September, I described my feelings about the future as being in a rowboat with a hole in the bottom, in the middle of a pond with two oars, but I don't know which way to row.

After pulling out of Naples, we steamed for a few days conducting flight operations, and then pulled into Beirut, Lebanon. In Beirut we pulled alongside the pier, so there was no need to ride liberty launches. We received a nice welcome when the ship pulled in; a band was playing, with hundreds of people welcoming us. Most of the men wore turbans, and the women had their faces covered. We were warned that there were many Soviet newspaper reporters around, and to be on our best behavior. The city was clean and "odor free," compared to Naples. There were large hotels located on beautiful clean beaches. There were many tourists from different European countries. In the cafes, and bars we were offered snacks of carrots, and olives. I remember walking through an Arab grocery store, looking at all the boxes and cans with Arabic writing on them, and there on one shelf amongst all the foreign looking cans were a couple of cans labeled "*Lindsay Ripe Olives*[14]." The olives were from my hometown. A friend, B.J. Milam, had worked for many years at this olive plant. It felt good seeing a little bit of home halfway around the world.

We were cautioned about going into certain sections of town because of occasional hostilities between Arabs and Jews. I enjoyed seeing camels, and one night a group of us went to a buffet, which featured a belly dancer. We enjoyed Beirut, and the people were friendly and seemed to like Americans. We confounded the Russian reporters, as there was not one incident from the thousands of sailors that went on liberty. Many of the guys took advantage of tours to the Holy Land. I've always regretted missing that opportunity, but at the time I was saving money for my discharge from the Navy.

After another period at sea we pulled into Taranto, Italy, which is located on the top of the inside heel of the boot shape of Italy. This city seemed cleaner than Naples, but there were gangs of children begging here also. We tried pizza and spaghetti but it was terrible. We did enjoy the bakeries.

In Taranto a group of us decided to tour a famous catacomb that was under a Catholic Church. After paying an entrance fee, we entered an underground tunnel dimly lit by light filtering down through grates high on the tunnel walls. There upon a raised ledge on both sides of the tunnel were rows of mummified bodies of men and women, some in clothes, some in rags. Some were skeletons; others were fairly well preserved. Interspersed throughout the rows were children's bodies. There were thousands of bodies, most with heads down with chins resting on chests, with eye sockets looking down toward we living who were walking between them. The bodies were held in place with wires wrapped around them and around posts that kept them upright. It was a gruesome sight. There had not been any bodies placed here for a number of years. In the past, the dry, constant temperature of the catacombs had made it popular for families to place deceased loved ones here, because it was cheaper than burial. There were six of us walking unescorted through the catacombs. Jerry Hecko, who had quite a bit of Italian wine that day, went down a corridor that had a rope across it. We followed him, and after many turns, and reversing of directions, we became lost. In this section of the catacomb, there were stacked coffins, and the bodies were in disarray. The number of bodies was unbelievable! It was like being in a horror movie; we finally stumbled onto the right tunnel that lead to the tour route, and we quickly left the catacomb. At the end of the tour there was an attraction on display.

It was a casket with a glass top that had been shattered. Within the casket was a small five-year-old girl in a pink lace trimmed dress, and she looked asleep. She had been dead for almost 100 years. The glass top of her coffin had been struck by a falling piece of the roof that had fallen during a bombing attack in World War II. It was considered a miracle that she was so well preserved, even after her body was exposed to air.

One night Jerry Hecko "hijacked" a horse and buggy taxi, and drove the horse and buggy several blocks with the taxi owner and shore patrol chasing him, he got away. On another night I and another W Division sailor saw a line of sailors almost a block long, we asked those standing in line what was going on. They said it was a "house of ill repute," there were two girls working. We didn't get in line.

I enjoyed Taranto more than Naples. One afternoon on the liberty launch going from the ship to the pier, I noticed a first class staring at me from across the boat, and his expression was murderous. A W Division sailor, Monte May happened to be sitting by him. This guy was talking to Monte out of the corner of his mouth, while his eyes threw daggers at me. This particular liberty launch was transporting not only *Independence* sailors, but also sailors from the destroyers that were anchored near us. The liberty launch pulled up alongside one of the anchored destroyers, and with one vicious look, the sailor got up and left the boat, climbing up the ladder that reached down from the destroyer's quarterdeck. Upon arrival at the pier, Monte came over to me and said that guy said he would like to kill you! He further said the guy told him his wife's name was Barbara, and they'd divorced. He had gone to the *Independence* to buy some uniforms from our ship's store, as he was stationed on the nearby anchored destroyer. I felt terrible; Barbara was the girl I had dated for a short while in Norfolk. She had originally told me she was divorced, and I was only one of the many sailors she dated. I didn't have a clue how he knew who I was, or why he thought I'd been the cause of his divorce. I knew from the look on his face I would not be able to reason with him. For the rest of that in port period I watched my back.

As time neared for my departure from the ship and I headed for Norfolk to be discharged, I dreaded saying farewell to my friends. One night at sea a group of us in W Division was playing poker, and I won hand after hand. The next day I bought a reel-to-reel tape recorder, mailed it home, and saved the rest of my winnings. A letter from home said the "Hells Angels" motorcycle gang had invaded the nearby town of Porterville, and disrupted the community for a couple of days. My brother Joe had the measles.

I was scheduled to leave the ship the next in port period, which was to be in Palermo, Sicily. My last at sea period I was busy packing my sea bag, and starting the checkout process. Just before the ship anchored I was given my last evaluation marks, which averaged 3.8 and the statement of my performance said, "Little has shown many of those qualities that are necessary in becoming a fine petty officer. He has been second class a relatively short time and does not have the experience that is so helpful in becoming a leader. Little is always neat in appearance, and wears the uniform with pride." An additional statement said: "Little's quiet and pleasing disposition contributes to and helps maintain the high morale of W Division." I didn't realize it at the time but the statements in my evaluations were pretty much "canned" statements. It was to eventually become a strong conviction of mine that evaluation forms were the most important piece of paperwork a supervisor in the Navy would ever complete.

Gary King and I agreed that we would meet in April 1964 when he was discharged. He was from Fullerton, California. Jerry Hecko also said he would travel from Indiana to see us both. I was anxious to leave, yet regretted leaving the friends I'd made. I was proud of the work my assembly team had done. We'd worked hard, completed a lot of difficult inspections, and gone through times of stress and hardship. We had shared good times on liberty, shared our dreams of the future, and had supported each other. Often it was felt that we younger "first termers" were alone against the establishment. I resisted all the "shipping over lectures", although deep down inside I enjoyed the prestige I had as a second class petty officer. I knew I would not have a comparable position in civilian life.

Fourteen November, nineteen hundred sixty three, the ship anchored at Palermo, Sicily, I went on liberty with my shipmates for the last time. Sicily was the birthplace of the mafia, so we imagined that we saw gangsters everywhere. Everyone was jealous of me; although I was envious they still had three months left on the Med cruise, with many more liberty ports to visit.

The morning of the 16th, my sea bag was packed; I had on my dress blues, with one Good Conduct Ribbon. My access badge to W Division was to be destroyed as soon as I left the ship. I went into W Division spaces, and with clenched teeth, and a forced smile, shook hands with my friends. This was a tough time saying farewell to shipmates who had become as close as brothers. And although it was never said, we loved each other as brothers.

After bidding everyone goodbye, with sea bag on my shoulder, I saluted the chief on the after brow, after he signed my transfer orders, and went down the ladder into the liberty boat. The ride to the pier was the roughest boat ride I'd ever had! Waves were coming over the bow, soaking everybody. I thought how ironic it would be to be drowned on the first leg of my trip to become a civilian! The boat finally made it to the pier. I looked out at sea for a last look at the huge gray ship that had been my home. I was to see her two more times in the coming years, the last time thirty-five years in the future, during her decommissioning ceremony at Puget Sound Naval Shipyard, Bremerton, Washington, September 30, 1998.

A group of thirty *Independence* sailors were leaving the ship. We boarded a bus and were taken to U. S. Naval Air Station Sigonella. We arrived in the early afternoon and were to remain overnight. In the morning I had breakfast in the most unusual Navy chow hall I'd ever been in. The tables were round with red and white-checkered tablecloths that seated four. Italian waiters would take your order selected from a menu, and deliver the meal to your table. It was the most unique chow hall I'd been in up to that point, and it was very pleasant. Our journey continued that day in a large transport plane to Naval Station Rota, Spain. In Rota we were directed to the dreaded transit barracks. In the morning I boarded a large transport plane, which took off and landed at an airfield in England called Green Fields. We remained in the terminal a couple of hours, and then took off again. At least I could say that I set a foot in England. After being in flight for a long time, we landed on the airstrip on the Azores Islands in the middle of the Atlantic. We had breakfast in the Air Force chow hall and then took to the air again. We landed at Bolling Air Force Base, Washington, D.C., and after a two-hour bus ride south, I was once again at the Norfolk Transit Barracks.

I had to have a complete physical before my discharge. If a sailor had an illness or injury while on active duty, a determination had to be made concerning the status of the physical condition of the sailor, whether he has any degree of disability. Most sailors in the transit barracks were anxious to get out of the Navy. They had the option of signing a release that meant the Navy would not be obligated to give them compensation, or medical treatment later on in civilian life for injuries or illnesses they had on active duty. I met a few sailors whose discharge had been delayed a couple of weeks. It was not wise to quickly sign a release as many of them did. During my three ½ years I'd seldom gone to sick call for anything other than colds, or the flu. I'd gone from 127 pounds to 155 pounds; I had occasional back pain from my mess cooking days on the *USS Haven*, but didn't complain.

One morning while walking to the chow hall for breakfast, another sailor and I were approaching an officer walking toward us. We saluted him, and he stopped us and chewed us out for not saluting him sooner. He was an ensign. Later in the barracks, on the third floor, looking out the window I saw the same officer on the path he'd stopped me on, chewing out other sailors. He was apparently walking back and forth feeding his ego by belittling enlisted men. This was a disgusting thing to see.

The times I went on liberty it was not the same without my shipmates. Sailors wore the name of their ship on the right shoulder of their dress uniform. I caused quite a stir among some of the women who saw the *USS Independence* on my right shoulder. Most were married women out on the town, with the assurance that their husbands were thousands of miles away in the Mediterranean. They were relieved to learn I was in Norfolk by myself, and the ship had not secretly returned.

A girl I'd known in the Peppermint Lounge, asked me one evening if I'd walk her home after work. She lived a few blocks away in a hotel. We walked to the hotel, and sat together in a little alcove in the hotel lobby. We were out of view, and began kissing. The vice squad was notorious in Norfolk. There were stories of them breaking into houses, and arresting sailors on the slightest possibility that there was a man and women, unmarried, and alone. I personally had seen two vice squad plain clothes men take a sailor into an alley and punch him unconscious. Anyway these two men in suits came into the hotel lobby, and told us to leave. The girl went up to her room, and I disgustedly left.

Another evening a girl I knew invited me to her house, which was a distance from the base. I took a city bus; stayed at her house a few hours, and then went to the bus stop to catch a bus back to the base. At the bus stop, a car pulled up, the driver leaned over and asked, "Do you want a ride?" I said, "I'm going to the Naval Base", he said, "Hop in." I was usually cautious about accepting rides, but he looked like a sailor. I got in the car, and after some small talk, he said, "You might be interested in some books I have in the glove compartment?" I opened the glove compartment, and it was full of books of nude women. Alarm bells started to go off in my mind! I looked over, and he was masturbating. I said, "Put both hands on the wheel and pull over, I'm getting out." He said, "OK, OK, don't get mad." I got out after he pulled over, I thought about kicking the car, but didn't. I walked until I found another bus stop. This event disgusted me.

I was not having good experiences since I'd left the ship! This intensified my desire to be discharged and get home. I missed W Division. We were a young group of kids that had worked hard together, and had good times. We had laughed and joked continually. There had been a lot of alcohol drinking, and looking back it seems the Navy encouraged drinking. There were happy hours at the clubs, where drinks sold for pennies. Drinking at divisional gatherings was encouraged. There was a work hard, play hard philosophy that included alcohol. Many of my old shipmates from that time now abstain from drinking, either because of health problems or life problems that were caused by excessive drinking.

I completed my physical, which was not too thorough. I signed my red ID card, which would be my Naval Reserve identification card, replacing my green active duty ID. It was not widely known, but every able-bodied man in America, between the ages of eighteen and thirty-two, at that time had a six-year military obligation. In my case, after three ½ years' active duty, I still had an additional two ½ years to serve. This time would be served in the Navy Reserves. This usually meant I would be in the inactive reserves, but could be called to active reserves at any time, which would mean monthly meetings, and a two-week active duty period each year. I was to report to my local draft board within sixty days' following my discharge.

There were a few sailors in the transit barracks that were not being given Honorable Discharges; some were awarded Administrative, or Undesirable Discharges. I recall one sailor who was being discharged, and because of his poor evaluations marks, was not recommended for re-enlistment. He was a Filipino seaman, and had enlisted originally in the Philippines for a six-year enlistment. Philippine enlistments had special conditions attached. A Filipino enlistee had six years in which to become an American citizen. If he did not pass the citizenship requirements, pass the test, etc., at the end of his enlistment he had to return to the Philippine Islands. This sailor was not aware of this requirement, or perhaps he didn't understand it. He was very upset; he did not want to return to the Philippines. We were told we could wear our uniforms home after our discharge, and after that only on special occasions.

On 20 November, 1963, a group of twenty sailors and I mustered in front of the administration building of the Norfolk Naval Base. One by one our names were called out, we stepped forward and were handed a white envelope that contained pages from our service records. Inside was one very important document, a DD-214, which was a proof document of our service. We were handed an Honorable Discharge pin to wear on civilian clothes. A lieutenant shook my hand, and said, "Thank you for your service to our country, good luck." I then saluted him, and walked away with my sea bag on my shoulder, toward a taxi cab which would take me to the Norfolk Airport. I had gone "a full circle": 30 June, 1960, a lieutenant had sworn me into the Navy, and now almost three ½ years later a lieutenant bid me farewell from the Navy.

The defense of our nation has a high price. The sailors who gave their tomorrows that we might have our "todays" while I was on board *Independence* were:

SN Peter R. White, USN	November 5, 1962
LT Bruce Holliday, USN	November 19, 1962
AN Robert J. Benedict, USN	July 3, 1963
Capt. W.E. Skinner, USMC	August 18, 1963
LT Steven E. Kadas, USN	August 23, 1963
Capt. Jackson Mize, USN	August 31, 1963
LT Theodore C. Garret, USN	September 19, 1963

My time in the Navy had truly been an adventure. I had seen much of the world. I was not sad to be leaving the east coast. My salary had gone from seventy-eight dollars a month, to $220 a month. My salary as a civilian would be zero dollars, until I found a job. These thoughts were going through my mind as I flew across country to California. I had gotten half a month pay upon my discharge, as I had sixteen days of unused leave.

Chapter 6: Beginnings of the Vietnam War

It was wonderful to see my family. They lived among an orange grove at the base of the Sierra Mountains, near Strathmore, California. I tried to look up some of my boyhood friends, but most had moved away long ago. I did find Butch Coley, who was now a milkman for a local creamery. Butch told me about a correspondence course on law enforcement he was completing. Butch went on to a highly successful career in law, achieving a master's degree from Pepperdine University, and becoming the elected Sheriff of Tulare County, California. Early one morning I went with Butch on his milk route. After he completed his route, we were sitting in his house in Lindsay; the date was 22 November 1963. Butch's wife, Janice came in and said, "The President has been shot." We turned on the television and learned of the assassination of President Kennedy in Dallas, Texas. The church bells were tolling in town, and after a while I left Butch and Janice's house. I had been out of the Navy for two days, I wondered if I would be called back on active duty.

I put in an application for employment at the state hospital where my mother worked and I began dating a girl I'd vaguely known when I was in high school. Allison Konrad had been a friend of my ex-fiancée, and lived on the same block as my ex-fiancée. I was celebrating my "freedom" as a civilian, with little thought of my future. The killer of President Kennedy, Oswald had been murdered, and we wondered if our country was falling apart. Many people remained glued to the television set watching the events unfold.

Twenty days after my discharge from the Navy, I made one of the worse decisions of my life: Allison and I drove to Las Vegas late at night, and were married in a Las Vegas wedding chapel on 10 December 1963, two days after my twenty-first birthday. In retrospect, the marriage was made on the rebound from my failed engagement with Donna, and with little thought of the future. The look of sorrow on my mother's face when I told her of the marriage remains frozen in my memory. She sensed as I did that I had made a serious mistake.

Allison's parents gave us a wedding shower at a church in Lindsay. Now I was really forced to consider the future. Allison did not have a job, and the only work available in the winter were "smudging" jobs, lighting oil pots in the orange groves during the night to prevent the oranges hanging on trees from freezing and spoiling. I passed written and oral exams at the state hospital, and had passed a physical exam. I was given a date to go to work, but I had a change of heart. I wasn't sure if I could do the job of changing diapers, caring for patient needs, and the compassionate things that my mother had done so well over the years.

I ran across a close boyhood friend, Ashley Caudle, who had just spent two years in the Army. We spent a lot of time talking about the good times we had in the service. Allison and I lived in her apartment, and the money I had saved in the Navy was becoming short. I had doctor bills, and my car needed work. My wonderful dreams of a carefree civilian life had turned into a nightmare.

At the time of my discharge I had been recommended for re-enlistment. If I should reenlist within ninety days following the date of my discharge, I would not have "broken service", which meant I'd be able to keep my second class petty officer rate. If I waited beyond the ninety days, I would probably be enlisted as a third class or seaman. By the end of January things was looking bleak, and my ninety days would be up on the 18th of February. The last of January, I got a haircut and went to see the Navy recruiter in nearby Visalia.

The recruiter arranged for me to travel to San Francisco for my physical exam and re-enlistment. Allison had gotten a job as a checker in a nearby grocery store. She was not happy that I had to leave for San Francisco, but she was going to have to adjust to times of separation in the Navy.

Before I left for San Francisco, Allison with my sister Linda went shopping in the Chevy convertible, and it stopped with engine trouble. I decided to trade it in. I got a 1963 Chevrolet Monza, one of the first American cars to have a rear engine. If I had the 56 Chevy convertible today, it would be priceless, as that model became a much sought-after collector's car.

On 4 February 1964, I boarded a bus at Visalia, California bound for San Francisco. In my suitcase I had a set of dress blues. In San Francisco, I checked into the YMCA, and spent a sleepless night with doubt and indecision running through my mind.

The next morning I walked three blocks to the federal building, where I underwent a physical. The recruiter in Visalia had checked with authorities to make sure I hadn't gotten into trouble as a civilian, and he had given me a green light. That afternoon I recited the same oath I had taken three and a half years previously. I signed an enlistment contract for six years. I received a re-enlistment bonus. This was a month's pay for each year I signed up for, and came to $1,320. I was also given thirty days' leave, and told my transfer orders to my next duty station would be mailed to my parents' address. Late that afternoon I walked back to the YMCA, and changed from civilian clothes into my dress blues.

All the doubts I had about going back into the Navy, disappeared as soon as I was back in uniform. I felt relieved to be back in uniform, it was almost like returning home. I rode the bus back to Visalia with $1,320 safely tucked in the inside pocket of my uniform jumper.

I paid off all my bills, and a couple of weeks later, a packet from the Navy arrived at my parents' mailbox. I was being assigned to *USS Ticonderoga*, (CVA-14), an aircraft carrier home ported in San Diego, California. I was very relieved not to be going back to the east coast. I especially did not want to go back to the *Independence* at this point, because I could imagine the teasing I would be subjected to now that I had become a "Lifer."

The *Ticonderoga* was much smaller than the *Independence*, and much older. She was an attack aircraft carrier[15]. She was the lead ship of modified 27,100-ton *Essex* class aircraft carriers, was built at Newport News, Virginia. She was commissioned in May 1944 and made a West Indies shakedown cruise prior to transiting the Panama Canal to the Pacific in early September. During the next few months, *Ticonderoga* transported aircraft to Hawaii, took part in underway ordnance replenishment experiments and trained her crew and air group for participation in the war against Japan. After steaming to the western Pacific in October, her first strikes were on 5 November 1944, hitting targets ashore and afloat in the northern Philippines area. As part of Task Force 38, she continued her attacks in the vicinity for the next two months, riding out a major typhoon in mid-December.

In January 1945, *Ticonderoga* took part in raids against Japanese assets in Indochina, China, Luzon and Formosa. Hit by two "Kamikaze" suicide planes on 21 January, she lost over 140 crewmen and had to go to the U.S. for repairs. *Ticonderoga* returned to the combat area in late May. For the remaining two and a half months of the Pacific War, her planes made regular attacks on the Japanese home islands. From September 1945 into January 1946, she transported veterans' home across the Pacific. Inactive after that, *Ticonderoga* was decommissioned at the Puget Sound Navy Yard in January 1947.

Five years later, *Ticonderoga* was temporarily reactivated and sent to the New York Naval Shipyard to receive an extensive modernization. Redesignated CVA-14, she recommissioned in September 1954 and served with the Atlantic Fleet for two years, making one Mediterranean deployment in 1955-56. More modifications followed in 1956-57, providing an angled flight deck and enclosed bow to fully suit her to operate high-performance jet aircraft. She then returned to the west coast, her home for the rest of her career. Up to 1962 she had completed four deployments to the Western Pacific as part of the U.S. Seventh Fleet. The name *Ticonderoga* was often shortened to *"Tico"* by her crew.

Allison and I left for San Diego the last of February. We rented a small apartment for a few days on Coronado Island, near the North Island Naval Air Station. The base had piers that the *Ticonderoga* tied up to. I learned that the ship was scheduled to get underway for the Western Pacific in six weeks. I also learned that Allison was pregnant.

I reported aboard *USS Ticonderoga* 15 March, 1964. I had brought my sea bag up to par by shopping at Lemoore Naval Air Station, near Visalia, California. As I said before, *Ticonderoga* was a large ship, but much smaller than the *USS Independence*, and not nearly as modern. The berthing compartment was not as comfortable as the *Independence*. The bunks on the *Tico* were stretched canvas with thin mattresses, and were stacked three and four high. The first and second class petty officers had a section separated from the common berthing area by a curtain.

I began my check in as soon as I reported to the personnel office. The ship had just undergone a series of inspections, and was scheduled for more prior to departure. There were thirty-five men in W Division. The Division Officer was Lieutenant (jg) Burkhardt; Electrical Officer LTJG F.L. Richardson; Junior Division Officer ENS. J.A. Gelsomino. The Leading Chief was GMTC Catron; our Leading Petty Officer was GMT1 Gaddley. W Division was somewhat top heavy, we had an unusually large number of second class. I'd not met any of the sailors before, except Dan Hoover, who I remembered being in a class behind me in Albuquerque A school. Compared to most W Divisions on carriers we were very well manned. Thirty-five men was twice the normal size of a W Division on a carrier the size of *Ticonderoga*.

As usual, my security clearance had to be confirmed, so I was put to work supervising cleaning of W Division berthing compartment. After a couple of weeks I was told some wonderful news; instead of getting underway with the ship, I would remain in the states and attend school for six weeks. A second class named T.J. Cherney and I were to attend loading school at Lemoore, California, and also a nuclear weapon refresher course at Nuclear Weapons Training Center Pacific, in San Diego, which was located on Coronado Island, a few blocks from where the ship tied up.

One convenient aspect was that Lemoore Naval Air Station was only a few miles from Lindsay, California where my new in-laws, Ernie and Effie Konrad, lived. Allison had returned to Lindsay and was staying with them.

On 12 April, Cherney and I left the ship for Lemoore. *Ticonderoga* was to get underway for the Western Pacific in two days on the fourteenth. In our absence, *Ticonderoga* would be undergoing an Operational Readiness Inspection (ORI); this was an inspection that was conducted on naval vessels before they went into potential combat areas to insure they were battle ready.

I was attending the loading school in Lemoore in order to be qualified as a technical monitor on *Ticonderoga* as I had on the *Independence*. The airplane types on *Tico* were different from those onboard *Independence*. *Ticonderoga* had the F-8 *Crusader*, a jet fighter; the A-1 *Skyraider*, a propeller driven fighter-bomber; the A-4 *Skyhawk* jet fighter-bomber, and the A-3 *Skywarrior* dual jet bomber, the biggest carrier-based aircraft in the Navy. *Tico* also had early warning radar planes, COD's, and helicopters. Cherney and I checked into loading school on Friday, and were given the weekend off, Cherney checked into the barracks, and I drove to Lindsay. On Monday I left my in-law's house at 5:00 a.m., and arrived at school at 7:00 a.m. The loading school was casual, and the only GMT stationed there, was also a GMT2 who taught us. Our school lasted two weeks, and we had an additional week before we were to report to San Diego, 320 miles south of Lemoore. After the class completion we volunteered to paint two of the weapon trainers that the school used for loading classes. The trainers' surfaces were scratched, and chipped. We sanded and painted the trainers during this last week. Our effort impressed the school. In reality we would have been bored sitting around for a week with nothing to do. Word about our volunteer work eventually got back to the ship, and it helped the reputation of *Ticonderoga*'s W Division.

I was becoming aware of a truth in the Navy. There were actually "two navies" within the Navy, the East coast Navy, and the West coast Navy. There were of course two different fleets, but the way tasks were performed, working relationships, and outlooks were very different. The East coast Navy was much closer to the Navy's origins, Portsmouth, Norfolk, Boston, etc., and steeped in tradition. It seemed there were more distinct lines of separation between officers and enlisted men. There seemed to be less emphasis on job performance, and more emphasis on military behavior. On the West coast it seemed that job performance, along with a "can do" attitude was the main goal. I enjoyed the West coast Navy, not only because it was nearest my home, but also because of the personality of the West coast Navy. There was a saying in the Navy, and particularly of the East coast Navy: "Navy; over 200 years of tradition unhampered by progress"!

I enjoyed the time at the loading school in Lemoore. This was to be the only time in the Navy I was able to return nightly to my hometown after work was over for the day. Cherney and I checked out of school, and drove south to San Diego, where we checked into Nuclear Weapons Training Center Pacific, one block from the main gate of North Island Naval Air Station. The school was within a large brick building surrounded by a tall fence. In order to get to North Island, or Coronado, you took a ferry that carried cars and passengers back and forth between San Diego and the island. Although in reality it was not an island, as a strand of land to the south connected with the mainland (called the Silver Strand). To drive this strand took about an hour, versus the ferry ride, which took about twenty minutes, and cost forty-five cents. There were also smaller boats that transported sailors back and forth between the island and the main city of San Diego, nicknamed "nickel snatchers." We attended these classes for four weeks. They were more structured than the classes at Lemoore, and covered warhead maintenance procedures. We had instructions on all the air-dropped weapons we would be working with.

One GMT2, who was a classmate, had completed Explosive Ordnance Disposal (EOD) School. He described an interesting aspect of his training: For one week during school he remained tied to another sailor by a short length of rope. This rope could not be removed for seven days, the purpose being to teach them the "buddy rule", or need to rely on each another, while scuba diving or defusing explosives.

We graduated from our course, and were directed to report to Travis Air Force Base, near Sacramento, the latter part of May, for a flight overseas to catch our ship. I spent the weekend at home, bid my parents and Allison goodbye, and caught a bus to Travis Air Force Base, where I met Cherney. We flew to Hawaii, Guam, and then on the Clark Air Force Base, Philippines.

It was 100 degrees, with very high humidity when the plane landed at Clark. Since Cherney and I were in transit, we had to wear our wool dress blue, which were miserably hot. We had a four-hour bus ride through the Philippine countryside to Subic Bay Naval Base where the *Ticonderoga* was alongside a pier. The bus was not air-conditioned, and the heat was almost unbearable.

The countryside was green and tropical, and we saw farmers plowing fields with caribous. The villages we passed through looked very poor. Most of the houses were built on stilts and had palm thatched roofs. Some homes were made of concrete with tin roofs. Children playing by the roadside were either naked, or scantily clothed. The open sewage was pungent to smell. Two hours into our ride the bus stopped at a small restaurant and bar called the Halfway House. I assumed their biggest customers were the travelers on the military bus between Clark Air Force Base, and the Subic Naval Base. There were two buses, with sixty sailors in each bus. The last hour of the ride we climbed steep, winding mountain roads, with thick jungle on each side of the road. We arrived at the naval base, and took a base taxi to the pier where the ship was. I was glad to finally be onboard; it had been a long hot journey, and I was exhausted.

I was assigned as an Assembly Team Leader in the after-magazine. Just as on the *Independence*, W Division was split into a forward and after magazine. The ship got underway the day after I arrived back onboard. *Ticonderoga* participated in a war game called *Operation Ligtas*, which lasted seven days. Afterwards, we anchored in the bay off the Philippine Capitol of Manila.

I did not know many people in W Division at this point. I went on liberty with Ray Steele and a couple of other second class GMT's. I noticed many World War II vintage jeeps that had been converted into taxis. These vehicles were called "jeepneys." The drivers decorated the jeepneys with flags, catholic statues, and all kinds of gaudy decorations; they were very colorful.

The currencies used in the Philippines were pesos. We were not paid with American currency while overseas, but with military scripts. This was paper money specially made for military payrolls. This method was intended to prevent black-market trading of American currency. We called the money "funny money." Each denomination, one, five, ten, and twenty dollar bill, was a different color; red, green, yellow, and so on. If we wanted to spend money off the ship, we had to change our "funny money" into pesos before leaving the ship. The disbursing office set up tables in the hangar bay for this purpose.

After we explored Manila for a couple of hours, we went to a bar where most of the W Division sailors were. Later that night I decided to go back to the ship alone; this was a mistake. It was about an eight-block walk back to the liberty boat pier. After I had walked three blocks, down a dark deserted street, a small Filipino came at me out of the shadows. He didn't look very old, perhaps sixteen. He had a knife, and thrust it forward toward my stomach. I grabbed the blade of the knife. At that same moment a hand came from behind me, and grabbed my billfold, which was hanging flap down from the right front pants pocket of my dress whites. Then in a flash the kid with the knife pulled it from my grasp, and he and the person with my wallet ran down an alley out of sight. I had grabbed the knife with my right hand and blood was seeping from my clenched fist. I kept my fist clenched to control the bleeding and continued walking toward the liberty boat pier. At the pier I found the shore patrol and explained what happened. A duty corpsman at the pier examined my hand, cleaned and bandaged it. Luckily stitches were not required, but it hurt. I was thankful the knife had not found its way to my stomach. My cut hand hurt, but I think my pride was hurt worse. I'd lost my driver's license, ID card, and about eight dollars in pesos. I didn't go ashore again in Manila during that in port stay. Never again in a foreign port did I take my driver's license, or anything other than my ID card, and I very seldom walked alone down foreign streets.

My sister Linda had just graduated from high school, and for my brother Joe's sixth birthday I had gotten him some toy golf clubs before leaving home. These were typical sacrifices in a sailor's life; missed milestones in our families' lives. With pro pay, sea pay, and family separation pay I was making $468 a month, before taxes. As a married sailor I was making a little more than during my single life. I was anxious for my baby's birth, which was to happen in November. The ship was due back in San Diego 16 October. Our next scheduled port of call was Sasebo, Japan.

The weather was hot and humid, and as on the *Independence*, one of the coolest places in *Ticonderoga* was W Division magazines. As well as performing the duties of an assembly team leader, I was also a technical monitor when the squadron loading teams would practice loading weapons. One requirement at that time was a drill held every three months simulating going to nuclear war. This quarterly drill on *Ticonderoga* was code named "Crew-cut." The ship would go to general quarters battle stations, and W Division would send up ordnance to be loaded. Everything was performed up to the point of aircraft launches off the ship, and then the drill was over. Timing was critical, and all those involved worked as quickly as possible.

We worked under a plan called a Strike Integrated Operation Plan, or "SIOP." This meant each carrier operating in the Western Pacific (West Pac), and other areas of the world might be assigned specific targets. Our planes could reach targets 600 miles away, and return.

We could steam at thirty knots for twelve hours and that range extended to 960 miles, steaming for twenty- four hours that range could be 1,320 miles. There might also be target missions that would call for the pilot to divert to other landing areas instead of returning to the *Ticonderoga*. We felt sympathy for the A-1 *Skyraider* pilots. They piloted the single prop bomber that was much slower than the jet bombers. They always asked if we thought they would escape the blast when they dropped their weapon. We always told them of course they would be safe, but it was questionable whether they would survive. We trained on our weapon trainers to keep our technical and mechanical skills sharp. We completed a full cycle of training operations once a month.

On 23 June we pulled into Sasebo, Japan. This was my first visit. The currency in Japan was yen and we changed our "Funny Money" into yen at the rate of $1.00 = 366 yen. Japan was somewhat how I'd imagined it. All the houses, streets, cars, etc., were very small by American standards, almost like a land of dolls. The odor of "benjoe" ditches was overpowering. These were sewer ditches in front of all the homes that were covered with concrete slabs that doubled as a sidewalk.

The ship tied up at a pier at the Sasebo Naval Station. On liberty I found everything was very inexpensive. As at other naval bases, shops and bars outside the naval base main gate catered to American sailors. The bars had names like, "American Bar", "Lucky Bar", "Rainbow Club", etc. We were busy during this in-port period because of a pending change of command ceremony. Captain Cooper was relieving *Ticonderoga*'s commanding officer, Captain Weinel. The change of command on a carrier is usually elaborate. Most of the crew changed into dress whites, and stood in ranks in the hangar bay during the ceremony.

One night Ray Steele and I were on liberty in a small Japanese bar, when suddenly the walls began swaying, bottles fell from the shelves, and the floor bucked wildly. It was an earthquake, and everyone ran out of the bar except Ray and me. We sat there for a long while, but no one returned, so we helped ourselves to drinks, and snacks. We even tried some pickled octopus tentacles; the suction cups were chewy. After we'd eaten to our capacity, we left some yen on the bar and departed.

A typical change of command ceremony pamphlet lists a biography of the departing C.O., and the new arriving Commanding Officer. Departing Captain Weinel's "bio" read[16]:

He graduated from the Naval Academy in 1939. Prior to being designated a naval aviator in 1942 he served in cruisers and destroyers. During World War II he was Executive Officer of composite Squadron 33 and later Commanding Officer of Fighter Squadron 22. Later he commanded Fighter Squadron 14, Fighter-Bomber Squadron 98 and Air Group 5. He served on the *USS Antietam* and *USS Valley Forge* as a ship's officer. He was Operations and Plans Officer Carrier Division Five Staff in 1956-57. He commanded the *USS Great Sitkin* in 1961-62. Captain Weinel is a graduate of the NATO Defense College, Paris, France, and the National War College in Washington, D.C. He assumed command of *Ticonderoga* July 20, 1963. He is married to the former Ann Mayhew of Coronado, California, and has three daughters.

I've included this biography as an example of the type of naval officers commanding aircraft carriers. Without fail they were naval aviators, and often following their tour as a commanding officer of a carrier, they would be promoted to rear admiral, or retire. An assignment as a commanding officer of a carrier is considered the apex of a naval aviator's career. It's necessary not only for naval aviators but for any naval officer, that they progress through a variety of jobs that give them the experience and job training to prepare them for command. This progression through jobs is called "getting your ticket punched." In other words, an officer had to complete each job before getting on the "train (commanding officer position)." To fail in a job, could mean a sudden and fatal stop in the climb toward command.

Also onboard *Ticonderoga* was Rear Adm. R.B. Moore, who was Commander Task Force 77 in the Seventh Fleet. He was the Task Force Commander of two or three carriers, and numerous vessels within the Seventh Fleet in the Far East. Admiral Moore had his own staff of nine officers, and a number of enlisted men. The admiral had his own living and working area for himself and his staff. Most of the senior officers, commander and above had been in the Navy during World War II. The number of enlisted men that had gone through that war was gradually diminishing as their twenty-year retirement approached; some would not retire until the thirty-year time frame – the Navy was slowly losing the sailors who had wartime experience, other than the Korean Conflict.

While in Sasebo, we had a change of command ceremony, and also a "visitor's day." All the Japanese civilians that wished could come on the ship on the designated day and tour the ship. Thousands of Japanese took advantage of the invitation to visit the ship. This was extra work for us, as many sailors were assigned tour guides to insure our visitors didn't go into unauthorized areas of the ship.

Around the middle of June Allison had an argument with her mother, and moved in with my parents. This was the first of many conflicts in Allison's relationships with others during our married life. At this time I also found out how small the world was, I discovered the brother of a high school friend was stationed on *Ticonderoga*. His name was Melvin Keith. He was a seaman scheduled to get out of the Navy in a year.

We pulled out of Sasebo on 28 June, and pulled back in on 2 July. We were scheduled to stay a week, but a typhoon was threatening the area, and we pulled back out to sea on the 5th. Our next scheduled in port visit was Hong Kong, China. We were to be there on 16 July. We didn't know it then, but we would not be in port again for fifty-seven days. On the 10th the captain addressed the crew over the 1MC, ship's loudspeaker, and said our visit to Hong Kong had been cancelled. We were to relieve a carrier that had been steaming off the coast of Vietnam. This was a surprise to us all. Vietnam had been in the news, North Vietnam and South Vietnam fighting had intensified the last couple of months. The carrier we were relieving had major problems, needing repair, we were stuck with their job. On our way to relieve the carrier off the coast of Vietnam, we were involved in a war game exercise. We anchored in an area called Buckner Bay for a few hours hiding from a fictitious enemy in the war game.

The war game was a training exercise that was a common training operation that was not uncommon to us. I had time to write letters, and turn my thoughts to home. My brother Jerry's latest comment was, while playing with brother Joe, "throw your gun down!" he had just started talking. My parents were planning a camping trip to an area called Mineral King in the Sierra Nevada Mountains of California.

Mid July found the *USS Ticonderoga* steaming in the Tonkin Gulf off the coast of Vietnam. On 2 August 1964, we were standing on the brink of history. Sailors in W Division were enjoying the relaxed routine we usually had on Sundays. Each Sunday at sea, unless the ship was involved in inspections or battle training, reveille would not be held, and sailors could sleep in. This was a day of relaxation, catching up on lost sleep, and attending church services. The church services were poorly attended. Sixty men out of 3,500 men attended protestant services, and about the same number for catholic services. After this day, however, church attendance increased dramatically.

Normally the chiefs and officers would not come down into W Division spaces on Sundays, so we enlisted men would relax in the coffee locker/break room. The daily requirements such as taking magazine temperatures and routine magazine security checks would be accomplished by whoever was on watch. There were always two W Division sailors on watch within the division, standing a four-hour watch. The launching and landing of aircraft were a sound you soon got used to. Thuds, thumps, and the squeal of catapults became everyday sounds of our life on the ship.

On the evening of the 2nd, the captain announced over the ship's loudspeaker that our aircraft were involved in protecting one of our destroyers from a PT boat attack. This was exciting news to us. Everyone was excited about the prospect of being in combat. Rumors flew about the ship. We wondered if it were North Vietnamese, or Red Chinese attacking our ships. We all thought about what we would do in the event *Ticonderoga* was torpedoed. W Division compartments were under the water line of the ship. Our battle stations were on the fifth and sixth deck below the hangar deck. We very seldom talked about it, but we all wondered what it would be like being deep within the bowels of the ship after an attack, sinking down to the bottom of the sea, knowing that when you used up all the oxygen within the compartment your life was ended. I think we all hoped we would be courageous and die like men.

Our Weapons Department divisions supplied the Zuni air to surface rockets that *Ticonderoga*'s planes launched at the fleeing PT boats that day. The F-8 *Crusaders*, hit two of the PT Boats with rockets, but they zipped through the boat's wooden hulls without exploding! The rockets were fused to explode against steel hulls, not wooden ones. After the 2nd our ordnancemen made fusing adjustments so the Zuni rockets would explode when striking the wooden communist boats. The evening of the 2nd, someone brought a box down to W Division that contained 20mm shell casings of the bullets that had been fired at the PT boats. I got two of them for souvenirs.

That night we all slept restlessly, wondering what the future held. The squadrons were flying many more sorties than the previous day. That day we went to general quarters for a couple of hours.

We all ran to our battle stations a little faster, and took extra pains to get into battle dress with our pants legs tucked into our socks, our shirts fully buttoned, and our gas masks ready for use. We tightened the dogs (levers) on the hatches a little more tightly, and took general quarters much more seriously than we had in the past few months.

On Tuesday, 4 August, we went to general quarters at about 2200 (10:00 p.m.). The weather was not good, and the ship was rolling a little more than usual. Our hearts beat faster when we heard the general quarter's announcement over the 1MC loudspeaker. Normally the announcement from the bridge would be, "This is a drill, this is a drill, general quarters, general quarters, all hands man your battle stations." But the announcement this night was, "This is NOT a drill, this is NOT a drill, general quarters, general quarters, all hands man your battle stations." We raced to our battle stations. Down in W Division magazines we could hear aircraft being launched off the flight deck. Each night at 2200 one of the ship's chaplains would say an evening prayer over the 1MC loudspeaker, just before "taps." This evening we listened closely as the chaplain said a prayer for our comrades who were in combat that very instant. After midnight the captain came over the 1MC and informed us that another attack against our destroyers had been beaten off. We remained at general quarters at our battle stations all night. Prior to this, when we underwent readiness training or practiced general quarters, we would not remain at battle stations for more than four hours. We wouldn't have believed it at the time, but we were to remain at our battle stations for two weeks!

The next day, the 5th, the ship was buzzing with activity. The ordnance divisions in Weapons Department were busy breaking out conventional bombs, rockets, and ammunition from magazines. Squadron loading crews were busy loading and arming aircraft. We didn't know about the air strikes that were carried out that day, until later when the captain came over the 1MC and told us of the success of the attack against the Quang Khe oil storage depot.

Being at general quarters kept the ship battle ready, and at the highest defensive level possible, but it drastically changed our normal shipboard lifestyle, and restricted our freedom of movement. All hands had to remain at battle stations twenty-four hours a day, which in my case was the after W Division magazine. Being in the magazine twenty-four hours a day meant sleeping there, and living on a diet of sandwiches and coffee. Food was brought to us from the mess decks, and we assigned a man to pick it up at designated times. There was "no smoking" on the ship, but we cheated by smoking in our coffee locker, without fear of being caught by the master at arms, who could not get into our marine guarded spaces.

As is always the case, we knew very little about what was happening in Vietnam, or the world? We speculated a lot. I was looked upon somewhat as a "veteran", as I had gone through something like this on the *USS Independence* during the Cuban Missile Crisis. I couldn't offer much insight; the Cuban situation had been tense and exciting, yet *Independence* had not gone to general quarters for days on end. This was somewhat alarming to us, because none of us had ever heard of an aircraft carrier being in such an advanced state of readiness.

We were proud of the successful attacks made by our planes on the 5th of August. We were sad about the news that the *USS Constellation*, an aircraft carrier with us in the South China Sea, had lost a couple of planes during air raids in the north. One concern that was bantered about the ship was the possibility of attack from the Red Chinese Air Force. There was a Red Chinese squadron based on the island of Hainan, which we were steaming in the vicinity of. It was thought that the jets based there were not very sophisticated. The bodies of the jets were made of wood, not very reliable, and after a few flights were scrapped. There was always the threat, and remembrance of the Japanese kamikaze attack that our ship had experienced in World War II.

During the day there were few periods of relaxation, lasting only a few minutes that permitted those sailors who did not have access to heads, to make head calls. We in the after magazine did not have a head, so we greatly appreciated these periods when we could relieve ourselves. The days dragged on, we had few opportunities to shower or shave, and it was difficult sleeping on the steel decks. We had a few "mail calls", and we got a few "*Stars and Stripes*", a daily armed forces newspaper that was published daily overseas. This paper was hungrily read when we could get it flown aboard on the mail COD. We wondered what our families were being told, and what the citizens of America thought about what was happening.

Many sailors wrote anxious letters, wondering if each letter might be the last they would write to their family. The days ground on. Finally after two weeks, we went into a modified readiness status. Passageways throughout the ship were reopened, and life returned to a somewhat normal routine. We had been scared, but also determined to do our job. We felt we were "in the right." Our ships had been attacked on the high sea in violation of international law, and we were defending our flag, and our country's honor.

For years after the "Tonkin Gulf Incident", there was speculation that it was contrived in order to involve the U.S. more deeply in the Vietnam War. I cannot address this speculation, other than to say I saw bullet holes in our aircraft, and heard pilots talk of firing on attacking boats. From my limited viewpoint, it happened!

The importance of these days in August was recorded in *Ticonderoga*'s cruise book[17] as follows:

> The first week in August gave us a chance to demonstrate why we are here, and to prove why the attack carrier is so important to the Navy. And because we were ready, Defense Secretary Robert McNamara, through Chief of Naval Operations Admiral David L. McDonald, recommended us for the Navy Unit Commendation Ribbon. The Navy Unit Commendation is awarded to units of the Armed Forces of the United States for outstanding heroism in action against the enemy or by extremely meritorious service not involving combat but in support of military operations. Admiral McDonald added a "well done" to the officers and enlisted men involved in Gulf of Tonkin operations, stating "The courage, skill and outstanding state of operational readiness displayed by our sailor men was in the finest tradition of our Navy and a source of supreme pride to me, their families and all other Americans."
>
> *Ticonderoga* emerged into world news prominently at 1608 Sunday, 2 August, when she came to the assistance of the *USS Maddox* (DD-731), operating on special assignment some distance from the Task Force. *Maddox*. While operating in international waters some thirty miles off the coast of North Vietnam in the Gulf of Tonkin, *Maddox* had flashed the message that she was being attacked by three high-speed PT type boats launching torpedoes and firing machine guns. The destroyer had answered the unprovoked attack with gunfire from her five-inch and three inch guns.
>
> Within minutes after the attacks began, *Ticonderoga* advised she was sending four already airborne F8E *Crusader* jets armed with rockets and 20mm machine guns to assist in repelling the attacking PT Boats.
>
> On arrival at the scene, *Ticonderoga*'s aircraft commenced attacking the boats with Zuni rocket runs and 20mm strafing attacks. Two of the PT's were damaged; the third was dead in the water after receiving a direct hit from *Maddox*'s 5-inch gun. Neither the *Maddox* or the *Ticonderoga*'s aircraft sustained any personnel or materiel casualties. President Johnson, commenting on the response to the attack, stated, "The performance of Commanders and crews in this engagement is in the highest tradition of the United States Navy."
>
> Following the attack of 2 August, the destroyer *Turner Joy* joined the *Maddox* in the Gulf of Tonkin patrol, and at 2130 hours, 4 August, a second deliberate PT attack was directed against these ships. *Maddox* and *Turner Joy*, steaming in international waters sixty miles off the North Vietnamese Coast, reported rapidly closing surface radar contacts and then stated they were under continuous torpedo attack and engaged in defensive counter fire. Aircraft from *Ticonderoga* again were immediately on the scene and joined in repelling the enemy torpedo craft. As the result of the engagement, two PT Boats were reported sunk and two others damaged. Once again, neither the destroyers nor the Air Wing Five aircraft from *Ticonderoga* suffered any personnel or materiel casualties.

In retaliation for the unprovoked aggression on the high seas, President Johnson on 5 August directed the Navy to conduct strikes against the bases used by the North Vietnamese naval craft.

During the day, sixty attack sorties were launched from the *Ticonderoga* and *Constellation* against four North Vietnamese patrol boat bases and an oil storage depot supporting these bases. The oil storage depot was ninety percent destroyed and, in addition to the damage to the torpedo boat bases, twenty-five of the boats were damaged or destroyed. The objective of the air strikes? To make clear the United States' intention to maintain our right to operate on the high seas. Mission accomplished!

Aboard *Ticonderoga* the ordnance crews jumped into action after the initial attack of Sunday, 2 August. The flight deck ordnance and aircraft handling crews were continuously readying aircraft for all missions from 2 August until well after the strikes of 5 August. *Ticonderoga*'s air wing personnel responded magnificently. With the full assistance of the ship's air department, Carrier Air Wing Five's Squadrons and Detachments flew 130 sorties over the Vietnam area in Wednesday's strike, not a singular effort by any means, the teamwork displayed by all Departments in supporting the Air Wing was impressive. Communications, as a result of the increased activity, handled 16,000 messages in the month of August compared with 9,000 in July. Radio and Teletype circuits throughout the Pacific flashed situation reports of the deliberate attack and generated response. Senior Commanders were immediately linked by a special "hot line." The Engineering Department maintained maximum speed capability and plant materiel readiness throughout the around-the-clock operations. In Operations, plans were readied and response actions were assigned.

Under the aggressive direction and experienced coordination of Commander Carrier Division Five, the response to the unprovoked attack was swift, calculated, and undeniably successful. Today, aboard ship, men and officers of the Air Wing and ship's company work in endless preparation for that time when we shall again be called upon to enforce our national policies. For *Ticonderoga*, it is a new generation of professionals who renew her pride in accomplishment – for the men and officers who serve on her, she is a ship beyond compare.

This was what was to become known as the "Gulf of Tonkin Incident," the first direct clash between U.S. and Communist armed vehicles since Korea hostilities ended. The *Ticonderoga* had been the only aircraft carrier in the Tonkin Gulf when the *Maddox* was attacked. The *USS Constellation* was in port Hong Kong when the attack took place, and the ship was ordered to cut its port visit short and join the *Ticonderoga* prior to the air strikes against the PT boat bases. While the air strike was underway, President Johnson went on nation wide television, and reported to America what had happened. He ended his talk with, "Our response for the present will be limited and fitting. We Americans know, although others appear to forget, the risks of spreading conflict. We will seek no wider war."

The anti aircraft fire was heaviest at Hongay, the northernmost target, on 5 August. From *Constellation*, ten A-4 *Skyhawk* jets, two F-4E *Phantoms*, and four A-1 *Skyraiders*, attacked patrol craft docks with bombs, rockets, and 20mm cannon. Five A-4 *Skyhawks*, Three F-4E *Phantoms*, and four A-1 *Skyraiders* from *Constellation* hit Loc Chao with the same ordnance used at Hongay.

Ticonderoga sent six F-8 *Crusaders* to hit Qunk Khe. The biggest attack was at Phuc Loi, carried out by thirty-two aircraft from *Ticonderoga*. The bombs and ordnance from *Ticonderoga* set dozens of oil storage tanks on fire. During the raids more than twenty-five North Vietnamese Patrol Craft were sent to the bottom, more than half of the North Vietnamese Navy!

LTJG Richard Sather, twenty-six, of Pomona, California, piloting an A-1 *Skyraider*, off the *USS Constellation*, was hit at Loc Chao, and crashed into the sea giving his life for his country. LTJG Everett Alvarez, Jr. of San Jose, California, flying an A-4 *Skyhawk*, from the USS *Constellation*, radioed he was bailing out. Hanoi later announced that he had been captured, and he began life as a prisoner of war (POW), the longest in the Vietnam War (eight ½ years).

This then was the beginning of the Vietnam War for me. It is said each generation has its war, and this was to be my war for many years to come. My parents, sister, brothers, and wife Allison had been vacationing in Arizona, and during the events of the Tonkin Gulf, they had listened anxiously to the radio reports.

Ticonderoga pulled out of the Tonkin Gulf on 31 August, and steamed toward Subic Bay, Philippines. We pulled into Subic for one day on 2 September, ending our fifty-seven day period at sea. Vietnam was becoming more prominent in the news. We headed north for Yokosuka, Japan, and pulled alongside the pier at Yokosuka on 8 September, where we were to stay until the 19th, for a much needed rest and recreation period.

Yokosuka catered to American sailors, much more so than Sasebo. The base was huge, the on- base clubs were gigantic, and the meals they served were fit for a gourmet! I enjoyed going to the Acey Ducey Club and ordering frog legs. I had gone "frog gigging" with my parents as a child, and enjoyed frog's legs, but none like these; they were as huge as chicken drumsticks!

Everyone "blew off steam" in Yokosuka. It had been a long, tense time at sea. W Division congregated in a bar called New Yokosuka, located in an area outside the base called "Thieves Alley"; this was also called the "Honcho District." There were blocks and blocks of bars catering to American sailors. Also outside the main gate of the Yokosuka Naval Base was a Navy-managed service club called Club Alliance. This club had many restaurants, bars, and slot machines for the enjoyment of sailors. Much of the sailors' liberty revolved around alcohol. The standard operating procedure or "SOP," was to buy a fifth or more of the preferred drink, (W Division's was Four Roses whiskey), at seventy-five cents a fifth, and then take it to the New Yokosuka bar, and "check it in." Each Japanese bar had a woman, called the "Mama-san." She was the owner, or manager of the bar. The Mama-san was usually an older woman; she took care of all the money transactions, and also ruled over everyone who worked in the bar, with an iron fist. To check a bottle in meant you paid the Momma-san a few dollars; she put your name on the bottle, and provided mix and ice for your entire stay in the bar, which often was twelve hours or more.

Outside the side-by-side bars in Thieves Alley, stood crowds of Japanese women dressed in every fashion imaginable, evening dress, casual dress, scantily clad, even some in nightgowns. They would try to entice sailors walking by into their bar. Some would grab the arms of sailors and try to drag them into the bar. If a sailor entered a bar, a girl would immediately grab your arm, and remain by your side throughout your stay. If a sailor did not approve of the girl who grabbed him initially, he could request a different girl. The girls would try to get sailors to buy them drinks, which had inflated prices, and were usually weak tea. Each drink bought for a girl, was counted, and the girl with the highest count at the end of the evening had the highest ranking in the bar society. The Mama-san would permit a girl to leave the bar with a sailor, if the sailor "bought her out," which meant paying the Mama-san a few dollars so the girl could leave the bar and forgo working the rest of the day or night. All the bars had jukeboxes that blared out American music. The streets were crowded with sailors, and shore patrol. Yokosuka was a wild, wide-open liberty port.

I noticed a common sight on Japanese streets, and sidewalks: blind or crippled Japanese men in World War II Japanese Army uniforms begging. Japanese soldiers received few or no benefits after the war, so many had become beggars. I would always contribute a few coins to these men's begging baskets. I don't know what they thought about military victors contributing to them, but to me it seemed the right thing to do. They had gone to war for their country, and flag, probably with little choice, and they now had very little dignity. They stood or lay on the streets with what pride they could muster. These Japanese veterans must have been secretly appalled, and disgusted to see Americans lusting after Japanese women, and spending more money than they could ever hope to have. Most Japanese felt we were "guyjeans" or barbarians, but in 1964 everything was exceptionally cheap, and our dollars were very much in demand.

I had felt an instant kinship with another second class on the ship, named Ray Steele, and we usually went on liberty together. We roamed up and down Thieves Alley. I had resisted the offers of bar girls to sit with me, when one afternoon in the New Yokosuka bar, a girl came over to our table. She was one of the most beautiful Japanese girls I'd seen. She said she had seen me the last couple of days, and would like to sit with me. I became good friends with her; she was half Japanese, and half another nationality (I'm not sure which one). Her name was Tamiko. She never asked for drinks, or asked to be bought out.

The Mama-san never argued with her, as she did the other girls. All the girls within a bar held "rank," with "number 1" being the highest rank. In the New Yokosuka bar, Tamiko was the number one girl. When the Japanese spoke us to, they added a "san" on the end, such as, "Jim-san," or "Ray-san." The bars we frequented would even send us Christmas cards, or birthday cards, if they knew the birth date.

I don't know if Tamiko was trying to avoid being bought out of the bar. She knew I was married, and our relationship was purely platonic. She always seemed to be overjoyed to see me, and I enjoyed her friendship. She certainly didn't make any money from me, as I heard from other sailors. The girls were expert at separating sailors from their money.

We all tried to master the use of chopsticks. Ray and I enjoyed getting a huge plate of shrimp fried, or ham fried rice, at the end of our liberty each night.

A couple of months previously I'd earned the right to wear a "hash mark," which was a stripe seven inches long, worn diagonally on the lower left sleeve of my uniform. This stripe indicated four years service. After twelve years (three hash marks), if a sailor had unblemished service, or three Good Conduct Medals, he was permitted to wear a gold crow, and gold hash marks. My first hash mark was earned 30 June 1964, and marked me as a "lifer."

On 19 September the ship pulled out of Yokosuka for two days, conducting flight operations, and then back into Yokosuka for two days' liberty. We got underway for a few days, and then pulled into Beppu, Japan, on the 28th for three days. We anchored of the coast of Beppu, and took liberty launches back and forth.

One night in Beppu, Ray Steele and I were walking down an alley, when a Japanese guy said, "Hey G.I.'s you want to see good show? Only 700 yen (two dollars)." We said "OK"; he then led us up a set of stairs, into a small room. There were about twelve other *Ticonderoga* sailors sitting within the room, on folding chairs, which faced a small stage. Everyone started clapping and stomping their feet, calling for the show to start. The Japanese guy we had seen on the street appeared, and said, "OK, OK we start show." The lights went out, and it was completely dark. Then a small light in front on the stage came on. There was a nude girl sitting in a chair on the stage. The lights only stayed on a few seconds, and then were turned off again. After a few more seconds the lights came back on and she had shifted to a different position. The light-turning on and off continued, but the girl was very homely. The sailors started booing and saying, "We want our money back." The lights came on, and the Japanese guy reappeared and said, "G.I.'s be nice or I call shore patrol." The show then resumed. Ray saw a cat near where we were sitting; he picked the cat up, and said to me "Let's liven the show up." He waited until one of the dark periods, and then threw the cat toward the stage. There was a loud scream, and yelling noises in Japanese, the lights came on, and the Japanese guy, and girl were running around hollering. Now that was a show! Everyone ran out laughing.

It wasn't long before we learned how each person behaved on liberty. One W Division sailor named Ted Brine, from Arizona, was well liked on the ship; he would go on liberty and look for fights. This was his recreation. We tried to look out for each other, and keep each other out of trouble, but Ted was continually fighting, and eventually he got into trouble over this enough times that he lost his security clearance and was kicked out of the division. Billy Gilbert was a young sailor who was absolutely girl crazy, and spent most of his money on girls in all the ports we visited. John Munson, from Oklahoma was another young sailor who was a hard worker, but was wild when he got a little alcohol inside.

GMT1 Gaddley was one of the least liked sailors in W Division. He was the division leading petty officer. It certainly wasn't a requirement of the job of leading petty officer that he makes friends, and he didn't. His temper was legendary: he would scream, rant and rave if he didn't get his way. He was transferred off the ship the latter part of September, while we were at sea. He was supposed to fly off the ship, but was "bumped" out of his seat by an officer. I remember him ranting and raving at our Nuclear Safety Officer, LCDR Chevalier about being bumped out of his seat. None of us would have dared cursed and screamed at an officer as he did. Not many in the division were sad to see him leave. When Gaddley left, GMT1 Reese, who was very popular, assumed the role of leading petty officer.

In Beppu, many in the division went to a large bar that had a big bandstand. A sailor in weapons department was a gifted drummer, and we enjoyed hearing him play. One afternoon a group of us was sitting at a table in this place, and up at the bar sat Ray Steele, and Charlie Miller, with two girls they had met. The Japanese girls were dressed in beautiful traditional geisha costumes. Unlike Yokosuka, girls who were interested in sailors were scarce in Beppu, and Ray and Charlie had been getting "cozy" with the two girls. Suddenly there was a huge disturbance at the bar. Ray was punching the girl, and Charlie was gagging, and cussing, but they had both been kissing the girls a few moments before.

The shore patrol rushed in, and after everything had settled down, they let Ray and Charlie go. Ray was steaming! They had discovered the girls were not what they appeared to be. They were "benny-boys," or men dressed up like women. We would have teased Ray and Charlie about it, but they were very angry.

We learned that those of us who had been on the ship 2 August were to be awarded two medals, the Armed Forces Expeditionary Medal, and the Navy Unit Commendation. The Citation accompanying the Navy Unit Commendation stated:

> The Secretary of the Navy takes pleasure in commending United States Naval Task Group 77.5, consisting of *USS Ticonderoga* (CVA-14), *USS Edson* (DD-946), *USS Berkely* (DDG-15), *USS Harry E. Hubbard* (DD-748), and *USS Samuel N. Moore* (DD-747), for service as set forth in the following:
>
> For exceptionally meritorious service in support of operations in the Gulf of Tonkin during the period 2-5 August 1964. By participating in immediate, determined, and successful air strike counterattack operations against the North Vietnamese Torpedo boats and supporting facilities. Task Group 77.5 demonstrated the firm intent of the United States to maintain freedom of the seas and to take all necessary measures in defense of peace in Southeast Asia. The outstanding professional and technical competence and effective teamwork displayed by all members of Task Group 77.5 in carrying out this action were in keeping with the highest tradition of United States Naval service
>
> All personnel attached to and serving on board Task Group 77.5 during the above period, including Commander Carrier Division Five, Commander Destroyer Squadron 13, and members of staff, air groups, squadrons, and detachments actually present and participating in the above action, are hereby authorized to wear the Navy Unit Commendation Ribbon." The citation was signed, Paul H. Nitze, Secretary of the Navy.

It was pleasing to receive a couple of medals acknowledging our presence in the South China Sea during the Gulf of Tonkin Incident. From 1 October to the 24th we were once again steaming off the coast of Vietnam. Our schedule kept changing during this turbulent time. We were supposed to visit Hong Kong the 3rd of November, and then after a short visit to Yokosuka, Japan, steam toward San Diego, and arrive in the U.S. 25 November. This time in the South China Sea, it was not nearly as hot.

The ship flew many missions in support of the South Vietnamese Army. During this time an A-4 *Skyhawk* lost power while being launched off the flight deck by the catapult. The plane slowly dropped down toward the surface of the sea. The pilot "punched out," the ejection seat shot into the air, his parachute deployed and he drifted safely down, while his plane crashed into the sea. This sequence of events was caught on film, and published in the ship's cruise book.

While the pilot of the A-4 was unharmed, there were others that were not so fortunate. Pilots LT Donald V. Hester, Jr., LTJG Gerald W. Taylor and LTJG Richard L. Evans, Jr. lost their lives during this cruise. A Chief, SKC Edward W. White died in his sleep. A death that greatly affected Weapons Department was the death of AO1 Joe Lee Williams, who was highly liked throughout the ship. He was a squadron ordnanceman who worked on the flight deck. He accidentally walked into the turning propeller of a double engine E-1, early warning aircraft, nicknamed a *"Willy Fud"* that was turning up its engines. He had been working for over twelve hours, and was on his way to disarm a plane that had just landed. He was struck in the head, and only survived a couple of days before passing away in sickbay. Another sailor, PN3 Wilmer A. Bolton, Jr., simply disappeared while the ship was at sea. It was assumed that he fell overboard late at night. It was a curious fact that so few men are named "Junior," and yet so many "Juniors"(3) lost their lives during this cruise.

I was busy during at sea periods studying for my first class exam that was to be conducted in November. This would be my first crack at first class petty officer. A name for the expected baby had been chosen, either Bradley, or Sandra. My parents sent me a form to apply to the California Department of Vehicles for a replacement driver license as mine had been stolen along with my wallet in Manila.

On 25 October, we steamed toward Hong Kong, China; we anchored in Hong Kong Harbor on October 29. From our position in the harbor I could see huge buildings rising up among crowded hilly terrain. The harbor was full of Chinese junks, and anchored merchant ships of every description. Motorized boats were under contract to transport us back and forth to the fleet landing on the pier, where we could change our "funny money" into Hong Kong dollars.

Hong Kong was a British Colony leased from China for 99 years. The lease was to expire in 1997. The most memorable thing about Hong Kong was the mass of people. It was very crowded. Chinese people were everywhere; some were "boat-people" who spent most of their lives living onboard floating junks. The harbor water appeared to be very dirty. Garbage barges were positioned alongside the ship, and we would dump our garbage and trash into these barges. One section of the garbage barges was reserved for food only where leftovers from the mess decks were dumped. Groups of Chinese women would carefully comb this food section for useable food. The barges and women were under the control of a woman called "Hong Kong Mary," who had combed the garbage of American and British ships for many years.

Poverty was very apparent in many sections of Hong Kong, with people sleeping on mats on the sidewalks, and beggars working the crowds on the streets. In other sections of the city there were no appearances of poverty, but to the contrary what appeared to be a modern beautiful city. As in many Asian ports, there were sections of Hong Kong that had clubs and bars which catered to American sailors. Many sailors on the ship took advantage of the excellent, inexpensive Chinese tailors, and ordered hand-made suits.

There were many British sailors in Hong Kong. Their initial enlistment in the British Navy was for a six-year period. A popular saying was, "We do four years for England, and two years for the queen." We were warned about speaking disrespectfully of the Queen of England; although the British sailors did continually, they didn't like disparaging remarks about the Queen from non-British. We visited a few British sailor service clubs. They liked warm beer, loved to fight, and played darts almost continually.

One afternoon, a group of us visited an area of Hong Kong, called Kowloon. We visited a large floating ferry that had been converted to a restaurant. The dining area was on the upper deck. Prior to being served, or ordering dinner, we visited the lower deck, which contained aquariums holding large varieties of live fish. It was here that we selected our dinner. Your selected fish was scooped out of the aquarium tank, you then returned to your table, and soon the cooked unlucky fish was served to you on a platter.

Because of the English-speaking population, and the British influence throughout Hong Kong, the city seemed more civilized than other Far East cities the ship visited. The ship contracted ferryboats to transport sailors back and forth from the ship at anchor and Fleet Landing. One large double deck ferry would make the trip between the ship and Fleet Landing once every hour. The ferry would pull alongside a floating platform that was tied to the hull of the ship. A ladder extended down from the ship's quarterdeck to the floating platform. Sailors would enter and disembark the ferry through an opening in the railing on the lower deck of the ferry. Directly above this opening in the lower rail, was a large steel ramp that was secured by ropes in the up position. This ramp was used when the ferry pulled alongside an elevated pier; it would be untied, and let down, then the upper deck would be used as an embarkation, and disembarkation point.

One evening a couple of W Division sailors, and I were returning to the ship on the ferry, along with about 300 other *Ticonderoga* sailors. We three left the ferry, climbed up the quarterdeck ladder, saluted the OOD, and then entered the hangar bay. While walking toward our berthing compartment, an announcement blared out from the 1MC, asking the duty corpsman to report to the quarterdeck immediately. We eventually learned that the ferry upper deck steel ramp had fallen and struck a sailor on the head as he was stepping through the open railing of the ferry onto the floating platform. The sailor was a second class petty officer in the Master at Arms force. He had a reputation for being obnoxious, and sometimes abusing his authority, he was one of the most disliked sailors on the ship. He was very seriously injured, and was taken off the ship. We heard different stories about his condition, ranging from critical to serious. Some said he would never recover. At the time of the incident, there was still a large group of sailors on the upper deck of the ferry, and the victim was the last sailor to leave the lower deck. It was determined that the steel ramp had been purposely untied and allowed to fall. All the sailors on the ferry were questioned, but it was never determined who may have untied the steel ramp.

As much as the second class Master at Arms was disliked, on the other end of the popularity scale, W Division's Leading Petty Officer GMT1 R.D. Reese was popular throughout the ship, or at least very well known. He reminded me of the television character Sergeant Bilko played by Phil Silvers, in the series "*The Phil Silvers Show*[18]." Reese always had a scheme, or plan for making money.

He sold illustrated Bibles throughout the ship, and also had what was called a "slush fund" which was illegal and was his capital for a kind of loan shark business. He lent five dollars for seven, ten dollars for fifteen, and twenty dollars for twenty-seven dollars. The loans would be between paydays, and for a two-week period. He was always at the end of the pay line collecting debts. He also had a used-car lot in Albuquerque, New Mexico. He was always conducting whispered, secret business deals. He was "silver tongued," able to talk an Eskimo into buying a freezer. An example of one of his deals, while the ship was in Sasebo, Japan he arranged to purchase 1,500 pairs of binoculars from a Japanese factory. He told the Japanese factory that he would pick up the binoculars when the ship returned to Sasebo. He then began selling the binoculars throughout the ship, giving receipts to the customers promising to deliver the binoculars when the ship returned to Sasebo. The binoculars sold for twelve dollars a pair. I ordered two pairs. I don't know what profit Reese was making, probably at least double. He didn't count on the Gulf of Tonkin Incident, the ship's extended stay at sea, and the cancelled return trip to Sasebo. Reese was worried about promises he made to the Japanese factory. His solution: he talked an A-3 *Skywarrior* pilot (the largest dual jet engine plane on the ship), into flying to Japan, landing at the Atsugi Naval Air Station, picking up the binoculars from the factory, and flying back to the ship in the South China Sea. When the plane flew aboard Reese organized a working party, brought the binoculars down to W Division berthing compartment and distributed the binoculars to the buyers. All of this was illegal, unauthorized use of government planes and manpower, selling items on the ship, and so on, but he got away with it. I often thought he looked upon the Navy as a part time job. If he'd put as much effort into his Navy career as he did his money making schemes he would have become an admiral. At this time he was unmarried, and was the older brother of Chief Tom Reese with whom I'd been stationed with on the *Independence*. As W Division leading petty officer on *Ticonderoga*, he was not very strict militarily and had a cheerful, friendly demeanor. He grumbled about chiefs and officers, and he tried to befriend everyone from petty officer down to seaman. He was as lax about discipline, as GMT1 Gaddley had been strict. Their two leadership styles were as different as night and day.

GMTC H.L. Catron was our Leading Chief Petty Officer, and he ruled with an iron fist. He was very technically knowledgeable; he had previously been an instructor in Albuquerque. The W Division Officer was LTJG Burkhardt, who was a Naval Academy graduate. He knew very little about the technicalities of nuclear weapons. He was assigned as W Division Officer in order to "get his ticket punched," a means to experience as many management positions as possible on his climb up the Navy career ladder. This was a situation that I was to see over and over again: an officer placed in charge of a nuclear weapon activity, who knew very little about the business of nuclear weapons. This situation resulted in the senior Gunner's Mate Technicians expending large amounts of time trying to educate the officer about the technicalities of nuclear weapons, instead of spending time on day-to-day tasks.

ENS J.A. Gelsomino was assigned as W Division, Junior Division Officer. This was his first duty station assignment following graduation from the Naval Academy. He was very green, and anxious to succeed. He was the same age as many of the enlisted men, twenty-one to twenty-three years old. He tried to be accepted, and yet maintain a proper distance because of his officer status. The wisest thing for an officer such as Ensign Gelsomino to do is to listen closely to the chiefs. Often a chief will take a young ensign "under his wing," and teach him, and guide him in the right direction. If the young ensign is prideful, or refuses to heed the advice of chiefs, it will take him much longer to assume the role of a leader, if he ever does. Without the respect of his men, an officer has a difficult life.

LTJG F.L. Richardson was assigned as W Division Electrical Officer; he was an older officer, and a Limited Duty Officer (LDO). The LDO program was a program in the Navy that permitted certain enlisted men to achieve commissioned status. LDO's and Chief Warrant Officers, who had come up through the ranks, as I said before, are called "Mustangs". LTJG Richardson was not well liked. He was a very strict disciplinarian, and his nickname among the enlisted men was "Fire and Lightning Richardson," for his initials "F.L." His favorite tactics were to rant and rave, and be all around obnoxious. Instilling fear was his main leadership style; however, he was the most knowledgeable officer in the division concerning technical matters, and the Navy. As an enlisted man he had been an aviation electrician; he had been a first class petty officer before being commissioned an ensign. One of his usual methods of making our lives miserable was to put a padlock on the division coffee locker if he was angry about something. This meant we didn't have a place to take breaks during working hours, or a place to relax after working hours. I recall one occasion when he kept the coffee locker locked while we were at sea, for two weeks.

I'd seen him lose his temper, throw his hat on the deck, and stomp on it, but there was a method to his "madness"; he was disliked, and feared, but when he gave an order, sailors usually "jumped" to carry the order out.

I was assigned the collateral duty of W Division Damage Control Petty Officer. This job was one of the larger collateral assignments. This meant I was responsible for the W Division watertight hatches, doors, and fittings that were closed to make the compartments of the ship watertight. I was also responsible for the firefighting equipment, first-aid equipment, and Oxygen Breathing Apparatus (OBA) equipment, and other equipment. Also within each compartment there was a compartment check off list that listed all of the equipment I was responsible for. Fire hoses were especially difficult to care for. They had to be stored properly, tested frequently, and maintained very diligently. Fire is a very serious matter onboard ship, and especially on an aircraft carrier. A carrier carries flammable propulsion fuel, and also the highly flammable JP5 aircraft fuel. Carriers also carry many more explosive bombs, ammunition, and pyrotechnics, than other ships. The only other type of ship carrying equivalent amounts of explosives would be the ammunition ship whose job it is to supply Navy ships at sea.

One of my weekly duties as damage control petty officer was to tour all of the division spaces with LTJG "Fire and Lightning Richardson." This chore would take two to three hours, and was usually accomplished on Friday afternoon. This was the job that no one in the division envied me having as I spent more time alone with "Fire and Lightning" than others in the division. One embarrassing thing he would do was during our weekly tour of spaces. Our route would take us past three or four enlisted men's heads. Each head contained six to ten toilets. There was an obscure ship regulation that prohibited reading books, while sitting on the toilet. This was supposedly to prevent hemorrhoids. LTJG Richardson and I would walk into the heads, all the toilets had open stalls without doors, and if he saw anyone reading on the toilet, he would grab the book out of the sailor's hand, and then would lecture the sailor about violation of the ship's regulation. The embarrassed sailor would usually be speechless. "Fire and Lightning" would confiscate the book, or reading material, and keep it. When walking out of the head he often would wink conspiratorially at me, but I was very uncomfortable being with him when he did this. He did complement me occasionally about my work as damage control petty officer. Although few and far between, the ones he gave me were unique. The best indication of his reputation on the ship occurred when he was transferred. When an officer transfers off a ship, it is customary, that the OOD on the quarterdeck, have the Boatswain's Mate of the watch ring however many bells the officer rated and then announce "Lieutenant United States Navy departing," when his foot touched the pier the Boatswain's Mate rang one bell. Everyone on the ship was anxious for LTJG F. L. Richardson to receive orders, and depart the ship. This happened while we were in port San Diego. I happened to be in the chow line for lunch, on the mess decks, when the 1MC announced LTJG Richardson's departure from the ship. A loud cheer rang out throughout the ship, and sailors threw hats in the air. We in W Division had been pitied because he was in our division. I did however learn much about being diplomatic, and about damage control from him. I saw LT F.L. Richardson (he had been promoted to lieutenant) once more after he left the ship. I ran across him at Nuclear Weapons Training Command, Pacific, North Island, California. He was stationed there, and during our brief reunion, it seemed he was a different person, much quieter and more reserved. To his credit he certainly had a strong personality; "Fire and Lightning" was a well-earned nickname on the *USS Ticonderoga*.

While the ship was at anchor in Hong Kong, on 8 November, at 2100 (9:00 p.m.), I received some horrible news. I was given a telegram by the communications division informing me that Allison had lost the child she was carrying. This was devastating news.

During this period I also got some other bad news. The ship schedule was changed drastically. Instead of returning to the States, the ship was directed to return to cruising up and down the coast of Vietnam. The ship that was supposed to relieve us, the aircraft carrier *USS Ranger*, had broken down, and was unable to steam. She was in Yokosuka, Japan, for an unknown period of time. It was assumed that we would not return to the United States until at least the middle of December. Our deployment extension, due to the breakdown of the *USS Ranger* was depressing for *Ticonderoga* sailors. One thing that did raise our morale somewhat was a cartoon a sailor on board made, that showed the *Ticonderoga* (with a raccoon tail hat on), with a towrope attached to the *USS Ranger* (with a cowboy hat on), trying to pull them out of port to sea. Thousands of the cartoons were printed, and loaded on an A-3 *Skywarrior*. The A-3 took off while we were in the South China Sea, and flew over the *Ranger* in the Yokosuka Naval Shipyard, and bombed them with the cartoons. Just as individuals have reputations, so do Navy ships. The *Ticonderoga* had a fighting, dependable, solid reputation. She was an older carrier, yet met all of, and often exceeded, the mission requirements asked of her.

The *Ranger* on the other hand was known for breaking down, and being unreliable, with an unhappy crew, although she was more modern, and a larger carrier than *Ticonderoga*.

In November President Johnson was re-elected as president over the Republican Candidate Senator Barry Goldwater. I took the November Navy wide advancement 150-question exam. I would not know for three months whether I passed or failed.

This was what I said in a letter to my parents on 26 November 1964:

> I guess the Navy is going to maintain carrier patrols down here indefinitely, until the war is decided one way or another. When we were down here for sixty days, it appeared we were close to war with China. I think even more so than with Cuba a year ago. It sure did shake everyone on this ship up! Quite a few nights we stayed up all night maintaining battle readiness, and a couple of times it was almost positive that we were going to be attacked by Red China planes. I doubt if the United States will get anywhere with this war in Vietnam. I think the only way we could win, would be to turn this into another Korea. It's exasperating knowing that our boys are getting killed daily over here, of course they get their name in the paper, but the big concern in the States seems to be civil rights, etc., and the war doesn't take on any importance until election time.

Everyone on the ship began to wonder if we would be home for Christmas. The 1964 *Ticonderoga* cruise book printed an article called "Why carriers?" and reads as follows[19]:

> The mission of the United States Navy is the protection of national interests on the high seas. In time of war the word protection is synonymous with control. Of the many varieties of control one of the most important is martial in nature, the exercise and deployment of power. For the modern Navy control includes not only the neutralization of the high seas but also that of the coasts and interiors of the lands that open on them. The combination of air power and sea power has made the land subject to sea in a curious reversal of logical order. The lands that open on the seas are now as important a strategic object as the seas themselves.
>
> Our early history was made possible by the protective insulation the seas afforded, and it is obvious that our more recent history has been determined by the degree we could maintain that natural isolation for national advantage. Our seas have protected us, and our Navy has protected the seas. This is no less true in the era of missiles and long-range bombers, since the ability to jump oceans and continents with nuclear weapons is not the same as tactical, day-to-day control. There is little advantage bombing Moscow when the issue is being decided in Saigon. While it is not intended to minimize the long-range striking power of the modern aircraft carrier the fact remains the unique capabilities of a carrier strike force are best used in the disturbances that plague the vast borderland between Russia and the Asian seas. Ever since De Gama's voyage around the Cape of Good Hope in 1499 this land has been the area of East-West confrontation and the aircraft carrier has proven the most effective weapon for the implementation of Western policies. The carrier fleets are ubiquitous reminders that treaties will be upheld and commitments met.
>
> This threat of an ever-present force in depth has virtually strangled overt aggression in the fluid stream of Afro-Asian relations whether the pressure comes from within in the case of Vietnam or is directed from a distant capital.

A beleaguered country has only to call for assistance and, as Lebanon discovered in 1958, that call is swiftly answered.

The capability of a fast, pinpointed show of military strength anywhere in the Asian periphery is the modern-day answer to the old British policy of containment. At the height of imperial power the foremost concern was to prevent a Russian seizure of vital lines of communication. It was an unending duel between land and sea power, between heartland and rimland.

As long as there is a power center in the heart of Asia and an equal center of power outside it, the conflict will continue. Undoubtedly the present situation is quite different than when Britain built her empire, but the fact of confrontation remains the same. Nonetheless the differences are worth noting, for in them lies the ultimate justification for a carrier oriented Naval establishment. Unlike the British the United States does not have imperial interests to defend. Through diplomacy or ideological persuasion we have established a chain of strategic alliances around the periphery of the communist world. Although these ties often hamstring us, mutual interest now affords a foundation for survival rather than imperial gain.

We consider that the very lands that once fell to Britain remain vital to our own security. If our objective is a potential control of the seas, we cannot afford to lose the coasts that surround them. We cannot abandon Iran for fear of losing India, and with India the Indian Ocean. Vietnam is on the road to Malaysia, Indonesia, the Philippines, and points east.

The second difference is political: communism versus capitalism. Things have simplified, two ways of life struggling for the exclusion of the other. Each seeks to win the uncommitted people to their own cause, and the balance is so delicate that the augmentation of one is at the expense of the other. Between the two powers the people of the rimlands have become spiritual commodities, the collection of which adds to the wealth of an ideal.

The ideological and nature of the conflict gives a peculiar impermanence to the accomplishments of diplomacy. Governments topple, insurrections become endemic, and the people alternately clamor for peace, bread, and war. The residual fear of colonialism, fumbled intentions, and the rising spirit of nationalism besmirch our position. We cannot occupy a country in the same way Britain garrisoned an imperial outpost, even when stability requires our presence. The American carrier fleets are the free world's major force in the Asian rimland, and with their independence of land bases they effectively prevent overt aggression within this troubled area. While unwilling to violate national borders and internal affairs they are at the disposal of our allies and friends.

The communist leaders know that there is a world to conquer under the nuclear umbrella, but they also grasp the futility of such an action under the sharp eyes of the Sixth and Seventh Fleets.

Time has not confirmed some of the ideas in the cruise book article, but this was the view held in 1964.

The first of December, we finally left the South China Sea, after being relieved by the repaired *USS Ranger*. We pulled into Yokosuka, Japan, for two days, and then began the transit to San Diego. By coincidence the ship crossed the International Date Line on 8 December, my birthday. The ship was steaming east, so 8 December was repeated, therefore I had two birthdays in 1964! I was twenty-two years old.

The quarterly evaluation marks I received for my first period on the ship averaged 3.6 in Professional Performance, Military Behavior, Leadership and Supervisory Ability, Military Appearance, and Adaptability. The description of assigned tasks read: Crew leader of special weapons assembly team, Technical Monitor. Evaluation of Performance read: "Little reported aboard 14 March 1964 and attended school six weeks thereafter. His performance at school was very good and his work as a crew leader in the after magazine has been well organized and efficient. He has adapted himself to shipboard life and duties very well and appears to show promise of becoming an outstanding Petty Officer."

When the ship reached the midpoint of our journey to the United States, something happened that was to repeat again and again as aircraft carriers crossed the Pacific. The Russians sent three long-range bombers (called *Bears*); out toward the ship to see how close they could get before being detected. Upon detection, and interception by the ship's fighter planes, they would wheel around and head back for their base in Russia. It was as though the Russians were saying, "We know where you are, and we want you to know it."

As I previously described, in the world of nuclear weapons, accidents or damage to weapons are classified according to severity, and when reported, set into action many preplanned actions by many local and national authorities. The level of severity is identified by a codeword. The most serious incident is called a "Broken Arrow". This heading on a message would alert authorities that a weapon had been lost, detonated, stolen, or caused radioactive contamination. By coincidence the code word "Broken Arrow" was also used by the Army when an American unit was about to be overrun by enemy forces, and meant all American aircraft were to immediately respond to support the troops that were in peril. In some cases this meant bombing the position of the overrun troops, even though it was likely to harm and kill friendly troops, along with the enemy. The *Ticonderoga* was to experience a Broken Arrow in the future. The next lower category of severity is a "Bent Spear"; this might be an accident with a weapon that caused the weapon to be returned to AEC for repair. The lowest severity is a "Dull Sword," which might report an electrical malfunction, or an unsafe handling practice, etc.

Throughout the history of nuclear weapons, the United States safety record has been admirable. The Navy has had the fewest accidents, and the Air Force has had the most. It should be explained that the Air Force has been much more involved with alert flying, (flying in Strategic Air Command (SAC) with bombs in the bomb bays, such as B-52's, etc.), than the Navy. Many accidents have been the results of aircraft crashes. This description of classes of accidents is very brief and not all-inclusive. A big part of a GMT's technical knowledge and training was directed toward what to do in the event of an accident, fire, or contamination, and minimizing the spread of damage.

The reporting of a Broken Arrow, Bent Spear, or Dull Sword was by electronic, instantaneous method, by message within minutes of the accident. A message called a "rainbow message" was transmitted by the highest priority within five minutes of the happening. The rationale behind the rapid sending of a rainbow message, was that if a weapon were involved in an accident, fire, etc., and detonated, and the ship or base suddenly vaporized, disappearing off the face of the earth, this would prevent higher command from starting to press buttons and beginning World War III, thinking an attack had been initiated by our enemies. The rainbow message would inform higher authority that the command's demise had been caused by an accident. The addresses on the accident messages began with the White House, the Joint Chiefs of Staff, and included the entire military chain of command.

On 16 December, the *Ticonderoga* pulled alongside the pier at North Island, San Diego. Bands were playing; banners and flags waving, and there were hundreds of people waiting on the pier. Ray Steele and I left the ship together. Allison and Ray's wife, Marie, had rented houses on the same block in San Diego. I didn't know it at the time, but shortly after Allison's miscarriage while living with my parents, Allison had decided to move, with her brother's help, back in with her parents, she made the move without telling my parents, and at a time when they were gone. I was to learn this erratic behavior was common with Allison.

Everyone was happy to finally be home. I discovered the Corvair was running poorly, so I had it tuned up. The house Allison had rented was a large two-bedroom house; Ray and Marie lived directly across the street.

Not all homecomings were happy and joyous occasions. GMT2 Charlie Miller's wife was not on the pier when the ship pulled in. He went to his San Diego apartment, and found all of his furniture gone, with nothing in the apartment other than his wife's wedding dress hanging in the middle of the living room with a note attached telling him "goodbye." He was to find out that she had left him for a woman!

Upon the ship's return to the states, we were granted a liberal liberty period. Until after the New Year we worked every third day, and were granted liberty on the other two days.

Allison, and I traveled to Strathmore to visit my parents; it was wonderful to see them. The boys had grown, and sister Linda was busy with college. My parents were planning to move to another house that they had built ½ mile from their current home. My parents told me how they had listened closely to the news reports, while on vacation to Arizona, during the time the Gulf of Tonkin Incident was taking place.

When we drove back to San Diego from Strathmore, a trip of about 300 miles, it was often very foggy. Each time I drove home I had to request an out of bounds pass, which was required anytime a sailor left the 100 miles imaginary circle encircling *Ticonderoga*.

On 22 December, while seated in my San Diego living room, and with Allison in the bedroom, at 1:00 p.m. an earthquake struck. I hollered to Allison to get outside. We ran outside, and everyone in the neighborhood including Ray and Marie were outside in the middle of the street. We waited outside for a long while to see if another earthquake would come. There was no major damage, other than a few things knocked over, and pictures' falling off the wall, but it was unnerving for a few days.

I had duty on Christmas Day, so we were not able to travel home to be with our families. Following New Years, W Division was busy with off-loads, and preparation for a yard period. The yard period was to take place at Hunters Point Naval Shipyard, San Francisco. I did not look forward to this as I had experienced the noise, dirt, and discomfort, and all around unpleasantness of living on a ship during a yard period, while on the *Independence* in the Norfolk.

I and two other W Division sailors, GMT2 E.J. Carroll, and ET1 R.E. Meyer, were informed that we were to attend Shipboard Instructor Training School at the San Diego Naval Training Center. We began school on 11 January 1965. This was the first time I'd returned to the training center since my graduation from boot camp four and a half years previously. There were boot camp recruits walking through the area our classes were held, and we were told to return any salutes the recruits gave us. We three car-pooled each day. This was a two-week school that was to teach us the proper way to prepare a lecture, and how to conduct a class. All of the students were second, first, and chief petty officers. It was an interesting class to me, and I learned much from it, such as the proper way to ask a question while conducting a lecture, (always ask the question before calling on an individual, so each individual in the class tries to formulate an answer, instead of relaxing when they hear someone else being called upon to answer). We learned techniques used to keep the attention of a group, and the proper way to prepare a lecture. We were told the two-week course had been condensed from a two-month course. The homework was grueling, and each night I remained up until near midnight completing my assignment for the following day. Our final exam included presenting a forty-five-minute lecture on the subject of our choice. My topic was the different types of nuclear bursts, and their characteristics. I was pleased to receive an "A" on my lecture; at least no one fell asleep. We three graduated on 22 January.

Allison and I enjoyed living in San Diego. My Uncle Hubert and Aunt Kay visited us for one enjoyable day. Marie Steele would knock on our door late at night almost weekly, and beg me to go look for Ray and ask him to come home. The W Division bar in San Diego was a place called the Hula Hut. I would usually go to the bar, talk with Ray for a while, and then return home, usually without Ray. Quite frankly I was thankful for the opportunity to get out of the house. Marie bought Ray a beer keg machine for his birthday, thinking it would keep him home; it didn't, and they were eventually divorced in 1965.

We moved out of our San Diego apartment the latter part of February, as the ship was soon to move to San Francisco. Allison had a huge fight with the landlord; I never did learn what the argument was about. Allison went to stay with her parents until I could arrange for a place to stay in San Francisco. There were a number of substandard housing units available at Hunters Point for *Ticonderoga* sailors, and I hoped to get one. The squadrons and planes had left the ship when we pulled into San Diego, and many sailors brought their automobiles on board for the trip to San Francisco. It was strange to see cars tied down in the hangar bay where aircraft were normally tied down. The trip to San Francisco was uneventful, I went up on the flight deck and watched the underside of the Golden Gate, and Oakland Bay Bridge slid over the bridge of the *Tico*. The ship went into a large concrete "bath tub," the water lock was closed, water pumped out, and the ship was in dry dock.

Shortly after the ship's arrival in Hunters Point, Ray Steele and I were picked as nuclear weapons inspectors, and told to report aboard the aircraft carrier *USS Midway* (CVA-41), for a week, while she was underway off the coast of California. *Midway* was participating in an exercise called "Silver Lance." Ray and I detailed a number of discrepancies. *Midway* was much larger than the *Ticonderoga*, and Ray and I were only required to watch a few of *Midway*'s W Division operations. At the time I could not have imagined what part the *USS Midway* would play in my future.

With the ship's change of ports, I was given a change of jobs. I was reassigned from the after magazine, to the forward magazine as the Technical Repair, Assistant Division Training and Classified Publication Petty Officer; I kept my collateral assignment as Damage Control Petty Officer. These new jobs covered a variety of tasks, the calibration of test and handling equipment, updating of technical publications, and innumerable other tasks.

I was successful getting a base house on Hunters Point, which was actually a Quonset hut that had a partition in the middle; so two families could live in either end. Each end contained two bedrooms, a small kitchen, living room, and bathroom. The Quonset hut we had faced out toward San Francisco Bay and toward Candlestick Park baseball stadium. The substandard huts with partitions were not very private. Families could hear everything being said or done in the adjoining family area. The rent was pro-rated according to rank; I paid thirty-eight dollars a month. The units contained a stove, refrigerator, basic furniture, and beds.

Hunters Point Naval Shipyard was located in a very rough part of town, and was one of the most depressed neighborhoods of San Francisco. We were advised not to walk through the area outside the main gate, but to drive. From time to time shots were fired at the sentry booth at the main gate. Although it was illegal, I bought a small twenty-two-caliber pistol that I carried in my car.

The latter part of March, I discovered that I had not passed my first attempt to make first class petty officer. "Not passed," is not entirely a correct term. I did not have enough accumulated points to be advanced. A sailor was given points for time in grade, medals awarded, time in service, points made from the correct answers to the questions in the exam, and points given for the average of all quarterly marks; these all combined for a "point total." The sailors to be advanced during the promotion cycle were the lucky ones with the highest point totals. One of the first class in the division H.E. Dunn got a big promotion. He made chief.

During the yard period I was busy remodeling the instrument shop, which was to be my office. I was also busy working on damage control equipment, getting ready for the day we would once again be underway. During my off duty time I enjoyed fishing in the bay just outside the front door of our Quonset hut house. It was also a pleasure to have a place away from the noisy, dirty environment of a ship in the yards.

Every third night I had duty and remained overnight on the ship. Since there were no weapons onboard, usually only one person would sleep in the forward division spaces in the coffee locker, on one of the couches. Often late at night I would hear strange noises, and what sounded like footsteps, along with a feeling of not being alone. Many in the division shared the same experiences when alone at night in the coffee locker. We joked that the division spaces were haunted. There had been many sailors in the past that had lost their lives on *Ticonderoga*.

During this yard period there were many transfers in and out of the division. The weekends I had off, we would travel to Strathmore and Lindsay to visit our parents. Driving the Corvair on these trips of about 300 miles, I noticed a very disturbing characteristic of the car. When passing a truck, or encountering wind, it was very difficult to control the car. I tried putting a heavy weight in the front trunk compartment, but this didn't help. I decided after one especially windy trip back to San Francisco from Strathmore that I would not endanger our lives again. I traded the Corvair for a 1963 Ford Galaxy, two door fast back. It was a pleasure to drive, and felt much safer than the little Corvair, although the gas mileage was not nearly as good.

After completing all the work on the ship in the yards, *Ticonderoga* had a change of command, along with a personnel inspection: Captain D.W. Cooper, who had taken us through the Gulf of Tonkin, and the busy times off the coast of Vietnam was being relieved by Captain R.N. Miller. The new commanding officer's biography said he was a 1940 graduate of the U.S. Naval Academy. He served on various ships during World War II, and became a naval aviator in 1943. During the Korean War he served in Attack Squadron 44 aboard *USS Midway* (CVA-41). He served at a multitude of commands before assuming command of *Ticonderoga* in May 1965.

The personality of W Division was changing as the "old guard" left, and new men came onboard. The most drastic change of course was the departure of "Fire and Lightning" Richardson. Also departing were Chief Catron, GMT2 Charlie Miller, and my best friend and "running mate" GMT2 Ray Steele. Our new division officer was an LDO, Lieutenant R.E. Hailey. Our new leading chief was GMTCS R.E. Morgan; his personality was much different from his predecessor GMTC Catron. Senior Chief Morgan always wore long sleeve khaki shirts regardless of the heat. He was not proud of all the tattoos he had gotten in his younger days in the Navy, which covered his body, other than his face and hands. He was quiet, and reserved, and also an ordained minister. GMTC Dunn was more of a motivator and kept the division in line, along with ET1 Meyer, and GMT1 Reese. Not only was the personality of the division changing, but also the physical appearance. A new regulation was published that permitted the wearing of beards.

Many of the younger sailors tried to grow beards, but were not very "manly" looking, mostly peach fuzz, and straggly wisps. I remained clean-shaven, as did most of the senior petty officers and officers. The evaluation marks I received for the period November 1964 to May 1965 were higher than the previous ones.

Shortly after the ship's arrival in San Diego, Ray Steele and Charlie Miller transferred off the ship. They both were going to Naval Weapons Station, Lake Mead, Nevada. Charlie Miller drank heavily; I don't think he ever fully got over his wife leaving him. In later years, I heard a story from Ray about a time in Nevada when Charlie drank until almost passing out one night in a Nevada bar. The bartender made him leave, and he fell asleep behind the bar in a ditch, which was on the edge of the desert. In the morning he woke up with a swollen arm. During the night he had rolled over on a rattlesnake! Charlie died of cancer in 1979.

When the ship moved from San Diego to San Francisco, Ray and Marie had separated. Ray wanted to remain on the ship, and since I was also a second class and due to receive shore duty orders in the near future, Ray called our detailer and said I could have his orders to Lake Mead, as he wanted to stay on the ship. The detailer in Washington didn't agree, and said Ray had to go. Ray prepared to leave the ship, he had a small pickup truck, and loaded his beer machine in the bed of the truck, threw his sea bag in, and we shook hands goodbye. It was hard to say goodbye to Ray, he was a true friend, and I always trusted him to "watch my back," just as I watched his. We had some great times together at work and at play. I had admiration and, respect for his technical knowledge. Over the years he made huge contributions to the nuclear weapons program.

Years later Ray told me some interesting stories about when he was stationed at the Lake Mead Base. He said many of the GMT's that worked at the base got part time jobs at nearby Las Vegas, working in the casinos. Ray got a job as a blackjack dealer and working on the slot machine floors. Another GMT named Fred Goshen was also working at the same casino (I was to be stationed with him in the future). Fred turned in a number of casino employees for cheating the casino out of money. There was a big scandal. The employees were forbidden employment in other casinos. Many of the fired people had gangster "connections" in Las Vegas, and there were threats against Fred's life. For years afterwards, he would occasionally receive a plain envelope in the mail; inside was a plain piece of paper with the imprint of a black hand, which was a symbol of the Italian Black Hand Society. Fred got out of the Navy before the twenty-year point, and moved to the Midwest. One day he was found in an isolated area locked inside his car, dead from a shotgun blast to his head. It was ruled a suicide.

While working as a blackjack dealer, Ray became acquainted with another dealer who worked with him; Don was his name. Don said he had purchased a couple of trailers, stocked them with slot machines, and had purchased some property on the Colorado River, with the intention of making a stop-off place for gamblers traveling the long trip from Los Angeles to Las Vegas. Don asked Ray if he would be interested in going into this business venture with him. Ray declined, saying he was going to remain in the Navy. Today this "stop-off" place is one of the major resort-gambling areas of Nevada. His full name was Don Laughlin, and the stop-off place is called Laughlin, Nevada.

One evening GMT2 Lloyd Wilson and I went on liberty to the W Division hangout Hula Hut in downtown San Diego. When we went in there was a new girl working behind the bar named Betsy. Upon seeing her, Lloyd said, "I'm going to marry that girl." I thought to myself, "Yeah, sure," Frankly Lloyd was homely, and this was an attractive, nice girl. Lloyd was persistent in his courtship of her, and they did get married! In the following years when I would run across them, Lloyd would always say to me "Please don't tell anyone that Betsy worked in a bar." They were a happy couple, with two children.

In July, *Ticonderoga* had a dependents' day cruise. This was a day when the sailors' wives, children, and parents could board the ship and go to sea for a day. Allison quickly became bored.

From 6 July, to 26 July, a group from W Division attended refresher training courses at Nuclear Weapons Training Group Pacific, which was located a couple of blocks from the pier. Before going to school Chief Dunn approached me, and said since we were going to school together, his wife Marilyn and he would like for Allison to come down from Lindsay, and stay with them in their Navy base house, which was located just south of North Island. This was a surprise, as Chief Dunn and I had not been particularly close. I accepted his offer, and Allison came down from Lindsay and stayed with the Dunns. The chief and Marilyn had a boy two years old, and we lived together for three weeks. We all got along together very well. Chief Dunn told me he thought I was one of the best sailors in W Division. This was very gratifying to hear. He also said I didn't have to call him "Chief" while we were off the ship, but could call him by his first name "Harold." I told him I couldn't do that, because to me he was always "Chief". Although we were good friends, while on the ship it was all business. I expected no favors, or special treatment from him.

I was discovering this was a sign of professionalism, realizing the importance of maintaining the chain of command while on duty, showing respect to higher ranks, and maintaining an awareness of when it's time to work, and time to play.

During this time the Los Angeles Watts riots took place. We watched it unfold on the television. Thirty-four people were killed, and over 800 injured. It was a chilling picture to see armored tanks and troops moving on American city streets.

One day at school, while in the coffee locker during a break, Chief Catron walked in. He had walked over from the ship. He saw me and said out of the blue, "There's that son of a bitch." He went on to say he'd been looking for a certain test set, and couldn't find it. I explained to him where it was, and the system I had set up to locate T and H Gear. He was satisfied, and I'm sure he didn't intend to, but I was very embarrassed to be called a name by a senior in front of the other sailors in the break room. I made a vow that I would try to not embarrass someone who worked for me in that manner.

Chief Catron was scheduled to transfer, and he and his wife scheduled a division party to be held at their house in Chula Vista, which was a town south of North Island. Wives and families were invited and we had a great time. Chief Catron's wife, Pat, was a wonderful hostess, and made everyone feel welcome. Most W Divisions were like a family, some happy and well adjusted, some dysfunctional, some all business. *Ticonderoga*'s W Division for the most part was a functional, happy family. Much of this was due to Chief Catron's leadership, and vast technical knowledge. Sadly, Chief Catron died of bone cancer in 2004.

The division party was a success, although one of our sailors almost got into serious trouble. GMT2 F.P. McAleer (Mac) was the oldest sailor in W Division in his early fifties. He had joined the Navy late in life. He also loved alcohol. During the party at Chief Catron's, after more than a few drinks, he wanted to take a motorcycle for a spin, which belonged to one of the partygoers. He rode the bike a few blocks, and then noticed a police car following him. He stopped the motorcycle at a stop sign, but forgot to put his foot down on the ground to balance the bike. He toppled over, the policeman in the car behind him, got out and helped him up. The policeman gave him a ride back to the party, and a group went to retrieve the motorcycle. The policeman talked to Chief Catron and then gave Mac a warning. Mac was famous for drying out periods when the ship went to sea. Often after being at sea for a few days, Mac would take a shower shoe and begin beating his bunk, and holler for help "killing all the bugs on his bunk!" Many times prior to going to sea he would bring onboard a case of Scope mouthwash, which had high alcohol content. He would drink bottles of Scope to get through the sea periods. All in the division knew of Mac's heavy use of alcohol, but we never saw it affect his technical performance working on weapons. He retired as a second class after twenty years and for a short while worked as a taxi driver in San Diego. Mac passed away in the mid 1970s.

While in San Diego, Allison and I would often drive to Strathmore and Lindsay on the weekends I had off. Many times we would stop at Camp Pendleton Marine Corps Base, and pick up Allison's brother Kenny Konrad, who was a Marine Corporal. One weekend we picked up Kenny early on Friday, and upon arrival at Allison's parents, Kenny and I went trout fishing in a mountain stream near Lindsay. Allison was upset when we returned home (she was seldom happy). I went to bed; in the morning when I awoke I had a pain in my chest over my heart. Looking down I saw what appeared to be a hole in my chest, encircled by a dark black and blue circle. My first thought was that Allison had shot me with my twenty-two-caliber pistol! Upon closer examination, I saw it was a huge tick that had burrowed into my chest. I'd apparently gotten it during the previous evening fishing trip. I went to the Lindsay hospital, and my childhood doctor, Doctor Clark removed it, by cutting it out. He said it was one of the largest ticks he'd seen.

On another occasion traveling north from San Diego, just south of the town of Porterville while negotiating a curve, a Volkswagen that was ahead of me going too fast, left the road and flipped end over end about three times. I stopped, as did a truck driver. Two young men crawled out of the wrecked Volkswagen, very drunk, and uninjured.

Allison's parents accepted me well. They were very different from my parents. Effie Konrad had many physical ailments, either real or imagined, she always complained about her health. Allison and her mother did not get along well at all. Allison and I had a very stormy relationship. She was jealous of my relationship with my family, and seemed happiest when she was in an argument with someone, or imagined she was being persecuted. I truly did not know her, until it was too late after we were married. The feeling I recall most clearly was the feeling of being trapped, but I was determined to be a good husband and father to the baby Allison was expecting in November.

August we were busy preparing for the upcoming deployment to the Far East. We were also preparing for the round of upcoming inspections. The anxiety and stress experienced preparing for Navy Technical Proficiency Inspections was always very high, from the lowest ranked GMT all the way to the commanding officer. I took the GMT1 rating advancement examination again on the first of August. Sadly on 22 August, I received word from my mom that my grandmother had passed away. I was thankful I had seen her while home on leave. Emergency leave was not normally granted for a grandparent's death.

A military pay bill was passed by Congress, which meant an additional twenty-five dollars a month for me. I had been toying with the idea of applying for Explosive Ordnance Disposal (EOD) School, which would mean an additional $110.00 a month. One sailor in the division, GMT2 Clark applied for EOD School, and received orders. We discovered later that he broke his leg during school, and washed out.

The ship received a message informing the captain that the ship had been awarded the "Battle E." This was a very significant achievement. All enlisted men first class and below wore "*USS Ticonderoga*" on their right sleeve, now we were to wear an "E" on our right sleeve below our ship's name. The Battle E was given annually to each ship within a class, i.e., cruisers, destroyers, submarines, etc., and in our case aircraft carriers, that had the highest marks in battle readiness inspections. The "E" in Battle E stood for Efficiency. In the preceding five years the *Ticonderoga* won the "E" four times. We wore three slash marks under "E" to indicate four awards. This meant she was the most battle efficient aircraft carrier among all the Pacific Fleet carriers.

The following statement by the captain was placed in the service records of all the sailors on board:

> You were attached to and serving in the *USS Ticonderoga* (CVA-14) during all or part of competitive cycle 1 March 1964 to 30 June 1965 during which the *USS Ticonderoga* won the coveted battle efficiency pennant. In addition the Communication Department green "C" and Operation Department green "E" were awarded for standing first in the Communications and Operations Department excellence during the competition cycle. Competition was among all attack carriers assigned to Naval Air Force, Pacific Fleet.
> The winnings of these awards for standing first in battle efficiency and for standing first in communications and operations is the result of teamwork and cooperation by all hands. In each Department each officer and enlisted man made a vital contribution by hard work, attention to duty and doing his job to the best of his ability. Teamwork, cooperation and mutual respect have paid off. It is a privilege and a pleasure to extend my sincere and heartfelt thanks, congratulations and a deserving, well done.

Weapons Departments were always in competition annually for the black "W," but we didn't make it this year. I was pleased that the condition of my damage control equipment played a part in the receipt of the "E." W Division didn't receive any discrepancies in the damage control area.

The ship was scheduled to leave San Diego, and steam toward the waters of Vietnam 27 September. Our schedule called for us to return to the United States 9 June 1966, which meant our deployment would last ten months. We were to be in San Diego on 3 September and remain alongside the pier until our departure. In W Division we were preparing for our big inspection. As an assembly team leader, I was pleased with the way my team was working together.

Around this time the captain mailed a newsletter to the families of the crew that said[20]:

> As the Commanding Officer of *Ticonderoga* and it's dedicated crew of *Tico* Tigers, this message is being sent to each of you on the eve of our departure to the Western Pacific on a cruise which will last for some months. During this time *Ticonderoga* and its embarked air wing, Air Wing Five, will join the mighty Seventh Fleet, and take its place on the front line of freedom.
> Our task will be a formidable one requiring long, hot hours of hard, dirty work, little rest, and prolonged periods at sea. I am confident in the ability of "our" Tigers to do the job. In my twenty-nine years in the Navy, I have never had a command in which I had more confidence or pride than *Ticonderoga* and her crew.

Last week this ship was awarded its fourth battle efficiency "E" in five straight years. I am proud to command her and serve with your men who make her crew.

Your cheerful letters from home will do wonders for the morale of your "Tiger." Mail will be flown to the ship almost daily and usually takes only a week to reach us from the states. Write often, and be cheerful, this is the ticket. If it is necessary to send an emergency telegram to your Tiger, send it to him by name, rate and division, *USS Ticonderoga* (CVA-14) Naval Communication Station, San Francisco, California.

Ticonderoga is equipped with a hospital, pharmacy, doctors, dental lab, and dentists to keep your Tiger healthy. The crews mess serves "chow" sixteen hours a day to keep him fed. There is also a soda fountain, hobby shop, library, and two chaplains to keep him happy. I will keep him busy, and your letters will keep him cheerful.

I hope this letter will reassure you, in some degree, about the well being of your *Tico* Tiger. I am proud to serve with him, R.N. Miller.

Allison came down from central California to stay in a motel on Coronado Island until the ship pulled out on the 27th. On Saturday 4 September, I had liberty over the weekend. Early in the morning I left the motel to do some shopping on the base for some uniform items I needed prior to the ship's deployment. Allison didn't feel well, and was staying in bed. I was gone about an hour, and then returned to the motel room.

When I returned, Allison was in the bathroom in pain, and saying the baby was coming! I ran downstairs and asked the people in the motel office if they would call an ambulance, but then I decided I should take her to the base. Since the motel room was on the second floor, I carried Allison down the stairs and to the car. The car was parked alongside the curb, and the door was locked. In order to unlock the door, I had to lay Allison on the ground, remove the keys from my pocket, and unlock the door. I finally got her positioned in the passenger seat. She was in much pain, and kept saying "Hurry, Hurry." I broke the speed limit driving to the base main gate, the sentry waved me through, and I sped to the base dispensary. A few days previous I had checked out the location of the dispensary for such an emergency as this. I ran into the dispensary, and told the corpsmen sitting there that my wife was having a baby. Four people ran outside with me. The only doctor at the dispensary was a young LT Flight Surgeon. The doctor directed the corpsmen to put Allison in a nearby ambulance, he then said "We'll take her to the Balboa Naval Hospital, stay right behind the ambulance." Balboa Hospital was across the bay in San Diego, so this meant taking the ferry. With lights flashing, and siren sounding the ambulance took off, I was close behind. We went through the base main gate, and sped toward the ferry landing area. As soon as the ambulance went through the ferry gate, the gatekeeper closed the gate. I yelled, "I'm with the ambulance," but he ignored me! The ambulance drove up the ferry ramp, and immediately the ferry began moving away from the pier. As the ferry moved away from the pier, I could see the ambulance with flashing lights slowly moving out of sight. I sat in my car stunned; another ferry would not be arriving for thirty minutes. The only other option was to drive south on the strand, and then east to the hospital, which would take almost an hour! This was to be an agonizing wait, wondering what was happening. Finally another ferry appeared, and the ferry gate opened for boarding. I gave a stern look to the gatekeeper, and drove on board after paying the fare. It seemed like a long ride across the channel, and finally the ferry was on the San Diego side. I drove the twenty-minute drive to the hospital. I parked, and not being sure where to go, I went to the emergency entrance.

I explained to the nurse at the reception desk who I was, and suddenly people who said they were reporters, surrounded me. They asked, "How does it feel to be a father?" I was overwhelmed. Then a doctor came in and led me to a room, explaining, "Your wife had a baby boy on the ferry that was bringing her here." The flight surgeon that had been at North Island Dispensary and on the ambulance came into the room. He was all smiles, and said the baby had decided to be born while they were on the ferry. He was congratulating me, and was as happy, as I was relieved! This was the first baby he'd delivered as a doctor.

I was directed to a waiting room, and soon a doctor came in to brief me. He said Allison was fine, but there was some concern for the baby. He was premature, weighed only three ½ pounds, and was being kept in an incubator. I was taken to see him, and he was a beautiful sight. He looked like a perfect baby in every aspect, except for his tiny size. My heart filled with love for him, the moment I saw him.

The doctor said they were watching him closely. He was inside a glass box, with many tubes attached to his small body. I watched him for a long while, and then was taken to the ward where Allison was. She was pretty much out of it from all the painkilling drugs she'd been given. A nurse came into the ward and asked for birth certificate information. We gave his name as James Stewart Little, Junior. Everyone was "buzzing" about the baby born on the ferry. I called the people at the motel, and told them what had happened and that I would be back soon. They said, "Don't worry we're a Navy family too." I also called my parents and Allison's parents and told them of the birth.

Before leaving the hospital, I returned to where James, Jr. was being kept in the incubator. The doctor and the nurses were very concerned about his breathing. He was breathing rapidly, his little chest rising and falling quickly. I finally left the hospital around 10:00 p.m., after giving the doctor my phone number. I then left for the motel, upon arriving I fell into bed. At 3:30 a.m. the phone in the room rang, I had a bad premonition when I heard the ringing phone. It was the doctor at Balboa Hospital, He said they had done everything they could, but James had just died. This was a horrible moment in my life. There is something very wrong and unjust about children dying before their parents. My joy over having a son now turned to pain and sorrow. I made the trip back to the hospital. When I arrived at the hospital, a chaplain was with Allison. I tried to comfort her. The chaplain was not much help, but I appreciated his efforts. I stayed with Allison until the sun came up. I went to the nurses' station and asked if Allison could be moved out of the maternity ward, as there were a number of women there that were having their babies brought in, and this was upsetting for Allison. They agreed and moved her to a private room. Everyone at the hospital was very helpful. It is said that the Navy is a family, and this was one of the times I felt that family kinship.

I waited until later in the morning to call my parents and tell them of James's death. I met with an officer called a Casualty Affairs Officer, and the attending doctor. The doctor explained that James had been unable to expel a membrane covering his lungs that were normally expelled by babies at birth. He said they would like to perform an autopsy to insure this was the cause of death. This was a painful decision but I agreed that an autopsy could be performed, in the hope that it might help future childbirths. This might in some small way prevent this from happening to others, and his death might not have been completely in vain. They said the autopsy would be completed with dignity, but there could not be an open casket. This was all right, as I preferred to remember him as I'd seen him in the incubator.

The headlines in the Sunday edition of the San Diego newspaper carried news of the birth of James, Jr. on the Coronado ferry. On Monday I went to the ship and requested seven days emergency leave. Our W Division big NTPI inspection was to begin the following week, but my assembly team was ready. We had not planned to train the week prior to the inspection. Many in the division had seen the story of James, Jr. birth in the paper, but most had not heard of his death. My emergency leave papers were prepared quickly, and I left the ship. I then had to make funeral arrangements. The casualty affairs officer at the hospital was a tremendous help. I planned to have the burial in the Lindsay cemetery. My parents were a tremendous help. They arranged for a burial plot in the cemetery, and made arrangements for a graveside service. The first part of the week I visited a San Diego funeral home. I was shown a casket room with caskets of every description. I selected a small blue one, and filled out some required paperwork, as I planned to drive James Jr. to Lindsay, and needed a permit to transport the casket across county lines.

On Wednesday, Allison, and I checked out of the Coronado motel. I drove to the San Diego funeral home. The funeral home director carried the small blue casket out to my car. I opened the trunk; I had placed a blanket in the trunk. The casket was placed in the trunk, and I closed the trunk lid. It was a long silent ride from San Diego to Lindsay, a distance of almost 300 miles. I drove into the parking lot of the funeral home in Lindsay. The funeral home director had been waiting for our arrival. He took the casket from the trunk, and said the graveside service was arranged for tomorrow. We then drove to my parent's home.

In the morning as I was dressing in preparation for the graveside service, Allison shocked me by saying "I'm not going to the graveside service!" I did not agree with this at all, I felt that as James Junior's parents it was our responsibility to oversee his burial, and we should show respect for the memorial service. She flatly refused to go, so my parents and I left for the cemetery.

At the cemetery rows of chairs were set up under a sunshade, which also over covered the small blue casket, which was positioned by the grave. Reverend Ira Howden, of Faith Baptist Church of Strathmore, conducted the service. There were about thirty friends and family members seated under the sunshade. The short service conducted by the pastor emphasized that the Bible taught that children who had not reached the age of accountability and died, were taken to heaven. It was a nice service, and very fitting for my son.

It's strange how abstract thoughts run through your mind during important events in one's life. I remember sitting in the front row of the folding chairs which were all connected together and not very stable, thinking if someone on this row leans back too far, we'll all topple over. The service concluded, I'd manage to control my emotions, but I did shed tears while being hugged, and given words of sympathy. Allison's parents were not involved in the preparations, or conduct of the service, I believe this was one of the many times Allison was mad at her parents.

The local newspaper, the *Lindsay Gazette*[21], carried the following story:

"Cause of Little infant's death is disclosed"

Graveside services were held at Olive Cemetery on Thursday morning for James Stewart Little, Jr., who died the previous Sunday in San Diego, the day following his birth. He was born prematurely; weight 3 pounds and 5 ounces. The cause of his death was Hyaline Membrane Disease.

The birth of the baby made front-page news in San Diego, as he was born on the Coronado Ferry, with a Navy flight surgeon in attendance. Gunner's Mate Technician Second Class Little contacted the Naval Air Station Dispensary to report the impending arrival and the Navy dispatched an ambulance, a doctor and two corpsmen to take the expectant mother to the hospital. The ferry "which waits for no man" waited for the ambulance, but they didn't quite make it to the hospital in San Diego in time.

The baby is survived by grandparents, Messrs. and Mmes. Ernest Konrad of Lindsay and Stewart Little of Strathmore. The parents are in Lindsay now at the Konrad home and will return to San Diego on Monday. Little will leave for Vietnam on September 27, aboard the carrier, *USS Ticonderoga*, for a one-year duty, during which time Mrs. Little will live in Lindsay.

On Friday as I was preparing to return to the ship, Allison insisted that I stay longer. I really did not want to, as there was nothing more that could be accomplished by extending my emergency leave, but she was hysterical in her insistence. I wired the ship requesting an extension of my emergency leave. Within hours I was granted an additional seven days. This meant I would not be on the ship for the inspection I had worked hard preparing for.

During this time and for a long while afterward, I reexamined the events surrounding James Junior's death, to see if it could have been prevented. In the years to come, hyaline membrane's disease was conquered, and because of these medical advances very few babies died of the disease. A few years' previously President Kennedy and Jackie lost a newborn daughter to hyaline membrane disease. One negative fact was that both Allison and I smoked cigarettes, which couldn't have helped his fight for survival. I had many people comment to me "You're young, you can have other children." Since then I've never repeated that comment to anyone as a comforting effort. A child is irreplaceable and the loss is an indescribable pain. As events in my life unfolded, as cruel as it may sound, James's death may have been a God-sent act of mercy, as he would not have had a happy, secure, and normal life. When he died, and was buried, a piece of my heart was buried with him.

At the end of my leave period, I bid my family farewell, boarded a bus to San Diego, and finally arrived back on *Ticonderoga*. The division had passed the inspection with flying colors. I felt guilty about not going through the inspection with them, but my team did very well. The division had sent flowers for the graveside service, for which I thanked them.

On 27 September the ship got underway. This was the third time I'd departed the United States for a deployment, but this time it was different; it was with a sense of foreboding. There was the possibility of never returning. We were off to war, and we did not know what the future held for us. These thoughts went through the minds of most sailors as the coast of our country disappeared from view. In the years to come I experienced these same thoughts and apprehensions each time I deployed to Vietnam.

The next couple of weeks were busy, which was good for me as it kept my mind off the sorrow and pain I had experienced. The aircraft squadrons had returned aboard in August, and now there was a lot of flying, and battle drills. The letters I received from home were discouraging.

Allison's letters were full of complaints, and much griping. I was becoming aware that she was an extremely moody person, even more so since the death of our son.

On 14 October the ship pulled into Pearl Harbor, Hawaii, for a few days' liberty. While there W Division contacted Barbers Point Naval Weapons Station, where a large number of GMT's were stationed. They challenged us to a softball game, so most of the division loaded into a Navy bus and rode to Barbers Point for a picnic and ball game. We had a good time, and even won the softball game, primarily because GMT2 Wayne Knowles was an outstanding pitcher. On the bus ride back to the ship the bus passed through a sugar cane field. We persuaded the bus driver to stop and we all picked some sugar cane to chew on. Another day I went on liberty and explored Waikiki Beach. It was a beautiful place. During this in port period I got word that I'd once again not made enough points on the rating exam held in September to promote to GMT1. At least I had company in my disappointment, four other GMT2's that took the exam with me also failed.

On the 18th the ship got underway from Pearl Harbor, and headed for Subic Bay, Philippines. A few days out of Hawaii a serious sabotage incident occurred. Someone went through the hanger deck with wire cutters, and reached up into the wheel wells of many of the jet fighters tied down in the hangar deck and cut as many wires as he could reach! The captain ordered marines to stand watch on the hangar deck to protect the planes. It was not a comforting thought that someone in our midst would do such a thing. The guilty person was never caught.

The Russians once again sent out their long-range bombers to see how close they could get to us without being detected. We in W Division were told we would be working with conventional bombs and ammunition when we began steaming off the coast of Vietnam. We were given a number of familiarization and safety classes on bombs and rockets.

The latter part of October we pulled into Subic Bay. Wayne Knowles, "Mac" McAleer and I had liberty one day, and we decided to do some golfing. We went to the Subic Naval Station golf course. We had to have a Filipino caddy, because if we hit a golf ball into the rough (jungle), we were not permitted to search for it, as there were cobras and vipers in the rough. The caddy was the only one permitted off the fairways. The ninth hole of the course was a bar that sold cold San Miguel beer. After we three played eighteen holes (not very well), we went to the clubhouse. It was a beautiful tropical night. We sat at a table in the clubhouse, and had dinner. Most of the people seated around us were high-ranking officers with their wives, enjoying drinks and dinner. After we ate dinner, we three began playing a dice game called "Ship, Captain, and Crew." We were betting a quarter on each game. After time passed, Wayne and I were constantly winning, with Mac losing every hand. Wayne and I were teasing Mac, after he lost another round; he said in his gravelly "whiskey" voice, "Boy, you're a bunch of hungry sons a bitches." His voice carried throughout the entire dining area. Wayne and I gasped, the entire room became silent, and you could have heard a pin drop. Mac looked around the room and said "Well they are!" The whole room erupted in laughter.

The first of November we headed for the war zone, we were once again in the hot, humid area off the coast of Vietnam. Some of what I wrote to my parents in a letter dated 9 November 1965 follows:

> We got into Subic Bay the last of October then pulled back out, right now we're back out by Vietnam, flying about 150 combat missions a day, and boy, am I tired! My division is split into two crews and we're helping push, load and store conventional bombs. I work for twelve hours, and then off twelve hours. I can't tell you how many bombs our planes drop a day, but its tons and tons. We have to replenish our ammunition about every other day from ammunition ships, because we drop all we have onboard. We've only been here seven days, but it seems like we have dropped enough to wipe out all of North Vietnam, and there are two other carriers out here. I work down in a bomb magazine, and you wouldn't believe how hot it gets, usually around 105 degrees! After working a few minutes I'm completely soaked in sweat! I think I've had a couple of heart attacks from seeing bombs dropped accidentally, they are very rugged, and not supposed to go off, or so they say.
>
> I guess the war over here must seem unreal to the people back in the States.

I read a newspaper article that said the war being fought from carriers was being carried on in an antiseptic world of crisply starched dungarees, and buttered popcorn! If the character were here that wrote that article, I think I'd punch him in the nose! He couldn't have been onboard this carrier. I get so tired and miserable at times, I don't think I can move! I don't know if the people over here will ever try to take a carrier, but a lot of people say that they'll have to, because that's where the majority of the bombs are coming from.

Today we had an officer killed by a net load of bombs, while an ammunition ship was replenishing us; the net fell on him, crushing him to death. It was ironic because he was a safety observer for the on-load!

One of the benefits we were given by Congress while off the coast, or in Vietnam, was free postage. When we mailed a letter while off the coast, instead of placing a stamp on the upper right corner of an envelope we wrote the word "free." Our return address had to include our complete address as well as rate, and service number. We also would eventually get hostile fire pay, which amounted to about sixty dollars a month. Also, while in combat zones we did not pay federal income tax on our earned wages. Underway replenishments, or "UnRep's," were conducted when an ammunition ship pulled alongside the *Ticonderoga*, and while steaming at the same speed, a line was shot across with a shotgun, with this small line as a beginning, eventually larger lines and cables were strung across the span over the sea between the two ships so bombs and ammunition could be passed across. There were also Vertical Replenishments "VertRep's," which involved helicopters flying back and forth between the supplying ship and the *Ticonderoga*. Our work as ordnancemen deep within the bowels of the ship was hot, dirty, and grueling. Our life was not as glamorous, or exciting as that of the pilots. In *Ticonderoga*'s 65-66 cruise book there is written a "pilot's story[22]," by John Bates, which I'll partially quote from:

One breed of flier is employing the latest in modern war technology and flight strategy in the Vietnam War effort today. He is the Navy Attack Pilot operating from the mobile air base of the high seas, the attack aircraft carrier.

LTJG Robert W. Sturgeon, a fledgling twenty-four-year-old pilot of Attack Squadron Fifty Six (VA-56) aboard the attack carrier *Ticonderoga* is such a pilot.

A redhead from Atlanta, Georgia with a deep southern drawl and a quick sense of humor, Sturgeon jockeys A-4E *Skyhawk* jets twice daily in raids over hostile Viet Cong installations in Vietnam.
His daily routine seldom varies; it's mostly hard work-and risky. His job is to deliver his bomb payload on target and return to his Mother ship.

Bob Sturgeon has undergone intensive training in such technical fields as aerodynamics, higher mathematics and structural mechanics to prepare for his job. His ability is exceptionally high; his dedication absolute, he is bound by the Navy flier's creed: "I am a United States Navy flier. My countrymen built the best airplane in the world and entrusted it to me. They trained me to fly it. I will use it to the absolute limit of my power.

With my fellow pilots, aircrews, and deck crews, my plane and I will do anything necessary to carry out our tremendous responsibilities. I will always remember we are part of an unbeatable combat team-the United States Navy.

When the going is fast and rough, I will not falter. I will be uncompromising in every blow I strike. I will be humble in victory.

I am a United States Navy flier. I have dedicated myself to my country, with its many millions of all races colors and creeds.
They and their way of life are worthy of my greatest protective effort.

I ask the help of God in making that effort great enough."

Sturgeon was commissioned Ensign in the U.S. Navy in 1963 after graduating from Georgia Institute of Technology with a degree in aerospace engineering. He attended flight training school for nearly two years.

His first assignment after flight training was VA-125 where he was introduced to the A-4 *Skyhawk*. His second assignment was VA-56, a unit of Carrier Airwing Five, presently operating off the *USS Ticonderoga* (CVA-14) in the Pacific. He has been flying strike missions over Vietnam for three months.

The plane he pilots is a single engine, lightweight bomber, the smallest jet-powered combat aircraft ever built for the United States. The stubby A-4E is thirty-nine feet long and has a wingspan of twenty-seven feet. The plane carries a two-ton payload at speeds of over 600 miles per hour.

The average day would find the Lieutenant Junior Grade hustling through an early morning: reveille at 0600, shower, breakfast, possibly a chat with his fellow pilots in the officer's wardroom. His first briefing for the day goes at 0700. This day finds him preparing for a major strike at 1030.

"The morning briefs give us the big picture of what to expect in the target zone," says Sturgeon. "The pilots are given the weather forecast around the target area, enemy and friendly forces distribution and "rules of engagement." Rules of engagement specify just how the pilots are to attack.

At 0800 the pilots gather in the squadrons "Ready Room" for a secondary briefing. "This" explains Sturgeon "is where we find out how our "hop" will be conducted, what radio frequencies will be used, emergency procedures and plans of attack." Sixteen A-4's forming flights of four *Skyhawks* each will bomb a railway bridge in North Vietnam.

One half hour before the flight, Sturgeon dons his flight gear. The bulky outfit includes an oxygen breathing unit, life vest, a survival vest, a torso harness for the parachute, an anti-"G"suit, a portable emergency radio transmitter-receiver, pistol, ammunition and a crash helmet. All together it weighs about fifty pounds. Dressed, he works his way to the flight deck via ladders, goes through an inspection of his A-4 with an enlisted plane captain who maintains the plane and then clambers into the cockpit. The signal to start the jets is given fifteen minutes before launch.

"A flight deck full of strike aircraft preparing for a launch," relates Sturgeon, "is quite an impressive display of American might." Flight deck personnel are rushing about making last minute checks and counterchecks. Loose tools and gear are tied down or put away-a hammer or chisel could become a deadly missile if caught in the exhaust blast of a jet. The deafening crescendo of twenty jets turning up lends an air of immediacy to the operation.

The 42,000-ton *Ticonderoga* pivots slowly and majestically into the wind to aid in giving the planes the air speed needed to lift them aloft. The jets, one after another, are positioned on two powerful steam catapults forward and launched in rapid succession.

One can feel the carrier shudder as 125,000 pounds of thrust slams the aircraft off the ship-one "cat" at full power can throw an automobile one-mile in the air.

Bob Sturgeon is the eighteenth pilot to go off the cat. He taxis into position and his plane is hooked up to the catapult harness. He jams the throttle forward to full thrust and checks his cockpit instruments. "Here's where I get a bit excited," says Sturgeon. "The cat shot that begins each hop has a sensation all its own."

Sturgeon salutes the catapult officer signifying he is ready for launch. The cat officer returns his salute and signals the cat crew to fire the catapult. In a little over 200 feet, the 23,000-pound A-4 is accelerated to 175 miles per hour and launched into the sky. The cat shot takes about two seconds and Sturgeon is busy raising his landing gear and flaps as he scans the horizon searching for the other planes in his flight.

Sighting his flight ahead, Sturgeon joins up and the planes head for the coast of North Vietnam. "The carrier is usually 100 or 150 miles from the coast," reveals Sturgeon. Today it was closer because of the distance to our target." The planes fly at about 400 miles per hour until they reach the target zone.

The pilots approach the railway bridge at about 10,000 feet. "We began to pick up some flak as we neared the target," recalls Sturgeon. "The muzzle flashes were clearly visible on the ground and the shells left small gray-black puffs of smoke as they exploded around our aircraft. Since we were constantly changing our altitude, heading, and airspeed, the gunners on the ground couldn't track us. Only a lucky hit would have downed us. "As we rolled in on the target, I didn't have time to worry about enemy defenses-my hands were full just concentrating on delivering my weapons on target." Accelerating to over 500 miles per hour, the A-4's swoop down on the railroad bridge and release their loads. They level off by about 3,500 feet, pulling five"G's" in the process.

"We were "jinxing" or flying irregular flight patterns" Sturgeon says, "All the way back to the coast today to elude enemy retaliation."

One A-4C pilot from VA-144, a fellow squadron aboard *Ticonderoga* does not make it back this day. He was shot down by enemy anti-aircraft fire over the target. "After we reached the coast" Sturgeon recalls, "we headed for home."

Sturgeon approaches *Ticonderoga* in a landing pattern making a large orbit of the ship to begin his approach to the carrier's flight deck.

"We're on a frequency with the landing signal officer who guides us down, but a flight deck landing is strictly solo. It's the pilot who handles the controls," Sturgeon explains. "From on high, the carriers flight deck looks the size of a postage stamp," says the young pilot. "It doesn't look any bigger from astern as you approach for the landing. Unlike a stationary runway, our "landing platform" isn't always steady. A carrier sometimes pitches and rolls in heavy seas."

Sturgeon makes the approach at approximately 150 miles an hour-slow enough to be caught by the arresting cables on the flight deck, fast enough to take off again if he misses.

Today Sturgeon snags the number two arresting cable on the first try is thrown forward violently in his seat as the plane is slowed to a stop in two seconds from 140 mph. He taxis forward to a "parking area," climbs out of his plane and goes down below to the Ready Room.

After the flight Bob Sturgeon will go down below to the ship's Air Intelligence Office to a "debrief." Here he gives a run-down on what he experienced on the mission and his opinions-both pro and con. Sturgeon will probably take an hour or so break for coffee after the debriefing. Later, he may find time to write a letter home. At 1330 the flight routine begins again for the afternoon hop scheduled for 1530.

"Why do I fly?" asks Sturgeon, "well it's like this. I like flying and I like the Navy. Out here "on the line" I get a lot of personal satisfaction using the skills and training I've acquired for some tangible reason-to support our national policy."

The middle of November marked the end of another evaluation period for me. My "evals" for this period averaged 3.8. In November I was on a very static work schedule. One week I'd work from noon to midnight on conventional ordnance tasks, then the next week from midnight to noon. The third week I'd work an eight-hour day in W Division trying to catch up on the work I'd not been able to do while working the twelve-hour conventional bomb shifts.

The usual routine when we bombed targets further north, would involve steaming in a northerly direction, with the ship at general quarters battle stations. The planes would launch for the air strike, then return. At that point we would steam south, and finally secure from battle stations. Sleep was a precious commodity and scarce. When the ship went to general quarters, regardless if it was your sleep period, you had to be awake and man your assigned battle station. There was always the constant concern about air attacks, especially when we were in the northern section of the South China Sea. We had a few anxious moments when the ship would go to general quarters because of a "bogey" (unidentified airplane) flying toward the ship. It usually turned out to be an Air Force plane, or a commercial airliner.

The news from home was that Allison had a job at the stationary store in Lindsay. Brother Joe had a case of the measles; Dad had a new job at the Lindsay-Strathmore Irrigation District. Mom was beginning work again at the Porterville State Hospital. I wondered if there was something "going on" with Allison. Her letters were full of complaints, she was fighting with her mom, and I also got word that she was seeing one of her old boyfriends. I sensed I wasn't being told the whole story about what was going on, but I couldn't do anything about it.

In mid-November our planes attacked large numbers of North Vietnamese Regular soldiers fighting the U.S. 7th Calvary at Ia Trang Valley. This was the first major battle between U.S. and North Vietnam regular forces in the war. Our troops were overrun by the North Vietnamese, and the commanding officer of the 7th Calvary called in air strikes to save his troops. The battle November 14-17 left 234 American soldiers killed. A total of 305 were killed in action during the Pleiku campaign in the highlands, October 25 – November 21. As I have said, the code word used to warn of an American unit about to be overrun by enemy forces, is "Broken Arrow", the same code word used to report a serious accident with a nuclear weapon. This battle between regular U.S. troops, and North Vietnamese regulars, is described in a book called "We Were Soldiers Once…and Young©[23]," written by LTGEN (ret) Harold G. Moore, and Joseph L. Galloway. The battle was also portrayed in a movie™©[23] with the same name, starring Mel Gibson.

The different work schedules, from noon till midnight, and midnight to noon, were used to rotate bombing requirements between the carriers stationed off the coast of Vietnam. There were always at least two carriers off the coast. The South China Sea was split into two sections of responsibility at different times during the war. The northern section became known as "Yankee Station", and the southern section, "Dixie Station". Steaming off the coast was called "being on the line."

The latter part of November we broke away from being on the line. One big relief we experienced when leaving the South China Sea was that the weather became cooler. When we were on the line, the uniform was a T-shirt (skivvies), and dungaree pants, which without the dungaree shirt made the heat much more bearable. Chiefs and officers however remained in full khaki uniforms. Our schedule called for the ship to pull into Subic Bay, Philippines for a few days, and then to Yokosuka, Japan.

After Japan we were to be back on the line, and remain on the line during Christmas. On 27 November a large anti-war demonstration took place in Washington, D.C. involving over 25,000 demonstrators.

The Philippines, Subic Naval Station, and Cubi Naval Air Station (as well as Anderson Air Force Base) had been U.S. Bases since the end of World War II. These three bases were the largest bases on the island. There were also smaller bases scattered about in the Philippines. Subic and Cubi were all within one huge fence that encircled the base. Within the base there were a Ship Repair Facility, and Naval Magazine. The base had large clubs, and recreational facilities such as bowling alleys, horseback riding, skeet shooting ranges, and much more. Many Philippine nationals worked on the base, as shipyard workers, grounds keepers, waiters, bartenders, taxi drivers, and in the many occupations necessary to keep a base functioning. One unique job within the clubs on base was the "rent a girl" in each club. Young Filipino girls dressed in evening gowns, or casually dressed, would sit in a designated section of the club, and dance with sailors for ten cents a dance.

There were many restaurants that catered to sailors and their dependants. The restaurants offered a variety of food, fast food such as hamburgers, and pizza, to traditional Filipino food, also steaks. A restaurant called the Spanish Gate served the best filet mignon steak I've ever tasted for a dollar. One thing the sailors on the ship all craved was fresh milk. On *Ticonderoga* we were served recombined or instant milk that tasted horrible.

Marines manned the gate that led to Olongapo, the city right outside the main gate. Filipino soldiers also manned the gate with the U.S. Marines. In order to leave the base you had to show your ID card to the marine guard (non-rated sailors had to show liberty cards as well). The marine also inspected sailors for uniform correctness, haircuts, and general appearance. We were always in dress white uniforms in Subic. Just beyond the gate were money exchange windows where "funny money" (military script) could be exchanged for pesos. After leaving the money exchange windows, you immediately stepped on a bridge that spanned a river. The first thing you noticed was the sewer smell, and the odor was horrible. This four-lane bridge crossed over Subic River, which was known to sailors worldwide as "Shit River," because frankly that's what it smelled like! The water was brown and filthy, with human feces floating on the surface. However, all along the water under the bridge were canoes with young boys, some naked, others with swimming trunks on, shouting for sailors on the bridge to throw pesos into the water. If a coin were thrown, there was a mad dash by all the swimmers to retrieve the coin. When the coin was found, the boy would rise to the surface holding the coin aloft, usually with a big smile, encouraging the sailors to throw more money. It was amazing that they could find anything at all in the filthy water! In the evening hours young girls dressed in flowing white wedding gowns, often holding white parasols would stand on the canoes trying to attract sailors, and entice them to throw money so their young swimming helpers could dive for the thrown coins. The white gowns were a startling contrast against the murky, dirty water, and a sight that I've never forgotten.

Lining the bank of the river across from the naval base was a large community of tin and cardboard shacks, homes of people living in unbelievable poverty. The main street of Olongapo was Magsay Drive. This main street was lined with literally hundreds of bars. Some of the bars were "holes in the wall," while others were exotic nightclubs. These bars were entirely supported by American sailors and marines. The city looked a lot like the towns of the American Wild West must have looked. Each bar had two or more heavily armed Filipino security guards, many with sawed off shotguns, and bandoliers of shells draped across their chest. The streets were filled with gaudy, brightly painted, decorated jeep taxis, or "jeepneys." The jeepneys had covered bench seats that could transport twelve or more persons. The drivers drove up and down Main Street, honking their horns looking for fares. There were also motorcycles with sidecars that would transport people for a few centavos. There was the constant sounding of jeepneys horns, and smoke hung in the air from all the vehicles belching exhaust fumes. This smoke mingled with the smoke from vendor's barbeques that lined the street, selling meat that was skewered on a wooden stick. The meat was usually very tasty, some type of pork or beef (we hoped it wasn't dog or monkey). A nickname for this barbequed meat was "monkey on a stick." As sailors walked down the sidewalks of Olongapo, dodging all the vendors trying to sell food, cigarettes, or trinkets, the calls of the bar girls would ring out from each bar trying to entice sailors to come in. Olongapo was like no other city in the Far East.

Each of the hundreds of bars in Olongapo had its own group of girls. When word was spread that a carrier was in port, sometimes two at a time, which meant thousands of sailors with pockets full of money, girls from all the surrounding provinces would rush to Olongapo to try and get their share of pesos from the free spending American sailors. American rock and roll music and country music blared from jukeboxes. There were small children begging for money, or cigarettes. Pickpockets and thieves were everywhere.

Sailors were cautioned about leaving the "main drag," as law enforcement was not apparent just a couple of blocks off the bar-lined street. Here you could be robbed, just as I discovered the hard way while in Manila when I had my wallet stolen. It was common for sailors who strayed away from the main street to be beaten, or even killed. There were bars that catered only to black sailors that white sailors did not frequent. There was entertainment of all types, trying to entice sailors into particular bars. Many of the bands that played in the bars were very good at mimicking American bands. One Filipino singer who was famous for many years, sounded exactly like the singer Johnny Cash. One bar not far from the main gate had a large concrete pit near the sidewalk, which contained a crocodile. At certain times of the day the crocodile was fed live baby ducks, sailors could buy a duck for a few pesos and fed it to the reptile. Crowds would gather to watch this gruesome meal.

One potent concoction prepared by Olongapo bars upon request was an alcohol punch, usually made by the gallons, called "moejoe." This was a mixture of vodka, rum, and fruit juice, which was the downfall of many sailors who drank it. Moejoe did not taste like an intoxicating beverage, and this lead to over indulgence. There were stripper acts of every description. There is no delicate way to describe what was a common act displayed on stage in many of the bars. There were girls called "peso pickers," who would be on stage completely nude, and would call for sailors to throw money on the stage, and they would pick up the money with their private parts! They would also pick up a stack of pesos and expel the coins' one at a time, or "smoke" a cigar or cigarette. There were also dancers that would dance with boa constrictors. The depravity of Olongapo was as I said like the old west, but I don't think the "old west" would have tolerated the nudity and x-rated entertainment that was geared to entice young men to spend money freely. The contrast of poverty, and wealth was evident throughout the country. Apparently Olongapo was very much aware of where its cash flow came from, as everything was geared toward accommodating sailors. Girls working in the bars were required to undergo periodic exams for venereal disease; they were then issued a card, which was referred to as a "blue card," which proclaimed their clean health, until their next physical exam. Venereal disease was common; sailors were warned not to solicit streetwalkers, as these were usually girls who could not get a blue card. Sailors were also advised not to wear wristwatches in Olongapo. Wrist watches were favorite targets of thieves who were expert at pulling wrist watches with expandable wrist bands off wrists, or cutting the leather strap of a wrist watch and running away with the watch, often cutting the owner's wrist. Pickpockets frequented the streets of Olongapo. The local police tried to deter pickpockets with severe punishment if they were caught. While standing shore patrol duty one night I saw a room at the Olongapo Police station that contained a table upon which there were two parallel boards. An accused pickpocket would be forced to lay his fingers across the span of these two boards. While the pickpocket was held, a policeman would swing a steel bar down across the fingers with enough force to break the four fingers. The pickpocket would then be released. Olongapo doctors and medical clinics were forbidden to treat broken fingers without checking with the police station, as it was against the law to set the broken fingers of a pickpocket.

As in Japan, the girls in Olongapo were experts at separating a sailor from the contents of his wallet. There was an established "buying out the bar" procedure. All the Olongapo hotels issued two cards at the time of registration, one for the sailor paying for the room, and the other for any companion he might find during the day or night. Room service was available in all the hotels, providing both food and drink. There were restaurants on the main street interspersed between the bars. The only beer sold was a Philippine brew called San Miguel. The alcohol content of this beer was not as consistent, nor regulated as American beer. One bottle of San Miguel might be as potent as water, while the next might have very high alcohol content. San Miguel also had a laxative effect until a sailor's digestive system got used to it after a day or two. Sailors were cautioned not to drink the water, or use ice in drinks, while off base.

Many young, (and a few old), sailors "fell in love" with a bar girl, which was what most of the girls were looking for, "a ticket" to the United States. The "grapevine communication" system of the bar girls was amazing! Most were very possessive of a particular sailor (and his money), and became very jealous if their sailor sat with, or bought drinks for another girl. They called this disloyal behavior being a "butterfly." If a sailor walked through the main gate headed for a bar a mile or so down the main street, by the time he got to the bar, the girl he had been dating would know what time he came through the gate, where he may have stopped, and eaten, or perhaps if he stopped at another bar.

As in other liberty ports, W Division hung out in one particular bar. The bar's name was "The Australian." GMT's could not afford to get into trouble, so we tried to watch out for each other. Sometimes this was a full time job, as in the case of Ted Brine who was from Arizona, and always looking for a fight.

Anything could be bought on the Olongapo "black market." Many sailors bought drugs that supposedly would cure venereal disease, because they didn't want to go to sickbay and be restricted to the ship while in port. One sailor in W Division was constantly trying to cure himself with these illegally bought drugs.

One group of people we were warned about was the "Huks." They lived in the jungles surrounding Olongapo, and wore loincloths. They were heavily tattooed and heavily armed, most carried huge machetes, and even the police gave them a wide berth. They were considered vicious, merciless fighters, and many of the sailors stationed on the base that had homes in Olongapo would hire Huks to guard their house, and possessions. The Huk would often stand guard in a nearby tree. Any house guarded by a Huk was untouchable. On infrequent occasions the head of a decapitated sailor would be found near the main gate. Perhaps the victim of a robbery, or perhaps the sailor insulted a machete welding Huk warrior? Most of the married sailors resisted the temptations of Olongapo, and the very real possibility of catching a venereal disease. They tried to "ride herd" on the single sailors. A very dangerous time on liberty was when it was time to return to the ship late at night either by liberty boat, or liberty bus. This involved hundreds of sailors, most inebriated, and some looking for a fight, trying to get back to the ship. In Subic Bay the ship often tied up at the Ship Repair Facility Pier, which was about ten miles from the main gate. The ship would contract semi-trucks pulling large-covered trailers with benches inside to run on a specific schedule back and forth between the main gate and the ship. The sailors called these vehicles "cattle cars." You haven't experienced excitement until you climb into a cattle car full of drunken sailors, and the doors close, then it's every man for himself. There was no effort to try and enforce order. Only the senior petty officers attempted discipline. They tried to identify those who started fights, and would report names, if known, to the ship's master at arms in the morning. Friends would sit back to back and try to watch for swinging fists. We in W Division would stay near our marine friends. Upon arrival at the ship, everyone would disembark, and often the ship's corpsman would be called to tend to those that might be hurt. Not all the cattle car rides were violent; many were cheerful with sailors singing and in good spirits. Fortunately I was never hit too many times, or hurt seriously on a cattle car ride, but one year in Subic I was at a liberty boat landing awaiting a boat to get back to the ship when a huge drunken brawl broke out; many sailors were hurt, and one marine was choked to death by someone with a coat hanger!

The expiration of liberty was "prorated" just as the commencement of liberty was. Higher ranked sailors left the ship earlier than junior sailors, and the reverse was true when liberty was over. Junior ranked sailors reported aboard sooner after liberty than those senior to them. Liberty expired overseas earlier than liberty expiration in the states. This was primarily because it was often dangerous to be on the streets after dark in many of the Far East ports we visited. Also considered were the political agreements made between the host countries and America. The times liberty was permitted in Olongapo varied greatly over the twenty-five years I visited there. In order for sailors other than chiefs and officers to spend over night ashore, a special request chit had to be submitted to a sailor's division officer. During the years of President Marcos's reign, martial law and a nightly curfew were in effect. This meant no one was permitted on the streets or in public between midnight and 6:00a.m. During the times of Philippine elections, sailors were not permitted off the base until after the polls closed, as the election voting periods were often violent, and sometimes deadly. During most of the years I visited Olongapo, a political dynasty was in charge. The first member of the dynasty was Mayor Gordon. After many years he was assassinated, and was replaced by his wife Mrs. Gordon. After she served a few terms, the Gordon's' son became Mayor. Just as President Marcos ruled with an iron fist, so did the Gordons. They would often be seen about Olongapo escorted by heavily armed guards carrying submachine guns.

There was a large population of retired Navy sailors living in Olongapo. Many had married Filipino women, and now made Olongapo their home. They were able to get medical care at the base hospital, and shop at the base commissary and exchange. The cost of living was cheap and they lived well on the Philippine economy. There were two large Veterans of Foreign War (VFW), and Fleet Reserve Association (FRA) clubs located on the main street of Olongapo.

As well as being cautioned about drinking water, streetwalkers, and going on liberty alone, sailors were warned about being invited to sit down at the poker games that were in many of the clubs. Most of these games were crooked, with marked cards, and other cheating tactics. Some even went so far as to make a small slit in the palm of one hand, and slip a small mirror in the slit so the cards that were being dealt face down to all the players could be read by the dealer with the small mirror. Sailors, who thought they were experienced poker players on the ship, would soon become losers in Olongapo!

In 1965 liberty in Olongapo, although cheap, cost a little more than liberty in Japan. While the ship was in the Philippines, many sailors would remain onboard preferring to save their money for liberty in Japan.

In the years to come this economic strategy was to change, as Japan eventually became much more expensive, and Olongapo became the liberty port of choice. Olongapo was an economy based on sex and alcohol.

Many young sailors were away from home for the first time, and being in a city with few restraints created a situation that required long hours of counseling, and advice, as well as discipline from senior petty officers and officers. The free flowing, cheap San Miguel beer, hot tropic sun, abundant availability of women, combined with young male egos (often looking for fights) resulted in the writing of many, many report chits, which would keep the division officers, executive officer, and the captain busy for many days after pulling out of Subic Bay. The *Ticonderoga* 65-66 cruise book[24] contains a very revealing statement:

> Olongapo, and the bar community outside Clark Air Force Base, was not representative of the people of the Philippines, it is disappointing to have so little space (in the cruise book) for the Philippines. Certainly by the end of a Western Pacific cruise Subic Bay is the port most often seen by American sailors. Unfortunately the Philippines are hard to know. To judge the entire nation by the port town of Olongapo is hardly fair, and, after all, one is hardly escaping anything just outside the gate. In fact whatever Olongapo has is most likely catching.

I agree wholeheartedly with this statement. I had many Filipino friends that were honest, polite, hardworking, and morally upstanding. Some of the hardest working and most patriotic sailors in the Navy were Filipinos. Olongapo was an exceptional city in the country, a city that was driven by greed for money, and fed upon the loneliness, frustration, lust, and exuberance of young American sailors.

The first part of December we left Subic Bay, and headed north. It was time for our quarterly readiness exercise. This exercise involved loading strike aircraft, pilots manning their planes, and positioning on the flight deck just as though they were about to fly off on a strike. Then the exercise would end and the planes would be unloaded. Something happened during this exercise that I was unable to talk about for twenty-four years until it was made public in 1989.

It was a clear, sunny autumn day the day of the exercise. The sea was calm with occasional rolling waves. The word "Crew-cut" had been passed over the ships 1MC loudspeakers, setting the exercise in motion. W Division had been preparing a week for this busy exercise. My assignment was as a technical monitor, roaming the hangar deck, observing the loading crews on the aircraft, and watching movement of the loaded aircraft in the hangar bays up to the flight deck. The loaded planes were lifted up to the flight deck by means of aircraft elevators, which were platforms that hung out over the water. These platforms moved up and down between the hangar deck and flight deck level. Planes were moved and positioned on the ship by small yellow, four wheel, motor powered carts hooked to the front landing gear of the airplanes. Planes were also moved by "muscle power": men called "plane pushers" moved the planes by pushing just as you would push a stalled automobile. The plane pushers were on the lowest rung of the ship's chain of command ladder. These sailors pushed planes all day. In the hot, humid tropical climates this was a very physically demanding job. A plane-handling supervisor directed the plane pushers. The handling supervisor was assisted by sailors watching the plane's wing tips and tail to ensure the plane didn't strike anything, including other planes, while moving in the close quarters of the hangar bay area. The handling supervisor directed the plane pushers by blowing on a whistle, which was carried around his neck on a chain. Two plane pushers always carried "U" shaped blocks of wood that were placed around the two wing landing gear wheels, and served as chocks, or wheel stops, when the plane came to a stop. The plane pushers also carried heavy tie down chains that were used to hold the plane in place any time it was parked or stationary for any length of time. Tie down wells were generously placed on the hanger deck, and flight deck as attachment points for the tie down chains. When a plane was being moved, either the enlisted plane captain (a squadron sailor assigned to a specific plane who cleaned, waxed, and accomplished various maintenance tasks) or the pilot assigned to the plane would be in the cockpit to apply brakes on the landing gear when called on to do so by the handling supervisor directing movement of the plane.

As the aircraft loads were completed in the hangar bay, the plane pushers pushed out the loaded planes onto the aircraft elevator. Two armed marines accompanied each plane. After sounding a warning horn, the aircraft elevator operator would push the "UP' button and the elevator would begin rapidly moving the loaded plane, pilot, plane pushers, and marines up to the flight deck.

Another GMT and I were technical monitors on the hangar deck; there were also two technical monitors on the flight deck. GMTCS Morgan was the roaming technical monitor supervisor.

From time to time the word would be passed "Now stand by for a roll to starboard (or port)." And we would experience a roll of the ship in the direction of the announcement. The sea was a little rough, and the ship was making turns trying to keep itself as stable as possible during the exercise.

A loaded A-4E *Skyhawk* was being pushed out onto the aircraft elevator. The pilot was in the cockpit, and the cockpit canopy was in the up position. As the plane was being pushed out onto the elevator, the ship began a roll to starboard, accelerating the rolling plane. The handling supervisor blew his whistle loudly indicating the command for the pilot to apply the landing gear brakes. The two plane pushers on each side of the plane stood ready to throw the wheel chocks on the rolling wheels. The pilot's head was down in the cockpit and the plane was accelerating faster. The handling supervisor blew his whistle wildly, and all the plane pushers trying to hold back the accelerating plane, began hollering "brakes, brakes," as the plane rolled closer and closer to the edge of the elevator. The pilot continued looking down into the cockpit and was oblivious to the loud whistling and shouting. Two of the plane pushers threw the wheels chocks around the wheels, but without the brakes being applied the momentum of the heavy plane could not be stopped. The tail of the plane extended out over the edge of the aircraft elevator, and then the wheels jolted off the edge, tearing out a portion of the safety net that encircled the elevator. The plane pushers' efforts were futile trying to hold back the rolling plane, and they leapt clear of it to keep from falling into the sea. As the body of the plane slammed against the deck of the elevator, the pilot finally looked up. I'll never forget the startled look on his face. He grasped the edges of the open cockpit, and appeared to attempt to stand up, but he was restrained in his seat by the seat harness. All of this happened in a matter of seconds, but it was as though it was happening in slow motion; the plane pushers, marines, and all of us stood there in stunned shock. The plane's nose lifted, and the plane rolled off the elevator with the shocked pilot struggling to stand up. The plane flipped completely upside down, and fell toward the sea. There was a huge splash, and as the ship moved away, the plane and pilot disappeared under the blue-green surface of the water.

I glanced around for Chief Morgan who had been there a moment ago, but he was gone. I immediately ran to a phone in the hanger bay, called the W Division office, and told them I was preparing a "rainbow message." All technical monitors carried a blank rainbow message that just needed blanks filled in. I filled it in, read it to the division officer, and then ran up the many ladders that led to the ship's bridge. As I had been calling the division, the word was being passed over the ship's loudspeakers, "Man overboard, man overboard, starboard side." The ship had slowed, and made a turn to starboard to move the ship screws away from anyone who might be in the water. It had been a miracle that none of the plane pushers had fallen into the sea with the plane.

I arrived at the bridge, gasping for air, and explained to the officer of the deck, that I needed the captain's release signature for the message. The captain called me over to his bridge chair, and I showed him the rough message that detailed the loss of the loaded plane in the sea. The captain took his time, and after looking at the high level of addresses, which were from the White House down, finally said "Well, I guess we have to send this one?" There was a five-minute time limit on messages of this type: but we didn't make it, it was twenty minutes before the message was released. There was a reason for urgency, because if there had been a nuclear detonation and our entire task force disappeared in a fireball, the White House thinking we had been attacked might begin pressing buttons starting World War III. After the captain signed, I ran to the communications office, where the message was sent by "flash precedence." The message informed the entire military chain of command what had happened. A "Broken Arrow" report was also prepared, the beginning of a small "mountain" of paperwork that was associated with this accident.

The *Ticonderoga* and our escorts circled the area where the plane had gone over the side for a long while, hoping to find the pilot. The plane had dropped off the ship into one of the deepest areas of the Pacific Ocean. Finally the search ended. There was no hope of finding the pilot.

I've often thought of the horror of those final moments of that young pilot's life, as he plunged down into the dark depths of the sea, with the sunlight on the surface rapidly disappearing, knowing that he was entombed within his coffin plummeting to his grave. It was speculated that as the plane hit the water, the cockpit canopy slammed down upon him, pinning him in. We also hoped that the canopy's slamming down also mercifully rendered him unconscious. The horror and helplessness of those few moments have remained burned into my memory.

During this cruise we lost a number of pilots to hostile fire over Vietnam. This young pilot was also a victim of war, as he was killed while perfecting the readiness for nuclear war. We learned it was LTJG Douglas M. Webster, and he was married, which made the tragedy even worse.

I recalled those occasions when he would come into W Division to sign the custody paperwork for the weapon he would use in the event of nuclear war. He was a cheerful, likeable officer who we enjoyed working with. The exercise was completed in a somber mood as we realized one of our shipmates had just been killed.

Twenty-four years after this accident, in May 1989, the incident was made public, and newspapers reported:

> The United States told Japan that a hydrogen bomb lost overboard
> from an American aircraft carrier 24 years ago almost certainly burst
> under intense water pressure and spread radioactive plutonium on
> the ocean floor. A team of American weapons designers from
> several national laboratories assured Japanese officials that there
> was "no environmental impact" from the accident. American
> officials offered no indication that radiation had escaped during the
> accident. The disclosure came after the Pentagon confirmed reports
> that it lost the bomb eighty miles from a small Japanese island in
> December 1965, when an A-4 aircraft carrying the weapon fell off
> the aircraft carrier *Ticonderoga*. The pilot was killed and the bomb
> immediately sank.

Those that gave their lives for our country that 65-66 cruise were:
CMDR John C. Mape
LT Richard W. Hastings
LTJG John V. McCormick
LTJG Gerald L. Pinneker
LTJG Douglas M. Webster
LTJG Stephan G. Richardson
AN Charles O. Dixon

LCDR Render Crayton was declared missing in action, but was captured, and survived the war.

On the 8th of December I celebrated my twenty-third birthday. We were to spend Christmas "on the line." After being on the line for a few days, we were told there was to be a lull in the bombing. There was also to be a thirty-hour truce during Christmas, and an overall slowdown of bombing strikes. The first visitor to fly aboard on 22 December was the entertainer Martha Raye. She gave two shows, one in the forecastle, and one on the flight deck after dark, and after completion of flight quarters.

Our cruise book reads[25]:

> On December 22 we had the pleasure of two performances given
> by Miss Martha Raye, the woman who, (except for age that is in no
> way excessive,) could be called the Grande Old Lady of the
> American Stage. She has been delighting audiences for years and
> years.
>
> Aboard the *Ticonderoga* the audience was similar to one she had
> performed before many times since her arrival in the Western Pacific
> Theater. At the conclusion of her last show Miss Raye told the
> appreciative crew, "I want you to know why an American woman should
> be proud she is an American...it is because of men like you." And she
> meant it. Everyone was sorry to see her go, and we all wished she could
> have stayed indefinitely. With her example of spirit and gumption we would never flag.

I watched the evening show, and it was very enjoyable. On Christmas Day it was a day much like any other, except for the huge turkey dinner, and free cigarettes handed out on the mess deck.

Francis Cardinal Spellman, Cardinal Archbishop of New York, was flown aboard the ship the 26th. The cruise book says about this visit[25]:

> His Eminence, whose advanced age enhanced the significance of
> his visit, offered mass in Hangar Bay One while attack aircraft were
> launched to their targets in Vietnam. The roar of the jets often
> obscured the sound of his words, but the meaning of his benediction
> was not lost on *Ticonderoga*'s men, some of who were fortunate
> enough to talk to him. Cardinal Spellman departed later that
> afternoon to continue his Christmas visit to servicemen in Vietnam.

On the 27th, Bob Hope's show flew aboard. His show was to be on the 29th. I looked forward to seeing the show; however, I was not destined to see it. The show troupe included actresses Carroll Baker, and Joey Heatherton, singers Kaye Stevens, Jack Jones, and Anita Bryant, Miss USA-World 1965 Diana Battsa, the dancing Nicholas Brothers, Jerry Colonna, Peter Leeds, and a large support crew. There was an incident on the 28th, the night before the show that was reported worldwide. The 28 December 1965 Sacramento Union newspaper[26] is partially quoted here.

"War mishap stuns Hope Troupe"

Aboard the USS *Ticonderoga* (UPI)-Comedian Bob Hope and his troupe got a taste of war Monday when they saw a U.S. Navy A-4 *Skyhawk* miss a recovery cable and plunge into the darkened sea in a ball of flames.

The incident cast an immediate gloom over the showstoppers, but a few moments later the cast cheered when the pilot, who had ejected, was pulled from the water. Dancer Joey Heatherton ran into his arms and planted a big kiss on his cheek. The rescued pilot Lt (j.g) William Braugher of Newark, Ohio; grinned and added "It was almost worth it."

During the suspense-filled minutes, while the carrier and its two escort Destroyers the *USS Turner Joy*, and the *USS Swanson* scoured the water for the pilot, Miss Heatherton said the cast was "stunned" by the incident. "This really brings the war home to you," she said.

Hope and his cast came to the aircraft carrier after Christmas weekend shows for G.I.'s at various posts in Vietnam.

The group of entertainers watched jets roar off into the tropical sunset for strikes against Viet Cong bases in South Vietnam. "This is the biggest treat of the trip,"Hope said. The girls with him shouted "whoopee" and "boy-oh-boy" as the jets thundered down the deck and soared into the air.

Hope and Capt. Willy House, Chief of Staff of Carrier Division Nine, played a golf tournament on the carrier deck. They drove golf balls off the carrier into the sea. "I was aiming for the 13th white cap," Hope said.

Jan King, Hope's traveling secretary, who has made ten trips with the comedian, said this trip was different from any of the others. "This is the first time we felt there was any danger" she said. Bob's family felt it too. "Each time he goes on one of these trips his four kids ask him to bring back gifts.

This time they asked for camouflaged helmets. Then Nora, she's nineteen, grabbed my arm and said "Make sure Poppa gets back safe."

I was looking forward to it, but was destined to miss the Bob Hope show (see photograph page). On the 27th I saw him and his accompanying crowd on the mess decks, which was the same day I received a telegram saying that Allison was seriously ill, and I was needed at home. The Red Cross had confirmed the telegram. I was very worried. This had been a complete surprise; I'd not heard anything from home about Allison being ill. On the night of the 27th, after hurriedly packing a suitcase, I was flown off the ship on a COD with emergency leave papers in hand. This was the second time in 1965 I'd gone on emergency leave. In Subic Bay, I took the long bus ride to Clark Air Force Base. As soon as I showed my emergency leave papers at the terminal desk, I was given the highest possible travel status. Before long I was on the long trip across the Pacific Ocean. After stopping in Guam and Hawaii, my plane landed at Travis Air Force Base in California. I called home as soon as the plane landed. Allison said she was fine! I don't recall which day I arrived in the states. My internal clock was messed up from all the travel, and I was groggy. When I got to Lindsay, Allison looked healthy and well. Allison said she had been in the hospital for a couple of days.

I was baffled why the doctor had asked that I be brought home. My parents could not understand it either. I was to find out the true reason I had been called home a few years later.

In December the American casualty count in the war was over 1,300, with 6,100 wounded Americans. After a week at home I checked into the Naval Receiving Station, Treasure Island, and went to the dreaded transit barracks in preparation for the long trip back across the Pacific. I checked in on 16 January, and reversed my direction of travel back to the ship. I had an uneventful trip back, except that when the plane was dropping for a landing at Clark Air Force Base I experienced one of the worst headaches I'd ever had. The pain was unbearable, but subsided when the air pressure in the plane's passenger compartment changed.

At Clark Air Force Base Terminal I had a surprise. GMT1 Reese was in the waiting room. I expected him to be on the ship. I greeted him, but he was acting strangely, and very secretive. He said the captain had kicked him off the ship, and he was headed for San Francisco for reassignment. When I arrived back at the ship, I was to discover that the captain had learned of his "slush fund" business, lending money for profit. He had finally been caught in one of his moneymaking schemes. This was to be the last time I saw GMT1 R.D. Reese. Over the years I heard stories about him, one being the time he was traveling across country with a pickup truck that had been severely damaged on one side, and he sold it to a guy he met at a gas station, without ever letting the guy see the damaged side! He sold the truck, and quickly left. I also heard a story that he was caught in an insurance scam with a mutual friend, Fred White, and Fred ended up in prison for it. Some time after his retirement from the Navy, Reese and his wife were traveling to meet his brother Tom Reese (the chief I'd been with on the *Independence*), in their recreation vehicle. They hit black ice on the roadway and both were killed in the accident. Years later at a reunion get together Tom Reese took me aside and asked me if I knew why his brother was kicked off the *Ticonderoga* those many years ago. I told him the truth. Tom said he had never told him the reason, but he had always suspected that it was because of one of his schemes. Tom joined him in death in 2002 succumbing to cancer.

Fortunately I didn't have to catch the ship at sea when I arrived at Subic Bay by bus. The ship was tied alongside the pier at Cubi Point; I walked aboard on 22 January. I had a surprise waiting when I returned to the division; my transfer orders had come in. I was being transferred to Naval Air Station Whidbey Island, Washington. I was to go first to an intermediate station, Naval Nuclear Weapons Training Center Pacific, North Island, California for a two-week school. This meant I would be leaving the ship in a little over a month, and retracing my long trip across the Pacific Ocean. I also had a letter from GMT1 Wiesenhahn, who had been with me on the *USS Independence*. He was now stationed at the Naval Air Station Whidbey Island. He told me a little about the Advanced Underwater Weapons (AUW) Shop that I'd be working in with him. It sounded a lot like the AUW Shop I'd been at in Iceland.

The ship's schedule called for us to return to the line for thirty days, and then back to Yokosuka for a port call. When the ship had last been in Yokosuka in December before I left on emergency leave, I happened to be in my bunk one night a little after midnight, unable to sleep. My bunk was a bottom bunk in a tier of three. A young sailor who had been moved into W Division berthing from the engineering department came into the berthing compartment. We had extra bunks that were used by other departments from time to time. I had gotten to know him because he was from a town close to my hometown in California, the town I had been born in, Porterville. That night, however, he did something that shocked me and that I found hard to believe. He put his hand into the pockets of a pair of dungarees that were hanging on a Second Class GMT's bunk. He rummaged through the pockets of the other sailor's pants, and it looked like he removed something. The next morning I asked GMT2 Baxter, whose pants had been the ones the sailor had been looking through, if he was missing anything. He said "yes," he'd lost fifteen dollars out of his pants. I then put the sailor I'd seen in the berthing compartment on report for stealing.

On the same subject of thievery, a number of things within W Division had disappeared. Not only within the berthing compartment, but also within our working spaces, it was someone who could only enter with a security clearance and a badge. The thief had been operating for a long while. A number of times immediately after something were reported missing, such as dishes bought in Hong Kong, pool sticks bought in Japan, etc., and then everyone would undergo a surprise locker inspection to see if the thief could be caught. This was a very uncomfortable situation, and everyone suspected everyone else. There was someone in our midst that could not be trusted. A thief is despised on board ships, because you live in such close quarters with everyone, you have to trust each other to respect your possessions. In history most navies dealt out the harshest punishments to thieves, often the death penalty.

The thief was never caught, but there was one person that was strongly suspected, and after his transfer the thefts stopped. I'll not say his name, but he was a high-ranking petty officer!

Returning to the sailor I'd put on report for stealing, upon my return from emergency leave I learned that there was to be a summary court martial, which is one level below the most serious court martial, a general court martial. GMT2 Baxter and I were the only witnesses for the prosecution. I testified how I'd seen the sailor digging through Baxter's pockets. I was asked about the lighting in the berthing compartment, and if I were sure about what I'd seen, etc. The end result was that, the sailor was found innocent, because there were not enough witnesses. I was disgusted, and ashamed that he was from my hometown. He was moved out of W Division berthing compartment. However, in the end justice was served. He continued getting in trouble, such as going AWOL, and committed many other infractions, and was eventually given an administrative discharge.

On the first of February, I didn't feel well, and began coughing up blood. I went to sick call, which was in the ship's medical department, and held at 8:00 a.m., and 1300 (1:00 p.m.) each day. The doctor committed me to sickbay and I was required to bunk in the compartment that was the ship's hospital. I had x-rays, a blood test, etc.; the doctor said that it might be acute bronchitis. Anyway, I was diagnosed as having "hematology of an unknown etiology." I didn't like lying in bed all day, or all the shots I was given.

While in sickbay, a marine friend of mine was brought in with his hand heavily bandaged. While preparing to assume the watch at the after W Division magazine, he had accidentally jacked a round (bullet) into his forty-five-caliber pistol, and shot himself in the palm of his left hand. I saw the wound as a corpsman was dressing it. The bullet had caused a huge hole in his hand. His Marine Captain was very displeased with him, because of his careless handling of a firearm.

A friend of mine, GMT2 E.J. Carroll, from W Division visited me in sickbay. He was the only sailor from the division to visit me in a week's time. This experience made me realize how important it was to visit people when they are hospitalized. I vowed that I would visit people I knew in the future when they were hospitalized. Finally after a week in sickbay, I was released and given a prescription of vitamins. It was never clearly determined what the problem was, but I think it was a ruptured sinus from the flight back from the U.S., associated with the pain I felt during that flight.

In February I got word that my sister Linda had been married. She had married Walt Wilson, a guy who had gone to the same high school in Strathmore that I had attended. They were living in Fresno, California, while Walt attended college.

We pulled off the line, and went to Sasebo, Japan, arriving there 21 February. The middle of February I'd once again taken the first class exam; I'd not learn the results until May. I was anxious to leave the ship for my new duty station. I was not happy about my last visit home; it seemed to have been one continuous argument between Allison and her mother, Allison and me, and Allison's mother and father. I was uncertain about the future of our marriage. Allison was not inclined to change. She had not saved any of the money I had asked her to, and she seemed to thrive on arguments and strife.

Sasebo, Japan, was the last liberty port I was to enjoy with my shipmates. I was anxious to leave the ship, but not anxious to leave the friends I had made. The entanglement in the war seemed to be never-ending. It was backbreaking work. We complained amongst ourselves, but never to outsiders. A constant question and topic of discussion was what did our countrymen think about our efforts in the war? We hoped we were supported, and thought of as defenders of freedom, but the newspapers read differently. A common saying was, "We trained for war, and Vietnam is the only war we have." As is most common, men engaged in war did not fight with conscious ideas of patriotism, or glory, but fought consciously to help and protect friends. We were a group that looked out for each other, against the communist Viet Cong, and even against our own bosses, as was the case with "Fire and Lightning." We'd gone together "to the brink," during the Gulf of Tonkin, and at times on the line, seen death first hand. We'd experienced the boredom, and infrequent terror of warfare. We'd worked hard, and played hard together.

On 18 March, 1966, I wrote to my parents of working twelve hours a day, and sometimes more, in a magazine during ammunition on-load. I and two other sailors brought aboard, and stored fifty tons of 500-pound bombs. "500 pounders" were the most commonly dropped Navy bombs. Some of the bombs we were handling and dropping were very old. They had been manufactured during and before World War II, thirty or more years previously! Years later I read of how short the U.S. supplies of conventional ordnance were during this time, and there was real concern that our stockpiles would run out. An intense bomb manufacturing effort was instituted to build our national supplies up. When *Ticonderoga* returned to the states after this cruise, sixteen planes, and five pilots had been lost in combat.

My last evaluations on the *Ticonderoga* read: "Little is a mature, motivated Petty officer. With his technical competence and demonstrated practical abilities, he is an effective GMT. Accepting orders and commands cheerfully, tasks assumed by Little are completed with thoroughness. Wearing the uniform with great personal pride and with a cheerful disposition, he promotes good morale while maintaining effective supervision."

I was to leave the ship on 27 March. After a checkout process, I bid everyone farewell. I was flown off the ship, my last experience on *Ticonderoga* was a jolt and I saw a blur of gray as the plane was catapulted off. As I began the long trip across the Pacific, leaving the war zone was a great relief, yet mixed with these feelings of relief was the nagging feelings of missing out on the action! Also I had feelings of concern for my friends who I was leaving behind, but I was looking forward to shore duty.

On 1 September, 1973, the *Ticonderoga*[27] was decommissioned after a board of inspection and survey found her to be unfit for further naval service. Her name was struck from the Navy list on 16 November, 1973. The ship was disposed of, sold by Defense Reutilization and Marketing Service (DRMS) for scrapping 1 September 1975. It wasn't the glorious end I would have wished for her!

Chapter 7: The "O.H.T."

At home in California, I was pleased to see my parents' newly built house. After thirty days leave, and attempts to return to a normal life, after spending time on the line, I reported to San Diego to begin school. On 29 April, soon after receiving security clearance confirmation, I began attending a two-week AUW refresher-training course at NWTGPAC. In San Diego I was painfully reminded of the events surrounding James Junior's death. While on leave, we had made arrangements for a headstone to be placed on his grave.

In San Diego I was staying in the enlisted barracks while attending school. One night I took the "nickel-snatcher" boat across the channel between Coronado and San Diego, and walked to the Hula Hut, which had been the W Division hangout. I didn't see any familiar faces, so I walked next door to an upstairs Chinese food restaurant. I ordered a small plate of fried rice. My bill for the meal was two dollars. I went to the cash register, and gave the Chinese man behind the register a twenty-dollar bill. He put the bill in the cash register and gave me three dollars in change. I said, "I gave you a twenty." He spoke very little English, and tried to ignore me. I told him I was not leaving until he gave me the correct change. He kept saying, "Go, Go," and then walked through a door in the rear of the restaurant. I sat down near the entrance thinking he had gone to get his boss. After a few minutes two policemen suddenly appeared, and said I was to come with them. I tried to explain that I had been short changed, but they did not want to hear my story. The San Diego police were notorious, in their dealings with sailors. Sailors were always guilty, even if they were proven innocent. I was taken to the San Diego police station in the back of their car. They did confess to me that this had happened a number of times in the past in the Chinese restaurant! At the police station I emptied all my pockets, took off my belt and shoestrings, and was put in a cell by myself. I did not sleep. I was disgusted. Early in the morning the cell door was unlocked, and I was directed to a shore patrol van. There were three other sailors inside the van, we were taken to the North Island Master at Arms Office, and given our personal belongings, and released. I was upset, it was a humiliating experience, and I'd not done anything wrong, I was out seventeen dollars, and had been treated like a criminal. I'd made friends with a Second Class Yeoman at the school and had lent him money in the past. He said the police would send a report to the school command, but he'd take care of it, and the report would end up in the trashcan. The incident went unknown. This emphasizes a fact of Navy life, that a wise sailor would be smart to make friends with yeomen, corpsmen, and disbursing (pay) clerks. I passed my two weeks' school, and graduated without further incident.

I rented a small trailer, hitched it to the Ford, and Allison, and I packed our meager belongings, and headed north toward Whidbey Island. We began our trip early in the morning. After crossing the California/Oregon border, we stopped at Canyonville, Oregon, to see my Uncle Ralph Little. He was not at his house (see photo page), so I left a note telling him we had missed him. We also stopped in Vancouver, Washington, for a short visit with a cousin. After leaving Vancouver we stopped for the night. In the morning, we continued our journey, passed through Seattle, and over Deception Pass Bridge that connected Whidbey Island with the Washington state mainland. On this road we passed a small lake amongst pine tree named Deception Pass Lake, which was one of the most beautiful lakes that I'd ever seen.

I found GMT1 Dave Wiesenhahn's house, and we stayed with him and his wife Doris for two nights. They had a son named Duffy.

Whidbey Island was a beautiful place. The island was covered with pine trees and ferns, with vegetable and dairy farms scattered throughout the Island. The main town was Oak Harbor; a smaller town named Coupeville to the south was the county seat. Oak Harbor was a Navy town populated mostly by sailors and their families. Dutch farmers had been the pioneers of Whidbey Island, and their influence was evident throughout the Island. There were two Navy bases on the island, the Naval Air Station, and the Navy Seaplane Base.

After I checked in at the AUW Shop on the Naval Air Station, the AUW Shop Officer told me to take as long as I needed to check in and get settled. I found a three-bedroom house to rent near the main gate, which was ninety-eight dollars a month. The furniture we had was being moved north from Lindsay.

After checking in, and finding a house, I began the long waiting process that always began when I first checked into a new command. I had to wait for my security clearance confirmation. I sat around at the armory on the seaplane base each day. During this time, one afternoon a First Class, GMT1 Doyle Howell invited me to the Naval Air Station Marine Enlisted Club, where a number of the GMT's were gathered. He drove me to the club, we both were in uniform, and I was "set up".

I walked in the club with my white hat on, and a bell rang. It was explained to me that because I had entered "covered," it meant I had to buy a round of drinks for everyone! I gritted my teeth, and paid for the drinks. It cost me twenty dollars, which I really couldn't afford.

I met the leading chief of the AUW Shop, GMTC McKenna. There were nine other GMT's assigned to the AUW Shop, along with twelve Torpedomen. I learned I would have six-section duty, which was the most liberal duty status I'd ever had in the Navy. This meant every sixth night I would be required to remain overnight at the AUW Shop.

While at the armory, I studied an explosive driver's handbook; I was to be licensed as an explosives truck driver. My security clearance was finally confirmed. I had an access badge photo taken, and was given an access badge for the AUW Shop. The shop was laid out almost exactly like the AUW Shop in Iceland. The shop was on the east side of the base, separated from the main base by the base runway. The shop was encircled by an alarmed fence, and guarded by marines twenty-four hours a day. Not far from the AUW Shop was the magazine area, where two magazines were surrounded by an alarmed fence, and also guarded by marines. In order to gain access to either area, our access badge was presented to the marine guard, who exchanged the badge for a clip-on badge that was worn at all times within the fenced areas. We were forbidden to bring matches or lighters into the fenced areas.

During this time I discovered I had passed the GMT1 promotion exam, but did not have enough points to be promoted. I enjoyed the relaxed pace of shore duty, compared to the frantic, hectic wartime environment I'd just come from. I was assigned to one of the two assembly teams in Shop 2. Dave Wiesenhahn was my assembly team leader. A Navy Technical Proficiency Inspection (NTPI) was scheduled for August, so I had a lot of training to do to be prepared for the inspection. The AUW Shop had four different weapon system capabilities. Each assembly crew was responsible for two weapon systems.

On July 4th, I was surprised how large the 4th of July celebration was. Oak Harbor went all out with a big parade, carnival, and fireworks demonstration. The local Jaycee's, was an organization of young businessmen under the age of forty, who managed all of the holiday's activities.

My 1963 Ford was not running well, and it almost became a "hobby" working on it. Dave Wiesenhahn enjoyed working on cars, so we did a lot of car work together, at the Seaplane Base Auto Repair Shop.

One GMT who worked in the shop, GMT2 Jeff Carlson, did a lot of salmon fishing. I was anxious to try salmon fishing. Jeff won a local fishing contest by catching a fifty-one-pound salmon. The grand prize was a fishing boat and motor. Jeff and his wife had two children, and we spent a lot of time with them. Jeff also raised and sold Beagle dogs.

At the AUW Shop, we spent July and August preparing for our NTPI. The inspection took a week to complete, and we passed with a numerical grade of 98%. Everyone from the captain down was pleased.

One evening Allison and I were in a Chinese restaurant, seated at a table. Allison's mom and dad walked in! They had planned to make a surprise visit to our house, and had stopped at the restaurant to ask for directions. They visited for a week. I also ran across a boyhood friend, Ronnie Cox, who was stationed at the naval air base.

Dave Wiesenhahn and I began golfing almost daily. I enjoyed the beautiful Navy golf course, and it only cost one dollar to play eighteen holes, or three dollars a month for unlimited golfing. Dave and I both did not have very happy homes lives. We enjoyed each other's company, and enjoyed getting out of our respective houses. His wife was as moody as Allison. He often would take his son Duffy, and we three would go to the golf course and hunt for golf balls. Duffy enjoyed it, much like an Easter egg hunt. We found so many that we never had to buy golf balls. In October, I got word from my parents that my little brother Jerry had run through a glass door, and cut his arm badly, requiring many stitches. It was expected that he would recover OK.

During the fall months on Whidbey Island the daylight hours shortened, and the night hours lengthened. Also, in October I experienced some excitement. Two other GMT's and I were performing some work within the magazine compound. It required two men or more to enter a magazine. So we had exchanged our badges with the sentry at the gate, and then walked to a magazine bunker, unlocked both padlocks on the magazine door and entered, after giving the code word over the magazine telephone. We were in the magazine a few minutes when we heard a gunshot! We walked outside the magazine, and looked toward the fenced compound gate, where the sound had come from. We saw one marine lying on the ground and another marine running back and forth holding a forty-five-caliber pistol. We immediately went back inside the magazine, and closed the door. We had a phone inside the magazine that connected to the front entry gate.

We rang the number, and the marine finally answered the ringing phone. We asked what was going on. Was the magazine under attack? The marine said, "Help me, I just shot my buddy!" We then cautiously went out of the magazine, one GMT ran to the front gate, while two stayed behind, waiting for his signal. He signaled and we ran to the fallen marine. He had a large bullet hole in his shirt in his stomach area. There was very little blood, and he was ashen white. He kept asking "Am I going to die, am I going to die?" I told him, "No, you're going to be OK, we're getting you help." We called an ambulance, and covered him with a blanket that we found in the alarm control center building. He didn't appear to be bleeding heavily, but we applied pressure to the wound and told him to lie still. The marines responded to the scene before the ambulance, and two of them assumed the guard duty of the wounded marine, and his guard companion. The marine who had shot him was much shaken. When the ambulance arrived, the marine was still conscious. We'd been reassuring him that we'd be OK. When the corpsmen carefully rolled him over, they discovered an exit bullet wound directly in the middle of his right rear pants pocket. The entry and exit hole were about the size of my thumb. The wounded man was placed in the ambulance, and taken to the base hospital.

An investigation of the incident determined that the marine who had fired the shot, had been demonstrating the safety features of the forty-five-caliber pistol to his friend. There are seven specific safety features, one being when the barrel of the semiautomatic pistol slides back toward the shooter, when the trigger is pulled, the pistol will not fire. The marine was holding the pistol against the stomach of his friend, pulling the trigger, when the marine who was shot stepped back, the barrel slide forward and the pistol went off. They both were not aware that a round was in the firing chamber. This was unauthorized "horse play," and both marines were punished. The marine who was shot was very lucky. The bullet entered just below his navel, and exited his right buttocks without striking anything vital! He remained in the hospital for only one week, and recovered fully.

I was enjoying the slower pace of shore duty, and the six-section duty, versus the three-section duty I'd had on the ship. It was nice to wear civilian clothes to and from work. Once inside the shop, we would change into our dungaree working uniforms, with white hats. In the winter months we also wore a dungaree working jacket, or a foul weather jacket. In December we only worked half a day each workday.

The war in Vietnam was in the news every night. Most of the marines stationed on the base were assigned as a security force for the AUW Shop. Many of these marines wanted to go to Vietnam, but a few were glad to be stationed in the States.

My first evaluations at Whidbey Island were all 3.8's, and one 4.0. I was busy studying for my upcoming first class exam, which was to take place in February. I was determined to pass it although not many GMT1's were being promoted.

One day we were tasked with off-loading a seaplane tender, the *USS Puget Sound*, which was anchored at the seaplane base. An incident happened on the ship that delayed the off-load. The GMT's on the ship were positioning a trainer into its storage container with an overhead hoist. The weapon was rotated 180 degrees when it fell from the hoist! The nut holding the hoist hook to the hoist cable had become unscrewed from numerous rotations. The cotter key holding the nut was missing. No one was hurt, but the ship's GMT's were embarrassed. I filed this away in my memory, as something to always check when using a hoist. It was to save me grief in years to come.

The first of 1967, Allison and I moved into a nice house in the country, about five miles from the base main gate. The house was on a farm that was owned by an older couple. It was a newer house with a double garage. The house had two bedrooms and a fireplace, and it also had a built in kitchen. It was fortunate that the house had a garage, as the Ford blew a head gasket. A garage in Oak Harbor wanted $100 to fix it, but I bought a head gasket for seven dollars and fixed it myself. While the Ford was broken down, I rode to work with Dave Wiesenhahn, who lived about a mile away. We eventually formed a car pool with a First Class Torpedoman that lived close by. He was unique because he had seat belts installed in his car, and he insisted that passengers in his car wear them. At this time very few people wore seat belts. He'd been in an accident a few years previous, and a seat belt had saved his life.

In March my mom, and brothers, Joe and Jerry, came by bus from California for a visit. We had a wonderful time exploring the island and being together. I found out in April that once again I did not make first class. This time it was especially painful, as I'd missed being promoted by 33/100th of a point! I began studying again for the next exam.

An unexplained event happened while we were living at the house in the country. One night at about 10:00 p.m., I was preparing to go to bed. Allison was in the living room knitting.

A long series of windows was on the two walls of the bedroom; the bottoms of the windows were about five feet from the floor, with the tops near the ceiling. I walked into the bedroom, walked around to the side of the bed nearest the windows, pulled the sheet and covers back, and then walked around to the other side of the bed where the light switch was located. I turned off the light, walked around to the other side of the bed, lay down on the bed, and pulled the covers up. I immediately felt pain in my leg; I got out of bed, turned on the light, and saw there were pieces of broken glass in the bed. I then saw a hole in the window that appeared to be a bullet hole. I immediately turned off the light, ran into the living room, and turned off all the lights. I told Allison someone was shooting at the house. I left the house darkened, and called the sheriff. After about fifteen minutes a police car arrived. The officer came to the door, and I let him in and turned on the lights. I showed him the hole in the window. Logic says the hole was made during the time the covers and sheet were pulled back, because there were no glass shards on the blanket covering the bed, the glass pieces were inside the sheets. The police officer looked for a bullet hole in the opposite wall, which contained a large closet, but there was no evidence of a bullet. After an hour investigating, he left. I felt nervous in the bedroom long after that incident. Around this time there had been numerous UFO sightings in the Northwest. Whatever it was, I was thankful it missed me.

The Whidbey Island AUW Shop was almost identical to the Iceland AUW Shop. AUW Shops were located worldwide, with the mission of supplying torpedoes and special weapons to antisubmarine aircraft such as P2V *Neptunes,* and helicopters. GMT's and Torpedomen had their own separate working areas, Torpedomen working in Shop 1, while GMT's worked in Shop 2. Both jobs were technical and precise, but GMT work on nuclear weapons was very different from work on torpedoes. We worked together on some projects, and GMT's had free access to Shop 1, but Torpedomen were not allowed into Shop 2. Each group's clip-on badges were different colors to indicate our level of access.

One of the Torpedomen, a second class, had the sad distinction of being a brother of one of the sailors who was lost at sea in the submarine *USS Thresher* (SSN-593) when she sank into the Atlantic Ocean beyond her crush depth, killing all 129 souls on board. This had happened three years before on 10 April 1963.

The number of sailors assigned to the AUW Shop fluctuated between twenty and twenty-five men. GMTC McKenna was our leading chief. Our division officer was Lieutenant Thompson, who reported to our Weapons Officer, Lieutenant Commander Quinn, who reported to the base commanding officer.

All the doors and vents in the ceiling of the AUW Shop were alarmed. The fence was also electronically alarmed. There were no windows in the building, and just as in Iceland, the roof "sat" on the walls of the shop, so in the event of an explosion the roof would blow off venting the force of the explosion upward, so that the building could be reused.

The "two man rule" was becoming a very strict requirement. This was the requirement that no fewer than two persons are present near a nuclear weapon, in order to prevent access to a weapon by a lone individual. This was not a hard requirement in the early days of nuclear weapons. An incident that pointed out the need for the "two man rule" happened on Wake Island. Lieutenant Thompson, who was on the Island when the incident happened, told this story to us.

At the Wake Island AUW Shop, sailors stood duty as armed guards. One sailor was fond of the gooney birds that populated the Island, and was often teased about it. The armed guard's supervisor drove to the AUW Shop one afternoon on a routine security check. When he arrived at the AUW Shop gate, he found it wide open! Near the gate lay the body of a sailor shot to death, with the dead body of a gooney bird nearby. Inside the AUW Shop were two more sailors shot to death. One of the armed guards was missing. Wake Island was put on alert, and a search began for the missing sailor. He was finally found holed up in a cave, where he had committed suicide. It was speculated that he had "gone over the edge," when teased.

In 1967 the "two man rule" was faithfully complied with. One violation during an inspection would mean failure of the entire inspection. There were two padlocks in place on all access doors, and two man rule procedures became a fact of life with GMT's.

The first of the year I got a "free" car. A seaman on the base wanted to tow the car off base, so he gave it to me. It was a four-door 1956 Chevrolet. It needed engine work, so Dave and I rebuilt the engine. Dave also had a 1955 Dodge station wagon which we worked together on, when not golfing. Allison got a job at a local grocery store, as a cashier. On 16 June, I got word that my sister had given birth to a baby girl; her name was "Lisa."

We had our annual NTPI inspection in July. Dave Wiesenhahn had transferred in June, and I was filling the billet of a first class petty officer. I was also performing a "juggling act," the chief and first class in Shop 2 didn't get along at all, and I was caught in the middle. One would tell me to do one thing, and the other would tell me to do the complete opposite. I tried to please both of them. This was not the last time I was to be in this uncomfortable position in the Navy. It was so obvious that during our inspection, one of the inspectors took me aside for a talk, and said, "I know you're in a difficult situation working for two bosses, but it won't last forever, you're doing a good job." This comment encouraged me. Shortly after the inspection, Chief McKenna retired from the Navy, and went to work for the phone company. GMT1 Doyle Howell then became the Shop 2 supervisor.

We moved out of the house on the farm, not by choice, but because the Dutch farmer's wife was becoming senile, had the keys to the house, and would walk into the house whenever she felt like it. Allison and the farmer's wife got into some terrible arguments, so we moved to a house in town near the Seaplane Base gate. The landlord of the new house wanted the house painted, so I painted it for a month's rent. I took the first class exam again in August. Also in August the blackberries were plentiful on the Island, and I enjoyed picking them, although I often would eat more than I would pick.

One day Chief Harold Dunn of the *Ticonderoga* called me. He came to the house for an overnight visit. He was stationed in Hawaii, and had come home on emergency leave, and was passing through. It was great to see him, and we had a good visit.

In September I bought a 1937 Chevrolet from a kid in Seattle. It was a two-door coupe, and had a 1955 engine in it. I began work restoring it. Also in September I was awarded my second Good Conduct Medal. This was for four years good conduct, and meant I now wore a star on my medal, and ribbon. The first of November I called Allison from work, and said, "I've invited a first class to come over for dinner." She said "OK." When I arrived home, she said, "Where's your friend?" I said, "I'm the First Class!" As of 16 November, 1967, I was promoted to GMT1. This meant I had become a true supervisor, my paperwork increased, and even more daunting was the fact that GMT1 Howell was transferring in seven months, and I would become the Shop 2 supervisor.

We moved once more in November. This time to the house Chief McKenna had lived in since he retired. He was moving to another town. It was a nice house, but had a huge yard that took hours to mow. I'd quit smoking for a few months and my weight shot up to 180 pounds, so the extra exercise did me good.

When I was promoted to first class in November, my "crow" was "tacked on," (a hard punch in the arm over the insignia), by the other first class petty officers in the shop. Junior sailors did not "tack on" the crows of seniors. I now wore one "hash mark" on the lower left sleeve of my dress uniform. This hash mark indicated four years service. After September 1968, I would wear another hash mark indicating eight years in the Navy.

When I was promoted, I received a document signed by the Commanding Officer, Captain Beecher Snipes, which announced my promotion, and also contained the following statement:

> Your appointment as a Petty Officer in the United States Navy carries with it the obligation for you to exercise additional authority and willingly accept greater responsibility. You have not only the authority, but also the responsibility to ensure that subordinates comply with the provisions of United States Navy Regulations, General Orders, and supporting orders and directives. You have the obligation to report to proper authority all offenses committed by persons in the Naval Service which you may observe, and have the authority, as delineated in the Uniform Code of Military Justice, to apprehend known offenders. These responsibilities apply whether you are in a duty or liberty status. You are legally and morally obligated to show in yourself a good example of subordination, courage, zeal, sobriety, neatness and attention to duty. Your every action must be governed by a strong sense of personal moral responsibility in order that this personal leadership will strengthen the character of subordinates so that they will contribute their utmost to the effectiveness and efficiency of the United States Navy.

The latter part of November I bought a bear-hunting permit, and planned a hunting trip with a young third class, who said he had hunted for bear before. We planned to go on a weekend, so early on a Friday morning, with guns, tent, and food, we packed my '63 Ford, and headed east of the town of Mount Vernon, to the Cascade Mountains. We hunted most of the day, and then set up camp that night. I noticed that the sailor that was with me was very careless about where he pointed the barrel of his gun, and didn't seem to know anything about hunting, or setting up camp. I set up the tent, and we slept in sleeping bags. In the morning it was very cold, and when I peeked outside the tent I saw that it had snowed overnight. I set up a gas stove inside the tent, and began cooking breakfast (without any help). I gave my hunting partner a plate of food first, and then began cooking my breakfast. He gulped his breakfast down, and then before I could eat, he accidentally knocked down the center supporting post of the tent, which collapsed on top of us. By the time I got the tent set back up, my breakfast was cold. At that point I called it quits, and we cancelled the bear-hunting trip. I took him back to the barracks, and I went home, and tried to get warm the rest of the weekend.

Christmas of 1967, we had a terrible snowstorm and everyone was snowbound. I couldn't get to the shop for a couple of days.

In December the casualty count of the Vietnam War reached 17,000 killed.

The first of 1968, I joined the Jaycees. I was the only sailor. All the rest of the members were local businessmen, or business owners. They were a fun group, and I made a lot of friends around Oak Harbor, including the chief of police, and the mayor.

All the sailors at the AUW Shop, and the entire Navy were concerned about the capture of the *USS Pueblo* by the North Koreans, and the fate of her 83 crewmen. In February GMT1 Howell and I went fishing in his boat, and I caught my first salmon. It weighed seventeen pounds and was a thrill to catch.

I had five young eighteen to twenty-year-old sailors to supervise at the shop, and they were a "handful." I previously described the second class rate as an "in between" rate, as second class petty officers have some authority, and responsibility, but they are not held as accountable as a first class petty officer. It usually took at least four years to be promoted to first class. "Slick arm" first class, or first class petty officers without a four-year hash mark were very rare. In my case it had taken seven years to be promoted. For the year and a half prior to being promoted, I had studied my rating during my spare time, and on every duty night. One disadvantage GMT's had studying for advancement, or increasing our technical knowledge, was that the subject of our studies was classified. We could not discuss our job outside of a secure area. We had to discipline ourselves to be silent about our job the minute we stepped outside the compound gate, or off the ship. In my year and a half study I had saturated my mind with all the technical publications held by the AUW Shop.

In mid 1967, Lieutenant Thompson had transferred, and a Limited Duty Officer (LDO), Lieutenant McClain transferred in as our AUW Shop officer. Officers and enlisted men generally rotated to different duty assignments on different time cycles. Officers normally transferred every two years, and enlisted men moved every three years. Enlisted men moved under a program called Shorevey/Seavey. Different ratings moved at differing time frames. GMT's stayed on board ship for three years, and shore duty in the U.S. three years, and at differing lengths, overseas shore duty. The frequent movement of officers every two years was primarily so they could experience a large number of different jobs as their careers progressed.

The latter part of 1967 the AUW Shop received a warrant officer. He was a W-1, which meant he'd just received his promotion to warrant officer, and would be on probation for a year before receiving his commission as a chief warrant officer. He was assigned as the Assistant AUW Shop Officer. His name was MacPhearson. He had been an Aviation Ordnanceman First Class, and knew nothing about torpedoes or nuclear weapons.

The war in Vietnam was a constant topic among the sailors at the shop. I had been out of the war for a year and a half, and the tempo, and involvement of the U.S. in the war had increased greatly. The Army was trying to entice Navy first class petty officers into the Army by offering to train them as helicopter pilots, and making them Army warrant officers. The Army warrant officers had a different status than those in the Navy. Army warrant officers received their commissions from the Secretary of the Army, while Navy warrant officers received their commissions from the president; however the pay was the same. The biggest problem with the Army job offer was that the life expectancy of an Army "helo" pilot in Vietnam was very short. The helicopters in the war were called "flying targets." It was a tempting offer for many first class petty officers, and many took the Army up on the offer. The Navy was also asking for volunteers from the first class petty officer ranks, to be trained as captains of 31 foot, water jet propelled, Patrol Boats Riverine (PBR), in the delta river waters of Vietnam.

This also was a tempting offer, as it would be very prestigious to be a captain and have a crew of five or six men. The problem with this offer was that while helos were called flying targets, gunboats were called "floating targets".

Oak Harbor was a Navy town, and Whidbey Island was an isolated community. We were somewhat insulated from the rest of the country, the antiwar demonstrations, draft card burning, and lack of patriotism on college campuses.

I never forgot attending the funeral of a marine who had been a guard at the AUW Shop, and had transferred to Vietnam for a tour of duty of thirteen months (the Army tour was twelve months.) After only three months he was back, in a casket. His hometown was Anacortes, a town near Whidbey Island. The memorial service was held at the Whidbey Island Base Chapel. A number of us from the shop attended. I don't know why they had an open casket; he had been hit in the chest by machine gun fire, and the mortician had done a horrible job. He was prepared for burial in his uniform, and his chest was badly sunken, and his face was not prepared well at all for viewing. The war was remote for all in the country except for those who had been in Vietnam, or those who were training to go. I thought often of those long, endless, hot days in the South China Sea.

After Dave Wiesenhahn transferred, I golfed less. I had tried salmon fishing from the bank with little success, and I continued working on my 1937 Chevy in my garage. I had gotten a young female beagle from Jeff Carlson, just before he transferred to the Philippines. She was a beautiful dog, and I named her "Lady." I often took her to a spot on the base that had a large field of bramble bushes and blackberry bushes with rabbit runs all through the thick bushes. The first time I took her, I went with a Torpedoman from the shop who had an adult beagle. His dog taught Lady how to follow a rabbit's scent. After that I would take her alone about once a week. She would run and bark for about an hour, and then she would crawl back to where I would be waiting for her. Often she would be so tired (but happy) that I would have to carry her back to the car.

I and another sailor attended a three-day class that would qualify us for a 10mm movie projection license so that we could show training movies at the AUW Shop. I particularly remember being cautioned about the dangers of the projector set up. There was a small power cable nicknamed the "cobra," which had electrocuted projector operators in the past, and required cautious handling. After I left Whidbey Island I never "advertised," or let it be known that I was a qualified projectionist, as the projectionist is the sailor always hollered at when something goes wrong during the movie.

I was the second in charge, after GMT1 Howell in Shop 2. In Shop 2 there were also two GMT2's, and five GMTSN's. There were fewer men than when I had first checked in. In January 1968, A GMT1 named Don Parker arrived. It quickly became apparent that he was not mechanically inclined, and not well accepted by the junior men. Howell assigned him to the front office as an administrative assistant. Don was an excellent typist. The job requirements in Shop 2 had been drastically reduced. When I first checked in, GMT's had been responsible for four weapon systems, but our responsibilities had since been reduced to two systems. I enjoyed my increased responsibility but was apprehensive about the future when I would be in charge of Shop 2.

In February I tried steelhead fishing a couple of weekends. Steelheads are rainbow trout that migrate to the ocean and annually return to the fresh water rivers of the Pacific Northwest. These fish can grow to more than thirty pounds in weight. I didn't have the proper gear for fishing for steelhead, so I checked out a rod and reel from the base special services gear locker. One afternoon, after fishing all day without a bite, I was about to quit, as it was illegal to fish after dark, so I made one last cast. I immediately got a bite, and the pole bent almost double. It was a huge fish, I fought it for almost five minutes, and then the line broke. I was heartbroken. The line on the checked out reel was old, and weak. That was the closest I came to catching a steelhead.

In April, Martin Luther King was assassinated. It seemed as though assassination was becoming a common event in America. In addition to the visit from Chief Dunn, I had a surprise visit from Steve Gable who was also on the *Ticonderoga* with me. He had been a GMT2, and had since divorced his wife Jan, and gotten out of the Navy. Another friend, Julian Lindstrom, who was a GMT2 at the AUW Shop for a year, had transferred to an aircraft carrier stationed out of Bremerton, Washington. He also visited me.

Allison and I were friends with a couple we'd met in the Jaycees, named Dave and Lu-Ann. Dave was a realtor, and he and Lu-Ann had a five year old son. We played cards with them once or twice a week. We also helped them refurbish older houses, which Dave would then sell for a profit. The Jaycees would meet monthly, and we made many friends within the club.

One day all the GMT's were to receive training on the proper way to set up explosive charges, for emergency destruction of weapons.

We assembled in a remote area of the base, and the Explosive Ordnance Disposal (EOD) sailors set up an explosive demonstration. They set a charge under a large metal container, and then the EOD sailors had us withdraw to what they said was a safe distance. They detonated the charge, and then we began hearing the "thump," "thump" sound of shrapnel hitting the ground all around us, we froze, and then ran for a small concrete bunker that was nearby. The EOD sailors were embarrassed; we had been too close to the explosion. I never forgot the sound of that shrapnel hitting the ground all around us.

The AUW Shop had a mascot. It was an old Labrador Retriever dog that had been at the shop for as long as anyone could remember. He got along with everyone. His name was "Red," he had gotten into a fight with a crane, and as the result was blind in one eye. Occasionally I would take him home overnight and spoil him. He liked playing with my beagle Lady.

GMT1 Doyle Howell was fond of taking off in the afternoon once a week, going to the Acey-Duecy Club, and "talking shop," and drinking beer. I would accompany him from time to time, and at least we made decisions during these sessions. An establishment in Oak Harbor famous Navy-wide, is the Oak Harbor Tavern, or as it's commonly called the "O.H.T." It was a bar owned by a retired sailor, which catered to sailors. I remember one afternoon; Howell and I were in the O.H.T., when a fight between two guys broke out. The bartender didn't do anything, and the fight continued for about fifteen minutes, with no one attempting to break it up. They finally stopped, and both were bloody, and bruised. The bartender said they were brothers, and fought often, they also always paid for any damages to the O.H.T. caused by the fight.

GMT1 Howell transferred in June. I became the Shop 2 Supervisor, reporting directly to the AUW Shop officers, both Mr. MacPhearson, and Lieutenant McClain. I was responsible for the conduct, training, and technical performance of all the GMT's in the AUW Shop. I was also expected to be the technical source for all matters concerning nuclear weapons. I was in a position unlike any other I had ever been in the Navy. I was free to supervise, and carry out tasks in any manner I chose. I was also the one responsible for the success or failure of the shop in any upcoming inspection. One immediate change I made after Howell left was to re-file inspection weapon records, and organize much of the paperwork that was in disarray. All the GMT's attended morning quarters with the Torpedomen at 0800 each day. At this gathering we were read the plan of the day, by the leading chief, who was a Torpedoman. I instituted an additional morning quarters that was held with just the GMT's in Shop 2. I used this meeting to make daily work assignments, and to discuss any topics I felt the men should know. I also used this time to acknowledge jobs well done, and to recognize exceptional performance. I was copying the style of Gunner White on the *USS Independence*. I tried to be as consistent as possible so the men working for me would know what to expect, and I tried to praise in public, and correct in private.

A presidential candidate, Robert Kennedy was assassinated in Los Angeles. I was shocked, and wondered what the future held for our nation. Demonstrations against the war continued, and burning of draft cards. There seemed to be a general anti-military feeling throughout the country. I was thankful that my family was supportive of my service in the Navy.

I had to contend with the tendency of the younger sailors trying to grow their hair longer than Navy standards permitted. Long hair was the younger generation's statement against the older "establishment." I made arrangement for a mobile "barber-van" to visit the AUW shop parking lot every two weeks. I instituted a requirement that all GMT's get a haircut each time the van visited. At first there was a lot of resistance to this, but eventually they realized if they got a haircut biweekly, I and the AUW Shop officers were satisfied, and even overlooked it if their hair was "borderline long." I tried to keep my uniform and appearance as perfect as possible, as I wanted to set a good example. I insisted that all the GMT's study for advancement, and I set aside time each day for this study. I also created a number of collateral jobs, and insured that everyone had a "job" he could call his own, and demonstrate individual success, or failure, and also show whether he should be given additional responsibility and authority.

Our main efforts were directed toward training to work as a team on nuclear weapons operations, and operations we would be required to demonstrate to inspectors during our inspections. We trained insuring that technical steps were read properly; that the team members accomplished the step correctly and when finished proclaimed, "Check." In order to impress anyone watching the operation, I used a technique I'd learned from Dave Wiesenhahn. The technique was to exaggerate the discipline shown during operations. An example being when a sailor completed a read step, he normally casually stood and waited for the next step to be read. Our technique was at the completion of the step the sailor would step back, and stand at parade rest, with his hands clasped behind his back.

There were many other touches of "show business" in our operations. We ordered blue lab coats for all the assemblymen to be worn during operations. The cleaning man, who was responsible for cleaning all metal, rubber, and plastic parts disassembled, and assembled during an operation, wore a white smock, and rubber surgical gloves. Another touch was tools were handed to the assemblymen upon cloth-covered trays, such as a doctor might be handed surgical tools during an operation. We hoped this exaggeration emphasized how focused our attention was on the task of performing an operation on a weapon. I also wore a white smock, as did GMT1 Parker, who read silently through a technical manual, as a backup, while I read the check sheets out loud. Another touch was a podium, emblazoned with the AUW Shop emblem on the front. The podium had rollers, and I would position the podium at different locations around the weapon we were working on, as I supervised the operation. We trained not only on all the routine maintenance operations, but also emergency procedures, such as what to do in case of a fire, or the dropping of a weapon from a hoist, personnel injuries, and anything that might go wrong during our job efforts.

In June, I traveled to the Washington state capitol, Olympia with a Jaycee friend. The purpose of our trip was to invite the governor to our annual Oak Harbor 4th of July parade and celebration. We met with Governor Evans. He said prior commitments would prevent his attendance, but would send the state attorney general in his place. I enjoyed meeting him, and he seemed to enjoy meeting us. The 4th of July celebration in Oak Harbor was a success. Around this time we had a party at one of the Jaycee member's house, Dave Harrington, who today is one of the largest realtors in Oak Harbor. We watched in amazement the televised riot at the Democratic Convention in Chicago. The turmoil in our country seemed never ending.

In August I attended a Nuclear-Biological-Chemical (NBC) warfare class for two weeks. Our instructors were from San Diego, who traveled up and down the Pacific Coast teaching classes at various bases. We were taught the protective measures to take in the event of a nuclear, biological, or chemical attack from an enemy. It was an interesting class. We learned, for example, that an enemy using chemical agents might first apply a spray to produce vomiting. This would make the use of gas masks practically impossible, rendering the troops exposed and vulnerable to deadly nerve gas. We studied chemical agents such as blister gas, mustard gas, as well as nerve, and blood gases. Some of the gases were harassing gases causing blisters and burns, and others killed almost instantly. One day we were put into a gas chamber, and exposed to tear gas. It was as I remembered tear gas in boot camp, painful and unpleasant.

An antidote for nerve gas is atropine. The antidote was self-injected by the person exposed to nerve gas by a needle thrust into the thigh or buttocks. In order to graduate from the NBC class we had to jam a "training syrette," which was a hollow needle about three inches long with a small tube containing water, into our thigh or buttocks, and squeeze out the contents of the tube into the selected injection site. After we squeezed out the contents of the tube, and before we removed the needle, the instructor had to see the inserted syrette. This was not for the squeamish. I chose my left thigh. Two sailors refused to do it, and thus did not graduate. One marine in the class fainted. It was painful but bearable, the hard part was waiting for the instructor to come around and look at the syrette, as I had to wait a couple of minutes. Along with our graduation certificate we received a certificate, which I have framed on my wall. The certificate reads:

> Associated Society of Self Aid Men (Syettificate of membership).
> This is to certify that on 20 August 1968 GMT1 James S. Little did
> with trepidation but without wincing, voluntarily uncover, puncture
> the seal, insert to the hilt and discharge the contents of one training
> syrette into a selected portion of his anatomy. By act of courage and
> devotion to duty he has hereby earned and is awarded membership
> in the A.S.S.A.M., signed DCCS Dewey E. Sherwood, USN.

In September, I submitted a request to my detailer in Washington, D.C. asking for a twelve-month extension on shore duty. Shortly after my request was mailed, I received an answer, my request was denied, and I was scheduled to transfer June 1969. I was disappointed, but at least I had asked the question.

Also, in September, my Uncle Don and Aunt Pearl Downing came from California for a visit. They were traveling with their camping trailer, and stayed a few days. I enjoyed their visit, although I had to work each day. We did have a nice drive around the island enjoying the beautiful scenery.

Physical fitness in the Navy was still not a serious program. We had horseshoe stakes at one side of the AUW Shop, and we passed horseshoe playing off as physical fitness training. We would quit our normal work at 3:45 pm, and play horseshoes for forty-five minutes each day, if it wasn't raining. After Lieutenant McClain checked in, we began daily volleyball games, which was much more realistic physical training.

On 10 November, the marines had their annual Marine Corp. birthday party celebration. Each year at this time the marines would ask if we would stand their security watches for a twenty-four-hour period so all the marines could attend the party. I stood a four-hour watch from midnight to 4:00 a.m., in the alarm control center in the magazine area. I gained an appreciation for the lonely, boring job this was for the marines who stood this watch each day. There were anxious moments though, it was very dark, and quiet in the woods surrounding the fenced area, and at every sound, I imagined intruders lurking in the shadows waiting to attack!

In November, Allison, and Lu-Ann (our civilian friend) and her son, traveled down to California to visit my parents, and Allison's parents. They were to spend two weeks visiting. After a week, Lu-Ann and her son unexpectedly returned to Oak Harbor. Lu-Ann wouldn't talk to me. My parents did not know what was going on, other than Allison was staying in a motel in Porterville. I called the motel, and Allison wouldn't talk to me. I was baffled about what was going on. I requested leave, and on 13 November, boarded a plane in Seattle and flew south to California.

In California I confronted Allison, and she confessed that she had an affair with Dave, Lu-Ann's husband, and she'd told Lu-Ann, who naturally left and went home. On top of this the car needed repair. I was shocked but not surprised. I told her I couldn't afford for her to stay in a motel, and she would have to stay with her parents. I stayed at my parent's house, and the next night I met her in Lindsay, we talked for a short while, then I returned to my parent's house. About midnight the phone rang at my parents; it was the Porterville police station; they wanted to see me. I went to the police station, and there was an old friend of mine, Butch Coley, it was good to see him. He was now a Porterville city police officer. He said Allison had been making a telephone call at a phone booth, and a drunk had attacked her (or so she said), anyway he said everything was OK now. We talked for a long while, and then I returned home. This was a hectic time; I appreciated my parents' support as always. One morning I was taking a shower, in my parent's home. Without warning, or knocking Allison came storming into the house grabbed my car keys, and ran out of the house. I had intended to return to Washington the next day. I rushed outside from the bathroom in an attempt to catch Allison. She was backing the car up, all I was able to do was to unlatch the hood and throw it up, but she continued driving and escaped. In the future I wished I'd not lost my temper, as this certainly wasn't an adult thing to do. The only enjoyment I got out of this leave period was that it was the first time I'd seen my niece Lisa, and I enjoyed being with my two young brothers.

I flew back to Whidbey Island on the 27th. It had snowed heavily, and I discovered I'd forgotten the key to the house (it was on the car key ring), and left it in California. Luckily I found a bedroom window that had been left unlocked, and I was able to get into the house. The only transportation I had was a 250cc motorcycle I'd had for a couple of months. It was very cold riding a motorcycle in the snow.

I found a lawyer, and began divorce proceedings on the grounds of adultery. Allison did not arrive back in Oak Harbor until 8 December. On that same day, I moved on base into the barracks. It was also my birthday, and I was twenty-six years old.

Allison hired a lawyer, and I was not aware of it at the time, began racking up credit card bills, until all card limits were reached. I learned that the reason Allison had insisted that I come home on emergency leave in December 1965 while I was deployed to Vietnam, was because she feared she had gotten pregnant during my absence on the ship. A family relative revealed to me that he had caught Allison and a man parked in an orange grove in a compromising position while I was overseas. I felt the marriage was ended, and there was no need to continue it. I explained the whole situation to my boss, WO1 McPhearson. He was very understanding, he said to take off any time I needed. I had him somewhat over a barrel, as I was the only supervisor in Shop 2, and our big inspection (NTPI) was scheduled for April. I did have concerns about my security clearance, because any reports of indebtedness to the commanding officer, could put my clearance, and job in jeopardy.

In mid-December I found a 1959 Chevrolet, which I bought for $175. I now at least had a way to get around, instead of freezing on the motorcycle. I went to the same insurance agent I had used for the Ford, and 1937 Chevy, for insurance on the new car. I asked the lady agent if my insurance rates would go up when I divorced. Her attitude before I asked the question was a little cold, after the divorce question her whole attitude changed. She said she had always wondered how I managed to live with Allison. Allison had caused a lot of trouble with the insurance office, when she had a fender bender in Seattle. I had not been aware of how nasty Allison had gotten with her. I apologized, and I ended up with very reasonable insurance rates.

I sold the '37 Chevy Coupe I'd spent so much time working on. I got $250 out of it, and a promise from the sailor I sold it to that he would continue working on restoring it. My beagle puppy "Lady" had disappeared in October during a visit we had made to Allison's cousin in Seattle.

We had been gone a few hours, and Lady was on a leash in the back yard. Upon our return the leash and Lady were gone. A few dogs in the neighborhood had disappeared at the same time. I advertised for her in the paper, but never saw her again.

In December the topic of discussion was the Apollo 8 mission that orbited the moon. This same month I received my first evaluations as Shop 2 Supervisor. They were the highest evaluation marks I'd ever received, 4.0's in all six categories. Oddly enough I was to find out years afterwards that these great evaluations, which were supposed to be copied and sent to Washington, D.C., were never sent from the Whidbey Island Personnel Office, as they should have been. Our country could send men around the moon, but a piece of paper could not find its way across country.

On 27 December, I was scheduled to go to family court to meet with a judge and Allison. Her attitude had not changed; reconciliation was out of the question. I was busy trying to keep ahead of the bills she had made. I learned that Allison had written bad checks while in California. My plans for the future, and emotional state were at a low point. I was depressed about the low salary I was making in the Navy, even though I'd advanced to a senior petty officer rank, my income for 1967 was $4,900, or $408 a month. I wasn't completely convinced that I wanted the Navy as a career? To top it off I stubbed my little toe on a bedpost in the barracks, and broke it. I had it taped at sickbay, and took aspirins.

The middle of January, a GMT2 who worked for me, invited me to go with him over a weekend to visit his sister and brother-in-law in Seattle. This was one of the first football super bowl weekends. The second class was named Walt Graham. Walt was a lot like Pappy Warren on the *Independence*, a career second class. He was unable to pass the first class exam, and was to retire in the future after twenty years as a GMT2. I agreed to go with Walt, and we traveled to Walt's sister's house. They lived on Queen Anne Hill, which was a very exclusive section of Seattle. Their "house" was a mansion, seven stories high. Walt's sister was one of the lead designers for the interior of the 747 jets built by Boeing; her husband had a realtor business in Seattle. They said their house, which had been built around the turn of the century had a friendly ghost who scared their cat, opened and closed doors, and threw things around. The ghost didn't appear while I was visiting. I had a very pleasant weekend, it was a welcome respite from the troubles I was having. Our country also had a new 37th president, President Richard M. Nixon.

February I was busy training in Shop 2 preparing for the big inspection in April. Much of my time was spent trying to educate WO1 MacPhearson about the nuclear weapons program, and what to expect during the inspection, since he had never gone through an NTPI. GMT1 Parker, who worked in the office was an immense help keeping the warrant officer "off my back," so I could concentrate on the training that needed to be accomplished. During this time I was also adjusting to single life. One benefit was that the meals in the chow hall were much better than any I'd gotten during my married life. All first class petty officers ate in a separate section of the chow hall.

In the latter part of 1967 a promising young GMTSN had checked into the AUW Shop, his name was Kaminski, we naturally called him "Ski." In 1968 he was promoted to GMT3. One weekend he and a friend were hiking near a beach on Whidbey Island, and he slipped and fell 150 feet down a cliff. The rescuers had to rappel down the cliff to get him. He had a number of broken bones. The worse injury was to his left leg. He remained unconscious for more than three weeks. Remembering my short hospital stay on the *Ticonderoga,* and because it was the right thing to do, I visited him in the hospital often. His parents flew out from Wisconsin, and his mom stayed for a few months. After he regained consciousness, he could not remember his name, and much of his past. He had to relearn many things including how to walk. He never did regain his full memory. He came back to work at the AUW Shop in February 1969. He still walked with a limp. We put him to work in the front office with Don Parker, who took him under his wing

The last of February, I had a weekend off, so I drove to Canada, and spent one night. I watched a curling game, visited an aquarium, saw a killer whale, and played tourist. I had a nice time, but Canada did not "feel" like the United States, and I felt better when I crossed back over the border.

The middle of February, GMT2 Walt Graham who lived in a small house three miles from the naval base back gate, was sitting in his living room when a large rock came crashing through his front window, barely missing him. He grabbed a twenty-two-caliber pistol he had nearby, and running outside, he fired four shots at a car that was speeding away. It turned out that inside the car were two young seamen from the base who were always courting trouble. Walt was charged with attempted murder, and scheduled for a general court martial. I was called as a character witness for Walt, and one morning I took the witness stand in the courtroom on base. I told the court that Walt was an outstanding sailor whom I enjoyed supervising, which was the truth.

Walt was found not guilty, primarily because he testified that he was trying to hit the gas tank of the car as it was speeding away. His statement was further verified by the fact that the four bullet holes in the car were right above the rear bumper, in a pattern no larger than a hand spread. It goes without saying that Walt was a very good marksman. The two sailors who threw the rock were charged and convicted in a subsequent court martial. Walt was very thankful for my testimony.

In March I was informed where I was to be transferred to in June. I was being assigned to Naval Magazine, Guam, Marianas Islands. Also, in March my relief checked in. His name was GMT1 John Milton, and he could be the topic of an entire book. John was six feet, eight inches tall, and weighed 260 pounds. In the past he had been in the Navy commando branch of the Navy, the SEALS. John, I believe was born too late in history; he would have been a great mountain man, roaming the woods, or a lawman, (or outlaw) in the old west. He wore a huge handlebar moustache. He was married, but his wife did not accompany him, so he moved into the barracks, sharing my room. John was somewhat intimidating in appearance, mostly because of his huge size. I'd never met anyone like him, nor have I since, and we become friends.

When John first met WO1 McPhearson, the warrant officer gave him a lecture about the length of his moustache, it didn't bother John, and few things did. They did not get along well from the very beginning. John lived life to the fullest, and seemed to thrive on getting a reaction out of people, whether it was a positive or negative reaction, he didn't care. Considering the things that were going on in my life at this time, the divorce, upcoming inspection, and my transfer to Guam, friendship with John certainly took my mind off these problems.

John drove a Ford pickup, and when he drank a can of beer, or the infrequent can of coke, after he finished, he would throw the empty can into the bed of the pickup. There were always hundreds of empty cans in the pickup bed. He carried a forty-five-caliber double shot derringer. He had some wild stories about his time in the SEALS, and after I got to know him, I believed these stories. He often drank straight shots of 151 proof rum, which would have killed anyone else. John's wife was in Idaho, with his three daughters. His wife was a red head, and John called her "Big Red," she was going to join him in Oak Harbor in a year.

John had just come from the AUW Shop in the Philippines, where he had been stationed with Jeff Carlson who had transferred from Whidbey. John had some news about Jeff; he said Jeff had lost his security clearance. Jeff and the wife he'd left in Oak Harbor had divorced. He had gotten in trouble by killing some ducks in the Philippine AUW Shop compound. He'd frozen their necks with a fire extinguisher, and then broken them off!

John Milton would enjoy "grossing people out" with juvenile pranks. For example, he'd go up to a stranger in a bar, and ask the guy "Would you like to see my new socks?" The person would look at this giant with a handlebar moustache, and could only say, "Yes." Then John would pull his pants all the way down to his ankles, and say, "See," the shocked guy would usually say, "Nice socks," then John would laugh and buy the guy a drink. When we were drinking, which was most of the time, I thought about trying to keep John low-keyed, but never could. Early one morning John and I were in a diner about 2:30 a.m. having breakfast. John had a plate of bacon and eggs. He cut a long strip of clear fat off one strip of bacon, and said, "Watch this." He stuffed the strip of fat into one of his nostrils, then got up and walked over where two guys were seated having breakfast. He said "Excuse me, can I use your salt shaker?" They said "yes," then John said, "Oh, wait a second," and wrinkling his nose, he pulled out the strip of fat from his nostril, and ate it. The two were too shocked to say anything; John picked up the saltshaker, walked back to our table, shook out some salt, and returned the shaker, saying, "Thanks a lot."

John always carried a goatskin wine bag, full of wine. This was the type of bag you could squirt a stream of wine into your mouth when the bag was squeezed. He was an expert with it. One night in the barracks, after drinking a considerable amount of wine, John said, "I wonder what it would be like to swallow Alka Seltzer." He then got two Alka Seltzers, and promptly swallowed them, followed by liberal squirts of wine. After a few moments, pink foam (he was drinking red wine), began bubbling out his mouth and nose. He began belching and burping loudly; I was worried that I might need to take him to sickbay. He just kept drinking wine, and finally stopped burping. He was miserable the next morning and for a couple of days afterwards. I think this would have killed an average sized man! John had two nicknames in the Navy, one was of course "Big John," and the other was "Animal." He called everyone whether he knew them or not, "shipmate." It was an adventure being around John!

Since John would be taking my job as shop supervisor when I transferred, he stayed by my side while we trained for the big inspection.

It would take four days to complete all the technical operations we would be demonstrating during the NTPI. There was an immense amount of details to consider. This was to be the first time I was wholly responsible for a success or failure.

We had to demonstrate absolute perfection, but I accepted this effort for perfection realizing that's all that could be expected considering the horrific destruction the weapons we were working with were capable of. I had three GMT2's, Williams, Graham, and Raper, two GMT3's, Mitchell and Dodge, and three GMTSN's Bertolin, Smith and Knutson, as well as GMT1 Don Parker, and his assistant GMT3 Kaminski to get through the inspection.

I prepared a schedule of events for the inspection, as well as a large stack of other documents that would be used by the inspectors. I also tried to help WO1 MacPhearson prepare for the inspection. He became increasingly nervous as the date for the inspection drew closer. I felt he was trying to patronize me, because about three weeks prior to the inspection, he said I was doing a great job, and before I left for Guam he was going to recommend that I be awarded a Meritorious Captain's Mast, where I would be congratulated by the commanding officer. He also said he was going to recommend me for the warrant officer program. He realized that his future to a large extent depended on how well I did my job during the inspection. I didn't tell him, but I was determined to do my best not because of fear of negative consequences, but because I wanted the men in Shop 2 to be recognized and rewarded for all the hard work of preparation they had done. I had experienced a small sense of relief from my personal problems by wholly dedicating myself to a purpose I considered being much more important than myself; contributing to the defense of my country. I did have some fear of failure, but not for myself, rather for the men I was leading and responsible for. Two weeks before the NTPI inspection date, we were told that the AUW Shop would also undergo a Defense Nuclear Surety Inspection (DNSI). This was a group of inspectors from Albuquerque, who conducted inspections for the Joint Chiefs of Staff (JCS), of one fourth of all nuclear-capable commands each year. This was not our scheduled time, and was what was called a "surprise inspection," which happened to an unlucky ten percent of Navy nuclear capable commands each year. I thought the warrant officer was going to have a heart attack! I told him we were ready; I secretly hoped he would stay out of the way.

The week before the inspection I didn't schedule any training, and concentrated on touching up paint, and small details. I told everyone on the Monday morning of the inspection I wanted them all to be in their best dungaree uniform, with good haircuts, and spit-shined shoes. I wanted to give a good "first impression" as all the inspectors were military men (DNSI inspectors were from all services, Navy, Marines, Army, and Air Force). The inspectors would primarily be observing our technical abilities, but a squared away, military appearance should impress them favorably. During this pre-inspection time, I tried to appear confident, and unworried, and tried to hide any nervousness. WO1 MacPhearson couldn't understand why we didn't train the week before the inspection began. I told him, if we weren't ready now, we never would be.

The day of the inspection arrived; the first event in the morning was a briefing by the inspectors in the commanding officer's office. I wasn't invited, so my crew and I waited in the AUW Shop. At 8:45 a.m. all the inspectors arrived and were issued visitors' badges. This was a huge crowd; we had to insure the "personnel limits" that were posted in each room of the AUW Shop were not exceeded. Only a certain number of persons could be in any specific room. This was so that in the event of an explosion, only a limited number of people would be lost.

The pre-inspection briefing was conducted in the large working bay of Shop 1 with the inspectors, and weapons officer before the official start of the inspection. During the briefing, a large alarm bell went off. It was Shop 2's air monitoring equipment alarm. The test set had malfunctioned. Another GMT and I immediately raced to the test set, and turned it off. This was not a good way to begin an inspection! I thought WO1 MacPhearson was going to have a heart attack.

We began our technical operations, with six or seven inspectors looking over our shoulders, watching every move. Their eyes widened when they saw our smocks, and methods of passing tools, along with the "show business" of our operations. The inspection was scheduled for four and a half days. At the end of each day I would brief WO McPhearson, LT McClain, and LCDR Brown (Weapons Officer), on the day's progress, and my perception on how we were doing. They would then brief the commanding officer. The inspectors never let on how we were doing. Normally the only time inspectors would speak would be to ask a question, or in the event of a major discrepancy, they would stop the operation, and proclaim a failure.

At the time of an announced failure the inspection would stop, and an inspection date would be set, usually a month later, often with newly assigned senior GMT's, and depending on how serious the failure was, the captain might be relieved which would signal the end of his career. A captain in this predicament would also see to it that those under him went down with him.

On the third day of the inspection, during a technical operation on a Lulu Mark 101 trainer, an electrical test indicated that a hydrostat was faulty. This had never happened before. The inspectors kept asking me what I was going to do. WO1 MacPhearson was absolutely panic stricken. I made a decision, and said, "I'm going to replace the hydrostat", as we had spares in our storeroom. We were authorized to replace it as far as I could tell; even though this was probably the first time in the history of the weapons system a hydrostat was found to be faulty. We replaced it, and this created much additional paperwork. I told the weapons officer that I was sure I'd done the right thing; at least the inspectors didn't stop the inspection. Regardless, it was my decision and my responsibility alone, although secretly, I wished I were more positive that I was right in the action I had taken. The end of the fourth day the inspection was over, we had completed ahead of schedule. We had demonstrated a weapon's movement from the AUW Shop to the magazine, we'd undergone scrutiny during a simulated weapon's accident, and all the technical operations we were required to demonstrate had been completed. All of our test and handling equipment had been inspected, as well as all our files, and paperwork, and much, much more. Now the suspense began. We would be briefed on the fifth day, which was Friday at noon. Everyone would be told the results at the same time, from the captain, down to the junior GMT. On Thursday night I told my crew that whatever the results I was proud of them. WO1 MacPhearson was a nervous wreck; he was smoking three packs of cigarettes a day.

Friday at noon, we assembled in the shop where we had assembled five days previously. The chief inspector of the NTPI stepped up to the podium and addressed the captain, and the rest of us. He began reading the official report: there were some discrepancies in the administration, and security areas, and then he began reading the technical areas I was responsible for, which were about fifteen specific areas. There was not one single discrepancy, and each area received a grade of "Outstanding" the highest possible grade! I couldn't believe my ears. This was an unbelievable achievement. I'd never heard of a perfect inspection. But we were not out of the woods yet, because this was an inspection by two different agencies, and the DNSI Inspector had yet to read his report. He stepped to the podium, and to my relief his report read exactly the same. However, the second he completed reading his report, an Air Force LTCOL, stood up in the audience. He said, "First Class Petty Officer Little, speaking on behalf of all the inspectors, we'd like to tell you that during this inspection you demonstrated the most impressive technical operations seen since Hiroshima!" I was stunned; everyone in the room began clapping, when the applause finally stopped, I said, "Thank you, but all I did was stay out of the way of my crew," at which point everyone clapped again. I can't properly describe the pride and relief I felt learning the outcome of this inspection. Even today this compliment ranks as one of the highest I've been honored to receive, and this is why I previously listed the names of the Shop 2 crew. WO1 MacPhearson was as excited as I'd ever seen him. I told him I planned to give the crew liberal liberty for the next couple of weeks, and he agreed completely. Following the meeting, the captain and the inspectors congratulated all the GMT's. After they left, I shook each man's hand, told each one I was proud to be stationed with him, and thanked each man for his outstanding work. WO1 MacPhearson hosted an impromptu celebration party at the base enlisted club.

The following week, on 25 April, I was scheduled to appear in divorce court, in the county seat, Coupeville, Washington. On this day it was snowing heavily, and I was worried about the fifteen-mile drive to the courthouse. I made it to the courthouse at 9:00 a.m., and then was told I had to wait until 1:00 p.m. Allison did not appear, but was represented by her attorney. Prior to this date I had signed a property settlement which basically said Allison got the car and household effects, and I got all the bills. At 1:00 p.m., in the courtroom, I was directed to the witness box, and after being sworn in, I testified about Allison's adultery, and marital problems. Allison's attorney was basically hostile, asking mostly about my financial status. The judge declared a final divorce. I also was required to provide Allison alimony for a year, and I was also required to pay Allison's lawyer bill.

As I left the courthouse, I felt a sense of relief, but also a sense of failure. As with all divorces there were two sides in the breakup, and I was not entirely blameless. I vowed this would never happen in my life again. I went to Allison's house and told her the divorce was complete, since she had not been present at the burial of our marriage, just as she had not been present at the burial of our son.

She said she had loved me up to today, because she thought I would not go through with the divorce. I did not believe her, for being untruthful was a way of life with her.

In May the pace was much slower in Shop 2. The afterglow of the "Outstanding" grade on our inspections was relished. I concentrated on writing complimentary evaluations on the GMT's that worked for me. A couple of weekends, John and I went cat fishing with a group of Torpedomen who camped at a nearby lake. John and I also visited a beach on a popular swimming hole at another lake, where I met a girl who said she tended a bar at a restaurant in Oak Harbor. Her name was Alma, and she said to come and see her at work some time.

I was having car trouble with the '59 Chevy, and trying to keep ahead of bill collectors. One day John asked me to go with him to Seattle. He was going to visit his married sister who lived there. He explained she had married late in life, as she had been a Catholic nun for fifteen years before turning in her "habit" and marrying. John drank beer all the way to Seattle, which was a two-hour drive. I was curious what his behavior would be like around his sister. As it turned out, he acted the same as always. His sister and husband were very nice people I enjoyed meeting. They were much more reserved than their brother and brother-in-law.

On the subject of driving and drinking, since Oak Harbor was a Navy town, drinking and driving was tolerated, and often overlooked. One night after leaving a party at the house of one of the AUW Shop sailors, I had more than my share of drinks; I was headed for the base. The headlights of an oncoming car passed going in the opposite direction. I saw in my rear view mirror that the car turned around, and soon red lights flashed. I pulled over; A Washington state trooper came to my window, and said, "Hello, you weaved over the center line, where are you headed?" I explained that I was headed for the base. He asked for my registration and license, which I gave him. After what seemed like a long time, he reappeared, gave my license and registration back, and said, "Drive very carefully back to the base, we don't want any head on collisions tonight." I breathed a sigh of relief and returned to the base. I'm not proud of the drinking I did at this time, and I'll not flinch from detailing it. Unfortunately heavy drinking was common among sailors, and most didn't give a second thought to driving while intoxicated.

I visited the bar where Alma, the girl I'd met on the beach worked. I began going to this bar almost every night. She introduced me to an older man who was often in the bar. Everyone called him "Commodore"; he was a retired admiral, and a prominent person in Oak Harbor. He was starting an electric component manufacturing company in Oak Harbor. We became friends, and he tried to persuade me to get out of the Navy, and come to work for him. There were times I considered it, but I still had over a year to go on my current enlistment.

Late one night at the barracks I got a call from Alma. She said her and her ex-husband had gotten into a fight and she wanted to see me. I met her, and tried to comfort her, and our relationship continued from that point. She quit the bar tending job at the Oak Harbor restaurant and bar, and began working at the Fleet Reserve Association Club. I had been an active member of the FRA since being in Oak Harbor. John and I began hanging out there nightly, with Alma supplying free drinks. I continued to date Alma, I did not plan to become too serious with her, as she seemed bent on a path of self-destruction, and she drank heavily, and at times was impossible to be around. She drove a new Dodge Charger that had a powerful engine, and was almost too much car for her to handle safely.

I began having more trouble with my car, so I went to see a friend from the Jaycees who was a car salesman. I'd had very little to do with the Jaycees since my divorce, but he gave me a good deal on a1962 Mercury. It was a four door and in good shape. My transfer date was drawing closer, and being my last few weeks at the AUW Shop, I was taken off the watch bill. This meant I did not have to stand duty every sixth night. One morning during this time, I attended departmental quarters, and was surprised to hear the weapons officer, call out my name, and order me to come forward. I went forward, stood before him, and saluted. He then read a commendation letter addressed to me from the Naval Air Station Commanding Officer, Captain Beecher Snipes. The letter read:

> For the past twelve months, you have served as Leading Petty Officer for the Special Weapons Assembly, Test Crew of the MAUW (Modified Advanced Undersea Weapons) Division of the Weapons Department. During this period, your continued efforts, attention to detail and conscientious and enthusiastic performance of duty have contributed significantly toward the increased operational readiness of the Weapons Department and Command.

> As Shop Supervisor, you were instrumental in your unit receiving an evaluation of outstanding in the technical and safety areas of a recent Navy Technical Standardization Inspection. This unique achievement is indicative of your day-to-day performance and reflects your qualifications for a position of great trust and responsibility. Your constant attention to duty, coupled with your administrative, technical and leadership abilities, has established the criteria for both seniors and subordinates, and is in keeping with the highest standards of Navy performance.
>
> In view of the above, it is with pleasure that I commend you for your outstanding performance of duty while attached to this command. In recognition of your professionalism and dedication, this letter shall be made a part of your official record.

The weapons officer shook my hand, congratulated me, and gave me the letter. I saluted, and returned to my place in ranks.

I began making preparations for my trip to Guam. I didn't know much about Guam, John said he had gone through the island one day, and the climate was a lot like the Philippines. Don Parker and his wife Mary-Ann had a going away party for me at their house. I appreciated them doing this. Don was a good friend. He was more inclined to paperwork, and administration, than technical work. He eventually applied for the limited duty officer program, and was commissioned an ensign. One day I began the checkout process, going to sickbay, the library, personnel office, and all the places I'd checked into three years before. At noon I was in the barracks, and I got a call from Warrant Officer MacPhearson. He said he was going to kick John Milton out of the AUW Shop! A couple of days previously, John had been conducting a training operation since he had taken over my position as shop supervisor, and a cable had been connected improperly. John had caught the mistake, but MacPhearson had been in Shop 2, and made a "big deal" about it. The mistake was inconsequential, and had been corrected, but the warrant officer had been looking for an excuse to get rid of John. He asked me to confirm to the weapons officer that this was a serious mistake. I refused, and told him John was a technical professional, which he was. John was wild, and when on liberty he didn't appear to care about anything, but on the job he was all business, a professional GMT, and serious about the nuclear weapons program. He was highly liked by all at the shop except WO1 MacPhearson. I was to see John in the future in the company of his wife "Big Red." He was a completely different person around her, subdued and polite. He'd always told me that she ruled the house with an iron fist, and after seeing the nice effect she had on John I believed it! Frankly I think John intimidated the warrant officer. I learned after my transfer to Guam that WO1 MacPhearson finally succeeded in his effort to get John kicked out of the Shop, but it was only for six months. When WO1 MacPhearson transferred John came back to the shop. In the interim GMT1 Don Parker was the Shop 2 supervisor.

I received all 4.0's on my transfer evaluation, and had a glowing write-up. I was pleased with them, as these and the previous evaluations were the highest a sailor could be given. I'd learned much about the Gunner's Mate Technician rating in the past three years, and more important, I learned effective ways to lead men. I'd learned that I relished positions of responsibility, and welcomed difficult or demanding tasks.

Finally I was packed and ready to go, although not anxious to leave Whidbey Island. I was going on thirty days transfer leave before departing for Guam. Alma did not want me to go; she was trying to arrange her work schedule, so she could see me in California while I was on leave. I planned on driving the Mercury to my parent's house. I left the base on 1 July 1969. I had said my goodbyes to all my friends the previous day, 30 June, which marked the ninth year I'd been in the U.S. Navy.

Allison had moved from Oak Harbor to Everett, a distance of about thirty miles, where she was taking a class to become a keypunch operator. I still had some clothes and other items that Allison had said I could get before I departed to Guam. It was with apprehension that I drove to her house before beginning the long trip to California.

This was the last time I was to see Allison. I had regrets, but was relieved that our lives were no longer yoked together. It was terrible that the marriage had failed, but it was doomed from the start. We both had made mistakes, the biggest being not knowing each other before marrying. Although it's cruel to say it was probably a blessing that the two children of our marriage had not survived, as they would have had a broken home.

Allison was not destined to have what I'd consider a happy life. She remarried, was arrested a few times, had restraining orders against her parents, and refused to attend her parents' funerals, and other things I'll not mention.

Chapter 8: Guam is Good

I began the long trip to California. Prior to going across the border, I stopped for gas in Oregon and as I'd always loved to eat them, I bought some cherries. When I stopped at the border fruit inspection booth, the inspector saw the cherries on the front seat, and said he had to take them, as fresh fruit wasn't allowed through. I stopped and got more cherries in California. It was very hot the further I drove south. After more than 800 miles, I finally arrived at my parent's house in Strathmore.

I had an enjoyable leave. One weekend, my parents, brothers, and I went backpacking in an area in the Sierra Nevada Mountains, called Mineral King. It was good being with those I loved, and camping outdoors, I enjoyed it thoroughly.

Alma flew down from Washington to visit her mother in Salinas, California, which was west of Strathmore, and I drove over to see her for a few days. One evening we watched the landing on the moon, and Neil Armstrong setting foot on the moon's surface. A friend of Alma's owned a gas station, and I worked for him a couple of days earning extra money.

The first part of August, with packed sea bag, my mom drove me to Travis Air Force Base where I would depart the United States for Guam. I bid mom farewell and boarded the plane; after a brief stop in Hawaii, we landed at the International Airport, Agana, Guam. Upon stepping off the plane, passengers saw the words painted above the terminal door, "GUAM IS GOOD." The heat and humidity hit me like a blast furnace when I stepped off the plane. It reminded me of the South China Sea climate, on those times the *Ticonderoga* pulled into the Philippines. The heat was made more unbearable by the fact that I had on my wool dress blue uniform, which we were required to wear when traveling between duty stations. After undergoing a customs inspection of my sea bag, I called the quarterdeck of the Naval Magazine, and asked for transportation. A little over an hour later, a sailor arrived in a van, and after a ride lasting about thirty minutes, we arrived at the marine guarded front gate of the Naval Magazine. It was dark, so I couldn't see much of my new duty station, other than it was surrounded by jungle. I handed my orders and records over to the petty officer on watch in the administration building quarterdeck. The sailor I'd traveled with walked with me to the barracks that was to be my new home. I was in the first class section of the barracks, which was located on the second floor of a two-story barracks. The Naval Magazine Marine Detachment occupied the rest of the barracks. My "check in" date was 8 August 1969.

I knew very little about Guam, other than it was a battlefield during World War II, and it was hot and humid. I was to learn later that Guam is a United States unincorporated territory, and Guamanians are U.S. citizens. The "pure" natives of Guam are "Chamorros." No one knows for sure when or how the original Chamorros arrived on the island of Guam, or where they came from? Guamanians are best described as Polynesians, with light complexion and jet-black hair. Spanish conquerors in the mid seventeenth century were unable to defeat the Chamorros for twenty-five years! Finally, muskets and gunpowder versus slings and spears won, and they subdued the Guamanians, only by eliminating the entire male population! Widowed women and their daughters married Philippine and Mexican troops stationed in Guam. Most of Guam's population practices Roman Catholicism.

In 1898 America captured Guam at the start of the Spanish-American War. The Treaty of Paris (1898) allotted Guam to the U.S. to be administered under the Department of the Navy. The U. S. sold the rest of the Marianas Islands to Germany. After Germany's defeat in WW I, Japan was granted a mandate to the Marianas. During World War II, 5,000 Japanese who quickly forced 400 U.S. military men and women to surrender, invaded Guam. Guam remained under Japanese rule until 21 July 1944 when U.S. forces liberated the Island. Admiral Chester Nimitz was made governor. Without a doubt World War II was the most significant happening on Guam, in the 20th century. An interesting history note, Ferdinand Magellan landed in Guam in 1521 on his historic around the world sailing trip.

In 1969 the population of Guam including military members was close to 85,000 people. Guam is the largest of 2,000 islands scattered between Hawaii and the Philippines. The annual average rainfall is eighty-five inches; the rainy season is from July to December. The average high temperature is eighty-five degrees, the average low seventy-five degrees. The humidity averages eighty percent. Typhoons occur near Guam, in 1962 a destructive typhoon named Karen, struck Guam with winds up to 150 knots. This typhoon destroyed seventy-five percent of the island's structures.

Guam is shaped like a footprint, thirty miles long, the width at its narrowest is four miles across, and its widest twelve miles across, and the island is 225 square miles in size.

The following is a local legend about the formation of Guam[28]:

In the old days, when much of the earth was still covered by water, two huge giants lived in the Western Pacific area. The first was Puntan, said to have been the strongest man in the world, and the second was his sister, Fuuna. When Puntan was ready to die, he willed his magical powers to his sister and told her to take his body, once he died, and divide it into separate parts. These he said could be used to make different parts of the earth and sky.

After her large brother had died, Fuuna did as she had been commanded and took his body apart. She tossed his breast into the air to make the sky and then his two eyes to make the sun and moon. Once this had been done, she turned the body over on its stomach, placed it in the water, and created the island of Guam.

Today, according to some people, you can see how much the island looks like a giant's back by climbing Mt. Santa Rosa in the northeast. Local names have been applied to parts of his anatomy. Barrigada (side) is his side, nearby Tiyan (belly) Hill, is his stomach, and Hilaan (tongue) Point, his mouth and tongue, just to name a few. The highest point on Guam, is Ritidian Point, which is 600 feet above sea level, Guam's center is 200 feet below sea level. Scientists say Guam was formed when a pair of volcanoes sank beneath the ocean, and left two separate chunks of land. The lava remains eventually fused together, and a huge coral polyp community formed the majority of the land. The island is a lush green jungle populated by various creatures, which I'll describe later.

Words I noticed at the airport and on license plates was "HAFA ADAI," pronounced "Hah-fah day." I learned it was Guam's equivalent of Hawaii's "Aloha." "Hafa Adai" like "Aloha," is a catch all phrase meaning "Hello," "How are you?" and "Gee you're looking good today!" It's a friendly, easy expression, that appears everywhere in Guam.

The next day after my arrival, I began the check-in process. I was a little weary with jet lag. My trip had taken twenty-six hours. To my dismay I discovered that one of my creditors had written a letter of complaint to the Naval Magazine Captain about non-receipt of a monthly payment. I was scheduled to talk to the captain about it! This was not a good way to start at a new duty station! The creditor was a company called Interstate Securities; I was to discover that they were unscrupulous, and my opinion was confirmed a few years later when they defaulted on loans, and went bankrupt.

The Naval Magazine was isolated from the populated areas of Guam, purposely so, in the event of an accidental explosion. Naval Magazine was a considerable distance from the main naval station, which was a much larger base. It was good to discover that there was GMT's stationed at Naval Magazine that I'd been stationed with before. There was George Holden, who I'd gone to "A" school with. We had been class leaders when our class traveled across the country from Great Lakes to Albuquerque. George was also a first class, and now married to Anita. GMT2 Lloyd Wilson, who I'd been with on the *Ticonderoga*, was also stationed at the magazine. It was always a relief to see familiar faces when I checked into a new command.

The commanding officer of the magazine, CDR D.G. Blodgett required every sailor in the command to have a crew-cut haircut. Naval Magazine sailors were not permitted to get a haircut at any barbershop other than the Naval Magazine barbershop. This was a requirement that was immensely disliked by the younger sailors.

For me Naval Magazine Guam was a drastic change from the Whidbey Island AUW Shop. At the AUW Shop, I had been in charge, had almost unlimited authority, now I was just a "face in the crowd." There were more than forty GMT's stationed at the magazine. I was now on an isolated base reminiscent of Iceland except for the climate. The only transportation I had was a Navy bus that served the bases on Guam on weekdays during working hours and with infrequent schedules on weekends. There were a variety of things for married sailors, to do, and also for those with transportation. My pastimes were very limited, as I was struggling with a never-ending parade of bills, and I had no transportation.

The first class section of the barracks was nice. There was six single first class that lived in the barracks. We had a television lounge, and a refrigerator with soft drinks, and beer. We even had a "houseboy." He was an older Guamanian in his sixties who had been promised by the United States that he would always have a job as a reward for the underground work he had done for our country during World War II. The Japanese had tortured him, and it affected him mentally, he had a childlike personality. His name was Zeus.

He would clean and sweep our section of the barracks, as well as make our beds daily. We were supposed to give him fifty cents a payday, but most gave him more. He would also take our clothes to the laundry, and return them.

We all had single bunk beds, and several metal, stand up lockers for our uniform and civilian clothes storage. The lockers had electric heaters inside that were supposed to retard the natural occurring mildew on our clothes, and leather items such as belts, and shoes. All the windows had screens, and we had electric fans, the only air-conditioned area was our television lounge.

What follows is a magazine history, and explanation of the magazine's mission; U.S. Naval Magazine, Guam had a primary mission to provide ordnance support to units of the Pacific Fleet operating in the Western Pacific. Logistic services provided, to the Fleet have undergone considerable change since the Japanese at this location commenced ordnance operations during World War II, the Navy ammunition storage area was a major ammunition supply base for the Pacific Fleet with more than double the present (1969) storage requirements. Forty officers and 1,300 enlisted men were assigned here by the end World War II. The workload and number of personnel dropped off sharply after 1945, while the Korean conflict created a substantial increase in the workload. Early in the Vietnam War, the Naval Magazine shipped nearly all ordnance on board to forward areas and thereby reduced ammunition stock levels to an all time low. I witnessed this shortage when working with the World War II ordnance on the *USS Ticonderoga.*

The activity was officially commissioned as U.S. Naval Ammunition Depot, Guam in February 1945 and re-designated as U.S. Naval Magazine, Guam in August 1949. The Naval Magazine is located in the south central portion of the island fairly well isolated from populated areas and occupies an area of 8,800 acres. The mission, of the Naval Magazine was to receive, renovate, maintain, store and issue ammunition, explosives, and expendable ordnance materials. Earth-covered magazines numbered 236, available for storage of conventional ammunition and classified ordnance. The entire military reservation was designated as a wildlife refuge. The command was authorized 16 officers and 165 enlisted personnel.

Two tenant activities performed their primary tasks at Naval Magazine, Guam. Guard Company, Marine Barracks, Guam provided security for Naval Magazine. Explosive Ordnance Disposal (EOD) Group One, Detachment, Guam was assigned to support Naval Magazine operations and also support other military activities, Government of Guam and the Trust territories of the Pacific in explosive ordnance recovery and disposal. U.S. Naval Magazine Guam was a major ammunition storage point for support of U.S. contingency plans in the Western Pacific.

My evaluations from Whidbey Island recommended me for the warrant officer program, which involved a lengthy application submission, an oral test, a physical, and a recommendation by the commanding officer. I would also have to extend my enlistment for a year; I declined.

I met with the executive officer about the letter sent to the command by Interstate Securities. I tried to assure him that I was meeting my obligations to creditors, and this was not indicative of my management of personal affairs. He seemed to be satisfied with my explanations.

My first job was the same as it had been in the past when I checked into a new command, the "job" of waiting for my security clearance confirmation. Daily I went to the armory near the barracks, sat around, drank coffee, and tried to stay out of the way of the people who worked in the armory.

One weekend Lloyd Wilson invited me to his house. His wife Betsy, stepdaughter and two-year-old son were living in a "booney shack" (Guamanian concrete house), while waiting for base housing to be available. Lloyd and Betsy took me on a tour of the island. They had a '62 Chevy Impala. Most cars on Guam had severe rust problems if they were over a couple of years old. I enjoyed my tour of the island. Palm and coconut trees covered the island. The Guam villages we visited all had a huge Catholic church in the town square. Many of the homes were made of concrete, the poorer sections of the town, had tin roofs. There were a lot of chickens running about. Each town, and at frequent intervals there were "Sari-Sari" stores, or small local neighborhood grocery and hardware stores, that sold a little bit of everything. The scenery was beautiful, thick green jungle, white clean beaches, with the blue-green ocean glimmering in the sunlight. Lloyd showed me a lot of interesting sights such as Magellan's monument in the town of Umatac, which marked the area he landed on Guam during his round the world trip. We also looked at the remains of a Spanish Army garrison, and a Spanish lookout point over the bay of Umatac. I saw Bear Rock, which was near the town of Inarajan, and looked very much like a large bear standing on his hind legs. We drove by the University of Guam, Anderson Air Force Base, and Agana, which was the Capitol of Guam.

Agana was the largest city on the island, with a few five and six story buildings. Apra Harbor, which was south of Agana, was home to the *USS Proteus* (AS-19), a submarine tender, whose mission was to repair and tend to Polaris submarines.

There were large numbers of sailors, Air Force airmen, soldiers, and Coast Guard members stationed on Guam. There were approximately 20,000 military and government workers on Guam, out of a population of 85,000.

The rains were like no others I'd experienced. Often the rain would come down in "buckets," for about fifteen minutes, then the sun would shine with a vengeance, and Guam would be like a huge steam room.

The scars of World War II were visible throughout Guam in more ways than one. The explosive ordnance disposal team stationed at the magazine was constantly being called out to take care of bombs, ammunition, hand grenades, and all kinds of unexploded ordnance lying about Guam. During my road tour of Guam with Lloyd, we walked about fifteen minutes into the jungle to an area called the "tank field." Here there were three rusted Japanese tanks in a field. The hills and jungle were honeycombed with caves that had been used by the Japanese Army. It was hard to imagine the hardships, and difficulties of fighting a war in an environment such as Guam. I gained an even greater respect for the men of our country who fought World War II in such tropical places as Guam.

I continued going to the armory daily, while waiting for my security clearance confirmation. I was notified that I would be attending semi-truck, and forklift driving school during my wait. The schools began on a Monday, and were conducted on the naval station. Two other GMT's were scheduled to attend school with me. One of the GMT's was also a first class, and lived in base housing just outside the magazine gate, so the third class GMT and I were able to ride to the naval station with him in his personal vehicle each day to and from class. The class was held in a Quonset hut on the naval base, and conducted by a Guamanian, who had taught this class for many years. The first day and a half we had classroom lectures on the operation of an electric forklift, then for the next few days we practiced driving the forklift. On Friday, the last day of the forklift class we had to demonstrate our ability to drive the forklift by driving forward through an "S" shaped course outlined by empty oil drums, and then drive in reverse through the same tight course. We were not permitted to hit a drum, and everyone passed.

The following Monday, we began semi-truck driving school. The trucks we were to drive were old International Harvester trucks, fifteen to twenty years old, with seventeen forward gear transmissions. We had classroom lectures, and then were taken to an old Japanese airstrip, located in the jungle, on the base, where we practiced driving the semi-trucks. We practiced driving a semi-tractor with two trailers hooked up, backing the two trailers between rows of empty oil drums, from both directions. As in forklift school, we were not permitted to hit any of the drums in the rows with the trailers, or the tractor. Backing the trailers with control took a lot of practice, the truck cabs were not air conditioned, and the diesel engine put off a lot of heat. The temperature in the cab was more than 110 degrees, so we could only drive for about thirty minutes, then trade with another student, and cool off. On the final day of the class we had to demonstrate our backing skills to the instructor, and also go on a road trip with him. It was a chore to shift seventeen times, and also downshift when coming to a stop. We had to double clutch in order to shift the old transmission gears. The Guamanian instructor was a nervous guy, and shouted at the top of his voice throughout the driving test. All in the class of ten students passed, and were issued semi-truck licenses.

The latter part of August, although I had not yet received my clearance, I was invited to a division party and barbeque. I was to learn that this was a monthly affair. The party was held at a beach on the naval station called Gab Gab Beach. I borrowed a pair of swim fins, and goggles with a snorkel, and went for a swim. The underwater coral reefs were amazingly beautiful. As I swam, I saw a huge moray eel swimming a few feet from me; I quickly got out of the water. I was to learn later that moray eels were plentiful in the waters around Guam, and seldom bothered you, unless you bothered them. Still, it was unsettling to see a huge snake like creature with a mouth full of needle sharp teeth. The Guamanians considered eels a delicious delicacy. Their method of catching them was courageous. They would wrap a burlap sack around their forearm, dive down to an eel hole in the coral, poke a stick into the hole, and jab until the eel was irritated enough to come out biting. The eel would bite into the burlap wrapped arm entangling its teeth, and then the swimmer would rise to the surface, with the wriggling eel caught on the burlap, and cut off the head with a machete.

My family was faithful writing to me, and sending "care" packages, which I greatly appreciated. One welcome item included in the packages was mosquito repellant, as the mosquitoes on Guam were ferocious! My brother Jerry had gotten a bad dog bite while visiting our sister in Fresno, California.

The dog belonged to a neighbor and had unexpectedly attacked him. My brother Joe had gone to a summer church camp at Hume Lake, California.

President Nixon had ordered that the Navy be reduced 72,000 men by July 1970. This meant I might be discharged before my scheduled discharge date in May.

I happened upon an interesting sight one afternoon, on the naval station after my driving school class. It was a small cove called the "shark pit." A few years previously there had been a rabies scare on Guam, and many of the dogs on the island had been killed, and dumped into the cove. This cove was still used as a garbage dump, which attracted large numbers of sharks. It was rumored that an exceptionally large hammerhead shark was often seen here. I saw a few large shapes in the water, which caused me to think this would not be a good swimming hole!

A popular pastime among the sailors on Guam, was bowling. The bowling alley had the best air conditioners on the base, as it was important to keep the wooden alleys cool, and in good shape. I joined a bowling team with Lloyd Wilson, and five other sailors. We bowled once a week, and called our team the "Magazine Hamburgers." We had bowling shirts with our names on them, and a hamburger embossed on the back.

The Guam Naval Station had a large exchange, which I enjoyed shopping at. Many items from the Far East were offered for sale. I bought two wooden bowls, with wood carved fruit, for my parents, and one for my sister.

The Naval Magazine movie theater, which was next to my barracks, showed a movie every night except Sunday night. The "theater" was rows of wooden benches, with a roof without walls. It was actually an open air shed. Moviegoers were always attacked by mosquitoes, and large moths, which were attracted by the flickering light of the movie projector.

The acey ducey club, which was open to second and first class petty officers only, showed a movie every Sunday afternoon. The senior chief of my division "ORT Division," Master Chief St. Onge managed the acey ducey club. He was married, but his wife had not accompanied him to Guam, so he was only serving twelve months on Guam, instead of twenty-four months.

The acey ducey club closed nightly on weekdays at 12:30 a.m., and on weekends at 2:00 a.m. As I mentioned the Naval Magazine was a game preserve, and there were large herds of caribous, that roamed throughout the magazine jungles. Jesuit Missionaries first brought caribou, or water buffalo, also found in Asia and Africa, to Guam in the 1700's. There was one large rogue male caribou, identified by the fact that he had one horn missing who delighted in lurking in the shadows by the acey ducey club, and chasing unsuspecting sailors toward the barracks at closing time. It was about 400 yards from the club to the barracks. Usually if a sailor was chased, upon reaching the barracks they would call the club and give the warning, "George is out tonight." This was the name given to the one horned caribou, "George." He never gored or harmed anyone, but would run just fast enough to scare sailors that had been drinking at the club to become sober, and run as fast as possible. He chased GMT1 Larry Walters and me one night. It was frightful to hear a loud snort, and see a huge creature weighing close to a ton come charging out of the shadows with a lowered head coming straight at you! When George became too much of a nuisance, he would be herded away from the base administration area, but would usually be back after a couple of months. Since he had a broken horn, and was an older caribou, it was thought that younger males had chased him from his herd?

Along with caribous, there were other unusual creatures, as well as a few oddities about Guam, which I'll discuss. There was a special reference to time on Guam; it was called "Guam time," or "island time." On Guam time is never an important factor. An example, if someone invites you to a party that starts at 7:30 p.m., what they really mean is to be there at 8:00 p.m. or 8:30! On Guam no one is punctual, and no one seems to mind? There is perpetual tardiness, even in government offices. Everyone is always at least thirty minutes late. Newcomers eventually get used to "Guam time." Guam has a well-publicized saying "Guam is where America's day begins." Guam is the westernmost possession of the United States, and is located west of the International Date Line. Flying to Guam from America, you lose a day passing over the International Date Line, therefore Guam's "today," is America's tomorrow.

On the Marianas Islands most of the natives chew betel nuts. The nut is a mild intoxicant, and an important part of traditional culture. This nut is chewed, as others chew chewing gum. The nut comes from the fruit of a palm called "pugua." The nuts vary in color, depending on maturity, from deep yellow to deep red. Inside the husk, the meat is either white, or red. The white is milder, but older people seem to prefer the bitter red variety, which is quite a bit stronger. Once the fibrous husk is broken off, the nut is usually sliced, frosted with slaked lime and then wrapped or chewed with tobacco or the leaf of the "pupulu" or piper betel.

This creeping vine is part of the pepper family and is often cultivated near houses on Guam for betel chewing. Betel nuts apparently had a negative impact on dental health, because the older Guamanians that had chewed betel nuts most of their lives had black stubs for teeth. Betel nuts are also addictive, and not permitted in the United States. Many sailors acquired a taste for betel nuts. I tried to chew one I bought in a Guam market, but it was very bitter, and I soon spit it out.

On the subject of intoxicating items, Guamanians version of America's "moonshine liquor" is a drink called "tuba." Catching the sap of certain coconut trees makes this drink. I'm not clear on the exact procedures? But tuba was very potent and ranged in color from clear to milky white. One sip would cause your head to spin!

Sometimes called the "robber crab" because of its knack for entering an open house and carrying off small objects, the coconut crab is another one of Guam's wonders. Nocturnal creatures, the crabs have the appearance of a large brownish-red spider! Their six long, slender spike-like legs and two front claws enable them to easily climb trees. The coconut crab climbs coconut trees for coconuts. Its claws are unbelievably powerful. There are stories of the crabs cutting their way out of empty steel oil drums. The crabs return to the sea to spawn, and the young coconut crabs remain in the sea several months until old enough to migrate to shore. Guamanians consider the crabs a delicacy, and relish eating the crabs; however some Guamanians also have missing fingers from being careless when catching a crab for dinner.

Geckos are among the first animals a newcomer to Guam notices. If you spot a tiny three to four inch lizard skittering across the ceiling, don't scream it's a gecko, Guam's answer to the common cricket. These harmless lizards eat insects and are considered by all on Guam as loveable neighbors. They perform their acrobatics and scurry across smooth ceilings, thanks to five flattened toes that sport microscopic clinging hairs. Geckos live in the wild but seem to prefer inhabited areas. Unlike other lizards they make a chirping sound, hence their name. Geckos lay two tiny white eggs in inconspicuous places that hatch a short time later. While they may be startling to newcomers, most Guamanian residents consider geckos' friends and allies against pesky insects. If you see a two-tailed gecko, according to Guamanian custom, you're living in a lucky house. If you kill a gecko, it's considered bad luck!

Other unique reptiles on Guam include the monitor lizard. These monsters reach as long as six feet, and are seldom seen by residents. There are numerous species of snakes, but none are poisonous. Snakes often caused power outages by climbing up power poles into power transformers and shorting them out. Many years in the future from 1969, a certain species of snakes caused tremendous problems on Guam by killing all bird life, and becoming very aggressive toward humans.

As well as caribou on the Naval Magazine property there were also herds of wild pigs, and deer. The deer were unique because they made a barking sound like a dog. Speaking of dogs, there were packs of wild dogs running wild in the jungle. The marines and sailors were authorized to shot any wild dogs that were seen.

At night on Guam, toads would come out by the thousands. They helped keep the insect population down, but many met their end on the roads of Guam. While driving in your automobile at night you would hear "pop, pop, pop" as your wheels ran over toads. People who had pet dogs had to watch them to insure they didn't bite the toads, as they were poisonous to canines. Snails were numerous on Guam; the Japanese Army had introduced them to Guam during the war, as Japanese included snails in their diet. The snails flourished in Guam's tropical climate, so as well as hearing "pop" which signaled a toad's demise, you often heard a "crunch" when running over a snail in the road.

On the subject of driving, Guam's roads were made of coral, and when it rained making the roads wet, you had to drive very cautiously, because the roads became as slick as ice. Something in the coral composition became very slippery when wet.

Tropical fruit was plentiful in the jungles of Guam. There were bananas, mangos, papayas, coconuts, star apples, and many other varieties of fruit. A friend of mine, GMT3 Joe Murphy enjoyed going into the jungle and finding betel nut trees, banana trees, and others. One day he showed me a star apple tree that had a deeply worn path underneath it that was in the shape of a circle that had been made by wild pigs trying to reach the sweet star apples hanging on the limbs.

There were very few creatures or things on land in Guam that could cause humans harm, but step a foot in the ocean and it was an entirely different matter. There were many creatures in the ocean around Guam that could harm or kill a person.

The first hazard was the coral reef. If you were scratched by the coral, or cut by it, small pieces of the coral would be dislodged into the cut or scratch, and continue to grow, preventing healing of the wound. We were advised to never walk in the surf, or swim bare footed, but to wear tennis shoes.

This was a precautionary measure against stonefish. These were fish that lay on the ocean floor, often in the surf, that looked exactly like a stone lying in the sand. If disturbed, spines on the back of the stonefish would be erected, and these spines contained a potent poison. A stonefish could kill a small child; an adult would suffer a severe illness, and tissue loss around the spine puncture.

There were sharks in the ocean, mako or tiger sharks, and hammerheads, which are considered man-eaters. There were barracudas, and moray eels, many with bodies as large as your leg. There were also sea snakes whose venom was more powerful than any land-based snake. The sea snakes mouth however is smaller than most snakes, and they bite few people. In Guam's ocean there were lionfish, and scorpion fish, which were beautiful fish, but deadly, the spines on their bodies contained venom, that they would inject into anyone who brushed against them. There were deadly seashells that had stingers, which would inject poison into a person's hand, unless he or she knew the proper way to handle the shell. The proper way to pick up a live cone shaped seashell is to grasp the shell by the large end of the cone, as the shell's stinger comes out the small opening at the small end of the cone, and the stinger only comes out a short distance. Stingrays were plentiful in the water; they would lay partially covered in the sand, and if disturbed would whip venom tipped tails. There were stinging jellyfish, and many other creatures in the sea that could be hazardous. You had to have an adventurous spirit to go into the ocean surrounding Guam. The island also is a famous Pacific Blue Marlin fishing spot. A large blue marlin weighing 1,153 pound was stuffed and displayed at the Guam International Airport, and was a former world record caught fish.

As I mentioned, the Naval Magazine was a game preserve. Located in the middle of magazine property was a large man made fresh water lake. This was Fena Lake, the largest body of fresh water on the island. It was against the law for Guamanians to fish or hunt on magazine property. The marines patrolled the property boundaries, and often caught poachers, and upon occasions had shots fired at them. Many Guamanians were understandably resentful about having an off-limits area in the middle of their island, where they had roamed freely in the past without any restrictions.

Shortly after my graduation from driving school, my security clearance confirmation came in, and after my badge picture was taken, I was issued my security badge, which was to be worn anytime I was within a specific area of the magazine. Just as at other commands I had been stationed at, marines provided security, and controlled the entry and exit points, exchanging badges for the GMT's.

Sailors assigned to the magazine were permitted to fish in Fena Lake. The magazine had a large houseboat, capable of accommodating ten or more people, powered by a twenty-five-horse power engine, called the *Fena Queen*. There were also a couple of twelve-foot outboard motor boats available for the use of sailors and marines. These boats were issued on a first come, first serve basis. One weekend ten of us checked out the *Fena Queen*. Lloyd Wilson lent me a fishing pole. The fish we were after were called Tucanery, a bass originally from South America that had been planted in Fena Lake a number of years previously. They were a very colorful fish, with red, yellow, and black stripes. Tucaneries had a marking near their tail that looked like a huge red eye. They looked a lot like a large mouth bass. Some weighed as much as six pounds. Also in Fena Lake was Tilapia, which looked like huge black perch. The most common bait used were worms, which was used with a bobber, also red yarn was used for Tucaneries. My first fishing trip, we didn't catch anything except a few fresh water eels. These eels were very large, and aggressive. When brought into the boat, they would try to bite anyone within range of their needle sharp teeth. Guamanians considered fresh water eels more of a treat than the saltwater eels. We saw a lot of bats zipping around Fena Lake, catching insects, I learned these bats also ate fruit, and were naturally called "fruit bats." The Guamanians also relished these bats as eatable. Earthquakes were common on Guam. Most were barely felt, but occasionally there would be a good "jolt."

Monthly after paying bills, I had around $109 a month spending money. I got news from home that my sister Linda was expecting a second baby in February. She was living in Fresno, California while her husband attended college. The personnel office told me that my discharge date would be around the first part of the year. At this point I was not sure about my future? I realized that ten years in the Navy was a large investment of time, but I was not happy at all in Guam.

There were forty enlisted GMT's assigned to the magazine. Our work area was Technical Ordnance Division, or "ORT Division," within an area of the magazine called the Limited Area. This area was three miles from the main administrative area of the base. My transportation to my work area from the barracks was a Navy pickup, with a covered bed, which provided cover from the frequent rains.

This pickup would also transport the single sailors back and forth for lunch, which was in the mess hall located in the administration area. Married sailors drove their personal vehicles back and forth to work. In order to enter the Limited Area we had to exchange our personal security badges for the clip on security badges which were worn at all times within this area. Armed marines, who were authorized to use deadly force against any intruder, guarded this area. Armed marines also patrolled the outermost boundaries of the magazine, watching not only for intruders, but also game poachers. Within the fenced Limited Area was a bunker, which housed a Marine Reaction Force, and Alarm Center. There were also lookout towers at corners of the Limited Area, which were manned by armed marines twenty-four hours a day. There was a large building which was the working headquarters for about ten GMT's who conducted maintenance on the outside grounds, and individual magazines within the Limited Area. They also transported ordnance to and from the magazines to the Main Assembly Plant. This group of sailors was called the Outside Handling Crew. The assembly plant housed about thirty GMT's as well as the ORT Division Officer. It was within the assembly plant that operations were conducted at periodic intervals, for maintenance and required inspections. The assembly plant building contained a number of working bays, which was the assigned working area of assembly crews. These bays were called "Hooks," where each assembly team would work. The plant also contained offices for the division officer, and assistant division officer, leading chief petty officer, two other chiefs, and George Holden who was the leading petty officer. Within the building was also a coffee locker, and head facilities.

I saw a GMT2 in the plant office named Buzanski. I thought he was a GMT I had attended school in Albuquerque with. However he told me I was mistaken, he was the brother of the guy I'd gone to school with. He was younger, but looked exactly like his brother. He then told me a sad story about his brother. He had stayed in the Navy four years after school, and then got out. One night after a fight with his girlfriend, he committed suicide by rigging the exhaust hose inside of his car, and running the engine until he died of inhaling the fumes.

The plant had three assembly teams, and I was assigned as Hook Leader, of one of the assembly teams. As the senior first class within the assembly bay, I was also responsible for the cleanliness of the assembly bay, and I supervised all field days. The systems I was assigned to work on were unfamiliar to me. One of them was a surface to air missile, which I'd only seen in A school. I felt uncomfortable about my lack of knowledge, and did a lot of studying of technical manuals on the weapons I was responsible for. I had four GMT's working for me, a second class, third class, and two seamen.

My previous Albuquerque classmate George Holden was as I said, the leading petty officer, and held daily morning quarters, which involved all of us standing in ranks, while he read the plan of the day. From time to time the division officer, a lieutenant, would inspect us for proper uniforms, and haircuts. The chiefs would then give out our daily work assignments each morning.

Standing duty was a way of life in the Navy, and Guam was no exception. I stood duty for twenty-four hours every sixth day. This involved staying overnight within the outside handling building, and handling any emergency that might arise after normal working hours. We also made security tours within the fenced area.

Of all the duty assignments I had in the past ten years, I was most uncomfortable, and felt like a round peg trying to fit into a square hole, in this assignment on Guam. All of my peers, my rank, and age, were married and lived an entirely different life than I did in the barracks. I was struggling to pay off the divorce bills I had, and I'd gotten off to a bad start with the negative letter that was sent to my new commanding officer. There were also a number of cliques within the plant, none of which I felt included in.

The middle of October a tropical depression passed over Guam. The winds weren't severe enough to rank this as a typhoon, but there were a lot of rain, and strong wind. After the weather calmed down, all the GMT's were busy cleaning out a security grate that was over a small creek, which passed through the Limited Area. The grate was full of palm leaves, coconuts and trash. Everyone talked about typhoon Karen that had devastated Guam a few years' prior.

The first of November, I went on another fishing trip on the *Fena Queen*, with GMT2 Buck Harrell and his wife. This time I caught a "mess" of fish, about twenty-five tucanery (see photo), and many tilapias.

Mid-November, a sailor that worked for me, GMT3 Ted Heck, had his 1956 Buick shipped to Guam, and while driving through a Guam village called Umatec, struck and killed a two-year-old girl walking in the street. He had been drinking, but was not charged with anything. The girl's mother shared some of the blame, as she always let her daughter play in the street.

Mid-November GMT1 Larry Walters checked in. His wife was to follow him to Guam in about six months. She and his children were in San Diego, and they would wait until the children were out of school on summer vacation, to move. Many married sailors tried to time their transfer between duty stations to coincide with their children's summer vacation period, to minimize the disruption of family life.

Larry lived in the barracks during this waiting period. He had his car shipped to Guam, a 1969 Plymouth Road Runner with the largest engine Plymouth made that year. Considering most of the speed limits on Guam were thirty-five miles per hour, and the island was only thirty miles long by twelve miles wide, the Plymouth was too much car for Guam.

On Thanksgiving I ate a big Thanksgiving meal at the chow hall. The chow halls both ashore and afloat in the Navy always tried to prepare special meals on holidays.

I had a blind date in October, with a girl that Betsy Wilson knew. My blind date was a Japanese girl who was teaching grammar school on a government contract. It turned out she was from Fowler, California a town not too far from my hometown of Strathmore. We knew many of the same people back in the states. I only had one date with her. This was to be my one and only date during my time on Guam.

The Naval Magazine supplied conventional bombs to Anderson Air Force Base, where B-52 strategic bombers were stationed. Frequent bombing strikes against North Vietnam were being flown out of Guam. This bomb supply effort involved driving semi-trucks twenty-six miles over island roads with truckloads of 500 and 1,000 pound bombs. I drove for a week doing this, driving three trips a day. It was a long, hot, dangerous drive.

On 8 December I reached the age of twenty-seven, and was still undecided about my future? The one thing I was sure about, I did not like being stationed on Guam! I enjoyed life in the service. I felt good serving my country. It was a life of sacrifice, with very little monetary reward, but there were the rewards of achieving difficult tasks. I still felt pride in my past service, and it was rewarding for me, seeing the men I led improve and mature. I enjoyed the considerable prestige given to a first class petty officer. Many of the kids I'd grown up with, and gone to high school with, had either gone on to college, or completed their military service, and were earning salaries three or four times what I was making in the Navy. I thought about getting out and going back to school, or trying to join the California Highway Patrol. In all of my thoughts and deliberations, I was somewhat depressed thinking about the "high" praise, and sense of accomplishment I'd gotten at Whidbey Island, compared to the "low" treatment, and loneliness of Guam. The commanding officer of the magazine ran it like a boot camp. As I said everyone had to wear crew cut haircuts, and there were very few privileges given to senior petty officers. The commanding officer used to watch the Limited Area, from his office on the hill, with binoculars to make sure no one left the area before the 1630 quitting time! He gave the impression of not trusting his chiefs and officers! Sailors stationed elsewhere on Guam pitied the sailors stationed at the magazine, because of the iron fist rule of our commanding officer.

My hook assemblymen and I repainted a weapon trainer that received praise from all who saw it. The division officer made a deal with us; he had an old rusty Ford that he needed painted. He gave the five of us a week off, to paint his car, and he would furnish the soft drinks and beer. We took his car to the back yard of GMT2 Buck Harrell's house, which was in the naval station base housing area. We masked and sanded the car in preparation for painting, and then painted it in the magazine motor pool garage. We used epoxy paint, the color was eggshell blue, and it came out beautifully. The paint job lasted the entire time the lieutenant was on Guam, although there was a problem a couple of days after we painted it. His wife parked the car at the exchange, and someone slammed a car door into the side of her door, and a large paint chip came out. We repainted the door.

Rust was a constant problem in the tropical climate of Guam, especially on automobile metal. American-made cars with U.S. steel resisted rust much better than Japanese built cars. Regardless, the life of all cars was much shorter in Guam.

On 17 December I was told by the personnel office that I would be leaving Guam between the 1st and 10th of March, for San Francisco, and be discharged from active duty. I did not look forward to spending another Christmas away from home. My family was very faithful writing to me during this time, which I greatly appreciated.

There were five first class living in the barracks, myself, Larry Walters, GMT1 Bean who was assigned to the Explosive Ordnance Disposal Shop. Also there were two Seabees, EO1 Riggs, and EO1 Walker, who worked in the transportation garage; they were EO's (Equipment Operators).

One unusual physical feature of Larry Walters was that his left nipple was missing! He had been assigned to a carrier on a Med cruise.

During an in port period in Naples, Italy, while in a bar, he got into a fight with a communist agitator, who suddenly stabbed him in the chest with a knife. The blade of the knife entered his chest through his left nipple; the tip of the blade nicked an aorta of his heart. Larry said at first he thought the guy had just hit him in the chest with his fist, but he said then it felt like a piece of ice had entered his chest. He said it was an odd feeling of "cold," he said he now knew why the saying "cold steel" came into being! He fainted after being stabbed, and was rushed to an Italian hospital where was operated on, for required repair to his heart, which included removal of his nipple.

EO1 Riggs was a completely different person. He was an older first class who had been in the Army, and served as a paratrooper in the Korean War. In the war he had been in combat behind enemy lines. He showed me a knife that he kept from his Army days. The knife had been invented for the gruesome job of sneaking up behind sentries and killing them soundlessly. The knife was called a "kidney knife." The blade was sharp on both edges, and flared out widely in the middle. It was generally thrust into a sentry's kidney. The wide blade insured the cutting edge would slice the organ. The pain of being stabbed in the kidney would be so intense that it paralyzed the sentry's vocal cords, and he would not be able to cry out an alarm.

Riggs did not sleep on a mattress. He slept on a one-inch thick plywood board. His hands, and feet were heavily callused, and he held a black belt in a number of martial arts. Riggs intimidated the marines, after a certain incident. Riggs liked to drink Mateus wine, a wine made in Spain (he seldom got inebriated), and one night after returning to the barracks from the acey ducey club, instead of walking up the stairway to our first class section in the barracks, he walked through the Marine Barracks, at 2:00 a.m. in the morning. He turned on the lights, and said he could whip all of them. After nine or ten of them tried, and ended up on the floor, the marines agreed with him.

He was one of the deadliest men I've known. He was soft spoken and polite. He had gone what sailors called "Asiatic." He'd not been in the United States for fifteen years, and had no desire to leave the Far East. He was married to a Japanese girl in Okinawa, who he'd visit once a year. He ate all meals with chopsticks, and preferred rice. He would often sit Asian style, with his feet flat on the floor, on his haunches, arms across his knees. I saw him sit in a lotus position immobile for hours. I enjoyed talking with Riggs, and I went on liberty with him a number of times.

Another first class that lived with us in the barracks, an equipment operator, was not admired, or respected by anyone. It would not be an exaggeration to say he was treated with disdain! This treatment was because of the way he achieved his rank, and his complete ignorance of the Navy, and lack of leadership traits and abilities.

This was a time in the Vietnam War when the Navy was extremely short handed in the construction trades, or Seabee ranks. The Navy offered a very generous payment of $5,000, and the rank of first class (E-6), to anyone that had a degree in a related construction skill. The enlistee did not go to boot camp, but a two-week Navy orientation class, and then put on a first class crow! We resented anyone who earned his rank in this manner instead of earning it as we had. This first class wore a straggly beard, and always appeared wrinkled, and unkempt. He was like a fish out of water. We did not feel sorry for him, and felt it was wrong for the Navy to have such a program. He was not respected by junior or senior ranks, and certainly did nothing for our morale. The only thing good about this program was that the initial enlistment was only for two years. I doubt that many sailors in this program shipped-over, as most did not adapt to the Navy at all.

Lloyd Wilson invited me to his house for Christmas. We had a very nice turkey dinner, and I enjoyed watching his kids tear into their wrapped Christmas presents. I only had two months before my enlistment was over, and I wanted to quit smoking. Cigarettes in California cost fifty cents a pack, which at the time was very expensive. I was anxious to get home. During the holiday period we worked shortened hours, which caused the time to drag slowly by. I was relieved when we began working regular hours again. From time to time my back hurt, and I noticed small bumps on the back of my hands, which I thought must be some sort of tropical skin fungus?

The first of January, Zeus our houseboy, invited all the first class to the wedding reception of his daughter. Most of his village, about 300 people, was at the wedding and reception. It was a huge Guamanian fiesta. Guamanians always had huge weddings, and the bride's father would usually go into debt trying to insure a proper celebration was held. Larry Walters and I went, and we had a great time.

My W-2 Form for the year of 1969 indicated I had made $5,367 dollars. Much of this salary was used paying for my divorce. One day while in the exchange, I ran across Lieutenant Thompson, who I had worked for at Whidbey Island. He had just arrived in Guam, but was preparing to return to the United States.

There had been a tragedy in his family, his wife, son and mother had just been in a car accident, his wife and son were seriously injured, and his mother had been killed. He was buying a few things before going on emergency leave. I offered him my condolences, and sympathy. He did seem happy to see me, I felt bad about his family who I had met while stationed with him on Whidbey.

I wrote a letter to my detailer in Washington, D.C., Chief Ford. He was the person who issued transfer orders, and determined where GMT's were stationed. I asked that I be transferred to any ship, or shore station in California. I eventually received a letter from him, saying he could not help me. It was a cold factual letter that discouraged me.

The middle of January, GMT3 Joe Murphy, who lived in a small shack in the Guam village of Umatec, invited me to spend the weekend with him. He rode a motorcycle, so I rode with him to the village on the back of his motorcycle. He introduced me to many people who lived in the village. It seemed if you knew one family in a Guam village, all in the village were friendly to you. Joe and I were invited by one family to eat supper with them. We were served chicken killigan (chicken cooked in lemon juice, and hot peppers), and pancit, a type of small noodles. It was a very delicious meal. There were two boys our age in the Guamanian family, and the mom treated Joe and me like we were part of the family. The next day there was to be a big chicken fight. One of the boys had a rooster he was going to fight. We were invited to stay overnight, so we accepted, and slept overnight in hammocks.

The next morning we were served breakfast. Around noon many people began gathering in a large clearing in the jungle behind the house. One Guamanian guy was the expert at taping and tying the razor sharp blades on the roosters' legs before they fought. He would tape a blade about three inches long on each of the chicken's legs. Bets were made before the fight—if your chicken won, you doubled your money, if your chicken lost, you got nothing. The fighting roosters were beautiful birds, with black, red, green and blue feathers. Some of the roosters were veterans of many fights, and were considered favorites. Our Guamanian friends told us which ones to bet on and we did very well.

There were about sixty people in the clearing, when suddenly there were shouts of, "police, police, run, run." Everyone scattered, including me! I didn't know this was illegal, and I certainly didn't want to get in trouble two months before my discharge. As I ran through the jungle, I glimpsed a blue uniformed Guam policeman. I ran in a large circle, and eventually returned to my Guamanian friend's house. Most of the people from the clearing had regrouped there. Joe was also there, he said the police had taken the "blade man's" box, and had not arrested anyone. They all got a big laugh, saying they had never seen anyone run as fast as I had with shower shoes on. Shortly the chicken fights resumed in the back yard, but this time lookouts were posted on the roads around the village.

The fights would begin with the owners of the roosters holding them by the body, facing each other, only inches apart, and raising them up and down to get them into a fighting mood. Then both chickens were released facing each other. Most fights only lasted a few seconds, with a flurry of wings, and bladed legs flaying, the winner's blade would fatally cut the loser. Our friend's chicken fought twice and won. The only reward the loser got was a chicken dinner. I could see why this cruel sport was outlawed in the United States. I saw true sorrow on many of the loser's faces, holding the dead body of their rooster. There were legally sanctioned cockfights on Guam, but this particular one Joe and I attended was illegal. Except for the fright in the jungle clearing, I had an enjoyable weekend. I gave Joe a carton of cigarettes to give to the Guamanian Mother, who had opened her home to us, and shown us such generous hospitality.

I was anxious to leave Guam, in preparation for my return home; I requested that the carpenter shop on base construct a "cruise box" for me, which I would use to ship clothes and other items home to California, so I wouldn't have such a large load of luggage to carry on the plane. This was an accepted practice, and I was shocked when my request chit was disapproved, but I accepted it. Then I learned that a third class, and a second class that were married, had gotten a cruise box from the carpenter shop, after my request had been turned down! I immediately put in a request chit asking for captain's mast, so I could find out why I had been discriminated against? This request caused a number of hurried phone calls, and then I was told my cruise box would be ready in a day or two. I never did find out why my original request had been turned down. It turned out to be a nice large wooden box that I packed and shipped. I still have the wooden box to this day.

Marriages of sailors stationed on Guam, were strengthened, weakened, or in some cases dissolved by life on the island. The isolation, limited recreation, and heavy alcohol use was hard on most marriages. One GMT had a wife that was notoriously promiscuous.

Her name was Lisa, and her nickname was "Lovely Lisa." Sailors, who were invited to stay overnight, would sleep on the couch, and she would rendezvous with the sailor on the couch while her husband was sleeping in bed! There was eventually a divorce. The divorce rate amongst sailors was very high, especially those couples that had never been away from the United States before.

I always looked forward to the monthly division parties, which were usually held at Gab Gab Beach. We would spend all day relaxing, playing volleyball, swimming, and barbequing steaks.

The first of February I received word that I would be leaving Guam 2 March, and fly to San Francisco for discharge processing. I did a lot of fishing around this time, and managed to catch a lot of fish. On 22 February I received a letter telling me I was an uncle again, I had a niece, and her name was Betty. She had been born 17 February.

My evaluation had been filled out in December, and would be the only evaluations I would receive prior to my discharge. My marks were all 3.8's, and 3.6's, and the write up was very lackluster, a far cry from the glowing evaluations, and 4.0's I'd been given on Whidbey Island. I was not pleased with them, and said so when I sat down with the chief to review, and sign them.

The last of February I began the checkout process. When it came time to get the executive officer's signature on my checkout sheet, he was shocked that I was leaving, and being discharged. I explained to him that I had requested reassignment from my detailer, but had been turned down. He tried to convince me to ship-over, and he also drafted a letter to Washington, D.C., asking if something could be worked out? I wasn't too enthusiastic about his concern, he had seen my original request a few months previously, and this was the first time he had ever talked to me civilly. I truthfully did not desire to remain in his command. I finished checking out, and finished packing my bags. The day before I was to leave, I was presented with a plaque, which was customarily given to departing sailors. The plaque had crossed cannons, with my rate symbol on it, along with a brass plate with my name, and the dates: "August 1969 – March 1970". It was fitting and symbolic of my tour on Guam, as my name was misspelled! The brass tag was embossed "GMT1 James F. Little," it should have been "James S. Little." Everything else had gone wrong on Guam; this was the way I expected my assignment to end!

On 2 March 1970, I was driven to the Guam International Airport. Lloyd Wilson, and his wife Betsy, George Holden, his wife Anita, and a few others came to the airport to bid me farewell. I finally boarded the plane, and left Guam with few regrets.

I once again crossed the Pacific, landing in Hawaii, and then on to Travis Air Force Base, California, then by bus to that dreaded place all sailors detest, a transit barracks, on Treasure Island, San Francisco, California. It was here I was to begin the process of being discharged. Although it was March, the drastic change in the climate from Guam to California, felt like the North Pole to me! The discharge process I was to undergo was much different from the process I went through in 1963. I sat through a number of lectures, and classes covering topics of the naval reserves, benefits I was entitled to, methods of job hunting, how to prepare a resume, etc. This new discharge program was called "Project Transition," which had come about because of the larger military since the Vietnam buildup. Project Transition was an effort to help servicemen make the change to civilian life a little smoother, and easier.

I also underwent a thorough physical exam. After my chest x-ray, I was scheduled to speak to a doctor who was concerned about my lungs. The doctor said I had considerable scarring on my lungs. After he questioned me; he came to the conclusion that I apparently had Valley Fever at one time in my youth. Valley Fever is unique to residents of the California San Joaquin Valley, where I spent my childhood.

My heart was not really into giving up on a career in the Navy, and in retrospect I think I was depressed about the drastic change from Whidbey Island to the isolated atmosphere of Guam. Also the death of my son continued to haunt me. The lack of appreciation for we who fought the Vietnam War, and the constant bombardment of bad news about the war were very discouraging to me and other senior petty officers. The atmosphere of the transit barracks was very depressing, being treated like a seaman recruit, which affected my decision to remain steadfast in my wish to quit the Navy.

Project Transition was definitely an improvement over the discharge procedures I'd gone through in 1963. There were a number of presentations from organizations that were interested in hiring ex-servicemen. There was a pitch to join the Central Intelligence Agency (CIA). They were looking specifically for people who were fluent in a foreign language, and could type. There were also talks by representatives from the San Francisco, and Los Angeles Police Departments, and other government agencies.

Finally the process was completed, I lined up with a few other sailors, was given a handshake, and discharge papers. I was honorably discharged 6 March 1970. I flew from San Francisco, to Fresno, where my Dad picked me up in his car.

Chapter 9: Tonkin Gulf Yacht Club

I began my new civilian life, and I was happy to see my family. I stayed at my parent's house, and I enrolled at the employment office. I began work on two job applications, one for the Tulare County Sheriff's office, and one for the California Highway Patrol. The employment office didn't have much to offer in the way of employment, except for a few manual labor jobs. I received unemployment checks for two weeks. To me it was demeaning to stand in line for a "hand out." Just a few weeks previously I had been working in a critical job that was supposed to be one of the most important in the country, and had been told that the fate of my country depended on how well I performed my duties, and now the only job I could get was digging ditches!

I had decided that I would remain in the Naval Reserves, and had signed papers enlisting in the reserves with my present first class rate. This meant I would be required to attend weekly training meetings, and once a year I would be required to go on active duty for two weeks. Most active duty sailors' look upon reserve-sailors with disdain, calling them weekend warriors, or not real sailors, lacking the complete dedication, those active duty sailors have. I felt odd being in the reserves, but it was the only way I could preserve the ten years active duty I had. If I remained in the reserves, I would be able to draw retirement pay at the age of sixty.

My mom worked at the state hospital with a reserve sailor who attended the weekly meetings in Dinuba, which was about twenty-five miles from my parent's home. Each Thursday night I would ride with him, and another sailor, to the reserve unit we were assigned to. The sailors in the reserve unit did not impress me. Most wore sloppy uniforms, and needed haircuts. Our commanding officer was a mortician in civilian life, and he certainly had the personality of an undertaker. I was the only GMT assigned to the unit. We were supposed to have four hours of training each week at our meeting, but most of the time we played volleyball. It did feel good when I put on my uniform once a week. I planned to take the chief promotion exam in September.

The employment office phoned me about a temporary job opening at Food Machinery Corporation (FMC), a machine manufacturing plant, in Lindsay, a town about ten miles from my parents house. The job description was an inventory clerk, and paid three dollars fifteen cents an hour. The job was to last as long as it took to complete an inventory of the plant's supplies and equipment. I took the job, and went to work for a guy named Ed Reeves. Ed, I and another guy worked in the plant storeroom area, which was enclosed by a large mesh screen.

I had to punch in and out of work at a time clock, with a time card. The majority of the men working there were welders and steel workers involved in the manufacture of machinery for orange packing houses in the Lindsay, Strathmore, and Porterville area, and other parts of California. I had to join the steelworker's union, and my days were spent inventorying hundreds of shelves containing various machinery parts. My boss Ed, liked my work, and offered me overtime many weekends, during which I would be paid time and a half for my hours at work.

The Mercury I'd bought in Washington was still running well. The work at FMC was completely different from my job in the Navy. I had no authority, or any significant responsibilities, and the task of inventorying was not mentally challenging.

One day at lunch, two welders whom I'd made friends with (one was the union shop advocate), asked if I'd like to stop after work at a bar about a mile from the plant for a beer. I said I would, and after about thirty minutes in the bar after work, I left the bar to go outside and get in my car. I was surprised to see two little boys with crew cuts sitting in the front seat of my car waiting for me! It was my two little brothers, Joe and Jerry. My mom had seen my car parked in front of the bar and dropped them off. I think this was a not too subtle hint that I was not setting a good example for my brothers by spending time in a bar!

It seemed odd to me how far away the war seemed, and it was seldom talked about other than occasional news reports. I listened closely to all the news about the war, as I had many friends fighting. It was sad to me how little civilian support there was for our military fighting half way around the world.

I submitted job applications for the California Highway Patrol, and the Tulare County Sheriff's Department. My friend Butch Coley was a deputy sheriff for the county, and he introduced me to the sheriff, in May during the annual Strathmore High School reunion gathering.

Often during my lunch hour at the plant, I would spend lunch with my Uncle Dean, and Aunt Lois Clark who lived in Lindsay. My boss was not happy with the other worker in the storeroom area. He was an older man who delivered supplies to other locations in town, or would run errands with a company van.

He often would return late, and many times smelling like whiskey. Ed told me that he would like to hire me permanently as a replacement for the other guy. My employment was supposed to end when I was completed with the inventory.

I had talked to the Navy Recruiter, a first class, in Porterville shortly after joining the reserve unit in Dinuba, and he said if I stayed out of the Navy more than ninety days, and tried to go back on active duty, I might not go back in as a first class, but as a third class!

One morning I went to the county courthouse for my scheduled interview and fitness test for the sheriffs' department. There was eight other men there applying for deputy sheriff positions. My name was called, and I got a surprise, I was told that I did not qualify because of the lung scarring on my chest x-ray! This was very disappointing, I'd pointed out what I'd thought was a minor problem on my discharge x-ray in my application, at that point I wished I'd not been so honest about it! When I told Butch Coley about what happened, he was very upset, he told his coworkers, that the Sheriff's Department had lost a good man.

The inventory was completed at FMC. Ed said I did a great job, and to keep in touch, because he was going to work on getting me a permanent job at the plant. My Aunt Edna told me of a job at a Lindsay orange packinghouse as a night watchman. I applied, and got the job. It was lonely work, walking about a huge dark packinghouse. The hours went by slowly each night. As I made my nightly rounds, I had time to reflect on all that I had accomplished in the Navy, all the friends I'd made, and the places throughout the world that I had seen. I worked as a night watchman for almost a month. During this time, I had a conversation with my father about the future. He felt that ten years was a lot of time to "throw away." I agreed with him. One day I went to Porterville to get a haircut, and while sitting in the chair, I suddenly said, "Cut it short." I then walked a couple of blocks to the Navy Recruiter's office, and told the recruiter I wanted to go back on active duty. I only had two days to get my enlistment processing done, or I would lose my first class crow! I was to be sworn in at the Fresno Armed Forces Induction Center, where I'd begun life in the Navy ten years previously. Two days later on 5 June 1970, I recited the oath of enlistment I'd recited twice before. Just as I felt in 1964 after re-enlisting, it felt good to be back in my uniform. The Navy was my home!

There was a negative, painful side to my re-enlistment. I'll never forget the afternoon I sat with my mother in her living room and I told her I was going back into the Navy. She cried. I think there are few things more painful for a son than seeing his mother tears! It saddened me deeply to have hurt her. I had enjoyed living with my parents, and two brothers, and being near my sister, and aunts and uncles, and getting to know my two nieces' Lisa, and three month old Betty and watching them grow up. But considering all this, I missed what I was destined to be, a sailor. I was very fortunate to have kept my first class crow, had I waited one more day past the ninety day deadline, I might have reverted to a second or third class!

When I went to the packinghouse, and told the boss that I was quitting, as I had reenlisted in the Navy, he threw a full-blown tantrum that I would expect from a three-year-old! It didn't bother me, as it was well known that he was a draft-dodger, his father had gotten him a deferment from the draft. As I was leaving the packing house, an older guy I'd gotten to know since working there, shook my hand, after the boss left the room, he congratulated me, saying "Don't worry about him, he's a jerk, I'm proud of you serving our country!"

I had two weeks leave before I was to report to Long Beach Naval Station. I decided to drive to Whidbey Island before reporting to Long Beach, and visit John Milton and my other friends. I had gotten $500 re-enlistment money, which helped finance my trip. It took a day and a half to drive north to Whidbey Island, Washington in the '62 Mercury.

The island and town of Oak Harbor had not changed much during my absence. I dropped by Allison's house and checking at the grocery store where Allison was supposed to work, no one knew where she was? I went to the AUW Shop, and discovered it was in the process of being closed! The shop was to be completely locked up in a couple of months. John Milton was still there, and he invited me to his house for dinner. That night I got to meet his wife, Big Red, and his daughters; he was a completely different person when with his family. I had an enjoyable evening, and the next day left the island to return to California.

I stayed the night at Portland, Oregon, and the next morning noticed the Mercury was becoming increasingly difficult to steer. The power steering was apparently failing. I drove 450 miles to Fresno without power steering. I arrived at my sister, and brother-in-law's house, and the next day went car shopping. I car shopped all day, and finally found a 1968 Pontiac Firebird. I left the Mercury as down payment, and drove off in the Firebird. It was burgundy in color, with black leather interior, four-speed transmission, with a 350 cubic inch V-8. It was very fast and I enjoyed driving it. At Long Beach Naval Station, I was to be in a dreaded transitbarracks awaiting orders to my next duty station.

Bidding my family goodbye, driving the firebird, with my packed sea bag in the trunk, I drove to Long Beach on 19 June 1970 and reported in. The transit barracks was somewhat better than previous transit barracks I'd been in. I was assigned to a two-man room, with another first class, who was a cook also awaiting assignment orders.

During the day all transit first and second class petty officers were assigned to work at the base legal office. We were told we were to be prisoner escorts. We were to escort prisoners brought to the legal office, to various offices, and locations on base, and often to their final destination the base brig. One statement that motivated us to prevent any escapes was the statement that if a prisoner escaped while in our custody, and was not recaptured; the escort would serve out the remainder of the escaped prisoner's prison sentence!

Many of the sailors brought to the legal office had been captured while AWOL (absent without leave), or as in the case of one longhaired sailor, a deserter. When a sailor is absent from his command without authorization for a specific period of time, he may be declared a deserter. Being a deserter carried more severe penalties than being AWOL. One deserter that was brought in while I worked at the legal office had been on the run for over four years.

Handcuffs were used in our escort duties. Escorts were handcuffed to a prisoner, and would walk with him to a specific location on base. Often we would walk to the base brig, where the Marine Sergeant of the Guard would unlock the handcuffs and take charge of the prisoner. Escorts did not have keys to the handcuffs, only the marines, and the legal office had keys, so we remained handcuffed throughout our travels about the base. Much of my time was spent sitting around the legal office. I did escort a few sailors. Some were destined for the brig, and after being handcuffed together we would walk to the base dispensary where a doctor would give the prisoner a physical examination while handcuffed to my wrist. We then would walk to the barbershop, where the sailor would be given a haircut, and then to the base exchange where I would cash a certificate from the legal office, so the sailor could purchase toilet articles. We would then walk to the brig, where the marines would unlock the handcuffs, and take charge of the prisoner. Many of the sailors were scared and nervous about being taken to the brig. I tried to distract them with small talk, and tried to encourage them.

I do remember one American Indian sailor that was close to seven feet tall, and so big that I had to lift the arm I was handcuffed by, up to reach his wrist. While walking to the barbershop, prior to walking to the brig, he looked at the fence that surrounded the base, and said to me, "What would you do if I crawled over that fence?" I said, "I wouldn't have a choice, I'd follow you wherever you go, I don't have any keys for these handcuffs." Thankfully he didn't try to escape, and we arrived at the brig without incident, I wished him good luck.

One day I was called to the personnel office, and told my orders had come in. I was going to be stationed at Naval Air Station Atsugi, Japan. I was to be assigned to the base calibration laboratory. I was excited about this assignment. I'd enjoyed Japan when I'd visited the country while onboard the *Ticonderoga*. I was told I'd be able to ship my car overseas, and I would be transferring in a week and a half.

One day my roommate and I met two girls from Huntington Beach. I dated one of the girls for a few nights. One night she took me to a party that was being hosted by a Hollywood producer, or director, I don't remember which, and I don't remember his name? But was told one of his movies was "*Mutiny on the Bounty*[29]" with Marlon Brando. He was interested in the girl I was dating, and he acted very stuck up and aloof. The girl was about ten years older than I, and I never contacted her again after leaving Long Beach. While in Long Beach, I drove to Lancaster, and had a nice visit and overnight stay with my Uncle Hubert and Aunt Kay.

I was busy preparing for my move to Japan. I made arrangements to have my car shipped to Japan. It would take about a month to arrive by ship. I was to pick up my orders in two days at the personnel office, when I received a call in the morning from the personnel office asking me to report to the office. When I arrived at the office, the yeoman that had been working on my transfer orders said, "I've got some bad news for you, we got word this morning that the job billet at Atsugi has been cancelled, and instead of orders to Japan, you'll be transferred to an aircraft carrier, the *USS Oriskany*." One of the "red tape" requirements of transfers in the Navy was that a job billet had to exist before a sailor could be assigned to a specific command. The yeoman said if I'd gotten my orders yesterday, even though the billet had been cancelled, I'd still transfer for a normal tour of two years, so I missed going to Japan by two days. It was a disappointment, but at least I knew what to expect on an aircraft carrier. In two days my orders were prepared. I was to report to *USS Oriskany* (CVA-34). She was currently deployed, so this meant I was going back to war. The *Oriskany*'s homeport was Alameda, California. In order to get to the ship, I was to fly out of Travis Air Force Base, and catch the ship wherever she might be.

I left the Firebird at my parent's house, and my brother-in-law, and sister Linda drove me from Fresno to Travis Air Force Base on the day I was to depart the United States. We arrived at the base in the early afternoon, and since my plane was to leave in the evening, we found a unique Mexican food restaurant off base, located in a plum orchard, and had a farewell dinner. At the base terminal we said goodbye, and I boarded a jet airliner bound for the Philippines. After a short stop at Hawaii, I was once again at Clark Air Force Base, Philippines. It was as hot and humid as I remembered it, and I felt very uncomfortable in my wool dress blues. I took the four-hour bus ride from Clark Air Force Base to Subic Naval Base, (after a stop at the halfway bar and restaurant), and finally arrived in Subic. I was once again at a dreaded transit barracks. I'd never been through the Subic Bay Transit Barracks, and it was by far the worse one I'd experienced.

The barracks area was fenced with barbed wire. The barracks had been used as a Japanese soldier detention camp after World War II, and not many improvements had been made since then! In order to leave the fenced compound we were required to request a "walking pass" from the master-at arms office. This was a "belittling" experience, I understood the need to keep track of younger non-rated sailors, but I and the other senior petty officers were disgusted at the prospect of needing a "walking pass" to leave the barracks, we were being treated like children!

I went into Olongapo a couple of times on liberty. I ran across many people in town that I'd met while on the *Ticonderoga*. The town had grown and seemed to be prospering, as the result of the frequent port visits made by the carriers busy off the coast of Vietnam. The river that flowed under the bridge outside the main gate was still as odorous! San Miguel beer still flowed freely, and the number of Olongapo bars had increased.

I was awakened early one morning before the daily morning muster, and told I was to leave immediately with twelve other sailors trying to catch the *Oriskany*, and board a plane which would fly us to Da Nang, Vietnam. I donned my wool dress blue uniform, and the group of us was taken by bus to the base terminal where we got aboard a C-130 transport plane. After a few hours the plane's wheels touched down on Da Nang Airfield, South Vietnam. We were herded into a terminal, where a soldier addressed us and said we were in a hostile environment (as if we had to be told!), and we were to turn in any American money we might have, so it could be exchanged for military scripts (funny money). We were then loaded into a personnel carrier, along with our sea bags, and taken to a wooden transit barracks. I did not say anything, but I was not sure about the legality of my presence in Vietnam? I had been told in the past that GMT's were not permitted ashore in Vietnam, because of the sensitive information we possessed, and the possibility of capture. I decided it would be wise for me to keep my mouth shut. There were whispered statements about GMT's stationed at secret locations in Vietnam who were involved with the maintenance of nuclear ordnance artillery shells, but I could not, or would not confirm this, even if I knew it to be true. This was on par with the existence or nonexistence of what was called in the GMT world, the "Gray Ghost," a small ship loaded with nuclear weapons that was supposedly kept off the coast of Japan for use in war contingency plans.

Being dressed in wool dress blues made it unbearably hot. The transit barracks were informal, with bunk beds. I was given a bed on the second floor of the two-story building. There was a sandbagged bomb shelter next to the barracks we were told to use in the event of an attack. We were told rocket and mortar attacks took place frequently.

Also next to the transit barracks was the Noncommissioned Officers Club, for E-4's through E-9's. We were to learn that this club, as well as the Officer's Club was favorite targets of the Viet Cong, who would climb a hill overlooking the base, called "Monkey Hill," and try to hit the clubs with rockets during times of "high population" such as during USO shows, or on Fridays and Saturdays.

One thing that stands out in my mind about Vietnam was how red the dirt was in some areas. There was red dust on the uniforms of the soldiers and marines that had been in the jungle areas around Da Nang. It was the reddest dirt I'd ever seen, almost as though it was blood soaked. We *Oriskany* bound sailors spent our days roaming about the base, or waiting in a small Quonset hut that served as a terminal for Navy carrier planes.

The *Oriskany* was steaming off the coast, but it was too far out to sea for us to be flown out and land aboard her. At almost every intersection of the base there were sandbagged fortifications containing armed South Vietnamese soldiers. The entire base was ringed with sandbagged bunkers, complete with firing positions. The base appeared to be very heavily defended.

Water was scarce, and I found it difficult to find a drink, other than in the mess hall. The Army mess hall had the biggest variety of food I'd ever seen in a military chow hall! At every scheduled lunch and dinner time, an alternate food line was set up serving steak and lobster, this line was for those that had been "in-country," or out on patrols, or special operations. The days were calm, but the nights were anything but calm.

Often at night there were both distant and near explosions, gunfire, and flashes of light would illuminate the sky and hills around Da Nang.

One night the sound of the base siren and a huge explosion awakened me while I was asleep in my bunk in the barracks. Another *Oriskany* bound sailor named Tom, was the only other person on the second floor of the barracks with me. We debated whether to run downstairs to the bomb shelter or stay put? After a very loud and close explosion, we got under our bunks. We heard shouting and gunfire. I imagined the Vietcong storming the barracks, and we had nothing to defend ourselves with! Finally the sounds of explosions, and gunfire seemed to be moving away from the barracks. Tom and I got out from under our bunks after a few minutes. We later laughed about how embarrassing it would have been if the barracks had been hit, and our parents were sent telegrams stating "The Navy regrets to inform you that your son was killed while hiding under his bed!" We remained awake most of the night watching the flashes of gunfire, and sounds coming from Monkey Hill overlooking the base. It was an ideal launching area for the Vietcong to use for their inaccurate rocket attacks, and although the hill was heavily patrolled, these attacks often came at night after the VC had sneaked into position. Being shot at prompts many unusual emotions and thoughts. One thought that ran through my mind, "These people are trying to kill me, and I haven't done anything to them?" I don't remember being scared until after the attack was over. The next morning we toured the base to see what damage had been done. No buildings were hit, but there were a few small craters that the Army had roped off. I picked up a few pieces of shrapnel.

Many of the soldiers and marines were armed, while we *Oriskany* sailors were not. We were cautioned about small children throwing hand grenades into bars, and buildings and warned not to kick any cans we might see laying on the ground. A favorite trick of the VC was to place an unpinned grenade inside a can, knowing that Americans often kicked cans they saw laying on the ground, this would dislodge the grenade, which would then explode.

There was a sense of excitement about the base. We also saw the sobering sight of filled body bags, and also coffins being loaded on planes for the final ride home. The war had been going on for almost six years. There was the certainty that we would eventually have victory. We never gave any thought to the possibility of defeat. There was grumbling that the military was not being permitted to fight the war on an even playing field. The North Vietnamese were finding sanctuary in Cambodia, and Laos, and we were not permitted to take the battle to them. Rules of engagement from Washington, D.C. meant our troops had to be attacked before taking aggressive action. Our military had trained for years for war in Europe against Russia, and many of these tactics did not work well in the jungles of Vietnam. Many military officers did not respect Secretary of Defense McNamara. He was perceived as a mathematician, not a military leader.

The Vietnam War had its own military "language." Vietnam was shortened to "Nam." To be in hostile territory was called to be "In country." The enemy was "Charlie, VC, Cong, or the derogatory "Gooks." Distances measured in kilometers were called "clicks," bullets, mortar rounds, or artillery directed at you was called "in coming." To be killed was to be "bagged, or zapped." The United States was "Stateside, or "Land of the Giant PX." A "tour" was an assignment of twelve months in Vietnam for Air Force, Army, and Navy, for the marines it was thirteen months. Days were always counted until that day you got on a plane and flew home to the U.S.; anyone with less than sixty days was called a "short-timer." There were many other terms, often a mixture of Vietnamese and English. Anything negative was "number ten", anything outstanding, or acceptable was "number one".

Finally we were told the *Oriskany* was close enough to Da Nang, to send a plane to pick us up. We were all anxious to leave, although we weren't quite as anxious when told that the Vietcong liked to shoot at departing and arriving aircraft. We boarded a two-engine "COD," and took off, clearing the base without being shot at. After an hour's flight, the plane's wheels slammed onto the flight deck of the carrier. I was now onboard my new home the *USS Oriskany*. The date was 21 August 1970.

Oriskany was an "*Essex*-Class" carrier, the same size as the *USS Ticonderoga*, but considerably smaller than the *USS Independence*. *Oriskany* got her name from a Revolutionary War battle fought on August 6, 1777, at Oriskany Creek near Rome, New York. The America Militia under General Nicholas Herkimer was ambushed by British and Indian forces attempting to come to the aid of Fort Stanwix, New York. Although General Herkimer was killed in the furious battle, it ended in an American victory, preventing the British occupation of the strategic Mohawk Valley and neutralizing General Burgoyne's Army at Saratoga.

Oriskany[30] was launched on 13 October 1945 at the Brooklyn Naval Shipyard in New York. She was commissioned on 25 September1950. World War II had ended, so she was laid up at Brooklyn, delaying completion and eventual commissioning until the Korean War.

A few "facts" about *Oriskany*: She is 911 feet long or about the length of three football fields placed end to end. *Oriskany* displaces more than 45,000 tons. She is capable of speeds in excess of thirty knots, *Oriskany's* four turbine engines; fed by eight boilers, deliver 150,000 horsepower to the ship's four screws. *Oriskany* consumes 90,000 gallons of black oil daily while she is steaming at thirty knots. *Oriskany* is comprised of eighteen decks. She is 186 feet 11 inches from the waterline to the top of the mast. Eleven of these decks stretch up from the hangar deck, and the other seven extend down. From the keel to the top of the mast she measures about the same height as a twenty-five-story skyscraper.

There are 2,056 crewmembers and 120 officers stationed aboard *Oriskany*. When the carrier's Airwing CVW-19, is aboard the ship's population increases by 1,500. *Oriskany* is organized into twelve departments. Each department is under the control of a department head and with a clearly defined area of responsibility. The departments are further broken down into divisions under a division officer and division leading chief petty officer. Lower ranking petty officers organize the remainder of the crew at what might be called the "grass roots" level.

Oriskany launches aircraft by means of two steam driven catapults, each 225 feet long. They are capable of launching a 48,000-pound dead weight at 105 knots. *Oriskany's* catapults launch the A-3 *Skywarrior*, which at 66,000 pounds, is the largest aircraft flown off any ship.

Oriskany's aircraft are recovered by means of four arresting wires, which are stretched across the flight deck and connected to separate hydraulic engines below decks. Each engine will arrest aircraft exerting up to 50,000 pounds. I was particularly thankful for this last fact when the aircraft I was in landed on the flight deck of *Oriskany*.

Another "claim to fame" held by *Oriskany* occurred five years before I reported aboard. Admiral James B. Stockdale (then a commander) was the Commander of Carrier Air Wing 16, on board the *USS Oriskany*, when he flew on a mission with Attack Squadron 163 on September 9, 1965. On that mission, Commander Stockdale's A-4E *Skyhawk* was hit by enemy AAA fire and he was forced to eject from the aircraft over enemy territory. He was captured by the North Vietnamese and imprisoned for 7½ years, during which he suffered hideous torture, horrible abuse, debasement, and starvation. Promoted to the rank of captain in absentia while a prisoner of war, Stockdale was released from captivity at war's end in early 1973. Subsequently, he was promoted to the rank of rear admiral, and then to vice admiral, the rank that he retired with. In the future (1992), Admiral Stockdale was a candidate for Vice-President of the United States of America. Also Senator John McCain was stationed in a squadron attached to Oriskany, flying A-4 *Skyhawks* when he was shot done and became a prisoner of war for five years(1967-1973). Senator McCain was a presidential candidate in 2008.

I got off the plane with my sea bag, and was directed off the flight deck, and guided to the personnel office below the hanger deck. I began the usual check-in process. As was always the case at a new duty station I would not be going to work in my rating in W Division, until my security clearance was confirmed.

During this interim waiting period, I was assigned to the Bomb Elevator Shop. This shop was involved in the maintenance and upkeep of the many bomb elevators throughout the ship, used to lift and lower ordnance in and out of the ship's magazines. I went to work with a renewed sense of purpose, and dedication. I felt I was fully committed to a career in the Navy, for better or worse. It seemed to be my lot in life to be a sailor, and I was determined to be the best sailor I could be. I was careful to wear pressed, clean uniforms, knowing that first impressions are important.

The berthing spaces, and mess decks were much like the *Ticonderoga*'s, and not nearly as modern as *Independence*. The mess decks had a First Class Section, and lounge set aside for first class petty officers. The first class mess charged seven dollars monthly dues, which was used to stock a small refrigerator with sandwich material, snacks, plus pay for coffee, and sodas. This was a small additional "perk" that went to those wearing a first class crow.

Shipboard life involved constant ladder climbing, and ladder descending (ladder: Navy term for stairs), and most sailors become very good at this. Going down a ladder, often so quickly, it almost appeared as though the sailor was falling down the ladder, only touching an occasional step to slow the fall. I became very painfully reacquainted with shipboard life, by hitting my head often on this or that steel overhead protrusion, or obstacle. Being six feet tall, I eventually assumed a hunched posture to prevent hitting my head. Tall sailors usually sported a head lump or two, and there were always those with head bumps in sickbay.

I also had to get accustomed again to sleeping with all the shipboard noise, the throb and hum of the ships engines, and the launching and recovery of aircraft.

It seemed the longer I stayed in the Navy, there were always old friends stationed at my new commands. Onboard *Oriskany* there was GMT1 Dan Hoover from "A" school, and the *Ticonderoga*, GMT1 Joe Schmidt from NWTCPAC School, and GMT1 Baldwin from NW school in Norfolk. W Division's breakdown was twenty-three enlisted, and two officers. There were two chiefs, GMTC Schofield, and GMTC Harry Chapbourne, five GMT1's, Baldwin, Goshen, Hoover, Schmidt, and myself. There were three second class, eleven third class, and two GMTSN's.

I was working a twelve-hour on, and twelve-hours off schedule in the bomb elevator shop. The shop had a leading chief, and a couple of Second Class Aviation Ordnancemen, and a large number of seamen. I was the only first class, and I did a little "organizing," and would take charge in the chief's absence. I enjoyed the work, and looked forward the ship's next liberty port, which was Hong Kong.

We pulled into Hong Kong on 27 August. I'd been to Hong Kong in the past, and the city seemed a little larger, with wider streets, the same overpopulation, and the same smell. Hong Kong Mary and her garbage-sorting ladies were still busy looking over the garbage barges that collected the garbage from the ships. The *Oriskany* was anchored in the harbor, which meant a thirty-minute boat ride from the ship to fleet landing. One change on *Oriskany* from my time on *Ticonderoga*, and *Independence*, was that I was permitted to leave the ship on liberty much sooner now that I was a first class. I now was permitted to be in line behind the chiefs. One sailor in W Division was hurt during this in port period in Hong Kong. GMT2 Blevins was in a bar, when someone threw a glass, which struck him in the head and eye. He was medically evacuated back to the U.S. It was never determined who threw the glass.

The bills I was paying off following my divorce were becoming more manageable, but my finances were still slim. My parents were faithful letter-writers. I also received letters from my little brothers. Joe wrote, and said, "Be careful with those "boms!""

On 3 September we pulled anchor from Hong Kong Harbor, and steamed toward Subic Bay. After a few days steaming we stopped at Subic Bay, and stayed a week. I'd had a cold since leaving the States, and was still struggling with it.

A "family gram" was an occasional letter written by the Captain of the *Oriskany* addressed to the crew's family and friends, one written 8 September 1970 said[31]:

Dear Families and friends of *Oriskany*;
With the appearance of this letter, *Oriskany* officially has gone past the halfway point in her current Western Pacific Cruise. Though all hands certainly look forward to the time three months from now when the Mighty "O" steams into San Francisco Bay and a well-deserved homecoming. There is still the second half of the cruise and many more operating days. The pace in the Tonkin Gulf over the ship's first three line periods has been quick and demanding, but everyone, from both ship's company and air wing, have done their jobs in a highly professional manner. You have much for which to be proud in the performances of your men on the Mighty "O" Team.

We are now in Subic Bay, Republic of Philippines, preparing for the fourth line period of air operations on Yankee Station. As I'm sure many of you know, we just completed a seven-day stay in the British Crown Colony of Hong Kong. We were anchored in the middle of beautiful Hong Kong Harbor, and everyone received their share of liberty in this beautiful and exotic city. The weather was seasonally hot, but pleasant enough for interesting tours and sightseeing. The city is a perfect mixture of oriental charm and western sophistication, making the visit most memorable.

Prior to visiting Hong Kong the *Oriskany*/Air Wing 19 team worked a twenty-seven-day line period in the Tonkin Gulf, our longest of the cruise.

Operations continued at a steady, precise pace, with our aviators doing an outstanding job of performing the ship's primary mission as an attack aircraft carrier.

While in the Gulf, one of the squadrons, Attack Squadron 153 had a change of command, with Commander Peter Fredrick relieving Commander Olaf Carlson, Jr. On our second day in Hong Kong Commander Jim Mauldin relieved Commander Edwin Adamson, Jr. of Attack Squadron 155. Just as this letter may be a first for many readers, these changes of command are indicative of the continuous changes in personnel on this ship with the never-ending task of training new people in critical jobs.

While enroute to Hong Kong, we had a cake-cutting ceremony on our hangar deck to commemorate several milestones. Two aviators, Lieutenant Junior Grade Mike Ellvy of Fleet Tactical Support Squadron (the people who bring our mail aboard) and Lieutenant Gary Crowell of Fighter Squadron 194 was recognized for making the ship's 156,000th and 157,000th arrested landings respectively. When we say cake cutting, incidentally, we are speaking of thirteen cakes, weighing a total of 250 pounds. We have a lot of people to serve, and the commissary men do a marvelous job every time in baking outstanding, tasty cakes.

In three days, on 11 September, I will be relieved as Commanding Officer of *Oriskany* by Captain Frank S. Haak here in Subic Bay. Though it saddens me to leave what has been the most rewarding assignment of my naval career, I leave this ship with a profound sense of personal fulfillment and professional pride. In the twelve months that I've commanded *Oriskany,* ten of those months spent at sea, I have seen 3,300 individuals perform in a uniformly outstanding manner. The tempo has seldom slackened. Soon after returning from the Western Pacific last November *Oriskany* was steaming again in February. New personnel had reported onboard, new training was necessary; skills for old hands had to be re-sharpened. Arduous drills and exercises preceded our current deployment in May. Never in that time did these men let up or lose their enthusiasm. The "can do" spirit that characterizes the crew of this ship and air wing is the finest I've seen, and their ability to perform their jobs as a team is what has made the mighty "O."

Oriskany's new skipper, an old personal friend and teammate (a halfback) brings an impressive record to his assignment. As an Ensign in World War II, Captain Haak commanded three minesweepers in the Pacific and served as Gunnery Officer aboard a destroyer prior to flight training. As a Naval aviator he served with various units, and was Commanding Officer of Heavy Attack Squadron Eight aboard the *USS Midway*. Other shipboard duties include assignments as Executive Officer aboard the *USS Forrestal* and Commanding Officer of *USS Point Defiance* (LSD-31) during combat operations in Southeast Asia. He comes to *Oriskany* from duty on the Staff of the Commander Naval Air Force, Pacific Fleet. I truly believe he will provide great leadership and dedication to his new job.

I would like to close by thanking each and every one of you for the commendable support you have given your men. Every *Oriskany*man is a professional sailor, and most importantly, a dedicated American.

It has been a rare privilege to have worked with them, and through them,
to have been acquainted with you, their loved ones. God bless you all.
Sincerely: John A. Gillchrist, Captain, U.S. Navy."

On 11 September, a change of command ceremony was held in the hangar bay, while the ship was tied to the pier. We pulled out to sea on the 15th, and soon were back off the coast of Vietnam, on the line, conducting bombing missions. I was told it would not be long before I would be given access to W Division, and start working as a GMT.

When we pulled out of Subic, the air-conditioning unit in our berthing compartment quit working. The temperature remained around ninety-five degrees and higher in the tropical climate. It was almost impossible to sleep, and rest. The sweat constantly trickling on your body made it difficult to fall asleep.

W Division was split into two working groups. One group built 500 pound bombs for bombing missions, while the other group worked down in W Division spaces. *Oriskany* was very "fire safety conscious," this was the first time I'd seen fire exit markings so prominently marked throughout a ship. Much of this fire awareness came from a tragic fire that had occurred a couple of years previously on *Oriskany*. This fire had killed forty-four sailors, and injured 300. A sailor who was working on an ammunition re-supply working party had caused the fire. He was part of a group of workers who were storing parachute flares in a magazine on the hangar deck. He was playing with a flare, and purposely pulled the initiation pin, and it ignited. The sailor panicked, and instead of throwing the flare down on the deck, or over the side into the water, he threw the flare into the magazine, and slammed the magazine door shut! The lit flare soon ignited all the other stored flares, and burned through the deck, and bulkheads igniting the explosive contents of other ordnance magazines.

Fire was a fairly common happening on a carrier, just as fires occur in any small city, but fire was feared on a ship at sea, because this was our only refuge on the sea, and the nearest land was always straight down a mile or two, at the bottom of the ocean! Our hearts always beat a little faster, knowing the potential for disaster, when the fire alarm was sounded over the 1 MC loudspeakers. Serious carrier fires had also happened on the *USS Enterprise*, and *Forrestal*.

I started wearing a moustache. I'd always been clean-shaven, but moustaches were popular. My mom wrote that she had gotten a number of calls from Alma, and often sounded like she was drunk. I hoped my parents would ignore the calls.

The heat and humidity were very uncomfortable. As usual the W Division nuclear weapon spaces were the coolest spaces on the ship. About this time three of *Oriskany*'s fighters "buzzed" a passenger plane flying in our operating area. I don't recall what the results of the investigation were about the incident? On 25 September, it was the ship's twentieth anniversary, which called for a cake cutting ceremony. A sailor who had been onboard the shortest time, RMSA Ricard (two days), and a sailor who had been onboard the longest, SD1 Santiago (ten years), cut the first piece of cake. After the cake cutting ceremony, it was back to the business of war.

The latter part of September my security clearance was confirmed, and I was permitted into W Division spaces. The magazine spaces were almost identical to the spaces on the *USS Ticonderoga*. My first job assignment was not within the W Division spaces. I was put to work assembling and building conventional bombs, working from midnight to noon. It was hot, dirty work. The bomb bodies came aboard while the ship was alongside a pier, or, as was usually the case, from ammunition ships steaming alongside while off the coast of Vietnam. This was called an UnRep (Underway Replenishment). The bombs were slung across the gap of the two ships with cables. The bombs were packaged in pallets. The bombs were stacked on the hangar deck, and then positioned on bomb elevators with forklifts, and sent down into the ship's magazine for storage. The bombs were securely stacked and tied down in the magazines so they would not roll with the motion of the ship, as we moved over the ocean waves. The bombs were painted olive drab with yellow rings painted around the nose area. There were Mark 82, 500-pound, and Mark 83, 1,000-pound, and Mk 84, 2,000-pound bombs.

During my time on the *Ticonderoga*, we dropped many bombs that had been manufactured during World War II. On *Oriskany* we saw a few of these older bombs; the majority was recently manufactured. As I explained previously, shortly after the intense bombing campaigns began in Vietnam, the U.S. stockpile of conventional bombs became dangerously low.

I would like to clarify for the reader what is meant by the term "bomb building," which I was involved with first on the *USS Ticonderoga*, and then on the *USS Oriskany*. Bomb building was completed in bomb assembly areas at specific locations on the ship. These assembly areas were on the second deck, or the deck immediately below the hanger deck.

These were unusually large compartments that were also used as alternate mess decks to feed the crew. The compartments contained large bomb building racks that were fitted with rollers on which the bomb bodies were placed. The bombs could then safely be rolled 360 degrees. The bomb racks were a little lower than waist high. An air-powered hoist and a manually operated chain hoist were on moveable monorails above the racks so bombs could be raised and lowered into place.

Magazine bomb breakout crews completed the first step in bomb building. These sailors within the magazines would cut the metal strapping holding the bombs onto pallets, and install two suspension lugs into each bomb body, and using a magazine overhead hoist, lift the bomb body out of the pallet and place it in a bomb hand truck. Tie down straps were used to secure the bomb body to the bomb hand truck. In the case of the Mk 8 Bomb Hand truck, two 500-pound, or one 1,000-pound bomb would be placed on the truck. The bombs would be wheeled onto a bomb elevator, and sent up to the bomb assembly area. Magazines were on the fourth, fifth, and sixth decks. The bomb pallets would be set aside for return to the ammunition ships for reuse.

The Mk 8 Bomb Hand Truck I mentioned was a two-wheeled truck, which looked like a wheelbarrow with a flat platform. One man could roll a Mk 8 Bomb Hand truck with two 500-pound bombs, but it took considerable strength (see photo page). When the hand truck was set down after moving, wheel brakes were automatically set. Four-wheel Mk 12 Bomb Hand trucks were used for larger 2,000-pound bombs, and also 500, and 1,000-pound bombs.

When the bombs reached the bomb assembly area, they were placed on the bomb racks, and we would install a nose fuze receiver, and tail fins. The bomb suspension lugs were also checked for tightness. We had two varieties of tails; there was a four finned tapered tail, and a tail that contained spring loaded flaps that would extend when the bomb was dropped so the fall of the bomb was slowed or retarded in order to give the dropping aircraft time to escape the bomb blast. These fins were called "snake eye fins." Snake eye fins were difficult to install, and had a nasty tendency to cut and pinch hands and fingers of bomb builders. After the bombs were "built," they were hoisted off the assembly racks, and placed in bomb hand trucks, and then positioned on a bomb elevator, and sent to the hanger deck for positioning, or sent to the flight deck to await loading on aircraft. On the flight deck loading crews would load the bombs on aircraft pylons, by lifting the bombs up to the pylon attachment points, with a hoist, or more often with a "hernia bar." This was a metal bar which was screwed into the nose of the bomb body, and then the bomb would be lifted with the bar, and by the tail by four men, about shoulder high, until the bomb suspension lugs locked into the aircraft pylon latches, and the bomb then hung from the plane wing, or fuselage, It was a full day's work to load 500-pound bombs in this manner for twelve hours.

There were sway braces that were screwed down against the bomb bodies to hold the bomb securely, and prevent any side-to-side motion that occurred during flight. Shortly before launches, ejector foot explosives were loaded into the aircraft pylons. These were small explosive charges that would initiate when the pilot "pickled," or dropped the bomb on target. The ejector foot would explode downward against the bomb body, and push the bomb away from the flying aircraft, and out of the slipstream caused by the speeding aircraft.

Also, shortly before flight the bomb fuses were screwed into the bomb nose cavities. The fuses had wind propellers, which had arming wires installed to prevent them from turning, until the time of release, when the arming wire was extracted upon dropping from the aircraft. Once the arming wire was extracted, the propeller would freely spin in the wind stream. The propeller was adjusted to spin a certain number of times to either arm the bomb for detonation upon contact with the ground, or to detonate at a certain height above the ground. The flight deck ordnance crew installed these fuses. This same crew would also immediately remove fuses from bombs that were returned by planes that had aborted bombing missions, and returned to the ship, or occasionally there would be a pylon release failure, and the bomb came back aboard with the recovered (landing) plane.

This was a unique experience for GMT's, being "bomb builders." We were considered the "Prima-Donna's" of the ordnance community. Our weapons were the most technically advanced, and sophisticated and destructive in our country's arsenal, and here we were building the basic, crudest weapons our country used. In addition this was one of the most dangerous and physically demanding jobs on the ship. It was on par with the hot, difficult job that the engineers did deep down in the ship's boiler compartments.

My crew usually had a quota of bombs to build each twelve-hour work period. The number was usually in the hundreds. W Division sailors were kept together in one crew, instead of being intermixed with ordnance men of other divisions. We worked well in the assembly line method of bomb building. Our habits of working fault free, safely, and natural drive for perfection translated well into the conventional ordnance world.

GMT's in W Division had been given this additional bomb building assignment, because the magnitude of the bombing at this point in the war was so high, it was beyond the capability of the usual G Division bomb builders. Often our twelve hours off duty time was interrupted by ammunition re-supply working parties, when ammunition ships came alongside to re-supply the ship with bombs, often as frequently as every other day. At these times we would help bring the palletized bombs onboard, and stow them in magazines. It was common to get only four or five hours sleep in a twenty-four-hour period. And that sleep was not restful sleep in a berthing compartment with the temperature hovering around ninety degrees plus, since we had no air conditioning.

As a first class I was placed in a supervisory position. I was thankful that I had some experience as a bomb builder on the *Ticonderoga*, and was able to give some leadership in this area. When working our seven days as bomb builders, we looked forward to our seven days back down in the secure, air-conditioned spaces of W Division, where the work tempo was much slower. We worked seven days a week, without regard to holidays, or weekends.

I quickly got to know the GMT's on board. I enjoyed working for the two W Division Chiefs, and got along well with the W Division Officer, Lieutenant Barber. Lieutenant Commander Salisbury was the Nuclear Safety Officer, or "NSO." This was a LCDR or CDR on a carrier that was directly responsible to the commanding officer on issues of safety during any operation, or handling action of special weapons that might be on board. His authority was absolute in the area of nuclear weapons' safety.

I got word in a letter from home that my dad had put the Firebird up on blocks until I returned. While off the coast of Vietnam, we had free postage. My parents also forwarded a letter that had been mailed to me at their address; it was from the California Highway Patrol. I'd been accepted as a California Highway Patrol Cadet, and was to report to the Sacramento California Highway Patrol Academy in September! It was a few months too late. A letter I wrote 3 October 1970 described my finances. My October first payday had been $450, which included hostile fire pay. Many of my bills from the divorce were being paid off. I had a total of $156 in monthly bills, which was manageable considering I had free "room and board". The ship was scheduled to pull into Japan in a couple of weeks, then another line period, then to Subic Bay, and finally in San Francisco on 19 December. While in Japan, I planned to go birthday present shopping for my sister Linda, and brother Jerry.

One first class, GMT1 Fred Goshen, was anxious to leave the ship in Japan. He was being discharged after ten years active duty. He was the sailor I mentioned who had been stationed with Ray Steele at Lake Mead, Nevada, and he was to later die under mysterious circumstances.

The second week of October, during a recovery (planes landing on the flight deck), an A-7 *Corsair* jet slammed into the ship's fantail, when the pilot came in too low. When the plane hit the aft portion of the ship, everyone felt the impact throughout the ship. The smashed plane and the killed pilot sank into the sea. Luckily the plane was not carrying any bombs. Crashing into the carrier's fantail was jokingly termed by pilots "landing in the spud locker." Because there is always a possibility of a plane coming in low and slamming into a carrier's rear end, the fantail does not contain magazines with explosives, or fuel storage tanks, and often are used as food storage areas, such as potato lockers. Unfortunately pilots did not normally survive a landing in the "spud locker."

I receive a letter saying my mom and two brothers had been in an automobile accident, no one was hurt, but I was anxious to hear more, as the letter did not go into detail. The ship left the line, and steamed toward Japan, which was to be a seven-day trip, during this time frame, the ship did not receive any mail. Finally on the 18th of October I received a letter from home saying my parent's car had been demolished, and thankfully no one was hurt. My brother Joe was playing football, and I wished I were home to watch him play.

I was tired after this line period. It had been an exhausting time. My duties included being a supervisor of a five-man bomb building crew, W Division Damage Control Petty Officer, and Forward Magazine Supervisor of eleven sailors. I was being "groomed" to assume the duties of W Division Leading Petty Officer, following the transfer of GMT1 Baldwin in January or February. I was also scheduled to take the Navy wide advancement examination for chief petty officer.

In Yokosuka, Japan, I was surprised to learn that many of the Japanese that had been there five years ago when I was on the *Ticonderoga* were still there. Tamiko was still working in the New Yokosuka bar, and we renewed our friendship. Japan had not changed too much since my last visit. The currency exchange rate was still 360 yen to one U.S. dollar. Items on Thieves Alley were a little more expensive. Club Alliance, the American run club outside the base had grown considerably, and seemed to be doing well. This was mainly due to the increased number of Navy ship visits carrying out the missions of the Vietnam War.

The ship needed extensive repairs, because of the damage that was caused on the fantail from the plane crash; this was completed in the Yokosuka, Shipyard. While in Yokosuka, we got word that we were scheduled to be back in San Francisco on 10 December, which was earlier than expected.

The first part of November we were back on the "line." We were by ourselves; this was the first time since 1964 that only one aircraft carrier was stationed off the coast of Vietnam. Normally since 1964 there were two or three carriers in the South China Sea.

My crew and I were back in our bomb building jobs. I noticed we were building more Mark 83 1,000 pound bombs (about 270 bombs daily), than we had during previous line periods. Instead of working from 12:00 a.m. to 12:00 p.m. or vice versa, we now were working from 8:00 a.m. to 8:00 p.m. We would work three hours and then take a fifteen-minute break. We were given salt pills, and we ate them like candy!

About this time frame, in November 1970, the "look" of the Navy began to change. If a person looks at pictures of sailors taken in 1970, and then looks at pictures taken in 1971, the change is very obvious. The "new look" came about because of proclamations from the Chief of Naval Operations (CNO). The CNO is the senior officer in the Navy, and advisor to the president on naval affairs, and is directly under the secretary of the Navy. This CNO was newly assigned, and his name was Admiral Elmo Zumwalt. He was considerably junior to a number of admirals that had been considered for the CNO job, and there was resentment among many officers that Zumwalt had "leap-frogged" over their heads for the CNO position.

Admiral Zumwalt began making sweeping and liberal changes in Navy regulations, and the way the Navy had operated for years. An example of the changes that lead to the "new look," was his proclamation that beards were now permitted to be worn by sailors, and sideburns could be worn much longer, which was the style worn by many men in civilian life. He abolished "out of bounds passes," which I mentioned before, were passes required to be in a sailor's possession if he went a certain distance away from his duty station. He abolished authority of petty officers to assign extra duty to junior men. He did away with property passes, and many more regulations that were often considered irritating by younger sailors. These proclamations of changes were issued by messages to all Navy commands from the CNO. The messages became known as "Z-grams." At the time I thought this was a breath of fresh air. Later however, and in retrospect, this method of change coming directly from the top, without going through the chain of command, caused damage to effective leadership, and discipline in the Navy for many years following the flood of "Z-grams." The authority of commanding officers was undermined, as well as the authority of senior petty officers. There was grumbling in the officer and chief petty officer ranks, along the line of, "Why should I give an order, when the CNO will probably reverse the order tomorrow?" The controversy over Z-grams would continue many years after Admiral Zumwalt retired. I often heard the comment "Admiral Zumwalt ruined the Navy." Perhaps there is a grain of truth in that comment, but it's also true that people resist change, and sailors are no different. Because of Z-grams all sailors were now permitted to have and store civilian clothes on board ships, which was previously a privilege only given to officers, and occasionally chiefs. This privilege was gradually phased in starting with first and second class petty officers, and over time extended down to the lowest ranks. This new Z-gram was a shock to locker clubs in Navy seaports. These clubs had made their living renting lockers for civilian clothes storage to sailors stationed on ships. Most locker clubs folded, and went out of business shortly after the civilian clothes Z-grams.

The permission to grow beards Z-gram was sent out to the fleet with limited direction, i.e., how long the beard was permitted to be, and what styles were allowed? It seemed like everyone on board the ship was trying to grow a beard. There was a lot of horrible straggly looking, facial hair growths. It should also be explained that this was a time when long hair was the fashion, and this along with a beard grown by young men was considered a statement of rebellion against the older generation, and the "establishment." Beards were also identified with those making protests against the government and the military. In groups of antiwar protesters, the beard was a common denominator. Before the beard Z-gram, officers and petty officers were constantly correcting young sailors who tried to get away with wearing their hair as long as possible. In the midst of this "hair battle," the beard Z-gram appeared. Many officers and senior petty officers threw their hands up and said, "If the CNO doesn't care what sailors look like, why should I?" and many stopped enforcing any military appearance standards.

Younger sailors waited anxiously for the next Z-gram, which were issued almost monthly, while commanding officers, and others were dismayed, and apprehensive about what the next Z-gram might say. During my ten years in the Navy, I had seen a dilution of the respect given to senior petty officers. My first few years in the Navy it had been unheard of to speak to a chief petty officer until spoken to.

All petty officers were generally respected, and revered, their authority was seldom questioned. Petty officers were able to enforce discipline by awarding extra duty and restricting liberty for violators. Z-grams took away much of the petty officer's authority, but did not take away the responsibility of petty officers to get the job done! The antiwar movement and demonstrations against our involvement in Vietnam created an atmosphere of questioning authority, which spilled over into Navy society. I was not comfortable with this increased questioning atmosphere. Another change over time I observed was the way sailors addressed one another. In the late 1960s it was becoming common for seniors to call juniors by their first name, something unheard of in the past. Even worse, some seniors permitted juniors to call them by their first name. I believed that this practice breed familiarity, and I also believed the saying "familiarity breeds contempt." The use of first names did have the effect of eroding respect. I always addressed others by rank or last name. On liberty off the ship, or base it was a different matter. This "name calling issue" was to me a matter of maturity. A sailor should be able to distinguish when it was all business or work, and when it was time to play. I made it very clear, that on the job I wanted to be addressed as either "Little," "GMT1 Little," or Petty Officer Little." Off the job (if the sailor was mature) "Jim." I never used the first name of a senior, either on the job, or off the job. To the reader it may seem I'm belaboring this point? I've always felt that a clear distinction of ranks is an important aspect of discipline. The "bottom line" reason for discipline, along with training, is to have a Navy that is battle-ready. The hard truth is that the ultimate aim of the Navy is to kill (or disable), enemies of the United States. This grim task is a hard and fearful job, and the most effective sailor is one who does his job in the midst of confusion, and horror of war without the hesitation or thought. He must be so disciplined, and well trained, that he does his job automatically without thought or desire to flee, when bullets are whizzing about, bombs exploding, and death is near.

On the 20th of November we were supposed to leave the line for Subic Bay, but instead we remained on station and were suddenly very busy building bombs, and preparing for a large strike against North Vietnam. There had not been many large bombing strikes in the north for some time, and we all felt something "big" was about to happen? We were also on edge because the ship was much further north than we had been for a long time. There were a number of bombing strikes launched with the bombs we built, and there was concern for our pilots flying over anti-aircraft batteries in the north that had been untouched for years during the war, and were probably built up and much more capable at this point in time. We learned a few days later that there had been an attempt by Special Forces, during the time of our increased bombing missions, to rescue some of our prisoners of war (POWS'), but when the rescue forces went in the POW camp was empty, so the rescue attempt was a failure.

We finally left the line for the last time during this cruise. After a short stay in Subic Bay, the ship began the long trip over the Pacific toward San Francisco. We were to be in Hawaii on the 3rd of December, because the Commander-in-Chief of the Pacific (CINCPAC), Admiral John J. Hyland wanted his change of command ceremony to be conducted on *Oriskany*. I don't know the reason for his desire to have the ceremony on the ship, but it caused a lot of resentment among crewmembers. This ceremony caused a lot of extra preparation work, and it delayed our return home, after a long cruise.

Twelve single sailors in W Division drafted a letter, and sent the letter to many colleges in America. The letter asked for college girls to write. The response was amazing; although there were a few insulting letters from "peaceniks," but the letters were mostly pleasant. In the years to come there were even a couple of marriages that took place between these girls and W Division sailors, who started their relationships in the mail!

The ship pulled into Pearl Harbor, and a few days later on 5 December the CINCPAC change of command ceremony was conducted. In some of the mail that came aboard in Hawaii, I received a wonderful box of cookies and candies, from the Ladies Missionary Circle, of my hometown church, Strathmore Faith Baptist Church. The cookies and candies disappeared quickly when I shared the package with the division. I did a little sightseeing while in Hawaii. I toured the monuments in Pearl Harbor. Many were preparing for the annual ceremonies that took place each year on the date of the Japanese attack, 7 December. This was to be the 29th anniversary of that attack.

The ship got underway after the change of command ceremony, and I spent my twenty-eighth birthday at sea. We were to arrive at the Naval Air Station Alameda pier on 10 December. As the ship sailed under the Golden Gate Bridge, *Oriskany* sailors stood on the flight deck in dress blues in formation, spelling out the words "NOEL POWS."

The men that lost their lives on that 1970 cruise were: LT John B. Martin, LT Joseph R. Klugg, LT Wiley H. Skidmore, and Comdr. Donald D. Aldern, who was declared missing in action.

Each deployment of a Navy ship is usually detailed in a "cruise book" which gives an outline of what happened over the deployment period, including pictures of the crew, and happenings on board, and ashore. The 1970 Cruise Book contained some interesting facts for the period 14 May 1970 to 10 December 1970 – 154 days at sea, 57 days in port. Number of aircraft launches: 7,983, Number of aircraft recoveries: 7,838, Number of underway replenishments: 77, Ordnance expended: 5,858 tons. Miles steamed: 67,743 nautical miles, Fresh water manufactured: 27,769,000 gallons, Mail handled: 492,746 pounds, Food consumed: 1,135 tons, Total payroll: $8,263,000.

The cruise book contained the following quote: "Our job is to keep the torch of freedom burning for all. To this solemn promise we call on the young, the brave, the strong, the steady, the fearless and the free. May those who hear it heed my call, come to sea, come sail with me. John Paul Jones."

The theme of the *Oriskany* 1970 cruise book was "Heritage 70", and began the first page with the following:

On August 6, 1777, a decisive, bloody battle raged in a valley called Oriskany Creek, located near Rome, New York. A group of American patriots, led by General Nicholas Herkimer, faced a combined force of British soldiers and Indian warriors loyal to King George III of England. The hard-fought American victory, though fatal to General Herkimer, averted a British occupation of the strategic Mohawk Valley and neutralized the strength of General Burgoyne at Saratoga, ultimately helping America gain its independence.

Oriskany was remembered some 166 years later when Congress authorized construction of an aircraft carrier, and named it in tribute to that significant battle.

Though work on the ship *Oriskany* began in 1944, the end of World War II halted progress, and it was not until 25 September 1950, with the Korean Conflict at hand, that she was commissioned as a fighting ship of the line in Brooklyn, New York.

In the twenty years since her commissioning *Oriskany* has undergone several changes, while building at the same time an impressive record of service and performance. Launched with a straight flight deck and open bow, *Oriskany* made one cruise to the Mediterranean in 1951. After being the first aircraft carrier to round Cape Horn, *Oriskany* became a Pacific warship in 1952, and promptly earned her nickname of "Mighty O" during two combat cruises off Korea.

In 1957 *Oriskany* was modernized, receiving the striking angled flight deck and enclosed hurricane bow that now highlights her profile. Now, more powerful steam catapults replaced the hydraulic variety, enabling the ship to handle the most modern jet aircraft. Her Western Pacific cruises resumed in routine fashion, and on 14 May 1970 *Oriskany* left her homeport of Alameda, California just six months after completing her 1969 cruise. Steaming for Yankee Station in the Gulf of Tonkin, *Oriskany* began her eleventh West Pac deployment, her fifth consecutive combat tour in the waters of Vietnam.

The cruise was doubly significant for *Oriskany*. Not only was it the twentieth year since her commissioning, but it was also her first cruise of the 1970s, the decade when America observes its double centennial.

Oriskany and the country she serves so proudly, enter the 70s committed to protecting the institutions and principles conceived two centuries ago. Yet both look forward to the prospects of progress and orderly, peaceful developments of tomorrow.

And it is to this, a welcome to the new decade, coupled with a salute to yesterday, that *Oriskany* dedicates the story of this cruise. This is Heritage 70.

Just as human beings have different personalities, it is the same with Navy ships! Just as blood flows through the arteries of a person's body, a ship's lifeblood are the sailors that flow through her passageways, and live within her. I had been very fortunate that all the ships I had been assigned to previously had good reputations and personalities. The *Oriskany* was no exception. I was proud to be part of her crew.

When the ship pulled alongside the Alameda pier, it was a time of intense excitement. I enjoyed watching the joy of couples and families reuniting. Although I knew there would be no one waiting on the pier looking for me, I secretly hoped I'd be surprised and there would be someone welcoming me home, although I knew it was a foolish wish. Regardless when the last of the huge crowd on the pier disappeared, and I'd not seen a familiar face, there was a feeling of disappointment. I think all the sailors far from home, and the single sailors felt the same sense of disappointment I did. We felt proud of the job we had done in the war, in a difficult and dangerous environment, and were relieved that we had survived to return home. What we really longed for was some sign of appreciation from our country, something like the veterans of World War II had received, but the only tangible appreciation was an occasional whispered thanks from older veterans, or a statement from someone that began " Everyone's against the war, but we're behind you." It was always a letdown to return to our homeland, and be greeted with indifference, or hostile opposition to a war that had been our life for month after long month. With these feelings, it was also a vast relief to be back in America safe and sound. A thought that always occurred to me when I departed on cruises, sometimes stronger than others, was "Will this be the last time I see home?"

The Oakland Tribune newspaper dated 11 December 1970 carried this article[32]:

"Pride and tears as Big "O" came home"

Alameda – The men of the *USS Oriskany* sailed into port Yesterday from the waters of Vietnam and waded into a sea of signs, binoculars and teddy bears.

Thousands of wives, parents and babes – some of whom had never met Daddy – lined the dock at the Alameda Naval Air Station to welcome back Oakland's flagship.

Many were anxious that they would not recognize their men, mainly because of the new Navy regulations that allowed long hair, beards, and moustaches. Some were right.

War seemed far away as the gangplank was lowered and goateed, sideburned sailors walked off carrying guitars and suitcases. But the anxiety of Vietnam showed itself in tears, the sobs and hugs.

The *Oriskany*, or "Big O" as she is known in the east bay, was returning from her fifth combat tour off the coast of Vietnam.

For the Kleindl family of Alameda, it was one of many homecomings. Eight year old Curtis stiffly held a hand-lettered sign reading, "Welcome home Daddy" as his Mother scanned the decks of the attack carrier looking for her husband, Machinist Mate Roger Kleindl.

He has been in the service for 16 years, so reunions are part of life.

The other Kleindl children – Kevin, 10; Diana 11; and Tammy, 18 months – waited patiently. Soon Daddy would be home again.

Another family stood nearby, the youngsters restlessly waiting for the welcoming ceremonies to subside, the wife thinking out loud about "his favorite dinner" that she was giving him that evening – tacos and cherry pie. "It may sound strange together, but that's what he likes."

A band played, cheerleaders danced, acrobatic pilots performed overhead and babies began to cry.

Pretty Gayle Sandra of Walnut Creek waved a banner reading "Colorado Kid". She smiled and explained she was welcoming her cousin, Jerry Cole, who was from Denver, Colorado.

"He's going to come home with us tonight and visit some of his relatives in the east bay and then tomorrow, he'll be flying home for Christmas."

A helicopter swooped overhead and dropped flowers on the decks and hundreds of balloons filled the air.

"Oh, I'm so excited," a red haired wife, clutching a pair of binoculars, murmured to no one in particular.

Electrician Technician Gary Goodwin in uniform was in the crowd with his wife, Kathy, and their son, Gary Lewis. He arrived here November 30 in an advance contingent to arrange the welcoming activities. He had been in Vietnam three times, but this trip was his first aboard the *Oriskany*.

Jim Gillentine of Hanford was in his civvies mingling in the crowd but he too was part of *Oriskany*. He took leave when the ship landed in Pearl Harbor and has been home with his wife Barbara, for a week.

LCDR Jon Dekker of Lemoore also belonged on *Oriskany* and also came home early on leave. Holding on to his wife, Jean, and children, Troy, 4, and Thor, 6, he was fighting his way through the crowd to get back on ship "to get my gear."

Some babes in arms hadn't seen their fathers in a long time and others not at all.

Eight-month-old Steven Charles slept soundly, cuddled in his stroller, as his Mother, Rebecca Denton, of Alameda, searched the deck of uniforms for her husband, Michael. She giggled as she went over her elaborate plans for a surprise party for him that evening. Steven slept through it all.

Little Jeannie Jumper seemed to take her Father's hugs and kisses for granted. She was born four days after her Father Ordnanceman Lester Jumper, shipped out. "Carol kept sending me pictures of her but she looks much better than her pictures"; he gushed as his wife stood by holding Jennie's teddy bear.

John Johnson had a big welcome party – his Mother, Mrs. June Empey of Oakland, his fiancé, Janice of Hayward, and his Pekingese dog, Kim.

So did LCDR John Siembieda of Fremont. His two daughters six-year old Amy and eight-year old Kathy shared a sign that said "Kathy and Amy say hi to our Daddy and the Mighty O." His wife, Marianne, wearing an orchid and holding another one, bubbled with happiness. She said he had been in the service for 11 years and had just been notified that this was his last cruise to Vietnam.
"We've had a lot of homecomings," she said, "but we're happier every time."

"Amy got up in the middle of the night to make sure her room was still clean for daddy. And Kathy went into the bathroom this morning and practiced smiling in the mirror."

The signs and the banners waved in the breeze. They listed names, ranks, titles like "Daddy" and "Uncle" and one that reflected the sentiment of the dockside mob. It screamed out "Welcome home Darling." The *Oriskany* was home."

My first evaluations on *Oriskany* covered the period 1 June 1970 to 1 December 1970. The evaluations detailed my assignment as a nuclear weapon technician, and as Periodic Maintenance System (PMS) coordinator for the division, and also as Division Damage Control Petty Officer.

There were not as high as the straight 4.0's I had gotten at Whidbey Island, but they were certainly better than the "lackluster" ones I'd been given on Guam.

I had duty the first day we pulled alongside the Alameda pier. The ship had a much-reduced workload over the holiday period. I went home to Strathmore, and it was wonderful to be reunited with my family, who I had not seen for six months. I learned that my parents and brothers had planned to surprise me and be on the pier when the ship pulled in, but on the way to San Francisco, their car broke down. The cold weather took some getting used to after being in the tropic climate, without air conditioning in W Division berthing compartment. Most of the division sailors ended up with colds and sniffles.

I was not able to spend Christmas with my parents, and brothers, but was able to spend the weekend before Christmas with them. I enjoyed visiting with my sister who lived in Fresno with her husband and two daughters. I drove my Pontiac firebird back to San Francisco, after my visit home. I had duty on Christmas day, and enjoyed a holiday meal in the ship's chow hall. We also were given free packs of cigarettes, because sailors were some of the tobacco company's best customers.

The ship's sailors and I enjoyed the relaxed tempo of life alongside the pier. Just about everyone onboard, while at sea, craved fresh vegetables, and fresh milk. The milk we were given at sea was a "recombined variety," that was only drinkable in the chocolate flavor. It was convenient having my car parked near the pier, although it was a long walk to the parking lot, about ½ mile from the after brow of the ship. I did enjoy having my car available, but I began to tire of the constant requests to take single sailors here and there, often without an offer to help pay for gas. The only thing that slowed down the requests was that I was a senior petty officer, and this intimidated some of the younger sailors.

I was scheduled to take the chief petty officer promotion examination in February, and I used much of my off duty time studying for the exam. Everyone was anxious about what the ship's future schedule might be? We apparently weren't going to get much of a "break" from the war, as we heard we were supposed to deploy again around the middle of 1971.

I was the division PMS (not the labeled female syndrome this was to become in future years) coordinator. This was a newly developed Periodic Maintenance System that placed all equipment and hardware on the ship, into a scheduled pattern of preventive maintenance. This was a complex system that included work orders, scheduling, and coordination with the ships main PMS office, as well as coordination with shipyard work planners and workers. I also had the responsibility of supervising all PMS actions within the division. I had a large office space in the forward W Division spaces that I used as my "PMS office."

As were the case in foreign ports, W Division frequented certain places all the time, usually bars. The desire to get off the ship on liberty was fed by the "imprisoned" feeling we'd sometimes feel on a ship. We lived within a steel boundary, with little privacy, and this world shrank after weeks and weeks at sea. Although we were driven to get off the ship, we were also driven to remain together as a group. We were shipmates, and lived closer together than most brothers in a family. In Alameda, a city close to the base, W Division would gather at a bar called the "Ready Room," which was named after the compartment on aircraft carriers where squadron pilots are briefed before missions. The Ready Room wasn't anything special, just a bar, two pool tables, and a jukebox. Another popular bar in Alameda was a place called "Johnny's," a club that had been in Alameda as long as the Navy had.

Not long after the ship returned to Alameda, The division had a new chief report aboard. He was a master chief, named GMTCM Reichman. He was also the senior enlisted man on *Oriskany*. Chief Schofield, and Chief Chadborne were a little easier going than Master Chief Reichman, and he soon made it clear that he was "in charge"!

GMT1 Baldwin made chief off the September 1970 promotion exam, and he "put the hat on" a couple of weeks before he was transferred off the ship bound for duty in Florida. The promotion from first class to chief petty officer is like no other promotion in the Navy, and is also unique in the Navy compared to the other military services promotion from E-6 to E-7. The actual promotion ceremony is shrouded in secrecy. The ceremony takes place within the Chief's Club, and no one is permitted to attend except chiefs, and a few invited officers. The social and professional gulf between enlisted chiefs and other enlisted men is wide, and almost as wide as the gulf between enlisted men and officers. It is a lofty goal for an enlisted man to make chief. Baldwin was required to carry around a "charge book" prior to his promotion that he had to give to any chief when requested. The chiefs would write accusations that would be used at his "trial" during his promotion ceremony. With the promotion of GMTC Baldwin, I became the senior first class in W Division, and therefore, the W Division Leading Petty Officer.

The W Division "hangout" across the Bay Bridge from Alameda in San Francisco was the "Carnival Club," a bar near O'Farrell Street in downtown San Francisco. The bar had an electronic bowling machine, and two pool tables. A unique feature about the Carnival Club was the many bowls of free salted in the shell peanuts that were kept for customers on the long bar at the front of the club. You were expected to drop the peanut shells on the floor while shelling and eating the peanuts. Peanut shells littered the floor, and they crunched each time a person walked about the bar. Of course the rationale behind offering free salted peanuts was the thirst they created, and thus the increased purchase of drinks.

An Italian man and his son owned the bar. The son worked at night, his name was Johnnie, and he was tough enough to also serve as a bouncer. Although anytime there were W Division sailors in the bar, they would help keep the peace, because we felt this was our territory. We were treated well in the Carnival Club, if someone was short on money, he was granted "credit" until next payday. This was a rough neighborhood, and we got to know about everyone. Two policemen that had a walking beat, would stop by every evening, and at a table in the back of the bar, would get "free drinks." They also got extra money "under the table" from the owner, for providing extra protection. We got to know all the prostitutes, and pimps that worked the streets, and also the beggars that asked for handouts. One black man about eighty years old, dressed in a tuxedo, would occasionally come into the bar very late at night, and Johnnie would turn down the lights, and this elder man would get on a small lit stage near the bar, and tap dance and play a harmonica. He called himself "Mister Bo Jangle." He was very good, and he appreciated our applause. He got no pay for this other than the small amounts we would give him, but he seemed to do it more for the pleasure he got out of performing than for the money. There was a parking lot I used directly across from the Carnival Club, and I got to know the owner. He had been raised in Oak Harbor, Washington and we both knew some of the same people. He was making a good living with his pay-for-parking business.

This was a rough section of San Francisco, and shootings and stabbings were common. One night in a place called the "High Ball," which was located across from the Carnival Club, Chief Baldwin and I were sitting together at the end of the bar. There were perhaps ten other customers in the bar. The bartender was an old boxer, with cauliflower ears, and a nose that was "all over his face." He was a little "punch drunk," but a very pleasant man. A woman, who was sitting at the bar, stood up and walked toward the restroom located in the back area of the bar. As soon as she came back out of the restroom, a guy she had been seated with at the bar, stood up, pulled out a gun, and said "Don't anyone move!" he appeared to be very nervous, and the hand holding the gun was shaking. The muzzle opening of the gun looked very large from my point of view, as he pointed it at everyone in the bar. The bartender started to move, and the gunman screamed again, "Don't move!" Finally after what seemed like a long time, he said, "I'm a police officer." He then kept his gun pointed at the woman who had come back out of the restroom. He stopped shaking enough to walk over to the bar's phone, and he placed a call. Soon there were about twelve policemen in the bar. They wrote down all of our names, and took the woman away. We never learned what the true story was? This was a common happening in that part of town.

In January the ship moved from the Alameda Naval Air Station pier across the bay to Hunters Point Naval Shipyard. This was the shipyard I'd been at during my time on the *USS Ticonderoga*. The ship was to undergo a short yard period before we deployed again to Vietnam. We all dreaded the inconvenience of living on a ship in a shipyard environment. The ship was not placed in dry dock, but tied alongside the pier at Hunters Point while the ship was worked on by the shipyard workers. Hunters Point was located near a low income, slum area, and a dangerous place to travel through, especially late at night. The area outside the base had not changed much since 1965, and if anything, seemed to be more run down, and poverty stricken.

It was wonderful to wear civilian clothes when leaving the ship on liberty. However this did cause a storage problem on the ship, because when the ship was built, it was assumed that there only needed to be storage room for sailor's sea bag uniforms, and not the additional civilian clothes everyone was now allowed to keep aboard. In W Division, we set up a common storage area within our Division spaces for civilian clothes.

One system we were always concerned about working properly, was the magazine sprinkler system. This was the ship system that had sprinkler heads in the overhead of all explosive magazines, and was operated by heat sensors, or remotely activated stations outside the magazine. This was a system that might save our lives in the event of fire. It was also a system that caused worries about premature activation, which would result in a flood within a magazine. The magazines also had flooding alarms connected to alarm panels at various locations on the ship, which would sound if there were six inches of water in the magazine compartments. The sprinkler system remote activation stations were tested monthly.

The hydraulic valves would be cycled monthly, with a mechanical wedge in the "dry aside" of the system that would prevent flooding during this monthly test. During the test it was required that commissioned officer be present. The water in this sprinkler system was salt water, or seawater, which was very corrosive to the steel, brass, and copper fittings that made up the sprinkler system.

One evening in San Francisco, a girl named Helen who worked in the Hi-Ball, asked me if I would walk her home after work? I agreed, and while walking to her apartment, at 2:30 a.m., about six blocks away, four men approached us from behind, and stopped us. They said they were police officers. They asked me my name, and if I knew the name of the girl I was with? After more questioning they let us go. They were very rude, and I think they were vice squad officers? I was relieved that they were not muggers, but I was angry about the rude treatment. Of course I should have expected something, being out on the street at that late hour.

While in Hunters Point, it was a noisy, dirty existence onboard *Oriskany*. Yard workers came onboard each morning, and shifts of welders worked twenty-four hours a day. One assignment disliked by the junior seaman, was "fire watch." This job along with mess cooking, and side cleaning, was considered a "bottom of the ladder" job. The fire watch sailors, armed with a fire extinguisher would position themselves in compartments adjacent to whatever compartment welding was taking place. The work was boring and tedious. The young seaman dreaded these assignments. My feeling was that all seamen should have a tour of at least one of the jobs. I'd had three months of mess cooking, and it certainly made me appreciate W Division work, and living conditions, as a "GMT."

Our "breather" from the fast pace of war operations didn't last long. The ship got underway from Hunters Point the last of February. I'd taken the chief's exam the middle of the month, but didn't feel like I had passed. We went alongside the pier at Alameda, and began periods of underway training each week. We'd usually pull back into Alameda after steaming off the California coast, on Friday afternoons. We would get underway early on Monday mornings. We stood four-section duty, thus every fourth day; we were required to remain onboard twenty-four hours. This was called a "duty day," and I stood a variety of duties on my duty day.

Weapons Department was shorthanded, and short of chiefs, so as I was a senior first class, I often stood duty as Weapons Department Duty Chief. I was responsible to the Weapons Department Duty Officer, for all of the Weapons Department spaces, after normal working hours. My duties more than anything else were ensuring all weapons department divisions made required reports to Damage Control Central, and compartments were kept trash free by dumping trash before taps, which was held at 2200 (10:00 p.m.). I occasionally stood shore patrol duties.

Since returning to the States, there had been many transfers from the ship. The division numbers were dropping, and we had fewer new men come aboard. One of the most tedious jobs was removing the thousands of screws in deck pads, in the magazines, cleaning the threads in the deck, and oiling the threads. These threads accepted the bolts that were used to hold the storage and handling frames, and weapons, to the deck. We also would have our annual NTPI before the deployment. Along with all this preparation, Master Chief Reichman was arranging the division to his liking.

The middle of March the ship visited San Diego. The city had not changed much since my time on the *Ticonderoga*. While in San Diego I tried to contact my cousin David Sylvester, who had recently joined the Navy and was at Balboa Naval Hospital working as a Hospital Corpsman. I didn't have success finding him.

A first class in the division, Dan Hoover who I'd been with on the *USS Ticonderoga*, was getting married in April. He asked Chief Harry Chapbourne if he would be his best man, and he asked me if I would be an usher, and also stand with him in the front of the church during the wedding. I was honored that he asked me. The church was to be in a huge Catholic church in Oakland. His future wife was Scottish, and the wedding was to have more than 500 guests. We had a rehearsal, and were fitted for tuxedos. The day of the wedding, on a Saturday, Dan made it through the wedding vows okay, and then there was a huge reception. Harry Chapbourne and I worked as bartenders, and general helpers. After the reception one of the maids of honor, said she'd like to go out on the town with me, so Harry, she, and I went to a lot of different places in San Francisco that night. I took her home, and she said she would call me. A few weeks later, I saw her in the Navy Exchange. She had three children with her, and was very nervous. Then I realized she was married. Just as there were Med (Mediterranean) widows, she was a WestPac (Western Pacific) widow, and I never saw her again.

W Division had been very busy preparing for our annual inspection. The first of May, I was able to attend my high school reunion/homecoming at my hometown of Strathmore.

Although it had been nine years in the past, when I happened to see my ex-fiancée Donna at this gathering, my heart pounded, and the old feelings of rejection and disappointment returned. At the reunion dance a classmate of mine introduced me to a girl named Teresa. I remembered her from my high school years. She was the same age as my sister Linda. I definitely remembered her brother, who was a couple of years ahead of me in grammar school and had been the school bully. I dated her a few times, and prior to deployment took a few days' leave, and we dated for a while. She said she would write to me.

The Navy was going through a period of transition, the sailors of World War II were gone, there were a few Korean veterans, but not many. Admiral Zumwalt was forcing a lot of changes upon the Navy. There was talk of changing our uniforms. We, as well as society, were coming to grips with a widespread illegal drug use problem, as well as struggling with race relations. The military was looked upon with mistrust by many of the younger generation in America.

Our annual inspection was held before deployment overseas. As I mentioned before every aspect of our operations with nuclear weapons was inspected. I was the forward magazine supervisor as well as leading petty officer. One operation that had to be demonstrated for the inspectors during our inspection was the movement of a weapon. It was required that a weapon on its wheel container be under positive control at all times when it was not bolted to the deck, or tied down with tie down chains. "Positive control" meant at least two men pushing or physically touching the weapon. During the demonstration a training weapon was positioned on an elevator during a movement to the hangar deck, with armed marines in attendance. Two W Division sailors were on the elevator with a weapon, and tie downs had just been removed. One sailor took his hand off the weapon for about fifteen seconds, at that point the operation was graded a failure! The sailor who did it was a "problem sailor." He was not mechanically inclined, and was not a good GMT. He eventually was kicked out of the GMT rate. He gave me a lot of extra work. Anyway, we passed our inspection except for this small section, which marred our attempt to complete a perfect inspection. We had to be re-inspected in a couple of weeks.

Near the day of our departure for deployment overseas, I drove my car home to Strathmore. My parents and two brothers drove me back to Alameda in their car. We arrived early in the morning. I took them on board as guests, and we toured the ship. We sat for a while in the First Class Mess. There were a lot of people on the ship, and pier in anticipation of our departure. The ship was to leave at 10:00 a.m., so my parents and brothers went down to the pier, the gangways and lines were removed. I was up on the flight deck waving goodbye. The departure of the ship was not smooth. The ship was turned too sharply pushing a camel into the pier destroying a number of pilings. It was near where my family was. This scared people standing on the pier, luckily no one was hurt. The captain came over the loudspeaker, and thanked everyone for seeing us off. He said, "Pray for us, we're off to war." As I looked down at my family as they disappeared from view, I wondered, "Will this be the last time I see them?"

The months prior to deployment we had trained at sea going to general quarters, firing our guns, and general warfare drills. On the way to Hawaii we did a lot of nuclear weapons aircraft loading training, and me and others worked as technical monitors on the hangar, and flight deck, overseeing the aircraft loads.

There were three first class in the division: Dan Hoover, Charlie Galbreath, and I. Dan had put an application in for the warrant officer program, which if accepted, he would be commissioned a warrant officer. I had considered applying, but instead wanted to make chief petty officer.

On 22 May we pulled into Hawaii. Our berthing compartment air conditioner was acting up again. I kept complaining about it to the chiefs, and our division officer. We expected the men to work hard, and I felt it was important, that at the very least they have a comfortable place to sleep. The part to repair the air conditioner was unavailable, so the division officer agreed to let people sleep in the coffee locker. We set up cots, and mattresses. It was not the best arrangement, but at least it was cool down in the division spaces. The berthing compartment temperatures hovered around 100 degrees.

Charlie Galbreath and I went on liberty in Hawaii. We walked along the beach, and visited a place called the International Marketplace. Hawaii was still an expensive port. He and I decided we would visit Hotel Street. We'd never been there; it's an infamous street that catered to sailors. Hotel Street was also patrolled by the HASP's, which stood for Hawaii Armed Services Police. They had the toughest reputation in the Navy, as far as being a "by the book shore patrol." They would arrest sailors for any minor infraction of military appearance or behavior. Most sailors were in civilian clothes. We went into a bar that was almost deserted. The place apparently became busy in the evenings. This was in the early afternoon; there was a huge dance floor, with chairs and tables. Charlie and I set at the bar.

I got up and walked to the restroom that was located way in the back of the dance floor. After using the restroom, and as I was about to walk out the door, two black guys appeared at the door. They were looking for trouble. One of them began cursing at me, and struck me in the chest with his fist. Then the fight began. I managed to force both of them out of the restroom onto the dance floor. Chairs and tables were flying, and after what seemed like a long time, they ran out of the bar. I went to the bar where Charlie was still sitting, and said, "Charlie why didn't you help me?" he said, "Huh, what are you talking about?" He had conveniently ignored the fight. As I said before many sailors were given nicknames on the ship, from that day on I called him "Backup Charlie." I was not injured during the fight except for a few cuts and bruises.

We got underway from Hawaii and steamed toward Subic Bay, Philippines. The fighter planes on the ship conducted flight operations daily, and bombers also flew almost every day. Sailors were permitted to line up on a catwalk area, about three decks above the flight deck, near the bridge. This was a wonderful viewpoint from which to watch flight deck operations, and takeoffs and landings. The viewpoint was called "vultures row," because just as people often go to car races with hopes of seeing a crash, so did some of the sailors who watched flight operations watch for an aircraft crash, thus, the nickname vultures row. The fighters, F-8 *Crusaders*, were our protection from enemy aircraft. During each transit of an American aircraft carrier over the Pacific Ocean, the Russians would make their presence known. The following is an excerpt from a letter that I wrote to my parents 4 June 1971:

> Yesterday, we had a little excitement. We had the usual visit from long-range Russian planes. Every time a carrier hits this area in the ocean, they send their planes out. It's really a sort of huge "game," although it's deadly serious. When we hit this area, our fighters are on constant alert, and the Russians usually try to see how close they can get before being detected and we try to intercept them before they get into missile range, of the ship. I went up on the flight deck, after they were intercepted, they usually make a couple of low passes over the ship, they flew over, with our fighters trailing them, within gun sight. They were huge planes, (2), one had six turbo jet engines, and one was a four-engine jet, each was silver, with the red star on the tail. In a way this can all be interpreted as the Russians saying, "We know you're there, and we can sink you, if we wanted." We're saying, "You can't get close enough to us, we'd shoot you down before you got the ship." Anyway it always breaks the monotony of the long crossing.

My mother showed this section of the letter to a neighbor named Greta Stewart, who was a newspaper reporter, and she published it in my local hometown paper, The *Lindsay Gazette*.

It took eleven days to travel from Pearl Harbor to Subic Bay. We would be back in the war soon. The annual battle efficiency award competition period ended 1 June, and we were to discover shortly afterward that we had won the "Battle E" in competition with the nine carriers in the Pacific. Weapons Department also won the black "W" as the best carrier weapons department in the Pacific. This was a feather in the cap for all *Oriskany* sailors. We now got to wear an "E" on our left arm. It was an exceptional honor for us in the weapons department to have won the black "W." Everyone in weapons department was very proud of this achievement! We in weapons department also got to wear a black "W" on our left arm below the "E." We had beat out the other nine weapons departments on the other nine carriers. Our guns had scored higher on graded shots, we had received the highest marks on our inspections, including our NTPI, and had been selected as the best. The pride in our ship, and weapons department sailors was intensified by the fact that most of the carriers we were competing with were newer, more modern warships, and some even powered differently than *Oriskany*. We competed against nuclear-powered carriers such as *USS Enterprise*.

In W Division our numbers were down, we only had twenty enlisted men in the division. In mid-June we were back off the coast of Vietnam. June marked the eleventh year since I joined the Navy, my next birthday I would be twenty-nine. I was somewhat depressed, about the "march of time." Most of the sailors my age were married. I'd been getting a lot of mail from Teresa, and all this prompted me to make a bad decision. I planned to send Teresa an engagement ring from Subic. I didn't know her that well, and after about a month a half I wrote her and told her it was a mistake and I didn't want to be engaged. I felt bad about misleading her, and I also felt it in my wallet, as she kept the ring.

On the way to the Western Pacific, we in W Division were busy preparing to begin building conventional bombs again. This cruise we were to build a lot of Mark 36 DST Destructor Mines (DST's), which are basically a Mark 82, 500-pound bomb, when fitted with a fuse, battery, and special electronics became a mine. When DST's were dropped, the bomb would not explode, but create a magnetic field, and any metal object such as belt buckles, tooth fillings, vehicles, etc. could approach the bomb lying in the earth or jungle, but when the metal disruption began to move out of the magnetic field the bomb would detonate. Certain aspects of the bomb were classified at this time, so we GMT's were selected to assemble these bombs. The EOD team onboard did not like the prospect of having to disarm the DST's if the need ever arose, they were difficult to make "safe."

After a month on the line the ship pulled back into Subic Bay. I bought a few wooden fruit bowls, and mailed them home. I also sent sister Linda a wooden mask and my Dad a coat of arms plaque for his birthday.

We had only been in Subic Bay two days, when we had to get underway very quickly. There was a typhoon threatening Subic. After being at sea a couple days we pulled back in. I bought a buffalo leather coat, with fringes. It was like the one worn by Dennis Hopper in the movie "*Easy Rider*[33]," and weighed about twenty pounds. I never wore the coat and eventually gave it to my cousin Jay Clark.

In Subic most W Division sailors hung out at a place called the Upstairs Lounge, it was next to the Golden Hotel where you could get a room for nine pesos, which amounted to less than an American dollar. We had to observe the midnight curfew, which President Marcos had imposed. Olongapo was as wild as it had been during my time on the *Ticonderoga*. There were a few more paved streets, and there seemed to be more clubs, if that were possible? Some of us would occasionally take a jeepney to Subic City that was about five miles from Olongapo, and was also a community of retired sailors. Here the pace was a little slower than Olongapo. We had a division party at a beach resort about ten miles from town called White Rock, which had a popular huge swimming pool. My financial outlook was much better at this point. The ship had made a deal with a few Japanese motorcycle companies, and was offering motorcycles at greatly reduced prices. The ship was scheduled to pick up the bikes in Japan just before returning to the states. I ordered a 650 CC Yamaha. A few sailors in the division ordered motorcycles. I had enjoyed motorcycle riding in Washington, and looked forward to riding one again. This liberty period in Subic was one of the more relaxing inport periods.

We returned to Japan on 12 August, and on 22 August we were back on the line, where we continued to build bombs. Living conditions were better, as the air conditioner in the berthing compartment was now working. This helped division morale immensely. I was enjoying my leading petty officer job, and although we worked hard, we were still a happy crew. My morale was raised by overhearing a conversation between a few younger division sailors, who said they would follow me through the "gates of hell," if I asked them to! I tried to look out for their interests, and I felt they were loyal to me. I did a lot of "homework" on each of the division sailors. I studied individual's service records to learn as much about each sailor as I could. I also kept what was called a "wheel book," which was a small green notebook carried in my shirt pocket, in which I noted commendable jobs, and information I should share with the division. I tried to praise in public, and correct in private.

We were hungry for news, and looked forward to the only newspaper available to us, the *Pacific Stars & Stripes*, a military newspaper I'd looked forward to while onboard *Ticonderoga*. This newspaper began during World War II as a means to get GI's news. It cost a dime, and came aboard with the mail. We were always anxious to read about how the people in the states felt about our war effort. Much of the news was discouraging, such as draft card burning, and college demonstrations against the war. It seemed as though the war had split our generation, and our nation. We all agreed in our hatred of Jane Fonda, pictures of her with anti-aircraft gunners that likely had shot down and killed men from her own country, labeled her as a traitor in our estimation. To this day I will not watch a movie featuring Jane Fonda. I do not feel she deserves to be a citizen of America, but that's only my opinion. Previously in April, U.S. Navy LTJG John Kerry, who was to be a future Senator, and presidential candidate, testified before congress about war crimes, and false atrocities committed by the military in Vietnam. This added to our feelings of rejection not only by our countrymen, but also a sense of being betrayed by one of our own.

It was during this line period, the ship had a close call. After we would build the DSTs, they would be stored on the hangar deck in bomb trucks at various locations about the hangar deck, out of the way of aircraft movements until the time they would be moved up to the flight deck and loaded on planes for bombing missions. One temporary storage area was on a sponson, which was a weather deck that projected out of the side of the ship on the hanger deck level.

This exposed deck with a lifeline encircling it was also a favorite place for sailors to go to get some sun and a breath of fresh air. DST's had a fuze in the nose of the bomb that had a propeller, which turned, in the wind stream (a lot like the propeller on a stick that children play with). This propeller rotated a number of specific times, and then the bomb would be armed. The propeller was prevented from turning, after being assembled, and before dropping from the aircraft, by a long wire that was inserted through a hole in the propeller, and attached to a suspension lug. Upon dropping from an aircraft, the wire was extracted, and the propeller would then spin, and arm the bomb. One afternoon a young sailor, who worked on the mess decks, was given a break, and went out on the sponson where there happened to be a number of DSTs in bomb trucks waiting for the time for them to be taken up to the flight deck. He extracted one of the DST's arming wires, and began absent-mindedly spinning the propeller while daydreaming. An ordnance man happened to walk out on the sponson and saw what the mess cook was doing. He screamed at the mess cook, scaring him half to death, and immediately notified the EOD team. It was a tense situation, as it was not known if the bomb was armed at this point are not? This would mean any magnetic disruption could set it off. The bomb was safed, and it was emphasized to all hands onboard to keep hands-off ordnance stored about the ship.

Since the *USS Pueblo* incident in Korea when North Korean forces captured a Navy ship, the Navy had been trying to implement, or improve emergency destruction procedures. The emergency destruction of nuclear weapons was a new program that we in the division had to be proficient at. In the event the ship was about to be boarded by hostile forces, or about to sink in shallow waters, the division would be tasked with setting up explosive charges. This was so any weapons we might have on board would be destroyed and not recovered by the enemy and used against us. We in W Division would be among the last to leave in the event of abandon ship. Once our destruction charges went off, it was anticipated the bottom of the ship to be blown out, and the ship would sink like a rock. We trained setting up destruction charges, using dummies or training wooden explosive material, once a month.

During my eleven years as a GMT, I'd seen a number of weapons systems retired, and new ones become part of the stockpile. One of the newest was the B61 Bomb (see photo page), which was nicknamed the "silver bullet," because of the silver metal color the bomb case was made of. It was a special material that resisted heat that might be experienced when the weapon was being carried by a high-speed aircraft, suspended from an aircraft wing. We were required to apply special wax to the bomb case to prevent corrosion. It was like waxing a car. These were early production bombs that were eventually replaced by bombs with a special coating that did not need waxing, so we eventually put up the wax and wax rags, as they were no longer needed.

About this time we learned we been awarded the Meritorious Unit Commendation Ribbon. A citation was placed in each *Oriskany* sailors' service record and reads as follows:

> The Secretary of the Navy takes pleasure in presenting the Meritorious Unit Commendation to *USS Oriskany* (CVA-34) and Attack Carrier Air Wing Nineteen (CVW-19) for services set forth in the following: For meritorious service from 1 June to 9 December 1970 while participating in combat operations in Southeast Asia. As a member of the Task Force Seventy-Seven, *USS Oriskany* and embarked Attack Carrier Air Wing Nineteen conducted sustained day and night interdiction operations against the enemy in support of the Republic of Vietnam and United States national policy. Effectively utilizing all available assets, the ship/airway combat team inflicted extensive damage to the enemy's logistics and communications network, thereby significantly reducing the flow of men and material from North Vietnam into the Republic of Vietnam. Their efforts provided vital support to the United States and allied ground forces and enhanced the prospects for achievement of United States goals in Southeast Asia. The professional, dedicated performance of the officers and men of *USS Oriskany* and her embarked Air Wing throughout this deployment reflected credit upon themselves and their ship and was keeping with the highest traditions of the United States Naval service. For the Secretary, E.Z. Zumwalt, Jr., Admiral, United States Navy, Chief of Naval Operations.

We pulled into Yokosuka, Japan on 12 August, and on that morning I once again took the chief's advancement exam. That afternoon I bought a nineteen-inch Panasonic color television at the Yokosuka Navy Exchange. This was the first color television I'd owned. I planned on mailing it to my parents, but later decided to let the division use it until we got back to the states. The ships closed circuit TV station broadcast throughout the ship. An anxiously anticipated event was the movie that was shown each night. The catapult launches, recoveries, or landings were also shown on the closed circuit TV system.

On this day (12 August) also, Jim Feller, a second class in the division, asked me if I'd come with him to meet his mother and sister, who had flown to Japan from Baton Rouge, Louisiana to visit him while the ship was import. I wasn't too excited about going all the way to Yokohama, which was about forty miles away, when I had planned on going on liberty in Yokosuka which was right outside the base, but I agreed to go with him to please him. I enjoyed meeting his mom and sister. His sister Mildred was my age, and we got along very well. We had a brief romance, and visited a few tourist spots together. Also a group of us rented a Japanese fishing boat, and tried fishing for a day, however we didn't catch anything. The ship stayed in Yokosuka for almost two weeks. I accompanied Mildred to the airport when she left. One of the last comments she made to me was "Promise to please take care of my brother." I did keep that promise, as he was safe all the way up his discharge the next year, but I was committed to keeping all those in my charge safe.

She had been engaged during the time she had been in Japan, and she wrote me a few times, but I never saw her again, although she asked me a couple times if I would come to the Mardi Gras. I also got a number of letters from my cousin David Sylvester; who was enjoying the Navy, and had just made third class.

We pulled out of Yokosuka, and went back to Subic for a short visit before pulling back on the line. We were to go to Hong Kong after this line period. I'd not heard any word about when I might expect shore duty orders? Although only a little over a year, it seemed like I'd been off the coast of Vietnam forever? We'd been on the line a couple days, with something happened that would drastically change the remainder of the cruise for W Division, and would increase our workload drastically!

The first week on the line, I had a crew of seven men building DSTs. We worked from midnight to noon. We had just gotten off work, and I was in my bunk in the berthing compartment, having just fallen asleep, suddenly all the lights when on. The compartment was normally darkened so we could sleep. Charlie Galbreath knelt down at the head of my bunk and said, "Jim, the Master Chief wants everybody up, the after magazine has been flooded!" This certainly woke me up, I quickly dressed, and went to the after magazine. The marine guard was at his post on the second deck, I gave them my access badge, he gave me my clip on badge, and I went down the ladder to the fourth deck, where the magazine hatch was open. A fire hose snaked out of the opening and down to the seventh deck bilges. Water was lapping at the bottom edge of the magazine hatch. Shoes were scattered just outside the door. I removed my shoes, rolled up my pants legs, and waded in. The magazine bulkheads, the overhead, and everything were dripping wet. A de-watering pump was going, pumping out the gallons of water that covered the deck. It was a mess. When the water was finally pumped out, the captain and weapons officer came down into the magazine. The captain was very upset! Something like this could be a "career-ending event." We organized a bucket brigade, and brought buckets of water down into the magazine to wash down the magazine. The floodwater was salt water that had come from the magazine sprinkler system. It was revealed to us that an officer, and a couple of men from a different division in weapons department, had been conducting monthly magazine sprinkler station checks. These checks were conducted with a wedge inserted as I explained before, so water would not flow into the magazine overhead pipes and out the sprinkler heads into the magazine. They mistakenly had initiated the wrong sprinkler valve that went into the W Division magazine, instead of the magazine sprinkler valve they were supposed to be testing. The seawater spewed from the sprinkler heads, and reached a water depth of about three feet. The flooding alarm went off, alerting Damage Control Central of the flooding problem. A message immediately left the ship describing what happened. This message was lower in urgency than a "Broken Arrow," notifying Washington of the problem. It was not long before instructions came back, informing us we would have to disassembly material, and inspect for damage. This was to be an unbelievable workload, which involved working sixteen-hour days. It was exhausting work, but at least we were happier working in our own spaces, versus building DST bombs.

The captain was displeased, and we felt his displeasure toward us was misdirected. The officer that set off the sprinklers was CWO Duprew (not his real name); he was not well liked on the ship, had a constant smirk on his face, and acted very conceited. We heard that the captain restricted him to his stateroom for one-week while we were at sea. All the work we were faced with made us feel the punishment did not fit a crime.

Master Chief Riechman asked me to prepare a plan, and schedule for going through the complex inspection procedures. He was very obviously ignoring Chief Schofield and Chief Chapbourne in the chain of command. So this placed me in the uncomfortable position of the being in the "middle." The two chiefs would come to me to find out what the master chief's orders were! I'd been in this undesirable position before on Whidbey Island, and other places, so it was not a new experience for me.

The messages flew back and forth between the ship and McAlester, Oklahoma, directing what actions to take. We disassembled material far beyond the point we normally were permitted to, in order to inspect for any saltwater damage. We cleaned every square inch of internal parts. We also had to document everything we did, and all of this was time consuming.

The last of September, *Oriskany* was once again the only carrier off the coast of Vietnam. We would quickly steam north, conduct bombing raids, and then steam south. After a short preparation period we would then repeat the run to the north. This cycle was repeated over and over again.

On 13 September 1971, I received my third Good Conduct Medal. This meant I would now wear two bronze stars on the burgundy colored Good Conduct Ribbon I wore on the chest of my dress uniform.

The first of October Dan Hoover learned some good news. He had been selected to be promoted to officer status as a chief warrant officer. Normally when an enlisted man is to be commissioned, he is transferred from his current duty station immediately. The rationale behind this instant transfer was because in most cases he would become senior, or the boss of those that had been his seniors, or bosses the previous day. This sudden shift of position would place a tremendous strain on the social order of most commands. In Dan's case he was to remain onboard a couple of months before he could be transferred. We had been friends, and it was a little uncomfortable to suddenly address him as "Sir," or "Mister Hoover," but we both handled it well. I was a little jealous; as I'd gotten word that once again I had not passed my chief's promotion examination. Dan was a very intelligent sailor. I wished him luck at his transfer, and felt he would be a good officer.

The last of September and the first of October, the ship was at anchor in Hong Kong. One favorite hangout was the Hong Kong British Navy Club, where English and American sailors intermingled. They were "Limeys," nicknamed after the British Navy's past when British ships carried limes for the crew to eat and prevent scurvy. We were called "Yanks." The British sailors enjoyed playing darts, and were much better at it than American sailors. Most British sailors drank bitter ale that was served at room temperature. We got along well, but were cautioned not to say anything disparaging about the Queen of England, as I had been cautioned on previous visits while on the *Ticonderoga*, even though they often spoke very disrespectfully of her. It was OK for them to slander the crown, but not outsiders.

Hong Kong had not changed much from the time of my visits while onboard the *Ticonderoga*. One day Charlie Galbreath (Backup Charlie) and I took a tour to see the Red Chinese Border. We also visited Victoria Peak, which overlooked the city and harbor. Victoria Peak was reached by a suspended cable car. I took a break from the ship, and stayed a couple of nights in the Hong Kong Hilton. I also had two tailor-made suits made, as well as two pairs of tailor-made shoes.

After our port visit to Hong Kong, we returned to Subic Bay. The ship had spent so much time in Subic it was beginning to feel like our homeport! I spent most of my liberty time in a place called the Dolphin Club. This club was small and much quieter than the larger, noisy clubs. A girl named Flora, in the Dolphin Club was trying to teach me the Filipino language, but I was not grasping it very well.

Venereal disease was common in Olongapo. The Navy even helped the city in efforts to eradicate, or lessen the frequency of the most common affliction, gonorrhea. Among the younger sailors it was thought to be "macho," or a sign of manhood to catch gonorrhea, or "clap" as it was often called. This was not a healthy attitude. There was concern in the ship's medical department, and other medical agencies over a new strain of gonorrhea that appeared to be resistant to the often-used cure of penicillin! As I explained previously, the city of Olongapo required that all girls working in the bars undergo a monthly medical examination, to check for any evidence of venereal disease. The girls were issued a card each month showing their compliance with the medical exam requirement. These cards were blue, and naturally were called a bar girl's "blue card." There were thousands of Filipino girls working in the bars, and there were almost an equal number of "street walking" prostitutes. Sailors were repeatedly warned not to solicit the services of the street walkers, as they were not required to have the monthly VD examination, and the chances of contracting a disease was very high. Condom use was emphasized, and frequent medical lectures were given by the ships corpsmen. There were also unannounced, surprise medical inspections held in berthing compartments from time to time. These inspections would usually be conducted shortly before reveille, prior to everyone getting out of their bunks.

The lights in the berthing compartment that had been selected for a surprise inspection would be turned on by Corpsmen from the Medical Department. All the sailors would be ordered out of bed, and each one would be inspected for signs of venereal disease discharge. These surprise inspections were nicknamed "short arm inspections." A crude common name for the Corpsmen was "pecker-checkers." I had seen the official attitude, and treatment of venereal disease change over the years, during my time in the Navy. When I was onboard the *USS Independence*, and the *USS Ticonderoga*, those sailors that reported to sickbay with symptoms of VD, were immediately placed on restriction and could not leave the ship. The sailor's name was given to the captain, and his division officer, and the sailor was given remedial lectures about venereal disease. All of these punitive measures had the effect of driving VD into the Navy's "underground." Sailors would try to hide the fact that they had contracted VD, and not report to sickbay, but instead try to get medical treatment or pills on the black-market, or from a civilian doctor. On board *Oriskany*, the above treatment actions were not taken. The medical condition of sailors reporting to sickbay was kept confidential, except in the case of officers. The captain was informed of the name of any officer who contracted VD.

About the middle of our Westpac cruise, a memo was issued from the medical department stating that ten percent of the *Oriskany*'s crew was required to participate in a medical survey. These sailors were to report to sickbay every two weeks during the cruise. In W Division, this meant that two sailors had to participate. Names were drawn out of a hat, and I was one of the unfortunate ones picked! I discovered when I reported to sickbay for the first survey appointment, that this was not to be a pleasant medical procedure. We all had a metal wire inserted into our penis, which was very painful. We were told this was to obtain a laboratory culture. Nothing was entered into our medical records, and I've often wondered if we were all being used for some type of medical experiment? Every two weeks I endured this "treatment," and was very relieved when the "medical survey" was finally over at the end of the cruise.

The ship was back on the line 29 October. We in W Division were still inspecting material that had been involved in the "flood," and also continued to build bombs for the bombing missions. We were scheduled to remain on the line until 19 November, at which time we were to steam for Singapore. After Singapore, and a few more port calls, we were to be back in San Francisco on 18 December.

My family was faithful sending letters, and letting me know what was happening at home. My brother Joe was playing football, and brother Jerry was playing baseball. Sister Linda was in Fresno with her family, my niece Lisa was ill with the flu, and niece Betty was beginning to walk.

I began studying for my chief's advancement exam, which was in February. I continued with my efforts to quit smoking. This was a difficult task, as the coffee locker where we took breaks, and our berthing compartment was always filled with cigarette, cigar, and pipe smoke. Most sailors smoked. We were only permitted to smoke when the "smoking lamp" was lit. The smoking lamp was out at specific times throughout the ship, such as during refueling, and ammunition replenishment. Also the smoking lamp was out during general quarters, and while at battle stations. During a couple of cruises there were complaints on the ship about the quality of the cigarettes sold in the ship's store. The cigarettes appeared to be very old! The tobacco was dry, and the cigarette papers had brown spots on them. The ships store sold cigarettes for one dollar a carton, or ten cents a pack. In all the foreign ports we visited, everyone wanted American cigarettes.

The first part of November, during an aircraft launch, a plane's landing gear collapsed and the plane crashed into the sea, killing the pilot. During all launches and recovery of aircraft, the ship's helicopter was in the air hovering near the ship ready to affect rescues if necessary, but in this case the plane sank immediately upon hitting the water.

I ordered an 8mm movie camera, and projector from the ship's store. Prices on many items made in the Orient were on sale at greatly reduced prices.

I was considering renting an apartment when the ship returned to San Francisco. The ship was scheduled to go back into the yards upon our return to the states, and I dreaded living in the miserable conditions while in the shipyard. On 20 November the ship left the line for the last time on this cruise. There was a festive mood on the ship. We were all happy to finally be out of the war zone.

On the way to Singapore after leaving the coast of Vietnam, the ship's path would take us below the equator. This would prompt one of the oldest traditions in Navy. Sailors that had never been beneath the equator were called a "pollywog," and were to be initiated by those sailors that had been beneath the equator at one time or another. These experienced sailors were called "shellbacks." There was a holiday atmosphere on the ship. Almost everyone on the ship was a pollywog, even the captain and executive officer. In W Division, Chief Chapbourne was the only shellback.

The evening before the scheduled initiation, a huge ceremony was held on the flight deck. This was the time when King Neptune, and his royal court, along with Davey Jones, came aboard! The shellbacks were dressed as pirates, and King Neptune was dressed as a "King." The pollywogs put on a show for the entertainment, and pleasure of King Neptune. Most of the entertainer pollywogs were officers. There was a chorus line, comedians, etc. It was fun, but many of the pollywogs were apprehensive about what might occur the next day? That night the shellbacks harassed us. We had "watches" assigned to us, such as sitting near a toilet bowl, continually flushing it, and announcing which way the water was circling. Supposedly when the ship crossed the equator the direction of the swirl would reverse. There was a box in the hangar bay with a sign on it that said "sea bat inside." Pollywogs were made to bend over and look inside the box. At that point a shellback with a paddle, would give the bending over pollywog, a "bat" to the behind.

The morning of the initiation, all pollywogs were instructed to put on their shirt and pants backwards! We also wore shower shoes. We were to remain in our division spaces, supervised by a shellback, until we were told to report to the hangar deck. The announcement finally came over the 1MC ship's loudspeaker for W Division to report to the hangar bay. On the hangar deck level, we were told to remain on our hands and knees, and commanded to do pushups, while shellbacks dressed as pirates walked through our midst, administering lashes with hand-held whips (not too hard). All the pollywogs in my group (about eighty) were then directed to crawl out on an aircraft elevator, which then lifted us up to the flight deck.

During our ride up to the flight deck, we were sprayed with a fire hose. At the flight deck we had to crawl through a gauntlet of shellbacks that lashed our backs with whips. We also had to crawl about the flight deck blowing water out of the aircraft tie down wells (indentations in the deck used as attachment points for tie down chains which held aircraft securely while the ship was underway) that covered the flight deck. The pooled water was from the fire hoses we had been soaked with. It took a lot of huffing and puffing to blow all the water out of a tie down well! After this we had to crawl single file through a series of "torture points." First was the Royal Barber, who poured a sickening, foul-smelling mixture all over our heads. Next we had to crawl past wooden stocks, which held pollywogs head and hands securely, while shellbacks rubbed grease and foul-smelling mixtures on their faces. I was not put into the stocks, but when the captain and executive officer crawled by, they were put in the stocks, and got the full treatment. This was one of the few times on the ship, officers and enlisted men were treated the same, which was with disdain by the shellbacks! After passing the stocks, there were the royal caskets. These caskets were filled with garbage, and a foul mixture of fire extinguishing liquid, which was made up of reconstituted animal blood, they smelled horrible! Each pollywog took turns getting into the caskets, and then the lids were placed on for a few minutes. After we soaked for a few minutes inside, the lids were removed, and we were instructed to crawl out. The next obstacle was a long sixty-foot tarp tunnel covered inside with grease. We had to crawl through this dark slimy tunnel to the surprise that awaited us at the end of the tunnel. Seated at the opening at the end of the tunnel, was the "Royal Baby." Seated on a chair was a pot-bellied shellback, without a shirt on, and his belly was smeared with grease. We were told to kiss the Royal Baby's belly. The "kiss" took place when the Royal Baby grabbed your head, and rubbed your face all over his grease-coated belly! After this we stood up and approached King Neptune, bowed, and he then proclaimed us "shellbacks."

We were filthy, and smelled badly. Showers were set up on the flight deck, and after showering we walked naked down to the heads to finish cleaning up. It took a lot of time and work to get all the grease and gunk out of our hair, ears, and body crevices. It was a fun time, and most enjoyed it except for the sore knees from crawling on all fours. Now that I was a shellback, I could look forward to the time when I would initiate pollywogs in the future.

Everyone on the ship had an entry placed in his service record, and issued certificates to prove their initiation. I knew sailors that carried an initiation proof, wallet sized card in their wallet as faithfully as a driving license, for their entire Navy career!

After seven months had past everyone got a large sixteen by twenty inch certificate. My decorative certificate states:

> To all sailors wherever ye may be: and to all mermaids, whales, sea serpents, porpoises, sharks, dolphins, eels, skates, suckers, crabs, lobsters, and all other living things of the sea greeting: Know ye: that on this 22nd day of November 1971 in latitude 00000 and longitude 105 - 40E there appeared within our royal domain the *USS Oriskany* (CVA-34) bound SW for the equator and for Singapore. Be it remembered that said vessel and officers and crew thereof have been inspected and passed on by ourself and our royal staff.

And be it known: by all ye sailors, marines, land lubbers and others who may be honored by his presence that James S. Little, GMT1, having been found worthy to be numbered as one of our trusty shellbacks he has been duly initiated into the solemn mysteries of the ancient order of the deep. Be it further understood that by virtue of the power invested in me I do hereby command all my subjects to show due honor and respect to him wherever he may be. Disobey this order under penalty of our royal displeasure. Given under our hand and seal this

12 July 1972. The certificate was signed by Davey Jones, and Neptunus Rex.

The day after the initiation, the ship anchored off Singapore where the British influence was very evident. It was a large city filled with turban wearing Indian men, and Indian women with dots in the middle of their forehead, dressed in long colorful dresses. I did a little shopping. Singapore, as well as many other Asian countries sold items and wares by a "barter system." Very seldom was the customer expected to pay the price that was listed on an item, but instead you bargained with the seller for the lowest price he would agree with.

On one liberty day I took a tour through a beautiful botanical garden called Tiger Garden. I also toured a crocodile farm. I happened to tour during the feeding time of the crocodiles. They were fearsome looking creatures. At the end of the tour, we looked through a store filled with items made from the crocodile's skin, such as wallets, purses, luggage, and shoes.

We were cautioned that many Singapore women were not what they appeared to be! Many were men dressed in women's clothing! On Thanksgiving, I went ashore and had a shrimp curry dinner. The ship got underway from Singapore on the 29th.

We pulled into Subic Bay, which was as I said, becoming more and more to feel like the ship's homeport! Since leaving the "line" everyone's spirit was high. We celebrated surviving our time on the line. I was a close friend to two sailors who worked for me—GMT2 Mike Jackson, and GMT2 Jim Feller. This would be the last time we would be in Subic Bay together. As was the case with most in W Division, they were "first termers" and would be discharged, and get out of the Navy soon after the ship returned to the states.

My latest evaluation period ended 1 December. I received 4.0's in all categories, except military appearance in which I received a 3.8. This was lower than my previous 4.0, and I think it was because during this period I had tried to grow a beard, and although authorized, it was frowned upon for a career sailor to have any facial hair. I once again celebrated my birthday on 8 December, on a warship headed away from the war zone, steaming toward the United States. I turned twenty-nine years old. One more year and I would be thirty, and as the popular saying went, "I could not be trusted."

As the ship approached the mid-Pacific, the Soviet long-range bombers once again tested our defenses. The ship made a short stop in Hawaii for fuel and supplies, and then got back underway.

On 18 December 1971, the ship steamed under the Golden Gate Bridge, with escorting tugboats spraying water, and an acrobatic plane flying above us. There was a huge crowd on the pier, along with a band playing, and Santa Claus waving welcome. We tied up alongside the Alameda Naval Air Station pier. The long cruise was over.

In *Oriskany*'s 1971 cruise book there is the following statement, "It is said that war does not always begin or end. That war does not always have a winner or loser. And that war has only one truth: that some who go to war shall not return." Those *Oriskany* sailors that did not return that cruise were: CDR Thomas P. Frank, CDR Charles D. Metzler, LT James R. Borst, LT John R. Painter, LTJG Raymond V. DeBlasio, ADJ2 Barry A. Bidwell, and FA Steven M. Stark

This had been a hard, long cruise, with the added work of cleaning up after the flood, and the extra bombing missions, I was relieved to see the cruise end. We had five-section duty in Alameda. I caught a plane to Fresno, and my parents picked me up at the airport. It was a wonderful homecoming. I drove my car, which had been stored at my parent's house, back to San Francisco.

To demonstrate the diversity of the twenty-two officers and men that made up that 1971 W Division, I'll write a short description of each one.

Commander J. S. Salisbury - He was the Nuclear Safety Officer, and oversaw many aspects of our work. He was an aviator and flew an A-6 *Intruder*. He flew just enough to draw his monthly flight pay. He and the Division Officer, Lieutenant Barber managed the Personnel Reliability Program (PRP). This was a massive administrative program that was a tool to help insure that only reliable sailors were given access to the nuclear weapon program. He was well liked, friendly, and approachable, unlike many officers we enlisted sailors related to. He always kept us informed of ships schedule changes, and war news we would not have heard of otherwise. He was directly accountable to the commanding officer on all issues of nuclear safety.

LT A.D. Barber - The W Division Officer. He was a Limited Duty Officer (LDO), who'd come up through the enlisted ranks. He had been an Aviation Ordnanceman First Class before being commissioned. He also was well liked by the crew, and approachable. He seldom went down into the magazines, and permitted the chiefs and me to enforce discipline. He enjoyed smoking cigars. He was directly accountable to the weapons officer, who was the department head of weapons department.

GMTCM Vincent L. Reichman - Master Chief Reichman was the Leading Chief of W Division. He was as I mentioned before, also the Master Chief of the ship, which meant he was the senior enlisted man onboard *Oriskany*. He was a strict disciplinarian, and left no doubt about being in charge. He had a temper, which he would occasionally show. He was feared and respected by most in W Division. There were very few master chiefs in the Navy, and they were highly revered. Master Chief Reichman had an impressive amount of technical knowledge. At one point in his career he had been an instructor in Nuclear Weapons School Albuquerque. As W Division Leading Petty Officer, I worked closely with him, planning division work, training, division problems, etc. I was impressed with his leadership skills, although at times I felt he was a little sterner than he needed to be. He worked and planned more with me than the other two division chiefs, which placed me in an awkward position. I never spoke negatively about him in front of other W Division sailors, and he always backed me up, which I greatly appreciated. He was a heavy smoker, recently divorced, and had a girl friend that lived in Long Beach. He was authorized direct access to the commanding officer on all matters concerning the enlisted members of the crew. Located at various locations about the ship were suggestion boxes that the crew could use to address questions to him. From time to time Master Chief Reichman would appear on the ship's television station and answer the suggestions and questions from the crew. His time was split between the two jobs of W Division Leading Chief, and Command Master Chief. The other two chiefs in the division Chief Schofield, and Chapbourne were fearful of him, and often talked negatively about him. He was of German descent, and some of the junior sailors in the division called him "Herr Reichman," or "Vince," and would give a German salute (behind his back). I heard in future years after his retirement from the Navy he went to work for an aircraft company in Los Angeles.

GMTC C. E. Schofield - He was the next senior chief under Master Chief Riechman. He was a very quiet, private person, and was very seldom in the working spaces. He was always in the division at morning muster, and would usually disappear shortly after morning quarters were held. I was to meet him again in the future.

GMTC H. T. Chapbourne - He was the junior chief in the division. He was a couple of years older than I. He was a jovial, well-liked chief. He identified more with the younger generation of sailors, than the older generation of chiefs. He went on liberty with many of the lower rank sailors. He was always looking for a girlfriend, and was legendary concerning the failures in his love life. Master Chief Riechman intimidated him. Often when he was about to talk to the master chief about some problem or topic, he would come down into the forward magazine where a group of us would be working, and he would say, "I'm going to talk to the master chief, so I'm going to practice talking to the bulkhead!" This inferred that the master chief would pay the same amount of attention to him that the bulkhead did. I'll never forget an incident that occurred during a training disassembly operation I was conducting one day. I was directing the crew to remove the nose of a training weapon. This particular weapon had a special shock absorbing nose that was designed to absorb the impact energy a weapon would experience when it was dropped from an aircraft in the parachute retarded option. In this option the weapon would hit the ground and lie there prior to detonation. The crew was having difficulty removing the nose. The mating surfaces of the nose section and warhead section were binding. We were struggling to remove it following removal of the securing screws. Chief Chapbourne happened to be in the magazine. He said, "Let me try something." He got a rag, and a rubber mallet. I started to object, but before I could say anything, he placed the rag on the surface of the nose, and struck the nose with the mallet in an effort to free the nose. The nose didn't budge. He removed the rag, his face turned white, and a look of horror came over his face. There was a large dent on the surface of the nose. He said, "Oh no, oh no, my career is over, what's the master chief going to say?" as he futilely tried to rub out the dent with the rag. It was serious, but it was all we could do to keep from laughing at his overreaction. It was surprising that such a light blow could cause such a dent. The master chief asked me if I thought we could repair the dent without reporting it, but I said, "No, that is not the right thing to do, we have to report it." We ended up rejecting the nose, and shipping it back for repair. Chief Chapbourne received a chewing out from the master chief, and that was as far as it went. His nickname was "Harry T.," and many of the younger sailors called him this while on liberty with him, I did not, as I always called him "Chief." He had an older Volkswagen "bug" that he kept a detailed diary on. He would record when the oil was changed, when he drove it, and how many miles.

The oddest detailing effort was that he would record each time he made a right or left turn. He would make an effort to keep the turns to the right and left at an even number. One night at Hunters Point, in the fog, he ran over a highway concrete divider and tore out the underside of the Volkswagen, it was totaled. I thought he was going to cry when he described the accident to me! Dan Hoover and he were close friends, and I considered him a friend. One time in Subic he was infatuated with a certain bar girl, and he bought her some false teeth that she needed. He didn't tell anyone about this. He didn't know that she was "dating" a few other sailors in the division when he had duty on the ship, and she had told everyone about his generosity. The bar girl had gotten a picture of him from one of the W Division sailors, and had commissioned a Philippine artist to paint an oil portrait picture of him. This was an effort to repay him for the teeth. The painting was horrible. One of the sailors told her he would give it to Harry T. A few days after we left Subic at the morning division muster, the master chief told Chief Chapbourne that he was to receive a special presentation. Chief Chapbourne didn't have a clue what it was about? The master chief said he had put forth a wonderful effort on behalf of the United States to further international relationships with the Philippines, by purchasing false teeth for a needy bar girl, and in appreciation he was awarded a beautiful hand painted oil portrait. I can't emphasize how horrible the huge framed painting looked. It didn't look at all like him! He was speechless and red faced. He was the good-natured brunt of a lot of practical jokes. Often when he would try to pull a practical joke however, it would often backfire! One day Dan Hoover's reenlistment ceremony was to take place in the forward magazine (this was before he was commissioned). The division was in ranks at attention, while the division officer administered the reenlistment oath. Immediately after the oath, Harry T. had hidden in his shirt; a battery powered "laugh box." He pressed the laugh box button, and sounds of laughter filled the magazine. The division officer and master chief glared at him. He got a severe chewing out for this prank. I was to meet Chief Harry T. Chapbourne again in the future after the *Oriskany*.

GMT1 C. J. Galbreath - Charlie and I, and another First Class, Tommy Jones, (who came aboard late in the cruise), were the only first class petty officers in W Division during the 1971 cruise. Charlie was married to a Japanese girl, and had a young daughter. His family lived in Alameda. He was called "Combat Charlie or "Backup Charlie after the incident in Hawaii. He was a good friend, and we shared a lot of time on the hangar deck and flight deck overseeing weapons loading. We often went on liberty together. He eventually went into the Explosive Ordnance Disposal (EOD) program. I was to meet Charlie again in the future.

GMT2 M. E. Jackson - A first termer from Minnesota. He was a natural leader. He could be relied upon to perform any job assigned to him in an outstanding manner. He was highly liked by all in the division, and was sorely missed when he was discharged and left the ship. An outdoorsman, he planned to return to Minnesota to live with his widowed Father. He was one of the few sailors that looked good in a full beard. I know he would have gone far in the Navy, but he was anxious to get out. He and I, and Jim Feller went on liberty together often. His nickname was "Mike."

GMT2 J. T. Feller - He was from Louisiana, and a friendly, easy-going sailor. He was a lot of fun to be around. Although considerably younger than I, we spent a lot of time on liberty together. His nickname was "Fal." He was a first termer, and only spent four years in the Navy before returning to Louisiana.

GMT2 G. L. Freeburg - another first termer and pleasant sailor who was a hard worker. He was married, and his wife lived in Alameda. They struggled to live on his second class salary. His nickname was "Burg." He was from Illinois.

GMT2 S. G. Kitson - Steve Kitson was an easy going, slow moving, but hard working sailor. He was a happy, cheerful person. He was also one of those guys you could put a $500 suit on, and he would still look like a bum! He always tried to grow a beard, but it always turned out straggly, and sparse. He was from South Dakota. I went on liberty with him often. One day, he and I and two girls drove to Reno and back in twenty hours. His nickname was "Kit Carson." He was a first termer, who eventually made the Navy a career, and I was to be stationed with him again in the future.

GMT2 J. E. Rohrkemper - A jovial, quiet sailor. Jim Rohrkemper kept to himself, and smoked nasty smelling cigars. He was from the town of Corcoran, California, which was close to my hometown. He enjoyed reading, and playing chess. He struggled with a weight problem, and his nickname was "Big Forty," because he wore pants with a waist size of forty inches. He made a career out of the Navy, retiring as a GMT1 after twenty years.

GMT2 C. E. Scriver - He was married, a first termer from California, who was always scheming about ways to get out of work. He was likeable, but resisted the discipline of the Navy. His attitude did change slightly when he was placed in supervisory positions. If there was ever a voice of dissent, I could count on it being his.

He always wore the straggliest beard in the division. Later I ran across him after he'd gotten out of the Navy, and he was still struggling with the hard realities that even in the civilian world there were orders he had to obey.

GMT3 C. E. Bairn - A married first termer from Utah. He was a hard-working sailor who was well liked by all in the division. He was a devout Mormon, and to his credit, I never heard him utter a single word of profanity. His nickname was "Chuck." He got out of the Navy after four years

GMT3 J. W. Barth - A first termer. A big, redheaded, quick-tempered sailor I liked. He was somewhat rebellious, but one of the hardest working sailors in the division. I went on liberty often with "Big John." He was married after our 71 cruise, which I'll describe later. He was from Detroit, Michigan. He and his wife moved to Michigan after he got out of the Navy.

GMT3 C. L. Haight - A sailor from Washington, that was only in the division a short while before becoming ill with an incurable disease. He was transferred to Oakland Naval Hospital for eventual discharge.

GMT3 F. Lieser - A first termer from Nebraska. He was a "misfit" in the nuclear weapons program. He was a "round peg" trying to fit into a "square hole!" He was almost impossible to supervise, mainly because he wouldn't listen to instructions, and was hopelessly clumsy. When I assigned him to do simple tasks such as painting, he would usually spill the paint and make a mess. He was "scary" trying to handle tools. I felt he had no business being in the nuclear weapons program. I gave him innumerable chances, and counseled him almost endlessly. Eventually he was removed from W Division, because he made a serious technical error during an operation. He was reassigned to the data processing division on the ship, where he was much happier, and became a productive sailor. His nickname was "Furd."

GMT3 P. M. McEvoy - A first termer from the east coast, who was a quiet, hard worker. He wore a very thick, black beard. He was a very talented guitar player, who said he once played with the rock band Chicago. His nickname was "Mac."

GMT3 P. J. Pastor - A first termer who considered himself a "ladies man." He always tried to get by growing his hair as long as possible. He was the one in the division told most often to "get a haircut." He had trouble conforming to the Navy, and required more than normal supervision. He dated a girl who worked in the Playboy Club in San Francisco. I'm not sure how he could afford to date her? He was always in debt to different people about the ship. He looked like a twin to one of my cousins, John Sylvester.

GMT3 G. A. Sparrow - A big, rawboned kid from Montana. He was the opposite of GMT3 Pastor. He was bashful, and shy around girls. He was a hard working, naive sailor that was polite, and well liked. He'd grown up in an isolated part of Montana; so far in the woods that he lived in a boarding house in a town called Wolf's Head while going to school, and would then return home during summer vacation. He always tried to please those he worked for. I enjoyed being around him. His nickname was "Bird."

GMTSN M. D. Gavin - An extremely quiet sailor from Arizona, so quiet it was not normal. He was a loner like Rohrkemper, and they got along well together. He was a hard worker, and always did exactly what he was told to do

GMTSN E. Monte – A cheerful, easygoing kid from back east that was a pleasure to be around. I felt he would go far in the Navy.

SN D. J. Robinson - The Division Yeoman. He was outgoing and cheerful, and one of two black sailors in the Division. We had to be cautious and not talk about technical weapon topics around him, because he did not have a "need to know."

This was the W Division crew of 1971. Each sailor was different, with very different personalities, and likes and dislikes. They put up with hardships, lack of freedom, and comforts that few men would. We often worked sixteen to twenty hour days for weeks at a time, and worked under the threat of death or injury from explosive ordnance. I considered them all patriots, brave, and courageous. As their leading petty officer I was very proud of them. They always did what I asked of them, and never let me down. We watched out for each other, and knew we could depend on each other as brothers. I was proud to be numbered among them, as well as being tired after the long cruise.

Shortly before our return to Alameda, W Division had a new GMT1 report aboard. His name was Tommy Jones. He was unique, as Ramsey was on the *USS Independence*, as he was black. Black sailors were very conspicuous in their absence from the nuclear weapons program. Tommy was married with two children. He was very upset upon our return to Alameda. He discovered that after he left home to report to the *Oriskany*, his wife had gone on a number of gambling trips to Reno, and had depleted the family savings! He was teased about a saying that he constantly used.

Before he said any statement about a technical problem he would say "The book say...." Surprisingly in the months to come, the game of chess became a very popular past time in W Division. Tommy had never played chess before, and within a few months of learning, he won a ship wide chess competition, and became a champion chess player.

I was able to spend Christmas with my family. My brothers' Joe and Jerry had grown into boys, and nieces' Lisa and Betty into little girls.

Since being on the ship, one of my efforts in W Division had been to train the second and third class working for me to be effective leaders and managers. I began assigning lectures to the second class, but before I did, I gave a series of lectures on the proper way to give a lecture. The information in the series of lectures was based on what I'd learned during instructor's training school a few years previously. At first there was grumbling and resistance to this, but some of the petty officers eventually became very good at lecturing.

I insisted that all petty officers understand how to evaluate, and write evaluation reports on the men that worked for them. I also explained that they should be able to justify any mark they assigned to sailors working for them. I also expected them to be able to sit down with their subordinates and review the marks they had given, and explain how they could improve, or congratulate them on performance. This was a painful effort at first, because I kept refusing to accept lackluster reports, and some of the second class had to do the reports over and over again. The evaluation instructions read that peers, or those of equal rank within a division are to be compared in each trait, and ranked, or in other words assigned as number 1, 2, 3, etc. At evaluation time, we had long, long discussions on these "ranking numbers" about who was numbered one or two in Military Appearance, Technical Ability, and so on. I know I was thought of as "hard-nosed" about evaluations, but I looked upon the evaluation reports, as the most important piece of paper that they or I could touch in the Navy! I tried to be as objective and as fair as possible filling out evaluations, as they described a sailor's service in the Navy, what kind of person he was, and was capable of becoming. These reports would become a permanent record of a person's service in the Navy Department of Records. I was very angry with supervisors who spent little time or thought evaluating those that worked for them. They expected obedience and action from their juniors, and the least they could give them in return was a thoughtful, fair, and objective evaluation.

The Ready Room, in Alameda, and Carnival Club in San Francisco, was happy to see *Oriskany*'s W Division back in port; this meant their cash registers would be fuller! I was the only single sailor in the division with a car. I cancelled my order for the Yamaha motorcycle, as I wanted to first pay off the Firebird. Three sailors in the division, Jim Feller, Mike Jackson, and Steve Kitson did get motorcycles. They soon discovered riding motorcycles on California's freeways was dangerous, and they had a few close calls.

A large group of us spent New Years in the Carnival Club. It was hard on all of us to adjust to the cold weather in San Francisco, after spending months in a hot, tropical climate. Most of us had sniffles, and colds.

The ship's schedule was very uncertain. President Nixon was talking about an end to the war, but the fighting was continuing. There were frequent cease-fire periods. We in the Navy sensed almost continuous resentment against the war and the military from civilians, although we were only carrying out the will of our government. Often sailors in uniform would be called "war mongers," or "baby killers." Nearby University of Berkeley was a hotbed of dissent and protest.

The Navy as a reflection of American society in 1971 was certainly a different Navy from the Navy I'd joined in 1960. There seemed to be much more questioning of authority, and less respect for senior ranks. In the 1960s I'd never have thought of treating a first class petty officer as casually as I, and other first class were now treated. In my younger days I'd never spoken to a first class, or chief, unless spoken to! Society and the Navy were changing, and I tried to accept that fact.

Illegal drug use was rampant throughout the Bay Area, and sailors were often involved. We as GMT's could not afford any involvement with illegal drugs, as we would immediately lose our security clearances, and thus our jobs. I suspected that a few of the junior men in W Division were using marijuana, but never caught them. Drugs were not a part of my teenage years, and quite frankly we in the older generation knew very little about illegal drugs. Our "drug" had been alcohol. It was pretty much accepted throughout the ranks that there were illegal drugs in the Navy, just as there was in the civilian society. During my time on *Oriskany*, I was given one lecture on illegal drugs. This lecture was given to all the first class petty officers on the ship. We were told what to look for in the cases of illegal drug usage such as personality changes, and work habits. We were shown what a heroin kit looked like, and how marijuana smelled. As a group, we older petty officers could not understand why anyone would take drugs?

Race relations were also very much on the minds of sailors during this time. Of all the military services, the Navy had resisted integration more than the Air Force, or Army. For many years black sailors and other minority races had only been permitted to work in the steward rating. This was the rating that worked in the wardroom, and served officers, which was almost akin to slavery! Minorities were not in positions of high authority. A black officer was a rarity. I do not recall seeing a black officer during my first four years in the Navy. Putting all these groups together in close proximity on board ships, where there was less privacy than in prison, caused strong pressures, and sometimes an undercurrent of resentment. More black sailors were in the Navy, and in different ratings than ever before, and the Navy and individuals were having trouble adjusting. There had been a few race riots on aircraft carriers that had been hushed up. In one instance black sailors took over a ship's mess deck, demanding better treatment, and privileges. This bordered on mutiny, and marines were used to break it up. The Navy was very concerned about these incidents. On *Oriskany*, in the mess decks, junior black sailors sat in their own section, and there was very little intermingling. There seemed to be a strong sense of distrust between white and black sailors. A few instances occurred on board when roving bands of whites or blacks would attack lone individuals late at night in darkened passageways, and beat the person up. When something like this happened, just as when crime occurs in a large city, the master at arms division, which was our police force, would increase security watches who would roam the ship looking for troublemakers. We in W Division had a tremendous advantage by having working and living spaces that were restricted, and could only be entered by GMT's, so we had a natural isolation that we enjoyed.

In the midst of these problems, the Navy was trying to change enlisted men's uniforms. Perhaps it was an attempt to distract sailors from the internal problems, by focusing on our uniforms? There was strong resistance to any uniform change. Bell-bottom pants were in fashion, and most liked the uniqueness of our sailors' uniform. The proposed uniform changes affected first class petty officers down. Our white hats, jumpers with back flap, square knot neckerchief, and thirteen button bell-bottom pants, were to be replaced with a suit type jacket, straight pants, and a visor cap. The uniform was exactly like the Army and Air Force enlisted uniform. This uniform change would blur the distinction between the petty officer first class ranks down, and the chief petty officer and officer ranks, as our uniforms would be basically the same. Sailors in Washington, D.C had worn the new uniforms in a yearlong test. There was grumbling in the Navy that the new uniforms were being test worn by sailors that were primarily desk workers, and in administrative jobs, instead of being tested in a real Navy environment, at a naval base, or on board ships. There was expressed concern about storage space on board ships for the new uniforms. The new suit type uniforms would have to be hung on hangers, whereas our current uniforms were folded, and placed into storage lockers that took up very little room. There were small groups of sailors, mostly first termers who liked the idea of looking more like chiefs and officers. It was felt generally that this uniform change was being forced upon us, because a few admirals wanted it. Eventually, the old uniform stayed. For many years following this time there were mixtures of the old and new uniforms in groups of sailors, as the uniform controversy continued.

I wore seven ribbons on my dress uniforms at this time. I rated the Navy Unit Commendation Ribbon, Good Conduct Ribbon, National Defense Ribbon, Armed Forces Expeditionary Ribbon, Vietnam Service Ribbon, Vietnam Gallantry Cross Unit Citation, and Vietnam Campaign Ribbon. The ribbons were worn in two rows, three in each row, with the senior ribbon on top. Each of these ribbons was also represented by a medal. Medals were worn on special occasions, such as changes of command, or ceremonies involving heads of state.

As I mentioned, a group of us celebrated New Years in the Carnival Club. The news at the Carnival Club was that the bar on the second floor above the Carnival Club had changed ownership during the ship's absence on the cruise. The bar upstairs catered to homosexuals. There were many homosexual bars scattered throughout San Francisco that we steered clear of, and this was the first one in this neighborhood that we considered our own. The owner of the Carnival Club was upset about it, as well as many who lived and did business in the neighborhood.

Ushering in 1972, I did not know what lie ahead for me? I was due to receive shore duty orders, but I had no idea when, or where it would be. The ship was to return to Hunters Point Shipyard, which I did not look forward to. It looked like I would be returning to Vietnam. I did not look forward to more time on the "line." It seemed like I had been in the war for years, which I had been since 1964. I was beginning to feel bitter, and having feelings of resentment about the lack of appreciation, or thanks from the countrymen and women, for whom we were fighting. I was also anxious about the dangers and hazards we would face once again building bombs. I'd had close calls in the past, and I wondered if the next cruise would be the one I might not return from? I was anxious not only for myself, but also those in my charge.

I'd not lost anyone to death or serious injury, and I'd worked hard to stress safety and caution while working with items that were designed to kill and harm the enemy. There was a sense of frustration within me that our youth as men was being spent working to the point of exhaustion, and sacrificing our freedom and liberty for citizens that did not appreciate it, but to the contrary treated us like criminals. All these feelings and thoughts, and my disappointment over not making chief petty officer, as well as my approaching thirtieth birthday, caused me to be very pessimistic about the future. In retrospect it certainly wasn't wise or healthy for me to spend so much time in a bar environment, I'll make no excuses, that was my lifestyle in 1971, drink and be happy, as I'll probably not be here tomorrow.

W Division worked and played hard, but I accepted no excuses for not being one hundred per cent ready to go to work at 7:30 a.m. every morning. If alcohol affected a sailor's work, then I had a serious talk with him. As for myself, I was staying up almost every night I did not have duty onboard, until 2:30 a.m. every night. I did this for many of the first months of 1972.

While overseas, and on the line, I dreamed about fishing. I had enjoyed fishing for salmon and steelhead on Whidbey Island. I bought a couple of books on steelhead fishing in Northern California. I wanted to go on a fishing trip along the Russian River, which was north of San Francisco. I had visited this area when I had gone on a drive while on the *Ticonderoga*.

One weekend in January, Mike Jackson, Jim Feller, and I took off early on a Saturday morning, with fishing poles, tent, and sleeping bags loaded into the Firebird. It took about two hours to drive to a little town called Guerneville, along the Russian River. We fished all day without any luck. It was cold that night, and wearing civilian clothes we left the spot by the river, and drove into town. We were wearing our dungaree working jackets, which had our petty officer crows sewn on the left arm. We went to an area where there were a lot of people our age. There was a dance being held, but we more or less got the "cold shoulder." There were a lot of hippies, and "long hairs" at the dance. We finally got tired of all the cold stares, and left. We then stopped at a little bar located on Main Street. When we walked in, at first we thought we were getting the cold shoulder again, but then everyone started buying us drinks. People in the bar were upset about the "hippie dance" we'd just come from. A couple of men, who looked like loggers, said they'd like to go down and clean out the hippies. Anyway we got a lot of free drinks, and steelhead fishing tips. We returned to our camping spot, and put up the tent in the dark. Although it was cold, we managed to stay warm (probably because of all the alcohol in us?).

The next day we fished all day. I had taken along my new 8mm movie camera, and hoped to get some pictures of fish. It was late in the afternoon, and I'd given up on catching any fish. I told Jim Feller I'd take a picture of him fishing. This may sound like a "fish story," but I have the picture to prove it. As soon as I began filming him fishing on the bank of the river, he got a bite, and after a short fight, landed a sixteen-inch trout! That was the only fish caught during the entire trip. Later that winter, Jim, Mike, and I took off on a three-day weekend, and drove up near the Oregon border, and fished along the Klamath River. We didn't catch anything, but it was a wonderful vacation from the ship. I took a few movies of the trip.

I tried to take advantage of all the liberty I could, as I felt it would not be long before the ship headed back overseas. There was a lot of work that needed to be done on the ship, after all the steaming she had done over the past months. In W Division we had to paint, strip, and replace most of the insulation in the after magazine, because of the water damage from the flood. This was also a busy time for me as I had to schedule, and document all the work completed within W Division, as the PMS-maintenance supervisor.

Not long after December the ship was back at Hunters Point in dry dock. Hunters Point was depressing not only because it was a shipyard, but also because it was situated in a depressed, slum area. I previously mentioned a bar a few blocks from the gate called the Horse and Cow. This was the only white owned bar within the black neighborhoods for a number of square miles. A retired chief submariner owned the bar. Next to the Horse and Cow was a barbeque rib's diner. We'd often go to the Horse and Cow, and ordered ribs from the diner next door. One night Jim Feller and John Barth returned to the ship from the Horse and Cow at a late hour. Jim was shaking and white faced. He said him and John had been in the Horse and Cow, he had gone to the rest room, and just returned to his table, when a young black man appeared at the entrance to the bar, and quickly fired three shots from a pistol into the room, then ran out. Everyone dove for the floor. The police were called, and luckily no one was hit. However one of the bullets fired had struck the wall in the back of the bar, penetrating the wall and exiting directly above the urinal where Jim had been standing just a few moments before. I would not have been able to keep my promise to his sister, to take care of him, if he'd delayed his exit from the bathroom!

I was a "taxi service" for most of the W Division single sailors. Most sailors would begin their leave time one minute after midnight, because the first day of leave was free, and not counted against accrued leave. I don't know how many nights I drove sailors to the airport after midnight so they could start their journey home on leave? The Pontiac Firebird was running rough, so I took it to a garage in Oakland. The mechanic tuned it up, but said I should replace the timing chain. The timing chain was a Teflon coated chain that was not performing well. The mechanic said it would cost more than $400, but I could wait a while. I also had trouble with the color television I'd bought, and let the division use. While at sea it had been a nightly affair to gather in the W Division Forward Coffee Locker and watch the movie that was broadcast by the ship's television station. While in port we watched TV programs that were broadcast by whatever country we were in.

In the midst of all the scheduled shipyard work, we still had to maintain our nuclear weapons technical competence and we conducted frequent training operations. Our Navy Technical Proficiency Inspection was to be held sometime in 1972, but we didn't know when.

This period in Hunters Point was one of the busiest times in the history of the shipyard. There were three aircraft carriers in the shipyard at the same time, the *Oriskany*, *Coral Sea*, and the *Midway*. I had a surprise one day. The quarterdeck called down to W Division and said I had a visitor. I went topside, and there was Walt Graham, who I'd been with at Whidbey Island. He was the one I'd spent a weekend with, at his sisters' in Seattle, and also gone to a court martial with, after he fired his pistol at a car. He was stationed on the *USS Midway*, and still a second class. He was retiring in a few months after twenty years. We went on liberty a few times together before he retired. With three aircraft carriers in the shipyard, and the GMT rating being so small, often at lunchtime W Divisions would be intermingled at the base exchange cafeteria. We would also see each other on liberty, often at the Carnival Club.

I dated a number of girls out of the Carnival Club. One girl whose name was "Boots" (because she always wore boots), one evening she asked me to drive her to see her mom. Her mom lived in Petaluma, north of Frisco. I drove her there, and was shocked to see that her mom lived in a mansion. Boots lived in a shabby apartment with another girl. Her story was that her parents disowned her because she didn't want to go to college, and wanted to live in the city, and work in the Carnival Club.

While in Hunters Point on 3 March, we had a change of command, and had a new captain. Our new captain was Captain John C. Barrow, a 1949 graduate of the Naval Academy. He had been in a squadron on the *USS Independence* when I had been onboard in 1962 and 1963.

Upon our arrival in Alameda, the Air Wing had left the ship. The planes had flown off prior to *Oriskany* steaming under the Golden Gate. They had flown to either Lemoore Naval Air Station, or Alameda Naval Air Station. This is where the planes would stay until our battle readiness training prior to our next deployment. All the supporting sailors in the air wing departed with their sea bags, and equipment upon arrival at the pier. This meant a decrease of about 1,500 sailors, or a third of the crews' population! We in the ships' company were never sad to see the air squadrons depart. This meant the chow lines would be shorter, as well as various other lines throughout the ship, such as sickbay, ships' store, etc., all in all the ship would be less crowded. There was some resentment toward the squadron "airedales," because while in port they would be living in relative luxury in nice clean, roomy barracks, while we would have to live in the dust, noise, and discomfort of a ship being worked on in the yards. There was not much "love lost" between ships' company sailors, and squadron sailors. From my point of view, it was good to see them leave.

The personality of W Division was changing. Upon our return to the states, eleven sailors out of the twenty-two that were on board upon our return would not be on the 1972 cruise. There were to be seventeen new men, mostly young men that had to be trained. And they had to be trained well, because going to war we could not afford mistakes.

I dreaded going back on the line, while at the same time I looked forward to it with anticipation. These conflicting feelings were because I did relish the responsibilities I had. I was proud of doing a job that few could do, I also enjoyed seeing younger sailors mature, and become a team. I must also admit that I enjoyed my position of authority as leading petty officer. My sense of dread came from not knowing what would happen in the war? There was always the possibility that the ship would be attacked, and that there would be the beginning of World War III. There were also the unbelievably long, hard work hours, and danger. As it turned out my apprehension was somewhat justified, as the '72 cruise turned out to be the hardest, and most dangerous war cruises I'd had thus far!

In the late 1960s and early 1970s, onboard aircraft carriers, the danger of fire were foremost in carrier sailor's minds. There had been a number of tragic fires on carriers.

Large fires had occurred on the *USS Enterprise, USS Saratoga, USS Forrestal* and on the *USS Oriskany*. In the aftermath of these fires it had been discovered that many of the sailors died needlessly. They had died with protective devices nearby that they did not know how to use, or had been unfamiliar with fire fighting techniques. The decision was made in the upper echelons of the Navy that all officers and enlisted men assigned to duty onboard an aircraft carrier would be required to attend a five-day fire fighting school. The schools were located in San Diego, and Treasure Island, California, and Norfolk, Virginia.

I was very familiar with fire fighting, and damage control equipment, as I had been assigned as the Damage Control Petty Officer on the *Independence*, and *Ticonderoga*. I had been responsible for the maintenance and upkeep of this equipment for a number of years. The most common shipboard personal fire protection equipment was the Oxygen Breathing Apparatus, or as it was commonly called the "OBA." This was a dual bag device, which looked like two lungs, with a mask, and hoses leading to the two "lungs." When a person had the OBA on, he looked like a scuba diver, with two exterior lungs hanging in front of his chest. The OBA had a cavity that held an OBA canister, which was a metal container with solid chemicals inside, which when lit by pulling a starting candle, burned the canister chemicals creating oxygen. This canister created oxygen for a period of about forty-five minutes. The OBA also had a timer, which would inform the user when it was time to remove the used canister, and install a new one. There were specific ways to insert an OBA canister. Many of the dead sailors in fires in the past had been found with an OBA on, but had failed to insert the canister properly, and sadly had died unnecessarily with a life saving device on. The majority of deaths in carrier fires were due to smoke inhalation. OBA's could keep a person alive for many hours in a smoke-filled compartment, so it was a very important piece of life saving gear.

In February W Division was scheduled to attend fire-fighting school. One third of the division would attend the five-day school at a time. The school was on Treasure Island. This was an island that the Oakland Bay Bridge rested upon, as it spanned the bay between Oakland, and the city of San Francisco. I had been on Treasure Island a number of times while I was in transit, and also for a couple of weeks while I was being discharged in 1970. I was with the last group to attend school. Enough sailors with cars were in each group to give the sailors without cars transportation back and forth from the ship at Hunters Point to the Treasure Island school which was a trip of about ten miles. W Division sailors were intermixed with other sailors from the ship. The first few days were spent in the classroom, studying types of fires, and various firefighting equipment.

One very important piece of fire-fighting equipment on board ships is the "all-purpose nozzle" that attaches to the end of a fire hose. The nozzle can produce either spray fog, or a solid stream of water. Also important is the "Handy-Billy," a light weight, gasoline driven pump, used for pumping fire fighting water, and also used for de-watering flooded compartments. A Handy-Billy was used when our W Division magazine was flooded.

Without a doubt the most exciting time in the firefighting course was when students had to actually fight fires! At the school there were two isolated brick buildings that had been constructed to be set on fire. The brick buildings had separate rooms within, and instead of solid floors, there were steel grates students walked on, under these grates were huge trays that could be filled with flammable diesel fuel.

It took a minimum of three sailors to control a one and ½ inch diameter fire hose. An unattended charged fire hose with water surging through it would flay about wildly, and was capable of breaking arms and legs, and causing injuries to bystanders. At school, seven men, strung out along the hose length, manned each fire hose. Before entering the burning buildings, we were given gas masks, cloth fire resistant pants and jackets, and heavy rubber boots and gloves. After students suited up, and manned the fire hoses, the instructors would light the filled fuel trays within the building. Two hose teams at a time would charge into the building. The first team in was supposed to fight the fire, while the second team was to keep the front team cool by drenching them with water. The teams were required to stay in the building until the fire was completely out.

It took courage to enter the building while flames were roaring out of all the windows and doors. The most fearful fires, were those burning underneath our feet, it felt as though flames surrounded us, with smoke blinding us completely. The heat inside the building was almost unbearable, and most of the students singed hair on various body parts. Two sailors in our class, panicked and dropped their section of the fire hose, and ran out of the building (thankfully not W Division sailors). These two had to repeat the course. After the class was completed, it took a couple of days to finally clean all the soot from our nostrils, ears, and hair.

We graduated on 25 February. We all were given a graduation certificate. This was certainly not the most pleasant school I'd attended, but it did give me confidence that I could utilize firefighting equipment properly, and I felt I could handle fire fighting situations, having undergone a "trial by fire."

Also in February, Charlie Galbreath, Chief Chapbourne, and I attended a boring, but necessary class at Treasure Island, on Preventive Maintenance System (PMS) paperwork.

One day while down in the W Division forward coffee locker, I received a call from the after brow chief of the watch, who said I had visitors on the quarterdeck. I went topside, and greeted George Holden, from A school, and Guam, and Lloyd Wilson, From *Ticonderoga*, and Guam. They both were stationed on board the aircraft carrier *USS Midway*, who was in the shipyard with us. This was a nice surprise, and we had a nice afternoon, catching up on what had been going on in our lives since we'd last seen each other.

Many in W Division began hanging out in a bar called the Velvet Glove. The attraction of this bar was that it was located near Pepperdine University, all girls' college. Another attraction was an aquarium that ran the length of the wall behind the bar. Within this aquarium were "fish eating fish," many South American bass such as the ones I had fished for in Guam. Each evening at 6:00 p.m, it was feeding time. The bartender would put goldfish into the aquarium, and a feeding frenzy would take place.

As I mentioned, living conditions on a ship in a shipyard are very uncomfortable, because of the noise, dirt, and inconvenience, many sailors rented apartments off the ship. Usually to save money, sailors would go in together and rent an apartment. This multiple renters' situation often didn't work well, as sailors tended to party, and make more noise than the normal renters.

One night I met a girl in the Velvet Glove who was very friendly, she said she had a few apartments she managed, right around the corner, and one was empty. It was only fifty-five dollars a month. I took a look at it, and said I'd take it. It was a one-room place with a kitchen, bath, and foldout sleeper couch. I moved my TV off the ship, put a few clothes in the closet, and looked forward to having a place I could stay off the ship. My new apartment did not work out well however, I only stayed in it a couple of nights. The long drive back and forth to the ship, was too much, and not long after moving in, I moved out.

The end of the 1971 cruise, I had a persistent premonition that I would not survive another cruise? I realized this was an irrational outlook, but looking back, I think my weariness, and the pressures of preparing, and training for yet another deployment fueled this attitude. I had no word from my detailer about when to expect my orders transferring to shore duty.

This was also a time of frustration for me, as I was hearing that many of the sailors I'd been stationed with who were my age were being promoted to chief. I felt like I was being left behind "promotion-wise." This was as well a time of rejection and bewilderment. The Vietnam War had split the country. This war was unlike any other our country had been involved in. We read newspapers filled with stories of protests against the war, many protests were in the San Francisco area. The Selective Service was a common target of protest, draft cards were burned in public, and servicemen were called cruel names. As sailors we had envisioned ourselves as guardians of our country, and protectors of freedom, and had dreamed of being hailed as honorable, courageous warriors. We had dreamed this, because this had been the case in World War II, and to some extent the Korean War. It was repulsive to us who had responded to our nations call to duty, to see stories in the media of draft dodgers that were portrayed as heroes! As GMT's we were getting a "double dose" of rejection, as there were not only Vietnam War protests, but also the anti nuclear protests. Most of the younger generation sailors wore civilian clothes on liberty, but I began making it a point to wear my uniform in preference to civilian clothes. I felt this was a statement that I refused to be ashamed of my uniform and my service. As the war drug on, it began to seem like we in the military were being reviled, and treated like the lowest class people in American society, not only by citizens who were turning their backs on us, but also those in our countries leadership! Restrictions were in place concerning how the war was fought, often for the enemy's advantage. In many situations, we could not fire back, if fired upon. It also appeared that in order to placate antiwar factions in the country, all of our accomplishments and victories in the war were not highly publicized, but were either not mentioned, or kept low-keyed.

Often while in public places while I was in uniform, people would be rude, refuse to sit near me, or stare sternly. I heard insults, or felt cold indifference. There were rare occasions, when I was given words of encouragement, or support. These words most often came from World War II veterans. I began to develop an affinity for this generation, men who had responded to America's call to duty, and had not shirked from this call to arms. I wished that my generation had responded as they had.

As a method of coping with our hurt and disappointment, we began to build impenetrable psychological walls around ourselves, as a group, and as individuals. It seemed as though it was us against the rest of the world.

We could not trust anyone that was not a part of our group, and we began to isolate ourselves from the rest of society. Although I dreaded another Vietnam cruise, in another way I looked forward to departing America and all the complexities of a society which seemed to be in constant turmoil, and rejected me.

In the years following the Vietnam War a condition known as Post Traumatic Stress Disorder, or "PTSD" affected many veterans. While I did not experience the horrors, and trauma many of the soldiers and marines did on land, I can appreciate the shock they felt when we returned from Vietnam, and were not respected for their service. I think to some degree I suffered from PTSD? I do know that after the war I had insomnia, had morbid thoughts of death, drank excessively, and was callous toward others around me. I know that some Vietnam veterans used PTSD as a means of getting attention, or sympathy from others. I make no excuses for my behavior, although I regret some of it, I have pride in the fact that I did the best that I could as an American sailor.

The Vietnam War did make me cynical about the way America treats her veterans, and those that shed their blood for her. Lip service is paid to veterans, with very little material benefit. I'll take pity on the reader, and not belabor this point any longer. Suffice to say, war veterans have not been treated as shabbily as Vietnam War veterans, since the Spanish American War, and the Philippine Insurrection, which can also be labeled as a time of national shame.

During the ship's yard period, without any ordnance aboard, nor any aircraft, or squadron sailors, we worked eight or nine hour days, and stood twenty-four-hour duty every sixth day. Every liberty night, I was off the ship, usually in the Carnival Club. The statement "it's lonely at the top" has a thread of truth in it. I certainly was not at the "top," but as leading petty officer, I was in a critical leadership position. A position of supervision in the Navy is vastly different from a position of supervision in the civilian world. In corporate America, or in the business world, managers work for eight hours, and then leave work for home. In the Navy, on board ship, I was on the job twenty-four hours a day, seven days a week. The men that worked for me spent their lives within arm's length. We ate, slept, worked, and played together. Every word I spoke, every action of mine affected their opinion and attitude toward me, and how they would carry out the orders I gave them. I took extra pains to make sure I showed appreciation for jobs well done, and gave public praise when possible. Many of the younger generation, or their peers were involved in protests, or were indifferent to the war in Vietnam, so the dedication, and patriotism, of these sailors made them a "breed apart."

I was staying up each liberty night until after 2:00 a.m. each night. If I didn't have a watch on my duty night, I would catch up on sleep. On the weekends I didn't have duty, I often would drive the 200 miles plus, south, and visit my parents, sister, and brothers. We had not gotten the word on when our next deployment might begin? We watched the news for happenings in the war. President Nixon and Secretary of State Kissinger were busy in negotiations with the North Vietnamese.

W Division spaces had gotten a lot of attention during this yard period in Hunters Point. We had painted all our work and living spaces. The after magazine bulkhead asbestos insulation that had been damaged during the "flood," had all been replaced. We had all moved out of our berthing compartment, and stayed in a barracks on base for a week while our berthing compartment was being painted.

There were only five civilian yard workers that were permitted into W Division spaces. A couple of the yard workers were tasked with overhauling our magazine overhead bi-rail hoists. The hoists were on an overhead rail system that we used for positioning over weapons, and used for raising and lowering weapons. These yard workers spent the majority of their time sleeping, or sitting around drinking coffee, and smoking. They knew they were safe slacking off, as their boss couldn't come into the spaces to check on them. We let them do this, and in return they would get us supplies, and yard work done that we would not have gotten otherwise.

There is an underground "supply system" that has always existed on Navy ships, and Navy shore stations, this system is maintained primarily by chiefs, and petty officers. A primary component of the underground supply system is coffee. An example might be that W Division needed green tiles to re-tile the instrument storage room. The yard workers had access to a warehouse full of tiles. We couldn't get the tile through the regular Navy supply system, so for two five-pound tins of coffee (which was regularly issued to each division on the ship), the coffee was traded for the tile. This underground system used between divisions, and between shipyards, and the ship, is called "comshaw." Someone who is good at trading or bartering is called a "comshaw artist." This is not a legal method of obtaining material or services, but in many instances nothing would be accomplished if it were not for the "comshaw system."

Yard workers were called by the slang term "sand crabs" by the sailors. Just off the dry dock pier there was a large restroom that was famous as a congregation point for yard workers avoiding work.

Chief Harry Chapbourne had a loud speaker on his Volkswagen, and he would enjoy pulling his car up by the restroom, and using the loudspeaker say things like "OK you men get back to work," or "the last man out of the restroom is fired." He would laugh as workers poured out the restroom door.

Just as ships have reputations and personalities, so do shipyards. Hunters Point did not have an admirable reputation. It seemed to take longer to get various jobs completed, and the yard workers seemed to work at a leisurely pace. Each worker had a specialty, and would not do a task if that task did not fall within his job description. A common statement was "the union won't let me do that." It was often frustrating to see five or six men sit around all day, waiting for ship fitters, welders, or some other specialty worker, so the job could continue. This was not the case in many foreign shipyards. In shipyards like the ones in Japan, there was no sitting around, or halted work because of union regulations, all workers worked to complete the job.

There was little love lost between most sailors and the "sand crabs." I think a lot of this disrespect was because sailors associated the miserable living conditions in the shipyards, with the people we associated with the shipyard, the shipyard workers. I should also say that there were many workers that were hard working, and dedicated to doing a good job, but it seemed in Hunters Point they were in the minority.

John Barth, a third class in the division had been dating a girl that was a friend of "Boots." They had met in the Carnival Club, and one weekend they got married at city hall. A number of us in the division went with them, and were at the ceremony, that was presided over by a justice of the peace. His new wife, Pat had an unusual roommate; he was a homosexual, so I guess it was like having a female roommate? Not long after the wedding, since they did not have a car, I drove them down to the town of Salinas where Pat's parents lived. While in Salinas, I visited Alma. She had called the ship the previous year, while the ship was in Japan, and begged to see me. She had not changed, and it was not an enjoyable reunion. This was the last time I was to see Alma. Not long after this trip to Salinas, John was discharged, and he and Pat moved to Michigan.

A movie called "*Dirty Harry*[34]", starring Clint Eastwood was released; it was filmed in San Francisco, in many of the places we in W Division frequented. A group of us went to see the movie, and enjoyed it. In the Carnival Club, a popular song was "*Okie from Muskogee*[35]," by Merle Haggard, and also his song "*Fighting Side of Me*[35]." Both songs were pro-U.S., pro-military, and anti hippy. A popular band that the younger generation liked was Credence Clearwater.

Shortly after the ship left Hunters Point Shipyard, and returned to our pier at Alameda Naval Air Station, the personality of W Division began to change drastically. The 1971 W Division had twenty enlisted men, and by the first part of 1972, twelve of them had left, most of them first-termers being discharged. The 1972 crew consisted of twenty-five enlisted men, seventeen of which were new men. I regretted seeing most of the 1971 crew leave. We'd experienced a rough cruise together. There were a lot of sad farewells, beginning with John Barth, Mike Feller, and then Mike Jackson. As leading petty officer, I was supposed to be impartial toward all those working for me, but these three were the closest to me. I remember Mike Jackson's departure. A number of us bought him an expensive bottle of brandy. We gave it to him the night before he left the ship. Mike said he would take a small sip of it each year in remembrance of us. I'm sure he was successful in whatever he pursued in civilian life. I've often wondered if he has any brandy left in the bottle we gave him.

My anxiety about the upcoming "72 cruise," was partially based upon the fact that most of the W Division crew would be "green." They would need to be trained, and there probably wouldn't be much time to train before we were once again on the line.

Our Division Officer, Lieutenant Barber was transferred; our new division officer was Chief Warrant Officer 2 Jackson. He had previously been an enlisted Aviation Ordnanceman. He had very little knowledge about the nuclear weapons program. I had become increasingly aware of the lack of knowledge, or experience of commissioned officers that were assigned as division officers, or supervisors of sailors working in the nuclear weapons programs. Much of Master Chief Riechman, Chief Chapbourne, and my time, were spent trying to educate CWO2 Jackson.

W Division now had five first class petty officers, Terry Morrison, Tommy Jones, Charlie Galbreath, Ted Trimble, and me. Terry Morrison and I had the same seniority, but Master Chief Riechman wanted me to remain the leading petty officer, until I transferred. Ted Trimble was an oddity, in that he had made first class in the Naval Reserves, and had just signed up for active duty. As leading petty officer, although we five were the same rates, I was the supervisor of the other four. I had to be sensitive to their egos, yet insure they realized I was in charge. I never had any problems in this area, and we all worked well together. Terry Morrison and I had taken the chiefs test in February, he had made it and was scheduled to "put on the hat" later in the year. I had not passed, and this was discouraging to me.

I'd scored higher than Terry in many areas of the exam, and my record was as good, if not better than his. As I explained previously, the exam score only counted fifty percent toward promotion, while the selection by the Chief Petty Officer Selection Board in Washington, D.C., counted for the remaining fifty percent. I was at a loss concerning what more I could do professionally to improve my chances for promotion to chief?

While in Oakland one night, Steve Kitson and I met two girls playing pool. I began dating one of the girls. Her name was Pamela. She lived in Oakland in a house in the middle of a predominantly black neighborhood. She had two small twin boys, and had been divorced for a year. She and her brother had moved to California from Kentucky, at the same time as her divorce. Pamela was a bartender, and I would frequent the particular bar she worked in (seldom paying for drinks). This was becoming an unhealthy and dangerous pattern in my life, dating bartenders, and spending time in their place of employment.

Pamela was outspoken, and a little "rough" around the edges. One weekend she and I traveled to Fresno, where she met my sister, and mom. One week the ship steamed to San Diego for a port call and Pamela flew down to San Diego for a day, along with a girlfriend of Harry Chapbourne's, we four toured San Diego, spending most of the time at the San Diego Zoo.

One evening I went to a bar in Oakland that Pamela was working in. I was surprised to see a huge hole in the wall opposite the bar that had been boarded up and covered. The bar foot rail was badly dented. I was told what had happened earlier in the afternoon. An automobile driver on the road outside the bar had lost control of his vehicle, crashed through the wall and the car had come to rest against the bar. The car slid the bar a couple of feet. Pamela had been behind the bar, and luckily no one was hurt. One regular bar customer, who was in the bar every day, happened to be sitting at one end of the bar when the car crashed through the wall. He had been holding a drink in his hand, and the crash knocked him off his barstool. To everyone's amazement, he didn't spill a drop of the drink in his hand, which he promptly drank, and immediately ordered a double shot!

Pamela changed jobs to a bar in Alameda. In addition to her regular neighborhood customers, there was one "biker" that was a Hell's Angel. Each time I'd come in the bar, he would accuse me of being a policeman, apparently because of my short military haircut? No matter how many times I told him I was not a cop, and even though he saw me in my uniform, he swore I was a cop. He was always polite and respectful, but one night when I had duty on the ship, Pamela said he got drunk, made a scene, was belligerent to the other customers, and she made him leave the bar. To force a member of the Hell's Angels to do anything against his will was a dangerous thing to do in Alameda, or Oakland. About one week later, Pamela got a call at the bar from a Hell's Angel, saying the leader of the Oakland chapter of the club wanted to talk to her. Pamela asked me to go with her, I reluctantly agreed. We went to a particular house in Oakland, where we were supposed to be at 1:00 p.m., we arrived at noon. The couple that lived in the house made us welcome. Promptly at 1:00, one of the biggest black men I'd ever seen knocked on the door and came in. Two other rough looking guys were with him. He carried a large cane that had a silver lions head on the top. He was extremely polite to us, and apologized to Pamela for the insults, and trouble a member of his club had caused in the bar. I had expected the three to come roaring up to the house on motorcycles, but they had arrived in a white Cadillac. Pamela kept talking to him, while I wished she would just shut up. The primary thought going through my mind was, I'd rather be somewhere else at this particular moment! Finally they bid us a friendly goodbye, and I heaved a sigh of relief. I never saw the Hell's Angel that had caused the problems in the bar again. Pamela wanted me to move into her apartment, and during a short trip to Reno, wanted to get married. I'm very thankful that I resisted both these requests.

From March to May the ship underwent battle readiness training. We would pull out to sea on weekdays, practice general quarters, shoot our guns, and do all the things that would prepare us for deployment, and then pull back in on Friday for the weekend. The majority of the crew was new, including our new captain, who was Captain Barrow. He had assumed command in March. In April instructors from San Diego Nuclear Weapons Training Group came onboard, and gave W Division a course of instruction in Limited Life Component Exchanges, or as it were called "LLC" operations. As well as changes taking place in society, and the Navy, changes were happening in the nuclear weapons program. An emergency destruction plan was being formulated at each nuclear capable activity. The quarterly requirement to practice load weapons on attack aircraft was deleted, primarily to minimize the handling and movement of weapons, and thus reduce the chance of accidents, such as occurred on the *Ticonderoga*, when a loaded plane and pilot fell into the sea. LLC operations, which in the past had been accomplished at shore stations, were now being completed on carriers. An additional new requirement was a vastly expanded quality assurance program.

The "Two Man Rule," and later when women GMT's came into being, the "Two Person Rule," was a way of life around nuclear weapons. Now there were additional safeguards or "quality assurance" points during weapons operations. Senior petty officers within W Divisions, or shore duty weapons stations, were designated as "quality assurance inspectors." An example of a quality assurance point might be; during a weapons operation the check sheet reader (Hook Leader), would read, "Insure the ready safe switch is in the safe green position." After being checked by two assemblymen, they would both respond, "Check, ready safe switch is in the safe green position." Then the Quality Assurance Inspector would also check the switch, and initial the check sheet. So with the addition of this extra assembly team member, in many critical mechanical or electrical steps, we had a "three person rule." This may sound redundant, or time-wasteful to the reader, but it is my belief that we could never be too safe, or overly conscientious with nuclear weapons. The GMT Quality Assurance Inspectors at many activities often had a different chain of command from the normal GMT's chain of command, which was a strengthening factor in the quality assurance program, as the inspectors could perform their work without fear of reprisal if they were overly critical. Another new program that came into being concerned the handling, and movement of weapons. Any time a weapon was removed from its storage location, or storage chocks, a "Movement Supervisor" had to be present. A Movement Supervisor was usually a first class, chief, or officer, and was required to have a letter of designation from the commanding officer.

Marines were authorized to use "deadly force," which meant they were authorized to shoot to kill to protect nuclear weapons. Another fact we as GMT's were aware of, and had to be prepared for if a situation occurred where we were taken hostage. The marines were under orders "not to consider the lives of the hostages!" In other words if someone, or a group took us as hostages in an attempt to gain control of a nuclear weapon, we were considered expendable, and to be shot as quickly as the "bad guys."

Our NTPI inspection was held, and it went off with very few problems. CWO2 Jackson was at a loss how to prepare for the NTPI, so he relied on Master Chief Riechman and me, and the other petty officers to prepare, and get through the inspection. The inspectors noted that some flammables were stored in one of our elevator pits; this was written up as a discrepancy. The master chief suspected that the instructors we'd had onboard in April had told the inspectors about the flammables, since the instructors and inspectors worked in the same command.

There were a lot of rumors about when the ship would leave on deployment. The most persistent rumor was that it would be 30 June. My brother Joe was about to graduate from the eighth grade. I enjoyed letting him practice driving while I visited home. I remember one Sunday, Joe, Jerry and I were headed home after church, and I had Joe drive. He was going very fast (more than eighty mph), and Jerry who was in the back seat, became very worried.

The last of May there was a sense of urgency on the ship. There were daily working parties bringing supplies aboard. Then on 3 June, we were told we would leave for Vietnam in forty-eight hours. We were told not to tell anyone but our families. I didn't have time to return my car to my parent's house, and I didn't want to take my television on another cruise. I put my car on blocks behind Pamela's house, hoping it wouldn't be stripped, if and when I returned? I also left my television at her house. I'd not been able to tell my parents I was leaving, because we were not permitted to talk about our deployment over the telephone.

The ship pulled away from the Alameda pier, early on the morning of 5 June 1972. Once again I wondered if I would see my homeland again. This marked my fifth deployment to Vietnam. There had been a number of accidents with the DST bombs we would be building. In one incident, a destroyer had been severely damaged by steaming over a DST that had been dropped in shallow water, in another incident; one that detonated prematurely had killed an Air Force crew.

After the ship had been at sea for a few hours, the captain spoke over the 1MC; apologizing for all the false rumors we'd heard. He admitted he did not know for sure when we were leaving until forty-eight hours before our departure. The captain said the reason our deployment was kept secret was because President Nixon didn't want it known that another aircraft carrier was leaving for Vietnam during the peace talks with Russia, and North Vietnam. In a letter I wrote on the 6th, I told my brother Jerry he could start praying for me again, he had said he stopped when I had returned last December! Our time in the States had seemed very short. The sailors that had been on the '71 cruise were shocked that we were headed back to the war so soon. I was in a weary physical state, the constant late hours, and burning of the candle at both ends was beginning to take a toll on my health.

My evaluations for the period December 1971 to June 1972 contained all 4.0's in all evaluation areas. One statement in my evaluations said, "He posses many qualities of a natural leader of men. During the ship's pre-deployment period his tactful leadership was particularly evident during the arduous ordnance on-load. Petty Officer Little at all times maintains the bearing and carriage of a true military man. His personal concern for the welfare of his shipmates has helped keep the division a close-knit unit. He has never hesitated to offer help to a shipmate whether during working or liberty hours." CWO2 Jackson and Master Chief Riechman sat down with me behind closed doors to review these evaluations. The master chief paid me a compliment saying he considered me his "right-hand man," even though there were two chiefs in W Division. I was pleased with my evaluations, and I wondered how much longer I would be on *Oriskany*? The NTPI before our deployment had been a grueling, exhausting job. I was hopeful I would not have to go through another one in 1973.

The ship made a short stop at Hawaii for a couple of hours. No one was permitted off the ship, and we were soon underway. The previous cruise I had bought an 8mm movie camera. I had taken pictures of launches and recoveries of aircraft, fishing trips, and Christmas at home. I was determined to take more pictures during this cruise. The captain let us know that the ship would be stopping in Guam for twelve hours, and the crew would be permitted a few hours liberty. I think he later regretted this decision to let the crew go on liberty?

The ship pulled alongside the fueling piers in Apra Harbor, Guam at 8:00 a.m. The crew was permitted to leave the ship in dungarees. I was anxious to see if Guam had changed in the two-½ years I'd been gone? I explained to Charlie Galbreath and a few others in the division that the coolest place on the base was the bowling alley. The bowling alley had to keep the inside of the building cool; in order to keep the wooden bowling lanes in shape. A few of us went to the bowling alley, while most of the crew went to the enlisted club. We were only permitted six hours of liberty. We bowled a few games, and then caught a bus headed back for the ship. The bus Charlie and I got on was full of drunken sailors. The combination of tropical heat, hurried drinking, and pent up emotions of sailors had created a volatile situation. Charlie and I were the only first class on board the bus. Someone threw a beer bottle from the back of the bus, which struck a sailor in the head. Charlie and I had to stand up, and maintain order, by threatening to put any troublemaker on report. The sailor that was struck in the head was bleeding profusely. When we arrived at the ship, we found an aid station to look after him. The scene at the pier shocked us. There were hundreds of inebriated sailors. The base was also selling beer on the pier. I had enjoyed seeing a little of Guam again, but was ashamed of the behavior of *Oriskany* sailors. This was an historic visit, as it had been many years since a carrier had tied up to a pier on the island of Guam, but was marred by the *Oriskany* sailors' wild liberty. After pulling out we learned there had been a huge fight in the base enlisted club, and thousands of dollars of damage had been done. It was my thought that many of the sailors were blowing off steam, because of the frustration many of us felt over not knowing when we were deploying, not knowing when we would return, and in general an uncertainty about our future. The captain was not happy about the behavior of the crew, and he let us know the evening we departed, by giving a long lecture over the 1MC. Many sailors ended up on report. Although there were W Division sailors that visited the club, none were involved in the fight.

Our "secret departure" from the states was apparently a success, as this was one of the few times we were not buzzed in mid-ocean by long-range Soviet bombers. Near the Philippines we steamed through a narrow channel with tropical islands visible on both sides. I took movies of this area, as well as the three destroyers with us that were strung out in a single file behind us.

We were scheduled to be in Subic Bay for two weeks before reporting to the line. Bomb builders were to attend a two-day school on the base covering DST's, and the building of the newest conventional bomb, the laser-guided bomb. The division had not had an opportunity to celebrate the passing of our NTPI. While Master Chief Riechman and I were talking one evening, we came up with the idea of chartering a fishing boat on the base, and having a division fishing party.

After pulling into Subic and after the division had attended the bomb school at the Subic Naval Magazine, we reserved a fishing boat for two days. Half the division would go on each day. We were able to get sandwich material from the mess deck, and everyone brought cases of cold drinks. The first morning there were fourteen of us on the pier. The fishing boat was forty feet long, and manned by a Filipino boat crew of three. We loaded the food onboard, as well as five cases of soda, and twenty cases of beer. This was a case of "extreme overkill," as there was no way twelve sailors could consume all these drinks. I took movies of the fishing trip.

On the way out of the harbor, we had a serious moment that brought the reality of war back to us. The cruiser *USS Newport News* (CA-148) was steaming into the harbor and passed by us. She had just come off the line, and was returning some marine casualties to Subic for further transportation back to the states.

As ordnancemen we appreciated the fact that sudden death was always a possibility, and as the cruiser slid by, we gave her a silent tribute. Later on in the month of October, *Newport News* was bombarding Vietnam coastal targets, when one of her gun turrets exploded killing twenty fellow ordnancemen.

We fished all day, and caught a few bottom fish. Around 3:00 p.m., we pulled into a small cove close to the shore, and we all went swimming. At 4:30 we headed back to the pier. We were trolling with two poles on the way back to the base pier. "Mac" McEvoy was sitting by the poles, half asleep, having put a considerable dent in a case of beer. Suddenly the reel of one pole buzzed. Something big had hit the trailing lure. The Master Chief ran for the pole, but Mac was in the way. We then saw a huge sword fish leap out of the water behind the boat. He was about fifty feet behind the stern of the boat, and he came completely out of the water, he was huge. The Filipino boatmen were wide eyed! Then the line went slack, and he was gone. Perhaps if the hook had been set right away, we might have caught the fish? The boatmen said it was one of the biggest they had seen! After that day, the master chief fished almost every day the ship was in Subic. The Chief's Club on base had their own fishing boat. We all had a good time, and left the small fish we had caught, leftover food, soda and beer with the boatmen.

The laser-guided bomb we had been given a class on was a relatively new piece of ordnance. It was basically a 2,000-pound bomb fitted with motorized moveable fins, connected electrically to a light-sensing eye. The "eye" locked onto a laser beam of light that was directed at the intended target, and would transmit signals to the fins, to adjust the fall through the air so the bomb struck the point of light. Normally one plane would focus the light on the target, while the aircraft carrying the laser-guided bomb would release the bomb. This precision bomb was most effective against bridges, and hardened targets.

Each morning the ship was in a foreign port, our EOD Team, which consisted of a chief warrant officer, and a first and second class, would don SCUBA gear, and inspect the hull of the ship for any suspicious devices. We also posted security watches on the ship, and pier, who had been instructed to watch for bubbles in the water that might indicate divers, or swimmers in the water near the ship.

It was a constant and ongoing effort to keep the ship clean, and keep trash off the ship, and thereby reducing fire-hazards. "Sweepers' and "trash dumpers" were assigned daily to ensure ships spaces were kept trash free. Trashcans were to be dumped frequently to prevent the possibility of a lit cigarette being carelessly thrown into a full trashcan. For duty sections this was the biggest chore, ensuring that spaces were trash free. The Command Duty Officer or the officer in charge of the ship in the captain's absence was always emphasizing the need to dump trash. Trash dumpsters were positioned on the pier, into which trash from the ship was to be dumped.

A frequent task of the base office of Naval Investigative Service (NIS) agents was to don rubber gloves, and aprons, and sift through the trash dumpsters to see if they could find any classified material that might have been thrown away. If any classified material were found, they would try to trace it back to whoever might be responsible for throwing it away. In severe cases this could mean prison time for offenders. In W Division we were very cautious about classified material disposal. Writing check sheets, making work schedules, storage plans, etc., generated a lot of classified paperwork, ranging from "For Official Use Only" to "Top Secret."
In W Division forward spaces, we had a classified paper shredder, which shredded paper into 1/16th inch strips. This shredded paper was kept in sealed plastic bags. All documents that were to be destroyed were listed on a "Classified Document Destruction Form," which was signed by two persons at the time of destruction.
From time to time, the division officer, accompanied by an enlisted man would take the filled bags of shredded documents to the ship's incinerator and burn all the paper. Before anyone dumped trash out of our working spaces, we insured no classified paper was included. Thankfully while I was onboard, we were never involved in compromising classified material. On one duty day, I was assigned to rummage through the dumpsters with an NIS agent. It was not pleasant work in the tropic heat, inside a smelly dumpster! We didn't find anything.

We knew it would be only a few more days and we would be back in the middle of the war, on the line. Everyone took advantage of liberty in Subic. Over the years the liberty restrictions overseas were eased, and petty officers were permitted to remain off the ship overnight in most overseas liberty ports. Seaman, and below had to report back to the ship at midnight, so there was an incentive to advance to third class petty officer, and higher. The privilege to remain off the ship overnight required mature behavior. In Olongapo there was a national curfew imposed by Philippine President Marcos. Everyone had to be off the streets at midnight. Many sailors, after drinking San Miguel beer all day in the heat, were quite inebriated. All sailors had to be back onboard ship at 7:30 a.m. Most W Division sailors stayed overnight in the Golden Hotel.

There were a few mornings, after I held musters on the ship, I had to send someone, or go myself into town to get a sailor that had overslept. Usually this meant that sailor's liberty was cancelled for the rest of the time the ship was in port. It was a much more serious matter to miss ships' movement. Anyone who missed the ship's departure from port was automatically scheduled for captain's mast, or court martial.

As leading petty officer, I was the "motivator" to ensure everyone in W Division kept within the liberty hour limits, and obeyed the muster times. This was a difficult task keeping rein on a group of eighteen to twenty year olds that wanted to "cut loose" after being at sea for weeks at a time. As I said, the personality of W Division had undergone a change with the departure of the '71 cruise sailors, and the arrival of the new GMT's. The new sailors were in many ways immature, and "untried, or untested" in the job of war, and bomb building, and also lacked the experience of serving on the line. The feelings of weariness, uncertainty about the future, and the persistent thoughts of "living on borrowed time," combined to cause me to spend much of my liberty time in more isolated surroundings. There is truth in the saying "familiarity breeds contempt," and also as I said "it's lonely at the top!" I had fun with the W Division sailors on liberty, and tried to always be open and approachable, but I expected respect from them as their leading petty officer, just as I respected them as capable sailors. Much of my liberty time was spent in a small "hole in the wall" place in Olongapo, along with other first class petty officers Charlie Galbreath, and Terry Morrison. This place was very basic, not flashy and glittering as many of the nightclubs in Olongapo. The mama-san appreciated our business, and the few girls that worked there waited on us hand and foot.

San Miguel beer was the safest thing to drink, and we couldn't drink the local water, or any drink with ice in it. As always, until your digestive system became used to San Miguel, it had a laxative effect. Olongapo was booming. The war meant many carrier visits, and sailors freely spending in town. More dirt streets were being paved, and new bars kept sprouting up. It was always amazing to me how a small, wild town such as Olongapo could swallow up 4,000 men on liberty? Mayor Gordon had been assassinated recently, and his wife was now the mayor, this was a common method of political change in the Philippines! Each bar had its own heavily armed guard. When we traveled any distance outside the town of Olongapo, every few miles there were Army checkpoints where all vehicles were required to stop, while armed Philippine soldiers checked identification cards, and inspected vehicle contents.

While Olongapo bar business seemed to be flourishing, there was still much poverty evident. Children begged for money, and cigarettes and we were cautioned about thieves, and pickpockets. One night Terry Morrison was headed back to the main gate, and the ship, before the midnight curfew. He caught a motorcycle sidecar taxi about six blocks from the gate. Instead of going directly down the main street to the gate, the driver zipped down a side street, and stopped. Six or seven men immediately surrounded the motorcycle with knives. They demanded Terry's money, about $100 dollars, which he gave to them. They also took his wristwatch off his wrist. He begged them to return his wristwatch, and surprisingly, they gave it back to him, probably because they had gotten so much money from him? He put his wristwatch on, and the robbers returned his empty wallet to him. Terry dejectedly walked back to the main street, and walked toward the main gate. Then a block and a half from the gate, a little kid ran up from behind him, and snatched his watch off his wrist! It definitely was not his night!

Since I had been robbed in Manila eight years previously, I had always been cautious overseas. I never carried anything off the ship that I wouldn't mind losing. I didn't wear rings, or expensive watches, and as far as documents, never carried anything other than my identification card. If a sailor wore a wristwatch with an expandable wristband, the thieves were expert at quickly pulling the watch off your wrist. There was a hazard involved with wearing a wristwatch with a rubber, or leather band. As I said before, thieves would sometimes cut the band with a sharp knife or razor, and you would not only lose your watch, but also have a cut wrist. I often wore a metal rigid watchband, and a very inexpensive watch. As always, the "buddy system" was encouraged, as it was much safer to go ashore in two's, so you could watch each other's back.

Terry Morrison was to be promoted to chief, and would "put on the hat," in August. As I explained before, he carried around a charge book that he had to produce anytime a chief requested it. The chief, would then write some comment, and return the book to him. This charge book was to be used during the secret initiation ceremony. I was slightly jealous, as this promotion had eluded me for three years.

In the "hole in the wall" bar that Terry and I frequented often, there was one girl who often sat with me. One day in the base exchange, Terry suggested to me that I buy the girl a cigarette lighter. I bought a Zippo lighter, with the ship's emblem on the side. I had duty the next day, but Terry had liberty, and he went to town. The next day on my liberty day, Terry and I went together into town.

Terry mentioned that I should present the lighter to the girl. We were sitting at a table, and I handed her the lighter, but instead of taking it, she said, "No thank you, I already have a chief petty officer lighter." Terry laughed so hard he almost fell out of his chair. He had given her a lighter with a chief's emblem on it the previous day, and prompted her what to say when I gave her the lighter. He thought this was hilarious, and talked about it for years in the future!

We left Subic and headed for the line. We formed crews for building bombs, manning W Division spaces, and for completing maintenance on our weapons. Our berthing compartment air conditioner began acting up again. It was an ongoing effort to repair, and keep the air conditioner working. In the berthing compartment, I slept in a bottom bunk that was near a pipe with a cap on it that went into a huge fuel tank underneath our berthing compartment. This pipe was a fuel sounding tube that was used when the ship went alongside a tanker for refueling. A sailor from engineering division would enter our berthing compartment, put on a sound powered phone headset, open the sounding tube, and periodically drop a sounding tape into the fuel tank, and report how full the tank was during the refueling operation. Although the sailors would make an effort to be quiet, this would always awaken me, and the odor of fuel oil would fill the berthing compartment.

If we believed in omens, we had a bad one just prior to our first line period. An ammunition ship, *USS Nitro* (AE-23) came alongside *Oriskany* for ammunition replenishment two days after we left Subic. The USS Nitro started her approach alongside at about 7:00 p.m. (1900). I happened to be in the forward W Division spaces, when the collision alarm sounded over the 1MC ship's loudspeaker. We all grabbed a stanchion, or hugged a bulkhead, bracing for a collision. We all felt a small thump, and held our breath waiting for an explosion. Thankfully there were no further movements or sounds. There was certainly a less hazardous ship than an ammunition ship to have a collision with! There was only slight damage to both ships, and after a short time the replenishment resumed. The collision was caused by a short in the *Oriskany*'s engine telegraph system. When coming alongside *Nitro* the command from the bridge to the engine room was to reverse engines 2, 3, and 4, but the faulty system signaled engine 4 to run at flank speed, which steered the *Oriskany* into the *Nitro*.

The next day bomb building and bombing sorties began. This was shortly after 30 June 1972, which marked the twelfth anniversary of my enlistment in the U.S. Navy. The bomb building was a little slow the first few days, as the majority of the sailors were new at this, but they learned quickly. I still had the persistent feeling that something was going to happen on this cruise?

Our new captain had an unusual hobby. Each evening in the tropics, he would watch for a "green flash" at sunset, and would try to get a picture of it. A "green flash" was a rare occurrence, and happened only if conditions were perfect. The sky would briefly flash a vivid green immediately after the sun dipped beneath the sea's horizon. Soon everyone on the ship was trying to get a picture of the green flash! I saw it once, but failed to get a picture. Speaking of the color green, the South China Sea off the coast of Vietnam seemed greener in color than the rest of the ocean. A term coined by the sailors that spent the Vietnam War years off the coast of Vietnam, and identified us as sailors that spent many months in the South China Sea, was "The Tonkin Gulf Yacht Club." I would go topside from time to time, on the sponson deck, to get a breath of fresh air. I recall one afternoon seeing hundreds of sea snakes in the water while we were on the line. I did not relish the thought of being in the water with these creatures, whose bite was more venomous than a land snake. We would often see dolphins playing, and swimming alongside the ship as we steamed through the water.

As well as practicing manning our battle stations, we would also practice abandon ship drills. There were always a few "non swimming" sailors. These sailors were assigned to a buddy who knew how to swim. When I came in the Navy if a sailor could not be taught to swim in boot camp, then he would be discharged. This was not the case now, if a sailor was a "non swimmer," he still continued on his Navy career regardless.

The bombing strikes continued almost nonstop. We worked seven days a week on the line, and slept when we could. My parents sent me a new "plain English" Bible, which I enjoyed reading. They continued to write me faithfully.

W Division's berthing compartment was located on the fourth deck, which was below the water line of the ship. One bulkhead of our berthing compartment was the outer hull of the ship, and if it was quiet enough, you could hear the sound of water rushing by. We could also hear the "pinging" sounds of the sonar's operating on the destroyers that were our escorts. The "pings" seemed to be particularly loud at night, or when sailors were trying to sleep. While on the line, the lights in the berthing compartment were out twenty-four hours a day (except when the decks were being swept), as there was always a crew shift of bomb builders trying to sleep. It was hard to sleep knowing that general quarters or some other alarm might sound at any time. I also had to contend with the engineering sailor taking fuel soundings by my bunk, every other day.

Much of our liberty time was spent catching up on lost sleep. It is said that a sailor can fall asleep anywhere. They are often seen asleep in a bus station, or airport, while sitting up. Irregular watches and varying work hours teach sailors to grab sleep when they can.

Water conservation is very important on board ships. Fresh water was converted from salt water by the engineering department, and was monitored closely to insure that the demand did not exceed the supply, or the ability to keep up with the water usage throughout the ship. If water were in short supply, then "water hours" would be enforced. Water hours meant that water for showers would only be turned on during specific hours. We were also required to take a "Navy shower," meaning in the shower, you would wet down, turn off the water, soap up, turn on the water and quickly rinse off, then turn off the shower. Often Masters at Arms were stationed in the showers to insure water was not being wasted. Anyone showering too long was put on report. Taking a longer than necessary shower was called taking a "Hollywood shower." There were times when the water would be shut off unexpectedly, or without any announcement. This unexpected shut off seemed to often occur when a sailor was in the shower, and had soaped up, and there would be no water to rinse off! This happened to me a number of times, and was uncomfortable having soap in your eyes, and soap drying on your skin with no water to rinse off!

I was becoming an "old timer" on the ship, having been on three cruises. As W Division Leading Petty Officer, I had gotten to know many of the ship's LPO's in the first class mess, and was able from time to time to accomplish work between divisions by coordinating with them. It was nice to have a special retreat in the first class mess. Sandwich material was always available in our refrigerator, and we had our own coffee pot. The "mess" was actually a curtained off area on the enlisted mess decks, with about ten tables within. A nightly movie was shown in the mess, although most watched the nightly movie shown over the ship's closed circuit television station.

An underground activity that often took place on the ship was the showing of pornographic movies. These were called "skin movies," and shown at various isolated areas on the ship. Sailors who owned the movies showed these movies, and they would charge admission. It was illegal to have obscene material on board, so the movies were illegal.

Some divisions had pin-up pictures of women, some very explicit, posted all over the bulkheads. A few W Division sailors tried to post a few pictures in our coffee locker, and I made them remove them. I explained that the pictures were not appropriate for our workspaces, and if they wanted pictures of this type they could keep them inside their personal lockers which were locked at all times. I put out the order at quarters one morning that there were to be no posting of pictures, etc., without my approval. A couple of months after this, the captain issued orders that pin-ups were not to be placed on the bulkheads of ships' compartments. I was pleased with his orders, which confirmed the position I had taken.

The first liberty port after our first line period was Hong Kong. One night Charlie and I went to a movie with two girls. The popular movies in Hong Kong were James Bond movies, or any movies with karate or martial art themes. Following the movie we went to a restaurant and had a Peking duck dinner. After dinner we hailed a taxi. I was the last person to get in the back seat, and as I closed the door, I had the thumb of my right hand in the doorjamb. I pulled the door closed and it latched with my thumb caught in the door. The cab driver took off right away. I could not get the door open to release my smashed thumb. The girls were jabbering in Chinese, and I was hollering for the driver to stop. Finally the driver realized I was hollering in pain, and stopped. With help I was able to open the cab door. My thumb was black and blue, and "flat," I was sure it was broken. The Chinese girls gave directions to the driver, who took us to a small out of the way shop that looked like an herb store. The girls directed me to the back, where there was an old Chinese lady. The old lady did not speak English, so the girls interpreted. She took a foul-smelling mixture out of a jar, and smeared it on my thumb. She massaged my thumb, for about ten minutes. It was very painful. She then put a tight bandage on my thumb, with instructions to remove the bandage after a couple of hours. Two hours later, I remove the bandage, there was no pain, or swelling, and I was amazed over this miraculous cure!

One snack that was popular in Hong Kong that was tried by Charlie and I was pickled chicken tail. We were not too enthusiastic about the pickled treats! Another popular snack in Hong Kong, and the Philippines was a "balut." This was an unborn chicken embryo that was placed in the ground to "ripen." They were foul smelling, and foul tasting, and on one occasion, on a dare I foolishly choked one down.

Hong Kong Mary and her women were still sifting through the garbage that was thrown into her garbage barges alongside the ships in port. Hong Kong had a great diversity of people, British, Americans, and Chinese, rich and poor.

There were people starving to death on the streets, while in the high finance areas of Kowloon, the streets appeared "paved in gold!" All sailors were warned that an area called "The Rooftops" was off limits. These were extreme slum areas of Hong Kong, and many of the residents of this area were refugees from Red China. A favorite tourist spot was Victoria Peak, I'd visited before, and which had one of the best views of the harbor and the city. I'd visited these Far East ports so many times that I was beginning to recognize each port by its particular smell.

After our Hong Kong visit, we were once again back on the line. Our daily quota of DST's kept increasing. Occasionally we would build laser-guided bombs. Our only source of war news at sea was the *Pacific Stars and Stripes* newspaper, which was usually flown aboard weekly by the COD. The mail COD was anxiously awaited by everyone. When the COD came aboard, there was always an announcement over the 1MC, and then it would take about four hours for the mail to be sorted. After the post office sorted the mail by divisions, "Mail Call" was sounded. At that point each division mail petty officer would go to the post office and pick up the divisions mail. After the mail petty officer returned to the division he would sort the mail and place each sailor's mail into a box, which was maintained in the forward spaces. This was a box in which we kept our cigarette lighters or matches, or small personal items. Large packages were left in the coffee locker. Packages could not be opened in private. Sailors usually hung around a person opening a package, like vultures around a piece of meat, hoping for cookies or candies inside the package that might be shared! My parents were very faithful about sending packages with cookies, candies, and snacks, although the contents of these wonderful packages didn't last very long! The sailors who received very little mail, greatly appreciated the sharing of packages, and the packages were a wonderful respite, and distraction from the hard grueling work of bomb building, and the monotony of being at sea.

One evening, a sudden loss of propulsion mystified the engineering department, so all engines were ordered stopped, and EOD divers went into the sea to investigate. It was discovered that one of the ships four propellers were missing! The propellers were about eighteen feet across with four huge fan vanes. The propeller shaft attachments had apparently loosened allowing the propeller to drop to the bottom of the South China Sea. There was some speculation the collision with the *USS Nitro* had somehow caused the loss of the propeller? The ship was still able to maintain the required speed in order to launch aircraft, with the remaining three propellers. We finished out the line period, and when we were relieved, steamed toward Yokosuka, Japan for replacement of the propeller. In Yokosuka, we went into a large concrete dry dock; the water was pumped out, the ship settled on huge blocks, and the yard workers set about replacing the propeller, and repairing the damage from the collision with the Nitro.

Terry Morrison had been stationed in Atsugi, Japan for three years. He could speak some Japanese, and knew more about Japanese customs than I did. We went on liberty together to a number of places in Japan I had not been before. We visited Kamakura, which was famous for a large Buddha shrine. The Buddha shrine was hollow inside, and for a few yen, we climbed the stairs inside up to the head of the shrine. I took movies of the Buddha, and people leaving food offerings in front of the shrine. After our visit to the shrine, Terry and I visited a bar that had a microphone, into which people would sing. This was called karaoke, and Terry and I were the worse singers in the place.

One night in Yokosuka, after a bar closed, it was late, and a girl said we could sleep overnight at her house, so we didn't have to go back to the ship. The street that led to her house was about four blocks from thieves' alley, and then about ten blocks almost straight up. She kept waiting for us as we huffed and puffed up the hill. The next morning our legs were so sore we could hardly walk. I began to understand why many Japanese have strong legs.

We were soon back on the line after the repairs to the ship were completed. A surprising past time began, in place of acey duecy, cribbage, poker, and other card games, playing chess became very popular throughout the ship. My mother had taught me the basic moves when I was a child, but I was very rusty. As I said before Tommy Jones, a first class in the division became a ship wide champion.

Terry went through the chief's initiation in Subic, at the base Chief Petty Officer Club, and he moved out of W Division berthing, into the ship's chief's quarters. The line periods, and short in port times became a "blur" to me. That cruise we built more than 40,000 bombs for strikes in Vietnam.

One evening on the line, there was a hard "thump" that was felt throughout the ship. It originated from the aft section of the ship. The chief's berthing compartment was jarred, and a few chiefs were thrown out of their bunks. Once again the engineering department reported a loss of propulsion power. As soon as the sun rose, the EOD divers went into the water, and inspected the area where the thump occurred.

Another propeller was missing, but this one had struck the hull of the ship, before sinking to the bottom of the sea. It was very unusual for a propeller to spin off, and unheard of for this to happen twice within a couple of months!

The first of October we once again headed for Yokosuka. The place was beginning to feel like our homeport! The previous September marked twelve years of unblemished service for me. This meant I was authorized to wear gold hash marks, and a gold crow, instead of the standard red, on my dress uniforms. I decided to wait until I got back to the states to have the "gold" sewn on my uniform. In Yokosuka, the ship once again went into the same dry dock we'd been in a couple of months previously. I stood Junior Officer of the Watch (J.O.O.D.) watches while in port. This watch was normally stood by a chief petty officer, but there was a shortage of chiefs on the ship, so senior first class were also used. This was a four-hour watch on the after brow, which was the gangway enlisted men used to arrive and depart the ship. I was required to inspect the men departing on liberty to insure they were dressed properly, had good haircuts, and so on. I refused permission for sailors to depart the ship if they did not meet dress and grooming standards. The JOOD answered to the Officer of the Deck (O.O.D.), who was the officer in charge of the ship in the absence of the commanding officer, he stood watch at the quarterdeck, where commissioned officers arrived and departed the ship. The weather was very cold this time of year, and after standing four hours exposed on the after brow, I was frozen. I was usually so busy during my four-hour watch; I didn't have time to think about being cold. Little did I know that many years in the future, I would become very familiar with Yokosuka, and quarterdeck watches.

I decided to call my detailer in Washington, D.C., while the ship was in Yokosuka. It was a chore to place a call like this. I had to go to a building on the base at midnight, because of the time difference between Japan and Washington, and use a phone system called the AUTOVON system. This is a Department of Defense worldwide phone system. Calls are made at differing priority levels. The priorities range from Routine to Flash priority. My call to the detailer was Routine priority, so my low priority could be cut off by a higher priority call at anytime, and this happened frequently. It was not unusual to try and complete a call for many hours, and often it was impossible to get through. Fortunately I was able to get through to my detailer on my first try. He said he was about to send a message to the ship addressed to me, and he was glad I called, so he could give me some information about my transfer. He said, "I've got some good news, and some bad news. First the good news, you can have transfer orders to your first duty choice, Nuclear Weapons Supply Annex, Oakland, California. The bad news is the Navy is out of transfer money, and for you to have these orders you must be in Oakland by December. This means you'll have to pay for your transportation costs from the ship to Oakland out of your own pocket. You could go on leave, and take a military "space available" flight back to the States, for no cost, and the odds are you shouldn't have any trouble getting back. If you decide not to accept these orders, you'll have to stay on *Oriskany* for another year." He told me to think about it and call him back in two days. Now I'm not a "rocket scientist," but it did not take much "thinking" on my part to make a decision about the orders. I felt like I had done my duty concerning the war, and while I enjoyed my status on the ship, I was ready for shore duty. I called the detailer after two days, and told him I would take the orders to Oakland, and take my chances getting back to the states. He said he would issue the orders. I could expect them to be on the ship in about a week, and I would be scheduled to leave the first of November.

Charlie Galbreath, a few years previously had met a Japanese girl in San Francisco, and they had married. His wife's parents and relations lived about eighty miles from Yokosuka. He had never met them, and he planned to visit them and asked me to go with him when he visited. I agreed that I would, and on a day we both had liberty, we went to the Yokosuka train station. Charlie had gotten directions from his wife about how to get to her parent's house. After a long train ride, and then a taxi ride, we arrived in a rural country part of Japan.

We walked up a dirt path to a wooden framed house surrounded by some kind of green shrubs that were not familiar to me. Charlie knocked on the door, and an elderly woman answered the door, and the excitement began. There were four other people in the house. We took our shoes off at the entryway, and entered the house. There were profuse bowing, and handshakes. They recognized Charlie from a picture that had been taken during his marriage to their daughter. They were extremely happy to see him, and they accepted me as family. The older people did not speak English, but soon other people began pouring into the house, after the mother made a few phone calls. Most of the younger people spoke English and acted as interpreters. I'm not sure of the exact number of relatives that filled the little house, and I don't believe Charlie knew either? Charlie's mother-in-law insisted that we eat, and also insisted that we drink Japanese beer. All during our visit there was a full plate of food, and full glass of beer before us.

One of Charlie's brother-in-laws' was a world ranked lightweight boxer. At this time he was ranked number twelve. He lived at a nearby boxing stable and school, and led a Spartan life. It was interesting listening to him talk about the fights he had in his career.

Charlie's Father-in-law also had an interesting background. He looked like a rough, durable man. He had been in the Japanese Army during World War II. When the war ended he had been in China, and had been imprisoned in a POW camp. After the war ended it took him twelve years to work his way back home. For eight years following the war his family had no idea if he was dead or alive.

The time flew by, and then it was time for Charlie and me to leave. We planned to catch the train back to Yokosuka. One brother-in-law would not hear about us returning on the train, but insisted on driving us all the way back to the base in his car. The family had treated us royally, and I truly felt their welcome was genuine. When we left the mom and dad gave me a gift of a mustard seed encased in plastic, which was to symbolize good luck. Charlie said this was a special gift not given to everyone, but someone special. They even shed tears at our departure, which was very "un-Japanese." This remains one of the best memories of my "war years."

I began preparing for my transfer. Charlie would take over the LPO position, and Tommy Jones was going to take over the PMS work center. No one wanted to see me go, but I was ready. I sent a package containing most of my civilian clothes to my parent's house. I started the check out process three days before my departure. The reality of leaving *Oriskany* had not hit me yet.

My sea bag was packed, and I'd gotten my transfer orders from the ship's personnel office. I was to go on thirty days leave before reporting to Oakland. The morning I was to leave, at division morning muster, the division gave me a farewell card they had all signed, and a few "gag gifts." I told them all I would miss them, and to be careful. Charlie insisted on carrying my sea bag off the ship. I bid them all farewell. I'd been through a lot with many of them. Charlie carried my sea bag off the ship, and all the way to the taxi stand. We shook hands' goodbye, and I got my last look at *Oriskany* as the taxi pulled away.

In the 1972 cruise book, listed in memoriam were: LT Leon F. Haas, LT Richard B. Lineberry, SA Peter Chan. Missing in Action: LT Daniel V. Borah, Jr. Also, in the cruise book was the following quote: "And a firm will, and deep sense, which even in torture can descry its own concenter'd recompense; Triumphant where it dares defy, and making death a victory." Byron, Prometheus.

I felt a great weight lifted from my shoulders, my premonition of death, or tragedy had not proven to be true. I had resigned myself to completing the entire cruise, and it felt odd leaving the ship before the cruise was over. The ship was not scheduled to return to Alameda until after December. I did not know it at the time, but the Vietnam War, as far as United States involvement, was about to end. A peace treaty was to be signed between North Vietnam, and the U.S. in Paris, France, 27 January 1973. I had not informed my parents about my transfer from the *Oriskany*. I thought it would be fun to surprise them. Before I left the ship, I wrote a number of letters, and predated them. I asked Charlie to mail the letters, one by one on specific dates, so my parents would think I was still on the ship.

I caught a bus on the Yokosuka Base that took me to Yokota Air Force Base. After waiting a couple of hours in the Air Force terminal, I was told I could catch a plane the next morning that was flying to Travis Air Force Base, California. I stayed in the transit barracks overnight, and at 8:00 a.m. the next morning the plane took off with me onboard.

When I got on the plane, I discovered it was a Medical Evacuation (MedEvac) flight. It was a C-130, and most of the rear of the plane was fitted with medical bunks along the side of the fuselage. There were about twenty bunks filled with mostly marines, and a few Army soldiers. Many had IV's inserted into their arms, or were fitted with oxygen masks. Other than the patients, there were a few nurses and corpsmen, and about ten passengers. Also, toward the front of the plane there were four caskets. Three hours after the take off, one of the nurses asked if any of the passengers would like to help feed the patients. A few others and I helped with the meal and the following meal later in the flight. Quite a few of the wounded men were drugged heavily, and slept most of the flight. I talked with a number of marines. I remember one marine from Idaho, who had been injured by an anti-personnel bomb. Both of his legs were in casts, and he was anxious to get home. The plane made one stop in Alaska, and then flew onto Travis Air Force Base. At Travis I caught a bus to Oakland, and caught a taxi to Pamela's house. At Pamela's house, I took my Firebird down off blocks, and then drove to Visalia. Linda and her husband had moved from Fresno to Visalia, where my brother-in-law had taken an engineering position with Tulare County. It was good seeing them and my nieces. That evening, we drove to my parent's house in Strathmore.

At my parent's house, my brother-in-law and Linda rang the doorbell. I waited behind them in the darkness. They told mom, "We picked up this hitch hiker up on the way over here." I then stepped out of the darkness, and walked up on the porch. My mom's face drained of color, and I was afraid she was going to faint, before I hugged her! This scared me, and I swore I'd never surprise her again like that.

The "O-boat" as her crew fondly called her, was decommissioned in 1976. A plan to sink the retired *Oriskany* off the Florida coast to serve as an artificial reef was carried out 17 May 2006; she sank in thirty-seven minutes. She was the first vessel in a new program designed to dispose of obsolete warships by sinking them as a cheaper alternative to the scrap yard. The ship also serves as an underwater memorial.

Chapter 10: First Class Rest Home

All the time overseas and on the line, my favorite daydream was fishing for the steelhead and rainbow trout in the Northern California coastal streams. My parents had a nice pickup, with a cab-over camper on the bed. After I'd been home a few days, I borrowed the pickup, and drove up to the Russian River above San Francisco. I also drove up the northern coastline on highway 101, fishing in streams along the way. I didn't catch one fish, but being outdoors, and relaxing was wonderful therapy, and after a week I felt more "human," and less "wound up" with the war daily becoming less of a reality.

I had an enjoyable thirty days leave. Just prior to checking into my new duty station, I found a studio apartment in Alameda. I was to sign a lease, but after being in the apartment for a few days, I decided it was not a place I wanted to live in. It was freezing in the one room apartment, the only heat being a small electric wall heater. I had a slight hassle with the landlord, but I had not signed the lease yet. I agreed I would stay in the apartment for one month and then move out in January.

On 9 December, one day after I had turned thirty years old, I checked into the Nuclear Weapons Supply Annex, located on the Oakland Naval Supply Base. The base was located near the Oakland bay piers, and across the bay from the Alameda Naval Air Station. The base was surrounded by run-down neighborhoods, and impoverished looking homes. Civilian government guards guarded the base, and civilian government employees populated the base. The Navy Nuclear Weapons Supply Annex, referred to as "NWSA," was about half a mile within the base. It was a large metal warehouse, with working and storage areas, as well as office spaces. An eight-foot fence, topped with barbed wire, encircled the building.

I was not sure what my duties would be at NWSA? I'd never met anyone that had been stationed at Oakland. In the past I'd spoken often to the civilian director, Mr. Norm Howell, when the *Oriskany* needed parts, or assistance with supply matters. I'd requested NWSA as a duty assignment because of its geographical location near my family, and because it had a reputation as a "rest home" for first class petty officers!

I was to discover that there were eighteen enlisted men assigned to NWSA, two chiefs, GMTCS Grabow, and GMTC Halterman, the majority were first class petty officers of the GMT rating, a storekeeper, a couple of electricians, and machinist. Our division officer was a LCDR in the Supply Corp. There were also twenty civilian employees led by Norm Howell, who was a government civilian employee with a GS-14 rank.

At all of my previous duty stations, the commands had very specific missions. As a GMT1 I had been involved with maintenance of nuclear weapons, and insuring they were ready for use in the event of a nuclear war. Nuclear Weapons Supply Annex had a different mission from those duty stations I'd been assigned to previously. NWSA Oakland was the primary supply source for non-nuclear and nonexplosive spare parts for nuclear weapons. It was a "spare parts store." The stowage and issue of spare parts, shipping, and supply logistics, was taken care of by the civilians. NWSA's customers were all the nuclear capable activities on the west coast, and all the commands in the Western Pacific. A Navy supply center in Norfolk, Virginia took care of the east coast, and the European Theater.

The GMT's job at NWSA was different from the jobs the civilians were involved in. Navy pilots and Navy bombardiers had to be trained, and remain proficient in the job of dropping nuclear weapons on targets. Of course this training could not be accomplished by dropping real weapons, or war reserves. This training was accomplished using Bomb Dummy Units, or "BDU's." A BDU is a metal and concrete dummy bomb that looks like the real thing externally, but internally is a dummy containing no nuclear components, or explosives. These dummies are recycled, or reusable after a drop from an aircraft. The BDU's also have electrical connections and electrical components that interface with the carrying aircraft, and "fool" the Aircraft Monitoring and Control (AMAC) panel in the plane's cockpit into thinking a real nuclear weapon is hanging on the aircraft pylon. Many of the BDU's contained parachutes, the same type of parachutes that are installed in war reserves. In the parachute retarded BDU a small explosive device is used to deploy the parachute at the time of release from the aircraft.

The BDU's were dropped at various bombing ranges, the most common area being Naval Station China Lake, California. After the practice bombing runs, crews would go into the desert bombing range and recover the dropped BDU's. They would place them on flatbed trucks for return to NWSA. Upon return to NWSA the GMT's would begin refurbishment of the BDU's. This rework often involved major bodywork. Most BDU's were mangled, or badly dented as the result of the drops. We had to hammer out dents, in some cases body putty rips, and tears, and repaint the BDU's. We were basically running a huge glorified body shop, such as a car body repair shop!

The GMT's worked in three adjoining areas, each about twenty by twenty feet in size. Each area shared a long workbench along one side of the room. Three different teams, or as they were called "Hooks," worked within each work area, on different types of BDU's. Each Hook consisted of four or more GMT1's. Most of the GMT's were career sailors. The majority of the sailors was married, and had considerable time at sea in the past. There was a relaxed atmosphere, with no stress, and few deadlines to meet, thus the nickname "First Class Rest Home."

I'd celebrated my thirtieth birthday just prior to checking in. My firebird was running rough. I'd paid it off earlier in the year. I'd doubled up on the car payments while at sea, since I was getting additional pay in the form of sea pay, and hostile fire pay. I visited a Pontiac dealer in Oakland. They had a special sale on a 1972 two-door hardtop Pontiac that had a "Raider Package." The car was gray and black, which were the uniform colors of the Oakland Raiders football team. On the front side panels, the word "Raiders" was painted. This car had low miles on it, as it had only been used by the dealership to drive around inside of the football stadium during the Raider's home games. I tried the car out for a couple of days. I wasn't fully sold on it, as it was quite different from my Firebird. Noting my hesitation, the dealership knocked off a lot on the purchase price, so I traded the Firebird in for it.

Life ashore was as different from life onboard ship, as night from day. Traveling to and from work, we wore civilian clothes, and then at work changed into dungaree working uniforms. When involved in sanding, painting, or dirty work we wore coveralls. In the past when I checked into a new duty station, I usually ran across someone I'd known before. At NWSA I'd not met anyone before, so all were strangers to me. I was assigned to work on a hook, and since I was the senior first class, I was assigned as the mechanical bay supervisor. There were three other first class petty officers on my "Hook." We were responsible for the BDU's that were dummies for the Mk 43 (see photo page), Mk 57 (see photo page), and Mk 61 (see photo page) bombs.

I was a bit unlucky in the area of upcoming inspections, as NWSA was scheduled to have an NTPI inspection the next April. This inspection however was not as intense as an inspection on board a ship, or a shore station that had custody of war reserves.

Single sailors were a minority at NWSA. One other sailor on my hook, Gaylen Ashton was also single. Gaylen invited me to his house in Hayward on the day of the super bowl football game. Gaylen and an ex-sailor named "Wild Bill," rented the house together. Wild Bill had been in the Navy as a GMT for ten years, and then had gotten out and now worked for the Southern Pacific Railroad. I remember Wild Bill showing me an illegal AK-47 sub machine gun that he kept in his attic. I was careful not to leave fingerprints on it.

I visited the *Oriskany* "hang-out", The Carnival Club a couple of times, but it was not the same without my shipmates. Also the son of the owner had been badly injured when a customer attacked him with a knife a few months previously.

The town of Hayward seemed to be a slower-paced city than Oakland, and I decided to rent an apartment in Hayward. I found a large apartment complex that had recently opened. I rented an apartment, and having learned my lesson in Alameda, I did not sign a lease. The apartment was unfurnished, so I rented furniture from a "rent to own" furniture company. It was a single bedroom, upstairs apartment.

Ever since Pearl Harbor, the Navy has had duty sections on board ships, and at shore stations, to insure there were always sailors available to maintain security, fight fires, and be prepared to defend the command. NWSA was not an exception to the "duty rule." We were in fourteen-section duty, this meant every fourteenth day (or more if more sailors were available), one of us would have duty. "Duty" consisted of being the last one to leave during the work day, and securing the building, setting the alarm system at the base police station, and then remaining available at home by the phone, ready to respond in the event the base police notified us of any emergencies. The following morning, we were required to open the building before the civilians and sailors arrived for work. In the event of a duty day on weekends, we had to remain at home by the phone for our twenty-four-hour duty day.

The *Oriskany* pulled alongside the Alameda pier, following their cruise in January. I took the day off, and was waiting on the pier when she pulled in, remembering how important it was when my position was reversed, and I was standing on the ship, looking to see if there was anyone on the pier that awaited my arrival, and supported what I'd been through. I welcomed Master Chief Riechman, Chief Chapbourne, Charlie, and many other W Division sailors home.

In February I once again took the promotion examination for chief. This was becoming a semiannual affair for me. I'd take the exam again in August. With the large number of first class at NWSA, and most eligible to take the chief's exam, we did a lot of studying together.

One morning in March during morning muster; I got a surprise. Our Division Officer Lieutenant Commander Mckenna, who normally didn't attend our muster, came in, brought the division to attention, and said I was being awarded a letter of commendation from the Commander of the Seventh Fleet. He then read a letter, which said:

> For outstanding performance of duty while attached to and serving in *USS Oriskany* (CVA-34) as an ordnance assembly quality assurance inspector from 16 June 1972 to 8 November 1972 during combat operations. Petty Officer Little through tireless personal effort and expert supervision ensured that the excellent quality of ordnance assembled by his assigned team was maintained throughout the deployment. His foresight and willingness to work long hours, and his extremely high standards for teamwork played an important part in the timely availability of ordnance for combat missions despite changing commitments. Petty Officer Little's skill and judgment contributed significantly and directly to the successful accomplishment of the ship's mission and to the United States' effort in the Republic of Vietnam.

J. L. Holloway, Vice Admiral, United States Navy, signed the letter.

This was a nice surprise. I had been told by the W Division Officer, and the chiefs that they were recommending me for a commendation, when I left the ship, but I had not thought any more about it. This recognition somewhat dulled the pain of the rejection and indifference I'd experienced from some of my countrymen during the war. This letter of commendation has remained one of my most precious mementoes. My parents had an article published in their local newspaper that reported the awarding of the letter.

Just as at other commands, while inside the NWSA complex, we wore a clip on security badges with our pictures on them. One additional assignment chiefs and first class petty officers shared were the duties of armed Navy couriers. From time to time we would arm ourselves with a forty-five-caliber pistol, and ride in the cab of a truck with a truck driver. The trucks were loaded with classified material that was transported off the Oakland Naval Supply Center through the civilian community to another base, usually Alameda Naval Air Station. The material most often was scheduled for further air transportation from Alameda to a location in the U.S., or overseas. While off base, we were charged with the safe keeping of the classified material. We carried courier cards with our photograph on the card, and a statement that said, "The person whose name, photograph and signature appear on the reverse of this card is an authorized courier for inert highly classified material for the NWSA. He is authorized to bear arms for the protection of escorted material. The convoy contains Restricted Data under the provisions of Public Law 585 (Atomic Energy Act of 1954). He is prohibited from revealing the contents or nature of the material entrusted to him to anyone other than the individual to whom it is consigned. Any person who without proper authority acquires or examines any "Restricted Data" in possession of this courier may be subject to penalty of law. In the event of an accident rendering him incapable of performing his mission, it is requested that a responsible person on the scene take custody of all documents and materials and without studying the contents thereof, contact by long-distance telephone, collect (....)" the statement continued giving the phone number of the base duty officer.

We had a special arrangement with the base police, the local Naval Investigative Service (NIS) agent, and our division officer. We drove through some very rough sections of Oakland, which could be described as slums, to enter the main gate at the supply center; these were high-crime areas it would not be wise to stop in. Our Division Officer, Lieutenant Commander McKenna said we could carry firearms in our vehicles, driving back and forth to work. If stopped by the police, we were to explain that the firearm was in our vehicle because we were either going to, or completing an assignment as a Navy courier. We were to show our courier card, and if need be tell the police to call the LCDR and he would confirm our courier assignment. It was comforting to have a gun nearby in some of the areas we drove through.

I spent a lot of time on liberty with the other single sailor, GMT1 Gaylen Ashton. I was almost a permanent chauffeur for him, as he drank almost a fifth of vodka each day! We often went to a western bar in Hayward. I dated Pamela a few times, and a girl from Hayward. I only dated the Hayward girl a few times. She had a son in the Air Force that was only a few years younger than I. Our age difference was too great.

Gaylen and Wild Bill had to move out of the house they were renting, because the owner wanted to sell it. They found a nice apartment complex that offered furnished apartments for half the rent I was paying for my unfurnished apartment. One weekend my mom drove up from Strathmore to pay me a surprise visit. It turned out to be a surprise for her, as I was spending the weekend helping Wild Bill and Gaylen move, and we missed seeing each other. I discovered the note she left on my apartment door on Sunday evening.

The end of February I prepared for my third move since being on shore duty for three months. I rented an apartment in the same complex that Gaylen and Wild Bill were in. I returned the rented furniture, and moved into a one bedroom, furnished, comfortable apartment. My front door opened into a courtyard that contained a swimming pool. My drive to and from Oakland was a forty-mile round trip.

In March, I went to sickbay complaining of fatigue. I'd felt tired and weak every since returning to the States from the ship. A blood test revealed that I had an extremely high white blood cell count. After being examined by a doctor, he could not figure out why the white blood cell count was so high? I began a daily routine of going to sickbay each morning so a corpsman could draw a sample of my blood. This daily "puncturing" lasted for many weeks. My arms stayed black and blue, and were full of punctures. I was beginning to look like a drug addict! In an effort to find out what was wrong I underwent a very unpleasant procedure. I was strapped to a table underneath an x-ray machine. The table was moveable so my body could be placed at different positions under the machine. A special dye was then injected into my veins. The doctor could then observe the dye traveling throughout my system. The unpleasant thing about this procedure was that I was warned that my body would naturally try to reject the dye being injected into me. During the injection of the dye, and during the whole procedure, I had uncontrollable convulsions. I was relieved when I was finally taken off the table. Nothing was detected that could explain my high white blood cell count?

One weekend Gaylen wanted to visit his brother, who was a Navy lieutenant, going to graduate school in Monterey. One Friday night before driving to Monterey, which was one hundred miles south, we attended a singles dance. It was a boring affair. Gaylen did meet a woman named Lucy, who was about twenty-five years older than he. Gaylen got plastered as usual, and I ended up driving all the way to Monterey that night. We went deep-sea fishing with his brother the next day, and caught many fish.

Gaylen had been leading a dangerous life for a few months at work. He had been having an affair with a wife of one of the first class who worked with us. Everyone knew about it except the husband. He was also dating a girl named Gloria, who was a civilian worker at NWSA. He finally began seriously dating the woman named Lucy that he had met at the singles dance. Lucy was a real estate agent, and she was constantly involved in various schemes to make money, many of the schemes seemed to be on the "shady" or just barely on the legal side of business, and she had many friends that could best be described as "outlaws."

One afternoon she asked Gaylen and me, and another GMT1 that worked at NWSA, to accompany her to a motel in Oakland that she owned. She said the manager that worked for her was skimming money, had threatened her, and she wanted to scare him a little bit. The motel's customers were mostly prostitutes who brought their customers to the motel throughout the day, and night. In retrospect what we did was foolish, but we dressed up like hoodlums, and had pistols not too well hidden under our jackets, and we accompanied Lucy to the motel. It definitely frightened the guy, because he packed up his things immediately and left.

As a large group of sailors with equal rates, everyone was interested in who was senior to whom? I had been promoted to GMT1 in November 1967. This was before anyone else at NWSA; therefore, I was once again placed in the position of the Leading Petty Officer (LPO). The most visible requirement of my job as LPO, as it had been on the *Oriskany*, was standing before the ranks of sailors each morning at quarters, calling muster, reading the plan of the day, and passing on any information from the chain of command.

Two of the first class at NWSA, were highly involved with firearms, and pistol shooting, GMT1 Julian Lindstrom, and Ron Forth. As I mentioned it was unusual to go to a new duty station, and not know any of the GMT's. Julian Lindstrom reported to NWSA shortly after me. He and I had been together at Whidbey Island working in the AUW Shop. In the future he became a member of the U.S. Navy Target Shooting Team, who toured the United States, and also participated in the Olympic Games. Both Julian and Ron had gunsmith licenses, and also managed the base shooting range. They had a friend who worked in the Alameda Naval Station Armory. This friend had a huge bin filled with forty-five caliber pistol parts. He permitted Julian and Ron to help themselves to the parts. The only pistol part he did not have was a crucial part called a "receiver." Julian and Ron ordered a large number of receivers, began building forty-fives, and selling them for twenty-five dollars a piece. I ordered one; I wish I had ordered more, because in the future the pistols were worth well more than $500!

The 1911, forty-five was the Navy's standard sidearm for more than seventy years until the 9mm automatic pistol replaced it in the 1980's. Designed by John Browning, the pistol was originally a thirty-eight caliber, but the Army wanted a larger caliber, so it became a forty-five. The pistol was invented because the Army was involved in the Philippines fighting tribesmen who would attack soldiers' positions after getting high on opiates, and drugs. A powerful firearm was needed to knock down these drug-crazed attackers wherever it struck a person's body. A person struck by a forty-five bullet, in the arm or leg, usually is knocked flat. The pistol was adapted in 1911, and was a mainstay through World War I and II, Korea and Vietnam. In my opinion it's the best pistol that has ever been manufactured. Julian and Ron sold many of the forty-fives to various people throughout the San Francisco area.

Talking to Julian years later about our time at NWSA, he told me of a concern he had about his firearm business. In 1975, in Sacramento, California, President Ford narrowly escaped an assassination attempt made by Squeaky Frome, (a Charles Mansion follower) when she fired a forty-five pistol at him. When Julian heard the news accounts of the attempted assassination, and the use of a forty-five pistol, he felt it was a very strong possibility that the pistol was one he and Ron had sold! He lived in fear for many months. Each time he heard a knock on his door, he thought it might be the Secret Service or the FBI! As it developed the pistol used in the attempted assassination was a forty-five that had been manufactured in Spain.

I was busy with the two chiefs preparing for our NTPI, which was a much "scaled down" inspection compared to the ones I'd gone through in the past. The inspection was mostly an administration inspection, with limited observations of our mechanical work. I put together "welcome aboard" packages that were to be given to the inspectors when they began their inspection. The captain of the base was very pleased with the packages. After much preparation, the inspection began. The inspection only lasted three days, and we did extremely well, much to the relief of Lieutenant Commander McKenna, and the two chiefs.

Gaylen and I spent a lot of time with another first class named Albert Fessenden. His nickname was "Fuzz," he was married and had two small children. Fuzz had a nineteen-foot outboard motor boat. Often on Saturday mornings, Gaylen and I would get up early and drive forty miles to Pittsburgh where Fuzz lived, launch the boat, and fish for sturgeon. There were specific length requirements for the taking of a sturgeon. The fish had to be at least forty inches long, and not more than six feet in length, in order to keep it. It was common to see fish others had caught, just less than six feet long. The fish is prehistoric looking, with armor plating, and an ugly looking demeanor, they are however, delicious eating. I caught many in the forty-five-inch range, and one day Gaylen caught a five footer. Gaylen also had a sixteen-foot boat he kept at Fuzz's house, which we used occasionally. At Pittsburgh where we launched the boat there was a marina, and bait shop that were owned by a friend of Gaylen and Fuzz's. This friend had been in the Navy in World War II, and he greatly enjoyed seeing us, and telling sea stories. Often when we went into the bait shop after a fishing trip and reloading the boat on the trailer. The bait shop owner would lock the door to the bait shop, put out a "closed" sign, and open his liquor cabinet. I would usually end up driving Gaylen back to Hayward, as he would not be able to drive.

Gaylen and Lucy often tried playing "cupid," by setting me up to meet a girl. Before Gaylen met Lucy, he and I often went to a large country music bar and dance hall in Hayward. This bar was patterned after a famous bar in Houston, Texas named Gilley's Bar. The main trouble with our outings was instead of meeting any women; I'd usually end up "baby-sitting Gaylen, as his daily liquor intake was a fifth of vodka just to get started! Lucy was a reformed alcoholic, and she managed to slow Gaylen down a bit.

Go-go clubs were popular throughout the bay area. They featured girls that danced on stage in varied outfits, to music that blared from a jukebox, or in some places' bands. The drinks were sold at highly inflated prices. One night Lucy told me about a girl she had met. She had been in a go-go club in Newark, called The Foxy Lady, with a real estate client. A girl dancing had caught her eye. The girl danced with much more style and grace than any others in the club, and was one of the best dancers she had seen. Lucy said she had talked to her and asked how long she had been dancing, as she danced at a much higher professional level than any of the other girls. She said she had danced for many years. Lucy then asked if she would be interested in meeting a friend of hers. The girl said she had recently broken up with someone, and yes she would be interested. Her name was Carmen, and she was originally from Puerto Rico. She said she wasn't looking for a relationship, but she would meet me as a favor to Lucy. I was continuing to have blood drawn daily at sickbay each morning, and my arms looked a mess. The doctor at the base clinic was stumped. He could not make a diagnosis. All he knew was that I had an unexplained high white blood cell count. He said he was going to refer me to the Oakland Naval Hospital. One statement he made worried me, he said I might have leukemia.

One evening after work, I put on my gray three-piece suit that I had bought in Hong Kong, drove to Newark, found the Foxy Lady, and went inside. Lucy had said Carmen had long black hair, and I couldn't miss her. Lucy was right, I could not miss her, she was beautiful. This marked the first time I set eyes upon Carmen Oquendo. I was somewhat "overdressed" for this first meeting, but I wanted to make an impression. The Foxy Lady was a large place with pool tables, and a large elevated stage, upon which girls took turns dancing in a variety of beautiful costumes. The crowd was a mixture of businessmen dressed in suits, and those that dressed informally. Carmen was definitely the most experienced and talented dancer in the place. When she danced, all eyes in the room were upon her. When her dance was over, I told her who I was, and we talked for a while. I asked her if perhaps we could go out together sometime. She said yes, and I gave her my phone number. I was excited at the prospect of dating her in the future. I stayed for about an hour and a half and then left.

I was still adjusting to the radical change in my environment, from the intense, nonstop tempo of shipboard life, to the easy relaxed and sometimes boring tempo of shore duty at NWSA. The peace treaty with North Vietnam had been signed the first of the year, and President Nixon had ordered massive troop withdrawals. The South Vietnamese Army carried on with the war. I continued following news about Vietnam closely, it was a topic of discussion at work, as many of the GMT's had been on a carrier, on the line at one time or another in the past. We often speculated about whether our efforts fighting the war, and the bloodshed in Vietnam, meant anything to our country? It seemed as though the war had been fought without a clear objective, as wars had been in the past, that objective being the goals of victory, and the liberation of oppressed people. We thought of ourselves as sailors in the most powerful Navy on earth, but the Vietnam failure tarnished, and diminished this image. Congress had passed a number of laws adversely affecting our promotions, and salary. We were also very concerned about the talk, and impending regulations about re-computing our retirement pay, which would greatly reduce our pensions. This did not improve or raise our morale at all!

Our leading chief, Senior Chief Grabow, changed our working hours, so we would miss the daily traffic jams we all experienced trying to get back and forth to work. We had morning quarters at 7:00 a.m., lunch from 11:30 a.m. to 1:00 p.m., and knock off work at 3:30 p.m. With these new hours we missed the majority of the morning and afternoon rush hour traffic.

An enlisted club, the Sergeant Gilbert Club, was a block away from NWSA. Most of the first class went to the club for lunch. Many of the truck drivers, who worked on the base, also had lunch there. The sailors got to know many of the regular truck drivers. The club did a brisk business selling beer during the lunch hour. Many of the truck drivers would place bets with bookies over the phone, on the daily horse races.

There was also a small four-lane bowling alley in the club. The lanes were not automated, but used two pinsetters, men who sat at the pin end of the lanes who would clear, or set up pins after the bowling ball was thrown. Shortly after I checked into NWSA, Norm Howell, the civilian director, recruited me to be a member of the NWSA bowling team. Norm was an avid bowler, and always on the lookout for team members. I'd not bowled since my time on Guam, but I managed to maintain a 175 average. The NWSA team always managed to finish in one of the top three finishing positions.

A week after I'd met Carmen, she called and asked if I'd like to meet her at a place she knew, on the west side of the Dumbarton Bridge, which was located across the bay from where I lived. I said "of course," we were to meet on the following Saturday night.

On the Saturday I was to meet Carmen, I went on a drive with Gaylen and Lucy to the Pittsburgh area where Gaylen and I fished for sturgeons. Lucy was looking at some property that was up for sale. We returned to Hayward and my apartment around 4:30 p.m. I showered, got dressed, and arrived at the restaurant that Carmen and I were to meet at. I arrived a little before 7:30, the time we were to meet. I'd waited for about thirty minutes, when a waiter approached me and asked if I were Jim Little? He said I had a phone call. It was Carmen, she said she was sorry, but she was unable to make it, and promised we'd get together another time. I was disappointed, but didn't feel completely "stood up," as she had called and apologized.

After a week, on a Monday, I called Carmen at work, and we agreed that we would meet at the same restaurant the upcoming Friday night. The next Thursday the doctor on the base, made an appointment for me to the Oakland Naval Hospital for an ominous sounding procedure. I was to have some bone marrow extracted so it could be examined under a microscope. I wasn't to eat anything before the procedure, and the doctor wrote a prescription for castor oil, which was to "clean me out" before reporting to the hospital. When I went to the pharmacy to pick up the castor oil, I was to discover later that the corpsman made a mistake, and instead of giving me one bottle of castor oil, he gave me two, and directed me to drink both that night! That night, I spent most of the night in the bathroom, and felt horrible in the morning when I reported to the hospital.

A few weeks earlier I'd had a bad experience at the hospital. I'd reported there to have blood drawn, and an inexperienced corpsman couldn't find a vein with the needle. After she had stuck my arm more than six times, suddenly everything went black! I awoke lying on a couch. I had passed out! On the last needle poke, the corpsman had found a vein, and allowed me to fall. During my fall, I had hit my head, and blood had spurted all over my dress white uniform.

The morning I reported to the hospital feeling very "empty," I was told I had two choices. The bone marrow could be withdrawn from my sternum, or hip. It may have been a mistake, but I chose my hip. I didn't like the idea of having a hole drilled into my chest. I was given a hospital gown to put on, then directed to lay face down on a table. A corpsman swabbed a large area on my lower back with an orange disinfectant. A doctor entered the room, and said he was giving me a shot to deaden the pain, but he said it would not completely get rid of the pain, and it would be painful when my bone marrow was
extracted. A hole was drilled into my hip, and the doctor was right, while the bone marrow was being extracted, it was very painful! I clenched my teeth, and after what seemed like a long time it was finally over.

I left the hospital, and was back at NWSA at 1:30 p.m. Senior Chief Graybow noticed me limping, and asked what was wrong? He knew that I'd had an appointment at the hospital, but did not know what I was having done. After I explained that I'd had some bone marrow taken out, he said, "Go ahead and take the day off, and don't bother coming in tomorrow (Friday). I went home to my apartment, and the next morning my hip was so sore I could barely walk. I took aspirin, and stayed in bed. That afternoon I decided as much as I wanted to, I would not be able to keep the date with Carmen. I called the Foxy Lady, but she was not there. I waited until the appointed time we were to meet at the restaurant, and called the restaurant. Carmen was there, I apologized for not being able to make it, and once again we agreed that we'd met in the future eventually.

The examination of my bone marrow did not reveal anything unusual, and the doctor finally gave up. More than thirty years later, I discover a medical study that may explain why I had the mysterious high white blood cell count? A medical study[36] in 1999, by Dr. Joseph A. Boscarino, of the New York Academy of Medicine, revealed that Vietnam veterans with post-traumatic stress disorder (PTSD) were more likely to have abnormally high T-cell counts and white blood cell counts. Both were signs of a highly active immune system."

Finally after a couple of weeks Carmen and I did go on our first date at the restaurant we'd failed to meet at two times previously. We had a wonderful time telling each other about ourselves (trying to emphasize all good things to impress). I learned that she left Puerto Rico at a young age, lived in New York, and then in San Francisco for a number of years. She had been a professional dancer, and model for most of her life. Just a couple of years previously she had her own dance troupe, and had been a "head liner" at many of the San Francisco, Reno, and Las Vegas Clubs. She was six months younger than I, and had three children. Carmen had a 1965 Ford Mustang, and at the end of the evening I followed her east across the Dumbarton Bridge that spanned the bay. At the Newark side she pulled off the side of the road, as we agreed, we would say goodnights there. We both got out of our cars. I thanked her for a wonderful evening, and then kissed her forehead.

About a week and a half later, Carmen and I met at an apartment complex in Fremont, which was about ten miles south of Hayward. The complex was called "Tara Hill Apartments." She was moving into this apartment complex, and I helped her carry in a few boxes from her car into the apartment. We sat on the couch in the apartment, about the only furniture that had been moved in, and talked long into the night. That was the first time that we kissed (on the lips).

On one of the first dates I had with Carmen, we went to an Egyptian museum in San Jose, with Gaylen and Lucy. Gaylen and Lucy were becoming increasingly serious. One weekend, Gaylen and I spent the entire weekend painting an apartment in a motel that Lucy owned. We split one hundred dollars we earned on this painting job. One afternoon, Carmen brought her three children, to my apartment to meet me. There was Peter who was eleven years old, Roger seven, and Mary five. I was very impressed with their good behavior and manners. The first of May, I drove south to my parent's house for the weekend. I attended the annual homecoming affair at Strathmore. I was enjoying shore duty, and the relaxed pace at NWSA.

On 1 June, I received my first performance evaluations at NWSA; I received all "4.0's" and a very favorable write-up. I was spending half my time at Carmen's new apartment, and the other half at my apartment in Hayward, ten miles to the north. One night Carmen came to my apartment for dinner, and I gave her some pinto beans. I'd gotten the bean recipe from my sister, Linda, and this was about all I knew how to cook. Carmen was kind, and didn't criticize my cooking efforts. After I'd eaten a few of the meals she prepared, and learned she was a fantastic cook, I realized she had the right to criticize my cooking if she wanted!

The refurbishment and repair of dropped bomb dummy units continued at NWSA. During the summer months we usually received more truckloads of the dropped units, as the bombing practice tempo seemed to increase during the summer. The dummy bombs would arrive at NWSA lying in wooden skids, secured with metal strapping wrapped around the bomb and the skid. The nose and tail sections, which were hollow, would usually be dented or smashed from the impact with the ground. The warhead sections, which were either concrete or solid metal usually, were not too damaged, and would only require paint touch-up. The fins on the tail sections were almost always damaged beyond repair, requiring replacement. The three air dropped systems that we worked on contained parachutes that deployed when the BDU's were dropped from aircraft, in the retarded mode. The deployed parachutes would arrive with the BDU's recovered from the bombing ranges. These parachutes were packaged and sent to parachute repack facilities for repack, and reuse.

Each "Hook" working area had a large overhead electrically operated hoist that was used to hoist the units out of the wooden skids onto trailers, which were then wheeled into sanding rooms, and a paint booth. The dented and damaged bombs were moved off the arriving trucks, and positioned on the hook areas by forklifts driven by one of the three civilian warehouse men.

Compared to shipboard duty, I had a huge amount of liberty. And as I've said repeatedly, the "laid back" tempo was refreshing to me. Most of the sailors had NWSA had eight to ten years in the Navy, and a constant topic of discussion was whether to remain in the Navy for twenty years or not, in order to qualify for a lifelong pension? Overall Navy morale was not very high. Our pay was low, and as was the case during peacetime, there was little chance of our pay or benefits being increased. Our traditional thirteen button pants, with bell bottoms, jumpers with a flap, along with the white hat uniform that most liked, was being phased out in favor of suit type uniform. I described this uniform change earlier. Most sailors liked the distinct difference of our uniform, and now that difference was being taken away with the pending uniform change. As well as demoralizing, the uniform change was expensive, as we were required to buy the new uniforms. Our pay included a small amount as a clothing allowance, but this was only a few dollars a month.

On the subject of money, many of the first class petty officers, especially the married ones, "moonlighted," or held additional jobs after NWSA working hours to supplement their meager pay from the Navy. Some sailors worked at gas stations, or as security police, or "rent-a-cops" for security companies. Special permission was needed to be employed outside the Navy. Sailors were not permitted to have jobs that might bring discredit upon the Navy

My time to reenlist or "ship-over" was one year away. I was coming up on my fourteen-year point. Although I'd not been happy when I'd gotten out of the Navy three years before, I still was toying with the idea whether I wanted to remain in, and go to sea again. Also the promotion to chief kept eluding me. Since the end of the Vietnam involvement, and the slowdown of wartime activity, the Navy seemed to be a "ship without a rudder." It seemed as though the bureaucracy of the Navy was going through something that was popular for individuals to say during that time in U.S. history, "Try and get in touch with your inner feelings."

The Navy without the busy work of Vietnam seemed to be going through a time of self-examination, ignoring the morale and well-being of its life blood, sailors, almost like someone trying to redefine his goals and purposes in life. I guess my thoughts about whether or not to stay in the Navy were a reflection of what was going on in the upper echelons of the Navy?

Gaylen was planning to marry Lucy. She did not care for military life, and was encouraging him to get out of the Navy. At the same time she was talking to him about getting out of the Navy, she was trying to persuade me to also get out, and help Gaylen manage a marina in the delta area of Pittsburgh, she was planning to buy. I was not fully convinced that I would be happy doing this.

Carmen was working part time as a hostess for a fashion show at various locations, in the evening hours. I would often go to her apartment when she had these jobs, and baby-sit the kids. In the apartment complex directly below Carmen's apartment, there lived a woman named Martha, who Carmen became friends with. Martha had a daughter named Remedy, and a son named Wayne. The kids spent a lot of time with Carmen's kids, and they all spent so much time together, it became a family of five kids. Being boys, Roger and Wayne spent a lot of time in trouble of one kind or another. Often in the evenings, there were loud thumps, and noises coming from an adjoining apartment. Sadly the husband who lived next door used his wife as a punching bag about once a week. They would break up, and then make up weekly. I enjoyed being around the kids, and we went on a number of fishing trips. Peter and Wayne fished at a nearby lake, and often had good luck catching blue gills, or small bass.

One weekend Gaylen and I went on a charter boat fishing trip out of San Pablo Bay, during striped bass season. We happened to go when five other men in their seventies and eighties charted the boat also. They were retired postal workers. We got into a good school of fish weighing twenty pounds or more each. The fish were ferocious fighters, and it would take fifteen or twenty minutes to land one. Gaylen got seasick soon after the boat left the pier, and the older men soon tired reeling in the big fish. I ended up bringing twelve fish into the boat. It was a lot of fun, but I was very tired by the time the charter boat returned to the pier.

As LPO, I had more responsibilities than my fellow first class petty officers. I was expected to conduct the daily muster, read the P.O.D., and pass on pertinent information. If the senior chief wished to inspect the ranks, then I would accompany him, and record names and discrepancies in uniforms, and appearance. I also was expected to insure that the identified sailor corrected whatever uniform or appearance problem, such as a haircut, poorly shined shoes, etc., the chief pointed out. I also filled out the daily muster report, which was then sent to the base personnel office. Anytime a sailor wanted time off during regular working hours, it was called "special liberty." Special liberty required permission from the division officer, the two chiefs, and me. This permission was granted, or disapproved when the requestor submitted a request chit. Some types of requests required approval from the base commanding officer. In all cases, the request chits flowed up the chain of command for signatures, and then back down to me. I was the one who informed the sailor of the results of whatever his request might be. I was also the one who announced the commencement of liberty. Once a month we would take a "Rope Yarn Sunday," which is a traditional day off that goes back to the days of sailing ships. Rope Yarn Sunday, was time off from normal shipboard chores, so sailors could work on mending uniforms, and mending sails. Our Rope Yarn Sunday was usually on a Wednesday afternoon, in the middle of the month. Everyone was given liberty at noon to do whatever he wished.

I relayed any information that came down the chain of command. I was also expected to relay up the chain of command any information that might be needed to judge the morale of the division, and also good, or bad performance by sailors. As leading petty officer, it was expected that I serve as an example by working as long as or longer than anyone else. I was expected to be exceptionally squared away in behavior and military dress. All of this was not new to me, as I had been a leading petty officer at Whidbey Island, Guam, and the *Oriskany*. As LPO it was wise to learn as much as I could about the sailors that worked for me. I tried to learn each man's home state, who his immediate family was, his interests and ambitions. I had learned if I paid attention to taking care of what might seem to be small personal problems for each person, then larger or bigger problems seldom developed. In this regard I tried to always remain approachable, and always tried to take time to listen to anyone that had a question or problem. Many sailors carried a small pocket sized, green, government-issued notebook. This notebook was usually carried in the left shirt pocket of the dungaree shirt. This notebook was nicknamed a "Wheel Book." I always carried a wheel book, to keep notes on daily happenings, and information I needed to remember.

I was very thankful to have Carmen in my life, and I had fallen in love with her. In July I asked her out for dinner. After we had eaten, I asked her if she would marry me. I was very relieved when she said "yes." I'd done a lot of thinking about the matter, before asking Carmen if she would marry me. Thinking about risking another divorce, and repeating all the problems of the past, but I felt in my heart that we were meant for each other. One very positive factor was that Carmen was enthusiastic about the Navy, and the prospect of traveling about the world. The three children were a big responsibility I'd thought long and hard about. They seemed to have accepted me. Peter and Roger visited their father frequently on weekends, and I realized I shouldn't try to take their father's place, but it would place me in a difficult position. I wanted to be a good father figure to all three. I was marrying not only Carmen, but also the kids.

Not long after Carmen and I became engaged, Gaylen and Lucy made plans to go to Reno and get married. One weekend, a large group, Gaylen and Lucy, Lucy's family, and Carmen and I traveled to Reno. Gaylen and Lucy were married in a wedding chapel. I was Gaylen's best man, and the wedding went off well.

During this summer of 1973, the Far East oil embargo caused a gas shortage throughout the U.S. This was a problem for sailors who lived any distance from Oakland. My drive to and from work was a forty mile round trip, and keeping enough gas in the Pontiac's gas tank was a constant concern. The lines to gas stations were blocks long. One restriction was on certain days only cars with license plates with numbers ending with odd numbers could purchase gas, on the alternate day; only cars with license plates ending in even numbers were permitted in the gas line.

One unforgettable story in the San Francisco area at this time was about a man who had been waiting in a gas line for a couple of hours. The line was a few blocks long, and moved slowly toward the gas station.

As the line stopped he would turn off his car engine, until once again the line moved forward. About five car lengths from his turn at the pump, before he could start his car and move forward, a woman in a car, suddenly appeared and cut in front of him instead of going to the rear of the line many blocks to the rear. He patiently got out of his car, walked to the car ahead of him, and tapped on the closed window. The woman inside ignored him as he told her the back of the line was to the rear. The car that had cut in front of him was the same model as his. She continued to ignore him; he walked back to his car amidst the shouts of angry people behind him, who were also upset at the woman for jumping the gas line. He unlocked the gas cap on his car, which was a lock and key type, took it off, walked forward to the woman's car, and removed her gas tank cap. He then placed his cap on her tank, and locked the cap. He walked to the front of her car, and dangled the key to the gas cap in front of the windshield, and then with a big flourish, and a mighty heave, he threw the key into a thickly weeded vacant lot across the street from the gas station. There were cheers from the motorist waiting in the line, as the woman drove away. I doubt that she ever cut in front of people at a gas line again!

One Saturday early in the morning, Martha lent us her Dodge camper van, and baby-sat the kids while Carmen and I made a day trip north to the Russian River. On the way back that night, we ran out of gas in an area called Niles Canyon. It was said that Niles Canyon was haunted by the souls of people who had been murdered in the past in the canyon. It was very dark, and although I did not believe rumors of ghosts, nevertheless it felt comforting to have my forty-five with me. After walking three miles to a phone, a friend rescued us by bringing a gas can. We also took a camping trip to a campground near Mount Shasta. We took movies of the campground and beautiful scenery. I managed to catch a very nice sixteen-inch trout. Peter also caught a couple of trout. He was an enthusiastic and patient fisherman.

I had become interested in gold panning, and after doing some reading on the subject, I bought a gold pan. Carmen and I made a few trips to the American River, in California's gold country located east of San Francisco. I found a lot of "fool's gold," which is a form of mica that looks a lot like gold, but not the real thing. The American River is located in a beautiful mountainous area, and we enjoyed the scenery.

A first class at NWSA named Bill Ooten, had three boys, two were the same ages as Peter and Roger. Bill and his wife June lived in base housing on Hamilton Air Force Base, which was located in Marin County, north of San Francisco. Bill and I made plans for a camping trip to the American River. He would take two of his sons, and I would take Peter and Roger, Martha's son, Wayne, and a friend of Peter's that lived at the Tara Hill apartments. One weekend, Bill and I and six boys, loaded Martha's van with camping gear and took off for the American River. We had a good time fishing, gold panning, and telling ghost stories around the campfire at night. Bill and I had our hands' full keeping track of six boys!

GMT1 Charlie Brewster was one of the first class that "moonlighted" on an extra job after work at NWSA. He worked as a part time orderly at the Oakland Naval Hospital. During coffee breaks, and during lunchtime, Charlie would tell us of his experiences on the job at the hospital. One of his jobs was to wheel patients out of arriving ambulances, and about the hospital in wheel chairs for various appointments within the hospital. One story he told was almost unbelievable, but he swore it was true. One night the ambulance arrived with a retired marine sergeant. The sergeant's "recreation activity" for a number of years had been the hobby of inserting various objects into his rectum. Over time he'd been able to insert and remove objects of increasingly larger sizes, such as broomsticks, cucumbers, mustard jars, etc. He had called for an ambulance, because he had inserted a mayonnaise jar into his rectum, and could not remove it! The doctor faced with the task of removing the jar, finally had to break the glass jar, and remove it piece by piece.

Troop withdrawals from Vietnam had been going on all year. The American bases, and defensive positions had been turned over to the South Vietnamese. Aircraft carriers were no longer conducting bombing campaigns. For the Navy, the mission of fighting the Vietnam War was no longer. Discipline problems, and illegal drug use in the Navy were on the rise. At this point in history, group therapy was a popular concept. The Navy began attempting to restore good discipline, and educate its sailors in socially acceptable behavior, by a series of group therapy sessions. These sessions were called "Upward Seminars."

Senior petty officers, and officers that had been in the Navy for a while, did not welcome these upward seminars with open arms. Most were very skeptical, and felt they were a waste of time. It was the opinion of this group that discipline was suffering, primarily because the chain of command had been weakened by the "Z grams" from Admiral Zumwalt. Additionally the lack of support from our civilian leaders during the war had demoralized many career sailors. Boot camp tour lengths had been shortened, and boot camp had become lax and easy compared to what it had been in the past. An example of the laxity was the use of washers and dryers by recruits, whereas in the past, recruits had been expected to wash clothes by hand.

From the descriptions we heard of boot camp, it had become more like a college dorm experience, instead of a molding experience for sailors. We saw a change in the caliber of new recruits coming out of boot camp, and it did not bode well for the future of the Navy.

Along with the change in our uniforms in 1973-74, another very important change took place. The quarterly performance evaluation form for petty officers that had been in use for many years was drastically changed. The old form had five areas in which petty officers were judged, Professional Performance, Military Behavior, Leadership and Supervisory Ability, Military Appearance, and Adaptability. The new form was greatly expanded, the areas we were to be evaluated in now were, Directing, Counseling, Individual Productivity, Flexibility, Reliability, Conduct, Personal Appearance, Cooperation, Equal Opportunity Achievements, Inter-Cultural Relationships, and Overall Performance. The grading system of 3.0 to 4.0, with 4.0 the highest mark, was done away with. A new grading system ranging from UNS "Unsatisfactory" to STU "Stands out from virtually all others" was placed in effect.

It was generally accepted that the old performance form was abused, and over inflated. It had gotten to the point, if a sailor received anything less than a 4.0, he was considered to be below average. The new form was an attempt to bring the median, or average marks back down to a baseline of reality. In the past few years, I consistently had been given "4.0's". What was to happen on the first evaluation period on the new form was to prove disastrous for me, and other first class petty officers at NWSA.

My first year of shore duty had gone by quickly. I did not relish the idea of going back to sea. Gaylen had gotten out of the Navy in November. He had been in the Navy for eleven years. He was not sure what he was going to do? Carmen and I had not set a wedding date. We both wanted a lengthy engagement. She and the kids had met my parents, and family. In December I turned 31 years old. Beards were permitted in the Navy, so for the first time, I decided to grow a beard for Christmas. I felt more comfortable growing a beard, and wearing one since the division officer, and both NWSA chiefs wore beards.

On 11 December, I and five other sailors from NWSA drove to Treasure Island Naval Base, where we attended an upward seminar for three days. The previous week a few NWSA sailors had attended the seminar, and they did not have any positive things to say about it. All the sailors attending the meeting sat in chairs in a large circle. There were two sailor instructors acting as moderators. We discussed various subjects such as race relations, chain of command, personal responsibility, and so on. There were twenty-five sailors in the class, and the junior sailors were the most vocal. From listening to the conversations, I realized this new Navy was far different from the Navy I joined thirteen years before. Race relations were a serious matter of concern for the Navy. For the first time in history, sailors were being evaluated on how they related to, and worked with people of other races. Everyone in the Navy was required to attend the upward seminar sessions, and this was documented on the new evaluation form.

I spent Christmas at Carmen's apartment. We had put up a tree, and she cooked a turkey with all the trimmings. We celebrated New Years Eve, 1974 together. We had tentatively set a wedding date sometime in June. The expiration of my enlistment was the first part of June, so I planned to "ship over," three months early in March. Sailors were permitted to ship over ninety days in advance of their enlistment expiration date. This was advantageous for career sailors, as this advance re-enlistment knocked off ninety days, each time you did it, for computing time served for pension purposes. A sailor, who did this twice in his career, meant getting credit for twenty years, after serving an actual time of nineteen years, six months. I asked my Division Officer Lieutenant Commander McKenna if he would administer the re-enlistment oath. He agreed. Many sailors try to come up with unique locations or circumstances to ship over, places such as, in flight in a plane, at the bottom of the sea in SCUBA gear, and other different locations. I had attended a number of shipping over ceremonies within nuclear weapons' magazines. I did not desire to have the ceremony in a unique setting. The division officer's office was fine for me.

The second set of evaluation marks I was to receive at NWSA, covered the period 1 June 1973 to 28 February 1974. They were filled out in the new form, and in the new format. Chief Halterman made out the marks. It was the goal of career sailors to make chief, and this had been the goal of most of the first class at NWSA. Many chiefs in the Navy wore the "badge of office" which was a potbelly, and Chief Halterman was no exception. He was overweight, and was extremely difficult to approach. He was not respected by most of the NWSA sailors. He seemed to be more interested in liberty than the job. He evaluated all the first class, and the marks he gave were devastating. We all received the equivalent of a 3.0 in all areas, which killed any opportunity any of us might have had making chief in the next promotion cycle. I protested the low marks, and also as leading petty officer, I protested on behalf of the other first class.

He refused to change the marks, saying the Navy needed a realistic system for evaluating sailors. Our marks were so low that there was an inquiry from Naval Personnel Command, Washington asking if the marks were correct. On the next evaluation cycle, Chief Halterman tried to correct his mistake, but the damage had already been done. I don't believe he fully understood the evaluation system? He apologized to me prior to his transfer, but I did not fully accept his apology. He mangled the career and promotion opportunity of every first and second class petty officer at NWSA. His contribution to the command was mostly negative, and he lacked most leadership skills. In retrospect, I probably should have protested the evaluations more strongly, but no one was familiar with the new form, and none of us at the time fully realized the damage Chief Halterman had done to us.

My evaluations read: "Petty Officer Little has continued to demonstrate his technical expertise during this evaluation period. His crew has exceeded the productive requirements of the department with no decrease in product quality. Petty Officer Little has continued to display his initiative and has shown a definite trend toward more effective leadership through the delegation of tasks to subordinates. Petty Officer Little has an excellent command of oral and written English. Petty Officer Little's impressive appearance, on and off the job is indicative of his pride in himself and the Naval service."

There were misspellings throughout the evaluations, and basically the same statements appeared on all the first class evaluations at NWSA. Even reading these evaluations years later, I'm still disgusted with them. I know that Chief Halterman put very little thought into preparing our evaluations; his goal was to complete them and get them out of the way so he could go on liberty. All the blame cannot be laid on Chief Halterman's shoulders, as they were reviewed, and approved by Senior Chief Graybow, and the division officer. There was complete unfamiliarity with this new system. Thinking back, although it is harsh to say, I think Chief Halterman was the least effective chief I ever worked for.

In the months following, and the years to come, I studied everything written about evaluation reports. I tried to become an absolute authority, and expert on performance evaluation reports. I've said this before in this book, and I'll say it again, I tried to insure that those working for me understood that I believed the most important piece of paper they ever touched in the Navy was the performance evaluation report. I know that I was called names, and grumbled at when evaluation report time rolled around. It was not unusual for me to return rough evaluation reports that petty officers made out on subordinates, to me for approval, six or seven times until they were completed properly. After the "Chief Halterman" affair, just as I had at previous commands, I gave a series of lectures on performance evaluation reports. I also had numerous "closed door" sessions with the first class working for me, on the subject of evaluations.

Lieutenant Commander McKenna was, as I said, a supply officer, and our division officer. He was well liked by the GMT's. He was an expert in the area of naval supply, but he knew very little about the nuclear weapons program. He let the two chiefs run the shop as they saw fit.

On 5 March 1974, I stood in Lieutenant Commander McKenna's office in dress blues, along with Carmen. I had shaved my beard, leaving a moustache. Standing before Lieutenant Commander McKenna with right hand raised, I repeated the oath of enlistment. I signed the documents obligating me for six years service in the Navy. Carmen and I, and the LCDR had our picture taken, and then I was given the rest of the day off. Carmen and I went to Jack London Square, where we celebrated by having lunch. I received a re-enlistment bonus of $600, and was "locked in" the Navy until I reached the twenty-year point.

Carmen and I began planning our wedding, which was to take place on 25 May 1974, in the naval chapel, on the Treasure Island Naval Base. There were hundreds of details, we had planned on a small wedding, but it seemed like the invitation list kept growing.

I asked my brother-in-law, to be my best man, and Carmen asked Martha to be the maid of honor. We had decided we would buy a house, and move into it after we were married. A house would be better than an apartment for the kids and us. We found a house for sale in a unique neighborhood in the town of Concord, which was twenty-five miles north of Oakland. What made the neighborhood unique was that all the houses were built "Cape Cod" style, or in the style of New England houses. Naturally the street in Concord was called Cape Cod Way. The house had four bedrooms, and also a large back yard, with a small above ground swimming pool. The rooms were rather small, but we felt it was larger than an apartment and just right for the five of us. Carmen and I were shown the house by a Concord realtor. We agreed that we would like to buy the house, and I gave the realtor $500 earnest money. The owners were scheduled to move out in March, which would be good timing for us.

Much of the news in March was about the kidnapping of Patty Hearst. It seemed like everyone in San Francisco imagined Symbionese Liberation Army (SLA) Terrorist behind every tree and bush. The Watergate scandal also dominated the news.

In March I received a letter from the Internal Revenue Service (IRS). The letter stated I was to report to the local IRS Office for an audit. The letter was threatening in tone, saying a warrant for my arrest would be issued if I did not appear for the appointment. I reported to the Oakland office at the appointed time. Carmen went along with me for support. I did not see one smiling face in the large office? I discovered that the meeting was to determine why I had not paid taxes on the alimony I had sent monthly to Allison in the past. I explained that at the time of our divorce, Allison had agreed that she would pay the taxes on the alimony she received from me. She had not paid the taxes, so I was required to pay all the back taxes along with a substantial amount of interest. This whole affair was not pleasant, mostly because of the way it was handled by the IRS; I was made to feel like a criminal.

The date we picked for the wedding was originally 25 May, but we discovered that the chapel had already been reserved for that date, so we decided on the 26th. This would also be on Memorial Day weekend, and we hoped this would make it easier for friends and family to travel to the bay area. I was going to take two weeks leave following the wedding. The first months of 1974 were spent making preparations for the wedding. We were to be married by a Navy Chaplain, named LCDR David L. Windle, who was a Lutheran. Carmen had been brought up as a child in the Catholic faith; she had agreed to enter my faith, as a Baptist. We had two meetings with the chaplain prior to the wedding.

The wedding was to be at 3:00 p.m. on Sunday, with a reception afterward in the base Acey Duecy Club. There was Carmen's wedding dress to consider, as well as the cake, flowers, invitations, and the many things that go together to make up a wedding.

In April, we asked the realtor a number of times if we could get into the house, since the owners had moved, and get some measurements, and make plans for our eventual move in. For some reason he kept avoiding us, and stalling. Finally after asking for two weeks, he said we could pick up the key on one afternoon, and look in the house. When we went to the house, and unlocked the door, we were shocked. It appeared that the house had been "trashed!" There were crayon scribbles on all the walls, the sink was rusted, doors were falling off the hinges, and the back yard was full of holes, as though someone had been digging for buried treasure? The swimming pool had stagnant water in it, and in general the house looked abused. Carmen was upset, and so was I. After returning the key to the real estate office, I called the realtor and told him I did not want the house. He suddenly became interested in communicating with me. He said he would look at the house and then meet with me. The next day he called me and said the damage to the house was nothing. I did not agree it would take a lot of money, and time to restore the house to the condition it was when we first looked at it. I again stated I did not want the house, and he said we would lose our earnest money. I wrote to the State Real Estate Commissioner, explaining the situation. I eventually did get the earnest money back, minus twenty-five dollars. So our plans for a house were down the drain at this point. We planned to live at the Tara Hill apartment after the wedding, and arrange for better living conditions later.

We estimated there would be about eighty-five people at the wedding. We reserved the Acey Duecy Club, and ordered a light buffet, two cases of champagne, and punch. Martha, and a couple of Carmen's girlfriends helped with some of the preparations, but Carmen and I did most of the preparation. I planned to wear the new style dress blue uniform, with gold crow and hash marks on the sleeve. We sent out the invitations well in advance of 26 May.

The first part of May, Carmen and I and the kids drove south to my parent's house at Strathmore. We attended the activities of the annual high school homecoming reunion. On Saturday evening there was a dance in the Veterans Memorial building, which Carmen and I, and my sister Linda, and brother-in-law attended.

The week prior to the wedding, we had a short rehearsal at the Treasure Island Naval Chapel. All the kids were involved in the wedding. Roger was to be the ring bearer, Mary, the flower girl, Peter was to walk his mom down the aisle, Wayne was wearing a tuxedo, and his sister Remedy was wearing a formal dress.

The evening before the wedding, my parents, and sister and brother-in-law had a dinner at a Mexican food restaurant. My dad graciously picked up the tab. I was to spend the night at Martha's apartment, since I had moved out of my Hayward apartment. Martha, Remedy, and Wayne were staying at Carmen's apartment.

**Uncle Hubert & me
Armed and Dangerous**

**Strathmore High School
1960**

Boot Camp, San Diego 1960

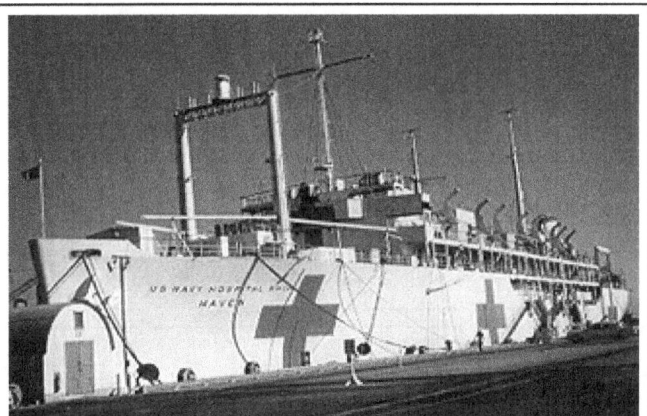
**USS Haven (AH-12), Long Beach Naval Station,
Calif. Photo by Imogene Little 1960**

**USS Independence (CVA-62), anchored
off the coast of Cannes, France**

**Fishing, Fena Lake
Guam**

**USS Ticonderoga (CVA-14)
Refueling off the coast of Vietnam**

**Flight of A-4 Skyhawks over
USS Ticonderoga**

Bob Hope onboard "Tico"

USS Oriskany enroute to Western Pacific

Bombs for Vietnam (unk. ordnanceman)

Wedding Day May 26, 1974

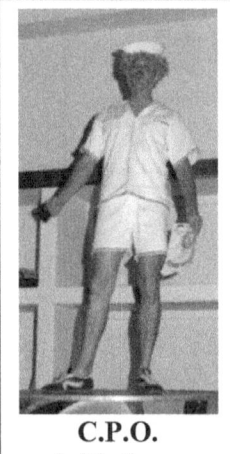
C.P.O. initiation

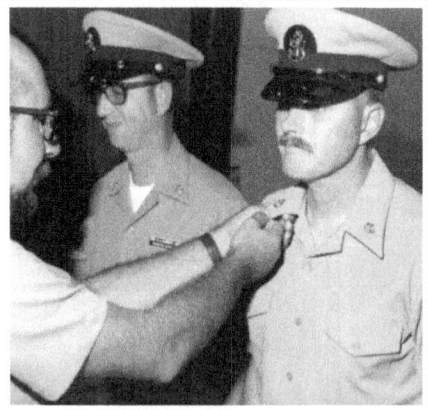
GMTC Margenson pinning on my Chief's collar anchor

Felt tip pen mural on wall of Guam Base House

USS Midway (CVA-41)

Yokosuka, Japan Officer's Club

Bombs of WWII, left to right, Little Boy (Hiroshima), Fat Man (Nagasaki), Atomic Museum, Albuquerque, N.M.

(COD) C-1A, USS Midway Museum, San Diego, Calif.

A-6 Intruder, USS Midway Museum, San Diego, Calif.

A-4 Skyhawk, USS Midway Museum, San Diego, Calif.

Mark 7 Bomb, Atomic Museum Albuquerque, New Mexico

Mark 43 Bomb, Atomic Museum, Albuquerque, New Mexico

Mark 57 Bomb, with parachute, Atomic Museum Albuquerque, New Mexico

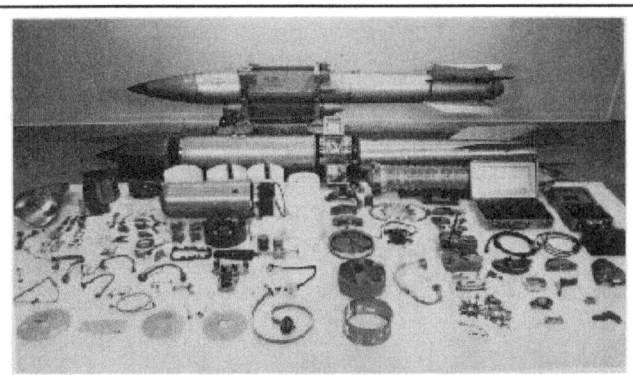
Mark 61 Bomb, with assembly parts, Atomic Museum Albuquerque, New Mexico

Mark 28 Bomb, external & internal configuration, Atomic Museum, Albuquerque, New Mexico

Mark 27 Bomb, one of the largest in the Navy stockpile Atomic Museum, N.M.

Arlington National Cemetery, Arlington, Va.

Artillery Shot, Nevada test Site

Uncle Ralph's cabin, Days Creek, Oregon

John Paul Jones House Museum, Portsmouth, New hampshire

My command, Coos Head Charleston, OR

"Piping over the side" Retirement Ceremony

Little Clan, Standing left to right Jim, Linda, Mom, Dad, left front Joe, right front Jerry

Retirement home on North Umpqua River, Oregon

Nuclear Weaponsman (NW1) 1957-1961   **Gunners' Mate Technician (GMT) 1961-1986**   **Weapons Technician (WT) 1987-1997**   **Chief Warrant Officer Surface Ordnance**

I should explain that I Martha was a very poor housekeeper. Martha had given me the key to her apartment. When I unlocked the door, the night prior to the wedding, and walked in I was shocked. I thought the apartment had been broken into, and ransacked by burglars? The apartment was a mess, clothes scattered everywhere, drawers opened, and doors ajar. Martha also kept a dog, a cocker spaniel, and a cat in the apartment; there were dog droppings everywhere. I cleared a spot on the couch, on which to sleep. As soon as I started to doze off, the dog would begin licking my face. I tried putting the dog in another room, but as soon as I lay down on the couch, the dog would begin to howl, and whine. I got very little sleep that night.

In the morning, I put on my uniform, and drove to the motel where my parents were staying. Shortly before noon we all drove to Treasure Island Naval Base. It was a beautiful day, with perfect weather. The photographer we hired took a number of pictures as family and guests arrived. I was becoming more nervous as the clock moved closer to 3:00 p.m. Finally it was three, Walt and I, the Minister, and Roger the ring bearer, stood at the front of the chapel. The music began, and Mary, Martha, Wayne, and Remedy walked down the aisle. Then Carmen and Peter entered, and everyone rose to their feet. Carmen looked beautiful, as she moved toward me with the music of "Here comes the bride".

We exchanged vows, and rings. Carmen did have a little trouble slipping my ring on, as she was crying during much of the ceremony. Finally the Chaplain said, "You may kiss your bride," which I happily did. The Chaplain then said, "Ladies and gentlemen may I introduce you to Mr. and Mrs. James S. Little." There was applause, and we walked back down the aisle. After a few photos, (see photograph page) and the signing of documents, we left for the Acey Duecy Club, which was four blocks away from the chapel. The reception was held in a large meeting room in the club. It was a happy joyous time. We cut the wedding cake, threw the bouquet (caught by a girlfriend of Carmen's), and garter, which was caught by my cousin Jay Clark. There were a number of toasts, and we ended up buying an additional case of champagne.

When Carmen and I left the club we were greeted with a shower of rice. Our car, the "Raider" Pontiac had been decorated "Just married," with balloons and streamers. We left waving at everyone, and thanking him or her for being there. As we drove down the freeway, cars honked, and the occupants waved happily at us. We had not told anyone where we were going, mostly because some of the sailors at the wedding might want to pull something mischievous on our wedding night. We'd reserved a motel room at "The Islander Motel," about six blocks from Carmen's apartment. We went to the motel room, changed clothes and had dinner at a restaurant in Fremont.

The next morning, we called mom and dad and thanked them for everything. We also called Martha's house to check on the kids, as she was baby-sitting. We then drove to Lake Tahoe, Nevada were we stayed at the "Blue Chalet Motel," in the bridal suite. This room was quite expensive, so we only stayed two nights. We drove down through the California gold country, and finally to Strathmore, where we visited with our family. While at my parent's house, we picked cherries. While picking cherries in the orchard, my new wedding ring slipped off. Unknown to me Carmen had found it lying on the ground. I frantically searched for it until she felt I'd suffered enough, and told me she had picked it up. By coincidence, in the foothills above my parent's house, a plant called a century plant was blooming at this time. The plants only bloom every fifty years. We took pictures of the blooms. Sister Linda also took pictures of us in her back yard, while I demonstrated how I had carried Carmen over the threshold at the motel on our wedding night.

We returned to Fremont, I checked in off leave, and I began life as a married sailor. The apartment was very small for the five of us. Carmen and I did not have a bed, and since the craze at that time was waterbeds, we bought one. We sold Carmen's Ford Mustang, in retrospect, the Mustang has become a classic, and we should have kept it.

Carmen knew that I wanted a pickup, and she surprised me one afternoon. She asked me to look at a pickup she had found in Hayward. A fireman who had been injured in an accident, and could no longer drive owned the pickup. He had been working on the pickup for a number of years, and was forced to sell it. The pickup was a1952 Dodge, with a 1960 Chrysler V-8 engine. It had a three-speed transmission with a hydraulic clutch. He was asking $400, and Carmen had secretly saved $400. She said if I wanted it, she would buy it for me! Of course, I happily said I wanted it.

With the marriage came my awareness of increased responsibility, and need to be a good provider. My wish for promotion, and increase in salary was multiplied. I was also aware that I needed to be an example for the children, and it was my responsibility to take care of their material needs, as well as their spiritual needs. I had never held the role of a father, but now I found myself in that important role.

The distance to work at NWSA was about ten miles further south than the distance from my Hayward apartment. This meant in order to be at NWSA by 7:00 a.m., I had to leave Fremont by 6:00 a.m. One morning after I'd been at work a short while, I got a call from Carmen, she was very upset about something that had just happened. She described it to me. I then asked Chief Graybow for permission to return home. He gave me permission to leave. Carmen said after I left for work, she had just awakened, and started to get up and begin the routine of getting the kids off to school. She saw a grotesque creature standing at the foot of the bed, saying in a low garbled voice, "I will have your soul." She felt like she was being strangled, and no matter how hard she tried she could not move. A mirror in the room appeared to be three dimensional, and the room was very cold.

When I arrived back at the apartment, the bedroom felt eerily cold, and there was a bruise on Carmen's neck! We called my mom, and related what had happened. She suggested we drive down to Strathmore, the upcoming weekend. We agreed we would. The following day, Carmen was preparing for the trip south. She had been doing laundry in the apartment laundry room, and when she went to the laundry room to retrieve clothes that had been drying in the dyers, the laundry room door was inexplicably locked. This occurrence and others were as though obstacles were being placed in our path to prevent our trip south?

On Friday afternoon, we all left for Strathmore, 250 miles to the south. On the next Sunday morning, we attended church services at Faith Baptist Church of Strathmore. Providentially, or as the result of heavenly arrangement, a visiting speaker was there on this morning. He was a former Catholic priest, who had converted to the Baptist faith. After the morning service, Carmen and I asked if we could have an appointment with him that afternoon. He agreed that we could, and we met with him at 3:00 that afternoon. Carmen described to him the happenings of last Thursday morning. He said it was probably a demonic materialization, as he was familiar with them. He then asked Carmen if she understood the plan of salvation as it was presented in the Bible. He went on to say that he had not realized the truth of the Bible as a Catholic priest. He said he had come to a point in his life where he realized that he had to merely accept what Jesus had done for him on the cross of Calvary, and that was to die for his sins. He realized there was nothing physically he could do in the Catholic Church for salvation, all he had to do was personally believe in Jesus. At that point he experienced spiritual birth, or what some call being "born again." He showed Carmen verses in the bible that explained what a person must do to be saved, and have eternal life. This rebirth also protects souls against demonic, and evil designs, and plans. Carmen agreed she wanted to receive Jesus as her Lord and Savior. This was not news to me, I had been raised in a Christian home, and church, and had made this same decision at a young age, and had been baptized as a teenager. I also recommitted myself to the principles of Christian life.

That Sunday night after the evening service, Carmen and I went forward before the congregation and publicly acknowledged our decisions. I drove back to the apartment that night, leaving Carmen and the kids at my parent's house for a week. I worked that week, and returned the following weekend to pick them up. Carmen had an enjoyable week, spending much of it with her new nieces, Lisa and Betty. It was indeed miraculous the way events, and people all worked together at the right time for the good of us all.

We found a nice church in Fremont, and attended regularly, often Wayne and Remedy went with us. In September, mom and dad sent all of us beautiful Bibles, with personalized names on the covers. Also in this month Carmen was baptized, during a baptismal service in the church. I had been baptized at the age of thirteen, but I felt it important to identify with Carmen's decision, and I was also baptized.

Two sailors, GMT1 Bill Ooten and GMT2 George Erath, at NWSA lived north of San Francisco in Navy housing on Hamilton Air Force Base. They told me there was a very short waiting list of military people waiting to get a house on base. This seemed like a good option to get out of the small Tara Hill apartment. In the civilian community there are a number of misconceptions about military life, one of them being that military members are given free housing. This is not true, married sailors receive an increase in salary called Basic Allowance for Quarters, or "BAQ." This amount varied depending on a person's rank. As a first class my BAQ amount was $105 a month. When a sailor moved into base housing with his family, his BAQ was forfeited, and his salary decreased by that amount. Although not free, it was usually a bargain, because all utilities are paid, and it is usually much cheaper than renting, or buying a house.

One thing I had to consider was the length of my daily drive. The distance from Hamilton Air Force Base to Oakland was a little more than forty miles. Bill and George agreed to car pool if I should move to Hamilton Air Force Base. I took liberty one afternoon, and drove to Hamilton to apply for housing. In years past the base had been a "showplace" for the Air Force. All the buildings were white stucco, with red Spanish tiles on the roofs. The entire base was beautifully manicured with nice trees and hedges.

The houses were not built in rows, as are most military base houses, but built randomly, in an effort to blend in with the landscape. When the base was built shortly after World War II, it appeared that no expense had been spared. When the Air Force hosted dignitaries, or important government officials, they always tried to include Hamilton Air Force Base on the trip itinerary.

There was a piece of little known nuclear weapon history about Hamilton Air Force Base. Near the end of World War II, a C-47 transport plane from Albuquerque carrying components for the first atomic bombs used against Japan, landed here before continuing on to Tinian Island.

In 1974 Air Force operations at the base were greatly reduced. The Navy took over management of the base housing. The Air Force occupied a few buildings, and maintained sentries on the main gates, but most of the operations buildings on the base were vacant. There was a large commissary (a grocery store), exchange (a general store), gas station, and chapel on base, and many other clubs, and activities for families. There was also a school for grades one through six. It appeared to be a nice place to live.

We had no way to know when a house might come available for us to move in. The waiting list was rather short and we were number twenty-five. I was told to check with the housing office on a weekly basis. After our wedding, Carmen and the kids had all been issued Identification Cards (ID's). They were now military dependents, and had to show the cards each time they entered an exchange, commissary, medical clinic, base movie theater, and so on. We were hopeful that our wait for housing would not be long, and that there would be minimal disruption of school for the kids.

It was soon September, and time for the Navy wide advancement examinations. On the designated morning, all the eligible first class petty officers gathered in a room on the base in preparation for the 150 question exams. Prior to the exam, we all were sitting in the room talking. There were mostly GMT's, but there were also Boatswain's Mates, Electricians, and a few other ratings. I had wanted to become a Boatswain's Mate early in my Navy career on the *USS Haven*. Boatswain's Mates however, were thought of as "deck apes," or "knuckle draggers," a rating that required more brawn than brain! Ratings in the Navy also have a seniority level. Boatswain's Mates are at the top of the seniority list, with Gunner's Mates second on the list. Gunner's Mate Technicians were often called "glorified Gunner's Mates" because of the technical, and security aspects of our rating.

In the exam room there was a large coffee pot brewing, nearby there were styrofoam cups for our use. When the red "ready" light came on the coffee pot, there was an exodus toward the coffee pot. The coffee pot was positioned in the middle of the table, and there was a problem. The coffee pot spigot was located near the bottom of the coffee pot, and it was lower than the tops of the Styrofoam cups. In order to get a cup of coffee, we had to tip the cup, slid it under the spigot, fill the cup up halfway, and then tip the cup to slide it out from under the spigot. A full cup of coffee would have spilled during the tipping process, so we all had half a cup of coffee. Everyone got a half a cup of coffee, and sat down, all except a Boatswain's Mate First Class in the back of the room. He stood up walked to the table where the coffee pot was, and said, "I thought all you GMT's were smart? I'll show you how a Boatswain's Mate gets a full cup of coffee." After saying this, He picked up an empty cup, slid the coffee pot to the edge of the table, with the spigot hanging over the edge, and holding his cup under the spigot, filled his cup to the brim! We all got a laugh out of this even though it was at our expense.

My name moved quickly to the top of the Hamilton Base Housing waiting list. Carmen and I looked at an available house the first of October. It was a three bedroom, two-story house, with a basement, in an older section of the base. This was one of the houses that had been built in the 1940s for high-ranking Air Force enlisted men. The homes in this section were only offered to E-6 and above rates. The houses had fireplaces, beautiful oak stairs, large basements, and made so two families lived side by side, separated by a sand-filled wall to deaden any noise. The address of the house we looked at was 240 San Jose Drive. We told the housing office we would take it. The next couple of weeks we were busy packing, and preparing for the move.

On our moving day, I took liberty. A moving van, with furniture movers, and packers, moved everything out of the Fremont apartment, and drove the sixty miles to Hamilton Air Force Base. Our new house had a large yard with oak and palm trees scattered about. In our block there was a mixture of military families. Across the street from us there lived an Air Force family, named Shumpert's, who we got to know very well. Also, across the street were a Coast Guard chief and his family. Right next door to us there lived an Army sergeant, and his family. At the very beginning of our block, GMT1 Bill Ooten, his wife June, and three boys, Shawn, Jessie, and Mike lived.

On Halloween we were given a small gray-stripped kitten. After many family discussions we named him Waldo. He was an unusual cat from the beginning.

He liked to hide under couches, chairs, or behind doors, and then leap out and swat at the ankles of people walking by (usually Carmen), and then run back to his hiding place.

We adjusted quickly to our new home on San Jose Drive. The church in Fremont had recommended a church in the town of Larkspur about twelve miles south of Hamilton called Calvary Baptist Church. We began attending this church. The pastor's named was David Tucker. It was a small church, and many in the congregation were security guards at nearby San Quentin Prison.

Bill Ooten, George Erath, and I began car-pooling back and forth to NWSA. We took turns driving for a week at a time. George drove a '71 Ford Mustang; Bill had an older Volkswagen station wagon, which he eventually traded for a '75 Volkswagen van. I would drive either the Pontiac, or the '52 Dodge pickup. The drive was forty-five minutes, to an hour in length, depending on the traffic. In order to make the 7:00 a.m. muster, we had to leave Hamilton at 5:30 a.m. This meant getting up at 5:00 a.m. or earlier each morning. If one of us had duty, which we had every fourteen days or so, it meant we would have a late start home, as the building had to be locked up after everyone went home, alarms set, and the keys turned into the base police office.

It wasn't too bad during the winter months, but during the summer, Bill and George dreaded riding back and forth to work in my pickup. The V-8 engine put out a lot of heat, and the firewall was not insulated. It would get very warm inside the cab, and they would fight over who had to sit in the middle. It was a long commute, but the peace and serenity, as well as the security we enjoyed at Hamilton Air Force base was well worth the drive. Back and forth from NWSA we drove each day through the double-decked freeway (called the Cypress Freeway) that would collapse in the future during the 1989 earthquake, killing many motorists.

Carmen and I had not seen much of Gaylen and Lucy since he had gotten out of the Navy. Gaylen was training to become a welder, and had not yet found a steady job. Chris Van Diven, a mutual friend of Gaylen and Lucy, told me one day that Lucy's father was critically ill in the hospital. Lucy had asked Chris if he would witness her father signing a new will, she wanted him to sign before he passed away? Chris said her father was not aware of anything and he did not want to be part of a "new will signing." Lucy was always walking a fine line between legalities.

On 8 December, I became thirty-two years old. The Larkspur Church was preparing a special Christmas program. The Pastor asked if I would be the narrator. I agreed, Peter, Roger, and Mary also had parts in the program, and it was well received.

Carmen had been encouraging me to develop my art and drawing talents, so I designed a Christmas card that depicted the five of us sitting before our fireplace in our new home. We sent this card to family and friends.

My performance evaluations for the period from February 1974 to January 1975 once again were "lukewarm" evaluations, and most of the first class were not happy. As a testament to the poor quality, and lack of thought that went into the writing of evaluations, there was no one promoted during my three-year tour at NWSA!

February was the month of my stepson Peter's birthday. He was becoming a teenager, achieving the age of thirteen. I chartered a fishing boat out of San Francisco, and we went fishing together all day. We didn't catch anything, but had a good time. The fishing boat sailed under the Golden Gate Bridge, bringing back memories of the times I sailed under that bridge on aircraft carriers, returning from deployments.

We had talked about having a family dog. The last dog I'd had was a beagle, when I was stationed at Whidbey Island. Since we had a large yard, with plenty of running room, and many families on base had dogs, I mentioned having a dog often. One day arriving home from work, Carmen surprised me. There was a dog on the porch. It was an adult beagle she had gotten at the county cat and dog shelter. It was a beautiful beagle, but not overly friendly. Waldo the cat was not happy about the intrusion of a dog in his territory. I enjoyed walking the beagle on a lease in the evenings. One afternoon while upstairs, I heard a huge commotion in the kitchen downstairs. I rushed downstairs. Carmen and Mary were on one side of the kitchen, and in a corner on the other side of the kitchen was the beagle, snarling viciously. He growled at me when I tried to grab his collar. He was so upset, that he was foaming at the mouth. He had snapped at Carmen for no reason. I didn't want a dog with that kind of temperament around the family, so the next day the dog went back to the shelter. Waldo was very happy over this turn of events.

The "Hook" working areas at NWSA were open to the view of anyone who might be walking through the building. A few nude pictures of women from men's magazines appeared one week, posted on the walls of the hook working area.

I let it go for one day, and then at morning quarters, I said the pictures were inappropriate, and offensive, and additionally we had women working in the building, I ordered that they be taken down. Senior Chief Graybow, and Chief Halterman were hesitant backing me up on this, but they reluctantly finally did. A few days later, one of the woman employees of NWSA, thanked me for taking this stand. Surprisingly, the married sailors were the ones who grumbled the most!

With spring approaching, I considered planting a garden. The only place available was in the middle of our large back yard, which was planted with grass. I marked off a plot fifteen feet by twenty-five feet I could use. I then asked permission from the housing office to plant a garden within this area. They gave me permission; I dug up the grass, and tilled the soil. Carmen and I planted corn, lettuce, carrots, radishes, and cucumbers.

Far back in a dark forgotten area of the NWSA warehouse there was a huge fir log. It had been cut squarely, and was about twelve feet long. It had been in the warehouse for many years. No one knew how it came to be in the warehouse? The Director Norm Howell was going to have it thrown away, when Bill Ooten saw it, and asked if he could have it? Norm said, "Yes, as long as you get it out of the warehouse." Bill planned on making a large table out of the log. The log was large enough for many tables, so he recruited me to haul the log to a lumberyard for cutting, with my pickup. In return I could have enough wood for a table. There were eventually three tables made out of the fir log. My table took two months to build. I glued and pegged three of the boards together. I also positioned brass straps on each end of the tabletop. The top measured four ½ feet by nine feet. The finished table was extremely heavy. It took me, and three other men to move the table from the garage up to the dining room on the floor above. My other carpentry efforts included building a large storage cabinet for pots and pans, out of pine boards, and pegboard, for Carmen's kitchen.

In the spring of '75, Pastor Tucker asked me if I would be a Sunday school teacher for the junior high class. I agreed that I would. It was not a large class, usually eight or ten teenagers. I enjoyed it, and I learned as well, from teaching the class. Pastor Tucker was my age, and we developed a close friendship. He planned an overnight church camping trip in the spring. He asked if Carmen and I would go, and help with the kids from the church that would be going. There were fifteen kids, and five adults. We had tents and sleeping bags. The day of the camping trip, we traveled a short distance from Larkspur to a Marin County Park. It was much too early in the year for a camping trip. Everyone almost froze that night, as the temperature dropped close to thirty-two degrees. Many of the kids ended up sleeping in cars. Carmen, who could not tolerate cold well, wanted me to breathe on her feet to keep them from freezing! I spent much of the night huffing and puffing on her cold feet.

The year of 1975 was busy. We had visits from mom, dad, Joe and Jerry, and a family friend, Mildred Anderson. Walt and Linda, and their girls also visited. When they visited over the weekend, we all went to the San Francisco zoo. I also painted a watercolor picture for Linda and Walt, which I'll explain more in detail later. Aunt Lois and Uncle Dean visited us one weekend, which also happened to be their wedding anniversary. Carmen surprised them by getting up earlier than anyone else, and decorated the dining room with balloons, and "happy anniversary" signs. She then fixed a huge breakfast. It surprised, and touched Aunt Lois so much that she cried.

All the neighborhood kids went to school together, and played together. We enjoyed the "Ooten kids," Shawn, Jessie, and Mike, and the "Shumpert kids," Darnell, and Mike. We all shared birthday, and holiday celebrations.

Snakes were common on Hamilton Air Force Base, and a story that circulated that year, that I can't confirm if it were true or not, was about a rattlesnake. A father on base was busy mowing his lawn, when his three-year-old daughter walked up to him, after playing in a nearby field. He glanced at her, and it appeared she was dragging a rope, but when he looked closer he was horrified to see that it was a rattlesnake! The snake had a large bulge in the middle of its body that was apparently a swallowed frog, and in its mouth was another large frog. It was unable to strike because of the frog in its mouth. The father quickly dispatched the snake by running over it with the lawnmower.

On 29 April 1975, the last American troops left Saigon, Vietnam, while North Vietnamese soldiers surrounded the city. Nineteen seventy-five, as a year of celebration of the Navy's 200th birthday, was also a year of disbelief over the fall of Vietnam to Communism. It was hard for me to accept that Vietnam had fallen. It seemed as though after all the effort our country had expended, my personal hard work, the people injured, and lives lost, it had all been for nothing. I was shocked when I heard that Da Nang had fallen, I had seen personally how well it was defended. I felt physically sick and depressed for a month or more after Vietnam fell. This sense of failure has persisted in my mind over the years.

President Kennedy said in his inaugural address in 1961, "Let every nation know, whether it wishes us well or ill, that we shall pay any price, bear any burden, meet any hardship, support any friend, oppose any foe, to assure the survival and success of liberty." We in the military had kept this commitment, but not the politicians, and American society. We in the military were not permitted to be victors. We had won all the battles, but lost the war. America was not able to hold its collective head up in pride, and I'm not sure if our nation's resolve and commitment to other nations have been fully trusted after Vietnam? Along with the sense of failure, nevertheless I felt pride having answered my country's call, and I knew in my heart that I had done the best I could do in my part in the war. I had spent a large part of my adult life trying to analyze the motivations of the sailors I worked with, and more importantly the motivations of those that I was responsible for, and who I was expected to lead. Americans, probably more than any nationality, like to compete, and like very much to win. Many times after completing a job, sailors would ask, "How did we do? How did we do?" In Vietnam we wanted to be winners, but were not permitted to fight to win. We did not understand our nation's lack of resolve, which lead to us ultimately becoming "Losers," not "Winners."

In May Hamilton Air Force Base had a surprise visitor. President Ford in Air Force One, landed for a couple of hours. Carmen was in the crowd when he got off the plane. She got to shake his hand, and she got a couple of pictures of him.

I had quit smoking the previous summer, and Bill Ooten and I began jogging each day at noon. I worked up to three miles. Bill had been jogging for a number of years. Before coming to NWSA, he and his wife June had been stationed at Adak, Alaska. The jogging helped me regain my wind after years of smoking.

Our church scheduled a "Vacation Bible School," which would take place during the summer school vacation. A contest was promoted by the church, whoever invited the most guests to the Vacation Bible School, would win an all expense-paid week at a special church camp. Roger busily invited many boys and girls, and won the contest. Our pickup or car was always full of kids, going to or from the base to the church.

At work when someone would transfer, I would often draw a cartoon of him or her, and we would all sign it as a "going away remembrance." Occasionally I would draw a pencil sketch at the request of someone. Carmen encouraged me to keep drawing, and she told me about a watercolor class that was convening in an art store located near the base. I enrolled in the class, bought a small water coloring set, and attended class once a week. I practiced on one particular painting, a still life of a wine bottle, pear, apple, wine glass, and knife. Carmen came up with the idea of putting the year of a couple's anniversary on the painted wine bottle label, as well as the name of a couple, and the place of their wedding. Thus, the "anniversary painting" was born. This painting hangs on innumerable walls about the world, as a gift given to many couples during my Navy career. I eventually gained a copyright on the painting. The first painting was given to my sister Linda, and brother-in-law. I enjoyed the watercolor painting class, but it quickly became apparent that the instructor wanted everyone in the class to paint in the same style she did. I developed my own painting style, and experimented with felt tip pens, and mural drawing. I painted a large, almost life-sized leopard (cheetah) with black spots, chasing a gazelle (African deer), on our dining room wall. I planned to paint over the mural when we moved.

On 8 July 1975 there was to be a change of command ceremony, at 10:00 a.m. The Oakland Naval Supply Center was getting a new commanding officer. All the sailors at NWSA were to wear dress blue uniforms in ranks during the ceremony. This was part of our military duties to participate in change of command ceremonies, but we were told that the current commanding officer, the one being relieved, wanted all sailors in ranks to wear white gloves. This was not an authorized uniform, white gloves with dress blue uniform. White gloves were optional uniform items that we weren't required to have in our sea bag. This meant we had to buy white gloves just to satisfy the "whim" of this officer. There was a lot of displeasure over this. I doubt that the admiral realized the unpleasant thoughts the men in ranks had about him during the ceremony! After the change of command ceremony, I took off my white gloves, and never wore them again with my service dress blue uniform.

As Waldo the cat aged, it became more and more apparent that he had an "attitude." He was very territorial, and would not permit any intrusion into our yard by any cat, or dog. I saw dogs much larger than he, run out of our yard with their tail between their lags! He had a very independent, aggressive personality. Waldo was more tolerant of Roger than anyone else in the family. We had three bedrooms in the upstairs portion of our house, but Roger wanted a small room in the basement as his room. Waldo usually slept in Roger's room. During warm weather he stayed outside overnight. Waldo's tomcat urges caused him to howl at night during the summer. Often someone in the family would have to holler at him late at night, and tell him to shut up!

One afternoon while I was at work, Carmen found Waldo in our yard badly hurt as the result of a fight he'd had the previous night. His stomach was torn open. Carmen took him to the veterinarian, and he underwent surgery. The doctor also neutered him, so he would be less combative in the future. He recovered quickly, but I always wondered if in fact he had been truly neutered, as he was still a very aggressive cat?

Carmen and I celebrated our first wedding anniversary. It was over a year since we'd had anything resembling a vacation, so I took two weeks leave; we borrowed mom and dad's pickup with camper, and drove to Edison Lake. This is a remote lake high in the Sierra Mountains, east of Fresno, California. The last section of the road to the lake was a narrow, winding, one-way road. We had been to the lake once before with my parents, and Uncle Dean and Aunt Lois. The lake and surrounding mountains were beautiful. Mom and Dad shared a few days with us. We caught some very nice trout. Carmen sunburned her hand badly, while patiently holding her fishing pole, waiting for a fish to bite.

On 13 September, I was awarded my fourth Good Conduct Medal. I received a certificate from the Oakland Supply Center Commanding Officer, and the occasion was acknowledged at morning quarters.

Since the signing of the peace treaty with North Vietnam, and the return of the Navy to a "peacetime attitude," it had become difficult to be promoted. Emphasis was being placed on after-hours education, social involvement, and activity in community affairs. Sailors being promoted were the ones heavily involved in education and social activities outside the Navy. This was not well accepted by my peers, who felt more emphasis should be placed on improving our job as nuclear weaponsmen, and becoming skilled in the "art" of conducting war, after all wasn't this our main purpose in life? We were not exempt from the problems American society was dealing with, racial relationships, and tainted leadership of our country, the Watergate scandal, and the elevation of education to solve life's difficulties. There were a lot of conversations amongst the first class concerning what we needed to do to look attractive to the Chief Petty Officer Selection Board, which met semiannually after each promotion examination. As the result of one of these conversations, another GMT1, Charlie Cushman and I agreed to enroll in a night school class, in an effort to "look more like promotion material" for the CPO selection board. We enrolled in an Oakland Merritt College night class called "Elements of Supervision." We attended evening class twice a week, for three months. The course teacher was a black man, and many of the students were younger than Charlie and me. After a few classes it was very apparent that our experiences as supervisors gave us a definite advantage over our classmates. During a class one evening, while discussing an imaginary supervision problem, Charlie and a black student who always wore militant type apparel, and always acted "angry at the world," got into a heated discussion. The discussion deteriorated into a shouting match between the student and the teacher. The black student accused the teacher of being an "Uncle Tom," playing favorites, and differing to the white students. He finally walked out, and never attended class again. After this, I always teased Charlie of starting a rebellion in our class. This was very far from the truth, as Charlie was a Christian, and very considerate of those around him. It was an enjoyable class, and I received an A plus for my final paper, and an A for the course. Charlie received an A as well, and I don't think it was because the teacher was "playing favorites!"

Nineteen seventy-five was a special year for the Navy. This year marked the 200th anniversary of the Navy! Carmen and I dressed up, I in my dress blue uniform, and she in a formal dress, and we attended a Navy ball on the anniversary date, 13 October. The Navy ball we attended was held on the island we were married on, Treasure Island. The celebration included a dinner and a dance with a band playing. A cake cutting ceremony was a highlight of the evening, with the youngest sailor present, an eighteen-year-old seaman, and the oldest sailor, a fifty-two-year-old admiral cutting the anniversary cake.

All the sailors at NWSA were given a special certificate following 13 October, which had the heading, "United States Navy 200th birthday building on a proud tradition 1775 - 1975", my certificate reads:

> To all who shall see these presents, know ye that on the occasion of the United States Navy's two hundredth year of service, commemorating the date in 1775 that the Continental Congress first ordered outfitting of a naval vessel, that James S. Little was on active duty and serving in support and defense of his country against all enemies at a significant moment in our nation's history, on board Naval Supply Center, Oakland, California. Certified by my hand this 13th day of October in the year of our Lord nineteen hundred and seventy-five.

The Chief of Naval Operations, Admiral J.L. Holloway, and Naval Supply Center Commanding Officer, Captain C.L. Culwell signed the certificate.

In July and August a large fenced storage area next to NWSA, which was a block in size, had been filled with large boxes and equipment that had originally been destined for Vietnam. These boxes and pieces of equipment had been on ships at sea steaming toward Vietnam, when the country had fallen to the communists. The ships had turned around in mid-ocean, and returned to the Oakland piers, and offloaded. With the coming of fall and winter, and rainfall, the items in the uncovered storage lot were being repositioned inside warehouses. A couple of sailors from NWSA had made friends with the civilian workers, who were working in the storage lot repositioning the material. These sailors asked our division officer if they could rummage through the material. Surprisingly, he said they could. For a number of days, forklifts would come into NWSA's building from the storage lot with pallets of material that was to eventually be loaded on semi-truck trailers for transportation to warehouses. Sailors converged on the pallets like ants on a sugar pile, sorting through the material for anything of value. I did not approve of this, and it was difficult for me to protest, as my superiors approved of what amounted to, thievery! As far as I know, Senior Chief Graybow and I, and a few others were the only ones that did not take anything from the endless chain of forklift loads. There were items such as ship's compasses, tents, field mess kits, bayonets, and many other things worth thousands of dollars that disappeared. There was a standard joke in the Navy about sailors that had "sticky fingers," or misappropriated government property. The comment was, "Don't ever holler "attention" in his house, or everything will stand up!" My conscience was clear on this point, as I tried my best not to misuse government property. On this same subject, I drew a cartoon of one of NWSA's most notorious "appropriators," who I'll not name. The cartoon shows him leaning against the wall smoking a cigarette, but his shadow is shown sneaking away with a bag full of tools, and government property. Everyone got a laugh out of it, but I think it embarrassed him?

One Friday a group of ten NWSA sailors took a day off and went deep-sea fishing out of Half Moon Bay, south of San Francisco. We stopped at a restaurant for breakfast before arriving at the boat. Most ordered mushroom omelets. Charlie Cushman got deathly seasick. As I said before, when a sailor gets sea sick, he can expect very little sympathy from his fellow shipmates! I did feel sorry for Charlie, but he turned some interesting shades of green. We caught a lot of fish, and had a division fish fry a couple of weeks later.

A week after the fishing trip, I typed up a phony certificate, called "El Facto Vomitus Mushromatic Chumley Award." The machine shop made up a wooden model, of the aft end of a fishing boat, with Charlie hanging over the rail. One morning at quarters, Charlie was called to the front of ranks. I read the certificate, and presented the wooden model to him. The letter was typed on official NWSA letterhead stationery, dated October 28, 1975 and read:

To: GMT1 Charles B. Cushman
From: Maintenance Head, NWSD Oakland
Subject: El Facto Vomitus Mushromatic Chumley Award, Presentation of:
1. Since the very beginning of the great United States Navy two hundred years ago, men that have gone down to sea in ships have always been in the position to throw themselves wholeheartedly, and with utter disregard for personal comfort into the act for which you have distinguished yourself. Good taste and prudence prevent this act from being accurately described. It is however called unofficially the act of "chumming."
2. Many brave and fearless sailors have preceded you throughout history in the performance of "chumming," however in the past it has been the expressed desire of these men not to seek public acknowledgment, and a wish to remain anonymous, combined with a desire to forget the accomplishment of "chumming." With the presentation of this award, the unheralded facts and obscurity that go hand in hand with "chumming," shall hopefully be abolished.
3. On 16 October 1975 at approximately 0800 hours, while onboard the S.S. Miss Princeton (hull number obscured), while serving in an unofficial capacity as a fisherman, and in the company of ten shipmates, and a various assortment of individuals from the civilian community. While exiting the breakwater area of Half Moon Bay, California, into slightly choppy seas, you were observed to rapidly change your complexion from ruddy pink to ghostly white, and then to a rarely seen tint of light green. Without hesitation and utter disregard for your surroundings, or thought about the effect your behavior might have on the traditions or heritage of the United States Navy, you assumed the position at the handrail necessary for "chumming." Your contributions to the volume of seawater present at the time are noteworthy. Your devotion to duty, continuing for almost seven hours, is probably a fact you hold as one of your fondest memories.

Your "head down attitude," and attempt to pay the Captain $2,000 to return to land is also noted in this letter of presentation. The consoling and comforting efforts and words of your shipmates did not hinder your consistent and continuing performance of "chumming." Upon return to land you demonstrated such joy, and performed such a rapid debarkation, that words cannot describe it.

4. This award is presented to you with the expressed desire that you do not duplicate the act of "chumming" again in the near future.

5. You can be assured that 16 October 1975 will not be forgotten, or lost in history. This letter will NOT be made a part of your official record. Written and presented with good cheer and a smile. Congratulations.

The letter was signed "Sincerely?, GMTCS James M. Barr." It should be explained that "chumming" is the act of throwing large amounts of bait into a body of water to attract fish. We all had a good laugh, and it was much more enjoyable, because Charlie was such a good sport.

The morale at NWSA the latter part of '75, and during 1976 was much improved. This was due to the transfer of sailors and the assignment of new men such as Charlie, and to a very large extent the assignment of an experienced leading chief, GMTCS James Barr. Also Chief Halterman was transferred to Adak, Alaska. I enjoyed working for Senior Chief Barr, and learned much from him.

In many organizations there's often one person that becomes a target for practical jokes, and unfortunately a person others ridicule, and not always harmlessly. At NWSA it was a civilian worker named Steve Darland. Steve acted somewhat feminine, was more than thirty years old, never married, and lived with his mother. He was teased and made the target of many pranks pulled by the rough masculine brotherhood of sailors at NWSA. Senior Chief Barr and I tried to discourage the practical jokes, with little success. Steve had difficulty relating to people, I believe he had led a sheltered life before going to work at NWSA. I think he also enjoy the attention, although much of it was negative. Just to mention a few pranks, someone would clip all of the paper clips in a bowl on his desk, into one long chain. Glue his coffee cup to the top of his desk, put red ink on his telephone phone ear receiver so he would smear red ink on his ear when he answered the phone. Marbles were put inside the hubcaps of his car, creating a rattling noise when he drove down the road; this was a prank that went on for many days with sailors offering phony car repair advice about what the noise could be. One prank that went "over the top," someone poured concrete into his desk drawer one night, and by the morning it was hard. I knew Steve for little over a year, and I saw him mature considerably. He was encouraged by some of us to join the Naval Reserves, and surprisingly he did join! I think part of his motivation was that he wanted badly to be accepted. After he joined the reserves, the practical jokes stopped, at that point the sailors wanted him to make good in the reserves, and he was given a lot of advice, and help about how to become a good sailor. The last I'd heard he had made Yeoman Third Class Petty Officer.

The previous couple of years I'd enjoyed gold panning as a part time hobby. I bought a few maps of an area called Grass Valley, near the American River, in the gold rush area of California. This area was famous for gold mining by the Forty-Niners in the 1800s. After the continental railroad was built across America, the Chinese laborers who built the railroad track were out of work. The Chinese scoured the gold country that had been mined by the Americans in the past. They searched with greater diligence, and thoroughness than the Forty-Niners, and found a considerable amount of gold. Searching my maps, I found an isolated area called Grizzly Flats that could be reached only by foot. At Grizzly Flats there was a stream I thought would be a good location for a gold panning trip.

In the fall, I had a three-day weekend off work, so Bill Ooten and I packed my pickup with camping supplies, and drove one hundred miles east to Grizzly Flats, which was east of Sacramento. The beginning of our camping trip was painful for Bill. A wasp flew into the pickup, and stung Bill on the arm.

After traveling a winding mountain road for many miles, we parked the pickup off the side of a dirt road, at the foot of the foot trail we were to take. I locked the pickup, and we put on backpacks, which contained sleeping bags, food, cooking utensils, and fishing poles. We walked through the woods for about an hour. We came to a clearing by the river; in the middle of the clearing was a fire pit someone had built with large rocks. We supposed that it had been built by cattlemen for use during roundups of cattle that roamed through the area. It was here that we set up our camp.

The next day we explored the area around our camp. I had brought my forty-five pistol, and Bill had a Ruger twenty-two pistol. We did some target shooting, and climbed a couple of hills. In the afternoon I caught a couple of small trout. They were small so I let them go.

I also did some gold panning, but did not find any gold flakes. The next day I planned to walk upstream and do some serious gold panning. We crawled into our sleeping bags early, so we could get up early in the morning.

In the morning after breakfast, we began walking along the stream. I would stop from time to time, and pan for gold. We had walked a long distance upstream, where we discovered an area where the stream flowed over solid rock, and had created over time a huge deep hollow in the rock streambed. The pool in this hollow, contained crystal clear water and I could see sand on the bottom. The water was about fifteen feet deep. I knew if any gold were in the stream there was a good chance there would be some at the bottom of this hollowed out rock. Gold would likely sink down through the sand, and come to rest on the rock bottom. I had a rope, which Bill tied around his waist so he wouldn't be washed down the stream. While I held the rope, Bill dove down to the bottom of the pool, and using my gold pan, he scooped out enough sand to reach the bedrock. He scooped up some of the sand on the bottom, and brought it to the surface, where I sifted it with my gold pan. I worked the sand until I had mostly what is called black sand, or the material at the very bottom of the pan. I did not see any gold, but I saved the black sand in a number of small glass bottles that I used for this purpose. I would examine the sand closer at a later time for any evidence of gold.

We walked back to our camp after walking and panning the river all day. This was our last night in the woods. We built a large campfire, and sat in the dark telling sea-stories. Bill was pouring hot coffee into my cup from a coffee pot we kept by the fire, when a noise in the darkness startled him, and he turned while still pouring the coffee. He poured hot coffee into my lap; I dropped my cup, and jumped up so fast that I jumped all the way over the campfire! It must have looked funny, because Bill laughed so loud and hard that I thought he was going to hurt himself! (Not that I minded at that point, the hot coffee burned terribly). I didn't let him pour me any more coffee, and the rest of the night passed without incident. The next morning we packed up our gear, and walked back to the pickup. At home I enjoyed a hot shower and a comfortable bed that night.

The next day was Monday, a workday. I took five bottles of black sand to work with me. At NWSA I put the glass bottles filled with sand on our large workbench. On the workbench we had a large magnifying glass. The magnifying glass was mounted on a flexible steel arm, and a neon light bulb encircled the glass. We used the magnifying glass to examine miniature electronic circuits. I planned to examine the black sand during a break. This was a busy Monday morning, and there were a number of things that kept me busy. I completely forgot about the bottles of sand. At our lunch hour, I ate the lunch Carmen had packed for me, and then remembering the sand, went to the work bench, and sprinkled some of the black sand on a white piece of paper, turned on the magnifying glass light, and slid the paper under the light. I immediately saw the glinting, glowing, color of gold throughout the small pile of black sand some pieces were very large. My heart was racing, and thoughts of striking it rich ran through my mind. I hollered for Bill Ooten, I was already thinking about how we could go back to Grizzly Flats and stake a claim. Then out of the corner of my eye, I saw a group of sailors giggling, and then laughing out loud. I "smelled a rat." A few of them, with Bill as the ring leader, had gone to our machine shop and gotten some very small brass filings, and during the morning while I was away from the work bench, they had sprinkled the filings into my bottles of black sand! That was the only time during my gold prospecting hobby; I thought I'd struck it rich.

Winter was around the corner, and during a visit to mom and dad in Strathmore, they loaded their pickup with firewood, and permitted us to drive the pickup back to Hamilton. We were very thankful for the firewood and used it all winter. While we were using the pickup, the transmission went out, confirming the natural law, if a person borrows something from another person, it will probably break while he has it!

A popular movie that year was *"Jaws[37],"* a movie about a huge man-eating white shark. Carmen and I went to the theater to see the movie. This movie did not make me anxious to go back to sea. My transfer time was rapidly approaching, and there was a strong chance that I would go back to sea, although my natural rotation should be overseas shore duty.

One fall weekend Carmen and I planned to go away for a weekend. Myra, the friend that lived across the street, watched the kids, and we drove to Lake Tahoe. We stayed in the same motel we'd stayed in after our wedding. Saturday evening we went to a casino called Harrah's Club, and Carmen played a slot machine. I tired of watching her, and told her I was going to the other side of the casino, where I had spotted a couple of the new poker machines. These were electronic machines that accepted one to five quarters, and then dealt five cards, with a draw option to improve the hand, and possibly win a jackpot. A hand with a pair of jacks or higher paid a jackpot, with higher hands paying increasingly larger jackpots. The highest jackpot was $1000 for a royal flush.

I played for about an hour, and was ahead by about forty dollars. There were not many customers, and one of the security guards started a conversation with me. He was a retired sailor, and we were enjoying talking about the Navy. A hand came up on the poker machine, which needed a ten of clubs to become a royal flush. I commented to the security guard, "wouldn't it be nice if a ten of clubs came up?" I punched the "draw" button, and a ten of clubs appeared! The jackpot bell ran, and the light on the machine flashed. A girl came over to where I was seated, and said, "You hit the jackpot!" Soon a man appeared, and as the machine was dispensing $100 in quarters, he counted out $900. I played a few more hands, and the security guard I had been talking to said, "Be careful when you leave here, there are people who watch to see who hits jackpots, and then they rob them in the parking lot." I told him thanks for the tip, I gathered my quarters, and cashed them in for bills. I then went to where Carmen was playing the slot machine, and watched her eyes widen in amazement when I showed her the handful of $100 bills. I explained to her what had happened. We then walked about the casino, insuring no one was following us, then walked quickly to our car, and returned to our motel.

The next day, we had about thirty dollars in quarters, so we decided to go back to Harrah's, and spend the quarters before we drove back home. In the daylight the parking lot was not as foreboding as it had been the night before. We went to the machine I had been playing the previous evening. I was about forty-five dollars in quarters ahead, when I decided to try one hand on the machine next to the one I was playing. A hand came up requiring a ten of clubs for a royal flush, just as it had last night on the machine I had been playing. I commented to Carmen, "Wouldn't it be something if I got a royal flush?" I pressed the draw button, and a ten of clubs appeared! This time however, the bell rang for a few seconds, and the jackpot light only flashed for a couple of times, then the machine went dark as though the power had been turned off? The machine poured out 400 quarters, and then was silent. I waited, and after a long while signaled a casino attendant. The attendant, a girl, came over to the machine I was seated at, and I told her I had hit the jackpot, but the machine shut off. She said, "OK, I'll get someone." Soon a man appeared, and said "Sir, the machine has already paid you." I pointed to the machine next to the one I was seated at, and said, "Last night I had the same hand, and was paid $1,000." He said, "Oh, I'll have to check on this." He then left. While he was gone, a group of people gathered around Carmen and me. An older man, moved close to me, and said, "If they want to open the machine, tell them you want an official of the Nevada Gaming Commission present." Soon the man returned, with another man who had on a very expensive suit. The man in the suit said, "Sir, we'd like to open the machine." I then said, just as though I knew what I was saying, "I'd like a member of the Nevada Gaming Commission present." This caused a flurry of whispered conversations among the casino officials. By this time there was a large crowd standing around us. Finally the well-dressed man said, "Sir, we are going to pay you your jackpot, then we'll need to open the machine." I was then given $900, and the machine was opened. After a lot of interior examination, they closed the machine up, and said they were putting the machine out of service. We immediately left Lake Tahoe. Carmen gave Myra a generous amount of money for watching the kids for us. We used our jackpot money to pay off our Pontiac.

Martha, along with Remedy and Wayne visited us a number of times at Hamilton Air Force Base. Martha had traded her Dodge Van for a Datsun 280Z. Remedy was doing very well in school, and we were proud of her. Wayne was still all boy, and struggling with school. He and Roger were often mischievous. An example was an incident while we lived at Tara Hill apartments. We had warned Roger about taking candy out of the kitchen cupboards without asking. One evening, Carmen and I were seated in the living room. Wayne and Remedy were staying overnight, and the kids had all gone to bed. We heard a loud commotion, and then Roger, pounding on the bathroom door hollering for Wayne to unlock to door and let him in! We went into the hall that led out of the bedroom, where Wayne and Roger had been sleeping. There was a trail of brown foul-smelling liquid leading to the bathroom door. We took Roger to the other bathroom. After the two had made their bathroom calls, and we began questioning them, we discovered that earlier in the evening, they had found some chocolate candy in the kitchen. They should have read the label, because it was chocolate covered ex-lax, a powerful laxative! They stayed up most of the night. For a long while afterwards, neither of them asked for any chocolate.

The Navy had an art collection, called "Navy Combat Art," that toured the country, and was shown at various locations. The collection was hung for display; with security guards watching over the paintings while the public viewed the pictures. NWSA was tasked with providing security guards, and Bill Ooten, and I got this assignment for a couple of days. We stood around in our dress blue uniforms, and greeted the public. Bill and I both received a letter of appreciation from Oakland Naval Supply Center, Commanding Officer. The letter was made part of our service records.

One thing I did while at Hamilton that did not necessarily contribute to marital harmony was an incident that occurred in late fall. Our neighbors the Shumpert's across the street, were close to retirement from the Air Force, and they planned to move to Sacramento. Myra had always talked about the delicious cheeseburgers she got at a special diner in Sacramento. She promised that she would bring Carmen one someday. One weekend I was home alone, while Carmen was at the commissary shopping, I looked into the refrigerator. I saw that someone had left a cheeseburger in the refrigerator. I made "short work" of the cheeseburger, and it was delicious! I was to find out upon Carmen's return, that the cheeseburger was given to Carmen by Myra, one she had always promised her, and Carmen had planned on sharing it with me later in the day. I never forgot the look of disbelief on Carmen's face when she realized the cheeseburger had been eaten by me! I don't think she has ever forgotten the incident, especially since Myra was not able to get her another cheeseburger before we transferred!

Carmen had been experiencing pain in her chest for a long while, and it was finally determined that she would have breast surgery in December. I still had no word on where I was to be stationed next?

The next evaluation report given to me covered most of 1975. The evaluation marks, and statements of performance were a leap upward from the two previous evaluation reports, mostly due to the administration experience of Senior Chief Barr.

Carmen was scheduled to undergo surgery on 9 December, at Letterman Hospital. Letterman was one of the largest military hospitals in the nation. The hospital was located at the "Presidio," near San Francisco Golden State Park. The hospital was one of the primary treatment centers for the wounded from the Vietnam War. Since the end of the war, there were many idle surgeons at the hospital. Carmen's breast surgery was to be severe, and the surgeon told Carmen that silicone breast implants would be used for reconstruction purposes.

On 8 December, I reached the age of thirty-three, and Carmen was admitted to the hospital on the same day. My mom came to visit, and also help watch the kids during Carmen's surgery. I took a week leave. Carmen remained in the hospital overnight on the 8th, and was scheduled for surgery at 8:00 a.m. the following morning. I went to the hospital at 7:00 a.m., went to her room, and she was not there? I was told she had been taken into surgery at 6:00 a.m. This was a shock. She had wanted to see me before going into surgery. It was a long wait; finally she was wheeled out of the operating room. She was pale, and looked drawn. In her room there were four other beds, all separated by curtains. Two other beds were occupied. Mom and I felt sorry for a young 16-year-old girl that was in one of the beds. She was about to undergo surgery that was one of a long series of surgeries she had undergone. A little over a year ago she had been accidentally shot in the stomach with a flare pistol! She had an amazingly cheerful outlook, and personality.

Carmen had a friend named Elshia, originally from Holland, who visited a number of times while she was in the hospital. One memorable thing about Letterman Hospital was the lack of parking space. I often had to circle the parking lot like a vulture, for an hour or more, waiting for someone to come out of the hospital, and leave, so I could take their place!

A couple of days after the surgery, mom and I were in Carmen's room at her bedside; she was not feeling well at all. She was pale, and breathing rapidly and suddenly passed out. We called for a nurse. When the nurse arrived in the room, she became very concerned, and immediately called for help. Many people rushed into the room, and mom and I were asked to leave. After an anxious twenty minutes we were allowed back into the room. We learned that Carmen had lost blood pressure, and the nurse had been unable to find a pulse. From this time on, they maintained a close watch on her. It was surmised that this episode was because of the large volume of blood she lost during surgery.

Finally Carmen was discharged from the hospital, after remaining for a week. Mom returned home, I was very grateful for her help during this time. Carmen still had a long recovery period. During the day while I was at work, and the kids were at school, our neighbor Myra kept watch over Carmen.

Christmas was right around the corner, and I had been busy making a few surprise gifts for the kids. One gift for Roger was a wooden battleship I was making at work during my lunch hour. While working on the battleship at work one day, at a band saw, the saw blade band broke, whipped around and struck my hand. My hand bleed heavily, and one of the sailors at work drove me to sickbay. Luckily the wedding band I wore on my left hand absorbed most of the force of the broken saw blade. Otherwise, I may have lost a finger! The corpsman at sickbay dressed the wound, and it healed quickly over the next few days. I finished the wooden model before Christmas, and named it "Roger the Great," that was what Roger liked to refer to himself as.

Before Christmas I drew another Christmas card, which we mailed to family and friends. Bill and June Ooten invited us to their house on Christmas Eve for oyster stew, which was a family tradition for them. Carmen and I were not crazy about oyster stew, but our two families had a wonderful time together.

Ray Gillip, Charlie Cushman, Bill Ooten and I studied together prior to the promotion exams for advancement to chief. The next exam was to be in February. Due to the classified nature of the GMT rating, much of our studying had to take place at work. Much of the information we were expected to know was in confidential and secret manuals. In order to read a classified manual, it had to be "checked out" of a safe by signing a check out/check in Log Book, noting the date and time. When the manual was returned to the safe, another individual had to confirm the return, and sign the check out/check in Log Book. Manuals were periodically page checked for any missing pages, and examined after any change was entered into the text of the manual. While the manual was checked out, it was expected that the sailors who checked it out, be responsible for the safe keeping of the manual, and that the contents not be revealed to anyone that did not have an appropriate security clearance, and a "need to know."

At NWSA we were not working with weapons we would normally be working with onboard ships, or at weapon storage sites ashore. Our primary mission at NWSA was the refurbishment of BDU's. There were very few, if any questions on our promotion exam about BDU's. The only way to keep abreast of our rating was to study the technical manuals. As well as completing the Merritt College course I mentioned, I also completed a Navy correspondence course entitled "Equal Opportunity in the Navy." These efforts were not only to increase my professional knowledge, but also to look "promotable" to the Chief Petty Officer Selection Board.

GMT1 Charlie Cushman had an unusual collateral assignment. He was assigned the duties of a Casualty Assistance Caller. If the death of an active duty sailor occurred within the local area of Oakland, he would go with an officer, usually a Chaplain, and call upon the next of kin of the deceased sailor. They would offer assistance on behalf of the Navy, with final arrangements, funerals, and so on. Charlie shared with us many tragic, sad stories. It was shocking to us how many drug related deaths in the Navy happened during this time frame.

After Christmas, I called my detailer in Washington, D.C. He told me where my next duty station would be. I'd asked for a carrier out of the Oakland/San Francisco area, or overseas in Hawaii, or Guam. I was secretly hoping I would not be going back to sea. As it turned out, I was not going back to sea. My next assignment was to be Naval Magazine, Guam. I was thankful for this news. This meant I was not to be separated from my family, as they would be going with me. This was to be a two-year assignment. I would attend a six weeks, advanced warhead maintenance school in San Diego, before reporting to Guam. I was also pleased with the school assignment, as this meant an additional fifty dollars a month salary increase following my graduation from school. This increase was called proficiency pay. I was permitted to ship one car to Guam. We decided to sell the pickup, and ship our Pontiac. I sold the Dodge pickup to a sailor for the same $400 I'd paid for it. I'd become attached to the pickup, and it was difficult seeing it being driven away.

Although we did not have a large amount of furniture, we were told it would be best to put the majority of our furniture into storage while we were in Guam. We would be able to use Navy-issued furniture while on Guam. I was to have thirty days leave before departing for Guam. Carmen and the kids were going to remain at Hamilton while I completed my six-week school in San Diego.

I began the checkout process from NWSA the second week in March. Charlie Cushman was to assume the duties of leading petty officer. Most of the first class petty officers had taken the promotion exam for chief the previous month, and for once I felt confident about my chances. My last evaluation report was very good, and I was sad to leave NWSA. While there I had become married, gained supervision experience, and enjoyed the relaxed pace of shore duty.

I had also enjoyed working with the civilian employees, especially the civilian director Norm Howell. Norm had been in this position for many years, and I learned much from him about the supply side of the nuclear weapons program. I had a high regard for his technical knowledge, and the many job decisions he made. Many sailors did not fully appreciate the importance of civilian employees, or as they were called "sand crabs," to the functioning of the Navy. Sailors were usually assigned to shore activities for three years at the most, officers for only two years. The civilians provided important "continuity" to shore stations. Civilians worked at the same base for twenty, thirty, or forty years, and could often accomplish things sailors could not, because of the civilian "network" that they had used for so many years. On many different bases, little civilian ladies, wearing tennis shoes, seated behind desks, were the ones that were very important "cogs" in the large scheme of the Navy nuclear weapons program, and the Navy.

I received a pleasant surprise just before my departure from NWSA. A few days before I was to leave, I was called up in front of the ranks and given a letter of appreciation from the commanding officer of the Naval Supply Center, which was made an official part of my service record. I checked out of NWSA feeling a sense of accomplishment, and with the knowledge that my efforts were appreciated. I bid everyone farewell, knowing that many would probably cross paths with me some time in the future. Senior Chief Barr promised he would keep in touch with me.

A few years previously the Navy had started a new program that was to help sailors adjust to a new duty station when they transferred. This program was called "The Sponsor Program." When transfer orders were issued to sailors, the prospective receiving command would assign a "sponsor sailor" who was the same rank, and married (if the incoming sailor was married), or single (if the incoming sailor was single). The sponsor sailor was expected to write a letter to the incoming sailor and tell him about his new duty station, what to expect for housing, schooling for children, what to expect as far as duty at the new command, and detail the surrounding community. The sponsor sailor was also expected to meet the sailor, and his family upon arrival at the new duty station, and help him with the initial settling in. Shortly after I received my orders for Guam, I received a letter from my sponsor. My sponsor was GMT1 Dick Clark. I had the advantage of knowing all about Guam from my previous assignment there. I doubted that Guam had changed much from my last visit, which had been on the *USS Oriskany* four years before. Carmen and the kids were anxious to know about Guam, I told them all I could remember about the island, and I showed them the books I had describing Guam.

I was issued an "Entry Approval Letter" from the Commanding Officer, Naval Magazine Guam. In this letter, it reconfirmed my sponsor's name, gave some information about the command, and approved the entry of my family onto the island. We had been anxious about receiving this letter, because it had only been a few weeks since Carmen's doctor had approved her health for travel. Before wives or children could accompany a sailor overseas, their medical condition had to be reviewed for any medical situation they might need care for. At some overseas bases medical care for dependents was limited. There was also a review process that looked at whether or not dependants had mental problems, legal problems, or a history of behavior that might embarrass the United States overseas. The entry approval letter also explained that there were restrictions on the shipping of certain household effects. I was limited to shipping a very small amount of furniture. I was permitted to place some furniture and personal property in storage in the United States while we were in Guam. The use of government furniture was available in Guam. The letter also explained a number of other things, such as a "Temporary Lodging Allowance," or "TLA," which I would be given to help defray the cost of hotel lodging while government family housing was being obtained. TLA was granted in ten-day increments. I would also be required to keep all meal receipts for reimbursement. The wait for government housing was seven to eleven months. I was surprised that the wait was so long! The cost for civilian housing for a three or four-bedroom houses was $175 to $400 a month, with utilities costing $50 to $150 a month.

I had an interview with the Oakland Supply Base Housing Office to schedule the household packing and shipping schedule. The plan was that I would attend my six-week school in San Diego, while Carmen and the kids remained at Hamilton. I'd return after school. We'd have our household effects packed, and shipped. We would check out of our Hamilton Base house, go on thirty days leave, and then fly to Guam.

The week I checked out of NWSA, I spent Saturday at home, and then Carmen packed my suitcase, drove me to the San Francisco airport, and I flew to San Diego. I took a taxi from the airport to North Island Naval Air Base, located on Coronado Island, where I'd been many times in the past. A large four-lane bridge had replaced the ferry that used to operate between Coronado Island and San Diego. I checked into Nuclear Weapons Training Group Pacific (NWTGPAC), which was a large brick building surrounded by a high security fence. The building was located a block from the main gate. I'd gone to school here while on the *Ticonderoga*, and *Oriskany*. The last time I had been in San Diego was in 1966 prior to going to Whidbey Island.

Each time a sailor officially checks into, or out of a command, his orders are stamped with the date and time of day, and signed by the Officer of the Deck (OOD), or Junior Officer of the Deck (JOOD). The NWTGP JOOD was a chief who directed me to a barracks about two blocks away, where I was to stay. He kept my orders, and service records. I checked into the barracks. The first and second class petty officers had rooms on the first floor of the three story barracks. I was shown the room I was assigned to. There were two bunks on each side of the room. Each room had large wooden lockers, and writing tables. I had a surprise when I walked into the room.

My new roommate was an old shipmate I had not seen for thirteen years! It was Monte May who had been on the *USS Independence* with me. He was now a second class, and had just recently come back into the Navy after being out for ten years. He had gotten out of the Navy after his time on the ship, moved to Washington State, managed a 7-eleven store, and then gotten a divorce. He had decided to come back into the Navy. He was permitted to reassume his old rate of second class. We had fun recalling the times we'd shared on the *USS Independence*.

In the morning, which was Monday, I had breakfast in the chow hall located next to the barracks. There was a special section in the chow hall where only first class sat for their meals. After breakfast I checked into NWTGPAC, and as was usually the case, it would be a few days before I could begin classes, as my security clearance had to be confirmed.

The GMT "A" school I had attended in 1961 in Albuquerque had been closed in the late 1960s. GMT's were now trained at NWTGPAC, San Diego and Nuclear Weapons Training Group Atlantic (NWTGLANT), in Norfolk, Virginia. The common appreciation of Albuquerque, New Mexico now only existed among older sailors such as me. The New Mexico "A" school had been thirteen weeks long, preceded by six weeks of electronic school at Great Lakes. This new GMT school was only a total of nine weeks long. What was also shocking to the older generation of GMT's was that Waves were being permitted to strike for GMT. The first female GMT had graduated from A school in the mid-70s. There were ten Waves attending A school during my class at NWTGPAC. There were hard feelings among many GMT's concerning the inclusion of women in the rating. GMT's rotated between sea duty and shore duty, and at this point in time, Waves were only assigned to shore duty stations. This meant they filled shore duty jobs, leaving fewer jobs for sailors coming off sea duty.

There were only eight students in the class I was attending. The class was an advanced warhead maintenance course, which would give us the job code and qualifications to go further into warhead mechanical and electrical areas to exchange limited life components. It was always an exciting time for GMT's to attend classes at NWTGPAC, or NWTGLANT, because the chance of running into old shipmates was very high.

A couple of days after I started my class, one morning while in the coffee locker on a break, in walked Ray Steele! He was my shipmate from the *USS Ticonderoga*, and we had not seen each other for almost ten years. It was great seeing Ray. He was now a chief, and assigned to the Inspection Branch of NWTGPAC, which was located in the upper area of the NWTGPAC building. After that day, we spent many evenings together catching up on what had been going on in our lives. Ray was in the midst of getting a divorce. He had been stationed on a few ships after his assignment at Lake Mead Base. We attended Sunday services together at the base chapel.

The town of San Diego had changed, it was still a "sailor town," but many of the old "haunts" had changed, or were gone. The old Hula-Hut, Ray and I used to frequent, and where Lloyd Wilson met his wife, was still there, but drastically changed.

One weekend, Carmen drove the long distance from Hamilton Air Force Base to San Diego, which was a distance of more than 600 miles, so we could spend the weekend together. A unique incident took place on her trip. On the way to San Diego, she stopped at a gas station in Los Angeles, and there was a friend we knew from Fremont that we'd not seen for a couple of years. We toured the San Diego Zoo, and took in the sights. I also introduced her to Ray.

The weekend prior to my graduation I flew from San Diego, back up to Hamilton, and then drove the Pontiac back down to San Diego. On 30 April, I graduated from the Advanced Warhead Maintenance Course, and checked out of NWTGPAC on thirty days leave.

I left San Diego in the afternoon, driving the Pontiac north on Interstate Highway Five. I was about 200 miles south of San Francisco, at 8:00 p.m., when the alternator light on the dashboard began flashing, indicating trouble. I pulled off the freeway into an isolated gas station. A mechanic happened to be on duty at the station, and after looking at the Pontiac; he said the alternator had burned up. While at the station, a guy with a sea bag walked up and began talking to me. He was a sailor hitch hiking to San Francisco. I told him I'd give him a ride, if I got the car running. The mechanic at the station said there was a town ten miles to the east of the freeway that had an auto parts store that would be open in the morning. The sailor hitchhiker and I drove the ten miles to the town, with the light flashing on the dash. We found a motel, and shared a room together. The sailor was a third class, and had only been in the Navy for two years, he asked me a lot of advice about Navy life. In the morning I found the parts store, bought an alternator, borrowed some tools from the store, and the sailor and I installed the new alternator. We were on the road and in San Francisco by noon. I dropped off my passenger in Oakland, he was very thankful for the ride, and I refused his offer to pay for the ride.

While I was in San Diego, Carmen had accidentally smashed a finger in the car door. She had been busy packing with a smashed bandaged finger. When a military family vacates a government house, the base housing office inspects the house for any damage, and also cleanliness. The service member must pay for any damage, and if appliances such as refrigerators, and stoves, are dirty they must be cleaned to an acceptable level before the final inspection form document is signed. Also the floors all had to be waxed and polished, and all lights had to be working. Until this document is signed off by base housing, the member does not get his monthly Basic Allowance for Quarters pay restarted, which in our case this meant $105 a month.

I filled in our garden plot in the back yard, and seeded it with grass seed. I got the paint color of the interior walls from the housing office, and bought a gallon of paint so I could paint over the cheetah, and gazelle I had painted on our dining room wall.

We were all very busy the next couple of days. The packers came in and packed all of our belongings into cardboard boxes. The following day the movers arrived and moved all of our furniture that would be going to Guam into a large truck. This effort took two days. The kids stayed overnight with the Shumperts' and Ootens'. Carmen and I borrowed sleeping bags from the Ootens and slept in the bare house. We cleaned for two days. I painted over the mural in the dining room, and then began working elsewhere in the house. An hour later I happened to walk through the dining room, and there on the wall was the mural as bright as ever! I had used felt tip markers to paint the mural, and it had apparently bled through the paint I'd used to cover it up! I repainted the wall, and this time it took as little longer for the cheetah and gazelle to reappear. I painted the wall four times, each time delaying the "bleed through" a little longer. Our housing inspection was the next day, so I decided to wait and paint the wall again just before the inspection.

The kids were half-heartedly helping clean around the house. Peter was goofing off, and avoiding work. After warning him many times, I gave him a spanking. We all continued working around the house, and a couple of hours later, we discovered Peter was missing? Finally Roger said that Peter had told him that he didn't want to go to Guam, and he was going to live with his father. This was a very traumatic situation for us. It appeared that Peter's father had been encouraging Peter to come and live with him for a long while.

The next morning, the day of our inspection, a young girl from the housing office arrived at our front door. This girl was notorious as having the personality of a snob, treating enlisted families as inferior, while deferring to officer families, and giving them lax inspections compared to the strict inspections she gave to enlisted families. She was not friendly at all as she looked about the house. In the bathroom she peered about, using a white glove to rub over surfaces looking for a speck of dirt. I had the impression she was anxious to find some fault. The house was much cleaner than when we moved in, as Carmen was always an immaculate housekeeper. I held my breath as we walked through the dining room; the mural remained hidden by the sixth coat of paint I had put on that morning. In the kitchen, with her white glove, she began rubbing and probing on the surface of the stove. Inside the oven she got a light smudge on her white glove. She said the stove was not clean, and began to say we'd failed the inspection. This was the wrong thing for her to say. Carmen immediately began reading her the "riot act," saying the stove was spotless, and she could clean it herself. (The stove was indeed spotless). Carmen told her she was irresponsible and foolish. The inspector left in a hurry, in a "huff," and I think a little frightened. This was a bad time for Carmen, dealing with an immature person, right after being upset by Peter's childish departure. I called the housing office and told them we would like to be inspected by a different person. They agreed to send an inspector the following day.

The next day, the different inspector agreed that the house was spotless. I once again held my breath in the dining room. I had just put a seventh coat of paint on the wall just to be safe. We passed our inspection with no problems. I've often wondered if the next family that moved into 240 San Jose Drive, one day sat in the dining room, and suddenly there appeared on the wall a cheetah chasing a gazelle!

Bill and June Ooten offered to let us stay at their house while we tried to resolve what to do about Peter. I talked to Peter's father, as did Carmen, and she talked to Peter, trying to confirm that he really wanted to remain in the United States. In retrospect, perhaps we should have forced him to come with us, as we had the legal right to, but his father probably would have hidden him until we were forced to leave for Guam. Had Peter gone with us, he would have had a much better future than he was to have with his father.

After a couple of days, we left Hamilton Air Force Base. While on leave, we returned for a visit to Lake Edison in the Sierra Mountains. We enjoyed being with our family knowing that we would be in Guam, away from them, and our homeland for a number of years.

Chapter 11: Guam is Good (again)

Waldo the cat was very happy in the country. He adjusted quickly to being a country cat on my parent's ranch. Being smart, Waldo became very attached to my father. My parents agreed to keep Waldo while we were in Guam. There were many firearm restrictions on Guam, so I gave my father the forty-five-caliber pistol I'd gotten in Oakland.

We were to leave Travis Air Force Base on 17 May, bound for Guam. My parents followed us in their car while we drove the Pontiac to Oakland, where we left it to be shipped to Guam. I did not know it at the time, but the "Raider" Pontiac would not be returning to the United States. We then drove to Travis Air Force Base. Mom and Dad treated all of us to dinner at McDonald's before going to the base airport terminal. Mary, thinking she would not have an opportunity to go to MacDonald's for a couple of years, overate and ended up getting very sick on the plane.

In the previous couple of months we had all gotten the necessary inoculations we had to have before entering Guam. These were recorded in our shot record books, and they were all checked, as well as our luggage, for loading on the plane. Our plane was to take off at 9:15 p.m., so at 9:00 we bid our parents farewell, and boarded the plane. Mom and Dad gave us farewell cards, and said we were not to open them until we were on the plane. After we settled into our seats on the plane, we opened the cards, and discovered there was money they had placed inside the cards! While we lived at Hamilton, on one occasion while visiting our parents, mom had fixed us sandwiches for the car drive back north to Hamilton at the end of the weekend. On the drive home, we stopped at a rest stop to eat the sandwiches. Upon biting into the sandwiches, we discovered she had wrapped money bills in cellophane and placed them in the middle of the sandwiches! I've always been thankful for the wonderful, loving parents I've been blessed with, who have supported and encouraged me throughout my service to our country.

The plane ride was long and tedious. We landed in Hawaii for a couple of hours, but could not leave the terminal. We soon re-boarded the plane and resumed our flight toward Guam. Mary was ill most of the trip, and Roger kept busy exploring the plane, including the cockpit, when the pilot let him in the cockpit area. After fourteen hours on 19 May, at 5:00 a.m., we were near the island. The stewardess spoke over the plane's intercom, and said we were about to land. As I watched out the window, the lush green jungle of Guam appeared. Upon landing, I saw through the window, the sign on the terminal that is known throughout the world, "GUAM IS GOOD." After the plane stopped moving, shortly the plane door was opened, and an Air Force man came in, and spoke over the intercom. He said, "Guam is currently in typhoon condition II, and this is the last airplane to land until this typhoon condition is lifted. We need to get you all cleared through customs as quickly as possible." We claimed our luggage inside the customs clearance area in the terminal. All the passengers lined up waiting for the customs inspector to look through our suitcases and bags. Roger's suitcase was first. The customs inspector had it on the table, opened and was rummaging through Roger's clothes and underwear, when he gasped, withdrew his hands from the suitcase, and jumped back! He was a brown Guamanian, but he turned white. There lying in the bottom of Roger's suitcase was a very large brown snake! I recognized it immediately as a toy rubber snake of Roger's. After we assured the inspector it was a rubber toy Roger had placed, unknown to us into his suitcase, he quickly closed Roger's suitcase. He motioned the rest of us through without looking at any more of our luggage.

As soon as we had stepped out of the plane, I felt the heat, and humidity of Guam, and smelled the musty, damp, unique odor of Guam. I remembered that it took a while to get used to the heat, and high humidity of the island. Outside the customs inspection area, a man walked up, and introduced himself as Dick Clark. We loaded our luggage, and got into his car, which was parked near the terminal. It was an older model, four door Chevrolet. Dick drove us to the Naval Magazine, which was a thirty-minute drive to the south. He said there was a typhoon named "Pamela," that was headed toward Guam.

After going through the Naval Magazine main gate, which was guarded by a marine, we went to the quarterdeck so I could check in. When I walked into the quarterdeck, I had a surprise. There behind the quarterdeck desk was GMG1 Ritchie, who had been at the magazine in 1969-1970. He had come back just as I had. I handed in my records, and Ritchie said I couldn't do much right now as most people were home preparing for the arrival of the typhoon. The island was in Typhoon Condition II, which meant the typhoon was expected to hit the island in twenty-four hours. A typhoon is described as having surface winds of 75-150 miles per hour. A super typhoon is one having winds in excess of 150 mph.

Typhoon conditions are described as; Typhoon Condition IV: a typhoon could hit the island in seventy-two hours (Guam is always in this typhoon condition), Typhoon Condition III: a typhoon could hit the island in forty-eight hours, Typhoon Condition II: a typhoon was expected in twenty-four hours, and Typhoon Condition I: a typhoon was expected in twelve hours, only emergency vehicles were permitted on roads, and all gates to military bases remained closed.

Dick drove all of us from the magazine to his house at the naval base. All over the base we saw people busily nailing plywood boards over windows, and doorways. The weather was calm and quiet without a hint of the approaching typhoon. We met Dick's wife Donna, and his three children, a boy and girl, who were twins, and an older daughter. The base house they lived in was a single story, three-bedroom concrete blockhouse, typical of the enlisted base houses on the naval station. At noon the wind began to pick up to around thirty miles per hour.

Dick drove us all to a nearby Guam village called Agat, where we checked into the Jahame Motel. We were in a small upstairs three-bedroom apartment, complete with a small kitchen. I had been given a check in sheet at the magazine, so while Carmen and the kids settled into the motel apartment, Dick drove me to a couple of places that I was to check in, although most places were closed because of the approaching typhoon.

I was back at the hotel after a couple of hours. I was tired after the long plane ride. We listened to the radio in the motel room, listening to the news of the approaching storm. My previous tour on Guam, I had experienced a number of typhoon alerts, but nothing serious. The last major typhoon to strike Guam, and cause death and destruction had been Typhoon Karen fourteen years before, in November 1962. The power flickered on and off, and it rained off and on throughout the afternoon and evening. Carmen and the kids were anxious, and all of us spent a restless night. This was not a good way to start a new life at a new duty station. Early in the morning the telephone rang. It was the GMG1 Ritchie at the magazine quarterdeck. He said the island was now in Typhoon Condition I, and we had to evacuate from the motel to a typhoon resistant building. It appeared that Typhoon Pamela was going to hit the island in the afternoon. We were told to go to Dick Clark's base house during the storm. Shortly after the phone call, we had repacked our suitcases, and Dick arrived in his car to drive us back to his house. When we arrived at Dick's house, Carmen and the kids settled in, and I helped Dick board up windows around the house. The wind was gradually increasing in intensity. There were nine of us in the house, including Clark's family dog, a small male collie. The date was 20 May 1976.

Anything lying loose outside was blown about by the wind. At noon the wind was blowing close to 100 miles per hour. The noise of the wind, and the rain beating against the house created so much noise, that we had to shout at each other to be heard. We kept busy trying to stop the water that was being blown into the house through any small crack the windblown water could enter. We used all the towels in the house, and for a while had a "bucket brigade" soaking up water flowing in under doors, and window seams. We would wring water soaked towels into buckets, and then the full buckets were dumped down the bathtub drain.

This busy time was a blessing and a distraction, which kept us from dwelling on our fear over the noise and fury of the storm. The adults kept assuring the children that we were going to be all right. Carmen and I were pleased that Donna was a Christian, and we all said many prayers out loud, and silently. We listened closely to a battery-powered radio, which periodically broadcast damage reports, and the typhoon's progress. The radio reported that the wind speed was approaching 200 miles per hour. The electricity throughout the island had gone off in the early morning hours, and remained off.

Suddenly at 5:00 p.m., the wind stopped, it quit raining, and the sun shone brightly. It became oddly quiet. The eye of Typhoon Pamela was passing over Guam. We all went outside into the front yard. Palm tree branches, loose pieces of wood, and power poles, were scattered everywhere. The streets were filled with fallen trees and debris. We saw two sea gulls flying about, caught in the eye of the typhoon. People were in their yards looking about in amazement at the destruction. Dick and I busily re-nailed many of the plywood boards over the windows, and plugged up the cracks and holes where water had entered the house. It was an eerie experience to have such peaceful weather, immediately after such powerful, and horrific forces had struck just a few minutes before. After about an hour and a half, the wind and rain began again. This time the wind was blowing from the opposite direction it had previously. The other "side" of the typhoon was striking the island. This time we did not have the flooding of the previous five hours, as the wind and water were hitting the side of the house that did not have doors, or cracks which water could flow through.

With the increasing fury of the wind, night began to fall. We only had candles, and flashlights for lighting, and the noise from the wind seemed much louder in the darkness. We all huddled in our beds. The noise grew so loud that it sounded like a huge freight train going directly over the house on the roof.

The concrete house walls shuddered from the force of the wind. Many prayers were said that night, asking that we survive. In the early morning hours, the winds gradually subsided; Typhoon Pamela had passed over Guam.

Saturday morning, 21 May, after a sleepless night, we all walked out on Dick's front yard into bright sun light. With wide-open eyes we gaped at the debris lying all around—palm trees uprooted, with power lines, and power poles lying about. We could hear the surf pounding the nearby shore, stirred up as the result of the departed typhoon.

Electricity had gone out the previous day, and the radio reported that it would probably be weeks before power could be restored. Acting upon the advice given over the radio, we filled every container in the house with fresh water. Dick and I worked at removing the plywood sheets that had been nailed over his house windows. That evening we played games by candlelight. We began to appreciate how much we relied on electricity now that it was gone.

Sunday evening, the weather was very calm, and the stars at night were specially bright and visible in the dark sky. Carmen and Roger were in the back yard looking up at the bright stars, when they saw an amazing sight. Three bright points of light moved from different areas of the sky to one central point, they appeared to move in a circular orbit, and then just as rapidly sped off to different areas in the sky and disappeared. The movement of the lights was very rapid, and some of the lights flight paths ninety-degree turns, and movement speed were unbelievable. There could be no explanation for these moving points of light and to this day remains a mystery?

An Associated Press News article written on 23 May, three days after Typhoon Pamela hit Guam, told of the damage of the storm[38].

> President Ford Saturday declared Guam a major disaster area in the wake of typhoon Pamela that killed at least three persons and wrecked at least eighty per cent of the buildings on the American Island Territory in the Pacific. The Presidential declaration, which would permit use of federal funds in relief and recovery efforts in a typhoon ravaged areas of the 210-square mile island, came in response to an appeal from Gov. Ricardo J. Bordallo.
>
> Federal Disaster Assistance Administration in Washington said its regional officials were meeting with the Joint Military Commanders of the Pacific in Hawaii to determine how best to provide disaster assistance to Guam, an island of approximately 90,000 population. All shipping in the Pacific area was being diverted to assist Guam, officials said.
>
> There were three known dead, including a two-month-old baby, officials said. They said eight vessels sunk in the Guam Harbor, one containing over 100,000 gallons of fuel oil, which is leaking, and about 1,000 military families were homeless.
>
> The Guam Governor's appeal to Washington came after he declared a state of emergency in the island and said damage from the typhoon would be well over $100 million. The authorities said the tropical storm wrecked more than eighty per cent of the buildings on the South Pacific Island, at least half of them beyond repair. Bordallo said he had not yet made an assessment of the damage but said from preliminary inspection the damage would amount to as much as that caused by Typhoon Karen, which hit the island in November 1962.
>
> Guam, where giant B52 bombers took off after targets in Vietnam during the heat of the war, was rebuilt following Karen with $150 million federal rehabilitation funds. The full force of the typhoon, which on its path struck Truk, in the Western Caroline Islands 600 miles southeast of here, and killing at least ten persons, lashed the 210 square mile Guam Island between noon Friday and 4:00 a.m. Saturday. At the height of her fury, Pamela hit the island with gusts up to 190 miles per hour.

On Monday we got word that one road was clear enough for us to drive to the Naval Magazine. Dick and I changed into dungarees and drove in his Toyota pickup to the magazine. It was an eight-mile drive. The destruction caused by the storm was very apparent. Most striking was the lack of vegetation on the hills, and the jungle that had been there a day or two before was now gone. In the days following the typhoon, people found caves that had been dug during World War II by the Japanese Army that had been hidden and never discovered, because of the dense jungle foliage that was now gone. Dick and I were also shocked to see a huge Navy tug that had been picked up from the harbor by the typhoon, and deposited astride the road just outside the main gate of the naval station, a distance of about 200 yards.

We were to learn later that there were two large tankers that had been pushed high upon the reef just off a beach on the naval station called Gab Gab Beach. These tankers remained aground, and stuck on the reef for all the time I was on Guam. The road was littered with debris, but we were able to get through.

At the Naval Magazine, Dick dropped me off at the quarterdeck, and he drove away headed for the Limited Area. As always I would be waiting for confirmation of my security clearance before I could go to work in my rating in the Limited Area. I was told at the quarterdeck that the mess hall had been flooded and the carpet and the tile on the mess hall deck (floor) were ruined and buckling. The mess hall could not be used until the floor could be fixed, so this effort had first priority. Everyone available was to help with this job. I went to the mess hall, and a chief there introduced himself as GMTC Margeson. There was a group of chiefs, and first and second class petty officers standing around watching a number of sailors stripping the soggy carpet up, and ripping the loose tiles up. I could see that the job was going to take a long time. There were a lot of petty officers standing around doing nothing. I organized a couple of second class into the job of moving the chairs and tables in the mess hall outside. I then got a metal bar, and began ripping the tiles up with the seaman that were working. It was hard, dirty work, and the other first class petty officers that had been standing around, all left rather than help as I was. The seamen were very appreciative of my help. They were amazed that a first class would get down on his hands and knees with them and help get the job done. I ruined the pants and shoes I had on, but this was the right thing to do. I also gained a good initial reputation, and gave a favorable "first impression" at my new duty station. One of the first things I was told by my new division officer, and the chiefs I would be working for, when I met them, was that they were impressed to hear how I jumped in and helped clean up the flooded mess deck so it could be used, instead of standing around avoiding work.

Carmen and I knew that our parents would be concerned about our safety. The Red Cross had phone lines set up for families to use. Carmen called mom and dad and told them we were OK.

I learned that Joe Murphy, who had been here at the Naval Magazine in 1969-1970, was stationed here again. He was the one I'd had the "chicken fight" adventure with six years before. Joe was now a first class. Steve Kitson, who I'd been on the *Oriskany* with, was also here, and he was also now a first class. I also learned that Billy Gilbert, who had been a seaman on the *Ticonderoga* with me, was stationed here. The shocking news was that he was now a chief! This was depressing news, it seemed as though everyone was passing me by, promotion-wise. I learned that I was the senior first class at the magazine (I'd been a first class for ten years), and I would once again have the additional duties of leading petty officer once I went to work in the Limited Area.

Zeus, the Guamanian who cleaned the barracks was still here, and he remembered me. He was the one promised a lifetime job because of his underground work during the Japanese occupation of Guam. He was becoming senile, and limited in what he could do, so he only worked a couple of days a week.

The Acey-Duecy Club that had been here in my 1970 tour, where George the water buffalo had waited nearby to ambush unsuspecting sailors, had been completely destroyed by Typhoon Pamela. The club was reduced to a pile of broken wood and roof shingles. A few of the Naval Magazine buildings had been damaged, but none as severely as the leveled Acey Duecy Club.

I had a surprise a couple of days after the typhoon. While on the quarterdeck, I saw a chief warrant officer, and it was Stan Stanwick, the Mineman First Class I'd been stationed with on Iceland, fourteen years before. He was still unmarried, and had just been commissioned a chief warrant officer a year before. He had been at the Naval Magazine for a year and a half, and worked in a section of the magazine called, Mobile Mine Assembly Group Eight. He was scheduled to transfer in a couple of months. We had a great time catching up on what had been happening in our lives.

Carmen the kids and I stayed with Dick and Donna Clark for a little over a week. The motel we had been staying in had taken a beating in the storm, and was not ready to have customers. We didn't have electricity, and we took showers in the back yard with a garden hose. It was much like camping for a week. A big challenge was keeping the ice chests containing food that we shared, supplied with ice. Ice was in short supply, and Dick and I made a number of trips in his pickup to the capital city of Agana for ice. We all got along well, but it was crowded in the small base house with nine people. After a week we were relieved when we finally moved back into our motel room. It was a very happy occasion when the electricity was finally restored.

The Red Cross had set up a number of disaster aid stations around the island. We heard a lot of stories about people exaggerating their losses in the typhoon, and taking advantage of the Red Cross. The Navy exchange warehouse had been damaged in the typhoon, and much of the merchandise inside had gotten wet.

One weekend the exchange had a huge sale, so Carmen and I stood in line for a couple of hours, and got a great deal on a freezer, and a few knick knacks, that we would pick up from the store once we got into base housing.

After I'd completed my check in sheet with the help of Dick Clark, I was assigned to the personnel office. I did nothing but sit around all day with another GMT1 who was also waiting for his security clearance confirmation. This first class had a bad experience. He and his family had arrived on Guam a week before we had. One afternoon he had walked from the hotel he and his family was staying at, to the corner grocery store to do some shopping. While walking back to the hotel carrying two grocery bags, a car with two Guamanian men had stopped by him, they got out, punched him, breaking his nose. They then took the groceries, and his wallet, and sped away. It was boring sitting in the personnel office. I passed the time drawing cartoons, which the five people who worked in the personnel office appreciated.

My previous assignment at Naval Magazine in 1969 and 1970, I'd had a difficult commanding officer. Things had not changed. My new commanding officer, Commander Gerrard was legendary for the temper tantrums he threw, and the insulting names he called officers and enlisted men in his command, names that would have made Captain Blue Beard blush!

Carmen and the kids and I were trying to adjust to the heat and humidity of Guam. Each morning the crowing of roosters behind the hotel awakened us. Since we did not have transportation, Dick Clark acting as our sponsor would pick me up in the mornings for a ride to the base, and he would drive me to the hotel in the afternoons. The base housing office said it would not be long before we were offered a house to live in.

On the main highway to the city of Agana, on one side of the road there was a large fenced compound that contained many barracks. At one time this had been a Japanese prisoner of war camp. Dick and some of the other sailors, who had been stationed on Guam when Vietnam fell, told stories about this now deserted camp. The refugees, who had fled from Vietnam, when the communist overran the South, fled the country by boat, plane, or whatever means they could find. The Vietnam refugees had been housed inside these old barracks, until further arrangements were made for them to travel on to the United States. Many of the refugees had escaped with suitcases of gold. They often would gather at the fence, as they were not permitted to leave the compound, and offer gold to the Guamanians and sailors standing outside the fence, for cigarettes, tooth paste, and other necessities. A lot of gold was dumped onto Guam's economy during this time. As a result of this there were many gold traders in business on Guam.

After a couple of weeks the base housing office called, and said they had a house for me to look at. Dick drove Carmen and me to the house so we could look at it. The house was not in good shape. There was water on the floor, broken doors, and generally the house was dirty. This was a bad moment for Carmen, and she began to cry. I assured her the house would be repaired, and cleaned before we would move in. The house was a three bedroom, one bath, small house of about 1,200 square feet. It was a single story made of concrete blocks. The house was not air conditioned, so we were faced with either buying air conditioners, or the discomfort of living in the heat and high humidity. We eventually bought three window air conditioners. The house was not nearly as nice as the one we had on Hamilton Air Force Base. It was a very "basic house," with tiled floors, a refrigerator and stove. We were provided a wooden frame couch, a cushioned chair, and a kitchen table with six chairs. I understood Carmen's tears that flowed down her cheeks when we looked at what was to be our house. This house did not compare to the house we had at Hamilton. We'd had our lives threatened by a super typhoon. The heat and humidity of the climate we were trying to adjust to were unbearable. She also was trying to accept the shock of Peter running away from home. Carmen did enjoy some of the things in Guam that were common with her homeland of Puerto Rico. One day she was excited about finding a mango tree, such as the ones in Puerto Rico.

Carmen and I were invited to Chief Gilbert's going away party. He was being transferred, and the party was taking place at his house. I was thankful to hear that he was transferring, so I would not be working for him. It had been a huge blow to my ego to hear that he was now a chief. I had trained and supervised him on the *USS Ticonderoga*. At the time he had been immature, difficult to supervise, and had been constantly in some sort of trouble. The thought that I was almost placed in a position to be supervised by him was difficult to swallow. My failure to make chief was becoming a major distraction in my life. I was beginning to feel that I was a failure in the Navy! It was humiliating to fail to be promoted each February and November.

After a few days, the housing office notified me that the house we had looked at had been cleaned up, and repaired. I went a second time to the house, and walked around making a lengthy list of any faults, so when it came time for us to move we would not be blamed for pre-existing damage.

I gave the housing office a copy of my list. Our new address was 25 Pacifico, North Tipalo, Naval Station, Guam. Our new house was ten miles from the Naval Magazine.

Our household effects, which had been packed at Hamilton Air Force Base, were delivered to our new house. Unpacking everything, and arranging our stuff, took Carmen a few weeks. One big job I had after work at the magazine was assembling our waterbed, which took a couple of evenings work. Mom sent some curtains in the mail, and Carmen got some curtains from a next-door neighbor who was moving. This was something military wives had to contend with, at each move, the house windows always had differing widths and lengths, usually requiring new curtains.

We were finally notified that our Pontiac had arrived. It had been shipped to Guam by ship. I picked it up at a fenced compound, near a pier in Agana. I had to arrange for insurance before driving the car. The Pontiac was running well, but it was apparent that some of the interior door paneling had been taken apart, probably as part of a customs inspection? I was not pleased that the paneling was not reinstalled well. I had to tighten many loose screws.

All motor vehicles on Guam had to undergo a safety inspection every two years. Guamanian Police in the capital city of Agana conducted this inspection. We had been told that women had a better chance passing the inspection than men, as the Guam Police Inspectors were famous for flirting with women drivers, and ignoring the finer technicalities of the inspection process. Not to boast, but Carmen is a beautiful woman, therefore she drove the Pontiac to the inspection garage, and the Pontiac easily passed the safety inspection. The inspection cost five dollars, and a decal was issued which had to be displayed on the front windshield. There was a lot of "red tape," to register and license a vehicle on Guam. Carmen was required to obtain a Guam driver's license, by passing a lengthy written test. My California driver's license was legal to use.

While waiting for my security clearance confirmation, I attended driving school, and was given a government driver's license allowing me to drive government vehicles up to five tons. I also attended forklift school, which was very easy, and a "snap," as this was the same school I'd gone through on my previous tour on Guam.

One weekend I decided to wax the Pontiac, as I'd already noticed a few rust spots on the body. Fighting rust on vehicles in the humid, salt air of Guam was a constant battle. American cars built with American steel seemed to resist rust, much better than the Japanese built vehicles, which would rust away in a very short time. On this weekend I donned a tank top, the type with a small strap over each shoulder, and waxed the entire Pontiac under the afternoon sun. The waxing effort took about four hours. That night I noticed that my shoulders and neck were burning from the exposure to the sun. This turned out to be the worse sunburn of my life. Eventually hundreds of blisters, ranging in size from pin points, to silver dollars arose on my neck and shoulders. It was agony to wear a shirt after the blisters burst leaving raw flesh. It was very painful sitting in the personnel office during the day. I could hardly wait to get home each day so I could take off my shirt, which rubbed against the raw wounds. As odd as it may seem, I could not go to sickbay, or complain about my sunburn. If a sailor got sunburn that was severe enough to keep him from duty, he could be placed on report for "damaging government property," his body being "government property." I gritted my teeth and bore the pain for a week. The sunburn was so bad that to this day I have on my shoulders the faint outline of the tank top I wore that day.

The 4th of July 1976 was special as it was the 200th anniversary of America's Independence. Guam had a huge fireworks display, which we enjoyed. Finally the first part of July, after waiting a month and a half, my security clearance was confirmed, my picture was taken for my security badge, and after being given the badge, Chief Margeson escorted me to the Limited Area. The limited area and the plant building had not changed from my 1969-1970 tour. I met my new Division Officer Lieutenant Hume, and the Leading Chief, Senior Chief Smith. The ORT Division had forty sailors assigned, and the number of first class was almost unbelievable! There were sixteen first class petty officers, of which I was the senior one. The Army shared the building and their comparable "GMT's" worked on Army weapons.

There was an additional building in the Limited Area that had not been there on my previous tour. This was a Torpedo Shop that was manned by seven Torpedomen. These sailors were assigned to ORT Division. The Torpedo Shop had been under construction for over a year. The building contained a huge air conditioner. The torpedoes that would eventually be worked on within the building following its completion could only be disassembled in a low humidity environment. TM1 Richard Burton supervised the Torpedomen.

The outside handling crew of GMT's, whose job it was to maintain the grounds, and the magazines, and also deliver items to the plant for maintenance operations, were supervised by GMT1 Denny Richards, and eventually GMT1 Jack Osilka.

As leading petty officer I was responsible for conducting morning quarters along with the chiefs, and the division officer. I had to fill out a daily muster report, and I was also responsible for the military conduct of the thirty-five plus sailors. There were a few women in the division, and this would be my first experience supervising women in the Navy.

Researching the division's instructions and directives, I discovered there were many missing, and I worked at updating them. I wrote GMTCS Jim Barr, at NWSA Oakland asking him for copies of evaluation guidance I knew he had. He promptly replied, as I knew he would. He gave me news of what was going on at NWSA. Bill Ooten had transferred to the east coast, Chris Van Diven had received orders to Guam, and the good, but somewhat depressing news was that my friend Charlie Cushman was being promoted to chief. An Electrician had taken over my old job as NWSA leading petty officer. Senior Chief Barr said the Electrician didn't have experience leading people, but he was learning.

Shortly after I reported to work in the limited area, it was discovered that there were three previously undiscovered caves within the eighty acres of the fenced and guarded limited area. The entrances of the caves had been covered with thick brush and vegetation, and the passing typhoon had uncovered the openings. The discovery of these caves caused a serious concern that the caves might extend under the fence, which meant a person or group who might want to get into the limited area would be able to dig down and enter the caves, and travel under the fence, to get into our secure area. The caves needed to be explored quickly. Dick Clark, Denny Richards, Richard Burton, Chris Reed, Steve Cline, and I were assigned as the cave exploration team. We donned old clothes, and carried flashlights. We tied a rope around our waists, in groups of three, leaving twelve feet of rope between each person. The first cave we entered only went in a very short distance, but we discovered that it became very dark just a few feet from the entrance of the caves. There was no evidence of anyone ever being in the first cave. The second cave was a little deeper, and at the end of the cave there were a few pieces of wood that at one time may have been wooden ammunition boxes. We could not tell whether they may have been American, or Japanese ammunition boxes? The cave did not go a horizontal distance far enough to go underneath and beyond the fence.

The third and last cave proved to be the most interesting cave, in more ways than one. At the entrance of this cave the opening quickly narrowed down to a sloping slot of about three feet in height. We had to inch our way through this slot on our stomachs. This was not a place for a person who might be concerned about running into a snake, or suffering from claustrophobia. After scooting along for about forty feet, the cave opened up into a large room, complete with stalactites hanging down from the cave ceiling. We discovered a series of rooms connected by a single tunnel large enough to walk through standing erect. There was no evidence of human presence. We continued walking, until we reached the end of the cave, which we estimated went about 200 yards beyond the security fence in the earth above us. The cave ended in a large room, and here deep within the bowels of the earth, we all directed our flashlights up on one large rock wall and all gasped in amazement. Someone had burned on the wall with a torch, large letters and numbers, a date, *25 August 1951*. The date we stood there was 25 August 1976. Someone had burned the date on the cave wall exactly twenty-five years before on this same day. After seeing this we all were anxious to get out of the cave, as this was a coincidence a little too eerie for us. The cave was eventually surveyed and blocked so the limited area could not be entered through the cave. Since that day in August, I've not had an urge, or desire to go cave exploring.

In an effort to dress up the drab white walls of our base house, I began painting murals throughout the house. I painted a cheetah, as I had on the Hamilton Base house wall. I painted a cave man, and cave woman, a deer, polar bears, a warrior on a horse, and an alligator in the bathroom. I also painted a very large mural that covered one entire wall in the living room. The mural was of astronauts landing on the moon, along with the lunar landing craft, and a moon rover vehicle (see photograph page).

As I've said, the first question a GMT would ask when reporting aboard a new duty station was "When is the next NTPI Inspection?" The next inspection for Guam was to be January 1977. The island continued to recover from the destruction caused by typhoon Pamela. There were a couple of typhoon alerts in August and September, but in both cases, the typhoons veered away from Guam.

In October we received a letter from Remedy, Martha's daughter. She missed us, and it sounded like she was doing OK in school. My brother Jerry was having a problem in high school.

He and a couple of classmates had set off a small explosive in a locker as a prank, but it had created a larger "bang" than they expected, and blown out a couple of school windows. The school officials were blowing this harmless prank way out of proportion, and my parents were considering sending him to Guam to live with us, as a way to escape the unreasonable actions of the local authorities in Strathmore. We would have welcomed Jerry, but as it developed things finally cooled down at home.

The kids were adjusting well to life on Guam. Roger joined the Boy Scouts. He and I also joined a taekwondo class, which is a Korean form of karate. A first class I worked with named Bill Cannon also took the class with us. The class would meet on Tuesday and Thursday afternoons. A small Korean named Mr. Kim taught us. Our instructor reeked of kim-chee, which is fermented cabbage popular in Korea. Kim-chee has a powerful smell, and Mr. Kim's breath was overwhelming. The students dreaded receiving instructions from him at close range. We had to wear a loose-fitting cotton jacket and pant uniform called a "gee" for our taekwondo classes. A cotton belt was tied around our waist. The color of the belt denoted ones rank, or level of ability. The beginners wore white belts. We learned and practiced the basics of kicking and striking with the fist and feet. The majority of striking movements in Taekwondo were executed with the legs; they were kicking motions that used the thigh muscles. After much stretching and practice I was able to kick above my head. Roger soon lost interest in the class, but Bill and I continued on. Bill was a Mormon. I often wondered how Bill endured wearing the underwear that Mormonism required, under his uniform in the heat of Guam. Bill wore a beard, as did most of the GMT's in ORT Division. I preferred to discourage the wearing of beards, but this was difficult since our Division Officer Lieutenant Hume wore a beard

In order to advance in the art of taekwondo, or be promoted to new belt level, students had to demonstrate a specific set of movements, or "kata." Bill and I were able to demonstrate the kata's and kicks required to advance to yellow belts at the end of three months. After a couple of weeks, a new class began, and Bill and I enrolled. At the end of this class period of three months, the class had a meet with a class group from Agana. This meeting was a full contact match, with each fighter being matched with a person of equal size and ability. I was matched with a younger person, and unfortunately lost, as did Bill. Although we lost, since we had fought, we were advanced to green belts. This was the end of my taekwondo career, as other interests took up my time following my loss at the match. I did gain an appreciation for those disciplined enough to study the martial arts of Judo, Aikido, Taekwondo, and Karate. To this day I am registered with the Korean Taekwondo Association as a green belt.

Dick Clark transferred a few months after our arrival in Guam. His family wanted to keep the family dog, a collie, but did not want to take him with them at the time of their departure from Guam. They asked us to keep him until they got settled at their new duty station at which time we would ship him to them. The keeping of the dog did not turn out to be a pleasant task. The collie had a habit of barking to be let out so he could relieve himself each morning at 3:00 a.m. One day while he was alone in the house he destroyed Carmen's new living room curtains. We were not sad the day we shipped him to the Clarks', on a plane destined for the United States.

We had two television stations, a local TV station which broadcast from Agana, and an Armed Forces Television Station which broadcast from 4:00 p.m. to 12:00 midnight each day. All the programs on the armed forces network were actually broadcast a few days before, and had been taped in the United States for later viewing in Guam. Carmen enjoyed watching the annual Miss America beauty contest, and other beauty pageants. I played a little trick on her prior to the broadcasting of each contest. Since all of the contests took place a few days prior to viewing them, I would scan the newspapers to see who won, and would make sure that Carmen didn't see the articles. When we would watch the programs together, at the very first of the program I would proclaim who would be the winner. Carmen was always amazed that I could consistently pick the winning contestant out of fifty or more girls. I did not admit this deception until after we had left Guam.

At the Naval Magazine, as was the case at all Navy bases, all sailors were assigned to a duty section, and stood twenty-four hour duty at specific intervals. As a first class I stood six section duty. Every sixth day and night, I remained at the Naval Magazine. I was one of six of the most senior first class petty officers on the magazine that were assigned the duties of section leader. On duty days I also stood a watch on the Naval Magazine Quarterdeck. This watch was called "Petty Officer of the Watch." As section leader, I had a number of additional military duties that did not fall upon the shoulders of other petty officers. I prepared watch bills that assigned four-hour watches to individual sailors in my duty section.

These watches were Petty Officer of the Watch, which I mentioned, Messenger of the Watch, who stood his watch on the quarterdeck with the Petty Officer of the Watch, Barracks Master-at-Arms watch, and the Barracks Fire Watch. Also on duty days there were two GMT's who stood a roving, and sleeping watch, which I'll explain later.

One of my duties as section leader was attending "Eight o'clock Reports." This formal meeting and report are held daily at all naval commands, and onboard all Navy ships. The reports are used as a method of ensuring that the command is secure for the next twelve hours, a time when most of the sailors are asleep. At 8:00 O'clock Reports, each division, or department was represented by the senior petty officer or officer on board at the time. Each person formally reports to the command duty officer, who represents the commanding officer. Reports are given on any information relevant to the security or administration of the command. Eight o'clock Reports were held on the quarterdeck with reporting sailors standing at attention in ranks before the command duty officer. These reports are a tradition passed down from ships routine. The reports were held at 1900 (7:00 p.m.), so it was a misnomer to call them 8:00 o'clock reports. As section leader I also was required to attend the nightly showing of the movie, which began at 2000 (8:00 p.m.). I was to maintain order, and oversee clean up of the movie theater at the conclusion of the movie. I got very little sleep on duty nights, as I also had to close the base enlisted club at midnight on weekdays, and at 1:00 a.m. on weekends. I accompanied the Officer of the Deck, who was a Naval Magazine chief petty officer, during these "closing duties." We didn't actually close the club, but had to be present at the closing to ensure there were no discipline problems, such as fights, or rowdy behavior. The duty Marine Sergeant accompanied us. The naval magazine had more than 200 marines assigned, who provided security for the magazine, by patrolling the magazine perimeter, and protecting the limited area where the GMT's worked.

On duty nights I slept in the duty bunkroom that was located in the old Naval Magazine Bachelor Officer's Quarters (BOQ). This was a long building that contained twelve individuals' rooms, and was no longer used by officers as living quarters. In mornings following a duty night, I had to awaken early enough to check the quarterdeck area, and the captain and executive officer's offices to make sure they were clean and squared away. There were hundreds of details associated with the job of section leader. One of the more important jobs was insuring that the quarterdeck petty officer of the watch was stood in a professional, military manner. The four-hour watch began at 1600 (4:00 p.m.) on workdays, and on weekends, and holidays for a twenty-four-hour period. GMG1 Ritchie stood the watch during workdays, from 0800 to 1600. The most disliked watch was the midnight to 0400 (4:00 a.m.) watch, called the "mid-watch." When I prepared the watch bill, assigning sailors to specific watches, I did so without preference to individuals, and included myself. I stood a four-hour watch, which many section leaders refused to do.

The petty officer of the watch was stood behind a large desk, behind a counter that had a view of the main entrance doors to the administration building. Inside the main doors a long hallway to the left, led to the captain and executive officer's offices, the hallway to the right led to the personnel office, and post office.

The messenger of the watch had a desk positioned behind the petty officer of the watch. There were a number of telephones on the quarterdeck desk, which were direct connections to various commands on the island. There were also a radio transmitter and receiver that were used to communicate with the marine security guards, commanding officer, command duty officer, assistant command duty officer, and duty GMT's. We used call signs, and radio code while using the radio system. We used strict radio procedures, and this was a subject of constant training. Before a sailor could stand a four-hour petty officer of the watch, he or she had to stand a number of training, or break in watches. If a petty officer of the watch made a mistake, I was the one taken to task over it, and expected to correct the problem, whatever it was.

One sailor in my duty section, named GMG2 Abad, a Filipino sailor always complained about standing the mid-watch, even though everyone took their turn, and I took pains to ensure everyone was treated fairly, and equally. He complained that he wanted to transfer to another duty section. After he'd been in my section for six months, I finally approved his transfer, as there were a lot of sailors who wanted to get into my section. Shortly after he transferred to another section, he wanted back, but there was no one in my section that wanted to trade with him. He eventually apologized for his complaints, and said I ran the best section on the "Mag," and wished he could get back into my section. As a side note, Abad completed a successful career in the Navy, eventually receiving a commission as a chief warrant officer.

The sailors in my duty section were conventional ordnance men, construction men, personnel men, and yeomen, as well as GMTs. By assigning myself to watch, and helping carry the load, I gained loyalty from the sailors in my section.

My section gained a good reputation, and handled a few after work emergencies very well, which I'll detail later. After a duty day I was often exhausted, but usually had to put in a full workday in ORT Division after my duty day.

Military members of services other than the Navy or Marines are always amazed at the extra work and hour's people in the Navy and Marines spend on "duty days." As I've said before the tradition of duty days is grounded in the determination of the Navy to never again suffer defeat like that experienced at Pearl Harbor. Navy ships, following the Japanese attack disaster at Hawaii, always kept enough of the crew aboard by way of duty sections, to get the ship underway, and fight in a moment's notice. The effort to keep ships battle worthy carried over to shore stations, so sailors in the United States Navy will probably always have a "duty section."

Carmen usually came to the magazine on my duty days, and we would eat supper together in the chow hall. We paid seventy-five cents each for this meal. She often would watch the evening movie with me, as I was required to watch it, and help maintain order during the movie. If the movie were rated "G," the kids would come to the movie theater with us. As I described previously the movie theater was actually just rows of wooden benches, with a roof overhead to keep the rain of our heads. Since there were no walls, and we were exposed to the tropical night, we had to have a liberal supply of mosquito repellant.

Foremost in the minds of all the GMTs was the upcoming NTPI. We kept busy running training operations, practicing what we would be demonstrating to the inspectors during the weeklong inspection.

At the Naval Air Station located near Agana, which was about fifteen miles north of the magazine there was an Advanced Underwater Weapons (AUW) Shop, such as the one I'd been stationed at in Iceland, and Whidbey Island. The AUW Shops in the U.S. and around the world were being shut down. A couple of GMT's who had been assigned to the Guam AUW Shop, were reassigned to the Naval Magazine, they were GMTC Bud Wilkins, and GMT1 Sotile. The AUW Shop itself would be deserted, and unmanned, but the building was preserved for possible future use. With the closing of the AUW Shop, the GMTs at Naval Magazine were tasked with preparing a "deployment box." This box was to contain all the necessary tools and equipment that might be needed in case the AUW Shop had to be reactivated, and manned during a future period of increased readiness, or war. This was an area we were scheduled to be inspected in during our upcoming NTPI. Chief Margeson was in charge of constructing the large wooden deployment boxes, and gathering the proper tools, and equipment.

As I mentioned our commanding officer, Commander Gerrard led by intimidation and fear, and was not highly respected by the sailors in his command. One day Commander Gerrard was visiting the production plant, looking at the deployment boxes that were being prepared. He was talking with Chief Margeson when he lost his temper, as he often did. It made no difference that there was a large group of sailors standing nearby in listening range. He shouted at Chief Margeson, "You're as f***** up as a soup sandwich!" After a long stream of profanity, he walked out of the room. We all suspected that he was drunk, as was often the case. From that day on Chief Margeson's nickname was "Soup."

One workday in October, GMG1 Ritchie, the sailor whose permanent job was as the petty officer of the watch on the quarterdeck during normal working hours, had the afternoon off. This meant my duty section, which had duty that day, was to start standing the petty officer of the watch earlier than the normal time of 1600. I left ORT Division early, and went to the quarterdeck to assume the watch, so Ritchie could go on liberty.

I had been sitting behind the quarterdeck desk for about an hour, the time was 1400 (2:00 p.m.), and all was quiet. Suddenly the main double doors, in front of my desk, and counter, flew open, in rushed a young sailor, who I recognized as a mineman that worked in the mine shop. He was wide-eyed, pale, and blood covered the front of his shirt, and both hands. He was screaming, "My division officer has been shot, my division officer has been shot!"

My first concern was that he was hurt. I asked him, "Have you been hurt?" he shakily replied, "No, my division officer has been shot." He frantically pointed toward the front of the building. I looked through the glass doors, and saw at the end of the long covered walkway, at the front of the building where there was a driveway that circled by the building, was a gray Navy pickup, with the passenger, and driver's doors open. At the end of the walkway was a sailor in dungarees lying on the ground. I told the panicky sailor to go down the hall to the personnel office, and get help attending to the sailor lying outside. He ran down the hall, and I immediately called the naval station and asked for an ambulance. I then called the commanding officer's office, which was at the opposite end of the hall. When Commander Gerrard answered, I said "Captain this is GMT1 Little on the quarterdeck, we have an emergency on the quarterdeck."

During my calls the bloody sailor, who had rushed in, ran outside with a personnel man from the personnel office. Both sailors had hands full of paper towels. Commander Gerrard arrived at my desk, and I explained what had just happened, he then rushed outside to where the sailor was lying. As soon as he went outside, I called the main gate that was guarded by marines, and told them to expect an ambulance, and to hold all outgoing and incoming traffic until further notice. The captain rushed back in, and asked me if an ambulance had been called. I told him, I had called for one, and also explained what I had told the marines at the main gate. He replied "Good." There was pandemonium for a while, with people rushing outside to where the sailor was lying on the ground. I called the Naval Magazine sickbay, where we had a corpsman assigned. The sickbay was in the BOQ, which was only a block away from the quarterdeck. The ambulance I had called for would be arriving from the naval station dispensary, which was about twelve miles away. Our corpsman usually wasn't in the BOQ in the afternoons, but luckily today he answered the phone! His name was HM1 Brown, and I told him we needed him at the quarterdeck right away as a sailor had been shot. Right after my call to HM1 Brown, the naval station dispensary called and said the ambulance had not left for the magazine yet. I told them we needed them right now without delay. The captain said the sailor had a bullet hole in the lower back, was bleeding heavily, and was having trouble breathing. HM1 Brown arrived where the wounded sailor was lying, but there wasn't much he could do other than control the bleeding. We still didn't know the circumstances of the shooting? The captain asked me to call the security officer, and the marine's commanding officer. I placed these calls, and told them their presence was required at the quarterdeck. I then recalled the dispensary, and the dispensary said the ambulance was on its way.

The ambulance finally arrived, and the wounded sailor was loaded into the back, and the ambulance sped off to the naval hospital. In the meantime, the security officer and I were questioning the young seaman that had rushed into the quarterdeck covered with blood. He was very shook up, and almost in shock. The story we got from him was that he and his boss, a First Class Mineman, had been driving in the pickup on one of the many gravel roads that went through the jungle on the Naval Magazine property. It was their lunch hour, and they were sightseeing. The first class was the driver, and the seaman was a passenger. The seaman said they heard three gunshots behind the pickup, and then the first class slumped over in the seat. The seaman managed to hit the brake pedal and bring the pickup to a stop. He didn't see anyone behind them, so he crawled over the first class and got behind the steering wheel. He did not know how to drive, but he managed to get the pickup, in first gear, and drove almost eight miles to the quarterdeck, where he rushed in screaming at me.

The marines deployed immediately to the shooting area, after getting a location from the seaman. The captain also directed the marines to patrol the perimeter of the magazine property, because at this point it was not known if the magazine was under attack or not? There were three bullet holes in the back of the pickup cab, in a vertical line, with one bullet entering the cab in the area where the first class was struck. It looked like the shooter was purposely trying to hit the driver.

I was the main communication point over the radio with the deployed marines, and I passed information back and forth between them and the captain. The marines at the scene found three empty shell casings, and found a trail leading away from the shooting scene. They also discovered what appeared to be a campsite. The trail ended at the perimeter of the magazine property near the town of Santa Rita. I also notified the Guam Police Department of the shooting. My messenger of the watch, a seaman, and the security officer, a lieutenant, was helping me with the phone calls, and radio calls. The security officer, who had a well-deserved reputation as a jerk, was more of a hindrance than help.

I had to keep a running written commentary, by recording all events, as they happened in the quarterdeck watch log. I had to be very correct, and precise in my comments, as a Navy log is considered a legal document, that is relied upon as a true record of events.

The intensity of the shooting, and the happenings around it did not calm down until six hours later, around 2000 (8:00 p.m.). I remained on watch, until things were calm. I was exhausted by the time I turned the watch over to a relieving petty officer. After this night, Commander Gerrard always went out of his way to acknowledge me, talk to me, or just say "Hello." He thanked me for the job I had done, and said he appreciated me remaining cool, and calm when things had gotten tense. He referred specifically to the Personnel Officer (a Wave Lieutenant), who got hysterical, and started crying when she came to the quarterdeck, and saw the wounded sailor. The captain had ordered her off the quarterdeck.

The next day it was learned that the wounded sailor was in critical condition, and might be paralyzed if he survived. Rumors were flying about the magazine, about what had really happened?

Guam was a popular illegal drug distribution point for drugs coming out of the Far East headed for the United States. A common illegal drug was marihuana, arranged on a wooden stick, and then dipped into a cocaine mixture. These were called Thai sticks, as most originated in Thailand. There was a lot of speculation about whether this shooting had been a drug deal that had gotten violent?

As I mentioned previously, the Naval Magazine was a game preserve, where hunting was prohibited. After the shooting, the marines began patrolling more aggressively, and "joy riding," by anyone off duty was not permitted for a number of months. One of my duties as section leader was a tour of the magazine area, with many of the checkpoints deep within the jungle. After the shooting, I was much more alert during my drives through the jungle. The marines patrolling often saw Guamanian poachers, and sometimes exchanged shots with them. There were a number of firefights between marines, and trespassers on the magazine. Fortunately there were no reports of injuries after these confrontations.

Following a six-month investigation of the shooting, three Guamanians from Santa Rita were arrested and charged with the shooting. They had apparently shot at the pickup for no apparent reason. They had been hunting illegally on magazine property. In Guam criminal court, they received very light punishment, over the Navy's objections. One man was given a six-month prison term, while his two partners were given probation. The wounded sailor was given a medical discharge, and the last word received at the magazine was that he would be confined to a wheel chair for the rest of his life. The quick action of the seaman, who didn't know how to drive, was credited with saving his life. The Personnelman, who rushed outside to give the wounded man aid, was also acknowledged as helping save his life.

On 20 November, my cousin David Sylvester, his wife Carolyn, and two children Michael and James arrived on Guam. David was a Second Class Hospital Corpsman, and was an x-ray technician. He was assigned to the naval station dispensary. David and I, a cousin Howard Worley, and an Uncle, Richard Durbin was the only ones in my parent's generation, and my generation to serve in the Navy. We four were unique in that aspect.

Carmen and Mary were part of a Tahitian dance group, and the group would give exhibitions at various places about the island. One afternoon they were driving to an exhibition, when Carmen, hit a slick spot in the road, and the car slid off the road and struck a stop sign. The roads were made of coral, and extremely slick when wet. Our insurance paid for the small dent in the car, and the road sign.

December was the month of my thirty-fourth birthday. In December the magazine also had a captain's personnel inspection. These were frequent inspections, where we would stand in ranks at attention, in dress whites, in front of the outside quarterdeck area, while the captain walked through the ranks inspecting us. Commander Gerrard had completed his walk through the ranks, and returned to the front of the assembled command. I was shocked when my name was called out "GMT1 Little, front and center." I stepped out of ranks, not knowing what to expect, marched to the podium behind which the captain stood. I saluted him, he returned my salute, and then he began reading a letter. "From Chief of Information, to Commanding Officer, Naval Magazine, Mariana Islands. Subject, All Navy Cartoon Contest, The Chief of Information takes pleasure in forwarding with congratulations enclosure (1), and (2) awarded to GMT1 James S. Little, USN. It is requested that an appropriate presentation of this award be made." The captain then read enclosure (1), which was a letter, and said' "Dear Petty Officer Little; Congratulations. Your cartoon submitted to the 1976 All-Navy Cartoon Contest has been awarded honorable mention. Your wit and artistic ability will add to the quality of All Hands Magazine and will give our readers an opportunity to laugh. The ability to recognize and enjoy humorous situations in our profession often is an important ingredient of good leadership. Again, thank you for your participation and congratulations on your selection as a winner in the 1976 All-Navy Cartoon Contest." Rear Admiral David M. Cooney signed the letter.

Enclosure (2) was a certificate called "Half Hitch Award," and said, "Half Hitch Award is presented to GMT1 James S. Little, Honorable mention. In recognition of outstanding artistic talent and humor created for the 1976 All Navy Cartoon Contest." Hank Ketchum, the cartoonist, and creator of *Dennis the Menace*, and *Half Hitch* signed the certificate.

This was a nice surprise. I had submitted three cartoons for this contest, while at NWSA. I'd completely forgotten about my submissions. "All Hands" was a monthly magazine that was distributed Navy-wide and always had one page devoted to cartoons with a Navy theme. Unfortunately this was to be the last year the magazine published cartoons, and I never learned which cartoon I submitted won, or if it was ever published?

Our commanding officer, as I said was well known for his unreasonable rages, and loss of temper. During these times, his eyes would bulge, his face would become vivid red, and the profanity that spewed from his mouth was unbelievable!

One duty day while I was standing watch on the quarterdeck while Ritchie went to lunch, the captain was in a rage, in his office, chewing out the security officer for something he neglected to do. The captain's shouting could be heard throughout the large administration building. The captain called me into his office, and said he wanted me to hear what a jerk, and many other profane names, the security officer was. I stood in his office listening as he dressed the lieutenant down. I thought this was very inappropriate for a commanding officer to discipline an officer in front of an enlisted man. As I said his officers and men did not revere him, but feared Commander Gerrard because of his irrational behavior. Unfortunately the executive officer, the second in command at the Naval Magazine, was in the same category. He was a LCDR who was an odd, quirky character, disliked by most of the crew. He often displayed his odd behavior during the conducting of captain's mast. This was a formal court of discipline conducted by commanding officers when an enlisted man or officer was charged with a violation of the Uniform Code of Military Justice (UCMJ). This was called "being placed on report." The accused would stand before the captain in his or her dress uniform, and accompanied by his division officer, division chief, and often I as the leading petty officer, would be standing with the accused. The magazine master at arms, and any witnesses associated with the case would also be present. The captain would be facing all of us as he listened to the facts and statements, and judged the accused sailor. He stood behind a large podium in his office, with the executive officer standing behind him. The "XO" was unseen by the captain, but all standing before the captain could see the executive officer standing to the rear of the captain. He would often make faces, and gestures throughout the proceedings, unknown to the captain, but seen by the accused and everyone else. The faces and gestures were made primarily when the sailor on trial was talking, trying to justify, or defend him or herself. The executive officer would roll his eyes, or draw his finger across his neck, as if he were cutting it with a knife. He would also act like he was choking, being hung with a rope, or pretend to muffle a laugh. This unprofessional behavior was very unnerving, especially to the sailor that was being judged. I saw the executive officer do this many times, and I felt it was improper and inappropriate behavior during a formal discipline trial.

   The few months before a nuclear capable unit has an inspection, the training efforts escalate, and the hours of work increase. As the inspection date draws closer, tempers are often shortened because of the pressures of preparing to be scrutinized under a microscope. I held the view that it was unrealistic to announce a specific inspection date, many months ahead of time, which everyone anxiously prepared for, and then after the inspection relaxed for the twelve or eighteen months until the next inspection. I thought that all inspections should be unannounced, or surprise inspections, in order to truly evaluate whether a command was capable of maintaining nuclear weapons in a safe and reliable manner. A certain number of inspections each year were surprise inspections, but usually only ten percent, or less of the total commands inspected.

   In the production plant there were three Hooks (teams), of GMT's that were responsible for specific systems. Each hook had to demonstrate all the maintenance operations we were capable of doing. One safety violation or numerous minor deficiencies would result in a failing grade. This would mean a re-inspection within a month, loss of the commands nuclear capability, and often a "shake-up in the chain of command, relief of the commanding officer, and many others beneath him.

   To describe all the details and items that had to be ready for scrutiny would take volumes, and volumes of books. But this is as it should be, for with nuclear weapons, mistakes could not be tolerated. The constant pressure, and stress to be perfect, required a special breed of sailors. We felt we were the guardians of the most precious, and peculiar treasure of our country. We were a misunderstood group, often called "prima donnas," "glorified Gunner's Mate's," "glow in the dark twidgits," and many other unmentionable names. I always took pride in the fact that few men could tolerate the pressures, and insistence of perfection that we lived with daily, and few understood. In a manner of speaking, the power and might of the United States had materialized in the form of nuclear weapons, and we special individuals in a distinctive brotherhood had been entrusted with their care. These weapons of mass destruction were capable of destroying all life on our planet. We were a special unique "Brotherhood of Doom."

   I was becoming more involved with the paperwork aspect of the nuclear weapons program, versus the wrench and screwdriver work, as I moved up the seniority ladder. As the assistant plant supervisor, and leading petty officer, I was tasked with preparing the schedule of events for the upcoming inspection, as well as numerous other pieces of paperwork associated with the NTPI. I'd noticed over the years that each command had a different attitude, or approach to a scheduled inspection, and to the inspectors who conducted the inspections. Some commands rolled out the red carpet, while others treated the inspectors with indifference, sometimes bordering on hostility.

Some held the idea that catering to the inspectors was undignified, or making any special arrangements for them was an act of "brown nosing." I felt the red carpet treatment was appropriate. Anything that would give us an edge, I did it. I prepared "welcome aboard" packets for each inspector, and worked hard to ensure that the living quarters they would be staying in were a "step above" what they expected. I had new coffee cups, with each inspector's name on them, and many other small things that would make them feel welcome, and "important." While the "bottom line" was that we had to demonstrate our technical knowledge, expertise, and ability, treating the inspectors respectfully, and even royally, might save us from having a minor deficiency written on the formal report. Instead the deficiency might be overlooked, or we might be told about it "under the table."

In December, the Navy Exchange displayed a large shipment of Christmas trees from the States. Families quickly grabbed the trees up, including the Little family.

One day in December, shortly after I'd sat down with the Leading Chief, Senior Chief Smith, and Lieutenant Hume to review my evaluation report, Senior Chief Smith asked if I'd ever written to the Naval Personnel Command in Washington, D.C., and asked to be given a copy of my service record? I said, "No, it had never occurred to me that I needed to?" He said the copy of my service record in Washington, D.C. was the one that was reviewed by the Chief Petty Officer Selection Board, when they met to deliberate who to select for promotion to chief, after the semiannual promotion tests were given. Senior Chief Smith, said he was baffled why I had not yet made chief? He said it was possible that someone else's information may have gotten misfiled into my record, or my service record could be missing information. That same day, I sent a request through the Magazine Personnel Officer, asking that a request be sent to Washington for a microfiche copy of my service record that was held in the Naval Personnel Command, Washington, D.C.

We were expected to demonstrate all of our capabilities during our NTPI. One requirement was that we were capable of destroying all weapons that might be present by carrying out an emergency destruction plan before they fell into enemy hands, or control. This destruction effort involved the entire Naval Magazine GMT's, all the marines, and most of the sailors assigned to the Naval Magazine. It was required that we hold an emergency destruction drill once every three months. This was a surprise drill that was usually held at 1:00 a.m., or 2:00 a.m. in the hours of darkness. This required a telephone recall of all sailors, including those asleep at home. At least once every ninety days, I'd get a call early in the morning, often shortly after midnight, given a code word, then I would rush the twelve miles to the magazine, and we would go through emergency destruction procedures. These procedures involved setting explosive charges on the training weapons, and simulating detonation of the destructive charges. We had a very short time frame within which to complete the destruction. A couple of drills during my time on Guam, we did not complete the drill within the required time frame, and we had to do it again within a week. The short time limit was due to a number of factors, but the most realistic was, in the event of war, Russian paratroopers might be dropped into the magazine in an effort to capture weapons, and use them against our forces. Considering an invasion by paratroopers, time was a very important factor in emergency destruction.

The day of our inspection arrived, and after a week, we had breezed through it. The ten inspectors from Nuclear Weapons Training Group Pacific were very impressed by our technical competence. Our inspection was marred by one incident. The debriefing at the conclusion of an inspection, which involved the reading of the inspection report, was held primarily for the benefit of the commanding officer. The debriefing was held on Friday afternoon, in the limited area. When Commander Gerrard arrived in his chauffeur driven car, he got out and was so drunk, that he fell down! He made inappropriate remarks during the inspection debrief, and in general insulted the inspectors. The inspectors were not pleased with him, but realized this was no fault of the GMT's who had gone through the inspection. We had a party celebrating our successful passing of the inspection that weekend.

I once again took the Navy wide promotion exam for chief in February. ORT Division was short one chief, so I was being assigned jobs as a first class that was normally given to a chief. One such job was as a "Weapons Movement Supervisor." Anytime a weapon was moved, a certified commissioned officer, or certified chief petty officer had to be physically present at the area of movement, observing all aspects of the task. I was the only first class granted this certification. While this was very gratifying to my ego, I was still in a fog of discontentment because of my failure to be promoted to chief.

The first part of February, Senior Chief Smith's prediction was proven to be true, and it was a shock to me! I received the copy of my service record that was on file in Washington, which was the service record the selection board reviewed during the promotion process.

The record on file in Washington was a mere skeleton of my service record that was kept in the Naval Magazine personnel office. The two records were supposed to duplicates, or exact "twins." Each time something was included or entered in a sailor's service record at his duty station, a copy of the entered information was supposed to be sent to Washington for inclusion into the service record maintained there. It was very obvious that over the years the personnel offices at my previous duty stations had not been doing their job, by keeping my Washington service record updated. Also, included in my Washington service record was the divorce paperwork of another sailor! A huge amount of information was missing, information that made me desirable for promotion to chief. There was no mention of the nine correspondence courses I had completed the last couple of years, nor of the five Navy schools I had attended and graduated from. Missing was fourteen awards, and letters of commendation I had received, and training seminars I had completed were not listed. There was a total of forty-two specific items missing in my Washington service record, and the inclusion of a negative document of another sailor. On 14 February, acting on the suggestion of Senior Chief Smith, I wrote a letter to the Chief of Naval Personnel, through the Naval Magazine Commanding Officer, requesting that my service record maintained in Washington be updated. I also sent a copy of the letter to the Chief Petty Officer Selection Board detailing the excluded items. The board would be meeting in the summer of 1977.

The magnitude of the missing forty-two items was unbelievable! It was no wonder I'd been passed over by the board looking at my record for the past seven years! I was disappointed with the "system" at this point. Never again would I blindly trust that personnel offices would carry through and keep records at naval headquarters updated. I was very thankful that Senior Chief Smith had suggested that I investigate this.

Many of the Navy wives worked in the large Navy exchange located on the naval station. Carmen got a job in the Navy exchange cobbler shop, working with leather making purses, belts, and various item. Only the shop owner and she worked in the cobbler shop, and often she managed the store in his absence. We decided that we needed two cars. Carmen found a "Guam bomb," (1967 Chevrolet Vega station wagon). A Guam bomb was usually an older car that passed from military family to military family at transfer time, and remained on the island and was used until it no longer passed the Guam safety inspection, or rusted away, or like a bomb, the engine blew up. The Vega was in good shape, owned by a sailor who was transferring. We bought it for $400. As Carmen did with the Pontiac, she drove the Vega to the Guam police auto safety inspection building, and the inspectors approved it and issued a safety inspection decal for the windshield.

In the production plant coffee locker where we took our coffee breaks, we had a large chalkboard that covered one wall. From time to time I would draw cartoons of various happenings in the division. I made caricatures of everyone so they were recognizable. Everyone enjoyed the cartoons, and if a few days went by, and I had not drawn a new one, I was always asked when was the next cartoon going to be drawn?

Since Typhoon Pamela had destroyed the acey ducey club, a new enlisted club was being built on the base. The club was to be completed, and opened in the spring of 1977. A contest was held to name the club, and the winning name selected was "The Silver Dollar Club." I was asked if I would label, and decorate the men and women's bathroom doors. I agreed, and painted both of them, a cowgirl on the lady's bathroom, and a cowboy on the men's bathroom.

The marines stationed in the Marine Barracks on the magazine, totaled 200. Each sailor assigned to the magazine was assigned as a member of the base defense force. We went through combat technique training, conducted by the marines. We sat through training lectures on the techniques of infantry fighting, composition of a fire team, and ways to attack a specific target.

Russian soldiers, we were told, trained in a more deadly fashion than American marines and sailors. Americans normally have war games in the field for a couple of days, or weeks, whereas the Russian's had war games in the field that lasted as long as six months. All the ammunition used in America's field training, was blanks. The Russians used blanks, mixed with live ammunition. Their rationale was if a Russian soldier were killed or wounded in training exercises, he probably would have been wounded or killed in real combat!

We practiced at the firing range with the M-14 rifle, and the M-60 machine gun. I was assigned as a fire team leader, with eight riflemen, as well as three sailors who manned an M-60 machine gun. A number of times we played war games with the marines. During these times we were issued our firearms with blanks, and wore helmets, and flak jackets, we also were given smoke grenades that were to simulate fragmentation grenades. Our most common training drill was attacking a position across an open field. Each fire team leader had to plan his attack before it took place. I learned much about tactics, and attack methods from the marines, training in these war games. We usually would attack across an open field in groups of three.

Two groups would lay down covering fire, as one group raced forward, and then fall to the ground. We would leap frog in this fashion, until we were close enough for an all out attack. I also had to position my machine gun team so they would be in a favorable position to lie down covering fire for us. We had to learn to conserve our ammunition racing across the field, for the final charge. We always attacked positions that were held by the marines, firing blanks at us.

There were five fire team leaders in my company, and we took turn attacking the marines. I remember my first attack; GMT1 Tommy Mize had trouble laying down covering fire, because the M-60 machine gun he was manning kept jamming. As we neared the marine's position, we threw smoke grenades simulating fragmentation grenades. It was exhausting work, running across an open field, with a heavy flak jacket, and steel helmet on, and diving for cover every few yards. The sailors usually didn't fare too well against the more experienced marines. One trick the marines pulled a few times before we caught on, was just before our fire teams over ran their position, they would abandon the defended hill and withdraw. They knew the tired sailors would often sit down and relax after the long charge across the open field. It was then the marines would counterattack and surprise the exhausted sailors. We learned the correct tactics were to continue chasing the retreating marines, and then set up a defensive perimeter before relaxing. On a couple of occasions we battled the marines in the jungle. During these exercises I gained much respect for the marines and soldiers who fought in the jungles of the South Pacific during World War II, and in the jungles of Vietnam. The sailor's victories in the jungle were few. These war games had the added benefit of reducing the amount of natural animosities that sometimes existed between sailors and marines. The sailors gained more respect for the marines abilities, fighting man to man, and the marines appreciated that at times the sailors did well fighting against them. After these war games, the things that happened in the practice field, and jungles were the topics of discussion for days afterwards.

A double fence topped with razor wire encircled the eighty plus acre limited area. Signs attached to the outer fence warned that any intrusion would be met with deadly force. The signs said in bold red letters, "DEADLY FORCE AUTHORIZED." The marines patrolled around the interior fence, and guard dogs were occasionally used inside the outer and inner fence. We had to insure that the guard dogs were well controlled, because goats were sometimes used inside the limited area, as natural lawnmowers. The marines also patrolled the outer perimeter of the 8,800-acre magazine. A constant problem with the patrolling marines, were vehicle accidents while patrolling. They drove Navy pickups, and were constantly having "fender-benders." During one month, the captain was so fed up with the number of accidents; he made the marines on patrol walk the perimeter of the magazine. After that month there were fewer accidents.

There were manned lookout towers inside the limited area. A lone marine manned these lookout towers for four hours, twenty-four hours a day. We heard many stories of marines, late at night seeing strange sights, and hearing eerie noises. One of the frequent sights was a lady gliding through the dense jungle, dressed in a glowing green dress. The people of Guam called these ghosts "taotaomonas." The Naval Magazine had been a fierce battleground during World War II; perhaps the marines were seeing ghosts of these long dead soldiers?

The marines had a barracks inside the limited area, which housed an Emergency Response Force. The barracks also contained an Alarm Panel Monitoring Room. This alarm system was connected to every building and magazine access point within the limited area. The two-person rule was a way of life for GMT's, and we had certain procedures, and code words for opening the magazines, and other buildings. In order to open an alarmed area, two persons had to communicate with the marines in the alarm panel monitoring room, over a telephone. Each person had physical control of a key, which opened one of the two locks that were always on the alarmed doors, when the magazine or building was not occupied. Just as at other commands, we had a duress word that could be used if we were being forced by someone to open an alarmed area. The duress word could be used in a sentence to the marines that would alert them that an unauthorized person was trying to gain access, perhaps holding a gun or knife on us. The duress code word changed each month, and we were required to memorize it. There were occasional mistakes made by the sailors, or marines when going through the opening, or closing procedures. The marine emergency response team would immediately deploy around the area that was being opened or closed. Anyone in the open had to freeze, and make no movement; there was a real possibility you could be shot if you moved. The standard procedure was, the GMT, or person in the open would be told by the surrounding marines to lay face down on the ground, with arms outstretched. The marines would check the badges we wore at all times within the limited area. The alert could only be secured by the ORT Division Officer, or after hours, the command duty officer.

Anytime a GMT made a mistake, it was not dealt with lightly. There was always an investigation afterward, by the division officer, or leading chief, to determine why the alert happened, and to correct any problem that might have been the cause. The alerts involved a large number of marines responding, and there was always the possibility of an accident while they were rushing to the scene. Also since live ammunition was used, there was the possibility of an accidental shooting.

In the hours of darkness, the limited area was lit up like a small city. Floodlights lit up the entire area. In the event of a power failure, which happened frequently on Guam, an emergency generator supplied power to keep the lights going. This generator ran nonstop for many days after Typhoon Pamela. At night one of the jobs of the two duty GMT's, was to drive around inside the limited area, and identify any burned out floodlights. There could only be a certain number of lights burned out. If this number was exceeded, a Navy public works truck with a basket lift, had to be dispatched to the limited area, to change the burned out bulbs, so the marine sentries would have good visibility around, and within the fenced area.

Grass growing within the limited area was a problem. It had to be cut often, so it would not provide cover for an intruder. GMT1 Jack Osilka and his outside maintenance, and handling crews worked with lawnmowers, over the eighty-acre area. The other grass cutting solution I mentioned was the goats that roamed inside the fence. The only problem with the goats was that sometimes, they spooked the marine sentries at nights who were on the look out for intruders.

One unusual security precaution that took place frequently was the unannounced arrival within the limited area of two Naval Investigative Service (N.I.S) agents, carrying two heavy suitcases filled with electronic equipment. They would not speak, but put their fingers to their lips indicating silence, and then show us a card that said, "We are conducting electronic surveillance to determine if any unauthorized eavesdropping is taking place. DO NOT say anything that would reveal that we are here, or that any type of surveillance is taking place. Please go about business as usual." They would listen over headphones for a few hours, and then leave.

The morale of ORT Division was much higher than when I'd previously been stationed on the magazine in 1969-70. We were pleased with the results of our NTPI. The sailors enjoyed working for Lieutenant Hume, and Senior Chief Smith, both were people oriented leaders. The commanding officer, and executive officer were not well liked, but this had the effect of causing us all to band together more closely, as we had a common dislike. We had monthly division picnics and barbeques, which everyone enjoyed. Many of the families socialized together after working hours. There was also a group of sailors that would play nickel-dime poker games at various houses. Often the game would go on all night.

Guam was a "testing ground" for some military marriages, and many marriages did not pass the test. Often young sailors and their wives were away from home for the first time, and homesick for life back in the U.S.A. Island life in Guam was foreign to anyplace in the States.

We knew a young couple that lived nearby us on base. He was a Third Class Radioman, and worked at the Naval Communication Station in the northern part of Guam. The young couple had always wanted a waterbed, and Carmen and I had considered selling ours. We made a deal with them, and sold it to them for a cheap price. One weekend, I spent all day Saturday disassembling the bed, putting it pieces by piece into the Vega station wagon, driving it across the base to their house, and reassembling the waterbed. Assembling the bed was a long involved task. Just filling it with water took a couple of hours. The young Radioman had duty that night. He was very anxious to use it. Carmen and I left the couple's house about 4:00 p.m. He had to go on duty at the communication station in two hours, at 6:00 p.m.

Early the next morning there was a knock on our door. I went to the door, and it was the young Radioman. He said, "I'm sorry but I can't buy the waterbed, I'll have to give it back." He then told me what happened the previous night. He had reported for duty at 6:00 p.m. He was very anxious to try the waterbed, so he found a sailor willing to take his duty, and at 10:00 p.m., he drove back home. He arrived home at 11:00 p.m., hoping to surprise his wife. He quietly opened the door of his house. What he saw baffled him; there on the living room table were two glasses, and a partially empty bottle of wine. He heard voices upstairs in the bedroom. Silently he climbed the stairs, and looked into the bedroom. He surprised his wife, but he also received a surprise. There sitting in the middle of his new waterbed, without a stitch of clothes on, were his wife, and the sailor who lived next door! He was devastated. His wife tried to tell him they were "just talking." The next couple of days I had to dismantle the bed, return it home, and put it back together. The young couple's marriage ended in divorce.

As I said in my narrative of my previous tour in Guam, the Explosive Ordnance Disposal (E.O.D.) Team, stationed on the Naval Magazine was kept very busy disposing of old World War II ordnance.

Bombs and ammunition were discovered almost daily, lying in the jungle, or buried in the earth. We knew a couple that lived on base with three young children, who were awakened one morning by the sounds of gunfire coming from their kitchen. They rushed from the bedroom into the kitchen where they found the children huddling in one corner of the kitchen in terror. On the kitchen counter, was a destroyed toaster that was smoking, and appeared to have exploded? They soon found out what had happened. Kids in the neighborhood had secretly found hundreds of old M-I rifle bullets, in an area nearby that was being bulldozed in preparation for construction of new buildings. Some kids had hidden huge collections of the rifle bullets in their rooms. In the toaster incident, one of the younger children had dropped a few of the old bullets into the toaster, and pushed down the toasting switch, which caused the surprising detonations. Parents in the neighborhood searched their kid's rooms after they heard about the toaster explosion.

One evening I had a nice surprise. I had a phone call from Charlie Galbreath, (Backup Charlie), who I'd been with on the *Oriskany*. He had completed E.O.D. School, and was now working in that program. He was temporarily assigned to Guam for a couple of days, and Carmen and I spent some time with him. Carmen fixed him dinner one evening, and we had fun reminiscing about the past. Charlie enjoyed his new job, and was stationed in Hawaii, where he and his wife and daughter lived.

The *USS Proteus* (AS-19), a Submarine Tender, had been home ported in Guam's Apra Harbor since 1964. She served as a repair ship for Polaris Submarines, as well as attack submarines operating in the South Pacific. The maintenance of Polaris, and later Trident ballistic missiles, on the submarines, included rotating the missile warheads back to the United States for necessary maintenance, or modernization. There was a regularly scheduled ship that steamed back and forth between Silverdale, Washington, and Guam, whose task it was to conduct maintenance on missiles. There were a few GMT's stationed on the *Proteus*, who worked on the missiles. One evening I got a call from George Erath. We had been together at Oakland. George was now stationed at Silverdale, and was making a trip on the ship that traveled back and forth between the *Proteus*, and Washington State. Carmen and I got to see George a couple of times, and on one occasion he attended a Guamanian fiesta with us. I also got a surprise call from John Milton (Big John), my shipmate from Whidbey Island. He was making a run with the ship from Silverdale. He was also stationed at Silverdale, and was now a chief. This was another blow to my ego. It seemed all my peers were now wearing a chief's hat.

Nineteen May 1977 was a happy day at Naval Magazine, Guam. This was the day Commander Gerrard was relieved by Commander Abrahams as the commanding officer. Commander Gerrard was retiring from the Navy. We later heard that he had gone to work managing a nursing and retirement home somewhere in the United States. We all chuckled at the idea of him trying to rule a nursing home with an iron fist, as he did at Naval Magazine.

Commander Abrahams was commissioned an ensign in June 1960, the same month and year I entered the Navy. He served at a variety of duty stations before being assigned as Naval Magazine's commanding officer, and he was also a bachelor. We saw almost immediately a change in the administration of the magazine, following his assumption of command. He was a people oriented commander, and unlike his predecessor, very "approachable." There was such a change in the attitude, and morale of everyone at the magazine, that Carmen and I agreed we would like to remain on Guam for an additional year. I requested an extension from Washington, and it was granted. This meant we would remain on Guam until June 1979.

A past time I enjoyed was snorkeling off the different beaches at the naval station. I'd found a few cowry shells, and I was amazed at the underwater beauty of the coral reef, and the variety of colorful fish. GMT1 Rick Leishner learned of a SCUBA class that was about to convene, and he talked me, and five others into joining the class with him. The class was to begin in May.

The course was taught in the classroom, swimming pool, and ocean. After each classroom session we were given a written exam. Our instructor, a First Class Constructionman, was very thorough, and safety conscious. We were taught what consisted of basic SCUBA divers' equipment. Stressed over and over again, was the importance of diving with a buddy, and to never dive alone. We were also told of the dangers of diving, which were many. The danger of developing nitrogen bubbles in the bloodstream, or "bends" had to always be considered. This danger did not exist if a diver dove no deeper than sixty feet. There was a complicated formula that involved waiting at specific depths, while surfacing after a dive of more than sixty feet. As I described in my description of Guam, during my previous tour on the island, there were many dangerous creatures in the ocean surrounding Guam. While walking in the surf, there was always the danger of stepping on a stonefish. As I explained previously, this fish would lie on the bottom of the ocean, often near the beach, and would usually be completely covered with sand, or partially covered.

The fish would look exactly like a stone lying on the ocean floor. If the stonefish were disturbed, it would raise poisonous spines that could penetrate the sole of your foot. A very basic item of diver's equipment was reef shoes. These were rubber slippers with very thick soles. Other diver's necessities were a mask and snorkel. The snorkel permitted divers to breathe while swimming or floating on the water surface face down and going from place to place on the surface. We also wore a weight belt, which had pockets that lead weights could be inserted into. The weight belt was needed to overcome the natural buoyancy of a person's body while in water. Each person's natural buoyancy is different, so we had to experiment to find out how much lead weight to add to our individual weight belts. Each diver wore a buoy compensator, which doubled as a life preserver. The buoy compensator was an inflatable vest, which could be inflated, or deflated as necessary to remain at different depths during a dive. We wore swim fins, which greatly increased the speed you could move through the water. We were advised to carry a diving knife, which was usually strapped around your lower leg in a sheath. The knife was not necessarily for defense from dangerous sea creatures, but for use in case we should become entangled underwater in seaweed, or other matter we needed to cut ourselves free from. The most important thing needed by divers underwater, is oxygen. Our air supply came from either single or double air tanks strapped on our back. A hose from the tank to our mouth supplied air through a mouthpiece. The tank or tanks also had a depth gage, so we could monitor what depth we were at. The tank also had a gauge that told us the amount of oxygen remaining in our air supply.

The tropic water in Guam was comfortably warm, so unless going on a deep dive, a rubber diving suit that was used in colder climates was not needed on Guam. Divers normally wore Levi pants to protect against coral cuts and scrapes, and a T-shirt to prevent sunburn.

A few weeks before we began our SCUBA class, there was a report in the newspaper about a diver that had been attacked by a tiger shark in Apra Harbor. The diver had been bitten on the upper arm. Our instructor knew the diver that had been attacked, and he said the bitten diver deserved the bite. He said prior to the attack the diver had been closely following the shark, pulling its tail, and pestering it. We were told if we gave sharks a wide berth, then they would usually ignore us. We studied the long list of creatures that could cause us harm while in the sea. There were poisonous lion fish, scorpion fish, sea snakes, sea shells, and also sharks, barracuda, sting rays, and moray eels, just to mention a few. Most of us taking the class planned to hunt for seashells. As I've mentioned before, many of the cone shells had poison stingers a diver had to be aware of. There was also the precaution of lifting a rock a certain way off the sea floor while looking for seashells. We always lifted the side of the rock furthest away from us so whatever might be hiding under the rock would swim away from us, instead of lifting the side nearest to us, and perhaps have a sea creature swim toward us. Moray eels liked to lurk underneath rocks.

After a few nights of classroom studies, our classes convened at a Navy swimming pool. Our instructor checked out students swimming ability. We were taught a deep-water survival technique, which is a method of conserving energy by bobbing up and down on the surface, rising slowly to gulp breaths of air. We had a contest during the class to see who could swim the furthest underwater while holding his breath. Although I had started smoking again, I won the contest easily.

The second night class at the pool, we donned air tanks and swam around the pool learning how to "buddy breath." This meant two people breathing out of one tank, sharing the breathing mouthpiece underwater. I teamed up with a friend, GMT1 Jim Porter. The next few classes were spent learning to breathe under water, and gaining confidence. We all dreaded the last class in the pool, which would be an exercise to see if we could control panic underwater! One by one, we were instructed to sit on the bottom of the deep end of the pool. We sat with an air tank on our back, breathing from the air hose. The instructor would swim up behind the student, and do varieties of things, such as a rip the mouthpiece away from your mouth, jerk your facemask off, or turn the supply valve on the air tank off. We had to remain calm, and without surfacing, hold our breath and solve the problem, of putting our mask back on, or getting our air supply going again. This drill had a very real purpose, teaching us confidence in our ability to solve problems that might occur underwater. I survived the harassment of the instructor, and solved all the problems.

Our first dive in the ocean, we went into the sea on the naval station, at Gab Gab Beach. On this day we all dove down to about 55 feet, and sat on the ocean bottom. This dive we were told to remove our air tank, and swim to the surface 55 feet above. A fact that was hard for us to accept, and learn, was when surfacing from a depth, we could not hold our breath, but to the contrary had to blow air out of our lungs as you surfaced. The reason behind this expulsion, was the air held in our lungs on the bottom, would expand as we surfaced, and the expansion could harm our lungs.

We were cautioned to rise from the bottom at a slow rate, no faster than the bubbles rising to the surface that were being blown out of our mouth. It was amazing how long that breath of air lasted, as I made that slow climb toward sunlight and the surface above. That first dive, the beauty of the underwater world was spell binding to us all. After this dive we had a final written examination. I was pleased with myself as I aced the exam without missing a question.

Before our instructor could declare us certified divers, we had a half-mile swim out to sea, and then a dive to fifty feet. After the dive, he issued us each a certification card, called a National Association of Underwater Instructors card, or most commonly called a "NAUI card." This card had to be shown anytime I rented an air tank, or had an air tank filled. My certification was placed on file at NAUI headquarters at Colton, California. My certification could have been upgraded to a higher certification called Professional Association of Diving Instructors (PADI), which meant I could instruct diving classes. This upgrade required five additional hours class work. I didn't desire the increased qualification.

Each dive in Guam I recorded in my personal diving logbook. Most of my dives were with Jim Porter, and to a depth of less than sixty feet. My first recorded dive was 11 June 1977, and the last was less than a year later on 17 April 1978. After Jim Porter retired, and left Guam, I didn't find a reliable diving partner I could trust.

I dove mostly in search of seashells, but the beauty of the tropical undersea world also fascinated me. It was much different from how I had imagined, or seen in movies. The world below was much quieter than the world above. The colors of the coral and sea life were brilliant, although at deep levels colors washed out, so the only visible colors were black, blue, and white. There was not absolute silence, as there were clicks, and shrill sounds made by various sea creatures. It was like entering a completely different world, and while it appeared peaceful, and serene, as air breathers we were aliens in this world. Jim Porter and I were never more than six feet away from each other, in the event one of us got into trouble and needed help. There was an invisible cord, a cord of safety connecting us.

On one of my first dives as a certified diver, along with three other divers, I saw a five-foot shark, and one of the largest moray eels I, or the other divers had ever seen. He was as large around as a telephone pole, and at least twelve feet long! We stayed as far as possible away from him.

The seashells we searched for were nocturnal creatures that mainly came out at night. In order to find the shells we searched under rocks, and looked into dark crevices where they hid during the day. We carried a shell bag tied to our waist, into which we would place the shells we found. Following the dives we would put the shells in the freezer, and once the animal inside was frozen, I'd place the shells on an anthill located near the house. It would take a week or longer for the ants to consume the interior of the shell. I would then place the empty shells in a Clorox and water mixture for a day or two to disinfect them.

The prize shell all shell hunters looked for was the golden cowry. This is a rare, precious shell that is golden in color, worth thousands of dollars. In the past islanders used the golden cowry to identify royalty, only kings and chieftains were permitted to wear the golden cowry around their neck. I had a friend who found a golden cowry during a dive in the morning. That afternoon, he decided to go snorkeling, and while walking on the reef out to deeper water, he looked down and there was another golden cowry! Most shell hunters never found one. I looked in vain for three years.

I had all the needed diving equipment, except for a weight belt, and an air tank, which I rented from a dive shop before each dive. Most dives were forty-five minutes, to an hour in length. While on Guam, I accumulated more than twenty-five diving hours.

One memorable dive was my first night dive. Four of us went on this dive. We took a small outboard motor board out to the area we wanted to dive at. We all had large dive lights. Diving at night in the darkness is thrilling due to the fact that is when most predators are out searching for food, and hopefully a shark won't consider you a meal. While diving, I continually flashed the light about, when I imagined some creature coming toward me out of the blackness. The advantage for shell hunters during night dives is that this is when shells are out of their hiding places, and easy to spot. After this dive we were all talking about what a beautiful dive it had been. Rich Logue had found a few rock lobsters. While motoring back to the pier, Jim Porter let out a yell, and something began flopping around in the bottom of the boat. We quickly found a dive light, turned it on, and found that it was a large flying fish. The fish had been flying along, when it hit Jim's forehead and fell into the boat. It gave Jim quite a scare!

As I mentioned before, when Jim Porter left the island, I didn't feel comfortable diving with anyone else. Two of my most memorable dives were going inside a sunken ship that had gone down during the war, and a dive exploring a Japanese Zero fighter plane that also went down during the war.

Diving was an experience I truly enjoyed. The beauty and "other world" quality of the tropical undersea environment are something I'll never forget. It is a sport that cannot be taken lightly, because man is out of his element underwater, and trouble can occur at any time. If I were to dive again in the future, it would only be after a lengthy training period, although with my NAUI card, I could dive today.

A bachelor friend I worked with, GMT1 Rubin Rassmusson visited our house after working hours often. He was tall and skinny, and Carmen and I were always amazed by how much he could eat. He was crazy about Carmen's cooking. One evening he confided in us some very dangerous information. He had secretly been dating an ensign Wave, who was the Naval Magazine's Supply Officer. This was a dangerous romance, because fraternization between an officer, and enlisted person was strictly forbidden. This could mean a court martial for them both. The penalties for fraternization were prison time, and dishonorable discharges! They had been dating for about a month, when Rubin told Carmen and me of their romance. Rubin told of visiting her one evening in her bachelor officer's quarter's room (he was forbidden to be in this building), when there was a knock on her door. Rubin immediately hid in her closet. She opened the door, and it was a lieutenant, who was the security officer at the Naval Magazine, and disliked by everyone. He was asking her for a date, and although the ensign kept telling him "no," he stayed and stayed. Rubin ended up staying in the closet for two hours. We had both of them over to our house a few times for dinner, and we double dated with them a couple of times. We were very cautious about where we went on these "dates," as it would have been catastrophic if we'd been seen by anyone from the magazine. Carmen and I were also concerned, because we could have been accomplices in the "fraternization." After a few months the romance ended, much to our relief. We had been very concerned about what might happen to both of them if their romance was discovered.

There was a case on the magazine involving a Limited Duty Officer (LDO) ensign who "set up house" with a Third Class Yeoman that worked in the limited area. The captain heard about it, and gave the ensign a direct order to cease the relationship immediately, or both would be facing a court martial.

Within ORT Division we had four women assigned. Two GMT's, one Yeoman, and a Torpedoman Second Class, named Paula Jones. A romance began between GMT1 Denny Richards, and Paula. When I held morning quarters, and the division was standing in ranks, I could never get used to seeing these two holding hands! A memorable thing about Paula was that she had the most unusual laugh I'd ever heard. Sailors would try to make her laugh, just to hear the odd sounds she made. One day in the coffee locker, Paula was sitting next to GMT2 Steve Cline who was known for his "colorful language." Paula handed him a written note that said, "Please do not use profanity in my presence." After reading the note, Steve let loose a loud repetitive string of profanity. I had to talk to both of them about using tact, and consideration. Richards and she were eventually married, but it was not a marriage made in heaven, and ended in divorce four years later.

In the past, women had not been permitted to strike for the GMT rating because of the concerns about a woman in pregnancy being exposed to radiation. The two Wave GMT's assigned to ORT Division, both wanted to work in the outside maintenance and handling crew. They caused a number of management problems for Jack Osilka. The two were failures as GMT's, as both were busted for illegal drug usage, and lost their security clearances. As their leading petty officer, I took pains to insure they were treated fairly, and as equally as their male counterparts. We had one head (toilet) in the production plant. Since there was only one head, it became a community head. Each sailor (or soldier), had to make sure a member of the opposite sex was not in the head (or in the case of the Army, latrine), before using it. Mixing of sexes in the division made management and leadership more complex.

In 1976 and 1977, the Army was experiencing a shortage of officers in its nuclear ordnance field. The Army tried to entice Navy first class petty officers in the nuclear weapons program, to join the Army, and become Army warrant officers. The Army warrant officer program is considerably different from the Navy and Marine Corps. warrant officer program (the Air Force discontinued its warrant officer program in 1972). Army warrant officers receive their commissions from the secretary of the Army, whereas the Navy and Marine Corps. warrant officer's commission originates from the office of the president. Also the Navy petty officers that were accepted into the Army warrant officer program did not go into the regular Army, but were placed in the Army Reserve. The Army also had the habit of issuing Reduction in Force (R.I.F.) orders, frequently. This meant at any time the Army could notify the warrant officers that their services were no longer needed, and they were "fired," or released, and often only a month or two advance notice was given. These RIF's could take place regardless how close the person involved was to retirement eligibility, or the twenty-year point.

The prospect of gaining a commission, even if it wasn't as prestigious as the Navy, was very tempting to many of the GMT's on Guam.

There were two Army warrant officers that worked in the production plant, side by side with us, and they encouraged many sailors to apply for the Army program. Following acceptance, and discharge from the Navy, the ex-sailors would be sent to an Army indoctrination course, then to Redstone Arsenal, Alabama for a school teaching the new officers the Army's nuclear ordnance program. Following training in Alabama, the most likely duty assignment would be at a remote duty station such as Turkey or an isolated post for a one or two year period, unaccompanied, without family. I and four first class applied for the Army warrant officer program. I was discouraged about my failure to be promoted to chief. With only three years to go before I completed twenty years' service and eligibility for retirement, I figured the risky program would be a way to increase my retirement pay. It was very hard for me to imagine leaving the Navy for the Army. The first four that applied, were accepted, GMT1 Richards, Cannon, Hutchinson, and Nehring. There were those among this group that did not have very strong leadership skills, and I wondered if they would make a successful transition to the Army? The one that I assumed would do very well was GMT1 Hank Nehring. Hank had six years previous Army experience, and I thought his temperament was well suited to becoming a good Army warrant officer. The sailors that were accepted into the Army, left Guam on a staggered schedule, one every couple of months.

The 515th Ordnance Company that worked in the production plant alongside the sailors, got word they would be relocating from the Naval Magazine back to the United States. This meant we would no longer be a host to the Army, and also all of their ordnance and equipment would be evacuated. At the same time of the relocation notice, one of the Army warrant officers that worked in the production plant received word that he was the victim of a RIF. Although he had enough years to retire, and draw a pension, this came as a shock to him.

The uncertainty of an Army career caused me to hesitate with the preparation of my application. I had started the application by preparing a history of my Navy assignments, and jobs. The final step was getting approval of the Naval Magazine commanding officer, and then sending the application to the Army channels. The commanding officer approved my application, but I pulled the application before it left the magazine, and I've never regretted this decision.

In the summer of 1977 we noticed rust problems on some of our equipment. We had documented these problems, and this resulted in an investigative visit from Naval Ammunition Depot, McAlester, Oklahoma who was the collection point for Unsatisfactory Reports (UR's) for the Navy nuclear weapons program. One of the inspectors was my old friend Senior Chief Ray Steele. Carmen and I had a good time showing Ray the island, although he had been stationed there early in his career. Ray had married a girl named Becky, and they were living in McAlester.

Carmen had worked in the cobbler/leather shop for a few months, when she applied for a job in the Navy exchange shoe department, which was located in the same building as the cobbler/leather shop. She was hired by the Navy exchange, and did very well, increasing shoe sales significantly. She received many award certificates, and was acknowledged for her salesmanship. She was promoted to the head of the shoe department.

In July I received a surprise. Each three months, one sailor assigned to the Naval Magazine was selected as "Sailor of the Quarter." The selected sailor's picture was posted on the magazine quarterdeck. The four sailors' of the quarter selected within a year were then eligible for selection as Naval Magazine "Sailor of the Year." I was notified that I had been selected as sailor of the quarter for the April/June/July quarter. A letter from the commanding officer, Captain Abrahams, notifying me of my selection was presented to me, and read at a captain's personnel inspection. Carmen enjoyed watching the ceremony of the personnel inspections, and she was present at this particular one. My selection as sailor of the quarter was reported in a number of newspapers.

Following the opening of the Naval Magazine Silver Dollar All Hands Club, and my painting of the bathroom doors, the chief who was the manager of the club, asked me if I would be interested in painting a mural in one section of the club. I said I would. The mural was to be painted in the club's poolroom. On those evenings I had free, which were seldom, I would paint on the walls of the poolroom. The mural was to be a moon-landing scene, such as the one I had painted on the living room wall of our base house. Carmen also helped me with this painting job.

After I had taken the Navy-wide promotion exam for advancement to chief petty officer in February, I received my exam result sheet from Pensacola, Florida, stating I had passed the exam. The points needed to pass, and be selection board eligible was 87.60. My final point total was 105.62. Passing the exam was nothing new to me; I'd passed the exam year after year, but had not been selected by the board.

The only difference this time was that I had updated the service record the board would be looking at, by having the other sailor's documents taken out, and adding the forty-two missing items.

After February's exam I continued studying for the next exam, which would be in November. The method of announcing the names of the first class that were selected for chief by the board was by electronic message. The personnel command in Washington, D.C sent out this message with selected names. The rough time period the message was due to be sent out, was always known within a day or two. This was always an anxious time of anticipation for me, and in past years, a time of bitter disappointment.

A neighbor of ours was a Filipino first class who had also taken the chief's exam, and was anxiously awaiting the publication of the announcement message. He had a friend at the Navy communication station that would be one of the first on the island to see the message, and he was supposed to call him as soon as the message came in. The evening of 10 August 1977, I got a call from my neighbor, and he asked Carmen and me to come over to his house. Carmen and I walked the half block to his house, and as soon as we walked in, my friend started yelling "You made it, you made it!" He said he had just gotten a call from his friend at the communication station, and my name was on the list of sailors to be promoted to chief petty officer. After waiting for all these years it was heard to believe I'd finally made it. Unfortunately my Filipino friend's name was not on the list, but he and his wife were very happy for Carmen and me.

It didn't really begin to sink in that I was to be a chief, until that evening when I began receiving phone calls from all the chiefs assigned to the Naval Magazine, congratulating me. Also that evening, I got a phone call from Senior Chief Smith, instructing me to call the senior chief on Guam, a master chief who lived on the naval station. After Senior Chief Smith gave me the phone number, I called the master chief, and told him I'd just been selected for promotion to chief. He grumbled, "I can hardly wait to see you at your initiation, you've disturbed me with this call!" This began my initiation.

I don't think I really believed it until the next day, when I saw my name in black and white on the announcement list. Twenty-five GMT's in the Navy had been selected for promotion, and the actual date each sailor was to be promoted, was to be published within a week. I was very pleased that the goal I'd had of becoming a chief, which began seventeen years before was finally coming to pass. I wondered how many years I'd been cheated out of achieving this goal by having a service record with so much missing vital information?

In the following week I learned my promotion date was to be 16 April 1978. This meant a nine-month wait! And it also meant a nine-month period of initiation. The chief petty officers' initiation was shrouded in secrecy, and the few things that did leak out about it were very ominous. There were rumors of physical abuse, high money costs, and fines. The initiation ceremony was a "rite of passage." There were stories of first class that refused to go through the initiation process, and as the result were ignored, or "black balled" by the chiefs in the Navy. These individuals were not welcomed in the Chief's Club, and chiefs in their command refused to work with them, or give them any respect. Other chiefs called these rare sailors "E-7's" instead of chief.

We heard of an unusual situation in ORT Division, our Leading Chief, Senior Chief Smith found himself in. This situation occurred shortly after I checked aboard the Naval Magazine. In the past Senior Chief Smith had been a W-1 warrant Officer. He had been promoted to warrant officer from first class petty officer. He had been a warrant officer for one year, when he was demoted to senior chief. This was not an unusual occurrence, and happened quite often, either because the warrant officer did not adjust to the officer ranks from the enlisted ranks, or because the officer ranks were being thinned. As he was demoted directly to senior chief, he never went through a chief's initiation. One unsuspecting day, he went to the Chief's Club to participate in the initiation ceremony for a number of first class petty officers. All chiefs on Guam were expected to be at initiations. It was announced before the initiation of the first class began, that there was an E-8 present that had never gone through the initiation process. Senior Chief Smith was given the option of going through the initiation, or becoming the object of disdain by other chiefs from that day on. He very wisely opted to go through the initiation.

One of the first things I was given as a prospective chief petty officer was a "charge book." This small green book had instructions glued inside the front cover. The instructions said I was to produce this book anytime a "real Chief" requested it. I was to carry it at all times, and never let it out of my possession.

I was to look forward to nine months of initiation "hazing," but my spirits were high, my faith in the promotion system had been restored. I didn't know what to expect at my initiation, but I was reasonably sure I would survive it. I was about to enter a world I knew little about, a world I had tried to get into for more than eight years. I'd worn a first class crow for ten years, and I'd gained valuable experience as a leading petty officer at my past commands.

I could hardly wait to put on the "hat," and be called "Chief Little," and enter the brotherhood of United States Navy Chief Petty Officers. My approaching promotion to chief definitely raised my morale, and improved my outlook for the future. April 1978 seemed far in the future, especially since I was now a target of initiation, and humiliation for all the chiefs stationed on the magazine, and all of Guam.

I was told there would be a trial at my initiation that would be held at the Chief's Club on the naval station. The book I was to carry from now on, the "charge book" would be used as evidence at my trial. I also had to have a defense lawyer. Most prospective chiefs asked their division officer to be their defense lawyer. I asked Lieutenant Hume, the ORT Division Officer if he would perform this duty? He said he would.

It seemed as though each time I saw a chief, he would ask for my charge book! An example of the type of entry in my charge book follows: "10 Sept. 1977 - This despicable, slimy, excuse for a Boot Chief was caught on this date trying to steal a real Chief's hat and try it on for size. This offense occurred at 15:46 - signed GMTC Ray Margeson." My book was quickly becoming filled, mostly with false charges.

One week I had to make a sign that read "Boot Chief," and wear it around my neck all week. All the other first class, and ranks below them watched all the harassment, and humiliations I was undergoing, with amusement, and bewilderment, as I had watched prospective chiefs in the past. There were unwritten and verbal rules that only chiefs, or officers who at one time had been a chief, be the only ones permitted to write charges in the charge book.

I would be wearing a completely different uniform as a chief. The only items of my first class uniform I'd wear were my underwear, shoes and socks. On the day of my promotion I would be given a clothing allowance of $400. This clothing allowance would only pay for a small portion of the new sea bag uniform items I was required to have. I had to study the Navy Uniform Regulations Manual[39] to determine what I needed. Ray Margeson helped me in this aspect. I also had to study the proper way to wear this new uniform. The most common uniform worn by chiefs was the working khaki uniform. The insignia of a chief, a gold fouled anchor, was worn on both points of the shirt collar. Each month I would buy a few items of the new uniform I would be wearing.

I continued my leading petty officer's duties. The first of November I and a couple of other first class petty officers were directed to attend a two-week Leadership and Management Training Course that was being held at ComNavMarianas Headquarters on top of Nimitz Hill. A lieutenant and chief gave this course from Naval Submarine Training Center, Hawaii. I was very impressed by something the chief instructor did the first day of the course. There were forty-five students attending the course, and we were asked to stand individually, state our name, where we were stationed, and tell the class a little about ourselves. This took quite a while, as each sailor stood and spoke. After everyone had spoken, the chief who had not been taking notes, but merely watching, went around the room, not in the order we had stood, but in a different sequence, repeated each person's name, their duty station, and a little about what they had said! We were very impressed by this. This was one of the first lessons we learned in this class. It was important to remember names, and important to use names. I enjoyed this course, and learned much in it. We completed eighty hours of instruction, and most of the petty officers were "energized," and anxious to try the leadership techniques we had learned.

Our new President, Jimmy Carter, had been a naval officer, and the Navy and all military services, hoped he would halt the slide toward weakness we seemed to be on. We also hoped our pay would be upgraded to compensate for the many years we'd been denied raises. As time passed however, our pay remained the same, and the militaries' strength lessened.

The first part of November another typhoon hit Guam. This was Typhoon Kim. It had been over a year since Typhoon Pamela. Kim's winds only reached eighty miles per hour, and caused no damage. We did lose power for twenty-four hours. We boarded up our windows, and the family had a "typhoon party."

Around this time GMTC Charlie Cushman was transferred in from Naval Supply Center, Oakland. At this point in time it meant there were four chiefs working within ORT Division, GMTCS Smith, GMTC's Margeson, Wilkins, and Cushman. GMTC Bud Wilkins was not assigned to ORT Division in a true sense, but was in a newly formed group called the Quality Assurance Division. This was a group of senior GMT's that were present as quality assurance inspectors anytime ordnance movement or ordnance work took place. I was pleased that I would once again be working with Charlie Cushman. He was a professional, a man of integrity and honesty, and also a friend.

When it was learned that I was to be promoted to chief, I was relieved as a duty section leader, and began standing Officer of the Deck (OOD) duties. The OOD was primarily an assistant to the command duty officer, who was a commissioned officer.

I welcomed this change in duty assignments, not only because of the added responsibility, but also due to the fact that I would now stand duty every twelve nights or so, instead of every sixth night.

The Vega station wagon I used as a work car was good transportation, but it had the unsettling habit of suddenly stopping without warning. The rubber timing belt would slip off the three pulleys it encircled. It was a six-hour job to reinstall the timing belt. The timing belt slipped off four times during my ownership of the car. Spare parts for cars were difficult to get on the island. There were two junkyards on the island that did a brisk business. I was lucky to find a 1972 Pontiac in one of the junkyards, and I cannibalized it to keep our car running. The heat and humidity of Guam shortened the life of many cars brought to Guam from the States. One first class, Chris Reed had brought a '73 Dodge van to Guam, and when his automatic transmission went out, he had to overhaul it himself. I helped him with this job. Many cars were repaired through a joint effort made by sailors of ORT Division.

Honda's were a very popular car on Guam. A number of sailors ordered them through a Honda dealership in Agana. Since we were permitted to ship a vehicle back to the states when our tour on Guam was over, a common thing to do was to buy a Honda just before leaving the island and have the new cars shipped home. The Honda's purchase price did not include the transportation cost all the way from Japan as it would if the car were purchased in the States. I was very impressed with the Hondas' and seriously considered getting one. Our Pontiac was showing signs of wear. I was continually fighting rust, and the air conditioner had quit shortly after we arrived on Guam. The electrical system was giving me trouble, and I was positive that we would be leaving the Pontiac on Guam.

My stepson Roger was doing very well in little league baseball on Guam. He had developed into a good pitcher. He did need to work on his sportsmanship, as he could not lose gracefully. A number of couples the same ages, as Carmen and I would get together often. Carmen's number of friends she made at the Navy exchange increased our circle of acquaintances. We also were friends with a Guam lady named Rose, who seemed to know everyone on Guam. Almost every weekend we had an invitation to a fiesta, wedding, or just regular party. All the food at these affairs was home cooked, and delicious. I definitely began getting a middle age spread. Many of the affairs Rose invited us to had guests that were island dignitaries, such as Governor Ricardo Bordallo, and various senators, and congressmen. Some of my favorite dishes at these affairs were pancit, and chicken adobe. Carmen mastered these dishes, and many more, preparing them better than a native Guamanian.

The Japanese had occupied Guam during World War II, and it appeared they were beginning to occupy Guam again! North of the capitol city of Agana where some of the most beautiful beaches on Guam existed, many resort hotels had been built. Many other hotels were under construction. This area was called Hotel Row. These hotels catered to Japanese tourists, and most of the hotels were either owned by Japanese, or funded by them. Hotel row was a popular honeymoon spot for Japanese couples. A Guam honeymoon was closer to Japan, and thus cheaper than going to the other popular Japanese honeymoon destination, Hawaii.

During World War II, 5,000 Japanese troops invaded Guam, and overwhelmed the 400 U.S. Military persons stationed on Guam. This was in 1941, and a First Class Radioman, George R. Tweed, who was assigned to the Naval Communication Station, fled into the jungle. He was the only American serviceman to escape detention throughout the entire Japanese occupation. He published a book *"Robinson Crusoe USN*[40]*."* His story was made into a motion picture called *"No Man is an Island*[41]*"* in 1962, released by Universal Pictures, starring Jeffrey Hunter. Many Guamanians were killed or tortured who helped Tweed remain hidden during the war.

On a number of occasions Japanese tourists would appear at the Naval Magazine main gate and ask permission to enter the Naval Magazine property so they could offer prayers for relative soldiers that were killed there during the war. These requests were denied, and they would pray outside the main gate.

December of this year, I turned thirty-five years old, and with my impending promotion to chief, I felt very good about the future. I made a 1977 ORT Division Christmas card, and sent it to other Navy activities throughout the world that had GMT's. These Christmas cards were shared each year, and it was always good to see names of old friends stationed around the world. ORT Division had thirty-eight persons assigned, counting enlisted men and women, and officers.

January 1978 marked the "halfway point of my assignment in Guam, I had a year and a half remaining before it was time to transfer. ORT Division was busy preparing for the departure of the Army. This meant we would be very busy transporting the Army material from Naval Magazine to Anderson Air Force Base, a distance of twenty-six miles. This required the formation of special convoys, with marine guard escorts.

This relocation or evacuation of the Army would mean emptying many of the magazines within the ORT Division fenced limited area.

Before the actual convoys took place, we ran a few "training convoys." A convoy was composed of three semi trucks pulling loaded trailers. At the head and tail of the convoy were personnel carriers, loaded with armed marines. Each semi-truck had a driver and an armed marine in the cab. The Assistant Convoy Commander, a chief petty officer, and an armed marine, were at the very head of the convoy in front of the personnel carrier. At the very rear of the group of vehicles was another vehicle with the Convoy Commander, a commissioned officer, and another armed marine. Far in advance of the convoy would be a "sweep vehicle" full of armed marines looking for road hazards, suspicious persons, or trouble areas. Far above the convoy was a surveillance helicopter, containing a pilot, copilot, two armed marines, and a first class assigned to ORT Division. The helicopter flew back and forth along the convoy route watching for problems along the twenty-six mile road. On the Naval Magazine, in the basement underneath the enlisted barracks was the convoy command post. Within the basement were the commanding officer, magazine security officer, marine barracks executive officer, and a chief petty officer that maintained radio contact with all members of the convoy. A large alert force of armed marines stood by the command post, ready to respond to trouble if need be. A Guam police car, with siren sounding, and lights flashing led the main body of the convoy throughout the trip. Radio contact was constant throughout the convoy trip to Anderson Air Force Base. Radio checks were made every five minutes. If radio contact was lost for more than five minutes, the marine alert force was ready to respond and investigate. This was a huge operation involving most of the sailors and marines of Naval Magazine.

In February Senior Chief Smith asked me if I would be able to finish the mural I was working on at the Silver Dollar Club by the middle of the month. I said I could, and worked a couple of weekends to complete it. I was to discover why he asked me to finish it the end of the month. I was surprised the end of February by being told that I had been selected as Naval Magazine sailor of the year for 1977! This was an unexpected honor, and I was flattered to receive it. My picture was to be posted on the Naval Magazine Quarterdeck, and remain there for a year.

My first assignment on the Army convoys that began in March was as the observer in the surveillance helicopter. The convoys would form on the magazine for the trip to Anderson Air Force Base, around 1:00 p.m., often on weekends during low traffic periods. Upon arrival at Anderson Air Force Base, the material would then be loaded on military aircraft for the flight back to the U.S. The convoy would then retrace its route back to the magazine main gate. I would report to the Agana Naval Air Station, an hour prior to the convoy's departure from the magazine. I would climb aboard the helicopter with two marines, armed with M-14 rifles. I was armed with a forty-five-caliber pistol. The helicopter would take off thirty minutes before convoy departure time. The pilot and copilot made five persons on board. The bench just behind the pilot and copilot had just enough room for the two marines and me. The doors at both sides of the bench were locked open. The only thing that kept me and the marine seated on the opposite end of the bench from falling out and hurtling to our death far below (the marine in the middle was sandwiched between us), was a seatbelt harness which went around our waists and shoulders. As the helo made violent turns, and pitched about in the sky, we checked our seatbelt harnesses often for tightness. Before the convoy left the confines of the magazine, the helicopter would fly along the highway that was to be traveled by the convoy. I watched for any unusual gatherings of vehicles, people, or road hazards the convoy commander should be aware of. We remained in the air all the time the convoy was out of the confines of Naval Magazine, and Anderson Air Force Base.

On one flight I had some excitement. The pilot had to make an emergency landing, because his instrument panel showed a sudden drop in engine oil pressure. We landed on a clear spot on top of a mountain surrounded by jungle. We sat on top of the mountain for half an hour, until the pilot determined that the oil pressure gauge was faulty. We then took off again. This particular model of helicopters had been grounded in the past, because of crashes that had occurred when the transmission driveline to the rear rotor blade froze up! On one flight I took motion pictures of the convoy, and our flight over the jungles of Guam.

The Navy began a program of weight control for all sailors. New instructions were issued from Washington concerning this new program. Everyone in the Navy was to conform to specific weight limits that were gauged on how tall a sailor was. There was a formula based on measurements taken around a sailor's neck and waist. We all were "measured" and those determined to be overweight were ordered to be weighed weekly, and had to show a pattern of weight loss until their weight limit was reached. Sailors unofficially called this weight control program, "the fat boy program".

Along with the weight control program, there were new directives on physical fitness training. I'd seen sporadic attempts at enforcing physical fitness in the Navy during my career. The first being the exercises we called "JFK's," after President Kennedy. It seemed like every time our country had an ex-sailor as president, such as Presidents Kennedy and Carter, the Navy placed emphasis on our physical fitness. Although President Johnson was an ex-sailor, his administration was preoccupied with the Vietnam War. America's Navy in the beginning was patterned after the British Navy. Bulging waistlines in the British Navy had been a sign of rank. The fatter the admiral, the higher was his rank. This was how side boys came into being. When honors are rendered to officers coming aboard ships, (or shore stations), sailors stand in line on both sides of the quarterdeck, or entrance to a building, and salute while the honored officer walks through the walkway created by the saluting sailors. The higher the rank of the officer, the more "side boys" he rates. This increase in side boy numbers has a base in history. Originally the side boys were posted on the wooden ship's quarterdecks to help the "fat" British admirals aboard; when they crawled aboard the ship they were visiting. The higher-ranking admirals were the "fattest" and needed more side boys to hoist them aboard! Bulging waistlines had also become a common sight in the chief petty officer ranks. Most ships and Navy shore stations fed sailors exceptionally well, so this contributed to weight problems.

ORT Division began having calisthenics for thirty minutes every morning. As leading petty officer, I led the exercises every morning after the muster and quarters were held. There was much grumbling, and complaining when these exercises first began. There were two young seaman apprentices that refused to do exercises one morning. All the sailors in ORT Division were watching to see what would happen after they refused to comply. I spoke to both of them individually and privately after quarters. I explained to them this was a mandatory program, and they did not have the option of refusing exercising. They both said they would not exercise, so I put them both on report for disobeying an order. These two had been suspected illegal drug users, and I had counseled them both many times in the past about discipline problems. This refusal was the final straw. Both were removed from ORT Division, and they went to work in another division on base. It was after they were reassigned, that they both expressed regret to whoever would listen; they wished they were back in ORT Division. Both sailors eventually were busted for illegal drug usage. I don't believe their rebellion was due wholly to their immaturity, but also due to laziness. They thought they would have an easier job in a division other than ORT Division. I held the view that GMT's while working under unimaginable pressure, and stress had better work conditions than other nontechnical jobs in the Navy. I also thought we would have fewer GMT's thrown out of the nuclear weapons program if after boot camp they were given a taste of mess cooking, side cleaning, and "regular sailor work," before being given technical training. This had been the road I had traveled down, and I felt it gave me more appreciation, and motivation for success in the GMT rating. I also felt this job assignment method would glean out the more immature, and irresponsible sailors.

I continued to pile up "charges" in my charge book. One day I mistakenly left my charge book lying on my desk. Someone gave the book to Chief Margeson, and he laid it outside in the rain for a few minutes. This was another "charge," that I left my book unattended! From then on I had to carry my book in a plastic baggie, to keep it from getting wet.

As 16 April drew closer, I prepared for the big uniform change with Carmen's help. As luck would have it, one day while we were buying khaki uniforms in the Navy exchange, Chief Margeson caught me! This ended up being another "charge," "buying chief's uniforms before I was a real chief."

In April I was faced with a real dilemma. My promotion date was 16 April, and this date was a Sunday. My initiation and congratulations from the captain were to be held on Monday the 17th. Normally I would have liberty on Sunday, and would not be wearing a uniform. The problem was, a convoy was scheduled for Sunday, and I was assigned to man the radio in the command center. My dilemma was that I would be wearing the uniform of a chief before my initiation! Chief Margeson, my primary advisor, said I should wear my chief's uniform. The Friday before this weekend, Chief Margeson had gone with me to the base disbursing office. The chief in the disbursing office handed Chief Margeson my chief petty officer clothing allowance, which amounted to a little more than $400. Both the chiefs said this would just about cover the fines I would be given at my initiation on Monday! I didn't know whether to believe them or not? I had counted on this clothing allowance to help me with the expensive uniform change.

Sixteen April, the official day of my promotion, I put on my chief's uniform for the first time. After admiring myself in the mirror, I went to the magazine, and reported to the basement command center. The captain, and others in the command center congratulated me, and the convoy operation went off without a hitch. I had hoped I would get back off the magazine and home without seeing any chiefs. I was not lucky.

I had to walk to the quarterdeck to turn in the keys to the command post room after the convoy. Chief Margeson, Cushman, and Wilkins met me at the quarterdeck. They made me stand at attention, wrote in my charge book, and in general humiliated me.

On Friday I had been given a song sheet with the words to the song, Anchors Aweigh, I was told I was to be prepared to sing this song upon request. I was also given a "Plan of the Day," patterned after a "real" Plan of the Day, which listed events that would take place on Monday.

It read:
>Boot Chief Plan of the Day," and was signed by Commander Abrahams, and Executive Officer Lieutenant Commander Dimalio.
>
>This Plan of the Day contains information for the Boot Chief and in that context it is as official as he could ever imagine. The Boot Chief is responsible for the complete knowledge of its contents. For this day only, the Boot Chief does not have the right to normal recourse.
>
>Date: 17 April 1978
>Duty Section: Him
>Sunrise: Unimportant
>Sunset: He'll never see it.
>Subject Boot Chief: James S. Little
>Orders for compliance by Boot Chief: When in the privacy of Chief Petty Officers, all real Chiefs and members of the court will be addressed in a loud, clear voice as follows:
>E-7.........."Chief Sir"
>E-8........"Chief Sir Sir"
>E-9......." Chief Sir Sir Sir"
>The Judge......"Your Exalted Honor, Chief Sir Sir Sir Sir Sir (as applicable)"
>The Prosecutor..."Oh Merciful Prosecutor, Chief Sir Sir Sir (etc. as applicable)"
>The Jury......."Hi fellow Chiefs"
>Officers........ Optional
>All Times Approximate
>0645 The Boot Chief will report to the Naval Magazine Chiefs at the Silver Dollar Club (in the uniform of the day) for inspection.
>0700 Commence welcoming all real Chief Petty Officers with a proper greeting, a good cigar, donuts. A cup of coffee and a smile.
>07– The Boot Chief will request (and surely received) advice on the proper wearing of his new uniform and recommended method of shining shoes.
>0845 The Boot Chief will report to the Silver Dollar Club in tropical white long Chief uniform for the 0900 advancement ceremony.
>---- (When directed) report to the Personnel Office (escorted by a real CPO) and then with the able assistance of your companion, report to the disbursing office to pick up your OUR money.
>1100 Report to the Harbor CPO Club, Naval Station Guam for indoctrination in "How to become a Chief Petty Officer - and may the jury have mercy on your soul."
>This Plan of the Day was signed by "The Real NavMag CPO's."

I had already been to the personnel office and disbursing office, but still my day promised to be very busy. I had to get up early on Monday to buy donuts. I'd already bought a box of cigars. On Sunday at the magazine I'd also been given a subpoena and summons that said:

>Subpoena and Summons Extraordinary, the High Court of Destiny, U.S. Naval Magazine, Guam, M.I. To Whom It May Concern, chastise and berate, James S. Little.
>
>Know all exalted and accredited Chief Petty Officers of the superior grades of "E-nine", "E-eight" and "E-seven" by these presents whereas the accused, fully and correctly identified above, did, on or about 1130, 16 April 1978, desert the lower pay grade(s) of GMT1 and did place upon his body the uniform of a Recruit Chief Petty Officer. And did publicly present himself in the Naval Magazine area in said uniform. This act in violation of good order and discipline, as the court is not now and has never been in proper or otherwise possession of the accused's application to wear the uniform of a Chief Petty Officer.

And, whereas the high court of destiny shows it to be high time, correct and proper, that you present your sad and wandering nautical soul before said court of justice at the time and the date indicated above. Other charges are also filed." Chief Cruz and Chief Margeson signed the subpoena.

Also on the document were these "additional charges,"

1. On or about 7 April 1978, the accused did draw a cartoon depicting the Honorable Judge and the incomparable court as being cruel, bloodthirsty, apelike and sadistic. He publicly stated that this was his conception of the Chief Petty Officers comprising the court (Exhibit "A").

2. On several occasions, the perverted accused was observed to be obscenely fondling the headgear of several NavMag Chief Petty Officers (24 March 1978, 5 March 1978, and 13 April 1978). This degenerate behavior deserves the merciful consideration of the court.

I was told there would be additional charges, and the reading of a document I'd signed (without being permitted to read), "Why I want to be a Chief," in the court.

Sunday night, 16 April, I was busy trying to memorize all the verses to "Anchors Aweigh." I was told that Carmen should be at the Chief's Club on Monday at 3:30 p.m. I wondered if this was so she could collect my body.

I did not sleep much the night of the 16th. I arose early enough to buy two-dozen donuts, on my way to the magazine. I was at the Silver Dollar Club at 6:30 a.m., made a pot of coffee, and had a box of cigars ready. As the chiefs came through the door, I greeted them "Chief Sir," or "Chief Sir Sir" depending on their rank. I stood at attention, and was treated with disdain. I shined everyone's shoes. I sang Anchors Aweigh about four times. After the first singing of the song, it was so horrible; there were not many requests for a repeat. My adrenalin was flowing, and I had a smile on my face, I had waited eighteen years for this day. At 8:00 a.m. the harassment stopped, and I was told to change into the tropical white uniform. There was a group of nine other magazine sailors being promoted on this day. GMT2 Jim Jacks of ORT Division was being promoted to first class this day. I was the only one being promoted to chief. Carmen arrived at 0830, and the captain arrived shortly afterward.

The captain read my appointment letter which said in part:

Certificate of permanent appointment, to all who see these presents, greeting: know ye, that reposing special trust and confidence in the patriotism, valor, fidelity, and abilities of James Stewart Little I do hereby appoint you a permanent Chief Gunner's Mate Technician in the United States Navy. Your appointment carries with it the obligation that you exercise additional authority and willingly accept greater responsibility. Your every action must be governed by a strong sense of personal moral responsibility and leadership. You will observe and follow such orders as may be given by superiors acting according to the rules, articles and provisions of United States Regulations, General Orders, Uniform Code of Military Justice, and supporting Orders and Directives. Given under my hand at U.S. Naval Magazine M.I., this sixteenth day of April in the Year of our Lord Nineteen Hundred and seventy-eight.

Commander Abrahams had signed the Letter. Carmen and I had our picture taken with the captain. There was also a group picture of all the sailors being promoted. After the ceremony, I bid Carmen farewell, and Chief Margeson and I left for the naval station Chief's Club.

At the Club, I and five other "Boot Chiefs," were herded into a small back room. We six were to be initiated this day. A few of the others looked wide-eyed and afraid. They told of being awakened at 4:00 a.m., and running behind a chief's car for miles. Charlie Cushman had told me before this day arrived, that this was my day, and to enjoy it, and I intended to.

We were given sandwiches, and then each of us was given "costumes" to put on. Most of the others wore costumes that were hanging in a metal locker within the small room, a pirate outfit, clown costume, and baby's outfit, etc. I however had a special costume that Charlie Cushman gave to me to put on. It was a costume his wife Ruth had made under his direction. It was a white uniform jumper lined with pink lace, a white hat lined with pink lace, and a pair of white shorts lined with pink lace. I had a baby's bottle I was to carry. On the back of the jumper were the embroidered words "TODAY I GET TO BELITTLE THE CHIEF." Shower shoes rounded out my costume, and I looked ridiculous! (See photo page)

We six stood by the main door as the chiefs walked in. We would loudly announce each chief's arrival, as "Chief Sir arriving," or "Chief Sir Sir arriving," depending on the rank. We were called names, and ridiculed by each chief that walked in.

When one o'clock arrived, we were taken one by one into the main room of the club. Both sides of this room were lined with seated chiefs. At the front of the room seated behind a desk, and dressed in a black robe and white wig, was the senior master chief of the naval station. He was the judge. Also standing close by the judge was the prosecutor, dressed as a pirate. My defense counsel, Lieutenant Hume, was standing by the desk. As I stood at attention in front of the judge, the first matter was the reading of the letter "Why I want to be a Chief" which I had signed, but not been permitted to read.

> I want to be a Chief. That is the most important position in the world. Only the smartest people can be called "Chief."
>
> The Naval Officer's Manual refers to Chiefs as being "sly and crafty and bears watching at all times." Some of the best thieves in the world are Chiefs. They have developed a fine art called "comshaw." That is taking someone's property and having them thank you for getting it out of their way. Chiefs run the Navy, which is a multi-million dollar business.
>
> They are so efficient; they can do it while setting on their backside with their feet up on a desk and a cup of coffee in their hand.
>
> The really good Chiefs set up little empires wherever they go. They have a group of people that work for them called "officers." These people do most of the work and assist the Chief in managing the Navy. Good help is hard to find so the Chief spends a lot of time training new officers. A Chief never drinks alcoholic beverages, but if he does he never staggers - but if he staggers he never falls - but if he falls, he does so in a military manner and covers his crow to look like an officer.
>
> I want to be a Chief so I can get on the "gravy train" too. Personally, I don't believe the rumor that Chiefs are undersexed and overpaid. Most of the Chiefs I know are only slightly perverted, and don't deserve their lousy reputation.
>
> The government was so pleased to hear that I was being advanced that they decided to give away the Panama Canal because I passed by it once in my career. When the kids in the neighborhood learned that I was going to be a Chief, they responded in typical Navy-brat manner. The insurance man said that the broken glass and dents from rocks and ball bats would be covered by my fifty dollars deductible.
>
> In closing, I would like it noted that my defense counsel, the incomparable Griff Hume, recommended a plea for leniency due to the fact that I have wanted to be a Chief for so long but I think that a plea of innocent due to insanity would be more appropriate.

After the reading of this letter, additional "charges" were read.

1. On or about 17 March 1978 and again on or about 27 March 1978. The legally wedded wife of the accused was observed wearing a necklace with the revered and exalted insignia of a Chief Petty Officer attached thereon. On both occasions, she replied to inquires about the necklace, "He made me wear it."

2. On or about 12 October 1977, the accused did submit a request for consideration into the Army warrant officer program which would make him a member of the Army reserve which, to quote his own words, would "....make me better than any Navy Chief."

This last charge brought gasps of outrage, and shouts of anger from the whole room, and I wished I could melt into the floor! Lieutenant Hume tried to plead in my defense, but he was fined five dollars for being my defense attorney.

All six of us were brought before the judge, and he said we'd all been found guilty. We were going to have to drink "truth serum," but first there was to be a "talent contest," and the winner would not have to drink "truth serum." The prosecutor brought in the "truth serum". It was a large pitcher filled with what appeared to be tomato juice, on a silver platter. As we watched, the prosecutor poured in a bottle of Tabasco sauce, jalapeno pepper juice, and a few raw eggs into the pitcher. After seeing this, I wanted to win the "talent contest." A few sailors tried singing, and a couple danced. When my turn came, I asked for a large poster board, and a black felt tip marker. I quickly drew a flattering picture of the Judge and Prosecutor. I won the contest, so I watched as my fellow Boot Chiefs choked down a glass of "truth serum."

We were then told we were going to receive our punishment. One at a time we were brought into the large room, and given a series of "painful experiences," while the others waited in the small room we'd initially been taken into. The first was to be a lashing with a cat of nine tails.

I was brought into the room, and standing in the middle of the room was a chief with a horrible looking whip in his hand. The strands of the whip had glass, nails, and razors glued on it. I was then told to knell over a chair in the middle of the room. I noticed there were blood spots on the chair. I was told to raise my shirt, and then I was blindfolded. I heard the chief holding the whip, say, "Now the lashing begins." Something slapped my back, I jumped, and there was laughter! The blindfold was taken off, and I saw that the whip had been replaced with a wet towel that had struck my back. The next punishment, I was told to stand on the chair I had knelt over. Throughout this ordeal, I was reasonably sure I and the other Boot Chiefs would not be physically harmed, but I wasn't 100 percent sure of this. While I stood on the chair seat, barefooted, two chiefs carried in a large tray containing broken glass, and placed it underneath where I stood. The glass shards completely covered the bottom of the tray. A blindfold was once again tied around my eyes, and I was told to jump down into the tray! After much hesitation, and shouts from the chiefs in the room, I jumped. I felt crunching under my feet, and winched. I didn't dare move my feet. Once again there was laughter! The blindfold was removed, and I saw that the large tray filled with glass, had been replaced with a large tray filled with corn chips before I jumped.

After each sailor had gone through these "punishments," all six of us gathered in the large room for a contest of "skill." On one side of the room was a large block of ice. Directly on top of the block of ice was a single olive. Across the room directly opposite the block of ice was a chair, with a cocktail glass sitting in the middle of the seat. We were told to remove the olive from the block of ice, and place it into the cocktail glass across the room. We were to do this without using our hands, and in a very unique manner. We had to lower our pants, sit on the ice, squeeze our buttocks together grasping the olive, waddle across the room, and drop the olive into the glass. I managed to do it on my first try, but this was not the end of the "contest." After dropping the olive into the glass, we each had to eat our olive.

One of the last humiliations was "bombing practice." We had to lie flat on the floor, face up, with our mouths wide open. A ten-foot ladder was brought in, and each chief could pay a dollar for three raw eggs, climb the ladder, crack open the eggs and try to drop the falling raw egg into our mouths. If an egg fell into our mouth, we were told to swallow it. After countless raw eggs were dropped, the remainder of the truth serum was poured into our mouths. We were splattered from head to toe with raw eggs, and the tomato juice concoction.

After bombing practice, we were all taken back to the small room. We all took a shower, and got cleaned up. We were told to put on our khaki's minus collar devices. Some of the Boot Chiefs had been drinking liquor during the initiation. I did not. I did not want anything to dull the perception of this day that I had waited so long for. After we showered and dressed, we were paraded back into the large room. The room had been cleaned up, and all the chiefs were silently standing in ranks with hats on. The master chief who had been the judge began speaking after we had assembled at attention. Everyone was silent, and appeared very serious.

> The following is dedicated to all the Chief Petty Officers that have gone before you and is directed specifically at you.
>
> During the course of your initiation you have been caused to suffer friendly indignities to experience humiliation. This you have accomplished with rare good grace, and therefore, we now believe it fitting to explain to you just why this was done.
>
> There was no intent, and certainly no desire to insult you, or in any way demean you. Pointless as it may have seemed to you, there was a valid, time honored, yes, traditional reason behind every single deed and each pointed barb.
>
> By experience, by performance, and by testing, you have earned advancement to the grade of E-7. You have one more hurdle to overcome. In the United States Navy and only in the United States Navy, does an E-7 carry such unique responsibility. No other armed forces throughout the world grants the esteem and the responsibility, which you are now privileged to observe and fulfill.
>
> Your entire way of life and position in the United States Navy has now been changed. More will be expected of you, more will be demanded of you. Not because you are an E-7, but because you are now a Chief Petty Officer.
>
> You have not merely been promoted in pay grade, you have joined an exclusive fraternity, and as in all fraternities, you have a responsibility to your brothers, even as they have a responsibility to you.

Always bear in mind that no other armed service has rate or rank equivalent to that of the United States Navy. Granted that all armed services have two classes of service, enlisted and commissioned. However the United States Navy has four. Enlisted, bureau appointed Chief Petty Officers, and bureau appointed warrant and commissioned officers. This is why we can maintain with pride, our feeling of seniority once we have attained this position of Chief Petty Officer.

The privileges and responsibilities that we enjoy do not appear in print. In fact they have no official standing, neither can they be referred to by name, number or file. They exist because for nearly 200 years, Chiefs before you have freely accepted responsibility beyond the call of printed assignment, and have by their actions and by their performance demanded the respect of their seniors, and commanded the respect of their juniors.

It is now required that you become the fount of wisdom. The ambassador of good will, the authority (sometimes the "buffer") in personal relations, the technical advisor and finally the example (militarily, morally and otherwise) that your juniors look up to, and that they strive to emulate and one day become....."Ask the Chief".... a phrase that rings throughout the Navy...You are now that Chief!!!

The exalted position you have now achieved and the word "exalted" is used advisedly exists only because of the attitude, example, and the performance of Chiefs before you. It shall exist only so long as you and your cohorts maintain these standards.

So this then is why you were caused to experience these things. You were subjected to humiliations to prove to you that humility is a good, great and a necessary trait which cannot mar you. In fact it strengthens you. In the future as a Chief Petty Officer, you will be caused to suffer indignities and humiliations far greater that those imposed upon you today. Bear them with dignity and with the same good grace with which you bore them today.

It was our intention to prove these facts to you. It was our intention that you will never forget this day. It was our intention to test you, to try you, and accept you. Your performance today has assured us that you will wear your hat with the same feeling of great pride as the Chiefs who preceded you have honorably and proudly worn theirs. We take sincere pleasure in welcoming you to our midst.

After this reading, Ray Margeson, while other chiefs were doing the same to those standing by me, pinned one anchor on my collar (see photograph page), shook my hand, and said, "Congratulations Chief." Then Carmen along with the other wives was escorted in, and she pinned the last anchor on my collar. Ray had been taking pictures throughout the initiation, and he got a picture of the collar pinning. Carmen and the wives were then escorted back out, and while we new chiefs stood in a row, each chief walked up to us and shook our hands. The master chief then said, "This is the only time you will be permitted to wear your hat within the club, chiefs please remove your hats," which we did.

It's hard to verbalize the feelings of elation I felt that day. Charlie said I had a smile a foot wide all day, and they all said it was a great initiation. I was also glad it was over. I thanked Lieutenant Hume for being my defense attorney, although he was a failure. While we were all sitting around, we were given back our $400 clothing allowance, minus twenty-five dollars, which helped with the expense of the initiation, and paid for some of the chief's drinks.

Soon Carmen joined me, and us, Ray Margeson, his wife Mary, and Bud Wilkins and his wife Penny went to Agana, and had dinner at a Bavarian restaurant. Charlie Cushman had duty as Naval Magazine OOD, and didn't get to accompany us with his wife Ruth. Bud gave me a nice present during the dinner. It was a plaque with a brass chief's insignia, and a plate inscribed, "James S. Little, GMTC, USN, 16 April 1978." We had a very nice evening together, and I might add alcohol free. The previous few years there had been considerable criticism about chief's initiations getting out of hand. There had been some deaths from over drinking and drunk driving after initiations. The Navy was not anxious to interfere with the initiation process, but the word filtered down that good judgment was expected by those conducting the initiations, and that excess drinking was frowned upon. There had been one death, when a phony beheading was carried out on a blindfolded Boot Chief, when he suffered a heart attack. The word from the Chief of Naval Operations (CNO) was to "tone-down" the initiations.

There are memorable days in a person's life, and the day I was initiated into the brotherhood of United States Navy Chief Petty Officers, was one of my most memorable days. The next day, Tuesday, I was given the day off. I didn't argue, it had been a very busy couple of days, and I was thankful for a breather.

On Wednesday morning when I went to work, I was somewhat self-conscious in my new uniform of khaki's, and I was no longer, "Jim" or "Little," now I was always addressed as "Chief."

A very real, invisible wall was suddenly erected between me and the sailors in dungarees. I was no longer "one of them." I was now a chief, and elevated to almost the same category as officers, and my authority was not questioned.

I now wore a chief's hat, which was a visor type, with the gold plated fouled anchor device that identified a chief. This hat was much heavier to wear than the baseball style cap worn by first class petty officers and below, and took some getting used to. Many chiefs wore the cloth garrison hat, which was not as cumbersome as the visor style hat, and when not being worn could be tucked under your belt. I wore a khaki uniform each workday. I also wore a different belt buckle now. Belt buckles worn by chiefs were gold in color, and uniform in style and color. Most commands overlooked the wearing of personalized belt buckles, except during personnel inspections when E-1 through E-6 was expected to wear silver belt buckles, and chiefs and officers gold belt buckles. Many had everyday belt buckles with their name engraved on them, or in the case of GMT's a buckle with crossed cannons on it. I preferred a belt buckle with a chief's fouled anchor insignia on it. In the past, Carmen had always faithfully ironed my dungaree uniforms. Now that I wore chief's uniforms, I had to use a dry cleaner. I also preferred shirts that had a military crease, which are two extra creases that travel vertically down through both shirt pockets.

With the uniform change, there also came a job change. GMT1 Jack Osilka, prior to my initiation had been easing into the leading petty officer job. Charlie Cushman was the production plant supervisor. Ray Margeson had taken over the leading chief position, following the transfer of Senior Chief Smith. My new job title was "Technical Ordnance Production control Supervisor." I was responsible for the coordination of all weapon's maintenance work, issuing work orders, and responsible for the preparation and submission of all necessary paperwork. This involved the operation of a keypunch machine, and the submission of countless messages. I had two assistants, GMT1 Chris Reed, and GMT2 Steve Cline. As I had advanced in rate, I had gradually migrated from the nuts and bolts, wrench and screwdriver area of nuclear weapons maintenance, to the paperwork, or deskwork aspects of the program. My new desk was in the production plant office, but with the evacuation of the Army, their offices in another building, the outside handling building, became available. I would be moving into this building, which was about two blocks from the production plant.

With my promotion came jobs of increasing responsibility. One of these jobs was as assistant convoy commander. Charlie Cushman began taking the job of command post chief, which I had for a couple of months. After being given a certification letter signed by the commanding officer, I assumed duties as the assistant convoy commander. The job moving the Army material was a large one, involving more than thirty convoys.

As Naval Magazine's "Sailor of the Year," I was nominated to be Naval Forces Marianas Sailor of the Year. Also since the Naval Magazine was a command under Commander Naval Logistics Command, Pacific Fleet, I was nominated as ComNavLogPac Sailor of the Year. Sailor of the year is an annual honor in the Navy. At the top of the hill of all the sailors of the year, are the Pacific, Atlantic, Shore and Sea Sailors of the Year. The Fleet Reserve Association hosts these four selected sailors, and they and their spouses are given a free trip to Washington, D.C. They get to meet the Chief of Naval Operations, and other Navy and government officials. An added benefit for the selected sailors of the year is that they get an automatic promotion to the next rate.

On 29 April 1978, thirteen days after my promotion to chief, I was to attend the Guam Council of the Navy League, "Silver Plate Dinner," which was a social affair honoring all the selected sailors of the year on Guam. It was a formal affair held at the naval station enlisted club, the Club Macambo. I wore dress whites, and Carmen wore a formal dress. We got a free dinner, and the U.S. Naval Forces Marianas Sailor of the Year was announced. Rear Admiral David S. Cruden, who was the Commander Naval Forces Marianas, announced the sailor's name. A sailor stationed on the U.S.S. Proteus won it. I was secretly relieved that I was not selected. I was somewhat uncomfortable being praised for doing my job, knowing many worthy sailors that did their jobs just as diligently as I. The admiral and his wife sat with Carmen and me at our table, and chatted with us for most of the evening. A USO troop called "Twenty-first Century fox" put on a very entertaining show.

The first of May, I received a letter from Admiral Cruden that had been endorsed by the Naval Magazine Commanding Officer. The letter read;

> You are to be commended for your nomination as Commander U.S. Naval Forces, Marianas Sailor of the Year.

> Although you were not selected, you are among the truly "top notch" sailors on the island of Guam, and I am proud of your personal achievement and sustained performance at this point in your naval career.
>
> Since your commanding officer has chosen you from among your shipmates to represent your activity in the competitive award, you may indeed consider yourself a winner. Please accept my personal congratulations for a job "well done."

Not long after this, I received a letter from Rear Admiral R.S. Wentworth, Jr. Commander of Naval Logistics, Pacific that said;

> It was with great pleasure that I recently reviewed your nomination as Naval Logistics Command, U.S. Pacific Fleet Shore Sailor of the Year. This nomination is an honor, which is bestowed only on those who have exhibited the highest standards of initiative, professionalism and devotion to the command.
>
> To be selected as the best in your command is an achievement that fully expresses your commanding officer's trust and confidence in your performance and capabilities.
>
> I was particularly impressed by your record of achievements. To excel as you have requires long hours of hard work and a degree of dedication that is seldom matched by your contemporaries. You and others like you are the greatest assets we have in the Navy.
>
> I wish to extend to you my personal appreciation for a job well done and my best wishes for continued success in your future endeavors.

In June we had our annual NTPI inspection. All of the reports, and paperwork, which I was responsible for, were inspected, and no discrepancies were found. I was very pleased with these results. I was surprised to see GMTCM, Master Chief Dave Wiesenhahn on the Inspection team. We had been together on the *USS Independence*, and at Whidbey Island. Dave said if I wanted it, he could get me on a staff job on North Island Naval Air Station when my time on Guam was up. The only drawback to this assignment, Carmen and I were not excited about living in San Diego.

After the inspection in June, work at ORT Division slowed down, and since I had a lot of leave on the books, I took ten days leave in July. I didn't do anything special other than snorkel, and look for seashells. I had a respectable collection at this point, but still no golden cowry.

My parents had sent me a beautiful Bible as a gift of congratulations for my promotion. In the front portion of the Bible, they had written, "Hail to the Chief." In my new life as a chief, I was amazed at the kinship, and spirit of cooperation among the chief petty officer ranks. There did exist deference to senior chiefs, and master chiefs, but as a rule if a chief needed help, cooperation, or encouragement, all he had to do was ask another chief. Within the first class ranks there had always been a spirit of cooperation, but it did not compare to the brotherhood of chief petty officers. Master Chiefs were the elite of the chief's ranks. I had noticed over the years in the officer ranks, some of the most difficult officers to deal with were lieutenant commanders. I believe this was due to the fact that the move from lieutenant commander to commander was a big promotion, almost akin to the move from first class to chief. Lieutenant commanders were always anxious about the promotion to commander. The frustration, and anxiety I'd felt over my inability to make chief were now gone, and I began considering what I needed to do to be promoted to senior chief.

The Navy special services of the naval station had a large fishing boat that was manned by four sailors, and could be chartered by sailors for a one-day fishing trip. Just as I had taken my stepson Peter on a fishing trip on his thirteenth birthday, I chartered a fishing trip for stepson Roger and me as a birthday present. Roger and I boarded the fishing boat one Saturday morning, and got underway. We trolled lures behind the boat, and were fishing for mahi mahi, and Pacific blue marlin. The first few mahi mahi (a fish in the dolphin family, with a high forehead) would swim after the trailing lures, near the surface with raised dorsal fins, looking very much like sharks moving in for a kill. We did very well; Roger and I caught seven of the fish, which weighed about fifteen pounds apiece. There was another fisherman on the boat, a Filipino Navy Exchange employee, who had not caught anything. I was beginning to feel sorry for him, when suddenly his pole bent double in the pole holder. He had hooked a marlin. He fought the big fish for more than thirty minutes. The first part of the fight, the marlin "tail walked" on the surface of the water. He was finally able to bring the fish alongside the boat, and the boatmen gaffed the fish, and brought it aboard. It was more than seven feet long, not counting the swordbill, and weighed more than 100 pounds. The fisherman was exhausted. When the day was over, and we were back alongside the pier, the Filipino fisherman offered to trade the marlin for three of the mahi mahi Roger and I had caught. We agreed, and I called Carmen to come and pick Roger and me up for the ride home.

She picked us up in the Vega Station Wagon, and we loaded the big fish. He filled the back, and front of the car. When the marine sentry at the main gate of the naval station saw the big fish inside the car, his eyes got big. At home we took pictures of the fish, and then I began the most distasteful part of fishing, cleaning the fish. The marlin yielded pounds and pounds of swordfish steak. We froze it in our freezer, and gave most of it away to friends.

The convoys evacuating the Army continued. GMT2 Steve Cline, who worked for me, had taken leave the first of the year and returned to his home in Las Vegas, Nevada to visit his mother, and father. His father was very ill the first six months of the year. During one of the convoys, I was assistant convoy commander, and Steve was one of the semi truck drivers. Upon our arrival at Anderson Air Force Base, Charlie Cushman, who was in the magazine command center, called Lieutenant Hume, the convoy commander, and I, and informed us that word had been received at the magazine that Steve's father had just passed away. Lieutenant Hume and I had to break the news to Steve. We relieved him of driving duties, and had a pickup driver return him to the magazine so he could contact his mother. It so happened that both Steve and I had duty that night. He came to my duty room that night, and he was very upset, I tried to console him. I listened to him talk about his father until late that night. There were many occasions at different commands when sailors were informed of deaths in their families. Sailors were permitted emergency leave only in the case of a death in their immediate family, such as wife, children, father, mother, or siblings. Sailors on emergency leave were always given the highest priority transportation when returning to the United States from overseas. Thankfully I only had two occasions for emergency leave that being when my son died, and my ex-wife was ill. In Steve's case he left on emergency leave the following day.

One evening Carmen and I went to a Mexican food restaurant on Marine Drive, which was the main road between the naval station and Agana. In the restaurant we saw Admiral Cruden and his wife, who invited us to join them for dinner. We shared a nice evening with them.

The job of Commander U.S. Naval Forces, Marianas, held by Admiral Cruden, came about after Fleet Admiral Chester W. Nimitz, who was the Commander in Chief of the Pacific, defeated the Japanese on Guam during World War II. From 1944 to 1949 Guam was under a military government, and the admiral who was ComNavMarianas was charged with governorship of all the Marianas Islands, as I explained in my narrative about my previous tour on Guam.

Admiral Cruden was one of a long line of admirals to hold this important position. In 1975 he had been in charge of an operation called *"Operation New Life,"* which had the monumental task of receiving, supporting, and processing 111,919 refugees transiting Guam after their evacuation from Vietnam. He also directed and coordinated recovery efforts on Guam in the aftermath of super Typhoon Pamela. In 1978, Admiral Cruden wrote a letter that was addressed to all military members on Guam, which was published in the annual magazine *"Orders Guam"*. The letter said[42];

> Hafa Adai, The traditional Chamorro greeting, often used by the people of Guam to welcome old friends and newcomers alike, seems an appropriate phrase for this publication. It is, after all, one way to welcome you to Guam for a tour of duty, which can be at once demanding, exciting, and most rewarding. In the pages which follow, you will find information concerning many aspects of life and work on Guam, ranging from descriptions of the various commands on the island to maps of the many housing areas. I hope you will study it carefully, since it is designed to increase your understanding of Guam and the lifestyle you will be part of during your assignment here.
>
> That lifestyle can be one, which is thoroughly enjoyable. In few places I have been stationed have I found such a wealth of potential for personal involvement and professional fulfillment. One of the best ways to enjoy Guam is to become acquainted with native Guamanians; by establishing friendships with them, and by taking advantage of the beautiful outdoor life Guam has to offer, the warmth of "Hafa Adai" can be fully understood.

Admiral Cruden and his wife always went out of their way to talk to us when they saw Carmen or me. I painted an anniversary painting for them, which Carmen presented to him in his office. I have a picture of this presentation. When Admiral Cruden was transferred, Carmen and I received an official invitation to his change of command ceremony. The Naval Magazine Commanding Officer and we were the only ones on the magazine to receive an invitation. We were honored by his friendship.

As I said, we conducted more than thirty convoys moving the Army off Guam. We tried to keep a low profile by conducting the convoys on weekends, and avoiding high traffic periods.

As luck would have it, on the last convoy, on the return trip to the magazine, a group of people on a bluff overlooking the highway threw rocks at the trucks. A few people were arrested, and then released the next day. Also the next day, the island paper ran a front-page story with pictures of our convoy trucks, and a story speculating about nuclear weapons. Fortunately this was our last convoy.

In July a historic event took place on Guam. Three ships of the Japanese Maritime Self Defense Force (Japanese Navy) were scheduled to make a port call on Guam. This was the first time the Japanese Navy had set foot on Guam since World War II. The first evening in port, the officers of the three ships, were hosting various American naval officers onboard the ships.

The Japanese Navy has six grades of enlisted men. The highest sixth level functioned as chiefs did in the U.S. Navy. Each command on Guam was to send a representative chief to a formal social gathering on one of the ships, on the second evening of their port visit. Wives of the chiefs were invited, and encouraged to attend. As the junior chief on the Naval Magazine, I was asked if Carmen and I would attend. Although it meant wearing formal dress whites, I agreed, as Carmen and I enjoyed attending such gatherings.

On the designated evening, Carmen and I went to the pier where the Japanese destroyer was tied alongside. We went aboard. We were not prepared for what awaited us. First, as all the wives came aboard, they were given a ticket stub, and told to please keep it for a drawing later on. A Japanese Navy "Chief" was assigned to remain with us for the whole evening. As we walked about the upper deck of the ship, we discovered at six different locations there were portable stoves, cooking and offering different types of food. It was a huge variety of food. Tempura shrimp, filet mignon steak chunks on a stick, lobster, oysters and fish, and even caviar! The selection of beverages was endless. Our assigned host spoke very good English, and kept our glasses and plates full as we walked about the ship.

The Japanese sailors put on a special show welcoming us. A huge wooden sake barrel was brought out, and with chanting, and dancing by sailors in samurai costumes and ceremonial gestures, the barrel was broken with a mallet. Everyone was served sake in wooden cups, followed by many, many toasts to the American and Japanese Navy. After the toasts, there were drawings of the tickets, that the wives had stubs of. The prizes were unbelievable, wristwatches, fur coats, and jewelry. Carmen received an expensive Japanese doll as well as other items such as fans, and scarves. When we were ready to depart the ship, we had an armful of keepsakes, wooden cups, Carmen's gifts, and the fancy chopsticks we had used during the evening. As we were crossing the quarterdeck, an international incident almost happened! The deck was damp, and Carmen was wearing high heel shoes. She slipped and fell. Ten Japanese sailors rushed forward. She was unhurt, but they were extremely concerned, and only let us go after assurances that she was OK.

The following night, it was our turn to host the Japanese sailors at the Naval Station Chief's Club. I took a Naval Magazine wall plaque, which I was to present to the Japanese sailors that night. Carmen and I arrived at the club wondering how in the world the American Navy would be able to extend to the Japanese Navy the hospitality and generosity we had received the previous night.

As we feared, the Chief's Club could not possibly be the host the Japanese had been. There was a line for snacks that were little hot dogs on toothpicks, and Ritz crackers with small bits of cheese. This was pitiful compared to the lobster, steak and caviar we had been treated to. I was also shocked at the exchange of command plaques. Each chief representing his command gave a wall plaque to the senior enlisted sailor of the three ships. We were given plaques in return. The plaque I received from them was a beautiful gold-plated plaque, as well as a full sized samurai helmet on a silk pillow. The Naval Magazine, wood and plaster wall plaque paled in comparison. A microphone was passed throughout the club from person to person to express gratitude for the hospitality shown to us over the two evenings. I expressed thanks, and then when the microphone was passed to Carmen, she surprised me by saying she wished to sing a Puerto Rican song to honor the visiting Japanese. She then sang the most beautiful song I think any of us had ever heard. Although it was in Spanish, and none understood the words, and there were no musical instruments accompanying her song, it was sung from her heart, and it stunned everyone. As the last words of her song faded, there was absolute silence, and then a long and loud burst of applause. Carmen had never sung publicly, prior to that day, or since, but it was the high point of the evening. She received continuous thanks and praise for her song. Her song helped us immensely by "saving face," for our pathetic efforts to equal the hospitality we were shown by the Japanese. All the chiefs took up a collection, and told the Japanese sailors that for the rest of the evening they could drink Johnny Walker Red scotch on the house. This was their favorite drink, and very expensive in Japan.

The big disadvantage we suffered as American sailors hosting the Japanese sailors, was that their defense budget included dollars (or yen), for social gatherings, and functions that interfaced with other nations. This attitude toward entertainment and hospitality was consistent throughout Japanese society.

A big item for Japanese businesses was the entertainment expense account. The companies paid for the entertainment of clients, and prospective clients. In the U.S. Navy we had no funds, or entertainment account for the entertainment of foreign militaries, so as was the case in Guam, we were "outgunned."

Later that week during a chief's meeting with Commander Abrahams I presented the plaque, and helmet to him, that had been given to me by the Japanese Navy. Both items were placed in a glass display case on the magazine quarterdeck.

In July, I also completed a Navy correspondence course called "Uniform Code of Military Justice." This was an effort at self-education, and also an attempt to show education endeavors to the promotion board, when I was eligible for senior chief. In September I enrolled in a Bible literature course conducted by Simpson College, San Francisco. This was an extension course that gave me three college credits. As a coincidence, Charlie Cushman and I had attended a college course in Oakland together, during this class his wife Ruth attended the class. I enjoyed the class, and received an "A."

GMT1 Jim Jacks transferred in the fall. He left a "Booney Dog" with us that we had become attached to when we visited the Jack's home. His name was "Mooch," and he was an exceptionally good-natured dog. A Guam Booney Dog was an actual breed of dog that had specific characteristics. They were large about sixty to seventy pounds in weight, short hair, mostly an orange, brown and tan color. Their muzzle was a lot like a German Shepherd. However, unlike a German Shepherd their ears did not peak, but flopped over. One of the most unusual traits of a booney dog was the way they ran. They bounded almost like a deer when running. Booney dogs were almost extinct at one point in Guam's history. A rabies plague spread through the island in the 1950s, and most of the dogs on the island were put to death, because of the fear of rabies. Mooch had a very pleasing personality and he adjusted to our home quickly. He was very protective of everyone in the family, but never barked or threatened visitors in our home. He would bark when someone walked up the sidewalk toward our front door, so he was a good "doorbell." Mooch was bothered with an ear infection, so we had to doctor his ears often with medication we got from a veterinarian. Mooch had the upsetting habit of disappearing for a week or a two at a time. He would then reappear at our door "smiling," with his tail wagging one hundred miles an hour. We suspected he was running with other booney dogs in the jungle. This was a dangerous way of life for a dog, and although he wore a collar, a loose dog on Guam was a "target." Rabies was still a concern on Guam, and wild dogs were hunted and shot. On the Naval Magazine a shotgun was kept on the quarterdeck specifically for dispatching wild dogs seen on magazine property. On one occasion Mooch disappeared for over a month, and we were sure he had met his end. A long while after we had searched for him, and given up, he appeared at our door with a wagging tail. His fur looked a little ragged, and torn, it was a happy homecoming, and we gave him a long lecture about disappearing, from the look on his face, I think he understood, because he didn't disappear again for three months.

Three months after his long disappearance, we received a telephone call from a woman who was calling from Hawaii. She said she was returning to Guam shortly to claim Mooch! The woman had gotten our phone number from Jim Jacks. The lady explained over the phone that they had been previously stationed on Guam, and had left Mooch with the Jack's with the understanding they would be reclaiming Mooch in the future. Carmen and I were upset by this turn of events. Jim Jacks had not told us anything about these arrangements, and we assumed that Mooch belonged to us. We almost didn't let Mooch go when the lady came to pick him up, but we finally relented. We never told the kids of this situation, and let them think he had once again disappeared for a "jungle vacation." This was a painful affair, like losing a member of the family. Mooch left Guam with his previous owner, and began his new life in Hawaii.

Carmen became friends with a French woman named Jacqueline. She was married to a first class petty officer that was a crewmember on an antisubmarine patrol P2V *Neptune* aircraft. He was stationed at the Agana Naval Air Station, while Jacqueline and their four children lived near us on the naval station. They had a tumultuous marriage. One day when Jacqueline was angry with him, she piled all of his clothes in the back yard, doused them with lighter fluid, and burned them all.

They eventually moved from the Naval Station to the Naval Air Station. I had suspicions about Jacqueline's husband. He always talked about having large amounts of money, instead of living from payday to payday as Carmen and I did. He talked of having a lot of property in California. Drug smuggling in the Navy was a frequent offense among aircraft crewmembers.

P2V's flew from country to country, landing and taking off at military bases, very seldom going through customs inspections. He must have sensed my suspicions, because one evening while visiting him, he revealed the source of the wealth he bragged about. He said he had been stationed in Southern California, and while shopping one day in a super market an idea came to him.

He noticed most of the groceries shopping carts were dirty, and many had sticking wheels that made them difficult and frustrating to use. He began researching and reading all the information he could find on grocery carts. He wrote to grocery shopping cart manufacturers, and purchased spare parts. He also bought a steam compressor that was on a trailer, and could be towed. He then approached a couple of super markets with contracts that stated he would come once a month during late night hours, and inspect and repair all their carts, as well as steam clean them. He was so successful that he expanded to additional markets, and hired workers. When he transferred to Guam, he had a couple of workers remaining in California continuing the shopping cart business. This was an impressive story, but I still wasn't fully convinced that this was the only additional source of wealth he bragged about.

GMT1 Joe Murphy, who had been with me on Guam in 1969-70, had been stationed on the *USS Proteus*, and then had been once again stationed on the Naval Magazine. He had married a Guamanian girl, spoke the language, and lived in a Guam village. Joe had almost turned into a Guamanian. Most of his wife's family lived with him.

During one of the many festivals Carmen and I attended, we visited Joe's house. During this festival, there was a parade through the village, with Admiral Cruden at the head of the parade. He was glad to see us.

On 29 November 1978 there was another change of command at the Naval Magazine. Commander Abraham's time to transfer had arrived. We had welcomed him when Commander Gerrard had departed. Commander Abraham had kept a low profile compared to his predecessor, and was respected by the magazine sailors.

Our new commanding officer was Commander John W. Brown. He was unique in that he had come up from the enlisted ranks. He had been a Radarman First Class Petty Officer at one time. He had attended Officer Candidate School (OCS). He served in the Korean War, and a variety of assignment in the Far East. One of his most impressive assignments was as Commanding Officer of the *USS Garrett County* (LST 786), when he spent a year in the Mekong Delta, where his ship engaged in river warfare as a Patrol Boat Riverine (PBR) Support Tender, and as a Sea Wolf Helicopter gunship platform, during the Vietnam War. The PBR's were one of the most recognizable weapons of the Vietnam War. They were 31 foot, water jet propelled boats armed with 50 caliber machine guns, and other weapons, used to patrol the Mekong Delta River waters.

A couple of days after the change of command ceremony, Commander Brown had a meeting with all the chiefs and officers. He was a very personable officer. He said he did not plan any radical changes in the management of the magazine. He said he would like to have monthly, or perhaps more frequent meetings with the officers and chiefs to discuss how things are going, and to share his ideas and any directions he wanted carried out. We chiefs were very optimistic about Commander Brown. He sounded like a professional, and very approachable. We also were pleased that he was a "Mustang," or officer that's come up through the ranks. It was common knowledge in the Navy that usually those officers with experience as an enlisted man were some of the best officers. We were also impressed with his wartime experience in Vietnam. Those that served in combat units, or knew what it was like to work under wartime conditions, tended to emphasize priorities on jobs and training efforts that were realistic, and meaningful. They were interested in accomplishing a command's mission effectively while paying close attention to the needs and morale of their men. Commander Brown gained our respect immediately, and as time passed that respect continued to grow.

TM1 Dick Burton, the leading Torpedoman in ORT Division, made chief after the February '78 exam. He was initiated in November. I made a number of entries in his "charge book," and I enjoyed the initiation ceremony at the Chief's Club, on the "other side of the fence." One of his fellow Boot Chiefs at the initiation was a Wave. She withstood the initiation with "exceptionally good grace" as stated in the Chief's creed.

Dick's wife, Debbie Burton was a reporter for Guam's daily newspaper *"The Islander."* She wanted to publish an article about my artistic efforts, so she interviewed me, and took a number of pictures. The article was published on 17 December 1978. There were pictures of the murals I'd painted on the walls of our house, (see photograph page) and the Silver Dollar Club, as well as a number of cartoons I'd drawn. This article led to a job as a cartoonist. A couple of weeks after the article, the paper asked me if I would provide one cartoon a week for the Sunday paper edition. The section where my cartoon was printed was to be called "Little Looks at Guam." They would pay me fifteen dollars for each cartoon. I was excited about doing it.

My cartoonist job was short-lived. I only had five published, before the paper substituted something else. In this short time however, I gained a faithful following of people who collected my cartoons, and anxiously waited for each week's cartoon. The money I received was the first time I'd been paid for my artwork.

In December, my Uncle Hubert visited Guam to see his son David, and daughter-in-law Carolyn, and his grandsons. I was happy to see him one evening in the Navy exchange cafeteria. Some of my fondest memories as a child included spending time with my Uncle Hubert at the California country home I was raised in (see photograph page).

Carmen, while working at the Navy exchange shoe section, had been approached by a vendor who worked in the jewelry section of the exchange. The vendor asked her if she would consider working as an independent jewelry vendor for a jeweler named Marie Ross. Carmen accepted the position, and was paid on a commission basis. She did very well selling jewelry.

The transmission in our Pontiac went out unexpectedly. We had the transmission replaced at a cost of $500. We began considering a new car, which we would take to our new duty station, wherever that might be. We considered purchasing a Honda, as many sailors at the magazine had. The Honda dealership wouldn't give us very much for the six-year-old Pontiac, which had more than 100,000 miles on it. The gas shortage we had experienced in the states was fresh in our minds, so we preferred a car that used little gas. The Navy exchange had auto sales offices that sold cars for delivery when sailors returned to the United States. We decided to buy a Buick LeSabre, with a six-cylinder engine. We ordered it in 1978, and planned to confirm the delivery date when I received transfer orders.

We learned firsthand how dangerous stonefish were. GMT1Fegan had a five-year-old son that stepped on a stonefish while walking in the surf. A spine punctured his foot, which resulted in a large decayed spot on the bottom of his foot.

One afternoon, Carmen and I went fishing at Fena Lake. The lake was located in the middle of magazine property, and to fish there, required permission from the magazine quarterdeck. Fena Lake and the surrounding jungle was a game preserve, as I said before, patrolled twenty-four hours by marines. As part of my duties as officer of the deck, I patrolled this same area during duty days and nights. Always in the back of my mind was the shooting incident that left the First Class Mineman paralyzed. I often looked in the rear view mirror of the Navy pickup as I drove on these duty rounds. On this particular day that Carmen and I went fishing, we fished an area that was a huge pool below the lake spillway. The lake was very low at this time of year, and there was no water flowing down the spillway. We'd fished for a few minutes, when we saw movement under the surface of the brackish, brown water. We saw snaking through the water, what looked like a sea monster! Moving slowly through the water below was the largest fresh water eel I've ever seen, or have ever heard of since! It was easily as large around as a telephone pole, dark brown, and more than fifteen feet long. The eel had apparently come over the spillway, when the lake level was higher, and as the lake lowered it was trapped. Concrete walls encircled the pool at the bottom of the spillway, and we stood about twenty feet above the surface of the spillway pool. The eel took our bait a couple of times, and we had fun fighting it until our lines' broke. I had no intention of bringing this creature up the side of the concrete walls to where we were standing. I'd seen how vicious the eels of Fena Lake were. If you brought one ashore or into a boat with your fishing pole, they would snap at you, and try to attack you. They had needle sharp teeth, and I could imagine what terrible teeth this monster had. In a week or two the lake level rose, and the eel disappeared. During the low water period, many people tried to capture the eel without success. I've often wondered if there were even larger eels in Fena Lake. The fresh water and salt-water eels were considered a delicacy to the people of Guam. Joe Murphy used to sell the fresh water eels in the village he lived in with his wife.

It was time to prepare for another inspection. There were many details that would be examined by the inspectors, and we had to demonstrate many different operations that would come under their scrutiny. One operation to be demonstrated during our inspection, were the actions of our Accident Response Team, and the containment of any possible radioactive material. The accident response team sprang into action if there was an accident with a weapon. We had frequent training drills that were unannounced, involving most of the sailors on base, and taking an entire morning or afternoon to complete. A simulated accident might be, a fire in the production plant involving weapons. After the fire was fought, and put out, everyone had to evacuate the fenced limited area. This was a controlled evacuation that meant each person had to be examined with monitoring equipment for possible radioactive contamination. If radioactive material was found on a person's body, then he or she had to be decontaminated. The most common method of decontamination was to take a shower, before the person could be declared "clean" and permitted to leave the limited area.

While this was going on, the EOD Team would be suited up in protective suits, and enter the production plant and determine what steps to take to ensure the weapon (s) were safe.

I was in charge of a decontamination team of six sailors. These sailors and I would be dressed in airtight suits, with filter masks. We would set up tables and equipment after suiting up in our protective suits. As each person approached our decontamination site, we would go through elaborate procedures to monitor them for radiation. It took considerable time for everyone to set up equipment, get organized, and suited up. The suits were extremely uncomfortable in the heat and humidity of Guam. After a training drill of a few hours, we would be drenched in sweat.

After each accident response drill, all the chiefs and officers would meet in Commander Brown's office for a critique meeting. Problems experienced would be discussed, along with possible solutions to correct any problems that had arisen.

We had gone through seven drills over a period of two months, and during the last two, no one had said much during the critique meetings. Most of the officers were assuring Commander Brown that we were ready for our inspection, and didn't need any more training. From what I had seen, I felt we were a long way from being ready for our inspection. There had been a lot of personnel changes, and many of the new people were unfamiliar with the proper way to suit up, or the proper way to use the equipment. Most of the magazine sailors were unfamiliar with our magazine written instructions that spelled out in detail what was supposed to be done in the event of an accident.

After what was supposed to be our last training drill before our inspection, we all attended the captain's critique meeting. After everyone had spoken, the captain went around the room asking each person if they wanted to add anything before we were dismissed. I was one of the last to be asked this question. All the officers and chiefs said we were ready for the inspection. When the captain nodded at me, I said, "Captain, I don't mean to be a wet blanket, but if we perform like we have the last seven drills, and particularly like today, we'll fail the inspection." There was absolute silence in the room. I then described the long list of discrepancies I'd seen, and suggested that we needed more training. I also said we needed to reexamine our own instructions, as many people were not complying with them, and the inspectors would be inspecting us to see if we complied with our own written directives. The captain seemed concerned, yet pleased to hear this, and said we would have more training exercises. He thanked me for my input, although I got some dirty looks from some of the officers! These training drills were unpopular, because the decontamination suits were very uncomfortable, and each drill would take the majority of one working day. I had hoped someone would speak up before me, but they did not. It had taken a bit of courage, and a lot of thought on my part to speak against the others in the room. I didn't want the commanding officer to be misled, and faced with what I'm sure would have been an inspection failure. This was the first nuclear weapons program inspection Commander Brown had gone through. Those that have not experienced a nuclear weapons inspection find it hard to imagine how trivial and "nit-picking" nuclear weapons inspectors are. This is however, how they should be, as there can be no mistakes in the nuclear weapon program. The magazine had three more training drills, with more attention to details. I agreed after the last one that we were ready not only for an inspection, but ready in the event of a real accident, which was in reality the main purpose of our training efforts. At the time of our inspection, the Emergency Response Team received the highest grade possible, an "outstanding, with no discrepancies." I cannot take the credit for this. I just know that at the time everyone said we were ready, I knew we were not.

GMT1 Jack Osilka was the outside handling/grounds maintenance supervisor, as well as the leading petty officer. GMT1 Dick Johnson was the senior first class in the production plant. Dick was a strict disciplinarian, and the troops had given him a nickname. They called him "Commander Johnson," because of his direct manner, and inflexibility. Chief Charlie Cushman was more people oriented, whereas Dick Johnson was mission oriented. The two "bumped heads" often, with Chief Cushman as it should be, usually the winner. As I had been the leading petty officer just a couple of months before, I was often approached by junior men and asked if I could do something about "Commander Johnson." I did not wish to usurp Dick's authority. I was thankful to be the Production Control Chief, versus the Production Plant Chief responsible for thirty-two plus sailors. For the time being I was satisfied with supervising two sailors, after being a leading petty officer for ten years.

In December I turned thirty-six years old. We spent our last Christmas on Guam. Carmen had bought a "houseful" of furniture from a furniture store that was famous for selling Asian furniture for very reasonable prices.

She purchased a huge stereo cabinet, china cabinet, a carved coffee table, and two end tables, a curio display case, two grandfather clocks, roll top desk, a couch and love seat, and eight wood carved high back chairs. All of the items were hand carved, and made of exotic wood. The plan was to have all the furniture delivered to our house just prior to the pack out for shipment to our next duty station. During our time on Guam, we had used the very basic and plain Navy issue furniture, and we looked forward to using our new furniture.

Mom and Dad were interested in a grandfather clock. They had picked one out of a catalog Carmen sent them. They had sent the money for one of the clocks that was to be included in our household shipment.

Shortly after New Year's Day, 1979 we received an invitation from Commander Brown asking Carmen and I to visit him and his wife in his home one evening. This marked the first time I'd received an invitation from my commanding officer to meet socially. On the designated evening, and in civilian clothes, Carmen and I arrived at Commander Brown's house. He lived in a special house near the Naval Magazine that had always been the Naval Magazine commanding officer's residence. We had a wonderful visit. Carmen was gracious as always, and she and Mrs. Brown became instant friends.

Since the evacuation of the Army, a Navy Construction Battalion, also called "Sea Bees," had been busy within the limited area. These sailors were constructing a new security fence, strengthening security doors, reworking rain gutters, and much more, all with the goal of downsizing the limited area, since less room was needed now that the Army was gone. From an area of more than eighty acres, we were shrinking to less than ten acres. The Torpedo Shop, which had been constructed at a great price, and was to be used to work on the ASROC weapon and Mark 48 torpedoes, had a special air-conditioning unit that was supposed to keep the humidity within the building to below ten percent. This air conditioner was not able to accomplish the dehumidifying it was designed for in the heat and high humidity of Guam. The building was never used for its intended purposes, but instead became a warehouse.

It was providential that Carmen had become self-employed, as she suffered health problems related to the surgery she had at Letterman Hospital before we left California. There were frequent days she was not able to go to work. ORT Division enjoyed monthly picnics'. These picnics were normally held at Gab Gab Beach on the naval station. During one of these parties I got a scare. Roger ran to me, saying his mom had fainted. I ran to her, and she was lying on the ground surrounded by a group of concerned people. An ambulance was called. She had been accompanying a small three-year-old girl to the bathroom, when the little girl stumbled and struck her head on a rock. The little girl was not hurt seriously, but her head bled profusely. When Carmen saw the blood, she fainted. She did not awaken until the ambulance arrived at the hospital. Upon awakening, she asked how the little girl was. The little girl was just frightened, and after a bandage was placed on her forehead she was fine. Carmen had a number of fainting spells, a few at home, and once when Roger got a bad cut on his upper lip from a dog bite. During the stitching of his lip, Carmen fainted. I was concerned about her fainting, all the doctors said it was anemia, but I was not convinced that this was the real reason for her fainting spells.

We had come to know many Guamanian people. One weekend we went with a Guamanian family to a small island off the coast of Guam, called Coco's Island. This was a small resort island that was reached by a thirty-minute boat ride. There were palm-thatched shelters, and barbeque pits scattered about on the island. We took one of the mahi mahi fish we had in our freezer, and the Guamanian father cooked the fish over a fire Guam style. They were a poor family, but generous and hospitable. We gave them a lot of clothes that our kids had outgrown, and other items from our home. We attended a fiesta in their village one weekend, and they made us feel like part of the family, and part of the village.

In February I attended a Nuclear Emergency Team Operations course that was taught by Air Force instructors from Kirtland Air Force Base, Albuquerque, New Mexico. It was an educational course. The instructors had many interesting stories to relate. One interesting story was how the Soviet Union targeted their missiles for nuclear strikes against the United States. The Russians used women exclusively for targeting tasks, as it was felt that Soviet women were much more aggressive, assigning targets for destruction, and more ruthless than men.

The instructors also told anecdotes about President Ford, and Carter. President Ford, as did all American presidents, had a constant military officer companion. This officer carries a black briefcase, handcuffed to his wrist, which contains the authentication codes used by the president to declare nuclear war. President Ford was noted for his clumsiness, but in this story, it was his military escort who was clumsy. While at Vale, Colorado, on the fourth floor of a ski resort equipment sales store, the military officer slipped, fell on the floor, and in falling slammed the black suitcase on the floor.

When the briefcase struck the floor, it caused the ignition of a thermite grenade, which was inside the briefcase, which was used to destroy the codes in the event of unauthorized tampering with the briefcase. The officer quickly unlocked the handcuffs attaching his wrist to the briefcase. The briefcase burned through the four floors of the building before coming to rest on the bottom floor.

President Carter was on his plane, Air Force One flying to France, when he asked his military aides to send a message to the American Embassy in France, in Morse code. After the Air Force officer left the president to carry out his request, he returned a few moments later, embarrassed. He told the president that none of his communication officers knew Morse code. At that moment a Navy chief who was assigned to the president's entourage as a radio repairman, spoke up and said he knew Morse code. The chief then sat down in one of the Air Force officer's chairs and sent the message. From that day forward President Carter directed that all his communication officers be Navy officers.

The North Tipalo housing section we lived in included the earliest houses built on the naval station, and was the oldest houses still in use. The houses that had been built after the North Tipalo housing section were modern and had central air conditioning. We were informed that the houses in our section were to be remodeled, while we were living in the house. Interior walls of plywood were to be installed inside the existing concrete walls, leaving a three-foot space between the temporary wall and the permanent wall. The remodeling would take place within this space. The installation of these plywood walls meant we had to relocate all of the furniture within the rooms toward the center of each room. Before the installation of these plywood walls the rooms in our house had been small. After the plywood walls were in place, the rooms were smaller yet and cramped with furniture pieces stacked on top of each other, and jammed together with very little walking space. The Guamanian workmen, who were working on the remodeling, repositioned our three air conditioners from the existing windows to the plywood walls. The concrete walls were to be partially destroyed and re-concreted, and double pane windows were to be installed all around the house. There were no windows in the temporary walls, and dust and debris was created during the remodeling work. After the walls were in place, there was sporadic work as delays were experienced when a shipment of double pane windows from the United States was misrouted. One day the workers left an air conditioner drain hose inside the space between the walls instead of repositioning it to drain water outside. Water leaked into our living room all night, ruining one of our rugs. Inside our house it was very hot, as the air conditioners couldn't effectively cool the house within the plywood walls. Insects entered the rooms freely, and it was very dusty inside the rooms. It was a crowded, dusty, hot condition we were living in, that I doubt would have been tolerated by families in the civilian community. This situation also emphasized the gap of separation between the officer and enlisted community. The officer housing sections were not subjected to this inconvenience. The remodeling work on our house took two and a half months, and greatly discouraged me. It was depressing to realize that the Navy expected families to live under such deplorable conditions. To Carmen's credit she complained very little, and took the inconvenience as a matter of course. It was a relief when the job was declared complete, and the plywood walls were taken down.

After the first of the year I considered applying for the Navy warrant officer program. This was an annual program in which chiefs throughout the Navy could participate by filling out a lengthy application package, which would be considered by a selection board in Washington, D.C. Those selected, and approved by the secretary of the Navy, and congress, would be commissioned chief warrant officers by the president. This was a very competitive program, and less than three percent of those that applied were selected. There was a very lengthy application to work on, but first I requested permission to apply by submitting a request to the commanding officer. I submitted my request on 24 January 1979. My request was approved, and on the request chit, was a comment from the executive officer which said, "Be advised that one of the criteria for recommendation is the skill which the candidate puts his own package together."

After my request approval, I began by studying the instructions for putting the application together. These instructions changed each year, requiring that the most current instructions be complied with. I also checked out my service record from the Naval Magazine personnel office each weekend, and studied the contents.

GMT1 Charlie Upham was applying for the limited duty officer program at the same time I was applying for the warrant officer program. The same instructions were used for application to both these programs. If Charlie were selected, he would be commissioned an ensign. Charlie and I helped each other preparing our applications, and we proofread each other's application.

After many retypes, and rewrites my application was ready on 28 February 1979. I had to apply for a warrant officer "designator," or specific job.

My preference was a surface ordnance technician, with the number designation "7161." The job description of a surface ordnance technician says: "Officer technical specialist in naval guns, rockets, and rocket launchers, missiles, bombs, and related launchers, guidance and control systems. They train and supervise personnel in assembly, maintenance and repair of surface ordnance, equipment and components, and related systems; co-ordinate, plan, and direct logistics, handling and safety procedures for all phases of ordnance operations. They may serve as, but are not limited only serving as, supervisors in related ordnance repair and logistics, nuclear weapons, fire control, ordnance training and repair and ordnance inspection and instructor assignments, or in various operational and staff billets."

I was required to list on my application two preferences for a warrant officer designator. My second preference was an aviation ordnance technician. This was the same job as a surface ordnance technician except it related to jobs with aviation ordnance, and involved assignments to aviation squadrons. I was hopeful that if selected I would be given my first preference, as I had little experience with aircraft conventional ordnance. To give the reader a better understanding of what a naval warrant officer is, and what his or her duties are, I'll write the "official" Navy description of a warrant officer.

> The Chief Warrant Officers provide the Navy with a vital and invaluable form of leadership. Chief Warrant Officers are officer technical specialists, qualified by performance and experience, who possess the expertise and authority to direct the most difficult and exacting technical operations in a given occupational area.
>
> Chief Warrant Officers are technical officer specialists who perform duties:
> a. Limited in scope (in relation to other officers)
> b. Technically oriented
> c. Repetitive in nature
> d. Not significantly affected by advancement in rank and therefore amenable to successive tours.
> e. Normally progress to Division Officer level

My application was sixteen pages long. Included was my education history, Navy correspondence courses completed, extracurricular activities, a statement of service, an agreement to serve on active duty for three years if selected, list of awards and letters, a chronological list of all the jobs I'd held in the Navy (this was five pages long), and my certificate confirming my security clearance. Also, included were copies of all my training, and awards pages from my service record. One important section of my application was a personal statement, "Why I want to be a warrant officer." My statement was long, but I kept shortening it until I felt I could no longer. The statement read:

> I am a career sailor, with intentions of remaining in the Navy well beyond the twenty-year period. I obtain immense satisfaction from the successful performance of tasks that contribute to the completion of my assigned command's mission. I relish and look forward to supervisory positions that allow me to accomplish jobs through the correct application of leadership techniques that get the job done safely, expeditiously, and thoroughly, without waste of man-hours or material. I also consider it a rewarding challenge to train and motivate subordinates, while attempting to maintain a high state of morale regardless of the circumstances. I have served at a variety of activities, under peacetime and wartime conditions, during my naval career. I feel fortunate to have a background that few individuals in the GMT rating have been able to obtain. I have been in supervisory positions in the GMT rating since 1962, and have observed with pride and deep satisfaction the manner in which the special weapon program has progressed over the years. While many of the technical aspects of the GMT rating have become simplified, other aspects such as security, personnel management, and proper readiness posture, have become more complex. I have noted also as the naval service becomes smaller and more efficient; the requirement that every sailor perform to the utmost of his ability has become a matter of foremost importance. I have felt the need at many activities for a technically oriented officer such as a warrant officer. Time has been spent in training and orienting line officers in managerial positions in the special weapons program, instead of utilizing the time on personnel management, unit readiness, technical problems, etc. I feel I have the technical knowledge, and managerial abilities required to fill the billet of a warrant officer. My family is agreeable to my participation in the warrant officer program.

I am further encouraged to apply for the Navy Warrant Officer Program by association with the outstanding warrant officers of the Navy throughout my career, and by the favorable accounts of many former shipmates concerning their newly attained status of a Navy warrant officer. Part of my desire to apply for the Navy Warrant Officer Program arises from the fact of position and salary increases, but this is secondary; of primary importance to me is job satisfaction and being part of what I consider the best military organization in existence, the U.S. Navy.

Charlie Upham and I went over each other's application with a "fine tooth comb." After I felt satisfied that I had prepared my application properly, I submitted it to Commander Brown. He wrote a "glowing" endorsement on my application. I was pleased with Commander Brown's endorsement. I didn't feel I had much of a chance being selected. My education record was quite slim. I'd always put my energy into the job, and had very little energy or time left over for personal education efforts. I felt at least I could say that once during my career I applied for the warrant officer program. In 1979 the age limit of thirty-five years was dropped, so as I was thirty-six, this might be my last chance to apply. Perhaps I was also trying to redeem myself from the shame I felt at my chief's initiation when it was said that I had applied for the Army warrant officer program? I respected Charlie Upham's technical expertise, and leadership abilities, and felt he had a good chance being selected as an ensign limited duty officer.

The Warrant, and Limited Duty Officers, are probably the least known officers in the civilian community. What follows is a short history of these officers, as is written in the *Navy Limited Duty Officer/Chief Warrant Officer Professional Guidebook*[43].

The Chief Warrant Officer, and, in some sense, the Limited Duty Officers' communities are as old as the Navies themselves. Warfare, in the distant past, was conducted by the aristocracy whose livelihood depended upon the income from agricultural lands given to them by the King in exchange for their obligation to provide armed fighting men when called upon. The King or Prince might command an entire military expedition while various aristocrats commanded, as Captains, their own "companies" of men-at-arms. There were also junior officer's who would command in "lieu" of the Captain if the latter were killed or wounded - a Lieutenant.

Actual fights at sea were rare in the middle ages but if ships were needed, they were drafted into military service from traders and merchants. The ship would then be commissioned and a Captain placed in command. The land-bound, part-time soldiers knew nothing of piloting, ship handling or navigation. The Ship's Master, his principal officers and the sailors or "swabbers" were necessary for the success of the operation. Being commoners, employed for their specific skills, these expert seaman were issued royal warrants which bound them to serve the King in their special capacities. Being commoners, employed for their specific skills, these expert seamen were issued royal warrants which bound them to serve the King in their special capacities. Whether the Master could be called a Limited Duty Officer or commissioned Warrant Officer is a moot point, as rank, authority and precedence were less precise in those times.

At the outbreak of the Revolutionary War, the Colonies quite logically modeled the nucleus of the naval establishment after the British. Our history records that on 14 December 1775, Congress agreed to construct thirteen Frigates. The grades of officers to lead this force were as follows: Captains of Ships, Captains of Marines, Lieutenants of Ships, Lieutenants of Marines, Surgeons, Chaplains, Pursers, Boatswains, Gunners, Carpenters, Master Mates, and Secretaries of the Fleet.

Contrary to popular belief, most Warrant Officers of the 1800's were not sailors who had begun at the bottom of the Navy's ladder and worked their way up. Boatswains', Gunners, Carpenters and Sailmakers were often appointed directly into the Navy after learning their trades in merchant vessels or as privateers. In 1859 most Warrant Officers had as little as six months as enlisted men, some had none at all.

In 1862 the rank of Ensign was introduced. By 1865 the Navy finally had Vice Admirals, Rear Admirals, and Commodores. Master ranked between Ensign and Lieutenant until 1881, when the rank was changed to Lieutenant (Junior Grade).

From the end of the Civil war, until the year 1900, Warrant Officers were Boatswains, Gunners, Carpenters, Sailmakers and Mates. The duties of the Mates were simple, he will perform duties As assigned by the Commanding Officer." The Mate was junior to all Officers and Warrant Officers, but senior to all enlisted men and to Naval Cadets, as graduates of Annapolis were then known.

Commissioned Warrant grades (The Chief Warrant Officer to "rank with but after Ensign") were introduced to the Navy at the turn of the nineteenth century.

By the beginning of World War I we see the Warrant ranks being used to meet the demands of the rapidly developing technology of the time. There remained on active duty only one Chief Sailmaker, but there were added to the register 84 Chief Pay Clerks, 101 Pay Clerks and 52 acting Pay Clerks. In the past, Pay Clerks had received an appointment after having been selected by a Commissioned Paymaster to work for that Officer only. Very often they came directly from civilian life. Warrant Pay Clerks, on the other hand, had to be Chief Petty Officers before they could apply for promotion.

It was during this period that the responsibilities of the Gunner began to change, which eventually lead to the creation of several new Warrants. The Gunner was also assigned the duty of supervising the electrical system of ships. The original answer for this new specialty requirement was to split the Gunner Warrant into Gunner and Gunner (E) who was, despite his insignia, the Electrical Officer. With the introduction of wireless, Gunner (E) was further divided to include Gunner (W) which was later changed to Gunner (R). In 1910 Congress authorized the annual promotion of ten Warrant Officers to the rank of Ensign. After World War I, almost all Warrant Officers and Chief Warrant Officers were former enlisted men. The Warrant Officer Mess was the abode of long service enlisted men who had achieved First Class or Chief Petty Officer status before becoming Warrants.

On the eve of World War II a Chief or First Class Petty Officer could be advanced to Warrant if:

a. He was under 35 years of age on the date appointed
b. He had no proficiency mark lower than 3.4
c. He was able to read and write English with facility, understand the four rules of arithmetic and proportion, was able to keep account of stores and was thoroughly conversant with all instructions and regulations to the grade for which examined.
e. Had five years of sea duty, at least one of which was in the rate of Chief Petty Officer or First Class Petty Officer.

The demands of World War II forced the creation of several new Warrant specialties and by 1950 there were twelve: Boatswain, Gunner, Torpedoman, Electrician, Radio Electrician, Machinist, Carpenter, Ships Clerk, Aerographer, Photographer, Hospital Corps (formerly Pharmacist) and Pay Clerk. In addition approximately one fourth of the Lieutenant Commanders, over 1,000 Lieutenants and one third of the Lieutenant (Junior Grade) were permanent Chief Warrant Officers or permanent enlisted.

In 1948 the Navy had recognized that it often lost critical skills and knowledge, learned as enlisted men or Warrant Officers, when a sailor was finally promoted to commissioned status in the unrestricted line community. This "Mustang" Officer was often not competitive with other commissioned Officers. To retain these skills, and to provide a fair competitive position for Officers promoted from the ranks, the Limited Duty Officer Program was established. In 1948 the Limited Duty Officer category was established under the Officer Personnel act of 1947. The community was envisioned as a relatively small, elite group of Officers who would retain their specialties acquired as enlisted men and Warrant Officers and support the unrestricted line community during periods of personnel shortages or when technological advances required. They were not to compete with the Unrestricted Line Officers. Limited Duty Officers commissioned after the inception of the Limited Duty Officer Program through 1956 were given permanent appointments. As these permanent Limited Duty Officers progressed through the grade structure they were given a promotion opportunity equivalent to that experienced by unrestricted line Officers.

The defense Reorganization Act of 1949 created four Warrant Officer grade levels W1, CWO2, CWO3, and CWO4. Commencing with 1957, all initial appointments to Limited Duty Officer through 1965 were temporary appointments. The input to the program was increased markedly in 1957, so that of the 2,502 Officers comprising the total strength of the Limited Duty Officer temporary program in January 1959, 1,148 were temporary Officers.

The "Williams Board," convened in 1959, recommended that the Limited duty Officer Program be expanded to meet the shortage of experienced Junior Officers and proposed that the Warrant Officer Program be concurrently phased out utilizing Senior and Master Chief Petty Officers to assume their duties. Pursuant to this recommendation, input to the Limited Duty Officer community was increased, including the selection of Warrant Officers to Limited Duty Officer status. As a result, the Limited Duty Officer (T) structure reached a peak population of about 7,500 Officers, in all Limited Duty Officer designators, by the mid-1960's. Very quickly it became clear that technical specialist supervisors with a greater scope of authority, than that afforded to Senior and Master Chief Petty Officers, were needed and that their duties were quite separate from the managerial responsibilities of Limited Duty Officers.

The "Settle Board" concluded, in October 1963, that the Limited Duty Officer Program should be phased down and the Warrant Officer Program re-instituted. The Secretary of the Navy approved the majority of the Board's recommendations and plans were developed and executed to reestablish a Warrant Officer Program of about 5,000 Officers with a subsequent reduction in the size of the Limited Duty Officer Program to a total of 3,000. Consequently, there were no Limited Duty Officer accessions in 1966, 67, and 68.

Recommendations designed to improve the Limited Duty Officer and Warrant Officer Programs and to improve stability to those communities was approved by the Secretary of the Navy, on 5 December 1974.

In the 1970's the Warrant (W1) was abandoned and qualified enlisted personnel were promoted directly to Chief Warrant Officer, receiving commissions as Chief Warrant Officer CWO2. In 1980 the requirement that applicants for Limited Duty Officer and Chief Warrant Officer be under 35 years of age was abandoned and shortly after, Master Chief Petty Officers with up to 24 years of service were declared eligible for promotion to Chief Warrant Officer. In 2003, a new grade was established, with the promotion of ten Chief Warrant Officers to the grade of Chief Warrant Officer CWO5.

The duties and status of both communities have changed over the past 500 years of modern Naval history from common seafarers, reluctantly admitted to Officer status by aristocratic soldiers at sea, to becoming an essential element to the operation of modern and permanent Naval forces.

We placed a "for sale" sign on the Pontiac. It was only seven years old, but had more than 100,000 miles, and a few rust spots. We were asking $1,500, which was much lower than the suggested blue book price. A young Guamanian high school senior was interested in the car. One afternoon while I had duty, Carmen brought the boy and his father to the magazine to discuss terms. The father kept trying to barter, and lower the price. I relented, and lowered the price to $1,200. The boy was ecstatic. Before I signed the paperwork, the father said, "Of course you'll pay the transfer fee, and license fee." This amounted to about forty dollars, but I was irritated with his pushy attitude, so I said, "No, I won't pay those costs, you have an exceptional deal, so if you insist that I pay the fee, which is usually the buyer's responsibility then forget the deal." The boy was crest fallen, and then the father said, "OK, OK it's a deal, I'll pay the fees." The Vega station wagon was to be our only transportation until we departed Guam. We were sad to see the Pontiac go, but it had served us well.

As a chief petty officer I was assigned a job I'd not had previously. This job was as an Authorization Code Team Member. I was given training during a special class and an authorization letter from the commanding officer. This is a Department of Defense program that is a safeguard in the steps necessary to declare nuclear war. Without going into detail, it is a program that prevents a commanding officer or a lone individual from acting independently and starting nuclear war. The authorization to use nuclear weapons resides in the office of the president, and the way he would direct the use of nuclear weapons would be by electronic message. There is a coded system set up that is changed frequently, and this system requires two persons to verify that a message from the president authorizing the use of nuclear weapons is authentic. The message must be verified in the presence of the commanding officer, or his representative before steps to use the weapons could be taken. As you can imagine, this system is a very critical link in our nation's defense. These codes are highly classified, and the people involved in their use must be of unquestionable integrity. The penalties for careless handling of these code cards are very severe. American citizens should appreciate this system, as it is a foolproof system against the unauthorized use of our most powerful weapons

I was anxious to learn what my next assignment would be. In order to call the detailer in Washington, D.C., I had to go to the magazine at midnight to place a call, because of the time difference between Guam and the U.S. East coast. Often it was very difficult getting a clear line, or even getting through at all. After many attempts one night in February, I got through to the detailer. He said the only job he had for me at the time was an ammunition ship. He said he might have another job open in a week, and to call back then. When I called a week later, he said he had a job at White Sands Missile Range, White Sands, New Mexico. When faced with a choice between New Mexico, and an ammunition ship, I quickly said I'd take the White Sands assignment, although I'd not heard of a GMTC job at White Sands? On 15 March, I received orders from Washington, D.C. to detach from Naval Magazine Guam on 20 May, for duty at Naval Ordnance Missile Test Facility White Sands, New Mexico.

A surprise was the appearance of my old friend Ray Steele at Naval Magazine. He was being assigned to the magazine. He and his wife Becky had come from McAlester, Oklahoma. I'd always hoped we would be stationed together, but the timing was terrible. We were only able to be together for a couple of months. This was the first time Carmen and I had met Becky, and we liked her instantly.

In April we passed our annual inspection. Afterwards we had a celebration party at the Guam Fleet Reserve Association Club. We had a good time congratulating one another. I had a sense of accomplishment, having gotten through yet another grueling inspection. The big job of downsizing the limited area was complete. I had completed my first year as a chief petty officer. I was also relieved that I would not be returning to sea duty yet.

While on Guam one of our favorite picnic, and snorkeling spots, on the naval station, was a beach below an area called the "Spanish Steps." It was a difficult matter to get to the beach. There was a very steep path leading down a cliff that had at a few places, steps that had been cut into the rock face of the cliff. Spanish soldiers had cut these steps into the rock during their occupation of Guam in the 1700s following Magellan's historic voyage around the world. The step path ended on the jungle floor, and another path led to a secluded beautiful cove with a white sand beach. On the path to the beach there were stone ruins of an ancient Spanish barracks. I often thought that it was sad that no one had thought to preserve the steps, and historic ruins which had been ignored for centuries, and would eventually disappear. It was difficult and dangerous going down the steps, but it was also dangerous crawling up from the beach, because of another danger. To gain access to the path, you had to walk through the base skeet shooting range! Blasts from shotguns would fly over the path entrance. A large bell with a rope was positioned just under the lip of the cliff. Anyone coming up the path would loudly ring the bell to warn any skeet shooters to "cease fire." GMT1 Jack Osilka was a talented skeet shooter, and was immortalized by having his picture taken while skeet shooting, in the *"Orders Guam"* booklet that I mentioned previously.

There was island-wide excitement in April. A Guamanian prisoner in the island prison, who was a convicted murderer, escaped. He remained at large for a month, which was no easy feat on an island as small as Guam. Everyone remained on the lookout for him during this month. He was finally captured after a shoot out on the Guam Naval Air Station with two base policemen. The convict was shot seven times, but survived. A base policeman was also severely injured with a gunshot wound. The newspaper had warned that Guamanian escapee was a determined, violent individual, and this was proven by the severe injuries he sustained during the shootout, and yet refused to surrender. He was taken into custody only after the bullet wounds incapacitated him.

In April I was contacted by the auto sales office at the Navy exchange, and told the Buick LeSabre we had ordered would not be available for six months, as there was a delay at the factory in Detroit. The salesman said we could order an Oldsmobile that was basically the same car. We reluctantly agreed. For $7,000 we ordered an Oldsmobile Delta 88 Royale. We would take delivery in Reno, Nevada to avoid the emission control devices that would have to be installed if we were to take delivery of the car in California.

Also in April the furniture company delivered all the furniture Carmen had bought the year before. Our base house was now very crowded. One day during this month a couple that had recently arrived on Guam came to our house from the housing office. They were looking for a house to move into. They liked the murals I'd painted on the walls, and wanted to keep them. This was a relief, as I'd made an agreement with the housing office, if the incoming new occupants of the house wanted the murals, I didn't have to paint over them when we left.

In May I went with Steve Cline to the magazine shooting range, and qualified as a "Sharpshooter" with the forty-five-caliber pistol.

This authorized me to wear a blue ribbon, with an "E" on it, standing for "expert with a pistol." Steve and Chris Reed were scheduled to run the production control section of ORT Division following my departure.

We planned to stay in a motel, following our pack out, and evacuation of our house, prior to our flight to the States. When the moving men came to our door on the day of our scheduled pack out, their eyes got big, and they groaned in anticipation of moving all the furniture we had stacked in our small house. Each rank has a "household goods weight allowance" which is a specific total weight. The weight allowance becomes larger, the higher rank of the sailor. Any weight over this allowed weight, the sailor has to pay for the moving cost, which can be substantial. I was worried about the total weight, but the weighing of the loaded trucks revealed that we were 1,000 pounds under our weight limit. The movers struggled with the large pieces of our new furniture. We hoped the furniture wouldn't be damaged during the long trip to New Mexico. During the pack out of our household goods, there was a first class petty officer whose job it was to inspect our personal property for any government property that might be included, and thus illegally appropriated. He collected a couple of U.S. Government ink pens. I did not like this questioning of my integrity, but this was something that everyone who left Guam went through.

After the house was empty, we set about cleaning everything, just as we had at our Hamilton Air Force Base house. It was required that the tile floors throughout the house be waxed and polished before the "inspection" by an inspector from the housing office. The house had been in a mess when we had moved in after Typhoon Pamela; regardless we worked for two days making the house spotless. Our inspection was scheduled for 1:00 p.m. one afternoon. As soon as the Guamanian inspector walked through the door, I immediately noticed that he had a haughty, superior attitude. He said the wall murals would have to be painted over. I then showed him the written permission I had from the Housing Officer to leave the murals as they were. He did not like this, and grumbled. He then slowly looked throughout the house. I could tell his self-important, smug self-image had been damaged when I corrected him by showing him the paperwork permitting the wall murals. After looking and looking, and failing to find anything, he finally pointed to one of the bedroom floors, and said it wasn't polished enough. I told him we would correct it, and asked if he come back at 3:00 p.m. to re-inspect so I could get to the housing office before they closed. This would give me enough time to sign the final move out paperwork, otherwise we would have to wait until tomorrow to be inspected, and be a day behind in our schedule.

Carmen and I rushed around, waxed the floor again, and polished it, although we really could not see any difference from the other rooms in the house. The inspector returned much after the 3:00 p.m. time he had said he would. He reluctantly signed the final paperwork, and I rushed to the housing office, barely making it before their 5:00 p.m. closing time. We returned to the motel we had checked into a couple of days previously. The next day, Carmen and I decided we would drive by our old house. What we saw angered me. Workmen were inside the house tearing out all the old tiles we had worked so hard waxing and polishing, and replacing them with new tiles. If I'd had more time I would have complained to the housing office about the unnecessary work (and worry) we went through to sooth the ruffled ego of the housing office inspector.

Prior to our pack out, I had completed the check out process at the Naval Magazine. A couple of weeks prior to my check out, the magazine held its annual base picnic, with Mongolian barbeque, hamburgers, hot dogs, game for families such as sack races, toad races and so on. I took 8mm movies of the picnic, knowing this would be the last time I would see many of the sailors and their families. The gang of people that we played "bunko" (a dice game) with each month, gave us a beautiful inscribed pewter mug as a going away present.

My last evaluation report had marks in the top 1 percent, and the description of my duties read:

> GMTC Little is assigned the primary duty of Technical Ordnance Control Supervisor responsible for coordination of division work schedules, key punch operations and initiation of numerous reports. His collateral duties include Assistant Convoy Commander, Command Post Operations Chief, Weapon Code Team Member and OOD.

The evaluation comments said:

> GMTC Little has continued to perform his professional duties in an outstanding manner. His attention to detail and his efficient use of all available assets has ensured that timely and accurate production reports are generated from his shop. Chief Little's reports are concise, and his work schedules are thoroughly planned. His positive attitude and enthusiastic approach to tasks carry over to his subordinates, and has instilled in them a high sense of devotion that has been of enormous benefit to the command in successfully meeting its mission.

Furthermore, Chief Little maintains close liaison with division branches and other departments to ensure continuity of planning and coordinated execution of technical operations.

GMTC Little has a quiet personality that is tactfully persistent. He exercises the basic functions of leadership without fanfare, but with purpose that ensures desired results. He plans, directs, supervises and motivates his subordinates to perform enthusiastically and effectively. He has exhibited a high regard for the well-being and professional desires of each sailor with whom he deals. Chief Little, along with his family, has participated in numerous Chamorro gatherings, lending a helping hand when needed, and actively joining in a variety of community events.

Chief Little has an excellent command of the English language, which he has often demonstrated by his clear and concise lectures delivered before division personnel, and through his preparation of written reports. As one of two Chiefs in a division staffed with both male, and female members, and individuals of various racial and ethnic backgrounds, he has developed a close working relationship with all members of the command.

Chief Petty Officer little has spent the major portion of this reporting period preparing the division for the annual Navy Technical Proficiency Inspection (NTPI). These preparations have demonstrated Chief Little's keen ability to plan ahead and anticipate potential problem areas. The results of his efforts were reflected in the NTPI Inspection Team findings. The Inspectors found no major or minor discrepancies in his area of responsibilities. From counseling individuals to exercising his technical abilities, Chief Petty Officer Little has demonstrated mature judgment, professional discretion and the utmost degree of reliability. Most significantly, Chief little has accomplished the impressive record of performance with minimum supervision and only broad policy guidance from his superiors.

During a recent relocation of the Limited Area, GMTC Little was responsible for planning the movement to a new location. Given a limited amount of time, GMTC Little planned, staffed, directed and supervised this evolution, resulting in finishing the job two days early. This effort was planned and carried out with the same professionalism that Chief Little has demonstrated throughout his tour at Naval Magazine Guam.

At this point in my writings I feel I should say a word about the above evaluation report the reader labored through, and may wonder why I've included it. When I began this effort of writing about my naval career, I wanted to include not only my observations, experiences, and how I perceived others, but also how my superiors perceived my performance. I've also included the narrative of this evaluation report so the reader can picture what I was involved with during this specific period of time. The report also show how sailors are evaluated in the Navy, with these reports becoming a permanent record of a sailor's performance in the Navy long after that individual has passed from this earth.

As I mentioned, we stayed in a motel near the airport a few days before our departure for Guam. This was not a particularly happy time for our family. We were anxious to leave for our new duty station, yet sad to leave the many friends we had. Also one evening when we were about to have dinner at a restaurant, Roger threw a teen-age tantrum, and said he wanted to go live with his father, and said some foolish, hateful things. He remained sullen after this outburst.

We had sold our "Guam bomb" Vega station wagon to a young sailor I worked with on the magazine. He assumed the keys at the airport before we boarded our plane. At the airport we were seen off by a large group of our friends. We bid one another farewell, which is always a bittersweet time for military families. You say goodbye to friends who have been like family, knowing that this is probably the last time you will ever see them, or hear from them. We were anxious to see our homeland, which we had not seen for three years. I was grateful to Ray Margeson and Charlie Cushman for their comradeship, and guidance into the chief ranks. I was sad that Ray Steele and I had shared so little time together on Guam. All in all as I reflected on my time on Guam, it had been enormously more enjoyable than my first tour, mainly because I shared my life with Carmen and the kids, and I had learned much about my chosen profession. I felt the words, known around the world, painted above the Guam International Airport entrance were indeed true, "GUAM IS GOOD."

The airport was not the same airport we had arrived at three years before. The terminal had been rebuilt, and was much larger and modern. There had been a flurry of construction during our time on Guam. Two well-known additions to Guam were McDonald's, and Burger King fast food restaurants.

We waved farewell to the large group that was seeing us off, and boarded our plane for the long trip over the Pacific with a short stop in Hawaii. Looking earthward, as the plane climbed skyward, we saw the lush green island of Guam quickly fade from view, replaced by the vast blue waters of the Pacific.

This was not to be my last sight of Guam, as I was to visit again in the future. In fifteen years, shortly after 1995, the Naval Magazine was to be re-designated Ordnance Annex, Guam. The limited area and other ordnance functions were re-located to Hawaii, and other locations in the United States, ending over five decades of support for the Pacific naval forces.

Chapter 12: Land of Enchantment

Martha met us in the San Francisco airport following the long plane ride. She was living in nearby San Jose. Remedy was living in a nearby neighborhood also, and came to see us. We were thrilled to see her. No longer a little girl, she'd grown into a young lady. We were amazed how she and her brother Wayne had grown. As a testament to Remedy's intelligence, and maturity, at the age of sixteen (she looked much older), she had gone to work for an electronic company called ROLM, which was destined to be a very successful company in the future Silicon Valley of Santa Clara, California. She did not reveal her true age, until she had worked for the company many years later. She reached a very prominent position in the company.

I had forty-five days leave before reporting to New Mexico. We picked up our new car in Reno, Nevada. This marked the first time in my life that I purchased a brand-new car. It was a two-door coupe, painted silver, with a red velour interior. The engine was a V8. I noticed there was what appeared to be a rubbed spot in the paint on the roof. The dealership in Reno said to point it out to the Oldsmobile dealer in New Mexico.

Roger's sullen attitude changed somewhat, and we permitted him to visit his father in San Francisco. We had a wonderful time reuniting with my parents, brothers' Joe, and Jerry, my sister Linda, and the rest of the family. We were amazed how all the children in the family appeared to have grown in a three-year period. It was also interesting how our country had changed during our absence. Ronald Reagan was running for president against Jimmy Carter. The military had come to the conclusion that President Carter was not "militarily friendly." His "give away" of the Panama Canal was not popular, and the Iran hostage situation had gone on endlessly without a solution. Our countrymen were still being held prisoners in Iran, and it was becoming an embarrassment to Carter. Reagan promised to strengthen the military, and improve our fighting ability.

We noticed a change in the formats of television programs. Sexual situations depicted on public television, which had previously been considered poor taste, were now considered to be humorous. There was much more profanity, and we were shocked to see television advertising of female hygiene products.

Although it was summer, the weather in the San Joaquin Valley seemed cool after the heat and humidity of Guam. The first of July we bid our parents goodbye. We also bid Waldo the cat goodbye. He had become a country cat during our absence in Guam, and he had become very attached to my father. He was just as aggressive, and independent as ever. Our parents had two dogs, and Waldo acted much like a dog, hunting rabbits, and considering himself the ruler of the household. We couldn't uproot him from his happy home.

We drove across the Mojave Desert toward New Mexico at night. We stopped at the Grand Canyon in the morning, and then drove onto the town of Show Low, Arizona. This was a town near my grandfather's homestead. He had left the homestead to my parents before his death. Show Low is not situated in what most people consider typical Arizona landscape, with desert sand, and cactus, and barren surroundings. The town is located in the Arizona White Mountains, with beautiful surrounding pine trees, and crystal clear blue sky. My grandfather had homesteaded here in the 1920's, and farmed for a period, before moving on to California. We stopped at a motel in Show Low. We caught up on sleep, having driven all night; we rested much of the following day. After resting, we visited the homestead, which was about ten miles outside of town located in a rural area. It was much as I remembered, having visited here with my parents, during my childhood, and teenage years. We spent the day exploring the tree-covered property, looking for arrowheads, and ancient Indian pottery, which was scattered about. We left the homestead in the late afternoon, and while driving back toward Show Low, a pickup sped by us going in the opposite direction, with two men standing up in the bed of the pickup. As they went past, there was a loud sound of something striking the windshield. There appeared immediately a large crack in the windshield that went all the way from the driver side to the passenger side of the window. It was a horrible crack, horrible because it was the first damage to our new car.

We remained one more night in Show Low, and then the following morning traveled to Socorro, New Mexico. At Socorro, we had the choice of driving south to White sands, or north to Albuquerque. I still had a couple of days before I was to report to White Sands, so we decided to visit a friend from Guam who lived in Albuquerque. Our friend's name was Chris Pilger. She had been married to GMT2 Bernie Pilger while in Guam, and they had since been divorced. She and her children lived near her mother in Albuquerque. We called Chris, and got directions to her house. She was happy to see us, and insisted we stay the night. This happened to be on the 4th of July, and since fireworks were allowed in Albuquerque, it sounded like a war in town during the night, with all the exploding fireworks.

George Holden, a senior chief who had been my old "A" school classmate, and who had been stationed with me in Guam in 1969-1970, was stationed at Kirtland Air Force Base, in the Radiation Monitoring School as an instructor. I decided to give him a call since I was in Albuquerque, and as it turned out, I was very thankful I did. George, said he had been trying to find out where I was, because the officer in charge of the Naval Liaison Office on Kirtland Air Force Base had been trying to contact me. George said the officer wanted me to call him. He also said I would not be going to White Sands Missile Range for duty, but instead would be stationed and working in Albuquerque. Ever since I had learned I was to be stationed at White Sands, I'd not been able to find out what my job would be as no one in the GMT community had ever heard of anyone being stationed there. Even the detailer who wrote my orders had no idea what job I would be doing. George said I would be working in the Joint Nuclear Weapons Publications System (JNWPS) Office.

We had planned to drive the 200 miles south to White Sands that weekend, but since I had a lot of time before my report date, we waited until Monday. I called the JNWPS Office Monday morning, and LCDR Perry Roberts answered the phone. He said he was very relieved that I had finally called. He said my orders had been written wrong. I was to go to work in Albuquerque in his office. This was good news to Carmen and me. We had researched in the library what White Sands was like, and it was apparently in the middle of "nowhere," far from any populated center. I had always dreamed of returning to Albuquerque following my "A" school days and now apparently my dream was coming true.

Lieutenant Commander Roberts gave me directions to his office located on Kirtland Air Force Base (it had been an Army base when I'd gone to school here in 1961). His office was located in a building complex occupied by Field Command Defense Nuclear Agency (FCDNA). There were three buildings that were three stories high. The JNWPS Office was located on the third story of one of the buildings. In order to gain access to these buildings a person had to be on an access list. As I was not on the access list, I called Lieutenant Commander Roberts, and he authorized the Air Force guard who had greeted me, permission to give me a visitor badge. I climbed the stairs with the guard to the JNWPS Office, where Lieutenant Commander Roberts welcomed me. Within his office which was about twenty by fifteen feet, there were two desks, two combination safes, as well as a couple of full bookcases.

I learned that morning that I was to be the Naval Liaison Office, Joint Nuclear Weapons Publication System, Officer Assistant. This title was a "mouthful!" I was the first chief petty officer to be assigned to this position. Previous officers who had been assigned to the naval liaison office had worked without an assistant. I also learned that I was not the only one to have received orders to this job. Donn Green, who I'd gone to "A" school with, had been assigned to this office early in 1979, but before he could report for duty, he was selected to be commissioned a chief warrant officer, and he was assigned to the *USS Enterprise*. This would have been an ideal assignment for him, as his wife, who was also named Carmen, was from Albuquerque.

This was quite a pleasant surprise, and a nice turn of events. I began checking in, turning in my medical, and personnel records. A Navy personnel office that managed personnel affairs for all the sailors stationed at Kirtland Air Force Base would maintain my records. Military personnel from all branches of the service were stationed on the Air Force Base. The largest Navy organization on base was Naval Weapons Evaluation Facility (NWEF), which had 300 plus sailors stationed there.

My new "chain-of-command" was LCDR Perry Roberts, who reported to Naval Ordnance Station, Indian Head, Maryland. We worked jointly with Naval Ammunition Depot, McAlester, Oklahoma. We worked locally with the Army, and Air Force liaison offices, which were also, located inside the FCDNA buildings. Lieutenant Commander Roberts and I were essentially an independent command. In our small office, the two desks faced each other, and we also had a dual line telephone, connected to an answering machine.

When I checked into the base housing office, I was told I could move my family into a temporary house on base, until a base house became available for us to move into permanently. The temporary house was a large five bedroom house, with very nice Air Force supplied furniture, and kitchen items. George Holden and his wife Anita, and family lived on base, near our temporary house.

The weather in Albuquerque was warm, and as the city is located in the high desert area of New Mexico, the air was thin and dry. We gradually adjusted to this climate, after being in the humid, hot tropic climate of Guam. The high altitude of New Mexico was different from the tropical sea-level air we had been used to for three years. The thin, dry air dried out your nasal passages, and it was common for newcomers to experience bloody nasal passages, until becoming acclimated to the high desert climate.

We had been in our temporary house for a couple of days, when there was a knock on the door. Upon answering the door we discovered it was Rubin Rassmusson, who we'd been with on Guam. It was good to see him. He was stationed at the same school as George Holden.

In my new job, I had every evening, and weekend off. For the first time in nineteen years, I did not have a duty section. The orders incorrectly directing me to White sands, instead of Albuquerque, created some serious problems. First I was not able to get paid for a month and a half, so we had to be frugal during this period. Secondly, all of our furniture and household goods had been sent to White Sands, 200 miles to the south. The Navy was saying I would be required to pay the additional transportation costs to Albuquerque, even though I had nothing to do with the incorrect routing of our furniture shipment! We also could not apply for base housing until my orders were corrected stating that I was to report to the naval liaison office, versus white sands. Lieutenant Commander Roberts made many phone calls on my behalf, and sent a message to Chief of Naval Personnel, Washington, D.C. (The command that writes all transfer orders), on 22 July, I finally received my correct orders.

Not long after I placed my name on the base housing list on the 22nd, I was told by the housing office, that there was a house available for us to move into. The house Carmen and I looked at was much larger than our previous "Guam house." It was a brick, single level, three-bedroom house. The rooms were large and spacious, and a big improvement from Guam. We now would have two bathrooms, instead of one. We also had a large fenced back yard. In our new neighborhood, each house was a duplex or two homes in one. Each building had a common wall in the middle of the long houses, and a family lived in opposite ends, with each front door being at the opposing ends of the buildings. Each house also had a carport for vehicles.

We had our windshield replaced after notifying our insurance company. The Albuquerque Oldsmobile dealership reluctantly repainted the "rubbed" spot on the roof of the car, only after I'd written a number of letters to General Motors complaining.

My security clearance was quickly confirmed, and as at other nuclear weapons program facilities, my picture was taken, and I was given a permanent identification badge, which was shown to the Air Force sentry upon entering the FCDNA building. The badge was worn exposed on my shirt at all times I was within the building.

Lieutenant Commander Roberts was a Limited Duty Officer (LDO), who had been a first class petty officer before receiving a commission as an LDO ensign. His previous assignments in the Navy had been on board, and associated with submarines. His nuclear weapons experience was limited. He was married, and his wife Vera had a successful ceramic shop in Albuquerque. His two daughters were high school age. Perry Roberts wore a full beard, which irritated a Navy Captain who worked in the same building we did. This captain was the senior Navy Captain in the building, and did not permit officers under him to wear beards, although it was permitted by Navy regulations. Lieutenant Commander Roberts was not under the captain's control, and there was often friction between the two of them. The captain did what he could to make life uncomfortable for Lieutenant Commander Roberts. The captain would do such things as schedule painting of our office, and "forget" to inform us. There was also a running argument over a flag that was displayed in our office, which the captain would take down after working hours, and Lieutenant Commander Roberts would put right back up. Perry was busy attending college night class, striving for a master's degree in business. He planned on retiring in Albuquerque in a couple of years. He had no desire to make commander, and was not concerned about trying to appease the Navy Captain.

Within our office there were two combination safes that contained all the Special Weapons Ordnance Publications (SWOP's) in use by the Navy. These SWOPS's ranged in classification from Top Secret to Unclassified. I discovered immediately that the SWOP's had not been kept current by entering changes that should have been entered. Lieutenant Commander Roberts admitted that he had been unable to keep the manuals updated, and this was one of the many reasons he had campaigned to have an assistant assigned to the office. I began the monumental task of updating manuals that had been out of date for a couple of years. I inventoried them all, and began entering changes. This task was to take three months to complete.

It soon became apparent that my new position carried more authority and the ability to affect change in the nuclear weapons program, than any other GMT enlisted position in the Navy. Lieutenant Commander Roberts (also called the NLO Officer) worked closely with Field Command Defense Nuclear Agency (FCDNA), Stockpile Maintenance Branch, and Sandia Corporation, located on Kirtland Air Force Base, as well as the Army and Air Force liaison offices that were within the same building in which we worked. Our responsibilities covered approving or disapproving changes proposed to all the Special Weapons Ordnance Publications (SWOP's, or "technical bibles") used by the Navy worldwide.

We also reviewed all the retrofit, and modernization orders proposed by the Department of Energy (DOE) on all Navy nuclear weapons. These tasks I've described only scratch the surface of all the projects we were expected to monitor for the Navy. I was becoming increasingly aware of the workings of the upper echelons of the nuclear weapon's world.

My workday began at 7:00 a.m. We would take an hour and a half for lunch, and since my house was only a few minutes' drive from the office, I would often go home and eat lunch. We would close the office for the day at 3:00 p.m., or whenever Lieutenant Commander Roberts decided to quit, which was often earlier. I definitely enjoyed the lax, slow pace, although during slow periods in the afternoons, I'd try to find things to keep busy. I also had plenty of time to study for my senior chief promotion examination, which I was scheduled to take in September.

Albuquerque had grown tremendously since I'd been there more than eighteen years earlier. The town had expanded to the east toward the Sandia Mountains. Where there had been vacant land in 1961, there were now homes and businesses. When I was attending "A" school, anytime sailors wore their uniform off base, they were treated like royalty. This attitude toward sailors had changed after the Vietnam War. The barracks, and most of the buildings that had been in use when I went to "A" school, were still occupied. The Air Force was now using the old Navy "A" school barracks.

GMTC Julian Lindstrom, who I'd been stationed with at Whidbey Island, and NWSA Oakland, was also stationed at Kirtland. He was assigned to Naval Weapons Evaluation Facility. In September he and I took the GMT senior chief promotion examination. George Holden took the exam for master chief. Promotion wise, George and I should have been equal, since we both started our career in the Navy at exactly the same time. Since my record in Washington, D.C. had not been properly kept up to date, my advancement to chief had been delayed for many years, so at this point I was considerably behind George. I knew this shouldn't bother me, but it "ruffled" my ego.

September was also time for the annual New Mexico state fair. The fair is always held at the Albuquerque fair grounds, located in the middle of town. One Saturday, Carmen, Mary and I went to the fair. We walked through the fair displays and carnival area with thousands of other fair goers. Around 7:00 p.m. we walked to the restrooms, which were large concrete buildings near the middle of the fairground complex. Carmen and Mary went into the ladies' side, and I visited the men's restroom. I was out before the girls, and when Carmen came out, she said a guy had grabbed her on the buttocks, and he had walked into the restroom behind me! I said, "Point him out when he comes out." Soon a guy in his mid-twenties, with Indian features, walked out, and Carmen said, "That's him." I walked up in front of him, and I immediately smelled a strong odor of alcohol. I said to him, "I understand you molested my wife, I want you to remain here, because I'm going to get a policeman." About that time two men walked up beside the one I was talking to. They started shouting at me, and the one I'd been talking with took a swing at me. At that point the fight was on. My glasses were knocked off almost immediately. Three men were swinging fists at me at the same time, so I concentrated on the one I'd had the short discussion with, and punched him numerous times, until he was on the ground. I was "blind-sided" and hit from the side on the right cheek with a hard blow that staggered me. A large crowd gathered around us as the fight continued, and even though Carmen was trying to help, no one from the crowd tried to help us. I was concerned that Carmen or Mary might get hurt, and I also wanted to stay on my feet, and not get knocked down which could lead to me being kicked. The men finally had enough, and we managed to get away from the crowd. We looked for about twenty minutes for a policeman, and finally found one. We explained what happened and he walked with us to an aid station. I had a badly swollen right cheek, and sore knuckles. A medic took a look at my cheek, and checked to insure I did not have a concussion. The police at the aid station took our description of the Indian men, and said due to the time that had already gone by, the "hoodlums were probably long gone."

One of the policemen escorted us to the fair exit and we went home. The next day I made a report to the base police about what happened. I definitely looked like I had been in a fight! My right eye was almost completely swollen shut, and my cheek was black and blue. I hoped the others we'd hit looked just as bad. My face was grotesque for a week after the fight, and I had to explain over and over again at work what happened. Following this incident, Carmen was very anxious anytime we left the base, and her feelings toward Albuquerque were negatively changed.

On 28 September 1979, the Secretary of the Navy sent a message to all Navy commands that caught me unaware, and shocked me. This message was the list of those selected in the Navy for promotion to limited duty officer, and chief warrant officer.

I had been selected along with ten other chiefs for appointment to Chief Warrant Officer, W-2, Surface Ordnance Technician. The message also said, the intention was, depending upon acceptance, to appoint selectees on 2 April 1980. I had to pass a physical examination before I could be commissioned. I would also be required to serve for three years following my commissioning as a CWO2. This would mean I would have to serve until 2 April 1983. Before commissioning, I would be required to submit a duty preference card, and a personal information card, which would be used by the detailer in Washington, D.C.

This message brought about a time of decision. I was faced with three options: 1. Refuse the appointment and retire with twenty years active service in 1980. 2. Refuse the appointment to CWO2, and hope to be promoted to senior chief, after which I'd only be required to serve for two years, and then retire after twenty-two years service. 3. Accept the promotion, transfer after being in Albuquerque for less than ten months, and likely go to sea for at least two years.

For nineteen years I had looked to the future year 1980 as the year I would reach the twenty-year point. I'd be eligible for retirement, and enter the civilian world with ½ my base pay each month for the rest of my life. In 1979 I'd reached a hallmark. For the first time in my Navy career, my salary with entitlements had reached $1,000 a month. This was a modest salary, but certainly more than the sixty-four dollars a month I'd received in 1960. Although I had been serious when I submitted my application for the chief warrant officer program, I truly did not expect to be selected. My motivation for the submission had been a case of, I'd never applied, and many of my friends had in the past, so I applied just so I could say I'd tried to achieve officer status once in my career. Faced with the reality of being a selectee was overwhelming!

The wide gulf between officers and enlisted men and women is difficult to explain to those without military experience. The separation between the two groups is absolute. The life of an officer is filled with responsibility and authority, as well as privilege, unknown in the life of enlisted members of the Navy. The life of an enlisted member is one of increasing responsibility, and closely resembles a life of servitude. To a large extent the heavy burden of being the "person responsible" when there's trouble in a command, rests mostly on the shoulders of officers. Being an officer carries with it an air of mystery to enlisted sailors, as there is very little social contact outside the working environment between the two groups. There are strict rules against fraternization, which are rigidly enforced, more so in the Navy than any other military service. Obedience to an officer was not to be questioned. To reverse my role as an enlisted man for twenty years was no small matter. The thought ran through my mind, for twenty years I'd periodically complained about officers, and the Navy had finally gotten even with me, they wanted to make me one!

While mulling over my decision whether to accept a commission or not, I went on a trip to Guided Missile School, Dam Neck, Virginia. The meeting was to discuss the publication of Navy SWOP's for the Trident Missile System. Also from Albuquerque, attending the meeting was CWO4 Charlie Schmidt, who worked in the FCDNA, Stockpile Maintenance Branch, which was located a few doors down the hall, from Lieutenant Commander Roberts and me. The meeting was for a four-day period, and Chief Warrant Officer Schmidt and I sat together during the meeting. I tried to glean as much information from him as I could about the life he had as an officer. While at Dam Neck, I stayed in a motel at Virginia Beach. This marked the first time I'd returned to Virginia since my days on the *USS Independence*. From what I saw of Norfolk, and Virginia Beach they had not changed much. This trip was an enjoyable break from all my administrative work in the NLO Office.

Shortly after my return to Albuquerque, I received a letter from Commander Brown, the commanding officer of Naval Magazine Guam. Commander Brown congratulated me on my selection for chief warrant officer, and described a Meritorious Unit Citation Ribbon that had been awarded by the Secretary of the Navy to those that had been stationed at Naval Magazine Guam. The citation accompanying the ribbon said:

> The Secretary of the Navy takes pleasure in presenting the Meritorious Unit Commendation to U.S. Naval Magazine, Guam for service as set forth in the following citation:
>
> For meritorious service from 28 March 1978 to 19 July 1978 while participating in direct support of the 515th Ordnance Company, U.S. Army. As Guam's joint service explosives' transportation activity, the U.S. Naval Magazine, Guam, its Guard of the Day, "Delta" Company, U.S. Marine Barracks, Guam; U.S. Naval Air Station, Guam, Helicopter Crews; and ComNavMarianas, Guam, Armed Forces Police contributed significantly to the relocation of the 515th Ordnance Company, U.S. Army from Naval Magazine, Guam to the Continental United States. During this period, U.S. Naval Magazine Guam conducted thirty major ordnance convoys from the Naval Magazine to Andersen Air Force Base over the only feasible land route, a distance of twenty-six miles over narrow, winding roads and through numerous populated areas.

In support of this logistic tasking, U.S. Naval Magazine and its Guard Force expended in excess of 25,300 man-hours in preparation and manning of security elements, Accident Response Teams, ordnance transportation personnel, and Command/Control personnel. By their continuous display of precise professionalism, determination, resourcefulness, and steadfast devotion to duty, the officers and enlisted personnel of U.S. Naval Magazine, Guam reflected credit upon themselves and upheld the highest traditions of the United States Naval service.

Commander Abrahams and Brown had both promised they would campaign for recognition for the monumental job we had completed moving the Army off Guam. They had kept their promise.

One long weekend with three days off, George Holden, Rubin Rassmusson, and I, along with few sailors they worked with at their school, packed camping gear and fishing equipment into George's large van. We went on a trout fishing trip to Navaho Lake, located 100 miles north of Albuquerque. We camped out two nights, and had a good time around the campfire in the evening telling sea stories, and relating stories about the times we were stationed together in the past. The first night in camp, a skunk wandered into our camp, and one of the sailors made a big mistake, he shot the skunk, and the smell was so bad we had to relocate our camp in the dark. I caught a few small trout, and although no one caught many fish, we had a good time sharing the outdoors.

I also went fishing a number of times with an Air Force sergeant, Dave Knight, who was the fiancé of our Guam friend, Chris. We fished a lake on the Acoma Indian Reservation located thirty miles west of Albuquerque. We caught a lot of catfish in this lake. Due to the scarcity of water in New Mexico, fishermen had to travel long distances to enjoy their sport.

On another weekend we traveled back to Show Low, Arizona, and met my parents, who were visiting their property, which had been my grandfather's homestead. Their granddaughters' Lisa and Betty were with them. The occasion of our visit was the fiftieth wedding anniversary of relatives who lived near Show Low, Opal and Louie Simpson. We had an anxious moment during this weekend. My niece Betty, while playing in a tree, fell fifteen feet to the ground. She cried loudly, but was unhurt.

We enjoyed a visit by my parents for a few days. They picked up the grandfather clock we had brought back from Guam. During their visit we all drove to an interesting old mining ghost town, called Madrid, New Mexico.

As I mentioned, George and Rubin worked as instructors at a joint service school that taught courses in radioactive material monitoring, and decontamination methods. The primary objective of the school was to teach service members the proper methods of dealing with accidents involving radioactive material. George planned on retiring after twenty years of active service. He had been approached by a number of companies who wanted to hire him after retirement. One of the companies was the power company that had been involved in the Three-Mile Island power plant accident. George kept me informed about possible civilian jobs, as I might be retiring the same time as him in 1980.

George and Rubin taught both in the classroom, and "in the field." Teaching in the field involved students putting on decontamination suits, with self contained breathing apparatus, then going to a designated location on the base, and attempting to find radioactive sources scattered about, with detection instruments, or as the instruments were commonly called, "RADIAC Instruments" (Radioactive Detection and Computation Instruments).

One student who attended the school, and came to our house for dinner one evening, was GMTC Ray Margeson, who I'd been with on Guam. He had also been my "sponsor" when I was initiated as a chief. Ray was stationed on the east coast, and had plans to retire shortly. He planned to settle down in rural New York State. It was great to see "Soup" again, and we had a good visit. Other visitors we had from Guam were GMT1 Fegan and his wife. They were on leave in Albuquerque visiting family. One of their relatives was the famous racecar driver, Al Unser, who called Albuquerque his home.

One Sunday afternoon, Carmen and I went for a Sunday drive. We drove to the ghost town of Madrid, the town we had visited with our parents. There was a long deserted length of the highway between Madrid and Albuquerque, and we both needed to relieve ourselves. We stopped off to the side of the deserted highway. We got out of the Oldsmobile, and stepped over a fallen barb wire fence onto a dirt path that lead toward a dry stream bed, out of sight of any passing motorists. I stopped out of sight of the highway, and Carmen walked on further out of sight. I waited a few minutes, and then Carmen rejoined me. As soon as we took a step on the dirt path leading back to the car, we heard the sound that cannot be mistaken for anything else.

It was the rattle of a rattlesnake's tail. Carmen becomes very agitated near snakes, and after I got her calmed down, we walked around the snake, which was curled up by the path we had just walked down a few minutes previously. When we reached the car, Carmen had raced to the door and leapt inside. I picked up a rock, and threw it at the snake. The snake was very aggressive, and began crawling toward me. I wanted no further argument, so I jumped into the car, and drove away. This was not to be the last time we encountered a disagreeable reptile in New Mexico.

One of my pastimes was metal detecting. Carmen had given me a metal detector as a gift when we lived in the San Francisco area. I had used it around some of the old Spanish ruins in Guam, but had not discovered anything. I began using the metal detector on base, and discovered a considerable amount of lost dimes, nickels, and quarters. I metal detected some of the public parks scattered throughout the city. Many of these parks had been established around the turn of the century, when white men first began settling in Albuquerque. My metal detector did not have a can "pop-top" discrimination circuit, which many modern metal detectors have, so I dug up many pop-tops. I did find a couple of rings, and a few old coins.

During my time at Whidbey Island I had held memberships in the Veterans of Foreign Wars (VFW), and the Fleet Reserve Association (FRA). I had let both memberships lapse. At the encouragement of Chris Pilger's fiancé, Dave Knight, I joined the American Legion. The Post (as they are called in the American Legion), was located near the Albuquerque fair grounds, and had one of the largest memberships in the nation. I would often watch Sunday afternoon football at the American Legion Post. Rubin encouraged me to rejoin the Fleet Reserve Association, which had a club building near the base. I'd first joined the FRA while in Iceland eighteen years before. There were many retired GMT's in the Albuquerque FRA Branch. Many had returned to Albuquerque, after being charmed by the city when attending "A" school at the beginning of their careers. At the beginning of the Navy Nuclear Weaponsman's trade, the sailors had been permanently stationed in Albuquerque. These sailors populated commands called "U.S. Navy Special Weapons Units," these Albuquerque-based sailors would deploy on ships deploying on cruises, and upon the ship's return to the states these "Units" would return to Albuquerque. Many of these pioneer nuclear weaponsmen were members of the Albuquerque Fleet Reserve Association (FRA) Branch 200.

Prior to my assignment to the NLO Office, while in Guam, all GMT chiefs, and a few first class GMTs, had been informed that since they attended the weapons warhead maintenance course, they were being placed in a newly assigned category of security clearance designation. This new designation was for those who had knowledge of Critical Nuclear Weapons Design Information (CNWDI). When placed in this category, sailors were said to have a "sin-witty" clearance. In my job in Albuquerque, I was required to have a sin-witty clearance.

Lieutenant Commander Perry Roberts was very talkative. He had been in the position as the NLO Officer for over a year, alone, and I think he was thankful for my company. We talked about a variety of subjects, also since he had transited the gulf from enlisted to officer status, by going from first class petty officer to ensign, he explained much about what to expect if I should accept my commission. One subject he stressed over and over again was the difference in the enlisted society and the officer's society. As an enlisted person, if a fellow enlisted shipmate offered to help you, it was usually a sincere offer. In the world of commissioned officers the key to success was the "ranking" the commanding officer assigned to each officer under him. On officer's fitness reports, which were the equivalent of enlisted evaluation performance reports, each officer of the same rank was given a "ranking number" by the commanding officer. An example might be, in a group of ten lieutenants, a particular lieutenant might have a ranking of "four", on his fitness report. This meant the commanding officer had judged this officer's performance, and potential as "four out of ten." Each lieutenant's goal was to become "number one out of ten." This ongoing struggle to reach number one was called "breaking out of the pack." In order to break out of the pack, officer's wanted to be noticed favorably by the commanding officer. Lieutenant Commander Roberts said, with this in mind, anytime a fellow officer offered help, or advice, he had to be held in suspicion as there might be an ulterior motive, that of making you look bad, and him look good in the commanding officer's eyes. To me this sounded like a foreign and "cut throat world," unlike the Navy I had known for almost twenty years. Lieutenant Commander Roberts explained I could not make the mistake of trying to act like a chief, and look upon other officers as brothers ready to help, or lend a helping hand at the drop of a hat without considering motives. In a sense the officer's society sounded like a society of intrigue, and subterfuge, with each officer looking out for himself.

Lieutenant Commander Roberts also stressed that unlike an enlisted man, I would be expected to observe strict rules of protocol, and I would be judged in the area of social graces. Lieutenant Commander Roberts was sincerely trying to help, but the more I learned from him, the more apprehensive, and undecided I became as April 2, 1980 drew closer.

Lieutenant Commander Roberts was scheduled to attend a publication group meeting in Norfolk, Virginia for one week. He returned after a week and a half. After this trip, he was a very different person. For over a week he spoke very little, and seemed preoccupied, which was unlike him. I was worried that something serious was going on in his life, such as health, or marital problems. After days of this he finally confided in me and revealed what had been bothering him. During his trip to Norfolk, one evening he had gone to an old shipmate's house, they had a few drinks, and on the way back to his motel, a policeman had pulled him over. A taillight was out on the rental car he was driving. The policeman smelled alcohol, had given him a sobriety test, and then arrested him for driving under the influence of alcohol. He had spent the night in jail, and then gone before a judge the next morning. He had to pay a large fine, and promise to take a remedial driving course in New Mexico. His biggest concern was that his commanding officer in Indian Head, Maryland would find out. A drunken driving conviction could end an officer's career. He told the Virginia judge that all the paperwork concerning his case should be sent to our office, instead of Indian Head. I watched for the paperwork in the mail, and I swore to secrecy, and never revealed this to anyone, until now.

In the past, driving under the influence by military members was so common; it was often overlooked, or ignored if no one was hurt, or if there was no property damage involved in such incidents. This attitude had changed dramatically in the past couple of years. The human suffering and loss of life, due to irresponsible drinking and driving was no longer ignored by society. A charge of drinking and driving became a kiss of death for a sailor's career. In the case of a GMT it could also mean the revocation of his security clearance.

One day out of the blue, I received a phone call from Allison (Konrad) Stice. I'd not had any contact with her since our divorce, and my transfer from Whidbey Island, ten years ago. She said she had talked to a lawyer, and he said that I owed her additional alimony! Recalling her false promise to pay the taxes on the alimony, this was a disturbing turn of events. About three weeks after this surprising call, there was a knock at our door one evening. I opened the door and there stood two grim faced men in suits, and neckties. They asked, "If I were James Little?" To which I replied "yes." One of the men handed me a folded piece of paper and said, "We're from the sheriff's department, and we are serving you with this summons." He then said, "I'm sorry we're just doing our job." After they left, I examined the paper I'd been given. It was a summons to appear in court in Coupeville, Washington for an alimony hearing. Allison had initiated the summons. This was not good news. I called Whidbey Island, and retained a lawyer to represent me at the hearing. I paid a considerable lawyer fee, although eventually the case was dismissed.

Performance evaluation reports for chief petty officers' were due in September. Lieutenant Commander Roberts submitted mine, with all marks in the top one percent; the text said I had been specifically selected for the NLO job because of my superior performance over the years. The statement in my evaluation about being selected specifically for the NLO assignment was stretching the truth a bit, since my detailer in Washington, D.C. not only didn't know what the job entailed, but he also didn't know where the job was located!

We had planned to get a family dog since returning to the states. We had grown fond of Mooch the booney dog, and missed him. We saw in the paper an advertisement for free German Shepherd puppies, which were being given away by an Air Force family that lived on base. We went to the families address one afternoon, and the kids picked a puppy out of a litter of five. The owners said the dog shouldn't get too large, as the mother was an exceptionally small German Shepherd. The puppy was named "Shadow." We had a large back yard, to which Shadow soon became accustomed.

In December 1979, I turned thirty-seven years old. LCDR Perry Roberts was becoming anxious about my approaching commissioning date. It was normal policy to immediately transfer a newly commissioned officer who had served in the enlisted ranks. This transfer was logical for a number of reasons. As I explained before, the sudden elevation of authority could cause problems in the chain of command. Overnight the new officer would become senior to the chiefs, and senior petty officers he had been working for the previous day. There could be problems with jealousy, resentment, and other issues that could be detrimental to good morale at a command. I had experienced this sudden elevation by someone I worked with, in the case of Dan Hoover on the *USS Oriskany*, when he was promoted to chief warrant officer, and not transferred for a long while after his commissioning. In that case it had been handled well by all concerned, because we were all mature individuals. I could see however, that a situation like that could cause serious problems, and I felt it was a good policy.

Lieutenant Commander Roberts planned to talk to my detailer, and try to convince him to leave me in Albuquerque following my commissioning instead of immediately issuing transfer orders. Lieutenant Commander Roberts's rationale was, since we were a two-man office, the problems that were associated with instant commissioning such as I described would not be a factor. My new detailer was to be LT Ron Bench. He was the officer stationed in Washington, D.C. who assigned LDO's and CWO's to their future assignments, and also provided career advice, and guidance.

Shortly after I'd received word that I'd been selected for promotion to chief warrant officer, I had received a large packet of information from Lieutenant Bench. In the packet was an Officer History Card, on which I was to detail all my past assignments, and Navy service schools I had attended. Also there were an Officer Preference and Personal Information Card, which was somewhat like the Duty Preference Cards, I had filled out as an enlisted man, detailing where I would like to be stationed in the future (also called "dream cards"). Within the packet was a list of all the jobs in the Navy, which I could be assigned to; these jobs were called "billets." He also included a lengthy letter, which said, in part, "Dear James. Welcome aboard! Please accept my personal congratulations on your selection for Ordnance Technician (7161). The purpose of this letter is to provide you with information that will answer some of the questions, which will facilitate your first assignment as a commissioned officer of the U.S. Navy."

This was a much different relationship with the detailing system as an officer, compared to my experiences with a detailer as an enlisted man. Little did I know, or imagine in my wildest dreams what part the detailing system in Washington, D.C. would play in the years to come in my future.

As well as an immediate transfer upon commissioning, it was normal policy for newly commissioned chief warrant officers, and LDO ensigns to attend an officer orientation and indoctrination course in Pensacola, Florida. This course was six weeks long, and topics included social graces, and conduct, administrative tasks, and military drill review. This course was commonly called "knife and fork school." A few looked upon this course as demeaning, and as an insult to enlisted men's integrity. They felt this strengthened the idea that enlisted men were considered an uncouth, ill-mannered, ignorant lot that needed refining before they could join the officer ranks. This was not true as many of the topics would be new to the previous chiefs and first class, who needed to learn these few subjects in order to be an effective officer. A common joke was that the school taught you that it was not good manners to pick your nose at the wardroom dinner table. Most of the classes in the course were condensed classes of those taught at the Naval Academy, and Officers Candidate School. I assumed I would be going to Pensacola, Florida shortly after commissioning, and attending this school, regardless if I transferred to a new duty station, or remained at Albuquerque.

I reviewed the billet listing I'd received from Washington, D.C. I had a much larger and varied selection of jobs as a chief warrant officer, compared to a chief's possible assignments. I was hopefully that I would have a job assignment in the nuclear weapons program, and not the conventional ordnance field. My possible jobs also included such assignments as a Fire Control Officer on a guided missile cruiser, Gunnery Officer on a carrier, a Missile Systems Officer, and many more that was unrelated to the nuclear weapons program, and would require education, and familiarization on my part. I did not want to be placed in a position, where I was considered the "technical expert," and the enlisted men working for me had much more knowledge about the job than I did. I'd heard of ex-GMT's being placed in such jobs, and they were not happy, having to blindly trust that the men in their division were doing the jobs properly, while they tried to quickly learn enough their new job to do a competent job of supervising and leading.

My chance to be promoted to senior chief was excellent, and I was still waiting for word on whether I'd passed. Until I signed the dotted line on my commissioning papers, I still had the options of being promoted to senior chief, or retire.

Just as I had studied the *Navy Uniform Regulations Manual* before being promoted to chief, I studied the same manual to learn what new insignia and rank devices I would be wearing as a chief warrant officer. Many of the uniform items were the same as a chief petty officer, but there were still significant changes in many articles of clothing. Most significant would be the new hat devices. I would be wearing a naval officer's crest, which is an eagle perched on a shield with crossed gold anchors. I would also wear a gold braid above the hat brim. I would have a gold stripe on the sleeves of my dress blues, and on some uniforms be wearing shoulder boards, which would be a new experience for me. I would be required to pay for all my new uniform items, as there would be no clothing allowance for my promotion. There was a clothing allowance for the first class petty officers that promoted to ensign, because of the significant changes in uniform that was just as radical as when promoting to chief petty officer.

Rubin had been dating a Wave while stationed at Kirtland. Her name was Mary, and they were planning a wedding. Everyone attending the wedding was asked to wear uniforms. The day of the wedding arrived, and Carmen and I attended. It was a nice wedding, with a reception held at the Acey Ducey Club, for Rubin and Mary. When Carmen and I prepared to leave after the reception, I discovered my hat was missing. George Holden, who was also at the wedding and reception told me he'd had his hat stolen a number of times. He suspected Air Force people who wanted them as souvenirs had stolen them. This was upsetting, as my combination chief's hat was one of my most expensive uniform items.

In December, prior to Christmas, we loaded up the Oldsmobile, and drove to California to spend Christmas with the family. My brother Joe was working on overhauling his Volkswagen and brother Jerry was trying to grow a beard. While in California, Carmen called Martha in San Jose, and got news on what she, Remedy, and Wayne were doing. Roger also called his father in San Francisco. We'd gotten very little word about what Peter was doing, or how he was, which was a constant worry for us. We had a wonderful family Christmas. On the return trip to New Mexico, we ran into a lot of snow, but made it home all right. The Oldsmobile rear end had an unsettling habit of making noises during long drives. The radio antenna motor failed, shortly after we picked the car up, and various panel lights kept going out. There were a lot of small things about the car that irritated me, although it did get good gas mileage.

One afternoon, there was a scheduled chief's initiation, and I took an afternoon off work to attend. It surprised me, the large number of chiefs that were in attendance. George Holden was the "Judge" at the initiation, and he did a great job, it was a good initiation. There were a number of retired sailors at the initiation.

There were many legendary sailors that at one time or another worked in the nuclear weapons field, in Albuquerque. A man I mentioned previously was Rear Admiral William Deke Parsons, who could be considered the first Navy Nuclear Weaponsman. He was a captain, on board the B29 *Superfortress*, Enola Gay, on 6 August 1945, when the first atomic bomb detonated during war was dropped, on Hiroshima, Japan. He had worked on the Manhattan Project with Oppenheimer, and went on the bombing mission to arm the bomb before the drop on the enemy city. The bomb was a gun-type, officially called a Mk-1, and nicknamed "Little Boy." Captain Parsons climbed into the planes bomb bay to arm the bomb after the take off from Tinian Island. The two plugs that were used to arm, and safe the bomb, were recently auctioned off on the Internet site, e-bay, for $150,000.

On the day of the drop, Navigator Major Thomas Ferebee used a Norden bombsight to drop the "little boy" from the Enola Gay, 31,000 feet above Hiroshima. The Norden bombsight was one of the most closely guarded military secrets of World War II, used by the Army Air Force for precision bombing. My mother befriended an elderly lady in Lindsay, California, who upon passing away left my mother a Norden circular sight that now hangs on her living room wall.

An interesting memo dated 25 July 1945 addresses that first bomb. The memo is to General Carl Spaats, Commanding General United States Army Strategic Air Forces, from the War Department Office of the Chief of Staff,

> 1. The 509 Composite Group, 20th Air Force will deliver its first special bomb as soon as weather will permit visual bombing after about 3 August 1945 on one of the targets: Hiroshima, Kokura, Nidgata and Nagasaki. To carry military and civilian scientific personnel from the War Department to observe and record the effects of the explosion of the bomb, additional aircraft will accompany the airplane carrying the bomb. The observing planes will stay several miles distant from the point of impact of the bomb.
> 2. Additional bombs will be delivered on the above targets as soon as made ready by the project staff. Further instructions will be issued concerning targets other than those listed above.
> 3. Dissemination of any and all information concerning the use of the weapon against Japan is reserved to the Secretary of War and the President of the United States. No communiqués on the subject or releases of information will be issued by Commanders in the field without specific prior authority. Any news stories will be sent to the War Department for special clearance.
> 4. The foregoing directive is issued to you by direction and with the approval of the Secretary of War and of the Chief of Staff, USA. It is desired that you personally deliver one copy of this directive to General MacArthur and one copy to Admiral Nimitz for their information.

On that fateful day, no one knew for sure what would happen when the bomb detonated. It was possible the earth's crust might crack, or an unforeseen chain reaction might occur in the atmosphere.

When the plane's crew observed the effects of the bomb, it was tremendous, and awe-inspiring. Although the bomb completely destroyed Hiroshima, and resulted in the deaths of 200,000 people, Japan did not surrender immediately, and a second bomb was dropped on Nagasaki three days after the destruction of Hiroshima. Japan surrendered on 10 August 1945. Admiral Parsons became the director of the Los Alamos Ordnance Program after retirement from the Navy. He passed away in 1953.

In many ways 1979 was a year of national frustration for Americans. When the American Embassy in Iran was invaded, and American hostages taken, there was a feeling of shock throughout the country, and as time drug on without any action, the feelings of shock, and frustration turned to anger against President Carter and his administration for their lack of action.

We in the military felt impotent, and rejected by American society since the end of the Vietnam War. A sense of failure ran like a small thread through the armed services. In the future when the hostage rescue attempt failed so miserably, it was like the final nail in our coffin of shame. It was an embarrassment we all felt. The Air Force, Army, Navy and Marines, had all been involved in the rescue attempt. Everything had gone so wrong, with planes colliding, the needless death of pilots, and with the rescue team being lost in the desert. It sounded more like a comedic Keystone Cops episode, than a serious military operation. This had been an opportunity to redeem ourselves, and appear professional in the public's eyes, and we only confirmed that America's military performed like a defeated force!

Carmen and I, and the kids, frequently went to see a movie in the evening at the base theater. The theater was directly across the street from the barracks I had lived in nineteen years before, while attending Nuclear Weapons A School. A big difference between a civilian movie theater, and a military base movie theater, is before the showing of a movie, the National Anthem is played, and everyone rises and stands at attention.

Lieutenant Commander Roberts was not successful in his efforts to persuade my Detailer Lieutenant Bench, to leave me in Albuquerque following my commissioning in April. I called Washington in February, to talk to Lieutenant Bench, and he said he had a job at Nuclear Weapons Training Group Pacific, in San Diego, but would have to check it out before he could confirm that it was a job I could go to. He also said there was a job on an ammunition ship. I told him I preferred the San Diego job. He confirmed that I would not be staying in Albuquerque, primarily because I was in a chief's billet, and needed to be in an officer's job, to be groomed for future promotions. He told me to call him back after a week.

After a week, I called Washington again. Lieutenant Bench immediately told me I would be going to the *USS Midway* (CV-41), an aircraft carrier home ported in Yokosuka, Japan. *Midway* was a "forward deployed aircraft carrier." *Midway* was a new concept in the Navy. She had been in Japan for seven years. In the past, aircraft carriers with crews of 4,000 to 6,000 sailors had been home ported either on the East or West coast of the United States. On the East coast, the ships were home ported in Philadelphia, Pennsylvania, Norfolk, Virginia, and Mayport, Florida. On the West coast, carriers called San Diego, San Francisco, California, and Seattle, Washington home. A "forward deployed carrier," was a concept started in 1973 that involved relocating *Midway* to Japan, and also relocating their families to Japan. This relocation was supposed to eliminate the long separations of families during the usual six-month or longer cruises that aircraft carriers made. It was also thought that this forward deployment would place *Midway* in a closer position to respond to the crisis situations that seemed to happen often in that part of the world. Lieutenant Bench said I would not be attending Officer Orientation School (knife & fork school) in Florida, but instead attend a few classes at Nuclear Weapons Training Group Pacific, before reporting to *Midway*.

I was not ecstatic about going back to sea, or about leaving Albuquerque, but this was standard policy, sending newly commissioned officers to sea. My orders were to be issued after 2 April. I was pleased that my first job as an officer was to be within my technical field of nuclear weapons. My official job title was to be, "W Division Technical Monitor," the same job Chief Warrant Officer White had held on board the *USS Independence*.

In February 1980, the big news in New Mexico was a prison riot in the New Mexico State prison, located north of Albuquerque. Thirty-three convicts were killed and hundreds injured.

Not long after I'd discovered we would be moving to Japan, my youngest stepson Roger, told Carmen he wanted to go live with his father in San Francisco. His father had urged him to come live with him, when Roger visited him after our return to the states from Guam. Carmen and I told him to think this over very carefully. We had heard that his older brother Peter was not getting along well with his father and stepmother. Roger was sure he did not want to go to Japan. I did not feel he had considered all the consequences, but at the age of fourteen, he was sure that he knew everything.

George Holden was retiring after twenty years. He and I had started our careers in the Navy at the same time, and I still entertained thoughts of retiring. George had gotten a job in Silverdale, Washington working in the Polaris/Trident missile program, these were the missiles used in the Navy's intercontinental ballistic missile submarines. In the process of his family moving from New Mexico to Washington, his son was going to travel to San Francisco to visit his grandparents. Since George's son and Roger were best friends, it worked out so Roger could travel to San Francisco by bus with him. It would be Carmen, Mary, and I going to Japan.

The family German Shepherd "Shadow," who was supposed to be a small dog according to the people we had gotten him from, had grown into a monster. His coat was a beautiful black and silver color. He was so big; he could put his front paws on my shoulders and look me in the eye. I hated the thought, but we would not be able to take Shadow to Japan with us. It was almost impossible to bring a family dog into Japan and especially difficult for a dog as large as ours.

I became anxious as the date for my commissioning drew closer. I was about to step foot into a world I knew little about. Enlisted men were not permitted to associate socially with officers or be familiar with them in any way. On board ships the officer's berthing, and mess area was called "officer's country," which enlisted men were forbidden to enter. This separation between officers and enlisted men was more pronounced, and adhered to in the Navy than in any other armed service. This separation was a naval tradition; due to the absolute authority officers at sea have always exercised over the crew.

As I said before, Lieutenant Commander Roberts gave me valuable insight into the world of officers, as well as Chief Warrant Officer Four Charlie Schmidt who worked on the same floor as us, in the FCDNA Stockpile Maintenance Branch. I also thought often of Gunner White on the *USS Independence*, and the professional way he had conducted himself.

I underwent a physical examination before my commissioning. I asked Lieutenant Commander Roberts if he would swear me in on the day of my commissioning, and he agreed that he would. In order to be commissioned as an officer, I had to be discharged as an enlisted man. On 1 April 1980, I was honorably discharged from active duty as a chief petty officer. Technically I was a civilian for about eight hours, from midnight on the 1st, until my swearing in ceremony on the 2nd. The ceremony was scheduled to take place at 10:00 a.m. in an auditorium on the same floor as the Navy Liaison Office. I invited many of the military and civilian people I had worked with since being in Albuquerque.

The legal status of limited duty officers and chief warrant officers has been ever changing and even confusing over the years. Although I previously detailed the history of the LDO/CWO program that is not the entire story. I'll try to explain the program more in depth, as it existed in 1980. When I was discharged, I permanently lost my status as an enlisted man. 1980 was the first year newly commissioned LDO and CWO's lost their legal standing as enlisted personnel. Prior to this year the newly commissioned officers retained their status as enlisted men. This retention of enlisted status was a "safety net" for the sailors being elevated to officer ranks. This dual status of both enlisted and officer rank permitted the new officer an alternate career path in the Navy if he failed as an officer. If he failed, he could revert to his or her enlisted rank and continue in the Navy until such time he or she had the required length of time in service to retire. These "temporary" limited duty officers and chief warrant officers commissioned before 1980, continued to be promoted as "permanent enlisted personnel." They did not participate in the semiannual promotion examination, but were "promoted on paper" automatically when they had served the required time for their next enlisted rank. An example might be, a temporary Chief Warrant Officer 2, would be a permanent Chief Petty Officer, after a few years he would promote to temporary Chief Warrant Officer 3, and permanent senior Chief Petty Officer. After a twenty to thirty year career, he would most likely be a temporary Chief Warrant Officer 4, and permanent Master Chief Petty Officer. This dual status or safety net system was halted for chief warrant officers, as I said in 1980. So I was commissioned a Chief Warrant Officer 2 with no legal enlisted status to fall back on should I fail as an officer.

The dual status system was retained for limited duty officers. These sailors were commissioned temporary ensigns, with permanent enlisted status, and promotions continuing automatically, paralleling their officer careers. This dual status continued until the limited duty officer reached the rank of lieutenant. At this point the limited duty officer lieutenant had to convert to permanent officer status, and lose his enlisted status prior to promoting to lieutenant commander. If he did not go "permanent" then he would be forced to retire as a lieutenant. I have not described this complicated system in detail, but have merely scratched the surface. Perhaps this is enough for the reader to appreciate the complexity of the path that enlisted sailors must take to reach commissioned officer status.

A law passed by Congress in the mid-70's impacts upon the employment options of retired sailors. This law is commonly referred to as the "double dipping law." The law prohibits a retired commissioned officer from holding a government job, and receiving a retired military pension during the time of his or her employment, and greatly restricts the final pension amount following retirement from government service. This forfeiture of a military pension does not apply to enlisted men and women, who can hold a government job and still draw their monthly military pension, and thus at the end of retirement from their government job, draw two retirement pensions. This law has the effect of discouraging many highly qualified retired officers from seeking employment with the government work force, such as the post office, state department, federal law enforcement, etc.

Relating to my promotion in 1980, I would have much rather been promoted as a temporary officer and permanent enlisted man, instead of a permanent officer with no enlisted status. Then my options at retirement would have included a government job, since the anti double dipping law did not affect temporary officers. This dual path of promotion was fiercely disliked within the chief petty officer ranks. They considered it an insult that a sailor, who could not make it as an officer, was promoted in the chief petty officer ranks automatically without taking an examination, and working for it as they had. Technically the officer who reverted could be called a failure. I appreciated the disgust felt by chiefs toward this dual promotion program, although I understand the motive behind the program, to provide a safety net for sailors who cannot perform as officers. During my career I meet a number of chiefs who had been reverted from a previous officer rank.

The morning of 2 April 1980, I put on the uniform of an officer, and standing before LCDR Perry Roberts, and a room full of observers, recited the following oath. "I James Stewart Little, do solemnly reaffirm that I will support and defend the constitution of the United States of America against all enemies, foreign and domestic, that I will continue to bear true faith and allegiance to the constitution and the country whose course it directs, and that I take this obligation freely, without any mental reservation. So help me God."

Following the reciting of the oath, Lieutenant Commander Roberts shook my hand and congratulated me. I thanked everyone in the audience, saying I appreciated them taking time to attend this ceremony, which was a very important day in my Navy career. Everyone shook my hand, and congratulated Carmen and I. Pictures were taken of Carmen and me, and Mary. After signing the official paperwork that obligated me for three years in the Navy, I was given a large certificate, which had the seal of the President of the United States at the top.

During my assignment to the NLO Office, I had worked closely with civilians working in the Unsatisfactory Report Office in McAlester, Oklahoma. When I returned to the office following my swearing in ceremony, there were many very nice congratulation messages on the answering machine from this group.

Lieutenant Commander Roberts's wife Vera had a ceramic business in Albuquerque. Her most frequent customers were Indians purchasing vases and jars they would then paint and sell to tourists as Indian pottery. The morning of my commissioning, Lieutenant Commander Roberts gave me a very nice ceramic coffee mug Vera had made. The mug was decorated with a Navy Officer's crest, my new rank "CWO2," and the date 2 April 1980.

I had reached a higher goal than I had ever dreamed of achieving, and I felt it was important that I thank the people responsible for my achievement of a commission in the Navy, my wife Carmen, and my parents. The day I put on an officer's uniform, I wrote a letter to my parents, expressing my love and gratitude for them.

It has long been a tradition that officers give a silver dollar to the first enlisted man that salutes him following his commissioning. I had a silver dollar ready, as I walked toward my car that morning. I was saluted for the first time by an Air Force enlisted man. I stopped him, and shocked him by handing him the silver dollar. I then explained the tradition to him.

A few days after my commissioning, the base newspaper, published an article and picture of me, which was entitled, "From Chief to Mister". An enlisted Air Force airman who worked for the base newspaper had interviewed me. The picture he took of me was not very flattering, as it showed my "potbelly." Carmen "chided" me about the picture, and I went on a diet.

Lieutenant Commander Roberts had gotten word from Washington that my replacement was to be Chief McNair, presently onboard the *USS Proteus* (submarine tender), stationed in Guam. The bad news was that he probably wouldn't arrive in Albuquerque for a couple of months, so Lieutenant Commander Roberts would once again be alone in the office. I had met Chief McNair while in Guam.

The day of my commissioning I handed out the traditional cigars. As an officer it was expected that I host a "wetting down party."

This meant I was to arrange a party for all the officers in FCDNA (more than 100), and pay for all the snacks, and drinks consumed. Luckily three other Navy officers were being promoted in April, two lieutenants junior grade, and a lieutenant, so we all went in together for a cost of fifty dollars each. We reserved a hotel reception room in the downtown Albuquerque area, and the "wetting down" party was held on a Friday night shortly after 2 April. Also in April, Carmen gave me a surprise "congratulation party" at the American Legion Post, which was attended by twenty-five friends.

I received my transfer orders by message on the 5th of April. Just as many things had changed in my life, transiting from the enlisted man's world, to the realm of an officer's world, my orders were in an entirely different format from those orders I'd received as an enlisted man.

My orders in message format directed me to detach from the Naval Liaison Office in time to report to Commander, Nuclear Weapons Training Group Pacific, San Diego for five weeks of instruction. Then to Fleet Training Center, Naval Station San Diego for two weeks instruction to include Fire Fighting School, Damage Control School, and administration and operation of Ship's 3-M System.

I was authorized thirty days leave. An officer was always designated a relief for another officer. This was different from enlisted transfers, as enlisted sailors are transferred to a specific job. In the case of officers, officers are transferred to relieve a specific officer. I was to relieve CWO2 William A. Grizzard, on the *USS Midway*. My tour length on the ship was to be twenty-four months.

I had a month to prepare for my transfer. This was to be a frantic time. I had initially expected to be in Albuquerque for three years. Now nine months after arriving, we had to pack up and leave for overseas again. We had to find a home for the family dog Shadow, get port entry approval for Carmen and Mary, as well as passports for the three of us. We also had to consider what to do with our new car, as we had been advised not to ship a car to Japan, but instead buy one when we arrived in Japan. One problem with shipping an American car to Japan was that the steering wheel was on the wrong side, as Japanese drive on the left side of the road.

As an officer my performance was to be evaluated in a completely different manner, and on a different form than that used to evaluate enlisted sailors. My performance was to be evaluated on forms called "Fitness Reports." All fitness reports are filled out by an officer's commanding officer. It was required that there be a fitness report covering every day of an officer's career. Any gaps or skipped days were not permitted. Every day of an officer's life had to be accounted for and documented. Lieutenant Commander Perry Roberts began preparing my fitness report, which would be signed off by the commanding officer of Naval Ordnance Station, Indian Head, Maryland, and so it would be ready by the time I left in a month.

Before military dependants can accompany a military member overseas, they must undergo questioning, and have their medical records screened. This scrutiny is required, because at many overseas bases there was limited medical care, and it had to be ascertained if the dependants had any physical or mental problems that might need special attention. This process was called "port entry approval" which I mentioned previously. If a sailor had children that had special disabilities, criminal records, or behavior problems, then that dependant would not be given port entry approval, and could not accompany him or her overseas. There was also the matter of expenses to consider. The Navy couldn't afford to pay for transportation back and forth from overseas bases to the United States, every time a problem occurred within a family unit. We also had to get all the required immunizations required for entry into Japan. We all had "shot record cards" which contained immunization histories.

Shadow had grown up into a beautiful black and silver German Shepherd. We took him as well as a number of other household items we wished to sell, to the weekend flea market that was held each week at the Albuquerque State Fairgrounds. An Indian family approached us at the flea market, and said they had a large ranch, and a dog that needed a companion. They wanted Shadow, and we agreed that he would have a good home with them. They said they would come to our house to pick him up in a couple of days. When they arrived to pick him up, it was a sad parting, we had grown close to Shadow, but it was good that he would have a lot of space to roam. He had been an "escape artist" on two occasions, getting out of our back yard. The Air Force military police had brought him back both times, but not until they had given him petting and affection, and all dog biscuits he could hold.

One afternoon I had an appointment at the housing office to arrange for the pack out of our household goods for shipment to Japan. I met with an Air Force first lieutenant. After we talked about the details of the pack out, he said, "Wow, I've never seen a real Navy warrant officer." He then asked me to wait a minute, and he left the room. He returned with an Air Force major, and three Air Force enlisted people, who stared at me in awe.

They kept repeating, "We've heard about warrant officers, but have never seen a real one," and "this is amazing." This was somewhat embarrassing sitting there, being looked at as though they expected me to perform a miracle, or perhaps bless them.

Since my commissioning, I had to adjust to my new relationship with other officers, who were now my peers, and not the aloof, authority figures officers had been to me during my enlisted life. It was also strange to have all the enlisted people I came in contact with instantly become accommodating, attentive, and subservient to me. I tried to adjust to this new position gracefully. I vowed that I would try to always remember the feelings I had toward officers as an enlisted man, and the traits I admired in officers that I had worked for, and also the traits that I disliked. I determined that the path I would like to take as an officer would be one of leadership, and attention to the well being, and productivity of the enlisted men that would eventually work for me. I had heard Gunner White say, "If you take care of the small problems your men might have, then seldom do big problems develop." In other words "take care of the troops." Too many officers were primarily interested in the person they saw in the mirror, and getting ahead, even if it meant over the bodies of enlisted men. This was a new life, and journey in which I had taken the first step, I was anxious to continue, and see what the future held. I was also encouraged by our country's new President, Ronald Reagan, who seemed to be concerned about the country's defense, and strengthening the military which had not been done in the past four years during the President Carter administration.

I was busy buying the necessary uniform items I needed as a warrant officer for a few months before and after my commissioning. Many of the uniforms I'd worn as a chief, after a few alterations, I could wear as a CWO2. The uniform I would be wearing most onboard ship would be khaki's. As a chief I'd worn gold fouled anchors pinned on each collar of my shirts. As a CWO2, I wore my "specialty device," which was a flaming ordnance pot (signifying surface ordnance), on my left collar. On the right collar, a gold bar was worn, with three blue squares within it, signifying CWO2. My dress blues as a chief had a gold crow, with four gold hash marks sewn on the left sleeve. Those with continuing good conduct, and who had been awarded Good Conduct Medals wore the gold crow, and gold hash marks; all others wore red crows and hash marks. These gold items were very expensive to purchase. Since I no longer needed them, I gave them to Rubin Rassmusson as a gift, since he could use them on his chief's uniform. It wasn't possible to buy Navy uniforms on the Kirtland Air Force base, even though there were many sailors stationed on the base. Most sailors bought their uniforms through the Navy mail order system that mailed uniform items to sailors from Norfolk, Virginia.

I was advised by LCDR Perry Roberts, and my Detailer Lieutenant Ron Bench, that when I had a firm idea about the date I would be arriving in Japan, I should write a personal letter to my future boss on the ship, who in my case would be the weapons officer on *Midway*. The letter should describe my personal qualifications, the size of my family, my expected arrival date, and where I could be contacted while on leave.

LCDR Perry Roberts also advised me to have some calling cards made. I had entered a world with social requirements, and formal and informal rules and regulations I knew very little about. I would not be going to the Officer's Indoctrination School (knife and fork school), as my fellow newly commissioned warrant officers would be. If I had gone to this school, I would have been instructed about these unknown rules, regulations, and social protocol items. I tried to educate myself by asking questions, and studying a Navy-issued book I found in the NLO Office, entitled *"Social Usage and Protocol Handbook[44]."*

The calling cards I had made at the Base Exchange were small white 3" x 2 ½" cards with my full name "James Stewart Little," and "Chief Warrant Officer, United States Navy" printed on them. One use of calling cards by naval officers is described in the book I mentioned, and studied.

Traditionally, naval officers were expected to pay formal social calls on their commanding officers when reporting to a new duty station. The new officer, accompanied by his/her spouse would visit the commanding officer's home for twenty minutes or more and leave calling cards.

Times have changed, however, and the trend is toward less formality in social settings. The formal exchange of social calls is generally not required today. It is far more common for a commanding officer to host large scale receptions to welcome newcomers and bid others farewell. An officer should always inquire as to the command's policy.

Should formal calls be desired, the following general guidelines are observed. An appointment should be made, and the officer and spouse should arrive promptly at the residence of the commanding officer. Usually a social call lasts twenty to thirty minutes, with light, pleasant conversational exchange. The appropriate number of cards is left on a silver dish or tray located on a table near the door.

The officer paying the call leaves one of his cards for the husband and one for the wife, as well as one for each lady of the house over eighteen, but never for a man. A man can never make a call for his wife nor leave her cards, although she may make calls and leave cards for him, except in the case of a call on his commanding officer.

Not mentioned in the protocol book, is the tradition that after the before mentioned visit, within thirty days the commanding officer, either with or without a spouse, could appear unannounced at the officer's home for a visit. So the officer and his family had to be prepared for an unannounced visit from the commanding officer at any time within the thirty-day period.

The formal call system probably wouldn't be used by the *Midway*'s commanding officer, but I had to be prepared. "Hail and Farewell" parties were the most common way to welcome officer's reporting to a new command, and honoring those departing.

In April George Holden had been honorably discharged. He traveled by car to Silverdale, Washington where he would begin his new civilian job. When he arrived from New Mexico, he was informed that he had been selected for master chief. George was the only senior chief GMT selected for promotion off the previous September examination. He was told if he came back on active duty, and enlisted for two years, he would be promoted. George refused; he wanted to get started on his civilian career. I was also informed that I was selected for promotion to senior chief, but my acceptance of a commission to CWO2, invalidated the promotion.

It was an unusual coincidence that George and I had both started our careers as nuclear weaponsmen in 1961 at the "A' school in Albuquerque. We had joined the Navy on the exact same date, 30 June 1960, and had been co-leaders of our class. Now almost twenty years later, we both were starting new careers from Albuquerque, George to the civilian world, and me to the officer's world.

My work in the NLO Office continued until a few days before my departure. All of our household effects, except for the suitcases we would be carrying to California, and Japan, were packed by a moving company, and began the long trip to Japan. Remembering the hard work, and problems we had in Hamilton Air Force Base, and Guam when we went through our base housing office inspection prior to leaving, we hired a woman who cleaned base houses that had been evacuated prior to the housing office inspections. She guaranteed that the house would pass the inspection, following her cleaning.

After we had moved out of our house on Ranger Loop, we stayed in a temporary family lodging barracks on the base. Two nights before we were to depart, Lieutenant Commander Roberts, and his wife Vera, invited us to their house for a farewell dinner. Their house was in an exclusive area of Albuquerque, on a ridge of the Sandia Mountain range, looking down on the city of Albuquerque. Lieutenant Commander Roberts had been wise, at each place he had been stationed in the past twenty years plus, he had bought a house or two, and had rented them for an amount over the monthly mortgage payment. As the result he and Vera had a number of rental houses scattered about the country, and were able to enjoy the expensive house they now lived in. Carmen and I had an enjoyable evening with them, and prior to leaving they presented us with a beautifully decorated Indian vase, as a going away present.

As an officer, my performance was now detailed on a fitness report form. This form was vastly different, and much more detailed than any enlisted performance evaluation form. The fitness report form had areas of grading such as: Goal Setting Achievement, Subordinate Management and Development, Working Relations, Equipment and Material Management, Navy Organization Support, Response in Stressful Situations, Equal Opportunity, Speaking ability, Writing Ability, Sea-Manship, and Watchstanding. These areas were graded "A" through "F," "A" being the highest mark, and "F" the lowest, there was also an "N" for Not Observed. There was an area on the form for marking Trend of Performance, choices being, First Report, Consistent, Improving, and Declining. There were areas for recommendations for future duty assignments of the officer being evaluated such as, Command, Operational, Staff, Joint, and Foreign Shore. Also there were areas for the commanding officer's recommendation for future promotion, Early, Regular, or the dreaded "No." There was an area for marking personal traits of an officer, under the headings of, Judgment, Imagination, Analytic Ability, Personal Behavior, Forcefulness, and Military Bearing. The personal traits were graded with the "A" through "F" system. There was also a section that gave the officer's "ranking number" within his peer group of officers. This was the number I explained before, that was very important to officers who wanted to "break out of the pack." For example in a command with ten lieutenants, the number "1 out of 10" was what every lieutenant in the command wanted. There was a section on the fitness report form that was entitled, "Weakness Discussed?" and the selections, None Noted, Yes, or No.

There were other marking sections such as, Days of Combat, Deployment of Command, etc. Lieutenant Commander Roberts graded me "A's," or "N" for not observed. It was generally expected that warrant officers maintain a constant level of "A's" on their fitness reports. My first fitness report I received after reporting aboard *Midway* would be a good indicator of my chances to succeed as an officer.

On the back of the fitness report was a section that detailed an officer's duties, and a large area for specific written comments about the officer's performance. The comments on my first fitness report included the statements:

> His diligent efforts, cheerful military behavior, and resourcefulness displayed throughout his tour at this joint services manned base inspired all who observed him and not only contributed significantly to the mission of this office, but exemplified the image of a professional Navy-Man. CWO Little's exceptional ability, initiative, and loyal dedication to duty coupled with his technical knowledge, administrative ability, and personal compatibility make him a prime candidate and highly recommended for selection to the Limited Duty Officer community if he should apply.

This report was as I said, my first fitness report as an officer, and I was pleased with it. After a short check out on base, and prior to turning in my security badge, I bid Lieutenant Commander Roberts farewell. I shook his hand and thanked him for all the valuable advice, and the good times we had working together. I knew he was not happy with the prospect of being alone in the office again, but he seemed genuinely happy for me as I started on my officer career. The last few months I had been in the office he had taken more than two months leave, and enjoyed time off while I was manning the office. He was busy in the evenings attending college night classes in an effort to complete his master's degree in business. He intended to retire in Albuquerque, and work for Sandia Corporation. I wished him success, and promised I would write to him. I also said farewell to CWO4 Charlie Schmidt, who I'd worked with over the past ten months. In the previous days, I'd said farewell to the Air Force, and Army liaison office people who I'd worked with, and who did basically the same things for their respective services, that I'd done for the Navy and Marine Corps. I'd made a lot of civilian friends, who I also bid farewell.

After Carmen and I said all our goodbyes, our last farewell was to Chris Pilger (who we'd known in Guam), we packed the Oldsmobile, and on the morning of 1 May 1980 we drove west away from Albuquerque. I'd enjoyed my job in the NLO Office, it had been vastly different from any job I'd had thus far in the Navy. Lieutenant Commander Roberts and I had worked our own hours. I'd been far from the rules and regulations of active operational Navy commands. I'd worked with all branches of the services, and scientists and engineers that few Navy Nuclear Weaponsmen make contact with. I'd been the first chief petty officer assigned to the office, and I felt like I'd accomplished much, although I felt I'd also left much undone. There was still much organizing of files and publications that remained to be done by my relief. I'd had more authority, and ability to affect the nuclear weapons program, than any job I'd previously held. I'd changed a few things in publications that had a favorable impact Navy-wide, and I was pleased to have worked, and gained insight into the upper echelons of the nuclear weapons program.

My time in Albuquerque had been a time of reliving the past, reflection on my future, and a time of decision. I'd enjoyed seeing the base I'd left almost twenty years ago after "A" school. At the time I'd applied for officer status in Guam, I had not seriously considered making it, and in Albuquerque, I had to decide to go beyond the twenty-year point. For many years I'd looked forward to 1980 as the year of my retirement, and now I was about to embark on a new adventure.

As I said before a common dream of GMT's was to be stationed in Albuquerque, and I regretted leaving. It was with feelings of sadness, and oddly, feelings of "home leaving," as I watched the panoramic view of the town of Albuquerque in my rear view mirror disappear as the Oldsmobile passed over the last desert ridge headed west. I had tried to analyze my strong feelings for Albuquerque, and concluded they must exist for a variety of reasons.

I remembered traveling through Albuquerque as a child, with my parents while on summer vacation. As a little boy, I'd been fascinated with cowboys and Indians, so naturally I enjoyed seeing the Indian influence, and old west appearance of Albuquerque. When I had attended nuclear weapons school almost twenty years earlier, I'd been a young eighteen year old, idealistic, and anxious to be a success in the Navy. I'd been amazed entering a world few are permitted entrance, a world of secrecy, and amazing technology. Alamogordo, Los Alamos, and Albuquerque, all being in the state of New Mexico, cause the state to be recognized as the birthplace of nuclear weapons.

My grandfather had a special affection for the high desert county of the Southwest. Some of the happiest times of his life had been when he homesteaded in Arizona. He had also searched for gold around Socorro, New Mexico. Perhaps my attraction to New Mexico was inherited?

Even further back in my family tree, my Great Great Great-grandfather James Austin Sylvester had fought for the Independence of Texas, in the Army of General Houston. There has been some controversy in my family whether he was a relation or not, regardless he and I traveled a parallel path in life. His name was also James.

He gained fame as "the man who captured General Santa Anna," the general who directed the Mexican siege at the famous Alamo, and who was also known as the "Napoleon of the West." James Sylvester, as I did, rose up through the enlisted ranks to gain a commission. What follows is a historical account of the events he, played a part in when the Mexican Army was defeated by General Houston's Army in April of 1836[45].

Following the defeat of his Army, Caro's (Santa Anna's brother-in-law) account makes no mention of Santa Anna bogging Old Whip. According to the Secretary, they entered a thicket, dismounted, and turned their horses loose. They had two reasons for preferring to travel on foot. One was that they were in very marshy country and could make better progress without horses, and the other was that the shoulder-high sedge grass offered fair cover for men on foot. Santa Anna evidently thought he would do best by himself. For Caro said that after they dismounted "His Excellency left me."

Old Whip went off, with his reins dragging, over the boggy turf. The big horse, for years after a famous sire in San Jacinto country, had completed his mission. The President of Mexico was in a trap from which a man with a distaste for swimming couldn't very well escape.

Santa Anna had snatched up a few things when his party with Emily, the pretty slave, had been so rudely interrupted, by General Houston's Army over running his camp. When he jumped on Old Whip, he had on silk drawers, a linen shirt with diamond studs, and red morocco slippers. He carried with him, for some reason, a white cotton sheet, a box of chocolates, a gourd water bottle half full, and a fine gray cloth vest with gold buttons. When he dismounted from Old Whip, he took a blanket which one of his officers; Colonel Bringas had tied behind the saddle.

Santa Anna spent the night in tall grass near a bayou. Early on the morning of the twenty-second, by crawling around in the grass and working up enough nerve to ford a waist high creek, he found his way to the Vince Ranch. There he found the slave quarters deserted. He took off his wet silk drawers put on the cast away clothes of a slave, including a blue cotton round jacket, pantaloons of domestic cotton and a smelly hide cap. He still wore the linen shirt with the diamond studs and the morocco slippers. He'd eaten the chocolates, but he made a bundle of the sheet, silk drawers, and water bottle. He used a blanket as a serape.

Had the President walked from the Vince Ranch through the tall grass toward the head of Vince's Bayou he still might have gotten away, but he'd lost all sense of direction, so instead he crept along the bayou in the general direction of the Texan camp.

James A. Sylvester's own account of the capture of Santa Anna is as follows:

On the morning of the 22nd of April 1836, news came into camp that a portion of our cavalry had surrounded Santa Anna and a number of his officers in a mot of timber some miles from our camp, and called for reinforcements in order to capture them. Col. Edward Burleson, commanding the First Regiment of Texas troops called for volunteers, and mounting such horses as were under their control, they set out in search of the Mexican chief—after marching from the camp, near Lynch's Ferry to Vince's Bayou, where the bridge, but recently burned by Deaf Smith, impeded our further progress, and not knowing where our services were required, Col. Burleson called a parley. Some of the party were anxious to proceed by fording or swimming the bayou while others thought it useless to proceed farther after an ignis fatuus, when Col Burleson ordered myself to take charge of such men as were disposed to return to camp and the others proceeded toward the Brazos in search of any Mexican stragglers that might be found.

The squad under my command proceeded back to camp. We left the main road and took down the bayou. We had not proceeded very far before some of them proposed to skirt the timber in search of game. I took the straight direction promising to await their arrival at a certain point. After leaving the party, pursuing my course alone, I suddenly espied an object coming toward me, near a ravine. I immediately turned and made an effort to attract their attention.

When I again looked for the object, it had vanished. Riding in the direction in which I had seen it, I came up to the figure of something covered with a Mexican blanket, which proved to be Santa Anna. I ordered him to get up, which he did, very reluctantly and immediately took hold of my hand and kissed it several times, and asked for General Houston and seemed very solicitous to find out whether he had been killed in battle the day previous. I replied assuring him that General Houston was only wounded, and was then in his camp. I then asked him who he was when he replied that he was nothing but a common soldier. I remarked on the fineness of his shirt bosom—which he tried to conceal and told him he was no common soldier; if so he must be a thief. He seemed much disconcerted, but finally stated that he was an aide to General Lopez de Santa Anna—to affirm his assertion, he drew from his pocket an official note from General Urrea to General Santa Anna dated on the Brazos informing Santa Anna that he would be able to form a junction at or near Galveston and should immediately take up line of march to Velasco.

I was satisfied at the time, that in his official capacity of aide, such a paper might have been retained by him. At this juncture a portion of my squad came up, and as near as I can recall consisted of Messrs. Miles, Vermillion and Thompson. General Santa Anna, complaining very much of fatigue, asked to ride a part of the way into camp. I think Miles proposed to dismount and walk to a point of timber, while we, (with Santa Anna mounted on his horse), went around the head of the ravine. When we formed a junction, Mr. Miles requested him to dismount, but Santa Anna refused to do so unless I required it. I told him I had no control over the horse, and he would have to dismount, which he did. I then took him behind me and we all proceeded to camp. I left him with the camp guard. He was immediately recognized by his own soldiers, who were then prisoners in our camp, and was sent to General Houston's headquarters.

When I returned to camp (having been sent for by General Houston) I was ordered to report to headquarters in person. I proceeded to the place—a wide-spreading oak—and on presenting myself to General Houston, General Santa Anna immediately arose and came forward, embraced me, and turning to General Houston and other officers returned me thanks for my kindness while escorting him to camp and told me I was his savior.

On 3 August 1836, General Sam Houston presented James A. Sylvester with a printed pamphlet, containing the names of the men who had fought at San Jacinto. This was on the occasion of General Houston appointing him a captain. On the back the general wrote:

> Presented to James A. Sylvester by General Sam Houston as a tribute of regard for his gallant and vigilant conduct first in the battle of San Jacinto and subsequently in the capture of Santa Anna, whose thanks were tendered by Santa Anna, in my presence to Captain Sylvester, for his, generous conduct towards him, when captured.

For my grandfather's services to the Republic he was promoted from sergeant to captain, and given 640 acres in what is now the heart of Dallas, Texas. Before he had joined the Army, he had been a wandering printer, and he continued to be one. He swapped his Dallas acreage for a flea-bitten mule and rode the animal off to a new job on the *New Orleans Picayune* newspaper.

He died 9 April 1882, and was buried in the Odd Fellows Cemetery, New Orleans, Louisiana. His remains were removed from the Odd Fellows Cemetery at New Orleans on 5 November 1936, by the state of Texas and re-interred in the state cemetery at Austin, Texas. I'm sure he would rotate in his grave a number of times if he knew the value of the land today, which he gave away.

He was the color-bearer, and carried the only battle flag carried by the Texans at the battle of San Jacinto. This flag is now mounted as a painting behind the Speaker's desk in the Texas House of representatives, and is the most highly prized relic of the state of Texas.

As the Sandia Mountains that loom over Albuquerque faded from view, I doubted I would see Albuquerque again while in the Navy. I agreed whole-heartedly with the slogan that appears on New Mexico's automobile license plates, "New Mexico, Land of Enchantment".

Chapter 13: Midway Magic

It had been eight years since I'd been on sea duty. I knew very little about *Midway*, other than she was one of the older "*Saratoga*-class" carriers. Ray Steele and I had been onboard *Midway* for a week in 1965, when we had been inspectors for "*Operation Silver Lance*." Four years earlier, Ray had mentioned to me that he had gone onboard *Midway* as an inspector during an NTPI. He said he had been very impressed by the ship's W Division. Ray Gillip, (from NWSD Oakland) had been onboard at the time, and he (Ray Steele) said he would like to be stationed on *Midway*. This was an encouraging statement, as I highly regarded Ray's professional judgment; however, a W Division can change drastically over a four-year period, as there would be an entirely different crew onboard by now. I intended to question the inspectors in the inspection branch at Nuclear Weapons Training Group Pacific, when I attended classes there. I remembered Yokosuka Naval Base from my *Ticonderoga* and *Oriskany* days, as a large beautiful base, with a large shipyard work force.

We spent a couple of days in Strathmore with my parents. We then left for San Diego, 300 miles to the south, leaving Mary with my parents. It was still the school year, and Mary was going to attend Strathmore Elementary School for a few weeks, while I attended school in San Diego.

When Carmen and I arrived at the North Island Naval Air Station, Bachelor Officers Quarters (BOQ), there were no vacancies, and there was not expected to be any for a few months. The only other lodging option was the base Navy lodge. We checked into a motel off base until we could check into the Navy lodge the following morning. Navy lodges are base motels operated by the Navy open primarily to servicemen who are transferring between duty stations, and offer reasonable rates.

The following morning, I donned my uniform, and went to Nuclear Weapons Training Group Pacific (NWTGP). This was a building I'd been to many times in the past. After turning in my records, and getting my orders stamped with my arrival time, I was given a student badge, which I was to wear clipped onto my shirt at all times I was within the building. I was told I could go to the officer's coffee locker located on the second deck. I kept on the look out for anyone I might know. I saw some vaguely familiar faces as I walked up the stairs to the coffee locker. When I walked into the coffee locker, at the first table there sat Charlie Upham in his brand-new ensign uniform. Charlie and I had worked together on our officer's program applications in Guam. Charlie was scheduled to go through the same courses I was. I was very pleased to see him, and pleased that we would be going to classes together. Charlie was going to the aircraft carrier *USS Constellation* after school. Also sitting at the table with Charlie was another new CWO2, who had been commissioned the same day as I, named Charlie Haynes. He was also going to attended classes with us, and then he was bound for the aircraft carrier, *USS Coral Sea*.

Nuclear Weapons Training Group Pacific, as it was when I'd last visited, was still the GMT "A" school, taking the place of the old "A" school that used to be in Albuquerque. It was odd seeing women in the groups of young seaman attending "A" school classes. As I mentioned before women had been excluded from the nuclear weapons program in the Navy in the past, because of fears about possible radiation exposure to an unborn child, should a female GMT be pregnant.

We three officers expected to have only three different types of air dropped weapons on our respective carriers. We were to have classes tailored to our specific jobs within the "W" Divisions we would be assigned to.

Our room at the Navy lodge was beautifully located on a sandy beach on base. This was the same beach shared by the famous Del Coronado Hotel, located off the base in the city of Coronado. This hotel was one of the favorites of President Nixon, and had been visited by many famous persons in its past.

One evening Carmen and I heard over the news that grunions were running. These are small fish, which annually flop ashore on the beaches at low tide, lay eggs, and then go back into the sea at high tides. We watched this happen one night around midnight. It was an amazing sight seeing thousands of fish suddenly appear, jumping, and flapping on the sand, flashing silver in the moonlight.

One evening we went to the officer's club for dinner. The North Island Officer's Club on base is beautifully furnished with thick lush carpets, in marble columned rooms, with linen-covered tables. It was much more lavish than any enlisted, or chief's club I'd been in. This marked the first time I'd been in an officer's club. The officer's club on Kirtland Air Force Base in Albuquerque had been a "closed club," which meant only those officers that paid monthly dues to the club were allowed entry. An "open club" meant that any commissioned officer could enter the club, which was what the North Island Club was. The evening we went happened to be bingo night, and we played a few enjoyable games.

One weekend we visited Tijuana, Mexico as we had in 1976. It was interesting visiting Mexico, but depressing to see such poverty that existed just outside our countries border. Visits to that town make people appreciate the United State's living conditions.

The "two Charlie's" and I were adjusting to our new status as officers and gentlemen. When walking about, instead of remaining alert to give salutes to officers, now we had to stay alert to return salutes given to us by enlisted men and women. As officers we saluted much more often, than when we had been enlisted men, as there were many more enlisted people versus numbers of officers. It was also an adjustment being referred to as "Mister," or "Sir" all the time. It was refreshing, I must admit, to walk into a personnel or disbursing office and get immediate service, instead of the slow service enlisted men often received. While I enjoyed my position as an officer, as I said before, I vowed not to be abusive or overbearing, as had a number of officers I'd had experiences with, in the past. I determined that as much as possible, when dealing with enlisted men, I would try to put myself in their shoes, and remember what had motivated me as an enlisted man. I tried to keep in mind the traits, and attitudes of those officers I'd respected in the past. One advantage I had from my experience as an enlisted man was that I was wise to all the tricks and maneuvers that some enlisted men used to get out of work, or used to give the false appearance of hard work. The next person I ran into from my past was Chief Julian Lindstrom, from Whidbey Island, Oakland Naval Supply Center, and NWEF Albuquerque. He was assigned as an "A" school instructor at NWTGP. Julian was the one I'd bought the 45-caliber pistol from while at NWSA Oakland. The last time I spoke to Julian, he was pursuing his beloved hobby, and working as a gunsmith in northern New Mexico. Chris Van Diven from Oakland, and Guam was also at NWTGP. He was now a GMT1, and working in the NWTGP Publication Library. I was to see Chris again in the future. Chris Reed, from Guam was working in the Inspection Branch, and was now a Chief. I was also very pleased to see Charlie Cushman (from Oakland and Guam), who was now a senior chief, and going to school before reporting for duty on a ship home ported in San Diego. Charlie was to eventually retire as a master chief, and settle in San Diego. Another old shipmate, I ran across was Joe Victor of the *Ticonderoga*. Joe was now a GMT chief, working as an instructor at the school. Joe had aged considerably; I suspected he had been drinking hard. He was bitter about a divorce he had just gone through. It seems that a friend of his had started having an affair with his wife, and she wanted out of the marriage, to marry his friend. The divorce judge had awarded her half of Joe's retirement pay when he retired from the Navy. I enjoyed seeing Joe again, and catching up on our lives. I heard a few years later that after Joe retired half his retirement pay went to his ex-wife, but one of the most unjust situations occurred in Joe's life that I'd ever heard of. A couple of years after he retired, his ex-wife died, and a San Diego court declared that he had to continue providing half his retirement pay to her husband, the guy who had originally broken up the marriage, because Joe's retirement pay was considered common property of the deceased wife! I guess in the end Joe got back at the guy who had cheated with his wife, as Joe died of a heart attack, and his retirement pay stopped at the time of his death.

Yet another sailor from the past was Dave Wiesenhahn. We'd been together on the *Independence*, and Whidbey Island. One evening Carmen and I visited Dave, who was now a master chief. I'd last seen him during a visit he made to Guam. We went to his house in Coronado. Dave and his wife Doris lived in the same house they had bought when Dave transferred from Whidbey Island thirteen years before. I also got to see their son Duffy, who I'd not seen since he was five years old; he was now a college student. After retirement, Dave and Doris were divorced, and Dave began a new civilian career as a "government employed GMT," working at an ordnance maintenance facility on North Island. Unfortunately Dave passed away in 2003. He and a friend worked at electrically rewiring his Coronado house, and that night a fire started, and Dave died of a heart attack attempting to escape from the house.

The first couple of weeks at the school, Charlie Upham, Charlie Haynes and I attended "shop classes" that were being given to GMT's on the air drop weapons that might be on our ships. These classes were conducted on school trainers, with the students completing all the mechanical and electrical operations in the maintenance manuals. We three officers did not actively participate, but watched the instructor (a chief or first class), teach the student sailors.

The third week at NWTGP, we attended a weeklong class that was attended by about twenty other officers. This class was entitled "Nuclear Safety Officer Course." This course covered a variety of subjects, such as security clearances, physical security requirements, courier procedures, and paperwork required during transfers of weapons between commands. Most of this was merely a review, and refresher of what the "two Charlie's" and me had been doing all our careers. To the other officers attending the course, many who had little nuclear weapons experience, it was a difficult course.

We also studied the message reporting requirements associated with nuclear weapons. This was a complex subject. Message reporting to higher authority, anytime a weapon was transferred, or maintenance conducted on it, had to be reported to higher authority sometimes within twelve hours, and the reporting requirements were very strict.

This course caused me to consider the reality of my position in the future. Although the commanding officer of a Navy ship was responsible for everything that occurred on the ship, I would be the one ultimately responsible for the weapons program onboard. In the past this had not been a burden I had concerned myself with; there had always been chiefs or officers above me in the chain of command that bore the responsibility of answering to the captain, or higher authority. Now there was not going to be a source of answers above me, I was to be the source, and bear the brunt of praise, criticism, or punishment from the captain, or others in the chain of command. But I had sought a commission, and with the privilege, there came increased accountability.

One afternoon we were shown an interesting movie. The movie was a marketing presentation to the military from one of the major aircraft companies. They were trying to sell a supersonic, non-piloted aircraft that could be used as a bomber to attack the Soviet Union in the event of war. The planes could carry numerous warheads, and could be programmed to fly various routes. Some of the programmed planes could be flown as decoys, so the Russians would not know which aircraft carried the bombs. Other attacking planes would carry "chaff," or equipment to disrupt defensive electronic, and radar systems. The film depicted a war scenario, with attacking planes, destroying Russia's ability to wage war in less than an hour and a half. The promotion film apparently was not successful, as the Pentagon rejected the idea.

A large portion of North Island, San Diego (although it's not actually an island, but connected to Southern California by a thin strand that extends south for about ten miles), is a naval station, and naval air station, home to a number of aircraft carriers. When I had been in San Diego on the *Ticonderoga*, and *Oriskany*, the direct route to San Diego had been by ferry, the same ferry that my son had been born on many years before. The ferries had long been out of business, as a toll bridge had been built connecting North Island, and the city of Coronado, with the city of San Diego. Down the strand south a few miles near the town of Chula Vista, was the Mexican restaurant, "Lydia's" that Carmen and I had visited in 1976. One evening we again visited Lydia's, and had an enjoyable meal.

A few blocks from the naval station main gate, and on the main street of the city of Coronado, is a restaurant and bar that are known Navy-wide as a hangout for Navy pilots, called the "Mexican Village." The two brothers that own the Mexican Village, are also known as the inventors of the liquid dispenser that's on the end of a hose with buttons, that bartenders select for dispensing a variety of liquids such as soda water, plain water, ginger ale, 7-up, etc. This dispenser is used all over the world. In the Mexican Village there is a unique mural that covers one entire wall. It's a picture set in a Mexico town, with an obviously pregnant Mexican girl in a wedding gown, with an angry father standing nearby with a shotgun. Near the couple there is a long line of men, a Mexican gunfighter, farmer, cook, and so on, each pointing at the person in line behind them. At the very end of the line, a poor guy is looking frantically about, but there's no one for him to point to. In years past, in the afternoon when the Mickey Mouse Club TV program would come on the bar television at 5:00 p.m., an announcement would sound throughout the restaurant, "A training film for junior officers is now being shown in the bar." The Mexican Village's reputation spread throughout the Pacific. An enterprising Japanese bar owner from Sasebo, Japan traveled to the Mexican Village, and spent three months learning how to cook Mexican food. He then returned to Sasebo, and opened up a replica of the Mexican Village outside the Sasebo Naval Station. He had also taken pictures of the mural, and had it duplicated in his "Japanese Mexican Village."

After completing the Nuclear Safety Officer Course, the following week we were told we could do as we wished. We could talk to the group that conducted refresher training on board ships, which was a group of GMT instructors that traveled to nuclear capable commands (including ships), and conducted training classes, usually lasting a week or two. These refresher-training classes were normally scheduled shortly before a command underwent an inspection, so the command could evaluate what their shortcomings were, or what additional training needed to be done before the inspection. We also could talk to the NTPI inspectors, and look at the results of the last inspection held on our respective ships. At this time in 1980, there was considerable concern in the Navy over the aircraft carrier's W Division inspection failure rates, in the Pacific Fleet. I was shown the *Midway*'s past inspection reports. The discrepancy lists were long, they had not failed, but they certainly had not been outstanding.

Along with the pressure from the Commander of the Pacific, and higher echelons, to stop the inspection failures on carriers, another matter of concern in the Pacific Fleet, was the *USS Enterprise*. The *Enterprise*, which was the Navy's first nuclear powered carrier, had gone into the shipyard in Bremerton, Washington, for what was supposed to be a six-month yard period. There had been major problems with the ship's nuclear reactor, and other unforeseen problems. The carrier had been in the shipyard for almost five years, with no completion date in sight.

I also sat in on a few aircraft loading school classes. The *Midway* had onboard the A-6 *Intruder* (see photo page), and A-7 *Corsair* aircraft, as well as a number of other different aircraft, but the *Intruder*, and *Corsair* would be the planes capable of carrying nuclear weapons.

The end of May, Carmen and I drove to my parent's home, and attended my brother Joe's graduation from college. He was awarded a degree in forestry, and went on to graduate as an engineer from Fresno State University. We were very proud of him, and enjoyed the graduation ceremony. At the graduation gathering, I also saw my high school friend Butch Coley. It was he and his wife Janice who I'd been visiting when I learned of the President Kennedy assassination. Butch was now a professor, teaching criminal law at the Porterville Junior College, and as I said eventually became the Sheriff of Tulare County.

We had kept in contact with Josaline, the French woman we'd known in Guam. Since leaving Guam, she now lived in Simi Valley, a suburb of Los Angeles. Mary was now out of school, and Josaline wanted Carmen and Mary to come visit her, and stay with her while I finished the remainder of my training in San Diego. She said, since leaving Guam, she and her husband had divorced, and she and her three children lived in a large house. One weekend we drove to Simi Valley, and located Josaline's house. It was a huge mansion, located on a hillside, surrounded by a large iron fence. In the backyard was a gigantic swimming pool. The house was a two story, Spanish style home, with innumerable rooms. Josaline also had a large nightclub, and many other holdings. As I was in Guam, I was suspicious about the source of her wealth? Leaving Carmen and Mary at Josaline's house, I drove to San Diego, to finish my training.

Following my training at Nuclear Weapons Training Group Pacific, the commanding officer of the training command wrote my fitness report, covering this period. The report had no specific trait evaluations, and described the classes I had attended. This was a "canned statement" that was written for the officer students who attended the school. During my time at school, I had been on a very relaxed schedule. One afternoon, Ensign Charlie Upham and I went golfing at the Navy golf course, near the San Diego Charger's Football Stadium. Neither of us had golfed since Guam, and we didn't do very well, we quit after nine holes, but had a good time.

My school after NWTGP was Damage Control and Fire fighting School, which was located across the bay from North Island, at 32nd Street San Diego. This was a naval station where many destroyers tied up to the pier. This school location meant I had to relocate to the 32nd Street BOQ. Since Carmen and Mary were in Simi Valley, I checked into a single room. Charlie Upham and I would be attending the two-week school together. Charlie Haynes went to catch his ship, the *Coral Sea*, after the NWTGP training.

The first week of training for Ensign Upham and me was classroom instruction on the subject of damage control on board ship, and the Shipboard 3M System, which is a complex preventive maintenance program used on board Navy ships to insure that Navy equipment and material is always in good working condition. The damage control portion was basically just a review for me since I had been a damage control petty officer on the three carriers I had served on.

After the first week of school was completed, that weekend, I drove north to Simi Valley, where Carmen and Mary were staying with Josaline. This was to be a busy weekend for me. I did a number of small repairs around the house, or I should say the mansion, for Josaline. We attended a wedding of a friend of Josaline's daughter, who happened to be marrying a sailor. I also did an errand for Josaline, by showing her nightclub to a couple of prospective buyers. They were hoodlum types, and were not quite sure who I was? Josaline had asked me to unlock the club, and show it to them, as she felt they would not try to take advantage of a man. We also had a barbeque at a sailor friend of Josaline's who was stationed at Port Hyneme, a nearby Construction (SeaBee) Base. Carmen confided in me that she was concerned about Josaline's drinking. She said she drank herself into a stupor every night.

I returned to San Diego, following the weekend, to attend a portion of the school, I did not look forward too. This was to be a week of fire fighting school, which was a dirty, hard-working course of instruction. This was to be like the school I attended in San Francisco while on board the *Oriskany*. Charlie and I were the only officers in the class.

During one hour of instruction we were required to start a fire pump within a couple of minutes. The starting procedure took two men. Pairs of sailors took turns going in front of the class, and demonstrating the engine starting procedure. Not many in the class were able to do it properly the first time. Charlie and I were a team, and when our turn came, all the enlisted sailors in the class watched closely to see if the officers would make a mistake. Thankfully we started the engine perfectly.

Just as we had in the fire-fighting course in San Francisco that I described previously, students in the classes formed hose teams, and practiced charging into burning buildings to extinguish fires. In one fire situation the entire interior walls of the building, including flammable trays of diesel fuel under steel grates upon which we stood, were set on fire. We were to extinguish the fire before we could exit the building. We all wore OBA's (Oxygen Breathing Apparatus), and flame retardant clothing, and boots. Throughout all the fire situations, Charlie and I could see it coming; we were always placed at the very front of the hose, exposed to the most flames, and heat. But we were expected to be leaders, and we charged into each fire, successfully completing the course. On 19 June, Ensign Charlie Upham and I bid each other farewell, promising each other if our ships were ever in the same port in the Far East, that we would look each other up.

While at the 32nd Street School, I bought a set of "choker" (dress uniform with a high collar) dress whites, and dress blues uniforms. I also stocked up on the uniform items I'd not been able to get in Albuquerque. Upon completion of school, my transfer leave commenced. After the fire fighting school, it took a couple of days to finally clean the soot, and smell of fire out of my hair, ears, and nose. We had originally planned on staying at Josaline's house a couple of days, but Carmen had her fill of being around Josaline's destructive drinking, so we left shortly after I returned to Simi Valley from San Diego.

We spent time with my parents, brothers' Joe and Jerry, and my sister Linda's family. I knew I would be in Japan for at least two years, and I tried to relax, knowing this would be the last casual "free" time I would have for a long while. We decided to leave the Oldsmobile at my parents instead of trying to ship it to Japan. I borrowed my Mom's typewriter, and typed a letter to the *Midway*'s weapons officer, who was to be my boss. I told him that my family and I expected to arrive in Yokosuka around 30 July. At this point I was becoming anxious about the passports for Carmen and Mary. We had not received them in the mail yet, and Carmen and Mary could not leave the United States without them. I made a few phone calls, and was promised the passport-issuing agency would not delay our passports. We eventually got our passports in the mail one week before we had to leave for Travis Air Force Base, and Japan. During this leave period, we took a camping trip to Edison Lake. This was the lake east of Fresno, California that we had visited before. We were to remember this trip for many years afterwards; Carmen and I both caught some of the largest lake trout we had ever caught. My parents, Uncle Dean and Aunt Lois, also camped a couple of days with us at Lake Edison.

The last time I'd left the United States on an aircraft carrier, the Vietnam War had been raging, and I was uncertain about what the future held. At this point in 1980, Iran was doing a lot of "sword rattling." American hostages were still being held in our Iran Embassy. Also, in the news was the Russian Navy's effort to expand their carrier force. The Soviets had a new aircraft carrier deployed off the coast of Vietnam. Reports were, however, that Russian carriers were not very capable, and had a long way to go before they were comparable to the American Navy carriers. The following is a portion of an article "*USS Midway* First of a Kind, One of a Kind", in a ship's newsletter, written by LT Pete Clayton, and Robert L. Broaddus[46]:

> The aircraft carrier has long been the centerpiece of America's Navy Fleets. In the early months of World War II a logical progression of American carrier development produced the design for a class of large, heavily protected, battle carriers. The lead ship of this class, ordered as CVB-41 on August 1942, was named for the carrier battle that turned the tide of war at Midway Island.
> The keel of the *USS Midway* was laid in a graving dock on 27 October 1943 at the Newport News Ship Building and Dry-dock Company. Launched 20 March 1945 she was the largest warship in the world through her first decade of service. She was constructed with the most advanced damage control innovations possible, including a 3 ½ inch thick armored flight deck and extensive internal sub-division not found on any carrier or other combatant before or since. She utilized very extensive electric welding in her construction as did her sisters *Franklin D. Roosevelt* (CVB-42) built at the New York Navy Shipyard and *Coral Sea* (CVB-43), also a Newport News Ship. *Midway*'s overall length was 968 feet, which with an extreme beam at waterline of 121 feet at a maximum draft of 34 feet gave a full load displacement of 55,000 tons. Her twelve Babcock and Wilcox boilers fed four Westinghouse geared turbines, developing a total of 212,000 shaft horsepower for a design speed of thirty-three knots.

World War II decided once and for all that henceforth, the American Carrier, not the Battleship, was the American Navy's capital ship. The carrier had accomplished more than anything else to bring Japan to her knees. When the war was over, the U.S. scrapped most of her older carriers, leaving primarily the three new *Midway*-class CVB's and the *Essex*-class CV's.

The 1950's were a period of uncertainty for the development of aircraft carriers. A hot debate arose over the issue of whether or not the Navy should have a strategic nuclear capability. The Air Force was against it; the Navy was for it. It was the old Billy Mitchell affair all over again. To prove the feasibility of nuclear strikes being flown from carriers, tests were conducted using *Coral Sea* and *Midway*. A P2 *Neptune* aircraft, large enough to carry a payload of 10,000 pounds (the weight of the Mk 3, and Mk 4 bombs), and the largest aircraft ever to operate from an aircraft carrier, flew from both ships to prove that the bombs could be delivered from the decks of carriers. The tests were so successful that they shifted the advantage from the Air Force to the Navy, and plans were developed for the production of a new, larger class of carrier - the *Forrestal* and her sisters. This new class of carriers marks the first time in history a ship was developed for a bomb. Another factor that argued for the building of even larger carriers than the *Midway* class was the rapid development of jet aircraft. Larger and faster than propeller-driven aircraft, jets were making existing designs of aircraft carriers obsolete. The *Essex* carriers were chosen for modernization. *Oriskany*, the prototype, was given a strengthened flight deck, tanks for storing JP5, stronger cross-deck pendants and stronger catapults. Soon the other *Essex*-class carriers were given the same improvements.

Aircraft carriers played a vital role in the Korean conflict during the early fifties, Korea is mountainous and it was difficult to quickly establish airfields that were needed to support the ground fighting. Carriers were the only answer.

In 1951 the British developed a way to make the operation of aircraft carriers much safer - the angled deck. Historically, the greatest danger had always been overshooting the wires. Although the crash barrier provided the means of stopping the over-shooting planes, it was a rarity when neither plane nor pilot received damages. With the modifications of an angled landing deck, all that the pilot had to do was gun his throttle and take his plane around again for another pass. The solution was so simple; it's a wonder that it hadn't been thought of sooner. The *Antietam* became the first American carrier to be equipped with an angled deck in 1952.

Other improvements came quickly. Enclosed "hurricane" bows became standard. The development of the steam-piston catapult (also a British invention) made it possible to actually launch aircraft while at anchor! The Fresnel lens, or "meatball" greatly improved the safety factor of landing on carriers, as pilots now had available to them real time glide-slope and angle information. It would be proven in time that the combination of the angled flight deck and the Fresnel lens halved the accident rate that had existed before their development.

A few of the old CVE's were retained on into the 1960's in their new roles as ASW ships, carrying fixed wing as well as rotary aircraft whose only job was to hunt and kill submarines.

In 1952 the keels were laid for the first new aircraft carriers in seven years, the *Forrestal* and her sister *Saratoga*. At 60,000 tons, the *Forrestal*-class represented a quantum leap in carrier development, with four deck-edge lifts, a ten-degree angle deck, two steam catapults forward, and two cats on the angle deck. In 1954 the *Ranger* (CVA-61) came along, and a year later the *Independence* (CVA-62).

In 1956, even bigger (and better) designs came into being with the development of the *Kitty Hawk* (CVA-63) class carriers. One major change over previous carriers was the provision for the Sea Sparrow Missile for self defense rather than AA guns. Other ships of the *Kitty Hawk*-class included the *USS Constellation* (CVA-64), *America* (CVA-66), and *John F. Kennedy* (CVA-67).

The next logical step for aircraft carriers was nuclear propulsion. Nuclear power provided huge bonuses, chiefly the advantage of unlimited endurance and all that implied. The island could now be designed for maximum convenience to personnel and flying requirements. Radar antenna could be arranged for optimum performance without having to worry about them being corroded by stack gases. In 1958 the *Enterprise* (CVAN-65) was ordered. 85,350 tons, the *Enterprise* also had a unique radar system - the "planer array," which did away with rotating antenna. She also was equipped with the Navy Tactical data System (NDTS).

NTDS, now extensively used by ship and aircraft of all types, is a computer aided system for evaluating and processing information from the ship's own radar, those of her escorts and aircraft, as well as information from other sources. Datalink permits the operation of a task force as a single coordinated unit and permits the assessment of multiple threats quicker than ever before.

The main drawback of nuclear power is its high cost. At two billion apiece, these mighty ships were tremendous strains on the national budget. However costly they were, Congress approved funding for three additional nuclear-powered carriers. The *Nimitz* (CVAN-68), *Dwight D. Eisenhower* (CVN-69), and *Carl Vinson* (CVAN-70).

Even today in the twenty-first century, critics claim that the age of the aircraft carrier is over, and that these ships are obsolete and vulnerable "sitting ducks." This is a continuing debate, and it is unclear how long the carrier will remain the centerpiece of the Navy. The incomparable service they provided in areas of the world such as Afghanistan, and Iraq, projecting air power when and where it was needed, has silenced most critics.

The previous short history of the aircraft carrier, only covers up to the 1980's, and fails to mention the invaluable role aircraft carriers played in Vietnam, but perhaps it will give the reader a picture of how the carrier came to be such an important element in our country's defense. My life thus far had been intertwined with two World War II carriers, the *Ticonderoga*, and *Oriskany*, and with a post war aircraft carrier *Independence*. I was about to become a crewmember on a carrier whose construction had begun during World War II, and in many aspects was unique among carriers. Many "firsts" occurred onboard *Midway*. An example being *Midway*'s aircraft shot down the first and last enemy planes during the Vietnam War.

What follows is a detailed description of the life of *USS Midway* up to 1980. This should give the reader an appreciation of the "behind the scenes" work that goes on daily, week after week, month after month, and yearly on our countries warships, that is seldom publicized, or heralded, yet is vital to our nation's defense.

As I said before, the keel of *USS Midway* was laid 27 October 1943 at the Newport News Shipyard. She was the lead carrier of the "CVB Class" (large heavily protected battle carriers). *Midway* was commissioned on 10 September 1945 too late for service in the war. Her first commanding officer was Capt. Joseph E. Bolger. Getting underway from Norfolk on 12 October 1945, her first arrested landing was made by an F4U-4 *Corsair*. On her shakedown cruise from Norfolk to Guantanamo Bay, Cuba she carried 121 aircraft. By the second week, the 1,000th landing was logged. After this she entered the Norfolk Shipyard for post-shakedown repairs.

Midway's first operational assignment was "*Operation Frostbite*," a cold weather evaluation of carrier equipment including aircraft, personnel, and the ship itself. Among the aircraft tested was the Ryan FR-1 *Fireball*, helicopter air-sea rescue techniques were refined and even the infamous "poopy suit" (a protective suit, used to protect the wearer in sub-degree waters) was tested. During the tests the ship suffered heavy weather damage to the elevator hangar doors, but was still able to conduct refueling and flight operations despite having two or four inches of snow on the flight deck. The ship was at sea from 1 March to 28 March 1946 operating in the Labrador Sea, and Davis Straits.

The early part of 1947 was spent operating off the East coast. *Midway* was underway 2 September 1947 for "*Operation Sandy*" with a captured German V-2 rocket aboard. On 6 September a special Navy crew successfully fired the V-2 from the flight deck. The rocket traveled approximately six miles and exploded in flight, but conclusively proved that large missiles could be fired from surface ships. *Midway*'s first deployment was to the Mediterranean, and began with her departure from Norfolk on 27 October 1947. The four and one-half month deployment concluded in Norfolk, 11 March 1948.

Although the first carrier P2V *Neptune* launch was made 28 April 1948 from Coral Sea, on 5 October 1949, CDR. F.L. Ashworth flew a P2V from *Midway* at sea off Norfolk, to the Panama Canal, then northward over Corpus Christi, Texas, and onto NAS San Diego completing the 4,800-mile nonstop flight in twenty-five hours, forty minutes. The significance of this test and the earlier P2V carrier flights was the demonstration of a viable Navy strategic nuclear strike capability. The impact of this capability on controversies in Congress and the Defense Department resulted in support for and the eventual construction of the *Forrestal*-class carriers.

There were many deployments, and exercises, which effectively showed our countries strength to the world between 1949 and 1964

During the period July 1964 - March 1965, *Midway* participated in a carrier task force exercise "*Silver Lance*" which lasted for a week, this was a simulated nuclear strike by three carriers. This was the period of time when Ray Steele and I, from the *USS Ticonderoga*, were on board *Midway* as inspectors for the exercise.

The *Midway* left Alameda 6 March 1965 for her first combat deployment. She proceeded toward "Yankee" station to join other elements of Task Force 77. *Midway*'s aircraft engaged in combat for the first time in her twenty-year career with strikes against military and logistics installations in North and South Vietnam, while the carrier was on station in the Tonkin Gulf and South China Sea. On 16 April she struck Bai Duc Thon and Xam Ca Trong highway bridges. Her aircraft dropped the Phoson Bridge and hit the Xom Gia Highway on 23 April.

On 17 June 1965, while covering a strike at the Gin Phu Barracks, four MIG-17 *Frescos* engaged *Midway* fighters. CDR Lou Page and his Rear Instrument Operator (RIO), LT John C. Smith in VF-21, F-4B (*Phantom*), scored the first confirmed MIG kill of the Vietnam War when they shot down one of the MIG's. LT Dave Batson and his RIO, LCDR Robert B. Doremus got a second MIG-17. Three days later, 20 June, in a seemingly unlikely match two MIG 17's jumped four VA-25, A-1H's (*Skyraider*, prop driven aircraft). Setting up a defensive weave pattern, the *Skyraider*'s jettisoned their tanks and ordnance, and dove for the deck. As one of the MIG's doggedly pursued one of the *Skyraider*'s it slipped into the gun sight of two others. Their 20mm cannons made short work of the MIG and it nosed over at a low altitude into a ridgeline. LT C.B. Johnson and LT C.W. Hartman were credited with the kill. The other MIG pilot decided to literally "save face" and departed the arena. This was one of the few times a propeller driven aircraft shot down a jet.

When USS *Frank Knox* (DDR-742) went aground on Pontas Reef on 21 July, *Midway* helos lifted 155 crewmen to the carrier and then put a damage control party onboard. The ship, although badly holed, was salvaged and later returned to service. A number of *Midway* sailors were awarded Distinguished Flying Crosses for this action.

The carrier sailed from Subic Bay 4 November 1965, ending the nine-month deployment on 23 November 1964 in Alameda. After completing her stand down and the Christmas holidays, *Midway* again moved to Hunter's Point, where she was decommissioned on 15 February 1966. The modernization of *Midway* would prove to be a very complex undertaking, requiring over four years to complete, but which would yield a vastly more capable ship and extend her useful service by fifteen years. The most visual result of the modernization was the tremendous increase in flight deck area, from 2.82 acres to 4.02 acres. The modernization included catapults, aircraft elevators, arresting gear, Navy Tactical Data System (NTDS), Ships Inertial Navigation System (SINS), improved crew living conditions, central air conditioning, also the first ship to have the aviation fueling system completely converted from aviation gas to JP-5 jet fuel. No AvGas tanks remained.

Delays caused the modernization to initially proceed very slowly, resulting in the original time estimates and dollar costs being greatly exceeded. Delays in 1966 and 1967 were partially caused by the simultaneous construction in the yard of the USS *Horne* (DLG-30), the modernization of USS *Chicago* (CG-11), and the unscheduled repairs to the fire ravaged USS *Oriskany* (CVA-34), which was to become my home from 1970 to 1972. These and last minute changes, as well as an investigation into the delays, resulted in a cost increase from 87 million to 202 million.

The re-commissioning of *Midway* on 31 January 1970 gave the Navy what could readily be described as the forerunner of today's Service Life Extension Program (SLEP) for aircraft carriers. The ship was fully capable of operating the most modern fleet aircraft. She was expected to deliver at least another fifteen years of service life.

On 17 March 1970, *Midway* got underway for the first time in four years, conducting builders' trials. She underwent a vigorous trial agenda for a year, before her next deployment. After training, and battle readiness inspections, *Midway* deployed on her sixteenth cruise, 16 April 1971. She arrived at Yankee station off the coast of North Vietnam April 30th. Immediately commencing strikes, *Midway*'s Air Wing flew over 6,000 sorties in support of allied operations. The 4,500 men of *Midway* spent 146 days at sea on this deployment for which the ship was awarded a Meritorious Unit Commendation Medal. The ship returned to Alameda 6 November1971.

With less than a week's notice, in April 1972, the ship's Airwing, CVW-5 was loaded aboard *Midway*, and the ship returned to the war zone seven weeks prior to her scheduled deployment date. She hastily left Alameda 10 April 1972. This was the same time, my ship the USS *Oriskany* deployed unexpectedly to Vietnam.

Midway fighters quickly made their presence known in Vietnam. On 18 May, two VF-161, F-4B's piloted by LT Bart Batholomay/RIO LT Oran Brown, and LT Patrick Arwood/RIO LT Michael "Taco" Bell engaged two MIG-19's while flying MIG CAP (Combat Air Patrol) for the third Alpha Strike of the day against Haiphong. Spotting the MIGs at three miles, Bartholomay engaged the first MIG, while Arwood went high and "covered their six."

The MIGs punched off their tanks and started to out turn the F-4's. Arwood pickled off a sidewinder missile, but was out of the envelope and missed. After two 360 degree turns, the lead MIG departed the fight. Arwood was in position at that point to again fly cover for his wingman, but when the lead MIG returned to the fight, he apparently did not see Arwood's F-4. He was attempting to draw the two F-4 *Phantoms* off to the north to his leader but the leader overshot Arwood who fired another sidewinder, which detonated near the MIG. At first, it looked like a miss but then a big shiny chunk came off the MIG, which erupted in flames, then nosed up and the pilot ejected. Meanwhile, Bartholomay dove in on the bait MIG and shot him, he too ejected. After tanking (in-flight refueling) both F-4's returned to *Midway*.

Five days later, LCDR Ronald "Mugs" McKeown/RIO LT Jack Ensch also of VF-161, was flying MIG CAP between Kep Airfield and Haiphong. They were operating under control of *USS Biddle* (DLG-34); they were given a bandit call of 278 degrees, and thirty-eight miles. "Tallyho" (in sight) came at seven to ten miles but before it could even be determined which way the bandits were headed, two MIG-19's flashed between McKeown's F-4B and his wingman.

Halfway through a cross-turn with his wingman, the sky filled with MIG-17s who were laying in ambush for the *Phantom* pilots. With a MIG hot on his tail McKeown was in a turn and reversed his controls, resulting in the *Phantom* departing from controlled flight, tumbling end over end. Regaining control, he had a windscreen full of MIG-17 and fired off a sidewinder, which missed.

After firing a second missile and missing again, McKeown thought he could get the MIG to overshoot. He came out of afterburner, hit the speed brakes, pushed two negative G's and the MIG slid past him. Mckeown launched a sidewinder as the MIG turned but then reversed right back into the missile, the aircraft exploded and the pilot ejected.

Meanwhile, another MIG was on their wingman, LT Mike Rabb and LTJG Ken Crandell. McKeown called for them to break into the MIG and then extend drawing the enemy plane into McKeown's sidewinder envelope. He fired the last sidewinder and it flew right into the MIG-17. The pilot ejected just before the aircraft blew up. Bringing to a total of five kills for VF-161.

During the cruise what was to be the last MIG kill of the Vietnam War, LT Vic Kovaleski and RIO LT Jim Wise shot down a MIG-17 on 12 January 1973. Ironically *Midway* aircraft had shot down both the first and last Navy MIG kills of the war.

After the signing of the cease-fire on 15 January 1973, *Midway* was the first carrier to depart the combat zone. With over 250 days at sea on the deployment, she arrived in Alameda on 3 March. For their outstanding performance during the eleven-month deployment, *Midway*, and Air Wing Five were awarded the Presidential Unit Citation.

Following her thirty-day stand down period the ship moved across San Francisco Bay to Hunter's Point. From 2 April to 18 June repairs and alterations were made to ready her for overseas home porting.

Underway 11 September 1973, it was a special day for *Midway* and Air Wing Five, as the carrier moved to her new homeport of Yokosuka, Japan. Operating out of Japan as a continuously deployed carrier, the *Midway* was ready to reduce the deployment cycles of her sister Pacific Fleet carriers, allowing them to each receive extended in-depth overhauls and greatly increase their home port time for routine maintenance and training.

In April 1975, the fall of South Vietnam again brought *Midway* into Vietnam waters. Paired with *USS Hancock* (CV-19), *Midway* flew off CVW-5 and took aboard ten Air Force H-35's to perform her part of *"Operation Frequent Wind."* On 29 April 1975, the helos began shuttling refugees, sixty per flight, out of Saigon. The H-53's made over forty sorties that day, bringing 2,074 persons aboard *Midway*. Flying that night and into the morning of the 30th, a total of 3,073 refugees was rescued from the communists. All the refugees did not however, come aboard by helo. Some South Vietnamese pilots flew their aircraft out to sea and ditched near the American warships. One of these pilots had flown out to sea with his wife and five children in a Cessna O-1 *Bird Dog* observation plane. Because of the danger of landing in the water with his family, the pilot, Major Buong, elected to land on *Midway*. After several attempts he got a note written on a scrap of map, aboard asking permission to land. The angle deck was cleared and Major Buong flew a good approach and landed, rolling out with room to spare. Cheers from the crew greeted his landing.

With *Operation Frequent Wind* completed *Midway* immediately steamed south into the Gulf of Siam. Lying off the Thailand coast, over 100 American built aircraft, flown out of South Vietnam by their fleeing aircrews, were loaded aboard. This maneuver prevented them from being returned to the communists, after they had pressured the Thais into agreeing to return the aircraft.

In the fall of 1975, *Midway* departed Subic Bay 14 October and entered the Indian Ocean, operating there until 12 December. She returned to Yokosuka for the Christmas holidays. In late 1977, *Midway* made an 87-day deployment to the Indian Ocean where she was the principal participant in *"Midlink 77"* an exercise hosted by the Iranian Navy and including representation from Pakistan, Turkey, and the Royal Navy.

During 1978 and 1979 *Midway* was deployed a number of times, from Yokosuka, including an extended deployment to "Gonzo Station" in the Indian Ocean. Just as the Vietnam War had "Yankee Station", and "Dixie Station" in the South China Sea, the name given the patrol area in the Indian Ocean was "Gonzo Station", named after the Sesame Street TV program character.

Midway was awarded the Air Pac Golden Anchor Carrier Motivation Award for the twelve-month competitive cycle ending September 30, 1978. In addition, *Midway* was the recipient of the Battle Efficiency "E" as the best Pacific Fleet carrier for the eighteen-month period ending 31 December 1978. In 1979, *Midway* returned to the Indian Ocean and made two cruises there in over a year. The first was in April in keeping with the U.S. Government policy of maintaining a highly visible presence in the area. This "emergency" cruise earned *Midway* the U.S. Navy and Marine Corp. Expeditionary Medal. Then in September, she was back again in the Indian Ocean on routine operations and remained there till February 1980 due to events in the Middle East. During this cruise, she set a record of ninety-one days of continuous operations at sea. *Midway* deployed from Yokosuka to the Indian Ocean, 15 July 1980, fifteen days prior to my arrival in Japan.

This then was the story of *Midway*'s life up to July 1980. Her story is not unlike the life stories of other American warships. There are facts, and unspoken stories between the statements of deployments, home port changes, and shipyard periods. The deployments meant many long months of separation for sailors and their families. Each yard period or change of home ports meant thousands of families were required to move across country, or as in the case of the move to Japan, to a different country. Each yard period meant dirty, hard work, and living in a noisy, uncomfortable environment. These hardships and sacrifices involved in a sailor's life, often go unheralded, and are unknown to the majority of American citizens. Yet without the sacrifices, professionalism, and dedication of the thousands of sailors in the "*Midway* story," these same citizens would not enjoy the quality of life and freedom they enjoy as Americans. *Midway* was at the "head of the class," in the area of carrying out that part of the U.S. Navy's mission statement, which states in part, "To be prepared to conduct prompt and sustained combat operations at sea in support of U.S. national interests and the national military strategy."

In my past Far East duty assignments the South China Sea off the coast of Vietnam had been the "hotspot" in the world, now the Indian Ocean had the honor of being the danger spot. There were stories of rouge Iranian merchant ships, with reinforced bows, used for ramming and sinking ships, roaming the Indian Ocean trying to ram American warships.

Our passports arrived in the mail, and with passports, shot cards, and suitcases in hand; we were driven to Travis Air Force Base, located north of Sacramento, by my parents. We bid them farewell at the terminal, not knowing for sure when we might see them again. We boarded a commercial jet liner, which landed in Alaska before flying on to Japan. We got off in Anchorage for the short lay over. We were shocked at the prices in the airport terminal; a small coke cost five dollars. We flew on to Narita Airport in Tokyo. Having passed over the International Date Line, the plane landed on the 30th, at 8:00 a.m., this was the same date we had departed America, and eight hours earlier than our departure time.

The Japanese Customs Officers very carefully examined our passports and suitcases. There was a bus outside the terminal waiting to take us to the Yokosuka Naval base. This was a large military-chartered bus. There were about forty-five other people on the bus with us. This was a four-hour long drive, and Japan was as I remembered it. Everything seen from the bus window seemed "doll sized." The streets, houses, cars, and the whole country seemed miniaturized, because of the smaller stature of the Japanese people.

When we arrived at the base in the afternoon, I checked in at the *Midway* Dependants Assistance Team (DAT). This was a group headed by a Personnelman Chief off the *Midway*, who stayed on the Yokosuka base when the *Midway* got underway. The "DAT" assisted wives and families of the ship's crew. They said they would arrange my transportation to the ship, as she had gotten underway two weeks ago. The big news was on the previous day the 29th, *Midway* had a collision with a Merchant Marine ship, two sailors on the *Midway* had been killed, and three sailors were injured. It was suspected that the merchant ship had purposely rammed *Midway*. All the families on base were anxious, as the names of the dead and injured had not yet been released.

A room at the base Navy lodge awaited our arrival. Shortly after checking into the lodge, there was a knock on our door. Two women greeted us, Candy Grizzard, who was the wife of the officer I would be relieving, and Teddy Kellner, wife of the weapons officer, who was to be my boss on the ship. They were very friendly and helpful. Candy was anxious for me to relieve her husband Bill. He was being transferred to the Yokosuka Naval Magazine, and they would be staying in Japan.

After a much needed rest that night, the next morning I was told at DAT that I could expect to leave for the ship in about three weeks on 21 August, and catch up with the ship wherever she might be at that time. We also discovered it would be a considerable wait before we would be able to get Navy housing. There was a very long waiting list for base housing. This meant we would have to rent a Japanese house off base, until a base house became available.

We would have to get a special drivers license in order to drive on base, and in Japan. We would also have to buy a car. Carmen and I would be required to attend an inter-culture awareness class for one week. In the interim period while we lived off base waiting for a base house, we would be given a Temporary Living Allowance (TLA), which was an allowance above my normal salary amount, so we could afford to live off base. We (Carmen in my absence) would have to keep track of weekly expenses, and turn the listing in weekly to DAT.

In the lodge next door, we met a woman named Vicky Peters, and her daughter, and a son. Her husband's name was Norm. He was an LDO Ensign, and had left on the ship on the same day they arrived in Japan. Ensign Peters was in the same department I was destined for, the weapons department, so we would be working together. Vicky, her daughter Sheila, and son David were very lonely, and they seemed pleased to meet us.

One night Vicky persuaded Carmen to go to a BINGO night at one of the base clubs. Carmen wanted me to go, so reluctantly I went. I sat through all the games, not playing for about an hour. The last game of the night was announced. It was to be a black out BINGO for a $1,500 prize. I decided to spend fifty cents and play the last game. As the game progressed, I noticed I seemed to be getting a lot of numbers. Only fifty-two numbers were to be called, when number fifty was called, I yelled "Bingo." This game I'd been half-heartedly playing, earned me $1,500! This prize had been building for a number of months, with faithful Bingo players trying to win each weekly Bingo night. The majority of the players were Filipino Navy wives. I'll never forget the looks of anger and disgust I got, as these ladies filed past me going out the door of the club. I received very few congratulations from them. I was very thankful for my good fortune, and the unexpected windfall came at a time we needed help with the bills associated with getting settled in Japan

Carmen and I attended an inter-culture awareness class that consisted of five eight-hour daily classes. Although I had visited Japan a number of times in the past, I learned many things about Japan I had previously been unaware of. We were taught a few basic Japanese phrases, such as: "*Konban Wa*"-Good evening, "*Sayonara*"-Goodbye, "*Arigato Gozaimasu*"-Thank you, "*Gomennasai*"-Excuse me, and many more. Japanese children are taught English in school, and they often would walk up to Americans, and strike up a conversation so they could practice the language they had been taught.

As a military family in Japan, Mary, Carmen and I were considered to be in a different legal status, compared to a normal American visitor to Japan. While living in Japan we were covered by a Status of Forces Agreement (SOFA), signed by the governments of Japan, and the U.S. In general this agreement provides[47]:

- That the United States military authorities will have the primary right to try members of the U.S. Armed forces for offenses committed against the property or security of the United States, offenses solely against the person or property of another member of the U.S. Armed Forces or accompanying civilian employee or dependant, and offenses which occur in the performance of official duty.

-That Japanese courts will have primary jurisdiction over all other offenses committed by members of the U.S. Armed forces and accompanying civilian employees, and over all offenses committed by dependants.

-That U.S. military personnel, civilian employees, and dependants tried in Japanese courts will be entitled to many rights. These rights include (1) A prompt trial. (2) Full information on the charges placed against them. (3) A defense counsel of their personal choice and the services of a competent interpreter, and (4) Communication with representatives of the United States government.

The "SOFA" further states that all members of the U.S. forces, accompanying civilian employees and dependants must not take part in any Japanese political activity. Some aspects of Japanese justice were quite different from the American judicial system. First, a Japanese prison is not very pleasant setting for Americans, the foods served, fish, rice, and soups were foreign to the American diet. The prison living conditions were Spartan, and sparse, mats laid on the bare floor served as a bed. A concern in the military was the severity of punishment for illegal drug offenses in Japan courts, compared to the lax punishments handed out in American courts. An American military teenage dependant, involved in illegal drug usage, caught off base by Japanese police, might spend many years in a Japanese prison. Also, Japanese courts meted out punishments, and prison terms for the parents of children law breakers. Victims of crimes were viewed differently in Japan. For example in the case of an automobile accident, the person at fault is expected to visit any injured person(s) that were involved in the wreck. He or she is expected to bring flowers to the victim, bring gifts to their family, if need be drive the victim's family back and forth to school or work, and pay the salary of the injured person if they are unable to work. When appearing before a judge, or at a trial, all the effort, and money spent by the accused person helping the victim (s), is taken into consideration by the judge prior to passing the sentence. We were advised when using a Japanese taxi off base, if the driver was involved in an accident, if we were able, leave the fare amount, and get away from the accident scene. Japanese law rationalized that the taxi driver would not have been in the accident, if he hadn't been hired, therefore the accident could be considered the rider's fault!

The population of Japan was more than 100 million people. On a small island such as Japan, private space is precious. Automobile parking space was very scarce. The personal "bubble" of space around a person's body that Americans are used to is nonexistent in Japan. When in a crowd you are bumped into, jostled, and it seems as though you are among very rude people, because no one bothers saying "excuse me," or "pardon me" when they run into you, or bump you. This takes some adjusting to by Americans. It was best to avoid rush hours, especially when using the train. People would cram into the train cars like sardines.

When introduced to a Japanese person, saying "hello', or "goodbye," one constant in Japan is bowing. It seems like people are always bowing to one another for some reason or another. We never wore shoes inside a Japanese house. At the entrance of homes there was an area where shoes worn were removed, and a person either went bare footed, or wore slippers made for indoor use.

Another interesting point to keep in mind when riding a train in Japan was if standing and holding on to an overhead strap, it was expected that you stand facing the seated passengers. It is considered insulting to stand with your buttocks toward the Japanese people seated on the benches.

In order to graduate from the Inter-culture Awareness class, each married couple, or pair of single sailors, were given a destination outside of Yokosuka, and were expected to travel to the assigned destination and back to Yokosuka by train. This meant we would be on our own, and have to read the Japanese signs, and purchase the train tickets. Carmen, Mary, and I made it to our destination city, which was thirty miles from Yokosuka, and back without getting too lost.

A week after we arrived in Yokosuka, the names of the sailors who had been killed on *Midway* was released. They were MM2 (Machinist Mate) Daniel F. Macey, and MM3 Christian Belgum.

Our household effects, which had been packed and shipped from Albuquerque, were not scheduled to arrive in Yokosuka until 15 September, well after I was to leave to catch the ship. One document I was required to get, which most of the sailors on *Midway* had, was a power of attorney, so Carmen could sign paperwork such as household goods receipts, ID card renewals, and other documents in my absence. Another oddity about living in Japan, Carmen and Mary had Japan visas' in their passports, which would require renewing every year. In order to renew visas' dependants had to travel to Yokohama every twelve months.

One day during our inter-culture awareness class, I approached a lieutenant commander (dentist), who was taking the class with us, and destined for *Midway*. I asked if he knew what our mess bill on the ship would amount to. As an officer, I along with all the officers on board would be paying a monthly mess bill, which was used to pay for our daily meals. The lieutenant commander gave me a very obvious "snub," and acted as though I was far beneath him! His rudeness shocked me, but was a lesson in the fact that, along with the sharp dividing lines between officers, chiefs, and enlisted, there were "status levels," or I should say, "Self perceived status levels" within the officer's community. LCDR Perry Roberts, CWO4 Schmidt, and others had expounded on this before my commissioning. At the top of the status ladder were the U.S. Naval Academy graduates, or as they were called "ring knockers," because of the enormous graduation ring most wore, and some kept in sight of others as much as possible.

Within the ring knocker group, the aviators, or pilots were supposedly the "top warriors," above those officers with jobs on surface vessels such as destroyers, frigates, and so on. At the turn of the twentieth century, when battleships reigned supreme, the surface line officers were at the "top of the heap," but with the advent of aviation, and aircraft carriers, the aviators enjoyed being on top. As a side point, pilots were called "brown shoes," just as enlisted rates that worked in aviation. Surface officers were called "black shoes," as in the enlisted community. Next on the ladder of status were the sub-surface officers, or submariners. The submarine officers got a tremendous boost in prestige with the advent of the nuclear-powered submarine, and the Polaris, and Trident missile system. Admiral Rickover, called the "father of the nuclear submarine Navy" had a lot to do with this jump in status, as well as the importance placed on the missile system to our nation's defense. Next down the status level ladder step, are the Officer Candidate School graduates (OCS). These officers gain the majority of their college education in colleges other than the Naval Academy, and then a "finishing course" of naval classes. These officers also enter the fields of aviation, surface, or subsurface, just as academy graduates, as "line officers." All line officers wear a "star" on their rank designation marks, or insignia. Lower on the status ladder are the "service, or staff officers," such as the dentist I had spoken to, as well as chaplains, civil engineers, supply corp., nurse and doctor corp., etc. These officers wear their specialty device on their rank designations, and insignias. At the bottom of the ladder were the limited duty officers, and chief warrant officers, or as I mentioned before, are called "Mustangs." Even though I was supposedly in the group on the bottom rung, I was very pleased to be counted as a Mustang.

On 21 August, along with ten other officers, I had my orders stamped at the *Midway* DAT, and prepared to board a bus and begin my journey to *Midway*. I bid Carmen and Mary farewell. I did not know when we would be together again? This was to be the first time in our marriage we would be separated for months on end. Carmen had a large burden on her shoulders, adjusting to a foreign country, trying to cope with the bureaucracy of the Navy, and get settled into a new home by herself.

The ship was supposed to be back in Yokosuka by Christmas, but the situation in Iran could change our schedule, so it was difficult to say for sure when I would be back. The bus we boarded took us to the Naval Air Station Atsugi, Japan. We boarded a plane at the naval air station, and flew south to Okinawa, from there on to Cubi Air Station, Philippines.

I sat with LCDR Bill Walker throughout the trip. He was older than I, and very likeable. He said he had the distinction of being the oldest, fighter pilot in the Navy, still actively flying in a squadron. The sometimes sharp dividing lines, or self perceived status levels in the officer ranks were not observed by all in the officers' community. These exceptional officers very wisely realized that these prejudicial attitudes did not further the good order and discipline of the Navy, my traveling companion Lieutenant Commander Walker, was such an officer. I enjoyed his company.

When we arrived at Cubi Point, late at night, there were no vacant rooms in the BOQ, so Lieutenant Commander Walker and I went in together and rented a room at the naval station Navy lodge. The next morning, all the officers bound for *Midway* boarded a plane, and after a lengthy flight. The plane landed on the small island of Diego Garcia.

Diego Garcia is located in the heart of the Indian Ocean, south of India and between Africa and Indonesia. It is a tropical island, a narrow atoll of about eleven square miles. Its shape is that of a "V" drawn by a shaky hand. The island stretches thirty-seven miles from tip to tip. The island's mean height above sea level is four feet.

The island is part of the British Indian Ocean Territory, and since December 1966, the British and American flag have both flown over the island. At the above date the two governments signed a bilateral agreement making the islands of the British Indian Ocean Territory available for the defenses purposes to both governments. The island had been a vital link in the defense posture of the U.S. during the Yemen crisis of 1979-1981. The island has a number of support facilities, a communications station, airfield, and other activities.

When I arrived on Diego Garcia 24 August 1980, the facilities were not as modern as the present buildings and accommodations are. Six years after my visit, a $500 million construction program was completed. In 1980, plywood huts, and open screened barracks was the "norm."

Portuguese explorers discovered Diego Garcia in the early 1500s. It is the largest of fifty-two islands, which form the Chagas Archipelago, located in the heart of the Indian Ocean. The island's name is believed to have come from either the ship's captain or the navigator on that early voyage of discovery.

Once located, the island just as quickly disappeared from maps of the Indian Ocean for many years until it was relocated and claimed by the French in the early 1700s. Diego Garcia remained under French control until after the Napoleonic Wars (circa 1814), when possession was ceded to the British.

Until 1971, Diego Garcia's main source of income was from the profitable copra oil plantation. At one time copra oil from here and other "oil islands" provided fine machine oil and fuel to light European lamps.

The climate reminded me of Guam, hot and humid. Transient officers were billeted in a wooden barracks that had screens in place of windows. Canvas cots were our beds for the night. We were given woolen blankets for bedding. There was apparently a shortage of pillows, because only lieutenant commander and above were issued pillows, (without pillow cases).

Our living conditions were very basic. The chow hall served meals on paper plates, and we used plastic eating utensils. We took showers with cold water, and as I said slept on canvas cots. After remaining one more night, we were not saddened to learn that we all were to go to the airfield, and board a helicopter that had been dispatched from *USS Midway* to pick us up, and fly us to the ship. I remember one young lieutenant in the group who was always running about trying to arrange transportation for the group, trying to behave as though he were in charge. He was typical of an officer whose goal is to always be noticed; trying to act like a motivated leader, but often merely succeeds in being obnoxious.

One pleasant fact was that we were permitted to wear khaki uniforms during our travels. Enlisted men were also permitted to wear dungarees when traveling in the Far East. This was certainly much more comfortable than in the past when I had to wear my woolen dress blues in the tropic, 100 degrees plus temperatures.

After a short flight on the helicopter, I was finally on board my new duty station. When I climbed out of the helo onto the flight deck, I was met by a second class petty officer, who said he was from W Division. He carried my sea bag, and led me below decks to the ship Captain's Office, which was the personnel office for officers. I turned in my orders, and records, and was given the standard check-in sheet. My next stop was at the wardroom office, where I was given a meal ticket, that contained 100 squares, and I was told by the stewards' mate in the office, that the ticket cost was $105, and each time I had a meal in the wardroom, one square was punched. Additionally there were wardroom dues that would be collected monthly, used for hail and farewell parties, and other expenses incurred by the ship's officers. The monthly amount of wardroom dues was determined each month by the executive officer.

All officers' lieutenant commander and below on the *Midway*, bunked in either two man staterooms, or officer's bunk rooms, which contained as many as ten officers. Lieutenant junior grades and ensigns normally occupied the large bunkrooms. Ranks of commander and above lived in single occupancy staterooms. There were no empty bunks available for me when I checked aboard. I was scheduled to move into Bill Grizzard's bunkroom in his place, when he left the ship. In the meantime, I was given a commander's stateroom that was empty. The stateroom was spacious, with a large metal desk, one bed, a huge storage closet, and even a television. It was definitely the largest living area; I'd ever had aboard a ship.

Shortly after I entered the stateroom I had been assigned to, and as I was unpacking my suitcase, and sea bag, there was a knock on the door. I opened the door, and was greeted by a chief warrant officer, a chief, and a first class. The warrant officer was Bill Grizzard, and the big surprise was the identity of the chief and first class. The chief was John Munson, who I'd known as a seaman on the *USS Ticonderoga*, sixteen years in the past. The first class was Dick Clark, who I'd last seen in Guam four years ago. Carmen and I had stayed with him and his family during Typhoon Pamela. I had not known that these two were stationed on *Midway*, and it was a wonderful reunion. While it was wonderful to see them, in the back of my mind was the question, "How would these two friends relate to me now that I am an officer?" John Munson had just made chief, and gone through his initiation three weeks prior while the ship was in Subic Bay. Dick Clark was W Division's Leading Petty Officer. I was surprised that Dick had not yet made chief.

I had arrived on the ship on a day that holiday routine was being observed, which meant a day off for most sailors, so they could sleep, or do what they wished. Most ships' offices and stores were closed. Bill Grizzard was visibly anxious to be relieved, and get back to Yokosuka, and start his new job at the ordnance station on overseas shore duty. Bill had been *Midway* W Division technical monitor for two years. Although the ship was on holiday routine, CWO2 Grizzard accompanied me around to get as many signatures on my check-in sheet as we could.

He explained that an A-6 *Intruder* aircraft navigator, lieutenant, named Glenn Oelrich, held the W Division Officer job. GMTC Munson was the only chief in the division.

Another GMT chief on the ship was not working in W Division, as he had been "fired," and was working in the special services office. As was usually the case, W Division was undermanned, and short of the number of GMT's it was supposed to have.

One of the first persons I met was my boss, the weapons officer, or as he's called on carriers, the "Gun Boss." He was a very personable officer, named Commander Gary Kellner. He greeted me warmly, and I noticed that he and Bill Grizzard seemed to be close friends. I told Commander Kellner that his wife Teddy, along with Bill's wife Candy, had helped Carmen and me when we arrived on the Yokosuka Naval Base. I told him I was anxious to get to work, and he thanked me for the letter I had sent him prior to my arrival. The gun boss had a large office, which contained an outer office, and an inner office. The inner office contained two desks, one for him, and one for the assistant weapons officer, a lieutenant commander. The outer office had a desk for the senior chief petty officer in the weapons department, and three desks for administrative yeomen assistants. The weapons department contained more than 200 enlisted men, and eleven officers.

CWO2 Grizzard told me that Commander Kellner was an Annapolis Academy graduate, and he had played football for Navy, with Roger Staubach, who went on to become quarterback for the professional football team Dallas Cowboys.

It was only a couple of days before my security badge photo was taken, and my name added to the W Division access list, by the captain, so I could enter W Division spaces. This was "blinding speed" compared to the weeks and occasionally months, I had waited as an enlisted man to have my security clearance confirmed before I could enter my assigned classified work area. The reason my access was approved so quickly was my status as an officer, but also because Bill Grizzard was anxious to transfer, so he "walked" most of the paperwork through.

My check in sheet required that I talk with the two senior officers on the ship, the executive officer, and the commanding officer. My meeting with both officers was in the company of CWO2 Grizzard. My meeting with the Executive Officer, Capt. K.L. Carlsen, was short. He quickly described the way the wardroom mess dues were collected monthly, and welcomed me aboard. He had a spacious office on the second deck, or the deck below the hangar deck. It was unusual that the executive officer was a captain, as a senior commander normally held this position, but Captain Carlsen had just recently been promoted. He also was a naval academy graduate, and had been a naval aviator, with EA-6 aircraft. He had been assigned to a squadron at Whidbey Island in 1967, while I was stationed at the Whidbey Island AUW Shop.

It was a couple of days before an audience with the captain could be arranged. Bill and I sat down with him in his huge office one evening, and he welcomed me aboard. His name was Captain "E" Inman Carmichael. He said there would be a hail and farewell party during one of our in-port periods in the near future. Captain Carmichael was an academy graduate, entering the Navy five years before me in 1955. He had assumed command of the *Midway* September 1979. Just as the X.O. was, he was a naval aviator.

Each day at sea, and in port, a meeting I described previously would take place. It was "eight o'clock reports." This meeting, which took place not at the time the name infers, but at 7:00 p.m., was between the executive officer, and all the ships' department heads (also the commanding officers of each squadron assigned onboard *Midway*). At this meeting any information the executive officer, or captain wished passed to officers or the ship's crew was relayed. In turn each department head, and squadron commanding officer, would report the condition of his respective department, or squadron. The information discussed in these meetings was varied, and sometimes information for officers only.

Commander Kellner would attend these nightly meetings, which lasted anywhere from twenty minutes, to two or three hours. After the meeting, Commander Kellner would return to the weapons department office, where all the weapons department officers would be assembled, awaiting his arrival. Either a chief or officer represented each division. Upon the entrance of the gun boss, the exclamation "attention on deck" would be given, and we would all stand at attention, until he stated, "carry on," or "be seated." All would be seated, in chairs positioned in a semicircle around his desk. Commander Kellner would relay whatever information he had been given at eight o'clock reports, and also give out any specific orders or information he wanted passed out at a divisional level. After he finished speaking, each person was given an opportunity to speak, or ask questions, and give him feedback on what was taking place in each division. This meeting was held without fail, day after day.

All chiefs and officers on *Midway* wore a nametag attached over their right shirt pocket. This nametag had the person's name, rank, and division. Also on the nametag was the ship's medallion, which was a shield with a sword, and the ship's hull number "41".

Since *Midway* was the only forward deployed carrier in the Navy, the sword was a symbol of the ship, as "the tip of the sword" defending America. CWO2 Grizzard wore a nametag "Gunner Grizzard, W Division." I had to decide whether I wished to be addressed as "Mr. Little," or "Gunner Little," I had decided long before, that I preferred Gunner Little. I also told chief Munson that I preferred to be addressed as "Gunner" by the troops.

Each division on the ship held a morning muster each day at 0730. In W Division this muster took place in the forward W Division coffee break compartment. This compartment was often called the "I Shop," the "I" standing for instrument shop, which was used in the early years of nuclear weapons when large storage areas were required for all the instruments that were needed to maintain the early weapons. All W Division sailors were expected to be at this muster without fail, and if not present without a valid reason, or excuse they were declared an "unauthorized absentee." GMT1 Dick Clark would conduct the muster, and read the plan of the day. This was a job I had for many years at my previous duty stations as leading petty officer. Chief Munson would then usually address the crew, or pass any orders he felt the sailors should have. It was seldom that the technical monitor or division officer addressed the sailors, and then it was usually information that had been passed out at the previous evenings eight o'clock report meeting. At times, when flight operations were not being conducted, and there was room on the hangar deck, then divisions would conduct morning muster standing in ranks in the hangar deck area. This was an opportunity for the leading petty officer, chief, and officers to inspect the appearance, and uniforms of the men in the division. My first formal introduction to the W Division sailors was at a hangar deck morning muster.

Anytime a new officer reports to a division, there's speculation among the sailors, as well as anxiety, about what kind of officer he might be, and how his leadership, or lack of leadership will impact the sailor's day-to-day life. I remembered those times I experienced the changing of division officers, or other officers in my previous duty stations, and ships.

During a morning divisional muster on the hangar deck, a few days after I came aboard, standing before the ranks of W Division sailors, with Lieutenant Oelrich, CWO2 Grizzard, and GMTC Munson, I was introduced. I spoke a few words, saying I was pleased to be on *Midway*, and that *Midway* was the fourth carrier I'd been stationed on. I also told the sailors I'd been at Nuclear Weapons Training Group, Pacific before coming onboard, and I learned that W Division on *Midway* was highly regarded and respected, and I looked forward to being part of the division, and meeting each one of them personally.

When I mentioned *Midway* as my fourth carrier, there were startled looks of disbelief and amazement. I was cautious not to say anything that might make the sailors think I was going to change anything. Any changes I might make in the way the division operated, or any leadership changes would be done gradually, and subtly. Sailors in general, as do most human beings, resist sudden changes in routines. I could remember the turmoil in divisions I'd been in the past by newly reporting officers that began immediately changing routines, just for the sake of change, or doing things their way, without considering the disruptions they were creating.

My check-in proceeded at a record-breaking pace, urged on by Bill Grizzard who was anxious to return to Japan. The relief of an officer was normally a process that took place over a time frame of one month. The newly reporting officer and the officer being relieved would normally be given transfer orders that were timed for this month turn over process. As it developed Bill, and I had a five-day turn over.

Along with the checkout sheet, other pieces of paper required completion, before the "turn over" process could be called complete. One such piece of paper was my designation as an "Accountable Officer" by the commanding officer. This letter of designation was signed by Captain Carmichael, and said in part:

As Accountable Officer you are directed to:
a. Accurately record property transactions and maintain current all records pertaining to the stock record account.
b. Control debit and credit posting to the accountable records.
c. Promptly report any losses, damage, or other irregularities.
d. Accomplish all reports and records in a timely and accurate manner.
e. Provide effective management direction normally associated with an individual having responsibility for property.
f. Sign all accountable documents which evidence property receipts or which verify correctness of supply/shipping documents and issue/turn-in documents.
g. Control the transfer, movement of, and access to classified ordnance and classified components that may be in your custody.
h. Maintain custodial records and at least semiannually verify their accuracy.

i. Insure adequate safeguards and protection are provided
j. Familiarize yourself with those publications pertaining to accountability and logistics procedures.

When relieved, the Accountable Officer and his successor shall complete the certificate of transfer of accountability and file as necessary.

This letter signed by the commanding officer, laid an immense mantel of responsibility upon my shoulders. Any damage, loss, or irregularity that might occur within the classified weapon area on board *Midway*, I would be held accountable for it. This accountability would be solely mine until such time in the future when I would be relieved of it by another officer.

As well as assigned as the accountable officer, I signed along with Bill Gizzard, a relief letter. Bill's portion of the relief letter, which was addressed to the Commanding Officer, said:

In accordance with Navy Regulations, 1973, I hereby report being relieved this date of duties as Assembly Technical Monitor, *USS Midway* (CV-41), by CWO2 James S. Little, USN. In company with my relief, an inspection of equipment, material, and records under cognizance of the Assembly Technical Monitor was made. No discrepancies were noted. An inventory was conducted of all classified material in custody of the Assembly Technical Monitor, and all material is accounted for.

The W Division work is current and my relief is acquainted with the forthcoming schedule.

Below Bill's signature, my portion of the letter to the Captain said:

"I relieved CWO2 William A. Grizzard, USN as Assembly Technical Monitor this date and found conditions stated in the basic letter to be correct and satisfactory."

I arrived on board 26 August. The above letters were dated 29 August. Prior to the letters being signed, CWO2 Grizzard and I had toured all the W Division spaces, which included the forward W Division offices, and coffee locker, also the W Division magazines which were located on the second, third, fourth, and fifth deck of the ship. Just as on other carriers, the magazine spaces were in both the forward, and after sections of the ship, separated so if the forward section, or after section of the ship was damaged, there would remain an undamaged magazine. There was also a W Division berthing compartment, which contained bunks and lockers for thirty-six sailors. W Division was also responsible for a common use head that was located near the berthing compartment. I learned there were also two compartments amidships on the third and fourth decks that the division used for storage space. Along with touring W Division spaces, I verified the serial numbers of all associated accountable test and handling gear. This effort required twelve to fourteen hour workdays.

One of my big concerns was the poor condition of the magazine sprinkler system. The main valves in the magazines looked neglected, with corrosion, and dampness around the sealing joints. This concern was fueled by my memories of the magazine flood I'd experienced on *Oriskany*. I certainly didn't want a magazine flood on *Midway*, while I was aboard. In many ways the ship was beginning to show her age of almost thirty-five years. She reminded me a lot of the *Oriskany*, the way her compartments were laid out, although *Midway* was a much larger carrier than *Oriskany*.

In addition to the paperwork associated with the assumption of my new job as assembly technical monitor, I started work on my Personal Qualification Standard (PQS) Sheet for damage control. This was a qualification sheet, and a written test that had to be completed by every officer and enlisted sailor reporting aboard *Midway*. Many of the qualification areas, and questions on the test were on the subject of fire fighting on board carriers.

I was also told that I would be given an oral and written test to become qualified as an Officer of the Deck (OOD), inport. The ship's navigator would administer the tests. I was expected to be qualified by the time *Midway* returned to Yokosuka. There was pressure for me to become qualified, because there was a shortage of qualified OOD's on the ship. Due to the shortage, many OOD's had to stand as much as eight hours of watch, every fifth day while the ship was in port. The navigator, a lieutenant commander, told me that I would stand indoctrination watches during the ships next in port call at Mombasa, Africa.

A couple of days after my arrival, all the Weapons Department officers and chiefs were told to muster on the flight deck in dress whites. We were to have our picture taken for the ship's cruise book. We lined up in two rows, and our picture was snapped. The older chiefs were teasing Chief John Munson, because they noticed he was wearing black socks. Chiefs and officers while in the dress white uniform wore white socks. Since Chief Munson was a newly promoted chief, he had overlooked this small uniform requirement. Since he was the only chief, and leading chief in W Division, I wondered about his leadership capabilities?

When I had known him on the *Ticonderoga* years before, he had been a quiet sailor, and a little wild on liberty. I wondered how he had matured over the years. Although there was only three years difference in our ages, I being the older, back in 1964 this age difference had been more obvious, I being twenty-one, and him, nineteen years' old. I noticed that he accepted the teasing about his socks, graciously, and with good humor.

With CWO2 Grizzards's departure from the ship, I moved into the bunkroom he had vacated. It was a spacious room with four bunks, two on each side of the room. Large clothes' lockers served as a partition between the two sleeping areas. Each side of the room had a desk, chair, and wall safe. Also, in the room was a sink and mirror. I shared the bunkroom with three other chief warrant officers. CWO2 Mike Paoletti was in the weapons department, and worked in the flight deck ordnance shop. CWO2 Chuck Morgan was in the air department, and worked on the steam catapult system that launched aircraft off the ship. CWO3 C.J. Heard was also in the air department, and held the job of Flight Deck Crash/Salvage Boatswain.

My bunk was an upper bunk that Bill Grizzard had vacated. The bunkroom was located on the 02 deck, and as I was to discover the first night I slept in my new bunk, I was lying right under the flight deck, just beneath the starboard catapult. During flight operations the noise was deafening. I was also to learn that Chuck Morgan who slept in the bunk beneath me talked in his sleep.

The living conditions on board ships, as an officer, compared to enlisted living conditions, were as different as night and day. Each day a Steward's Mate came into our bunkroom, made up our beds, and cleaned the room. Twice a week he would collect our laundry, and deliver it to the ship's laundry, where our clothes would be washed, and our uniforms dry cleaned and pressed. This was like having a personal butler, or maid. Once a month, the four of us would put money together, and give it to the Steward's Mate that took care of our room. As four former enlisted men, we had a higher degree of appreciation for the work he did for us, than did most other officers.

After wishing me good luck, CWO2 Grizzard had departed the ship on 1 September, and I began my duties in earnest. I soon discovered, as was the case on most carriers, LT Glenn Oelrich, the assigned W Division Officer, had very limited nuclear weapons' experience. He was an aviator, and the W Division Officer job was a "ticket-punch" job to round out his progression as a career line officer. He had attended a couple of loading schools, and the Nuclear Weapons Safety Officer Course I had attended in San Diego. He was a likeable, friendly officer who was easy to work with. He recognized that his knowledge in the nuclear weapons field was limited.

I sensed from the first day in W Division spaces, that the sailors in the division were apprehensive, and anxious about what kind of officer I was to be.

A couple of days after 1 September, I had my first crisis to deal with. One of the sprinkler valves within the forward magazine began to leak. This brought back distasteful memories of the magazine flood I'd been involved in, and validated the concerns I had when I first saw the neglected and old appearance of the valves while touring the W Division spaces. The leak was bad, and the only way to repair the valve, was to disassemble the valve, and replace a large gasket that was between two bolted machine surfaces, which measured about two feet across. This repair effort meant all the water in the lines had to be turned off. This water was saltwater which was circulated throughout the ship, and used during firefighting efforts. Securing the water, meant shutting it off throughout the forward section of the ship, the same water used in our magazine sprinkler system, was also supplied to cool the jet blast deflectors used on the flight deck to deflect jet exhausts when planes were launched off the flight deck. We would have to attempt the repair when flight quarters were not being conducted.

Chief Munson and I watched as four sailors began removing the bolts holding the valve sections together, following the water shut off. We were only given ninety minutes to complete the repairs, between flight operations. Two sailors worked with swabs and buckets mopping up spilled salt water as the job progressed. The removed gasket was in bad shape. Using the old gasket as a pattern, a new one was quickly cut out of a rubber sheet, and put in place. When the men began bolting the sections back together, I left the magazine, and climbed up the ladder to my office on the third deck.

Ten minutes had passed since I left the magazine, when Chief Munson came into the office, and said, "Gunner we have a problem." I followed him back down the ladder into the magazine. The sailors were standing around the valve looking perplexed and worried. All of the bolts in the flange of the two sections had been replaced and had been tightened except for one. There were twelve large bolts and nuts that held the flanges together. They could not install the last bolt and nut because an open end wrench, and socket wrench could not be placed on the bolt head due to the close proximity of the bulkhead to the flange.

When they had removed the bolt and nut, they hadn't needed to hold the bolt head. If this bolt could not be tightened, then the flange would probably leak under pressure worse than before the repair. The time we had been given to repair the flange was rapidly coming to an end. They had been struggling with this problem for about ten minutes, before calling for me. When I entered the magazine, all eyes turned to me. I looked at the inaccessible bolt head, and immediately the solution came to me. I told them to remove the bolt and nut on a flange, located about one foot directly over the bolt and nut they were struggling with. After giving me puzzled looks, they proceeded to remove the upper flange bolt and nut. I then told them to put a long extension on a socket wrench down through the bolt hole they had just created. Since the bulkhead angled away at the upper end of the sprinkler pipe, there was clearance to install a socket wrench and hold the bolt head below while the nut was tightened. They all looked at me with astonishment and relief. The bolt and nut were tightened, and the removed bolt and nut on the upper flange reinstalled, and the repair was complete. After the water was turned on, the repair was successful, as the leak had been stopped. Providing the solution to this problem, increased my confidence, and I gained a small measure of respect from the men in the division.

The ship was holding flight quarters daily, flying many sorties. We were in a "tense" part of the world. Iran still had our embassy in its control as well as the fifty-two American hostages. Russian planes made their presence known by periodically flying close to *Midway,* and our escorting ships.

On 10 September, a milestone in the life of *Midway* was marked with a special cake that was served in the crew's mess. This was the thirty-fifth year since *Midway* had been commissioned in 1945.

I remained busy reviewing W Division records, studying the service records of the GMT's assigned to the division, watching training operations on training weapons, and formulating plans for the future. The first major inspection looming on the horizon for W Division would happen the first part of 1981. This was a fact that lurked in the back of everyone's mind. Inspections were a major part of a Nuclear Weaponsman's life; with the dread of failure and the disaster it represented always a topic of discussion.

On 22 September, the ship anchored off the shore of Africa. We were scheduled for a stay of five days in Mombasa, Kenya. The first day in port, everyone going on liberty was required to be in dress white uniforms. After the first day in port, the crew was permitted to wear civilian clothes on liberty.

Mombasa, the principal port in East Africa, lies on the shore of the Indian Ocean forty-three miles north of the Kenya-Tanzania border. It is Kenya's second largest city and its major Naval Base. It is the main gateway to Kenya and Uganda, with a population of 400,000 (in 1980), of which more than half are Africans, with lesser numbers of Indians, Arabs, and Europeans. It is a municipality, which comprises an island 5.5. square miles and an area of mainland of fifteen square miles.

In the fifteenth century Vasco De Gama landed at Mombasa. The Portuguese, realizing Mombasa was too rich a prize to be ignored, organized several strong expeditions against the Arabs and, in 1528 added Mombasa to their domain. In order to protect themselves against counter-attacks, they built Fort Jesus, which still stands at the southern tip of Mombasa Island. In 1730, after repeated attacks over two centuries, the Arabs finally ousted the Portuguese and managed to retain control of Mombasa until late in the nineteenth century. After a period as a British possession, Kenya became independent on 12 December 1964.

A couple of weeks before the ship's arrival off the shore of Africa, the crew was given a series of malaria tablets, which were furnished at meals on the crew's mess deck, and the officer's wardroom. Navy ships that had visited Mombasa had reported a few cases of malaria. A booklet that was prepared on the ship, describing Mombasa, and things to do there, contained an interesting comment on taking photographs in Mombasa[48].

> Religion plays a large part in deciding what you can photograph in Kenya, and what you can't photograph. By and large the culture in Kenya is Islamic. This means you don't take pictures of women, veiled, or unveiled. Especially this is true in the Arab quarter. Many of the African tribesmen still hold to animist beliefs, among which is the idea that a photograph enslaves a person's spirit. One never knows just what kind of action might be taken in such a case? The least would be anger and bad feeling; the worst might be an attempt to break the camera to free the imprisoned spirit. Since some of these men are more than seven feet tall, forewarned is forearmed. Politics is also involved, as photographing slum areas is considered to be a hostile act by the government, they feel we are being overly comparative and looking down on them. Snapping a picture of the president is also a "no-no." A smart idea is to ask before you shoot. Also be prepared to tip the Masai Warriors who are specially posed in tribal costume for your photo activities. (As long as they get a bit of your money, they evidently do not worry about their spirits). Forty percent of the population is Muslim, and there are forty-nine Mosques.

Mandhry Mosque is the oldest, built in 1570, and is one of many in picturesque old town, whose narrow, winding streets and black veiled women are reminiscent of such cities as Morocco or Tunisia. In the old harbor, Arabian dhow ships from Oman and the Persian Gulf tie up with cargoes of Arab silverware, Persian carpets, and chests with brass decorations, spices, dried dates, and furniture. You can photograph this harbor, and maybe arrange to board one of the dhows to photograph or bargain for some of the items they have for sale. If you get shanghaied, sorry about that!

At anchor off the coast of Mombasa, a ladder was attached to the side of the ship at the quarterdeck area on the hangar bay. It was here that sailors departed the ship, and boarded liberty launches that held 100 men or more, and would shuttle back and forth from the ship to the pier. The Officer of the Deck (OOD) and Junior Officer of the Deck (JOOD) stood four-hour watches on the quarterdeck. I was scheduled to stand two OOD indoctrination watches during our five-day stay.

The second day in port there was to be a social gathering of officers, at a large hotel in Mombasa. All officers not on duty were expected to attend. This was to be a "hail and farewell" party, and all newly reporting officers were required to be present.

The first day at anchor, I stood my first four-hour OOD indoctrination watch. I stood on the quarterdeck with a lieutenant who was the OOD, for a busy event filled four hours. I realized I had a lot to learn before I would be certified to stand this watch alone. My watch was from 1200 to 1600 in the afternoon. I was scheduled to stand another four-hour watch the last night at anchor.

The second day at anchor, all the officers were to report to a hotel that was located on the outskirts of Mombasa. My roommate CWO2 Chuck Morgan, Ensign Norm Peters and I caught a bus near the fleet landing pier where the liberty boats tied up. After a thirty-minute bus ride we arrived at a large hotel, built with white stonework, surrounded by palm trees. All of the *Midway* Officers were gathered on a large lawn at the side of the hotel. There was a large patio with tables laden with snacks and sandwiches. Near these tables were a podium, and microphone.

Shortly after the bus arrival at the hotel, Captain Carmichael stepped behind the podium, and addressed the gathered officers. There were twelve officers that would be transferring off *Midway* in less than a month, and each one spoke a few words of farewell. There were an equal number of officers that had reported aboard, and as the captain called out our names, we raised our hands to be identified, which I did when he said, "CWO2 Jim Little of Weapons Department." The hail and farewell party broke up about an hour after the captain had spoken.

The following day, Ensign Norm Peters, and Lieutenant Goglin, who was also in weapons department, and I walked about Mombasa, and looked at the sights. The poverty of this African nation was very apparent in the streets we walked. The streets were filled with beggars, and people who obviously had serious diseases. I was thankful for the malaria pills I had taken the weeks previously. I bought a large wooden carved giraffe, and gifts for Carmen and Mary. Norm wanted to find a bakery, as he had a craving for some Danish sweet rolls. It took a long time to locate one, but we finally did. All in all Mombasa was the dirtiest, most impoverished country I'd visited thus far in my visits to foreign countries.

On 26 September, the ship pulled anchor, and we were once again underway. I began to feel more at ease in my role as a Navy officer, as each day passed. Meals in the wardrooms were served at specific times, and actually served not only as an eating area, but also a social gathering place for *Midway*'s Officers. There were two wardrooms; one was the formal wardroom, while the other was the informal wardroom. In order to eat in the formal wardroom, an officer was required to wear a full khaki uniform, or on occasions a dress uniform. The tables in the formal wardroom were covered with white linen tablecloths, and set with chinaware, and silver eating tableware. Steward's Mates waited upon the officers seated in this room. Within the formal wardroom, there was a separate room, which contained a long table, with a setting at the head for the executive officer. There were place settings at the sides for each department head. The captain was normally served meals in his cabin, or upon rare occasions he would sit in the executive officer's seat at the head of the table.

The informal wardroom had a self-serve food line, with trays and self-seating at tables with four chairs each. Officers wearing flight deck jerseys (turtleneck, long sleeve pull over shirts), and pilots wearing flight suits were permitted in this wardroom. The hours of operation in the informal wardroom were longer than those of the formal wardroom. At sea this wardroom was usually open twenty-four hours a day. The meals served were very good, and as I mentioned, each time an officer ate a meal, his meal ticket was punched. Often the night before pulling into port, we would be served steak and lobster.

Steward's Mates would clear the tables of dishes when an officer was finished with his meal. These Steward's Mates were predominately Filipino sailors who cleaned all spaces within officer's country, and took care of all the staterooms in which officers lived.

Sailors working on the hangar deck, and flight deck, wore colored jerseys, which told an observer what his job was. As on my previous carriers, my flight deck jersey color was red. Stenciled on the front and back was a large "W" for W Division. When wearing a flight deck jersey, the only thing that distinguished officers and chiefs from enlisted sailors, was the khaki pants worn by chiefs and officers, while enlisted wore dungaree pants. Petty officers wore their rate stenciled on their left upper sleeve.

As I said, Lieutenant Oelrich was an A-6 *Intruder* aircraft navigator. He flew often in one of the squadrons, and was busy getting his qualifications as an underway OOD. He usually spent no more than a couple of hours daily in the W Division office. This was a normal situation I had seen in other W Divisions, a line officer with little nuclear weapons experience, getting his "ticket punch" for his career progress.

I was busy getting to know the GMT's in the division, trying to determine their level of technical expertise. I watched training operations, when the assembly teams would train, on one of the four systems we had. I tried to judge the division's preparedness for the upcoming inspection the first of next year.

One problem I gradually became aware of was that W Division was not well liked, or highly regarded within the weapons department. W Division sailors were often referred to as "prima-donnas," and not considered "team players." This was not an unusual attitude on carriers. W Division's job was shrouded in secrecy, with marines guarding our spaces, preventing free access, as was the case throughout the rest of the ship. W Division sailors generally kept to themselves, only socializing with each other or the marines that guarded their spaces. While secrecy was a necessary part of our job as nuclear weaponsmen, it was not right to ignore the fact that we were all shipmates together on the *Midway*. I felt it would benefit the division, if we took a more active part in weapons department tasks, and attempted to dispel this negative attitude other weapons department sailors had toward W Division. I had experienced this situation when on the *USS Oriskany*, when W Division sailors had pitched in and worked building bombs while off the coast of Vietnam. The morale in the ship's weapons department, and W Division was much higher during the times of these shared work efforts. One added benefit when W Division sailors worked outside their work spaces was that the GMT's usually gained an appreciation for the higher intelligence level of the sailors in W Division, and the nice spaces they enjoyed within W Division, compared to the other sailor's daily life on the ship. I discussed this with Lieutenant Oelrich, and he agreed with my perception that the division was not well liked within the department. I told him I would like to try and change this. He was agreeable, and let me have a free rein within the division. I discussed this at length with Chief Munson. He and I were Vietnam era sailors, and he understood the situation completely. I knew this effort would not be popular with the GMT's at first, but popularity wasn't my main concern. They would resist change, and grumble, but I knew in the end they and the division would benefit from my efforts. I began to look for opportunities to show weapons department that W Division could be counted on to help accomplish weapons department goals and jobs. Often during the nightly meeting in the weapons office with Commander Kellner after he returned from eight o'clock reports, he would ask for volunteers from the divisions for working parties for the following day. These working parties would perform various jobs such as breaking out food stores on the mess decks, doing different cleaning jobs throughout the ship, or helping bring supplies on board from supply ships steaming alongside. I began aggressively volunteering W Division help, when divisions were asked to provide men to help with these tasks.

At each morning muster, I would speak for a few minutes, gradually telling the sailors what I expected of them, and what they could expect from me. I explained that I would never ask them to do something I wouldn't do, or had not done in the past. I explained because of the nature of our work technical mistakes could not be tolerated, and I believed in a heavy training schedule, as a tool to keep everybody technically sharp. I told them they could approach me anytime concerning problems they might have, as long as they did not jump the chain of command, and leave GMT1 Clark and GMTC Munson "out of the loop." I told them I believed in a liberal liberty policy while in port, as long as we worked hard at sea. I assured them anytime the division was working, I would be working alongside them. I would acknowledge good work, and praise publicly, and as much as possible criticize, or correct privately. I explained that I would respect their privacy as much as possible within the limits of the Personnel Reliability Program. I told them illegal drug usage would not be tolerated, however, I would not go on "witch hunts," but respect them as adults until proven otherwise. I told them they could expect fair quarterly performance evaluations, and I would gradually show them what I meant by that.

I planned to insure that all petty officers knew the instructions concerning performance evaluations inside and out. From my review of the sailor's service records, it was obvious that this was an area that needed work. Additionally I let it be known that I expected each man in the division to work toward his next promotion in rate as much as possible. This meant completing correspondence courses, and studying for promotion exams. I privately liked the leadership philosophy, "Take care of those you lead and they will not only follow, they will take care of you as well."

As much as possible I wanted GMT1 Clark, and Chief Munson to manage the daily affairs of the division with minimal involvement from me. I only asked to be kept informed daily of significant happenings, and I promised to support them in their leadership roles. I felt it was difficult for anyone to effectively manage more than five people, and oversee the results of their work, so there had to be a "down flow" of leadership throughout the twenty-five plus man division. I wanted to spread out management tasks. I asked Chief Munson to prepare a collateral job list, listing such jobs as "Training Petty Officer," "Damage Control Petty Officer," "Flammable Materials Petty Officer," "Safety Petty Officer," and so on. I planned on assigning specific jobs to each petty officer, in addition to the regularly assigned jobs such as "Assembly Team Leader, Magazine Supervisor," etc. This was a busy time for me. It was also a busy time for Chief John Munson, as he was adjusting to his new role as leading chief of W Division. The other GMT chief that was on the ship working in special services that had been kicked out of the division by CWO2 Grizzard was actually a hindrance to the division in more ways than one. Because he was assigned to *Midway*, even though not working in W Division, until he transferred, Washington, D.C would not assign another GMTC Chief to the ship.

On 13 October, the ship declared holiday routine, and celebrated the Navy's 205th birthday. There were a number of activities scheduled for the day. There were to be foot races on the flight deck, sports competitions in baseball, basketball, and volleyball. Sports competition throughout the year was held between departments in a program called "The Captain's Cup." At the end of each year, the department with the most points gained through winning competitions, was declared the winner, and allowed to display the Captain's Cup, a gold colored trophy in their department office. In addition to the sports events scheduled for the day, there was to be a "steel beach picnic." The mess cooks would set up barbeques on the flight deck, and cook hamburgers and hot dogs for the crew. Sailors were also permitted to sun bathe on the flight deck throughout the day. I had been assigned the collateral duty of captain's cup representative of weapons department. This job was given to me because Bill Grizzard had held the job, so I inherited it. I told Commander Kellner I would decorate the T-shirts of the weapon department runners participating in the flight deck foot race. I got an old T-shirt from the five weapons department runners and with a felt tip pen, decorated the five shirts with the Disney character "The Tasmanian Devil," and inscribed "Weapons Department" on each shirt. The race was held in the afternoon, and weapons department was the only department with "designer T-shirts." The foot race was five times around the edge of the flight deck. Weapons department had an exceptionally fast runner on the last leg of the race, and he won. However, it was so hot that the perspiring runners caused the felt tip designs on their shirts to run, but in the excitement of victory no one cared.

On 4 November, LCDR Henry B. Meyers, Jr., a pilot assigned to a squadron on the ship, was killed. While flying with two other A-7 *Corsairs* in formation, during a descent toward the surface of the ocean, for some unknown reason his plane continued it's dive, and crashed into the sea. The plane and his body were not recovered. I had shared a dinner table with him in the wardroom a couple of times. A few days after his death, I put on dress whites, and attended a memorial service for him on the flight deck one evening.

I continued working on my OOD qualifications, and damage control qualifications. I passed the written tests on both subjects, as well as a verbal exam on OOD duties given by the ship's navigator. The ship published a daily four-page newspaper, which published a few of my cartoons.

On 6 November, we were relieved in the Indian Ocean by the carrier *USS Ranger*. This brought back memories of the time I was on the *USS Ticonderoga*, and the *Ranger* failed to relieve us off the coast of Vietnam, tacking on an additional month to our overseas deployment. This time, however the *USS Ranger* was on time. The *Midway* left the Indian Ocean and steamed for Yokosuka. Everyone's spirits were high, we were headed home, and it appeared the ship would be in our homeport for Christmas. The work tempo slowed down, and few flight operations were conducted, except for those times the ship's COD (see photo page) with the mail would fly aboard.

We got word that our country had elected a new president. President Elect Ronald Reagan would take office in January 1981. I had voted by mailing an absentee ballot to California.

I had voted for Reagan, as had many sailors, because he promised to strengthen the military, and build up the country's defense, as well as straighten out the hostage situation in Iran.

While steaming toward Japan, a massive ship cleaning effort was begun. Field days were to be held for a week, culminating in a ship wide material zone inspection. The hours prior to a zone inspection were always an inconvenience to everyone, as it was almost impossible to move about the ship with everyone busily cleaning each compartment. The ship was divided into zones, and designated officers, of which I was one, would meet in the wardroom and be given specific compartments about the ship to inspect. Two enlisted sailors accompanied each officer. One sailor was to transcribe the comments made by the inspecting officer, and the other sailor was a sailor assigned to the department being inspected, and served as a guide for the officer. After a briefing in the wardroom, all the officers spread out over the ship, inspecting for cleanliness, and condition of fire fighting, and damage control equipment. As the inspecting party entered each compartment, a sailor would stand at attention, and present the compartment, by sounding off with his name, and the compartment number being presented for inspection. After the inspection of the compartment, the sailor standing by and accompanying the inspection party would be told the results of the inspection. An entire zone inspection of the ship would usually take four or five hours, or an entire afternoon. Each inspecting officer completed an inspection results form, which was turned into a LCDR who was the head of the ship's PMS Office. Each compartment received a written grade. The highest grade was "Outstanding." A compartment graded outstanding was excluded from the next scheduled zone inspection. W Division magazines were spotless, and each time they were inspected they received an outstanding, which all in W Division took pride in.

This period of time was not a lax period for W Division; we were scheduled to undergo training that was conducted by GMT's from the Nuclear Weapons Training Group Pacific. This was called Refresher Training, which I had gone through many times in the past. This was training offered to W Divisions that helped them prepare for inspections by evaluating and training GMT's in the assembly operations they would be demonstrating during the inspection process. Chief Munson and I put together the operations schedule that we would be demonstrating to the inspectors at our inspection time. As I mentioned, the division was split into forward, and after teams. Each magazine assembly team would be demonstrating operations on the four assigned weapon systems. Two weeks before our return to Yokosuka, the instructors were scheduled to fly aboard and begin classes. The training would last for about one week.

I explained to the men in the division, although this was considered a training evolution, and not an inspection, we still needed to make a favorable impression, because the instructors from San Diego, worked in the same department as the inspectors who would be conducting our inspection next year. I knew from experience that what the refresher-training instructors observed in W Division would eventually be talked about in the inspection branch. If we gave a favorable impression to the instructors, it would be to our advantage when our inspection began.

There were to be three instructors from San Diego. I received their clearance information in advance. It was to be CWO2 Tony Lewin, and GMTC Tommy Mize, who I'd been stationed with in Guam, and a GMT1 whose name was not familiar to me. I made arrangements to insure they all had good bunks, and living arrangements. We did a lot preparation, to insure "we rolled out the red carpet" for these three. I explained why I wanted to give these three special treatments, and make them feel welcome, to both Lieutenant Oelrich, and Commander Kellner.

On the 13th the three were flown aboard, and the next day the training classes began. CWO2 Tony Lewin and I felt we had met at some time in the past, but could not recall where, or when? It was good to see Chief Tommy Mize again. The training progressed over the next few days, and at the end of each day I made a report to Commander Kellner following our nightly eight o'clock reports meeting.

At the completion of the refresher training classes, the instructors had watched all the assembly operations, and had scrutinized everything within W Division spaces, and it was now time for CWO2 Lewin to make his report to Commander Kellner. I was with him in the gun boss's office when he gave him his verbal report. He said W Division operations were outstanding, and the division morale was at the highest level he had ever seen in any division on board any ship. Commander Kellner was very pleased, and escorted CWO2 Lewin to Captain Carmichael's at sea cabin, where he repeated his report. I relayed all this back to Chief Munson, and told him I was pleased and proud of the work the men had done. I asked CWO2 Lewin to repeat what he had told the gun boss, and captain, to the W Division sailors the following morning at quarters, which he did. I thanked all three for their help, and kind comments after they had addressed the division.

All three said if they had to go to sea, they would want to go on *USS Midway*. I was pleased that apparently the division was prepared for the upcoming inspection. CWO2 Tony Lewin and I were to cross paths again in the future.

The ship had a television station that broadcast programs, including newscasts, and movies, throughout the ship via cable. During flight quarters, each aircraft launch, and landing was telecast over the television circuit. One popular broadcast was the nightly movie, which was shown at 8:00 p.m. We had a television in our bunkroom, and the four officers in the bunkroom, if not working, would watch the evening movie together. This was a pleasant diversion from my daily duties.

The evening before pulling into Yokosuka, the ship was filled with anticipation. I had only been away from home for three months, while the others on board had not seen their families for six months. On 26 November, *Midway* pulled alongside the Yokosuka Naval Base pier. The pier was crowded with wives and families anxiously waiting, and cheering, holding signs and banners, trying to spot their loved one among the 4,500 sailors. A band was playing on the pier, as the gangways were hoisted by cranes, in place on the quarterdeck, and after brow. The positioning of the gangways always seemed to be a long drawn out job, taking too much time to the impatient people on the pier, and those sailors anxious to reunite with their family. This was always a joyous and happy time for those sailors with families on the pier, and as I said before, a bittersweet time for those sailors that had no one waiting for them on the pier. As soon as the gangways were in place, the people on the pier came streaming on board. The hangar bay was filled with husbands and wives hugging and kissing, and children happily hugging their fathers, or in some case showing shyness, as they had not seen their father for over half a year. I bid CWO2 Lewin, Chief Mize, and the first class farewell, and looking on the pier saw Carmen walking up the gangway. We happily embraced, and were thankful to once again be together.

It was the day after Thanksgiving. Carmen had been very busy in my absence, finding a house to live in, unpacking our household goods, and getting settled in Japan. She had found a Japanese house located about twenty miles from the front gate of the naval base, in a community called Zushi-Numama. In order to travel from the ship to the house, we took a taxi from the ship to the train station, then boarded a train for eighteen miles, then at the train station boarded a bus, and finally getting off the bus at our bus stop, we had a 1/4 mile walk up a steep hill to our new house. The house was a wooden frame, two story, two-bedroom house. It was very well built, but not insulated as houses are in America. Everything in the house was built to a much smaller scale than houses in the USA. Covering the floor on the first floor was a thick straw woven mat, or straw rug. One room contained a sunken bathtub, which contained water that was heated to a high temperature for soaking. On the wall of this room was a water hose with a spray attachment. The Japanese method of bathing was to wash with soap, and rinse off your body with the spray hose, before getting into the hot bath, or as Americans called it "a hotsy bath," and then soak for as long as you wished. The bathroom on the first floor had a unique feature, an electrically heated toilet seat. The heat was turned on and off by means of a switch located on the wall near the toilet. As in all Japanese houses, there was a spacious entryway at the front door, used for shoe storage, when those entering the house removed their shoes. It was not possible to put all of our furniture that had been moved from New Mexico, into the small Japanese house, so much of our furniture remained in storage on the base, until such time we got into a house on base. This was a cold time of year in Japan. Heating was by a small gas heater, which we used to heat one room at a time. The heater could be moved from room to room, and connected to gas outlets located in each room.

As I said the ship arrived in Yokosuka the day after Thanksgiving, but Carmen had cooked a turkey in our new house, so we celebrated Thanksgiving one day late, as did most of the returning crewmembers.

A few days after our arrival back in Yokosuka, the *USS Midway* CV-41, 1979-1980 Cruise Books were given out to the sailors who had ordered them. I got one of the first ones to be handed out. After the first day of distribution of the books, the handing out of them was stopped by the executive officer. It had been discovered that in one of the group photos, of a group of sailors in engineering department, one of the sailors had exposed his penis. Special services, which were responsible for publishing the book, busily censored the remaining books, by blotted out the picture, before distribution of the books began again. The fireman guilty of exposing himself was taken to captain's mast and punished for his folly.

The first part of December chief warrant officers were scheduled to have fitness reports completed by the commanding officer. I did not know what to expect. Commander Kellner would write the report, and then the captain would review, and sign it. Shortly after the first of the month, the gun boss called me to his office to discuss my first fitness report on the ship. I was given an "A" in all evaluation blocks, was recommended for early promotion, and ranked number "2" out of the four CWO2's on board. This was my ranking in the "pack."

The report emphasized the good report W Division had received during our Refresher Training, and all the work I had completed since reporting aboard. I was very pleased with my first fitness report on *Midway*. Commander Kellner and I talked for a long while. He told me one of the things he did to be noticed by the captain, was to often volunteer for jobs the captain needed done, jobs that weren't necessarily pleasant jobs, but had to be done by someone. This reinforced in the captain's mind that he was a team player, and could be counted on. This was all tied to the philosophy of "breaking out of the pack," to be listed "number one" on the fitness report, and thus be noticed by the promotion boards, at promotion review times. This was the only negative area of my fitness report, being "number two."

On my birthday, I received what I considered to be one of the nicest birthday presents I'd ever received. I was to achieve a position I'd always dreamed of having, and on 8 December, it became a reality. For a couple of days I'd known that Lieutenant Oelrich was going to take over the job of weapons safety officer, which was held by a commander in operations department, who was transferring. I was to assume the duties of W Division Officer. I signed a relief letter assuming these duties on my birthday. The letter was then forwarded to the captain, and I was officially a division officer.

In mid-December I was surprised by a call from the executive officer. He wanted to see me right away. Baffled about what he wanted to see me for, I went to his stateroom. He told me he would like me to consider preparing a relieving book for Captain Carmichael, who was being relieved in February. He explained this would be a book that would list the ship's accomplishments since the captain had been in command of *Midway*. He said I would be assisted by a first class petty officer that worked in the public affairs office on the ship.

While I had more than enough to keep me busy, since I was now a division officer, and the only officer in the division, I nevertheless recalled the advice Commander Kellner had given me about assuming jobs that others often did not want. I told the XO, I would gladly accept the job of preparing the book. I only had two months to complete the book, as Captain Carmichael was scheduled to be relieved mid February. Some of the work on the book would have to be done while the ship was underway, as we were scheduled to pull out of Yokosuka 2 February, and return on 13 February. This short underway period was to be a familiarization cruise for the new captain. Following the change of command, we were to be underway for two and one half months. With Carmen's help, I bought a Japanese style scrapbook, which would hold the pages of the relieving/farewell book. I also painted a watercolor painting, of a wine bottle, and fruit still life, which had the captain's name, and the name of his wife, as well as the place and date of their marriage on the bottle label. This was a replica of the one I painted for Admiral Cruden in Guam, and others.

December and January were cold months in Japan, and as I said our Japanese house had non-insulated walls. We lived Japanese style, keeping one room at a time warm. Each officer reporting to *Midway* typically had a twelve-month wait until a base house became available. We had snow during the winter, and often I would walk the 1/4-mile from the house to the bus stop through fallen snow, going back and forth to the ship. Walking up the steep hill to my Japanese neighborhood, I began to realize again why so many Japanese people had strong, sturdy legs.

On 30 December, the ship's navigator, and the captain signed my OOD sign-off indoctrination book I had been working on since coming on board. The sign-off book contained a multitude of subjects such as: honors and ceremonies, rules of the road, internal ship's security, anchor watch, beach guard, shipboard emergency drills, man overboard, sneak attack, enemy boarding, what to do with people requesting political asylum and many, many more subjects. During each of my indoctrination watches, the officer I was standing watch with had questioned me. When he was satisfied that I knew a particular subject, he would date and sign my sign-off book. I was now a qualified Officer of the Deck, on a U.S. Navy aircraft carrier. In the absence of the captain, while on watch, I was his substitute, and in command of a crew of more than 4,500 men. During an OOD's watch, he issues orders that must be obeyed by all onboard, regardless of rank, just as though the orders came directly from the mouth of the captain. This was an awesome responsibility that I took very seriously. Anytime the ship was in port, alongside a pier, or at anchor in a bay, an Officer of the Deck was stationed on the quarterdeck, which was at the hangar deck level. This was the entry and exit point for ship's officers, and visiting dignitaries. There was also an after brow, which was on the after section of the hangar deck level, and served as an exit and entry point for enlisted men. Normally a chief petty officer was stationed here for a Junior Officer of the Deck (JOOD) four-hour watch. This was a watch I had stood in the past on the USS *Oriskany*. The JOOD had one or two messengers of the watch to assist him. As OOD, I had an armed marine sentry, a Boatswain's Mate, usually a third or second class, who was responsible for making announcements over the ship's public address system (one MC).

Announcements such as arrival/departure of the commanding officer, meal call, mail call, ringing the ship's bell on the hour and half hour, and other general announcements. A whistle on his Boatswain's Mate's whistle, called a "bosun pipe", preceded these announcements. I also had on the quarterdeck a messenger of the watch, normally a seaman from the deck department, who assisted the Boatswain's Mate of the watch, or who I used to run errands. The watches on the quarterdeck were usually very busy and event filled, and four hours went by very quickly. The night watches, such as the mid-watch from midnight to 4:00 a.m., and the 0400 to 0800 watch went by much slower. The turnover of the watch from the OOD being relieved, to the assuming OOD was a very formal ceremony. To assume the watch, I had to be on the quarterdeck fifteen minutes prior to the hour, in the appropriate dress uniform, and be briefed by the off-going Officer of the Deck. When I fully understood what had transpired on his watch, and understood any orders that were to be carried out, and he had answered any questions I had, then I would salute him, and state, "I relieve you Sir." He would return my salute, and say, "I stand relieved." At that point I would officially be the OOD. It was not uncommon to stand eight hours of OOD watches every fourth or fifth day, as the ship was often short of qualified officers. These watches were time consuming, and in addition to my duties as a division officer. There was a canvas roof over the quarterdeck to keep rain and snow from falling on the OOD, Marine Sentry, Boatswain's Mate of the Watch, and the Messenger of the Watch. We were all standing in an exposed area. The only source of heat was a small compartment just off the quarterdeck in which there was the ship's loudspeaker system, telephone for both the ship, and a line for calls ashore. There was also a small coffee pot, within this compartment. This was a cold environment to be in for four, sometimes eight hours, in the winter months. There was also no opportunity to make "head calls" (go to the bathroom), unless temporarily relieved by another OOD. While standing my OOD watch I often wore "long johns," or insulated underwear under my uniform.

Following four hours of this intense watch, I would be exhausted, yet it was exhilarating to think of the authority and responsibility of being in charge of one of the largest man-of-war ships of our country. An additional duty of the OOD during a morning, noon, or afternoon watch, was to sample the crew's mess. A special table was set up on the enlisted mess decks, where the Officer of the Deck would eat a meal served from the enlisted mess line. This sampling would take place after being relieved on the quarterdeck. Following the meal, a two-page questionnaire was filled out describing quality, taste, etc., of the food. This questionnaire was signed by the OOD, and reviewed by the food services officer, and the executive officer. The food on board *Midway* was generally outstanding. The food services divisions were awarded numerous Navy-wide awards for excellence.

As well as standing Officer of the Deck watch, each officer in weapons department stood Weapons Department Duty Officer on duty days. This entailed being responsible for anything that went on within weapons department in the absence of Commander Kellner. When the gun boss was off the ship, the weapons department duty officer attended nightly eight o'clock reports, with the Command Duty Officer, who was the substitute for the commanding officer. The command duty officer was normally a department head. This system of duty sections extended down to the division level. Within W Division, twenty-four hours a day, there were always two awake watch standers, in port, and at sea. This concept of watch standing, and duty sections is foreign to the other armed services. The Navy has adhered to the policy of always having enough sailors on board ships, as I've repeated before, to get underway in the event of an emergency, ever since the attack by the Japanese at Pearl Harbor, Hawaii.

In Yokosuka, wives could come aboard until 2200 (10:00 p.m.) On duty nights, if I did not have a quarterdeck watch in the evening, Carmen and Mary would often come on board and we would have dinner together in the wardroom.

When we had first arrived in Japan, in addition to the culture awareness class Carmen and I had taken, we also took a weeklong driver's education class that would prepare us for obtaining a Japanese driver's license. We had to learn how to read Japanese road signs, adjust to driving on the left side of the road, and pass a written exam, as well as a driving test. It was a difficult course, but we both passed. I accused Carmen of bribing the Japanese instructor, because she bought him a carton of cigarettes. The Navy wives had told her this was a sure way to pass the course.

We were anxious to have our own transportation, and luckily we soon found one, shortly before Christmas. A chief warrant officer who worked in the food services division was transferring and wanted to sell his car. It was a 1972 Toyota station wagon, in very good condition, and although only eight years old, we bought the car for $750.

As part of agreements between Japan and America, automobiles owned by servicemen did not have to undergo the extensive annual car safety inspections that Japanese auto owners were required to undergo. I did however, have a scaled down safety inspection each year which was of the horn, lights, and tires. I purchased auto insurance from a company located off base that specialized in selling auto insurance to sailors.

One task that was time consuming for division officers on the ship was the task of going to captain's mast with sailors. A sailor was placed on report for violating a regulation, or an article in the Uniform Code of Military Justice (UCMJ). Report chits contained a description of the violation, and statements of witnesses, and were processed by the ship's Master at Arms (MAA's) office, which was the ship's police force. The MAA's worked directly for the executive officer. When a sailor in W Division was placed on report, I as division officer was then required to interview the sailor, get his side of the story, and try to determine the facts of the offense. If the violation was serious enough to warrant a summary court martial or general court martial, which was above the level of captain's mast, then I had to involve the ship's legal office that was manned by naval lawyers. If the offense was one punishable by captain's mast, I gave the sailor advice about how to act during the mast proceedings. If it were appropriate, I would act as his defense counsel.

The executive officer held "XO's Mast" and reviewed all offenders' cases, prior to captain's mast to see if the case warranted mast. XO's mast was usually held once a month, and could involve as many as seventy to one hundred ship-wide cases. This meant waiting most of the day for a ten or fifteen-minute audience with the executive officer. XO's mast involved all the people associated with the report chit, and the accused, as well as myself. The executive officer stood behind a podium with his marine escort, and master at arms standing by. Often Chief Munson, as W Division leading chief would be standing at attention with me, with the accused sailor. If it was a minor offense, such as a few minutes late for muster, or a uniform infraction, the executive officer would dismiss the case, and award a minor punishment, or leave the discipline punishment up to me. But some of the cases were passed on to captain's mast, which was held at a future date.

One case that stands out in my mind was a young seaman in W Division that was placed on report for breaking a mirror in a Yokosuka Japanese bar. The details of the case were not clear, it seems there were many sailors in the bar, a beer bottle had been thrown, and a large mirror behind the bar had been broken, the shore patrol was summoned. The witnesses in the bar weren't sure who had thrown the bottle, but it had been thrown from the area where the seaman was sitting. Chief Munson questioned him first, and then I sat down with him. He swore that he did not throw the bottle. He was so strong in his denial that I felt he was telling the truth. I told him I would vouch for him at executive officer's mast, as he had not been in trouble up to this point, and had been a reasonably good worker. I emphasized to him that it was important that he be truthful with me. Up to the minute that we walked into the executive officer's cabin for XO's mast, he insisted that he had not thrown the bottle.

At the appointed time, Chief Munson and I walked into the XO's cabin. The seaman was escorted in by the MAA's, and he stood at attention before the XO while the MAA read the charges. The executive officer then asked him, "Seaman what do you have to say to these charges?" He immediately blurted out, "I did it Sir. I threw the bottle!" I was shocked, and from the look on Chief Munson's face he was shocked. The XO asked, if I as division officer had anything to say in his defense. I told him I didn't have anything to say concerning the case. The XO referred him to stand captain's mast. After we all left the XO's Cabin, I told the seaman I was very disappointed in him, and had he not lied to me, I would have helped him in any way I could, but now I had very little trust in anything he said. He was awarded a reduction in rate, and a fine at captain's mast. In a case like this I had to suspend his access to division spaces, and assign him work outside the weapon spaces, until such time he might once again be approved to work in W Division.

I was fortunate in W Division, because the GMT's had the additional pressure to avoid trouble, as they could lose their security clearance, and thus their job as a GMT. Also as a group they had a higher educational level than the majority of the ship's enlisted crew. Some of the officers in weapons department, such as Ensign Norm Peters, spent many hours with numerous sailors in his division that had been placed on report.

One day in January all ship and squadron officers were directed to muster in the forecastle, with the captain. This was a large enclosed compartment in the bow of the ship, from which the ship's huge anchors were dropped and retracted. This was one of the largest compartments of the ship that could hold the estimated 400 officers called to the meeting.

When everyone had assembled in the forecastle, we saw television sets positioned around the compartment. The captain addressed us over a microphone, and it was soon apparent what the topic was. It was about illegal drug use.

There had been an accident on an east coast aircraft carrier that had been prominent in the newspapers for a couple of weeks. A pilot had crashed his plane on the flight deck of the carrier, killing him, and a number of sailors working on the flight deck. Autopsies on the dead sailors revealed that most of them had been under the influence of marijuana, heroin, and other illegal drugs at the time of their death. Since the ship had been at sea for longer than a week, the amounts of illegal drugs in their bodies indicated that the drugs had been consumed while the ship was at sea. The Navy was being "drug over the coals" by the press, inferring that the Navy was filled with drug-crazed sailors defending the nation. Other than jobs such as mine, where drug usage was absolutely not tolerated, the enforcement of illegal drug usage was conducted half-heartedly. Some commands even looked the other way, with the attitude that since illegal drugs was so prevalent in American society; it was only natural that illegal drugs would be in the Navy ranks.

After the captain addressed all the officers, he then directed our attention to the television sets, located about the compartment. A VCR connected to all the TVs was turned on, and the Chief of Naval Operations (CNO) appeared on the screen. He spoke of the recent smear of the Navy in the press, and turmoil it had caused. He said there was to be a new "watchword" in the Navy, it was, "No drugs, not in my Navy." New guidelines were being issued for all Navy commands. He said there was to be a no illegal drug usage policy for officers and chiefs. Any illegal drug involvement was an automatic discharge, and loss of all benefits, and privileges. The same policy was to apply to petty officers. There was to be some latitude for lower ranks. Lower rank first time offenses would be met with harshly, with some corrective discipline. The main thrust of the new policy was that from this point forward there was to be "zero-tolerance" concerning illegal drugs in the Navy. This was a somber meeting, and welcome news to most of us; we now had clear directions. From that day forward the Navy began to "clean its own house" of illegal drug use in the ranks. Instructions eventually came down from the CNO directing periodic surprise urinalysis testing, and unannounced locker, and berthing, and barracks inspections. It was also directed that all service records be reviewed to identify those sailors that had past illegal drug violations in civilian or navy life, so warnings could be issued concerning any future involvement with drugs.

During this Yokosuka in port period there was a hail and farewell party, as there had been in Mombasa, the big difference being, that officer's wives were expected to attend. This gathering took place at the Yokosuka Naval Base Officer's Club. The weapons department officers would often get together, at Commander Kellner's house, with him and his wife Teddy as hosts. Carmen and I spent many nights at their house as guests. They gyrated toward us more so than many of the younger officers and wives, because we were closer to their age, and I like to think enjoyable company.

During January a number of officers who were to be assigned to weapons department checked aboard. One of the officers was Lieutenant Bill Essing. He was a pilot, and scheduled to be assigned as W Division Officer, so he could complete his "ticket punch." So my joy over being a division officer was short-lived. Bill was a unique individual. He was energetic, and anxious to learn about nuclear weapons, which he had no experience with. This was not a situation I was happy about. I only had a couple of months to ready the division for our big inspection, and being tasked once again trying to educate an inexperienced line officer was not an additional task I needed at this point.

The first part of February, the ship went to sea for a short period. We conducted flight operations, and general quarters. Weapons Department had a "gun shoot," which was a firing of the ship's five-inch gun batteries, and a "missile shoot," which was the launching of "ground to air" sparrow missiles. The missiles were fired at a target drone which was remotely controlled, and flown near the ship. All of this activity was for the soon-to-be new captain of *Midway*, Captain Robert S. "Rupe" Owens. He had been an A-6 *Intruder* aircraft pilot, and had made four combat deployments to Vietnam during his career. He had joined the Navy five years before me in 1955.

On 16 February, fifteen percent of the crew dressed in dress blues, mustered in the hangar bay, and stood in ranks during the change of command ceremony. I was not included in this group, so I continued working in W Division spaces. The approaching inspection date, in the latter part of April, was ever present in my mind.

The evening of the 16th, the ship reserved the base officer's club for a change of command party. The objective of the party was to honor Captain Carmichael, bid him farewell, and welcome Captain Owens. A program after dinner was served was hosted by the Executive Officer, Captain Carlsen. Much of the program was a "roast," poking fun at departing Captain Carmichael. Much of the teasing, and many of the humorous skits were directed at Captain Carlsen, who was short in stature. Both Captain Carmichael and Captain Carlsen accepted the satirical presentations in good humor.

At one point, I was called up to the stage located before the seated officers and their wives. I presented Captain Carmichael with the framed watercolor I had painted for him and his wife. One high point of the evening was when the XO presented Captain Carmichael the relieving book I had worked on. The executive officer had reviewed the book a couple of days previously, and told me he was very pleased with it. While working on the book I had given him weekly progress reports. I also made sure the executive officer was aware of all the people who had assisted me, especially the first class in the public affairs office. I also wrote a letter, via the executive officer to the public affairs officer, who was the first class's division officer, expressing my appreciation for all the hard work the first class had done.

Captain Carmichael addressed the crowd after the program and presentations were completed. Weapons Department officers along with wives were seated at one large table with Commander Kellner seated at the head of the table. At a table next to us, were a group of squadron pilots and their wives, who were very loud, and rowdy. One of the wives had obviously had too much to drink, and was talking loudly during the captain's speech. Finally after this loud talking had gone on for some time, Carmen turned in her chair, and told her to respect the captain, and shut up. She was immediately silent, and everyone looked somewhat shocked. No one mentioned the incident for the rest of the evening. The next day I happened to be in the weapons office, and Commander Kellner said he wanted to talk to me. I thought perhaps he was upset about the incident the previous evening. But he said he appreciated what Carmen had said, and he had spoken to the squadron's commanding officer about the rude, obnoxious behavior of his pilots during the gathering.

We were underway the day after the change of command and not scheduled to return to Yokosuka for two and a half months. A fitness report on my performance had been completed two months previously, but each time a change of command takes place; all officers receive a fitness report. I once again was given all "A's" and again ranked number "2" in the pack of four. Certain words and sentences in my fitness report were underlined for emphasis, and once again I was pleased with my fitness report. What I considered to be one of my most important jobs as an officer was the preparation of performance evaluation reports on my men. Early on in my job on *Midway*, I made it clear that I would not accept sloppy, or half-hearted written evaluations, or "evals" as they are commonly called. There were mutters, and displeasure among the W Division petty officers, because I was continually insisting that the evals they submitted to me be rewritten. Many of the third class, and second class petty officers had never written evals before as I had as an enlisted man. I conducted a number of classes on the proper way to complete the evaluation forms. I emphasized over and over again, that I considered the evaluation forms to be the most important piece of paper a leader would ever complete in the Navy. It was important not only to the man being evaluated, but also to the Navy. Evaluations were submitted at different time frames, spread out over the calendar year, for each rank. I was always involved each month in filling out, or evaluating evaluation performance forms.

Our Navy Technical Proficiency Inspection (NTPI) was scheduled for the last week in April. During this at sea period in February we were busy with magazine assembly teams training on the operations they would be demonstrating for the inspectors. Lieutenant Essing wanted to be fully involved, but he was interfering with many of our preparation efforts. Chief Munson relayed complaints to me about the lieutenant from the men. I tried to be a "buffer" between Lieutenant Essing and the crew. I tried to explain to him what to expect when the inspection began, and also how we should relate to and treat the inspectors. I personally liked Bill Essing, but his inter-personal skills were terrible, and he was not well liked by the officers, or the men.

The first of March the ship pulled into Subic Bay, Philippines for a couple of days. On one day I went with Chief Munson and Petty Officer Dick Clark to the base Fleet Reserve Association Club, where I renewed my membership, which had lapsed since leaving New Mexico.

Over the months I'd been onboard; my respect for the leadership qualities, and technical knowledge possessed by Chief Munson had grown. He was a firm effective leader, and as the sayings states, "Chiefs are the backbone of the Navy," Chief John Munson was the backbone of W Division. We had a mutual respect for each other, and I enjoyed his company on liberty off the ship.

March, found the ship at anchor off the city of Singapore. The city had changed since I last visited in the early 1970s. It was definitely more expensive, and crowded. After a four day stay the ship got underway.

On 27 March, a sailor was throwing a bundle of metal strapping off the ship, from a sponson that was an area used for dumping trash over the side while at sea. It was in the evening, and the sun had just gone down. His foot became entangled in the metal straps, as he was throwing a heavy bundle of the strapping off the ship. He was seen falling off the ship into the water far below. "Man overboard" was sounded throughout the ship. *Midway*, and the destroyers escorting us made a thorough search, but he was not found.

On 28 March, LT Bill Essing assumed the position of W Division Officer, and I once again assumed the position of technical monitor. On 29 March, I received a tremendous surprise. Commander Kellner informed me that I had been deep selected for CWO3. I had not been scheduled to be considered for promotion until after serving two years as a CWO2. I was being promoted a year ahead of time. CWO2 Mike Palotti, an aviation ordnance warrant officer in weapons department, and who lived in my bunkroom, was also deep selected to CWO3. This was something that happens to very few officers, so we both were very pleased about this surprise. The next day, Commander Kellner and I went to Captain Owen's at sea cabin, and the captain administered the oath of office of a chief warrant officer three. Before leaving Albuquerque in April 1980, CWO4 Charlie Schmidt, who worked in FCDNA, had given me a CWO3 collar bar. Captain Owens pinned this bar on my collar, after the oath was completed. Pictures of the ceremony were taken, and the gun boss and captain congratulated me. They both then said, in good humor, "Get back to work, getting ready for the inspection." The importance of passing this inspection was on everyone's mind, from the commanding officer down. I had to sign paperwork, obligating myself for service for two years. The good news was I had the title, and uniform devices of a CWO3, as I was in a "frocked status," which meant I had all the privileges, and authority of my new rank, but the bad news was I would not receive the increased salary of a CWO3 for another year.

On 31 March, the big news was that President Reagan had been shot! We anxiously awaited any additional news about this shocking event, hoping this was not a repeat of the Kennedy assassination.

The news from Yokosuka was that Carmen had been given a house on base. It was a three bedroom, older house, within walking distance of the base exchange and commissary. Also on base there were apartment towers, of twenty stories that families lived in, I was thankful that we had gotten a house. It's not entirely accurate to describe our new dwelling as a "house," it was more accurately a duplex, as there was a shared wall with a family that lived immediately next door. The other news from Carmen was that she had received word from San Francisco that Roger was in custody of a child protective agency. Our prediction had come true, as his father had abandoned him. We tried to figure out a way to get him to Japan, which involved a mass of red tape.

The magazine assembly teams continued to go through all the operations that would be demonstrated for the inspectors. All the operations would be completed on our training weapons, or those weapons that did not contain explosives, or radioactive material, but were realistic in every other aspect. An important list that needed to be prepared before the inspection was an inspection deviation list. This was a list that was provided to the inspectors prior to commencing the inspection that detailed specific things that were different from war reserve assembly operations. These specific things would be pointed out to the inspectors during the course of the inspection. An example of an item listed on the inspection deviation list might be a scratch or dent in a training weapon that would be overlooked during a weapon case visual inspection, and deemed acceptable. But if the GMT's had been working on a war reserve weapon the scratch or dent would have been considered unacceptable, therefore this was a deviation from a typical operation on a "real weapon." These deviation items had to be pointed out to the inspectors each applicable time. Chief Munson and I prepared a complete schedule of events. This schedule contained all the operations that would be demonstrated in both the forward and after magazines on the weapons systems. One important fact that was always a matter of concern was a violation of the two-man rule. Any time the magazines were opened and occupied, the two-man rule was in effect, with two W Division sailors in clear view of each other. The inspectors could never be considered one of the members of the two-man rule, so this was something the W Division sailors had to always keep in mind. A violation of the two-man rule was an automatic failure of the inspection.

During an inspection there were categories of minor deficiencies, and major discrepancies. Any action by an assembly team that would cause a weapon to have a decreased yield if it were used, if a cable was left disconnected, or any step neglected that might result in a weapon being a dud, or result in the weapon not performing as it was made to, meant an automatic inspection failure.

Along with the inspection deviation list, and schedule of events, a list of the minor discrepancies from the previous *Midway* inspection report, as well as corrective actions taken, was also prepared. Folders were made for each inspector that contained ships' information, and a ship's embroidered patch. I also insured there were staterooms available for the officers in the inspection team, and bunks available for the chiefs and petty officers.

In mid-April *Midway* pulled into Subic Bay. Carmen and Vicky Peters, Ensign Peter's wife, flew from Japan with a number of *Midway* wives to visit their husbands while the ship was in port.

The ship was to stay in port for five days. The Peters' and we stayed on a small island that was reached by boat, and had tropical screened huts for couples. This was a beautiful setting with palm trees, and beautiful tropical beaches. This was a wonderful respite from the intense inspection preparations we had been making. I made sure that W Division sailors had liberal liberty during this in port period.

The wild-west atmosphere of Olongapo shocked Carmen with the block after block of side by side bars, along with hundreds of women trying to entice sailors to come into the bars. She jokingly made the comment; "You're not coming to Subic again without me." Vicky Peters being Filipino knew what Subic was like. Not only was it her country, but also Norm and she had been stationed at the Subic Naval Base in the past, when Ensign Peters was an enlisted man. They told an interesting story about the time they were stationed here. Vicky's parents lived far to the south of Manila, on a remote island, with no electricity, or modern conveniences. Norm and Vicky assumed her parents would enjoy visiting them in their house on the base. They thought the parents would enjoy the pleasures of modern living with running water, air conditioning, all the things they did not have on their primitive island. The visit did not go well however. A couple of days into the two weeks visit, the parents were ready to return to their island. The air-conditioned base house was too cold and unnatural for them, and they missed sitting on their porch every evening chatting with neighbors in their village. Norm and Vicky thought they would be fascinated by television, but they were fascinated by the way people watching television appeared hypnotized by the screen. The parents didn't watch the screen, but watched Norm and Vicky, and their grandchildren intently watching programs. They were baffled why anyone would stare at a TV screen for hours on end. They were not impressed by civilization at all.

Norm and Vicky told us when they lived on Subic Base burglaries were common. Sailors and their families were cautioned about thieves sneaking through the base fence, breaking into homes stealing their valuables. One evening, Norm and Vicky, and their children were away from their house for a couple of hours. Upon returning to their house, the discovered their piano was gone! It was a mystery how the burglars managed to take an 800-pound piano out of the house and off the base without being detected.

After five days, Carmen returned to Yokosuka, and the ship got underway. We had a week before the inspectors would be flown aboard, and the inspection would begin. The division assumed I would have them working twelve hours daily training, as we had prior to pulling into Subic Bay. I told them all the morning we pulled out that we were going to have a relaxed work schedule for the week prior to the inspection, because if we were not ready now, we never would be. I told them I had confidence in them, and knew they would do well.

While in port, the ship had gotten a message listing the inspector's names. I knew two of them, GMT1 Rich Meredith who had been on *USS Ticonderoga* with me, and a senior chief I'd been on Guam with. I was surprised to see this senior chief's name on the list (I'll not mention it), as I'd known him as a first class, and at the time I didn't think he had the competency, or technical knowledge to ever become a chief petty officer.

The inspectors came aboard on the COD (see photo page) aircraft. A few days after the inspection was completed, the *Midway* was scheduled to pull into Perth, Australia. I'm sure there had been inspectors in San Diego fighting to be on this inspection team, and visit Australia. Few ships had the opportunity to visit Australia. It was rumored to be one of the best liberty ports in the world for American sailors.

A commander led the inspection team. The day after flying aboard, with Chief Munson and me insuring that they were settled comfortably in, there was a meeting with Captain Owens, who welcomed the inspection team aboard. Commander Kellner, Lieutenant Oelrich, Lieutenant Essing, and I represented weapons department at this meeting. After the welcome meeting, the inspection officially started. Lieutenant Essing was visibly nervous. I was anxious to get started, when finally the operations in both magazines began.

At the end of each day the inspectors would give Lieutenant Essing and me a briefing on how the day's operations went. We would be told of any discrepancies, or problems. After this briefing, we would brief Commander Kellner, who would then brief the captain.

On the second day of the inspection, Lieutenant Bill Essing did something I was not pleased about. He had been frustrated about not being actively involved in the preparations for the inspection, and now the conduct of the inspection. This was naturally because he had no experience with the nuclear weapons program, but it was not in his nature to passively stand by. He told me he did not like the senior chief on the inspection team that I had been stationed in Guam with. Lieutenant Essing had taken him aside, and given him a chewing out about needing a haircut. I did not need this added tension during my effort to complete the inspection. This also set the stage for what was to happen later.

At the end of each day's operation, the inspectors had very little negative news to report. The operations in the magazines were going very well. Each assembly team had to demonstrate emergency procedures to the inspectors at some point during the inspection. This was an emergency scenario that the inspectors would surprise the GMTs with. It could happen at any time, and everyone was expected to react appropriately. These simulated accidents would involve everyone on board *Midway*. In the event of an explosion, compartments of the ship would be sealed off, and the medical department would be called upon to treat casualties. The Explosive Ordnance Disposal (EOD) Team on board would respond to the accident site to assist in disarming, or safing any weapon involved. In all accident scenarios I had sailors that would don Oxygen Breathing Apparatus's (OBA's), and re-enter the magazine where the accident occurred. We naturally trained to be ready for a real accident, and we had practiced prior to the inspection on many varied scenarios. The inspectors sprung the simulated accidents on both the forward and after magazine crews, and they, and the ship reacted very well. I was pleased with the performance of all the GMTs thus far, and everything seemed to be going very smoothly.

The fourth day of the inspection, the last scheduled assembly operations were close to being finished in the afternoon. I was in my office in the forward spaces when I got word that the inspectors had stopped the assembly operation in the after magazine. The crew and the inspectors were coming forward to talk to Lieutenant Essing and me. After a few minutes, they entered the office; I knew it was bad news. The Assembly Team Leader GMT2 Halpin and the Quality Assurance Petty Officer GMT1 Clark was pale-faced, and silent. The inspectors said they were going to have to assign a failure grade on the weapon system the crew had been working on. This was disastrous news. All of the inspectors were apologetic, except the senior chief I knew from Guam, he appeared to be smirking at Lieutenant Essing, and me. I'll try to explain the operation the inspectors were observing, so the reader can understand what happened, and what was to happen later on.

Some weapons had warheads that were pressurized with dry air. The fuzing and firing section of the weapons were located within the warhead section. This section of the bomb needed to be pressurized to prevent a condition known as "high altitude arcing." This was to permit electrical components in the fuzing and firing circuits to operate properly when a weapon was flown at high altitudes hanging on an aircraft wing. The pressurization of this bomb section required an operation called "purging', which was accomplished with nitrogen. The assembly team would connect a nitrogen bottle to the weapon case with a rubber hose, and pressurization valves. The purging operation involved pressurizing the weapon case to a certain pressure, then allowing the case to remain at this pressure for five minutes, then letting the nitrogen bleed off for five minutes. This pressurizing and depressurizing were to be accomplished five times. This purging was to clear the warhead case of any fumes from the interior plastic parts, or any foreign gas that might be present within the case. Following the last purging cycle, the case was pressurized with dry air. Then the weapon tail was reinstalled. The tail installation made the pressurization valve on the warhead rear case inaccessible.

The assembly crew in the after magazine, had pressurized the training warhead case with dry air, and then installed the weapon tail. The inspector asked the crew leader GMT2 Halpin, if he had completed all steps up to that point? Both GMT2 Halpin, and GMT1 Clark replied, "Yes Sir." At that point the inspectors stopped the operation, and said they had reached a "point of no return," and had not completed the purging operation. They said based on this they were awarding a failure grade on this weapon system in the after magazine. I did not agree that the operation had reached a "point of no return." I questioned GMT1 Clark, why they had installed the tail and had not performed the purging operation. He said he didn't know, but they had just skipped it. I looked at the check sheets they had been using, and the purging steps had not been marked with a grease pencil, and initialed by GMT1 Clark, as they should have been. Had the inspectors allowed the operation to continue, at the end of the operation the team leader and QA inspector were required to review the check sheets to insure that all steps had been marked off with a grease pencil. I felt at that time they would have caught the omission of the purging, and backed up and completed the operation, but the NTPI inspector did not let the operation continue that far. I had also instituted a procedure that when a weapon operation was complete, paperwork was submitted by the crew that listed the times of the purging operations. There was a blank for each five-minute space of time. This paperwork was submitted by the crew to Chief Munson, who reviewed it, and then I reviewed it for final approval. Had the inspectors allowed the operation to continue, the crew, Chief Munson, or I would have caught the omission, and the purging operation would have been completed. Lieutenant Glen Oelrich, Lieutenant Bill Essing, and I immediately briefed the gun boss. Commander Kellner looked worried, I insisted that this was not a solid case for a failure, as the inspectors had not allowed the operation to continue to what I felt was a point of return.

I knew positively that we would have caught the omission with all the safeguards that we had in place. I did not say it, but I felt this was probably a case of the senior chief who had been humiliated by Lieutenant Essing, jumping on a situation so he could declare a failure, as he was the one who stopped the operation.

That night after eight o'clock reports in the weapons office, Commander Keller asked Lieutenant Essing and I to remain after everyone else had left the meeting. He was furious, he said the captain was very upset, and had told him if this affected his career, then Commander Kellner's career was finished. Commander Kellner said he would do likewise to our careers. I told him it was not fair to punish Bill Essing for the failure rating, since he had just reported aboard, and that I was the one responsible for all the preparation, and training prior to the inspection. I told him I took full responsibility for what had happened. He then curtly told us we were dismissed. Outside the weapons office, Bill told me thanks for what I had said. I was upset over this, and told Bill I would talk to him later. I took a long walk through the hangar bay. I felt this might be the end of my career in the Navy. Up to this point I had not known a technical failure in my job, with the exception of the one small failure on the *Oriskany* that I had no control over. I'd certainly not had failures when I was the one in charge. I did not sleep well that night.

There was one more day of inspection. In the morning I tried not to let my disappointment show, and encouraged the crew to keep up the good work, as the inspection was soon to be over. There was a somber atmosphere throughout the division. The end of the day the inspection was officially over, and the inspectors gathered to write the inspection results report which would be read at a meeting in the morning with the captain, and all those who had been at the welcome aboard meeting.

The next morning the group gathered in the captain's stateroom. I asked Chief Munson to be present also. The inspection commander read the report, and all areas were graded outstanding except the one weapon system, which was graded unsatisfactory. Lieutenant Oelrich and I had worked on a statement the previous night, which stated our objection to the grade as we felt the operation, had been stopped prematurely. We stated that the operation would not have been declared complete, until I had reviewed the paperwork, and at that point the omitted purging operation would have been caught. The statement was rather lengthy, and pointed out that the forward magazine team had completed the exact same operation, and we had reviewed the operation paperwork that we had not been given the opportunity to in the case of the after magazine. In retrospect, these many years later, I still feel it was a case of the senior chief, being vindictive toward Lieutenant Essing, looking for any excuse to fail the division. The grade stood however, even after our statement was read. The commanding officer of NWTGP San Diego would review the inspection report, and our statement, before a final determination was made about the grade. This review would take a considerable time, and in the mean time the after assembly team was decertified on this particular weapon system, and I would be required to show what corrective action I took to resolve the discrepancy. The overall grade was satisfactory, only "satisfactory," or "unsatisfactory" was given as an overall grade. An overall unsatisfactory grade would have meant the ship was decertified as a nuclear capable ship, with a re-inspection in a matter of weeks, most likely with a new commanding officer on *Midway*. Commander Kellner and I probably would have been relieved. In the majority of areas we received a grade of outstanding; there were very few minor deficiencies. All the inspectors told the captain this was one of the best W Divisions they had seen on a carrier in many years. The captain appeared to be very pleased. With the exception of the one black mark, I was very pleased.

I returned to the division and congratulated the division on a job well done. Commander Kellner also came into W Division spaces, gave the men his thanks. He said the captain was very pleased, and he appreciated their hard work. He didn't mention the meeting him and me and Bill Essing had during the inspection. Our relationship continued as before, if anything he seemed to be overly friendly with me following the conclusion of the inspection.

The ship steamed toward Perth, Australia, and as the ship neared the equator, preparations were made for a "crossing the equator ceremony." I was a "shellback," having crossed the equator while on the *USS Oriskany*. Chief Munson and GMT1 Clark were the only other shellbacks in the division, so we would be initiating all the "pollywogs" in the division. A unique situation on the ship, as had been the case on the *Oriskany*, was the fact that our captain, Captain Owens had never crossed the equator, so he was a pollywog, and subject to the initiation process. On the day the ship crossed the equator, all the shellbacks dressed as pirates, and we spent the day overseeing the initiation. The initiation was very subdued, compared to the one I had gone through years before on the *Oriskany*. In the past there had been a couple of accidental deaths during the initiations, so now all crossing the line initiations were closely supervised.

The pollywogs were still soaked with fire hoses, and required to get into coffins filled with garbage, and kiss the "royal baby's belly" which had been smeared with grease. Captain Owens was given special attention by all the shellbacks, and he participated in the ceremonies of humiliation graciously, and humbly. He was a good sport throughout the whole affair.

One unpleasant task I had after the inspection was to sit down in my office with GMT2 Halpin, and GMT1 Clark and discuss the ramifications of their mistake during the inspection. I told them I still had confidence in their technical abilities, but I was under pressure from the gun boss, and captain, and I was also required under the stipulations of the inspection report to show corrective action concerning their mistake. I told them I was placing a letter in their service records decertifying GMT2 Halpin as a team leader, and GMT1 Clark as a quality assurance inspector on the particular weapon system they had been working on. These letters would remain in their local service record (a copy would not leave the ship to be included in their service record on file in Washington, D.C.), until they completed a two month training cycle on the weapon system, participating in a few training operations. They both tried to object, as I knew this was a blow to their egos, but I assured them these letters would not leave the ship, and I would personally destroy them after two months. I also assured them this would not affect their performance evaluations, but I hoped this would serve as a lesson for them to be vigilant in the future, and not assume since things were going so well during an inspection, they could relax and not pay attention to detail. I knew they were both unhappy, and I personally liked both men. Clark had been a friend for many years, but I could not let that affect taking the action I felt was proper. The mistake they made had resulted in marring an otherwise perfect inspection, and although I hoped the inspection grade would be overturned, I had to assume it would not. The mistake had a far-reaching impact that went all the way to the Joint Chiefs of Staff, the highest-ranking officers in the military, as they reviewed the inspection reports. They had to realize that mistakes had consequences. I would not hesitate to back them up when they were right, but on the other hand, our business was so serious, that mistakes could not be tolerated. I also had to demonstrate to the other GMTs that they could not make mistakes without consequences.

We had a short slack period, but not for long, there was to be another round of inspections in a couple of months. We were scheduled for a Nuclear Readiness Inspection, which was part of the ship's Operational Readiness Inspection. There was also to be a Ship's Explosive Safety Inspection, and a Command Administrative, and Material Inspection. *Midway*, as a forward deployed carrier, unlike other carriers' home ported in the U.S., was expected to be battle ready all the time. Other carriers only underwent readiness inspections prior to deployments outside the United States. To insure our battle readiness our inspection schedule was very full indeed.

Another unique difference on *Midway* as a forward deployed carrier, and a difference I had begun to appreciate, was the fact that the squadrons of pilots, and squadron support sailors that made up the air wing were permanently stationed on board *Midway*. This was not the case on U.S. home ported carriers. Just prior to deployments on these carriers, the air wing would come on board, having been stationed at Lemoore Naval Air Station, San Diego, Alameda, Norfolk, or whatever naval air station was nearby the deploying ship's home port. The ship's company sailors and the air wing sailors, although "in the same boat," acted like separate commands. Working relationships took time to be established, and there was always some animosity between the "back shoes" (ships' company sailors), and the "brown shoes" (air wing sailors). As soon as these carriers returned to the U.S. following deployments, the air wing would pack up and return to the naval air station. The brown shoes or "airedales" would not have to contend with the difficult living conditions during yard periods, as I mentioned before, that the ship's company sailors had to contend with, so this was some source of the animosity between the two groups. Each deployment of the carrier there would be different squadrons deploying with the ship, so the ship and air wing would only have a six-month relationship. On *Midway* the air wing was permanently stationed on board, so we definitely were all "in the same boat together." The working relationships were much smoother than on the other carriers I'd been on, and the long-term relationship between the ship and air wing worked very well. The only time the planes were off the ship would be in the event *Midway* had to go into dry dock, then the planes would be flown to Atsugi Naval Air station. There was also the fact that we all lived together on the ship and together with our families on the base as neighbors, this contributed to the cohesiveness we experienced. Being in a foreign country brought all of us closer together than we would have been living in the United States. I had friends among the pilots and squadron sailors that I probably would not have had aboard any other carrier.

We anchored off the port of Perth, Australia. As I mentioned before, each country had its own odor, and Australia smelled much like the United States ports. I had duty the first day at anchor.

The following day I got onboard a liberty boat, and went ashore. There on the pier were fifteen or more scantily-clad show girls, such as you might see in Las Vegas stage shows, greeting each liberty boat, with a dance show. Also, tied up at fleet landing was the Australian aircraft carrier *HMS Melbourne*.

The country reminded me of America as it was in the 1950s. Perth was a very beautiful, clean city. I did some shopping, and found some opal jewelry, which are gems unique to Australia. I also purchased a couple of sheepskin rugs. All the W Division sailors reported that the Australian women were very friendly toward Americans. There was an underlying reason for this acceptance of American sailors. Australian men were known for their lack of manners, or consideration toward women. Most U.S. sailors would open doors, pull out chairs, and try to be gentlemen toward the so-called weaker sex. The Australian women enjoyed this treatment that they did not experience from their male counterparts. Carmen related a story to me about an incident that occurred while I was away from Yokosuka during an at sea period. An Australian Navy cruiser pulled into Yokosuka for a port visit. It was common for the *Midway* Officer's Wives to welcome ships of different nationalities to the Yokosuka Naval Base. She said the wives went aboard the Australian ship, and they were treated discourteously, and rudely. They all agreed they would not greet another Australian ship in the future.

There was an impressive World War II memorial high overlooking the city that I visited. Also, while in Perth, I treated Chief Munson to a dinner. After the inspection, I had told him I wanted to treat him to whatever kind of dinner he'd like, as a small appreciation for the wonderful job he had done preparing for the inspection. He said he would like a Mexican dinner. We looked and looked throughout Perth, but there were no Mexican restaurants. The closest we could find was a restaurant that served food from Spain. While we ate, we had a Spanish violinist playing near our table. Many sailors enjoyed visiting the ocean beaches of Perth filled with sunbathers. The main reason for their enjoyment was because many of the women sunbathers were topless.

The news from Yokosuka was that the paperwork for Roger's travel to Japan was finally complete. Carmen flew to San Francisco, and returned to Yokosuka with him. Mary was doing very poorly in school, and would probably be held back a year instead of advancing to the next grade. While in San Francisco, Carmen had seen Peter, and he was doing well. He was nineteen years old, and sharing an apartment with a friend. Judging from the pictures she sent me of him, he had grown considerably.

We pulled anchor from Perth after a week, and steamed north toward the Philippines. While underway, W Division provided training bombs to the squadrons for aircraft loading team practice. The loading teams performed loading operations in much the same way W Division assembly teams performed operations. The loading teams were made up of team members, who were read steps to accomplish, by a team leader. During each weapon load, there was a loading officer overseeing the operation. W Division also supplied GMT's as safety observers. The loading team leader, safety officer, and the safety observers used loading checklists. I had all first class petty officers in the division assigned as safety observers. I was the senior safety observer. This was a very familiar job for me, having been a safety observer (also called technical monitor) for many years, on my previous three carriers. As I explained before, safety observers had the authority to stop the loading operation at any time a safety violation, or problems were observed. Safety observers also filled out a critique sheet on each loading operation. I would review the critique sheets, and provide them to the squadrons commanding officers, so they could use the critiques as a tool to evaluate each loading team's performance. Squadrons periodically underwent NTPI's conducted by the same inspectors from San Diego who conducted NTPI's in W Division. These inspections were just as critical, and as important as the ship's NTPI's. Loading operations were not small evolutions. They involved much coordination between ships' company, and the squadrons. The loading training weapons were kept within W Division magazines, loaded on bomb hand trucks. These training weapons were wheeled onto the magazine bomb elevators and moved up to the hangar deck level when loading practice was to take place. The trainers were treated in exactly the same manner as the real ones, or war reserve weapons. The marines were positioned around the training weapons at all times they were out of W Division magazines. In order for sailors to have access to the proximity of a weapon, cleared, authorized sailors wore a loading badge, and the armed marines kept all others away. The whole ship was alerted when these loading operations took place, and warned to stay clear and also that cameras and picture taking were not permitted in the vicinity of loading operations. The engineering department also provided special fire fighting teams that stood by during the loads for fire protection. I spent many hours providing suggestions, and advice to squadrons concerning their loading operations, and how to prepare for their inspections.

We pulled into Subic for a four-day visit, and then on to Yokosuka. It was always a joyful time to watch for Carmen on the pier, as the ship edged closer and closer to the side of the pier.

This time there were three persons waiting on the pier, Carmen, Roger, and Mary. I had requested a twenty days leave for this in port period. I needed to unwind after the pressure of the inspection, and all that had happened during the time at sea. I had a relaxing time on leave although I frequently went to the ship, which was tied up to the pier six blocks from our base house. I often went to assist Lieutenant Essing with some problem, or difficulty he was having.

During this in port period we had a division party at our base house. We provided all the food and drinks. The younger sailors especially enjoyed Carmen's cooking, and stuffed themselves. Many of them were away from home for the first time in their lives, and most of them had been born long after I had been in the Navy a few years! I realized many of the younger sailors looked to me as a father figure; many came from a broken home that had no father. As a substitute father, I had a lot satisfaction from seeing these young sailors mature, and require less daily supervision.

Carmen and I visited the officer's club, as it was one of the few social gathering places for officers on the base. One evening we were having dinner with four other wives, who were pilot's wives, and were alone. Their pilot husbands were on flying duty at Atsugi Naval Air Base, located sixty miles to the north of Yokosuka. We were having an enjoyable evening listening to the band that was playing that evening, and occasionally dancing. There were two gentlemen dressed in suits at a table next to us. They seemed lonely, so we invited them to join us at our table. I didn't catch their names, as they introduced themselves, but enjoyed their company. I assumed they were older officers from one of the ships other than *Midway*, which was in port. We had an enjoyable evening. When the lights were turned up as a signal that it was closing time, the waitresses were having trouble awakening a young officer who had fallen asleep at his table who had obviously had too much to drink. The older of the two men in suits, who had joined us, and I, helped the waitress wake up the young officer. We discovered he was from one of the destroyers that were in port. We helped him outside the club, flagged a taxi, and directed the driver to take him to his ship. After we loaded him into the back seat of the taxi, we then reentered the club. Carmen and the other wives were walking toward us to exit the club. The man in the suit with me said "It's much too early to call off the party, would you join me as my guests?" We all said "OK." He then said, "Follow me," and walked toward a door within the club that was locked. He removed keys from his pocket, unlocked the door, and we all walked through, being somewhat baffled. We all walked down a hallway, toward an area called the "Plum Room." It slowly began to dawn on me that the only officers who stayed in this area were admirals, or flag officers. At this point I was very thankful that I had treated this man respectfully throughout the evening. We arrived at an elegantly furnished large room with overstuffed couches and chairs. He then told the man accompanying him, "Wake up the chief of staff, and we'll have a party." It soon became apparent who the mystery man was; he was Rear Admiral Huntington Hardisty. He was going to be Commander Battle Force U.S. Seventh Fleet, Commander Carrier Strike Force U.S. Seventh Fleet, as well as Commander Carrier Group Five; all these titles meant he was to be the on-scene commander of naval forces in this part of the world. He was about to check aboard *Midway* where he would maintain his headquarters in the flag stateroom that was even more lavish than the captain's Stateroom. His large staff of officers and enlisted men would accompany him. He was to check aboard *Midway* in a couple of weeks, the first part of July.

One of his famous achievements was as an F4B *Phantom* II aircraft test pilot; he had set a world low-level speed record in 1961, which remained unbroken for sixteen years. He asked what I did on *Midway*, when I told him I was in W Division; we discovered that we had much in common. He had been a W Division Officer early in his career, and had been stationed at one time at Naval Weapons Evaluation Facility in Albuquerque, New Mexico.

His chief of staff, a captain, sleepily joined us, and we all stayed up until the break of dawn. The admiral and I had a lengthy discussion about carriers, and our experiences in the Navy. We enjoyed each other's company, and shared many of the same views about life in the Navy. I think he would have liked us all to stay longer, but finally the party broke up, with promises that he would see Carmen and me again in the near future.

The ship was scheduled for three busy months, the months of July, August, and September. The three inspections I mentioned were to take place, in addition there were to be port visits to Hong Kong, Korea, and Thailand.

The ship left Yokosuka the last part of June. W Division had made an agreement with Engineering Department's, M Division, to make a compartment swap. M Division had a need for a larger storage space. W Division had a compartment that had been used in the past for storage of "bird cages," that I mentioned earlier in my story. These were storage containers for components used by the old Mark 7 warhead.

This system had long been obsolete. M Division wished to trade a much smaller compartment. W Division agreed, although we were getting the worst of the deal, we could not justify having this large storage compartment. We agreed to make the exchange in a week. I had a crew of four men moving items from our compartment to the new one, in readiness for the exchange. One evening I received a complaint from the petty officer that was in charge of this working party. He said an officer had appeared while they were working, and had started hollering orders at them. I immediately went to the compartment, and confronted the officer. It was Limited Duty Officer (LDO) LTJG John Adam, the M Division Officer. He was screaming at the men as I walked up, telling them to clear the compartment out right now. I jumped into the middle of his screaming, and told Lieutenant Junior Grade Adam to stop yelling at my men. I told him we still had three days before the compartment switch was to take place. I told the W Division sailors to stop working, and clear out of the compartment, and told Lieutenant Junior Grade Adam to leave. I then locked the door. Lieutenant Junior Grade Adam said, "I'm going to talk to my boss." I said, "Good, I'll talk to my boss also." I then went to the weapons office, and told the gun boss what had happened. I told Commander Kellner, as far as I was concerned, if the LTJG was going to behave this way, and abuse my men, then the compartment exchange was off. Commander Kellner, and the engineering officer, who was a captain, had a discussion over the phone, and said the compartment exchange would take place in three days, and Lieutenant Junior Grade Adam and I should remain clear of each other. I had a dislike for him from that day forward, but later I was to be thankful for the restraint I used toward him when we had our argument. As it developed, the compartments were exchanged, and we signed paperwork making it official. Chief Munson and the crew got busy making our new compartment habitable. The new compartment was to be used as a storage area for our excess equipment, and as a personal storage area for the GMT's that bought items ashore, at the various ports we visited. The compartment was in poor shape. M Division had neglected it. The deck was retiled, and the entire compartment was repainted and refurbished, bringing it up to the outstanding condition all other W Division spaces were in. After the compartment had been nicely redone, and was in use, one day a couple of M Division sailors happened to look inside the compartment while it was unlocked and in use. They complained to Lieutenant Junior Grade Adam that it was a much nicer compartment than the one they had gotten from W Division, and now they felt it was much more convenient to their working spaces. Commander Kellner said the engineering officer had asked him if we would trade the compartment back for the old one. I said "No Sir" we had worked hard to clean up the compartment we had gotten from them, and their attitude throughout the exchange had been one of non-cooperation. I said I would only agree to the exchange, if he gave me a direct order. Commander Kellner said he didn't blame me, and told the engineering officer we would not exchange the compartments again. I did get some satisfaction, knowing that Lieutenant Junior Grade Adam regretted the exchange.

The ship anchored in the harbor of Hong Kong, and I had a special mission. I had been secretly saving money for a surprise for Carmen. Furs could be purchased in Hong Kong for a fraction of the cost elsewhere, and I was going to shop for a mink coat. After looking through many shops, I found a nice one, and stored it in my stateroom for the trip back to Yokosuka.

I had a number of OOD watches while the ship was at anchor in Hong Kong Harbor. One afternoon the 1200-1600 watch developed into one of the most harrowing watches I was to stand as officer of the deck on *Midway*. It happened on an afternoon when both the captain and executive officer were ashore. The *Midway* was anchored near the middle of the harbor, and the tide was going out. There were many ships of various nationalities anchored at different location about the harbor near us. About an hour into my watch, I got word from the bridge that a large merchant ship appeared to have broken anchor and was drifting toward us. The merchant ship was still quite a distance from us, but with the tide going out, the ship was drifting steadily toward us.

Collisions of ships, or the grounding of a ship, are an extremely serious matter in the Navy. As officer of the deck, it was my responsibility to avoid a collision. It was no simple matter, getting *Midway* underway; the engines had to be started up, an anchor detail mustered, and a number of other things to consider. I notified the command duty officer, and directed a qualified underway OOD to man the bridge, and give me an update over the intercom system every five minutes. I also notified the engine room to standby. This was a very nerve wracking situation; the bridge was trying to notify the drifting ship, but had not been able to establish communication. The minutes ticked by, and the five-minute reports continued giving the merchant ship's position closer and closer to *Midway*. The bridge asked a couple of times, "Are we going to get underway Sir?" I knew once I made a decision to get underway, and move, it was irrevocable. I estimated it would take at least ten minutes to pull anchor, and then another twenty minutes to slowly move out of the way and re- anchor.

I told the bridge to give me a time of fifteen minutes before collision was imminent, and at that point I was going to give the order to get underway. I had visions of a collision, and then later giving my testimony before an investigation board, seated behind a long green-covered table. All eyes were upon me, waiting for me to give the order, when a call came down from the bridge, that it appeared the drifting ship was slowing, and appeared to be dragging anchor. I breathed a sigh of relief, and whispered a thankful prayer, when it was reported that the ship had stopped its drift. I told the bridge to send a message to the merchant ship that *Midway* would appreciate it, if they would wait until slack tide and re-anchor outside a drift line from *Midway*'s anchored position. I was emotionally exhausted when the officer assuming the next watch relieved me.

After Hong Kong, the ship visited Pusan, South Korea. This was my first visit to this country. I shopped for brass souvenirs, and bought two leather jackets for Carmen and me, along with gifts for the kids. We were warned of taxi drivers who cheated sailors by overcharging fares. This happened to a couple of W Division sailors while on liberty. Tennis shoes were very cheap, and the stores were filled with them. The country at this time was governed by martial law, and armed South Korean soldiers were visible on every street corner. One memorable thing about the Korean people, they smelled like kim-chee, the pickled cabbage that was a popular item in their diet. This was the cabbage smell my Korean Taekwondo instructor in Guam had reeked of.

After a few days in Korea, we sailed for Pattaya Beach, Thailand. This was another country I'd never visited in all my years in the Far East. *Midway* was my passport to visit many of the countries I thought I'd never see. At Pattaya Beach the ship anchored quite a distance from the beach area. In order to go ashore, sailors would ride liberty boats, which would stop short of a large sandy beach, where they would have to remove shoes and socks, roll up pants legs, and jump into the surf and wade ashore. Going back to the ship, we had to wade from the shore out to the liberty boats, and climb aboard. On the late night boats returning to the ship, there were sailors on duty in the liberty boats, who helped their shipmates aboard, that had drunk too much of the Thailand beer. Pattaya Beach was a beautiful resort town nestled by the ocean. The white sandy beaches were lined with palm trees. The side-by-side bars that catered to tourists were reminiscent of Olongapo. A few bars along the main street offered unusual entertainment. A large boxing ring was set up in the middle of the open-air bar, and featured kick boxers. Many sailors, after a few beers would challenge the kick boxers, and would be permitted in the ring for a few rounds. Jewelry was very inexpensive; much of the gold jewelry was eighteen karats, which is purer than the fourteen karat gold jewelry Americans are used to. A popular attraction on the beach was boats that offered parasailing. Boats would speed away from the beach with sailors in a para-sail that would soar hundreds of feet into the tropical sky.

In July the ship was back in Yokosuka. I got off the ship with an armload of packages. At home I enjoyed watching the kids and Carmen open the packages of gifts I'd picked up at different ports. Carmen had opened all the packages, but one, which was a box with cowboy boots, pictured on the lid. I told her to open it last, as I'd bought some boots, but didn't care for them. I told her she could look at them if she wanted. She opened the box, and there was the mink coat I had bought for her. She was shocked, and so surprised, that she cried.

During this in port period, we had visitors from the States. Our friend from Fremont, California, Martha, and a friend of hers visited us for three weeks. We were anxious to hear news of her children Remedy, and Wayne. I gave them a tour of the ship, and we had dinner in the wardroom a couple of times while I was on duty. Martha was always on the lookout for a way to make a "fast buck." When I told her the ship was scheduled for a return trip to Korea, she asked me to buy $900 worth of tennis shoes in Korea, and ship them to her. She planned to sell them for a profit in San Jose, California. I initially said I would, but after she returned to the States, Carmen and I reconsidered, and decided against the plan. There was import, and export rules we might unknowingly violate, so we mailed Martha's $900 back to her.

Prior to getting underway for the next at sea period, the inspection team from San Diego that was to conduct the squadron's NTPI came aboard. A Navy Captain was the senior inspector on the team, who had a reputation of being a stern, inflexible inspector. I'll not record his name, but merely say his nickname throughout the fleet was "Captain Cobra." When he came aboard two days before the ship got underway, he did indeed strike like a snake! Commander Kellner happened to be the command duty officer on duty when the inspection team walked aboard. A stateroom had been reserved for "Captain Cobra," but he was very displeased with it. He asked for Commander Kellner, and when the gun boss arrived in the stateroom, Captain Cobra had him standing at attention for fifteen minutes, chewing him out. He was given a stateroom that was normally reserved for Admiral Hardisty's Staff. Commander Kellner told me later that he now understood why he had the nickname "Cobra."

Roger was adjusting to Japan, after his trip from San Francisco with Carmen. He was doing fair in school, but Carmen said she saw signs that he might be involved in drugs. She said during an argument with him, he had told her he would use drugs if he wanted to, and no one could tell him differently. I talked to him, and explained that Japanese laws were not like American laws. If he were arrested by the Japanese police for illegal drug possession, he could end up in jail for many years, and there would be nothing his mother, or I could do. He acted sullen, and I didn't feel like he believed me. I was on a few days leave at the time, and one day I went to the naval investigative service office on base. I told a detective in the office about my concerns over Roger. He told me that drug usage in the Yokosuka Base High School was rampant. I ask him if he would talk to Roger, and perhaps scare him with the consequences of being arrested in Japan. He said he would. We also had poor relationships with our neighbors who shared the duplex we lived in. They had complained that Roger played music loudly when we were not home. Instead of talking to Carmen or me about it, they had complained to the base police. This did not contribute to peaceful living; with hostile neighbors on the other side of the common living room wall we shared. Carmen and I had a number of conferences with Mary's teachers. She was not doing well in school at all. They decided not to hold her back a year, which we did not fully agree with.

The latter part of July, the ship pulled away from Yokosuka pier, and the squadron's NTPI began. W Division would be graded for support during this inspection, since we provided the trainers, and safety observers for the inspected loading operations. The first day of the inspection, I was overseeing the movement of the four trainers that would be used by the squadron's loading teams, when I was told that Captain Cobra wanted to see me. When I reported to him, he was scowling, and wanted to know why our trainers were in such bad condition. He said they look terrible. I agreed with him. I explained I was not happy with the appearance of the trainers when I had reported aboard a year ago. I said these trainers had been aboard since 1973, and subject to heavy squadron training cycles. I also said I had been stationed at NWSA Oakland, and all the carriers stationed on the west coast had the luxury of rotating trainers every two years with the naval supply annex for newly refurbished ones. *Midway*'s trainers had been in use for more than nine years. I explained I stored the trainers the only place I was permitted to, within our magazines. I was not permitted to perform large painting jobs, such as the ones that would be needed to improve the appearance of the trainers within the magazines. I had eight trainers onboard, and I had plans to repaint them during an upcoming yard period. He appeared pleased with my explanation, and said, "We need to get you some new trainers. I'll write up what you've told me in the inspection report, and you let me know if there's anything I can do to help you." He also said, "Don't worry about the cost; we need to support you better, keep up the good work." We had a few conversations after that, all which I reported to Commander Kellner. The gun boss had stayed clear of Captain Cobra, after the run in they had, and was anxious to hear what Captain Cobra was saying about the inspection.

During the squadron's inspection, the training weapons were positioned on bomb hand trucks within a roped off area in the hangar deck. The ship's marines guarded this roped off area. When a training weapon was pushed in or out of this roped off, and guarded area by a loading team, access was granted at one area of the cordoned off storage area. One marine checked loading badges against an access list, to insure only authorized sailors were being permitted within the storage area. The trainers being used had a low-level security classification. Nevertheless, the marines were trained to react as though they were guarding war reserves. Armed marines were stationed at each corner of the roped off area, to prevent unauthorized entry.

As I mentioned previously, "A marine on watch has no friends," he is trained to observe all as potential intruders. One morning during the squadron's inspection, a sailor strolling on the hangar bay, apparently thought he could take a short cut through the trainer's roped off area. He ignored the marines shouted orders to halt, and one of the marine guards "butt-stroked" him, which means the marine struck the sailor across the face with the rear stock of his M-16 rifle. A corpsman had to be called to tend to the injured sailor, and the disobedient sailor was taken to sickbay with a broken nose. Captain Cobra was upset by this incident, and chewed out the marine detachment's commanding officer. I did not agree with this. The marine was merely performing his duty as a sentry. No disciplinary action was taken against the marine. Since he was guarding trainers, it had been emphasized that he was not permitted to use deadly force. He was expected to use "reasonable force" protecting the trainers, had he been guarding war reserves, the sailor could have been shot.

All in W Division were well aware of the "deadly force" authorized to protect nuclear weapons. As I mentioned before, we knew if we were ever in a hostage situation the marines entering an area were weapons might be stored, were to shoot to kill all persons within the area. They were not to consider the lives of the hostages. Considering the awesome power of the weapons, this was the only possible action to take.

The entry to both the forward, and after W Division magazines, was through a square, large metal box that jutted out into the second deck passageway. On each of the three sides there were small, darkened, bulletproof windows. On the front side of the metal box, there was a small slot used for dropping our access badge into. The marine inside the metal box would take the badge, examine it, and compare it with the access list he held. After the marine compared your face to the photo on the badge, there would be a loud clanking noise, as the marine inside opened the heavy armored door, to permit access inside the metal box. Once inside the metal box, the door would immediately be shut. The marine would hand you your "inside badge," which had a clip on it used to fasten the badge on shirt pockets, and remain visible all the time anyone was within W Division spaces. After clipping on the inside security badge, a heavy door inside the marine's metal box was opened. Once inside, after closing the door, there was another inner door, made of thick metal bars that contained a numbered keypad. The correct numbers had to be pressed, before the door would open, and allow access down a ladder, which lead to the third deck office, coffee locker, and storeroom. The fourth and fifth deck contained the weapon's magazines. This description has been of the forward spaces; the after spaces were identical, although somewhat smaller.

The marine metal boxes guarding access to W Division spaces were painted green. While I had been growing up as a teenager in the 1950s, there had been a popular song called *"Green Door."* The lyrics of the song were about a guy wondering what was going on behind a green door. Some of the lines of the song went, "Don't know what they're doing behind the green door? But they laugh a lot behind the green door, wish I knew what was going on behind the green door." When I mentioned this song to the sailors in the division, and said it could be our division theme song, they just looked at me blankly. It was a song that was popular before most of them were born. I looked for a recording of the song all the time I was on *Midway*, but never found one. It was certainly an appropriate song for W Division's green entrance doors.

At the conclusion of the squadron's NTPI, there was a meeting with the inspectors, the commanding officer, and commanding officers of the squadrons, Commander Kellner, Lieutenant Essing, Chief Munson, and myself, for the purpose of reading the inspection report. All the squadrons were given a satisfactory grade, and W Division was given an outstanding for support. There was also a lengthy statement I had supplied to Captain Cobra about a plan I had to upgrade our onboard trainers. This plan included a repainting effort at Naval Magazine, Subic Bay, Philippines, and exchanging a couple of our trainers with NWSA Oakland.

A couple of days after the squadron's inspection, I received some tremendous news. The ship received a message stating that W Divisions inspection report had been reviewed, and the "unsatisfactory" grade we had received on one weapon system during our inspection had been reversed, and a grade of "satisfactory" was awarded. The NWTGP San Diego commanding officer and review board had determined that the inspector had stopped the operation prematurely (just as I had insisted). This was fantastic news. It was unheard of that results were reversed like this. Commander Kellner was ecstatic over the good news, and somewhat sheepish.

On 29 July, I stayed up all night with Carmen, and we watched the televised wedding of Prince of Wales, Charles Windsor, and Princess Diana Spencer.

A couple of weeks after the squadron's NTPI, while at sea, the squadron's held a training day to review some of the discrepancies they had gotten during the inspection. Loading operations were scheduled, and I was on the hangar deck during these operations. One of W Division's safety observers ran up to me, and said, "There's a problem with one of the trainers." I quickly followed him to the plane being loaded, and guarded by a marine. After gaining access to the loading area, the loading team showed me the training weapon's ARM/SAFE switch. The trainer was hanging on the aircraft wing's pylon, and had the electrical cable attached. The crew had been going through the standard electrical checks with the Aircraft Monitoring and Control (AMAC) box located in the plane's cockpit. When a step was read to check the ARM/SAFE switch on the bomb, the switch was observed to be in the RED ARMED position.

This was a problem of the highest degree. The Joint Chiefs of Staff (JCS) have peacetime safety rules that all nuclear capable commands are required to comply with. One of these rules states that the ARM/SAFE Switch of a weapon will never be in the RED ARMED position while handled on the ground. The only time a weapon ARM/SAFE switch was to be armed was in wartime, just before the pilot released the bomb over the target. Although this was a trainer, without explosives or radioactive material, we were still obligated to treat it exactly as a war reserve. I immediately notified the Explosive Ordnance Disposal (EOD) team, and also called Chief Munson up to the hangar deck. Chief Munson and I, along with the EOD team performed safing procedures. While this was going on, I was dictating a message to a W Division first class petty officer that was writing my words on a message form. A message was required to be dispatched immediately in an event like this.

As I explained previously there are different categories of accidents, and incidents with nuclear weapons, that are supposed to be reported instantaneously to higher authority. This incident with the trainer was classified as a lesser incident codename, "Dull Sword." Just as I had transmitted a "Broken Arrow" report on board *Ticonderoga,* this "Dull Sword" report was to be transmitted off the ship within minutes. After I was satisfied the message was ready for the captain's release signature, I sent the first class petty officer on his way to the bridge. After a few minutes I got word from the bridge that I was to report to the admiral's stateroom right away. I quickly climbed up the many ladders that led up to the admiral's area near the bridge. I was quickly ushered into Admiral Hardisty's office. This was the first time I'd seen him since our meeting in the officer's club in Yokosuka. He greeted me, and said he just wanted to make sure we wanted to send this message to the high levels the message was addressed to. The addresses on a message of this type include the Joint Chiefs of Staff, and the White House. I told the admiral absolutely, we were required to release the message within five minutes of an incident of this type. (About twenty minutes had already expired). He said, "Good, I just wanted you to reassure me." He said it was good seeing me again, and said to carry on.

The reason for urgency in a case like this was that higher authorities had to be made aware of an ARM/SAFE switch malfunctioning, even though we were working with a trainer, the exact same procedures were used with the real bombs, and these procedures had to be letter perfect. The Dull Sword message was transmitted, and the trainer was suspended from use. The trainer was eventually transferred off the ship, and a determination was made that the internal wiring of the trainer was faulty.

It was almost time for another round of inspections. The ship was to undergo an Operational Readiness Inspection, by an inspection team from the Commander in Charge of the Pacific, based in Pearl Harbor, Hawaii. Part of the inspection would include the loading of training weapons on aircraft. I was hopeful we would not have another incident during the inspection, like the problem with the trainer ARM/SAFE switch. The primary purpose of this inspection was to test the ship's battle readiness. This was an inspection all carriers underwent periodically, and the results of the inspections were used to select the winner of the Battle Efficiency Award, or "E," such as the E's won by *Ticonderoga* and *Oriskany.* As it developed, we did very well on the inspection. In conjunction with this inspection, the ship underwent an Administrative, and Explosive Safety Inspection, which we also passed. It seemed to me that there was an endless parade of inspections to undergo, and it was as though when we finished one, there were two more to look forward to! In August our Executive Officer Captain Carlson transferred, after being relieved by Captain Newman.

Prior to Captain Carlson's transfer he was given a farewell party in the wardroom. Almost every month a hail/farewell party was scheduled for departing, and arriving officers. Prior to Captain Carlson's departure, one of the enlisted men in Ensign Norm Peter's division embarrassed Norm. Late one evening in Yokosuka, a sailor in Norm's division came aboard the after brow, and had obviously had too much Japanese beer. He spied the XO coming aboard via the quarterdeck. The sailor drunkenly walked over to Captain Carlson, and put his arm around his shoulder (as I mentioned the XO was short in stature), and said, "How is Mrs. Carlson's little boy Johnny this evening?" The captain didn't say anything, but walked away to his stateroom. The next morning, the sailor, and Ensign Peters were standing before the captain, at XO's Mast.

Mid September found *Midway* once again in Subic Bay. Carmen flew down with a few of the other *Midway* officer's wives, and we spent a few days together. One evening at the Subic Officer's Club, while we were having dinner with Commander Kellner and his wife Teddy, a group of squadron pilots loudly went from table to table serenading tables with a song that had very obscene lyrics. We didn't say anything, but the gun boss was furious. He talked to the pilot's commanding officer the following day, and the pilots formally apologized for their behavior.

It was the end of September, and time I received another fitness report. I wondered how I would fare after the blowup in the Commander Kellner's office during the inspection. When it came time for me to sit down with the Commander to discuss my fitness report, he began our discussion by apologizing profusely, saying he was sorry for losing his temper, and that he should have trusted my judgment and technical knowledge. I was given all "A's" in the trait boxes, and ranked number two out of five.

Commander Kellner was transferring to San Diego, and his replacement came aboard during an in port visit to Subic Bay. His name was Commander Steve Quinn. He had been a test pilot, and was quite young to hold the rank of commander. We had also gotten a new LCDR on board, about a month before Commander Quinn. He was an LDO named Jerry Burrows. He was assigned the job within weapons department as the Ordnance Handling Officer (OHO), who was commonly called "O" "HOE."

He was responsible for the storage and handling of all conventional ordnance on board *Midway,* and was considered to be the second in command behind the weapons officer. Carmen and I became close friends with Lieutenant Commander Jerry Burrows. Although married, he had reported aboard alone. His wife and two daughters were going to join him in Japan in a few months as soon as the daughters were out of school.

In September we had another officer report to weapons department, who was a C-130 *Hercules* pilot, and was scheduled to relieve LT Bill Essing as W Division Officer. The C-130 pilot's name was Ray Danske. He was a young officer. His uncle was the founder of a company in Oregon that made a popular brand of boots. I reluctantly looked forward to educating yet another line officer as a W Division Officer.

The first of October the ship was steaming toward Yokosuka, when I received a message from Carmen saying that Roger was uncontrollable. The ship was about three days out, and since there was nothing of importance going on in the division, the gun boss got me a seat on the mail plane that was flying to the Atsugi Naval Air Station. I was catapulted off the ship and after landing in Atsugi, took a bus to Yokosuka, and surprised Carmen by walking into the house three days ahead of time. She and two couples were in the house discussing Roger when I walked in. I quickly learned that she had discovered that Roger was selling drugs, and would not obey her, or listen to her. Another bit of bad news was that she had gotten word from California that my Aunt Lois was very ill in the hospital, and not expected to survive. When Roger walked into the house later that night, he was shocked to see me. I told him I had no option but to take him back to the states. Otherwise, he might end up spending much of the rest of his life in a Japanese prison. He said, "Good, I want to go back to the United States." This was a painful experience; I felt if I'd been able to be with him consistently, instead of being away on the ship, things might have turned out differently. All the time he had lived with his father in San Francisco, he had not had any discipline, or a structured family life, and it showed. I was very concerned about him getting in trouble with the Japanese authorities.

When *Midway* pulled in I was on the pier. This was the first time I'd seen the ship pull in from this perspective. The ship looked huge approaching the pier. I went aboard, and began the paperwork submission for an emergency return to the United States. I would have to bear the cost of plane tickets, but I couldn't let cost be a subject of consideration. Everything fell into place quickly. Commander Quinn had not gotten a house on base for his family, so he and his wife and two children agreed to stay in our house during our absence and housesit, and also babysit Mary. On the long plane ride to Travis Air Force Base, California, Roger refused to sit with Carmen and me.

In San Francisco there was a delay getting Roger a place to stay within the child protection agency, and we had very little time before we had to travel back to Japan. After Roger was settled in San Francisco, Carmen and I returned to Travis Air Force Base, to catch a plane for the return trip. There was one seat on a plane leaving for Japan, but no vacant seat for Carmen. She urged me to take the seat, I hated to leave her, but otherwise I would be late getting back. I arrived in Yokosuka in time, but it was a week before Carmen finally made it home. The flight desk at Travis had misdirected her, and she ended up stranded in Hawaii for two days.

During our short stay in the United States, I'd been able to visit my parents, and Aunt Lois in the hospital. She was recovering in the hospital, and it appeared she was going to be all right, for which I was very thankful.

On the ship, Chief Munson had kept everything under control in the division in my absence. LT Ray Danske was sitting in the W Division Officer's seat. Bill Essing had been promoted to lieutenant commander, and was now working in the weapons office. Commander Kellner told me confidentially that he had created a job in the weapons office for Lieutenant Commander Essing to keep him out of everyone's hair. Commander Quinn was now seated in the weapons department head chair. A few days after Carmen's return, all the weapon's department officers gathered and we bid Commander Kellner farewell, and welcomed Commander Quinn. Before he left, Commander Gary Kellner, once again apologized for the threatening words he had said during the NTPI. Commander Kellner was an honorable and fair leader, and a good man to work for, all in weapons department would miss him.

Midway was scheduled for a yard period from mid-December to mid-March. I was anxious to have the W Division sprinkler system overhauled. I also wanted to improve the W Division berthing compartment. It looked like it was going to be a busy yard period. I remembered the unpleasant living conditions on board ships during yard periods, often no hot water, the noise, and dust, and all the inconveniences. Thankfully the ship had made arrangements for the crew to live in berthing barges, and barracks on base during the yard period. We would stand watches, and work within our spaces during the day, and live ashore at night.

During October, Lieutenant Commander Ron Bench, who was my detailer, stationed in Washington, D.C., paid a visit to the Yokosuka Naval Base.

He was to be at the base officer's club one afternoon, for the purpose of meeting with officers and discussing careers and future assignments. I met with him, and he said it looked good for me to have an assignment in Puerto Rico. I was scheduled to transfer in about seven months, and at that time there would be a job available at Roosevelt Roads Naval Air Station, Puerto Rico. I talked this over with Carmen. She said she would like to return to Puerto Rico, but was concerned about the terrorist's activity there. A Navy bus had been attacked, and sailors had been killed and wounded by Puerto Rican terrorists in the recent past.

I began to think about the possibility of extending on board *Midway*. CWO3 Bill Grizzard, the officer I had relieved on the ship, and had gone to work at the Yokosuka Naval Magazine lived a few blocks from us. He was included in many of the *Midway* weapon department's get togethers'. His wife Candy, daughter, and son Alton were often at our house. I was always thankful for the outstanding *Midway* W Division Bill had left for me, and I remain thankful to this day. There was a warrant officer that worked at the magazine with Bill who was anxious to take my job in W Division, as he wanted to stay in Yokosuka.

A book was maintained in the W Division front office, called "The Division Officer's Notebook." This book was kept locked in the division officer's desk, and was a book all division officers were supposed to maintain. Within the book were all the vital statistics on each enlisted man in the division. As each sailor checked aboard, they were asked to fill out a page, which contained vital statistic blanks for the sailor to fill in. These pages contained information such as birth date, birthplace, parent's address, previous duty stations, marital status, family member names, and ages, personal education level, hobbies, and interests. I worked at keeping this book current, and would often check out a sailor's service record from the ship's personnel office to insure I had up to date information. I also kept in mind the way my service record had been mismanaged in the past. I wanted to be sure that the sailor's service records in W Division were being updated, as they should be. Once a week I would memorize some of the data in the division officer's notebook, on one sailor, and make a point of personally speaking to him during the week, perhaps about his family, home state, or personal interests. I was interested in knowing as much as I could about each sailor in the division. One concern I had was that each sailor was ready to take the next Navy-wide advancement examination, and be promoted as soon as possible. I also was on the lookout for opportunities to delegate authority, and the responsibility that went along with it. This was the main reason for the large collateral duties' list, I instituted when I first came aboard. I also looked for opportunities to let Chief Munson manage the division, and as much as possible, I tried to maintain a "low profile." I did not want to manage as I'd seen some officers in the past. Many had wanted to micro manage everything, which was impossible for anyone to do in a very large organization; all they managed to do was discourage initiative, and motivation of their workers. I did however; want the GMT's to know that I was very interested in their day-to-day work.

For the most part I was very impressed with the GMT's in W Division. They all worked hard and played hard. They had less personal living space on board ship than prisoners in a federal prison, yet they lived together harmoniously. One distasteful task I had every six months, was an unannounced, required inspection and search of W Division berthing compartment looking for illegal drugs. I would direct Chief Munson to order everyone out of the berthing compartment, and one by one, in the company of each sailor, I would look through his locker, and under his bunk. I tried to do this as quickly as possible and in a dignified way that was not humiliating to the sailor. After everyone's locker and bunk had been inspected, I would report the results to the gun boss. I did not discover any illegal drugs during any of my inspections.

I was interested in the daily affairs of W Division sailors not only from a leadership point of view, but I was also required to closely monitor the behavior of all the GMT's as a requirement of the Personnel Reliability Program (PRP). Any change in a sailor's behavior, habits, indebtedness, mental attitude, or anything that might make him susceptible to blackmail, had to be investigated. I could not permit anyone that might be unstable, or that had questionable loyalty have access to W Division. This concern was to be "brought home" to me in a real way within the next year.

On the subject of preventing access, W Division practiced perfecting our ability to perform emergency destruction. This was the same drill we practiced in Guam, and other commands I'd been stationed at. We had to be prepared to destroy weapons that might be on board if they were in danger of falling into enemy hands, and possibly be used against us. Emergency destruction would be accomplished by placing explosive shape charges on all the weapons. The shape charges were connected by an elaborate system of primer cord. W Division sailors would practice emergency destruction by using wooden blocks in the place of explosive shape charges, and rope instead of primer cord. The captain or senior man in command of the ship would be the person to order emergency destruction.

This would be in the event the ship was about to be captured, run aground in enemy water, or about to sink in shallow waters. It was anticipated that the detonation of ordnance in magazines would blow out the bottom of the ship's hull, and hasten sinking of the ship. W Division GMT's would detonate the shape charges at the last possible moment. We would be the last sailors to leave the ship, so our survival was not very likely. We demonstrated our emergency destruction capability during the many inspections we underwent.

Midway also practiced abandon ship drills. During these drills the entire ship would muster in the hangar bay, with life jackets on. Unlike the days I went through boot camp, when each sailor had to know how to swim, the sailors of this era did not have to be swimmers. Within W Division there were two sailors that did not know how to swim. These non-swimmers were assigned to a sailor in the division who was a swimmer. It was a joke that non-swimmers should always be very kind to their assigned swimmer. W Division's participation in abandon ship drills was an exercise in futility, as we would probably go down with the ship carrying out emergency destruction. An old joke that was circulated by mustangs (LDOs', and Chief Warrant Officers') was if the ship sank, we would just walk home, inferring that we could walk on water as Jesus did.

Weapons Department had to off-load all the ships' conventional bombs, missiles, and explosives stored by the weapons department divisions. The *Midway* was to anchor off the shore of Sasebo Naval Station, and off-load to ammunition barges, which would shuttle the ordnance to a pier, and from there the ordnance would be placed into storage magazines. Working in twenty-four hour shifts, the off-load would take five days. During this time the rest of the crew (with the exception of the weapons department and those involved in the work), were given liberty in Sasebo. Ensign Norm Peters and I were assigned as safety observers on the hangar deck, to oversee the ordnancemen working there. Most of W Division was assigned to various magazines, preparing bombs for shipment, by strapping them onto metal pallets, or bomb trucks, and pushing bombs onto, and out of bomb elevators. Many GMT's were assigned as bomb elevator operators. It was a very long five days, but finally the last ordnance item was off the ship, and loaded onto the ordnance barge. Commander Quinn reserved a large area at the Sasebo Naval Station Enlisted Club, and said the drinks were free for weapons department sailors, the day following the off-load. The next day the weapons department sailors that had duty, also were treated to free drinks. Everyone was happy that this huge job was over. All the weapons department sailors had a good time celebrating the successful off-load.

The morning after the celebration at the club, Chief Munson related something that had happened in the division. Commander Quinn had celebrated wholeheartedly, and enjoyed many beers, and was subsequently helped out of the club, and to the liberty boat pier, by two W Division sailors. They were all in civilian clothes, and since enlisted men were not permitted in officer's country, when the three arrived at the ship, the two W Division sailors took the commander down into W Division berthing, where they put him into an empty bunk. He awoke before reveille, and made his way to his stateroom.

While in Sasebo, I had a surprise phone call. It was Charlie Galbreath, my old shipmate from the *Oriskany*. He was now a chief, and stationed in Sasebo with his family. I'd last seen Charlie in Guam. He was still in Explosive Ordnance Disposal (EOD). He invited me to dinner at his base house, and I had a very enjoyable evening with him, his wife and daughter. I learned that his Japanese relatives whom we had visited together, when we were stationed on *Oriskany* were all doing well, and they visited often. I asked him to tell them "hello" for me, and to thank them again for being so kind to me during our visit that took place ten years before.

The ship was in a festive mood when we pulled anchor and began steaming toward Yokosuka. Then a mere twelve hours after our departure from Sasebo, the captain came over the ship's loudspeaker system, and announced there was a situation developing in Korea. North Korea's Army was massing near the North/South demilitarization zone, and we had been directed to on-load our ordnance and stand-by. We groaned, tightened our belts, and began to prepare to bring all the ordnance back on board; we'd spent five days offloading. This on-load, two ammunition ships would steam alongside while we were at sea, and restock all of our magazines. The on-load was completed in record time, working around the clock; it was done in three days. Weapons Department sailors including me were exhausted, but the important thing was, that it was done safely without injury to anyone.

Two days after the on-load, we were steaming toward South Korea. We were all preparing for bombing sorties, and wartime operations. It was then that the ship received word that the alert was off. It developed that the North Koreans had been conducting normal training operations without informing South Korea. This meant we would have to off-load again.

There was real concern that weapons department sailors would be able to do this safely, without incident, considering that we had been working almost nonstop for two weeks. To me this was reminiscent of the days off the coast of Vietnam.

The ship anchored again at Sasebo, and we began the off-load. It was getting close to the 25th of December, and everyone on the ship wondered if weapons department would off-load in time for the ship to make it back to Yokosuka in time for sailors to spend Christmas with their families? This was a question constantly heard about the decks of the ship. Weapons Department sailors were definitely going to be considered the Scrooges that ruined Christmas if we delayed the *Midway*'s return to Yokosuka. This time, instead of five days to off-load, we did it in three. The reason for the speedier time was the fact that much of the ordnance that was on-loaded while we were steaming toward Korea, had not yet been unpackaged, so most items just needed to be taken out of the magazines, and taken to the off-load point on the hangar bay. This time all the weapons department sailors were truly exhausted after the last explosive item left the ship. There was once again a party at the Sasebo Naval Base Enlisted club. We had redeemed ourselves with the rest of the ship. We would make it back to Yokosuka by 22 December.

I enjoyed being home at Christmas. I had not been home on my 39th birthday, on 8 December. A few days after the New Year Day of 1982, Carmen surprised me with a birthday present. My gift was a reservation she had made through the base special services office on a Japanese charter fishing boat. I had missed fishing while in Japan, so this was a wonderful surprise. Early one Saturday morning, I took my packed lunch, and with about twenty other sailors, some with their wives, caught a bus on base that was to take us to our Japanese fishing boat, for the start of our fishing trip. We all boarded a forty-five-foot wooden Japanese fishing boat. The crew spoke very little English. The women in the group were not happy at all about the bathroom arrangements we had on the boat. It was a hole cut in the deck, in the after section of the boat that opened to the sea below. In order to use this "bathroom," they had to squat over the hole, while all on the boat averted their eyes. The Japanese were used to this lack of privacy, but we were not. As we pulled away from the pier, we all wondered where the fishing poles were. The fishing trip reservation paper we all had, said that everything would be provided. Soon a Japanese crewman walked about handing out small rectangular pieces of wood with fishing line wrapped around them, and a few hooks attached to the end of the line. This answered our questions about fishing poles. After going a distance from the pier, the boat stopped in the water, and the crewmen brought out buckets filled with red liquid, with bits of what appeared to be fish floating in it. This liquid had the foulest smell imaginable. A couple in the group became seasick when they smelled this concoction. The crewmembers began dipping ladles into the buckets, and pouring the foul-smelling stuff over the side. Each person was then given small portions of fish bait to put on our hooks. After baiting the hooks we dropped our lines into the water. We began to catch fish, but it took forever to twist the rectangular pieces of wood winding the line around and around until the fish was at the surface, and could be brought aboard. The only fish we caught were Spanish Mackerels, about eight or ten inches long. Most of us ended up with sore and blistered hands from twisting the lines up and down. It was January, and very cold, so I was not too disappointed when the fishing boat finally pulled back alongside the pier. I'd caught ten fish, which I gave to a Filipino neighbor. I did not go on any more Japanese charter boat fishing trips.

As part of the effort to improve the appearance of the trainers the squadrons used for loading practice, we had off-loaded three trainers at the Subic Bay Naval Magazine. As soon as the ship pulled into Yokosuka, three W Division sailors had been flown down to Subic Bay, where they were to begin repainting the trainers. Many of the sailors in W Division had volunteered for this job, which was in a way a tropical vacation in sailors' paradise, away from the cold, winter of Yokosuka. Chief Munson selected GMT1 Bogner, GMT3 Clark, and GMT3 Tellings. The first class and one of the third class petty officers had girlfriends in Subic, which they eventually married, so this was an ideal assignment for them.

The division sailors were busy preparing the division spaces for repainting, and replacing tile on the compartment decks. There were plans to completely refurbish W Division berthing compartment, with new clothes storage lockers, and new bunks. W Division sailors moved into a barracks on base while the berthing compartment work was being undertaken. Chief Munson or I checked on the barracks frequently to insure living conditions were comfortable, and acceptable.

This was a very busy yard period. The ship was in dry dock, with the hull resting on huge supports in a gigantic, dry concrete "bathtub" type of enclosure. The entire outer hull of *Midway* was to be painted. I was very impressed with the Japanese yard workers. Comparing them to American yard workers or workers from other countries, they were far more industrious, and hard working.

To work on the outer hull of the ship, an elaborate framework of poles was erected, on which workers with rubber soled "slippers," that looked like socks with a gap between the big toe and the rest of the toes, would walk back and forth like tightrope walkers. They walked on this framework, hundreds of feet above the concrete bottom of the dry dock.

As with most aspects of Navy life, yard work required reams of paperwork. The Yokosuka Naval Base Ship Repair Facility was scheduled to perform a number of jobs within W Division spaces. During the yard period there was no longer a requirement for the spaces to be guarded by the marine detachment. The months leading up to the yard period, we had planned all the jobs that would need to be done. Work requests for these jobs had been submitted up the chain of command for approval. My first concern was the magazine sprinkler system, which had been neglected, and was in need of an overhaul. Another concern was the magazine overhead hoists. These were air-operated hoists that were used to lift and position ordnance within the magazines. It was obviously important that the hoist not fail while lifting. I scheduled weight testing, which was an annual requirement for any hoist or lifting device that might be used. The weight testing involved subjecting the hoists to a much higher weight than they would normally lift, to insure they would not fail, during normal use. This was a busy time, but I also wanted to insure that W Division sailors took full advantage of this in port time. I granted as much liberty as possible. A number of division sailors took leave for visits with their families in the States.

Mid-January, I flew to Subic Bay, Philippines for three days. I checked with the three sailors who were working on the three trainers we had off-loaded there. The work was going well, and they were enjoying their working "vacation." The Subic Magazine area was located in a part of the base that was in the midst of thick jungle. This jungle was populated with very aggressive monkeys. Sailors were cautioned about walking along the magazine roads on foot, as there were groups of monkeys that had attacked lone sailors in the past.

Although I had wanted to check on the progress of the trainers' refurbishment job, this was not the main purpose for my visit to Subic. I wanted to talk with the officers in the Commander Naval Logistics Pacific Office (ComNavLogPac). This office was responsible for making transportation arrangements for classified shipments throughout the Pacific area. W Division had an unusually high number of maintenance operations that would be due after the next at sea period. These maintenance operations would require the shipment of a large number of replacement-classified items, which would be used during the maintenance operations. I sat down with a lieutenant in the office, and we looked at the ship's upcoming schedule, and made up a tentative shipment schedule. The replacement items would be shipped from the U.S., and the removed items would be returned for reuse. While walking through the Subic Bay Exchange, I had a surprise. I ran across GMT1 Bernie Pilger, and GMT1 Paul Fegan, who I had been stationed with on Guam. They both were on a carrier, which was visiting Subic Bay.

I returned to chilly Yokosuka, and fell into the yard-period routine. This was a cold time of the year, and I used "long johns" under my uniform while standing OOD watches. Early in February, Chief Munson and I were given a short tropical holiday. A new message reporting system was being introduced into the nuclear weapons program, and we were flown to Hawaii for a three-day school on these reporting requirements. Nuclear Weapons Training Group Pacific and Sandia Corporation conducted the class. John and I enjoyed the sun, attended classes for three days, and then flew back to frigid Japan.

GMT1 Tonnon worked in the W Division front office. He was an excellent typist, and paperwork expert. He was invaluable keeping the paperwork river flowing. The new reporting system was a coded system detailed in a secret publication that was maintained and updated by the Joint Chiefs of Staff. This new reporting system would give the Joint Chiefs a complete picture of the United States nuclear weapons' readiness at any given point in time. Any change in a weapon readiness condition had to be reported within twenty-four hours. There was also a new report that required a response time of an hour. This new report was called a Stockpile Verification Report. This basically was an emergency inventory of the nation's stockpile, in the event of a theft by terrorists, or unexplained loss of a weapon. There were a number of other new reports, and GMT1 Tonnon took pride in keeping the reports error-free.

On 12 February, I decided that I would submit a request for a twelve-month extension on *Midway*. This request had to be submitted to Washington, D.C., with the captain's endorsement. The reason for my request read:

> My reasons for requesting an extension of my PRD (Projected Rotation Date) are as follows:
> My tour on the *USS Midway* has been one of the most rewarding of my career.

The high tempo of operations and the varied mission requirements of *Midway* have afforded me the opportunity to gain valuable experience that I could not gain elsewhere. The division I am assigned to have set many records of accomplishments, and the division has the highest rates of extension requests on the ship. My goal is to achieve a discrepancy free NTPI, which I feel can be achieved if my extension request is granted. My family is in complete agreement with this request.

Captain Owens forwarded my request most strongly recommending approval. I called my Detailer, Lieutenant Commander Ron Bench, and told him of my request. He sounded shocked, and said "Are you sure you don't want Puerto Rico?" I said "No." He said he would recommend approval of my request. The approval was dated 23 February 1982. My new rotation date was now August 1983.

My decision to extend had been tempered by a number of things. Most of the GMT's that were aboard that first part of 1982 would be going through the next inspection in September, they had always "gone an extra mile" when I asked them to do anything, and I didn't want them to feel like I had deserted them. I also felt a desire to "clear my name," after the last NTPI. Commander Quinn was very pleased that I would be onboard for the NTPI later in the year.

It was during the first part of the year that I also learned my ex-wife in Oak Harbor, Washington was reopening the alimony case. I received a legal letter from a lawyer in Oak Harbor that Allison had retained, saying I would be expected to pay for the entire doctor and hospital bills associated with an accident Allison had experienced. I hired a lawyer in Oak Harbor, by mail, to defend my position. The case was eventually dismissed, but it certainly was troubling that the ship had received such a letter. We had not heard anything from Peter or Roger, and Mary was failing most of her classes in Yokosuka High School.

During this yard period, GMT1 Dick Clark transferred off *Midway*. Carmen cooked him farewell dinner, and we spent an evening together at our base house. He was being transferred to a submarine tender home ported in San Diego. After he left the ship, I got word from him that he was picked up for chief, which I was very happy to hear about. It was sad to hear however, that he and his wife Donna, who we'd stayed with on Guam during Typhoon Pamela, were divorced shortly after Dick left the ship. GMT1 Bogner assumed the duties of leading petty officer after GMT1 Clark departed. As I said this was a hard-working yard period, but it was pleasant to be able to go home every evening. Every fifth night, I remained on board, and stood OOD watches, as well as weapons department duty officer.

The first of March, our yard work was completed. The dry dock was flooded, and *Midway* once again floated on seawater. We got underway, and held numerous battle drills, and damage control drills. The crew gradually readjusted to the at sea routine. The ship received welcome news around this time. *Midway* had been awarded the Battle Efficiency Award for the Pacific Fleet. In essence this meant we were the best aircraft carrier in the Pacific Fleet, beating out ten or twelve carriers for the honor. A large "E" was painted on the bridge, and all sailors on board were authorized to wear the Battle "E" ribbon on their chest. All first class petty officers and below, sewed an "E" on their right shoulder, underneath the *U.S.S. Midway* patch worn on the right shoulder. This was the third ship I'd been on that had won this award. The other two were the *Oriskany*, and *Ticonderoga*. There was a great deal of pride among the crew over this honor.

The ship anchored off Sasebo Naval Station and weapons department on-loaded all the ships' conventional ordnance. This was another five-day round the clock effort. Weapons Department again celebrated at the Sasebo Naval Base Club.

The first of April the ship participated in an annual exercise called *"Team Spirit."* This was a joint exercise with ships of the South Korea Republic. During flight quarters one day, the President of South Korea, Mr. Chun Doo Hwan was flown aboard for a tour of the ship.

April first, I'd been an officer for two years, and I received another fitness report. I received all "A's," and was still "ranked in the pack" as number "two." I was pleased with my fitness report. When I sat down with Commander Quinn to discuss my fitness report, he said he was well pleased with W Division, and thought it was the best division in weapons department. From time to time I would run into the commanding officer, Captain Owens, and he would always take time to stop and chat with me, asking how things were going in W Division.

On 14 April, I was once again the W Division Officer. Lieutenant Danske moved to the weapons safety officer position, working in the weapons office. I was very pleased with this turn of events, as I could now concentrate on preparing for the maintenance work that was to come, and for the big inspection in September. Chief Munson had extended for twelve months, for which I was extremely pleased.

Many other petty officers in W Division had voluntarily extended their time on board, which was rare, usually sailors are anxious to get off sea duty, and go ashore. I had a genuine affection for the sailors in W Division; they had worked hard, and never failed to accomplish what I asked of them. Many of them had been born long after I'd started my Navy career, so I was as old as, or older than their fathers. I appreciated the hardships of shipboard living that they endured. I also understood the sacrifices they made by giving up personal freedoms, always obeying orders, and living under the most rigid, strictest working and living conditions possible. There is a brotherhood among shipmates that is hard to describe, unless you've experienced it. Carmen and I both enjoyed being around these younger sailors and our home was always open to them. There were many officers that would not dare socialize with enlisted men, believing that familiarization bred contempt, and that enlisted men were a class beneath them. I did not adhere to these beliefs, and told all in the division that my door was always open to them. Our job was shrouded in secrecy, and could only be talked about among us, so this had the effect of bringing us closer together, than most divisions on the ship. I was always addressed as "Gunner," or "Sir," and the younger sailors addressed Carmen as "Mrs. Gunner." I like to think the reason so many sailors extended their tour of duty on *Midway*, was because I showed respect for them, and when they learned I had extended my tour, they wanted to continue on *Midway*, not only to improve their chance for promotion, but also because Chief Munson and I were always concerned about their working and living conditions. I always told them, we would try to have fun no matter what we did, and for the most part, we did have a happy group of sailors that made up W Division. Many of the division officers in weapons department, and on the ship, were jealous of W Division's high retention, and promotion percentages. I no longer heard the complaints I'd first heard when I came aboard that W Division didn't pull its share of the work load when it came to weapons department working parties, or other jobs the weapons department was tasked with. W Division sailors worked as hard as and often harder than others in the department during working parties, and ordnance on-loads and off-loads.

A highlight of the day while the ship was at sea, was watching the world news over the ship's closed circuit television system in the evenings. In April we all closely followed the events of the war between England and Argentina, over the Falkland Islands. Much of our interest was how the British carriers would fare in the war. The war was over in June. The war brought an interesting naval fact to light. Surface ships were in critical danger of being sunk by the French air to surface *Exocet* missile used by the Argentine Air Force to attack British ships. This missile was a real threat to all navies in the world, and brought about the installation of "Close In Weapon Support" (CIWS) gun mounts on many surface ships. These were rapid firing machine guns that would spew out bullets made of depleted uranium, and would destroy an incoming missile in midair.

The ship pulled into Subic Bay. Carmen and Vicky Peters were waiting on the pier. Ensign Peters and I took a few days' leave, and the four of us took a tour to Manila. We rode in a van through the Philippine countryside to the capital city of Manila. The van ride lasted five hours, and we got to see a lot of farmland, along with a lot of poverty that the majority of the people of this country lived in. In Manila, we stayed at a hotel called "The Admiral." Carmen brought a hair curler from Yokosuka that she planned to use one evening. She plugged it in, and after checking on it in a few minutes, discovered that it had melted! We had forgotten that the voltage in this country was 220 volts, twice the voltage used on base in Yokosuka. The four of us toured Manila for two days. We had lunch at the American Embassy compound, and visited a large international park that had replica villages of the different provinces of the Philippine Islands. This park had been the "brainchild" of Imelda Marcos, the president's wife. I admired President Marcos. He was a very intelligent man, and the most decorated Filipino soldier of World War II. But as events proved in the future, there was greed, and corruption in his administration. Norm was excited about finding some books he had been looking for, about the early history of the Philippines. We all agreed that we had a good time on the tour.

While in the Subic Officer's Club after the tour, Carmen and I bumped into Admiral Hardisty. He was happy to see us, and we had lunch together. Carmen and Vicky returned to Yokosuka, and the ship was once again underway.

On the first of July, the ship was in Yokosuka. One weekend, Norm and Vicky Peters, and their son and daughter, Carmen, Mary, and I traveled by bus to Tokyo, and visited the Tokyo Disneyland for a day. We got the Disneyland admission tickets through the base special services office. We were fortunate that the Navy was given an allotment of tickets each year. The waiting list for Japanese citizens to purchase admission tickets, for one day, was over a year long. It was an odd experience hearing Disney characters such as Mickey Mouse, and Goofy speaking Japanese.

W Division was busily preparing for the upcoming NTPI. For me this was a much easier time of preparation since I was now the only officer in the division, and did not have to "run interference," so to speak, or educated another officer. Commander Quinn expressed concern to me that Lieutenant Danske, who was now the weapons safety officer, did not seem concerned about preparing for the upcoming NTPI. I suggested to him that perhaps LCDR Bill Essing could give him a hand, since Lieutenant Commander Essing had gone through an inspection last year. Commander Quinn followed my suggestion, and I also helped Lieutenant Danske when I could.

In August the ship had a surprise visit from the Secretary of the Navy, Paul Lehman. Following his visit the ship got underway for a week. Upon returning to Yokosuka, Carmen related what happened after she left the pier, after seeing the ship off. She had car trouble, and a man in a suit, being driven in a Navy limousine, stopped and helped her push the car. From her description, it was apparently the Secretary of the Navy; I asked if he asked her name, and she said "No," I said "Good."

The weapons office had a visitor, GMGC Ritchie, who I'd been stationed with on Guam on two occasions. He was on another ship visiting Yokosuka. He was amazed that the last time I'd seen him two and a half years before I'd been a chief, and now was a CWO3. He also had some sad news, my old friend Ray Steele's wife Becky, had died of cancer while Ray and her had been stationed in Guam. (Ray succumbed to cancer and joined Becky in death in 2007)

I had a leave request from a third class petty officer in the division, who wanted to visit his family in the states. This was only a few weeks before our inspection, but he was well trained, and I approved his request without any reservations as he would be back a week before the inspection began. Captain Owens was scheduled to be relieved, and transferred, the week following the inspection. Our inspection was to be not only an NTPI, but also a combined inspection, including a Defense Nuclear Surety Inspection (DNSI), which was conducted at commands every fourth year. Inspectors from FCDNA Albuquerque would conduct the DNSI. We would have twice the number of inspectors we normally would have, looking at us under a magnifying glass. An alarming fact was for the past four years, all carriers on the west coast that had undergone a DNSI, had failed. There was real concern in the Navy about the readiness of carriers in the Pacific Fleet. There was intense pressure for W Division to do well with the inspection. Captain Owens often asked me how preparations were coming, and Commander Quinn asked to be briefed often on how things were going. Chief Munson and I reviewed every possible area the inspectors would be examining, and then reviewed them again.

Prior to Captain Owens transfer, there was to be a farewell gathering of *Midway* officers in the ship's wardroom. During this farewell gathering, there was to be a "roast" of the captain, and each department was expected to relate something comical, or humorous about Captain Owens tour as our commanding officer. Commander Quinn asked me if I could come up with something for this roast.

The ship was to get underway for our NTPI and DNSI. This at sea period was also a familiarization cruise for the new captain. The W Division teams had trained to a peak, and all was ready for the inspection, except for the third class petty officer I had granted leave. He had not returned from leave in the states. He was two days overdue, when I placed an overseas call to his parent's house. I spoke to his sister, who said he had left a few days previously. I was baffled by his absence, and also concerned about how his team would do without him. We shuffled some people around to cover his position on the assembly team.

On 7 September, a long line of inspectors came aboard. I presented each of them with a welcome aboard package that contained ship's information, and Yokosuka Naval Base information. The inspection was not scheduled to start until the 9th, when we got underway. Many of the inspectors visited the base exchange to purchase electronic, or camera equipment, they mailed home to either San Diego, or Albuquerque. VCR tape machines were a new popular item on the market, and less expensive in Japan.

On 9 September, the ship got underway, and the pre-inspection meeting was held with the captain, and the inspection began. The next eleven days we were busy with the inspections. Not only were W Division's two inspections to be conducted, but also the squadron's NTPI's, which W Division would support. There was a whirlwind of activity throughout the division, weapons department, and the marine detachment. The inspectors pulled two simulated emergencies, which W Division sailors reacted to. All of my accountability paperwork was examined, and the daily operations in the magazines continued. Daily after the end of the workday, I would brief Commander Quinn, who in turn would brief the captain. Finally the last operation in the magazines was completed. I breathed a sigh of relief, at least this time an operation had not been stopped, but I still did not have a clue about how well, or how badly we did.

To report how we did in the inspections, the large group of inspectors assembled with Captain Owens, Commander Quinn, and all the officers involved in the inspection in the captain's cabin. I and Lieutenant Danske, and others were seated in chairs lining the walls, all others sat at a large table in the middle of the captain's cabin. Captain Owens motioned for me to take a seat at the table next to him. I thought at the time, perhaps he wants me closer, so he can poke me if there's bad news in the inspection report! The chief inspector began reading the inspection report, which went very quickly, because there were no discrepancies! All areas received a grade of "outstanding." As I said only grades of "satisfactory or unsatisfactory" were awarded following these inspections, but in exceptional cases the grade of "outstanding" was awarded, and *Midway*'s W Division had received it! In the report, *Midway* was also praised as the first Pacific Fleet carrier to pass a DNSI inspection in four years! The inspectors gave the division high praise, and said it was definitely the best W Division any of them had seen. The captain was beaming, and congratulated me. After the meeting broke up, Commander Quinn continued congratulating me. I told him he had a great W Division crew, and Chief Munson, and all the men who had worked so hard deserved all the credit, all I did was stay out of their way, this was the same comment I made to the captain. I was given a copy of the report, and immediately returned to the W Division coffee locker, where all the sailors were anxiously awaiting the news. I gave the report to Chief Munson, and asked that he read it to the crew. After the reading of the report, they were all walking on air. We all congratulated each another, and I was as proud of them at that moment, as I have been of anyone in my life. They had achieved something I had sought for all during my career as a Nuclear Weaponsman, a discrepancy free inspection, and the rare grade of "Outstanding". I had achieved this at the Whidbey Island AUW Shop, but that inspection was not the magnitude of *Midway*'s inspection. This was definitely one of the high points in my naval career. This was a time for celebrating, but not relaxing. The same inspectors now turned their attention to the squadrons, as it was now time for their NTPI/DNSI. As always W Division supplied the trainers, and safety observers for the squadron loading teams, as they demonstrated their loading operations.

On the second day of the squadron inspection, I was standing on the hangar bay near the roped off area where the W Division trainers were kept when they were not being used for loading operations. I was talking to an inspector, when suddenly the hangar bay sprinkler system went off. Caustic liquid poured down from sprinkler heads located in the hangar bay overhead. All the sailors, marines, inspectors, planes, and everything in the hangar bay were immediately soaked. The inspector and I sought refuge under a nearby airplane wing. A marine sentry standing near the roped off area, was grimacing in pain, and wiping his eyes. I hollered for him to get under the wing with us, but he refused to budge. I finally grabbed his arm, and pulled him under the protection of the wing with the inspector and me. He was in severe pain with the liquid burning his eyes, I told him not to worry about stepping away and leaving his post, I would take responsibility. He continued rubbing his eyes in pain. After a few minutes the sprinkler system was turned off, and the liquid stopped its torrential downpour. Everything within the hangar bay was soaked with fire extinguishing liquid. I ran to the ordnance handling office, which was located on the hangar bay. I called W Division on the phone, and told GMT1 Tonnon, who was in the office, to double time up to the hangar bay, and I began filling out the second emergency "Dull Sword" message I had filled out on *Midway*. It was bad timing to have this happen during an inspection. The Dull Sword message reported two trainers being subjected to caustic firefighting liquid. This message was sent out within five minutes. The inspectors were somewhat in awe, as it was a rare situation to send a Dull Sword, and especially during an inspection. It was discovered that someone had deliberately set off the sprinkler system. The sprinkler system had been set off in one of the three hangar bays on the ship, the aft hangar bay where the loading operations were being conducted.

W Division sailors cleaned the exposed trainers with fresh water, and the ship and squadron sailors began cleaning up all the planes, and soaked equipment. I quickly got out of my soaked clothes, and took a shower. The liquid burned my skin, and eyes. Many of the marines were treated in sickbay for eye and skin burns. The loading operations were moved to a dry hangar bay. It was never discovered who purposely set off the sprinkler system, but watches were posted near the sprinkler initiation handles for the remainder of the inspection.

This was an unfortunate accident, but probably added to the overall favorable grade the squadrons received for the inspection. W Division was graded "outstanding' for the support we had given the squadrons. We had reacted properly during an emergency situation. The cleanup of the hangar bay took over a week. The hangar bay doors had to be kept closed during the change of command ceremony that took place in the hangar bay on 21 August.

Our new commanding officer was to be Capt. Charles R. McGrail. He was of course an aviator, and had been commissioned an ensign out of the Naval Academy in 1957.

At one point in his career he had been in a squadron on the *USS Ticonderoga*, in 1962, two years before I reported aboard. He had served a number of tours in Vietnam. He was unique, as he was a bachelor. *USS Midway* was known throughout the Navy as a "stepping stone," for a sailor's career. Most commanding officers were promoted, upon transfer from *Midway*, and Captain Owens was not an exception. Upon his departure from *USS Midway* as Commanding Officer, he was to be promoted to Rear Admiral (Lower-Half). I liked to think that the successful inspection results had a lot to do with his promotion.

Most of the officers in weapons department recognized that Commander Quinn did not seem happy in the weapons officer job, and was not the enthusiastic leader that Commander Kellner had been. Commander Quinn's "true love," was being a test pilot. He had campaigned to have an assignment as a pilot ever since being onboard *Midway*. About this time, we learned that he would not be on board for a full two years, but instead would transfer in the near future.

The evening before the ship pulled back into Yokosuka, a meeting in the wardroom was scheduled as a farewell party for Captain Owens; this was to be a farewell roast, with Captain Owens as the victim. I had prepared something for Commander Quinn to read as part of weapons department's portion of the roast. The captain was a tobacco chewer. As Commander Quinn read what I had prepared, I held up a Tab soft drink can (which was the captain's favorite drink while sitting in his chair in the bridge), which everyone could see had the bottom of the can cut out.

> Negotiations between the *Midway* Weapons Department and Coca Cola bottling company, along with the Tokyo Spittoon Corporation have recently been completed. These negotiations were undertaken to create a new product that should cause an explosion of excitement in the world market, and makes all previous spittoons obsolete. All dedicated tobacco and snuff chewers owe a debt of gratitude to our Captain, R.S. Owens, for his ingenuity and originality that lead to the creation of the "Captain Rube" Owens Tab Can Spittoon. The *USS Midway* Weapons Department takes great pleasure in presenting Captain Owens with the first spittoon to be manufactured."

At this point I handed the can to Captain Owens, and Commander Quinn continued reading.

> "The unique features of the spittoon are obvious. The happy tobacco, or snuff user can well disguise his tobacco or snuff use by declaring, "I'm drinking a Tab!" As the need arises to get rid of the tobacco or snuff juice, the convenient hole in the top of the can is utilized. A scientific breakthrough has created an unheard of feature that has been incorporated in the "Captain Rube" Owens Tab Can Spittoon. Regardless of how intense, or lengthy flight operations (or similar activities) take place, the spittoon can may be used over and over again. Looking at the bottom of the can, this unique feature can be observed. A word of caution however, field tests have revealed that the spittoon user and anyone standing in the near vicinity may require a shower and a change of clothes. Once again we thank you Captain, for without you, the "Captain Rube" Owens Tab Can Spittoon would never have been possible.

The presentation went over well, and received a long round of applause. I had worked on this when I could find time during the inspection. Commander Quinn began to retake his seat, but he was in for a surprise. The officers of weapons department had a surprise for him. He was also a "victim" of the roast. Lieutenant Commander Jim Goglin of the weapons department then read from a page, I had written, that described an incident that had occurred in October of last year.

> On 23 October 1981 on board *USS Midway*, something occurred that very few people are aware of. On that date the Weapons Officer; Commander Quinn visited the Captain in his inport cabin. Following Commander Quinn's departure, the Captain discovered his combination cap was missing. Very little is known about what transpired between Captain Owens and Commander Quinn, when the Captain discovered that Commander Quinn had his hat? The officers of weapons department have not attempted to analyze the reasons why Commander Quinn took the Captain's hat, because he is our leader, and his reasons are not to be questioned. We have observed that the cap incident may have been a "pass down item" to Captain McGrail, as its been noticed that when Commander Quinn visits the Captain; the Captain's Orderly positions himself near the Captain's cap.

At this point a hat, with flashing lights powered by batteries, and a large nametag "Gun Boss" attached to it was displayed, and the narrative continued.

The weapons department officers being ever faithful to their "Gun Boss," felt it appropriate to obtain an exceptionally sharp looking combination cap to present to him on the occasion of his departure. This cap is his to wear on future visits to his commanding officers. The cap is very distinctive, and cannot be confused with another cap, or if he has not returned Admiral Owen's cap, he can mail it to him as a replacement.

The presentations at the roast went very well. The success of the inspections contributed to the joviality of the wardroom gathering.

When the inspection team left the ship upon our return to Yokosuka, the captain of Nuclear Weapons Training Group Pacific, who had come onboard as the senior inspector, shook my hand, again congratulated me, and said he would like for me to come to work for him when I transferred. I was honored by his offer, as he was highly regarded in the nuclear weapons community as an outstanding commanding officer. The interest and importance of the inspection *Midway* had just gone through was emphasized by his presence. Normally he did not go on inspection trips.

After the change of command ceremony, the ship pulled back out to sea, after having been in port for only twenty-four hours. This change of commanding officer meant all officers were given fitness reports.
I received all "A's," and my rank was still number "two" in the "pack. I sat down with Commander Quinn to discuss this report prior to signing it.

The inspection had been over for a month, when the sailor who had gone on leave, and then gone AWOL, reported aboard. I was very disappointed in him, and he never gave me a straight answer why he went AWOL. His security clearance was revoked, and I took him to captain's mast. I explained to the captain how the third class had let the division down by being an unauthorized absentee during the course of the inspection. Prior to going on leave he had been scheduled to be promoted to second class petty officer in a couple of months. The captain cancelled his promotion, and pulled his access to W Division. He was assigned to another division within weapons department. One underlying factor may have been that he was one of only two black sailors in W Division. I had always been alert to any racial issues, and had never seen any evidence of racism. As I mentioned there had always been few black GMT's. The third class adjusted to his new division. There was no chance for him to be promoted beyond GMT Third Class without a security clearance. I would see him about the ship from time to time, and talking to him he seemed to regret being thrown out of the division.

In Yokosuka I had a wooden plaque made, which I mounted over the doorway leading into W Division spaces, which had a statement and a list of names. I'll list the names because these men accomplished something they should be proud of for the rest of their lives. The statement said:

During the period 9 to 20 September 1982 the below listed personnel successfully completed a combined Defense Nuclear Surety Inspection (DNSI)/Navy Technical Proficiency Inspection (NTPI), becoming the first "W" Division on a United States Aircraft Carrier to pass an inspection of this type in a four year period, and the first "W" Division to pass an NTPI in the year 1982. CDR Quinn, LT Danske, CWO3 Little, GMTC Munson, GMT1 Hartman, GMT1 Walbert, GMT1 Bogner, GMT1 Halpin, GMT1 Tonnon, GMT2 Smith, GMT2 Hamilton, GMT2 Hensley, SK2 Johnson, GMT2 Tellings, GMT3 Clark, GMT3 Stevenson, GMT3 Martin, GMT3 Hebbard, GMT3 Rodriguez, GMTSN Gomez, GMTSN Killingsworth, GMTSN McKernan, GMTSN St. Arnaud.

The plaque was lacquer coated with a brass plate listing the names. The agreement was that the last sailor leaving *Midway* whose name was on the plaque would take the plaque with him. This accomplishment was a huge source of pride for all of us, and in my mind what made it even more amazing was nineteen GMT's, and one SK (store keeper), achieved a grade of "outstanding" when W Division was considered undermanned. The division was supposed to have twenty-eight GMT's assigned! Years later I heard that Seaman St. Arnaud took the plaque with him when he transferred; I hope he has it in a place of honor.

After the change of command, the ship got underway on a secret mission. We were to link up with the nuclear powered aircraft carrier *USS Enterprise* in the Northern Pacific, and see how close we could get to the coast of the Soviet Union before being detected. The *Enterprise* had just gotten out of the shipyard in Bremerton, Washington after a six-year stay. There had been problems with the ship's nuclear reactor, but she was now operational. *Midway* sailors were cautioned not to tell anyone of our destination.

Steaming north, the new captain made an offer to the crew. Any crewman that saw a submarine near the ship, which had not been detected by our escorting ships, or other means, the captain would grant the sailor thirty days "basket leave."

This leave would be free, and not counted against the sailor's normally accrued leave total. After flight quarters, daily hundreds of sailors would roam the upper decks looking out over the seas surface surrounding the ship. The amazing thing was there were three sailors on three different occasions that saw submarines near the ship that had not been detected by electronic methods! This was proof that lookouts were valuable even in the so-called electronic age. The subs were all friendly, trying to penetrate, our defensive barriers.

I have an Arial picture[49] of the *Midway*, and *Enterprise* task group steaming together in the Northern Pacific, and on the back of the picture is a summary of this operation:

> Battle Group Alpha, *USS Midway*, and Battle group Foxtrot, *USS Enterprise*, conducted operations in the North Pacific Ocean and the Sea of Japan during September and October of 1982. The purpose of this North Pacific operation was to develop doctrine for a multi-carrier battle group, to gain valuable experience in working in a hostile environment, and to show our allies and potential adversaries that aircraft carriers can operate anywhere, anytime, under any conditions.
>
> On the twentieth of September, *USS Midway* with Carrier air Wing Five, *USS Reeves*, *USS Knox, USS Lockwood, USS Towers*, and *USNS Hassayampa* sped northward from Japanese waters to a rendezvous point near Attu Island in the Western Aleutians. Meanwhile *USS Enterprise* with Carrier Air Wing Eleven, *USS Bainbridge, USS Jouett, USS O'Callahan, USS Hepburn, USS Harry W. Hill, USS Hull, USS Sacramento,* and *USS Shasta* conducted a transit from their Hawaiian operating waters to the rendezvous point. The two task groups rendezvoused on the twenty-sixth of September. While in the Aleutian Island operating area, the Battle Groups participated in exercise *Kernal Potlatch*. This exercise included long-range reconnaissance flights and long-range strikes against islands in the eastern Aleutians. The *Midway* experienced harsh weather conditions while in the North Pacific. The seas were heavy, temperatures frigid, winds high, and the sky was continuously overcast. Green water was often taken over the bow. Foul weather makes flight operations extremely difficult and dangerous. On the evening of the twenty-ninth of September, *Enterprise* had become surrounded by fog making landings impossible. Darkness was approaching and aircraft remained to be recovered. Two F-14 *Tomcats* and an A-6 *Intruder* were low on fuel with no airfields within range. *USS Midway* was the only place that these aircraft could land. The situation was serious since the weather was deteriorating and *Tomcats* had never recovered on *Midway* before. In addition, the *Tomcat* aircrews were not accustomed to *Midway*'s small deck. Hard work, professional expertise, and *Midway* Magic brought the *Tomcats* and *Intruder* to a safe recovery.
>
> The Battle Groups transited the Tsugaru Strait on the second of October and entered the Sea of Japan, Battle Group Alpha exercised throughout the area, making it plain that the United States of America does not recognize excessive claims over the high seas.
>
> The Soviet Union reacted to the presence of the Battle Groups in an extensive manner. During the North Pacific and Sea of Japan operations Soviet aircraft flew numerous sorties against the Battle Groups. The Soviet Navy also maintained close surveillance on the Battle Groups with surface units. The dual battle group operations proved anew that multi-carrier task force operation in the Northern Pacific possible and practical with today's super carriers and high performance aircraft. The experience gained and lessons learned by Battle Group Alpha will form a base of knowledge multi-carrier battle groups will need to carry out their mission of protecting the United States of America and the free world.

I can confirm that during this Northern Pacific cruise it was very cold. *Midway* steamed mostly in a humid, hot, tropical climate, and sudden exposure to the extreme cold was brutal. Most of the crew came down with sniffles, and colds. It must have been a shock to the Russian leadership to awaken one morning, and have two huge battle groups at their back door. It was hoped that our presence would cause the Soviet Air Force to fly one of their newly developed TU-17 *Backfire* bombers out near the fleet. They didn't take the bait, and permit us to take a look at this secret aircraft. The future revealed that the *Backfire* bomber was not operational at this time, as our intelligence had assumed it was. The Russian plane was not operational until much later in 1982, and 1983. This was the bomber the Russians were building in response to America's B-1 Bomber program.

The ship steamed south after our joint operation with the *Enterprise*. I had a "hello" message from *Enterprise*'s W Division, the technical monitor on the ship was CWO2 Donn Green, who I'd gone to "A" School with twenty-one years before, and had served with on the *USS Independence*.

We were scheduled to pull into Singapore, after our "chilly northern cruise" for a three-day port visit. Prior to pulling into Singapore, Captain McGrail emphasized that no one on board *Midway* was to get a tattoo in Singapore. There had been reports from other Navy ships that sailors had come down with hepatitis, after getting tattoos in Singapore with dirty needles. This caution was stated many times in the plan of the day, and over the ship's loudspeaker. Sure enough after leaving Singapore, a few sailors were put on report for disobeying the captain's orders by getting tattoos. A young ensign I had come onboard with, had a sailor in his division that had gotten a tattoo, and he accompanied him to captain's mast. Standing before the captain, Captain McGrail asked the seaman, "Why did you get a tattoo, when I had publicized that anyone who did would be punished?" The seaman said, "Captain I thought it was OK since my division officer got a tattoo!" The captain said, "Oh," and asked the ensign standing beside the seaman, to show him his tattoo, which was small one on his chest. The captain dismissed the seaman without punishment, and immediately held mast on the ensign, telling him he hoped the tattoo was worth it, because it was going to cost him dearly. He restricted the ensign to his stateroom, relieved him of his division, and when the ship returned to Yokosuka, directed Washington to take him off the ship. This was a sad affair for me, because I personally liked the ensign, and had given him a lot of advice about being a division officer. He had a lot of potential, but because of one dumb mistake, his career was over.

During this time frame the list of names selected for commissioning in 1982 was publicized, by the selection board that had convened in Washington, D.C., Bill Ooten, along with Chris Van Diven who I'd been stationed with at Oakland had been selected for commissioning to CWO2. The previous year, Billy Gilbert who I'd been with on the *Ticonderoga*, had been selected for LDO Ensign. An unusually large number of my shipmates ended their naval careers as commissioned officers.

One of my roommates on *Midway*, Mike Palotti was selected for promotion from CWO3 to LTJG. He had applied for LDO status the previous year. I had been under pressure from many of the officers including the gun boss to apply for the LDO program. I had considered it, but with only seven years remaining before I would be forced to retire, it was possible I would not have enough time to retire as a lieutenant commander, but as a lieutenant, and thus have a lower pension than if I'd remained a chief warrant officer. I almost submitted an application, but in the end decided against it.

On 6 October, the ship's daily newspaper reprinted newspaper articles[50] initially published nine years previously when *USS Midway* first arrived in Yokosuka, her new homeport. The article spoke of a new era for American-Japanese relations, and of a stronger military presence in Japan. The Yokosuka Base population immediately exploded a few thousand upon the *Midway*'s arrival. The prices on the Honce, (Thieves Alley Bar District) doubled in one day. The waiting list time for base housing jumped from two to three months to twelve to fourteen months. The base exchange shelves were emptied within a few days. The commissary and exchange immediately submitted plans for new and bigger buildings. The yard worker population tripled.

On 27 October, the ship once again crossed the equator, and a day was set aside for crossing the line ceremonies, initiating "pollywogs" to "shellbacks." In weapons department, there were two sailors (none in W Division), who did not want to participate. I thought this was poor sportsmanship. They were not forced to go through the initiation, and had to remain in their berthing space all day during the festivities.

The ship pulled again into Pattaya Beach, Thailand. Carmen had flown to Bangkok, and was waiting at Pattaya Beach, when I "waded ashore." We shopped for jewelry. One popular thing for pilots to do in Thailand was to have jewelers make their pilot's wings, which were worn on their chest, made into rings. I had my warrant officer surface ordnance symbol, a flaming ordnance pot, made into a gold ring.

One evening Carmen and I had dinner in a converted railroad car restaurant, called the "Orient Express." The waiters were extremely attentive, to the point of distraction! A waiter was positioned standing behind both of us. Each time we took a sip from our glass, the waiter would immediately refill the glass; each time we took a bite of our food, and laid the fork down, the waiter would replace the used fork with a clean one. This was a case of too much service! I bought a stuffed cobra and mongoose that Carmen was not too fond of. I think she was pleased when a few years later it deteriorated to the point that I had to throw it away.

The ship pulled anchor, and we steamed together with the *USS Enterprise* for a short "war game." Both aircraft carriers were tasked with building five hundred 500-pound bombs, load them on aircraft and drop them. This was a timed event to be completed within twenty-four hours. *Midway* weapons department built 520 bombs, and they were dropped within twenty-three hours. *USS Enterprise* built 470 bombs, and it took forty-eight hours before their bombs were dropped. We took a lot of pride in besting the *Enterprise*, who was much larger, and newer than *Midway*.

On 22 November, the ship pulled into Subic Bay, and Carmen was able to meet the ship. We got a room at the Subic Bay Bachelor Officer's Club. I ran across the captain from San Diego, who had inspected the ship. He was traveling to another inspection site. He restated his desire for me to come to work for him some time in the future.

Commander Jim McDevitt was to be the new weapons department head. He was to relieve Commander Quinn, who was going to a test pilot assignment on the east coast. One evening Carmen and I traveled to the resort area of White Rock, and there in the restaurant spied Commander McDevitt, who asked us to join him for dinner. We enjoyed a dinner show that included a seven-year-old Filipino boy, who was a fantastic singer.

I was soon to celebrate my fortieth birthday. I was much older than the majority of sailors on *Midway*. Looking back at what I had accomplished thus far, and considering the experiences I'd had, I was well pleased at this point. I was very thankful for Carmen, and the life we shared. I was not pleased with the impact our nomadic life had on our children. I was very pleased with the records of accomplishment that *Midway*'s W Division had set. I was not happy about the lack of acknowledgment that the captain and Commander Quinn had given W Division sailors. They had been intensely interested in W Division prior to the inspection, and then seemed to forget them after the inspection was over. I was very disappointed that Commander Quinn had not come down into the division, after they had done so well for him, and at least verbally thank them. My reflections included my amazement that I had exceeded the goals I had set for myself when I decided to make the Navy my career. I had hoped to become a chief petty officer, and to have achieved the status of a commissioned officer was far above my expectations.

The Navy was very serious about weight control. This was in strict contrast to the Navy's casual attitude toward overweight sailors during the first few years of my career. Along with new enforcement regulations against illegal drug usage, the Navy issued new weight control program guidance. Every sailor's height was compared to his weight to see if he or she were to be declared overweight. Gone were the days when a "pot belly" was considered standard issue for chief petty officers, and senior officers. *Midway*'s executive officer was very serious about enforcing the new weight standards. Sailors identified as overweight were weighed weekly, and the medical department gave the recorded weights to the executive officer for his review. This was nicknamed, as I said before, "the fat boy program." If a weight decrease didn't take place over a specific time period, then disciplinary action was taken. Disciplinary actions might include suspended promotions, or withdrawal of promotion recommendations and in severe cases, an administrative discharge from the Navy. In W Division I had four sailors that were put into the fat boy program. In the case of two sailors, this was a difficult situation, because they were senior petty officers, who had exceptional records, except for the overweight problem. One complaint I had from these sailors was that they were given orders to lose weight, but given very little guidance from the medical department how to do it. Chief Munson and I counseled these sailors each week, and tried to suggest ways to lose weight. It was difficult to lose weight in a shipboard environment, with meals available twenty-four hours a day, and limited space for exercise. The executive officer made it clear to everyone on *Midway* that he was going to strictly enforce the weight control program.

Working with other division officers, and socializing in the wardroom, I made a number of friends outside the weapons department, the ship's meteorologist, supply officers, and squadron pilots just to name a few. I often shared a dining table with the Protestant Chaplain. I attended church services each Sunday; work permitting, when the ship was underway. Attendance at the church services was very low, usually a group of sixty sailors out of a crew of 4,500. The chaplain's office was struck with a scandal the latter part of 1982. A Catholic Chaplain that had been onboard for about six months was charged with making homosexual advances toward a number of sailors. One of these sailors was a seaman that worked in the weapons office. After these accusations were confirmed, the captain threw the chaplain off the ship, at the next port call. The chaplain held the rank of commander, but I doubt that he remained in the Navy.

In *Midway*'s homeport of Yokosuka the *Midway* Officer's wives were a busy group. During Captain Owen's time on *Midway*, his wife had frequent "teas," and meetings with the wives. Carmen was active in this group. The wives interacted with various Japanese women's groups. The Navy wives did such things as put on fashion shows that raised money for different Japanese charities, and causes. Carmen made many Japanese lady friends. With the departure of Captain Owens and his wife, and since the new captain was unmarried, the Navy wives' activities lessened somewhat. The incoming new gun boss, Commander Jim McDevitt was no stranger to Japan. He had previously been stationed on *Midway*, and in Japan as a pilot. Many years in the future, we discovered that we had been on the *Ticonderoga* at the same time.

His wife Kimi was from Japan, and her and Carmen formed a close and immediate friendship. Kimi was the "sparkplug' for many of the *Midway* wife's activities.

After the ship departed from Subic, W Division performed one of the many operations we were scheduled to complete that month. My policy was that the day after leaving port there would be no technical or critical work, as many of the sailors were likely to be tired, or have hangovers from liberty celebrations. I wanted them to be one hundred percent alert, and not prone to mistakes before picking up tools. After twenty-four hours of casual work, and rest, I would permit technical operations to begin.

The ship anchored in the port of Hong Kong for five days. I stood by for a number of weapons department officers who had wives visiting from Yokosuka. In Hong Kong, standing OOD watches, I always asked for ships' position reports anchored in our vicinity, every couple of hours. The merchant ship that was adrift on the one occasion in Hong Kong Harbor remained fresh in my mind.

Midway pulled anchor and we got underway. After the usual day of recuperation, the forward magazine assembly crew went below into the magazine to begin a maintenance operation. After about an hour, Chief Munson came into my office and said, "Gunner, we've got a problem, one of the classified maintenance kits is missing." I immediately went below into the magazine. Before pulling into Hong Kong we had fourteen cans with maintenance kits stored inside. Now there were fourteen container cans, but one kit was gone. All sailors were searching the magazine. I directed that all division spaces be searched. I was in disbelief, and I could not imagine how a classified maintenance kit could be missing? After an hour with no results, I told everyone to take a ten-minute break, think about where the kit might be, and then search the compartments again. Everyone was worried, but not to the extent that I was. I thought of the in port period, and how a classified item could have been smuggled off the ship. I thought also of the garbage barge that daily came alongside, and the possibility of the kit ending up in the garbage barge. This could cause an international incident with huge ramifications. After the second search failed to turn up the kit, I told Chief Munson, I had to inform Commander Quinn. I left the division, and walked toward the weapons office on the second deck. Images of the end of my Navy career flashed before my eyes. It was unthinkable that a classified component could disappear. I was the custodian of all classified components on board *Midway*, and responsible for their safekeeping. I would be fortunate to only get a court martial. This could mean prison for dereliction of duty, and huge monetary fines. I reached the weapons office; Commander Quinn was in a conference with another officer in his inner office, so I had to wait. While waiting, I rehearsed how I was going to break this terrible news to him. Just as the visiting officer was leaving Commander Quinn's inner office, and I was about to go in, Chief Munson arrived breathlessly at the weapons office door, and said, "Gunner we found it." I asked where, and he said "Hidden in the overhead behind some pipes in the forward magazine." I followed Chief Munson back to the W Division spaces, and he showed me where the kit had been found. It appeared undamaged, and I told the sailors not to handle it excessively as we might need to fingerprint it. I was extremely relieved, but this revelation caused other serious concerns to surface. I apparently had a dangerous sailor or sailors in the division. It always took two sailors to enter a magazine, observing the two-man rule. Whoever the culprit or culprits were, he or they had no problem violating security rules. After I made sure the kit was secured, I returned to the weapons office, and informed Commander Quinn what had happened. I then told him it was imperative that I find out who the guilty sailor was. I intended to interview all W Division sailors, and I might need the help of the Naval Investigative Service civilian detective who was stationed onboard *Midway*.

I began that same day interviewing each W Division sailor, in my office with Chief Munson, behind a closed door. Before the interviews, I reviewed the magazine access logs, with times, and names of those that entered the magazine during our in port period. The magazines were entered twice daily, by two sailors in the duty section, for the purpose of taking magazine temperatures, and checking the security of the magazine. I also had to take into consideration that two sailors might have entered the magazine without recording their names and the times on the access log. I also reviewed the marine's access log, which showed the times the magazine alarm system was turned off to permit entry. The logs all appeared to detail each entry and exit without any discrepancies. I began by interviewing the senior petty officers, and worked down.

I had no indication who may have hidden the kit, until Chief Munson and I began interviewing the Seaman GMT's. One man confessed to me he knew who did it, and said if after I'd spoken to everyone, the person hadn't confessed, he would tell me who it was. A few interviews after this one, a GMTSN admitted to me that he had hidden the kit. He was one of the sailors that were in the weight control program. He said he was upset about being in the program, and thought he would "get back at the Navy" by hiding the kit. I then questioned who the other sailor was with him in the magazine.

He told me who it was, although I already knew from looking at the access log. He said the other GMTSN didn't see him hide the kit, and had nothing to do with his plan. I was not pleased with this revelation because it meant in this instance the two-man rule had not been complied with. Each person was to remain in sight of each other at all times in the magazine, and be aware of what the other person was doing.

My first concern was to get the guilty sailor out of the division. There was real anger against him. I was worried what the other sailors in the division might do to him. I directed Chief Munson to hold everyone in the coffee locker. I then accompanied the seaman to the berthing compartment, and had him empty his locker, pack his sea bag, and gather all his personal belongings. I then took him to another berthing area in the ship, in a division out of weapons department. I removed his name from the W Division access list, and informed the weapons officer what action I had taken. I placed the sailor on report for failure to comply with a lawful order, i.e., the two-man rule, and mishandling of government property, and additional charges of endangering. When I accompanied the sailor to captain's mast, I was disappointed when the captain dismissed the charges, but instead recommended an administrative discharge. A few months later the sailor was out of the Navy. I saw him frequently and tried to understand what caused him to take such a drastic action. He was somewhat of a loner. I could never understand how he felt such an action would resolve the inner-turmoil he felt because of the weight control program. I also was worried that there may have been signs that the petty officers or I may have missed that could have prompted us to somehow help him.

I was upset with the man who had been in the magazine with the guilty sailor, and told him I was considering putting him on report. I let him worry about this for a couple of days before letting him off with a warning. I also lectured the entire division on the importance of the two-man rule, and emphasized that they could never let their guard down.

The division continued the maintenance work, minus the help of one GMTSN. The ship pulled into Yokosuka for one day, and the following day we got underway with sailor's families for a special dependent day cruise. Carmen and Mary enjoyed the day at sea, which included a flyby of the ship's planes, and a barbeque on the flight deck. Many of the families quickly got bored, and gained an appreciation for the way their husbands and fathers served day after day at sea. The ship was to remain in Yokosuka until 12 January. There was a lot of talk about oil shortages the last part of 1982, and it was not yet clear how this might affect *Midway*'s operating schedule. There was also talk of extending assignments, so my transfer time in 1983 and the transfers of others on the ship were questionable. One transfer I was not looking forward to was to happen in March 1983. Chief Munson had orders to Jacksonville, Florida. His relief had not been identified. I knew it was going to be difficult, if not impossible to replace him. Carmen surprised me on my birthday with a ten-speed bicycle. I was to use the bike to go the eight blocks back and forth from the house to the ship. Prior to Christmas we had a division get-together at our house. The younger sailors, who were thousands of miles from home, and family, enjoyed and appreciated this gathering.

Mary's problems at school were escalating, and the help we were getting from the local family services was not very professional, in particular a LCDR psychologist, who's ideas I did not agree with. Discipline and illegal drugs were a large problem in the base dependant school on the Yokosuka base. During January, three teenagers were killed in an automobile accident on base, after attending a glue-sniffing party. Without going into details, it became necessary for Mary to return to the States, and live with my parents until I received transfer orders. Sailor's families are subjected to difficult living conditions, and stresses that are hard to be understood, or appreciated by the American civilian population. The Navy divorce rate is much higher, than the rest of society, and I can attest to this from my personal experience, and from what I observed in the Navy. Family relationships are strained and often broken. This can be added to the list of sacrifices made by men and women who don the uniform of the United States Navy.

As time passed since our inspection, I was becoming frustrated by the lack of recognition the division had received for the NTPI/DNSI. This prompted me to write a letter to Commander Quinn, dated 23 January 1983, concerning a memorandum I'd written four months previously, which said:

> On 22 September 1982 I submitted a memorandum listing those W Division personnel I felt deserved recognition for their part in the DNSI/NTPI, along with proposed write-ups. On 12 October 1982 I submitted a memorandum expressing concern over the time span between the DNSI and recognition efforts. The weapons officer assured me that recognition would be forthcoming. I resubmitted write-ups and justification in November 1982. I submitted further justification to Lieutenant Junior Grade Dickinson (weapons officer assistant) in December 1982.

As of February 1983, five men of the nineteen that participated in the DNSI will have transferred. I feel that some transfer or discharge decisions are being affected by the lack of recognition for the DNSI/NTPI. For the past four months I have been assuring W Division that personal recognition for their part in the DNSI/NTPI would shortly occur, it has become a mute point. I am beginning to perceive an effect on divisional morale and individual/divisional motivation that was at a peak in October 1982.

    I respectfully suggest that if approved I initiate personal recognition letters for the W Division members' currently onboard, and mail letters to those individuals that have since been transferred.

    I estimate this project could be completed the latter part of February 1983.

    Very Respectfully CWO3 James S. Little.

I was prompted to write this letter not only because it was the right thing to do, but also because an officer within the weapons department, who I'll not name, had submitted a recommendation to Commander Quinn that he be awarded a Navy Achievement Medal for his part in the inspection. This not only upset me, but infuriated me, as this particular officer had very little to do with the preparation or conduct of the inspection. If anyone deserved recognition and a medal it was the men in the magazines. This was a case of the officer in the rear asking for a medal for what the men in the trenches on the front line had done. I never knew for sure if this officer was awarded a medal, because there was no formal presentation, as there was in normal cases. He must have known in his heart this was a selfish, cowardly thing to do.

    The elation, and satisfaction I had felt after the inspection was being replaced by frustration and disappointment, from the lack of recognition I felt my men deserved from higher up the chain of command. I had spent more than two years leading, preparing and encouraging W Division sailors to reach their highest potential. All of my waking hours, and energies had been concentrated toward this goal. The W Division sailors had risen to the challenge, and proven themselves to be perfect, by undergoing the intense inspections, and coming through faultless. They had not received the praise, and recognition I felt they deserved; I had to come up with a way to give them a proper reward. The gun boss gave me the go ahead with my recognition efforts, after he read my memorandum.

    This may not be fair to Commander Quinn, and I'm not qualified to judge him, but I felt, as did others that he acted like the weapons department head job on *Midway* was a delaying point in his career, as his true desire, was to be in the cockpit of an airplane. I saw a difference in the brand of leadership he provided, compared to his predecessor Commander Kellner, and his relief, Commander McDevitt.

    In Yokosuka from the first part of December to February 1983, minor shipyard repairs were accomplished on the ship. Over the past years of *Midway*'s life, more and more equipment had been brought on board and installed. Her hull had originally been constructed for a battleship. Thick armored plating encircled her hull around the water line, for protection from torpedoes. *Midway* had gradually over the years taken on a permanent list to the starboard side. One day during this in-port period, everyone except the duty section was ordered off the ship. Then the yard workers and squadron personnel moved weights and airplanes about to different positions while measurements were taken, to determine what ballast would need to be needed to correct this ever-increasing list of *Midway* to starboard. The next major yard period was to be in August 1983.

    In February, I had a "heart to heart" meeting with all the sailors in W division. I told them of my pride in the division, and in each of them as professional sailors. I told them I felt they should have received more recognition for their outstanding performance of duties during the inspection, but as I explained this was not an unusual situation, as those outside our division spaces did not understand the pressures and requirements of our jobs. I said this was mostly because our jobs were shrouded in secrecy. I also said we had received praise from those who understood our job the best, the NTPI and DNSI inspectors. They had many years of experience doing the same jobs we did, day in, and day out.

    I went on to say I would reward them where it counted, in their performance evaluation reports. I told them I was requesting a Navy Achievement Medal for Leading Chief Munson, Assembly Team Leaders GMT1 Hartman, GMT1 Bogner, GMT1 Halpin, and Administration Petty Officer GMT1 Tonnon. I was also submitting letters of appreciation to be signed by the captain, for the assembly team leaders. I planned to include letters of appreciation from me to each GMT that would be placed in each sailor's service record. I felt the men in this meeting appreciated my efforts, although many shared my disappointment in the lack of recognition from the command. I'm sure if we had failed the inspection, we would have gotten all the attention we could stand!

    As it developed, only Chief Munson, and GMT1 Bogner were approved for the Navy Achievement Medal.

One of the sailors I had recommended was in the "fat boy" program, and did not have a chance of making it through the approval process. Sadly, the executive officer, recommended this same sailor, who was squared away in all other aspects, for an administrative discharge. He left the ship in February, very bitter. I heard that later he was able to lose weight while out of the Navy, and came back in to finish his naval career. I completed all the letters of appreciation I'd promised. For the rest of my time onboard, I ensured that the sailors, who had gone through the inspection, received the highest justifiable marks on their performance evaluations. Most of these sailors were promoted at the earliest point possible. In Chief Munson's case he was promoted to senior chief the same year in 1983, and eventually ended his career as a master chief, having been promoted to the highest possible level for an enlisted man.

The ship got underway from Yokosuka 26 February. We were to be away from Yokosuka for two and a half months. One Sunday morning while underway, I went down to W Division office after breakfast in the wardroom, at 0730, as was my usual routine. I often permitted the crew to have a slack day on Sunday, although underway, Sunday was considered a normal workday. A little before 10:00 a.m., I left the W Division spaces, and walked to the compartment on the second deck where Sunday church services were held. After the church service, I had lunch in the wardroom, and returned to the W Division Office. Around 1430 (2:30 p.m.) while sitting at my desk, with Chief Munson sitting at his desk nearby, heavy black smoke suddenly began pouring out of the ventilation air outlet in the overhead. I immediately called the crew that was working in the magazine below, and asked if they were experiencing smoke? There were three men in the magazine, and after they quickly checked all the vents, they said "No." The smoke was becoming so thick that it was difficult to breathe. I told the men in the magazine over the intercom that we were going to have to evacuate the third deck office, and coffee locker area, and go up to the second deck. I told them to remain in the magazine, and frequently feel the bulkheads to see if they felt any heat. At the same time I was talking to the men in the magazine, Chief Munson was reporting the smoke to the bridge. It was a matter of seconds before Chief Munson, and me and four other sailors who were in the coffee locker had to leave by going up the ladder, and closing the hatch so the smoke would not spread to the upper deck. It was impossible to see in the thick black smoke. I was thankful that we had training drills from time to time, blindfolding the sailors to see if they could find their way out of the spaces in darkness. The fire drills we had held in the past had assumed that the third deck office area would be the command center, using the division intercom, directing the sailors within the magazines to take certain actions. The sailors down in the fourth deck magazine were now cut off from us. They could not move up through the smoke-filled third deck. The only way they would be able to evacuate, was through a small escape hatch within the magazine that lead to another compartment on the fourth deck. I positioned myself directly above the closed second deck hatch that was within the marine sentry's security room. Chief Munson went outside the "green door," and called the after magazine on the ship's telephone, and told the crew there to maintain contact with the sailors in the forward magazine. It was a roundabout method of communication, but at least we had communication. The bridge sounded the fire alarm, and the ship's fire party responded to W Division entrance, they could not enter unless it was an absolute emergency. Two of the sailors on the second deck with me had donned OBA's; I double-checked their equipment to make sure they had the breathing apparatuses on properly. I then had the other two sailors attach tending lines to the belts of the men with the OBA's on. The lines would be used to drag the men out of the smoke-filled compartment if they got into trouble. I continued shouting to Chief Munson what we were doing, so he could relay it to the fire party. The two sailors with OBA's on, with battle lanterns in their hands, quickly opened the hatch as smoke billowed out, and in seconds they were gone, and the hatch was closed just enough for the tending lines to slip through. The two young sailors holding the lines were wide eyed, and pale faced. The two sailors within the compartment below were trying to find any evidence of heat and fire. I remember thinking; "it's good that I attended church services this morning." I was becoming concerned about the men within the smoke-filled compartment below, when after what seemed like an eternity, the two sailors reappeared. They reported they could not find any source of fire, and the smoke seemed to be thinning. About this time, Chief Munson shouted from outside the door, that the fire fighters had found the source of the fire. It was within a small storage compartment, adjacent to our W Division office that shared the same ventilation system. Someone had stored a sea bag against steam pipes, which got so hot the sea bag smoldered for many days, and finally burst into flames, burning other sea bags stacked near it. The fire was quickly put out, and we all breathed a sigh of relief. The forward office was aired out, but the odor of smoke lingered for many weeks afterward. This was a lesson for me, and all in the division. Living on a warship, during an emergency you can never assume you'll have access to the same compartment all the time.

After that day, I created a few emergency training scenarios that involved directing magazine crews from areas other than the third deck office area. This emergency also emphasized the responsibility I had for the welfare and safety of the men working for me. They were willing and eager to leap into danger when I gave the word, and I did not take this authority lightly.

One of the things I insisted the GMT's do was submit Unsatisfactory Reports (UR's). I had always felt this was something GMT's could do that improved and bettered the nuclear weapons program we all worked in. At previous commands I'd been at, when a UR was submitted up through the chain of command, and finally sent to McAlester, Oklahoma, and FCDNA, Albuquerque New Mexico, there was a block on the form entitled "submitted by." The division officer usually signed this block, or the commanding officer. I instituted a new policy, that the sailor, who discovered the problem, or error in the manuals, has his name in the "submitted by" block, when the form left the ship. I was hopeful this "pride of authorship" would prompt more UR submissions. The path to perfection was improved by GMT's always looking for imperfections. For a short while, I gave an UR quota requirement to each magazine supervisor. This quota was not well liked, but eventually the GMT's began a steady stream of UR reports leaving the ship. When the answer to the UR was received back, the sailor submitting the UR would read the answer to the crew. Little did I know at the time what a large part Unsatisfactory Reports would play in my future?

During the February and March at sea period, *Midway* was at one time alongside a destroyer tender, when I got a message down in W Division that I had a call from the ship that was alongside, over a phone line that was strung between the two ships. I went to the hangar deck, and took the phone receiver from the boatswain's mate. It was Senior Chief Graybow, who I'd been stationed with at Oakland Naval Supply Center. After we exchanged "hellos and greetings" he asked if I could calibrate some torque wrenches he had. I told him "sure." The wrenches were sent over the unrep line connecting the two ships. I directed a W Division sailor to take the wrenches to *Midway*'s calibration lab, and after the calibration sent the wrenches back to Senior Chief Graybow. One afternoon, we connected up to an ammo ship, and it was asked that I fly aboard the ammo ship on their helicopter. I boarded the helo on Midway's flight deck, and after a very short flight landed on the ammunition ship's landing deck on her stern. There to meet me after I climbed out of the helo was Terry Morrison, who I'd been on the *Oriskany* with. He was now a CWO2, and assigned as the ammo ship's gunner. After a short reunion, and a meeting with the captain, I returned to *Midway*. Terry said his tour on the ammo ship was about to end, and he was transferring to Subic Bay Magazine.

Chief John Munson left the ship in the latter part of March. W Division gave him a farewell party. Carmen and I had enjoyed times with him and his wife Louise. I thanked him for all his hard work. We had known each other for twenty years, since the days of the *Ticonderoga*. Chief Munson was a true professional, a good shipmate, and friend. I was to miss him sorely. After he left the ship, GMT1 Bogner sat down at his desk.

The last of March, I was given another fitness report. On this report, I received all "A's," and was ranked number "one in the pack" for the first time on *Midway*.

In April the Battleship USS *Iowa* came alongside *Midway*. The past couple of years, the Navy had been reactivating the World War II era battleships. One reason for this reactivation effort was that these huge ships looked very impressive as a warship, much more so than any surface ship presently in the Navy. The battleship's sixteen-inch guns turrets looked huge, and foreboding. When an American Battleship pulled into a foreign port, its appearance projected our military presence in a more forcible manner than a destroyer with a single barreled five inch gun on the bow. The sixteen-inch guns were fired using black powder propellants in canvas bags. The Navy brought a number of retired Gunner's Mates back on active duty to teach the present generation of Gunner's Mates how to fire sixteen-inch guns using black powder bags. These guns were extremely accurate. There had been a plan at one time to fit the sixteen-inch gun turrets with a sophisticated radar system, and place the turrets at various locations about the U.S., as a system that would be used to shoot down incoming intercontinental ballistic missiles.

Armored hatches were at locations about the *Midway*, mostly on the second deck. These hatches weighed hundreds of pounds, and protected specific compartments from explosions, or the intense heat produced during oil or aviation gas fires. The armored hatches were primarily protection for magazine areas that would hopefully prevent the stored bombs beneath the hatches from detonating. These hatches were so heavy that counter balance weights attached to a pulley system were used to help sailors open and close the heavy hatches. The Navy had focused special attention on these armored hatches, because there had been a number of injuries, and deaths when the counter balance systems failed, permitting the hatches to fall on unfortunate sailors.

W Division had two armored hatches over our forward and after magazines. A sailor who worked in the after magazine badly smashed his finger while closing the armored hatch. Since his injury involved an armored hatch, there was an investigation conducted by the ship's safety office. This was a Navy-wide requirement anytime an injury was reported with a hatch of this type. Periodic maintenance records were examined, and it was determined that all periodic preventive maintenance had been held properly. The investigators came to the conclusion that the sailor had not been cautious enough when closing the hatch and the blame for the accident was on his shoulders. Nevertheless, after the accident, and during the investigation, I had been anxious about the sailor's injury, and the outcome of the investigation. Had the investigation revealed that the periodic maintenance had not been completed, or completed improperly, I could have been held responsible, and most likely punished. This small incident emphasized that while I had authority over men, much more so than any position in civilian life, as W Division Officer, I also had responsibility, and accountability for all that occurred within W Division This responsibility and accountability increased in scope with the weapons officer's accountability extending throughout all of weapons department, and the captain's accountability extending to all of *Midway*.

Just as cities on land experience daily fires that require dispatching of fire departments, *Midway* had daily fires that the ship's fire fighting party would respond to. When the rapid ringing of the fire bell sounded over the ships announcement system, all activity came to a halt, while everyone listened for the announcement of the location of the fire. If a fire was in any adjacent compartment to W Division compartments, then W Division was required to man that compartment. Everyone in W Division had to memorize our compartment numbers. On each sailor's bunk there was a plastic hood with an attached can that would supply fifteen minutes of air, during an emergency escape from smoke filled berthing compartments. My bunkroom was located in the worse possible location on an aircraft carrier, considering fire possibilities. The bunkroom was on the 02 deck, right under the flight deck, the overhead (or the ceiling) was actually the flight deck. The deck (or the floor) was the roof of the hangar bay. Fires on the flight deck usually involved aircraft fuel, which would naturally flow down into the 02 deck. Fires in the hangar bay would cause smoke that would fill the 02 level. I and the three other officers that lived in the bunk room would always listen closely to fire alarm announcements, not only to hear if our divisions were involved, but also for our personal survival.

One day in April I received a call to report to the weapons office. Upon arriving in the office the weapons officer told me I was to pull the access of a GMT3 that had been aboard for little over a year. I was to supervise him packing his sea bag, and then escort him to the master at arms office. The gun boss explained the ship had gotten a message saying this sailor had enlisted under a false name. He had been in the Army, and had gone AWOL. At the time of his disappearance, he had been implicated in an illegal drug smuggling operation, and a murder. Up to this point he had been an outstanding sailor, and had given me no reason to question him, or his technical performance. I wondered from that day on, how reliable the security system truly was, to have let a person with a false name, and on the run from legal problems, become a Nuclear Weaponsman.

This situation sent shock waves through W Division, and the weapons department. While I walked with the sailor to the master at arms office, he apologized to me, and said he enjoyed working for me. He was taken off the ship within twenty-four hours, and I never saw him again, nor heard what happened to him.

In April the ship paid a return visit to Pusan, Korea. Carmen and her frequent traveling companion Vicky Peters flew to Korea to meet the ship. Carmen and I bought some silverware from a Korean silverware manufacturer that were decorated with a popular Korean diet item, ginseng. Carmen and I were strolling down a Pusan street with Norm and Vicky one afternoon, when air raid sirens sounded. The streets and sidewalks were immediately vacant. People leaned from doorways, and windows, shouting at the four of us in Korean. We finally understood they were telling us to get off the street. We ducked into an alleyway, and a Korean standing there motioned for us to stay there. We remained in the alley for about fifteen minutes, perplexed about what was going on. Then the sirens sounded again, and people began filling the street. We learned later that this had been a weekly air raid drill. South Korea was a country with a siege mentality since the Korean War cease fire that divided the country into two different nations. Armed South Korean soldiers were on almost every street corner. This was very intimidating to Carmen and Vicky, and the other *Midway* wives visiting Korea.

Everyone stocked up on tennis shoes while in Pusan. One night Carmen and I ran across some W Division sailors out on the town. They insisted that I try some Korean plum wine they were drinking, foolishly I did, and was sick for most of the night. The ship got underway from Pusan, and Carmen and Vicky returned to Japan, going first through Seoul, Korea.

CDR Jim McDevitt, and his wife Kimi had many Japanese friends and acquaintances, which in turn, Carmen and I got to know. I truly enjoyed working for Commander McDevitt, and Carmen and I became close to him and Kimi, and their family of a girl, Tami, and two boys, J.J., and David. The gun boss and a number of Japanese shipyard contractors founded a Japanese/American Appreciation Society. The officers of weapons department were all members of this society. Informal social gatherings are an important ingredient in Japanese business affairs. The weapons department officers were treated to a number of elaborate dinner parties. Hosted by Japanese businessmen whose companies worked on *Midway* shipyard projects. We could not accept gifts, but were permitted to accept food and drink.

I recall one occasion in Sasebo, Japan, when Commander McDevitt, and about eight of us were guests at a Japanese restaurant, hosted by a number of Yokosuka businessmen. We all knelt on pillows around a low table piled high with various snacks, and fruits. Positioned behind each officer was a geisha girl, dressed in an elaborate kimono, whose task it was to keep our glasses full, and hand us snacks, and bits of food. There were numerous toasts with sake. After a few speeches an army of restaurant waiters brought in the main dinner course. There were mountains of food, and one dish in particular I remember, was a large fish, that was whole, with slabs cut in its sides. This was sushi, or fresh fish. This fish was very fresh, and must have been prepared skillfully, and quickly, because the fish was still moving when it was carried in on a large plate.

In April, my detailer informed me where my next assignment was to be. I discovered that CWO4 Charlie Schmidt had asked that I be his replacement at Field Command Defense Nuclear Agency (FCDNA), when he retired in 1984. This was a CWO4 job assignment, and even though I was a CWO3, Charlie had told the detailer that he had worked with me, and I would be the best man for the job. I was not to transfer until October, which would mean I would spend thirty-eight months on *Midway*.

The ship was in Yokosuka in mid-May, and one evening Kimi Mcdevitt, Carmen and I had an interesting evening together. Commander McDevitt had duty as the command duty officer on this particular evening. Kimi took us to a unique Japanese café in Yokosuka. The stools for customers were positioned around a curving, twisting table upon which an electric train was moving. The train's cars contained various food in small bowls, which constantly moved by the seated customers. If you saw a dish that you wanted, you grabbed it from the moving train, and dug in with your chopsticks. After customers had eaten their fill, the restaurant cashier totaled up the empty dishes in front of the customer, and that was the bill.

Shortly after the end of May, I received word that I had a niece, born to my brother Jerry, her name was Monica Leigh Little, and Carmen and I were anxious to see her, when we returned to the States.

There were sixteen chief warrant officers on *Midway*, and only one of them was a CWO4. This CWO4 did not stand duty as an OOD, but stood duty as command duty officer, in company with the ship's department heads. CWO4 was considered a lofty position, and on many ships they were exempted from standing duty, as it was considered that they had stood more than their share of duty days in the Navy. On some ships' wardrooms had an area set aside as the warrant officer mess, but this was not the case on *Midway*. The CWO4 would occasionally call a meeting of all the chief warrant officers to discuss any issues that we felt needed discussing. We were a special breed of officers, and tended to look out for each other, just as we had in our "previous lives" as chief petty officers.

CWO2 Chuck Morgan, who lived in my bunkroom, worked on the ship's catapults. As I mentioned, he slept underneath me in a bottom bunk, and often talked in his sleep. It would not have been so bad, but when he talked he often answered himself. Chuck had been married six times, and was married for the seventh time while on *Midway*. Another member of the bunkroom CWO3 Carl Snow, who worked in the operations department, was a talented oil painter. For the 1981-82 ship's cruise book, he painted pictures of the planes used by the squadrons on board. He painted dual pictures, one of the very first plane flown by the squadrons, mostly propeller driven aircraft, and pictures of the current plane used by the squadrons.

W Division day-to-day work continued, with GMT1 Bogner standing in as leading chief petty officer. With the departure of Chief Munson, I became more involved in the daily routine of the division as GMT1 Bogner was not nearly as experienced as Chief Munson.

The latter part of May, a P-3 *Orion* aircraft pilot, LT Charlie Wittenburg checked into weapons department. He had attended the Nuclear Safety Officer Course in San Diego, and was to be the W Division Officer. I liked Lieutenant Wittenburg immediately, and he was well accepted by the sailors in the division. In June I was once again "demoted" to the position of Technical Monitor.

The first part of June, a ship's hail/farewell party included welcoming Captain McGrail's new wife. He had married the widow of a pilot he had flown with in Vietnam.

On 18 June, the ship was in Subic Bay. Carmen, Kimi McDevitt, and Sue Burrows met the ship. One day we three couples visited CWO3 Terry Morrison, who was now stationed at the Naval Magazine, and lived on base with his family. Another day, Carmen and I visited with Kimi, and her children who were staying at White Rock Resort. This was the resort where I had attended W Division parties, and gatherings while on the *Ticonderoga*, and *Oriskany*. Carmen and I and Kimi, and her kids had a great time swimming, and getting sunburned.

On 16 June, GMT1 Bogner had extended his enlistment in the Navy four years, or as it was called, "shipped over." I held a formal shipping over ceremony in the forward magazine. I had also recommended him for a Navy Achievement Medal. The medal was presented to him by the captain during a ceremony in the Captain's At Sea Cabin. Lieutenant Wittenburg and I were present at this ceremony. When I first reported aboard *Midway*, Bogner was in a disciplinary status. He had been in Yokosuka, having checked in while the ship was at sea, and was awaiting its return to port, so he could check aboard. One evening he had gotten drunk, and could not find his way back to the transient barracks where he was staying. He broke into a base house garage, and fell asleep. The next morning the woman of the house, who happened to be the wife of the admiral in charge of the naval forces Japan, discovered him. Bogner was picked up by the shore patrol, but was not formally charged. His access approval to W Division was delayed, while a decision was made about whether he had an alcohol problem. At the time he was a second class petty officer. I had seen him promoted to first class petty officer, and mature into a leader, and excellent technician.

Bogner and a second class in W Division had married Filipino women while I had been onboard. There were many marriages between sailors and Filipino women. Some, sadly to say were cases of the women looking for a "ticket to the states," and the marriages would soon end in divorce when the women obtained citizenship. The Philippine government had taken notice of this exodus of its young women to the United States, and had made it very difficult for the women to obtain exit-visas, even after the marriage had taken place. The ship had a very effective program that tried to help sailors contemplating marriage to Filipino women. It was illegal for a sailor to marry a foreign national without command approval. A request chit for marriage had to be submitted to the captain for his approval. Following the captain's approval, sailors were required to attend a series of six classes given by the chaplain's office. The goal of these classes was to attempt to make the adjustment of the marriage between two different nationalities easier, and hopefully lead to a successful, happy union. The classes taught cultural differences. One class emphasized that marriage to a Filipino girl, meant not only marriage to the girl, but to her whole family as well. This meant the sailor might be expected to financially support not only his wife, but his new in-laws as well. Bogner and Clark had been married for over a year, and still had not gotten visa approval for their wives to leave the Philippines and join them. In Clark's case, it was not for two years, and six months after he was transferred, before his wife was able to join him.

GMT1 Bogner transferred Mid-June, and was selected for advancement to chief petty officer, as the results of the February 1983 promotion exam. He was transferred to Lualualei, Hawaii Naval Magazine. A couple of months later, Chief Munson related the following to me in a letter. GMT1 Bogner arrived in Hawaii, and it appeared he was finally going to get his wife out of the Philippines, and join him in Hawaii. Before going to work with the other GMT's at the magazine, while awaiting his clearance confirmation, he got a driving while intoxicated (DWI) ticket. As the result of his ticket, he attended alcohol awareness classes, and successfully graduated, and was a couple of days away from being promoted to chief. A surprise urinalysis was held on all the GMT's, and it was discovered that he had used marijuana. He admitted to smoking a joint a few days prior to the surprise test. At that point his career was over. He was punished under the zero tolerance guidelines since he was a senior petty officer. He lost everything, including his promotion, and possible retirement and benefits. He received an administrative discharge. He also lost command sponsorship for his wife to travel to Hawaii. This was devastating news to me, and I was very disappointed over his stupidity, and loss of his future. I never heard what became of him, or if he ever saw his wife again.

In July I discovered who was to be my relief on *Midway*. It was CWO4 Raymond Langley, who was on a submarine tender stationed in San Diego. I was appointed as his sponsor, and he was expected onboard in September.

In July the ship visited Hong Kong. Carmen baby-sat Kimi McDevitt's children while Kimi visited Hong Kong, to be with Commander McDevitt. A number of other weapons department officer's wives flew down from Japan. Much of my in port time was spent standing by for these officers so they could spend time with their wives.

In August the ship and weapons department received some wonderful news. The *Midway* had been awarded the Battle Efficiency Award, for the second time, and weapons department had been awarded the "Black W." The black W meant we were considered the best weapons department of all the aircraft carriers in the Pacific Fleet. This meant all sailors first class and below would now wear a black "W" on their upper left sleeve, under the "E" which now would be worn with one hash mark under it indicating two awards. Weapons department sailors were ecstatic about this recognition. Weapons Department wives were also excited about the black W. Our first return to Yokosuka, after learning of the award, Kimi McDevitt, Carmen and some of the other weapons department wives prepared a huge banner congratulating weapons department. They held it up for all on the ship to see when we moved toward our berthing pier. I felt that W Division had contributed much to the award decision, by the outstanding grades of the past inspections. Commander McDevitt wrote a congratulatory letter to every sailor in weapons department that was included in our service records.

I requested that the division be given a refresher training course by instructors from San Diego, such as the one given by CWO2 Tony Lewin when I first came aboard. The ship would undergo an NTPI some time after the first part of 1984.

I had been corresponding with CWO4 Charlie Schmidt concerning my approaching transfer. I learned I would be working for an Air Force colonel, and with a mix of Army and Air Force officers. I wrote to my future new boss, Colonel Smith, telling about him about myself and family, and that I should arrive in Albuquerque late October, or early November.

As the time for my departure from *Midway* approached, I felt I had accomplished the things I had set out to do when I first came onboard. I turned my attention to some areas I had not looked at. I also began maintaining a lower profile, letting Lieutenant Wittenburg do those things I had been doing as division officer for the past year and a half, thus beginning a shift of authority from me to him. I worked on a list of "lessons learned" that might be useful for the officers and chiefs that would run W Division in the future.

The ship pulled into Yokosuka for an extended yard period. On 21 August, the world news was that a Soviet SU-15 Fighter had shot down a Boeing 747 Airliner, killing 269 persons, including some Americans. The Russians said the airliner had violated their airspace. We on *Midway* anxiously watched the news, wondering if we would onload our ordnance and get underway. As the days passed, we remained in the shipyard, and the crisis cooled.

When the ship was in port, one thing I had to adjust to while at my base house was the silence. During flight quarters, the noise in my bunkroom was deafening. The starboard catapult was located about four feet directly over the head of my bunk. When a plane was launched, the sound was like a locomotive running directly over my bed. Along with this sound, there was the constant sound of the ventilation system, and other noises associated with a steel ship underway at sea. I also think a seaman who worked on the flight deck knew exactly where my bunk was underneath, because often just as I was about to fall asleep, someone up on the flight deck above me would drop a set of tie down chains on the deck, which sounded like a train crash! Off the ship it was difficult for me to fall asleep in the silence of my house.

I got a surprise one day when a GMT1 reported aboard for W Division. It was GMT1 Norm Woods, who I'd last seen as a seaman in Guam. The last time I'd seen him, he was about to be discharged, with plans to return to his hometown and marry his high school sweetheart. He said he had returned home, but the marriage had not taken place, instead he reenlisted in the Navy. He was married to a Filipino girl, and Carmen and I invited him and his wife to our house for a welcome dinner. I felt he would be a good addition to the division. My estimation was correct, as he would be a master chief in the future. Also reporting aboard was GMTC Plymel, who would be the division leading chief.

CWO4 Raymond Langley checked aboard, and we began "turn over procedures" which was much longer than usual, almost a month and a half, versus the couple of days I'd had with CWO2 Grizzard. Soon he and Lieutenant Wittenburg assumed complete leadership of W Division. This was somewhat painful for me, and also painful for the men of W Division. It was obvious from the beginning that CWO4 Langley was going to do things differently. He was more a disciplinarian than me. A week after he began holding daily musters, I began hearing complaints from the crew that they did not like working for him. Some of the GMT's asked if I would please talk to him. I told them I would talk to him, although this was to be his division, and he would run it as he saw fit, which was his right as a naval officer. I told Raymond, he now had an exceptional crew that had done everything I asked of them. I had regrets handing the fates of those I considered "my men" over to him. I was hopeful that the division would continue to be successful.

In the future, Lieutenant Wittenburg was to move to the weapons safety officer position, and CWO4 Langley would become the W Division Officer. I noticed friction between the two officers soon after their first meeting. In many ways Lieutenant Wittenburg, CWO4 Langley, Chief Plymel, and the new LPO, GMT1 Norm Woods had an immense advantage I did not have when I first reported aboard. They had well over a month turn over period, and they were not being thrown into an intense operational situation. These managers and leaders came aboard during a slack operational time, with ample time to get organized and comfortable in their new respective positions.

Along with the crackdown on illegal drugs in the Navy, added emphasis had been placed on physical fitness. Everyone in the Navy was now expected to complete a physical fitness test every six months. This fitness tests consisted of a specific number of pushups, sit-ups, and a timed run of two miles. Weapons Department sailors participated in the first test on the Yokosuka Naval Base. I had no problem with the pushups, and sit-ups, but the two-mile run left me huffing and puffing. This was the result of the years of smoking I had subjected my lungs to.

Prior to my transfer, there was a *Midway* hail/farewell party at the new Yokosuka Officer's Club that was less than a year old. Carmen and I often went to the officer's club on "seafood night," when the specialty was broiled lobster. At the hail/farewell as I was one of the departing officers, I said a few words of thanks to all who had helped me during my tour, and I wished Raymond Langley "good luck." In addition to this party, the weapons department officers and chiefs gave Carmen and me, a farewell party. During this party I was given a picture of *Midway* that all the weapons department officers had signed. I was also given a set of bookends with dummy 20MM shells, and the dates of my service on the ship, along with a ship's plaque with my name on it. With the arrival of our new gun boss Commander McDevitt, the weapons department chiefs had been included in all the officers' gatherings. I whole-heartedly agreed with his new policy, and wished his predecessors had thought of it. Kimi McDevitt often took pictures during our parties, which were enjoyed by everyone.

Our household items were packed for the trip to New Mexico. The Japanese furniture movers groaned and moaned when they strained to move the huge table I had built while stationed in Oakland. It took six men to move the table to the moving van. Carmen and I stayed in the base Navy lodge after vacating our house. I sold our reliable Toyota station wagon to a sailor in operations department, for exactly what I had bought it for three years previously.

My last fitness report on *Midway* was written in advance of the day I was to leave which was October 7, 1983. I received all "A's," and was ranked number one. I've included the written narrative of this one fitness report, so the reader can see how fitness report narratives are written:

Chief Warrant Officer Little is unquestionably one of the finest, most outstanding Chief Warrant Officers in the Navy. Highly motivated, thoroughly competent, and totally professional. He has rightfully earned a Navy-wide reputation for excellence among an elite corps of special weapons technical specialists. A gentleman in all respects. Responds with calmness and consideration to high pressure situations. Displays compassionate concern and understanding to personnel needs as well as logic and foresight in the intense planning required to maintain *Midway*'s outstanding special weapons program. His vast technical expertise, proven managerial skills, and solid administrative abilities are far superior to his contemporaries, and have been primary factors in our outstanding performance. Significant accomplishments include:

*Unprecedented completion of an exceptionally high number of limited life component exchanges during an extremely arduous underway period despite numerous logistics difficulties and a tremendous turnover of personnel.

*Outstanding grades earned in recent Nuclear operational Readiness Exercises, War at Sea Exercises and other major inspections which were crucial in *Midway*'s winning of both the ComNavAirPac Battle Efficiency "E" and the Weapons Black "W" Awards.

*W Division's enviable and unequaled reputation for extremely high retention and for 100 percent advancement of all eligible personnel (a ship-wide record for over three years).

*An exemplary PMS and material readiness program which has consistently produced spaces which are "second to none."

No other stands a prouder, more efficient watch as Officer of the deck (inport).
His wholehearted support of the Navy's Equal Opportunity and Goals Programs helps to create a command climate wherein the dignity and self-worth of all hands is respected.

> Chief Warrant Officer Little has been singularly responsible for the numerous successes enjoyed by this command through his adept execution of duties normally assigned to a Lieutenant. He is the mainstay of the special weapons program. A totally responsible and accountable Naval Officer. Ranked against other Chief Warrant Officers aboard, he stands as number one of this highly select group. He has my strongest possible recommendation for early promotion and assignment to duties which require the highest levels of performance, responsibility, and dedication.

I was pleased, and flattered by this last fitness report from Commander McDevitt, and Captain McGrail. I felt I had given them one hundred percent while onboard. This had been three of the busiest years of my life, and in many ways some of the most rewarding years of my life. I was most thankful for the young sailors of W Division. They were a dedicated, professional group of warriors. They had many of the feelings I had long ago onboard *USS Independence*, as the first line of defense protecting our country. Positioned where *Midway* was in the world, we would probably be the first in battle in the event of war, and possibly the first to be destroyed. They were determined to carry out their jobs to the best of their ability, for the preservation of their families, and country. They took their duties seriously, and accepted sacrifices cheerfully. They took pride in being members of the most powerful Navy in the world, as well as crewmembers of the best aircraft carrier in that Navy.

Finally the day of my departure arrived. All the accountability letters had been transferred to my relief. I had walked about the ship for two days, saying goodbyes, and getting my checkout sheet signed. I was going to miss being a crewmember of *Midway*, but I was not going to miss the nightly eight-o'clock meetings in the weapons office. These meetings, which were often enjoyable, but usually lengthy, seemed to make the day much longer. I had gone to these meetings every night at 7:00 p.m. for more than three years. My last morning on *Midway*, I spoke to the division during morning muster. I told them I was proud to have served with them, and told them to never forget that we had accomplished things no other W Division had done. I wished them all "smooth sailing." I told them Carmen and I would miss them all, and if any of them were ever in Albuquerque, our home was always open to them. They surprised me by presenting me with a *Midway* cigarette lighter as a going away gift. I had serious concerns, and forebodings about W Division, and future events proved my concerns to be correct.

I walked to the quarterdeck, where I had stood countless OOD watches, and asked the OOD on watch if he would announce my departure. This was a customary announcement when an officer transferring left the ship for the last time. I walked down the gangway after saluting the OOD and the flag on the stern. The ship's bell rang four times over the ship's loudspeaker, followed by the announcement "Chief Warrant Officer, United States Navy, departing," The bell rang once when my foot touched the pier.

As I walked the length of the pier, I looked at the *Midway* for the last time. I stopped walking, and took a long look at the large white "E" with a hash mark underneath it, which was painted on the side of the bridge superstructure, and the black "W" painted just under the "E." A catch phrase used on the ship when we were faced with difficult tasks, or jobs, was that we could do them with "*Midway* Magic." I think the true "magic" was the outstanding sailors who called *Midway* home. I felt I owned a large portion of these awards. I must admit I had feelings of elation, but also a lump in my throat. I mentioned before, that there is truth in the statement, "it's lonely at the top." While I certainly wasn't on the "top," while serving on *Midway*, I nevertheless had more responsibility than I'd ever had in my life. There was no one who shared my burden of responsibility, and no one who could give me advice about how to perform my duties. I had no one to confide in, other than the weapons officers that I worked for, and certainly no one I could shift blame to in the event of failure. There had been times when I had felt very much alone, yet I had weathered these times, and I felt a great deal of accomplishment in that.

In 1991, *Midway* was relieved as a forward deployed carrier home ported in Yokosuka, Japan by my old ship the *USS Independence*. This was not to be the last time I was to see *Midway*. I was to see her again, at the Naval Shipyard Bremerton, Washington in a decommissioned status. Happily she did not end her life as many aircraft carriers, scrapped, sold to a foreign country, or sunk by naval gunfire, or torpedo target practice. In 2004 she made her last voyage from Washington State to San Diego, California where she became the San Diego National Aircraft Carrier Museum.

The true heroes of *Midway* were those who lost their lives in the service of our country while I was onboard, they were:

    MM3 Christian J. Belgum
    MM2 Daniel F. Macey
    LCDR Henry B. Meyers
    AMEAN Joseph A. McGibson, Jr.
    MMFA James A. Watts
    AK3 Enrique T. Lazarte
    EM3 Troa H. Blevins
    LTJG John Murihead

The morning of our departure, Carmen and I had very little time to get to the bus that would take us to the Tokyo Airport. As soon as I returned from the ship to the Navy lodge, Carmen was waiting with our packed suitcases. There to see us off was Commander McDevitt, and Kimi, along with LCDR Jerry Burrows, his wife Sue, and a number of other friends. A few days previously Carmen had received many beautiful farewell gifts from her Japanese friends. We said our goodbyes, and we boarded the bus.

The bus moved away amid the waving, and shouting friends. Our trip by bus to Narita Airport in Tokyo was uneventful, as was our take off on the huge jet passenger airliner. It is said if you see Mount Fuji when you leave Japan, it means you will return. As the plane gained altitude after takeoff, Carmen and I both saw Mount Fuji.

Chapter 14: One-Third of the Nation's Stockpile

I had thirty days leave associated with my transfer, but as was the case with most transfers, this leave could not be classified as a vacation, as most of the time was spent preparing for our relocation. In San Francisco, we rented a car. I had an appointment with the office of the Commander Naval Logistics Pacific, located at Naval Supply Center, Oakland. I met with a commander who was on the staff of the admiral. We discussed my experiences on *Midway*, and I submitted some ideas I had for improvement of ordnance logistics in the Far East. I also dropped by the Nuclear Weapons Supply Annex, and said "hello" to Norm Howell, who was still the director there. He was soon to retire. There were a few civilians still there that had been at NWSA during my tour in the mid 1970s.

Carmen and I drove to Strathmore, and visited with my parents and family. I also enjoyed visiting the church (Strathmore Faith Baptist) that I had attended as a child. I found it hard to readjust to a slower tempo of life, after the intensity of the *Midway*. I "blew of steam," by pruning some of the ten acres of orange trees my parents owned. In the news on 23 October, was the tragic terrorist attack in Beirut, Lebanon that killed 237 marines. Soon we packed up the Oldsmobile we had left with my parents, and headed for Albuquerque, New Mexico.

At Albuquerque, I checked into the same building I had left more than three years previously. It was good to see CWO4 Charlie Schmidt again. I learned my old boss LCDR Perry Roberts had retired, and was now working on base at Sandia Corporation in the publication division. I was to be working in the Field Command Defense Nuclear Agency (FCDNA) Stockpile Maintenance Branch. One of my bosses was an Air Force major named Wally Meyers. Also in the office were Army, and Navy officers, along with civilian workers.

Checking with Kirtland Air Force Base Housing Office, I was told it could be as long as three months before a base house would be available. Carmen and I rented a one-bedroom apartment near one of the Kirtland base gates. Albuquerque had not changed much in the three years we had been gone. We renewed old friendships at the Fleet Reserve Association (FRA) clubhouse, and the American Legion Post. Many of the civilians at FCDNA remembered me from my previous job in the NLO JNWPS Office. A few of the military people I had worked with in the past, now worked for Sandia Corporation in the nuclear weapons program.

CWO4 Schmidt was scheduled to retire from the Navy in March, so I had four months to "learn the ropes" of my new job. It soon became apparent to me that this was an immense job that included more authority and responsibility in the nuclear weapons program than any other position a Nuclear Weaponsman could ever expect to hold.

CWO4 Schmidt was responsible for the maintenance of specific weapons in the nation's stockpile. He was responsible for resolving any problems with these weapon systems, or problems with the maintenance procedures. He was the single point of contact between the Department of Energy (DOE), Sandia Corporation, Los Alamos, and Lawrence Livermore Laboratories, and many other nuclear weapons' contractors, and the military services. He coordinated communications between the Army, Air Force, Navy and Marines and DOE and the nuclear weapons design laboratories. He also was a board member on groups involved with designing new weapons systems. His responsibilities extended over such a large area, I wondered if I would ever be able to grasp it all? CWO4 Schmidt had been doing this job for more than six years, and had gained an admirable reputation with all the military and civilian people he worked with. He had named me as his replacement, and now that I realized the scope of his position I was flattered, and a little fearful! This was a CWO4 position, so as a CWO3 this job was a "feather in my cap." My security clearance was confirmed in a couple of days, and after completing a short check-in sheet, I was once again working in my old building.

FCDNA published a book that contained a description of the background, and areas of responsibility of each officer assigned to FCDNA, along with a picture of the officer. One of my first tasks in my new job was to write this description.

My official title was "Nuclear Weapons Systems Project Manager." My background read:

> High school education plus 8 hours college level work in management/liberal arts. Nuclear Weaponsman Class A School August 1961. Aircraft loading Schools. Instructor Training School September 1964. Nuclear Safety Officer Course 1980.
>
> Enlisted assignments: *USS Haven* (AH-12); NAS Keflavik, Iceland; *USS Independence* (CVA-62); *USS Ticonderoga* (CVA-14); NAS Whidbey Island, Washington; Naval Magazine Guam, M.I.; *USS Oriskany* (CVA-34); Nuclear Weapons Supply Annex Oakland, CA; Naval Magazine Guam, M.I.; Naval Liaison Office, KAFB, NM.

Officer assignments: *USS Midway* (CV-41) W Division Officer 1980-1983.

Areas of Responsibility: Nuclear Weapons Systems Project Manager for selected weapons systems and related technical publications with the Department of Defense (DOD) stockpile. Provides technical guidance for the maintenance and modernization of selected weapons systems within the DOD stockpile. The DOD central point-of-contact and monitor for all Unsatisfactory Reports concerning weapons/technical publication defects. Central control and coordination point for all modifications to stockpiled weapons, Chairman of all related meetings concerning modifications to weapons systems. Nuclear Weapons System Project Manager for related nuclear weapons technical publications within the Joint Nuclear Weapons Technical Publications System (JNWPS). Chairman of the Joint Conferences during weapon development. Represents FCDNA at Project Officers Meetings for applicable weapons systems after initial weapons development.

I accompanied Charlie at all meetings he had at the huge Sandia Corporation within Kirtland Air Force Base. One day we drove to Los Alamos National Laboratory for a meeting. This was my first visit to Los Alamos. It is a unique town, located high in the mountains of northern New Mexico, which is considered the birthplace of nuclear weapons.

As Christmas 1983 approached, Carmen and I began adjusting to living once again in the United States. One thing we noticed immediately, was the language used on television was much more liberal, and bordered upon profane compared to when we left for Japan. We missed the friendships, and comradeship we shared in Yokosuka, and on the ship. We had shared our lives with many good people. As Americans we had gyrated toward one another, ending up in close relationships, being together in a foreign country. In Albuquerque I worked from 0730 to 1630, after work, everyone went to his family, and his own world that was mostly disassociated with fellow workers at FCDNA. My working schedule was very relaxed compared to the long hours I spent on the *Midway*, and the duty I stood every sixth day on the ship. At FCDNA I worked five days a week, and the only duty I stood, occurred once every two months, when I had to remain near my home phone, as FCDNA Duty Officer, and as a Nuclear Accident Coordinating Duty Officer. FCDNA had a Christmas party at the officers club, on 10 December, which Carmen and I attended. On Christmas Eve we were still living in our one bedroom apartment off base. It had snowed a couple of days before Christmas Eve, and about three inches of snow covered the city. We didn't have any family to share Christmas with, and not wanting to stay cooped up in our apartment on Christmas Eve, we went for a drive, hoping to find a restaurant we could have dinner at. All the restaurants were closed, but after driving for a long while, we found a Chinese food buffet open for business. We had a very different Christmas Eve dinner that year.

In mid-January, I was offered a house on base. It was an older three-bedroom house located near the Base Exchange. We began moving in, and were happy to finally be out of our small apartment.

The latter part of January, I was surprised when told the following day I was to report to my boss, Colonel Smith's office in dress blues, along with Carmen, to be awarded a medal. The next day while standing at attention before the colonel, with Carmen at my side, I was awarded a Navy Commendation Medal, for my duty on the *USS Midway*. A letter accompanying the medal was read out loud. Vice Admiral James R. Hogg signed the letter, for the secretary of the Navy. There were a number of officers gathered to watch this award ceremony, and after the colonel congratulated me, I said I would wear this medal on behalf of those who truly deserved it, the sailors who worked for me in *Midway*'s W Division. I was pleased to have been given this medal, and I suspected my previous boss Commander McDevitt had much to do with it.

The first part of March, I received an urgent message from *USS Midway*. The ship was undergoing an NTPI, and had received a failure grade, due to a discrepancy observed during a maintenance operation that was being demonstrated to the inspectors. I'll not go into specific details. However, the ship asked if I would investigate the problem with DOE and Sandia Corporation. I worked on this problem for two days, and the engineers at DOE and Sandia determined that the inspectors were incorrect, and the inspection results were reversed. Commander McDevitt was very thankful for my efforts on behalf of the ship.

I was to learn later that CWO4 Raymond Langley was relieved as W Division Officer, and he spent the remainder of his time on *Midway*, sitting in the wardroom, as an outcast from weapons department. I was sad to hear this, and concerned about the treatment the sailors who had worked for me might have received. The only good thing I could think of about this situation was that since Chief Warrant Officer Langley had changed many of the things I handed over to him, this was a validation of my leadership, and management practices within W Division.

Our new neighborhood on Kirtland Air Force Base had a mixture of both officer and enlisted families. This was in contrast to most Navy bases where there was a distinct separation between officer and enlisted neighborhoods. We became friends with an Air Force sergeant and his German wife, who lived next door to us. Their names were Art and Peggy Burkett. They had a three-year-old daughter, named "Jackie," who was often at our house, and whom we delighted babysitting. In the years to come she was to become a registered nurse. I got busy planning a garden as spring was approaching. I'd not had a garden since we lived at Hamilton Air Force Base in California.

In March a "dining-out" was scheduled. This was to be a new experience for me. A "dining-out" was a variation of a "dining-in." A dining-out included spouses, while a dining-in did not include spouses. This was a formal military dinner ceremony that has been a tradition observed by military services in the United States and Europe for hundreds of years.

The origin of the dining-in dates back to the early eighteenth century in Europe, where officers of various regiments of the established monarchies would gather together for the sole purpose of an evening of good food, drinking, fellowship and the honoring of feats of individuals and organizations. Down through the years, as governments and military organizations became more sophisticated, the mess night became a definite part of the officer's routine social program. In this country, only slightly more than sixty-five years ago, Dining-in was a regular military social affair. While the occasion for the mess night became less and less one of celebration of individual achievements within the particular command or service, the protocol of the event became more and more formalized. The uniforms prescribed were evening dress with orders and decorations. World War II forced many traditional social functions and the military dress to be set aside. Subsequent to the war, however many traditional amenities of the mess were gradually restored. One of those that have been reestablished is the formal dining-in/dining-out. The evening is sometimes called "Mess Night," "Regimental Dinner," or "Band Night." The general pattern, however, does not differ greatly. The primary elements are a formal setting, the comradeship of the members of the mess, a fine dinner, traditional toasts to the president and military services, martial music and attendance of honored guests.

There are two "officers" of the mess, the president and vice president. The president presides over the mess throughout the evening. The vice president is normally a junior member of the mess. Traditionally "Mr. Vice" is a person with a keen wit and a fine sense of repartee who can be expected to stimulate table conversation. CWO4 Charlie Schmidt was "Mr. Vice" for the dining-out. Carmen and I studied the "rules and regulations," I was given in the office. The evening of the dining-out, we dressed formally and attended our first dining-out. It was a very enjoyable evening, filled with laughter, and good humor.

CWO4 Charlie Schmidt retired after thirty years naval service shortly after the dining-out evening. The stockpile maintenance branch held a retirement party for him at a restaurant on Sandia Mountain's Crest, overlooking Albuquerque. Charlie wore a moustache, and glasses. One of our bosses, LTCOL Jim Waddell, handed out "Groucho Marx" glasses complete with noses and moustaches, which we wore during the party. At the time of his departure, I felt I had a very big pair of shoes to fill. Charlie and his wife Margaret had two small children. Margaret was a commander in the local Navy reserve center, and they planned to remain in Albuquerque following Charlie's retirement. He wanted to return to college, and perhaps in the future be employed in the special weapons program. I learned much from him and was always grateful that he recommended me as his replacement.

The last of March I received my first fitness report, signed by Admiral Aut, the commanding officer of FCDNA. I received all "A's," and since I was the only CWO3 assigned to FCDNA, ranking was not appropriate. The comments partially read:

> CWO3 Little was instrumental in bringing about the initial operational capability of the W84 Cruise Missile. Specifically he staffed development of the maintenance manuals for field use, and most notably, coordinated solutions to engineering problems on the warhead sections with Sandia National Laboratories in a thorough rapid manner. Without CWO3 Little, the W84 would not have been deployed on time.

I was pleased with my first fitness report. I felt much of the credit belonged to my predecessor CWO4 Schmidt, because after only six months on the job, much of my work was work that had been done on foundations Charlie Schmidt had created during his six years at FCDNA.

There was considerable traveling associated with my job. One of my first trips was to Davis-Monthan Air Force Base near Tucson, Arizona. Here I visited the W84 Ground Launched Cruise Missile (GLCM) Training School for the Air Force, for three days.

Another initial trip was to Kelly Air Force Base, near San Antonio, Texas. I made this trip with one of my bosses, Major Wally Meyers. An office on Kelly Air Force Base performed the same function for the Air Force that the McAlester, Oklahoma Unsatisfactory Report (UR) office did for the Navy. The Kelly AFB office reviewed all Air Force UR's submitted by Air Force nuclear weaponsmen on Air Force weapons. I was the point of contact with these offices, as well as a UR office in New Jersey that performed the same function for the Army. I would relay the UR's to the appropriate person for resolution in either Sandia, or DOE, and work with them on an answer, or resolution. During this trip to San Antonio with Maj. Wally Meyers, we visited the San Antonio Riverwalk, which is a famous tourist attraction.

As I mentioned the base house Carmen and I lived in was an older house, but it was comfortable. All of our household goods had made it from Japan relatively unscathed. My garden was doing well in the back yard, although I had to erect a chicken wire fence around it to keep out jackrabbits, which were thick on the base. Carmen became involved in a theater production in the base theater, presenting the play "Little Abner." Around this time we received some bad news. Our Uncle Dean Clark passed away. He had suffered with diabetes and poor health since falling into a rock crusher in the early sixties. I was unable to attend the funeral, as an uncle was not considered "immediate family" for emergency leave purposes.

Carmen and I became close friends with an Air Force wife named Jerrie that Carmen had met. Her husband was a sergeant who was attending an Air Force-sponsored college, and upon completion, he would receive a commission as an Air Force officer. Jerrie was expecting a baby. She spent a lot of time with us in our home. Her husband did not have any time for socializing as his college studies took up most of his free time.

In the summer of 1984 we had a number of surprise visits from people I had known in the past. Many nuclear weaponsmen would attend meetings, or classes on Kirtland Air Force Base, as the base was a gathering place for our trade. Dick Johnson, who I'd been stationed with on Guam, was one such visitor. He had retired from the Navy, and now worked for Lockheed Aircraft Corporation, Sunnyvale, California working in the Polaris and Trident missile program. Also GMT1 Tonnon, who had been with me on the *Midway*, visited. He was on his way to a new assignment in Hawaii.

Officers from different branches of the service worked in my office. Officers tended to stick together with officers of their respective service. The only other Navy Officer in the stockpile maintenance office was an Aviation Ordnance Limited Duty Officer, Lieutenant Dick Grass. There were two Army captains, an Air Force major, and a number of civilians.

The Navy had a unique promotion program that no other service had, and it was called "frocking." As I described before, I had been frocked when promoted to CWO3. Again this meant an officer notified of a future promotion date, could wear the rank he was being promoted to prior to the actual promotion date. The officer was afforded all the privileges of his new rank, but was not paid the salary of the rank, until the actual promotion date. In my case I had worn the uniform of a CWO3 for one year, before being paid as a CWO3.

Lieutenant Grass received some good news; he had been selected for promotion to lieutenant commander, and was to be frocked. At the time he received this news, an Army captain in the office was the senior officer under Major Meyers, and was in charge during periods of the major's absence. Lieutenant Grass's frocking to a higher rank than he, caused friction in the office. The Army captain was somewhat immature, and upset that he had lost his seniority.

The Fleet Reserve Association Branch I belonged to held a fishing contest each year at a lake called Bluewater Lake, located about ninety miles west of Albuquerque. The contest lasted three days, over the Fourth of July weekend. Most people took motor homes or camping trailers to the lake for the three-day contest. A mechanic at the FRA clubhouse, offered to weld a trailer hitch on our Oldsmobile, so Carmen and I could tow a camping trailer to the lake. It was a difficult job welding the hitch on the Oldsmobile, and took most of one day, but the mechanic only charged me for the cost of the hitch. For the weekend we checked out a camping trailer from the base special services office. We camped by the lake with the other FRA members, and fished each day. We caught a lot of Kokanee salmon, but Carmen or I didn't win a prize for the largest fish. For many years in a row a woman named Ruby won the contest. Many thought she cheated somehow, but I think she was just persistent and lucky. Carmen and I enjoyed the FRA fishing contest each year we were in New Mexico. Unfortunately, 1984 was the last fishing contest for the helpful mechanic who welded my hitch on the car, as he died of a heart attack the following year.

In September I attended a meeting at Lawrence Livermore Laboratory in California. The second day of my meeting, I was at my motel at 7:00 a.m., preparing to leave for the meeting location when I received a phone call from my Albuquerque office.

It was Major Donart, the major who had relieved Major Meyers upon his transfer a few months earlier. The major congratulated me, saying I had been selected for promotion to CWO4. This was a pleasant shock, as I was not scheduled to be looked at for promotion for another year. Once again I had been deep selected for promotion. Upon my return to Albuquerque Admiral Kersh, the commanding officer of FCDNA frocked me to CWO4. This promotion meant I had been promoted to the highest rank of a chief warrant officer. Another nice benefit of my higher rank meant I no longer stood any duties after normal working hours, as FCDNA Duty Officer as others did. I would not receive the pay of a CWO4 for over a year.

Many of the meetings I attended at various locations throughout the United States cannot be described in detail, as the topics, and some locations were classified. I put a lot of traveling miles under my belt during my time at FCDNA, and I became convinced that this job was the very apex of assignments for a Navy Nuclear Weaponsman. Being responsible for more than one third of the nation's nuclear weapons stockpile, and being a key member in the development process of our country's new weapons was a position, and level of authority far above any position I thought I'd ever hold, twenty-four years before, when I'd first enlisted in the Navy.

I was the project officer for twelve different weapons' systems. Each weapon system had a responsible person at DOE, and Sandia. These persons would convene meetings at various locations throughout the country. A popular meeting location was Las Vegas, Nevada. During one meeting in Las Vegas, a tour of the Nevada Test site, near Las Vegas, was arranged. The tour lasted an entire day, and I enjoyed this interesting trip.

About forty members of the meeting group gathered early one morning at the DOE Office in Las Vegas. We all were issued security access badges, and we boarded a large air-conditioned bus. We headed north from Las Vegas, toward the Test Site. We passed the Air Force base where the famous Air Force precision flying team "The Thunderbirds" practiced. Two years previously, four planes of the Thunderbirds had crashed into the desert floor here, killing all four pilots.

The bus entered the guarded Test Site, and we drove by an observation area with bleachers, that used to be used by reporters and observers during the 1950s when above ground tests of nuclear weapons were conducted. We then were given a tour of a huge complex of concrete buildings that were built during a cancelled DOE program that had attempted to develop a nuclear-powered aircraft for the military. We were also shown an underground project that was being undertaken as a place for the storage of nuclear waste from nuclear power plants, and the manufacture of nuclear weapons. I did not see the mysterious "Area 51," that many speculate is a secret military base.

After lunch at the test site cafeteria, we toured some of the ground zero sites of past above ground detonations. One was a surface detonation that had left an unbelievably large crater. The group then met some of the men involved in digging the shafts for underground test detonations. Most of the men had gained their drilling experience, drilling oil wells, and they now drilled for weapons underground test shots. We were then taken to a building where we were given overalls, gloves, rubber boots, and hats, which we were instructed to put on. We all then walked to a nearby cave entrance, which had railroad tracks leading into the cave mouth. We all boarded small railroad cars that seated six people in each car. The cars were pulled by a small diesel locomotive. The train traveled deep into the side of a mountain. Lights lined the side of the cave. After traveling for what seemed like a long while in a straight line, the tracks suddenly turned at a ninety-degree angle. After going a short distance following the turn, the railroad cars came to a halt. We all got off the train, and were shown a series of huge steel doors that went across the roof, sides, and floor of the cave. This steel door system was designed to slam shut at the time of the underground detonation of the warhead. The nuclear explosion would create a huge underground cavern, which would partially collapse the desert floor, or mountain above, as the surface fell downward into the cavity created by the explosion. This elaborate system insured that no radiation was vented to the earth's atmosphere. Some of the huge doors were warped from the nuclear blast in this cave that had taken place in the past. After we exited the cave following our train ride out, we were monitored for radioactivity, and we all came out clean. This was a very interesting tour, and gave me an appreciation for the pains and work our nation undertakes to conduct safe, reliable, underground nuclear tests. I am definitely in favor of nuclear weapons testing, not only as a nuclear weaponsmen, but also as a citizen that believes in a strong defense for our country. My position is strengthened by a story CWO4 Charlie Schmidt related to me.

Quality assurance is an important aspect of the nuclear weapons program. Periodically a warhead that has been under the control of the Air Force, Army, Navy or Marine Corp. was selected at random for an underground detonation at the Nevada Test Site.

This selection was of a specific type, as a method of quality assurance for that particular system. After the random selection, the weapon was transported to the Test Site, placed underground, and detonated. The yield of the explosion is gauged, and then estimates could be made concerning the reliability and performance of the weapons in the United States stockpile. During my assignment at FCDNA I was involved in a number of these tests, which were preceded, by a number of planning meetings before the weapons were shipped from military custody to the Nevada Test Site.

CWO4 Charlie Schmidt told me he was participating in such a planning meeting for the test preparation of a weapon that had as one of the methods of delivery, release from an aircraft wing pylon. Charlie suggested during the meeting that it would be logical to have the tested warhead cooled down to the temperature it would be subjected to hanging on an aircraft wing flying high in the atmosphere, prior to a real drop during war time. The engineers and scientists from DOE and Sandia in the meetings resisted his idea, and said this would be unnecessary as they were sure the warhead would detonate properly. Charlie insisted. He was the only military member in the meeting, and he did not have a long line of educational credentials, as did the other members of the meeting, so he was not given a lot of credibility by some of the members. I experienced this from time to time when working with some of these brilliant minds in the scientific community. They were very intelligent, but often lacked common sense. Charlie was persistent, and finally DOE agreed that prior to detonating the warhead underground, they would cool the warhead to the temperature it would experience on the wing of a high-flying aircraft wing.

The warhead was selected from the military stockpile and shipped to the Nevada Test Site. The underground tunnel had been prepared, and the warhead was cooled down with dry ice. The day of the test, the countdown commenced, the firing wires leading from the command center to the warhead deep underground were connected, and the firing button was pushed. The scientists and engineers received a shock. Only a fraction of the kilotons of energy that were supposed to be created occurred! After a frantic, and thorough examination of the warhead design, it was discovered that one component within the warhead would fail when subjected to cold temperatures. This failure received an extremely high level of attention. An emergency retrofit was performed on all warheads of this type in the stockpile, and changes were made to those warheads being manufactured. Had Charlie not insisted, this problem may never have been discovered. Had our country gone to war, the targets these warheads would have been used against, might have survived, and there's always the possibility we may have been defeated.

Another interesting place to visit was Amarillo, Texas. I visited the Department of Energy (DOE) Pantex Plant for five days. An engineer from DOE Albuquerque, named Tom was my host on this trip. The plant was a six-hour drive from Albuquerque, and Carmen accompanied me on this trip, so we could do some sightseeing when I was not working. We left Albuquerque on Sunday morning, a day before my visit was scheduled to start on a Monday. The first thing a person notices about Amarillo when approaching from the west, is the smell. Huge cattle stockyards are located just outside the city limits.

On Monday morning I met Tom at the motel office we were staying at, and together we drove to the Pantex plant. We passed the closed Amarillo Air Force Base. Tom told an interesting story about why the base closed. It seems when President Lyndon Johnson ran for election in 1964, Amarillo was the only county in Texas that did not back him for election. After his inauguration, one of his first acts was to close the Amarillo Air Force Base, and the economy of the county plummeted.

Upon arrival at the plant, I was issued an access badge to wear while within the complex. I noted that the plant was very heavily guarded. Once inside the plant, Tom introduced me to the Pantex Plant DOE Manager. This plant was where DOE built warheads, prior to the warheads being transferred to military control. The buildings of the plant were widely separated and connected together by long above ground-enclosed walkways. The buildings had been built in this fashion to minimize any damage that might occur in the event of an explosion. Many employees used bicycles transiting back and forth between buildings.

Much of my visit was spent watching a crew of civilian DOE technicians assembling a warhead. They used the same assembly, and work methods used by the military. There was a crew leader who read steps to be performed from check sheets, and assemblymen and women who performed the read steps. The assembly people would also respond, "Check" after completing a step. This work took place within concrete cells constructed to minimize any damage to adjacent cells in the event of an explosion. I enjoyed watching the team assemble the warhead, and was very impressed with the good discipline of the workers.

The year of 1984 was the year of a presidential election. There was much talk within DOE, Sandia Corp., and the military about how President Carter had decimated the military, and the nuclear weapons program.

Under President Reagan there had been a tremendous recovery, and the majority of the people in the nuclear weapons program had hopes President Reagan would be reelected. He had inspired us as no President in the past had. He had said out loud what we in the military had been saying for years, that Russia was indeed an evil empire, whose primary mission was our countries destruction. His faith in America's way of life, and confidence that we would prevail, was the kind of leadership we in the military understood and admired.

The week before our visit to Amarillo, the area had experienced a severe hailstorm. Many of the automobiles I saw had dents in the hood, roof, and top of the trunk, the size of golf balls. No one had been killed in this storm, but a few people had been injured. From the look of the damaged cars, it must have been a terrible storm.

The final day of our visit to the Pantex Plant, Tom gave a critique of his visit at a meeting with the Plant Manager, and other supervisors. I attended this meeting, and made the comment that I was very impressed with the Pantex operation, and I noted that the assembly teams were very disciplined. I said I had worked with assembly teams for more than twenty years, and the DOE teams were on par with some of the best I'd seen. The plant manager seemed very pleased with my comments. That evening, many of the DOE people I'd met during the week gathered for dinner at an Amarillo steak house. One of the DOE engineers had a very interesting hobby. Each weekend a number of people with the same hobby as he, would gather at a local pond, put model radio-controlled battleships with small motors, into the pond. They would engage each other in miniature sea battles. The small ships fired BB's from the air compressed gun turrets on the battle ship decks. The engineer had never been in the service, and was very interested about my experiences in the Navy

Carmen and I visited the Roadhouse Grill while in Amarillo. This restaurant is well known for its standing offer for a free steak dinner. If a person can eat all of one of their seventy-two-ounce steaks in one sitting, the eater does not have to pay for his meal. Pictures of those who had accomplished this feat lined the walls of the restaurant. We didn't try it. After this trip to Amarillo with Tom, he invited Carmen and me to his small horse ranch south of Albuquerque a number of times.

As I described, the Pantex Plant was DOE's bomb manufacturing plant. After completion, warheads were shipped to various locations throughout the country, and then turned over to the military. The warheads were transported by various means, one of which was by Safe Secure Trucks, or SST's. Specially trained armed guards escorted these trucks. The guards were civilian employees of DOE, and lived in a military type of environment. The home barracks for the guards was at Pantex, where they underwent constant training and physical conditioning. They accompanied the loaded trucks riding in Chevrolet Suburban vans, with darkened bulletproof glass. The guards were heavily armed, and also carried an M60 machine gun in the vans.

The trucks were unmarked, except for the required department of transportation explosive placards. These trucks were equipped with numerous security and safety devices. One security feature was large metal spikes, activated by explosive charges, which would ram downward from the truck undercarriage, impaling into the road, making movement of the truck impossible. The warhead storage area of the truck was enclosed with thick hardened steel. Access required two persons that had combinations to the dual combination locks. If an unauthorized attempted entry was made into the warhead storage compartment, or the wrong combination entered, there was immediate flooding of the storage compartment with sticky foam that quickly hardened, making removal of the warhead impossible. These devices plus many more I'll not detail, make the trucks a very safe secure method of transportation, and impossible to hijack.

While talking to a few DOE guards one day, they related an interesting story to me. They were taking an SST through a southern state, when they stopped at a small restaurant for supper. While three guards and drivers stayed with the parked SST and escort vehicles, three of the men entered the restaurant. One DOE guard sat alone at the restaurant counter, while two guards sat at a table behind him. A local deputy sheriff happened to walk into the restaurant, and saw a pistol under the coat of the guard seated at the counter. The deputy thinking he had the drop on a criminal, drew his revolver, pointed it at the seated guard, and loudly said "You, at the counter, put your hands' up." As soon as he had stopped speaking, behind him there came the sound of two pistols being cocked. The guards behind the deputy, asked him to please holster his pistol, as they were federal guards authorized to carry firearms. The shaken deputy quickly complied. In order to sooth the ego of the embarrassed deputy, they gave him a tour of the guard escort vehicles. At one time I had considered the job of a DOE guard, as a possible job after retirement from the Navy, as they hired many military retirees. The major drawback however was that they were never home, and constantly on the road.

Another transportation method from Pantex was by railroad train. Often the train route was from Pantex to Bangor, Washington, or North Carolina where the Trident submarines were home ported.

These shipments were classified, and carefully planned, but somehow anti-bomb activists would find out about the shipments, they called "death trains," and would try to stage protests. Much to DOE's credit, there was never an accident involving transportation of a nuclear warhead.

Field Command Defense Nuclear Agency Albuquerque was actually a branch of Defense Nuclear Agency (DNA) Headquarters located in Washington, D.C. Both commands were headed by flag Officers, which were appointed by the president. During my assignment as FCDNA the commanding officers were Navy admirals, but this position was rotated among the armed services.

I made a trip to DNA Headquarters with an Air Force captain from the FCDNA Air Force Liaison Office. I'd never visited our nation's Capitol, although I'd been stationed in nearby Norfolk, Virginia on the *USS Independence* for a couple of years. I had a free day during our meetings at DNA, so I looked forward to visiting the sights of the country's Capitol. The captain, named Tim, and I walked around an area called the mall, and visited many museums, and monuments for a full day. I purposely visited the National Space and Aeronautical Museum, and had Tim take a picture of me standing in front of a huge mural that I had copied and painted on the walls of my house on Guam (see photograph page), and in the enlisted club on Naval Magazine Guam. We must have walked twenty miles that day. I suffered for my enthusiastic walking that night. I had worn a pair of cowboy boots I'd bought in El Paso, Texas, and they were not made for extended walking. My feet were covered with painful blisters. The pain of these blisters did not lessen the thrill I had seeing all the monuments and buildings I'd only read about, or seen in pictures up to that point.

There was a small amount of "underground animosities" between Defense Nuclear Agency Headquarters, and Field Command Defense Nuclear Agency. Headquarters was thought of as populated by bureaucrats, while FCDNA contained the "real workers." I remember a cartoon that circulated through our office. It was a picture of a tree, with two branches extending away from the trunk. On the upper branch there was a row of birds sitting with their beaks raised in the air, with a superior, aloof attitude. This branch was labeled Headquarters DNA. The lower branch had a row of birds, chattering to each other, flying about, and looking very busy. This branch was labeled Field Command DNA.

The latter part of September I came down with a bad cold and at the same time injured my back while lifting weights. I was confined to bed for a week. At this time I finally quit smoking for good, which I had done for almost twenty-five years. My quitting effort was helped by the reading of an article which said to put a large rubber band around your wrist, and when you feel the urge to have a cigarette, stretch the rubber band, and pop it against the inside of your wrist, hard enough to cause pain. The theory was that your mind would begin to associate pain with the desire for nicotine. I'd tried many other "kick the habit" suggestions, and along with Carmen's encouragement the "rubber band trick" worked for me!

Our Aunt Lois visited us for a couple of weeks. She was terrified of flying, and on one of my trips to California for FCDNA; on the return trip to Albuquerque she flew with me. She held my hand so tightly during the flight that I lost feeling in my fingers for a while, but I was much honored that she loved Carmen and me so much that she fought back her terror of flying to spend time with us. She enjoyed visiting the Indian casinos that had recently opened west of Albuquerque. On the return flight to California, I was thankful that she found someone on the plane to chat with all during the flight, to keep her mind off her fear of flying. Aunt Lois passed away in 2003, and the memories of this visit remain precious to me.

The Navy continued to be serious about physical fitness, and FCDNA was no exception to the rule. Every six months all sailors on the base would gather and do our required pushup, sit-ups, and a timed two-mile run. LCDR Dick Grass, my office partner, had great difficulty completing the two-mile run in the required time limit. I practice ran with him often after work, trying to encourage him. Running in Albuquerque was more difficult than in many places, because of the mile high altitude of the base. Dick struggled complying with the run requirement throughout his tour at FCDNA. He was a smoker, and I thought perhaps that was his major obstacle concerning running. It was not until years later, that a doctor finally discovered that he was suffering from a disease that gradually weakened the major muscle groups of his body. I enjoyed jogging daily, and it felt good to use my lungs that had been abused by smoking for so many years.

1985 began with the reelection of President Reagan. In March, I received my second FCDNA fitness report. I received all A's, and one of the comments in my fitness report mentioned a task I helped complete for the Secretary of Defense. I wrote technical data for a handbook used by Nuclear Emergency Search Teams, or NESTS. These teams used the handbook to search for nuclear weapons perhaps hidden within a city by terrorists, or search for a bomb that might be stolen from our nation's stockpile.

Our neighbors' Art and Peggy had two dogs, a large Saint Bernard, and a small German Shepherd puppy. Behind their house, they had a fenced area, with two doghouses. Early one morning, Art went into the dog's fenced area, and he noticed both dogs were in one doghouse. The previous night had been cold, so he assumed the two dogs had gotten into one doghouse to keep warm. He placed some dog food in a bowl near the doghouse occupied by the two dogs, and then went to the food bowl by the other doghouse. He was startled by a growl that came from within the supposedly empty doghouse, and he also caught a glimpse of rows of white bared teeth. Art backed away from the doghouse, and a large coyote shot out of the doghouse, and squeezed under a gap under the backyard fence. That morning, Art filled in the gap under the fence!

In early March of 1985, I began planning and preparing for my annual garden. The previous year I'd had tomatoes, onions, okra, carrots, and many cucumbers. I planned to have a much larger garden in 1985. The winter had been colder than usual, and I was anxious to start on my garden. I called a guy that had an ad in the newspaper, advertising ground tilling. One Saturday morning he came to our house, and he tilled my garden area with his rototiller garden tractor. The garden was almost twice as large as the previous year. It took two hours to complete the ground tilling, after which I paid him fifty dollars. Thirty minutes after he left, and I was mentally planning how to plant the seeds for the garden, Carmen came to the back yard with a letter the mailman had just delivered to our mailbox. She said, "You're not going to like the letter we just received." The letter was from the base housing office, and each house in our neighborhood of twenty houses had received the same letter. We were being told that within sixty days we would be moved to a different house on base; because all the houses in our neighborhood were being torn down to make way for a new commissary that was to be built in this location. The whole block was in an uproar over this unexpected news. The letters said to check with the housing office for additional information. This was upsetting news to Carmen and me, on top of the fact that I had just spent fifty dollars for ground tilling needlessly.

The officer in charge of the stockpile maintenance branch at this time was a major I mentioned before, Air Force Major Jim Donart. Jim and his family lived in the same block on base, as Carmen and me. He was particularly upset about being told to move, as he and his family had moved into their house only two months previously. He organized a block party, and we all discussed the unexpected directions from the housing office. We all agreed to sign a letter asking the housing office to delay relocation of our neighborhood for at least a year. There was little hope that our letter would be seriously considered.

After Carmen and I talked to the housing office, we opted to move to a much larger house across the base that was located in an all officer neighborhood. Our new house had three large bedrooms, and two large extra storage rooms. The house also had a unique double-sided fireplace that opened both into the living room and dining room. An Air Force lieutenant colonel was vacating the house, and had a white shag carpet he had bought when he moved in. He offered to sell it to us, we accepted his offer and he left the carpet when he and his family moved out.

This was a busy time, preparing for the unexpected move. We moved most of our small household items across the base by ourselves. The base promised to use professional movers to move our large heavy items. Our friend Jerrie, had delivered a baby boy named Justin, a couple of months previously. Jerrie and Justin were often at our house helping us prepare for the big move. Justin didn't actually help of course, but Carmen and I enjoyed having him around, as he was a cheerful happy little guy. One evening during our moving efforts, Carmen and Jerrie needed to go to the grocery store. We were all at our new house, which was bare of furniture, as none of our large furniture items had been moved yet. Jerrie and Carmen left Justin in my care while they went to the store. Justin was in a car seat, which was positioned on the rug-covered floor. I was busy in the kitchen, which was open into the room Justin was in, by a breakfast counter. I was cleaning the sink, and Justin was cooing and making his happy baby talk, as I talked to him from the kitchen. Suddenly Justin was very quiet, I sensed something was wrong. I stepped around the counter, and there on the white rug, no more than a few inches from Justin in his car seat, was a large straw-colored scorpion. I quickly moved Justin away, and grabbing a jar lid, slammed it over the scorpion. I got a broom, and lifting the lid, I squashed the scorpion. I picked up Justin, and held him in my arms, until Carmen and his mom returned from the store. It was not encouraging to think we might be moving into a scorpion-infested house. I called the housing office the following morning, and they sent a man to the house to fumigate it. I showed the body of the scorpion to the fumigator, and he said this kind was the most venomous.

Surprisingly, after a couple of months the housing office agreed with the neighborhood letter that had been started by Major Donart, asking that the demolition of the houses be delayed. This decision was too late for Carmen and me however, as we had already moved, and settled into our new house.

One day in the office, I received a phone call from Commander Gary Kellner, who had been my boss as weapons officer on the USS *Midway*. He had retired, and was leaving his last assignment in the Navy in San Diego, and headed for Dallas, Texas, where his wife Terri and two children were waiting for him, so they could begin their new lives as civilians. He was flying through Albuquerque, and had an hour layover at the airport. He asked if I would come to the airport to see him. I said I'd be glad to, so the following day, Carmen and I were at the Albuquerque Airport. We greeted him at the arrival gate, and together we went to the airport coffee shop. We were pleased to see him; it had been four years since we'd seen each other. He said he was going to start a new career working for an insurance firm in Dallas.

We three sat in a booth in the coffee shop, and at one point Carmen excused herself to go to the ladies room. While she was gone, Commander Kellner once again apologized for the night on the *Midway* he threatened me with punishment when he thought the inspection had been failed. He said he deeply regretted doing that, and he should have trusted me, and my experience. He said I was one of the finest officers he had been stationed with in his career. I told him I appreciated all he had done for me, and an apology wasn't necessary. After Carmen returned, we chatted for a while, and then we saw him off as he continued his journey. I had the feeling that he purposely arranged this meeting so he could apologize to me again. It was a heartfelt apology, and one I think he had worried about for a long while. I respected him as a gentleman and officer of high integrity, and a man with courage to admit when he was wrong, or thought he had offended anyone. He was an officer I greatly respected and admired, and do to this day.

In July Carmen accompanied me on a trip to Las Vegas. I was to attend a meeting at the DOE office with Sandia engineers, and other military members concerning the B61 bomb. The meeting included observing a unique event. We all were to be seated on bleachers at the Nevada Test Site. An Air Force F-15E *Eagle* fighter, loaded with a B61 was scheduled to fly by in front of us, and drop the B61 in the retarded mode, which would drop to the ground on a parachute, and then detonate. One very important ingredient was missing in the bomb. There was no nuclear material contained. There were only high explosives within the bomb warhead. All components of this bomb were of war reserve quality; this was a quality assurance test that we as a group had been working on for many months.

We all assembled at the test site on the designated day. The F-15 was to take off from Kirtland Air Force Base, hundreds of miles to the east of Nevada. The scheduled time for the drop came and went. We were told the drop was delayed (for a reason I was to discover later). Finally the F-15 appeared racing toward us from the horizon. Then we saw the B61 drop from the aircraft. The parachute deployed, as the weapon drifted down toward the ground. A thought ran through my mind, what if a mistake had been made and this was a war reserve bomb about to explode; we all would be turned into vapor in a few seconds. I also imagined the terror anyone might feel seeing such a sight knowing that this would be the last scene his or her eyes would behold before annihilation. The explosion occurred shortly after the bomb struck the desert floor. It was a relatively small explosion, but it was of great relief to those seated in the bleachers, to realize that everything worked, as it should. This was as close to a real drop of a nuclear weapon, as I was to see in my career, as above ground testing ended in the early 1960's during the start of my journey as a Nuclear Weaponsman. I have a series of pictures of this drop, along with a certificate of appreciation from Sandia Laboratories, hanging on my wall.

A few weeks later I learned the reason for the delay at the drop site. The Air Force had the responsibility of loading the B61 for the drop. The Air Force loading crew discovered after loading the bomb on the aircraft wing, that the electrical cable between the bomb and the aircraft would not fit. The pin sockets on the bomb's electrical connector were slightly different from those of a war reserve. They were about to cancel the drop, which would be very embarrassing for the Air Force, when a sailor from the Naval Weapons Evaluation Facility at Kirtland heard of the Air Force problem. He informed them that the Navy had a cable adapter that could be used on the cable. After borrowing the adapter, the cable was connected, and the loaded plane was able to take off. I was proud of the Navy for "saving the Air Force's bacon," and hoped they would get recognition for this, I told everyone I knew about how they saved the day.

We had become settled in our new house. An Air Force Captain, who had been our neighbor in the old neighborhood, moved into the house next to us. His wife had the distinction of being a contestant on the television program Wheel of Fortune. This was in the early days of this popular TV game show, when the prizes were furniture and various gifts the contestants would select during the game when they won.
The captain's wife did well, and selected a large number of items. She complained however, that many of the items she selected during her wins on the show were substituted for cheaper items when they were delivered.

During the Christmas season, we traveled to California to spend Christmas with our family. We ran into very thick fog after crossing the Mojave Desert, and it was tense driving for many miles. We arrived back in Albuquerque before New Years Eve of 1986.

In March 1986 I received a fitness report covering the previous six months. I again received all "A's," and was ranked number one of three CWO4's. One day I received a phone call from George Holden, my old friend from my "A" school days in 1961, and from Guam, and Albuquerque. Following his retirement in 1980, he had gone to work for Lockheed in Puget Sound, Washington, and was now in charge of security for the Puget Sound Naval Base. He had some sad news, a mutual friend of ours, Lloyd Wilson who I'd been with on the *Ticonderoga*, and George and I had been with on Guam, had died of a heart attack. Lloyd had retired in 1979 as a chief, and settled on a farm in Arkansas, along with his wife Betsy, and two children.

One day in April, I was surprised to learn I had been selected as the 1985 FCDNA officer of the year. The evening of 26 April, Carmen and I attended an award ceremony, and dinner hosted by the Navy League, Albuquerque Chapter. There were nine Navy and Marine commands in the Albuquerque area that were represented by one officer, and one enlisted man or woman, that had been selected as outstanding for the year of 1985. I was awarded a plaque, and Carmen and I had a free dinner. This was an honor I appreciated.

In 1985, I had gotten a call from the weapons officer on the *USS Kitty Hawk*, an aircraft carrier home ported in San Diego. It was CDR Ralph Spangler, or as he was known by his friends "Rotten Ralph." Commander Spangler was a limited duty officer, and highly respected in the nuclear weapons community. He was one of the first LDO's to hold the prestigious job of weapons officer on an aircraft carrier. I had known him over the years, first when he worked in the ComNavAirPac Weapons Office in San Diego, as a lieutenant junior grade.

His W Division had just gone through a Defense Nuclear Surety Inspection (DNSI). The inspectors that conducted the inspection were stationed at FCDNA. I knew most of the inspectors from the past, and also from various command functions, and meetings. One of the chief warrant officers in the Inspection Branch had been my inspector while I was on *Midway*. Another inspector was CWO3 Donn Green who I'd gone to "A" school with, and had been stationed with on the *USS Independence* more than twenty years before. The captain of the Inspection Branch, was Captain Abrahams, who had been the commanding officer of Naval Magazine Guam, when I'd been there in 1978, and been promoted to chief.

The *Kitty Hawk* DNSI inspection results were in question, just as the NTPI inspection report had been questioned on *Midway* during my tour on board. This was also a situation identical to the time Commander McDevitt on the *Midway* had asked my help, with an inspection discrepancy shortly after I left the ship. Commander Spangler asked if I could coordinate with Sandia, and determine if the discrepancy the inspectors detailed was valid. This discrepancy resulted in an "unsatisfactory" grade for the ship. After I reviewed the discrepancy, it was my opinion that the inspector who wrote the discrepancy was wrong. My opinion pitted my technical experience, and knowledge against the entire inspection branch. The engineers at Sandia examined the discrepancy in the *Kitty Hawk* inspection report, and they agreed with me, that the discrepancy should never have been written. I can't describe the discrepancy as it was classified. The result of this was that the inspection results were reversed to "satisfactory." This was welcome news for Commander Spangler, and the ship, but not welcomed news at the FCDNA Inspection Branch.

This situation emphasized the authority I had in my position at the stockpile maintenance branch. This was more authority than I imagined I'd ever have in the nuclear weapons program. I was ever mindful to be careful and not abuse this authority, but always try to put myself in the position of the nuclear weaponsmen in the field, and try to determine what would be best for them, and our nation's stockpile. Reversed situations had happened in the past at FCDNA, when I backed the FCDNA Inspection Branch inspectors when there was a dispute over inspection reports. I hoped the nuclear weaponsmen in these inspector positions were the ultimate technical experts, and men who would not let personalities affect their inspection judgments. Inspections in the nuclear weapons program were an invaluable tool used to help keep activities' error and mistake-free. In the past I'd come in contact with inspectors who were not technical experts, and obviously used the inspector position to feed their egos, as was the case of the senior chief inspector during my first inspection on *Midway*.

There were also GMT's who had "homesteaded" at inspection commands, and had not been assigned to an operational command, or the "real world" for many years. There were a few in this category in FCDNA Inspection Branch. I did not know it at the time, but in the future I would be in a position to drastically change this "homesteading phenomena."

LCDR Dick Grass and I encouraged the inspectors to keep in contact with us, and if they had technical questions we would be glad to assist them. The inspection branch accepted this invitation, and there were many occasions when we would receive phone calls from inspectors in the field asking for technical guidance.

In the spring of 1986, a meeting of the same group that met in Las Vegas for the quality assurance drop of a B61, met in San Diego. We were scheduled to visit the *USS Kitty Hawk*, which happened to be in port during our conference. The day of the visit, I stepped on board the *Kitty Hawk*, after walking up the gangway. It felt good to set a foot on a Navy warship once again. CDR Ralph Spangler met the group on the quarterdeck. After being issued visitors badges, we all toured W Division magazines. After the tour of the magazines, we all had lunch in the wardroom. After lunch, Commander Spangler, sat with me, and we talked for a long while. He was very thankful for the help I had given him, and the ship, after last year's inspection. His thanks, and appreciation was very sincere. I was to see him again in the future. He was one of the few LDO's in the Navy to be promoted to the rank of captain. I did not know it at the time, but this was to be the last time I set foot in a ship's magazine.

Like other commands I'd been stationed at, security was a way of life at FCDNA. A badge exchange security system was in effect. All classified documents and papers were kept locked in safes. We were cautious about discussing classified information over the telephone. We were told our conversations might be monitored, to ensure classified information was not being discussed. It became evident that we were being listened to, when LCDR Dick Grass was cautioned about using profanity during phone calls, when he was shown a written transcript of his phone calls over a two-week period.

We had guests from the past who stayed with us for a couple of days. It was Norm and Vicky Peters, who we'd been with on the *Midway*. They and their two children were on a cross-country trip from their previous duty station Feller Naval Air Station, Nevada. Norm was being transferred to Loch Ness, Scotland. They were driving to New York, where their car would be shipped, and they would travel overseas. Norm and I, and his son David, attended a minor league baseball game, played by the Albuquerque Dukes. Since I'd last seen Norm, he had been promoted to lieutenant. He hoped someday to get a job on a carrier as the Ordnance Handling Officer (OHO). He did very well in the Navy, retiring in the future as a commander (and becoming an OHO). He had been urged to remain in the Navy, and be promoted to the rank of captain, but decided it was his time to retire.

Another visitor from the past was Dick Clark, who we had stayed with on Guam during Typhoon Pamela, and who also had been on the *Midway* with me. Dick had retired from the Navy after twenty years, and was working as a civilian weapon technician at Concord Naval Station, California. As I mentioned Dick and his wife had been divorced a few years ago, and he was now living with a woman who worked as a civilian supply clerk at NWSA, Oakland. Carmen and I had a good visit with Dick. He and a co-worker at Concord were attending a class at Sandia for a week. We did not know it at the time, but this was the last time we would see Dick. Our friend Jerrie was having a barbeque at her house, and Dick went with Carmen and me, and we had a great time. Jerrie and her Air Force husband had gotten a divorce, and she and her son Justin were making a life for themselves. We were to see Jerrie, and Justin again in the future, when years later, Jerrie was married to Dick Miller of San Diego.

Normally when I attended meetings outside the state of New Mexico, I would travel by plane. On one occasion however, I traveled to San Antonio, Texas by car. Carmen accompanied me on this trip. It took two days to drive from Albuquerque to San Antonio. Much of the road trip was across the desolate plains of west Texas. I attended a meeting at Kelly Air Force Base in San Antonio. One surprise attendee at the meeting was Bob Meyer, who had been on the *Ticonderoga* with me twenty years ago. He now worked for Lockheed Aircraft Corporation. While in San Antonio, Carmen and I visited the Riverwalk, and the Alamo. We also visited a unique restaurant that had girls dressed in 1800s costumes swinging on swings attached to the ceiling. They swung high over the customers seated below.

Home burglaries were common in Albuquerque. Luckily there were few on base, so this was not a concern for Carmen and me, but many of the people I worked with had experienced break-ins. An Army captain who worked in my office, discovered one day after work that his house had been broken into during his family's absence. The burglar didn't get anything, and had a surprise when he broke in. The captain had a German Shepherd dog that was kept inside the house. The burglar had gotten inside the house; by breaking a window located in the back of the house, and apparently was inside the house before he realized a dog was inside.

The dog was very agitated when the family came home, and there was blood splattered on the floor, and leading out the window. The burglar was not caught, but the police said he must have gotten a very painful lesson from all the blood they found.

During my assignment at FCDNA, many new devices were being incorporated into nuclear weapons. One new device was called Permissive Action Links, or PAL devices. These devices required the entering of a numerical code in a weapons circuitry before it could be used on a target. The codes were split into two sections, so it required two persons to activate, or deactivate the protective circuit. Sandia and DOE were developing devices that would render the bomb useless if someone entered the wrong code, or tried to bypass the PAL system. These devices could also be used as a method of emergency destruction if a storage site was about to be overrun by enemy forces. The devices also provided protection against the possibility of terrorist stealing a weapon, and detonating it.

The plan was, that eventually all the weapons in the stockpile would incorporate PAL devices. One war scenario that I was critical of, involved headquarters units sending PAL codes to military units in the field with nuclear weapons. For example, a ground launched cruise missile truck unit, would not have the PAL codes, until receipt of a message from headquarters, which would give them the proper codes. This plan was not encouraging to me, as it assumed we would have ample time to send the codes out from headquarters well in advance of hostilities. It would be easy, for example in Europe, for the Russians to render all our nuclear weapons useless. All they would have to do would be to launch a pre-emptive strike by detonating a high altitude, high yield warhead over Europe causing an electromagnetic pulse (EMP), which would make radio transmitting impossible. Without radio communications, there would be no code distributions to the cruise missile units. I welcomed the added safety that the PAL devices provided, but they were in a way a "two-edged sword." Each time an additional safety device was added to a weapon it decreased the likelihood that it would explode should the time arise we needed it to.

One day two Los Alamos scientists visited my office. They explained that the Veterans Administration (VA) was investigating the medical claim of a sailor who had been on a nuclear weapon loading team, on an aircraft carrier during his four-year enlistment. He had been diagnosed with cancer, and it was his claim that his exposure to the weapons had caused the cancer. His enlistment had been during the late 1950s. The VA had asked Los Alamos to investigate what levels of radiation the sailor may have been exposed to.

The Los Alamos scientists were frustrated in their efforts to answer the question from the VA, because they discovered there were no technical manuals in existence that detailed maintenance procedures on the older weapons of the 1950s. This was a surprising situation to me, because I had always assumed there was a historical library somewhere within the nuclear weapons program. Apparently over the years, as weapons' systems were retired, all associated classified manuals had been destroyed without thought of retaining copies for future historical needs? Sandia had recommended me as a source of help for the Los Alamos scientists. At this point I had twenty-six years of experience in nuclear weapons' maintenance. The two Los Alamos scientists and I discussed ways to track down information on the 1950s and 1960s air dropped nuclear weapons. I suggested that Chief Ed Boren, who worked down the hall in my old job in the NLO office, would be help, as he had close to twenty years nuclear weapons experience. I told the two scientists, to give me a week, and I would see what we could find for them.

The next week, Chief Boren and I looked through libraries, and film storage areas for any historical information on the older weapon systems. The Defense Atomic Support Agency or DASA that had been the predecessor of FCDNA had produced numerous nuclear weapon training films. We found a few applicable films at the joint military training school that taught officers of all services various nuclear weapons topics. We searched for any of the old weapons technical manuals, but it was apparent that they had all in fact been destroyed. The National Atomic Museum, which is open to the public, is located on Kirtland Base, and contains a number of the old retired weapon system trainers. The joint military training school has a more complete, classified, museum, which contains all the old weapon system trainers.

After a week of preparation I notified Los Alamos. The two scientists I had spoken to previously, brought six more with them. I had arranged a tour for the eight through the classified museum. Chief Boren and I demonstrated some of the maintenance procedures we had performed on some of the older weapons in the past. The group appeared horrified, and dismayed when we demonstrated how we used to examine the capsule balls of active material that was stored in "birdcage" containers. They had not been aware of the extent of exposure to radiation that maintenance procedures, had subjected nuclear weaponsmen to in the past.

Over the course of a few days, Chief Boren and I showed them all the DASA films we had discovered and we answered all the questions they had concerning the older weapon systems. They were very thankful for the help, and information we provided to them. I never heard what the outcome of the sailor's cancer claim was. I was concerned about the shock they expressed when Chief Boren and I explained the radiation exposure we had while working on older weapons. Over the years I wondered what effect my past exposure might have on my future health.

One afternoon at work, I received a phone call from Carmen. She was in our base house, and sounded terrified, she pleaded with me to come home, saying there was a snake in the house. I rushed home, and after parking in our carport, saw that the front door was wide open. When I stepped through the door, I saw Carmen standing on top of our dining room table, with a broom in her hands. Around the table and near the door there were a few straws from the broom. Her eyes were wide with terror. I coaxed her down from the table. She told me she had been walking by the front door with a broom in her hands, and did not have on her glasses, which she normally wore. She noticed something long, and black lying partially out from under the door, thinking it was part of the weather stripping from under the door, she pushed at it with her broom. It began moving, and that's when she realized it was a snake. That's also when the excitement began. Carmen flayed away with the broom, and the snake began to move about, finally going back under the door. Carmen got up on the table, reached across the kitchen counter got the phone and called me. I searched the house, and came to the conclusion that the snake had probably tried to crawl into the coolness of the house to escape the afternoon heat, and after the surprising encounter with Carmen and her broom, raced back outside. We notified the neighbors, and they all looked about their yards for the snake. The neighborhood occasionally had "snake alarms," when someone ran across one. I imagine to this day, the snake is still slithering away, trying to escape the flaying broom he felt! I tacked all the door weather stripping down, so there would be no further snake incidents. After the snake encounter, and considering we had found a scorpion in the house, we kept a wary eye out for any crawling creatures inside the house.

I earned thirty days leave each year, and each September, if I had more than sixty days on the leave "books," I lost them. The last few years I had lost a few days, and I was determined not to have that happen this year. In the spring I took a one-week leave, and Carmen and I drove north to Navaho Lake for a fishing trip. We spent the week in a fishing lodge near the lake. One day while fishing, the New Mexico Fish and Game Department stocked the lake with twelve-inch trout a few yards from where we were fishing on the bank. We came home with an ice cooler full of fish.

When I returned to the office after this leave period, LCDR Dick Grass said my detailer in Washington, D.C had called me. He had told him I was on leave. Then the Detailer CWO4 Bobby Hamilton, began asking Dick questions about me. Dick gave him glowing, positive comments, and praises about what an outstanding officer I was, etc., CWO4 Hamilton, then told him he was considering me as his relief in Washington, D.C. This caught me completely off guard. I hadn't begun to think seriously about my next assignment after FCDNA. I'd thought about extending for a year, or perhaps an assignment to Hawaii, Puerto Rico, or Guam, as an overseas shore assignment was my next scheduled duty. I'd certainly not considered being a detailer in Washington, D.C. CWO4 Hamilton, told Lieutenant Commander Grass to give me a message to call him as soon as I got back. It was with great apprehension that I called CWO4 Hamilton. He said his tour as a detailer was about over, and he had been reviewing records for his relief. He was very impressed by the variety of places I'd been stationed, and also was impressed by my good fitness reports. He said there had never been a surface ordnance officer in the detailer's chair, in the past it had been occupied by operations technicians. He said my assignment would have to be approved by the Chief of Naval Personnel, the senior admiral in the Navy under the Chief of Naval Operations. He went on to say my performance, as a detailer would have an enormous impact on the Navy, and the careers of the officers I would deal with. I asked Bobby to give me a week to think about it. Carmen was as shocked as me when I told her of the call. If I accepted this job, it would mean doing a job completely different from anything I had been doing over the past twenty-six years. I would no longer be in the nuclear weapons program. Also to consider, if I refused, since my assignment affected the officer who would be sending me to my next duty station, where would I be assigned? The standard assignment joke was North Pole, or Timbuktu.

After a week, I called CWO4 Hamilton, and told him "Convince me to take this assignment, because I have doubts." He said there was no other job in the Navy that had more impact on the Navy's performance, and future. On the other hand it was the most difficult job in the Navy, managing the careers of well over 1,500 naval officers. He said I would be the first in my officer's designator to ever hold the job.

It was with hesitation, and foreboding, that I told him I would take the job. Bobby said my record would be reviewed by the chain of command, and the admiral, and if approved he would call me. He called a couple of days later, and said I was easily approved. He said he would issue my orders shortly, and I would be transferring in August. This was three months earlier than I had expected. I had assumed I would be leaving in November, as that would be my thirty-six-month point at FCDNA. My relief at FCDNA had to be assigned also before I could leave.

One of my last trips for FCDNA was to Pease Air Force Base, New Hampshire. During my time there, I had a "free day" to do as I wished. I went on a drive in my rental car near the New London Navy Submarine Base. I stopped at the house where the "Father of the U.S. Navy" was honored, Adm. John Paul Jones. An Air Force Captain that was on the drive with me took a picture of me standing in front of the John Paul Jones House Museum in Portsmouth, New Hampshire (see photograph page). The day I boarded the plane headed back to New Mexico, I bought some live Maine lobsters packed in Styrofoam boxes with dry ice. Upon arriving home, Carmen and I boiled a couple, and I shared the rest with the officers in the office.

A month and a half before my transfer from FCDNA, my relief checked in, after being approved by the Admiral. My relief was CWO4 Tony Lewin, the officer who had come on board *Midway* in 1980 to conduct refresher training for W Division. When the admiral was considering him for my position, I had been asked if I would recommend him as my relief. I had concurred, that he would be able to do my job. When Tony checked in, he began accompanying me during various meetings with DOE and Sandia. I also introduced him to all the key people I had worked with for the past three years.

This was a time of preparation for Carmen and me, a time of getting ready to relocate to Washington, D.C. We planned to drive our Oldsmobile from Albuquerque, to D.C., stopping in Kansas, and Oklahoma to visit, relatives, and friends. This was also a time of reflection for me. I was somewhat nostalgic; as my next assignment would be completely different from anything I had done in the past. I would no longer be in the nuclear weapons program. I was vacating a position that I felt was at the top apex of the nuclear weapons program, the best job a nuclear weaponsman could find for himself. I had made decisions, and been part of decision-making processes that would affect the nuclear weapons program for many years into the future. I was very proud of my part in the deployment of the Ground Launched Cruise Missile (GLCM) throughout Europe. As W84 project manager, I had worked throughout my assignment at FCDNA, preparing sites throughout Europe for the deployment of this weapons system. The Russians were very concerned about the deployment of the GLCM sites. They realized it would take many more interceptor aircraft than they had to neutralize the cruise missile threat to Russia. They launched a frantic aircraft-building program. This sudden expensive effort, along with fear over President Reagan's plan to deploy Pershing II ICBM's, which had a huge range, spurred the Russian's to spend heavily, and unwisely trying to build their defenses. This eventually led to their economic failure, and downfall.

During my time at FCDNA, the name of my enlisted rating, "Gunner's Mate Technician," in 1985, had been changed to "Weapons Technician." The rating badge insignia of crossed cannons was also changed to a trident, with an encircling neutron. This was the third name change for nuclear weaponsman during my time in the Navy. The first being, "Nuclear Weaponsman" (see photograph page).

Most nuclear weapons in the stockpile were now considered to be "wooden bombs." This meant the bombs required very little hands on maintenance. About the only maintenance was the exchanging of limited life components, such as parachutes. The days of complete disassembly of fuzing, and firing sets, and removal and installation of detonators, such as I participated in were now things of the past. Most of the weapons now had PAL devices, and new technology was being incorporated almost daily.

An interesting example of old technology, becoming new technology is a case in point with the B61 bomb. One delivery method to a target, considered when the B61 bomb was being developed was delivery by a high-speed aircraft, carrying the bomb externally on the aircraft wing. One problem was that carriage of the bomb in this fashion would expose the bomb to the friction of the passing air stream, and the resulting heat. In an effort to reduce the friction of air passing over the bomb case, the bomb case was made of highly polished aluminum alloy. The first production of these bombs tasked the GMTs' to frequently polish the bomb cases to keep the bomb cases from corroding, or rusting. Eventually the bomb cases were painted with heat resistant epoxy paint. Another problem fighting the air friction heat was what method to use to hold the bomb nose, warhead, and tail sections together. The method used had to permit disassembly of the bomb by nuclear weaponsmen in the field for maintenance operations, and also the method of connection had to permit an unrestricted flow of air over the bomb case when it was assembled.

The connection of bomb assemblies methods used on the B61's predecessors was with clamp bands that encircled the bomb case and held the sections together. The clamp bands were held together by screws, which were tighten and torqued by nuclear weaponsmen. The B61 incorporated a new system, called high torque countersunk screws as a means of holding the bomb sections together. This type of screw was not new to the aviation community. Howard Hughes first used this type of screw on his revolutionary aircraft, the H-1B. The screw was invented in an effort to decrease the air drag over the surface of plane body and wings. Howard Hughes carried this effort to decrease wind drag to the extreme. He machined the heads of the high torque countersunk screws so the slots on the head of the screw were aligned fore and aft along the horizontal axis of the plane body, when the screws were installed.

As I said Howard Hughes used these screws in his Hughes 1B *Racer*, which was a single engine plane, made of polished aluminum. The plane was designed and built in the 1930's. On 13 September 1935, the plane set a speed record of 352 miles per hour. On 19 January 1937, the plane set an L.A. to New York nonstop record of seven hours twenty minutes. This plane represented a revolution in aircraft design. Howard Hughes attempted to sell this plane to the U.S. military, but America was not interested. The United States was to pay for this lack of interest in the future. The plane was sold to Japan, and the Japanese military incorporated many features of the revolutionary plane into the building of the Mitsubishi AGM2 fighter named *"Zeke,"* or better known as the Japanese *"Zero."* When World War II began, the *Zero* gave allied fighter pilots a shock. No fighter could match the *Zero*'s phenomenal maneuverability and climb, or its range. Even when the U.S. introduced faster and more powerful fighters later in the war, pilots could never underestimate the *Zero*. The Howard Hughes *Racer* was in many aspects the father of the Japanese *Zero*, and in the area of screw fasteners, a partial ancestor of the B61 thermonuclear bomb.

As a side comment, on 16 March 1998, Mr. Jim Wright of Wright Tools, Cottage Grove, Oregon began building a replica of the original 1935 H-1B. The original (the only other plane of this type in existence) is in the National Air and Space Museum in Washington, D.C. Building of the plane was no small undertaking, it took thousands of hours, and a cost of more than three million dollars. In 2001 I happened to be at the Cottage Grove, Oregon airport, with my friend Al Satterla. Al knew Jim Wright, and introduced me to him. Jim Wright was in his hangar where the partially assembled H-1 *Racer* was. He very kindly offered to give me a tour of the plane. I was very interested in the screws on the fuselage, and told him of the screw's connection to the nuclear weapons program. He was a very kind, and interesting man, one who people liked at first meeting. He was very obviously a compassionate man, because he found the original engineer who had worked on the H-1 with Howard Hughes, and he gave the ninety-year-old plus engineer a tour of his replica. As fate would have it, the engineer died a few weeks after the tour. Mr. Wright invited me to see the maiden voyage of the H-1, which I regret I was not able to attend.

The H-1 Replica flew its maiden flight in 2002. There were many plans for this historic replica. One plan was to include the aircraft in an upcoming movie "*The Aviator*[51]" directed by Martin Scorsese, and starring Leonardo DiCaprio, which is a film about Howard Hughes.

On the morning of 13 September 2002, Jim Wright piloted the Hughes *Racer* Reproduction to a new world speed record (category C-1.d) of 304.07 miles per hour at Reno, Nevada. The H-1 once again earned a place in the record books, but unfortunately Jim Wright and the H-1 replica were to have a tragic end[52].

> While on a cross country flight, on 4 August 2003, in the H-1, headed west toward Cottage Grove, Oregon, Jim Wright had reportedly had some propeller trouble, but after landing a couple of times during the trip decided to continue on to Oregon. While flying over National Yellowstone Park, Wyoming, it's not known why, but he apparently experienced an in-flight emergency, and had to land the plane. Witnesses say it sounded like the aircraft engine was failing. The only possible landing area was a place in the park called Midway Geyser Basin. While attempting to land, there were groups of tourist in the landing area, and instead of endangering them he sacrificed his life, by maneuvering the plane away from the people on the ground, and crashed into a nearby mountain, killing him, and completely destroying the H-1 *Racer*. Many of the people on the ground gave testimonies that they were spared, because of his heroic action. On 17 December 2003, the Cottage Grove, Oregon Airport, was rededicated and named "Jim Wright Field".

I began the familiar check out procedures, and the preparation for pack out of household goods. Talking to Bobby Hamilton, I was told it was very unlikely that we would be able to get into military housing in Washington.

We would probably have to rent an apartment, and rent cost was extremely high. We placed some of our larger pieces of furniture in storage, as we would probably end up with a small apartment. We began bidding farewell to friends and people we knew in Albuquerque. Carmen and I had enjoyed being on a bowling league, with retired and active duty Navy families that were members of the FRA, for three years. We also had a number of friends in the Air Force, and some that worked in the base exchange. It seemed the time had gone by quickly in New Mexico. I had lived the dream of many nuclear weaponsmen of my era, by being stationed in Albuquerque after Nuclear Weaponsman A school. I had been stationed here, not just once, but twice. I teased Lieutenant Commander Grass, by telling him "Thanks a lot for getting me assigned as a detailer, by bragging about me to CWO4 Bobby Hamilton!"

The stockpile maintenance branch gave Carmen and me a farewell luncheon, as was the custom for those departing FCDNA. After all our goodbyes, on 26 August 1986 I once again saw the town of Albuquerque fade from sight in the car's rear view mirrors. Once again I felt sadness as I drove away, I had a rewarding, and exciting job at FCDNA, and I was not sure what kind of job lie ahead. To say I was apprehensive about my assignment in Washington would be huge understatement. I had not sought this job, but it had, in a manner of speaking, been forced upon me. I would be in an administrative job, requiring skills, and abilities I hoped I possessed. I would be tasked with making decisions that would have an impact on sailors, and the Navy's future, which were as significant as the decisions I had been making for the past three years, about the nation's nuclear weapon stockpile. I also was concerned about the stories I'd heard about the high cost of living in the Nation's Capitol.

When it was known that my next assignment was as a detailer, my Navy comrades asked me constantly, "When I was getting the operation?" This was an old joke about detailers that had been around for years, it was said that detailers spoke with a forked tongue, inferring that what they said could not be trusted! So I was being teased about having an operation to split my tongue before assuming the detailer duties.

Chapter 15: Inside the Beltway

Leaving New Mexico, we drove northeast toward Kansas. We drove all day and stayed overnight in a small Kansas town. The next morning we stopped at a small café for breakfast. From the moment we stepped through the door of the café, until we left we felt everyone was staring us at. We guessed it was because of Carmen's dark hair, and brown skin. Anyway it was an uncomfortable atmosphere in the café. Perhaps they just weren't used to strangers.

The afternoon of the second day of our journey found us in Hamilton, Kansas, the birthplace of my father. He had been born in a farmhouse near Hamilton, in 1914. I called my father's sister, Aunt Marguerite, and after about an hour she met us in town. She was eighty-five years old, and looked much as I remembered her, when I'd last seen her almost twenty-eight years before. We followed Aunt Marguerite to her ranch located far from town, where she lived alone in the company of her dog. The house looked as I remembered it, when I'd visited with my parents during my boyhood. The house was situated in the middle of a large cattle ranch, which she now leased out to cattlemen. My Uncle Floyd, her husband, had passed away years before, and had built a number of fishing ponds throughout the ranch. One day Aunt Marguerite loaded Carmen and me into her pickup, and we raced across a field to one of the ponds. She did not drive like a normal eighty-five year old. Carmen and I hung on for dear life, as she sped over the bumps in the field. We caught many perch and catfish that day, and had a wonderful fish fry that night. I greatly enjoyed this visit. Aunt Marguerite relished relating family history to us. After a couple of days, it was time to continue our trip. As we were getting ready to go, Carmen asked Aunt Marguerite about a bump on one of her fingers. She said a few years ago while weeding a flowerbed in front of the house; she had been bitten by a small rattlesnake. Carmen immediately began looking about the ground near us. Considering her past experiences with snakes, Carmen was not sad to leave at that point! Aunt Marguerite was a true pioneer woman. She taught school in a one-room schoolhouse for much of her life. She spent years alone in the ranch house far from town, after her husband's death. This was to be the last time I saw her, in 2003 she passed away at the ripe old age of 102.

We drove south toward Oklahoma. We were going to visit another aunt, my Aunt Mildred Abbey. We arrived in the town she and my uncle lived in, Broken Arrow, Oklahoma, that afternoon. We stayed with our aunt and uncle for a couple of days visiting them and my cousins' Lenole, and Barbara, who lived nearby. During this time I noticed a few bites on my legs and groin area. It soon became apparent that I had a case of chiggers. These are small insects that burrow under a person's skin, and cause unbelievable itching. I counted sixty-eight bites, and for a miserable day or two had a fever. I had gotten the chiggers during the fishing trip at Aunt Marguerite's pond. Carmen was spared any bites. I teased her that chiggers must not like brown skin, but I was truly thankful that she did not have the misery I was having. This was also to be the last time I saw my Aunt Mildred, and Uncle John, as they passed away in the years to come.

Leaving Broken Arrow, we drove south to McAlester, Oklahoma. We were to visit Bill and June Ooten, who had been our neighbors at Hamilton Air Force Base, when Bill and I both worked at NWSA. We arrived at Bill and June's house in the evening. Bill was now a CWO3, and stationed at the McAlester Naval Detachment. He'd been on an aircraft carrier on the east coast, as a Technical Monitor/Division Officer before being assigned to McAlester. I had visited Bill and June earlier in the year during a trip to McAlester for FCDNA, and they had asked us to stop by on the way to Washington, D.C.

I also got to see Commander Russ Rhine who was the commanding officer of the McAlester Navy Detachment. He was an LDO I'd known for many years. I was to be Commander Rhine, and Bill Ooten's detailer. The news I was to be a detailer had preceded my visit, most of the LDO's and CWO's throughout the Navy had heard the news that I was to be the new detailer. We had a good day, and stayed one night with Bill and June, before we continued on our trip. Sadly this was to be the last time Carmen and I was to see June, she succumbed to ovarian cancer four years later.

We were driving through Western Tennessee on the interstate in the afternoon when we saw a terrifying sight. A car being driven by an older man was coming toward us going the wrong way in the left lane. We pulled over, and the car went by. We decided to stop for the day.

After a night in a motel, we drove on to Memphis, where we planned to visit Elvis Presley's Graceland mansion. In Memphis we paid a tour fee, and boarded a bus, which took us through the gates of Graceland. We were guided through the mansion. The fixtures and furniture were left in place, as they were when Elvis Presley died in 1977. We were shown the garage, with his cars, which included a pink Cadillac.

We toured his gym, and a special museum that contained his costumes, and golden hit records. The last stop was the gravesite where he and his relatives were buried. There was also a guided tour of his private jet, but we skipped this and continued on our way to Washington.

The following day, we arrived in Washington, D.C. It was Saturday, and we checked into a Navy Lodge, which was located near Andrews Air Force Base. Over the weekend, since I couldn't check in until Monday, we drove around sightseeing. We drove through an area near the Navy Lodge that can only be described as slums. We commented that it would be scary to have a car break down in this area. We drove by the Naval Military Personnel Command (NMPC), where I would be working. It was a series of seven large six-story buildings within a guarded fenced compound. The compound was positioned on a hill overlooking the Pentagon. The Washington Monument, Vietnam Memorial, Lincoln Memorial, and other capitol buildings were visible from this hill. On the opposite side was the Arlington National Cemetery.

On Monday morning I checked into the Navy personnel office, which was located in an area called Crystal City. This was the personnel office for all sailors stationed in the Washington, D.C. area. I was told to report to Naval Military Personnel Command (NMPC). I found a parking space near my new command, and at the guarded gate, was issued a visitor badge. Then the civilian guard called CWO4 Bobby Hamilton, who shortly appeared, and greeted me. From the gate, Bobby and I walked into one of the nearby buildings, down a long hallway, and into my new office. I met CDR Gene Perry, who was to be my boss. He was the head of the section of detailers I was now assigned to. I also met LT Bill Crooks an LDO Bobby worked with. Both Bobby and Bill were operation technicians. This was the same community as LCDR Ron Bench, who had been the lone detailer for many years. He had ensured that his reliefs were from the operations community, so there had been "a corner on the market" so to speak, in the detailer's office for many years. Lieutenant Commander Bench was still stationed at NMPC in another office.

I learned I would not only be detailing Surface Ordnance officers, but also Electronic Technicians, Operation Technicians, Oceanographic Technicians, and Radio Technicians, of ranks CWO2 to commander. This was a total of more than 1,500 Officers.

Within the office there were four cubicles, one in which Lieutenant Crooks and CWO4 Hamilton worked, and one containing Commander Perry, and a lieutenant, who detailed personnel and disbursing office LDO and CWO Officers. Another cubicle was home to a civilian employee, named Peg Slacta, a lady who had worked in the office for many years. The last cubicle contained CWO3 Mike Keegan, and a LT LDO who detailed boatswain's mate CWO's and LDO's, as well as engineering LDO's and CWO's. The big surprise was in the last mentioned cubicle. The LDO lieutenant was John Adam, the officer I'd had the furious argument with on the *Midway*, five years before, about a compartment exchange between W Division, and his engineering division. We greeted each other warmly. I was thankful that during our past argument, I'd used restraint, and we'd never said anything personally insulting to one another. This emphasized to me that it was important to treat all I met in the Navy with dignity, and a measure of respect, because you never knew whom you might work with in the future.

I noticed on this first visit to my new office, that the telephone rang constantly. I slowly became aware that the scope of this job was huge. Bobby began taking me around on my check in tour. I learned that in Washington, D.C., all sailors wore the dress uniform. This meant dress whites in the summer, and dress blues in the winter. CDR Perry directed me to take a couple of days, and do some apartment hunting. Carmen and I looked for two days with little success. We looked at a few apartments that were little better than slum apartments. We finally found an apartment located three miles from NMPC. It was an apartment within a huge apartment complex called "The Brittany." It was a small two bedroom, unfurnished apartment, with a washer and dryer, and rented for $1,200 a month. The D.C. area was a high crime area, and The Brittany had security features that we liked. The doors to the building were always locked. Each resident had a key for access to the lobby. The garage had a closed door that could only be opened with an access card. There were also security guards on duty twenty-four hours a day.

We were able to afford the high cost of rent on our meager salary, only because of the Cost of Living Allowance, or COLA, we and all other service members received while stationed in the Washington area. COLA was special pay given to military members who live in an area that has a higher cost of living than normal. Our apartment was located on the third floor of the apartment building, and we had a small storage area in the basement. I was able to ride a city bus to and from work. The apartment was located in the city of Arlington, in the state of Virginia.

As we began our new life in Washington, it was very obvious that this was a completely different pace, and lifestyle from New Mexico. My new job was definitely different from anything I had done in the past.

My day at work began at 7:00 a.m., with quitting time at 4:00 p.m. Since officers called us from all over the world, these working hours were widely published throughout the Navy. On the West coast, if an officer wanted to call us the beginning of the day at 7:00 a.m., he had to place his call at 4:00 a.m. Peg Slacta, the civilian secretary, and a seaman worked answering the phone. There was also an assigned yeoman who did paperwork for the office, and he also worked answering the phones. Each detailer had a telephone with two incoming phone lines, with "hold buttons." For a few days I watched CWO4 Hamilton, and Lieutenant Crooks work the phones. Most of the time without ceasing, they were talking to one person, while another person was on hold, waiting to talk.

As a detailer, I would be writing transfer orders, and estimate what the transfer would cost. This estimate included the cost of packing and shipping household effects of families. I would also write orders placing officers on "Limited Duty," if they were diagnosed with a disease, or suffered a physical injury. I would write orders transferring an officer to federal prison, if a court martial convicted him or her. I also wrote humanitarian orders for officers who may have had a death in his or her immediate family, or needed orders resolving personal problems, or issues.

By the telephones on the desks were large rotating rolodexes' containing metal pages that held cardboard strips upon which name, rank, duty station, Primary Rotation Date (PRD), and other basic information, on a particular officer, was written. The names within each specialty were further separated into sea duty, shore duty, and overseas shore duty. On the written strips there were also colored tabs that had meanings only the detailers knew. The different colors meant various things to us. Anyone looking at the strips would not be aware of the hidden meaning. For example, a green tab might mean the officer had poor fitness reports, a blue tab might mean the officer was on a legal hold, a purple tag might indicate an officers race. While it might sound discriminatory to list an officer's race, there were places in the world detailers had to use caution when assigning a black officer, or officers of a minority race, places such as Iceland, and Australia. The strips were arranged in PRD order, or the date an officer was scheduled to transfer. An officer approaching his PRD date could be transferred to his or her next duty station within a six-month window, three months before the officer's PRD, or three months after the officer's PRD. In order to issue transfer orders to an officer, he had to have an identified relief, with his orders in hand. Also to consider was an ideal one-month "turn over" period between the incoming, and outgoing officer. Each officer's transfer was dependant on many transfers prior to his. Each transfer sending an officer to relieve one officer, so he could in turn relieve another officer, and so on. Any break or failure in this chain of transfers would stop the whole process, such as one domino failing to fall in a line of falling dominoes. Each officer was allowed thirty days transfer leave, if he wanted, so this had to be figured into the chain of transfers. There were also unusual circumstances, such as a commanding officer might request a longer than one month turn over period or families with disabled children, and a myriad of other circumstances. Each technical specialty had a specific sequence of types of duty assignments. Normally sea duty to shore duty within the continental limits of the U.S.A., overseas shore duty, then the sequence started over again with sea duty, etc. Detailers had to also consider the fact that each officer should have assignments of increasing responsibility. These assignments of increasing responsibility were to encourage career growth, and also make the officer attractive to promotion boards. In addition to the tasks of writing transfer orders, detailers were expected to be career counselors, giving advice and direction to all the officers we detailed on how to best further their careers, and promote to the next higher rank.

My first week on the job after getting checked in, and finding an apartment, Lieutenant Crooks handled the phone calls, while Bobby taught me how to write transfer orders, and many other administrative tasks I needed to know. I had noticed that all the sailors at NMPC were clean-shaven, while I wore a moustache. While I was not told directly, it was "suggested" that it would be best if I shaved my moustache. One night after work I shaved, and the moustache I'd worn for sixteen years became a victim of my new assignment as a detailer. I was to learn that within NMPC, there was a definite dislike of facial hair on officers. During promotion board deliberations if two officers were alike in all aspects, or neck in neck for promotion to the next rank, the board would look at the picture of the officer in his service record, and the clean-shaven officer would get the promotion over the mustachioed or bearded officer. I was unaware of this prejudice, as were many officers outside the Washington, D.C. area.

CWO4 Bobby Hamilton was anxious to leave for his next duty station, which was the *USS Jouett*, a destroyer home ported in San Diego, California. One of the benefits of being a detailer was at the end of your assignment, a detailer got to write his own orders. Also, the detailer assignment was for only two years. This short assignment time was because of the intense, stressful, difficult nature of the job, considered by many as the most difficult job in the Navy!

From the moment I would walk into the office in the morning, until quitting time, it appeared that everyone was working at full speed. I usually had only thirty minutes to go to the NMPC cafeteria for a quick lunch. Before I knew it, Bobby Hamilton was gone, and I was sitting at the desk that had been his, and was now mine. It wasn't long before I began getting calls from officers I'd known in the past, saying "hello," or trying to "butter me up," by recalling times we may have had together, in an obvious attempt to get an inside track on getting orders they wanted. I suddenly had friends I didn't know I had, or calls from people I'd not heard from for many years! Bobby Hamilton had warned me of officers attempting to influence me by flattery, or other underhanded methods. I vowed that as much as possible I would be an impartial detailer, not giving favorable treatment to anyone because of friendship, and deal with everyone equally. The friends I might lose because of this approach were probably not friends in the first place.

In order for the reader to understand the detailing process, it should be explained that there were two other very important people in the detailing job, other than the detailer. One person was an officer who was assigned to NMPC as a "Placement Officer". Just as there were many detailers there were many placement officers. placement officers were spokesmen for specific commands. An example being, a placement officer might be responsible for the entire officer jobs on carriers home ported on the East coast. Another placement officer might be responsible for all naval air station officer jobs on the West coast. Each command had its own placement officer within NMPC. In addition to the detailer, and placement officer, the third important person in the detailing process was the commanding officer of a command. Commanding officers of a ship, or shore station had to approve the assignments of incoming officers. Commanding officers worked with placement officers to get the best officers they could for their command.

I as a detailer was considered a spokesman for, and a representative of the individual officer. All commands had "billets," or job descriptions, that described a specific type of officer that was supposed to be in that particular billet. Often there was a lot of negotiating, and sometimes compromising between detailers and placement officers, in order to get the right officer into the right job, and also, please the commanding officer. Obviously there were constant "politics" involved with this three-way effort. An example might be, as a detailer I might have an officer that wanted to be on a specific ship, but the billet description on the ship calls for an officer with a rank one step higher than him. I might tell the placement officer, "This officer may not be the correct rank, but I'm sure he can do the job. If you and the captain of the ship approve him, I'll make sure you get the best qualified officers I can find for the next couple of assignments." Often if commands had vacant officer billets, the commanding officers would pressure the placement officers, who in turn would pressure the detailers, to find qualified officers to fill the vacant billets.

The official description of my duties as a detailer, or as I was sometimes called "Assignment Officer," was spelled out in the *Naval Military Personnel Manual*[53], and said:

> The Assignment Officer represents the individual Officer and is responsible for insuring that the Officer's personal desires are considered. The Assignment Officer compares the individual with his or her contemporaries and is cognizant of overall billet requirements. He attempts to place each Officer in the very best possible job, considering the "needs of the Navy" their professional development, and their personal desires.

The placement officers that I worked with had a job description that said:

> The Placement Officer represents the activity and is responsible for ensuring the proper manning and orderly rotation of officers to the activity. He ensures that the correct number of officers of the proper rank with the requisite qualifications is assigned to the command. He reviews the experience level, performance record, and training background to ensure that each officer who is proposed by an Assignment Officer for a specific billet is qualified for the assignment.

Limited duty officers and chief warrant officers were in high demand from most commanding officers. Wise commanding officers looked to this group of officers as "problem solvers." They were respected for their many years of experience, and considered a definite asset to any naval command.

For the most part, LDO's and CWO's were not "yes men," and were not intimidated by the commanding officer, and they would not hesitate to tell the C.O. about problems, or suggested solutions to problems. This was not always the case with line officers coming up through the ranks that didn't want to "rock the boat," or "make waves', and be associated with bad news, or negative comments, even though the need existed. LDO's and CWO's had years of experience that gave them a tremendous advantage over line officers, and they had "inside knowledge" about enlisted men, having served in this position for many years. All things considered a "Mustang" was an invaluable help to any commanding officer.

An example of a commanding officer using the experience and technical knowledge of a chief warrant officer is a story CWO3 Bill Ooten told me. Bill as a CWO on board an east coast aircraft carrier, was the W Division Officer, and his division received an outstanding grade following an inspection. The commanding officer of an aircraft carrier from the same east coast port asked Bill's commanding officer if he could "borrow" Bill for two weeks, and have him take a look at his W Division, which was having problems. Bill's C.O. agreed, and Bill was given complete access to the ship's entire weapon department as an investigator. The commanding officer directed all his weapons department officers to give Bill full cooperation. At the end of Bill's two weeks, two officers in the weapons department were fired, and W Division was reorganized. The ship did very well in future inspections. Commanding officers were very aware that LDO's and CWO's were good troubleshooters.

I began cultivating working relationships with the placement officers I dealt with. My first effort was to get to know the civilian secretaries in each of their offices. These people are called in the Navy "little old ladies in tennis shoes" who maintain continuity in offices, versus the military members who are usually in the office for only two or three years. Many of these ladies had thirty years experience or more, such as Peg Slacta, and knew how to get things done.

One day shortly after Bobby Hamilton had left, LT Bill Crooks asked me to speak over the phone to an officer he was talking to. I picked the phone up, and heard a CWO2 who said he was in San Diego on a pier. He was stationed on a destroyer that was getting underway the following day. He said he wanted orders off the ship, because he didn't want to go to sea and leave his wife! I was dumbfounded, and speechless for a second, this was something I would expect to hear from a seaman recruit, certainly not from an officer who had come up through the ranks. I let him talk, and then told him he had to remain on the ship. It sounded like he was crying. I talked to him for about fifteen minutes, and basically told him to behave like a man, and officer. I told him, he had sailors that looked to him for leadership, and as an example. He calmed down, and said he would do his best. I told him he could call me anytime. I was concerned about an officer who would act so childish. The phone call ended, and I hung up the phone. As soon as the phone was in the receiver, the office erupted with applause, and cheering, it was then I noticed everyone in the office had been listening to my conversation. This officer had a reputation for making these kinds of phone calls, and Bill had given him to me to see how I would handle him. Everyone said I had done an outstanding counseling job.

In September the annual LDO and CWO Selection Board met to review the applications that had been sent in from throughout the Navy. When the board announced the new selectees, it would mean I would have 150 to 200 new officers to assign to duty stations. I sent letters to each of them introducing LT Bill Crooks and me as their new detailers. This was much like the letter I had received from Ron Bench, in 1980 when I was first commissioned. Most of the new selectees would be going to sea, just as I had gone to *USS Midway*.

Before the first assignment, all the new ensigns, and CWO2's had to go to the Officer's Indoctrination Course in Pensacola, Florida. As I mentioned before this indoctrination school was nicknamed "knife and fork school." This was the school I'd not been able to attend following my commissioning. During my time as a detailer, the school was mandatory for all new LDO's and CWO's. I spent a lot of time on the phone telling new selectees what to expect in their experience as a newly commissioned officer.

Since it was my job to place primary emphasis on individual officers, and be his or her voice in the assignment process, an important tool in my job was the Officer Preference and Personal Information Card, or as it was sometimes called, "dream card." This card was filled out by each officer, and provided to our office. The card listed the officer's personal desires for future duty stations, and personal information such as capabilities, and personal information on the officer's family that I as a detailer needed to know. These cards were on file in a large safe in the office. At each phone call, Peg Slacta, or an office worker, would hand the dream card to the detailer about to speak to the officer. Before picking up the phone with the flashing hold button, we would quickly review the card.

There were a huge number of things to consider when making an assignment. The officer's fitness reports were reviewed, his rotation had to be proper, i.e.: from sea duty to shore duty, etc., and the job hopefully was helpful for his promotion to the next rank. The placement officer or the commanding officer could reject an officer I nominated to the placement officer. There was a panel of senior officers at NMPC who would attempt to resolve disagreements between detailers and placement officers. Fortunately, I never had to resort to this panel during my assignment as a detailer.

Since I was the first surface ordnance officer to be assigned as a detailer, and the first one with a background in nuclear weapons, I paid close attention to the assignments of officers to nuclear capable commands. Often in the past I had seen LDO's and CWO's in the nuclear weapons program that had little or no weapons experience. I set about to try and improve the experience level at nuclear weapon activities.

As detailers, we called the officers we detailed, our "constituents." We also were expected to keep conversations with our constituents' private, and not made a part of the officer's service record. Officers would often reveal personal things to us that no other person in their life would hear, because they knew we could not violate their trust. Often we felt like priests, expected to keep silent after hearing "confessions." We encouraged officers to visit NMPC with their wives and families, so we could talk face to face, instead of over a telephone, and this gave us an opportunity to explain to families how the assignment of their husbands, or wives, worked. This helped dispel the old joke that as detailers we threw a dart with an officer's name on it, at a dartboard with duty stations listed.

The news from my hometown of Strathmore was that my brother Joe had married his childhood sweetheart Sherry Blua. My mother was preparing to retire from her position at the State Hospital she worked at, and my father was enjoying life as a retiree.

Physical fitness had become a permanent part of Navy life, unlike my first two decades in the Navy. In Albuquerque I had gotten into the habit of jogging daily and lifting weights. I continued this lifestyle in Washington. Near our apartment there was a long, city maintained jogging trail, which I used nightly. Every six months, my section of about 200 officers would undergo physical fitness testing, which involved running a mile within the time limit of your age group, and doing the required number of sit ups, and pushups.

One November morning our physical fitness testing was completed. Everyone was told to muster in the NMPC auditorium in the afternoon. I was surprised to be told that the muster was for the occasion of awarding me the Joint Service Commendation Medal, given by the Secretary of Defense, for my duties at FCDNA. I was given the medal by the captain who was the head of my section, and he read the citation, which detailed my work at FCDNA for three years. This was a pleasant surprise, and I told those assembled that my previous job was at the apex of assignments for a nuclear weaponsman, and I'd enjoyed going to work every day. I thanked them for witnessing the medal ceremony. The following day, I called Major Jim Donart, my old boss at FCDNA, and thanked him for initiating the medal request.

One familiar name on the new Chief Warrant Officer Selectee list was Jim Jacks. Carmen and I had known him as a GMT2 in Guam. He visited the office in early October. He wanted to be assigned to the *USS Yellowstone*, a destroyer tender home ported in Norfolk. CWO3 Richard Logue, who had been a mutual friend of ours in Guam, was also on the *Yellowstone*. Jim stayed overnight with us, and I told him I'd keep his request in mind. When he was commissioned the following May, as it worked out I was able to assign him to the *Yellowstone*.

During the course of my career, I had known an unusually large number of enlisted men who eventually became officers. Those that come to mind are, John Gaffey in Iceland, Robert Reese, and Donn Green on the *USS Independence*, Don Parker on Whidbey Island, Billy Gilbert, and Dan Hoover on the *USS Ticonderoga*. Harry Chapbourne and Terry Morrison on the *USS Oriskany*, and there was Ray Gillip, Chris Van Diven, and Bill Ooten at Oakland, Rich Logue, Jim Jacks, Charlie Upham, and Bill Borgelt on Guam. Considering the small percentage of enlisted men who achieve "mustang status," I had known a large number. And as fate would have it I was now the detailer of all these officers. I did not include the three sailors I knew in Guam who was selected for the Army warrant officer Program, which had significantly lower admission standards.

LT Bill Crooks, my working partner had been a detailer for a little over a year, when he learned that a unique ship home ported in Norfolk was about to be commissioned. This ship had a mission different from other Navy ships. It was being refitted to be an illegal drug interdiction ship. It was to be an important tool in the countries war against illegal drugs. Bill began campaigning with the placement officer for this ship, to be assigned as the commanding officer. There was one other ship of this type on the East coast, and it was commanded by an LDO.

There were very few ships that an LDO could step aboard as the commanding officer, and Bill wanted this job badly. One objection to his assignment came from our boss CDR Gene Perry. He said the officers' we detailed might view Bill's assignment as a commanding officer, as a detailer getting preferential treatment. In many aspects this was a true statement, because Bill would probably never get a commanding officer's job, or even be aware of the job unless he was a detailer, and had "inside information." Another hurdle for Bill to overcome was the fact that his relief had not been identified. If he got this job it might be as long as a year before a relief could sit down at his desk. I began being questioned if I could handle the job of detailing all the officers we both were responsible for by myself. After only being on the job for a little more than two months, I had no choice but to say, "I'd handle it by myself" (I'd either sink or swim).

The latter part of November I was scheduled to go on my first detailer field trip. CWO3 Mike Keegan, the Engineering detailer, and Lieutenant Ward, the Personnel Officer detailer was also to go on the trip. We were to visit Charleston Naval Base, South Carolina, Jacksonville, Florida Naval Air Station, and Mayport, Florida Naval Base. I was to learn that field trips involved long hours and hard work. Most officers looked forward to the opportunity to sit down with us, and go face to face with the detailer who held their future in his hands.

The three of us flew from the Washington, D.C. airport to Charleston on a Sunday. We stayed overnight in the Charleston Naval Base BOQ. Early Monday morning we went for a run, and then had breakfast. We then went to the base theater, and gave a slide show about the detailing process to about eighty assembled officers. After the slide presentation, we offered to sit down with our constituents, and discuss future assignments, career problems, or anything they wished to discuss. Prior to the trip I had xeroxed all the metal Rolodex pages, with names and assignments, and as I spoke to each officer I would show them the pages. I emphasized to each one that they needed to keep their duty preference "dream cards" updated. Each "sit-down took about twenty to thirty minutes. Often as many as ten or fifteen officers were waiting in line to speak to me. This first day, I took fifteen minutes for lunch, and stayed in the theater until 2000 (8:00 p.m.). Charleston was home base for a large group of officers I detailed. This was the East coast headquarters for minemen. This was the group of officers and enlisted men responsible for anything to do with explosive mines in the Navy. I leaned heavily upon the advice of an LDO commander stationed here as the commanding officer of the Mine Facility. The day after the appointments in the base theater, I had an appointment with the base commanding officer, and briefed him on the detailing situation in the Navy, and the things going on at NMPC.

After Charleston, we flew to Jacksonville, where we gave another presentation and held interviews. Following Jacksonville, we flew to Mayport, Florida, which was the homeport of the aircraft carrier *USS Saratoga*. I'd not been in Mayport since the Cuban Missile crisis of 1962. After Mayport, we returned to Washington, D.C. I had made personal contact with more than 200 officers in a four-day period.

The weather in Washington became colder and colder as Christmas 1986 drew near. In November a retired chief warrant officer named John Walker was convicted of spying for Russia. He had recruited his son and brother who were also in the Navy, to be partners in his spy ring. This was a subject of shame for our office, since CWO Walker as a radioman, had been detailed out of our office while he was on active duty. From time to time I talked to officers who knew Walker while he was on active duty. They said they suspected something was wrong, because he spent much more than a CWO made, and he was always throwing lavish weekend parties for the sailors he worked with. He cast shame upon every honorable naval officer, and especially chief warrant officers in the Navy. Many felt the death penalty; instead of the life prison sentence he got, would have been an appropriate punishment.

The week before Christmas a heavy snowstorm came through town, and brought everything to a standstill. I was snow bound and could not get to work, even though NMPC was only three miles from our apartment. Two days after the first snowstorm, another storm hit. No one was able to work, or move about the city for a week.

Carmen and I got to know many of the people who lived in our apartment building. There were government workers, military officers, workers in foreign embassies, and retired people. Most were fanatical Washington Redskin's football team fans. Every Sunday afternoon, during football season, the apartment party room was opened for the telecast Redskins game. The game was shown on a large screen television, and there were free drinks for everyone, and an informal potluck. Carmen contributed to the potluck, and everyone was always anxious to see what delicious item she had cooked up. This was the year the Redskins became Super Bowl Champions, led by Doug Williams, one of the first black quarterbacks in the National Football League. All of Washington was excited about this championship team. When they returned to town after the super bowl, all work in the Capitol came to a standstill, and everyone welcomed the team home.

The first of February 1987, Lieutenant John Adam and I were scheduled for a two-week field trip to the Far East. Back on *USS Midway* when I had arguments with John, and was angry over his actions, I never dreamed him and I would be fellow detailers traveling together, and supporting each other. This was a testimony to the twists and turns our lives can take.

We flew out of Washington, D.C. on a Saturday, for what seemed like a never-ending flight to Hawaii. At each of our Far East stops, our visit had been publicized, and we would give the standard slide presentation, then after the presentation, John and I would sit down with our respective constituents, and talk about future assignments, and give career counseling. Our first stop was at CincPacFlt (Commander in Chief Pacific Fleet) Headquarters, located on a hill near Pearl Harbor, Hawaii. In the future, my past acquaintance Admiral Hardisty was to hold this lofty position in the Navy. On most of my field trips I would run across old friends, and this trip was no exception. I greeted CWO4 Harry T. Chapbourne, who had been a chief while we were together on the *USS Oriskany*, sixteen years before. Harry was preparing to retire in a year. He had married since we'd last seen each other; he had married a lieutenant commander, who worked at CincPacFlt with him. It was good seeing him again. While in Hawaii, I had a reunion with a childhood friend; I'd grown up with in Strathmore, California, named Herman Low. Herman had a chrome plating business, and one evening I had dinner with him and his wife, and he gave me a tour of his company. We'd not seen each other for twenty-eight years.

From Hawaii we flew to Guam. We gave our detailers presentations and interviews at the naval base. From all outward appearances Guam had not changed much since my departure eight years previously. Many officers I spoke to said illegal drug usage on Guam had become a huge problem. One afternoon, I drove our rental car to my old command, U.S. Naval Magazine Guam. I had a few appointments with some of the LDO's and CWO's stationed there. The magazine had not changed at all, although I was disappointed that the mural I had painted on the wall of the Silver dollar Club had been painted over. I had a short meeting with the commanding officer of the magazine who was pleased to meet me. While at FCDNA, I had helped him with a problem that arisen during an inspection the magazine was going through, and he was very grateful. It was obvious, as when I last saw Guam in 1979, that the Japanese had reoccupied the island. There were many new large, expensive, beachfront hotels that catered mostly to honeymooning Japanese couples.

As I mentioned, eight years in the future, the Naval Magazine was to be re-designated Ordnance Annex, Guam. The limited area and other ordnance functions were re-located to Hawaii, and other locations in the United States.

After a few days on Guam, we flew to Clark Air Force Base, Philippines. From Clark Air Force Base we got a flight to Cubi Naval Air Station, Subic Bay. We gave our presentation and interviews at the Subic Naval Base Theater. I met CWO3 Terry Morrison, who had been on the *Oriskany* with me. He was stationed at the Subic Naval Magazine. I told him he was overdue for transfer, and he was going to be either transferring or retiring. One day Lieutenant Adam and I traveled by Navy bus to San Miguel Naval Communications Station located about two hours traveling time from Subic. This was a beautiful isolated base, where I met with a few LDO and CWO radiomen.

The Subic Base had not changed, but the city of Olongapo, outside the main gate had changed. Olongapo now had paved streets, whereas before the streets had been dirt, and after rains, mud. There were many fast food places such as McDonald's and Pizza Hut. The town looked cleaner than it had in the past, although the river under the bridge that connected the base with the town still smelled just as bad as it always had.

From the Philippines we flew to Tokyo, Japan, and then to our old homeport, Yokosuka that John and I shared while on *Midway*. We stayed in a newly constructed BOQ. We met with LDO's and CWO's stationed on the base, and we went onboard *Midway*, which happened to be in port, to talk with our constitutes. W Division on *Midway* was doing well. The division officer was a LT, assisted by a newly commissioned CWO2. One evening I drove to a house on base for a reunion with CDR Jim McDevitt, and his wife Kimi, who were still living in Japan. After he had transferred from the gun boss job on *Midway*, Commander McDevitt had gone to work on the Commander Naval Forces Japan Staff. He and Kimi, and the kids were doing very well, and we had a very nice evening together. When I left, they told me to give Carmen their love. In the years to come Jim went on to be the executive officer of Port Hueneme, California, Naval Base. Following his retirement from the Navy he worked as an engineer on the cruise missile program. Their youngest son, David became a naval officer, and J.J. became a nationally acclaimed chef, with restaurants in Arizona, California, and New York. Their daughter Tami had a successful career in real estate. Carmen and I always had a special place in our hearts for them and their family, and were always pleased to hear of the successes of their children.

It was much colder in Japan, compared to the tropical islands John and I had visited, and we both suffered with colds. For the most part, the field trip had been a sentimental journey for me, seeing the bases and places, and the ship I been stationed on in the past. This was to be the last time I was to see the Philippines. The eruption of a volcano devastated Clark Air Force Base, forcing its abandonment. In 1992 U.S. Naval Forces left the island, ending an American presence that had lasted for almost one hundred years.

A week after I returned to Washington, D.C., LT Bill Crooks transferred to the commanding officer position on the drug interdiction ship, and I became the lone detailer in our section. Bill's replacement was not scheduled to arrive for a couple of months. He was a lieutenant named John Sweeney, and his specialty was as an electronic technician.

The automobile traffic in D.C. was very heavy, with limited parking. All at NMPC were issued parking passes. The pass was a large serialized card that had to be displayed on the car's front dashboard visible from the outside when parked in the NMPC parking lot. The entrance to the NMPC fenced compound was a considerable distance from the parking lot. There were a few parking spaces near the entrance that were not reserved spaces, and taken on a first come, first serve basis. In order to get these spaces, a person had to arrive before 5:30 a.m. The traffic rush hours from 6:00 a.m. to 9:00 a.m., and 4:00 p.m. to 7:00 p.m. would congest the highways leading into and out of Washington, heavily. Many married officers lived a distance away from NMPC, mostly because houses within a fifty-mile radius were extremely expensive. These officers would typically leave home at 4:30 a.m., sleep in their car in the parking lot until the work day began at 7:00 or 8:00, and at night they might not arrive back at their home until long after dark.

There was a sense of excitement, or awareness living in the Nation's Capitol, a feeling of being close to history. There was always a politician being quoted, or something happening that was in the national news. It was said that life was different within the "beltway." The beltway was the highway system that encircled the Capitol buildings, with the Congress, White House, Supreme Court, and all the government buildings, being the centers of the beltway bull's-eye. There was some truth to the statement that people inside the beltway seemed out of touch with the rest of the country. Much of the power and authority of the United States was concentrated in this small area, and rubbing shoulders with it gave a person an inflated ego, and a self-important outlook.

Crime as well as power was concentrated in Washington D.C. Nightly on the local news there was a "body count," it was unusual to have a day pass without the report of a murder. The Major of D.C. at this time was Marion Barry, who was eventually convicted of illegal drug use, and was a failure as a serious leader. There were certain places in Washington, D.C. that a person did not venture into after dark. While in public, it was wise to always be aware of your surroundings. The most wealthy and influential people of America, lived side by side with the poorest, and most disadvantaged of our country, making Washington, D.C. a city of contrasts.

Marine Lieutenant Colonel Oliver North, Jr., was in the news daily, concerning his testimony before a congressional committee investigating Iran-Contra operations. During his testimony he was assigned to an office within NMPC. From time to time I would see him walking the halls of NMPC, often accompanied by civilian clothed bodyguards.

Carmen and I had a few visits by officers we'd been stationed with in the past, a lieutenant I'd been stationed with on the *Midway*, and an Army Captain I'd been with at FCDNA. We had enjoyable times with these visitors from the past. I was usually exhausted after working hours, as I was the lone detailer after the departure of Bill Crooks.

There was an interesting story told about the construction of the NMPC buildings during the years of World War II. The large building had seven wings, or extensions that extended out from the main building. As I said before the building was located on a hill overlooking the Pentagon, Lincoln Memorial, Washington Memorial, and all the other impressive Capitol buildings. Windows in the offices of the seven building extensions had views of these magnificent structures, and memorials of the United States. This view was especially impressive at sunrise, with sunlight glistening on the concrete and marble structures. On the opposite side of the building there was only one window, with a drastically different view. Through this window Arlington National Cemetery was viewed. Row upon row of white headstones that marked the final resting place of those who died in the service, and defense of our country (see photograph page). This window was in the office of the admiral who was the Chief of Naval Personnel. The story was that his office was purposely placed there.

It was hoped that this view would act as a reminder to the admiral the impact his decisions could have on the destiny of sailors in the Navy, and the importance of recognizing the serious price paid by those in the past for the freedom, and peace our country enjoyed. This was a somber sight that would temper the decisions of anyone looking through that lone window.

The first time I visited the Vietnam War Memorial Wall, and subsequent visits, were very emotional times for me. The sight of that stark black wall with more than 58,000 names chiseled into the black granite had the effect of bringing memories of the war back to me. Memories of the long, hard hours building bombs off the coast of Vietnam, my short time in Da Nang, and the ones killed on the cruises I made. It also caused me to recall the feelings of rejection, and frustration we who fought the war, experienced when we were insulted and looked upon with disapproval by our fellow countrymen, who we thought we were fighting for. I was pleased that the memorial had an atmosphere of honor for the men and women whose names were chiseled in stone.

The Lee Mansion located in Arlington National Cemetery was one of my favorite visiting spots. The mansion had been kept just as it was when General Lee and his family lived there. General Lee was one of my favorite historical figures, a man of integrity and great moral character. Near the mansion, which was located on a hill within the cemetery, were a number of secluded rest spots with benches. I enjoyed the solitude of these rest places, especially after a hectic week in the office. Where the phone would ring constantly and often emotionally charged conversations took place.

One aspect of detailing that we as LDO and CWO Detailers had to deal with that the other detailers in NMPC, such as line officer, and staff officer Detailers, did not have to consider, was the fact that our constituents had been in the Navy for long periods of time. They all had exceptional, outstanding past performances, and records. Most had at one time or another in their career, helped or impressed a senior officer they had worked for. Often this senior officer was an admiral. Many times if we detailed a CWO or LDO to an assignment they did not want, the next call we would get would be from an admiral or captain trying to persuade us to change the orders. Our response was always, "Admiral, (or Captain), I'll direct you to my boss Commander Perry," or Commander Perry would ask for the NMPC Admiral to speak to the caller. There was also the occasional call from a wife, upset that her husband had received orders to shipboard duty. A few would accuse detailers of breaking up their marriage!

CWO3 Mike Keegan, the Engineers, and Boatswain's Mate detailer in our office, one weekend took a trip to Atlanta, Georgia to visit his ailing mother. Mike and his wife of two months lived in an apartment in Arlington. He left on Friday evening, leaving his wife at their apartment. He returned to the apartment on Sunday night, and was shocked to find his apartment completely empty of furniture, and household items. The only thing in the apartment was his clothes, and a note from his wife saying the marriage was over. He said it was a terrible shock, and adding insult to injury, she had even taken the toilet paper roll in the holder in the bathroom. The marriage was annulled, and Mike married another woman before I left D.C.

A few months after Bill Crooks had left, LT John Sweeney reported aboard. I finally had help with the 1,500 officers I detailed. John quickly learned the ropes, and was soon taking phone calls. Matching the needs of the Navy with the personal desires of the officers was not always possible, and sometimes caused unpleasant conversations. There were also the occasional demanding officers who were difficult to work with. John and I worked well together from the beginning. We supported each other, to get through the difficult days.

One weekend I was resting after a particularly difficult week, as well as trying to recuperate from some medical problems. I was reading the *Washington Post* newspaper, and I turned to the "weekend section." There on the front page was a full-page photo that immediately caught my attention. It was a photo of an old grave headstone, and the name on the headstone was James Little! This was one of those times when a person feels he is being given a message that needs to be heeded. This happened to me on one other occasion while in Washington, D.C. One afternoon after visiting the Lee Mansion on the hill of Arlington Cemetery, I was walking down the path leading away from the mansion. I had an inexplicable urge to climb a nearby hill, and see what the view was like from the top of the hill. I walked up past the many white headstones. After reaching the top of the hill, I caught my breath, and I turned to look out over the landscape toward the Capitol buildings. My eyes were drawn toward the headstone that was at my feet. The name was Admiral James Little. In both these instances, I felt God was telling me that life here is short, and not to be wasted. The life I had was a gift, not only physical life, but spiritual eternal life because of what Jesus accomplished on the cross of Calvary. I certainly did not hear a voice of doom warning of my impending death, or anything of that nature. I can best explain my feelings and my behavior after this, by describing the sight of the headstones as a catalyst.

This was motivation for me to practice my faith more diligently, read my Bible often, and worship at church at every opportunity. This unsettling sight happened to me once again, while strolling across a cemetery to attend my cousin's burial service. I glanced down and saw another headstone marked, James Little. If my name were Smith, or Jones, I could say these instances were just happenstance, but Little is not a common name. The sight of your name on a headstone is definitely an "attention getter."

One problem we as detailers dealt with was fraternization. The Navy forbid officers and enlisted personnel from socializing, or mingling on fraternal terms. Specifically this meant it was illegal for officers and enlisted people to have romantic relationships, or any type of personal intercourse, other than on a professional level. Fraternization violations did occur from time to time, such as the one I personally saw in Guam between Rubin, and an ensign. These violations were punishable by court martial, and the guilty parties could be awarded discharges, and prison time. The punishments were particularly harsh if the fraternization happened between a commanding officer, and enlisted members of his command. A commanding officer was expected to protect and lead the sailors in his command, not exploit and use them for his or her personal sexual desires. Punishment meted out to commanding officers were often harsh, to serve as a warning to others in the Navy, that fraternization would not be tolerated.

I remember one LDO commander who was the commanding officer of a communications station on the east coast, and was found guilty of fraternization with a second class WAVE in his command. He was relieved of his command, and John and I had to find a replacement for him. He was given a dishonorable discharge, and the twenty plus years he had in the Navy did not count for anything, and he lost all retirement benefits. One day he came to visit the office before his dishonorable discharge went into effect. John and I could not pity him, or give him any consolation. He had known the penalties before he took his pants off. It was sad to see a promising career destroyed.

We had an LDO lieutenant stationed in Hawaii who was convicted of fraternization with a female in his command. He was sentenced to six months in Leavenworth prison, and a dishonorable discharge. I had to coordinate his transfer from Hawaii to prison, and write orders that directed him to report to prison. I talked to him often on the phone, and tried to encourage him. Not only had he been banished from the Navy, but also his wife and family had left him as the result of his affair. These were difficult conversations, and I think my voice was the only friendly voice he heard from the time of his conviction by court martial, until he walked through the prison gates. Fraternization penalties may seem cruel or unreasonable to the civilian community, but the rules against it are for the discipline, and good of the Navy.

In the summer of 1987, I had a very enjoyable break from detailing duties. My mother and father traveled from California, and together we toured all the sites of Washington, D.C. We visited the museums, Congress, the White House, George Washington's home on the Potomac River, and Arlington Cemetery. We also attended a patriotic celebration that the Army presents every year. My Aunt Edna from California was visiting her son Mike who lived in Pennsylvania at the same time, and I got to spend time with her. It was the visit of a lifetime, and we got to see just about everything a tourist can see in Washington, D.C. My mother liked to comment that while on this trip, she had seen one homeless man in the Washington, D.C. Mall, who seemed to be featured in all the newspaper stories she read concerning the homeless situation in Washington.

On one occasion friends from Strathmore happened to be in the Washington D.C. area, and I took a day off to show them the sights. There were three couples, and we toured Mount Vernon, George Washington's home. Something happened during this tour that I did not learn about until years later. While going on the guided tour one friend was missing from the group for a short while. I thought nothing of it. My friend finally admitted that when the tour group had passed by George Washington's bedroom. He had an irresistible urge to lie down on the bed! He confessed that he did lie down for a few moments, after the group left the room, and the bed was very uncomfortable. Had he been caught we probably would still be in jail!

Commander Gene Perry, the boss of our detailing section was transferring to England. He had a 1987 Ford Escort station wagon. He had tried unsuccessfully to teach his wife to drive it, as it had a manual shift she was not familiar with. He decided to sell it prior to his transfer. I had ridden in it a number of times, once on a 150-mile trip with the commander on a detailer field trip to Norfolk. It was a nice car, and the good gas mileage, forty miles per gallon, impressed me. Since I'd been having trouble with our Oldsmobile, and Carmen was using it to drive back and forth to her job as a hostess at the Virginia Radisson Hotel, I bought the Escort from Commander Perry.

After a year as a detailer, in September '87 I received my first fitness report. I received all "A's." Looking back over the year I had just completed, I was in full agreement with the statement that being a detailer was one of the hardest jobs in the Navy! I enjoyed attending a Baptist Church that was located close to the apartment. The pastor asked if I would consider driving the church van on Sunday mornings to pick up children in the local area, for Sunday School. I agreed, and became busy with this task each Sunday morning. I also taught a Sunday School class of high school age children. I made many friends in this friendly small church. Many church members were government workers, or retired government workers. One friend worked in the State Department, and was an expert on Cuba. There was a tragedy in his life, his wife who was in her late twenties, died suddenly of bone cancer. He asked me to be a pallbearer at the funeral, which was held in our church. His wife was from Venezuela, and her family traveled from South America to attend the funeral. After the funeral service, which was a closed casket service, the coffin remained in the church, prior to being taken to the burial plot in the cemetery. The people who had attended the funeral departed for the cemetery, while the pallbearers and the immediate family remained in the church, as the family wished to see her one last time. The casket was opened, and I'll never forget the heartbreaking scream of her sister when she looked into the casket.

One interesting job LCDR John Sweeney (John had been promoted to lieutenant commander shortly after arriving in the office), and I detailed was a job on the president's staff. A Navy lieutenant electrician made trips with the president and his staff, and oversaw the installation of communication equipment, and other devices. He traveled on Air Force One with the president's party. This job was highly sought after, and the candidates underwent a thorough security check.

As I mentioned, Ron Bench who had been the detailer when I was commissioned seven years previously, had a job within NMPC that he had gone to following his detailer assignment. He became friends with Carmen and me. He was always baffled why I turned down the orders to Puerto Rico, and remained on *Midway*. Ron was a close friend of Peg Slacta in our office. They had worked together for many years. Peg had been in NMPC for almost thirty years, and had turned down many promotions just to stay in the LDO/CWO Assignment Office. Ron Bench was promoted to commander, and invited Peg, Carmen and I, to a promotion celebration dinner at a small restaurant in Arlington. This was a small gathering of Commander Bench's friends. One of the guests was a Navy captain who was assigned to the staff of the top military officers in the nation, the Joint Chiefs of Staff. He and I had an interesting discussion about one of the hot topics of the time, President Reagan's so called "Star Wars project," which was a proposed missile defense system for the U.S.

Carmen and I met many interesting people while in D.C. One lady, who was the ex-landlord of Commander Bench, was the widow of a famous Washington Post reporter. A group of us, including Peg, would meet every month, attend a theater production, or gather at a restaurant for a social afternoon or evening. Remedy Martin, our "adopted daughter" from Santa Clara, California visited us for two weeks. She was on a sabbatical from her job at Rolm Communications Company in San Jose.

Bill Grizzard, the chief warrant officer I had relieved on the *Midway* and who then worked at the Yokosuka Magazine, and lived near us on Yokosuka base, was now assigned in Norfolk, Virginia. Bill was close to retirement. His son Alton was attending the Annapolis Naval Academy. This was the boy who had played with our kids in Japan, and had been heavily involved in sports. His involvement in sports paid off. From his sophomore year to his senior year at the Naval Academy, he was the quarterback of the Navy's football team. He was a very popular naval cadet, and naturally Bill was proud of him. I spoke to an LDO who was assigned at the Naval Academy, and asked him about Alton. The LDO said Alton Grizzard was an outstanding student, and highly respected by all at the academy. He was not large in stature as most football players, but made up for it in heart and leadership. He was one of the best Navy quarterbacks in history. He had a very bright future in the Navy, and the sky was the limit. After graduation, and promotion to Ensign, Alton entered the most elite, demanding program in the Navy, the SEAL's (Sea, Air, Land), who are the Navy's commandos. Following his graduation from the demanding SEAL school in San Diego, he was featured in promotional films about the Navy, and the SEAL's.

A few years later in December 1999, while watching an editorial program on television, Carmen and I were shocked to see Alton Grizzard featured in a tragic story[54]. He had run across an academy female classmate while shopping in a San Diego Navy Exchange, she was with another male classmate of his, and the three had a pleasant reunion. The girl was stationed in San Diego, and the guy was stationed on a ship that was soon to deploy overseas. The two were engaged to be married; all three exchanged phone numbers, and promised to get together in the future. One evening the girl called Alton, very upset, saying she and her fiancé had a fight, and could he please come over to see her at her BOQ room, so they could talk.

Alton was a very gracious person always ready to help a friend, so he went to her room. Shortly after he arrived at her room, there was a knock on the door, Alton opened it, and it was his classmate, who instantly shot him four times, then killed his fiancée and turning the gun on himself, committed suicide. This was a horrible story, Carmen and I was sick about it for a long time after we heard it. Alton was in the wrong place at the wrong time, just trying to help a friend. A promising, outstanding, young man's life was cut short, as well as two others. Lieutenant Alton Grizzard was buried at Arlington National Cemetery This story was prominent in the national news for a week, and a special half hour documentary was broadcast about Alton's short life.

The winter of 1987 was not as severe as the previous winter. I had gradually become accustomed to life in the big city. We seldom left the apartment after dark, and when we did we were very cautious. One night someone broke into the trunk of our car. Nothing was taken, but we reported it to the police, who said after investigating, that it was probably someone looking to steal something that could be sold to buy drugs.

One day LDO Lieutenants Charlie Upham, and Ray Gillip, old friends from Guam and Oakland came by the office to talk about future orders. It was enjoyable seeing them again, and like true friends they did not pressure me to give them preferential treatment. I did try my best to honor the personal desires of each officer when making assignments, but there were many times when the needs of the Navy took precedence over all other considerations.

From time to time officers were placed in a status called a "legal hold." Officers placed on legal hold, had a colored tag on their Rolodex name strip, which was a reminder to John and me, and not revealed to anyone else. Within NMPC, there was a legal office that worked with the Navy Judge Advocate General's (JAG) office, and would notify us of officers placed on legal hold. Often the officer placed on legal hold would not be aware of his legal hold status.

Working as a detailer, I learned many things in the upper bureaucracy of the Navy that I had not known before. One of these previously unknown things was concerning command surveys. Semiannually, or annually the Navy would send questionnaires to ships and shore stations, and direct commands to conduct surveys, by having all sailors at the command complete the questionnaires. I participated in many command surveys during my career. The questions were all to be answered, and sailors were not required to sign their name. The information collected was supposed to be kept confidential, and no one was to be penalized for providing information that might otherwise be punished under the articles of the UCMJ. Questions such as what the sailor thought of his commanding officer, or division officer, feelings about the readiness and training of the command, illegal drug usage, etc., were examples of the questions asked. Everyone was told this information was being collected for statistical purposes, and no one would be identified, or punished for providing answers. This was not entirely true. If a survey revealed a drug problem, fraternization, or illegal activity at a command, a secret investigation would be initiated. If an officer was suspected of an offense, he could not be transferred until the investigation was complete, and he or she was secretly designated as being in a legal hold. This was the first time in my Navy career, I was told officially to lie! If an officer was due to transfer, and waiting for me to issue his orders, and he or she was in a legal hold, we could not reveal this to them. We were told to make up an excuse for not getting the orders out, such as not enough money, or a problem at the command he was going to, or anything except the truth, that he or she was the subject of an investigation. I recall one officer I had to string along for six months after his transfer date. He was stationed in Alaska, and anxious to leave. He would call me almost weekly, and his tone ranged from pleading, to anger. Finally after six months the legal office notified us that he was off legal hold, and I immediately issued his orders. I could never tell him the truth for the delay, and I imagine to this day he still has hard feelings toward me.

Carmen and I received a sad letter from Dick Clark's girlfriend. Dick was the GMT whom we stayed with on Guam during Typhoon Pamela, and who had been the LPO of *Midway*'s W Division. We'd last Dick seen when he visited Albuquerque from Concord Naval Weapons Station, attending school as a civilian weapon technician. The letter from his girlfriend said Dick was sitting at the dinner table having dinner one evening, and fell from his chair. His heart had stopped, and he died before help was summoned. She said Dick always talked fondly of Carmen and I, and she felt we would want to know about his death. She was very unhappy. She and Dick lived together in a house they had bought together, but Dick had not updated his will. Dick's ex-wife was still listed on his will, and she was taking possession of his portion of the house they had bought together, which meant the girlfriend was going to have to sell her home.

As well as clean-shaven while working in NMPC, I kept my hair cut very short. This meant I made frequent visits to the NMPC Barber shop. I made friends with one particular barber. One day while cutting my hair, shortly after Christmas, he told me about a unique Christmas gift he had given his wife.

The barber and his wife had one child, a daughter who was in college, living away from home in another state. On Christmas morning the barber had given his wife a gift-wrapped box of Kleenex, and a VHS cassette tape enclosed in a box listing it as a Perry Mason movie, which she enjoyed. The barber then explained to me, those years ago before the birth of their daughter, he had bought an 8MM movie camera. He took pictures of their daughter in the hospital after her birth, pictures of her first steps, and many family gatherings. He never bothered getting a movie projector, so over the years as each roll of film was developed he would toss the roll of film into a box in the closet. Shortly before Christmas he took the box of unseen rolls of film to a film developing company, who converted all the 8MM film to a single cassette tape, which could be watched continuously, accompanied by sentimental music. He said his wife was baffled when she unwrapped the box of Kleenex, Christmas morning. On Christmas evening, the barber suggested to his wife that she watch the Perry Mason movie. She agreed and put the tape into the recorder. It was then that she discovered what the Kleenex was for. The tears flowed freely as she watched forgotten scenes of their daughter, and films of her family members, some who had since passed away. This was a wonderful story, and I thanked him for sharing it with me. His story prompted me years later, to compile old films of my sister's daughters, and films of her and her family that were taken years before, compile them together, and give the cassette to her (along with Kleenex), as a gift for her birthday. She was very pleased with the tape, and this became a sweet memory for me as my sister passed away a few years afterwards at the age of 55.

LCDR John Sweeney and I struggled filling jobs, with few officers, and a tight budget. We were told to try to conserve money by transferring officers' short distances. Any transfer across country had to have strong justification. We began looking at ways to conserve our transfer money. I did not agree with the current policy of assigning surface ordnance officers to an aircraft carrier for only two years, while assignments to all other types of ships were three years. This policy had been effect for many years, and did not make sense. An aircraft carrier assignment had many advantages over smaller ship assignments. The living conditions on carriers were much more comfortable, and the carriers rode the sea much smoother than smaller vessels. Carriers had larger stores and messing facilities not available on smaller ships. I assumed that the two-year policy was related to the time in the past when nuclear weaponsmen had been permanently stationed in Albuquerque, and deployed on carriers for six-month periods. This was not the present day situation. I had served on *Midway* for three years (after requesting an extension), and I felt a three-year assignment was reasonable. Another factor I considered was that all other officers assigned to carriers had three-year tours of duty. I made a decision that was not popular, but I felt it was the right thing to do. I made all LDO/CWO surface ordnance officer carrier assignments a three-year duration. I determined a cutoff date, and all officers with more than six months before his transfer date, was automatically extended on board his carrier for one year, making the tour a three-year stay. This was objected to by a few officers on carriers, but was a decision I still feel was right.

AIDS was a relatively new disease affecting society in 1987, and it affected the LDO/CWO community in a way that surprised me. Of the 1,500 officers John and I detailed, six of them had been diagnosed with AIDS.

I received messages from medical commands such as Bethesda Naval Hospital, Oakland Naval Hospital, and other medical facilities when any of the officers I detailed were placed on medical hold. A medical hold meant an officer with a medical condition that prevented him from being completely capable of performing his duties, such as a broken leg, disease, or the like, was placed in a limited duty status for six months. These six months were used to determine if the officer should be medically discharged, or could be returned to full duty. When a doctor placed an officer on limited duty, he was not expected to carry out his duties fully as he would if he were completely healthy. This often meant I needed to transfer an officer in to assume duties of the officer placed on medical limited duty.

One day I received a message that one of the chief warrant officers I detailed had been placed in a medical hold status. I was always concerned when I received a message of this type, but I was doubly concerned in this instance. The CWO was a friend of mine I'd been stationed with at various times in my career. I'll respect his privacy and not reveal his name.

Normally I would receive a phone call from the officer placed on medical hold a day or two after I received the initial message, but two weeks went by and I still had not heard from the CWO. Finally he called me, and said he had been embarrassed to call me. The reason he was embarrassed was because he had been diagnosed as having AIDS. This was shocking news. The policy of the Navy was to avoid seeking to determine if there was a homosexual connection with the disease of AIDS, unless the infected officer voluntarily stated he had homosexual relations. In the event he volunteered this information, he would be processed for a medical discharge.

In the event there was no homosexual revelation, or it was determined that the AIDS condition was not homosexually related, the officer was to be immediately transferred to another command. This immediate transfer was to avoid any speculation, or rumors within the officer's command. The only person to be told the reason for the transfer was the officer's commanding officer. He was not to reveal this information to anyone, just as placement officers, and detailers were required to keep the officer's medical condition confidential.

The CWO with AIDS was stationed on shore duty, and was scheduled within a few months for transfer to sea duty. Detailers were forbidden to transfer officers with AIDS to any overseas command, including ships that might visit a foreign port. Many countries had custom laws against persons infected with AIDS entering their borders. The only transfer assignments we could make were locations within the continental limit of the United States (CONUS). I wrote transfer orders for this officer transferring him from his current shore duty station, to another shore duty station. Since the surface ordnance LDO/CWO community was a small one, many knew of this transfer, but none of the reasons why it took place. It appeared that I as a detailer was acting with favoritism, since it was known that I was a friend of the CWO. I was strict, and inflexible with the rotation cycle of all officers from shore duty to sea duty. When I was asked from time to time why this particular CWO went from shore duty to shore duty, I could merely reply that it was none of their business. At this point I can honestly say that I wrote no transfer orders with favoritism, but this particular situation with my friend weighed heavily on my mind. Thankfully, I can say that he is still well today, and living in retirement.

As I said, the length of my assignment as a detailer was for two years. And as I also said previously, the job was among the most stressful, demanding in the Navy. The NMPC Commanding Officer, Admiral Mike Boorda, on one occasion told me if I successfully completed my two-year assignment as a detailer, and he didn't fire me, my reward would be the duty station of my choice at transfer time. I could put my finger on a map, and he would send me there. If there was not an open billet at the duty station of my choice, it didn't matter I would go there anyway. There had been two officers assigned in my office as detailers, who lasted a couple of months before being reassigned elsewhere (or fired) because they could not handle the job!

This was a position I'd never been in while in the Navy. For the first time I was able to control absolutely where I was to be assigned, and determine what my future job would be. One thing for sure, if I were not happy with my future assignment, there would be no one to blame except the person looking back at me when I looked into a mirror. I had considered possible future assignments. My next job in the Navy would be my last in the Navy, as I would only have two years before my thirty-year mandatory retirement. I was considering a job at an ammunition plant near Los Angeles, also a job at an ammunition plant near Reno, Nevada. I also considered Puerto Rico, and Hawaii. In the fall of 1988 I was still undecided. My transfer date was supposed to be in August, and I still had not identified my relief. Out of 1,500 officers there had only been one officer that asked for my job. This officer was rejected because of poor fitness reports. I finally found a CWO3 on a ship home ported in Norfolk, who was a good prospect as my relief. He was an electrician. None of my ordnance peers wanted the detailer job. His name was Tom Paige.

A wonderful piece of news from my brother Jerry in California was that a son had been born to him the middle of September. My nephew's name was Jacob Stewart Little.

One evening I had a call from an old friend, Rubin Rassmusson, who had been with me in Guam. Rubin was now a master chief. He had injured his knee, and was at Bethesda Naval Hospital, on limited duty. Carmen and I spent Thanksgiving with him at his house in Virginia. Rubin has since retired from the Navy, and for a short while worked for the Central Intelligence Agency (CIA).

President Reagan's missile defense program, dubbed "Star Wars Program" was in its infancy. John Sweeney and I detailed a group of officers whose specialty was oceanographic technicians. These officers were in a program called Sound Surveillance Underwater System (SOSUS). This system intercepted underwater sounds with undersea hydrophones, to determine where Russian, Chinese, North Korean, and any nation's submarines were at any given time.

The sea hydrophones picked up sounds from the ocean that were converted into lines on scrolls of paper, which looked liked marks made by an electrocardiogram machine. Oceanographic technicians whose job it was to determine what kind of vessel made the noise in the ocean examined these scrolls of paper with the electrocardiogram like etchings, which in Navy slang were called pieces of "dirty paper." For years this program had been highly classified. The general public first became aware of this Navy program by the publishing of the fictional book in 1984, *"Hunt for Red October*[55]*,"* by Tom Clancy, which is about the hunt for a Russian submarine, and its crew who have defected to the United States.

A proposed "star wars" plan was to use the technicians who worked in this underwater surveillance program, and train them to intercept hostile incoming ballistic missiles aimed at the U.S., and destroy them with lasers. These sailors would be deployed in special vans encircling America. John Sweeney and I since we were the LDO/CWO Detailers for "OT's" were invited to a number of meetings where this proposed plan was discussed. During one of these meetings, John and I brought up the problem we had with this proposal to use OT's was that there were severe shortages of people within this community. The overall LDO/CWO community was undermanned. Along with the shortage of LDO/CWO Officers in 1988, there was also a shortage of money to affect transfers. One solution for these shortages was to automatically extend everyone who was scheduled to transfer in 1988, at their current duty station for four months. This extension included me, so I would be staying in the detailer job, for at least an additional four months.

There were 4,500 LDO's and 3,000 CWO's in the Navy at this time, or about 11% of the total Navy officer force. Anytime there was an order from the top, to decrease the number of officers in the Navy, the LDO/CWO community usually took a larger cut, than the staff officers' community (supply, medical, dental, etc.). These cuts were also much larger than the line community (academy graduates). To make our jobs as detailers even more difficult, at this time there was also an increase in the number of jobs that needed filling on board ships, and a decrease in the shore duty jobs. Promotion opportunities were on the downslide. It was becoming increasingly difficult to promote to lieutenant commander, and the time for promotions for chief warrant officer ranks was raised from three years to four years between promotions.

I made a number of field trips in 1988. One trip to the west coast included stops at Seattle, Washington, San Francisco, California, Long Beach, California, and San Diego, California. While in Long Beach, my brother Joe who was an engineer for the city of Los Angeles met me at the Long Beach Naval Station. This was the same base I'd started my Naval career twenty-seven years before on the *USS Haven*. I was scheduled to have a luncheon meeting on the battleship, the *USS New Jersey* (BB-62). Joe went along with me, and a lieutenant LDO I detailed, took us on a very interesting tour of the ship, which included the huge gun turrets of the battleship. We had lunch in the wardroom, and one comment my brother made after the tour, was that sailors had their own language, that was difficult for an outsider to decipher. Thinking about his comment, I realized that all the acronyms, and abbreviations such as PCS, per-diem, dislocation pay, sea pay, limited duty, and so on that sailors use, would sound like a foreign language to a listener. While on the *New Jersey*, the lieutenant told us the problem, I mentioned before, when the battleships were re-commissioned there was a lack of knowledge about firing the huge guns with black powder. A lot of old sailors, some in their sixties and seventies, volunteered to help with the learning process. In my mind the battleships were the most impressive warships ever built.

I spent the night in Joe and Sherry's apartment, and one evening while we were sitting around the kitchen table, there was a small southern California earthquake. It was great spending time with my brother and sister-in-law. While visiting with them, we visited Sherry's grandparents, Mr. and Mrs. Jim Puppi, who lived nearby. They had a beautiful Italian villa on a hill in West Covina, in Los Angeles. Mr. Puppi had come to America as a young boy, shortly after World War I. As a young man he had unknowingly managed a large farm for the secret Italian Black Hand Society. He had been very successful farming, and had some of the most desirable land in southern California. They were very gracious people, and I enjoyed meeting them and corresponding with them after this visit. At the end of the weekend, Joe and Sherry drove me to San Diego, where I finished the field trip.

From time to time commanding officers from various commands would visit the office on behalf of a CWO or LDO in their command, or visit with the purpose of asking our help. A woman commander named Finley made one such visit. She was the commanding officer of Naval Facility Whidbey Island, Washington. She was concerned about an LDO lieutenant, who was the Officer In Charge of a detachment of her command, located at Charleston, Oregon, which was located near the town of Coos Bay. The lieutenant was in command of a detachment that had both sailors, and civilian workers. This lieutenant had been passed over twice for promotion, and there were disciplinary problems at the detachment. This LDO had been passed over because of his poor record, and below average fitness reports. He was to be discharged on retirement in the first part of 1989. Commander Finley said she would like a replacement officer in charge who could provide discipline. She did not necessarily need an officer who was in the OT field, but preferred an officer who she could rely on to run the detachment without problems. I told her, I was due to transfer the first part of 1989, and I might be interested. She said she would welcome my assignment.

I was still trying to decide what to do, resign and stay in the D.C. area, go to the ammo plant in Reno, or Los Angeles, take an overseas assignment, or take the job in the Pacific Northwest. I had often said, if I ever got to the point in my life in the Navy, that I dreaded getting up in the morning to go to work, then it would be time to think about quitting. There had been a few mornings as a detailer I had not looked forward to walking into the office, because there were almost insurmountable situations and problems awaiting me.

All detailers had to be cautious about relationships with the officers we detailed, to guard our integrity. On field trips, I often would be offered gifts, such as command ball caps, and novelty items. I had to report all such gifts. This was to discourage bribes, and the playing of favoritism when making assignments. I had a few officers who would send me postcards from the various ports their ship visited. They would write comments on the postcards such as, "Wish you were here," or "The liberty is great here," and so on. I thought this was a clever way to keep their name on my mind, and there was certainly no regulation against sending a postcard to your detailer.

I witnessed a surprising effort of an officer trying to influence his assignment one afternoon in my office. As I said, the detailers in our office were separated by six-foot partitions that made up our individual cubicles. The people in the adjoining cubicle overheard much of the business, and phone conversations that took place within the individual cubicles. Mike Keegan, the engineer detailer had the cubicle next to the cubicle John Sweeney and I worked in. The LDO/CWO engineering officers had a rough sea/shore rotation. The community was undermanned as we were, and because of the shortage of shore duty jobs, these sailors had to spend six years on sea duty, and only two years ashore. Their job on board ships was among the most difficult, working in the bowels of the ship in the engine rooms, in heat, and discomfort.

On this particular afternoon a lieutenant junior grade, along with his wife and three children ranging in ages from four to eight years old, visited Mike in his cubicle. The LDO was stationed in Norfolk on shore duty, and scheduled to report to sea duty on a ship in a couple of months. He had come to the detailing office to ask for an extension on shore duty, which was impossible considering the shortage of engineering officers. After talking for about twenty minutes, and not getting anywhere with his request to Mike for an extension, the officer said loudly, "I have to go to the bathroom." Addressing his wife, he said, "Honey, don't you have to go to the bathroom, also?" the wife said, "Yes, I do." They asked Mike to watch their three children, and left the cubicle headed for the bathrooms located down the hall from our office. As soon as the LDO and his wife left the cubicle, the three children encircled Mike, and began pleading, "Please don't send our daddy to sea," and "we don't want him to leave us." One even started to cry (not too convincingly). This continued for about ten minutes, until the parents returned, and then the children became silent. It was very obvious that this was a rehearsed plan, designed to play on Mike's sympathy. Shortly after the officer returned to the cubicle, Mike asked the officer to step out into the passageway alone with him. Mike told him if he ever pulled something like this again he could expect to be on sea duty for many, many years. After the dejected family left, we all had a good laugh over their failed theatrical presentation.

My relief, CWO3 Tom Paige checked in shortly before Christmas, and I began showing him the details of being a detailer. I had decided to take the Officer In Charge job in Charleston, Oregon. My decision was based on a number of things. This was one of the few officer in charge, or commanding officer jobs in the Navy available to a chief warrant officer or limited duty officer. I had always wanted to return to the Pacific Northwest following my assignment at Whidbey Island, Washington. Another factor was my eighty-year-old Uncle Ralph Little lived close to Charleston, Oregon at Days Creek, Oregon. He had been caring for his bedridden wife, for a number of years. There were no members of the family close by, other than my parents who lived 600 miles to the south, and I thought Carmen and I might be a help to him. When I put my name in as a nominee for this job, the placement officer for this job, told me that the commanding officer of Naval Facility Whidbey Island, the officer who would approve my assignment, and the officer I had spoken to during her visit earlier in the year, had changed her mind about wanting a disciplinarian for the job. She now wanted an officer who had experience in the underwater surveillance program. The placement officer told her she had no choice; Admiral Boorda had approved my assignment.

When I had been stationed in Albuquerque in the Naval Liaison Office with Perry Roberts, I had always wondered why an LDO submarine officer who had little nuclear weapons experience held this position. I felt an experienced surface ordnance LDO with nuclear weapons experience should hold the position. One of my last efforts as a detailer was to change this job from a submarine officer's position to a surface ordnance officer's billet. As it happened this job needed filling, and I had a commander anxious to go to Albuquerque.

I was pleased with this accomplishment, and felt it would enhance the overall functioning of the Navy's nuclear weapons program.

Tom Paige was gradually grasping the detailer's day-to-day tasks. As was the case when my time at a duty station drew to an end, I reflected on what I had or had not accomplished. I felt that I had contributed to the nuclear weapons program, by being the first ordnance man to hold the detailer position. I had ensured that the officers I assigned to nuclear weapon positions had in fact possessed nuclear weapons experience. I felt I had dealt fairly with all the officers I detailed, and had tried not to play favoritism.

A few officers had been difficult to deal with. I recall one officer who had been eligible for either sea duty or overseas shore duty in Guam. He pleaded with me to send him orders to Guam, so I did. After he had been on Guam for one day, he called me crying over the phone that he and his wife arrived on Guam, checked into the Navy Lodge; it was then that she saw a gecko (small lizard common on Guam). She picked up her luggage, returned to the airport, and bought a return ticket to the United States. He complained that he wanted off Guam, after being there a day. After a long discussion, I convinced him to stick it out. Eventually his wife did return to Guam. In another case, an officer broke his leg, on board his west coast ship. I placed him on limited duty for six months, and was required to transfer him off the ship. The only job I had was San Clemente Island off the coast of California. He wanted orders to the east coast, but I could not transfer him until his leg healed. He would call every few days complaining that he wanted to go to the east coast. I would listen to him, and then explain that he was going to stay in San Clemente for at least six months. After a couple of months the phone calls stopped. It was then I learned from an LDO officer friend of his that he had won the California lottery for three million dollars! I only heard from him once after that when I wrote his transfer orders. He did not mention the lottery win, probably because he knew if I hadn't insisted he stay there, he would not have won. It would have been nice if he had thanked me, and offered to share the lottery prize (oh well). I remember another officer who was so rude, obnoxious, and profane during an interview on board a ship in San Diego, that I told him the interview was over. I refused to deal with him in the future, and said he could talk to John Sweeney from that point on.

I remember the displeasure of some of the officers stationed on aircraft carriers when they learned I had extended their tour from two years to three years. There was also dissatisfaction when everyone was extended at his or her current duty station in 1988 for four months. As a detailer I had been under constant pressure to meet the needs of the Navy, while balancing the desires and needs of the officers I detailed. There was one thing I felt hypocritical about. As a detailer I urged all the officers I detailed to become Surface Warfare Officer (SWO) qualified. This was a lengthy, difficult qualification program that all line officers had to complete. This involved being a qualified OOD underway or being qualified to drive a ship. The qualifications covered every aspect of shipboard tasks, and took over a year for most officers to complete, and be able to wear a SWO badge on their uniform. I had never become surface warfare officer qualified, as my other duties on board ship as a division officer, and other duties took priority, and I never seemed to have extra time. It was much more difficult to achieve this qualification on an aircraft carrier, than other smaller ships. There were large numbers of line officers fighting for qualification time, and LDO's and CWO's could seldom find time to complete the qualification sheet. Also the captain on aircraft carriers seldom encouraged LDO's, CWO's, or staff officers to become SWO qualified. I felt hypocritical encouraging officers to get their surface warfare qualification completed, while they looked at my uniform chest, and did not see a SWO badge. The "other side of the coin," was that I had many officers thank me for helping them, or for getting the assignment they wanted. I often had to argue, or represent my constituents to placement officers, or commanding officers, and give assurances that the officer I was proposing could do the job. I had a number of officers who said, "They owed me." My job as a detailer had been one of the most difficult I had held in the Navy, and certainly the most stressful. I had learned much about the inner workings of the Navy, and I had gained insights into the Navy's leadership at the top.

President George H. Bush had been elected, and Carmen and I had invitations to one of the inaugural balls. I regret that we did not go, as we were busy packing and getting ready to transfer. Before reporting to Charleston, Oregon, I was to attend a school in Norfolk, Virginia to become qualified as a Communications Security Custodian, which would be part of my future job as an officer in charge. The school was one week in length.

The latter part of January, my last day at NMPC, Carmen and I were given a small going away party in the office. Peg Slacta had ordered a cake, and I said farewell to my fellow detailers. I was given a beautiful pen and pencil set, from those in my office. Engraved on them was "Gunner Little." Carmen and I visited with Admiral "Mike" Boorda, and he thanked me for the job I had done.

We talked about my future assignment, and what he saw in the future for the Navy. He gave me a signed farewell card, which I cherish to this day. Admiral Boorda was highly respected by Navy LDO's and CWO's. He was known as the "Sailor's Admiral." He started as they all had, at the bottom as an enlisted man. He rose up through the ranks, and was to become the top admiral in the Navy, the Chief of Naval Operations.
In this position he was the advisor to President Clinton on all affairs of the Navy. Seven and a half years later after Carmen and I had our farewell meeting with him, on 16 May 1996 he was found dead of a gunshot wound outside his Washington, D.C. residence. His death was ruled a suicide. He had supposedly ended his life over accusations that he wore a ribbon on his chest that he did not earn. I have serious doubts about how his life ended. I watched him in his job as Chief of Naval Personnel, and he was not the kind of officer who would shrink from controversy, or end his life over such a trivial matter. While I have no evidence that his death was not a suicide, I'm not fully convinced that he was not murdered. It was definitely a shock when Carmen and I learned of his death.

Also on this last day, I was told that I was to be awarded a medal. All the detailers and placement officers I had worked with gathered with Carmen and me, and I was presented with the Navy Commendation Medal, from the Secretary of the Navy (this was my second award of this medal). This was a pleasant surprise, and I thanked all the assembled officers for their help, support, and friendship. I also thanked the most important person, the Lord Jesus Christ, for his guidance, and help throughout this difficult tour of duty. I bid farewell to LCDR John Sweeney, who was genuinely sorry to see me go. We had been through a lot together.

In the future, NMPC was to be re-located to Memphis, Tennessee. This re-location did not make a lot of sense to me, as NMPC seemed to be located in the most logical area of the country, where the Pentagon, and other major Navy commands were located. Then I realized the re-location was mostly political, as the vice president at the time of the re-location order, was the past senator from Tennessee, Al Gore.

The detailers and placement officers also gave me a picture of the NMPC buildings that was signed, and a plaque engraved with my name, and time of my service as the LDO/CWO Detailer. Our car was loaded to the roof, and we soon saw Washington, D.C. fade in the rear view mirror, as we drove toward Norfolk, Virginia.

Chapter 16: Submarines and Salmon

We arrived in Norfolk after a three-hour drive. We had reserved a room at the Navy Lodge, where we were to stay while I attended school. I began the school on Monday morning. All of the other sailors were radiomen, or officers with a communications background. This was foreign water to an ordnance man. It felt good to relax somewhat after the intensity of the detailer's job. The school course of instruction Classified Material System (CMS), covered the management of codes that were changed every twenty-four hours by military communication activities, and the equipment used to decode messages. This was the first time I had seen any of this equipment, and much of the presented material was tailored to radiomen. In order to pass the course, a final quiz of 150 questions was given. On Friday when the test was given, and I barely passed, perhaps I had enjoyed the release from the intense atmosphere of the NMPC office too much. Also there had been a nightly western series on television called *Lonesome Dove*[56], and the main character reminded me a lot of my Grandfather Sylvester. Instead of studying I had watched this program each night.

The Friday afternoon after my last class of the CMS Custodian School, Carmen and I climbed into our loaded Ford Escort station wagon, and started our drive across country. We had originally planned to drive through Kentucky and see my Uncle John Little, but there were reported severe floods in Kentucky so we dropped these plans. We had an uneventful day of travel the first day. The second day we ran into a snowstorm in Tennessee, and had to stop for the night early in the day. The third day, we arrived in Albuquerque, New Mexico, and drove around town for a few hours to see the changes in town. Albuquerque had grown considerably in our absence. Two more days of driving, and we arrived at our parents' home in Strathmore, California.

After a few days visiting family and friends, we drove north 600 miles to Coos Bay, Oregon. While in Washington, D.C. I had spoken to the officer I was to relieve in Charleston, his name was LT Bob Barke, an LDO who had been passed over for lieutenant commander. We planned to spend two days in Coos Bay, and then travel 400 miles north to Naval Air Station Whidbey Island where I would check in with my new boss Commander Finley.

In order to get to Coos Bay located on the Oregon coast, we left interstate highway five, which cuts through the middle of California, Oregon, and Washington, and traveled over Oregon state road forty-two, which goes west for 100 miles. This road winds through pine tree covered coastal range mountains. We arrived in Coos Bay late in the evening, and got a motel room.

In my childhood I had visited Oregon annually with my parents to visit my Grandparents who lived in Azalea, Oregon, 100 miles east of Coos Bay. It was known on the west coast that Oregonians were not overly friendly to visitors from other states. They were particularly hostile to visiting Californians. We were to experience this "cold shoulder" attitude our first night in Oregon. Our car of course had Virginia license plates, and we discovered in the morning that someone had bent our rear license plate downward from the attachment screws, while our car was parked outside our motel room.

We drove around the town of Coos Bay sightseeing, and then to Charleston, which was located seven miles south of Coos Bay. Charleston, Oregon had been selected as a Navy sound surveillance system site because Charleston was the most western projection of land within the boundaries of the United States.

The Charleston Navy Base, called Coos Head Naval Facility, was built in the early 1960s, and was home base for more than 200 sailors. The mission of the base, which was listening for submarines off the coast of the U.S., was highly classified. In 1987, two years before my arrival, the base was disestablished, and down sized. The Oregon Air National Guard moved onto the base taking over the barracks, gym, motor pool, headquarters building, and mess hall buildings that made up the base.

The Navy's portion of the base collapsed into a three-acre fenced area within the former Navy base. The reason for the downsizing in 1987 was the advent of advanced communication systems that permitted all the sound data collected by the hydrophones at Charleston to be transmitted to a central location, Whidbey Island for analysis. In the past all analysis of the "dirty paper" which I explained previously, was analyzed at the Coos Head Navy Base. The downsizing was a move that resulted in a substantial saving of manpower, and tax dollars. The downsizing however, was depressing to the local Coos Bay economy, when suddenly the dollars 200 sailors spent every day disappeared.

Far to the north on the coast of Washington state, was another facility, which was a twin to the Coos Head Facility. An LDO lieutenant commanded the Washington state facility.

Bob Barke was the first officer in charge since the downsizing, and had overseen the collapsed move into the Navy compound, while the Oregon National Air Guard, 104th Air Control Squadron (ACS), had moved into the vacated base buildings.

After a day of sightseeing at Coos Bay, we drove north to Washington state, and Whidbey Island. The island had not changed significantly since my departure in 1969, but there was much more traffic on the island's roads. The Naval Facility on the Navy air base was an ominous looking concrete building encircled with a razor wire topped security fence. The fenced compound was guarded twenty-four hours a day, by a civilian guard force.

I checked in at the guarded gate, and was issued a visitor badge. CWO3 Bob Lockhart met me at the gate, He was pleased to see me, as his detailer I had worked hard to get him the orders he wanted, to Whidbey Island, and he was very grateful. I entered the building with him, and then was ushered into the commanding officer's office.

I'd not seen Commander Finley since our meeting in Washington, D.C. As soon as the door closed, she said, "I didn't want you as my Officer In Charge in Oregon, but I didn't have a choice." This was a shocking statement, and certainly not an encouraging way to begin a relationship with a boss! She went on to say, since our meeting in NMPC, the disciplinary problems she had discussed during our meeting had been resolved by substituting the sailors as a guard force, with a civilian agency called Burns Security. She said she now preferred having an officer experienced in the underwater surveillance program. Admiral Boorda had responded to her objections, by saying he had the utmost confidence in me, and if I wanted the job, I had it. I told Commander Finley, I hoped to change her mind about my assignment, and I would do the best job I could for her. She briefed me on upcoming events at Charleston, and then we both left her office, and walked to the basement of the building. In the basement was a briefing area, which had a large map of the entire Pacific Ocean displayed on one wall. A group of officers had assembled for the daily morning briefing. The commander introduced me to the assembled officers, and then a lieutenant conducted a briefing. He pointed out various dots on the wall map, which represented both American and Russian submarines. The tracks of each dot showed position changes from the previous twenty-four hours. After the briefing, and a short farewell from Commander Finley, with a promise from her that she would be at the change of command ceremony between Lieutenant Barke and me, I left the naval facility, not feeling too encouraged. Before leaving Naval Air Station Whidbey Island, I drove to the AUW shop I'd been stationed at twenty-three years before. The fenced compound was locked, and the long deserted buildings looked as though they had been turned into base storage warehouses.

The return trip to Coos Bay was uneventful, and I began the turn over process with Bob Barke. Apartments for rent were very scarce in Coos Bay. Carmen and I finally found one that was not very desirable, but would do until we found a house. The apartment was in an old house that had been built in the 1930s that had been converted into three separate apartments. We referred to the apartment as "the dump." We planned to buy our first house, and were anxious to find it.

I learned I would have four civilian technicians and six security guards in my command. I also discovered I was responsible for a large twenty-seven home housing area, north of Coos Bay, called Ridgeview Housing area. This housing base had been built by the Air Force. The houses were near a radar site on a mountaintop overlooking the coast. The housing area was in a beautiful setting among pine trees, with a distant view of the Pacific Ocean. This mountain was near a small Oregon town called Houser. When the Air Force closed the radar site, the Navy took over the houses. Sailors who worked at the Coos Head Naval Facility moved into the vacated homes. This housing area was self sufficient with its own water supply, and sewage treatment facility. In 1987 when the Coos Head Facility was downsized, and all the sailors transferred, the Government Sales Agency (GSA) of San Francisco put up the housing area for sale. The sale was a "highest bidder sale." One of the first things to happen when the houses and property were put up for sale was a legal action by the local Indian tribe asking for bid preference. This court action delayed the effort to sell the government property. Since Lieutenant Barke was the only active duty commissioned officer within a radius of a few hundred miles, he was assigned as the responsible officer for the property, and so I would assume this title when I assumed command of the facility. A celebrity had visited Coos Bay a few months previously, showing interest in the sale. It was Wayne Newton, but when he learned of the legal action of the Indians, he withdrew his interest. Fir, and pine and cedar tree-covered mountains surrounded all of Coos Bay. The climate was considered mild, with the average rainfall more than sixty inches. When we first arrived in Coos Bay, and went shopping it would often be raining. We would sit in the shop parking lots in our car waiting for the rain to subside.

Then we noticed people walking about ignoring the rain. Very few people used umbrellas. We soon learned to accept, and ignore the almost constant rain. Being near the ocean gave Coos Bay an air quality advantage. At one time air quality monitoring devices had been positioned around the town of Coos Bay to determine the air quality. After a year the devices were removed, as there was no detectable air pollution. The ever-present sea breezes and abundant trees provided clean air to breathe.

Bob Barke and I began the turn over process in earnest. In order to enter the Navy compound, I first had to enter the outer Oregon Air National Guard Base by entering a four numbered numerical code into an electrical box positioned at the base main gate. This box controlled a sliding gate, which would open and permit me to drive into the base. After a short drive I would arrive at the Navy compound parking lot. After parking, I would walk to the Navy pedestrian gate where I would enter another numbered code into an electrical box, which controlled the entry gate. After entering into the fenced compound, I would approach the main door of the large windowless building, where a monitor camera was positioned. A Burns Security guard, who was positioned inside the building monitoring the front door, would punch a button opening the door. Once inside the entrance, just as was the case in nuclear weapons capable facilities, the guard handed out a badge, which was to be worn at all times inside the building.

The office, which was to be mine, contained a large oak desk, a number of safes, a couch, and a computer, typewriter, and other office machines. Prior to entering the office there was a waiting room complete with a couch and coffee table. Next to the commanding officer's office was the security guard's post, with camera monitors, and telephones. Down a long hallway was another door that was entered by punching a code into the door-opening latch. In this large room was all the equipment that received the sounds picked up by the hydrophones, and the equipment that coded the sounds, and then sent the information to Whidbey Island. This was the working area of the four civilian technicians who tended the equipment. There was also a room containing a huge diesel generator, various storage rooms, and a bathroom and shower. Outside the main building there were a large satellite dish, and a building containing an emergency diesel generator, which would come on in the event of a power loss. This then was the extent of my domain. For the first time in my naval career I was a commanding officer, and this was to be my command.

The turn over included Bob Barke showing me the daily routine, this involved a daily trip to the nearby Charleston Post Office for mail pickup. We also prepared for the change of command ceremony, which included Bob's retirement ceremony. The ceremonies were to be held in the Oregon Air National Guard Base Theater.

The day before the ceremonies, Commander Finley arrived in Coos Bay, along with a group of sailors who would help with the proceedings. On 28 March 1989, the change of command ceremony was held. A newspaper article in the *Lindsay Gazette*[57] reported the event, and said:

> Chief Warrant Officer (W4) James S. Little, son of Mr. And Mrs. L.S. Little of Strathmore, assumed command of the Coos Head Naval Facility in Charleston, Oregon, March 28.
>
> About 150 persons attended the combined Change of Command and Retirement Ceremony. Former Facility Commander, LT Bob Barke, retired after twenty-one years of service.
>
> The Facility conducts oceanographic observations to provide the Navy with extensive information on currents, temperatures, salinity and other factors which compromise the oceanic environment and impact sound patterns in the sea.
>
> Little is a twenty-eight year Navy veteran. He and his wife Carmen were stationed with Naval Military Personnel Command in Washington, D.C., prior to Little assuming his new command.
>
> During a recent ceremony which honored both Little and his wife, he was awarded a Navy Commendation Medal (second award) for the performance of duty at the command. Little is a 1960 graduate of Strathmore Union High School.

During the ceremony Bob read his retirement orders, and I read my orders before the audience. I then told Lieutenant Barke that I assumed command, and he stated that he stood relieved. We both then reported to Commander Finley. After Bob's speech, I gave a short speech. I thanked Bob and his family. I told the crowd I was happy to be in Coos Bay, as opposed to Washington, D.C., where now the only gun fire I would hear would be during deer hunting season, and the only traffic jams would be waiting for the drawbridge operation over the Coos River which separated Coos Bay from Charleston. This brought a chuckle from the audience. Commander Finley was much more hospitable to me during this visit, and she promised to return in a few months.

I quickly settled into the much slower and relaxed work routine as a commanding officer, versus a detailer position. Carmen and I continued to search for a house. We also visited our Uncle Ralph Little, who lived in Days Creek, 100 miles to the east (see photo page), who had just turned eighty-one years old, and tended to his bedridden wife, our Aunt Freda.

As I adjusted to the community of Coos Bay, and met the people that were citizens of this Pacific Northwest town, I learned of the history, and recent past of this area I now called home. Coos Bay was named after the original Indian Tribe "Coos" that originated here. It was said throughout the region, if an Indian had a potbelly, he was probably a Coos Indian. This was because food such as salmon, deer, seafood, berries, clams and oysters were so plentiful. The climate was mild, and it was easy to survive. Leaning bark and branches against large trees, and getting between this material and the tree trunk made the tribe's living areas.

The first white men in Coos Bay were soldiers from San Francisco exploring the Pacific coastline. Their ship was wrecked off the coast and they were stranded in Coos Bay. The group of soldiers eventually made it back overland to San Francisco. In time, the ex-soldiers who recalled the beauty, and plentiful food and wildlife in the area returned to Coos Bay and settled in the area. It was difficult to reach Coos Bay because of the natural barriers surrounding it, a coastal mountain range to the east, and surrounding thick forests. There were also rivers to the north and south of the bay area, the Umpqua, Coos, and Coquille Rivers. In the 1800s a few efforts to reach Coos Bay from inland Oregon were made by determined pioneers. Timber and coal were the two main natural resources of Coos Bay. The discovery and mining of coal stimulated a major population increases in Coos Bay. Following the gold rush of 1849 in California, and the completion of the transcontinental railroad track, which was built with Chinese laborers, these same Chinese workers culled the deserted gold mine fields in California. Most of the Chinese settled in San Francisco. The town was an insatiable user of coal for energy and heat. With the discovery of coal in Coos Bay, and the fact that Coos Bay was the only deep water harbor between San Francisco, and Seattle, Coos Bay became the host to thousands of Chinese coal miners. For many years Coos Bay was the major source of coal for San Francisco. Many forgotten coal mine shafts honeycomb an area of Coos Bay called Barview. Newcomers from California have quickly bought up this area in recent years, and many old time Coos Bay residents chuckle that some day the new homes built in Barview, may someday collapse into an old, forgotten coalmine shaft.

When coal ceased being used for energy and heating, the Chinese settlements in Coos Bay disappeared. Near the turn of the twentieth century, an entrepreneur named Simpson became the "timber baron" of Coos Bay. He built a huge timber business, as well as a large mansion. He also built a beautiful botanical garden, Shore Acres, which today is a popular tourist attraction in Coos Bay.

The town that sprang up, supported by the timber industry was called Marshfield. The town enjoyed isolation from the rest of Oregon, and the country, due to the natural barriers surrounding Marshfield. Coastal Highway 101, which follows the western Pacific coastline, ran through Marshfield, and north of town, crosses a bridge built in the 1920s, which spans the Coos River. Roads to the interior of Oregon from Coos Bay are long and twisting mountainous roadways, taking hours to traverse. Fishing was also a major industry of Coos Bay, with fishermen harvesting the abundant salmon, deep-sea fish, crabs, and oysters. Sadly due to foreign fishermen, and mile long dragnets used by foreign nations, this industry has almost completely disappeared.

The fishermen and lumbermen were a rough, hard-working class of men. Many blue-collared and white collared professionals such as doctors, lawyers, and merchantmen settled in the northern portion of Marshfield, called North Bend. The ones who lived in North Bend wanted isolation from the southern portion of Marshfield, so they became incorporated, and the town of North Bend came into being. The southern portion of Marshfield was renamed Coos Bay. Although the city limits of both towns are right next to one another, over the year's efforts to consolidate, or combine the two towns have failed. So both Coos Bay and North Bend have separate mayors, fire departments, and police departments, and resist combining even though it would make good financial sense.

I was very pleased to be once again living in the Pacific Northwest. As I mentioned before, ever since visiting Oregon as a child, and living on Whidbey Island for three years, I had relished the idea of living among pine trees, with a mild climate, and fishing, and outdoor activities.

With the help of a real estate agent that Bob Barke recommended, we began looking for a house. This effort lasted a couple of months, until we finally found the house we wanted. It was a tri-level house built in the early 1960s, with fireplace, and a large family room with a wood stove. The person selling the house was a retired Coast Guard warrant officer who was moving to the east coast. We were able to move into the house on 26 May, which happened to be our fifteenth wedding anniversary.

The real estate agent, who helped us, became a longtime friend. Carmen and I were older than the usual first time homebuyer. Nevertheless we were very excited about having our own house, after living in Navy housing, and rental apartments all of our lives.

We called Uncle Ralph each week, and visited him and Aunt Freda, completing the 200-mile round trip, once a month. Since we were now closer to the family in California, than we had been in many years, we began having frequent visits from our relatives, which we enjoyed very much.

I enjoyed the independence I had as an officer in charge, and worked on strengthening working relationships with the civilians in my command, and with the 104th Air Control Squadron (ACS) who shared the base. I also worked with the Coos County Sheriff's Office, concerning security for the vacant Ridgeview Housing area, which I was responsible for. Oregonians were well known for their fierce independence, and distrust of outsiders. I soon discovered that my status as commanding officer of the naval detachment was a badge of instant acceptance. The base had been in Coos Bay for so long that it was thought of as part of the community. As commanding officer I was considered part of the community, just as family members who had been in the Coos Bay area for generations. There had been a scandal at the base ten years previously. The commanding officer had been sentenced to prison for molesting children. The Navy had worked hard to mend the damage this had caused between the relationships of the Coos Bay community and Navy; I was the benefactor of these efforts.

Other than an occasional phone call from Whidbey Island, I was pretty much left to my own devices. Most of my attention was toward the civilian technicians who worked with the equipment, in the "back room." A retired Navy chief, who had retired here at the naval base, led the team of four men. He was an outstanding supervisor, and thus made my job much easier. The Burns Security Guards also had an experienced supervisor, so my management tasks were minimal.

The base was located on a large bluff overlooking the ocean. At the bottom of the bluff was a road, and a sandy beach. The road led to a jetty, which was the southern border of the bay, which led to the port of Coos Bay. One Monday morning one of the civilian technicians told me he had gone to the jetty over the weekend to do some fishing. He had seen a young teenager crawling out of a cave mouth that was located at the base of the bluff directly under the base. The cave mouth had steel bars across the entrance, with U.S. Government No Trespassing signs posted. I was concerned about someone entering this cave, as they might have access to the hydrophone cables, which led from our equipment room out into the ocean. Someone might sabotage our equipment by entering this cave. The technician who had seen the trespasser and an Oregon Air National Guardsman volunteered to go into the cave and investigate. People had been going into the cave by digging out the dirt underneath the steel bars across the cave mouth. I agreed to their exploration trip, and with lights and rope, they entered the cave. After a couple of hours the cave explorers reported back to me. They said there was a huge cavern under the base. Inside the cave there were redwood tree trunks that had apparently been washed into the cave by the sea years or centuries before. They said they also saw a huge snake inside the cave. I considered this a serious security problem for the base, just as the caves discovered in the limited area in Guam had been. I immediately took steps to have the cave mouth filled with concrete, and from time to time I inspected the blocked cave entrance to make sure it was undisturbed.

My off duty time involved getting settled in our new house, and enjoying fishing. The salmon fishing was very good in Coos Bay, and one week my parents visited from California. We charted a fishing boat, and landed three salmon.

A few months after I had assumed command, I had an inspection by the Whidbey Island executive officer, and a group of enlisted sailors from Whidbey. The inspection was an annual inspection called a Remote Site Inspection. The inspectors looked at all the procedures the civilian technicians carried out daily, as well as the administrative tasks I was responsible for. They also inspected the security of my command. This was an intense inspection, but nothing like the meticulous, thorough inspections like the NTPI's, and DNSI's I had gone through in the past. The command received an overall grade of outstanding.

The old housing area, Ridgeview Village, that I was responsible for was cleared through the courts to be placed up for sale by the GSA Office in San Francisco. As I described earlier there were twenty-seven houses on thirteen acres, secluded among pine trees with a distant view of the ocean. The advertised open bid for the housing area was $150,000. The ad offering the property ran in all the major newspapers in the country. My telephone number was listed as the point of contact. My phone "rang off the hook" for a long while. For a period of six months I felt more like a real estate agent, than the commanding officer of a Navy detachment. Each week I would show the property to three or four prospective bidders.

Since the housing area was about twenty miles from the base, my real estate duties took up much of my time. I remained in close contact with the GSA Office in San Francisco, and kept them posted on the people who looked at the property. One of my concerns during this period, since I was the officer responsible for the safe keeping of the property, was the security of the property. Each house contained an electric stove, refrigerator, and water heater. A padlocked single wire cable strung across the access road blocked access to the houses. Ridgeview Village was in an isolated area, and with arrangements with the sheriff's office was patrolled occasionally by a sheriff's deputy. The sheriff's office recommended that I be armed when I checked on the property, which I did two or three times a week. I obtained an Oregon concealed weapons permit, and would take my .357 caliber pistol with me when checking on the houses.

As a testament to the law-abiding attitude of Coos Bay, during the one-year period I was responsible for the property, there was only one minor break in. A maintenance shed was broken into, and some paint was stolen, along with keys out of a key storage box. The sheriff's office that investigated the break-in was sure it was a juvenile crime. I took the precaution of changing all the locks on the houses. It was a big burden lifted when the property was sold in the latter part of 1989. The property was sold to a southern California developer for $247,789. He planned to refurbish the homes and rent the houses. The Air Force property located higher on the mountain the housing area was located on was to be turned into a minimum-security prison. The guards who worked at the future prison would be prospective renters of the Ridgeview houses.

I met a lot of interesting people, while acting as a "real estate agent". Most were courteous, and appreciative. However I did get a few rude and discourteous people who insisted that I drop everything and take them to see the property. I required a twenty-four hour notice before a tour of the property, and I refused to tour the property on Saturday and Sunday. I did not want this collateral duty as a real estate agent to interfere with my primary job as a commanding officer.

My Aunt Edna, and Uncle Richard from California visited us during the summer, and we had fun discussing the possibility of our family buying the houses and setting up an independent community. We assigned each member in the family an imaginary job, such as mayor, newspaper editor, entertainment chairman, etc.

The southern California developer who purchased the property hired a retired first class petty officer that lived in Coos Bay, and had been the housing manager of the houses when the Navy had occupied the homes. The first class lived in one of the houses while refurbishing the twenty-seven houses. A problem soon surfaced with the property after the sale. The Oregon Department of Environmental Quality (DEQ), refused to approve the sewer treatment facility that had been in use when the Air Force and Navy occupied the site. The sewage treatment and water supply problems at the housing area did not contribute to a successful business venture for the southern California developer. He eventually sold the property, and more than twelve years later only a few houses were rented by prison guards.

In November Commander Finley came down from Whidbey Island to visit the base. She visited with her mother who lived with her on Whidbey Island. We had them visit our home for dinner, and Carmen prepared a fantastic meal. We had a very pleasant evening. Following her visit, I received a nice note from her, which said:

> Dear Jim;
> Just a quick note to pass on BZ for my visit in November. I was impressed with the thoroughness of your preparation for the "inspection" and the condition of your spaces. I am also pleased that you have a solid plan to address known deficiencies or improve existing procedures.
> You have done well in your relatively brief time on board. Pass along my congratulations and appreciation to your folks and wish them all a safe and satisfying holiday. Signed, Sincerely Commander M.L. Finley.

With the attitude she had during her visit, and the nice note, I felt somewhat vindicated from our first meeting when she had been disapproving of my assignment.

As Christmas 1989 approached, and New Year 1990, I was acutely aware that 1990 was to be my last year in the Navy. It was an exciting prospect, yet I dreaded my exit from active duty. I'd known no other life since the age of seventeen, and would be forty-eight at the time of my retirement. One helpful aspect of my assignment at Coos Bay was the effect of "weaning" Carmen and me from the Navy. We'd always lived on bases, and associated exclusively with sailors, or members of the military service. The only military members in Coos Bay were the Coast Guard, Oregon Air National Guard, and the local armed forces recruiters. This lack of association with the military helped us gradually adjust to civilian life.

The Pacific Integrated Underseas Surveillance System (IUSS) was headquartered in Hawaii. The "boss" of the Pacific was a commodore named Crawford. Commodore Crawford was scheduled to visit me in January. He was to be the highest ranked officer to visit Coos Head Naval Facility for four years. I prepared a "welcome aboard" package for him; similar to the ones I use to prepare for welcoming aboard NTPI Inspectors. I "rolled out the red carpet" for him on his arrival. The commanding officer of the Oregon Air National Guard, and I had lunch with the commodore during his one-day visit. Commander Finley was happy, that the commodore reported to her, that he was well pleased with his visit to Coos Bay.

In April 1990, my parents celebrated their fiftieth wedding anniversary. My sister Linda worked hard making all the arrangements for the celebration, which was held in Strathmore, California. Their anniversary was celebrated in the church they had helped build, and had attended for many years. Carmen and I traveled to Strathmore for the gathering. This was to mark the first and only occasion I wore my formal dress white uniform, with a ceremonial sword. The family enjoyed honoring them, and congratulating them on this happy occasion.

Also, in April Commander Finley was relieved by Commander Peter Reinhardt as commanding officer of Whidbey Island Naval Facility. Carmen and I attended the change of command ceremony, which was conducted on the Whidbey Island Naval Air Station. During our stay in the Whidbey Island BOQ, I ran across my old executive officer on the *USS Midway*. It was Captain Carlson, who was now an admiral. It was a pleasant chance meeting, and he was impressed that I was now an officer in charge. The change of command prompted fitness reports for all the officers in Commander Finley's command. I received all "A's."

My main telephone contact with Whidbey Island was CWO3 Bob Lockhart, who was continually grateful that I had gotten him his assignment at Whidbey. I also talked often with the officer in charge of the Washington "sister" facility, as we often had the same issues or problems at our respective commands.

I kept in contact with the officer I had relieved, LT Bob Barke. After his retirement he had remained in Coos bay. He had an unusual retirement goal he wanted to pursue, and that was being a used car salesman. After his retirement he went to work for a local Honda car dealer.

Bob Dewey, the retired chief who was the lead technician, had worked for a short while as a cook in Coos Bay, and now worked for Research Planning Incorporated (R.P.I.), the company who had the contract to do the maintenance work at Coos Head. Bob, his wife Toni, and two daughters had lived many years in Coos Bay. Herman Barber was the second senior technician. He was from Kentucky, and enjoyed working with computers. Herman and his wife Cindy lived a few blocks from Carmen and me. Herman and his wife Cindy had been married for five years, and wanted a child. They had been working on adopting a baby from Kentucky for about a year, when they finally brought their baby girl home. When the adoption was complete, they were surprised to learn that Cindy was pregnant. They had a baby girl a few months later! The next technician was Jim Bush, who was also married with a little girl. Last was Charlie Margerum, who was the only single guy in the group. One of these technicians was always at the command for twenty-four hours, along with one of the security officers. Wayne Burkland led the Burns Security Officers. His men stood eight-hour shifts, monitoring the surveillance cameras.

Carmen and I socialized with the Oregon Air National Guard, 104th Air Control Squadron. They invited us to their social functions, picnics, and annual Christmas party. I also joined the local chapter of The Retired Officers Association (TROA). The chapter was made up mostly of World War II veterans, and Carmen and I were considered the "kids."

Navy ships would visit Coos bay infrequently. When the ships would arrive at the pier, I would usually go onboard, and as the only officer in charge in Coos Bay, would welcome the commanding officer to the Bay Area, and offer any assistance I might be able to provide. I occasionally would lend the ships the use of the detachment van while they were in port. The ships would normally remain in Coos Bay for only a few of days. Following one Navy ship visit to Coos Bay, I had a visit from a Naval Investigative Service (NIS) agent from the Seattle, Washington NIS Office. She said her office had received complaints from a black sailor on the visiting ship, about racial slurs while on liberty in Coos Bay. She remained in Coos Bay for a couple of days investigating, and came to the conclusion that racial discrimination was not common in the predominately white population of Coos bay, and the incident was an isolated one.

Some of the Oregon Air National Guardsmen, following retirement went to work for a family owned business in Portland, Oregon called PLEXSYS Interface Products Incorporated. Three Oregon air guardsmen brothers who had worked in the air traffic controllers' area had started this company. They were determined to make a realistic radar simulator that could be used to train civilian, and military air traffic controllers.

Their company became well established as a leader training the military in air combat techniques. I did not know it at the time, but I was to enjoy working for this company part time in my retirement years, but that's another story.

As I mentioned, we had many visitors our first year in Coos Bay. One of the most pleasant was Remedy Martin, who we'd last seen when she visited us in Washington, D.C. She visited with her fiancé Mark Early, who we liked instantly, and highly approved of. Both Remedy and Mark worked for Siemens Company in the San Francisco Silicon Valley. Mark's youngest son Ryan, in future years joined the Navy, and became a career sailor. Ryan would be a source of pride for me, and when I saw him, I always asked him "to take care of my Navy." He became a fellow ordnanceman as a Fire Controlman. In 2006 he was promoted to first class petty officer. He "took care of my Navy" far beyond my expectations!

My parents, and brother Jerry and his wife Mona, seven-year-old daughter Monica, and two year old son Jacob, stayed with us for a couple days, after we all visited with Uncle Ralph and Aunt Freda. Carmen had fun preparing an all seafood dinner of Dungeness crab, salmon, trout, and oysters. Monica and Jacobs' eyes got big when they saw the boiled crabs on each person's dinner plate.

I joined an artist club, which met monthly at the Coos Bay art museum. We shared paintings, and held art classes. Carmen enjoyed acting and working in the Coos Bay community theater.

Once a month I would travel from the base to the North Bend Coast Guard Air Station, which was a trip of about twelve miles. My task would be to pick up the classified codes used for transmission of data collected by the base's hydrophones to Whidbey Island. The transmission codes were changed throughout the military, every twenty-four hours. These codes were the ones the spy CWO John Walker had given to the Soviets each month of his traitorous career, which enabled them to listen to our coded radio transmissions. After picking up the classified codes at the Coast Guard base, I would call the Coos Head technicians and tell them I was on my return trip, so they could expect me within a reasonable time, or else suspect foul play.

Daily the twenty-four hour codes had to be entered into transmitting equipment within a certain two-hour time frame. If the daily codes could not be entered within this two-hour time frame, a high-level flash message had to be sent which would affect all the communication codes worldwide.

One day Technician Herman Barber rushed into my office, agitated and said, "Gunner we can't open the safe to get out the daily codes for the code change." I followed him into the equipment room where the other three technicians were dialing and re dialing the combination into the locked safe, without success. The clock was ticking, drawing closer and closer to the time when I would have to tell the world that Coos Head Naval Facility could not change its daily codes. Finally as a last resort, I told the men to lay the safe on its back, and hit the combination drawer with a hammer. I thought perhaps this might loosen any stuck tumblers in the combination dial. They did as I directed, and amazingly the safe opened, with minutes to spare the codes were withdrawn from the safe, and entered into the communications equipment. We put this safe out of commission, and used a different one from that day on.

In November the new commanding officer of Whidbey Island visited. He said he would be hosting my retirement, and change of command. I must admit I enjoyed working for Commander Reinhardt more than Commander Finley. Not only because of the rough start I had with Commander Finley, but also as a commanding officer in a male dominated Navy, she had a reputation for dealing harshly with subordinates, and being inflexible. With the commingling of men and women on board ships, I saw problems in the future that the Navy had not had to deal with during my time in the Navy.

The world seemed to be undergoing radical changes. The Soviet Union, who I had looked upon as our mortal enemy, was now crumbling, and making efforts of friendship with the U.S. There was also a major disarmament agreement being worked out between the two super powers. Many Chinese had been killed in Red China when demonstrators proclaimed the virtues of democracy. We had invaded Panama to capture Panama dictator General Noriega. The Berlin Wall was taken down, uniting West and East Germany. In August 1990, Iraqi invaded the country of Kuwait, and it appeared that war was on the horizon. I wondered what effect this would have on my retirement. I secretly hoped I would somehow be forgotten, and continue on active duty. By law, I was only permitted to remain on active duty for thirty years, and sixty-one days. The only exception to this law would be presidential or congressional action extending everyone in the military on active duty until the end of hostilities. It was very unsettling to me to be getting out of the Navy just when our nation was going to war. Daily at noon I would go for a three mile run, running over a road that went by a beach, and over a fir and cedar tree-lined roadway. I considered my job as an officer in charge, as one of the best I'd had in the Navy, and felt I lived in one of the most beautiful areas in America.

This I felt was an excellent place to end my Navy career. As I ran daily, and as my running shoes pounded the pavement, my mind would wander to thoughts of the past and present. I had been out of the nuclear weapons program for four years, but conversations with friends kept me updated on what was happening.

Weapons were no longer stored or deployed on aircraft carriers, and the Navy's surface ships. The new bomb in the stockpile was the B83, which I'd never seen or worked on. My old rating Gunner's Mate Technician had been phased out and the rate was now called Weapons Technician. There was talk of the job of nuclear weaponsman being done away with. It seemed that the wish that had been expressed years ago when I was first starting in the nuclear weapons program that there might come a day when our job would no longer be needed, was coming to pass.

A retired CWO, Fred Dyer, who worked at McAlester, Oklahoma, and whom I'd met in Albuquerque, was vice-president of an organization that had been in existence since 1983 to the present. The organization was an outgrowth of a fraternity of old nuclear weapon units that used to deploy from Albuquerque to aircraft carriers. These sailors would meet annually in September or October at various locations across the U.S. to reminisce with long-lost friends, provide support with veteran's affairs and medical information, visit historical sites, enjoy quality entertainment in hospitable environs, and salute the departed. They opened membership to all nuclear weaponsmen, GMT's, WT's, and to any military or civilian participants in the Department of the Navy nuclear weapons program in the past or present who had duties involving nuclear weapons. This organization is called Navy Nuclear Weapons Association©™[58] (NNWA). The slogan of the NNWA is the copyright slogan: *"Keepers of the Dragon©™"*. The membership consists of more than 500 members, and I gladly joined.

I became aware of a group of retired sailors who had been stationed on the *USS Haven*, who held annual reunions. I planned to attend a reunion, in 1991, the same year I was to retire. This was the ship on which I had begun my journey in the navy, thirty years ago.

I had been looking for a pickup since being in Coos Bay, and I found one through Bob Barke who was now a car salesman. It was a 1959 Chevrolet, in perfect condition. The seller, a man named Mr. Boggs, had purchased the pickup new, and was now having knee problems, and could no longer drive the pickup as it had a manual transmission. He was an interesting gentleman, a widower who had raised three children, and helped start one of the largest churches in the Coos Bay area. He loved his pickup, and I'll never forget looking back as Carmen and I drove away in his pickup, seeing him standing in his driveway with tears rolling down his cheeks. I enjoyed the pickup, and would drive by his house from time to time so he could see it.

The country had been preparing for war since August, with an invasion force building up in the Middle East. Bases throughout the world were beefing up security. Coos Head Naval Facility was no exception. I met with the Coos County Sheriff's Office, and requested increased patrols around the perimeter of the base fence during night hours. They agreed to have a deputy patrol around the base every three hours during hours of darkness. The Burns Security guards were not armed, so I prepared contingency plans in the event I needed to increase security. I worked with Captain Bill Nielson, commanding officer of the 104th ACS, as he was also beefing up security. I had plans to house armed sailors from Whidbey Island in the event they were needed.

In the midst of this heightened awareness, and tension, plans for my retirement ceremony continued. CWO3 Lockhart of the Whidbey Facility was assigned as the officer who would arrange the ceremony. I planned to have it in a large theater located on the base. I supplied a guest list to Whidbey Island, as they would send out invitations to the ceremony. I also arranged for a medical physical exam at the Coast Guard medical clinic, which would be my retirement physical. During this physical I made sure my radiation exposure in the past was documented, in the event of future health problems.

I learned that following my retirement, Coos Head Naval facility was to be headed by a GS-11 civilian employee. The civilian had yet to be identified, so in the interim I was to hand the detachment over to a chief petty officer named Mark Kohlman. He and I were to begin the turn over process in December.

December was a time for preparation, and reflection. I turned forty-eight years old, and was approaching a new phase in life, retirement. The invitation to the retirement ceremony had been sent out, close to 300. I had RSVP's from more than 200 people. Bob Lockhart asked for a list of all my duty assignments during my career, and also asked if I could identify eight side boys for the ceremony.

I had accrued a lot of leave time, and had the option of either selling it, or using it. I opted to sell some, and use some. My official retirement date was set as 28 February 1991. At midnight that day I would be officially retired from the U.S. Navy. I would be on terminal leave following the retirement ceremony. My retirement ceremony was to be held 24 January 1991.

New Year 1991 came, and the troop and equipment buildup in Saudi-Arabia continued, in preparation for invasion of occupied Kuwait. I as well as most of the country remained close to television sets watching the day-by-day developments. The buildup was called *"Desert Shield,"* and on 16 January, the operation became *"Desert Storm."*

On 17 January the CNO sent a message to all naval commands, which said:

> Once again our Navy is responding to our Commander in Chief's call to arms. The American Sailor's courage and bravery are a cherished part of our nation's honor and heritage. I am certain this generation of young Americans serving in our Navy will add their chapter to this distinguished history.
>
> In our democracy, there are, and always have been, some who oppose our country's going to war, but all are in full support of those serving in the armed forces. As the President and Congress have stated, you will be provided whatever is needed to get the job done.
>
> To those of you in harm's way, be certain you have the full support and resources of all of us in the Navy. We admire and respect your courage and dedication to your duty and to your country. Our prayers for your safety and strength of courage go with you. We are dedicated to take care of your loved ones. Get the job done so we can get you home. Let none of us rest until peace and stability are restored.
>
> Released by Admiral Frank B. Kelso, II.

On the 17th a local Coos Bay television station interviewed me. My face and comments appeared on the evening news. The following day the local Coos Bay, Oregon, newspaper The World carried the following story[59]:

> Threat Condition Bravo." Charleston-"The Coos Head Naval Facility has been placed on"Threat Condition Bravo," said CWO4 James S. Little. "Due to commencement of operation *Desert Storm* as of 5 p.m. the Coos Head Naval Facility has taken additional safety precautions along with other Naval commands in the Pacific Northwest," according to Little. The alert did not significantly change any of the normal activities at the base, Little explained. The Naval Facility is set to house additional forces if need be, Little added.

This then was the atmosphere in the Navy when before I knew it 24 January 1991 arrived. Commander Reinhardt, CWO3 Lockhart, and Master Chief of the Command OTCM Brodeur, and a number of other sailors, had come down from Whidbey Island on the 23rd for a rehearsal. My final ceremony in the Navy was to take place at 1400 (2:00 p.m.).

Thirteen years in the future, 22 November 2004, the federal government announced that the abandoned Oregon Air National Guard, and U.S. Navy site, Coos Head will be given to the Confederated Tribes of the Coos, Lower Umpqua and Suislaw Indians. The tribe said it would use the forty- three-acre base for educational and social enhancement. This was the epitaph for my command.

Chapter 17: I Request Permission To Go Ashore Sir

The list of people present at my retirement was long and varied, and I apologize in advance to the reader, who reads through this list. It probably is as laborious as the Bible book of Numbers to read through, but I feel compelled to list a few names. My Mother and Father, Mr. & Mrs. L.S. Little of Strathmore, California. Sister and Brother-in-law Mr. & Mrs. Walt Wilson of Visalia, California. Uncles and Aunts Mr. & Mrs. Hubert Sylvester of Lancaster, California, Mr. & Mrs. Don Downing of Reedly, California. Also Mrs. Jessie Wilson of Porterville, California, and Mr. George Neese of Strathmore, California. Mayor R. Gould, Mayor of Coos Bay. Capt. D. S. Lovett, U.S. Coast Guard, Commanding Officer of Coast Guard Group, North Bend, Oregon. CDR Russell Rhine, U.S. Navy, Officer in Charge, Naval Ordnance Station, Indian Head Detachment, Army Ammunition Plant, McAlester, Oklahoma, Mr. & Mrs. Phil Marlowe, President Navy League, Coos Bay Chapter. Mrs. Fran Capehart, Coos County Veterans Affairs Officer. LCDR Richard Grass, U.S. Navy-Retired, Albuquerque, New Mexico. GMT1 & Mrs. James Porter, U.S. Navy-Retired, Olympia, Washington, Oregon. LCDR & Mrs. Don Burdg, U.S. Navy-Retired, Coos Bay, Oregon.

My Mother and Father, Sister Linda, and Uncle Hubert and Aunt Kay, had been present at my boot camp graduation ceremony thirty years ago when I began my Navy career, now they were present to see that career come to an end.

All of the above listed persons and many more were gathered in the auditorium. As I mentioned, Carmen and I had met many interesting people in Coos Bay, and one of these was Mr. Ron Loffer. Ron was originally from Canyonville, Oregon where he began his occupation as a barber. He was almost the same age as our Uncle Ralph, and he had known Uncle Ralph while living in Canyonville, which is near Days Creek, Oregon. Ron liked to tell the story about the lost Scheifflin mine around the area of Days Creek, and Canyonville. Scheifflin was the man who discovered the gold and silver deposits in Tombstone, Arizona in the 1800s. Around the turn of the century he visited Canyonville, and began gold prospecting. He rented a cabin not far from town, and apparently found a rich source of gold, he wrote his sister saying, "I've found it and it's bigger than Tombstone!" He never shared the location of the gold, and was found dead of exposure in his rented cabin. People have searched in vain for his gold strike over the years. Ron as a young boy worked for an old barber in Canyonville who had met Scheifflin when he visited and began his search for gold. Ron had a barbershop in Charleston for more than thirty years, and had been the naval facility barber when the base was operating. He was my barber until ill health forced him to retire. Ron had one leg, having lost it after a shooting accident when he was sixteen years old. He used a wooden leg, and liked to joke that he could stand all day cutting hair on his wooden leg! He was a sincere Christian, and one of the kindest, thoughtful men I've met in life, and I came to respect, and admire him. He was a staunch pillar of the Charleston Community Church. Often, out of work fishermen would gather in his barbershop to talk, and gossip. Ron realized most of them were out of work, and he would say things like, "get up here in my chair, I need some practice Sir," and he would give free haircuts to the men who could not afford it. Following retirement, he and his wife moved to Texas to be near their daughter. Ron would write me often asking about Coos Bay, and Oregon. I could tell from his letters that he missed Oregon terribly. Sadly he passed away a few years after leaving Oregon. I know if there's a barbershop in heaven that he's the proprietor of the best one on heaven's golden streets. While Ron did not have a prestigious title, or impressive credentials, I felt very honored, and pleased that he attended my retirement ceremony.

Commander Reinhardt and I had been visiting in my office for about an hour, prior to walking to the auditorium. The commander was a very personable man, easy to talk to, and this conversation helped to ease my nervousness. Shortly before 1400 we walked together from the fenced compound to the auditorium where the crowd was gathered. The guests, who had arrived, had all been checked against a guest list by a sentry at the gate, because of the increased security caused by the war.

When Commander Reinhardt and I entered the auditorium, Carmen and Pastor Bob Meksch were seated on the auditorium stage. The Master Chief of the Whidbey Island Naval Facility stood on the stage behind a podium. He asked everyone to please stand when we walked in. After the commander and I climbed up the stairs to the stage, we all faced the flag positioned on the stage, and the National Anthem was played.

After the playing of the Star Spangled Banner, Commander Reinhardt approached the podium. He said he was not going to speak too long, as this was my day. He spoke of my thirty years service, and said two thirds of his command had not yet been born when I joined the Navy. This drew a laugh from the audience. He outlined the duty stations I'd been at.

He spoke of the importance of sailors' families, and congratulated Carmen on the help she had given me throughout my career. He mentioned the coordination efforts I'd made with the Oregon Air National Guard, Coast Guard, Sheriff's Office, and local community. He ended his speech by saying he appreciated my hard work, and he would welcome me working for him anytime in the future.

Then I was asked to stand, and was presented the Meritorious Service Medal, which is awarded by the President of the United States. The Master Chief read the citation, which detailed my assignments, and jobs over the past thirty years, and expressed appreciation from the President of the United States, George H. Bush. This was a pleasant surprise I did not expect. Then the master chief read a letter of appreciation from Commander Reinhardt, which said:

> On this occasion of your retirement from active service, I wish to extend to you my personal thanks and sincere appreciation of the United States Navy and the Department of defense for the thirty years of outstanding service you have given your country. You have helped to maintain the security of the nation, during a most important period in its history, with a devotion to duty and a spirit of sacrifice in keeping with the proud tradition of naval service.
>
> During your distinguished career, you have served at (the letter listed my many duty stations), and your final tour as Officer in Charge, Naval Facility Whidbey Island Detachment, Coos Head, Oregon.
>
> Over the years, your professionalism and performance have been recognized in you earning the Meritorious Service Medal, the Joint Service Commendation Medal, two awards of the Navy Commendation Medal, the Joint Meritorious Unit Award, the Navy Unit Commendation, two awards of the Meritorious Unit Commendation, three awards of the Navy "E" Ribbon, five Navy Good Conduct Medals, the Navy Expeditionary Medal, the National Defense Service Medal, the Armed Forces Expeditionary Medal. The Vietnam Service Medal (with star), three awards of the Sea Service Deployment Ribbon, the Navy Overseas Service Ribbon. The Republic of Vietnam Meritorious Unit Citation (gallantry cross color), the Republic of Vietnam Campaign Medal, and the Sharpshooter Pistol Ribbon.
>
> Your expertise, organizational skills, and leadership abilities were an inspiration and motivating factor in the successful completion of the command mission.
>
> As you depart from active service, you may be justly proud of your accomplishments, for they have identified you as a true leader. You are leaving behind a legacy which can only serve as an inspiration and challenge to those who follow. It is with a mixture of pride and sadness that I wish you "fair winds and following seas." For the future I wish you and your family many years of success and happiness. Signed Peter J. Reinhardt.

At this point, after the master chief had read aloud the letter of appreciation, he stepped back from the podium. I approached and acknowledged all the dignitaries, military members, family, and friends. I then said, "If I have enough breath left, I will now read my orders." As with any change of duty in the Navy, written orders were issued, retirement was no exception; I read my orders which were signed by J.M. Boorda, Vice Admiral, U.S. Navy, Chief of Naval Personnel.

I then turned to Commander Reinhardt, saluted and said, "I am ready to be relieved Sir." The commander returned my salute, and said, "You stand relieved."

I was then presented a letter from President George H. Bush, which was read by the master chief and said:

> Certificate of Appreciation for service in the Armed Forces of the United States, for CWO4 James S. Little. I extend to you my personal thanks and the sincere appreciation of a grateful nation for your contribution of honorable service to our country. You have helped maintain the security of the nation during a critical time in its history with a devotion to duty and a spirit of sacrifice in keeping with the proud tradition of the military service.
>
> I trust that within the coming years you will maintain an active interest in the armed forces and the purposes for which you served. My best wishes to you for happiness and success in the future. Signed George Bush, Commander in Chief.

After this reading, Carmen was asked to step forward, and Commander Reinhardt presented her with a certificate of appreciation, which said:

> Certificate of appreciation from the United States Navy, to all who see these presents, greeting; This is to certify that Carmen Little has earned grateful appreciation for her unselfish, faithful and devoted service during her husband's naval career.

Her unfailing support and understanding helped to make possible her husband's lasting contribution to the Nation. Given this 24th day of January 1991. Signed Peter J. Reinhardt.

She was also given a letter, which was read by the master chief, and said:

Dear Mrs. Little; On the occasion of your husband's retirement, I would like to take this opportunity to congratulate both of you on the culmination of a rewarding and fulfilling career in the service of you country. The unsung sacrifices you have so willingly made in the Navy's toughest job have been complemented by the public admiration and recognition afforded your husband during your long tenure together and serves as an inspiration for other Navy spouses.

Over the course of his career, your husband has faced many difficult decisions and situations, and has been guided in these decisions by the support, encouragement and love you have provided. You should feel a great sense of pride in what you have accomplished together, and I hope you are eagerly anticipating the future.

The enclosed certificate of appreciation is a small but sincere recognition for the contributions you have made to your husband's career. Thank You, Peter J. Reinhardt, Commander, U.S. Navy, Commanding Officer."

Carmen was then presented with a dozen red roses, which had been purchased by the Whidbey Island Naval Facility Officers. I was also given a naval facility wood and brass plaque, with my name, and dates of service engraved on it.

I was then presented with a beautiful shadow box, which had two compartments. One compartment contained metal rank insignia's of the ten ranks I had held, from seaman recruit, to CWO4. Within this same compartment was a metal plate listing all my duty stations in the Navy, and the dates I was assigned. Also in the compartment were all the twenty-six ribbons I had been awarded, and wore on my uniform chest. In the other compartment was a very special folded flag. This flag had been flown over the sunken battleship, *USS Arizona*, at Pearl Harbor, Hawaii. Along with the shadow box I was given a certificate, which at the head of the page had the ship's seal of the *USS Arizona*.

The master chief read the certificate, which said:

Certificate of flag presentation to CWO W-4 James S. Little, USN 30 JUN 1960-28 FEB 1991, Fair winds & Following seas.

In tribute to the American fighting men killed during the attack on Pearl Harbor, the National Ensign is flown daily over the sunken Battleship *USS Arizona* in its resting place in thirty-eight feet of water at the bottom of Pearl Harbor. The Battleship is no longer commissioned. It was stricken from the active list in 1942, but the Secretary of the Navy has granted special permission to fly the United States flag over the ship in memory of the brave men killed during the attack on Pearl Harbor on December 7, 1941.

The flag is flown from 8 a.m. to sunset. It appears to fly from the *USS Arizona* memorial which spans the sunken hull of the Battleship, but it rises from a flagpole mounted on the ship's mainmast, which is still visible above the waterline.

The United States flag accompanying this certificate was raised and lowered from this flagpole on 7 December 1990, at 1027. Signed and authenticated this date 8 December 1990. Donald E. Magee, National Park Service, Superintendent *USS Arizona* Memorial, and E.W. Earner, Rear Admiral, U.S. Navy, Commander, Pearl Harbor Naval Base.

This was a very special memento to me, not only because of the historical significance to the Navy, but because this flag was flown on the forty-ninth anniversary of the Pearl Harbor attack, at almost the exact time of day the attack took place forty-nine years before. Also, the certificate was signed on my forty-eighth birthday.

At this point in the ceremony, I approached the podium, and began my retirement speech.

"I've been shot at, been on planes that have taken off and landed on carriers, been in collisions at sea, been screamed at by very high ranking admirals and generals, and even had my wife angry at me (not too often), but I don't think I've ever been as nervous as I am today. I don't believe the reality of retirement has struck me yet. I have very mixed emotions about leaving the Navy during Desert Storm.

I'd like to share with you a few memories of the past thirty years. It doesn't seem as though thirty years has past. When I joined the Navy in 1960, President Eisenhower was in office. I was seventeen, weighed 120 pounds, my hair was one color, and I had all of it.

At that time many of my shipmates were World War II, and Korean veterans that were finishing up their twenty-year careers. They were good sailors that knew how to set priorities, and I learned much from them.

I remember the way my Father shook my hand and smiled when I boarded the bus for boot camp. I think he was thinking about the improvement in his grocery bill? As I said I weighed 120 pounds, but I still ate everything in sight.

I remember when I was given a wool blanket my first night in boot camp. I was allergic to wool. I usually didn't come within two feet of anything woolen. My boot camp commander was not as sympathetic as my mom would have been.

I remember attending Nuclear Weaponsman School in Great Lakes, and Albuquerque, New Mexico. I wished that I'd paid closer attention during my math and algebra classes in high school.

I remember getting paid thirty-seven dollars a payday, although I always seemed to have enough money. I remember the Cuban Missile Crisis. I was stationed on the aircraft carrier *USS Independence*, and at the time was a third class petty officer. I and another third class, and a lieutenant were detailed to evacuate some classified material out of Cuba, and onto Puerto Rico. We flew from the ship onto the base. Everyone on the Cuban base was armed, even dependants. It was expected that the Cuban Army was going to attack at any time. We had to remain overnight. The lieutenant got sleepy about midnight, so he left us to guard the material while he went to the BOQ to sleep. He left his forty-five-caliber pistol with us, but forgot to leave the bullets. That was one of the longest nights of my Navy career.

I remember being in the Gulf of Tonkin at the outbreak of the Vietnam War. I was stationed on the *USS Ticonderoga*, an aircraft carrier, when the *USS Maddox* and *USS Turner Joy* were attacked. Our aircraft attacked the attacking North Vietnamese gunboats. There's been controversy about whether this incident really happened. From my viewpoint, I can only say that we were being shot at and we shot back.

I remember my Father encouraging me to reenlist in the Navy at the ten-year point. He may have been thinking about his grocery bill again?

I remember the many cruises off the coast of Vietnam, from 1964 to 1972.

I remember being under my bunk in the barracks in Da Nang during a rocket attack, and crawling out from under it, because I'd be embarrassed if my parents received a telegram from the Navy, saying I'd been killed while hiding under my bed!

I remember Carmen and I being married at the Treasure Island Navy Chapel. I remember arriving in Guam just prior to the arrival of Super Typhoon Pamela, with winds of 200 miles per hour. Carmen and I were sure that might be the end of our naval career!

I remember being promoted to chief petty officer, which was the most memorable event of my Navy career. The most common refrain in the Navy is "Ask the Chief." Suddenly becoming the source for all those questions is a very sobering experience.

I remember being commissioned a chief warrant officer. For twenty years I had complained about officers, and the Navy got even with me and made me one.

I remember being a division officer on an aircraft carrier, the *USS Midway*, and appreciating the hard-working, dedication of the young sailors that worked for me.

I remember my assignment in Albuquerque, New Mexico after being at sea for three years. I'm proud of being the Project Officer on the Ground Launched Cruise Missile. I feel that the deployment of this weapon system was a significant factor in affecting the economy of the Soviet Union, and the resulting end of the cold war. A shipmate that was with me in Albuquerque is here today, LCDR Dick Grass. He was the project officer on the Tomahawk Missile that we hear so much about in the news.

I remember my assignment in Washington, D.C. as a detailer. A detailer is a guy that tells sailors where they will be stationed next, and when it's time to go to sea. I was amazed how many people I heard from, that I'd not talked to for years, saying how much they admired me, and asking me to remember what great friends we were.

I remember my assignment as Officer In Charge of Navfac Coos Head Detachment. It's a great feeling having your name on the door (see photograph page).

My mother has kept every letter I've sent her over the past thirty years, so I have a good source for recalling my memories of the Navy. (My mom had surprised me the night before, by presenting me with a ribbon-tied box, which I discovered contained every letter I had written to her and my father while in the Navy. This was one of the most pleasant surprises I've had in my life, and if it were not for her, these memoirs would never have been possible.)

I have many people to thank; the many good shipmates I've been stationed with over the years. I'm very honored that three ordnance men are here today, Commander Rhine, Lieutenant Commander Grass, and Gunner's Mate First Class Jim Porter. As you know, my specialty is surface ordnance. Ordnance men are part of a special brotherhood. We do things very deliberately, and carefully, and we do not like loud noises. I'm very pleased that they are here today to share in my retirement. Commander Rhine has traveled from Oklahoma. Lieutenant Commander Grass has traveled from Albuquerque, New Mexico, and Petty Officer Jim Porter from Washington, State. I have great respect for these men, and the outstanding job they've done for our country.

Commander Reinhardt, thank you for your leadership and support, and the outstanding service the detachment received from NavFac Whidbey Island, often same day service. Thank you for your conspicuous absence from the detachment, which indicated your faith in my ability to manage the detachment.

Thanks to CWO Bob Lockhart, as a shipmate who has helped me throughout this tour, and today. Thanks to Master Chief Broduer for being the master of ceremony. Thanks to Petty Officer Knipple. The Detachment head underwent an extensive remodel, and Petty Officer Knipple was in charge of that. Most Navy heads are painted haze gray, or perhaps Navy blue, but she chose whispering peach, and I wanted to tell her that color is starting to grow on me! Thanks to Chief Kohlman, I'm confident that the detachment is in good hands. Thanks to the dedicated professional people here at Coos Head, RPI Technicians Bob Dewey, Herman Barber, Jim Bush, and Charlie Margerum. They are professionals; they are the ones that make the detachment what it is. I appreciate the outstanding work they did, and the fact that we had fun doing it. Thank you Captain Nielsen, working with the air guard has been a pleasure. Thanks to the Burns Security Officers, thank you for your professional, hard work. Thank you Captain Lovett for all the help and support the Coast Guard has given the detachment. Thanks to LT Bob Barke for handing over an organization that basically ran itself.

Thanks Mayor Gould, and the Sheriff's Office. The good people of Coos Bay and North Bend, is the main reason Carmen and I are making this area our home. Thanks to our church, Bible Baptist, and Pastor Meksch, for your friendship and support. Thanks to Faith Baptist Church of Strathmore, California. They've been faithful praying for Carmen and me, and each year for thirty years at Christmas time they sent me a huge box of candy and cookies. I'm honored that Mr. George Neese is here, a World War II veteran, who would always welcome me to the church in Strathmore with a hearty handshake, and big smile. Thanks to my sister, brother-in-law, aunts and uncles, and family for their love and support over the years.

Thanks to mom and dad for their encouragement, support, and love over the years, and for teaching me the values and ethics that have served me well throughout my Navy career. Thanks for instilling in my heart a great love for this country.

Thanks to my bride, Carmen, for standing by me, for never complaining, sharing good times, and bad times, for being my love, my partner, and best friend. We finally made it! She has encouraged me, has supported me, and has truly been a model Navy wife. If we could, we would stay in the Navy longer, but it's time to move on. We look forward to discovering if there's life after the Navy. I may try selling my watercolor paintings, so if you see one in a store, and even if it's priced ridiculously high, please buy it.

Above all, thanks to the Lord Jesus Christ, because of his mercy, love, and watch care, Carmen and I have survived up to this point, and He has promised that He will continue to care for us.

I've had a fantastic time. It's been a privilege and honor to have served our country. God Bless you all, God Bless the United States Navy, God Bless America."

My voice faltered at the end of my speech. This was a very emotional moment for me and I was honored with a long period of applause.

Pastor Bob Meksch came to the podium for the benediction. He gave thanks, asked for blessings, and asked for protection for those fighting in *Desert Storm*.

After the prayer, the Master Chief addressed the audience and explained the custom of "piping over the side," and side boys in the Navy. He then asked everyone to rise, and ordered, "Side boys, post." I had asked a variety of people to be side boys, Navy, Coast Guard, and Oregon Air National Guard, eight men total, four on each side of the walkway I was to walk through.

I then faced Commander Reinhardt, saluted and said, "I request permission to go ashore Sir." He returned my salute and said, "Permission granted." I then moved next to the side boys. Four bells rang out, and Master Chief Broduer called out "Chief Warrant Officer, United States Navy departing." I then held a hand salute, and slowly walked through the saluting side boys, while a boatswain's mate, piped on a boatswain's pipe.

When I completed my walk through, I lowered my salute, and one bell rang. I then returned to the stage, and offered Carmen my arm. She took my arm, while the master chief explained that it was a custom at Navy retirements for the retiree to walk through the side boys a second time with his spouse. Carmen and I walked through the side boys while the boatswain's pipe whistled.

Then the ceremony was over. There was to be a reception in the club located right next door to the auditorium. Carmen and I, and Commander Reinhardt stood outside the entrance to the club while people shook our hands and offered congratulations, as they entered the club. This was an exhilarating time for me, but I was relieved to have the formal ceremony over. When I finally entered the club, I was shocked to see two pictures Carmen had secretly prepared. Both were eight by eleven inch photographs. One was the first picture taken of me in the Navy uniform of a seaman recruit in boot camp (see photograph page). The other was the last picture taken of me on active duty, in the uniform of a chief warrant officer.

Carmen had worked hard to prepare everything for the reception. She had hired a caterer, and there was a large cake, and food and drinks for all the guests.

Commander Rhine approached me in the reception room, and said he had a presentation for me. He gave me a plaque from his command, which had a metal plate, upon which was engraved, "Presented to CWO4 James S. Little, thirty years of professional service June 1960 - February 1991." He also gave me a letter of commendation, which said,

> On behalf of the Navy's tactical nuclear weapons community, I would like to take this opportunity to express our appreciation for the superior manner in which you have supported the United States Navy's mission and goals over the past thirty years of Naval service.
> You have served professionally in a number of challenging assignments aboard ship in both the Atlantic and Pacific Fleets as well as ashore involving conventional ordnance and nuclear weapons' responsibilities. Over the years you have progressed through the ranks as a technician, leader, and manager to Chief Gunner's Mate Technician and to your current grade of CWO4 in the Warrant Officer Program. You have epitomized the role model for our younger sailors coming up through the ranks seeking increased leadership, technical and management responsibilities.
> On behalf of our NAVSEASYSCOM, NAVAIRSYSCOM, and PEOCMPANDUAV sponsors, and the Warrant Officer and Limited Duty Officer Surface Ordnance community, I want to pass along a hearty "Bravo Zulu!" We wish you and your family happiness, good health, fair winds and following seas in your retirement years. Signed, Russ Rhine.

I greatly appreciated this compliment from my peers in the ordnance community. I also considered it a tribute from an officer I had immense respect for. Commander Rhine's presence at my retirement was a great honor.

Mrs. Fran Capehart, the Coos County Veterans Affairs Officer, approached me in the reception room, and presented me with an award of merit, which said,

> Award of Merit, by these presents it shall be known that James S. Little, CWO4 has rendered a service to the citizen's of Coos County by having discharged in a capable, diligent, and faithful manner the duties of the last active personnel, retiring from Coos Head. We hereby gratefully express the appreciation of the governing board of Coos County and its citizens." The award was dated January 24, 1991, and signed by the Coos County Commissioners.

There was another ceremony where Carmen and I cut the retirement cake with my Navy sword. This was the last official act of my sword. Carmen gave me a retirement gift of a sword holder, engraved with my rank, and dates of service, which now holds my sword over our fireplace.

Two Oregon Air National Guard sergeants approached me in the reception room and asked me to please come outside with them. Outside, they both said they wished to salute me one last time out of the respect and esteem they held for me. I was touched by this effort, and thanked them. I received gifts of a fishing pole from the Oregon Air National Guard; an embossed brass Navy bell engraved "U.S. Navy 1960-1990" from my mom and dad. A lighthouse, and cane from my sister, a myrtle wood clock from Bob Barke, and many other gifts.

The evening of the twenty-fifth, many of the out of town guests stayed late at our house after leaving the base. At the end of the day, I felt my farewell from the Navy had been very fitting. I'd seen many changes since 1960. I'd served with World War II, and Korean veterans, experienced the Cold War years, and the liberal Admiral Zumwalt times. There had been long, hard periods of deployments during the Vietnam War, where we won all the battles but lost the war.

There were the painful rejections from our fellow countrymen and women when we returned home. The only welcome we received was from our immediate families, and demonstrators. Looking back at the Vietnam War, I began to sense victory! Today I feel the United States won that war. We were resolved to stop the spread of communism, and I think historians will note we prevented many Asian countries from falling to that system. I definitely feel the Vietnam conflict contributed to the eventual fall of the Soviet Union. I was pleased that the men and women of Desert Storm were being praised and honored for their service.

I'd gone through the sparse years under President Carter, and the continuing "socialization" of the Navy. I'd seen strengthening under President Reagan, and the beginning of the end of the Cold War, which was largely due to Reagan's vision and leadership.

In 1997, the job of Nuclear Weaponsman ceased to exist. On 27 September 1991, President Bush directed tactical nuclear weapons removed from U.S. surface ships, attack submarines, and naval aircraft. This brought to pass the wish those of us in the nuclear weapons program had secretly hoped for—that someday our job might be done away with. In a few short years all the ships and commands I'd been stationed aboard, ceased to exist.

By the strangest of coincidences, on my birthday 8 December 1991, the Union of Soviet Socialist Republic ceased to exist. This was one of the nicest birthday presents I could have imagined. I was however baffled there was so little celebration and fanfare over the end of the Cold War, which had been such a large part of life, and caused so much dread in America. I prepared a list of the men that had given their life on the ships I served on (it totaled forty-three) and vowed each Memorial Day, I would carry this list in an attempt to honor these brave heroes.

As I reflected on my journey as a U.S. Navy Sailor, I thought of the models of leadership, and examples of men I admired and respected, such as Gunner White of the *USS Independence*, who said, "Try to leave a command in better shape, and more battle ready, than it was when you first reported aboard."

I have fond memories of all the exceptional men who served in the demanding nuclear weapons program. One of my most treasured recollections was the day I donned the uniform of a chief petty officer. I hoped I had made a favorable mark not only on the Navy in which I served, but also on the sailors I served with. Speaking of achievements, a source of pride for me was as an officer for ten years, I received all "A's" on each of my fitness reports.

After my retirement, I acknowledged a mildly embarrassing compliment that was still one of the nicest comments on my career I'd ever received. At an annual reunion of the Navy Nuclear Weapons Association©™[58], I was being introduced to a group of reunion attendees. When one man, who I did not know, said, "You're Jim Little, the original Gunner Jim Little? I thought you were a legend. I can't believe it!"

I've often thought of a quote attributed to President John F. Kennedy: "I can imagine no more rewarding career. And any man who may be asked in this century what he did to make his life worthwhile, I think can respond with a good deal of pride and satisfaction, I served in the United States Navy."

Thus at midnight 28 February 1991, I was officially retired from the United States Navy, proud and honored to have been included in the exclusive Brotherhood of Navy Nuclear Weaponsmen.

The End

Readers interested in learning more about Navy Nuclear Weaponsmen, Navy nuclear weapons, or to review eligibility in the Navy Nuclear Weapons Association©™, go to the Internet website: **http://www.navynucweps.com**

In Memoriam

August 5, 1964 onboard *USS Ticonderoga* (CVA-14), in support of combat operations, Aviation Ordnanceman First Class (AO1) Joe Lee Williams was killed in a flight deck mishap that occurred as he was enroute from the squadron's armory to de-arm the 20MM cannons of a VA-56, A-4 *Skyhawk* returning from a combat mission. After a delay of nearly 40 years, his name was finally engraved on the Vietnam Memorial Wall during 2004. This act was accomplished only after a group of concerned *Ticonderoga* sailors successfully lobbied the Navy to recognize that his death occurred as the result of combat operations. Homeland Security Secretary Tom Ridge, hosted the ceremony.

On April 17, 2006 during a ceremony at the Vietnam Veterans Memorial Wall in Washington, D.C, forty-one years after his death, *USS Ticonderoga,* A-4 *Skyhawk* pilot, LTJG Douglas M. Webster's name was included in the Vietnam War Memory Book. Doug's stepbrother Mike Rawl and his wife Mary attended the ceremony. A speaker at the ceremony was Tim Russert, host and moderator of NBC's program "Meet the Press". Mike Rawl, and Roger Ailes, who was Doug's best friend from Warren, Ohio High School, and is now the President of Fox News Channel, and chairman of the Fox Television Stations Group, has established a memorial fund in memory of LTJG Douglas M. Webster. Information about this charitable fund can be found at:

www.a4skyhawk.org/3e/va56/webster-memorial.htm

Or by writing:

Douglas M. Webster Memorial fund
Community Foundation of the Mahoning Valley
11 Federal Plaza Central
Youngstown, Ohio 44503

Endnotes

1. Big Picture: ABC Documentary series 1953-1959
2. Navy Log: ABC/CBS television series: 1955-1958
3. The Silent Service: Syndicated television series: 1957-1959
4. The Bluejackets' Manual: The Bluejackets' Manual 15th edition, by Captain John V. Noel, Jr., U.S. Navy. Copyright © 1959 by the U.S. Naval Institute, Annapolis, Maryland.
5. 568th Recruit Brigade Review Pamphlet: 9 September 1960
6. USS Haven history: Department of the Navy, Naval Historical Center, 805 Kidder Breese S.E., Washington Navy Yard, Washington, D.C. 20374-5060
7. Ben Hur: 1959 Metro Goldwyn Mayer movie starring Charlton Heston.
8. Navy Times: Weekly newspaper published by Military Times Media Group
9. USS Independence (CVA-62) General and Safety Regulations AIRLANT-AIRPAC CV INST. 5400.1
10. Moon River: 1962 song by Andy Williams
11. USS Independence Newsletter: USS Independence "The Declaration Newsletter" Volume VI, August 1963, Number VII.
12. USS Independence (CVA-62) Welcome Aboard Booklet: 1962, forward by Captain L.V. Swanson, Commanding Officer
13. Where the Boys are: 1960 Metro Goldwyn Mayer movie, starring Connie Francis, and George Hamilton.
14. Lindsay Ripe Olives: An olive company in Lindsay California, formed in 1916, suffered bankruptcy in 1992
15. USS Ticonderoga history: Department of the Navy, Naval Historical Center, 805 Kidder Breese S.E., Washington Navy Yard, Washington, D.C. 20374-5060
16. Capt. Weinel's biography: USS Ticonderoga Cruise Book, Far East Cruise 1964
17. Gulf of Tonkin Incident: USS Ticonderoga Cruise Book, Far East Cruise 1964
18. The Phil Silvers Show: CBS television series 1955-1959
19. Why Carriers?: USS Ticonderoga Cruise Book, Far East Cruise 1964, author unknown
20. Ticonderoga Letter: Undated letter by Captain Robert N. Miller
21. Newspaper Article: Lindsay Gazette newspaper, Lindsay, California, 15 September 1965 Mineral King Publishing
22. Pilot's Story: USS Ticonderoga Cruise Book 1965-1966, by John Bates
23. We were soldiers once…and young: © New York Random House, November 1992, copyright 1992, by Harold G. Moore, and Joseph L. Galloway, TM and © Paramount Pictures 2002
24. Olongapo statement: USS Ticonderoga Cruise Book 1965-1966, author unknown.
25. Martha Raye and Cardinal Spellman Story: USS Ticonderoga Cruise Book 1965-1966, author unknown
26. War Mishap, Stuns Hope Troupe: Sacramento Union newspaper, dated 28 December 1965, Writer unknown
27. USS Ticonderoga Scrapping: Department of the Navy, Naval Historical Center, 805 Kidder Breese S.E., Washington Navy Yard, Washington, D.C. 20374-5060
28. Guam Legend: Orders Guam Vol. 2, 1978, Glimpses of Guam C. Inc., ©copyright 1978
29. Mutiny on the Bounty: MGM Pictures ©1962, starring Marlon Brando
30. USS Oriskany description: USS Oriskany Cruise Book '72
31. USS Oriskany Family Gram: 8 September 1970, by Capt. John A. Gilchrist, Commanding Officer
32. Pride and Tears as Big "O" Came Home: Oakland tribune newspaper article written by Tribune writer Marlene Freedman
33. Easy Rider: 1969 Columbia Pictures Corporation Movie starring Peter Fonda
34. Dirty Harry: movie starring Clint Eastwood, directed by Don Seigel
35. Okie from Muskgogee, Fighting Side of Me: 1969 songs released by Merle Haggard
36. PTSD Study: 1999 study, Dr. Joseph A. Boscarino, a senior scientist at the New York Academy of Medicine, and Associate Professor of Medicine at Mt. Sinai School of Medicine
37. Jaws: 1975 Universal Pictures movie, directed by Steven Spielburg, starring Roy Scheider

38 Typhoon Pamela: Associated Press article dated 23 May 1976
39 Navy Uniform Regulations Manual: Department of the Navy NAVPERS 156651
40 Robinson Crusoe USN: ©copyright 1945 Whittlesey House Publishing, by Clark, Givens and Tweed
41 No Man is an Island: 1962 Universal Pictures, starring Jeffrey Hunter
42 Admiral Cruden Letter: Orders Guam Vol. 2, 1978, Glimpses of Guam Inc., ©copyright 1978
43 LDO/CWO History: The Limited Duty/Chief Warrant Officer Professional Guidebook OPNAV 130-1-85
44 Protocol Book: Social Usage and Protocol Handbook OPNAVINST 1710.7
45 James Sylvester story: ©1997-2001, Wallace L McKeehan, All Rights Reserved, reproduced with permission of Sons of Dewitt Colony, Texas
46 USS Midway First of a Kind, One of a Kind/dogfight stories/deployment history: "Launch" USS Midway newsletter, by LT Pete Clayton, and Robert L. Broaddus
47 Status of Forces Agreement (SOFA): A pocket Guide to Japan, NAVPERS 92785A, 20 March 1970
48 Welcome to Mombasa pamphlet: USS Midway newsletter, undated, author unknown
49 Aerial Picture of Battle Groups ALPHA and FOXTROT, The USS Midway, USS Enterprise and escorts in the North Pacific Ocean: undated, writer unknown
50 USS Midway Berths at Yokosuka Naval Base: Midway Mutiplex Special Edition, dated 6 October 1982
51 The Aviator: 2004 Miramax film directed by Martin Scorsese, and starring Leonardo DiCaprio a film about Howard Hughes.
52 Jim Wright Story: from family website: http://www.wrightools.com/hughes/
53 Naval Military Personnel Manual: MILPERSMAN-NAVPERS 15560
54 Alton Grizzard story: as related by his father, CWO4 Bill Grizzard and website http://www.arlingtoncemetery.net/algrizzard.htm
55 Hunt for Red October: Naval Institute Press, 1984, by Tom Clancy
56 Lonesome Dove: 1989 Television series, Artisan Entertainment. Directed by Simon Wincer, starring Robert Duvall and Tommy Lee Jones
57 Change of command ceremony: Lindsay Gazette Newspaper, Lindsay, California. Mineral King Publishing.
58 Navy Nuclear Weapons Association: Copyrighted 2000-2006, and Trademark. All rights reserved worldwide by the Navy Nuclear Weapons Association.
59 Desert Storm article: The World Newspaper, Coos Bay, Oregon

CPSIA information can be obtained at www.ICGtesting.com
Printed in the USA
BVOW09s1732110614

355920BV00003B/4/P